Robotics Research

The MIT Press Series in Artificial Intelligence
Edited by Patrick Henry Winston and Michael Brady

Artificial Intelligence: An MIT Perspective, Volume I: Expert Problem Solving, Natural Language Understanding, Intelligent Computer Coaches, Representation and Learning edited by Patrick Henry Winston and Richard Henry Brown, 1979

Artificial Intelligence: An MIT Perspective, Volume II: Understanding Vision, Manipulation, Computer Design, Symbol Manipulation edited by Patrick Henry Winston and Richard Henry Brown, 1979

NETL: A System for Representing and Using Real-World Knowledge by Scott Fahlman, 1979

The Interpretation of Visual Motion by Shimon Ullman, 1979

A Theory of Syntactic Recognition for Natural Language by Mitchell P. Marcus, 1980

Turtle Geometry: The Computer as a Medium for Exploring Mathematics by Harold Abelson and Andrea diSessa, 1981

From Images to Surfaces: A Computational Study of the Human Early Visual System by William Eric Leifur Grimson, 1981

Robot Manipulators: Mathematics, Programming and Control by Richard P. Paul, 1981

Computational Models of Discourse edited by Michael Brady and Robert C. Berwick, 1982

Robot Motion: Planning and Control by Michael Brady, John M. Hollerbach, Timothy Johnson, Tomas Lozano-Perez, and Matthew Mason, 1982

In-Depth Understanding: A Computer Model of Integrated Processing for Narrative Comprehension by Michael G. Dyer, 1983

Robotics Research: The First International Symposium edited by Michael Brady and Richard Paul, 1984

Robotics Research: The Second International Symposium edited by Hideo Hanafusa and Hirochika Inoue, 1985

Robotics Research

The Second International Symposium

Edited by Hideo Hanafusa and Hirochika Inoue

The MIT Press
Cambridge, Massachusetts
London, England

Publisher's note: This format is intended to reduce the cost of publishing certain work in book form and to shorten the gap between editorial preparation and the final publication. Detailed editing and composition have been avoided by photographing the text of this book directly from the authors' word-processor output.

This book was printed and bound in the United States of America

Library of Congress Cataloging in Publication Data

Main entry under title:
Robotics research.

(The MIT Press series in artificial intelligence)
Papers presented at the Second International Symposium on Robotics Research, held Aug. 20–23, 1984, in Kyoto, Japan.
Includes bibliographies.
1. Robotics—Research—Congresses. I. Hanafusa, Hideo, 1923– . II. Inoue, Hirochika, 1942–
III. International Symposium on Robotics Research (2nd: 1984: Kyoto, Japan). IV. Series.
TJ210.3.R64 1985 629.8′92 85-6
ISBN 0-262-08151-2

Contents

Series Foreword
Patrick Henry Winston and Michael Brady ix

Preface
Hideo Hanafusa and Hirochika Inoue xi

Introduction xiii

I
VISUAL PERCEPTION

1
Representation and Recognition of Three-Dimensional Objects 3

Describing Surfaces 5
Michael Brady, Jean Ponce, Alan Yuille, and Haruo Asada

Regular Pattern Projection for Surface Measurement 17
Kōkichi Sugihara, Kiyoshi Okazaki, Feng Kaihua, and Noboru Sugie

New Steps toward a Flexible 3-D Vision System for Robotics 25
O. D. Faugeras

A 3D Vision System: Generating and Matching Shape Descriptions in Range Images 35
Fumiaki Tomita and Takeo Kanade

Configuration Understanding in Range Data 43
Robert C. Bolles and Patrice Horaud

Recognition and Localization of Overlapping Parts from Sparse Data 51
Tomás Lozano-Pérez and W. Eric L. Grimson

2
Implementation of Robot Vision 57

Precise Manipulation with Endpoint Sensing 59
Russell H. Taylor, Ralph L. Hollis, and Mark D. Lavin

Segmentation by Object-Matched Low-Level Operators 71
John F. Jarvis

Converging Disparate Sensory Data 81
Ruzena Bajcsy and Peter Allen

Shape Recognition by Human-Like Trial and Error Random Processes 87
Makoto Nagao

A Flexible Multi Window Vision System for Robots 95
Hirochika Inoue and Hiroshi Mizoguchi

Computer Vision for Future Robots/Towards Real Time Sensory Feed Back 103
Jean-Louis Lacombe

Hardware Implementation for Robot Vision 109
Masatsugu Kidode, Hiroshi Hoshino, and Youkio Shiraogawa

II
ACTION CONTROL

3
Control Theory 117

On the Development of High Performance Adaptive Control Algorithms for Robotic Manipulators 119
Steven Dubowsky and Roy Kornbluh

Can Mechanical Robots Learn by Themselves? 127
Suguru Arimoto, Sadao Kawamura, and Fumio Miyazaki

Collision Avoidance in Multi-Robot Systems 135
E. Freund and H. Hoyer

Closed Loop Control of Robots with Local Environment Sensing: Principles and Applications 147
Bernard Espiau

Task Priority Based Redundancy Control of Robot Manipulators 155
Yoshihiko Nakamura and Hideo Hanafusa

Modeling Robot Contour Processes 163
Daniel E. Whitney and Alexander C. Edsall

Trajectory Control of Robot Manipulator based on the Preview Tracking Control Algorithm 171
Kenichi Yoshimoto and Hajime Sugiuchi

Manipulator Control Using Autonomous Trajectory Generating Servomechanism 179
Kensuke Hasegawa and Takashi Mizutani

Robot Motion Trajectory Specification and Generation 187
Richard P. Paul and Hong Zhang

4
Kinematics and Design 195

Control and Mechanics of Simple Manipulator Systems 197
Bernard Roth

New Concepts in Lightweight Arms 203
Wayne J. Book

Use of Redundancy in the Design of Robotic Systems 207
Charles A. Klein

Optimum Kinematic Design for a Seven Degree of Freedom Manipulator 215
John M. Hollerbach

Development of Simulation System of Robot Motion and Its Role in Task Planning and Design Systems 223
Masaharu Takano

Compensation of Positioning Errors Caused by Geometric Deviations in Robot System 231
Koichi Sugimoto and Takushi Okada

Kinematic Analysis and Design for Automatic Workpart Fixturing in Flexible Assembly 237
Haruhiko Asada and Andre B. By

Optimization of Mechanics for Force Generation by Using Pulleys and Spring 245
Tokuji Okada

III
ROBOT MECHANISMS

5
Manipulators and End Effectors 255

A Manipulation System Based on Direct-Computational Task-Coordinate Servoing 257
Takashi Suehiro and Kunikatsu Takase

Fine Motion Control for a Small Articulated Robot 265
Takashi Uchiyama, Tadashi Akita, and Makoto Araki

Skills for a Shearing Robot: Dexterity and Sensing 273
James P. Trevelyan

Application of Electromagnetic Impulsive Force to Precise Positioning Tools in Robot System 281
Toshiro Higuchi

Mechanical Analysis of a Gripper-Manipulator 287
J. C. Guinot, P. Bidaud, and J. P. Lallemand

On the Articulated Hands 293
Hiroaki Kobayashi

The Version I Utah/MIT Dextrous Hand 301
S. C. Jacobsen, J. E. Wood, D. F. Knutti, K. B. Biggers, and E. K. Iversen

6
Mobile Robots 309

Four-Legged Running with One-Legged Algorithms 311
Marc H. Raibert

Dynamical Walk of Quadruped Robot (COLLIE-1) 317
Hirofumi Miura, Isao Shimoyama, Mamoru Mitsuishi, and Hiroshi Kimura

TITAN III: A Quadruped Walking Vehicle 325
Shigeo Hirose, Tomoyuki Masui, Hidekazu Kikuchi, Yasushi Fukuda, and Yoji Umetani

Guide Dog Robot 333
Susumu Tachi and Kiyoshi Komoriya

Intelligent Robot System II 341
A. Ooka, K. Ogi, Y. Wada, Y. Kida, A. Takemoto, K. Okamoto, and K. Yoshida

Monitoring of a Building Environment by a Mobile Robot 349
Saburo Tsuji

IV
TASK LEVEL STUDIES

7
Modelling, Programming, and Monitoring 359

Robotics and Solid Modelling: A Discussion of the Requirements Robotic Applications Put on Solid Modelling Systems 361
A. P. Ambler

Aspects of Mobile Robot Visual Map Making 369
Rodney A. Brooks

The LM Robot Programming System 377
J. C. Latombe, C. Laugier, J. M. Lefebvre, E. Mazer, and J. F. Miribel

Task Execution Monitoring by Compiled Production Rules in an Advanced Multi-Sensor Robot 393
Malik Ghallab

Projection Derived Space Cube Scene Models for Robotic Vision and Collision-Free Trajectory Planning 403
R. A. Jarvis

Programming, Simulating and Evaluating Robot Actions 411
A. Liegeois, P. Borrel, and E. Dombre

8
Theory of Manipulation 419

Mechanics of Pushing 421
Matthew T. Mason

On the Motion of Objects in Contact 429
John Hopcroft and Gordon Wilfong

Manipulability of Robotic Mechanisms 439
Tsuneo Yoshikawa

Performance Evaluation of Manipulators Using the Jacobian and Its Application to Trajectory Planning 447
Masaru Uchiyama, Kunitoshi Shimizu, and Kyojiro Hakomori

V
PANEL DISCUSSIONS

9
Robotics for Future Industry 457

Design Concept of Factory Automation Systems 459
Minoru Morita

Views on Robotics for Future Industry 461
Masakazu Ejiri

Robotization in Shipbuilding Industry 469
Ryoichiro Sasano

Valuation of the Practical Use of SCARA Type Robots on Assembly Lines and the Future Robotized Assembly Systems 479
Akitaka Kato

Panel Discussion: Robotics for Future Industry 487

10
Key Issues of Robotics Research 491

Key Issues in Robot Vision 493
Thomas O. Binford

Two Key Problems in Robotics Research 495
R. W. Daniel and P. G. Davey

Key Issues of Robotics Research 501
Brian Carlisle

Key Issues of Robotics Research 505
Yoshiaki Shirai

Research Trends in Decisional and Multisensory Aspects of Third Generation Robots 511
Georges Giralt

Panel Discussion: Key Issues of Robotics Research 521

List of Contributors 525

Series Foreword

Artificial intelligence is the study of intelligence using the ideas and methods of computation. Unfortunately, a definition of intelligence seems impossible at the moment because intelligence appears to be an amalgam of so many information-processing and information-representation abilities.

Of course psychology, philosophy, linguistics, and related disciplines offer various perspectives and methodologies for studying intelligence. For the most part, however, the theories proposed in these fields are too incomplete and too vaguely stated to be realized in computational terms. Something more is needed, even though valuable ideas, relationships, and constraints can be gleaned from traditional studies of what are, after all, impressive existence proofs that intelligence is in fact possible.

Artificial intelligence offers a new perspective and a new methodology. Its central goal is to make computers intelligent, both to make them more useful and to understand the principles that make intelligence possible. That intelligent computers will be extremely useful is obvious. The more profound point is that artificial intelligence aims to understand intelligence using the ideas and methods of computation, thus offering a radically new and different basis for theory formation. Most of the people doing artificial intelligence believe that these theories will apply to any intelligent information processor, whether biological or solid state.

There are side effects that deserve attention, too. Any program that will successfully model even a small part of intelligence will be inherently massive and complex. Consequently, artificial intelligence continually confronts the limits of computer science technology. The problems encountered have been hard enough and interesting enough to seduce artificial intelligence people into working on them with enthusiasm. It is natural, then, that there has been a steady flow of ideas from artificial intelligence to computer science, and the flow shows no sign of abating.

The purpose of this MIT Press Series in Artificial Intelligence is to provide people in many areas, both professionals and students, with timely, detailed information about what is happening on the frontiers in research centers all over the world.

Patrick Henry Winston
Michael Brady

Preface

The papers contained in this volume are the record of the Second International Symposium on Robotics Research, held at Kyoto-Kaikan, Kyoto, Japan, 20–23 August 1984. The 65 invited participants from Japan, the United States, France, the United Kingdom, and West Germany attended the symposium and shared discussions on the state of the art as well as the future of the field. This volume reproduces the 62 papers and 2 panel-discussion summaries presented at the symposium, together with an introduction prepared especially for this publication.

Robotics is a young, fast-growing interdisciplinary field. It covers wide aspects of research activities: perception, action control, task level strategies, mechanisms, and so on. Those different disciplines, originally from other areas, are now converging into a new field that is called robotics. However, the structure of the field is not yet fully established. Many questions are still open to discussion among the different disciplines.

The series International Symposia on Robotics Research was initiated for the purpose of bringing the world's leading researchers together and providing extensive opportunities to discuss the current and future problems of robotics. The first symposium, held at Bretton Woods, New Hampshire, in August 1983, successfully established an international community and encouraged international collaboration through the exchange of views and personnel. The national committee for the second symposium was organized by several Japanese attendees of the first symposium in collaboration with domestic researchers. The committee planned and prepared the Kyoto symposium over a year. One of the most important but difficult decisions concerned the invitees. The total number of the participants was limited, to encourage scientifically rewarding interactions, and there are many researchers who are prominent not only in their respective areas of robotics but also in these areas' boundaries. An International Advisory Committee, consisting of M. Brady, R. Paul, G. Giralt, H. Hanafusa, and H. Inoue, had a meeting on this matter, in Kyoto, in December 1983. After consulting with members of the editorial board of the *International Journal of Robotics Research*, the advisory committee submitted a list of invitees. The list of candidates was also examined from the viewpoints of technical, institutional, and geographic balance. On the basis of this suggestion, the Japanese Organizing Committee decided to invite 65 participants. Half of them were new names.

The structure of this book does not follow that of the symposium. The 53 papers presented at the 12 technical sessions are grouped into four parts: Visual Perception, Action Control, Robot Mechanisms, and Task Level Studies. There are two chapters in the first part, focusing on these topics in visual perception: representation and recognition of three-dimensional objects; and implementation of robot vision. The two chapters in the second part are concerned with the computational aspects of action control: control theory; and kinematics and design. The two chapters in the third part examine these features of robot mechanisms: manipulators and end effectors; and mobile robots. The two chapters in the fourth part explore the following task level studies: modelling, programming, and monitoring; and theory of manipulation. A final (fifth) part presents in two chapters 9 papers debated at two panel discussions: robotics for future industry; and key issues of robotics research. This final part also includes the 2 panel-discussion summaries.

The cooperation of many people made the Second International Symposium on Robotics Research successful indeed. The members of the Japanese Organizing Committee were most helpful in planning, preparing, and running the symposium. Many thanks go to Suguru Arimoto, Tatsuo Gotoh, Kensuke Hasegawa, Hirofumi Miura, Makoto Nagao, Yoshihiko Nakamura, Yoshiaki Shirai, Saburo Tsuji, Yoji Umetani, and Tsuneo Yoshikawa. Tsuneo Yoshikawa of Kyoto University performed the difficult task of heading the symposium's secretariat, with the assistance of Yoshihiko Nakamura and Tohru Watanabe. Noriko Katayanagi and Hitomi Hashimoto were excellent secretaries, and we appreciate their efforts very much. We also thank Michael Brady, Richard Paul, and Georges Giralt for their valuable advice. The second symposium was supported mainly by 31 Japanese companies, and partly by the National Science Foundation of the United States and the CNRS and INRIA of France. And finally, we wish to thank all the participants who contributed to both the symposium and the book.

The International Symposia on Robotics Research were born in Bretton Woods, have learned to walk in Kyoto, and will go to Europe. The third symposium will be held next year near Paris.

Hideo Hanafusa
Kyoto, Japan

Hirochika Inoue
Tokyo, Japan

Introduction

Broadly speaking, robotics is a study of the intelligent connection of perception to action. It is a young, fast-growing interdisciplinary field, in which many researchers are challenged to create smarter machines. Some researchers are exploring the general principles of robotics, while others are devoting their efforts to the actual implementation of smart robots that work in a physical environment. There are experts who focus their interest on specific problems in robotics research, such as vision, tactile sensing, force sensing, control, mechanisms, task planning, and languages, and there are several groups who seek to combine the results of this research to produce integrated robot systems. So far, the problems of robotics have been investigated separately within several different fields of science and technology: computer vision, automatic control, mechanical design, artificial intelligence, and so on. And today, they are converging into a new field: robotics.

Robotics covers wide research areas, each of which may be relevant to producing integrated smart systems that work in real environments. Key elements of robots are perception, action, connecting strategies, and very friendly human interfaces. Perception is needed to understand the physical environments in which robots must interact—not only for the analysis of overall scenes before motion planning but also for guiding motion correctly. The role of action is to change the situations of the physical environments as required. Design of fine mechanisms and fine control with sensor feedback are important to facilitate good actions. Task strategies, the general way of connecting perception to action, is an essential problem for the robot itself. It involves the problem of task description, planning, programming, execution monitoring, and environment modelling. Moreover, the robot system must provide very friendly user interfaces in order to reduce the complexity of commanding a robot.

This volume reflects recent progress of robotics research raised at the Second International Symposium on Robotics Research. It is not our purpose to discuss in depth the structure of robotics. Rather we leave that to the many excellent papers presented by the experts at the symposium. In order to help the reader to understand the field of robotics, we arranged these papers into five parts: Visual Perception (I), Action Control (II), Robot Mechanisms (III), Task Level Studies (IV), and Panel Discussions (V). Part I is divided into two chapters: chapter 1 (six papers), which deals with the representation and recognition of three-dimensional objects, and chapter 2 (seven papers), which deals with the implementation of robot vision. Part II consists of chapter 3 (nine papers), which deals with the control theory of manipulators, and chapter 4 (eight papers), which deals with kinematics and design. Part III contains chapter 5 (seven papers), on manipulators and end effectors, and chapter 6 (six papers), on mobile robot systems. Part IV includes chapter 7 (six papers), on modelling, programming, and monitoring, and chapter 8 (four papers), which explores the theory of manipulation. Part V consists of two panel discussions: chapter 9 (four papers plus panel-discussion summary), on robotics for future industry, and chapter 10 (five papers plus panel-discussion summary), on key issues of robotics research. Brief summaries of all papers follow.

I Visual Perception

1 Representation and Recognition of Three-Dimensional Objects

Brady et al. discuss visual representations of three-dimensional surfaces. On the basis of the theoretical study of classes of surface curves as a source of constraints on the surface on which they lie, they analyze bounding contours, surface intersections, lines of curvature, and asymptotes. They demonstrate algorithms that compute lines of curvature of a surface, determine planar patches and umbilic regions, and extract axes of surfaces of revolution and tube surfaces.

Sugihara et al. propose a new method for recovering the three-dimensional structure of surfaces from visual images. Their method uses the projection of two-dimensional regular patterns, such as circles and squares, and analyzes the distortions of projected patterns to calculate local surface normals. When the patterns are projected by parallel rays of light, a local surface normal is determined uniquely from a single image. When the patterns are projected by radial rays of light, both a local surface and the associated range are determined from three images obtained by a fixed camera with three different positions of the light source.

Faugeras discusses the problem of representing three-dimensional scenes when dense range data are available. Rich symbolic descriptions are obtained by fitting planes and quadrics to the range data. A region growing algorithm working on a three-dimensional graph approximating object surfaces is described. He also discusses the problem of matching models and scene descriptions for recognition and positioning as well as an algorithm based on hypothesis prediction and verification in the case of planar primitives.

Tomita and Kanade describe a vision system for recognizing and locating three-dimensional objects from light-stripe rangefinder images. The range image is first segmented into edges and surfaces in three-dimensional space, and a scene is described by a set of surfaces, each of which is represented by a list of boundary edges. Object models are represented by component surfaces and edges in a similar fashion as scene descriptions. Matching between the input scene and an object model is based on finding appropriate coordinate transformations from the object models to the scene. A transformation is hypothesized by initial matching between a few features, and the transformation is then tested with the rest of the features for verification.

Bolles and Horaud describe range-based techniques for verifying and determining object configurations. Range images are predicted from hypotheses and compared with measured data. Differences between predicted and measured data lead to the rejection of hypotheses. As hypotheses are made and verified, a graph is built that describes which objects are on top of others. This graph, plus regions of unexplained occlusions, forms the basis for an understanding of the configuration.

Lozano-Pérez and Grimson discuss how sparse local measurements of positions and surface normals may be used to identify and locate overlapping objects. The objects are modeled as polyhedra having up to six degrees of freedom relative to the sensors. The approach operates by examining all hypotheses about pairings between sensed points and object surfaces and efficiently discarding inconsistent ones by using local constraints on distances between faces, angles between face normals, and angles of vectors between sensed points.

2 Implementation of Robot Vision

Taylor et al. describe an endpoint-sensing method for achieving very precise alignment of a part or tool to a workpiece. Their approach relies on the coarse joint of a robot to bring a tool or part within the "capture range" of a fine-positioning system carried by the robot, which is then used to null out sensed misalignments. The experiment reported used an extremely precise, high-bandwidth planar "wrist" and an industrial vision system to perform accurate alignment of small parts.

Jarvis describes a general method for implementing computer vision systems suitable for a variety of industrial and manufacturing tasks. The method, segmentation by object-matched low-level operators, is generally applicable where there is one or at most a few kinds of objects in the scene. However, many of the objects may be present in a single scene requiring the analysis of images of considerable complexity. The system is designed for strict bottom-up processing and does not require any global iterations or searching strategies in its interpretation.

Object recognition systems using single sensors are still limited in their ability to recognize correctly different three-dimensional objects. By utilizing multiple sensors (in particular, vision and touch), more information is available to the system. Bajcsy and Allen attempt to utilize multiple sensors and explore the problem and possible solutions to converging disparate sensory data for object recognition.

Nagao proposes a new approach to shape recognition by a human-like trial-and-error method. He develops a new system, which has nonalgorithmic feature detections and does not require procedural description for object detection. His system only requires the declarative description of an object structure. It uses a variable-size slit that is applied to the most plausible parts in an image by a top-down command from an object model and obtains the characteristic features of the object parts. This slit application is realized mostly in hardware and has some automatic ability to detect the best features by a sort of random search. The system interprets the declarative description and activates the slit application to obtain the features. If we give many alternative descriptions, the system can choose a description that is easily satisfiable and obtains the final whole description of object by a trial-and-error search method.

Inoue and Mizoguchi present a flexible multiwindow vision system for robots, which can perform color image processing. The window is a local rectangular region to be processed. It is not fixed on the screen. Location, shape, and resolution of each window can be controlled independently. The current prototype system has 16 windows, which are processed by microcomputer independently in parallel, and provides flexible hardware for investigating simultaneous control of visual attention for various hand-eye interactions.

Lacombe classifies the applications of computer vision to robot control and discusses the performance requirements of computer vision systems for real-time sensor feedback. He shows two typical architectures of computer vision systems and emphasizes the importance of developing very integrated operators, which are the key components of future powerful vision systems.

Kidode et al. introduce a high-performance image processor newly developed for robot vision. Several basic functions have been implemented by means of simple hardware that are efficiently used in object identification, position detection, and inspection. Not only can this vision processor execute basic functions at video-rate speed for 512 × 512 images; it also has technical features in image data access for more complex programming and in common bus structure for more flexible systems.

II Action Control

3 Control Theory

The simple constant-gain linear control system commonly used for current industrial manipulators compensates poorly for the nonlinear dynamic characteristics of manipulators and environmental changes. Dubowsky and Kornbluh present the development of an adaptive control algorithm that adjusts, in real time, the control parameters to compensate for manipulator nonlinear characteristics and changes in environment and payload. Experimental results are also presented for two devices showing that the algorithm is practical and capable of producing significantly improved system dynamic performance.

Arimoto et al. give an affirmative answer to the question, "Can mechanical robots learn by themselves?" They propose a betterment process for a motion control of mechanical robots. The process has a function of self-learning through an iterative structure. Computer simulation and experiment show that the betterment process betters the next operation of a robot in a certain sense and that the motion trajectory converges eventually to the one desired through automatically repeated operations.

Freund and Hoyer describe the collision avoidance problem for three robots with a common collision space. The strategy for collision avoidance itself is based on analytically described avoidance trajectories that serve in the hierarchical coordinator for collision detection as well as avoidance. The derivation demonstrates the usefulness of this design method even for a larger number of robots.

Espiau proposes a coherent approach to the problem of controlling a robot in an operating space by sensory information. He distinguishes two kinds of control by using dynamics and kinematics. The first one may easily be related to a potential model of the environment and is compatible with a dynamical analysis of the whole system. The second approach, which controls more finely the geometric trajectory, is velocity control. He also proposes a new formalism for dynamic modelling, compatible with the description at the sensor level, and allowing for the analysis of the behavior of a manipulator under closed-loop sensor-based control.

Nakamura and Hanafusa discuss the redundancy utilization of the robot manipulator. They introduce the concept of task priority into the kinematic inverse problem and divide a required task into subtasks according to the order of priority. Then they propose to solve the joint motion of robot manipulators in such a way that the subtasks with lower priority will be performed utilizing the redundancy on the subtasks with higher priority. Both the locally optimal redundancy control and the globally optimal redundancy control are formulated using the null space of the Jacobian matrix.

Robot contour processes include those with contact force, like car grinding or deburring of complex castings, as well as those with little or no contact force, like inspection. Whitney and Edsall describe ways of characterizing, identifying, and estimating contours and robot trajectories. Contour and robot are modeled as stochastic processes in order to emphasize that both successive robot cycles and successive industrial workpieces are similar but not exactly the same. The stochastic models can be used to identify the state of a workpiece or process, or to design a linear or nonlinear filter to estimate workpiece shape and robot position from robot-based measurements.

Yoshimoto and Sugiuchi describe an improvement in the preview tracking control algorithm. In their method, the ''ahead'' deviation is detected by comparing the predicted future position with the previewed trajectory, and the control signal is generated by the integral action concerning the ''ahead'' deviation. To predict the future position more accurately, prediction by the fast-time model is proposed, and the more precise simulation model that considers Coulomb's friction as well as joint flexibilities is used. Theoretical analysis gives the concrete design policy of this method for manipulator trajectory control.

Hasegawa and Mizutani propose a novel method for trajectory control of the end of a manipulator based on the autonomous trajectory generating servomechanism (ATGS) technique. The ATGS is a multivariable servomechanism including part of a trajectory planner in which the corresponding paths, the tangential motion rates, and the algorithm for path tracing are generated automatically without giving nominal trajectories.

Paul and Zhang discuss a consistent and efficient method of specifying and generating robot manipulator trajectories. They classify manipulator motion into four basic categories: joint coordinate, orthogonal coordinate, procedural, and tabular. Joint coordinate motion is appropriate when time must be minimized or when the manipulator is to change kinematic configurations. Orthogonal or straight-line motion is used when a well-defined motion is important, when sensors are used, or when making motions of accommodation. Procedural motion is used when the trajectory is geometrically defined. A tabular motion specification is used when direct teaching methods are employed. They present a method for the specification of all these forms of trajectories in a dynamic free manner, which is computationally efficient and provides for transitions between all possible forms of trajectories in both fixed and moving coordinate systems.

4 Kinematics and Design

Roth describes several of the research problems that are now under investigation by his group at Stanford University. Those problems involve the optimal design and placement, robust control, analysis of instantaneous kinematic properties, description of manipulators workspace, and mechanics of manipulation with multifingered dexterous hands.

The conflict in designing a robot that is fast for large motions and small motions as well as accurate can be alleviated by the bracing strategy described by Book. Larger motions are assigned to joints that move the major links. When these motions are completed, the arm is ''braced'' against the workpiece or a passive workbench. The small motions are assigned to other degrees of freedom that are referenced to the workpiece rather than to the base of the robot. In this way lighter arms are possible, without their disadvantages, for fast, accurate small motions. Book discusses the concept and its implementation.

A robotic system can be termed redundant if it contains more than the minimum number of degrees of freedom needed to perform a class of tasks. Klein discusses two aspects of the use of redundancy in robotic systems. The first aspect is obstacle avoidance as a criterion for the use of the homogeneous solutions of a kinematically redundant manipulator; the second is an examination of several different quantities that have been proposed as a measure of dexterity for a manipulator.

While today's general-purpose manipulators contain six degrees of freedom, effective reduction in degrees of freedom occurs from singularity regions and from workspace obstacles. Hollerbach argues that the future general-purpose manipulators will contain seven degrees of freedom and that one particular kinematic design is superior to other possible seven-degree-of-freedom kinematic designs. Considerations of elimination of singularities, mechanical realizability, kinematic simplicity, and workspace shape are taken into account in arriving at this design.

Takano presents a computer simulation system of robot motion that includes kinematics, inverse kinematics, statics, control system analysis, deflection, and its compensation. He also proposes a new method for solving the synthesis problem for a robot with six degrees of freedom, where position synthesis by the first three joints and orientation synthesis by the last three joints are carried out analytically; the solution is obtained by iteration of both synthesis procedures. The calculation time by this new method is decreased to about one-tenth of that by the 6×6 Jacobian method.

Sugimoto and Okada present a method for estimating errors in a robot mechanism, such as dimensional errors of kinematic pairs and the setting error of the robot with respect to work area coordinate, and for compensating for positioning errors caused by them. The deviations in the robot system are estimated by the least-squares method from displacement data of kinematic pairs when the robot is positioned at a number of preestablished points. They also show that the positioning errors can be well compensated within a limited work area by approximating the nonlinear effects of the deviations on the positioning errors to a linear projective transformation.

Asada and By present an automatic fixturing system for computer-integrated advanced assembly. The system employs reconfigurable fixture modules or elements that are used to locate and hold various workparts for assembly. The fixture configuration or layout can be changed automatically depending upon the workpart geometry and the assembly operations required. Based on a CAD database description of the assembly, the system determines the optimal layout for the reconfigurable fixture elements and builds the desired fixture automatically using a robot manipulator.

Okada proposes link mechanisms for force generation by using pulleys and springs. The mechanisms are based on a scissors structure having two arms and are effective in saving energy and in simplifying and miniaturizing a total system of force generation. He analyzes the relation between the motion of the mechanism and its output force to optimize structure and dimensions of the mechanisms. Experimental results show that eccentric noncircular pulleys make more accurate force-satisfying conditional relations between the force and displacement of mechanisms than do circular pulleys.

III Robot Mechanisms

5 Manipulators and End Effectors

Suehiro and Takase describe the implementation of a task-coordinate servoing system by direct computational approach, the application of the servoing method to a direct-drive manipulator, and the incorporation of a motion control system into a LISP system. In this integrated manipulation system, the position, velocity, compliance, and damping in a task-coordinate frame can be controlled by a program written in LISP language, and even dexterous manual operations can be described easily. A servoing routine, including the computation of dynamics and coordinate transformation, is executed every 0.0025 second by a high-speed microcomputer and fast computation technique.

Takashi Uchiyama et al. describe the development of a small articulated robot with six degrees of freedom that is intended for use in precision applications. It features high positioning resolution, smooth travel under new tracking velocity control, and fast trajectory calculation. The actual positioning resolution of 4 micrometers is achieved throughout the operating area with an accurate servo control designed on the basis of the state space control theory.

Trevelyan focuses his continuing research into the application of robotics to shearing sheep on sensing, shearing technique, programming, and dexterity. Important skills learned from expert human shearers have been transformed into improved sensing techniques and new programming techniques. An automatic "emergency" handling program can temporarily override the normal sequence of programmed operations. Studies for a new robot have highlighted the problem of dexterity, which is limited principally by the design of the wrist mechanism. Factors such as degeneracy, angular range of joints, and mechanical arrangement affect the usable workspace, and additional factors such as drive stiffness and size affect dynamic performance.

Higuchi describes a micropositioning method that uses electromagnetic impulsive forces. This electromagnetic impulsive force's waveform can be controlled by the electric circuit. The micropositioning method is utilized in two kinds of applications. In the first, the conductive plate is fixed to the object and the coil is attached to a hand of a robot; in the second, both coil and conductive plate are loaded on the object. In either case, the object can move step by step. Experiments show that a rigid mass of 3 kg can be moved from 0.1 to 200 micrometers by one shot of electric discharge, according to the charged energy.

Guinot et al. present a general analysis of a gripper-manipulator. During the grasping process, the prototype is a closed loop mechanism, having an isostatic condition with compatible displacements in the punctual contacts between object and fingers.

The kinematic equations give the control system and conditions for nonparasitic mobilities. The static equations after treatment give the stress screw applied to the object. Elastic transmissions are necessary for high resolution in force control as well as in displacements. In general cases the method of different object displacement control under unknown external stresses prescribes the simultaneous resolution of control equations and static equations.

Kobayashi discusses kinematic problems for articulated hands. He presents the necessary condition for grasping an object securely and for handling it freely. He also analyzes handling force and grasping force based on the principle of virtual work. By taking into account the expected external forces during the task, the most suitable posture is determined. Experimental results with a three-finger hand of twelve joints are shown.

Jacobsen et al. present the Utah/MIT dexterous hand, which is designed to maximize two characteristics: generality of operation and high performance. The finger is five to eight times faster than a human finger and generates approximately the same force levels as its natural counterpart. Its joint impedance is adjustable over a wide range, and the system is well behaved, even with the use of only a simple control system. Structures of the finger possess adequate room for the addition of sensor systems. Most important, it appears that this dexterous hand can become an important tool for the investigation of complex artificial manipulation.

6 Mobile Robots

Raibert's previous work resulted in a set of simple algorithms that control one-legged systems that balance as they hop on one leg. This year, he explores the generalization of the one-leg algorithms for the control of systems with several legs. The generalization is simple for the one-foot, a class of running gaits that sequences the support legs one at a time. Sutherland's idea of a virtual leg is used to reduce the gaits that employ the legs in pairs—the trot, the pace, and the bound—into virtual biped one-foot gaits. The symmetry of stepping is used to understand more complicated gaits, like the gallop and the canter.

Miura et al. report on the design concepts and construction of a four-legged robot developed for research into the dynamic walk of the quadruped. They argue the necessity for a real-time multitasking language to implement various sensor-action interactions and describe the control oriented language (COL), which supports concurrent processing, process status control, priority control, shared variables, feedback/feedforward control, and so on, in real time.

Hirose et al. discuss the comparison of walking machines with wheeled vehicles used for moving vehicles that travel on uneven ground. They also discuss the number of legs and the morphology of legs in relation to moving efficiency. Then they report on the mechanism, control system, and basic actions of the quadruped walking vehicle TITAN III.

Tachi and Komoriya present the design concept of the guide dog robot MELDOG, developed to enhance mobility for blind people. They describe the navigation method using an organized map and landmarks, an obstacle detection/avoidance system based on the ultrasonic environment measurement, and man-machine communication via an electrocutaneous stimulation system.

Ooka et al. report on an integrated intelligent robot consisting of a vision system, two arms, and a four-legged vehicle. The vision system has special circuits that can detect the edge lines from a gray level image within 200 milliseconds, and it can recognize the shapes of objects and measure the distances to them with a laser scanner. The locomotion system is a four-legged vehicle that can keep static balance walking slowly.

Tsuji describes model-guided monitoring of an inside building environment by a mobile robot. Prior knowledge of the environment is used as an a priori world model and constraints for image analysis. The world model is arranged in a hierarchy with three levels so as to provide coarse to fine structure of the environment. In preliminary experiments, a mobile platform with a television camera is driven around passages along a given route and reports the environment's changes to a human operator. It stops every few meters, takes pictures, and finds correspondences between line features detected in the image and those in the image model generated from the workspace model. Matched lines are further examined to detect changes in the scene.

IV Task Level Studies

7 Modelling, Programming, and Monitoring

Ambler discusses robotics and solid modelling. Conventional solid modelling systems are concerned with single, static objects. The essence of robotics involves moving things around and bringing objects into contact with each other. Robotic applications and, in particular, robot programming systems are therefore likely to require additional information from the solid modelling system. In programming a robot system, we shall be interested in questions of stability of structures, freedom to move in particular directions, and restrictions in others. We also need to take account of uncertainty, in both shape and position. As well as being able to represent this uncertainty in a usable way, coping with it could imply the use of sensors. Predicting and interpreting the information gathered from sensors involves novel use of solid modellers.

Mobile robots sense their environment and receive error-laden readings. They try to move a certain distance and in a certain direction, and do so only approximately. Rather than try to engineer these problems away, it may be possible, and may be necessary, to develop map-making and navigation algorithms that explicitly represent these uncertainties, but still provide robust performance. Brooks combines and extends two aspects of his previous work: the freeway representation for free space and explicit symbolic reasoning about uncertain quantities. A plausible new design for a mobile robot map-making and navigation system is developed. The key idea is to use a relational map, which is rubbery and stretchy, rather than try to place observations in a two-dimensional (2D) coordinate system.

Latombe et al. present the LM robot programming system, providing support for developing and debugging programs. The system includes a textual programming language, in both compile and interactive modes, augmented by program-by-showing utilities. It also incorporates a graphic simulator, which can be used both to debug and assess existing programs and to develop new ones. An extension to the programming language makes possible what they call geometric programming of robots, using a CAD data base. A motion planner is also available for computing complex trajectories described by symbolic equations.

The execution of a task by an advanced multisensor robot must be carefully monitored in order to take into account unexpected changes in the environment, uncertainties in the world model, and inaccuracies in the sensors and effectors. Ghallab reports on the design of a robot execution monitor using a rule-based system, together with a compiler that transforms the costly procedure of rule evaluation and chaining into a single traversal of a decision network. From an initial set of production rules whose antecedents are a conjunction of propositions, the proposed compiler suppresses the rules with only a "deduction" and transforms the remaining rules into a set of complete decision rules, which is subsequently translated into an optimized decision network.

Jarvis describes a semantic-free low-level approach to scene modelling for robotic vision and collision-free trajectory planning. Multiple silhouette and color image projections are used to create a space occupancy and surface colored model in a three-dimensional (3D) voxel array. 3D connectivity analysis separates the distinct object group in the scene. For each group, intensity/color-based segmentation needs only to contend with local variations to isolate individually discernible objects, each of which is as yet unrecognized. 3D distance transforms propagated from single or multiple goal points through unoccupied space provide a distance "potential field."

Liegeois et al. present methodologies and software developed for analyzing robot performance. His work makes use of a CAD/CAM system, which allows designers and users of robots to evaluate geometric capabilities (such as workspaces and interferences with environmental objects), the static and dynamic forces/torques required to perform a given task, and the robot's behavior in the course of a continuous path or a point-to-point motion. The three-dimensional models of the mechanisms, the environment, and the tasks are entered interactively into the database by means of a light pen and a keyboard. The mathematical models required for the applications are automatically generated. The system allows easy communication with the geometric database of parts to be handled, welded, machined, and so on, and is able to generate inputs for robot programs.

8 Theory of Manipulation

Effective robotic manipulation requires an understanding of the underlying physical processes. We need to know how the different elements of a manipulator operation combine to give a desired effect, under what circumstances an operation is appropriate, and how to select and tailor an operation to fit the task. Mason describes the mechanics of "pushing," which is an important element in some manipulator operations, such as grasping, but which is also an operation in its own right, as when rearranging the furniture in your living room. Pushing is a complex process, whose outcome is unpredictable in most practical situations. Nonetheless, the results presented in his paper provide a theoretical basis sufficient for analyzing and planning pushing operations.

An important aspect of reasoning about the design, manufacture, and manipulation of physical objects concerns the motion of objects in contact. Hopcroft and Wilfong investigate such problems and prove a fundamental theorem concerning the motion of objects in contact. The simplest form of this theorem states that if two objects in contact can be moved to another configuration in which they are in contact, then there is a way to move them from the first configuration to the second configuration in such a way that the objects remain in contact throughout the motion. This result is proved when translation and rotation of objects are allowed. The problem of more generalized types of motion is also discussed. This study has obvious applications in compliant motion and in motion planning.

Yoshikawa proposes the concept of manipulability measure of robotic mechanisms, which is a measure of manipulating ability of robots in positioning and orienting end-effectors. Some properties of this measure are obtained, and the best posture of various types of manipulators as well as a four-degree-of-freedom finger are given from the viewpoint of this measure. It is found that these postures have some resemblance to those taken by human arms and fingers. He also analyzes a four-joint wrist mechanism with respect to its ability to orient the end-effector and develops a control algorithm for this redundant mechanism.

Masaru Uchiyama et al. discuss the use of the Jacobian as a performance index for manipulators from the kinematic and static viewpoints. The Jacobian is an index for the evaluation of manipulator dexterity at a point in the workspace. The index takes the least value at singular points where the manipulator loses the capability of moving in a certain direction and is least dexterous. The distribution of the index value in the whole workspace, which is visualized on a color graphics display, gives an overall understanding of the manipulator performance. As an example of the application of this performance index, optimal trajectory planning using the index is presented. The trajectories obtained for several cases, such as turning a crank, show that the method generates a kinematically reasonable trajectory.

V Panel Discussions

9 Robotics for Future Industry

One of the most promising fields of application for robotics is advanced manufacturing automation. A panel chaired by Umetani discusses various aspects of robotics for future industry. Morita presents the requirements and the design concepts for the factory automation system. Ejiri gives his views on the future direction for research and development of robotics based on the three essential robot capabilities: task understanding, vision, and automatic decision making. Sasano, in treating the current problems of the shipbuilding industry, is optimistic that it will be possible to automate various heavy work by the intensive use of robots. Kato reviews his experience in assembly automation in the electrical industry and stresses the importance of peripheral equipment mated with robots themselves succeeding in cost effective robotized assembly. A summary of the discussions is also presented.

10 Key Issues of Robotics Research

This panel, chaired by Roth, takes up key issues of robotics research. Binford considers key issues in vision, recognition, and inference rules motivated by mobile robots. Daniel and Davey present two key issues: off-line programming for robot sensors and measurement and control of flexible arms. Carlisle comments on the need to reduce the complexity of programming robots, because of sensors, multiple robots, parallel tasks, and so forth. Shirai introduces the key problems of robotics involved in the Jupiter Project, the Japanese National Project for advanced robotics. Giralt presents research trends in decisional and multisensory aspects of the third-generation robots. Again, a summary of the discussions is presented.

I VISUAL PERCEPTION

1 Representation and Recognition of Three-Dimensional Objects

DESCRIBING SURFACES

Michael Brady, Jean Ponce, Alan Yuille,

Artificial Intelligence Laboratory,
Massachusetts Institute of Technology

Haruo Asada

Toshiba Research and Development Center,
Kawasaki City, Kanagawa 210
Japan

This paper continues our work on visual representations of three-dimensional surfaces [Brady and Yuille 1984b]. The theoretical component of our work is a study of classes of surface curves as a source of constraint on the surface on which they lie, and as a basis for describing it. We analyse bounding contours, surface intersections, lines of curvature, and asymptotes. Our experimental work investigates whether the information suggested by our theoretical study can be computed reliably and efficiently. We demonstrate algorithms that compute lines of curvature of a (Gaussian smoothed) surface; determine planar patches and umbilic regions; extract axes of surfaces of revolution and tube surfaces. We report preliminary results on adapting the curvature primal sketch algorithms of Asada and Brady [1984] to detect and describe surface intersections.

1. Introduction

Recent work in Image Understanding [Ballard and Brown 1982, Brady 1982, Marr 1982] has centered on the development of modules that compute three-dimensional depth, or depth gradients. Such modules include: stereo [Grimson 1981, 1984, Mayhew 1983]; shape from shading [Ikeuchi and Horn 1981, 1984] and photometric stereo; shape from contour [Brady and Yuille 1984a, Witkin 1981, Barnard 1983, Barnard and Pentland 1983]; and shape from motion [Bruss and Horn 1983, Ullman 1978]. Other work has concentrated on shape from texture [Vilnrotter, Nevatia, and Price 1981]. In applying vision to robotics, range finding and structured light have been investigated as techniques for recovering depth directly [Agin 1972, Holland, Rossol, and Ward 1979, Bolles, Horaud, and Hannah 1984, Faugeras et. al. 1982, 1984, Porter and Mundy 1982, 1984, Tsuji and Asada 1984] Although the work referred to in this paragraph is currently largely experimental, it is clear that robust, efficient, practical three-dimensional vision systems will soon be available.

Several authors have suggested that the output of these "shape from" processes is a representation(s) that makes explicit the surface depth $z(x,y)$ or the local surface normal $n(x,y)$. Barrow and Tenenbaum [1978] call such a representation an "intrinsic image", which emphasises that the representation has the same lack of structure as an image. Just as applications of two-dimensional vision depend upon the development of rich representations of shape (for example, Brady and Asada [1984]), so will applications of three-dimensional vision.

The representation that we are developing employs a hierarchy of descriptors from differential geometry. We may, for example, find a region of umbilic points that indicates that part of the surface is spherical. If there is a line of curvature or an asymptote that is planar or whose associated curvature (principal curvature or geodesic curvature respectively) is constant, then it is made explicit. We may associate a description with a curve that is a surface intersection; but only if it has an important property such as being planar. Figure 1 illustrates the representation of a lightbulb that can be computed by the algorithms described below. The stem of the lightbulb is cylindrical because it is ruled and because it is a surface of revolution. We can compute the axis of the stem. The bulb is a connected region of umbilic points, so it is part of a sphere. The stem is smoothly joined to the bulb.

In the next two sections we report recent theoretical developments and computational experiments. The theoretical component of our work is a study of classes of surface curves as a source of constraint on the surface on which they lie, and as a basis for describing it. We analyse bounding contours, surface intersections, lines of curvature, and asymptotes. Our experimental work investigates whether the information suggested by our theoretical study can be computed reliably and efficiently. We demonstrate algorithms that compute lines of curvature of a (Gaussian smoothed) surface; determine planar patches and umbilic regions; extract axes of surfaces of revolution and tube surfaces. We report preliminary results on adapting the curvature primal sketch algorithms of Asada and Brady [1984] to detect and describe surface intersections. The experimental results appear to contradict statements by a number of authors to the effect that second differential quantities such as lines of curvature cannot be computed reliably.

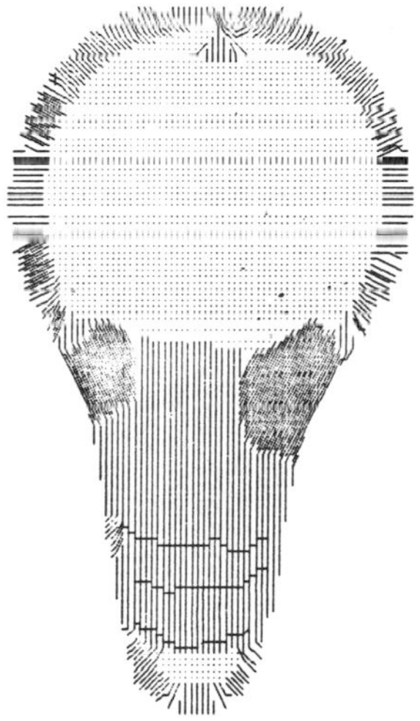

Figure 1. The representation of a lightbulb. The dotted region consists of umbilic points, indicating that the bulb is spherical. The parallel lines are the meridians of the cylindrical stem. The parallels, which are also rulings, are not shown. The significant surface changes are shown. They indicate the smooth join between the bulb and the stem and between the stem and the threaded end.

2. Surface curves

2.1. Introduction

A surprising amount can be learned about a surface from certain curves that lie upon it. Our theoretical work is an investigation of classes of surface curves as a source of constraint on the geometry of the surface and as a basis for description of the surface. The curves that we have studied are: bounding contours [Koenderinck and van Doorn 1982, Koenderinck 1984, Marr 1977, Barrow and Tenenbaum 1978, 1981, Binford 1982]; lines of curvature [Stevens 1982, 1983, Brady and Yuille 1984b]; asymptotes [Brady and Yuille 1984b]; and surface intersections [Binford 1982].

We begin by discussing (extremal) bounding contours of a surface, where the surface normal turns smoothly away from the viewer. First, we recall that the surface normal can be determined from its (orthographic) projection. Then we present a new proof of a recent result due to Koenderinck [1984] which states that the sign of the Gaussian curvature of the surface at points along the boundary curve is the same as the sign of the curvature of the projection of the boundary curve. We extend the result and show that, in general, points on the projection of an extremal boundary where the curvature is zero typically correspond to points on the surface that are locally flat (that is, where both principal curvatures are zero), or the boundary is locally aligned with a surface line of curvature whose curvature is zero. We suggest that these results may provide an alternative to line labelling for interpreting line drawings of curved objects.

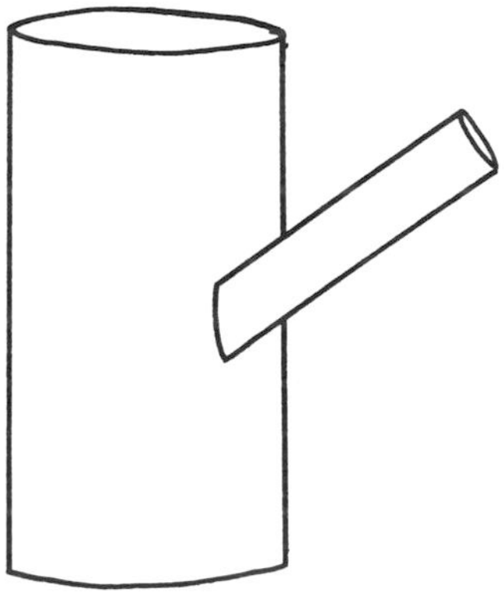

Figure 2. The curve that is the intersection of the two cylinders is not a line of curvature of either cylinder

The bounding contours of a surface are either extremal or they mark discontinuities of some order C_n. Depth discontinuities of type C_0 typically occur at occluding boundaries. Most surface intersections are of type C_1. Smooth joins are C_2 discontinuities that can only be perceived if the curvature in a direction orthogonal to the join changes substantially. Asada and Brady [1984] discuss the analogous situation for planar curves. A Theorem of Joachimsthal [Weatherburn 1927, page 68] implies that surfaces rarely intersect along their lines of curvature. The intersection of the two cylinders in Figure 2 is *not* a line of curvature of either surface.

The problem of detecting, localizing, and describing the discontinuities of a surface is analogous to computing the Primal Sketch representation for images [Marr 1976, Haralick 1983] and the Curvature Primal Sketch representation of the significant changes of curvature along planar curves [Asada and Brady 1984]. In Section 2.3, we show that Joachimsthal's Theorem can, under certain circumstances, be undone by Gaussian smoothing. More precisely, we prove:

Theorem Let $f(x, y, z)$ be a surface that is the cross product of a planar curve and a straight line. The lines of curvature of the convolution of f with a Gaussian are in the plane of the curve and parallel to the generating line.

The restriction that the straight line be orthogonal to the planar curve is severe and implies that the surface is cylindrical. We are investigating ways to weaken the assumption as part of our development of the Surface Primal Sketch.

In Sections 2.4 and 2.5 we turn our attention to curves that lie in the interior of the visible portion of the surface, though they may intersect its boundaries. At each point of the surface, we define a set of *intrinsic directions* $\theta_i(x, y)$ in which the surface change locally appears to be intrinsically important, and we associate a descriptor $\delta_i(x, y)$ with each such direction. The set of intrinsic directions that we have investigated so far consists of the directions of principal curvature, the asymptotic directions (directions in which the normal curvature is zero), and the parabolic directions, across which the sign of the Gaussian curvature changes. The corresponding descriptors $\delta_i(x, y)$ are the principal curvatures, and, for the asymptotes, the geodesic curvature. Currently, no descriptor is associated with parabolic directions. We may find it necessary to investigate additional intrinsically important directions in due course, though the directions of principal curvature, and asymptotic and parabolic directions suffice for a broad class of analytic surfaces that includes surfaces of revolution, ruled and developable surfaces, and generalized cones.

The directions and descriptors are *local* statements about the surface. For example, the directions of principal curvature give the locally flattest coordinate system intrinsic to the surface. We aim to describe the *larger scale* structure of the surface. Whereas local surface structure is thoroughly discussed in differential geometry, larger scale structure is not. To determine the larger scale structure of the surface, we link the local directions to form smooth curves. These curves are the lines of curvature, asymptotes, and parabolic lines of the surface, and they are discussed in Sections 2.4 and 2.5. We propose that these smooth curves are only made explicit when they satisfy additional constraints. Currently, these constraints are that either (i) the descriptors δ_i in the directions θ_i are (nearly) constant along the curve, or (ii) the curve is (nearly) planar. The need for constraints on the surface curves is illustrated in Figure 3, which shows the lines of curvature on an ellipsoid. Only three of the lines of curvature are planar, and they are the intersections of the symmetry planes of the ellipsoid with the surface. The surface is effectively described by these curves. We show how choosing a set of surface curves in this manner can automatically suggest a "natural parameterization" of a surface.

A surface curve is a geodesic if and only if its geodesic curvature is zero. A geodesic is planar if and only if it is a line of curvature. It follows that if the geodesic curvature is zero along a line of curvature then it is planar. However, planar lines of curvature are not necessarily geodesics, hence do not have zero geodesic curvature.

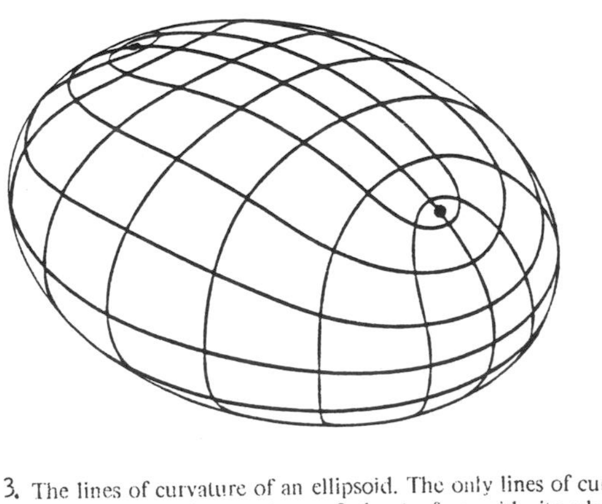

Figure 3. The lines of curvature of an ellipsoid. The only lines of curvature that are planar are the intersections of the surface with its planes of symmetry. Other lines of curvature do not seem to convey important information about the shape of the surface.

So requiring planarity is less severe than requiring that the curve be a geodesic. The more severe constraint is, however, an interesting subclass of curves.

Section 2.4 is mostly given over to proving a theorem about generalized cones, a theorem that relates surface curves to a volumetric representation proposed by Marr [1977]. Marr considered generalized cones [Brooks 1981, Brooks and Binford 1980] with straight axes. He suggested that such a generalized cone is effectively represented by (i) those cross sections, called *skeletons*, for which the expansion function attains an extreme value; and (ii) the tracings, called *flutings*, for which the cross-section function attains an extremum. (A tracing is the space curve formed by a point of the cross section contour as the cross section is drawn along the axis.) Figure 4 illustrates these terms. We prove the following Theorem:

Theorem If the axis of a generalized cone is planar, and the eccentricity of the cone is zero, then (i) a cross section is a line of curvature if and only if the cross section is a skeleton; and (ii) a tracing is a line of curvature if the generalized cone is a tube surface (the expansion function is a constant), or the tracing is a fluting.

The cone's eccentricity at a point is the angle between the tangent to the axis curve and the normal to the cross-section through that point. It follows that the flutings and skeletons of a (planar axis) generalized cone are implied by both consideration of surface curves and by Marr's considerations of volumetric representations. Lines of curvature that satisfy a large scale constraint, such as being planar, provide a natural basis for describing a surface. As is illustrated

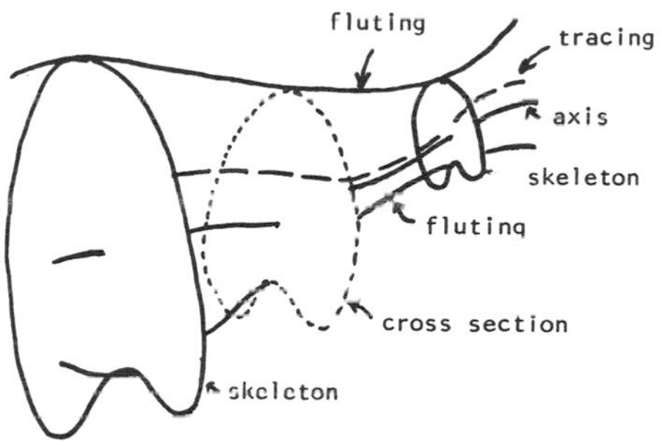

Figure 4. A generalized cylinder is formed by drawing a uniformly-expanding planar cross-section along a space curve.

by the ellipsoid shown in Figure 2, and generalized cones more generally, there may only be a small number of lines of curvature that satisfy the large scale constraints. Coupled to a suitable scheme for surface interpolation (for example, Terzopoulos [1984]), they may provide a natural parameterization of the surface. Brady and Yuille [1984b] call such a parameterization a *curvature patch* representation.

As we shall show in Section 2.5, however, lines of curvature are a poor basis for describing many surfaces. In particular, ruled surfaces are seldom usefully described in terms of their lines of curvature, which typically fail to satisfy the large scale constraints. In such cases, the rulings are a better basis for description. More generally, asymptotes are curves along which the normal curvature is zero. They are discussed in Section 2.4.

Section 3 reports some initial experiments on developing a *Surface Primal Sketch* representation of significant surface changes. Significant surface changes are found as follows. First, the surface is filtered with a Gaussian and its lines of curvature are found. These are projected into a plane and input to Asada and Brady's Curvature Primal Sketch program.

Parabolic lines are the smooth loci of parabolic points [Hilbert and Cohn Vossen 1952, pages 197 – 202]. Koenderinck's Theorem (re-proved in Section 2.2) suggests that parabolic points on extremal contours can be found. Figure 5 is reproduced from Hilbert and Cohn-Vossen [1952, page 197]. It shows the parabolic lines on the bust of the Apollo Belvidere. The footnote on page 198 of Hilbert and Cohn-Vossen has a familiar ring: "F. Klein used the parabolic curves for a peculiar investigation. To test his hypothesis that the artistic beauty of the face was based on certain mathematical relations,

Figure 5. Bust of the Apollo Belvidere with superimposed parabolic lines. (Reproduced from [Hilbert and Cohn-Vossen 1952, page 197])

he had all the parabolic curves marked out on the Apollo Belvidere, a statue renowned for the high degree of classical beauty portrayed in its features. But the curves did not possess a particularly simple form, nor did they follow any general law that could be discerned".

Consider, however, Figure 6a, which shows the regions of positive (white) and negative (black) Gaussian curvature on the surface of a lightbulb. The parabolic curves are planar and they mark smooth joins between significant parts, such as the bulb and stem. This suggests that, just like directions of curvature, a parabolic curve needs to satisfy additional large scale constraints in order to be made explicit by the visual system. The cross product (Figure 6b) of a straight line and a planar curve that is the smooth join of two curves whose (planar) curvatures have opposite signs (a smooth join in the terminology of Asada and Brady [1984]) is a simple surface that has a planar parabolic line. Asada and Brady point out that a smooth join is only perceivable if the difference between the curvatures of the flanking curves is sufficiently different. Few of the parabolic curves on the Apollo Belvidere have extended planar components. Those that do, such as the line on the forehead, are crossed by curves that do not have perceivable smooth joins. Two exceptions are the smooth join between the mouth and chin, and the smooth join between the nostril and the rest of the nose. In general, the Gaussian curvature is a divergence expression [Courant and Hilbert 1953, p. 196], which means that its Euler equation vanishes. Representations based on Gaussian curvature typically suppress spatial structure.

We omit analysis of certain classes of surface curve, particularly geodesics. There are at once too many geodesics, yet, in many cases, too few. There are too many since there is a geodesic through every point on a surface in every direction. The geodesics on a cylinder, for example, are all the helices $(R\cos\theta, R\sin\theta, k\theta)$, where R is the radius of the cylinder. On the other hand, only those meridians of a surface of revolution that are extrema of the surface width (skeletons, if it is thought of as a generalized cone) are geodesics. We have, moreover, proposed that to be made explicit, a surface curve must satisfy certain strong constraints. In particular, we would require a geodesic to be planar. However, if a geodesic is planar then it is a line of curvature [Weatherburn 1927, page 103].

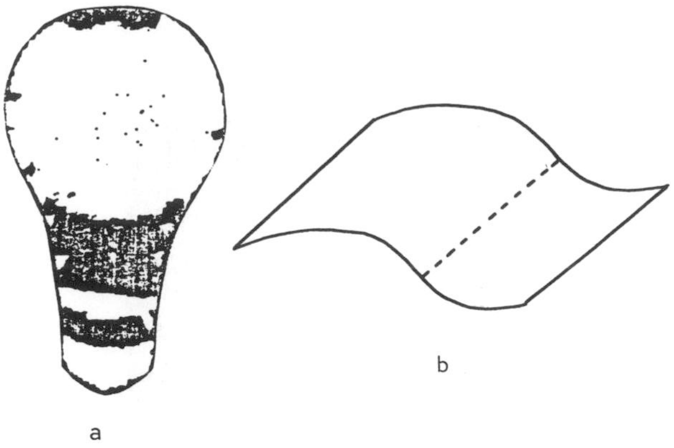

Figure 6. a. The parabolic curves on a lightbulb are the transitions from elliptic regions (white) to hyperbolic regions (black). b. The cross product of a planar curve with a smooth join and a straight line.

2.2. Bounding Contours

Barrow and Tenenbaum [1981] propose that there are two distinct types of contour that bound a surface, which they call *extremal* and *discontinuity*. At an extremal boundary, the surface normal turns away smoothly from the viewer. A discontinuity boundary marks the abrupt termination of a smooth surface, perhaps to intersect another surface (see Barrow and Tenenbaum [1981, Figure 3.1]). Since a discontinuity boundary could be produced by the edge of a ribbon that is oriented in an arbitrary direction, it is difficult to infer a great deal about the flanking smooth surface solely from the image of a discontinuity boundary. Brady and Yuille [1984a], Barnard and Pentland [1983], and Barrow and Tenenbaum [1981] offer some suggestions.

Extremal boundaries are a rich source of information. First, suppose that a surface $f(x, y, z) = 0$ is orthographically projected onto a plane whose normal is $\mathbf{k}$. Suppose that the surface has an extremal boundary, then its boundary rim curve contains $\mathbf{k}$ and lies in the tangent plane of the surface. That is, $\mathbf{k} \cdot \nabla f = 0$, which can be written $\mathbf{k} \cdot \mathbf{n} = 0$, where $\mathbf{n}$ is the local surface normal.

Let the boundary curve $\mathbf{r}(s)$ have tangent vector $\mathbf{T}(s) = d\mathbf{r}/ds$. Now $\mathbf{n}$ is orthogonal to both $\mathbf{k}$ and $\mathbf{T}$, from which it follows that $\mathbf{n}$ is parallel to $\mathbf{k} \times \mathbf{T}$. The image of the boundary curve is

$$\mathbf{r}_P(s_P) = \mathbf{k} \times (\mathbf{r} \times \mathbf{k}),$$

whose tangent is

$$\begin{aligned} \mathbf{T}_P &= \frac{d\mathbf{r}_P}{ds_P} \\ &= \mathbf{k} \times (\mathbf{T} \times \mathbf{k}) \frac{ds}{ds_P} \end{aligned} \qquad (1).$$

That is, the image of the tangent to the boundary curve is parallel to the tangent to the image. In fact, it is easy to see that

$$\frac{ds}{ds_P} = \{1 - (\mathbf{T} \cdot \mathbf{k})^2\}^{-\frac{1}{2}} \qquad (2).$$

Since the unit surface normal $\mathbf{n}$ is parallel to $\mathbf{k} \times \mathbf{T}$, it follows from Eqs. (1) and (2) that it is parallel to $\mathbf{k} \times \mathbf{T}_P$ and so the surface normal at an extremal boundary can be determined from the image if the (orthographic) viewing direction is known. This result is due to Barrow and Tenenbaum [1978].

An arbitrary curve parameterized by arclength s and lying on the surface satisfies (see, for example, [Millman and Parker 1977, page 103]):

$$\kappa(s)\mathbf{N}(s) = \kappa_n(s)\mathbf{n}(s) + \kappa_g(s)\mathbf{n} \times \mathbf{T}(s), \qquad (3)$$

where $\mathbf{T}$ and $\mathbf{N}$ are the tangent and normal to the curve (in the moving trihedron of the curve); κ is the curvature $|d\mathbf{T}/ds|$ of the curve; κ_n is the normal curvature of the curve, defined as the curvature of the curve that is the intersection of the surface and the plane that contains $\mathbf{n}$ and $\mathbf{T}$; and κ_g is called the geodesic curvature (Figure 7).

From now on, we restrict attention to the extremal boundary curve. Since $\mathbf{k} \cdot \mathbf{n} = 0$, Eq. 3 implies

$$\kappa \mathbf{N} \cdot \mathbf{k} = \kappa_g [\mathbf{k}, \mathbf{n}, \mathbf{T}],$$

where $[\ldots]$ indicates the triple scalar product. Since $\mathbf{k} \cdot \mathbf{n} = 0$ (and $\mathbf{n} \cdot \mathbf{T} = 0$), the triple scalar product is zero if and only if $\mathbf{k}$ coincides with $\mathbf{T}$. Similarly, $\mathbf{k} \cdot \mathbf{N}$ is zero if and only if $\mathbf{k}$ is parallel either to the tangent $\mathbf{T}$ or to the binormal $\mathbf{B}$. General position assumptions show that they are rarely zero. It follows that

$$\kappa = 0 \text{ if and only if } \kappa_g = 0. \qquad (4)$$

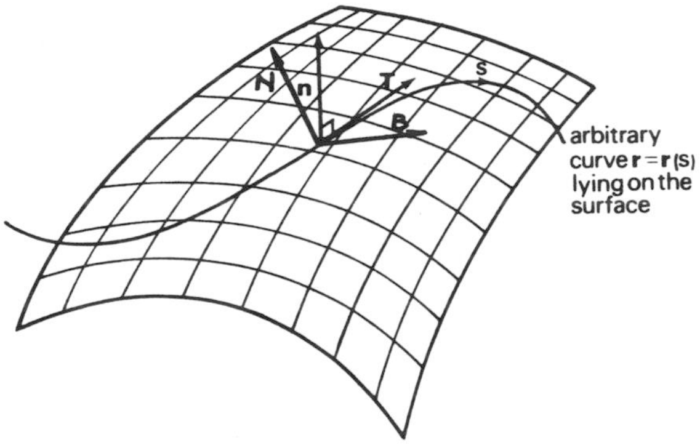

Figure 7. A curve lying on a surface. The vectors $\mathbf{T}, \mathbf{N}, \mathbf{B}$ are the moving trihedron of the curve, whose curvature is κ. The surface normal is $\mathbf{n}$.

Squaring Eq. 3 yields

$$\kappa^2 = \kappa_n^2 + \kappa_g^2. \qquad (5)$$

It follows that if $\kappa = 0$ then $\kappa_n = \kappa_g = 0$, and if $\kappa_g = 0$, then by Eq. 4, in general, $\kappa = 0$, and $\kappa_n = 0$. It is easy to show (see Appendix A) that

$$\kappa_P^2 = \frac{\{1 - (\mathbf{T} \cdot \mathbf{k})^2 - (\mathbf{N} \cdot \mathbf{k})^2\}}{\{1 - (\mathbf{T} \cdot \mathbf{k})^2\}^3} \kappa^2. \qquad (6)$$

where κ_P is the curvature of the projected curve $\mathbf{r}_P(s_P)$. It follows that, in general,

$$\kappa_P = 0 \text{ if and only if } \kappa = 0. \qquad (7)$$

We can now present a new proof of a recent result due to Koenderinck [1984] that relates the curvature κ_P of the projection of the boundary curve to the Gaussian curvature κ_G of the surface. The key is to choose an appropriate parameterization of the surface at a point on the boundary curve (Figure 8). Define the radial curve at a point on the boundary to be the (normal) intersection of the surface with the plane that contains the surface normal $\mathbf{n}$ and the view vector $\mathbf{k}$. Let the radial curve be parameterized by u, and denote points along the radial curve by $\mathbf{r}_r(u)$. Using s and u to parameterize the surface in the neighborhood of a point on the boundary, we find the first and second fundamental forms of the surface:

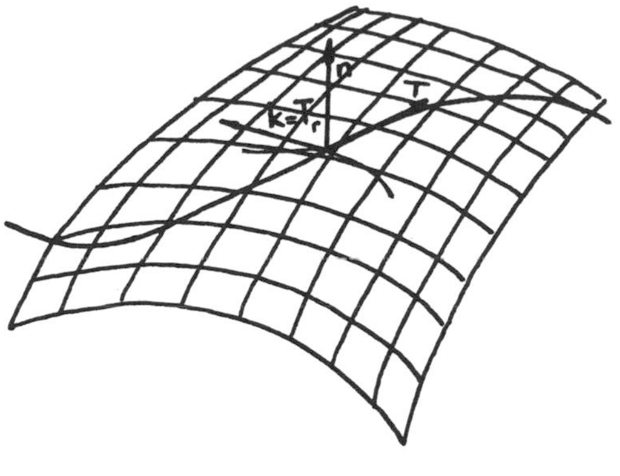

Figure 8. The rim and radial coordinate frame. The radial curve is the intersection of the surface and the plane that contains the view vector and the surface normal. The boundary curve defines the other parameter.

$$G = \begin{bmatrix} 1 & \mathbf{T}\cdot\mathbf{T}_r \\ \mathbf{T}\cdot\mathbf{T}_r & 1 \end{bmatrix}$$
$$D = \begin{bmatrix} \kappa_r \mathbf{n}\cdot\mathbf{N}_r & \mathbf{n}\cdot\frac{\partial^2\mathbf{r}}{\partial s\partial u} \\ \mathbf{n}\cdot\frac{\partial^2\mathbf{r}}{\partial s\partial u} & \kappa\mathbf{n}\cdot\mathbf{N} \end{bmatrix}, \tag{8}$$

where κ_r is the curvature of the radial curve. In order for the boundary rim to be visible, κ_r must be positive.

Note that, in general, $\mathbf{T}\cdot\mathbf{T}_r \neq 0$. Since the tangent $\mathbf{T}_r$ to the radial curve $\mathbf{r}_r$ lies in the plane spanned by both $\mathbf{k}$ and $\mathbf{n}$ (remembering that we are considering a boundary curve), and is in the surface tangent plane, we have

$$\mathbf{T}_r = \mathbf{k}, \text{ and } \mathbf{N}_r = \mathbf{n}. \tag{9}$$

It follows that $\mathbf{T}_r$ is constant along the boundary curve, so that

$$\begin{aligned} 0 &= \frac{\partial \mathbf{T}_r}{\partial s} \\ &= \frac{\partial^2 \mathbf{r}}{\partial u \partial s}. \end{aligned} \tag{10}$$

The second fundamental form reduces by Eqs. 9 and 10 to

$$D = \begin{bmatrix} \kappa_r & 0 \\ 0 & \kappa\mathbf{n}\cdot\mathbf{N} \end{bmatrix}. \tag{11}$$

Since

$$\mathbf{n} = \frac{\mathbf{k}\times\mathbf{T}}{\{1-(\mathbf{k}\cdot\mathbf{T})^2\}^{\frac{1}{2}}},$$

we find

$$\begin{aligned} \mathbf{n}\cdot\mathbf{N} &= \frac{[\mathbf{k},\mathbf{T},\mathbf{N}]}{\{1-(\mathbf{k}\cdot\mathbf{T})^2\}^{\frac{1}{2}}}, \\ &= \frac{\{1-(\mathbf{k}\cdot\mathbf{T})^2-(\mathbf{k}\cdot\mathbf{N})^2\}^{\frac{1}{2}}}{\{1-(\mathbf{k}\cdot\mathbf{T})^2\}^{\frac{1}{2}}}. \end{aligned}$$

The Gaussian curvature κ_G of the surface at points along extremal boundaries is given by [Faux and Pratt 1979, page 112]

$$\begin{aligned} \kappa_G &= \frac{|D|}{|G|} \\ &= \frac{\kappa_r\kappa\mathbf{n}\cdot\mathbf{N}}{1-(\mathbf{T}\cdot\mathbf{k})^2} \\ &= \kappa_r\kappa\frac{\{1-(\mathbf{k}\cdot\mathbf{T})^2-(\mathbf{k}\cdot\mathbf{N})^2\}^{\frac{1}{2}}}{\{1-(\mathbf{k}\cdot\mathbf{T})^2\}^{\frac{3}{2}}} \end{aligned} \tag{12}$$

It finally follows from Eq. 6 that

$$\kappa_G = \kappa_r\kappa_P \tag{13}.$$

Since κ_r is always positive, *the sign of the Gaussian curvature of the surface at points along the boundary curve is the same as the sign of the curvature of the projection of the boundary curve.* [Koenderinck 1984].

We can prove a slight extension to Koenderinck's result. If κ_P is zero, then the Gaussian curvature κ_G is zero. Also, recall from Eq. 6 that if κ_P is zero then (in general) the curvature κ of the boundary curve is also zero. It follows from Eq. 5 that the normal curvature κ_n of the boundary curve is also zero. Denote the principal curvatures at the surface point by κ_1, κ_2. The Gaussian curvature $\kappa_G = \kappa_1\kappa_2$ is zero, and so at least one of κ_1, κ_2 is zero. But, by Euler's theorem,

$$\kappa_n = \kappa_1\cos^2\theta + \kappa_2\sin^2\theta,$$

and so $\kappa_1 = \kappa_2 = 0$ or θ is zero or $\pi/2$. That is, points on the projection of an extremal boundary where the curvature κ_P is zero typically correspond to surface points that are locally flat, that is, where both principal curvatures are zero, or the boundary is locally aligned with a surface line of curvature whose curvature is zero.

We have assumed that it is possible to determine which bounding contours are extremal and which mark discontinuities. This is a reasonable assumption in the case of dense surface data such as that used in the experiments reported in the next section.

Figure 9. A line drawing that is perceived as the curved surface of a sail.

It is much more difficult in the case of line drawings such as that shown in Figure 9. Barrow and Tenenbaum [1981] propose that line labelling can suffice to make the distinction. We suggest that the results derived in this section hint at a more general approach that is based on an analysis of the surfaces meeting at a corner. For example, if the smooth contour curves are all extremal then the Gaussian curvature would be positive along the curve with positive curvature and negative along the curves with negative curvature. This would imply that the surface changes the sign of its Gaussian curvature. But there are no surface markings or other evidence that it does. A more parsimonious assumption is that the surface has the same (positive) Gaussian curvature everywhere, and hence that the contour curves with negative curvature are discontinuities. This is, in fact, what is perceived.

We can derive further results about the relationships between surface curves and the surface. For example, the sign of the normal curvature along the boundary rim can be determined from its projection [Yuille and Brady 1984]

2.3. Surface Intersections

In this Section, we prove the following Theorem:

Theorem The Gaussian convolution of a cylindrical surface is cylindrical. In more detail, let $f(x, y, z)$ be a surface that is the cross product of a planar curve and a straight line. The lines of curvature of the convolution of f with a Gaussian are in the plane of the curve and parallel to the generating line.

We begin with a Lemma, whose proof is simple and is omitted.

Lemma Let $\mathbf{r}(x, y) = x\mathbf{i} + y\mathbf{j} + f(x)\mathbf{k}$ be a cross product surface consisting of parallel instances of a curve $f(x)$ in the $x - z$ plane. The principal curvatures and directions of $\mathbf{r}(x, y)$ are zero in the y direction and the curvature of f in the $x - z$ plane.

Proof of Theorem. We assume that the surface has the form of the Lemma. Since the Gaussian is separable, the convolution of the surface is

$$G_\sigma(r) * f(x) = G_\sigma(y) * (G_\sigma(x) * f(x)).$$

By the derivative theorem for convolutions, it follows that

$$\{G_\sigma(r) * f(x)\}^{(n)} = G_\sigma(y) * \{G_\sigma(x) * f(x)\}^{(n)}.$$

Convolution with a constant is simply multiplication by a constant, and so the principal curvatures of $G_\sigma(r) * f(x)$ are the same as the principal curvatures of $G_\sigma(x) * f(x)$, which are given by the Lemma.

The Lemma can be extended straightforwardly to show that the Gaussian convolution of a surface of the form $z = f(x)(A + By)$ is a similar surface $z = (G_\sigma * f(x))(A + By)$ but the lines of curvature are not preserved.

2.4. Lines of Curvature

Brady and Yuille [1984b] argue that, in many cases, the lines of curvature give a natural parameterization of a surface. One practical advantage is that a computer-aided design (CAD) patch representation based on lines of curvature avoids problems of local flattening of the surface. Stevens [1982, 1983] has studied drawings consisting of a repeated pattern of "parallel" planar curves and the curved surfaces they suggest. He proposes that the given curves are often interpreted as lines of curvature of the perceived surface.

In Section 2.1 we noted that a line of curvature has to satisfy additional constraint if it is to be made explicit. For example, only the planar lines of curvature of the ellipsoid shown in Figure 2 are useful for describing the surface.

Consider a surface of revolution. Suppose that the axis is aligned with the $z-$ axis. The surface is formed by rotating the (one-parameter) curve $p(u)\mathbf{i} + z(u)\mathbf{k}$ about $\mathbf{k}$. The surface is

$$\mathbf{r}(u, \theta) = p(u)\cos\theta\mathbf{i} + p(u)\sin\theta\mathbf{j} + z(u)\mathbf{k}.$$

The principal curvatures (see for example Millman and Parker [1977, p86]) are the meridians and the parallels, all of which are planar. In addition, the parallels are circular, so the curvature along any one of them is constant. The curvature along a parallel is $\mathbf{n}^T\mathbf{r}^*/p(u)$, where $\mathbf{r}^* = [\cos\theta \; \sin\theta \; 0]^T$. The foreshortening of the expected curvature $p(u)$ exemplifies Meusnier's theorem [Weatherburn 1927]. On the other hand, the asymptotes on a surface of revolution are, in general, complex space curves and the geodesic curvature is a complex function of position along the asymptote.

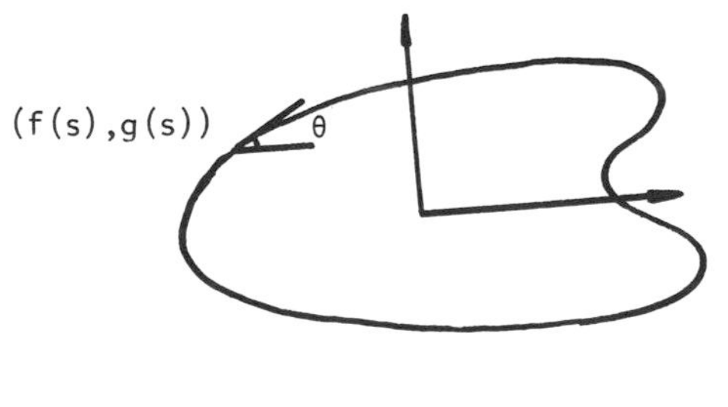

Figure 10. A planar cross-section curve

Surfaces of revolution are essentially one-dimensional in that their shape is completely determined by a planar curve. It is reasonable to ask whether lines of curvature are more generally useful. The theorem stated in Section 2.1 shows that they are. We first prove the theorem for the straight axis case originally studied by Marr [1977], relegating the more general case to Appendix B.

Theorem 2 If the axis of a generalized cone is straight, and the axis is normal to the cross-section, then (i) a cross-section is a line of curvature if and only if it is a skeleton; (ii) a tracing is a line of curvature if and only if it is a fluting.

Proof. To fix notation, we begin by analyzing a planar cross section (Figure 10). The curve is $(f(s), g(s))$, where s denotes arclength, and so its *radial distance* from the origin is given by

$$d^2(s) = f^2 + g^2. \tag{14}$$

Differentiating Eq. 14 with respect to arc length gives

$$\dot{d} = \frac{f\dot{f} + g\dot{g}}{d}. \tag{15}$$

Thus the radial distance attains an extremum where the numerator of Eq. 15 is zero. Now consider the orientation θ of the tangent to the curve.

$$\begin{aligned} \tan\theta &= \frac{\dot{g}}{\dot{f}}, \\ \sec^2\theta\dot{\theta} &= \frac{\dot{f}\ddot{g} - \dot{g}\ddot{f}}{\dot{f}^2}, \\ \cos^2\theta &= \frac{\dot{f}^2}{\dot{f}^2 + \dot{g}^2}, \\ \dot{\theta} &= \frac{\dot{f}\ddot{g} - \dot{g}\ddot{f}}{l^2}, \end{aligned} \tag{16}$$

where $l^2(s) = \dot{f}^2 + \dot{g}^2$. Notice that $\dot{\theta}$ is the curvature of the cross section curve.

We are now ready to prove the Theorem. Suppose, without loss of generality, that the straight axis of the cone is $\mathbf{k}$. Let the cross-section be $f(s)\mathbf{i} + g(s)\mathbf{j}$, as above. Suppose the expansion function is $h(z)$, and assume that the eccentricity of the cone is zero, that is, the axis is normal to the cross-section. The generalized cone is

$$\mathbf{r}(s, z) = h(z)f(s)\mathbf{i} + h(z)g(s)\mathbf{j} + z\mathbf{k}.$$

To save on notation, we suppress parameters. We find

$$\begin{aligned} \frac{\partial\mathbf{r}}{\partial s} &= [h\dot{f}, h\dot{g}, 0]^t \\ \frac{\partial\mathbf{r}}{\partial z} &= [\dot{h}f, \dot{h}g, 1]^t \end{aligned},$$

(where $[\ldots]^t$ denotes the vector that is the transpose of the given row vector) and so the first fundamental form of the surface is (using the notation introduced above)

$$\mathbf{G} = \begin{bmatrix} h^2l^2 & h\dot{h}d\dot{d} \\ h\dot{h}d\dot{d} & 1 + \dot{h}^2d^2 \end{bmatrix}.$$

The surface unit normal $\mathbf{n}$ is parallel to $\mathbf{h} = [h\dot{g}, -h\dot{f}, h\dot{h}(\dot{f}g - f\dot{g})]^t$. The second fundamental form of the surface is

$$\mathbf{D} = \begin{bmatrix} \frac{1}{|\mathbf{h}|}h^2(\ddot{f}\dot{g} - \dot{f}\ddot{g}) & 0 \\ 0 & \frac{1}{|\mathbf{h}|}h\ddot{h}(f\dot{g} - \dot{f}g) \end{bmatrix}.$$

The principal directions of curvature are the eigenvectors of the matrix $G^{-1}D$, and this matrix is diagonal if and only if

$$\frac{dh}{dz}\frac{dd}{ds} = 0,$$

from which the result follows.

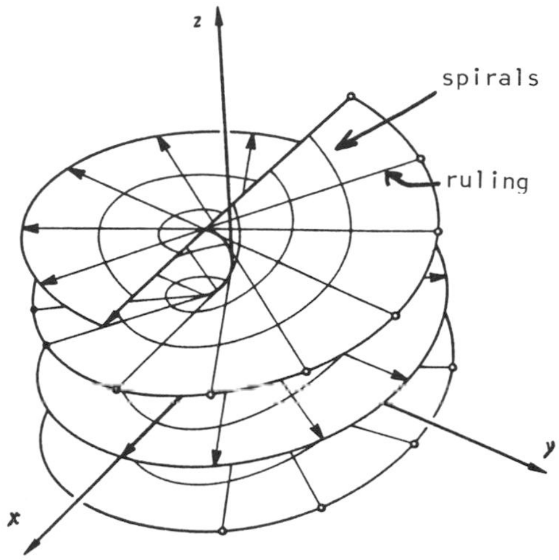

Figure 11. The helicoid of a single blade. (Reproduced from [do Carmo 1976, Figure 2-27 Page 94])

2.5. Asymptotes

We begin with an example that illustrates that lines of curvature are not always the best basis for describing a surface. Consider a helicoid of a single blade (Figure 11), which can be parameterized as follows

$$\mathbf{r}(l, \theta) = [l \cos \theta, l \sin \theta, m\theta]^t.$$

Denoting $\sqrt{l^2 + m^2}$ by d^2, and m/l by $\tan \psi$, we find

$$\mathbf{r}_l = [\cos \theta, \sin \theta, 0]^t$$
$$\mathbf{r}_\theta = [-l \sin \theta, l \cos \theta, m]^t$$
$$\mathbf{n} = [\sin \theta \sin \psi, -\cos \theta \sin \psi, \cos \psi]^t$$
$$\mathbf{G} = \begin{bmatrix} 1 & 0 \\ 0 & d^2 \end{bmatrix}$$
$$\mathbf{D} = \begin{bmatrix} 0 & -\frac{m}{d} \\ -\frac{m}{d} & 0 \end{bmatrix}$$

The principal directions of curvature are given by $\dot{l} = \pm d\dot{\theta}$, and the principal curvatures are $\pm m/d^2$. Since the parameter l varies in the principal directions, so does m, hence so does the principal curvature. It is easy to show that the lines of curvature are not planar.

Notice that the diagonal of $\mathbf{D}$ is zero. It follows that the normal curvature in the directions of the tangent vectors $\mathbf{r}_l$, $\mathbf{r}_\theta$ is zero. These are the asymptotes, and they correspond to the rulings and spirals that make up the helicoid. The geodesic curvature along the spirals is simply the curvature of the spiral considered as a curve. The geodesic curvature of the ruling is zero. (It is a curious fact that the lines of curvature cut the asymptotes at a constant angle of $\pi/4$.)

In general, ruled surfaces are poorly described by their lines of curvature. Examples such as the helicoid and the surface $z = kxy$ suggest that the asymptotes may be a better basis for description. The asymptotic direction can be found from Euler's theorem if the principal curvatures have opposite signs, that is, the Gaussian curvature is negative. Note that a given ruled surface may be generated by more than one set of rulings. Also, it is possible for a ruled surface to admit a significantly different description. For example, the hyperboloid $x^2 + y^2 - z^2 = 1$ is both a ruled surface and a surface of revolution.

In general, a ruled surface can be parameterized in the form

$$\mathbf{r}(s, t) = \mathbf{u}(s) + t\mathbf{w}(s),$$

where $\mathbf{u}$ is a curve called the directrix, and $\mathbf{w}(s)$ is the set of rulings. The theory of ruled surfaces emphasises a unique curve, called the line of striction, that lies in the surface and is orthogonal to the $\mathbf{w}'$. It is not clear what role, if any, it plays in perception.

The normal to a ruled surface is parallel to

$$\mathbf{u}' \times \mathbf{w} + t\mathbf{w}' \times \mathbf{w},$$

and varies with t along the ruling. The normal direction is constant along a ruling if and only if $\mathbf{n} \cdot \mathbf{u}'$ is constant, which is if and only if the triple scalar product $[\mathbf{u}', \mathbf{w}', \mathbf{w}]$ is zero. Along such rulings, the determinant of the second fundamental form $\mathbf{D}$ is zero, and this in turn implies that the Gaussian curvature κ_G is zero. If this condition holds for all rulings on a ruled surface, the surface is called developable and the Gaussian curvature is everywhere zero. Informally, a surface is developable if it can be rolled out flat onto a plane. For such surfaces the rulings are both asymptotes and lines of curvature. For developable surfaces, the descriptive bases of Sections 2.4 and 2.5 coincide.

3. Computational Experiments

In this Section we report on a number of computational experiments that investigate whether the surface curves and regions proposed by our theoretical analysis can be computed reliably and efficiently. The input to our programs are mostly (dense) depth maps obtained by the structured light systems at MIT [Brou 1984] and INRIA [Faugeras et. al. 1983]. Both systems are accurate to about $0.5mm$. The objects that we have worked with include: a bottle, an egg, a sphere, a styrofoam cup, a lightbulb, and a pen (all surfaces of revolution); a telephone handset (surface intersections and an approximately ruled surface); a coffee mug with a handle, a plastic container, a hammer, and a Renault part [Faugeras et. al. 1983] (complex surfaces with surface intersections). We have also conducted experiments with artificial data to which controlled amounts of noise has been added.

3.1. Gaussian Smoothing

Depth maps generated by structured light systems are noisy, as are image surfaces. In recent years, Gaussian smoothing filters have been extensively investigated for early processing of images. For example, Marr and Hildreth [1980] suggest Laplacian of a Gaussian filters $\nabla^2 G_\sigma$ for edge finding. These filters are closely approximated by difference-of-Gaussian (DOG) filters that can be efficiently implemented. Poggio and Torre [1984] and Canny [1983] have suggested directional edge finders whose first step is Gaussian smoothing.

Witkin [1983] has proposed *scale-space filtering* in which a (one-dimensional) signal is filtered at a variety of spatial scales to produce a hierarchical description. Witkin suggests that it is possible to automatically determine a discrete set of "natural scales" at which to describe a signal symbolically. Witkin's scale space representation is a ternary tree of zero crossings of G''_σ. He did not attempt to *interpret* the multiple descriptions in terms of primitive events. Asada and Brady [1984] have shown how scale space filtering can be used to generate a symbolic description of the significant curvature changes along a planar contour.

Yuille and Poggio [1983a] have provided some theoretical underpinning for the scale space representation. They have shown that the contour of zero crossings of second derivatives ("fingerprint") may preserve enough information to reconstruct the original signal to within a constant scale factor. They also show [Yuille and Poggio 1983b] that a Gaussian filter is essentially unique in having the property that zero crossings are not introduced as one moves to coarser scales.

In view of this background with images, the first processing stage of our program is Gaussian smoothing. Initially, we applied the

Gaussian filter at every surface point $z(x, y)$. This is unsatisfactory as it smooths across the depth discontinuities that are the bounding contours of an object (Figure 12b). This is an advantage in edge detection; but a disadvantage in smoothing within a given region. In our experimental data, the depth discontinuities are sharp and easy to find before smoothing. It is difficult to prevent smoothing across discontinuities with a straightforward implementation of Gaussians using convolution masks. It is particularly difficult when the distance between opposite sides of a surface is roughly the same size as the footprint of the convolution mask as it typically is in our data.

We appeal to the central-limit theorem and implement Gaussian filtering using repeated averaging with the 3×3 mask shown in Figure 13a (see Burt [1981, 1983]). Iterating n times approximately corresponds to filtering with a Gaussian whose standard deviation is proportional to $\sqrt{n}$. To prevent smoothing across previously marked depth discontinuities, we use the technique of computational molecules proposed by Terzopoulos [1983] in his application of finite-element techniques to surface reconstruction. In more detail, the mask shown in Figure 13a is viewed as the sum of the four

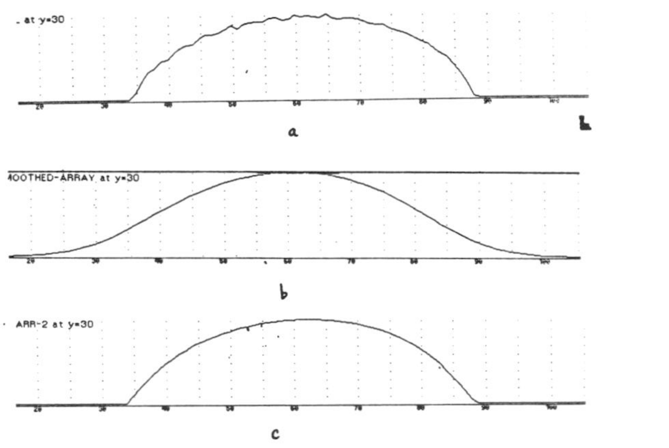

Figure 12. a. Raw data from a cross section of an oil bottle after scanning using the INRIA system. b. Smoothing across surface boundaries with a Gaussian mask that is applied everywhere. c. Gaussian smoothing using repeated averaging and computational molecules.

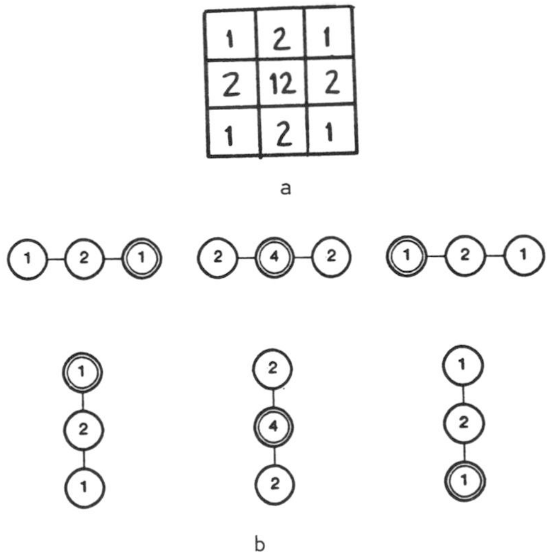

Figure 13. Gaussian smoothing. a. The 3×3 mask that is repeatedly applied to approximate Gaussian filtering. b. The computational molecules whose sum is the mask shown in a.

molecules shown in Figure 13b. To apply the filter to a surface point, only those molecules that do not overlap the set of points marked as discontinuities are used. Figure 12c shows the result of Gaussian smoothing using repeated averaging and computational molecules.

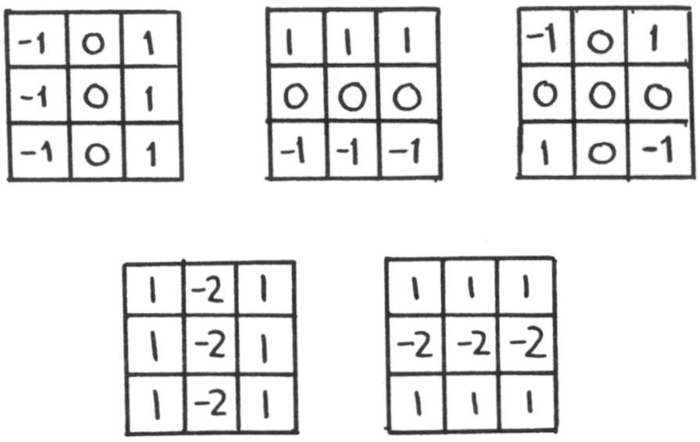

Figure 14. Operators used to estimate first and second derivatives of the Gaussian smoothed surface.

3.2. Lines of Curvature

Suppose that the (Gaussian smoothed) surface is $z(x, y)$. Its first and second derivatives can be estimated using the facet model [Haralick 1980]. We derived the finite difference operators shown in Figure 14 by least squares fitting a quadratic to a 3×3 facet of the surface. Although these operators are sensitive to noise in raw image or surface data, they perform well after Gaussian smoothing.

From these estimates we can compute the fundamental forms of the surface [Millman and Parker 1977, Faux and Pratt 1979]. The first fundamental form is:

$$G = \begin{bmatrix} \mathbf{z}_x^2 & \mathbf{z}_x \cdot \mathbf{z}_y \\ \mathbf{z}_x \cdot \mathbf{z}_y & \mathbf{z}_y^2 \end{bmatrix} = \begin{bmatrix} 1 + p^2 & pq \\ pq & 1 + q^2 \end{bmatrix} = \begin{bmatrix} g_{11} & g_{12} \\ g_{12} & g_{22} \end{bmatrix}$$

where p is the z component of $\mathbf{z}_x$ and q is the z component of $\mathbf{z}_y$. Similarly, the second fundamental form is:

$$D = \begin{bmatrix} \mathbf{n} \cdot \mathbf{z}_{xx} & \mathbf{n} \cdot \mathbf{z}_{xy} \\ \mathbf{n} \cdot \mathbf{z}_{xy} & \mathbf{n} \cdot \mathbf{z}_{yy} \end{bmatrix} = \begin{bmatrix} d_{11} & d_{12} \\ d_{12} & d_{22} \end{bmatrix}$$

where $\mathbf{n}$ is the unit surface normal. The (tangent) principal directions are the solutions of the quadratic equation [Faux and Pratt 1979]:

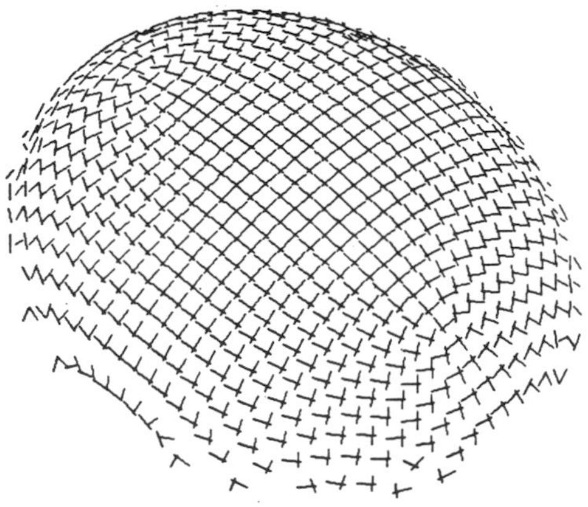

Figure 15. The orthographic projections of the principal directions of curvature for an ellipsoid.

$$(d_{12}g_{22} - d_{22}g_{12})\frac{dy}{dx}^2 + (d_{11}g_{22} - d_{22}g_{11})\frac{dy}{dx} + (d_{11}g_{12} - d_{12}g_{11}) = 0.$$

Suppose that $\lambda = dy/dx$ is a tangent principal direction. Then the unit vector lying in the surface tangent plane in the principal direction is parallel to

$$\mathbf{t} = [1, \lambda, p + q\lambda]^t.$$

By Euler's theorem, the surface tangent vectors $\mathbf{t}_{max}$ and $\mathbf{t}_{min}$ in the principal directions are orthogonal. Of course, their (orthographic) projections onto the plane $z = 0$ are not orthogonal, as Figure 15 shows.

The surface curvatures in the principal directions are the roots of the quadratic [Faux and Pratt 1979, page 112]:

$$|\mathbf{G}|\kappa^2 + (g_{11}d_{22} + g_{22}d_{11} - 2g_{12}d_{12})\kappa + |\mathbf{D}| = 0.$$

The curvature values can be used to extract planar patches of a surface and regions that consist entirely of umbilic points. To find planar patches, for example, we have adopted the simple approach of requiring the absolute values of both principal curvatures to be below a small threshold. Figure 16a shows the planar patches found by this technique for a Renault part used in experiments by Faugeras and his colleagues at INRIA. Faugeras et. al. [1982, 1984] have investigated a variety of techniques that exploit special properties of planes. Figure 16b shows the planes computed by the INRIA

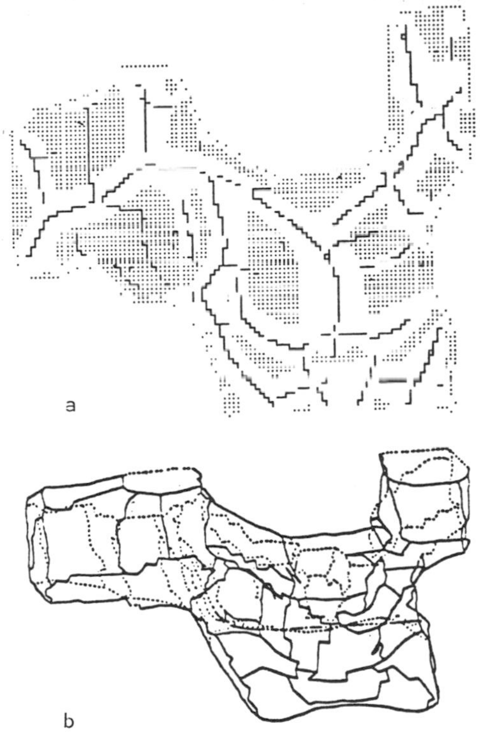

Figure 16. a. Planar patches on the Renault part found by simply requiring the absolute values of both principal curvatures to be below a threshold. b. The planar patches on the same part found by the INRIA group. (Reproduced from [Faugeras et. al. 1984, page 432])

group for the Renault part. The two methods appear to be equally effective.

A point is umbilic if its principal curvatures are equal. The principal curvatures define a best fitting ellipsoid in the local neighborhood of a surface point. In the case of an umbilic point, the ellipsoid is a sphere. To determine umbilic points, we simply require that

$$\frac{|\kappa_1| - |\kappa_2|}{\max(|\kappa_1|, |\kappa_2|)}$$

is less than a threshold. Figure 1 shows a region of umbilic points found for the lightbulb. It is well-known (for example, do Carmo [1976, page 147 proposition 4]) that if all the points of a connected surface are umbilic, then the surface is either contained in a sphere or in a plane. Since the curvatures are non-zero, the connected region that is the bulb of the lightbulb is a portion of a sphere.

In order to extract the lines of curvature, the directions at the individual surface points need to be linked. This is more difficult than linking zero crossings to form an edge for example since the principal directions form a dense set. Figure 17 shows that lines of curvature cannot be extracted by simply choosing the eight-connected neighbor with the nearest direction after projection onto $z = 0$.

Instead, linking is based on the vectors $\mathbf{t}_{max}(x, y)$ in the surface tangent plane. Initially, each point (x, y) can potentially link to its eight-connected neighbors. As the program proceeds, neighbors

Figure 17. A swirling pattern of principal directions shows that lines of curvature cannot be extracted by simply choosing the eight-connected neighbor with the nearest direction after projection onto $z = 0$. The direction closest to the point marked A is at the point marked B, but C is more consistent with global judgments.

become inhibited as they are linked to other points. The program conducts a breadth-first search. At each iteration, the point (x, y) for which a *closeness* evaluation function is minimized is chosen. If its minimizing neighbor is part of a growing line of curvature, (x, y) extends it, otherwise a new line of curvature is started. In either case, neighbors that are not minimizing inhibit their link to (x, y). The closeness function that is currently used is the sum of three dot products involving principal vectors at neighboring points in the surface tangent plane:

$$\begin{aligned} c(x_1, y_1, x_2, y_2) &= \mathbf{t}(x_1, y_1) \cdot \mathbf{t}(x_2, y_2) \\ &+ \mathbf{t}(x_1, y_1) \cdot \mathbf{r}(x_1, y_1, x_2, y_2), \\ &+ \mathbf{t}(x_2, y_2) \cdot \mathbf{r}(x_1, y_1, x_2, y_2) \end{aligned}$$

where $\mathbf{r}(x_1, y_1, x_2, y_2) = \mathbf{r}(x_1, y_1) - \mathbf{r}(x_2, y_2)$. Other evaluation functions could have used the curvature values as well as their directions, but we have not found this to be necessary. Figure 18 shows the lines of curvature found by the algorithm for a coffee cup and an oil bottle. The program gives similarly good results on all our test objects. Note that because of discretization it is possible for all the neighbors of a point to become inhibited before it is selected. Hence some points may not lie on the lines of curvature computed by the program.

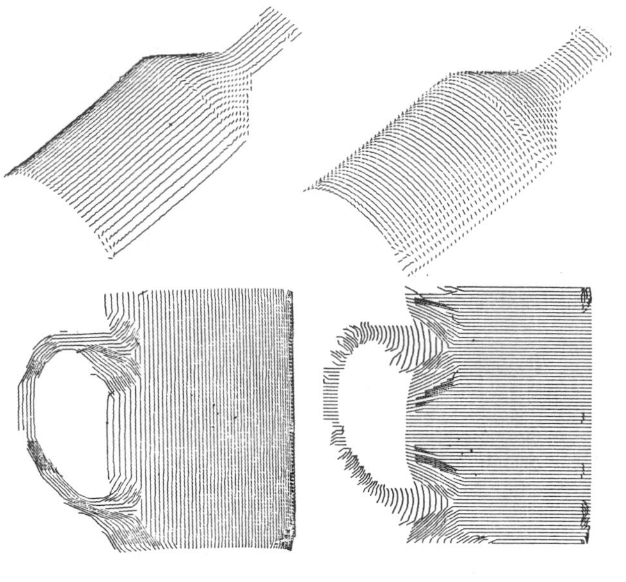

Figure 18. Linked lines of curvature found for an oil bottle and a coffee mug.

3.3. Using lines of curvature

Earlier, we showed that lines of curvature that are planar, or along which the principal curvature is constant, are important for describing surfaces. Given a linked list of surfaces points forming a line of curvature, we can determine the best fitting plane. If the set is $\{(x_i, y_i, a_i) \mid 1 \leq i \leq n\}$, then the least-squares fitting plane $ax + by + cz + d = 0$ is determined from a solution of

$$\begin{bmatrix} \operatorname{var}(x) & \operatorname{cov}(x,y) & \operatorname{cov}(x,z) \\ \operatorname{cov}(x,y) & \operatorname{var}(y) & \operatorname{cov}(y,z) \\ \operatorname{cov}(x,z) & \operatorname{cov}(y,z) & \operatorname{var}(z) \end{bmatrix} \begin{bmatrix} a \\ b \\ c \end{bmatrix} = 0,$$

where $\operatorname{var}(x)$ is the variance of the x_i's, and $\operatorname{cov}(x, y)$ the covariance of the x_i and y_i. We can determine whether a given population of points is planar by examining the condition number of the covariance matrix (compare Brady and Asada [1984, pages 341 – 342]). Similarly, we can compute the best fitting circle to a line of curvature and determine whether the population lies on that circle. Figure 19a shows the best fitting circles computed for the lines of curvature that are the parallels of a cup. Figure 19b shows the axis that is the locus of the centers of the circles in Figure 19a.

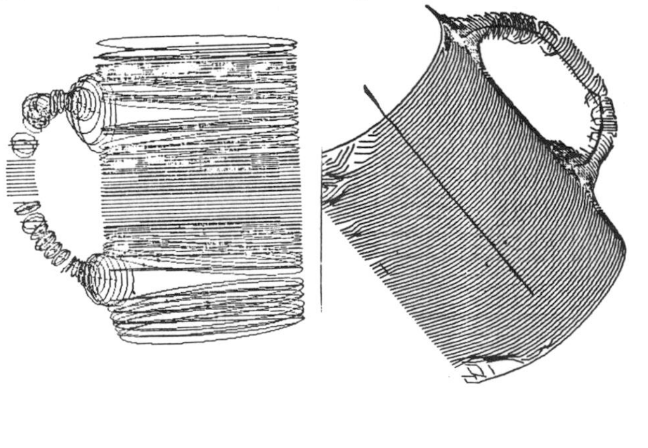

Figure 19. a. The best fitting circles to the parallels of the cup. b. the axis that is the locus of the centers of the best fitting circles shown in a.

We need to determine the significant discontinuities in a surface. The result would be a *Surface Primal Sketch* analogous to Marr's [1976] intensity change Primal Sketch (for image surfaces) and Asada and Brady's [1984] Curvature Primal Sketch for significant curvature changes along planar contours. In each case, the problem is to *detect* all significant changes, *localize* those changes as accurately as possible, and to *symbolically describe* the change. Yuille and Poggio [1983a, 1983b] have proved that, in principle, scale space filtering enables a discontinuity to be accurately localized. Canny [1983] uses the smallest scale at which a given intensity change can be detected to most accurately localize it. Figure 20 shows the surface intersections of a telephone handset found by a program described below after the surface has first been smoothed at a variety of scales. The increasing localization of the surface intersection flanking the elongated portion of the surface can be clearly seen. Canny's [1983] claim that signal to noise increases proportional to the scale of the filter can also be seen. We are currently working to integrate these separate descriptions to yield a single description.

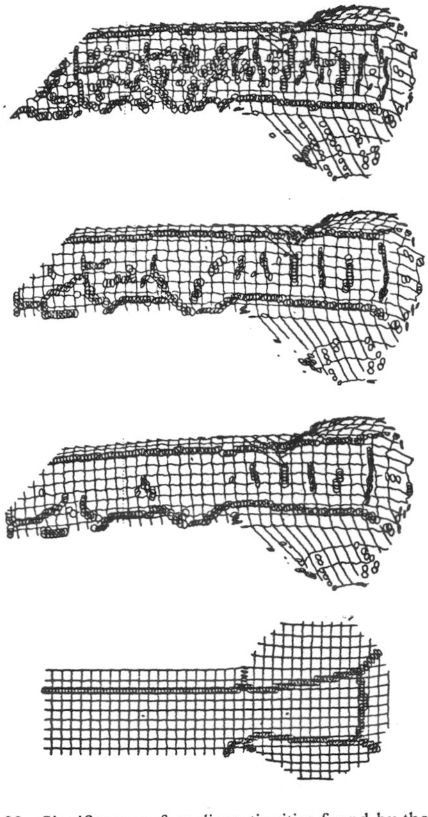

Figure 20. Significant surface discontinuities found by the curvature primal sketch program at multiple scales. The input to the program is the lines of curvature computed at each scale. The scales shown are 20, 40, 60, and 80

Earlier, we noted a theorem by Joachimsthal that shows that surfaces rarely intersect along their lines of curvature. We also showed that Gaussian smoothing overcomes this problem. So long as the curvature of the curve of intersection is small compared to the Gaussian filter, the lines of curvature of the smoothed surface lie parallel and perpendicular to the locus of curvature maxima of the smoothed surface. Asada and Brady [1983] filter a planar contour at multiple scales to detect, localize, and describe the significant changes in curvature. As an initial experiment, we have applied the curvature primal sketch program to lines of curvature after they have been projected into their best fitting plane. The results encourage us to extend the Asada and Brady program to two-dimensions. Figures 20 and 21 show some of the surface intersections found by this method.

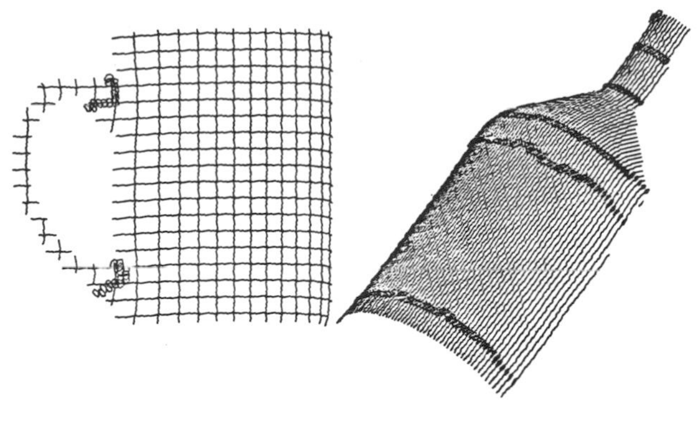

Figure 21. Surface intersections found by the curvature primal sketch program applied to lines of curvature after they have been projected into their best fitting plane.

4. Acknowledgements

This report describes research done at the Artificial Intelligence Laboratory of the Massachusetts Institute of Technology. Support for the Laboratory's Artificial Intelligence research is provided in part by the the System Development Foundation, the Advanced Research Projects Agency of the Department of Defense under Office of Naval Research contract N00014-75-C-0643, and the Office of Naval Research under contract number N00014-80-C-050. We thank several people have commented on the ideas presented in this paper, particularly Brian Barsky, Tom Binford, Jean-Daniel Boissonat, Philippe Brou, Olivier Faugeras, Eric Grimson, Berthold Horn, Joe Mundy, Tommy Poggio, Demetri Terzopoulos, and Shimon Ullman. We are indebted to Olivier Faugeras and the INRIA group for giving us access to their ranging system. More especially, we appreciate the exchange of ideas, results, and personnel with INRIA. Steve Bagley, Margaret Fleck, and Eric Grimson made valuable comments on drafts of this paper.

5. Appendix A

We derive Equation 6.

$$\begin{aligned}\kappa_P^2 &= \left(\frac{d\mathrm{T}_P}{ds_P}\right)^2 \\ &= \left(\frac{ds}{ds_P}\right)^2 \left(\frac{d}{ds}\frac{\mathbf{k}\times(\mathrm{T}\times\mathbf{k})}{\{1-(\mathrm{T}\cdot\mathbf{k})^2\}^{\frac{1}{2}}}\right)^2 \\ &= \left(\frac{ds}{ds_P}\right)^2 \frac{\{1-(\mathrm{T}\cdot\mathbf{k})^2-(\mathrm{N}\cdot\mathbf{k})^2\}}{\{1-(\mathrm{T}\cdot\mathbf{k})^2\}^2}\kappa^2\end{aligned}$$

and the result follows from Eq. 2.

6. Appendix B: The Generalized Cone Theorem

We prove a more general form of the Theorem proved in Section 2.3. We relax the condition of the Theorem to planar axes. As before, we assume that the eccentricity of the generalized cone is zero, so that the tangent to the axis curve is normal to the cross section. Without this assumption, the proof becomes quite complex.

Theorem If the axis of a generalized cone is planar, and the eccentricity of the cone is zero, then (i) a cross section is a line of curvature if either the generalized cone is a surface of revolution or the cross section is an extremum; and (ii) a tracing is a line of curvature if the generalized cone is a *tube surface* (the expansion function is a constant), or the tracing is a fluting.

Proof. Denote the Frenet-Serret moving trihedron of the axis curve by $(\mathrm{T}, \mathrm{N}, \mathrm{B})$. Since the axis is planar it has zero torsion, which simplifies the Frenet-Serret formulae:

$$\frac{d\mathrm{T}}{dt} = \kappa\mathrm{N}, \text{ and } \frac{d\mathrm{N}}{dt} = -\kappa\mathrm{T} \qquad (B2.1)$$

Note that the binormal B is constant, being the unit normal to the plane of the axis. Since the eccentricity of the cone is assumed to be zero, the tangent T to the axis is normal to the cross-section, which has N and B as a basis. Let the axis of the cone be $\mathbf{a}(t)$, where t is arclength, and let the expansion function be $h(t)$. As in Section 2.3, suppose that the cross-section is given by $f(s)\mathrm{N} + g(s)\mathrm{B}$. The generalized cone is defined to be

$$\mathbf{r}(s,t) = \mathbf{a}(t) + h(t)\{f(s)\mathrm{N} + g(s)\mathrm{B}\}. \qquad (B2.2)$$

The analysis proceeds as in Section 2.3. The first fundamental form is

$$\mathrm{G} = \begin{bmatrix} h^2 l^2 & h\dot{h}d\dot{d} \\ h\dot{h}d\dot{d} & \dot{h}^2 d^2 + (1-\kappa h f)^2 \end{bmatrix}.$$

As expected, this reduces to the expression in Section 2.3 in the case $\kappa = 0$. The second fundamental form hints at the complexity of the most general case, when the axis is not restricted to lie in a plane:

$$\mathrm{D} = \begin{bmatrix} \frac{1}{|\mathbf{n}|}d_{11} & \frac{1}{|\mathbf{n}|}d_{12} \\ \frac{1}{|\mathbf{n}|}d_{12} & \frac{1}{|\mathbf{n}|}d_{22} \end{bmatrix},$$

where

$$\begin{aligned} d_{11} &= h^2(\dot{f}\ddot{g} - \ddot{f}\dot{g})(1-\kappa h f) \\ d_{12} &= -\kappa h^2 \dot{f}\dot{h}(\dot{f}g - f\dot{g}) \\ d_{22} &= h\ddot{h}(\dot{f}g - f\dot{g})(1-\kappa h f) \\ &\quad - (1-\kappa h f)^2 h\kappa\dot{g} \\ &\quad f\dot{h}(\dot{f}g - f\dot{g})(\dot{\kappa}h + 2\kappa\dot{h}) \end{aligned} \qquad (B2.3)$$

We establish the result as before.

References

Agin, G. J, [1972], Representation and description of curved objects, Stanford University, AIM-73.

Asada, Haruo and Michael Brady, [1984], The curvature primal sketch, MIT Artificial Intelligence Laboratory, AIM-758.

Ballard, D. H., and Brown, C. M, [1982], *Computer Vision*, Prentice-Hall.

Barnard, S,"Interpeting perspective images," *Artificial Intelligence.*

Barnard, S., and Pentland, Alex P, [1983], Three-dimensional shape from line drawings, Proc. 8th Int. Jt. Conf. Artif. Intell., Karlsruehe, 1061 – 1063.

Barrow, H. G., and Tenenbaum, J. M, [1978], Recovering intrinsic scene characteristics from images, *Computer vision systems* Riseman, E. M., and Hanson, A. (eds). Academic, 3 – 26.

Barrow, H. G., and Tenenbaum, J. M, [1981], "Interpreting line drawings as three-dimensional surfaces," *Artif. Intell.*, 17, 75 – 116.

Binford, T. O, [1982], "Inferring surfaces from images," *Artificial Intelligence*, 17, 205 – 245.

Bolles, Robert C., Horaud, Patrice, and Hannah, Marsha Jo, [1984], 3DPO: a three-dimensional parts orientation system, *First International Symposium on Robotics Research* Brady, Michael, and Paul Richard (eds). MIT Press, 413 – 424.

Brady, Michael, [1982], "Computational approaches to image understanding," *Computing surveys*, **14**, 3 - 71.

Brady, Michael, and Asada, Haruo, [1984], "Smoothed local symmetries and their implementation," *Int. J. Robotics Research*, **3 (3).**

Brady, Michael, and Yuille, Alan,"An extremum principle for shape from contour," *IEEE Patt. Anal. and Mach. Int.*, **PAMI-6.**

Brady, Michael, and Alan Yuille, [1984b], Representing three-dimensional shape, Romansy Conf., Udine, Italy.

Brooks, R.A, [1981], "Symbolic Reasoning Among 3-D Models and 2D Images," *Artificial Intelligence*, 17, 285-348.

Brooks, R. A., and Binford, T. O, [1980], Representing and reasoning about partially specified scenes, *Proc. Image Understanding workshop* Baumann Lee S. (ed)., Science Applications Inc., 95 - 103.

Brou, P, [1984], "Finding the orientation of objects in vector maps," *Int. J. Rob. Res.*, **3 (4).**

Bruss, A., and Horn, B. K. P, [1983], "Passive navigation," *Comp. V. Graph. and Im. Proc.*, **21**, 3-20.

Burt, Peter J, [1981], "Fast filter transforms for image processing," *Comp. Graph. and Im. Proc.*, **16**, 20 – 51.

Burt, Peter J, [1983], "Fast algorithms for estimating local image properties," *Comp. Graph. and Im. Proc.*, **21**, 368 – 382.

Canny, John Francis, [1983], "Finding Edges and Lines in Images," *MIT Artificial Intelligence Lab. TR-720.*

Courant R., and Hilbert D, [1953], *Methods of mathematical physics*, John Wiley Interscience, New York.

Do Carmo, Manfredo P, [1976], *Differential Geometry of Curves and Surfaces*, Prentice-Hall, Englewood Cliffs, NJ.

Faugeras, O. D., *et. al*, **[1982],** Towards a flexible vision system, *Robot vision*, ed. Pugh, Alan, IFS, UK.

Faugeras, O. D., *et. al*, **[1984],** Object representation, identification, and positioning from range data, *First International Symposium on Robotics Research* Brady, Michael, and Paul Richard (eds). MIT Press, 425 – 446.

Faux, I. D., and Pratt, M. J, [1979], *Computational Geometry for Design and Manufacture*, Ellis Horwood, Chichester.

Grimson, W. E. L, [1981], *From Images to Surfaces: a Computational Study of the Human Early Visual System*, MIT Press, Cambridge.

Grimson, W. E. L, [1984], Computational experiments with a feature based stereo algorithm, MIT Artificial Intelligence Laboratory, AIM-762.

Haralick, R. M, [1980], "Edge and region analysis for digital image data," *Comp. Graph. and Im. Proc.*, **12**, 60 – 73.

Haralick, R. M, Watson, Layne T., and Laffey, Thomas J, [1983], "The topographic primal sketch," *Int. J. Robotics Res.*, **2**, 50 – 71.

Hilbert, D., and Cohn .Vossen, S., [1952], *Geometry and the Imagination*, Chelsea, New York.

Holland, Steven W., Rossol, L., and Ward, Mitchell R, [1979], CONSIGHT 1: a vision controlled robot system for transferring parts from belt conveyors, *Computer vision and sensor based robots* eds. Dodd, G. and Rossol, L. Plenum Press.

Ikeuchi, K., and Horn, B. K. P, [1981], "Numerical shape from shading and occluding boundaries," *Artificial Intelligence*, **17**, 141- 185.

Ikeuchi, Katsushi, Horn, B. K. P., et. al., [1984], Picking up an object from a pile of objects, *First International Symposium on Robotics Research* Brady, Michael, and Paul Richard (eds). MIT Press, 139 – 162.

Koenderinck, Jan J, [1984], What tells us the contour about solid shape?, Dept. Medical and Physiol. Physics, Univ. Utrecht, Netherlands.

Koenderinck, Jan J., and van Doorn, Andrea J, [1982], "The shape of smooth objects and the way contours end," *Perception*, **11**, 129 – 137.

Marr, D, [1977], "Analysis of occluding contour," *Proc. R. Soc. Lond. B*, **197**, 441 - 475.

Marr, D, [1982], *Vision*, Freeman.

Mayhew, J, [1983], Stereopsis, *Physical and Biological Processing of Images*, Braddick, O. J., and Sleigh, A. C.(eds.), Springer, New York, 204 – 216.

Millman, Richard S., and Parker, George D, [1977], *Elements of Differential Geometry*, Prentice-Hall.

Porter, G., and Mundy, J, [1982], Non-contact profile sensor system for visual inspections, *Robot Vision*, Rosenfeld A. (ed.), Proc. SPIE, 67 – 76.

Porter, G. B., and Mundy, J. L, [1984], A model-driven visual inspection module, *First International Symposium on Robotics Research* Brady, Michael, and Paul Richard (eds). MIT Press, 371 – 388.

Stevens, K. A, [1982], "The visual interpretation of surface contours," *Artificial Intelligence*, 17, 47 – 73.

Stevens, K. A, [1982], The line of curvature constraint and the interpretation of 3-D shape from parallel surface contours, Proc. 8th Int. Jt. Conf. Artif. Intell., Karlsruehe, 1057 – 1061.

Terzopoulos, D, [1983], "The role of constraints and discontinuities in visible-surface reconstruction," *Proc. 7th Int. Jt. Conf. Artif. Intell., Karlsruehe*, 1073 - 1077.

Terzopoulos, D, [1984], The Computation of Visible Surface Representations, MIT, Artif. Intell. Lab..

Tsuji, S., and Asada, M, [1984], Understanding of three-dimensional motion in time-varying imagery, *First International Symposium on Robotics Research* Brady, Michael, and Paul Richard (eds). MIT Press, 465 – 474.

Ullman, S, [1978], *The Interpretation of Visual Motion*, MIT Press, Cambridge Mass..

Vilnrotter, F., Nevatia, R., and Price, K. E, [1981], Structural analysis of natural textures, *Proc. Image Understanding Workshop* Baumann L. S. (ed.), 61-68.

Witkin, A., [1981], "Recovering surface shape and orientation from texture," *Artificial Intelligence*, 17, 17 – 47.

Witkin, A., [1983], "Scale-Space Filtering," *Proc. 7th Int. Jt. Conf. Artif. Intell., Karlsruehe*, 1019 - 1021.

Yuille, A. L., and Brady, Michael, [1984], Surface information from boundary projections, MIT Artificial Intelligence Lab (forthcoming).

Yuille, A.L. and Poggio, T, [1983a], "Fingerprints Theorems for Zero-Crossings," *MIT Artificial Intelligence Laboratory AIM-730.*

Yuille, A.L. and Poggio, T, [1983b], "Scaling theorems for zero crossings," *MIT Artificial Intelligence Laboratory AIM-722.*

REGULAR PATTERN PROJECTION FOR SURFACE MEASUREMENT[1]

Kōkichi Sugihara, Kiyoshi Okazaki[2], Feng Kaihua[3], and Noboru Sugie

Department of Information Science,
Faculty of Engineering, Nagoya University,
Furo-cho, Chikusa-ku, Nagoya 464, Japan

A new method for recovering three-dimensional structures of surface from visual images is proposed. In this method, two-dimensional regular patterns such as circles and squares are actively projected onto the surface of objects, and apparent distortions of the projected patterns are used for the recovery of surface structures. When the patterns are projected by parallel rays of light, a local surface normal at each point on the surface is determined uniquely from a single image. When, on the other hand, the patterns are projected by radial rays of light, both a local surface normal and the associated range are determined from three images obtained by a fixed camera with three different positions of the light source.

1. Introduction

The principle most commonly utilized in robot vision is triangulation. This principle has been implemented mainly in two different types of systems, that is, the camera-camera type and the projector-camera type.

The camera-camera type is usually called stereo vision or binocular vision [Moravec, 1979], [Grimson, 1981]. Like human visual systems, two cameras are fixed mutually at some distance, and the object surface is observed from both the cameras. A three-dimensional position of each point on the surface is measured from the triangle formed by the two cameras and the surface point.

The most difficult problem in this type of implementation is to establish the correspondence between the two images obtained by the cameras, that is, each surface point that gives rise to some observable feature in one image should be identified in the other image in order to determine the triangle. Usually local features are not enough to find a correct correspondence, so that a variety of mechanisms have been proposed; for example, a hypothesis-and-test mechanism [Yasue and Shirai, 1973], parallel processing suggested by a neural network model [Sugie and Suwa, 1977], active projection of textured light for feature generation [Nishihara, 1981], [Aoki, Yachida and Tsuji, 1984], the use of the third camera for verification [Omori and Morishita, 1982], and the use of dynamic programming for elastic matching [Ohta, 1983]. The correspondence problem is nevertheless still time consuming.

The other type of implementation, the projector-camera type, aims at circumventing the correspondence problem. One of the two cameras is replaced with a light source, from which bright light is projected in a selected direction onto the surface of the objects. The image of the projected light on the surface is observed by the remaining camera, and thus the triangle is determined [Shirai and Suwa, 1971].

This type of the implementation can indeed provide a way to get around the correspondence problem, but it requires much more time for the data acquisition because many images should be obtained, one for each projecting direction, in order to measure the whole surface. If a spot light is projected, only one point is measured at a time, whereas if a slit light (i.e., the light passing through a narrow slit) is used, many points along a line can be measured at a time. Hence, the slit light is usually used [Shirai and Suwa, 1971], [Agin and Binford, 1976], [Sugihara, 1979], [Oshima and Shirai, 1983]; the spot light is used mainly for the random-access measurement such as on-line edge tracking [Ishii and Nagata, 1974]. Even if the slit light is used, the projected light must sweep the scene to get the data about the whole surface, and hence the data acquisition takes much time. More than one slit image can be obtained at a time if the projected light is coded appropriately [Mino, Kanade and Sakai, 1980], [Sato and Inokuchi, 1984]; we have to take only $\log_2 n$ images in order to detect the positions of the slits projected in $n-1$ different directions. However, this method still requires, for example, 8 images for the slits projected in 255 directions.

On the other hand, quite a different principle has also been used for the detection of surface structures from visual information, that is, the principle called 'shape from texture' [Kender, 1979]. If we have *a priori* knowledge about textures on the surface, we can recover the surface structure from a very few images. Only one image is enough for us to find local surface normals if the surface is covered with regular patterns [Kender, 1979], [Ikeuchi, 1980], [Kanade, 1981] or with statistically homogeneous textures [Witkin, 1981], and three images are enough if a reflectance map is known [Woodham, 1977], [Ikeuchi, 1981]. However, this principle can not be used so widely because it is based on the strong assumption that we have *a priori* knowledge about the surface texture or the surface reflectance.

However, we need not give up employing the shape-from-texture principle, because the principle will revive if we generate artificial texture. Thus, it seems natural to use a projector, just as we did in the triangulation, in order to generate surface texture actively so that the shape-from-texture principle may become applicable.

Indeed some methods in this direction have already been found. One typical method is grid coding [Will and Pennington, 1972] or moiré topography [Idesawa, Yatagai, and Soma, 1977], and another is the use of a taper beam light [Wei and Gini, 1983] or its software version [Inokuchi, Nita, Matsuda, and Sakurai, 1982]. However, the former method can detect only relative ranges, and the latter requires much time for data acquisition.

In this paper we present a new method for extracting three-dimensional structure of the object surface from images of actively projected regular patterns. In this method, known regular patterns are projected onto the surface so that artificial textures are generated. From only three images of these textures taken by a fixed camera, we can extract both the local surface normals and the ranges. Moreover, the method does not require any global computation; each pattern is processed locally and independently for the extraction of the three-dimensional structures.

We first show in Section 2 that local surface normals can be determined from single images of orthographically projected patterns. On the basis of this observation, we will point out in Section 3 that both the ranges and the surface normals can be determined from three images of perspectively projected patterns.

2. Surface Normals from Orthographically Projected Patterns

2.1. Method

Let S be a planar surface whose unit normal $\boldsymbol{n} = (a, b, c)$ is unknown. In order to measure the normal $\boldsymbol{n}$, we project some known patterns by parallel rays of light onto the surface and observe its image from another angle.

Let $\boldsymbol{p}$ be a known vector on a slide film (i.e., $\boldsymbol{p}$ is part of the pattern), $\boldsymbol{q}$ be its 'shadow' cast on the surface S by a slide projector facing in the direction $\boldsymbol{m}$, and $\boldsymbol{r}$ be an 'image' of $\boldsymbol{q}$ obtained by a camera situated in the direction $\boldsymbol{l}$, as are shown in Fig. 1 (let $\boldsymbol{m}$ and $\boldsymbol{l}$ be of the unit length). Hence we get

$$\boldsymbol{m} \cdot \boldsymbol{p} = 0, \tag{1}$$
$$\boldsymbol{n} \cdot \boldsymbol{q} = 0, \tag{2}$$

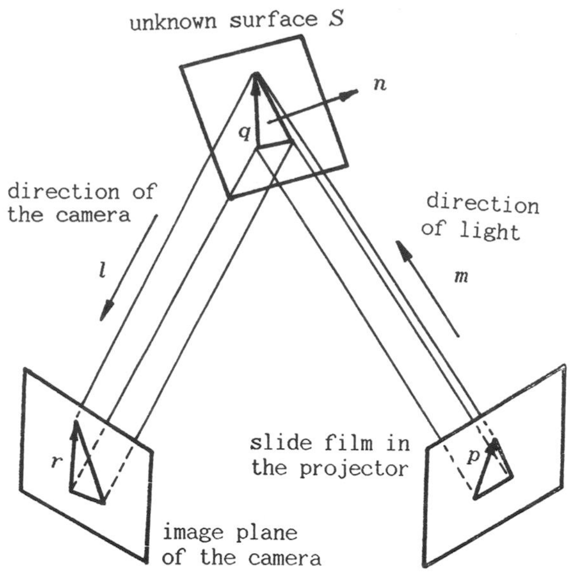

Fig. 1. Projector, surface, and a camera.

$$\boldsymbol{l} \cdot \boldsymbol{r} = 0. \tag{3}$$

Let us assume, furthermore, that the surface S is in large distance from both the projector and the camera, so that we can consider $\boldsymbol{q}$ and $\boldsymbol{r}$ as parallel projections of $\boldsymbol{p}$ and $\boldsymbol{q}$, respectively. Then, we get

$$\boldsymbol{q} = \boldsymbol{p} + t_1 \boldsymbol{m}, \tag{4}$$
$$\boldsymbol{r} = \boldsymbol{q} + t_2 \boldsymbol{l}, \tag{5}$$

where t_1 and t_2 are some reals. From (2) and (4) we get

$$\boldsymbol{n} \cdot \boldsymbol{p} + t_1 (\boldsymbol{n} \cdot \boldsymbol{m}) = 0$$

and consequently

$$\boldsymbol{q} = \boldsymbol{p} - \frac{\boldsymbol{n} \cdot \boldsymbol{p}}{\boldsymbol{m} \cdot \boldsymbol{n}} \boldsymbol{m}. \tag{6}$$

Similarly, from (3) and (5) we get

$$\boldsymbol{r} = \boldsymbol{q} - (\boldsymbol{l} \cdot \boldsymbol{q}) \boldsymbol{l}. \tag{7}$$

Hence, from (6) and (7) it follows that

$$\boldsymbol{r} = \boldsymbol{p} - \frac{\boldsymbol{n} \cdot \boldsymbol{p}}{\boldsymbol{n} \cdot \boldsymbol{m}} \boldsymbol{m} - \left[\boldsymbol{l} \cdot \boldsymbol{p} - \frac{(\boldsymbol{n} \cdot \boldsymbol{p})(\boldsymbol{l} \cdot \boldsymbol{m})}{\boldsymbol{n} \cdot \boldsymbol{m}} \right] \boldsymbol{l}, \tag{8}$$

which is the fundamental relationship between the original vector $\boldsymbol{p}$ and the observed image $\boldsymbol{r}$.

Now let us introduce an (x, y, z) Cartesian coordinate system in such a way that $\boldsymbol{l}$ coincides with the positive direction of the z axis and $\boldsymbol{m}$ is parallel to the x-z plane, say $\boldsymbol{m} = (m_x, 0, m_z)$. Let $\boldsymbol{e}_x$, $\boldsymbol{e}_y$, and $\boldsymbol{e}_z$ denote the unit vectors parallel to the x, y, and z axes, respectively. Then, (8) can be written as

$$r = [p \cdot e_x - \frac{(n \cdot p)(m \cdot e_x)}{n \cdot m}] e_x + (p \cdot e_y) e_y. \quad (9)$$

Particularly, if the original vector p_1 is parallel to the y axis, say $p_1 = (0, y_1, 0)$, then the resulting image $r_1 = (X_1, Y_1, 0)$ should satisfy

$$X_1 = -\frac{bm_x}{am_x + cm_z} y_1, \quad (10)$$

$$Y_1 = y_1, \quad (11)$$

where a, b, c are components of the unknown vector n. If, on the other hand, the original vector p_2 is perpendicular to the y axis, say $p_2 = (x_2, 0, z_2)$, then the corresponding image $r_2 = (X_2, Y_2, 0)$ should satisfy

$$X_2 = -\frac{c}{m_z(am_x + cm_z)} x_2, \quad (12)$$

$$Y_2 = 0. \quad (13)$$

Since, $n = (a, b, c)$ is of the unit length, we get

$$a^2 + b^2 + c^2 = 1. \quad (14)$$

Therefore, if the pattern on the slide film contains both vertical and horizontal vectors and they can be identified in the image, the surface normal $n = (a, b, c)$ can be determined uniquely from the three equations (10), (12), (14). (note that (14) is quadric and hence we have two normal vectors in a mathematical sense; however, they represent the same physical surface because one is a mere reversal of the other.)

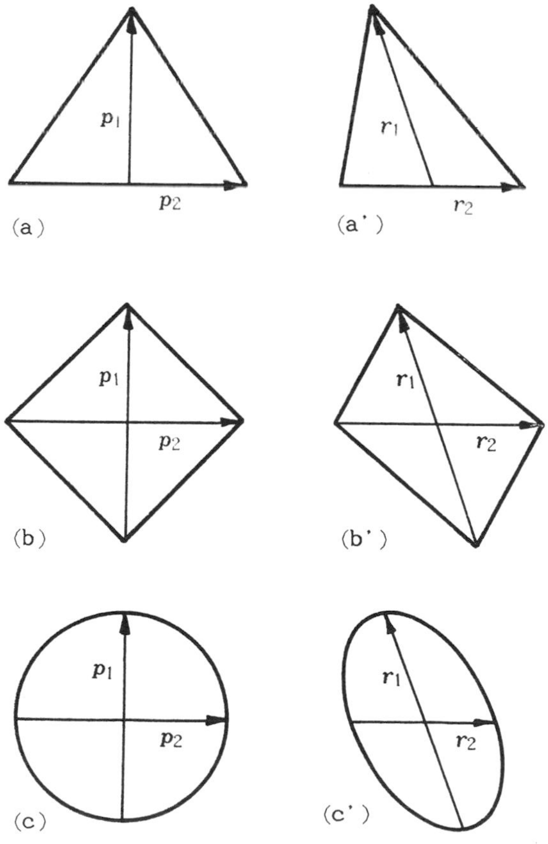

Fig. 2. Examples of patterns in which the vertical and horizontal vectors can be easily identified.

Fig. 2 shows some simple patterns having vertical and horizontal vectors that can be easily identified in the image. In the figure, (a), (b), (c) are original patterns and (a'), (b'), (c') are typical examples of the observed images. It may seem that in the circle pattern (c) the detection of the observed vector r_1 is sensitive to noise. Indeed if we directly extract the vector r_1 by connecting the lowest point on the observed pattern boundary to the highest one, we may not attain high accuracy. However, we can detect the vector r_1 in a reliable manner if we first find the equation of the ellipse that fits the observed pattern boundary [Okazaki, 1984]. Moreover, the circle pattern is superior in that we need not be careful to set the pattern vector p_2 to be parallel to the x-z plane. This point will play an essential role when we use perspectively projected patterns (see the next section).

In the implementation of the above method, we can use many patterns at a time; from the observed image we extract connected regions (corresponding to the patterns), process them independently, and thus obtain local surface normals at many points on the surface. This is where the present method differs from the triangulation.

2.2 Experiments

Some experimental results are shown in Photo. 1 and Fig. 3. Regularly arranged patterns are generated on 35mm slide films and projected onto object surfaces by a slide projector with a 180mm telephoto lens. Then, the photographs are taken by a camera with a 200mm telephoto lens. The objects used are (a) a planar board, (b) a cylinder, (c) a helmet, and (d) an electric megaphone. The picture regions are first partitioned into patterns and backgrounds by adaptive-threshold binalization [Otsu, 1979], and next the boundaries of the pattern regions are extracted. Fig. 3(a), (b), (c), (d) show the boundaries of the extracted pattern regions. Finally, the two vectors r_1 and r_2 in Fig. 2 (i.e., the results of the originally vertical and horizontal vectors) are extracted, and the associated normals are calculated by the system of equations consisting of (10), (12), and (14). Fig. 3(a'), (b'), (c'), (d') show the resultant normal vectors together with polygons that fits the observed patterns.

3. Ranges and Normals from Radially Projected Patterns

3.1. Basic Idea

As has been seen in the last section, the local surface normals at many points on the object can be measured from only one image if the patterns are cast by parallel rays of light and the image

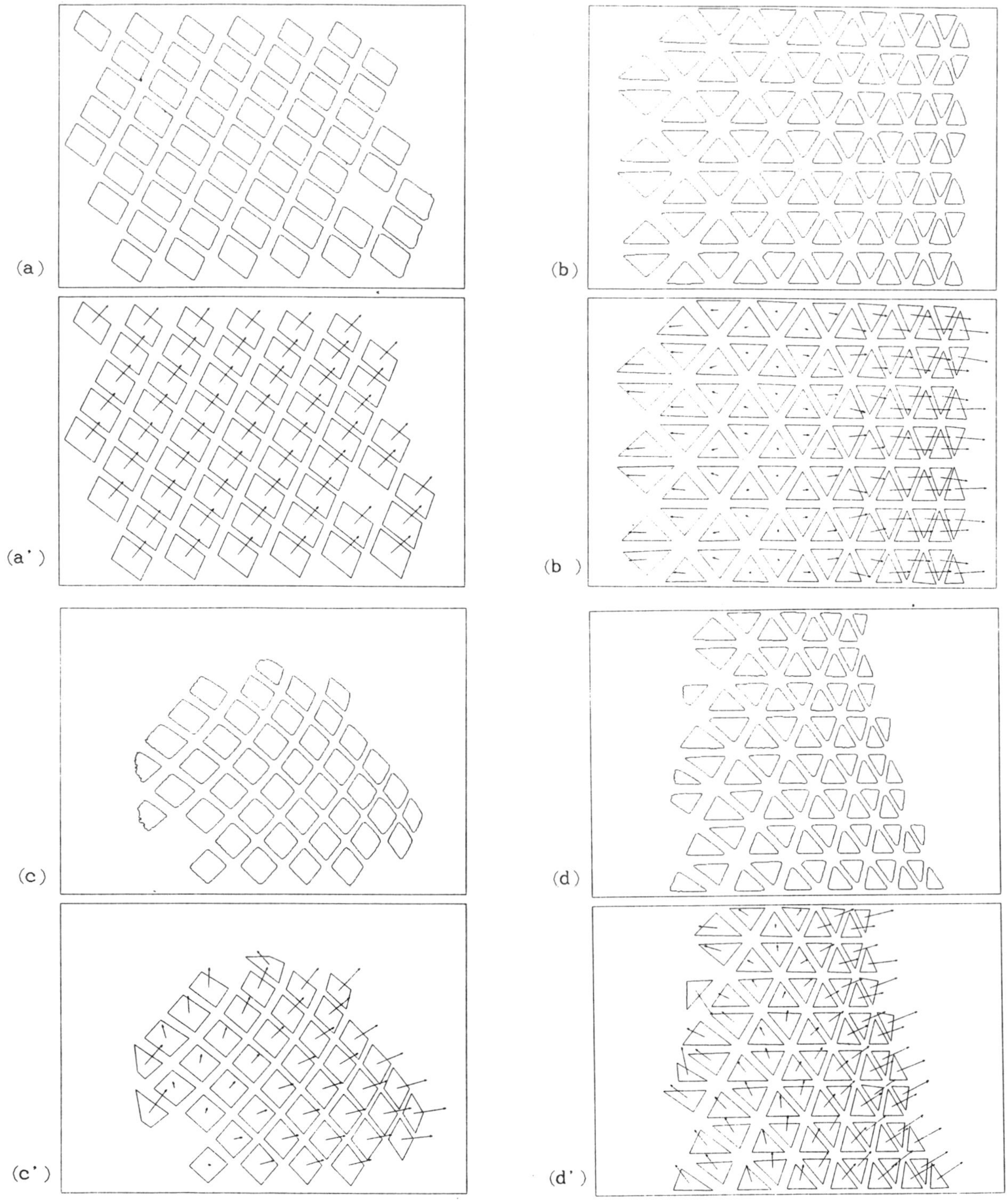

Fig. 3. Surface normals extracted from the data in Photo. 1.

is taken orthographically. Since the patterns can be made small, it seems sound, from an engineering point of view, to assume that each pattern is both cast and observed by the parallel projection. However, even if we use telephoto lenses, it is not easy to cast all the patterns in parallel or to take an orthographic image of the whole surface. That is, different patterns have different directions of the projection (i.e., the vector $\boldsymbol{m}$ in Fig. 1) and different directions of the observation (i.e., the vector $\boldsymbol{l}$ in Fig. 1).

In this section, we positively make use of the perspective nature of the projections, and establish a method for measuring both the normals and the ranges to the surfaces using three images taken by a fixed camera of projected patterns generated by three different light sources. The basic idea is the following.

Let us imagine a spherical surface having many small circular holes on it. If we put a light source at the center of the sphere, we get corn-shape beams of light emanating in many directions from the source. We shall call this type of light patterns *corn-beam patterns*. For the practical purpose, the corn-beam patterns can be realized by a usual slide film instead of a sphere; all we have to do is to generate elliptical patterns on the film in such a way that all the patterns look circular when seen from the position of the light source (note that the patterns themselves are, therefore, of different shape from each other).

Suppose that the corn-beam patterns are projected onto a smooth surface and they are observed by a camera. Let the resultant image be denoted by I_1. If the corn-beam patterns are small enough for us to assume that each pattern is cast onto a locally planar surface, then the observed patterns in the image I_1 can be regarded as ellipses. However, since there arise many ellipses in the image, we can not identify which ellipse results from which corn-beam pattern, and consequently we obtain no explicit information about the surface structures.

Now let us concentrate our attention upon any one ellipse in the image I_1 and study it in more detail. Let L be the half line starting at the camera center and passing the center of the ellipse, and let P be the point of intersection of the surface and the line L. Furthermore, let d be the range from the camera center to the surface point P. Of course we do not know where the surface is, and hence d is unknown. It should be noted, however, that if d is given, then the direction of the pattern projection $\boldsymbol{m}$ is determined and consequently the normal at P is determined by the method stated in the last section. That is, given the image I_1, we can consider the surface normal at the surface point on the line L as a function of the range d; see Fig. 4(a). Let us express this function by $\boldsymbol{n}_1(d)$, where the suffix 1 means that the function depends on the 'first' image, I_1.

Suppose next that the corn-beam patterns are projected from the second light source at another position, and the second image, say I_2, is obtained. Let us assume for simplicity that there is in I_2 an ellipse whose center is on the half line L. Then, using this ellipse together with the position of the second light source, we similarly obtain another function, say $\boldsymbol{n}_2(d)$, representing the surface normal at the surface point on the line L as the function of d, as is shown in Fig. 4(b).

The real point P on the object is to have a unique normal to the surface, and hence

$$\boldsymbol{n}_1(d) = \boldsymbol{n}_2(d) \qquad (15)$$

must be satisfied. Therefore, by finding the solution d^* to (15), we can determine both the range d^* and the surface normal $\boldsymbol{n} = \boldsymbol{n}_1(d^*) = \boldsymbol{n}_2(d^*)$.

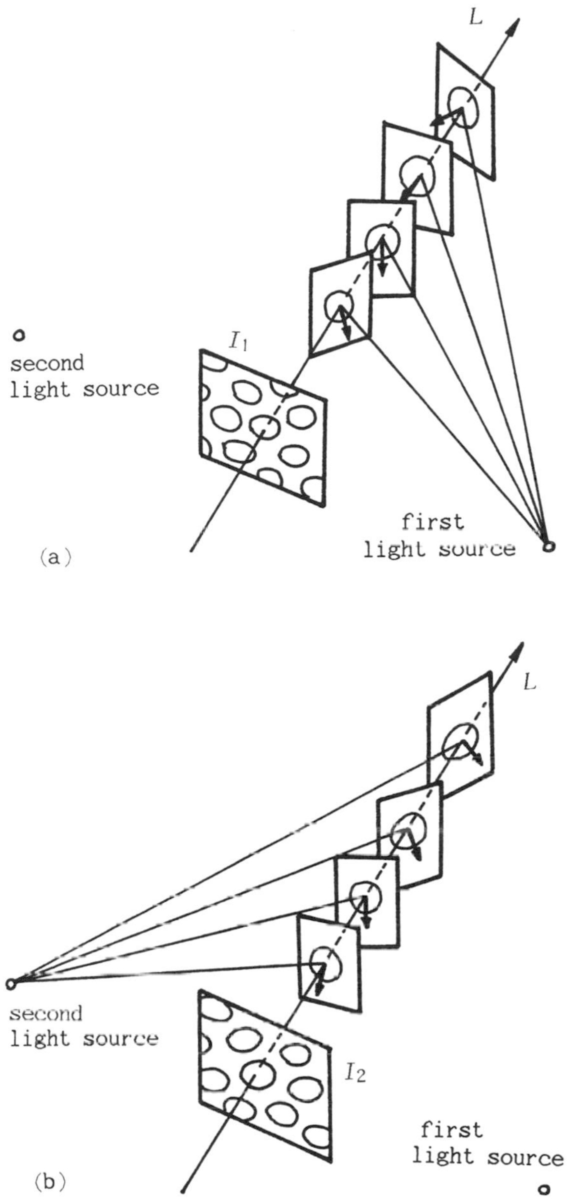

Fig. 4. Relationship between the range and the normal determined by the observed pattern projected from each of the two light sources.

However, it should be noted that Eq. (15) does not necessarily admit a unique solution. Eq. (15) is a vector equation consisting of three equations corresponding to the x, y, and z components, but they are not independent. Indeed, since $\boldsymbol{n}_1$ and $\boldsymbol{n}_2$ are unit vectors, one component is determined automatically from the other two components. Moreover, there is no assurance that the other two are independent (see the example in the next subsection). Therefore, it may happen that there are two or more solutions to Eq. (15) (note that $\boldsymbol{n}_1$ and $\boldsymbol{n}_2$ are nonlinear functions of d). In that case we take the third image generated by the third light source, and choose the solution that is consistent also with the third image. On the other hand, if we have a *priori* knowledge about rough ranges to the object, only two images are usually enough because Eq. (15) has a unique solution in a small range of d.

For practical implementation of this method, several comments should be stated here. First, the centers of the ellipses in the first image I_1 do not usually occupy the same positions as those in the second image I_2; we can not find in the second image any ellipse whose center is on the half line L. Therefore, we have to do some interpolation; for example, we can use a weighted average of neighboring ellipses in I_2. Secondly, because of inevitable noises due to digitization etc., we can not expect Eq. (15) holds exactly. Hence, instead we must search for d that minimize the difference between n_1 and n_2; for example, we search for the range d such that

$$|n_1(d) - n_2(d)|^2 \rightarrow \text{minimum}.$$

3.2. Computer Simulation

As a preliminary step for the verification of the validity of the present method, we made some computer simulation. One example of the simulation is shown in Figs. 5 and 6.

In this example, we consider the situation where at 180cm distance from the camera there stands a vertical surface slanting to the right of the camera by 10 degrees, as is shown in Fig. 5(a). We introduce a right-handed (x, y, z) Cartesian coordinate system in such a way that the z axis coincides with the optical axis of the camera and the y axis is vertical. Then, the unit normal to the surface is (0.174, 0.0, 0.985). Assuming that the corn-beam patterns are projected from two light sources at 80cm distance to the right and to the left respectively of the camera, we get a

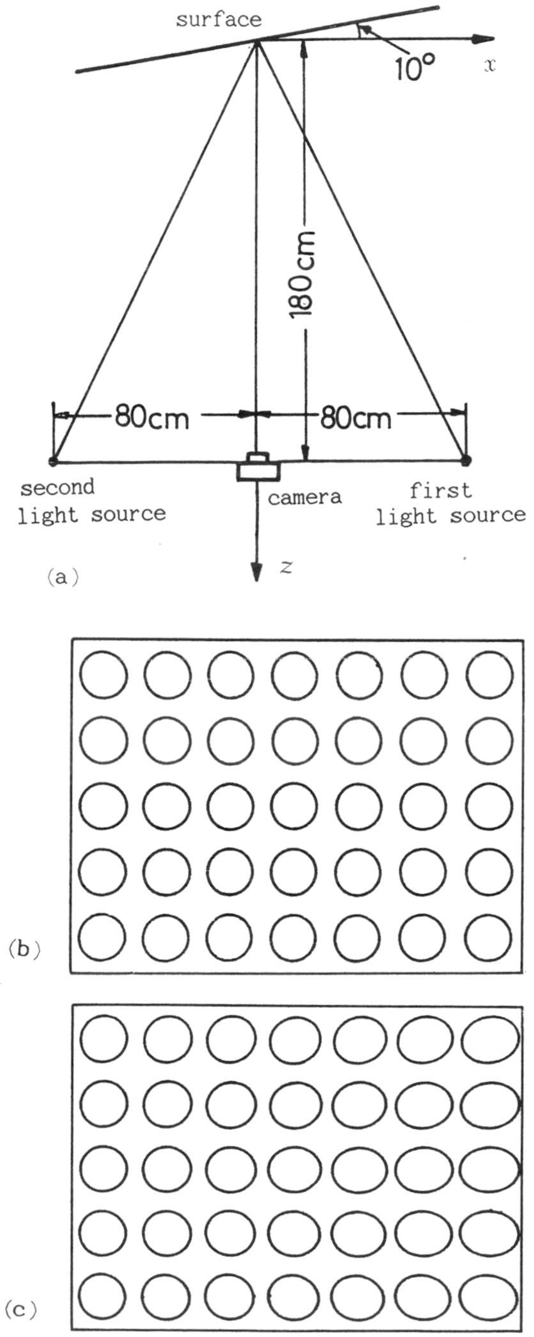

Fig. 5. Data for the simulation.

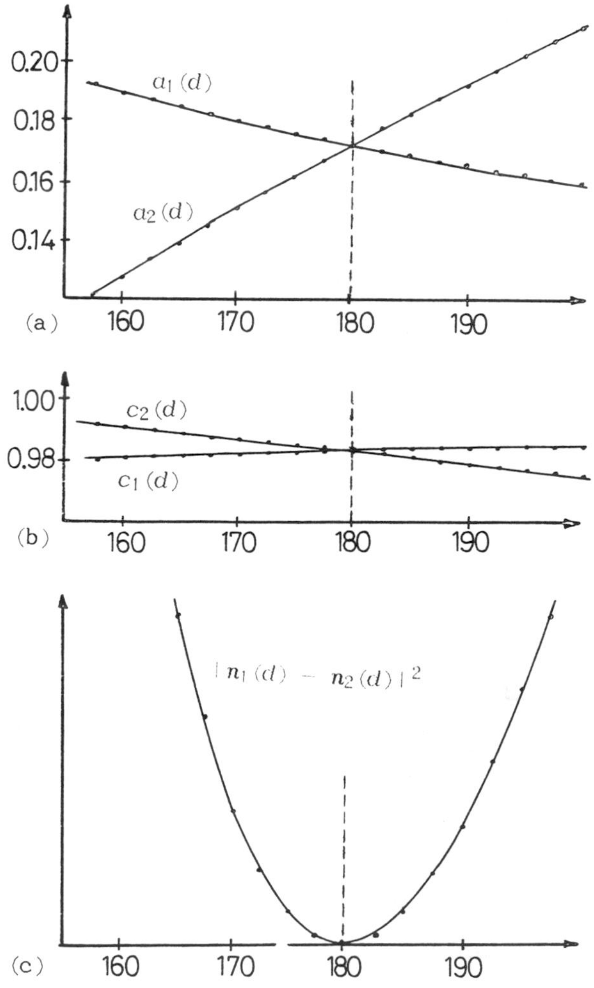

Fig. 6. Result of the simulation.

pair of computer-generated images I_1 and I_2, as are shown in (b) and (c).

Now we concentrate our attention to the pair of the ellipses at the center of the images. First, from the ellipse at the center of the image I_1, we obtain the predicted surface normal, say $n_1(d) = (a_1(d), b_1(d), c_1(d))$, for each value d of the range from the camera in the direction indicated by the center of the ellipse. In the present case $b_1(d) = 0$ for every d; only $a_1(d)$ and $c_1(d)$ vary as d changes. Those values are plotted in Fig. 6(a) and (b). Similarly, we obtain from the other ellipse (i.e., the one at the center of the second image I_2) another predicted surface normal $n_2(d) := (a_2(d), b_2(d), c_2(d))$. Here again we see $b_2(d) = 0$. The values of $a_2(d)$ and $c_2(d)$ are as plotted in Fig. 6(a) and (b). We can see that the curves $a_1(d)$ and $a_2(d)$ cross at the correct range $d = 180$cm, and so do the curves $c_1(d)$ and $c_2(d)$. Fig. 6(c) plots the quadric difference of the two vectors

$$| n_1(d) - n_2(d) |^2$$

for various values of the range d. We can see that the quadric difference decreases and forms a valley at the correct range $d = 180$cm. Thus, we can determine from the pair of the ellipses both the correct range and the correct normal.

4. Conclusion

We have proposed a new method for extracting three-dimensional structures of the surface from artificially projected texture patterns. The method has the following advantageous points.

1. Though it is mainly based on the shape-from-texture techniques, it can be applied to surfaces without textures, because artificial textures are generated by a projector.

2. We can extract not only surface normals but also surface ranges.

3. Unlike triangulation, we need not solve any correspondence problem or we need not process many images.

However, further experiments using real images are necessary in order to see the accuracy of the measurement attainable by this method.

Footnotes

1. The work is partly supported by the Grant in Aid for Scientific Research of the Ministry of Education, Science and Culture of Japan (Grant No. 59580023). Nagoya University Computation Center was used for the experiments.

2. He is now at Toshiba Ltd.

3. He is a visiting researcher from Faculty of Physics, Nanjing University, Nanjing, The People's Republic of China

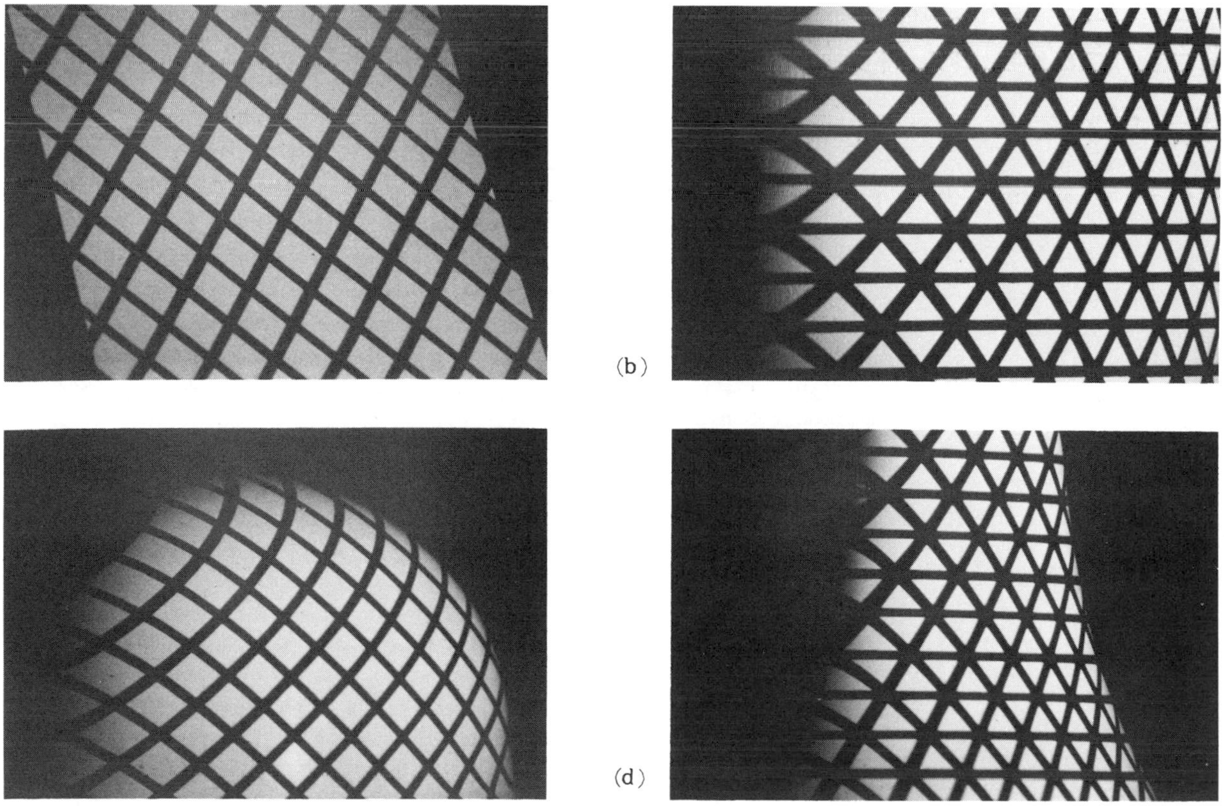

Photo. 1. Observed patterns used in the experiment in Section 2.2.

References

Agin, G. J. and Binford, T. O., 1976. Computer description of curved objects, *IEEE Trans. Computer*, **C-25**, pp. 439-449.

Aoki, N., Yachida, M., and Tsuji, S., 1984. Measuring of 3-d objects using a recorded image projection and 2 cameras (in Japanese), PRL83-85., Pap. Tech. Group Pattern Recognition and Learning of the Institute of Electronics and Communication Engineers of Japan.

Grimson, W. E. L., 1981. *From Images to Surfaces*, Cambridge, MIT Press.

Idesawa, M., Yatagai, T., and Soma, T., 1977. Scanning moiré method and automatic measurement of 3-d shapes, *Applied Optics*, **14**, pp. 2152-2162.

Ikeuchi, K., 1980. Shape from regular patterns: An example of constraint propagation in vision, AI Memo 567, Cambridge, MIT, Artificial Intelligence Laboratory.

Ikeuchi, K., 1981. Determining surface orientation of specular surfaces by using the photometric stereo method, *IEEE Trans. Pattern Analysis and Machine Intelligence*, **PAMI-3**, pp. 661-669.

Inokuchi, S., Nita, T., Matsuda, F., and Sakurai, Y., 1982. A three-dimensional edge-region operator for range pictures, Sixth Internat. Conf. Pattern Recognition, Munchen, pp. 918-920.

Ishii, M., and Nagata, T., 1974. Feature extraction of 3-dimensional objects with a laser tracker (in Japanese), *Trans. of the Society of Instrument and Control Engineers of Japan*, **10**, pp. 599-605.

Kanade, T., 1981. Recovery of the three-dimensional shape of an object from a single view, *Artificial Intelligence*, **17**, pp. 409-460.

Kender, J. R., 1979. Shape from texture: A computational paradigm, DARPA Image Understanding Workshop, pp. 134-138.

Mino, M., Kanade, T., and Sakai, T., 1980. Parallel use of coded slit light for range finding (in Japanese), 21th National Convention of the Information Processing Society of Japan, pp. 875-876.

Moravec, H. P., 1979, August 20-23. Visual mapping by a robot rover, Sixth Internat. Joint Conf. Artificial Intelligence, Tokyo, pp. 598-600.

Nishihara, H. K., and Larson, N. G., 1981, April. Towards a real-time implementation of the Marr-Poggio stereo matcher, DARPA Image Understanding Workshop.

Ohta, Y., and kanade, T., 1983. Stereo by intra- and inter-scanline search using dynamic programming, CMU-CS-83-162, Pittsburgh, Carnegie-Mellon Univ., Computer Science Dept.

Okazaki, K., 1984. Study on the method for extracting three-dimensional structures from actively projected regular patterns, Bachelor Thesis, Nagoya Univ., Dept. of Information Science.

Omori, T., and Morishita, I., 1982. Object detection using multiview stereo images (in Japanese), *Trans. of the Society of Instrument and Control Engineers of Japan*, **18**, pp. 70-76.

Oshima, M., and Shirai, Y., 1983. Object recognition using three-dimensional information, *IEEE Trans. Pattern Analysis and Machine Intelligence*, **PAMI-5**, pp. 353-361.

Otsu, N., 1979. A threshold selection method from gray-level histograms. *IEEE Trans. System, Man and Cybernetics*, **SMC-9**, pp. 62-66.

Sato, S., and Inokuchi, S., 1984. Range imaging by Gray coded projection (in Japanese), National Convention 1984 of the Institute of Electronics and Communication Engineers of Japan, Part 6, pp. 283-284.

Shirai, Y., and Suwa, M., 1971. Recognition of polyhedrons with a range finder, Second Internat. Joint Conf. Artificial Intelligence, pp. 80-87.

Sugie, N., and Suwa, M., 1977. A scheme for binocular depth perception suggested by neurophysiological evidence, *Biological Cybernetics*, **26**, p. 1-15.

Sugihara, K., 1979. Range-data analysis guided by a junction dictionary, *Artificial Intelligence*, **12**, pp. 41-69.

Wei, D., and Gini, M., 1983. The use of taper light beam for object recognition, *Robot Vision*, A. Pugh (ed.), U.K., IFS Ltd,. pp. 143-153.

Will, P. M., and Pennington, K. S., 1972. Grid coding: A novel technique for image processing, *Proc. IEEE*, **60**, pp. 669-680.

Witkin, A. P., 1981. Recovering surface shape and orientation from texture, *Artificial Intelligence*, **17**, pp. 17-45.

Woodham, R. J., 1977. A cooperative algorithm for determining surface orientation from a single view, Fifth Internat. Joint Conf. Artificial Intelligence, pp. 635-641.

Yasue, T., and Shirai, Y., 1973. Binocular stereoscopic vision for object recognition (in Japanese), *Bul. Electrotechnical Laboratory*, **37**, pp. 1101-1119.

NEW STEPS TOWARD A FLEXIBLE 3-D VISION SYSTEM FOR ROBOTICS

O.D. FAUGERAS

INRIA, Domaine de Voluceau, Rocquencourt, 78150 Le Chesnay, FRANCE

We discuss the problems of representing 3-D scenes when dense range data are available. Rich symbolic descriptions are obtained by fitting planes and quadrics to the data. A region growing algorithm working on a 3-D graph approximating object surfaces is described. The problem of matching models and scene descriptions for recognition and positioning is discussed and an algorithm based on hypothesis prediction and verification is described in the case of planar primitives.

INTRODUCTION

One of the most exciting goals for Computer Vision is the design and implementation of a general purpose Vision system. This goal is of course still far ahead of us and reaching it implies many more scientific discoveries and technical breakthroughs. But systems with sophisticated capabilities do begin to exist in many laboratories, operating on scenes of limited but certainly nontrivial complexities. Issues that are being addressed in these systems are how do we go about acquiring reliable range and motion data , how do we process this information to produce rich symbolic descriptions of the observed scene content in which information relevant to solving the tasks at hand is explicitely present, how do we acquire, learn and represent a priori knowledge about objects shapes, functions, relations, and finally how do we relate this knowledge to the processed sensor data to produce something we may call understanding and which in turn can be used to act in a reliable fashion on the environment.

Robotics is a fascinating application area of Computer Vision because of its tremendous industrial implications but also as a fantastic testbed for the theories of the field. It provides the researcher in Computer Vision with a large variety of problem environments from the most constrained ones like picking a few well defined objects to the most unconstrained ones like exploring an unknown planet.

In this paper we deal with the problem of modelling, recognizing and positioning rigid 3-D objects such as industrial parts when range information is readily obtained from a laser range finder. A great deal of effort is made among the Computer Vision community to develop algorithms for extracting range information by passive techniques (shape from stereo[12,23-25], shape from shading[18,21,28], shape from photogrammetric stereo[20,31], shape from texture[30], shape from motion, etc...). Obviously this work is very important and provides clues as to how range information can be recovered from a variety of image features. In some cases, however, it is possible to adopt a less anthropomorphic attitude toward the problem of acquiring range data and to design active techniques that work quickly and accurately.

This has been our approach in developing a laser range finder that produces dense range maps of scenes directly. A recent survey of techniques available for acquiring range data can be found in [22]. We discuss briefly the problems of preprocessing these data to produce a complete low level polyhedral representation of objects for model construction. We then address the question of generating symbolic descriptions of scenes and models and propose a solution based upon a functional approximation of the surfaces with planar and quadric primitives. This in turn raises the question of the representation of these primitives for recognition and positioning purposes. We show that one answer to this question is to use geometric features like the surface primitives equation which is both unambiguous and robust to occlusion. We demonstrate the use of such features in recovering object position. Finally we address the problem of relating models and scene descriptions and discuss a scene analysis program which, in its current implementation, deals only with planar primitives.

DATA ACQUISITION AND PREPROCESSING

The system which has been developed has been described elsewhere[10]. We briefly review its main features. It is composed of a laser and its associated optics, a system of cameras and a computer controlled table (Fig.1). It provides the z-coordinate of a point on the surface of an object as a function of the x-coordinate by active stereoscopy. The platform on which the object rests is equiped with step motors and can be raised and lowered along and rotated around the y-axis. The laser beam can be moved in the x-direction by means of a mirror steered by a galvanometer. The redundancy of the mirror sweep and the table rotation allows us to analyse concave objects.

The technique currently used for obtaining complete models of objects can be described as follows. For a given table height we combine the rotation of the table and the sweep of the mirror to obtain an accurate polygonal approximation of the object cross-section. We then connect the different cross-sections with triangles and obtain a polyhedral approximation of the object.

MODEL BUILDING AND SCENE SEGMENTATION

In our current system there is only a slight difference between the construction of image models and the segmentation of range scenes. This is because of the unavailability of convenient 3-D solid modellers capable of generating object descriptions adapted to the problems of recognition and positioning.

We have investigated two classes of segmentation techniques. One is based on the region growing paradigm and has been implemented on the polyhedral model graph and the scene range 'image'. The other one is an adaptation of the Hough transform to the detection of 3-D surfaces and has been implemented only on the scene range 'image'[15].

We concentrate here on the region growing method operating on the polyhedral model graph and only mention its variations when applied to the scene. The goal is to segment the object represented by the polyhedron with triangular faces obtained as explained above into significant surface primitives which are planes and quadrics. The algorithm knows about regions, adjacency of regions, planes and quadrics. A region is defined by a set of points, a border, a surface of approximation (plane or quadric) and the corresponding error. A point M is defined by its coordinates x_M, y_M, z_M sometimes arranged in a vector v_M. A border is a set of simple closed oriented polygonal lines the edges of which are edges of the original triangulation. A border is consistently oriented in such a way that the corresponding region interior is on the right of an observer who would be walking on the object surface along that border.

At the beginning the regions are defined to be the triangles of the original polyhedron and approximated by the corresponding planes with a zero error.

Regions are adjacent when their borders share a set of edges.

Planes are defined by their normal $\vec{n}$($\|\vec{n}\|=1$) and their distance d to the origin of coordinates. The equation of a plane is therefore given by :

$$P(v_M) = n^t v_M + d$$

Quadrics are defined by their equation :

$$Q(v_M) = v_M^t A v_M + v_M^t B + r = 0$$

with :

$$A = \begin{bmatrix} a & \frac{d}{\sqrt{2}} & \frac{f}{\sqrt{2}} \\ \frac{d}{\sqrt{2}} & b & \frac{e}{\sqrt{2}} \\ \frac{f}{\sqrt{2}} & \frac{e}{\sqrt{2}} & c \end{bmatrix}$$

$$B = (b_1, b_2, b_3)^t$$

Just as in the case of planes we impose the constraint $\|\vec{n}\|=1$ to the normal which is invariant with respect to translation and rotation, we impose a similar constraint for quadrics. As discussed in[8] a convenient constraint satisfying the above invariance property is :

$$tr(A^2) = a^2+b^2+c^2+d^2+e^2+f^2 = 1$$

where tr denotes the trace of a matrix.

The distance of a point M to a plane is given by $|P(v_M)|$ therefore the squared approximation error of a plane to a region can be defined as :

$$\Sigma\ P(v_M)^2$$

Just as in the case of conics[5,27] there is no such equivalent simple expression for the distance of a point to a quadric. We choose somewhat arbitrarily $Q(v_M)^2$ as an approximative squared distance for its simplicity (notice that it is zero when M is on the surface) and define the approximation error of a quadric to a region to be :

$$\Sigma\ Q(v_M)^2$$

Given these definitions, the problem of finding the best approximating plane (quadric) to a region can be readily shown[8] to be equivalent to the computation of the eigenvector corresponding to the smallest eigenvalue of a 3*3, (6*6) positive matrix.

The algorithm starts with a description of the region adjacency graph of the current segmentation. This contains for every region the list of adjacent regions, the list of points in the region, a description of the borders of the region, the type and parameters of the best approximating surface primitive. It then proceeds to merge pairs of adjacent regions in such a way that some error grows as little as possible. Various control options can be thought of in this grouping process. A global control strategy merges at every step the pair of adjacent regions that causes the smallest error increase. This implies exploring after every merge the whole list of candidate pairs of regions but guarantees the slowest increase of the error. This strategy has been implemented for the production of the model description. A local control strategy chooses the region with the smallest error and starts growing it until the approximation error reaches some threshold. It then goes to the region with the next smallest error... This implies that only the list of regions adjacent to the current region of interest has to be explored but does not guarantee the slowest increase of the error. This faster strategy has been implemented for the production of the scene description[14].

The most tricky part of the algorithm is certainly the one that deals with the borders of two adjacent regions and produces the border of the resulting region after the merge. For example, if we go back to Fig.3, region i has one border, region j two borders and their union has five ! The computation of borders can be put on a firm theoretical basis by the two propositions :

Proposition 1 : given two adjacent regions i and j, there is only one border of region i and one border of region j that can share edges. This is a direct consequence of the fact that regions are connected and places a strict upper bound on the complexity of the border building problem.

Proposition 2 : given the two adjacent borders B_i and B_j of two adjacent regions i and j, the new set of borders can be computed by traversing B_i and B_j once.

This is fairly obvious and restricts even further the complexity.

At this point one may wonder why we take so much trouble in computing these borders which are not really necessary to perform the merge. There are two reasons. The first one is related to the visualisation of results, an issue of utmost importance when dealing with 3-D data where displaying results is not as easy as with standard images. We found that displaying borders is a very effective way of presenting the results of the segmentation procedure. The second point is that we think that these borders may be important geometric features that can be useful for recognition and positioning even though we have not used them as such so far. Results of this algorithm are shown in Fig.4 and 5.

SCENE ANALYSIS

After the segmentation process, models and scenes are represented by a list of primitives (M_i) and (S_i). One of the tasks of the scene analysis program is to provide a list of matched model and scene primitives $M=((S_i,M_i))$. This is the identification or recognition task. In practice one is also often interested in positioning the identified model in the observer coordinate system. Our approach has been to solve both problems simultaneously but obviously this needs not always be the case.

The risks of computational explosion in solving such problems are well known to be very high and the control strategy must be carefully chosen to reduce the search to a small number of likely solutions. The efficiency of such a control strategy depends in turn quite heavily upon the type of features which are used to define model and scene primitives.

Given these observations and the task at hand, we can produce a list of requirements for the primitive features. They should be both unambiguous, that is allowing us to recover object position, and stable. Stable means that if (S_i) and (M_i) are regions corresponding to two observations of the same object, with S_i corresponding to M_i for all i, then there exists a function c such that $f(S_i)$ (the features of region S_i) is 'close' to $c(f(M_i))$ for all i. Moreover, the distance between f(S) and c(f(M)) should be independent of the observed object position and of its degree occultation. We show next that such features and such a function c exist for planes and quadrics.

But let us review briefly some commonly used features and measure them on our scale. Numerical features used in Pattern Recognition such as surface, perimeter, moments of inertia, etc... are obviously ambiguous, that is do not allow to recover object position, and unstable to occultation. They can at best only be used as a gross measure of the quality of a match. Topological features such as region connectivity, genus, number and type of neighboring regions are also ambiguous and unstable. Finally what we could call geometric features such as axis of inertia, region borders, and surface equation are more promising. Indeed they are very unambiguous but, except for the last one, unstable to occultation. This means that if we want to satisfy our previous requirements it seems that the desired features are the region surface equation independently of any other feature related to the size, shape of borders, etc... It may seem a bit exagerated but if we think of it a little, it is a direct consequence of the basic problem of occultation we have to cope with in 3-D Vision.

Since we address here the problem of recognizing and positioning rigid objects which are a large proportion of the everyday environment of a robot, the function c should exploit this constraint i.e. that there exists a rigid transformation D applying each matched model primitive onto its corresponding scene primitive.

Let us now review some of the main techniques which are candidates for matching model and scene descriptions.

Relaxation

Relaxation techniques[20,7,10] are ways to construct a coherent list of matched model and scene primitives. To achieve this, a measure p(S,M) of the quality of every potential match (S,M) is computed and used to define the original model to scene correspondence. Another measure $c(S_1,M_1,\dots,S_n,M_n)$ is also available to evaluate the compatibility of n-tuples of matches. Depending upon the type of problem we are solving, relaxation can be discrete or continuous. In the discrete relaxation paradigm, the functions p and c can take only the values 0 or 1. This does not apply readily to our problem. In the continuous relaxation model, they take real values and p(S,M) is often considered as something like the possibility that S corresponds to M. The idea is then to modify iteratively these pseudo-probabilities by combining those computed at the previous iteration with the compatibility measures c. When the process converges a decision is taken.

These techniques have been applied to a large number of problems in Vision including that of recognizing planar[1,4,6] and 3-D shapes[3,26]. We think they suffer of two main drawbacks. First of all the convergence depends heavily upon the initial probabilities p(S,M) which can only be computed from the above unstable numerical features. Second of all they provide only local compatibility checking (through the function c) whereas our constraint (rigidity) is global.

Hough transform

Several algorithms for the recognition of 2D[2] and 3D[16] shapes based on the principle of the Hough transform have been recently proposed. The basic idea is to use the quantized space of model to scene transformations as an accumulator where cells are increased when they correspond to the match of a model and a scene primitives. The maximum cell in the accumulator then yields the desired transformation. In the case of 3-D data the transformation space is 6-dimensional and separates in two 3-dimensional subspaces representing the translations and the rotations. The problems are then that in order to obtain a good accuracy on the estimation of the transformation one needs to quantize finely the accumulator thus yielding large memory requirements and that there is in general an infinity of transformationswhich map a plane onto a plane or a quadric onto a quadric and this makes the updating of the accumulator difficult.

Hypothesis prediction and verification

This is a generic name to encompass a class of techniques for the exhaustive search for the best solution. The general principle is at every step to attempt to augment the best partial solution with a new hypothesis. If none is possible one backtracks to another partial solution. The basic technique is thus to search the hypothesis tree, where to make an hypothesis is to match a model and a scene primitive. The size of this tree can be extremely large and it is necessary to control the search[13]. In the case where a cost can be associated with every solution then branch and bound techniques can be used. The rigidity constraint provides such a cost and can therefore be used to reduce the combinatorial explosion as we show later.

POSITIONING OBJECTS

We now consider the problem of estimating the rigid displacement D from one set of model primitives (M_i) to a set of scene primitives (S_i). D can be decomposed as a product of a rotation R and a translation T. This decomposition is not unique and we assume that the notation is applied first and leaves the origin of coordinates invariant. We now examine separately the case of planes and quadrics.

1) Planar primitives

As we saw before, a plane is defined by a pair $(\vec{n},d)$ where $\vec{n}$ is a unit norm vector normal to the plane and d the algebraic distance of the origin to the plane. Notice that this representation is not unique and that $(-\vec{n},-d)$ represents the same plane. This can be a very serious problem when attempting to estimate D. We therefore choose a canonical orientation of the vectors $\vec{n}$ for example pointing toward the outside of objects. Let now $(\vec{n},d)$ represent a scene primitive S corresponding through D to a model primitive M represented by $(\vec{n}',d')$. If we denote by $\vec{t}$ the vector of translation we can easily show that the following relations must hold :

$$\vec{n} = R\vec{n}'$$
$$\vec{t}.\vec{n} + d - d' = 0$$

in practice these relations are only approximately satisfied and the best transformation D applying the list of model primitives (M_i) onto the list of scene primitives (S_i) is found by minimizing the two criteria :

$$c_1(R) = \Sigma\|\vec{n}_i - R\vec{n}_i'\|^2 \qquad (1)$$

$$c_2(\vec{t}) = \Sigma|t.\vec{n}_i + d_i - d_i'|^2 \qquad (2)$$

Finding the translation vector $\vec{t}$ which minimizes (2) is a standard mean-square problem. Finding the rotation matrix R that minimizes (1) is a much more difficult problem because of the constraint $R^tR=I$. Iterative solutions such as projected or conjugate gradient can be used but they are bound to be slow and may converge toward a local minimum. As is pointed out in[14,9], the use of a different representation for rotation matrixes makes the solution much easier. The key idea is to use the quaternions as a means of representing the rotation matrixes. This representation which is a direct extension of the representation of planar rotations with complex numbers allows us to rewrite criterion (1) as a quadratic form in four variables and replace the constraint $R^tR=I$ by a much simpler one. The consequence is that the solution can be computed as the eigenvector of 4x4 definite positive matrix, associated to its smallest eigenvalue. We review briefly now quaternions and their use for representing 3-D rotations. A quaternion q can be throught of as a pair $(s,\vec{v})$ where s is a real number and v a vector in R^3. s and v can be thought of as the real and imaginary parts of the quaternion q. Real numbers s and vectors $\vec{v}$ of R^3 can be identified with quaternions $(s,0)$ and $(0,\vec{v})$. The product of two quaternions $q=(s,\vec{v})$ and $q'=(s',\vec{v}')$ is defined by :

$$q*q'=(ss'+\vec{v}.\vec{v}', s\vec{v}'+s'\vec{v}+\vec{v}\wedge\vec{v}')$$

This product is non commutative. Moreover, one can extend familiar notions from the field of complex numbers to the field of quaternions :

conjugate : $\bar{q}=(s,-\vec{v})$

magnitude : $|q|^2=|s|^2+\|\vec{v}\|^2=q*\bar{q}=\bar{q}*q$

wich satisfies $|q*q'|=|q|.|q'|$

inverse : $q^{-1} = \dfrac{\bar{q}}{|q|^2} \quad (q\neq 0)$

Just as there is an isomorphism between complex numbers of magnitude 1 and the set of vector plane rotations, we can associate with every quaternion q of magnitude 1 a rotation R(q) of R^3 such that if q and q' are two such quaternions, the associated rotation matrices R(q) and R(q') satisfy $R(q*q')=R(q).R(q')$ (group homomorphism). Inversely, to every rotation of R^3 defined by its angle a and its axis $\vec{w}$ $(\|\vec{w}\|=1)$ there correspond two quaternions :

$$q = (\cos(\tfrac{a}{2}), \sin(\tfrac{a}{2})\vec{w}) \text{ and } -q$$

to avoid this ambiguity we restrict ourselves to quaternions with a positive real part or equivalently to rotations with an angle a satisfying $0<=a<=\pi$. The last result we need is that for a given rotation matrix R, if q is its associated quaternion and if $\vec{v}$ is a vector in R^3 identified to the quaternion $v=(0,\vec{v})$, then :

$$(0,R\vec{v})=q*v*\bar{q}$$

We can now go back to criterion $c_1(R)$ and rewrite it as :

$$c_1(q) = \Sigma|n_i - q*n_i'*\bar{q}|^2$$

where vectors are identified with quaternions and euclidean norm with quaternion magnitude. Multiplying both sides of the equality with $|q|^2=1$ yields :

$c_1(q) = \Sigma|n_i*q-q*n_i'|^2$

From the definition of the quaternion product, $n_i*q-q*n_i'$ is a linear function of q therefore there exists a 4x4 matrix A_i such that :

$n_i*q-q*n_i' = A_iq$

(here quaternions are identified with 4-dimensional column vectors) and $c_1(q)$ can be rewritten as :

$c_1(q)=q^tBq \qquad B=\Sigma A_i^tA_i$

the constraint being $|q|^2=1$.

The best rotation is thus associated to the eigenvector of unit norm and with a positive first component associated to the smallest eigenvalue of the positive matrix B above. Expressing B as a function of the vectors $\vec{n}_i'$ and $\vec{n}_i$ is a simple matter. It should be noticed that the estimation of the translation and of the rotation are independent. Intuitively the method rotates the model planes until they become as parallel as possible to the scene planes and translates them to minimize the sum of the differences of the distances to the origin.

Quadric primitives

As we saw above , a quadric is defined by a triplet $(A,\vec{B},r)$ where A is a symmetric 3x3 matrix satisfying $tr(A^2)=1$, $\vec{B}$ a vector and r a number. Just as in the case of planes it is to be noted that this representation is not unique and that $(-A,-\vec{B},-r)$ represents the same quadric. Unfortunately there is no physically satisfying canonical choice of "orientation" and we simply impose the further constraint on A that its determinant is greater than or equal to 0. To derive an estimation of the transformation D, it is more convenient to assume some standard representation for the quadrics. We assume here for simplicity that matrix A is invertible.

Proposition 3 : given a quadric $Q=(A,\vec{B},r)$ there exists a rotation matrix P and translation vector $\vec{u}$ such that after rotating the coordinate system by P and translating it by $\vec{u}$ the representation of Q is $(\Delta,0,\varepsilon)$ where Δ is a diagonal matrix the elements of which are the eigenvalues of matrix A. The matrix P is made of the corresponding eigenvectors.

The proof is fairly obvious but the thing to notice is that matrix P is not unique. Even in the case where matrix A has distinct eigenvalues which have been ordered in decreasing order for example there still exist four degrees of freedom corresponding to the orientation of the eigenvectors (8 possibilities minus four since we impose $det(P)>0$).

Let now $(A,\vec{B},r)$ represent a scene primitive S,P and $\vec{u}$ being the attached rotation matrix and translation vector, corresponding through D to a model primitive M represented by $(A',\vec{B}',r')$, P' and $\vec{u}'$ being the attached rotation matrix and translation vector. We can easily show that the following relations must hold :

$$P = RP'$$
$$\vec{u} = R\vec{u}'+\vec{t}$$

again, in practice these relations are only approximately satisfied and the best transformation D applying the list of model primitives (M_i) onto the list of scene primitives (S_i) is found by minimizing the two criteria :

$$c_3(R) = \Sigma\|P_i-RP_i'\|^2$$

$$c_4(R,\vec{t}) = \Sigma\|\vec{u}_i-R\vec{u}_i'-\vec{t}\|^2$$

Having estimated the best rotation matrix $\hat{R}$ by minimizing c_3 the best translation vector $\hat{t}$ that minimizes c_4 is given by :

$$\hat{\vec{t}} = \Sigma(\vec{u}_i-\hat{R}\vec{u}_i')$$

The difficult part is to compute R. Criterion c_3 is very reminiscent of c_1 and poses the same problems. It turns out that we can use the same tools to find an exact solution. Let $\vec{n}_{i1}$, $\vec{n}_{i2}$ and $\vec{n}_{i3}$ ($\vec{n}'_{i1}$,$\vec{n}'_{i2}$ and $\vec{n}'_{i3}$) be the column vectors of matrixes P_i and P_i'. We can rewrite c_3 as :

$$c_3(R) = \Sigma\Sigma\|\vec{n}_{ij}-R\vec{n}_{ij}'\|^2$$

or, if we use the quaternion q associated with R :

$$c_3(q) - \Sigma\Sigma|n_{ij}*q-q*n_{ij}'|^2$$

noticing as before that there exists as 4x4 matrix A_{ij} such that :

$n_{ij}*q-q*n_{ij}'=A_{ij}q$

we eventually obtain :

$$c_3(q)=q^tBq \qquad B=\Sigma B_j \qquad B_j=\Sigma A_{ij}^tA_{ij}$$

Again the best rotation is associated to the unit norm eigenvector with a positive first component associated to the smallest eigenvalue of the positive matrix B. Expressing B as a function of the vectors $\vec{n}_{ij}$ and $\vec{n}_{ij}'$ is a simple matter.

There is a slight difficulty with this nice theoretical solution which does not exist with planes and comes from the fact that quadrics have rich groups of symmetry which planes do not have. Moreover, these groups can be discrete or continuous. As an example of a discrete group we can choose an ellipsoid with three different axis lengths a,b,c. Its equation is :

$$\frac{x^2}{a^2} + \frac{y^2}{b^2} + \frac{z^2}{c^2} - 1 = 0$$

The corresponding eigenvectors of matrix A are the three unit vectors $(1,0,0)^t$, $(0,1,0)^t$ and $(0,0,1)^t$. In fact the vectors $(a_1,0,0)^t$, $(0,a_2,0)^t$ and $(0,0,a_3)^t$ where $a_i=+-1$ and $a_1a_2a_3=1$ are equivalent descriptions of our ellipsoid corresponding to its various symmetries. As an example of continuous group we can choose an ellipsoid satisfying a=b. In that case the ellipsoid is invariant under all rotations of axis z which means that the vectors $(a_1\cos\theta,a_1\sin\theta,0)^t$, $(-a_2\sin\theta,a_2\cos\theta,0)^t$ and $(0,0,a_3)^t$ are equivalent descriptions.

These theoretical considerations have a very concrete consequence, namely that the program which diagonalizes the matrixes A and A' does not have any way of choosing coherently the eigenvectors (for example by using the difference between interior and exterior as in the case of planes) and this is a very serious threat to our proposed method for estimating the rotation matrix R.

We do not have at the time of this writing a complete answer to this problem. We now present some partial answers. First of all we restrict ourselves to quadrics with a matrix A having different eigenvalues (one possibly equal to 0) that is we restrict ourselves to discrete groups of symmetries.

We show that the rigidity constraint allows us to reduce the combinatorial explosion caused by the symmetries. Indeed the relation :

$$P_i = RP'_i \qquad (3)$$

must be rewritten as :

$$\tilde{P}_i D_i = RP'_i \qquad (4)$$

where D_i is a diagonal matrix with 1 and -1 on its diagonal satisfying $\det(D_i)=+1$ and $\tilde{P}_i$ is the matrix computed by the eigenvector program. Matrixes D_i are unknown. But relations (3) and (4) imply :

$$D_i^t \tilde{P}_i^t \tilde{P}_j D_j = P'^t_j P'_i \qquad \text{for all } i,j$$

This allows at best to determine all matrixes D_i, $i \geq 2$ as a function of matrix D_1 for example, therefore reduces the combinatorial explosion but cannot lift all ambiguities.

One way to reduce it further is to use the idea of "clusters of features". For example, if the sphere and the ellipsoid have been detected, we could agree that the eigenvector parallel to the line between the centers is oriented away from the sphere and so on and so forth. This structural information, implicit in the model, should be computed automatically and made explicit. We are presently working in direction. Still another way of going is to use the remarkable features that any quadric has, such as centers, axis and planes of symmetry, as constraints to reduce the search for D. Let us take the example of the strange object of figure 5, and suppose we have identified the sphere and the ellipsoid. We first translate the model so that the centers of the spheres do coincide, we then rotate it around this point so that the centers of the ellipsoids coincide. We then have one more degree of freedom for rotating the ellipsoid around the line between the centers. Of course if errors have been commited in estimating the various elements in the scene the final transformation will also be in error and the question must be asked as to how to compute the best transformation. Answers to these questions are provided by the preceding Section.

RECOGNIZING OBJECTS

We now describe the structure of the Recognition algorithm which has only been fully implemented for planes[14,9].

Model primitives $(M_1,\ldots,M_N)$ are sorted in decreasing surface order and we consider only the K primitives with a surface above some threshold. The algorithm can then be divided in four steps :

Step 1 : choosing a first match :
We associate to every model region M a list of possible candidates in the scene. As we pointed out previously it is not possible at this stage to use the rigidity constraint to help reduce the possible choices. Only region features can be used and we have seen that they are very non robust. In the present implementation we use only the region area and allow a 50% difference between model and scene regions to take care of possible partial overlap. This may cut down by 90% the number of candidates for model regions. This first match, even though it does not fully constrain the transformation D allows to eliminate a number of model regions as being invisible.

Step 2 : choosing a second match and prevision of possible solutions :

Having selected an initial hypothesis (S_j,M_i), where S_j is represented by $(\vec{n}_0,d_0)$ and M_i by $(\vec{n}'_0,d'_0)$, we look for the compatible matches (S_1,M_k) for k>i. If $(\vec{n}',d')$ and $(\vec{n},d)$ are the representations for M_k and S_1 we check that the angles between $(\vec{n}$ and $\vec{n}_0$ and $\vec{n}'$ and $\vec{n}'_0)$ are sufficiently close (.1 radian in the current implementation) and that if G, G', G_0, G'_0 are the centers of gravity of regions S_1, M_k, S_j and M_i, respectively, that the ratio of distances $G_0G'_0/GG'$ is sufficiently close to 1 (between .5 and 1.5 in the current implementation to allow for partial overlap).

The second hypothesis is chosen such that M_i and M_k are not parallel so that we can estimate the rotation R by the methods described above. It is now possible to predict fairly precisely the other hypothesis which are compatible with these two. We associate with each model region M_m (m>k) a list Cand(m) of compatible scene regions.

Step 3 : verifying the hypothesis :
We now verify the first two hypothesis by attempting to generate a complete compatible list of matches for all model primitives. A partial match M_p of order is a list of assignments

$$M_p=((S_{j_1},M_{i_1})(S_{j_2},M_{i_2})\ldots(S_{j_p},M_{i_p})) \text{ with}$$

$i_1<i_2<\ldots<i_p$ where S_{j_k} is neither a scene primitive or NIL indicating no match for the corresponding model primitive M_{i_k}. For a given pair of initial hypothesis we generate all compatible total matches by the recursive algorithm MATCH(M,p) which takes a partial match M and the index p of the model primitive to be matched. Initially M contains the first two hypothesis. MATCH works as follows :

. Look in Cand (p) for a scene primitive S_1 such that (S_1,M_p) is compatible with the current solution M. If γ_p is the rotation angle of the best rotation estimated from M_p by the above techniques, compatible means that the angle between the normals to regions S_1 and M_p must be close to γ_p.

. If no such primitive S_1 exists then we stop.

. Else if p=K (number of model regions) then we store the complete match (M,(1,p)) else we estimate γ_{p+1} and call recursively MATCH ((M,(1,p)),p+1).

We now see why we took so much trouble in finding an efficient way of estimating the rotation. The computation has to be performed many times in the tree search implemented by the algorithm MATCH.

Results of this algorithm on one scene are displayed in Figs. 6 and 7.

CONCLUSIONS

In one of our previous papers[11] we discussed a set of ideas for implementing a flexible 3-D Vision system oriented towards the recognition and positioning of industrial parts. We have pushed further and implemented a number of these ideas and reached several conclusions. Surface representations are powerful representations for 3-D objects and can be computed efficiently and accurately from range data if the surface primitives used in the description are simple (planes and quadrics). Analytical descriptions of these surface primitives are features which are both unambiguous and robuts to occultation. Line primitives such as borders between regions, lines of high curvature, etc... Are also most probably useful[17] but have not been yet incorporated in our system. Matching rigid objects models and scene descriptions is efficiently performed in this framework by hypothesis prediction and verification implemented as a tree search guided by the rigidity constraint. Computation times are quite acceptable and very close to industrial requirements.

Others groups are pursuing similar efforts[17] and have reached a number of similar conclusions.

Acknowledgements : the author is grateful to P. Bourgeois, M. Hébert and F. Pauchon for their contributions to the work reported here.

Footnote n° 1

This paper was invited to the Seventh International Conference on Pattern Recognition.

REFERENCES

(1) Ayache, N. 1983. Un système de vision bidimensionnelle en robotique industrielle, (in french). INRIA Technical Report ISBN 2726103456.

(2) Ballard, D.H. 1981. Generalizing the Hough Transform to Arbitrary Shapes. Pattern Recognition, Vol.13, N° 2, pp.111-122.

(3) Bhanu, B. 1981. Shape matching and image segmentation using stochastic labeling. University of Southern California, USCIPI Report 1030.

(4) Bhanu, B. and Faugeras, O.D. 1984. Shape matching of two-dimensional objects. IEEE Trans. on PAMI, Vol.PAMI-6, N° 2, pp.137-156.

(5) Bookstein, F.L. 1979. Fitting conic sections to scattered data. Computer Graphics and Image Processing, 9, pp.56-71.

(6) Davis, L.S. 1979. Shape matching using relaxation techniques. IEEE Trans. on PAMI, Vol.1, N° 1, pp.60-72.

(7) Faugeras, O.D. and Berthod, M. 1981. Improving consistency and reducing ambiguity in stochastic labeling : an optimization approach. IEEE Trans. on PAMI, Vol.PAMI-3, pp.245.

(8) Faugeras, O.D., Hébert, M. and Pauchon, E. 1983. Segmentation of range data into planar and quadratic patches. Proc. PRIP 83, pp.8-13.

(9) Faugeras, O.D. and Hébert, M. 1983. A 3-D recognition fand positioning algorithm using geometrical matching between primitive surface. Proc. IJCAI 83, pp.996-1002.

(10) Faugeras, O.D. and Pauchon, E. 1983. Measuring the shape of 3-D objects. Proc. of PRIP 83, pp.2-7.

(11) Faugeras, O.D. et al. 1983. Towards a flexible vision System. In Robot Vision, A. Pugh editor, IFS (Publications) Ltd., U.D.

(12) Grimson, W.E.L. 1981. From images to surfaces: a computational study of the human early visual system. Cambridge, Mass. : MIT Press.

(13) Haralick R.M. and Elliott, G.L. 1980. Increasing tree search efficiency for constraint satisfaction problems. Artificial Intell., Vol.14, pp. 263-313.

(14) Hebert, M. 1983. Reconnaissance de formes tridimensionnelles. (in french), INRIA Technical Report ISBN 2726103790.

(15) Hébert, M. and Ponce, J. 1982. A new method for segmenting 3-D scenes into primitives. Proc. 6th Int. J. Conf. on Pattern Recognition, pp.836-838, Münich, Germany.

(16) Henderson, T. 1984. The 3-D Hough shape transform. To appear in Pattern Recognition Letters.

(17) Horaud, P. and Bolles, R. 1984. Finding modeled objects in range data. Submitted to 6th ECAI, Pisa, Italy.

(18) Horn, B.K.P. 1975. Obtaining shape from shading information. In The Psychology of Computer Vision editor, P.H. Winston editor, New York, Mc Graw-Hill, pp.115-155.

(19) Hummel, R.A. and Zucker, S.W. 1983. On the foundations of relaxation labeling processes. IEEE Trans. on PAMI, Vol.PAMI-5, pp.267-287.

(20) Ikeuchi, K. 1981. Determining surface orientations of specular surfaces by using the photometric stereo method. IEEE Trans. on PAMI, Vol. PAMI-2, N° 6, pp.661-669.

(21) Ikeuchi, K. and Horn, B.K.P. 1981. Numerical shape from shading and occluding boundaries. In Computer Vision, M. Brady editor, Amsterdam, North-Holland, pp.141-184.

(22) Jarvis, R.A. 1983. Perspective on range finding techniques for computer vision. IEEE Trans. on PAMI, Vol. PAMI-5, N° 2, pp.122-139.

(23) Marr, D. and Poggio, T. 1976. Cooperative computation of stereo disparity. Science, 194, pp. 283-287.

(24) Marr, D. and Poggio, T. 1979. A computational theory of human stereo vision. Proc. R. Soc. Lond. B, 204, pp.301-328.

(25) Nishihara, H.K. and Poggio, T. 1983. Stereo Vision for Robotics. Proc. First International Symposium of Robotics Research, Brettenwoods, USA.

(26) Oshima, M. and Shirai, Y. 1983. Object recognition using three-dimensional information. IEEE Trans. on PAMI, Vol. PAMI-5, N° 4, pp.353-361.

(27) Pavlidis, T. 1983. Curve fitting with conic splines. Submitted to ACM-TOGS.

(28) Ray, R., Birk, J. and Kelley, R.B. 1983. Error analysis of surfaces normals determined by radiometry. IEEE Trans. on PAMI, Vol.PAMI-5, N° 6, pp.631-644.

(29) Rosenfeld, A., Hummel, R. and Zucker, S. 1976. Scene labeling by relaxation operations. IEEE Trans. on SMC, 6, pp.420-433.

(30) Witkin, A.P. 1981. Recovering surface shape and orientation from texture. In Computer Vision, M. Brady editor, Amsterdam, North-Holland, pp.17-47.

(31) Woodham, R.J. 1978. Reflectance map techniques

for analysing surface defects in metal casting.
MIT AI Report, AI-TR-547, Cambridge, MIT, USA.

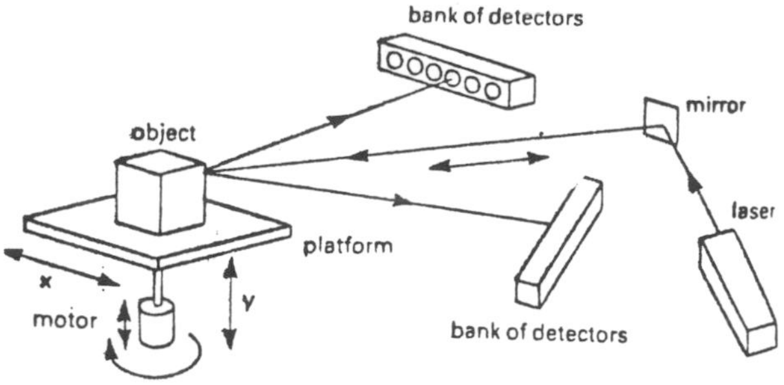

Fig.1. System for object digitalization.

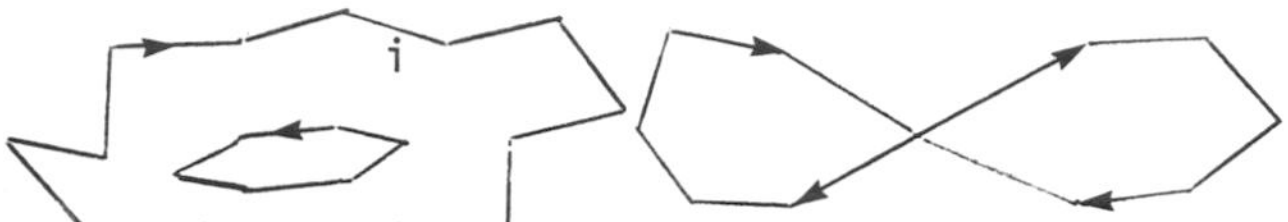

a) a region Fig.2. b) not a region

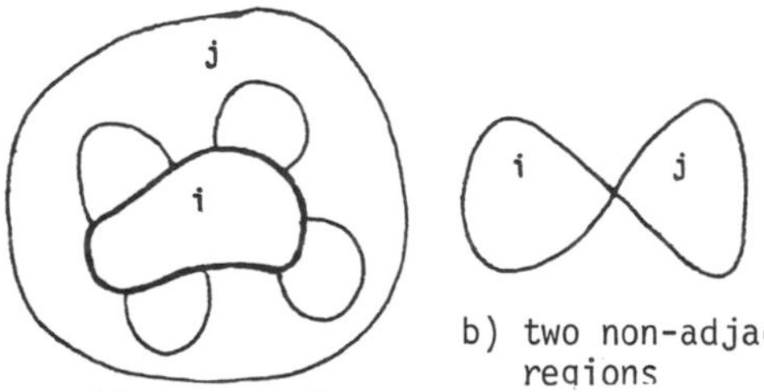

a) two adjacent regions b) two non-adjacent regions
Fig.3.

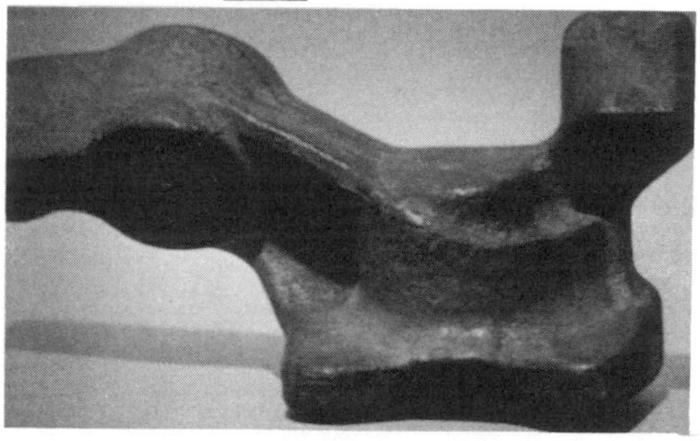

Fig.4. a) Photograph of a car part.

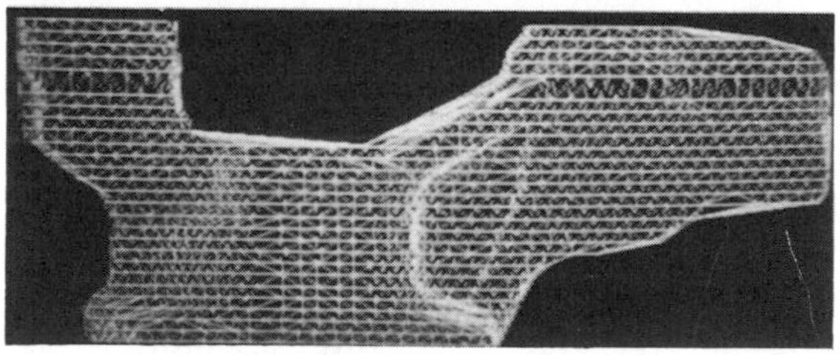

Fig.4. b) 3-D triangulation of the part in a).

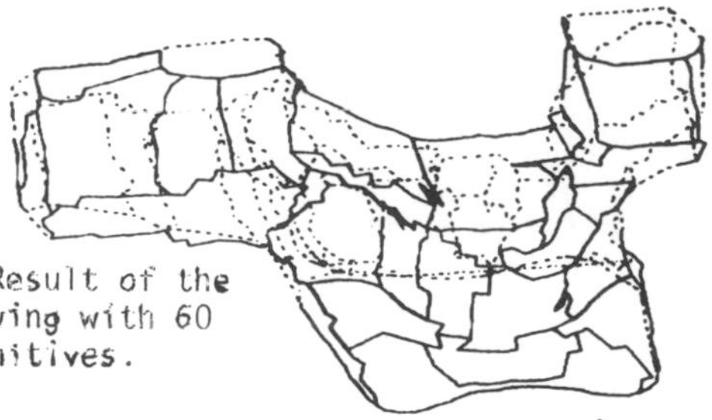

Fig.4. c) Result of the region growing with 60 planar primitives.

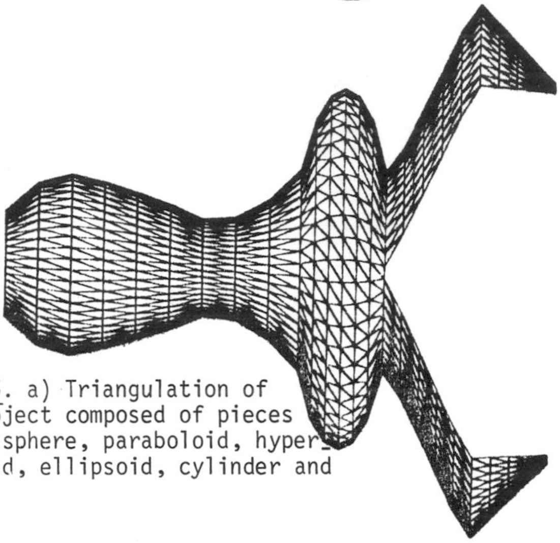

Fig.5. a) Triangulation of an object composed of pieces of a sphere, paraboloid, hyper-boloid, ellipsoid, cylinder and cone.

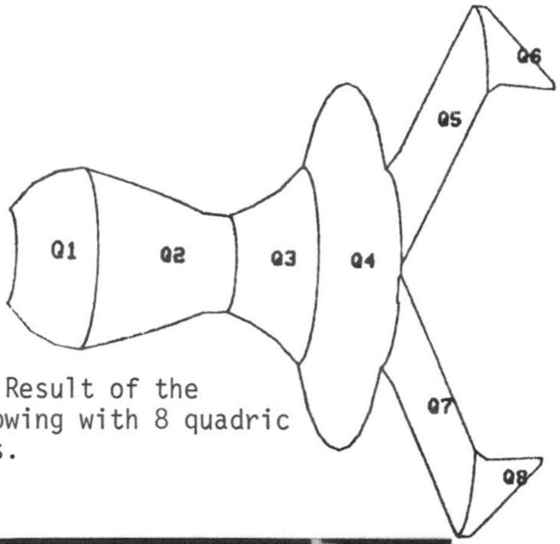

Fig.5. b) Result of the region growing with 8 quadric primitives.

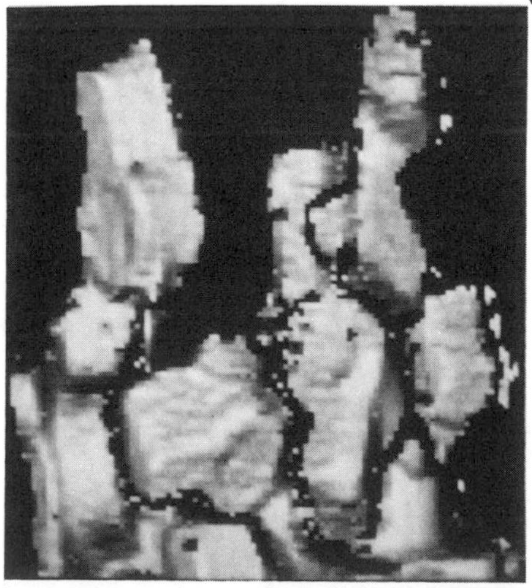

Fig.6. Scene to be analysed (x component of the normal).

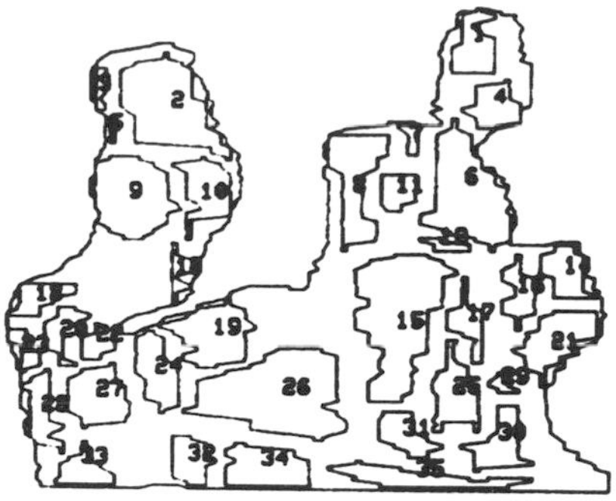
Fig.7a. Segmentation of Fig.6 with planar primitives.

Fig.7b. Model of Fig.4c as positioned.

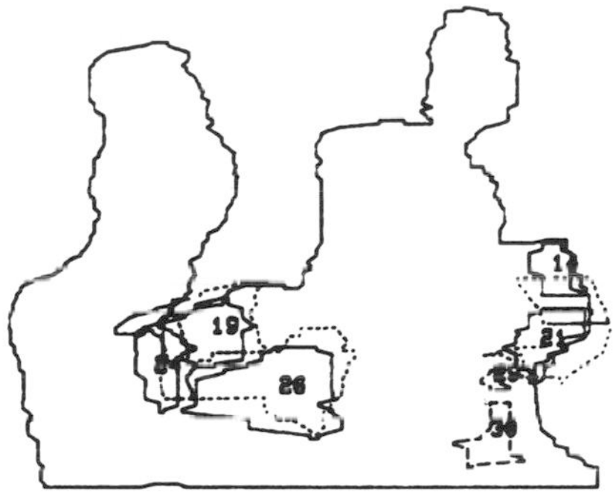
Fig.7c. Superposition of identified scene and model primitives.

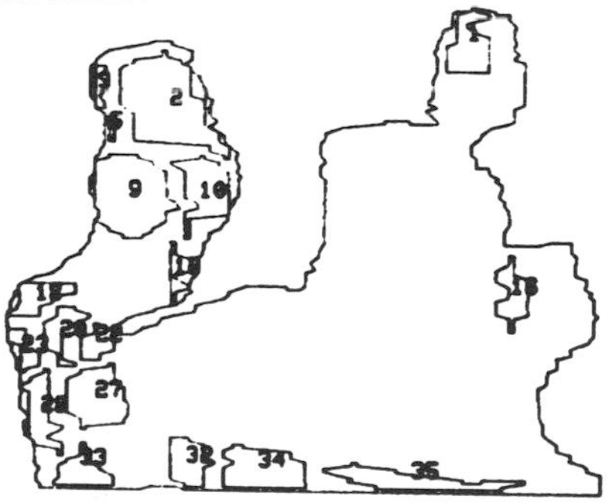
Fig.7d. Same as 7a.

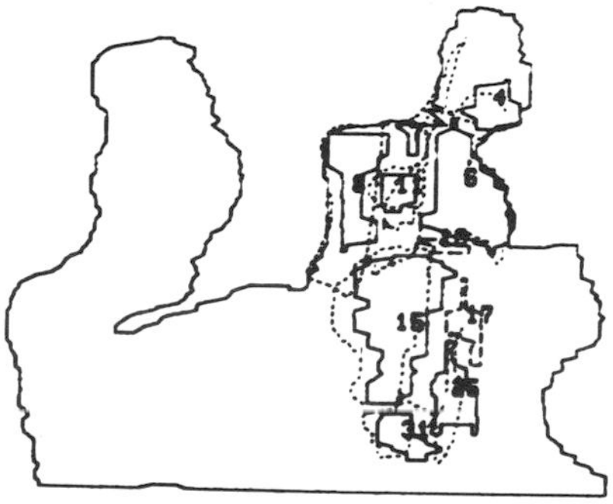
Fig.7e. Same as 7c.

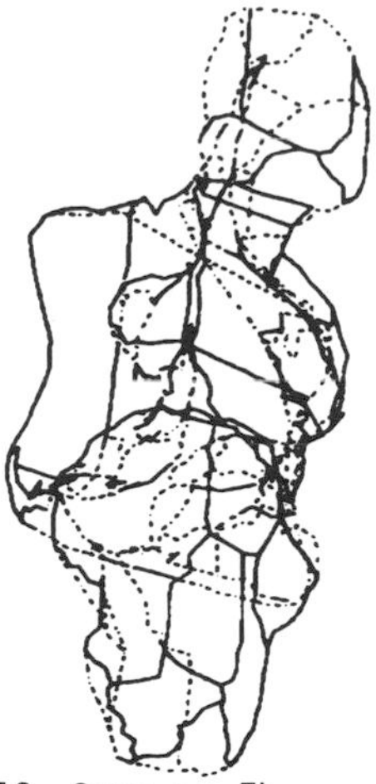
Fig.7f. Same as 7b.

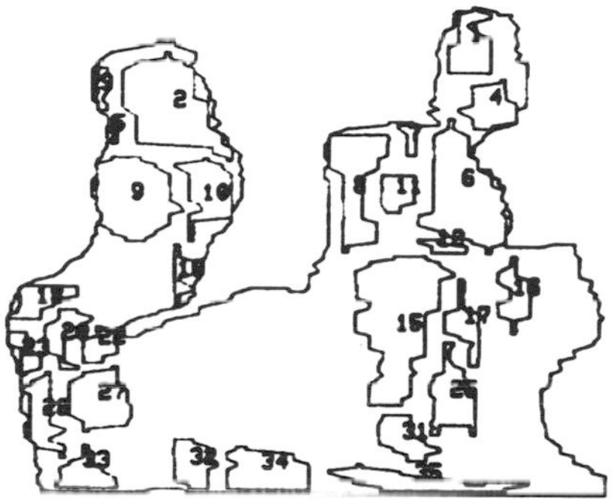
Fig.7g. Same as 7a.

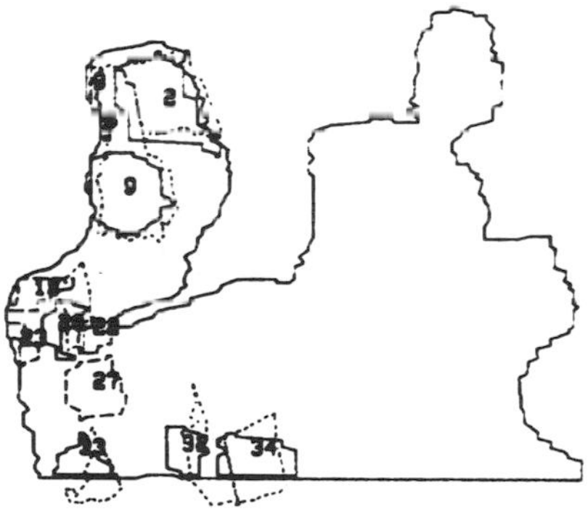
Fig.7h. Same as 7c.

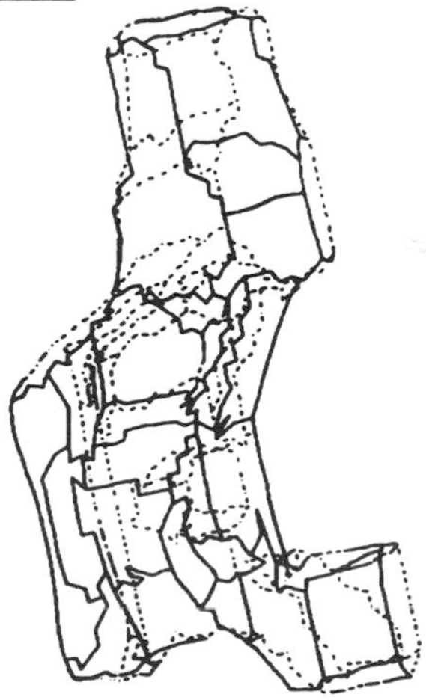
Fig.7i. Same as 7b.

A 3D VISION SYSTEM: GENERATING AND MATCHING SHAPE DESCRIPTIONS IN RANGE IMAGES

Fumiaki Tomita and Takeo Kanade
Department of Computer Science
Carnegie-Mellon University
Pittsburgh, Pa. 15213
U. S. A.

We have developed a vision system to recognize and locate three dimensional (3D) objects in range images. A light-stripe rangefinder image is first segemented into edges and surfaces. This segmentation is done in 3D space; edges are classified as either 3D straight lines or circular curves, and surfaces are either planar or conic. An object model consists of component edges and surfaces and their interrelationships. Our model representation can accomodate not only objects with rigid, fixed shape, but also objects with articulations between their parts, such as rotational-joint or linear-slide motions. The system supports interactive construction of object models. Using sample scenes, the object models can be generated and modified till they become satisfactory. The matching process is rather straightforward. A transformation from an object model to the scene is hypothesized by initially matching a few scene features with model features. The transformation is then tested with the rest of the features for verification.

1. Introduction

Three-dimensional (3D) information about a scene may be represented as a range image. We use a light-stripe rangefinder [Shirai and Suwa 71, Agin 72] to obtain a range image. The range image is first segmented into edges and surfaces. This segmentation is done in 3D space; edges are classified as either 3D straight lines or circular curves, and surfaces are classified as either planar or curved.

Since the descriptions obtained from the scene are to be matched with object models, the models must be described in similar terms. Methods to acquire objects models include programming in advance, using a CAD-type system [Brooks 81], or showing examples [Oshima 83, Herman and Kanade 84]. Our system supports interactive construction of object models. Using sample scenes, the object models can be generated and modified till they become satisfactory. In our system, the model can represent not only objects with rigid, fixed shape, but also objects with articulations between their parts, such as rotational-joint or linear-slide motions.

Matching between the input scene and an object model is based on finding appropriate coordinate transformations from the object model to the scene. A transformation is hypothesized by initially matching a few scene features with model features. The transformation is then tested with the rest of features for verification.

In this paper, the method for building edge-based scene descriptions from range images is first presented in Section 2. Next, the method for interactively generating object models from sample scenes is presented in Section 3, and then the method for obtaining matching object models with scenes is presented in Section 4. Finally, the experimental results and conclusions are provided in Section 5 and 6, respectively.

2. Scene Analysis

The first step in object recognition is to obtain scene descriptions from a range image. In our approach, edges are first detected from a range image and they are used to define the boundaries of surfaces. A scene is represented by a set of surfaces and each surface is represented by the boundary segments which are classified as circular curves or straight lines.

2.1. Range Image

A light-stripe rangefinder provides a range image of a 3D scene. It measures x, y, z values of the points on projected light stripes. Fig. 1(a) shows a light-stripe image as viewed from the camera. In this registration, however, the light stripe does not cover all the points in the scene uniformly; in the portions where light stripes are sparse, points between neighboring stripes have no range data. These gaps are filled by linear interpolation. However, those portions occluded from the light source are not filled. Fig. 1(b) shows the interpolated x, y, and z images.

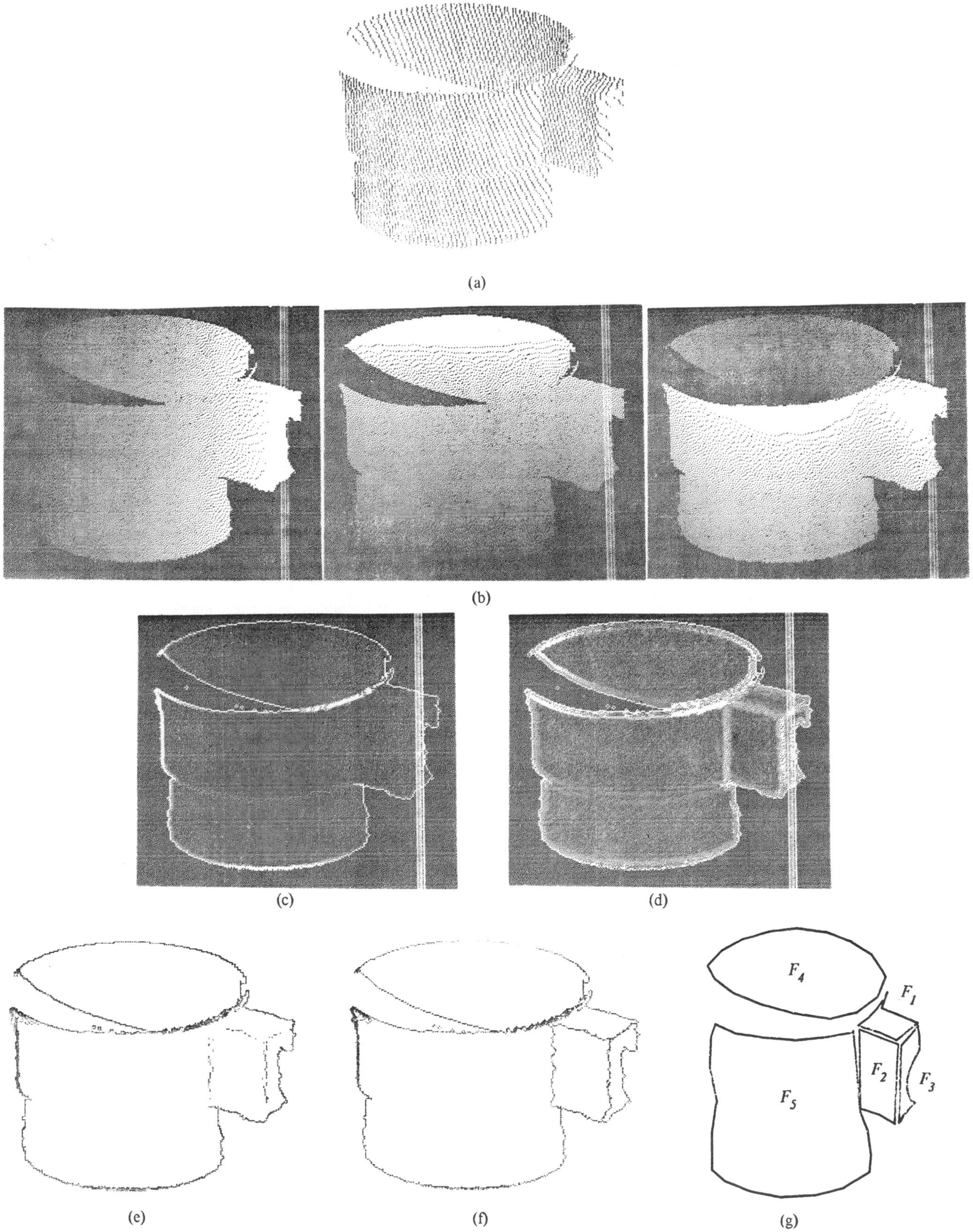

Figure 1: Scene analysis. (a) Light-stripe image of a cup. (b) Interpolated x, y, and z images. (c) Gap-edge strength image. (d) Corner-edge strength image. (e) Strong edge points. (f) Linked edge points. (g) Line and curve fitting.

2.2. Edge Detection

The range image is first segmented into edges. This segmentation is done by using 3D coordinates of points. We consider two kinds of edges: gap edges and corner edges. Gap edges are located where the depth abruptly changes. Corner edges are located where the surface normal abruptly changes. Therefore, gap edges usually correspond to contours of objects and corner edges to convex or concave edges. Let a range image be represented by three image arrays X, Y, and Z in which x, y, and z values are stored, respectively. First, gap edges are detected. This is done by calculating the gradient of the z-coordinate with respect to x and y. After the image is smoothed to reduce the noise with a $(2m-1) \times (2m-1)$ averaging operator ($m = 2$ is used in the experiments), the depth gradient at a point (i, j) is computed as,

$$Z_x(i, j) = \frac{Z(i+m, j) - Z(i-m, j)}{X(i+m, j) - X(i-m, j)}$$

$$Z_y(i, j) = \frac{Z(i, j+m) - Z(i, j-m)}{Y(i, j+m) - Y(i, j-m)}$$

The strength and the direction of the gap edge at a point (i, j) are defined as,

$$|E_g(i, j)| = \sqrt{Z_x(i, j)^2 + Z_y(i, j)^2}$$

$$\angle E_g(i, j) = \tan^{-1}\frac{Z_y(i, j)}{Z_x(i, j)} + \frac{\pi}{2}$$

Next, corner edges are detected. This is done also by using the $Z_x(i, j)$ and $Z_y(i, j)$ values. We define the surface normal as $N(i, j) = (Z_x(i, j), Z_y(i, j), -1)$. Let $\alpha(i, j)$ denote the angle between a horizontal pair of surface normals $N(i+2m, j)$ and $N(i-2m, j)$, and $\beta(i, j)$ denote the angle between a vertical pair of surface normals $N(i, j+2m)$ and $N(i, j-2m)$. The strength of the corner edge at a point (i, j) is defined as,

$$|E_c(i, j)| = \max\{\alpha(i, j), \beta(i, j)\},$$

where

$$\cos\alpha(i, j) = \frac{N(i+2m, j) \cdot N(i-2m, j)}{|N(i+2m, j)||N(i-2m, j)|}$$

$$\cos\beta(i, j) = \frac{N(i, j+2m) \cdot N(i, j-2m)}{|N(i, j+2m)||N(i, j-2m)|}$$

To compute the direction of the corner edge point, we compute the cross-product of the pair of surface normals whose angle has been the greatest. Let $(v_x(i, j), v_y(i, j), v_z(i, j))$ be the components of the cross-product at a point (i, j). The direction of the corner edge at a point (i, j) is defined as the projection of this vector onto the x-y plane,

$$\angle E_c(i, j) = \tan^{-1}\frac{v_y(i, j)}{v_x(i, j)}$$

Fig. 1(c) shows the strength of the gap edges and Fig. 1(d) shows the strength of the corner edges.

2.3. Edge Linking

Both gap edges and corner edges are thinned to suppress redundant edges, thresholded to extract reliable edges, and linked to obtain continuous edges.

The thinning process looks for local maxima of edge strength by examining the local neighborhood of each edge point. For a gap edge point, m points are examined in both directions perpendicular to the edge direction. For a corner edge point, $2m$ points are examined in each direction. If an examined edge point has greater strength than the central edge point, the central point is deleted.

The thresholding process deletes the edge points whose strengths are below some fixed threshold. Fig. 1(e) shows the strong edge points which have been extracted by thinning and thresholding. These points may not be continuous. They are therefore linked by reviving some of the deleted weak edge points. In this procedure, we consider a 3×3 window surrounding each strong edge point, and test three edge points which are almost in the same direction as the central edge point e_0 (edge points e_5, e_6, and e_7 in Fig. 2). Of these three edge points, the one that maximizes the following function is revived if it had been deleted in the process of thinning and thresholding.

$$f(e_0, e_i) = |e_i| \cos(\angle e_i - \angle e_0)$$

This function gives a large value when the strength of the edge point e_i is large and the direction is the same as that of the central edge point. This process is recursively applied to the edge point just revived until the linked edges run into an edge already found in the image or very weak edge points are continuously revived. A similar test is performed for the three edge points in the direction opposite to the central point (edge points e_1, e_2, and e_3 in Fig. 2). Fig. 1(f) shows the result of linking.

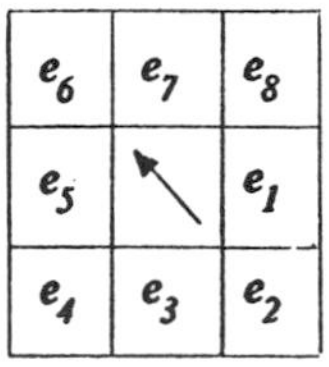

Figure 2: 3×3 window for linking (the arrow signifies the direction of the central edge point e_0)

2.4. Boundary Following

Surfaces are defined by their closed boundaries. The closed boundary of a surface is extracted by following edges in a direction such that the surface is always to the right. Here, the boundaries which are extracted based on gap edges are classified into either occluding or occluded; only occluding boundaries will be used for recognition. A plane is fitted to the 3D data points on the detected boundary, and the surface is classified as either planar or curved depending on the error in the plane fit. In our example, five surfaces were found as shown in Fig. 1(g). Three (F_1, F_2, F_3) were classified as planar and two (F_4, F_5) as curved.

The boundary of each surface is segmented into boundary components based on the curvature at each point on the boundary. Let p_i denote the i th point on the boundary. The curvature at p_i is defined by the angle between two vectors $p_{i-k}p_i$ and p_ip_{i+k} ($k = 10$ is used in the experiments). The boundary is segmented at the points where the curvature exceeds some fixed threshold and is locally maximal. The boundary components are approximated by circular curves by using a least-square method and are classified as either straight lines or circular curves based on the ratio of the length of the arc to the length of the chord. Fig. 1(g) shows the result of line and curve fitting.

2.5. Scene Description

A scene may now be described by a list structure such as shown in Fig. 3. In this description, a scene is segmented into a set of surfaces, and each surface is represented by a list of the boundary components. A surface node has value slots for surface normal of the fitted plane, error to the fitted plane, and perimeter. A a boundary-component node has value slots for starting point, ending point, orientation (used only for straight lines, defined as a vector from start to end point), length, curvature, center of curve, angle of arc, and surface orientation for circular curve (every circular curve determines the planar surface on which it exists).

3. Object Model

Object models are represented by component surfaces in a similar fashon as scene descriptions. The system supports interactive construction of object models using sample scenes.

3.1. Generation

The initial version of the model of an object is generated by extracting its boundary components in the first sample scene and defining the surfaces based on them. Successive versions of an object model are incrementally generated as follows. An object in a new sample scene is matched with the current model to give the coordinate transformation T between them (which is described in section 4). Once T is obtained, the boundary components in the new scene which are necessary to describe the object, but which are not yet contained in the model, are incorporated into the model using the inverse transformation T^{-1}.

As shown in Fig. 4, an object model is represented with a similar structure as that of scene descriptions. An object consists of parts, which are composed of component surfaces (which are in turn represented by a list of boundary components). The relation R between parts represents the geometrical relationship between them, including the articulated ones to be described next.

3.2. Articulations

The model can represent not only objects with rigid, fixed shape, but also objects having articulations between their parts, such as rotational-joint or linear-slide motions. For example, the scissors in Fig. 5 should be regarded as the same; it is composed of two parts which rotate around the joint. We consider five articulations: linear slide, rotational joint, combination of slide and joint, combination of two joints (which causes pan and tilt), and universal joint (combination of three joints). For an object having articulations between its parts, the parts are defined separately and the relations between them are stored in the object model. When the kind of

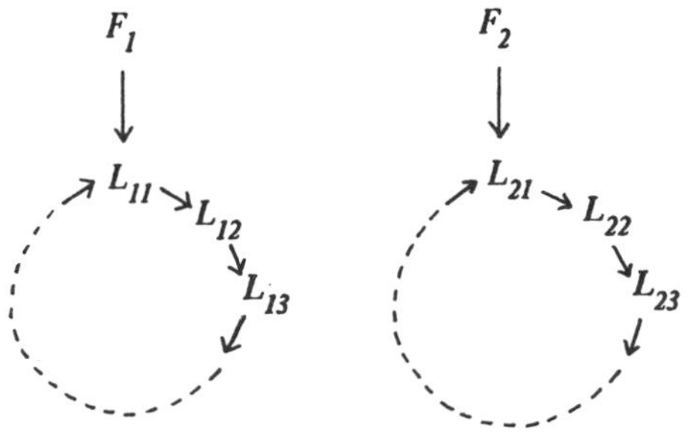

Figure 3: List structures for describing a scene (F: surface, L: boundary component)

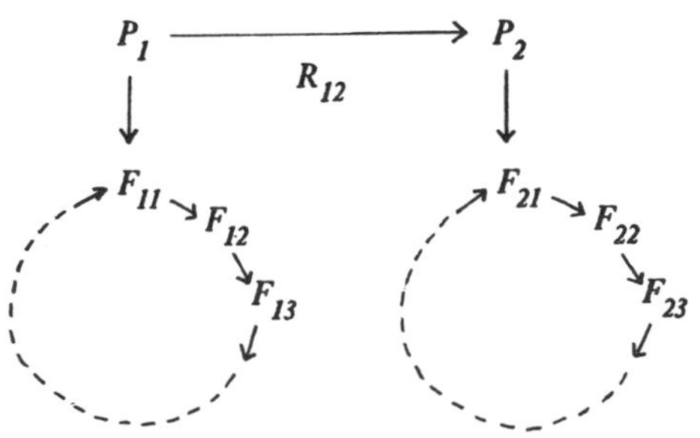

Figure 4: List structures for describing an object model (P: part of object, F: component surface, R: relationship)

articulation is specified, the parameters describing the relationship can be obtained by showing at least two good examples as follows.

Suppose that part P_1 is matched with two sample scenes a and b by two transformations $T_1(a)$ and $T_1(b)$, respectively, and similarly part P_2 is matched by two transformations $T_2(a)$ and $T_2(b)$. The coordinate system of part P_2 viewed from part P_1 is obtained from each scene by

$$R_{12}(a) = T_1(a)^{-1}T_2(a)$$

$$R_{12}(b) = T_1(b)^{-1}T_2(b)$$

These two coordinate systems determine the range of motion of part P_2 relative to part P_1 as follows.

1. In the case of a linear slide, the orientation of the two coordinate systems is the same but their origins differ. The line which links the two origins is the range of the slide (Fig. 6(a)).

2. In the case of a rotational joint, the origins of the two coordinate systems lie on a circle. The circle gives the center of rotation and the orientation of the rotation axis (Fig. 6(b)).

3. In the case of a combination of joint and slide, the origins of the two coordinate systems lie on a cylinder. The cylinder gives the rotation axis and the range of the slide (Fig. 6(c)).

4. In the case of a combination of two joints or a universal joint, the origins of the two coordinate systems lie on a sphere. The sphere gives the center of rotation (Fig. 6(d)). In the case of a universal joint, there is the rotation around the line which links the center of the sphere and the origin of the coordinate system.

There are shapes whose descriptions are invariant to rotation. For example, a cylinder's description will not change if rotated about its axis. When an object includes such an invariant shape as a part, the part and the other parts of the object can be considered to have the rotational-joint relationship. The cup in Fig. 1 is such an example. In this case, the handle can rotate around the fixed body of the cup. The body and the handle of the cup are defined separately in the model and the rotational-joint relationship between them is stored. Similarly, when an object includes a spherical part, the spherical part and the other parts are considered to have the universal-joint relationship. Tangential contours in cylinders and spheres are registered with the model in the same way as contours arising from real edges.

For example, Fig. 7(a) shows models of the body and handle of a cup. They have a rotational-joint relationship and the cup in Fig. 1 is one of the instances which satisfy the relationship. Fig. 7(b) shows models of the body and handle of a pan. They also have a rotational-

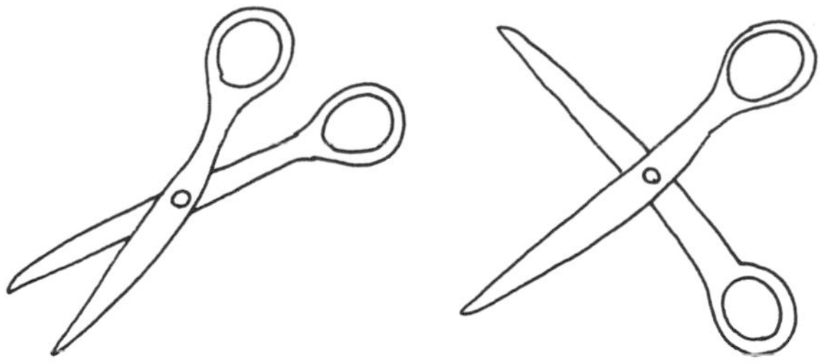

Figure 5: Scissors.

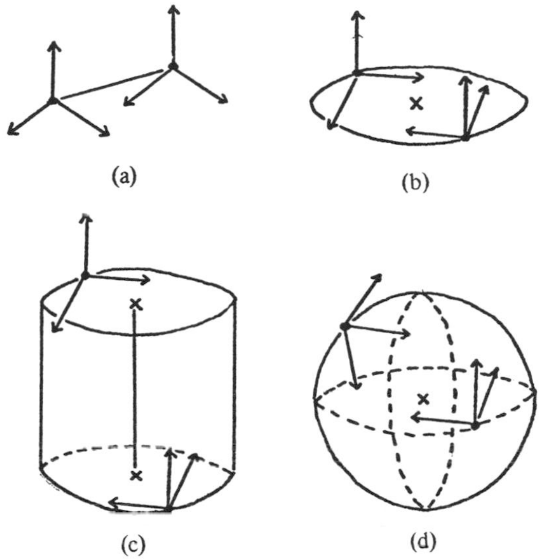

Figure 6: Range of motion of coordinate system. (a) Linear slide. (b) Rotational joint. (c) Combination of slide and joint. (d) Combination of two joints or universal joint.

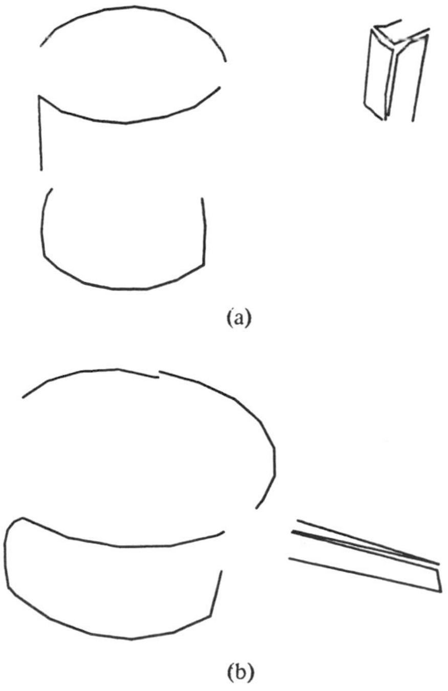

Figure 7: Object model. (a) Cup. (b) Pan.

joint relationship. The parameters for these relations are obtained from sample scenes.

4. Matching

Matching between the input scene and an object model is based on finding appropriate coordinate transformations from the object model to the scene. A transformation is hypothesized by initially matching a few scene features with model features. The transformation is then tested with the rest of the features for verification.

4.1. Transformations

A candidate transformation from an object model to a scene is generated by considering a pair of boundary components, one in the object model and the other in the scene. Let us assume that the i th boundary component in the model $L_m(i)$ be matched to the k th boundary component in the scene $L_s(k)$. We want to compute the transformation which transforms $L_m(i)$ to $L_s(k)$.

We must first know the local gradients of the surfaces on which the boundary components exist. When the boundary component is a circular curve, we already know the surface on which it exists (see Section 2.5). When the boundary component is a straight line and it is on a planar surface, that surface is used. When the boundary component is a straight line and it is on a curved surface, another point is necessary to determine the local planar surface. We choose this extra point as follows. For the boundary component of the model, the $i-1$ th boundary component on the same surface is chosen and when it is a straight line, its starting point is used, otherwise, the center point of the curve is used. For the boundary component of the scene, the j th ($j \neq k$) boundary component which corresponds to the $i-1$ th boundary component of the model must be searched for from the same surface.

Once the boundary components to be matched are identified, the transformation can be calculated as follows. For the case that they are both straight lines,

1. The line $L_m(i)$ is translated so that the starting point corresponds to that of the line $L_s(k)$.

2. The line $L_m(i)$ is rotated so that the normal of the local planar surface (obtained as described above) on which it exists corresponds to that of the line $L_s(k)$.

3. The line $L_m(i)$ is rotated on that local surface so that the orientation corresponds to that of the line $L_s(k)$.

For the case that both boundary components are circular curves,

1. The curve $L_m(i)$ is translated so that the center point corresponds to that of the curve $L_s(k)$.

2. The curve $L_m(i)$ is rotated so that the normal of the local planar surface on which it exists corresponds to that of the curve $L_s(k)$.

3. The curve $L_m(i)$ is rotated on that local surface so that the orientation from the center point to the starting point (or the ending point) corresponds to that of the curve $L_s(k)$.

Pairing of boundary components are done basically by an exhaustive search. To reduce the search space, surfaces having about the same perimeter are paired and then only boundary components having about the same length are paired.

4.2. Matching of Boundary Components

Once a transformation T is determined, its validity is tested by determining whether the other boundary components in the object model, when transformed by T, actually match the boundary components found in the scene. The degree of match between a transformed boundary component in the object model and a boundary component in the scene is measured as follows.

1. When matching straight lines, the orientation of the line is first tested, and the distance of each terminal point of the scene line to the transformed model line is measured as the error. When the error is below a threshold, the length of overlapping portion is measured as the degree of match.

2. When matching circular curves, the radius of the curve and the orientation of the surface normal are tested, and the difference of the center point is measured as the error. When the errors are below a threshold, the length of the overlapping portion is measured as the degree of match.

The errors can be used to adjust the transformation by a least-square method. The degree of match is accumulated as the amount of match for each object.

4.3. Test for Occlusion

The matching is executed for each boundary component in the object model except for those on occluded surfaces. The system can know occluded surfaces by rotating the surface normals according to the transformation T. Surface normals are outward pointing. If they point away from the sensor system, the surface is occluded by parts of the same object.

When a part of a boundary component in the object model can not be matched with any boundary components in the scene, we try to determine if the part is occluded by some other objects. This is done by comparing the z values of the points on the transformed boundary component of the object model and those of the corresponding points in the Z image. If the part is found not to be occluded, the transformation is regarded as wrong.

4.4. Control of Matching

There are three classes of parameters which control the matching process. These parameters are used not only to get reliable results but also to speed up the matching process.

1. Amount of error (reliability) — This gives the threshold for errors.

2. Amount of match (plausibility) — When the amount of match exceeds the threshold, the object is regarded as found. If the amount of match at any point during the way of matching is not expected to exceed the threshold, that matching is not performed any more. Thus, longer boundary components on larger surfaces in the object model are matched first because rejecting an incorrect transformation should be done as early as possible.

3. Rank — The parts of an object are ranked to order the matching process. The parts with higher rank are found

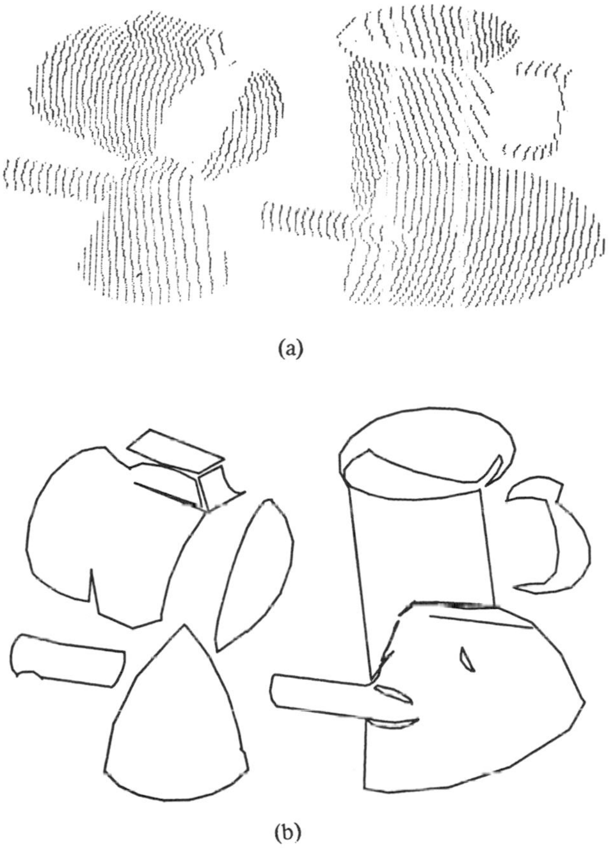

Figure 8: Input scene containing a cup. (a) Light-stripe image. (b) Line and curve fitting.

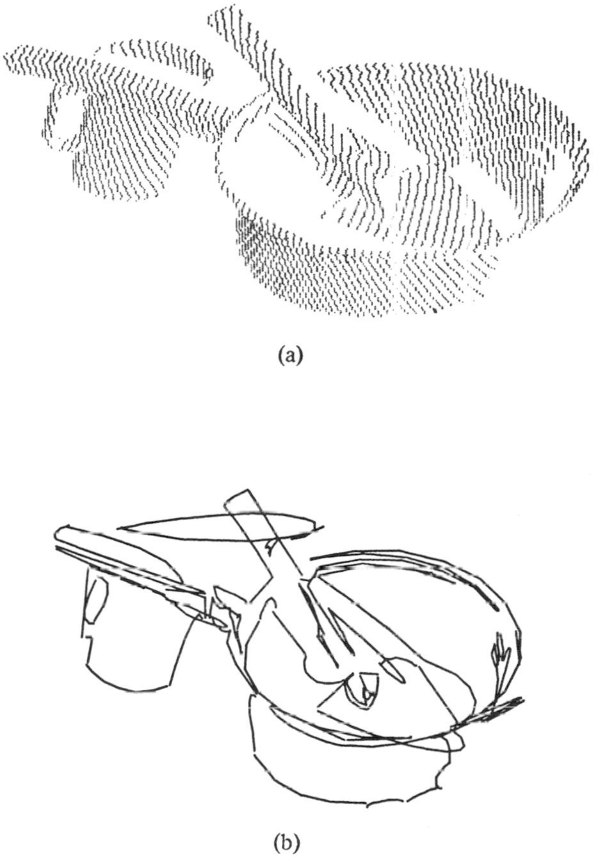

Figure 10: Input scene containing a pan. (a) Light-stripe image. (b) Line and curve fitting.

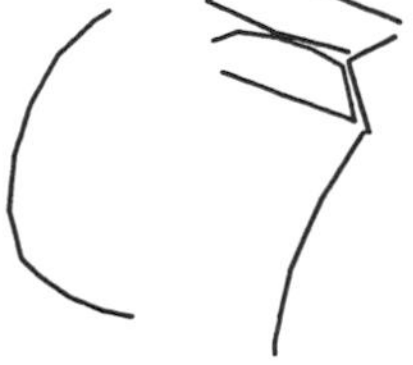

Figure 9: Recognition of a cup.

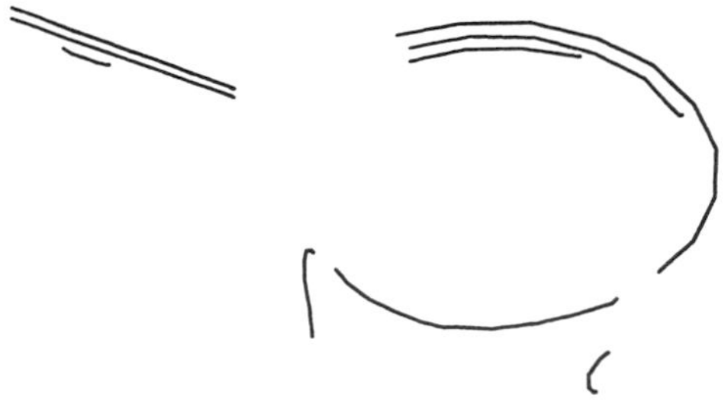

Figure 11: Recognition of a pan.

first and the parts with lower rank are found later by testing the relationship to the parts with higher rank. Parts with simple shape should be ranked low because they may match many parts of other objects in a scene without any constraints.

The matching begins with high thresholds for parts with higher rank. If some parts are not found, the thresholds are decreased and the matching is retried. When some parts with higher rank are found, relevant parts with lower rank are then searched by testing the relations to the objects with higher rank which are already found; a transformation which does not satisfy the relationship is excluded in advance. This reduces the amount of unnecessary shape matching.

5. Experimental Results

Fig. 8 is an example scene for which the recognition is applied. When the scene is matched with models in Fig. 7(a), one body and one handle of the cup which satisfy the rotational-joint relationship are found, as shown in Fig. 9. The amount of match and the maximal error for each object are listed below.

object	amount of match	maximal error
handle	0.82	28.33
body	0.59	22.86

The scene in Fig. 10 is matched with the object model in Fig. 7(b). Since the shape of the handle of the pan is simple, its rank is set lower than that of the body (see in Section 4.4). Fig. 11 shows the result of matching. If the rank of the handle is not set low, many candidate objects are found. Thus, the relations between parts not only reduce ambiguity in shape descriptions but also make recognition flexible.

6. Conclusion

The matching process is based on a depth-first search of possible corresponding pairs of boundary components. It is necessary to reduce the search space to speed up the matching process. The current efforts to reduce the search are summarized below.

1. Parts of objects are ranked and parts with lower rank are searched by first testing the relationships with parts with higher rank (Section 4.4). This reduces the amount of unnecessary shape matching.

2. When obtaining a transformation, surfaces with about the same perimeter are paired and then only the boundary components with about the same length are paired (Section 4.1).

3. When matching boundary components, those on occluded surfaces are excluded in advance (Section 4.3).

4. When matching boundary components, longer components on larger surfaces in an object model are matched first so as to reject using an incorrect transformation as early as possible (Section 4.4).

5. The boundary components in the scene that are to be matched are retrieved based on the orientation for a straight line and on the surface normal for a circular curve.

In the future, we will examine quantitatively how much these methods reduce the search space. Furthermore, the idea of precompiling [Goad 83] may be used to speed up the matching process. Once an object model is completed, the matching procedure can be systematically tuned for a particular object model using the shape constraints.

We performed test runs on several scenes. We will try more data such as industrial machine parts. Furthermore, we plan to extend the system to recognize 3D objects in 2D gray images using the 3D object models which are generated from 3D scenes. Also, we plan to use a CAD-type system to generate object models.

Acknowledgement

The authors would like to thank Marty Herman and David Smith at Carnegie-Mellon University for their helpful discussions.

References

[Agin 72] Agin, G. J.
Representation and Description of Curved Objects.
PhD thesis, Stanford University, October, 1972.

[Brooks 81] Brooks, R. A.
Symbolic Reasoning Among 3-D Models and 2-D Images.
PhD thesis, Stanford University, 1981.

[Goad 83] Goad, C.
Special Purpose Automatic Programming for 3D Model-Based Vision.
Proc. ARPA Image Understanding Workshop, June, 1983.

[Herman and Kanade 84]
Herman, M., and Kanade, T.
The 3D MOSAIC Scene Understanding System: Incremental Reconstruction of 3D Scenes from Complex Images.
Technical Report CMU-CS-84-102, Department of Computer Science, Carnegie-Mellon University, Pittsburgh, PA, February, 1984.

[Oshima 83] Oshima, M., and Shirai, Y.
Object Recognition Using Three-Dimensional Information.
IEEE Trans. on Pattern Analysis and Machine Intelligence PAMI-5(2):353-361, July, 1983.

[Shirai and Suwa 71]
Shirai, Y., and Suwa, M.
Recognition of Polyhedrons with a Rangefinder.
Proc. IJCAI-71 :80-87, 1971.

CONFIGURATION UNDERSTANDING IN RANGE DATA

Robert C. Bolles and Patrice Horaud*

SRI International, EK290
333 Ravenswood Avenue,
Menlo Park, California 94025, U. S. A.

Range-based techniques for verifying hypotheses and determining object configurations are described. Range images are predicted from hypothesized objects and compared with measured data. Differences between predicted and measured data lead to the rejection of hypotheses. For example, a hypothesized object implying that the sensor saw through a solid object is rejected. As hypotheses are made and verified, a graph is built that describes which objects are on top of others. This graph, plus regions of unexplained occlusions, forms the basis for an understanding of the configuration. A detailed example of this approach, currently employed as part of the Three-Dimensional Part Orientation (3DPO) system for recognizing moderately complex castings in a pile, is presented.

INTRODUCTION

After an object recognition system has hypothesized a pose (i.e., a position and orientation) for an object, there are three things it can do to increase an arm´s chances of acquiring the object correctly:

* Verify the hypothesis
* Refine the pose estimate
* Determine the configuration of objects.

Most object recognition research has concentrated on making hypotheses, not refining them. Recent systems for recognizing objects have been proposed by Oshima and Shirai [1981], Faugeraus and Hebert [1983], Horaud and Bolles [1984], and Grimson and Lozano-Perez [1984]. In this paper we describe range-based techniques for verifying hypotheses and ascertaining object configurations. Although the pose refinement step is an essential component of a complete system, it will not be discussed here. We simply observe that one approach to pose refinement described by Rutkowski and Benton [1984].

VERIFICATION

There is only one way to check a hypothesis: compare predictions based on it with data gathered from the scene. Predictions may differ in type, but the process is nonetheless identical. If too many predictions disagree with the data, the hypothesis is rejected.

Predictions can be object features, such as holes, corners, or surface patches, or they can be sensor data, such as the expected intensity of a point on the surface of an object. Most matching strategies have feature-level verification built into the matching process. They use the first few features to narrow the number of possible matches down to one -- which is equivalent to making a hypothesis -- and then match additional features to increase their confidence in that hypothesis. These systems generally report the hypotheses that contain the most matching features to be the best matches.

Data-level comparison is another level of verification that can be done. In this kind of comparison the program employs a hypothesis to predict the data that would been measured by the sensor if the object had been in the hypothesized pose, and then compares these predictions with the data actually measured by the sensor. In this paper we describe data-level techniques that complement traditional feature-level techniques. We concentrate on range data because they encode the geometry of an object directly and are relatively easy to predict.

The experiments were performed within the 3DPO system, which locates objects jumbled together in a pile (such as the one shown in Figure 1). In a typical task the 3DPO system uses the three-dimensional model of a casting illustrated in Figure 2 to locate castings in the range data shown in Figure 3. The system forms one hypothesis at a time (such as the one shown in Figure 4) and then tries to verify it.

To check a hypothesis, the program predicts the range data, compares it with the actual data, and then makes decisions based on the relationships between the predicted and actual data. The predictions are an estimate of what the sensor would have seen if the objects had been in the hypothesized poses. To make the predictions, the

---

* Patrice Horaud is now at the Laboratoire d´Automatique de Grenoble, BP 46, 38402 Saint-Martin d´Heres, France.

program uses the planar-patch model shown in Figure 5, which consists of a list of points on the surface of the object and their outward-pointing normals. Given a hypothesis or set of hypotheses, the program builds an image by painting in regions corresponding to the surface patches in the scene that are closest to the sensor. This is essentially the same as the Z buffer technique used by computer graphics systems. Figure 6 shows a predicted range image that corresponds to the measured data shown in Figure 3. It was produced from seven hypotheses.

When a measured range value is compared with a predicted value, three situations can occur:

(1) The measured data are approximately equal to the predicted data.
(2) The measured data are significantly farther from the sensor than the predicted data.
(3) The measured data are significantly closer to the sensor than the predicted data.

These situations are illustrated in Figure 7. In the first case, the measured data agree with the prediction, and the system increases its confidence in the hypothesis that led to that prediction. In the second case, the sensor appears to have seen through the predicted object because the measured data are farther from the sensor than the predicted data. This is strong negative evidence, since the objects are assumed to be opaque. In the third case, there appears to be an object between the sensor and the hypothesized object. By itself, this situation is inconclusive. It neither supports nor refutes the hypothesis. However, given a set of hypothesized objects for a scene, it is possible to determine whether or not the measured data belong to any one of them. If so, the program marks the data as explained and treats them as neutral evidence. If not, it marks the data as unexplained and treats them as weak negative evidence. The three types of predictions are referred to as positive, negative, and neutral evidence, respectively.

To illustrate the classification of predicted surface patches, let us consider the range image in Figure 8(a). In the middle of the image there is a casting that is different from the model. It has a pipelike portion that is about the same diameter as the one on the expected casting, but it is significantly longer. Assume that the system finds the end of that pipe and hypothesizes a pose, such as the one shown in Figure 8(b). Since the hypothesis is based on the data near the end of the pipe, the predictions in that region agree with the measured data. In some of the other regions, however, the predictions disagree. Figure 8(c) shows the negative evidence (i.e., the predicted data that are farther from the sensor than the measured data). Figure 8(d) shows the neutral evidence (i.e., the predicted data that are closer than the measured data). This hypothesis would be rejected because of the large region of negative evidence.

The 3DPO system makes hypotheses one at a time, checking each one as it is formed. Figure 9 depicts a good hypothesis. Figure 9(a) shows the

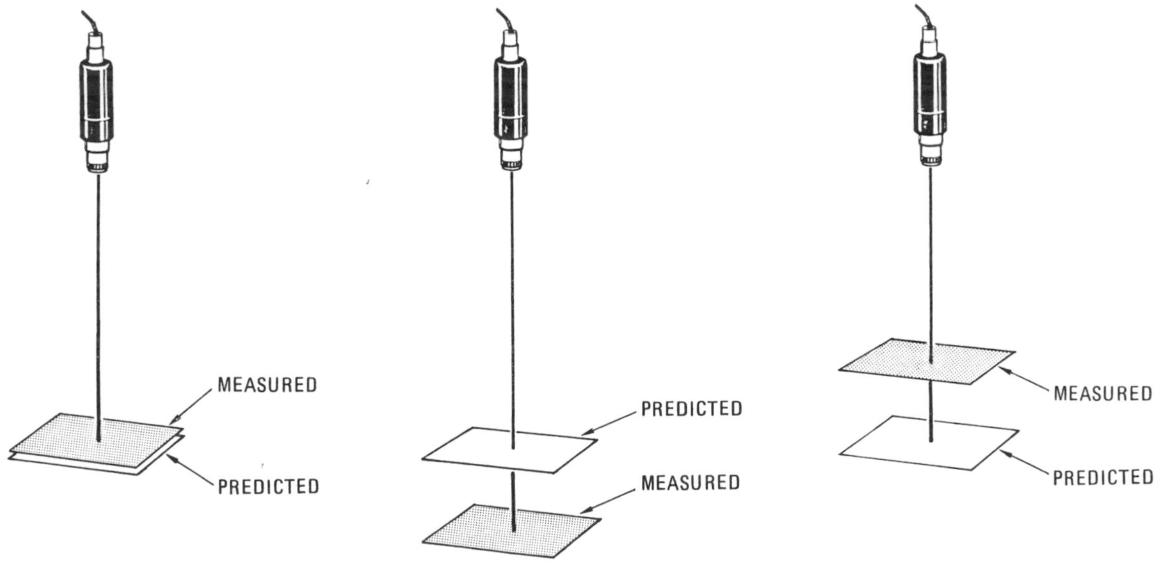

FIGURE 7(a) The measured data are approximately equal to the predicted data

FIGURE 7(b) The measured data are significantly farther from the sensor than the predicted data

FIGURE 7(c) The measured data are significantly closer to the sensor than the predicted data

FIGURE 7 Possible relationships between predicted and measured range data

range data, Figure 9(b) the hypothesis, Figure 9(c) the negative evidence, and Figure 9(d) the neutral evidence. There are several small discrepancies along the edges of the object that are due to a slight misalignment of the hypothesis. Because there are no large discrepancies, however, the system still accepts this hypothesis. Nevertheless, the large number of edge effects emphasizes the need for a technique to refine pose estimates. A better pose estimate would eliminate most of the discrepancies.

CONFIGURATION UNDERSTANDING

There are several reasons it is better to pick up an object from the top of a pile than one that is partially buried. First, the top object usually has more surfaces exposed and hence provides more ways in which it can be grasped. Second, its relatively accessible location minimizes the force required to extract it. This also tends to minimize the forces that might change the object's pose in the hand of the robot. This is important because the goal of the 3DPO system is to ascertain the pose of an object before grasping it so that the arm can select a grasping position that will be compatible with the pose required at the time the object is set down. If the pose of the object in the hand changes as the object is being pulled out of the pile, the system loses some positional information. A third reason for selecting the top object is that its removal generally causes minimal disruption in the rest of the pile, thus simplifying the analysis necessary for selection of the next object to be acquired.

The 3DPO system determines which object is at the top of a pile by predicting a range image from all the verified hypotheses, tagging each projected range value with the number of the hypothesized object it was derived from, and then checking to see which one is on top whenever two predictions are made at the same place in the image. As it makes predictions and compares them with the partially completed image, the program gathers statistics on the number of overlapping patches between each pair of objects. After completing this analysis it uses the statistics to build a graph that represents the significant occlusions.

Figure 10 illustrates a typical occlusion. In this example, at least four range values would be predicted along the indicated ray, which corresponds to one pixel in the synthetic image. It is easy to determine that at this particular pixel Object 2 is on top of Object 1. However, when three or more objects occur along a ray, the amount of configurational information extracted depends on the amount of data the program stores for each pixel. The current program keeps track of the range value closest to the sensor and the object it belongs to. When a new range value is predicted, the program checks the synthetic image to determine whether a value has already been predicted for that pixel. If not, it inserts one. If so, it compares the object identification numbers of the old and new predictions. If they are the same, the program updates the predicted range value, if necessary, and continues. If the objects are different, it notes which of them is on top and updates both the range value and the object number.

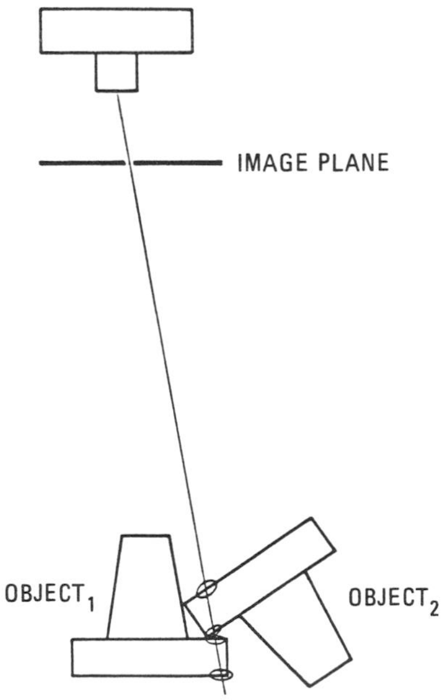

FIGURE 10 One object occluding another

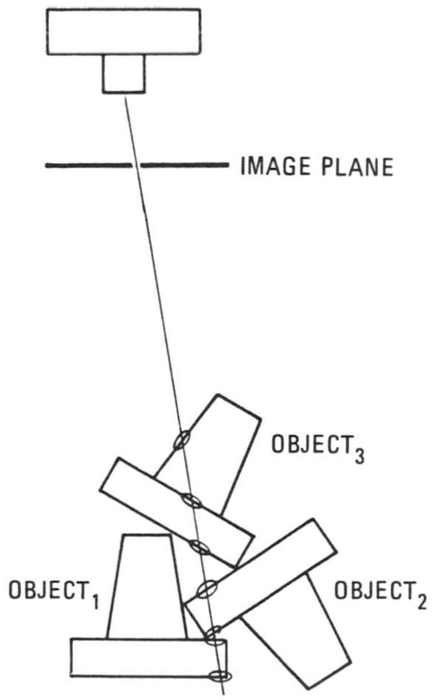

FIGURE 11 Stack of three objects

This process gathers all the occlusion information if there are no more than two objects along any one ray. If there are three or more, however, the occlusion relationships obtained depend on the order in which the hypothesized objects are processed. For example, let us consider Figure 11. If Object 1 is processed by the range prediction software first, Object 2 second, and Object 3 third, the relationships that would then be computed are that Object 2 is on top of Object 1 and that Object 3 is on top of Object 2. The fact that Object 3 is on top of Object 1 is missed. If the program kept track of all range values along each ray, together with their objects, it would be possible to compute all such relationships. However, the data structures required to store this information are unwieldy. Fortunately, since the two top objects usually completely occlude lower objects, stacks of three or more objects are not often detected in range images. In addition, missing an occlusion relationship at a pixel is normally not crucial because the relationship generally occurs at other places in the image where the program can detect it. In this case, missing one occurrence of a relationship simply reduces the estimate of the amount of overlap between the two objects -- which is significantly less detrimental than missing the crucial fact that they are overlapping.

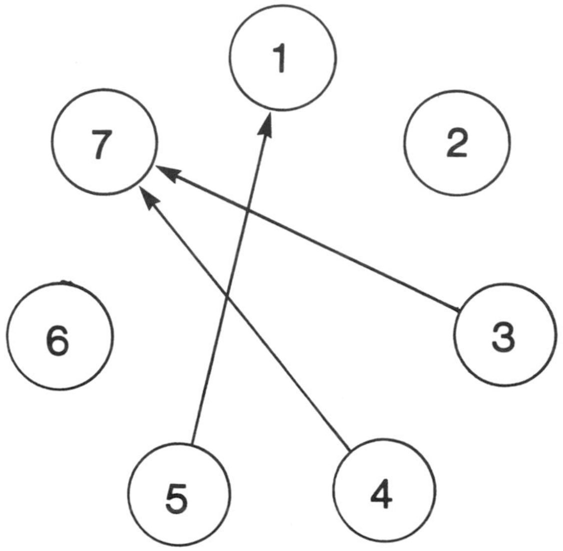

FIGURE 12 Graph of the on-top-of relationships for the hypotheses in Figure 13

After the program has gathered statistics about occlusions in the image, it builds a graph to represent object interrelationships. Figure 12 displays the graph constructed for the seven hypotheses of Figure 13. Figure 14 shows the information from that graph in terms of arrows superimposed upon the intensity image returned by the range sensor. An arrow points from an occluded object to the occluding one. The arrows indicate, for example, that the object at the top center of the image is lying atop two other objects. The three objects at the butts of the arrows would not be good choices to be picked up first because other objects are known to be on top of them.

It should be borne in mind that there might not even be an object on top. All of the objects might be partially occluded by other objects. In that case, the graph would be cyclic. Figure 15 shows two configurations of objects in which none of them is on top. In Figure 15(a) two concave objects are arranged so that they overlap each other. In Figure 15(b) three convex objects are arranged so that all of them are partially occluded.

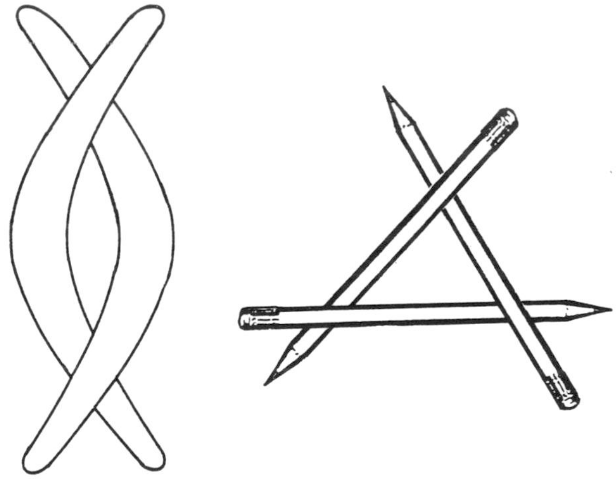

FIGURE 15(a) Two concave objects that overlap each other

FIGURE 15(b) Three convex objects that overlap one another

FIGURE 15 Cyclic occlusion relationships

The information as to what is on top of what represents the first-level undertanding an object configuration. A second level might be a specification stating exactly which objects are resting on or leaning against other objects and where they touch one another. This information would make it possible to perform a more detailed analysis of which objects would be moved when one of them was lifted out of the pile. Unfortunately, it appears to difficult to compute these relationships from predicted range images or from three-dimensional models without a spatial-reasoning system that understands gravity and the geometric constraints associated with mutual contact between objects.

DISCUSSION

The feature-based approach to hypothesis verification is convenient because the features have already been detected as part of the matching process; essentially, all one has to do is match a few additional features. However, there are at least two disadvantages. First, this method requires that the objects have several distinct features. It doesn't work very well for smooth objects such as an apple. Second, it places a burden on the feature detectors in that they must locate all the features and describe them in a canonical way. If any features are missed or incorrectly described, a more complicated matching strategy will be necessary. For example, if a feature is missed, the program may have to apply a specially tuned feature detector to find the feature so as to include it in the verification process. (We have used this approach in the 3DPO system to find such things as concentric circles.) If a feature detector happens to describe the low-level data in a way that is different from what was expected, the matcher will have to be smart enough to recognize alternative descriptions. For example, if the line-and-arc fitter should segment an arc predicted from the model into a sequence of short line segments, the matcher would have to recognize the pieces as parts of the arc.

One of the advantages of a data-level approach to hypothesis verification is that it is a homogeneous process that works for all types of objects. Another advantage is that it produces explanations in terms of regions, which is a convenient form for deciding how much of a scene is explained by a set of hypotheses. One disadvantage is that this approach requires a detailed model of the physics of the sensor. While this is relatively straightforward for range data, our current capabilities cannot handle intensity images. We can of course predict the locations of edges in an intensity image, but even then we lack models of the detectors employed to locate the edges. Since each detector has side effects, such as displacing edges and inserting new ones, precise predictions are still not possible.

A second disadvantage of data-level verification is that it is sensitive to misalignment. Slight offsets lead to discrepancies along the edges of the object. One way to reduce misalignment is to apply an iterative technique that assigns measured data points to surfaces of the object, uses these assignments to update the pose estimate, and then repeats the process until it minimizes the sum of the errors. Given a good estimate of the pose, the program can reject the hypothesis if the sum of the errors is too large or, alternatively, it can make the data-level comparison to perform a more structural evaluation of the match.

In the future we plan to investigate ways of combining feature-level verification with data-level techniques. This combination would utilize features to help develop a region-based explanation of a scene. For example, the location of a feature could be used for local correction of a global pose estimate so as to avoid the edge effects produced by an unguided data-level comparison. Such a system would also provide a way of extending the technique to gray-scale analysis when it is impossible to predict absolute intensity values, yet possible to predict intensity edges and approximate intensity values.

REFERENCES

Faugeras, O. D., and M. Hebert, "A 3-D Recognition and Positioning Algorithm Using Geometrical Matching Between Primitive Surfaces," Proc. of the Eighth IJCAI, Karlsruhe, Germany, pp. 996-1002 (August 1983).

Grimson, W.E.L., and T. Lozano-Perez, "Model-Based Recognition and Localization from Sparse Range or Tactile Data," to appear in the International Journal of Robotics Research (1984).

Horaud, P., and R. C.Bolles, "3DPO's Strategy for Matching Three-Dimensional Objects in Range Data," Proc. of the International Conference on Robotics, Atlanta, Georgia, pp. 78-85 (March 1984).

Oshima, M., and Y. Shirai, "Object Recognition Using Three-Dimensional Information," Proc. of the Seventh IJCAI, Vancouver, British Columbia, pp. 601-609 (August 1981).

Rutkowski, W. and R. Benton, "Determination of Object Pose by Fitting a Model to Sparse Range Data," Interim Technical Report of the Intelligent Task Automation Program, Honeywell, Inc., pp. 6-62:6-98 (January 1984).

FIGURE 1 Pile of castings

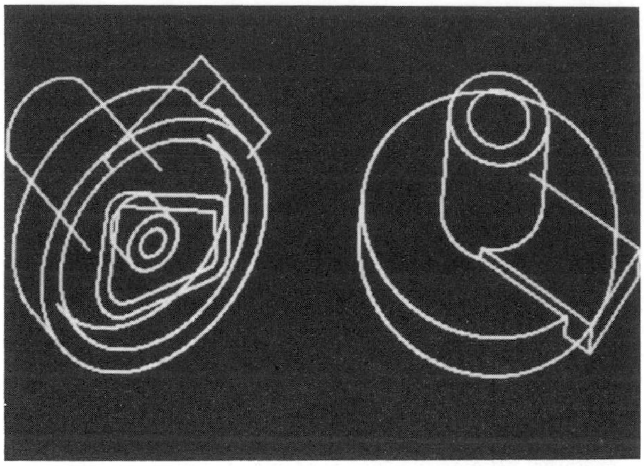

FIGURE 2 Model of casting (bottom and top)

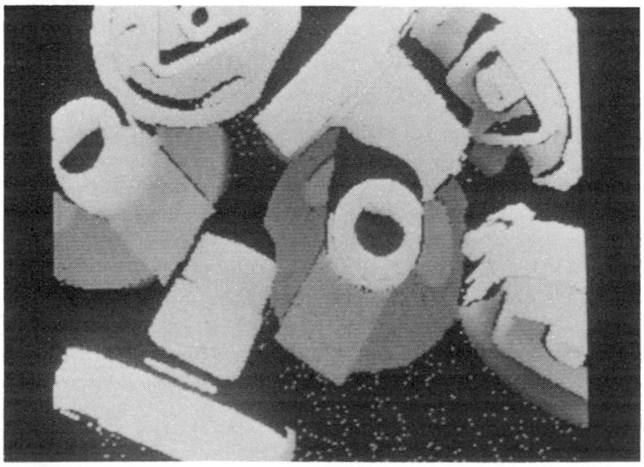

FIGURE 3 Height image of a pile

FIGURE 4 Hypothesized casting

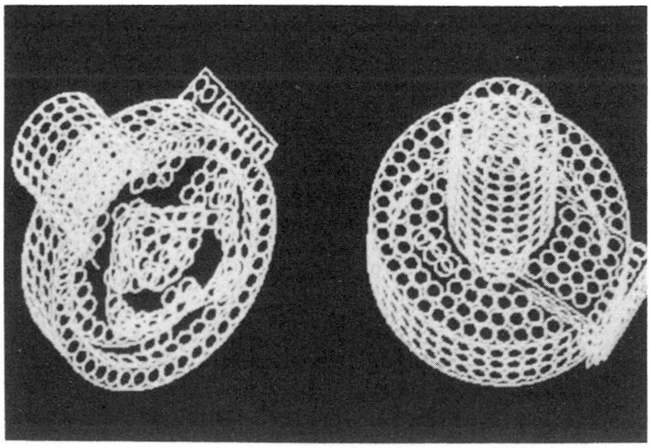

FIGURE 5 Planar-patch model of a casting (bottom and top)

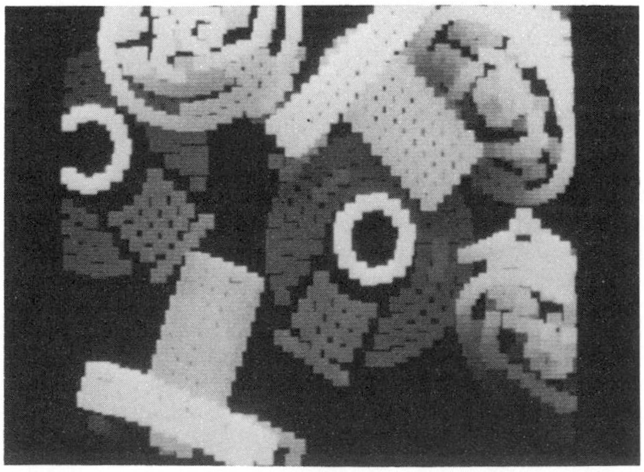

FIGURE 6 Synthetic height image (corresponding to Figure 3)

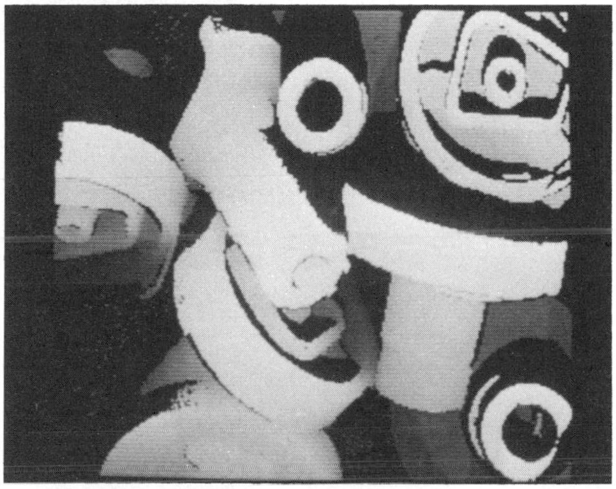

FIGURE 8(a) Measured range data

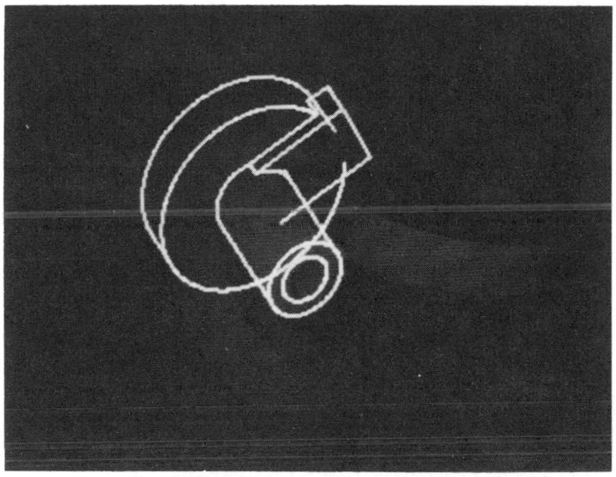

FIGURE 8(b) Hypothesized casting

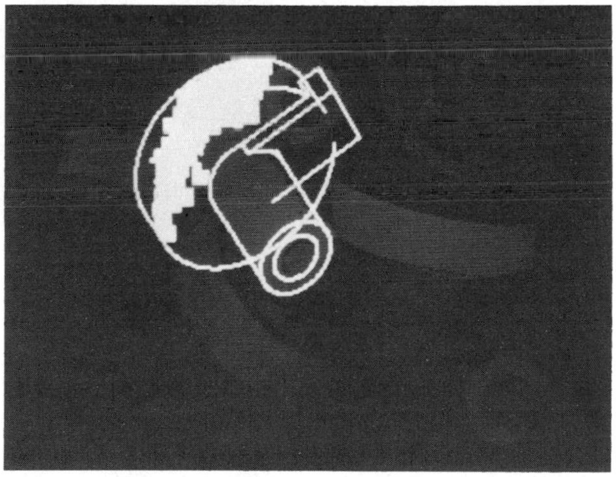

FIGURE 8(c) Negative evidence

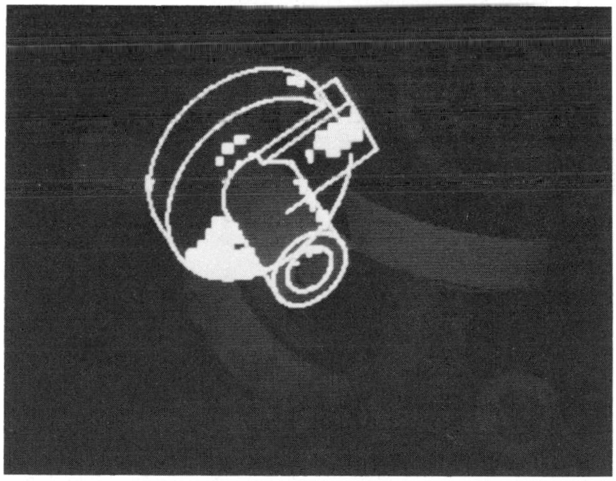

FIGURE 8(d) Neutral evidence

FIGURE 8 A bad hypothesis

FIGURE 9(a) Measured range data

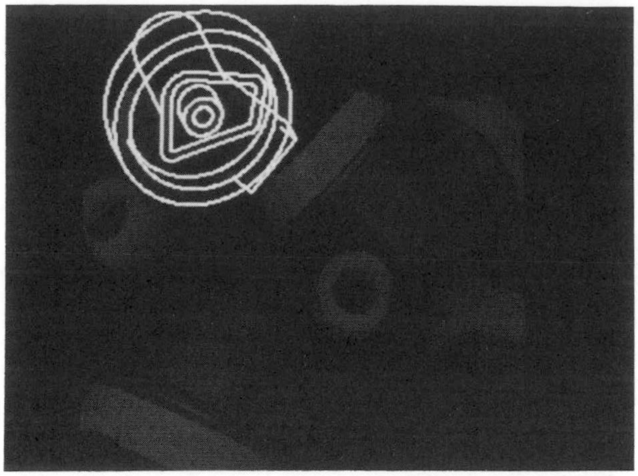

FIGURE 9(b) Hypothesized casting

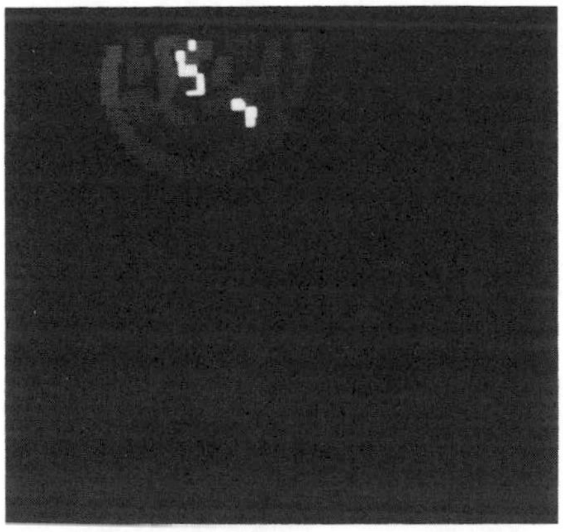

FIGURE 9(c) Negative evidence

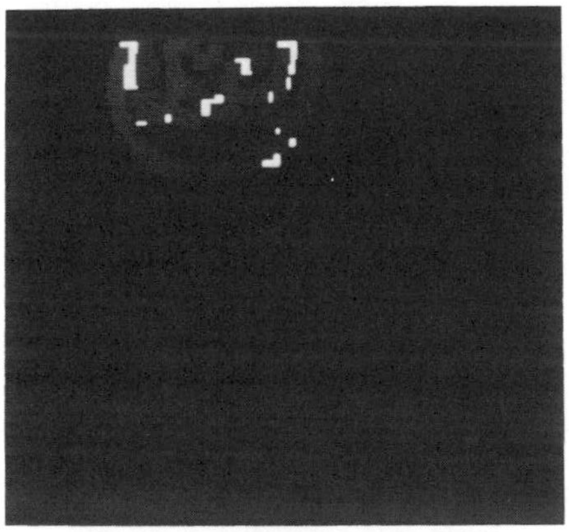

FIGURE 9(d) Neutral evidence

FIGURE 9 A good hypothesis

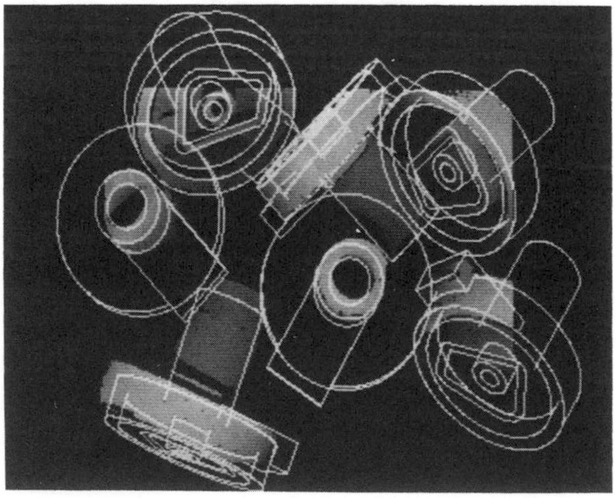

FIGURE 13 Seven hypothesized castings

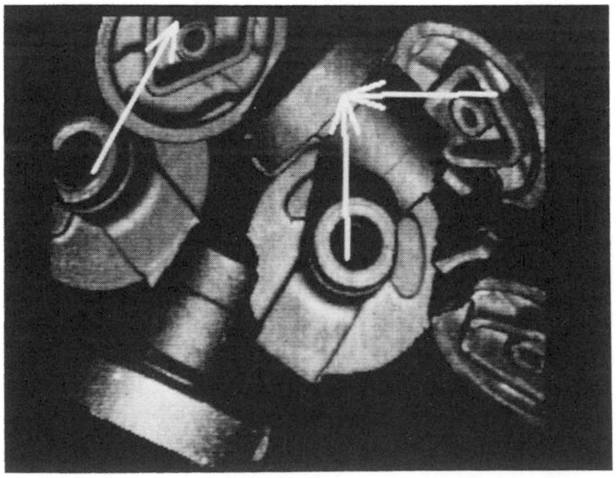

FIGURE 14 Arrows point from occluded castings to occluding ones.

RECOGNITION AND LOCALIZATION OF OVERLAPPING PARTS FROM SPARSE DATA

Tomás Lozano-Pérez
W. Eric L. Grimson

Massachusetts Institute of Technology
Artificial Intelligence Laboratory
545 Technology Square
Cambridge, Massachusetts

This paper discusses how sparse local measurements of positions and surface normals may be used to identify and locate overlapping objects. The objects are modeled as polyhedra (or polygons) having up to six degrees of freedom relative to the sensors. The approach operates by examining all hypotheses about pairings between sensed points and object surfaces and efficiently discarding inconsistent ones by using local constraints on: distances between faces, angles between face normals, and angles (relative to the surface normals) of vectors between sensed points. The method described here is an extension of a method for recognition and localization of non-overlapping parts previously described in [Grimson & Lozano-Pérez 83, 84] and [Gaston and Lozano-Pérez 84].

1. Problem Definition

The specific problem we consider in this paper is how to identify a known object and locate it relative to the sensor using relatively few data points. The object is assumed to be overlapped by other (unknown) objects, so that many of the data points do not arise from the object of interest. The object may have up to six degrees of freedom relative to the sensor (three translational and three rotational).

We assume that a polyhedral model is available for the object to be located. Importantly, the model may simply be an approximation of a curved object since only weak use is made of the edge and vertex structure of the polyhedral model. Only the individual plane equations and face dimensions of the model are used for recognition and localization. Furthermore, the polyhedral model does not have to be complete or connected; it may be missing many of its faces.

Acknowledgements. This report describes research done at the Artificial Intelligence Laboratory of the Massachusetts Institute of Technology. Support for the Laboratory's Artificial Intelligence research is provided in part by a grant from the System Development Foundation, and in part by the Advanced Research Projects Agency under Office of Naval Research contracts N00014-80-C-0505 and N00014-82-K-0334.

The sensor is assumed to be capable of providing information about the position and local surface orientation of a small set of points on the object. If the object has only three degrees of freedom relative to the sensor (two translational and one rotational), then the position and surface normals need only be two-dimensional. If the object has six degrees of freedom, the position and orientation data must be three-dimensional.

The sensor is processed to obtain:

1. Surface points — On the basis of sensor readings, the positions of some points on the sensed object can be determined to lie within some small volume relative to the sensor.
2. Surface normals — At the sensed points, the surface normal of the object's surface can be recovered to within some cone of uncertainty.

Our goal is to use local information about sensed points to determine which subset of the sensed points are consistent with some position and orientation of the object of interest.

In this paper we do not discuss how surface points and normals may be obtained from actual sensor data. Our aim is to show, instead, how such data may be used in conjunction with object models to recognize and localize objects. It is important to note that many sensory modalities can be used to obtain this type of data. Depth data can be obtained from laser triangulation, ultrasonic range finders, binocular stereo, or tactile sensing. Surface normals can be obtained by local fitting of the depth data to a plane. In two dimensional problems, edge segments obtained from gray-scale or binary images can be used to provide position and normal information. In fact, data from two or more of these modalities can be used simultaneously, as long as it is embedded in a common coordinate system.

A survey of related work in sensing and recognition can be found in [Grimson & Lozano-Pérez 83, 84].

2. Approach

Some recent papers [Grimson & Lozano-Pérez 83, 84] and [Gaston and Lozano-Pérez 84] have introduced a new approach to recognition and localization based on exploiting simple geometric constraints between sensed data and a model. The inputs to the recognition process are: a set of sensed points and normals, and a set of geometric object models for the known objects. In the earlier papers, the assumption was that all the sensed data arose from a single object. In this paper, we show that a simple extension of the earlier approach can be used to deal with the more general case of overlapping objects.

The recognition process, as described in the earlier papers, proceeds in two steps:

1. *Generate Feasible Interpretations:* A set of feasible interpretations of the sense data is constructed. Interpretations consist of pairings of each sensed point with some object surface of one of the known objects. Interpretations inconsistent with local constraints (derived from the model) on the sense data are discarded.
2. *Model Test:* The feasible interpretations are tested for consistency with surface equations obtained from the object models. An interpretation is legal if it is possible to solve for a rotation and translation that would place each sense point on an object surface. The sensed point must lie *inside* the object face, not just on the surface.

The first step is the key to this process. The number of possible interpretations given s sensed points and n surfaces is n^s. Therefore, it is not feasible to carry out a model test on all possible interpretations. The earlier papers showed, primarily by simulation, that the number of feasible interpretations can be reduced to manageable numbers by the use of local geometric constraints. In particular, the papers investigated the effectiveness of the different local constraints and the impact of measurement errors on their effectiveness.

In the presence of data from multiple objects, the generate step of the process must be modified to select a subset of the data to assign to model surfaces. This is equivalent, within this framework, to *segmentation* in computer vision. Another analogue is the identification of maximal cliques in the *Local Feature Focus* method [Bolles and Cain 82]. Our approach to this problem will be described in the next section.

3. Generating Feasible Interpretations

After sensing a scene involving several objects, we have the positions of up to s points, P_i. We are seeking some object that has n faces. If all the points came from the desired object, the range of possible pairings of sensed points and model faces can be cast in the form of an *interpretation tree* (IT). The root node of the IT, has n descendants, each representing an interpretation in which P_1 is on a different face of the object. There are a total of s levels in the tree, level i indicating the possible pairings of P_i with the faces of the object (see Figure 1). Note that there may be multiple points on a single face, so that the number of branches remains constant at all levels.

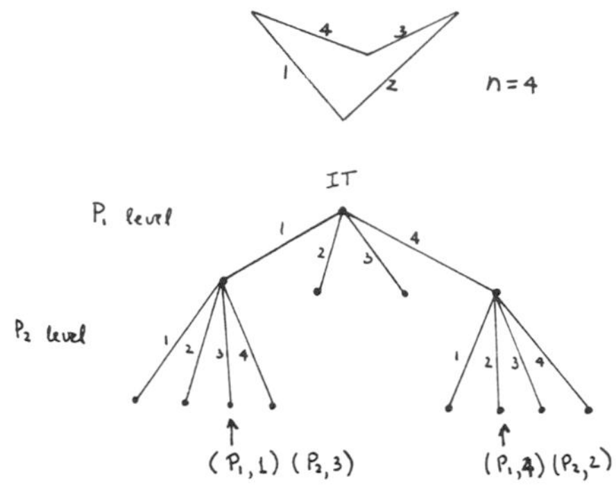

Figure 1. Interpretation Tree

3.1. Pruning the IT by Local Constraints

Only a very few interpretations in an IT are consistent with the input data. We can exploit the following local constraints to prune inconsistent interpretations:

1. Distance Constraint — The range of distance between each pair of P_i's, taking into account the measurement error, must overlap the range of possible distances between the faces paired with them in an interpretation.
2. Angle Constraint — The range of possible angles between measured normals at each pair of P_i's must include the known angle between surface normals of the faces paired with them in an interpretation.
3. Direction Constraint — The range of values for the component of a vector between sensed points ($P_i \mapsto P_j$) in the direction of the sensed normal at P_i and at P_j must intersect the range of components of possible vectors between points on the faces assigned to P_i and P_j by the interpretation.

A detailed description of these constraints and their implementation can be found in [Grimson and Lozano-Pérez 83, 84].

These constraints typically serve to prune most of the non-symmetric interpretations of the data. It is important to realize, however, that these constraints are not guaranteed to reject all impossible interpretations. Let d_{ij} be the distance between two sensed points, P_i and P_j. This measured distance may be consistent with the range of distances between faces f_u and f_v, but only if the sensed points are inside of small patches on the candidate surfaces. This progressive restriction of candidate positions for the sensed points is ignored in the generate phase of the recognition process. Consider what happens when adding another point–surface pairing, (P_k, f_w), to an interpretation that already includes (P_i, f_u) and (P_j, f_v). The tree generation phase considers adding this pairing only if the distances d_{ik} and d_{jk} are consistent with the range of distances between f_u, f_w and f_v, f_w, respectively. In doing this, however, it uses the ranges of distances possible between any these pairs of faces. It does not take into account the fact that only small patches of f_u and f_v are actually elegible. The model test is then applied to interpretations surviving pruning so as to guarantee that all the available geometric constraint is exploited.

We have focused on the three constraints above, primarily because they are simple to implement while being quite effective. In particular, they can be used to prune partial interpretations of length 2 or greater, thereby collapsing whole subtrees of the IT, without explicitly exploring all the nodes of that subtree, yielding a large computational savings. It is surprising, considering the relative weakness of the constraints, how effectively they can prune the IT; refer to [Grimson and Lozano-Pérez 83] for results of extensive simulations that bear on this point.

3.2. Data from Multiple Objects

Assume that all of the sensed points, except one, originate from a single object. Let P_i be the extraneous sensed point. Most of the time, it will be impossible to find an interpretation that includes this point. Unfortunately, it is not always possible to differentiate between a violation of the constraints due to assigning a point to an infeasible surface from a violation due to an extraneous point. It is not the case that all interpretations will fail at level i in the tree; it may require adding a few more data points to the interpretation before the inconsistency is noted. It is only when all possible single-object interpretations fail that we are certain to have at least one extraneous data point.

It may still be possible to find an interpretation of all the sensed points, including extraneous points, that is consistent with the local pruning constraints. In fact, it is even possible, by a fortuitous alignment of the data, for interpretations involving extraneous points to pass the model test. There is nothing within the approach described here to exclude this possibility. Of course, the larger the number of point–surface pairings in the interpretation, the less likely this is to happen. In many cases, it may be necessary to attempt to verify the interpretation obtained by acquiring more data. We will not pursue this point here; we will assume, instead, that the presence of extraneous points will cause all interpretations to fail either the local constraints or the model test.

One straight–forward approach to handling extraneous data points is to apply the recognition process to all subsets of the data points, possibly ordered by some heuristic. But, of course, this approach wastes much work determining the feasibility of the same partial interpretations.

Consider, however, how we could consider all subsets of the data without wasting the work of testing partial interpretations. The simple way we have done this is by adding one more branch to each node of the IT (see Figure 2). This branch represents the possibility of discarding the data point as extraneous. Call this branch the *null face*. The remainder of the process operates as before except that, when applying the local constraints, the null face behaves as a "wild card"; assigning a point to the null face will never cause the failure of an interpretation.

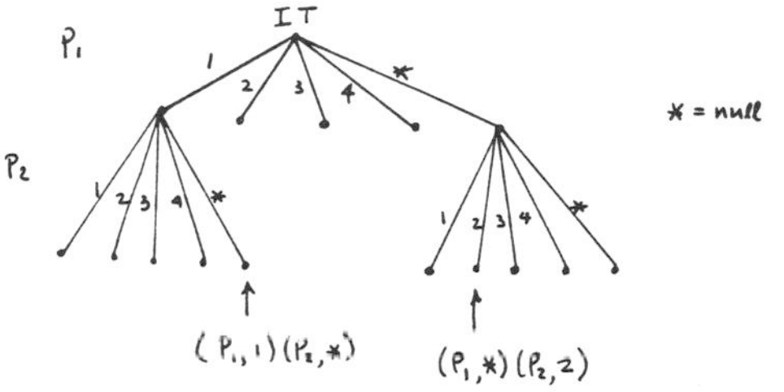

Figure 2. Adding a null branch to the IT

It is easy to see that if an interpretation is legal, the process described above will generate all subsets of this interpretation as leaves of the tree. This is true of partial interpretations as well as full interpretations. Every combination of assignments of the null face to the sensed points will still produce a valid interpretation. This condition guarantees that if any subset of the data points is valid, then a valid interpretation will be obtained as a leaf.

The same condition that ensures the validity of this process guarantees its inefficiency. We do not want to generate all subsets of a valid interpretation. In general, we want to generate the interpretations that are consistent with as much as possible of the sensed data. The following simple method guarantees that we find only the most complete interpretations.

The IT is explored in a depth–first fashion, with the null face considered last when expanding a node. In addition, the model test is applied to any complete interpretations, that is, any that reaches a leaf of the IT. This choice of tree traversal has the effect of considering the legal interpretations by length order (where length is taken to be the number of non–null faces paired with sensed points by the interpretation).

Now, assume an external variable, call it MAX, that keeps track of the longest valid interpretation found so far. It is only worth assigning a null face to point P_i, if $s - i \geq MAX$. Otherwise, the length of the interpretations at all the leaves below this node will be less than that of the longest interpretation already found. If we initialize MAX to some non–zero value, then only interpretations of this length or longer will be found. As longer interpretations are found, the value of MAX is incremented, thus ensuring that we find the most complete interpretation of the data. Note that an interpretation of length s is found, then no null-face assignments will be made.

4. Testing the Algorithm

In order to test the efficacy of this algorithm we have run simulations as well as applied versions of the method to actual data from three sensory modalities. As of this writing, we have not yet systematically collected statistics on the performance of the extended method, but we have carried out a large number of simulations as well as a number of experiments with real data. We will first describe these tests and then discuss our conclusions from these experiments.

4.1. Simulations with Two-Dimensional Data

We have done extensive testing of the algorithm with simulated two-dimensional data of the type illustrated in Figure 3. A number of polygons, representing the outline of parts, are overlapped at random. The position and orientation of a number of data points are determined by computing the outermost intersection of randomly-chosen rays with the polygon boundaries. The position and normal information is then corrupted by random errors designed to simulate the effect of imperfect sensors (see Figure 3, the small circles indicate the sensed points).

The algorithm performs quite well in this application. As along as enough points are sensed on the desired object, the algorithm can locate it. Furthermore, the time to do the recognition and localization is relatively low: on the order of one or two seconds on a Symbolics 3600 Lisp Machine. The time grows when the measurement error grows, in the manner illustrated by the simulations reported in [Grimson and Lozano-Pérez 83].

4.2. Edge Fragments from Gray-Level Images

A modified version of the algorithm described here has been applied to locating a simple object in cluttered scenes, using edge fragments from images obtained by a camera located (almost) directly overhead. The images are obtained under lighting from several overhead fluorescent lights. The camera is a standard vidicon located approximately five feet above the scene. The edge fragments are obtained by linking edge points marked as zero crossings in the Laplacian of Gaussian-smoothed images. Edge points are marked only when the gradient at that point exceeds a pre-defined threshold; this is done to eliminate some shallow edges due to shadows. The algorithm is applied to some pre-defined number of edge fragments sorted by their length.

The application described above has some characteristics that require an extension of the method described earlier. One point to notice is that since we are now using edge fragments rather than points, we can use the length of the fragments as an additional local constraint. In our implementation, we will not assign edge fragments to model edges that are shorter than the measured fragment. We do allow assignment of small measured edge fragments to long model edges.

The most difficult problem faced in this application is the inability to determine the sign of the vector normal to the edge. That is, we do not know which side of the edge contains the object. The algorithm was modified to keep track of the two possible assignments of sign and to guarantee that all the pairings in an interpretation have consistent assignments of sign. This extension, however, causes a noticeable degradation in the performance of the algorithm, since it reduces the effectiveness of the angle and direction constraints.

The algorithm succeeds in locating the desired object in images where the edge data is very sparse (see Figure 4). The speed of performance under these circumstances is not yet acceptable for practical applications; it can take several minutes of elapsed time on an MIT CADR Lisp machine to process an image with 20 edge fragments. This is many times slower than the performance of the algorithm when the sign of the normal is available. We are currently investigating extensions of the algorithm to improve this performance.

4.3. Range Data from an Ultrasonic Sensor

Michael Drumheller [Drumheller 84] has implemented a modified version of the algorithm described above and applied it to data obtained from an unmodified Polaroid ultrasonic range sensor. The intended application is navigation of mobile robots. The system matches the range data obtained by circularly scanning from the robot's position towards the walls of the room. The robot has a map of the walls of the room, but much of the data obtained arises from objects on the walls, such as bookshelves, or between the robot and the walls, such as columns.

The algorithm first fits line segments to the range data and attempts to match these line segments to wall segments. After matching, the robot can solve for its position in the room. An example of the operation of the algorithm is shown in Figure 5. Note that the data obtained from the sensor is far from perfect. In particular, the beam width is approximately 10 degrees, which leads to significant errors on the length of data segments as well as a wide "penumbra" around nearby obstacles.

5. Discussion

We have described an extension to an earlier approach to model-based recognition and localization, described in [Gaston and Lozano-Pérez 84] and [Grimson and Lozano-Pérez 83, 84]. This extension significantly expands the domain of applicability of the method. In particular, it allows the algorithm to tolerate extraneous data and data from multiple objects. Predictably, the performance of the method is degraded in this more general context. We can summarize the results from our testing up to now by saying that if the data is reasonably accurate, then the degradation in performance is small. When the data is significantly degraded, such as in the case of missing sign on the normal of edge fragments or large measurement error, the performance is severely degraded. This follows from the exponential increase in the size of the search space due to the addition of the null face. We are currently exploring the effects of adding tighter local constraints than we have described here. These constraints require more computation at each node, but are significantly tighter than the current local constraints. It remains to be seen whether the increased constraint justifies the increased computation.

References

R. C. Bolles and R. A. Cain, "Recognizing and Locating Partially Visible Objects: The Local-Feature-Focus Method, *Int. J. Robotics Research,* vol.1, no.3, pp. 57–82, 1982.

M. Drumheller, "Robot Localization Using Range Data", S. B. Thesis, Dept. of Mechanical Engineering, MIT, May 1984.

P. C. Gaston, and T. Lozano-Pérez, "Tactile Recognition and Localization Using Object Models," *IEEE Transactions on PAMI,* Vol. PAMI-6, No. 3, May 1984.

W. E. L. Grimson, and T. Lozano-Pérez, "Model-Based Recognition and Localization From Sparse Range or Tactile Data," MIT Artificial Intelligence Laboratory, Report AIM-738, 1983. To appear in Int. J. Robotics Research.

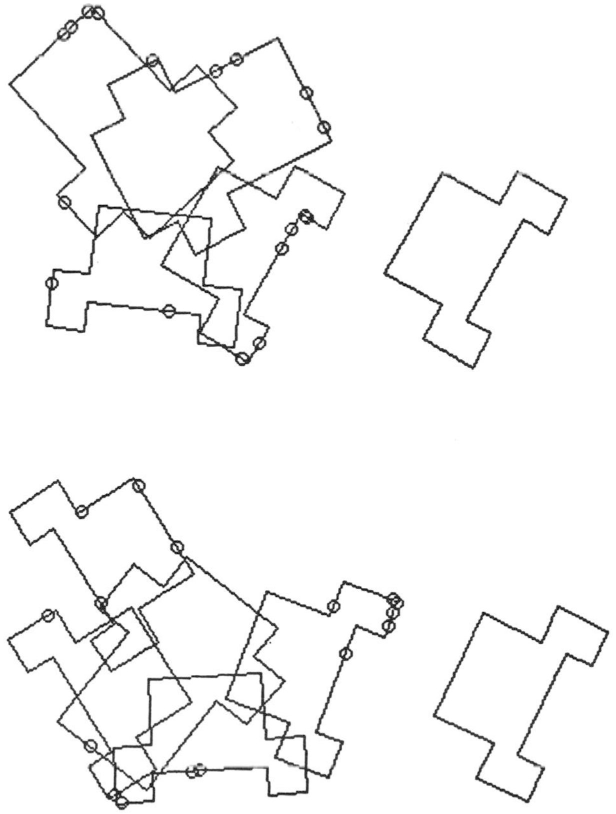

Figure 3. Two-Dimensional Simulations of Overlapping Parts

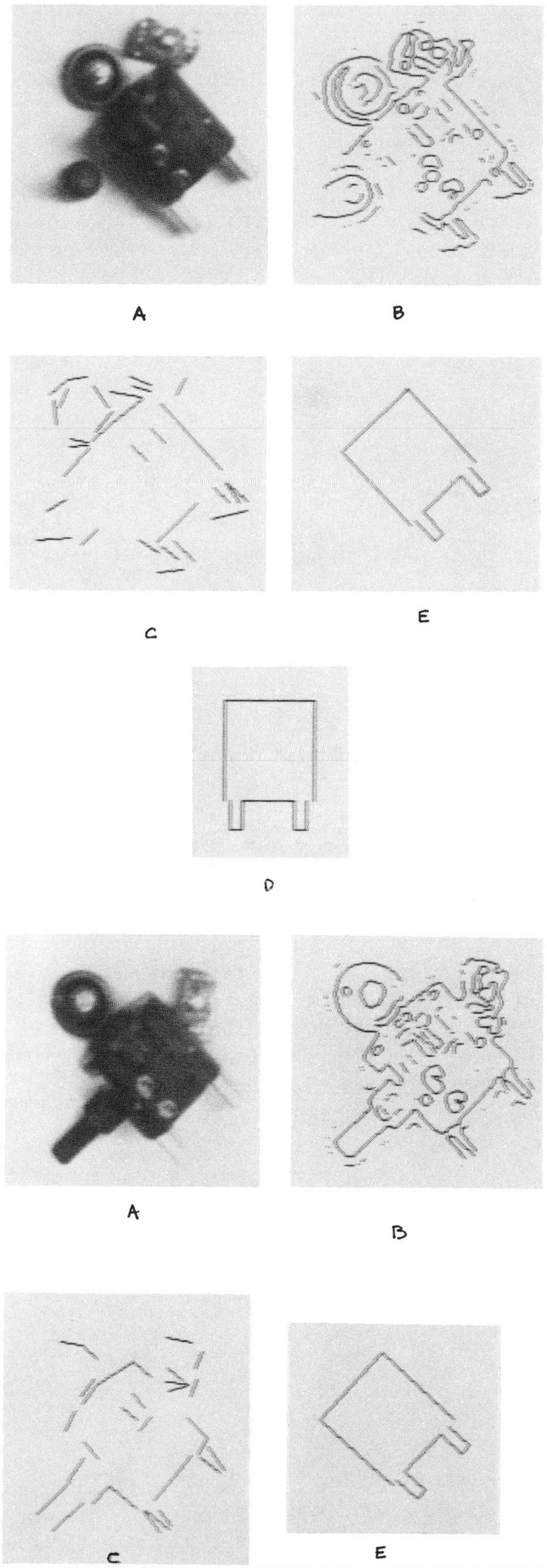

Figure 4. (a) Gray-Level Images, (b) Zero Crossings, (c) Edge Fragments, (d) Model, and (e) Located Object

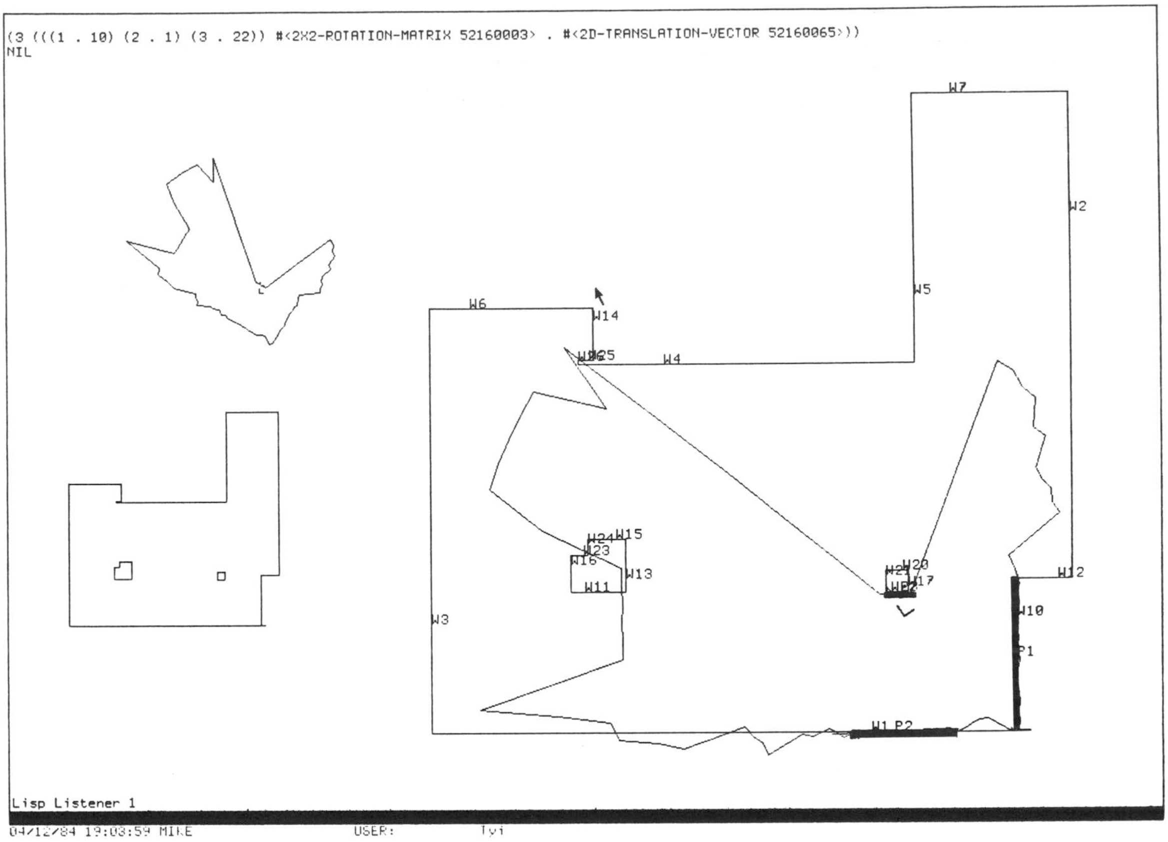

Figure 5. (a) Range Data from an Ultrasonic Sensor (b) Room Model (c) Data and Model Overlapped

Acknowledgements

The idea of using a null face to handle multiple objects was first suggested to one of us (TLP) by V. Melenkovich of CMU; we are very thankful for his remark. The image processing was done on a hardware/software environment developed by Keith Nishihara and Noble Larson. We thank to Mike Drumheller for the data reported in Figure 5.

2 Implementation of Robot Vision

Precise Manipulation with Endpoint Sensing

Russell H. Taylor
Ralph L. Hollis
Mark A. Lavin

Manufacturing Research Center
IBM T. J. Watson Research Center
Yorktown Heights, New York, 10598 USA

This paper describes recent work at IBM Research on manipulation strategies that rely on "coarse-fine" robot hardware and direct sensing of part-workpiece relationships. The experiments reported use an extremely precise, high bandwidth planar "wrist" and an industrial vision system to perform accurate alignment of small parts. The system architecture, experimental hardware, and programming methods employed are all discussed.

Introduction

Industrial robots have traditionally been used as general-purpose positioning devices. In a typical application, the robot is moved through a sequence of positions so that a tool or part held by the robot achieves a desired relationship to a workpiece whose position is fixed or known relative to the robot. Although textual programming methods and languages for robots have been around for some time [1], the overwhelming number of robots are still programmed by "teaching" a sequences of points under teleoperator control. When a robot is programmed in this manner, the most important requirement for successful accomplishment of its task is the *repeatability* with which it can return to the taught positions and with which successive workpieces can be presented to the robot. This method of using a robot is easily understood and many people have developed considerable expertise in designing the necessary end-effectors, fixtures, and setup procedures to go with it.

Unfortunately, reliance on simple repetition of taught points is inadequate for several increasingly important classes of robot applications, especially automatic assembly and "data-driven" manufacturing in which position goals must be computed directly from design data. Assembly tolerances are often at the extreme limit of a robot's repeatability, and small variations in parts can have a big effect on successful task completion. Part presentation equipment and workpiece fixtures often represent a significant fraction of the total system cost for an assembly robot. Even in cases for which teaching "works", the necessity of reteaching at least some points any time the robot or a fixture is changed (or even subjected to routine maintenance) can create significant operational difficulties.

Data driven automation is especially important in the aerospace industry and in electronics manufacturing applications such as printed circuit card assembly and testing. These applications often require both the ability to align a part or tool very precisely relative to a workpiece with the ability to move through a large work envelope. The requirements are likely to become more and more stringent in the future.

A major goal of robot research and development over the past fifteen years has been finding techniques for improving the *effective accuracy* of the manipulator, i.e., the precision with which it can place a part or tool at a computed position relative to a workpiece. Several major themes have emerged from this work.

Calibration methods use sensing to measure and correct for the inaccuracies of the robot. A typical approach [*e.g.*, 2] commands the robot to move nominal positions relative to an accurately constructed calibration fixture. Sensors are used to measure the corresponding alignment errors, and the data is then used to update a mathematical model of the robot. Although these techniques are frequently effective in improving manipulator accuracy, their usefulness in any particular application depends somewhat on the number of calibration points required, the dimensional stability of the robot, and the difficulty of installing the calibration fixture. A related technique is to use the workpiece itself as the calibration fixture. For example, the robots used in testing IBM 303x backpanel wiring used touch sensing to locate the corners of each printed circuit board. Commanded positions for features on a board were then computed by interpolation. This method has the advantage of automatically accounting for small variations in workpiece dimensions or orientation, but has the drawback of requiring that the robot spend time calibrating itself before beginning each job cycle. This is tolerable so long as the calibration time is short compared to the rest of the job (as here) or where sensing incidental to normal execution can be used to update a calibration model [3].

Compliance methods are widely used in automatic assembly. The robot simply moves through a nominal path, and the manipulator structure, the workpiece, or a cleverly designed mechanism [*e.g.*, 4] provides the necessary "give" to make up for any positioning errors that result. Limiting factors for this approach include the design time and cost associated with special fixtures and the fact that different steps in a task may require different compliances. To get around these limits, there has been considerable attention to controlling the *force* exerted by the robot, rather than its position, and then relying on software to synthesize whatever effective compliance is required [*e.g.*, 5,6, 7, 8, 9]. Friction and inertia create practical difficulties for implementing these methods on existing robots. There has been considerable recent activity in building "direct drive" manipulators that substantially eliminate friction [*e.g.*, 10, 11] and in designing wrists with redundant actuators to avoid the inertias associated with "big" joints [*e.g.*, 12, 13]. These research activities may be expected to have a significant effect on future industrial robots, but they are not a panacea for applications which are not well-adapted to force compliance. These difficulties are particularly relevant in electronics manufacturing, since electronic parts are often small and delicate and since it may not be possible to design parts with chamfers or other features to facilitate force-compliant assembly.

Endpoint sensing methods rely on sensors to measure part-workpiece or tool-workpiece misalignments directly and then move the robot accordingly. If force sensing is used, this reduces to a compliance method. However, many other forms of endpoint sensing have been used, including vision [*e.g.*, 14, 15, 16], touch [*e.g.*, 14, 17], proximity [*e.g.*, 18, 19], and so forth. The principal factors limiting the alignment precision that can be achieved with endpoint sensing methods are the resolution of the sensing system and the motion resolution of the robot. The motion resolution of robots used in present-day electronics manufacturing (i.e., the size of the smallest incremental motions that they can reliably make) is typically a bit better than 0.1 mm. However, many future applications are likely to require precision on the order of 0.01 mm [16]. The difficulty of achieving these precisions with existing robot designs is exacerbated by the need to retain a large working volume and high motion speed.

The manipulation approach reported in this paper uses endpoint sensing to measure part misalignments and a fine-positioning "wrist" to get around the resolution limitations of the robot. This approach may be summarized as follows:

1. Use the coarse joints of the robot to bring the tool or part into approximately the desired position and orientation relative to the workpiece.
2. Use the fine-motion joints to null out the sensed misalignment.

Subsequent sections of this paper describe the architecture of our experimental system, the fine positioning wrist, and two application experiments illustrating the approach.

System Architecture

Objectives

Experience with an earlier system [20] and with a number of applications within IBM convinced us that the key problem with industrial robots was not so much manipulation as the integration of a broad spectrum of capabilities, including manipulation, sensing, computation, and connections to factory control systems and data bases [3]. Addressing this problem required a control computer and powerful software, providing three main classes of function: configurability, flexible user interfaces, and reliability.

Components

The principal components of the system are a system controller, operator interface hardware, robot and sensor hardware, and system software. Each component is described briefly below.

System Controller

The system controller is responsible for coordination of all activity at the robot workstation. It consists of an IBM Series/1 minicomputer, together with data processing peripherals and workstation interface electronics. Data processing peripherals vary somewhat according to the particular application requirements but normally include such items as keyboard, display terminal, printer, diskette drives, hard disk, and teleprocessing attachments to other computer systems.

The workstation interface electronics perform a number of functions, including positional control of robot joints, safety interlocks and robot power controls, input of sensor values, and output of control signals to miscellaneous devices at the workstation. The original Research and IBM 7565 implementations of these functions used non-programmable custom-designed electronics. The robot had analog position feedback, and joint control was accomplished by analog "PD" loops with some compensation for the nonlinearities of the hydraulic actuators.

In order to facilitate experimentation with more advanced control methods and to simplify problems associated with interfacing many different robots and sensors to the system, we developed a family of programmable attachments, called "RRA cards". Each attachment has a standard base, consisting of a Series/1 channel interface, a 4 K-byte shared memory, a Motorola M68000 processor, timers, and miscellaneous support chips, and a custom sensor interface area. These attachments have been used for a number of robot and device control applications.

Operator interface

Operator interface hardware includes an operator's console on the robot and a hand-held pendant containing a small display and a number of switches and lights. Except for safety-related functions, the interpretation of all operator input/output is determined by application software.

Robot and sensor hardware

The key design objectives for both the robot and sensors were modularity and configurability. The system architecture makes no assumptions about the kinematic structure of the manipulator, which it views simply as a collection of position-controlled "joints" together with associated power and safety interlocks. The system provides coordinated straight-line motion in configuration space, and kinematic transformations are handled by built-in subroutines.

This approach has been fairly successful in allowing us to use a number of different robot configurations with the system. The most common configuration has been a cartesian structure similar to the IBM 7565. Other configurations have included an IBM 7535 SCARA-type robot and a number of specialized structures put together for particular applications.

The present robot in our laboratory is a two-armed cartesian electric-drive manipulator developed for use in IBM clean room manufacturing. Each arm consists of three linear actuators providing *X*, *Y*, and *Z* motions, three rotary actuators providing *Roll*, *Pitch*, and *Yaw* motions, and a gripper with linearly actuated fingers. For the application experiments described in this paper, the *Pitch*, *Roll*, and *Gripper* actuators of one arm have been removed and replaced with an extremely accurate planar wrist providing fine motions in the *X* and *Y* directions.

Sensors typically include force transducers and a light beam presence sensor mounted in the fingers, several solid state television cameras, and miscellaneous application-specific sensors, such as empty-feeder indicators.

Software

One component of the system controller software provides an interactive programming environment for a high level programming language, AML [21,23], which is used for all application programming. A second software component performs trajectory planning, motion coordination, sensor monitoring, and other real time activity in response to commands from the AML interpreter. A third component supplies standard supervisor services, such as file and terminal I/O.

AML Language

Objectives and overview

The principal programming interface to the robot workstation is the AML language [3,21,23]. AML was designed to be a well-structured, semantically powerful interactive language that would be good for robot programming. The central idea was to provide an expressive base language with simple subsets which would be usable by programmers with a wide variety of experience. Although the language primitives have been chosen to provide a natural way of describing manufacturing applications, we make a clear distinction between the language constructs and the semantics of the application environment. No special syntax is supplied for robotic concepts. Instead, all access to system functions is accomplished through calls to system-defined subroutines that are called exactly like those written by a user. This transparency provides a natural mechanism for system extensibility through the use of subroutine libraries for customization of the runtime environment for particular application domains.

Language summary

AML supports a number of "scalar" data types, including *INT*eger, *REAL*, *STRING*, and provides the usual unary and binary operations on them. A number of auxiliary types useful in construction of application subroutine libraries and debugging packages are also supported. The language supports ordered lists, called "aggregates", of scalar and/or aggregate AML objects. The language includes constructs, somewhat reminiscent of APL's [24], for generalized indexing of aggregates and for uniform mapping of scalar operations over aggregate objects. Variables are typed and are declared by binding an identifier to the value produced by evaluating an expression. For example,

```
var: NEW 2+<<1,2>,3.5>;
```

would bind the identifier *var* to an aggregate data object whose initial value is *<<3,4>,5.5>*

The language is expression-oriented, in the sense that every legal AML construct produces a value which may be used as a part of some other expression. Expressions are evaluated left-to-right, and the grouping of expressions is determined by operator precedence and parentheses as in most common programming languages. The normal constructs of structured programming,

```
IF e1 THEN e2 ELSE e3
WHILE e1 DO e2
REPEAT e1 UNTIL e2
BEGIN e1; ... ; en END
```

are supported by the language and also produce values.

AML subroutine definitions have the general form

```
subr_name: SUBR (formal_1, ... , formal_n);
  statement_1;
  statement_2;        -- Comments are preceeded
     :                -- by a "--", as this
  statement_k;        -- example indicates.
  END;
```

and are called by expressions with the general form

```
subr_name (expression_1, ... ,expression_n)
```

The lanugage supports both "by value" and "by reference" passing of parameters and has a number of special constructs provided for builidng subroutine packages.

Vision System

Our system supports attachment of up to four 128×128 solid state binary cameras to the Series/1 controller. The programming interface, AML/V [22], is an extension of AML. It was designed to provide the power and ease-of-use of AML for machine vision application development, and to allow close coupling of robot control and vision sensing. The latter capability is very important if endpoint sensing is being used to improve robot accuracy, since communication delays can have a significant effect on system throughput and since application data may be used to provide input to the vision system.

AML/V images are stored as AML strings and may be packed binary, run-length coded binary, or gray-scale representations of the TV input. System-defined subroutines provide a number of image processing functions. *Image I/O Functions* allow the user to define "logical vision input devices", control their operating parameters, and acquire images. Additional I/O functions support display of images on raster output devices (such as TV monitors) and storage/retrieval operations on disk files. *Image-to-image* functions perform boolean operations on packed-binary and run-coded binary images, image windowing and shifting on runcoded images, arithmetic operations on gray-scale images and conversion between the various representations. *Image analysis functions* provide histogramming and binary region analysis functions.

Planar Fine Positioner

We decided to concentrate initially on precise motion in the *XY* plane, since many of the principles of coarse-fine motion could still be studied, and since a planar fine positioner could be applied to several practical problems in electronic testing and assembly. We wanted a device that was fast, strong, and as free as possible of backlash, friction, or hysteresis.

We used a single direct-drive two-dimensional actuator rather than coupling a pair of linear actuators together to achieve two dimensional motion. This parallel arrangement maintains symmetry between the *X* and *Y* axes, offering the advantage of nearly identical inertia for each axis, while eliminating the problems of serial kinematics stack buildup and resulting error accumulation.

Figure 1 shows an overall view of the fine positioner. The design combines four major elements: an electromagnetic drive, flexure spring suspension, lateral effect device position sensor, and digital control system. Subsequent sections provide a brief description of each design element and summarize its operational modes. A fuller discussion of the design may be found in [25].

Design

Two-Dimensional Motor

Many actuator technogies can be considered, including shape memory alloys, magnetostriction, piezoelectrics, pneumatics, hydraulics [26, 12], electrodynamics [13], and electromagnetics. The need for high actuation speed, contamination-free operation, large motion range, good stiffness range, and controllability narrowed the choice to either an electrodynamic or electromagnetic drive. A further need to generate fairly high forces in a small package led to the selection of an electromagnetic drive based on the Sawyer motor principle [27]. The Sawyer motor is really a linear stepping motor which operates by permanent magnet flux-steering. In the fine positioner device, it is used as a direct-drive analog positioner with a total range of one step.

Flexure Spring Assembly

A flexure spring assembly supports the moving armature without friction or backlash. This assembly allows motion in the *X*- and *Y*-directions, but is rigid in the *Z*-direction and in torsion about *Z*. As the springs bend in a slight arc, some *Z*-motion (worst case 14 μm) occurs which can be compensated for in most robotic applications. We are considering alternative flexure arrangements that would practically eliminate this deflection, but that may be less compact.

Position Sensor

A commercially available semiconductor lateral-effect cell [28] provides non-contact position sensing in two dimensions. A light emitting diode (LED) attached to the moving armature produces a spot of light whose position is measured by the fixed lateral effect cell. The position of the light spot on the cell's surface is determined by measuring the generated photocurrents in four electrodes arranged on the periphery of the square active surface of the cell.

In addition to the built-in position sensor, the fine positioner is normally operated in a manner which requires a separate external sensing means. External sensors can take many forms, including fiber optics, image sensors, or other means appropriate to the task, and may sometimes be used in place of or together with the internal sensor in servocontrol of the fine positioner.

Controller

The fine positioner open-loop response is very underdamped due to the frictionless suspension, and can be closely modeled as a second-order complex pole with natural frequency $\omega_n = 17.5$ Hz and damping ratio $\zeta = .03$. After amplification, voltages proportional to the lateral effect currents are sampled by a multiplexed 12-bit analog-to-digital (ADC) converter and M68000-based microcomputer on the RRA card. The control algorithm running in the microcomputer computes the required control efforts from commanded and measured positions, establishing proper values of currents in the drive coils through a pair of 12-bit digital-to-analog (DAC) converters on the RRA card. We have experimented with z-transform direct design algorithms as well as analog and digital proportional integral derivative (PID) controllers. Figure 2 shows the response obtained for large and small step position commands with a digital PID controller. Since peak dynamic performance depends greatly on the detailed characteristics of the servo controller, we are continuing to refine the algorithms.

Fine Positioner Operation

A brief table of the fine positioner specifications appears in Figure 3. Our primary emphasis has been on using the device as a high-precision positioner attached to a general purpose robot. Other modes of operation include use as a variable compliance device, variable forcing device, or as a measuring device.

We have already mentioned the device can be used to execute rapid sub-micron motions in X and Y over a total range of approximately 2mm, which is large enough to accomodate most errors in robot positioning. The ability to execute fine motions has many applications in science and engineering, as well as robotics.

Alternatively, by varying the closed loop gain parameter (in our implementation this is done simply by changing coefficients in the computer control program) the compliance can be varied over a range from much greater than to much less than the natural spring compliance.

In some applications, it is desirable to exert known forces on a workpiece. If negligible motion occurs, the force exerted on the armature is proportional to the coil current. For direct force measurement an external transducer can also be mounted on the armature.

Using the built-in sensor, the device can be used as a a passive measuring device, in a mode where the coil drive currents are disabled. Applications such as parts profiling can be accomplished by sensing the relationship between a mechanical probe or stylus attached to the moveable armature and the fixed part of the device.

Since the device incorporates digital control, operation can be switched between the various modes described above as may be necessary to perform a given task.

Application Experiments

Trace Probing

Application Overview

The electronic components of IBM mainframe computers are packaged in high density Thermal Conduction Modules (TCMs), each of which can accommodate up to 118 chips. The TCMs have 1800 I/O pins and plug into special high-density printed circuit boards ("TCM boards") with zero-insertion-force connectors. The TCM boards are 600 mm × 700 mm and contain twelve power planes and six signal planes, each of which can contain several thousand signal lines [29].

In order to improve system reliability and to reduce the cost of rework, it would be very desirable to perform exhaustive electronic testing of the signal planes before they are assembled into the TCM board. Testing requires that electronic probes be placed at the ends of each signal line. If a defect is found, then it must be localized by probing points along the line. The lines are only 80 μm wide and can be spaced as close together as 150 μm as illustrated in Figure 4.

The probes must be placed within ± 20 μm of a line's center in order to avoid damage to the product. Maintaining this accuracy over a large area is quite challanging with a conventional robot. The problem is exacerbated by the manufacturing tolerances in producing the sublaminates [30]. Consequently, a coarse-fine manipulation strategy that relies on a robot to get the probes "close" to their targets and direct sensing of the lines coupled with fine manipulation to "home in" seems natural.

System Overview

A robotic system for electronic testing of TCM boards is illustrated Figure 5. The robot has two arms, each of which has three coarse actuators, providing X, Y, and Z motions, and a fine positioning mechanism providing fine XY motions. Each fine positioner carries an electronic test probe and a fiber-optic sensor for detecting circuit wires, as shown in Figure 5.

The sensor is quite simple. Light from an LED source is passes through the optical fiber and shines on the TCM board. A photodetector then measures the amount of light reflected back up through the fiber. Figure 6. shows the sensor output when the fine positioner is used to scan it over two closely-spaced TCM board wires.

Job cycle

The application consists of two phases: a setup phase, in which a sublaminate is placed under the robot and an initial calibration is done to determine the transformation relating sublaminate coordinates to robot coordinates, and a test phase in which each wire is tested as follows:

1. Read design data for next wire.
2. Place the probes at the endpoints of the wire, and conduct the test (see below). If the test is successful, then go on to the next wire. Otherwise, conduct a binary search along the wire to determine the location of the defect to within a few millimeters. Note that the possibility of multiple defects in a single wire cannot be ignored.

The method for conducting each electronic test may be summarized as follows:

1. Using the board-to-robot transformation determined in the calibration phase, compute the robot coordinates corresponding to the circuit features to be probed.
2. Move both arms to these coordinates.
3. Use the fine positioners to scan the optic probes rapidly across the circuit features. Use the resulting data to determine the center of each feature.
4. Move each fine positioner so that the electronic probes are centered over the features.
5. Conduct the electronic test.

Probe Placement Sensitivity

One difficulty often encountered with endpoint-sensing methods is that of finding an *independent* means of verifying that the method is achieving its desired result. We used the apparatus illustrated in Figure 7 to investigate the ability of the fine positioner and fiber-optic sensor combination to compensate for small variations in wire placement and robot inaccuracies. A lateral effect cell was attached and a small piece of TCM-sublaminate were affixed to a micrometer stage. A probe attached to the fine-positioner armature carried both the fiber-optic sensor and a LED so arranged that the light spot from the LED fell on the lateral effect cell when the fiber-optic sensor was centered over a sublaminate wire.

The robot was then repeatedly moved to a nominal wire position, the optic probe was scanned over the wire, and the resulting data were used to center the optic probe over a line, as described in the previous section. The lateral effect cell was then read to determine the relative placement of the probe to the sublaminate board. After five trials, the micrometer stage was used to displace the sublaminate by a known amount, and the process was repeated. Figure 8 shows the results obtained. The probe placement relative to the line varied by at most about 10 μm when the wire was displaced over 75 μm, well within the ± 20 μm precision required by the application.

Disk Slider Assembly

Requirements

The high storage density of IBM 3370 and 3380 disk products requires that the distance between the recording head and the spinning magnetic disk be extremely small and almost constant. To accomplish this, the head is supported by a small "slider" which rides on an air cushion created between the slider and the disk [31,32]. The slider has two rails and is supported by a leaf-spring suspension, as shown in Figure 9. It is approximately 3 mm wide and 4 mm long. Since the alignment of the slider to the suspension can have a significant effect on its flying characteristics, both its position and orientation must be tightly controlled during assembly. In this application experiment, we wish to place the slider on the suspension so that its center is displaced at most ± 10 μm in relative to its nominal location in the XY plane, and its orientation about the Z-axis is controlled to within $\pm 0.15°$.

Hardware

The experimental setup is shown in Figure 10. A standard carrier is used to dispense sliders, and a specially constructed carrier was used to hold both suspensions and completed slider-suspension assemblies. For this experiment, we simply bolted the carriers to the table. An actual production application would include provisions for replacing them at appropriate times, and would probably include some sensing scheme to locate them relative to the robot.

A standard vacuum pen was mounted to the the fine positioner and was used to transport both sliders and suspensions. This required us to make some undesirable compromises in the vacuum head design. The small size required for picking up the sliders made it difficult to hold the suspension firmly enough to prevent it from rotating about the pen axis while being moved to the assembly fixture. In a production application, two pens would probably be used. This would permit better design, and would improve thruput, since both parts (the slider and the suspension) could be brought to the assembly fixture at the same time.

The assembly fixture is a translucent block, which is backlit to provide a high-contrast image for the binary vision system. The field of view of the TV camera is approximately 7 mm × 7 mm, so each pixel corresponds to a square approximately 55 μm on a side. The camera is rotated relative to the fixture so that the slider and suspension are tilted in the image. This tilting is necessary to achieve sub-pixel resolution for the slider-suspension alignment (see below). The block was machined to provide a small "platform" for the suspension, and a suction port is used to hold the suspension in place during assembly. In order to get around the difficulties encountered in transporting the suspension, several alignment pins were added to the fixture, so that the suspension is approximately oriented. These could probably be eliminated in a production application.

Job Cycle

An AML program for performing slider-suspension assembly is shown in Figure 11. The execution steps are as follows:

Step 1 Get a suspension.

Using the vacuum pen, pick up the next suspension from the suspension carrier and place it in the assembly fixture. Turn on the fixture suction to hold the suspension in place.

Step 2 Locate the suspension.

Use the vision system to locate the suspension.

Step 3 Apply a drop of glue to the suspension.

For this experiment, we used a heat setting epoxy. Since our primary interest was in demonstrating visual alignment of the head to the suspension, we chose to do this step manually with a hypodermic needle. In an actual production application, any one of a number of techniques could be used to automate it.

Step 4 Get a slider.

Using the vacuum pen, pick up the next slider from the slider carrier. Using the coarse joints of the robot, move the slider to its approximate final position relative to the suspension.

Step 5 Use visual feedback to adjust the slider relative to the suspension.

Step 6 Cure the glue.

Step 7 Return completed suspension.

Using the vacuum pen, pick up the completed suspension assembly and return it to the suspension assembly.

Getting a Suspension

The AML code for picking up a suspension and transporting it to the assembly fixture is shown in Figure 12. A common subroutine, *pen_pickup*, is used for picking up both suspensions and sliders. This subroutine moves the arm to the pickup point, turns on the pen vacuum, waits for a specified time, then lifts the pen by a specified amount. The code for placing a suspension into the assembly fixture is also straightforward. The arm is moved through an appropriate approach trajectory to the setdown point, the fixture vacuum is turned on, and the pen vacuum is turned off. The fine positioner then makes several quick back-and-forth motions to break the pen suction, and the arm moves up to a clear plane.

Locating the Suspension

The 2D position and orientation of the suspension is determined as follows:

Step 1 Acquire a runcoded binary image *rc* of the suspension; a typical image is shown in Figure 14.

Step 2 Extract a "center-line" image of the suspension (shown superimposed on the original suspension image in Figure 15) by evaluating the AML/V expression:

```
rc_suspension_center =
    RCOR(RCSHIFT(rc,suspension_half_width,WHITE),
         RCSHIFT(rc,-suspension_half_width,WHITE))
```

where *suspension_half_width* is a vector that would span slightly less than half the small dimension of the rectangular suspension. This vector is obtained during calibration. The technique is insensitive to up to $\pm 5^\circ$ variations in its orientation.

Step 3 Perform binary region analysis on *rc_suspension_center*; from second moment features of the white centerline region, determine the suspension orientation.

Step 4 Perform binary region analysis on *rc*; use the centroid of the white region lying most nearly on the centerline (the locating hole in Figure 14) as the *XY* coordinates for the suspension.

Sub-pixel resolution is obtained for both position and orientation parameters since region features are derived from sums of values over all pixels in the region (cf., [33]).

Getting the Slider

The AML code for picking up a slider is shown in Figure 13. The principal complication arose because the clearance between the rails of the slider and the tip of the vacuum pen was only 0.2 mm. This is comparable to the potential slider-vacuum tip misalignment at the pickup point. In order to assure that the vacuum tip is not cocked on the rails, the fine positioner makes a small "scrubbing" motion before the robot lifts the slider out of its nest. This motion takes almost no time and has the added benefit of squaring up the slider somewhat, thus significantly reducing rotational misalignments at the assembly fixture.

Locating the slider

The 2D position and orientation of the slider is determined as follows:

Step 1 Acquire a runcoded binary image *rc* of the slider; Figure 16 shows a typical image.

Step 2 Extract a binary image of the slider's "minor axis" (shown in Figure 17, superimposed on the slider image) by evaluating the AML/V expression

```
rc_slider_minor_axis =
    RCOR(RCSHIFT(rc,slider_half_length,WHITE),
         RCSHIFT(rc,-slider_half_length,WHITE))
```

where *slider_half_length* is a vector that would span slightly less than half the long dimension of the rectangular slider

Step 3 Compute X, Y, and θ parameters for the minor axis using first- and second-moment features derived from binary region analysis of *rc_slider_minor_axis*.

Step 4 Extract a binary image of the slider's "major axis" (shown in Figure 18, superimposed on the slider image) by evaluating the AML/V expression

```
rc_slider_major_axis =
    RCAND(RCNOT(RCSHIFT(rc,slider_half_width,BLACK)),
          RCNOT(RCSHIFT(rc,-slider_half_width,BLACK)),
          RCSHIFT(rc,1.1*slider_half_width,BLACK),
          RCSHIFT(rc,-1.1*slider_half_width,BLACK))
```

where *slider_half_width* is a vector that would span slightly less than half the short dimension of the rectangular slider.

Step 5 Compute X, Y, and θ parameters for the minor axis using first- and second-moment features derived from binary region analysis of *rc_slider_minor_axis*.

Step 6 Compute slider X, Y from the intesection of the minor and major axes, and θ from the orientation of the minor axis.

As with the suspension, sub-pixel resolution is obtained for both position and orientation parameters since region features are derived from sums of values over all pixels in the region. By experimentally moving the slider by known amounts, we were able to verify that resolutions on the order of 0.2 pixels, corresponding to displacements of about 10 μm, were obtained.

Adjusting the slider

The AML code for aligning the slider to the suspension is shown in Figure 19. An iterative approach is used:

Step 1 Determine the position and orientation of the slider, using the method described above. Compute the displacement and orientational misalignment relative to the suspension.

Step 2 If the slider is correctly oriented relative to the suspension, go on to step 3. Otherwise move the coarse *X*, *Y*, and θ joints to correct for the misalignment while keeping the slider in the camera's field of view, and go back to Step 1.

Step 3 If the slider's displacement relative to the suspension is small enough, then stop. Otherwise, move the fine positioner *X* and *Y* actuators by an appropriate amount to correct for the misalignment, and go back to Step 1.

The principal complications with this approach arise from using the coarse joints to correct for angular misorientations. The distance from the axis of the θ motor to the tip of the vacuum pen is about 14 cm. Thus each 1° of rotation correction introduces an additional 0.24 mm lateral displacement of the slider. In principle, up to 4° orientation could be compensated by using the fine positioner axes. However, we found that the θ joint was slow enough so that it made sense to move the coarse *X* and *Y* motors as well, and to reserve the full range of the fine positioner for Step 3.

The final motions are made using the fine-positioner actuators. For various reasons, we found it most convenient to compute the desired displacement in camera coordinates. The necessary camera-to-fine-positioner transformation is determined by using the fine-positioner to displace a slider by known amounts and then calling the *find_slider* subroutine. The transformation is then computed by ordinary least squares.

Conclusion

This paper has described an endpoint-sensing method for achieving very precise alignment of a part or tool to a workpiece. Our approach relies on the coarse joints of a robot to bring a tool or part within the "capture range" of a fine-positioning system carried by the robot, which is then used to null out sensed misalignments. To investigate this approach, we have developed a compact "wrist" mechanism capable of making fast and extremely precise motions in two directions, and have used it in several application experiments. These experiments demonstrate the feasibility of achieving roughly an order of magnitude improvement in the effective precision of a robot (from about 0.1 mm to 0.01 mm) while retaining a large working volume and high speed for long motions. The principal requirement is that it be possible to sense the misalignment between the tool or part and the workpiece.

Many applications require the ability to correct small rotational misalignments, as well as displacement errors. In this paper, we used a "coarse" wrist motor to supply these corrections. Work is proceding on an $XY\theta_Z$ model of the fine positioner that will allow fast rotational motions through small fractions of 1°. Work is also proceeding on additional endpoint-sensing experiments, and on investigation of other operating modes, such as force compliance.

Acknowledgements

Many people contributed to the success of this work. We are grateful to all of them. We would like to express our particular thanks to Bela Musits, who assisted in the detailed design of our first batch of fine positioners, to Frank Morgan, who constructed them, to Richard Perrone, who was responsible for constructing their control electronics, to Patrick Muir, who built electronic interfaces for the first fine positioner prototype and who implemented an initial prototype of the TCM-board testing application, to Mark Johnson, who developed the fiber-optic sensors for locating the wires, and to Friedrich Fischer, who built the fixtures for the disk slider mounting experiment.

References

[1] T. Lozano-Perez, "Robot Programming", *IEEE Proceedings*, July 1983.

[2] R. Podoloff, W. Seering, and B. Hunter, "An Accuracy Test Procedure for Robotic Manipulators Utilizing a Vision Based, 3-D Position Sensing System", *Proc. American Control Conf.*, San Diego, June 1984.

[3] R. H. Taylor and D. D. Grossman, "An Integrated Robot System Architecture", *IEEE Proceedings*, July 1983.

[4] S. Drake, *Using Compliance in Lieu of Sensory Feedback for Automatic Assembly*, D.Sc. Thesis, MIT, 1977.

[5] C. C. Geschke, "A System for Programming and Controlling Sensor-Based Robot Manipulators", *IEEE Trans. on Pattern Analysis and Machine Intelligence*, January, 1983.

[6] M. T. Mason, "Compliance and Force Control for Computer Controlled Manipulators", *IEEE Trans. Syst. Man Cybern.*. SMC-11(6):418-432, 1981.

[7] M. Raibert and J. Craig, "Hybrid Position/Force Control of Manipulators", *J. Dyn. Syst. Measurement Contr.*, 102:126-133, 1981.

[8] N. Hogan, "Mechanical Impedance Control in Assistive Devices and Manipulators", *Proc. of the Joint Automatic Control Conference*, San Francisco, 1980.

[9] T. Lozano-Perez, M. T. Mason, R. H. Taylor, "Automatic Synthesis of Fine-Motion Strategies for Manipulators", *Int. J. of Robotics Research*, Vol 3, No. 1, 1984.

[10] H. Asada and T. Kanade, "Design of Direct-Drive Mechanical Arms", Carnegie-Mellon University Robotics Institute Report CMU-RIi81-1, 1981.

[11] H. Asada and K. Youcef-Toumi, "Development of a Direct-Drive Arm using High-Torque Brushless Motors", MIT Laboratory for Manufacturing and Productivity, 1983.

[12] Andre Sharon and David Hardt, "Enhancement of Robot Accuracy Using Endpoint Feedback and a Macro-Micro Manipulator System," *American Control Conference proceedings*, San Diego, California, June 6-8 1984. pp. 1836-1842.

[13] K. Asakawa, F. Akiya, F. Tabata, "A Variable Compliance Device and its Application for Automatic Assembly", *Proc. Autofact 5 Conference*, Detroit, November 14-17, 1983.

[14] R. Bolles and R. Paul, "The Use of Sensory Feedback in a Programmable Assembly System", Stanford Computer Science Report STAN-CS-396, October 1973.

[15] Y. Shirai and H. Ionue, "Guiding a Robot by Visual Feedback in Assembling Tasks", *Pattern Recognition*, Vol 5, pp 99-108, Pergamon Press 1973.

[16] G. Beni, S. Hackwood, and W. S. Trimmer, "High-Precision Robot System for Inspection and Testing of Electronic Devices", *Proc. IEEE Int. Conf. on Robotics*, Atlanta, March 1984.

[17] P. Dario, D. DeRossi, C. Domenici, and R. Francesconi, "Ferroelectric Polymer Tactile Sensors with Anthropomorphic Features", *Proc. IEEE Int. Conf. on Robotics*, Atlanta, March 1984.

[18] G. L. Miller, R. A. Boie, M. J.. Sibilia, "Active Damping of Ultrasonic Transducers for Robotic Applications", *Proc. IEEE Int. Conf. on Robotics*, Atlanta, March 1984.

[19] T. Kanade and T. Somer, "An Optical Proximity Sensor for Measuring Surface Position and Orientation for Robot Manipulation", *Proc First Int. Symposium on Robotics Research*, 1983.

[20] P. Will and D. Grossman, "An Experimental System for Computer Controlled Mechanical Assembly." *IEEE Trans. Comput.*, C-24, (1975), 879.

[21] R. Taylor, P. Summers, and J. Meyer. "AML: A Manufacturing Language." *International Journal of Robotics Research*, Vol. 1, No. 3, (1982).

[22] M. Lavin and L. Lieberman, "AML/V: An Industrial Machine Vision Programming System." *International Journal of Robotics Research*, Vol. 1, No. 3, (1982).

[23] -----, *IBM Manufacturing System: A Manufacturing Language Reference Manual* No. 8509015, IBM Corporation, 1983.

[24] -----, *APL Language*, No. GC26-3847-4, IBM Corporation, 1978.

[25] R. L. Hollis, "Fine Positioner Increases Robot Precision", IBM Research Report, 1984.

[26] M. R. Cutkosky and P. K. Wright, "Position Sensing Wrists for Industrial Manipulators," *12th International Symposium on Industrial Robots*, 1982, pp. 427-438.

[27] B. A. Sawyer, "Magnetic Positioning Device," U.S. Patent No. 3,457,482, issued July 22, 1969.

[28] For specifications of the lateral effect position sensor, see data sheets from Silicon Detector Corporation, Newbury Park, California.

[29] R. F. Bonner, J. A. Asselta, F. W. Haining, "Advanced Printed-Circuit Board Design for High-Performance Computer Applications", *IBM J. Res. Develop.*, Vol 26, No. 3., May 1982.

[30] J. R. Bupp, L. N. Chellis, R. E. Ruane, J. P. Wiley, "High Density Board Fabrication Tolerances", *IBM J. Res. Develop.*, Vol 26, No. 3., May 1982.

[31] S. A. Bolasna, et al., "Air Bearing Support of a Magnetic Recording Head", *IBM Disk Storage Technology* IBM Corporation, February 1980.

[32] R. B. Watrous, "Transducer suspension mount apparatus", U.S. Patent 3,931,641, 1976.

[33] J. Hill, "Dimensional Measurements from Quantized Images", *Machine Intelligence Research Applied to Industrial Automation (Tenth Report):EHP1, SRI International, pp. 75-106, November, 1980.*

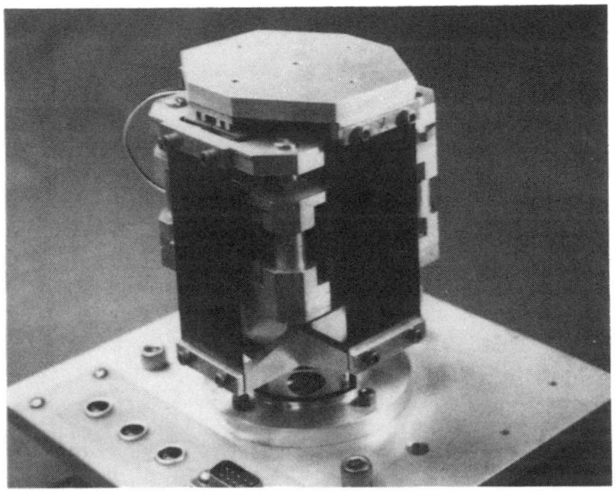

Figure 1. Two-dimensional Planar Fine Positioner

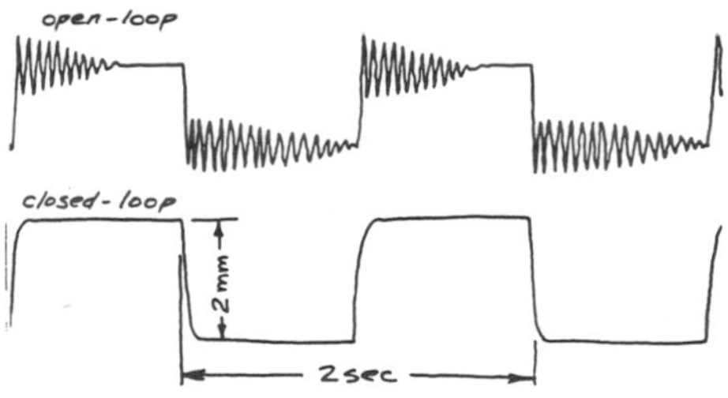

(a)

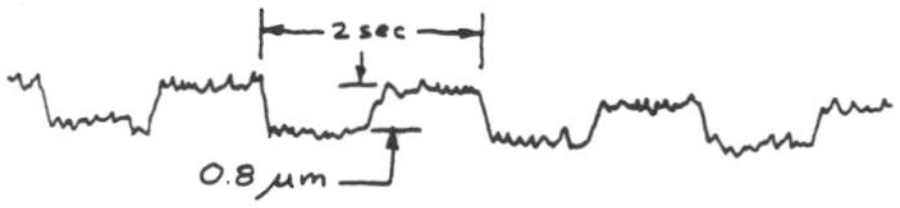

(b)

Figure 2. Position vs Time Trace: (a) large step response; (b) small step response

Approximate physical dimensions	7.6 cm on a side
Approximate mass	1 Kg
Force	27 N
Motion Range	± 1 mm
Positional resolution with internal sensor	0.5 μm
Closed loop bandwidth with PID controller	52 Hz
Rise time (10% to 90%) for 1 mm move	8 msec

Figure 3. Planar Fine Positioner Specifications

(a)

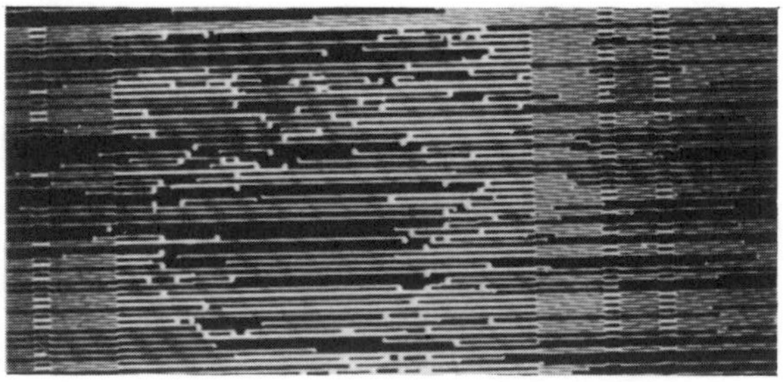

(b)

Figure 4. TCM Board: (a) Assembled Board; (b) Signal Plane Traces

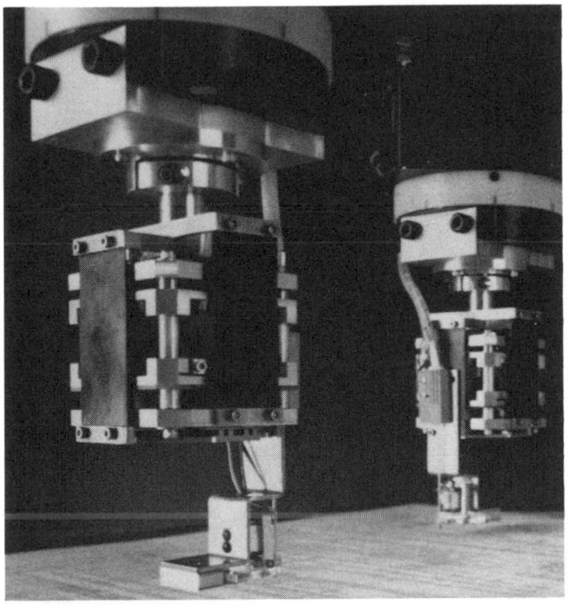

Figure 5. Robotic System for TCM-Board Probing

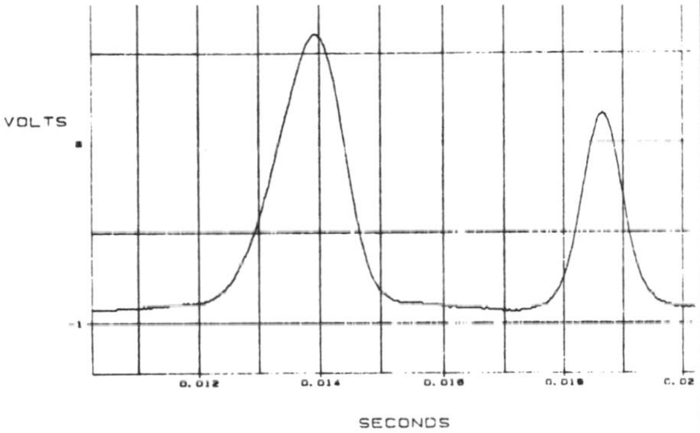

Figure 6. Fiber-Optic Sensor Output: This figure shows the output of the fiber-optic sensor when it is swept past a pair of TCM board wires spaced 0.15 mm apart.

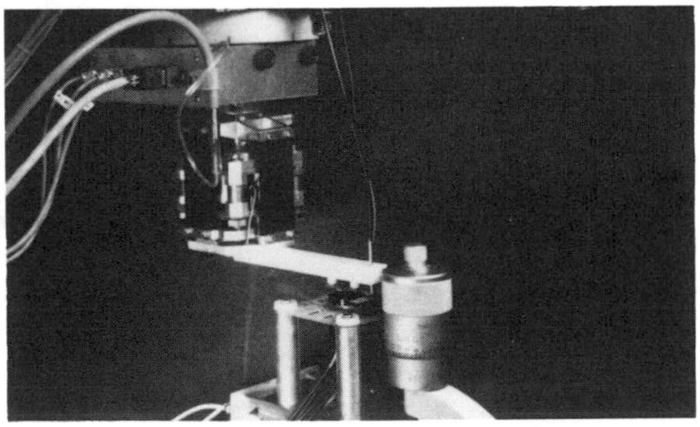

Figure 7. Probe Placement Sensitivity Experiment Apparatus: The micrometer stage is used to displace the small section of TCM board by known amounts, and the lateral effect cell is used to measure the probe displacement after the wire is located.

Wire Displacement (μm)	Lateral Cell Reading(μm)
0	730.1 ±1.6
5	723.7 ±2.1
10	730.9 ±1.1
15	731.2 ±0.9
20	725.1 ±2.6
25	728.2 ±1.4
30	731.9 ±1.4
35	732.0 ±0.9
40	732.9 ±0.7
45	732.9 ±0.7
50	732.5 ±0.8
75	732.8 ±0.4

Figure 8. Probe Placement Sensitivity Experiment Results: Five trials were made for each displacement value. Mean and standard deviation lateral cell readings are given.

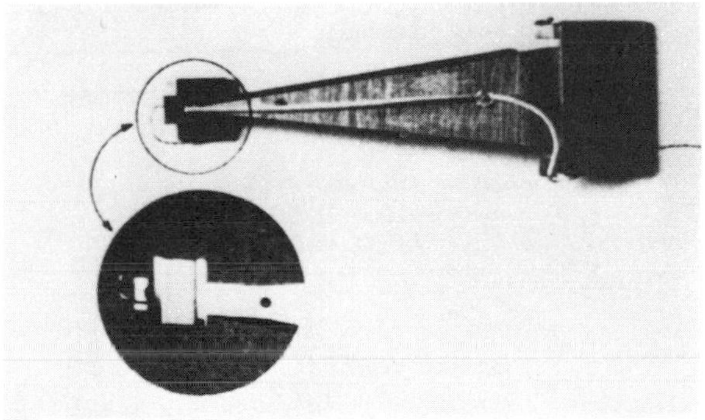

Figure 9. IBM Slider-Suspension Assembly

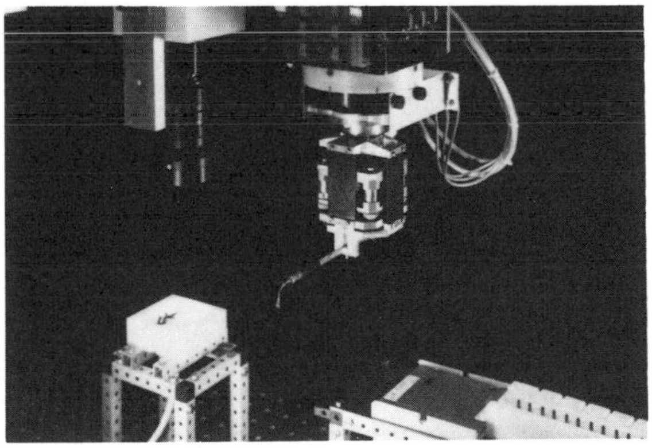

Figure 10. Slider-Suspension Assembly Experiment

```
job_cycle: SUBR;
 step_1:   next_suspension;
           get_suspension;
           susp_to_fixture;
 step_2:   susp_xyw = locate_suspension;
 step_3:   apply_glue;
 step_4:   next_slider;
           get_slider;
           safe_z_move(ARM,tv_station);
 step_5:   adjust_slider;
 step_6:   cure_glue;
           pen_vacuum(OFF);
 step_7:   replace_suspension;
           BRANCH(step_1);
  END;
```

Figure 11. AML Program for Slider-Suspension Assembly: Significant subroutines are shown in subsequent figures. An actual production program would include a number of other elements, including operator interfaces, links to the production control system, and error recovery procedures.

```
get_suspension: SUBR;
  pen_pickup(suspension_pallet(susp_no),0.05,
                    susp_dwell,0.3,<0.02,0.1,0.1>);
  MOVE(ZJT,safe_z,,<SPEED,0.5,0.5>);
  END;

pen_pickup:SUBR(loc,
                    approach_dz DEFAULT 0.020,
                    dwell_time DEFAULT .25,
                    depart_dz DEFAULT safe__z-loc(3),
                    depart_ctl DEFAULT DEFAULT);
  safe_z__move(ARM,loc+<0,0,approach__dz,0,0,0>);
  MOVE(ZJT,loc(3));
  pen_vacuum(ON);DELAY(dwell__time);
  DMOVE(ZJT,depart_dz,,depart__ctl);
  END;

susp_to_fixture: SUBR;
  safe_z_move(arm,fixture+fixture_app1);
  MOVE(ARM,fixture+fixture_app2);
  MOVE(ARM,fixture);
  fixture_vacuum(ON);
  pen_vacuum(OFF); delay(.5);
  scrub_fp(4,.2);
  MOVE(ZJT,safe_z);
  END;

scrub_fp: SUBR(n,df);
 i: NEW 0;
 f0: NEW QGOAL(fp);
   WHILE n GE i=i+1 DO
       BEGIN
       MOVE(fp,f0+df,,<1.,1.,1.,0>);
       MOVE(fp,f0-df,,<1.,1.,1.,0>);
       END;
   MOVE(fp,f0,,<1.,1.,1.,1>);
   END;
```

Figure 12. AML Subroutines for Getting a Suspension

```
get_slider: SUBR(loc DEFAULT slider_tray(slider_no));
                    pen_pickup(loc,,slider_dwell,.02);
                    scrub_fp(3,<0.,0.05>);
                    MOVE(ZJT,safe_z);
                    END;
```

Figure 13. AML Subroutine for Getting a Slider

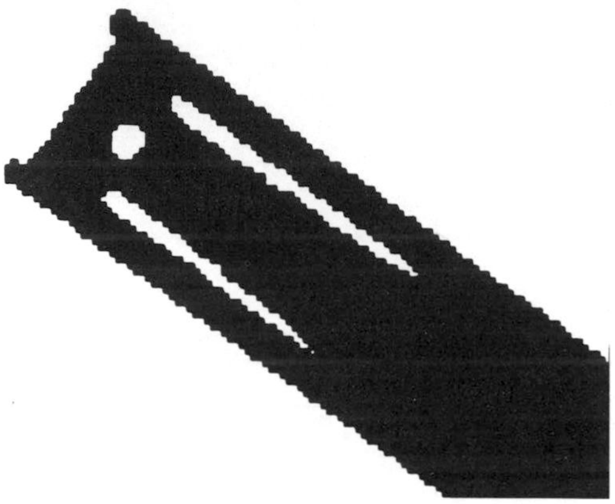

Figure 14. Binary Image of Suspension

Figure 15. Suspension Centerline, Superimposed on Suspension Image

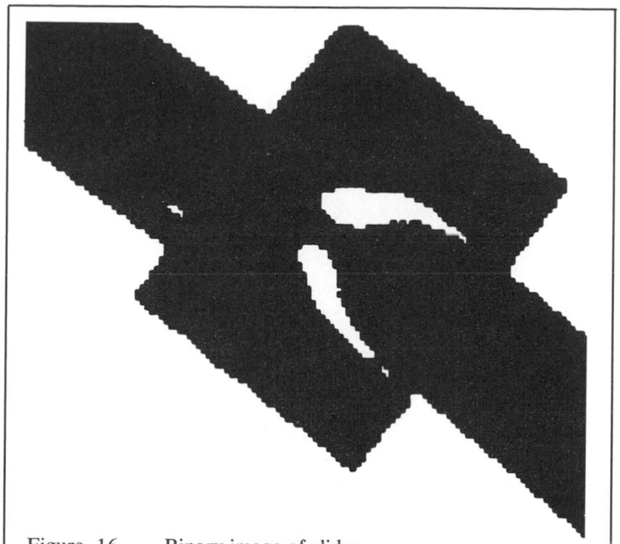

Figure 16. Binary image of slider

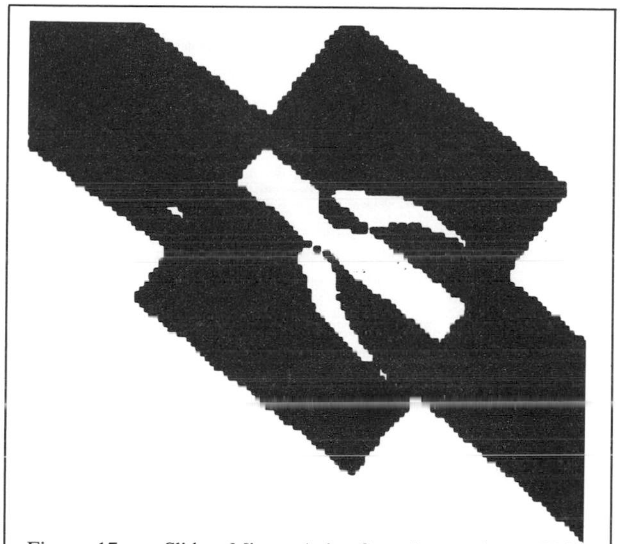

Figure 17. Slider Minor Axis, Superimposed on Slider Image

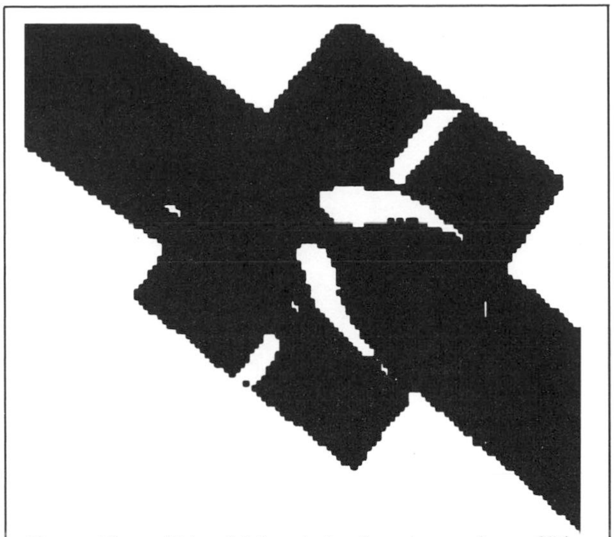

Figure 18. Slider Major Axis, Superimposed on Slider Image

```
adjust_slider: SUBR;
 slider_target: NEW susp_xyw + slider_offset(susp_xyw(3));
 e_xyw: NEW slider_xyw;
 tvw: NEW tool_vect(qgoal(6));
 loop:
  slider_xyw = find_slider;
  e_xyw = slider_xyw - slider_target;
  IF ABS(e_xyw(2)) GT r_tol THEN
          BEGIN
          DMOVE(xyw,
                    (-tvw+tvw=tool_vect(qgoal(6)-e_xyw(2)))
                                                  #<e_xyw(2)>);
          NULL, OUT(ARM(6));
          BRANCH(loop);
          END;
  IF DOT(e_xyw(1),e_xyw(1)) GT xy_tol*xy_tol THEN
          BEGIN
          dmove_in_cam(-e_xyw(1));
          BRANCH(loop);
          END;
  END;
```

Figure 19. AML Subroutine for Adjusting Slider

Segmentation by Object-Matched Low-Level Operators

John F. Jarvis
Bell Laboratories
Holmdel, New Jersey 07733

A general method for implementing computer vision systems suitable for a variety of industrial and manufacturing tasks is described. The method, SOMLO, is generally applicable where there is one or at most a few kinds of objects in the scene. However, many of the objects may be present in a single scene requiring the analysis of images of considerable complexity. SOMLO is designed for strict bottom-up processing and does not require any global iterations or searching strategies in its implementation.

The method is described and applied to three different visual image processing tasks: location of a Rubik's Cube, locating wire-wrap pins and wires on a wire-wrapped circuit board and tracing two different types of conductors, aluminum and polysilicon, on a silicon integrated circuit.

INTRODUCTION

Computer vision systems have found significant usage in the manufacturing domain. Such systems are used for parts identification, determination of position and orientation and for implementing various forms of visual inspection. This paper presents a technique potentially useful for solving more complex problems than the currently available commercial systems can in all the mentioned applications areas. The acronym SOMLO, for image Segmentation by Object-Matched Low-level Operators, was given to the technique in recognition of the principle technical approach used.

The industrial vision environment has several characteristics that tends to make it a distinctive applications area within the computer vision discipline [1]. In general, the object or objects to be examined by the vision system are known. In many cases, only one type of object may be presented to the vision system. However, many instances of that one object may be present in the image leading to images of considerable complexity. The illumination and viewing conditions can be carefully structured and controlled. It is this latter property that has enabled the development and use of the present generation of binary vision systems. Often the approximate location and orientation of the part is known. Finally, an objective measures for assessing the performance of an industrial vision system are available, a prerequisite for the continued development of more competent systems. Parts that are inspected are either good or bad according to an independent method of evaluation. When used for providing orientation and position information, the precision required can be well characterized [2].

The industrial vision environment is also subject to constraints that limit the choice of algorithms and techniques that are suitable for building functional systems. The major constraint can be loosely characterized as a performance to cost ratio. If the system can not meet throughput, accuracy and reliability requirements while subject to a simultaneous cost constraint it simply is not a solution to the original problem.

This paper will describe the SOMLO method that has been designed to both take advantage of the unique features of the industrial environment and to meet performance requirements. Simply stated, SOMLO uses lexical operations to search for prespecified object features in suitably coded one dimensional projections computed from the original image. Performance issues are approached by a careful partitioning of the processing steps into individual modules amenable to a pipelined implementation by using only bottom-up or feed-forward data flow. SOMLO also uses judicious sampling as a means of performance enhancement and is naturally implemented for processing raster oriented image data. The initial, computation intensive steps require only integer arithmetic and Boolean operations minimizing the cost of constructing dedicated processors.

Historically, this work can be viewed as a generalization of techniques successfully used in a variety of industrial inspection tasks [3,4,5,6,7]. In each of these applications, techniques such as projections, straight line approximations, symbolic representations and syntactic analysis were shown to have utility. The SOMLO technique uses all these methods in a coordinated and systematic way to provide a significant computer vision capability while satisfying externally imposed cost constraints and performance requirements. The following sections will describe SOMLO in detail and illustrate its application to three specific vision problems. In order of increasing complexity the three examples are location of a Rubik's cube viewed against an uncluttered background, tracing individual wires on a wire-wrapped circuit board and tracing two different kinds of conductors in an image of a SIC chip.

METHOD

The scheme followed in each application of SOMLO is the same with many of the operations performed common to all three examples. The general flow of data and the individual processing steps are shown in Figure 1. The most computationally intensive operations are the common low-level steps. These will be described once with minor differences in each applications noted as needed. The processes used rely on simple steps operating at the high rates characteristic of video data graduating to complex model based processes operating on greatly reduced quantities of highly abstracted data representations. Following the discussion on the common low-level steps each of the three examples will be described in detail.

Processing starts with the acquisition of an image. Data used in this study were derived from standard resolution monochrome industrial grade vidicon cameras using lighting and optics specific to each example. The TV images were digitized to 512×512 pixels spatial resolution and 6 bits of intensity resolution using an Adage RDS-3000 graphics system. Typically, images were saved in files that were normally used instead of live images. Enough testing with online images was done to insure that the processing results claimed are not artifacts of the stored images.

The first processing step, an optional one, was to filter the image with a smoothing filter, usually a 3×3 box filter. The filtering reduces the noise in the image and increases the number of grey scale levels present. Obviously, this type of processing does not result in any reduction of data.

The first data reducing operation in SOMLO is generating two sets of one dimensional projections. In these examples, the natural identification of projections with rows (horizontal scan lines) and columns of the digital image was made. In both cases, a one pixel wide projection, every N_{th} line or column was used. While any set of projections could be used, there are obvious computational advantages to the use of rows and columns as projections. Along each projection, all image data is used preserving the spatial resolution of the image. A slightly more complex projection would vertically average N adjacent rows or horizontally average N adjacent columns where N is the sampling interval. This latter technique would provides most of the benefits of a 3×3 smoothing filter while preserving the spatial resolution along the projection.

The projections operation creates two sets of intensity waveforms expressed as a function of distance along a row or column. The second abstraction or data reduction step in SOMLO is the approximation of the intensity waveforms by a set of connected straight lines. Many such techniques are possible [8] differing in the error criteria used, control of the number of segments and methods for locating the breakpoints between segments. A particularly simple method that needs only one adjustable parameter, the maximum error allowed before starting a new segment, described by Tomek [9] was used in this project. Data is processed serially and no iteration or backtracking is used to improve the locations of the breakpoints between segments. This approximation admits the possibility of pathological results but such things have not been a problem. Clearly, if the number of segments is comparable to the number of data samples in the projection, no advantage accrues to this method. Requiring that the number of segments be significantly less than the number of image samples in the projection sets a limit on how closely the straight line approximation can match the original data.

Next, a further abstraction is made by representing each line segment by 1 of 11 symbols according to Figure 2. There are five orientations with two length divisions except for the horizontal line category that has an additional short length division. While the parameters governing this conversion were obtained empirically, it has worked well in each of the three examples. Even though the angular and length division points can be adjusted to optimize the performance of the system for specific objects, the recognition performance in each of the three examples does not depend strongly on the values chosen.

There is an implicit geometric scale factor in this mapping: The intensity space codes 256 values while there are 512 samples along a line or column. Equating one intensity step to one geometric increment defines this scale factor.

Replacing each line segment with a symbol results an a character string that represents the original waveform. This string is part of a data representation that also includes the geometric (intensity, coordinate) data corresponding to the end of each symbol. This symbol string is the final abstraction of the data and is the input for the recognition steps of SOMLO.

An alternative symbolic representation to the one just described is the chain code [10]. Although usage of a chain code is conceivable for this type of problem, the total number of symbols cannot be less than the number of intensity samples and may be significantly greater if substantial intensity resolution is needed. While some experiments with chain codes have been done [7], this representation tends to result in more complex processing steps in the recognition phases than those used in SOMLO.

At this stage in the processing a useful, but optional, consolidation step is performed. Using a lexical analyzer, runs of symbols corresponding to to lines with similar orientations are identified and are replaced by the single characters representing the run if it were considered a single straight segment. While this is potentially an object dependent processing step, each of the three examples has employed the same segment combination rules. This process is roughly equivalent to allowing a less stringent error criteria for long segments than for short ones. The resulting compacted strings also have the parallel geometric data updated to correspond to the new endpoints. The set of lexical rules used for this compaction operation can be stated as follows:

[abj][abj]+	[bk][bk]+	[ak][ak]+	[dm][dm]+
[em][em]+	[em][em]+	[den][den]+	[cfl][cfl]+

where each expression is the specification for an allowed combination of segments. The implementation language used for this task is LEX [11]. In this language each specification is a regular expression. In the expressions given, the [] pair encloses alternate matching characters while the + operator specifies one or more of the preceding character or class of characters. The first specification matches strings of 2 or more of the characters a,b,j appearing in any combination.

LEX is a compiler-compiler that generates C programs that search for the specified strings in an input stream. As such, it is particularly convenient during the developmental stages of a project. Obtaining adequate performance in a production system would require more optimal implementations of the lexical analyzers.

Following the production of the set of compacted strings representing the original projections, the first truly object dependent recognition step is taken. This is a search for substrings corresponding to particular object features within each projection string. This is done for each example with another LEX specified lexical analyzer using a grammar that is related to specific object characteristics. Given the recognition of an object feature substring, geomètrics tests are made as a conformation that the recognition step succeeded. This step follows the notion of attributed grammars [12]. The feature recognizers described here are the object-matched low-level operators referred to in the SOMLO acronym.

In this description, no distinction has been made in the processing given to the horizontal and vertical projection sets. While both sets are processed identically in the three examples in this paper, there is no reason in principle requiring identical treatment. Given objects that are approximately oriented, asymmetry in the projections processing and object recognition stages is a natural procedure to implement.

The final canonical step in SOMLO is to correlate the features recognized in the projection strings into a suitable object description. Processing of parallel features from adjacent strings as well as the matching of features from perpendicular scans can both be used in this task. As with the feature recognition step, the object recognition step is highly application domain dependent and requires an appropriate model of the object or objects being viewed. Details of the types of models used will be given with the examples.

Two lexical analyzers have been used in the processing steps outlined. Both have the same basic structure: an input string is searched for a class of patterns, which, if one is found that satisfies simple parametric tests, is replaced by a single character in the output string. The parallel geometric data structure is preserved. That is, a (intensity, coordinate) pair describing the endpoint of the segment matched is associated with the output symbol. Since the lexical analyzers differ only by the parsing rules, both lexical and parametric, a single design for a special purpose processor could be used for both string processing steps.

EXAMPLE: RUBIK'S CUBE

The first example of an object to be located in an image using SOMLO is a Rubik's Cube (Figure 3) which is viewed by a camera situated to view two adjacent faces of the cube. The viewing position results in an image consisting of 18 individual facets, small uniformly colored squares, arranged in three columns by six rows. Red, green and blue images are recorded using a color wheel assembly mounted in front of a standard monochrome TV camera. Specifically, the task is to locate each of the 18 facets visible in the images and compute a red, green and blue (RGB) triplet characterizing the color of each facet. While conceptually simple, there is substantial variability in the images since any of the six cube colors can appear in any location on the cube resulting in widely different monochrome images. There are also variations in the background and the device holding the cube is also visible. Figure 4 shows the intensity waveforms corresponding to the cursor overlaying the image in Figure 3.

Each image could be processed independently to obtain the 18 facet intensities for its color. However, the images are registered thus knowing the coordinates of the facets in one is sufficient. The first processing step is to choose or derive a single image for the analysis leading to the cube location. Choosing one image as representative (the green channel), summing the three images on a pixel by pixel basis, a procedure producing the perceived monochrome intensities or choosing the brightest pixel at each location were tried. While the performance of the search did not depend strongly on the method used, the maximum pixel intensity method appeared to be more robust and was used.

The production of the horizontal and vertical projections, straight line approximations, conversion to symbol strings and string compaction steps were performed as outlined in the Method section. Object recognition in the one dimensional scans was performed by a matching specification designed to locate a single object, the characteristic pattern of intensity of a scan across a single facet. Typically, a facet is characterized as a roughly constant intensity between a step or a dark line. Both the horizontal and vertical scans were processed by the same matching specification that is coded as the lexical analyzer given as:

facet: [ajbkdmen][bdkmfcl]+[ajbkdmen]

in the LEX regular expression language. Qualitatively, this describes a portion of the intensity waveform with a minimum of three segments. The center segment(s) can not include any high slope lines (ajdn) while the end segments can not include any of the horizontal segments (cfl). The geometric test performed after recognition is a maximum and minimum range test on the length of the center segment or segments of the matched string. Separate limit values are used for the horizontal and vertical scans since there is some foreshortening of the vertical dimensions owing to the oblique viewing angle. While it may be claimed that the lexical specification for the object recognition step is almost all inclusive, the results obtained justify its use. Although a single regular expression could be written to match the entire trace across the cube, the great variability of the appearance of the individual facets makes this a practical impossibility. The lines in Figure 5 show the location and extent of the matches obtained from the facet lexical analyzer. Table 1 tabulates the various stages of approximation of the projections corresponding to the cursor in Figure 3. In the table the segment intersecting the cursor is highlighted with between a pair of '+' symbols.

In addition to a horizontal position obtained from the location of the matched segment in the string, there is a vertical coordinate corresponding to the position of the scan line. A complimentary situation exists for vertically oriented scans. Facets are located by finding overlapping groups of the one dimensional facet indicators from sets of vertical and horizontal scans. Each group, generally consisting of more than one each of horizontal and vertical facet symbols, is assumed to indicate the location of one facet. Requiring that a facet be defined by at least one horizontal and one vertical object match successfully excludes most spurious matches.

The final step in locating the cube is to edit the preliminary facet indications with the three column by six row model. This step allows rejection of the remaining spurious matches while missing facets can be identified and their locations interpolated (Figure 6). With this step, the "computer vision" processing is completed. The resulting 18 locations are used to obtain a RGB intensity triplet for each facet by averaging intensities in a rectangular area centered on the computed coordinates. This method works $\pm$ 15 *degrees* of vertical and has proven to be insensitive to background image variations. Processing three such views enables the color of each of the 54 cube facets to be determined. The center facet of each of face has a unique color thus the remaining 48 facets can be grouped into similar colors by nearest neighbor matching using the center facets as the prototype values.

EXAMPLE: WIRE-WRAPPED CIRCUIT BOARDS

In this particular example of SOMLO, images of considerable complexity must be analyzed. In spite of the total complexity, only two specific types of objects are contained in the images, wires and the wire wrap pins. The specific problem addressed is the locating the pins and tracing individual wires. An initial report on this work has been given [13] which contains additional information on the inspection task that prompted the research effort.

Single monochrome images were obtained of one inch square areas of a wire-wrapped circuit board. The 512×512 spatial resolution image results in pixels having a 0.002 *inch* size. Wire diameter is about 0.015 *inch*. Lighting is diffuse and symmetrical about the camera axis. Surfaces normal to the camera axis appear the brightest consequently intensity traces across wires show a pronounced maximum at the wire centerline (Figures 7 and 8).

Simple approaches to segmenting individual wires from the mass of wires present in the image do not work adequately. Shading caused by the vertical depth of wires in the overall wiring pattern prevents the use of simple thresholding as a segmentation technique. Edge detection approaches result in pairs of edges for each wire resulting in considerable ambiguity in associating pairs with a specific wire even with the help of edge polarities.

As in the first example, the initial processing steps of obtaining projections, straight line approximations, conversion to symbol strings and string compaction were performed as described previously. The sampling interval for the projections was every sixth scan line or column, about the diameter of the wires.

The final processing in the low level segmentation is to identify one dimensional objects in the strings resulting from processing the projections. For the wire-wrap circuit board images only two object classes need be recognized, wire segments and pins. The 1D object recognition is done by a simple lexical analyzer defined by the following regular expressions:

```
wires:   jf?n   af?e   jf?e   af?n

pins:    j[^f]n   j..n   j...n   j....n
```

The general interpretation of the wire specification is for an approximately symmetric peak with an optional, short horizontal segment at the peak. Two additional LEX language operators have been used, the ^ meaning all characters except those contained in the bracket pair and ? that matches 0 or 1 instances of the preceding characters. The pin detector specification requires a larger amplitude intensity increase, up to four segments of structure excluding a single short segment followed by a larger amplitude intensity decrease. A wire location along a projection is defined by the location of the breakpoint at the peak, which usually is very close to the maximum in the intensity at the top of a wire. Table 2 lists the stages of approximation for the traces in Figure 8. The segments intersecting the cursor position are enclosed between a '+' pair.

The definition of a pin in the symbolic representation includes instances of valid wire definitions. This ambiguity is difficult to remove in the 1D case as the two classes of objects are virtually the same when viewed as 1D images. Some of this ambiguity is resolved by requiring that pin symbols satisfy geometric screening tests described in Figure 9. The usage of lexical analysis to propose and geometric analysis to dispose of objects is embodied in the attributed grammars [14].

Following the generation of the horizontal and vertical lists of 1D objects, the two lists must be merged to extract a two dimensional, model based, description of the image. Simply, perpendicular scans are processed to yield pin locations while parallel scans are analyzed to trace wires. Detection of pins is done first so 1D wire segments overlapping pin descriptions may be removed from further consideration. Both the pin detection and wire tracing algorithms work incrementally with the raster oriented data and make no reference to earlier data representations and thus do not require global searching. The recovery of the two dimensional image description fits within the pipelined architecture framework.

Pins are recognized by the presence of overlapping 1D pin objects in horizontal and vertical scans. Generally a cluster of both horizontal and vertical 1D pin objects is found, since a pin is normally detected in 2 or 3 adjacent parallel scans. The pin location is given as the mean location of all the 1D symbols comprising the cluster. This simple process is both fast and effective since a pin is limited in extent. While pin locations are known in principle, this knowledge is not used now in this system. Since the pins are at accurately known locations on the board determining their location could provide the basis for a calibration procedure relating board coordinates to vision system coordinates.

Tracing of individual wires, since they are extended objects, is considerably more difficult than finding the wire wrap pins. Intrinsic problems that complicate the tracing include wires crossing over and under each other, changes in direction, termination of wires on pins, shadowing of wires by pins and different wire colors. In addition, the implementation requirement of raster processing introduces several additional complications resulting from the asymmetry in the treatment of horizontal and vertical wires. Color might be viewed as an additional parameter available to reduce ambiguity. However, the processing requirements at the lowest level make this an expensive addition to the system.

The raster processing of the original image data forces the primary restriction on the wire tracing algorithm. Each wire segment, a single 1D wire object from a single scan, must be dealt with as it is detected. Possibilities include adding it to an existing wire, starting a new wire, joining two existing wires or discarding the segment. When comparing a new segment to the existing wires only the last M (M is usually 2 or 3) segments of the wire can be used for comparisons. Finally, a segment is assigned irrevocably to a wire with no reassignments are allowed even if later segments could be used to show a different assignment would have been better. These significant restrictions on the design of the tracing algorithm have been made in order to insure rapid processing of the image data. As a side issue, the demonstration that a workable algorithm can be created under these restrictions is one of the achievements of this project. Finally, the knowledge of the amount that these restrictions must be relaxed to obtain acceptable accuracy is also a goal of the project.

Wires that are being traced are kept on one of three lists: horizontal, vertical and diagonal. New horizontal segments may be added to wires on either the horizontal or diagonal lists. Similarly, vertical segments can only be added to wires on the vertical or diagonal lists. This three list structure exists to prevent extraneous matches between segments and wires perpendicular to segment direction. After each addition of a segment to a wire, the resulting slope is examined and the wire is moved to the appropriate list. This procedure allows tracing of wires around corners. The method of assigning a segment to a wire requires locating all wires whose extrapolation include the segment. The details of the extrapolation imply a simple linear model of wires. The extrapolation definition is the primary controller of the radius of curvature that may be followed and also defines the size of gaps that may be bridged when tracing wires. If a single wire extrapolates over the segment, it is added to that wire. If no wires extrapolate to the segment, the segment starts a new wire. If two or more wires extrapolate to the segment, several actions are possible including joining the two wires, adding to the wire that gives the best match or ignoring the segment.

Wire lists are kept ordered on their horizontal coordinate minimizing the time taken to determine the set of wires extrapolating over a segment. When a wire has not been added to for a vertical distance equal to the maximum extrapolation distance it is finished and moved from the active list to an output list. The output of this process is a list of wire-wrap pin centers and a list of partial traces of wires suitable for input to a fault detection procedure (Figure 10).

EXAMPLE: SILICON INTEGRATED CIRCUIT

This application represents an attempt to understand the visual world of SICs and is an extension of SOMLO to a third applications domain. The work described in this section was done by Ellen L. Walker of CMU during summer employment at AT&T Bell Laboratories.

There are many distinctive visual features present in SIC images (Figures 11 and 12) including diffusion regions, contact windows and two different types of conductors. The small scale of features in SICs yields far greater variability in the local appearance of the circuit features than has been evident in the other applications. The SIC images were recorded using a conventional monochrome vidicon camera viewing a portion of the circuit through a microscope. Illumination details and magnification used are not available. The processing steps leading to the compacted string representations for the sets of horizontal and vertical projections were made following the same procedures as the previous two examples.

The lexical analyzer was designed to locate two classes of objects, aluminum and polysilicon conductors, using the following regular expressions:

aluminum: j[cf]?n
polysilicon: [demn][cf]?[abjk][cf]?[demn][cf]?[abjk]

Qualitatively, an aluminum conductor has the same signature as the wires in the wire-wrap circuit board example: an abrupt transition from the background intensity to a narrow peak followed by an abrupt transition to the background intensity. The polysilicon definition is similar to the aluminum conductor except for the added requirement that a small dip in intensity relative to the background precede and follow the main peak. At the minimum and maximum intensities points, a short constant intensity line segment is allowed. The transition between intensity levels is also allowed to be more variable in the polysilicon recognizer than the aluminum conductor recognizer. Table 3 contains the symbolic approximations of the projections indicated in Figure 12.

Geometric tests used following recognition include a minimum intensity for aluminum conductors and an intensity range specification for the difference between the minimum and maximum values in a polysilicon object. The conductors do not have a single width thus no useful range checks can be made on the width of conductor segments.

This processing is made more complicated by several effects visible in the SIC image. First, there is considerable variation in the visual appearance of either type of conductor as a function of distance along the conductor. A conductor that crosses any other circuit feature on the chip has its appearance significantly modified. The other most notable feature present is the boundary of diffusion areas. Secondly, manufacturing processes at the scale of SIC production are intrinsically variable when compared to macroscopic objects such as wires or smooth plastic objects. This intrinsic variability must be accommodated in both the analysis of symbol strings and in the reconstruction algorithms used to create the object description from the projections sets.

A model based reconstruction of the two classes of conductors has not been done for the SIC problem. However, the following considerations would be relevant to building a model directed reconstruction of the two classes of conductors. First, the SIC conductor patterns are rectilinear with sharp corners between horizontal and vertical paths. Having only two orientations of conductors as opposed to the continuous range of orientations possible in the wire-wrapped circuit case will significantly simplify tracing algorithms. Complicating factors in building the model include variable conductor widths, the presence of two conductor types, tees and crosses of conductors and transitions from one conductor type to the other. These local variations in conductor appearance occasionally result in an error in conductor type assignment from the low level recognition process. The type assignment of a conductor run will have to be made by a statistical or voting procedure. The distances needed to extrapolate conductors to bridge crossover areas is limited. These considerations suggest that a simpler tracing procedure than used in the wire-wrap example would allow adequate reconstruction of conductor patterns. Figure 13 shows the results from the conductor recognition process applied to the compacted symbol strings, the data that would serve as input to the tracing process.

CONCLUSION

The visual environment for many of the routine tasks performed in manufacturing is well structured and controllable. This paper has described a general method for approaching a subset of industrial vision automation problems that is called image Segmentation by Object-Matched Low-level Operators (SOMLO). Three examples illustrating the application of SOMLO to images of varying complexity also show that it can be implemented using only a bottom-up data flow thus it offers the possibilities of economic implementation.

REFERENCES

1. J. F. Jarvis, "Research Directions in Industrial Machine Vision: A Workshop Summary," *Computer* **15**(12) pp. 55-61 (1982).
2. C.-S. Ho, "Precision of Digital Vision Systems," *IEEE Trans. Pattern Analysis and Machine Intelligence* **5**(6) pp. 593-601 (1983).
3. J. F. Jarvis, "Automatic Visual Inspection of Western Electric Series 700 Connectors," *Proc. Pattern Recognition and Image Processing Conf.*, pp. 153-159 (June 6, 1977).
4. J. Van Daele, A. Oosterlinck, and H. Van Den Berghe, "The Leuven Automatic Visual Inspection Machine (LAVIM)," *Proc. SPIE* **182** pp. 58-64 (1979).
5. J. F. Jarvis, "Automatic Visual Inspection of Glass-Metal Seals," *Proc. Fourth Int. Conf. Pattern Recognition*, pp. 961-965 (Nov. 7, 1978).
6. J. Mundy and R. E. Joynson, "Automatic Visual Inspection Using Syntactic Analysis," *Proc. PRIP 77, IEEE Computer Society Conf. on Pattern Recognition and Image Processing, Troy, NY*, pp. 144-147 (1977).
7. J. F. Jarvis, "Feature Recognition in Line Drawings Using Regular Expressions," *Proc. Third Int. Conf. Pattern Recognition*, pp. 189-192 (Nov. 8, 1976).
8. T. Pavlidis, *Structural Pattern Recognition*, Springer-Verlag, New York (1977).
9. I. Tomek, "Two Algorithms for Piecewise-Linear Continuous Approximation of Functions of One Variable," *IEEE Trans. Computers* **C-23**(4) pp. 445-448 (1974).
10. H. Freeman, "Computer Processing of Line Drawing Images," *Computing Surveys* **6** pp. 57-97 (March 1974).
11. S. C. Johnson and M. E. Lesk, "Language Development Tools," *Bell System Technical Journal* **57** pp. 2155-2175 (1978).
12. W. H. Tsai and K. S. Fu, "Attributed Grammars - A Tool for Combining Syntactic and Statistical Approaches to Pattern Recognition," *IEEE Trans. Syst. Man. Cyber.* **SMC-10** pp. 873-885 (1980).
13. J. F. Jarvis, "Computer Vision Experiments on Images of Wire-Wrap Circuit Cards," *Proc. Industrial Applications of Machine Vision (IEEE-CS)*, pp. 144-150 (May 3, 1982).
14. K. C. You and K. S. Fu, "Distorted Shape Recognition Using Attributed Grammars and Error-Correcting Codes," *Computer Graphics Image Processing* **13**(1) pp. 1-16 (1980).

FIGURE CAPTIONS

(1) A flow diagram showing typical image processing by the SOMLO method.

(2) The definition of the coding of line segments to symbols. With the left end of a line segment placed at the origin of the diagram, the symbol chosen is specified by where the right end of the segment is found.

(3) An image of two faces of a scrambled Rubik's Cube.

(4) The intensity traces corresponding to the cursor overlaid on the cube image in Figure 3. In each plot, the upper trace is the compacted straight line approximation while the lower is the original intensity waveform. The upper traces have been offset vertically for clarity.

(5) The result of the lexical search for objects in the coded projection strings. Each line is shown at the locations of the matching point.

(6) The 18 facets of the cube determined from the facet object matches. The squares containing the X's were interpolated.

(7) An image of one square inch of a wire-wrapped circuit board.

(8) The intensity traces corresponding to the cursor overlaid on the circuit board image in Figure 7.

(9) A diagram showing the geometric constraints that must be satisfied if a group of line segments is considered to be a pin symbol.

(10) The results of processing the wire-wrapped board image. Pins are shown as circles and wire are shown as line segments.

(11) An image of a portion of a silicon integrated circuit.

(12) The intensity traces corresponding to the cursor overlaid on the SIC image in Figure 11.

(13) The results of processing the SIC image. Individual vectors corresponding to objects recognized in the compacted symbol strings are plotted. Single lines indicate aluminum conductor matches while double lines indicate polysilicon conductors.

Table 1. RUBIK'S CUBE REPRESENTATIONS		
HORIZONTAL TRACE		
PHASE	SYM	STRING
Initial	35	kjklncdbnjjlnnfjjjlnnnnn+l+jdjn lklmnl
Compact	27	kjklncdbnjlnfjln+l+jdjnlklmnl
Objects	11	k=n=f=+=+djnl
VERTICAL TRACE		
PHASE	SYM	STRING
Initial	27	ljjjlnnn+l+jmjjjlnnbjlnjjjlnnlc
Compact	18	ljln+l+jmjlnbjlnjlnl
Objects	11	l=+l+==b=n=nl
Legend:	= facet	

Table 2. WIRE WRAP BOARD REPRESENTATIONS		
HORIZONTAL TRACE		
PHASE	SYM	STRING
Initial	129	knmkjjdnjjnbbbjenejjennajncjnjj bnmbjnejanbjdjnndnjnjcjnnjjndjj dnnnjanbjjdnjnbjnncjnjnnn+j+jen mkcjjenbncnbjdncbbjdnjnjbnjnnbj ncldjnm
Compact	80	knmkjnjnjnjnjncjnjnmjnjnjdjnjnj cjnjnjnjnjnjncjnjn+j+nmkcjnbn cnjncjnjnjnjnjnldjnm
Objects	51	knmk%%%%%c%%m%%*jd%%*jc%%%%%%%c %%+%+mkc*%bncn%c%%%%%ld%m
VERTICAL TRACE		
PHASE	SYM	STRING
Initial	64	mjenklmjjnjlcfjncjnkldjenckljnj n+l+jnnmljdnjjandljjnjjendklnjj nnbm
Compact	48	klmjnjljncjnkldjnckljnjn+l+jnml jnjnljnjnklnjnbm
Objects	35	m%klm%jl%c%kld%ckl%%+l+%ml%%l%% kln%bm
Legend:	% Wires, * Pins	

Table 3. SIC INTENSITY REPRESENTATIONS		
HORIZONTAL TRACE		
PHASE	SYM	STRING
Initial	122	adddadjnbeadjdebjenejnajanbanbd jncjjenccnajanbanajdncjjendbbje ndj+d+najandjnbanajandjdnajeebe ajjaennebeajenbjeeajencjjanndje
Compact	71	amadjnbeadjejnjnjnanbdjncjncnjn anjncjnjnj+m+jnjnjnjnjnbejnbe jnjnjncjnje
Objects	38	ama#eadj##nbdjncjnc#j#nj+#+nj## e%b#%c%je
VERTICAL TRACE		
PHASE	SYM	STRING
Initial	109	ennjjbcnnnajaenddnbjeeajaenebea adleajacnnajaennajaceneajaennaj jen+d+bnbacddajaendaddjdcdjjaen ejjbdndjjaendbnbac
Compact	51	njcnjnjejnbejdlejcnjnjcnjnj+n+b nbcdjnamjdcdjnjnjnbnjc
Objects	36	n%%je%bejdle%%%%+%+bnbcd%amjdcd %%%bnjc
Legend:	% Aluminum, # Polysilicon	

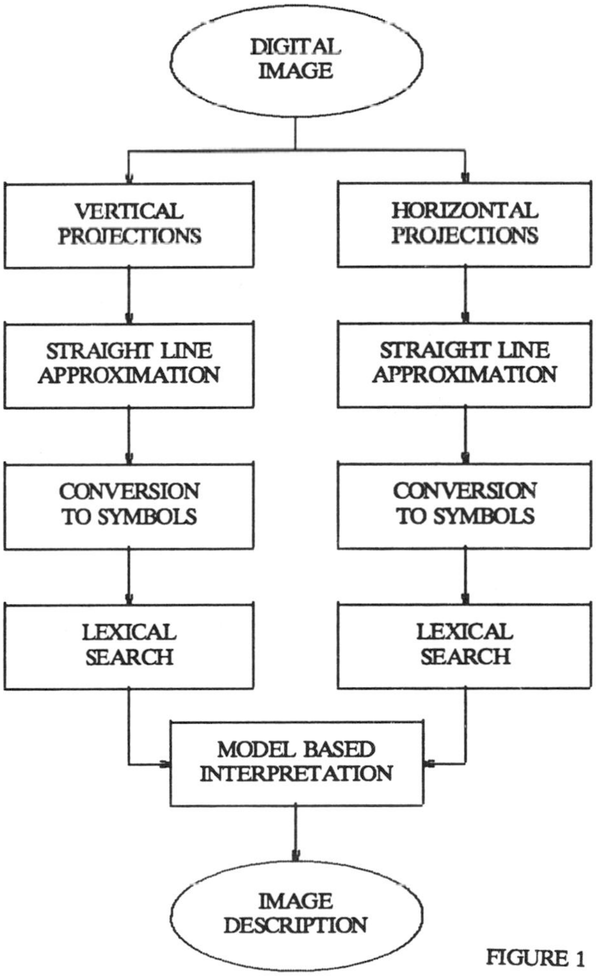

FIGURE 1

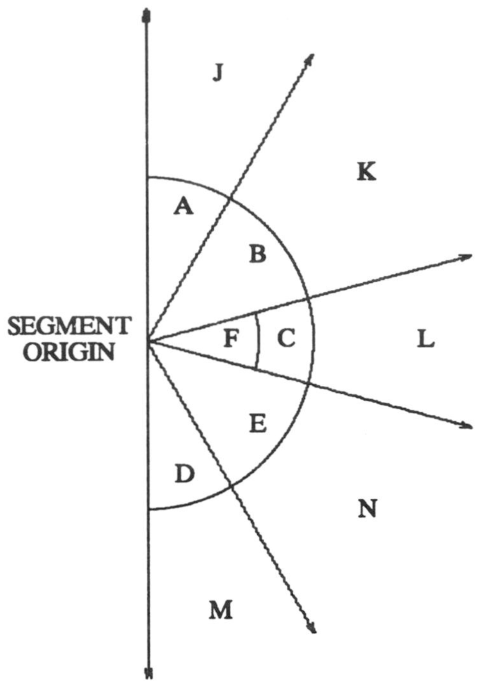

FIGURE 2

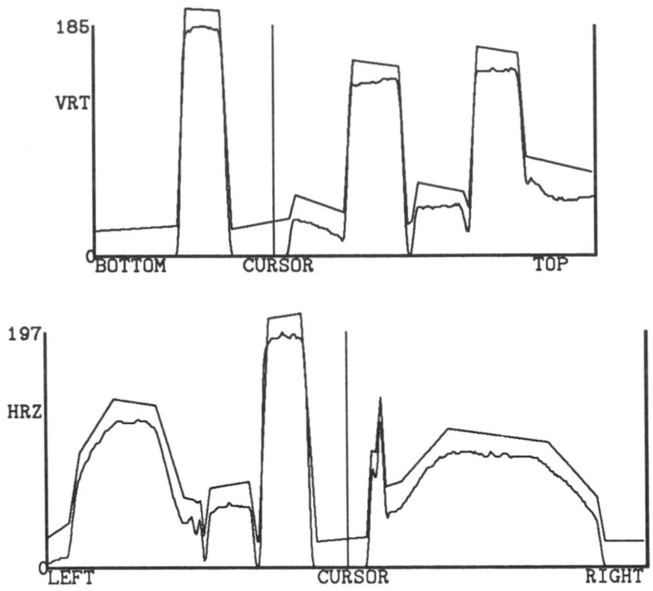

FIGURE 4

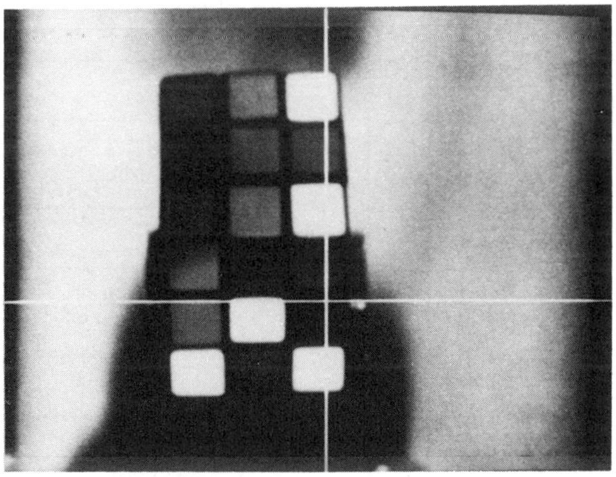

FIGURE 3

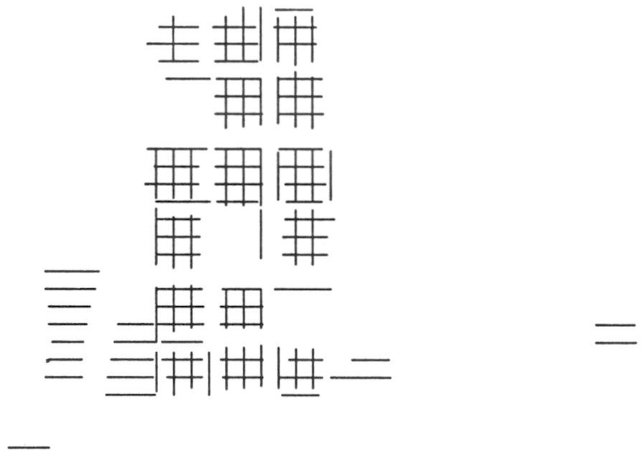

FIGURE 5

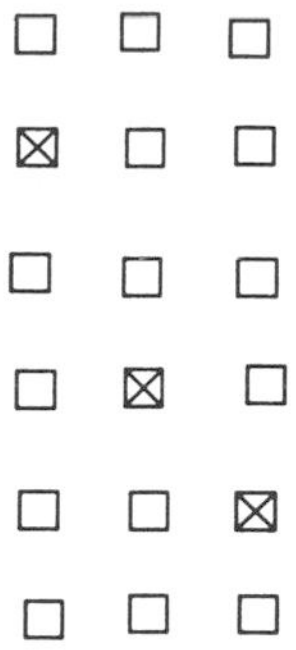

FIGURE 6

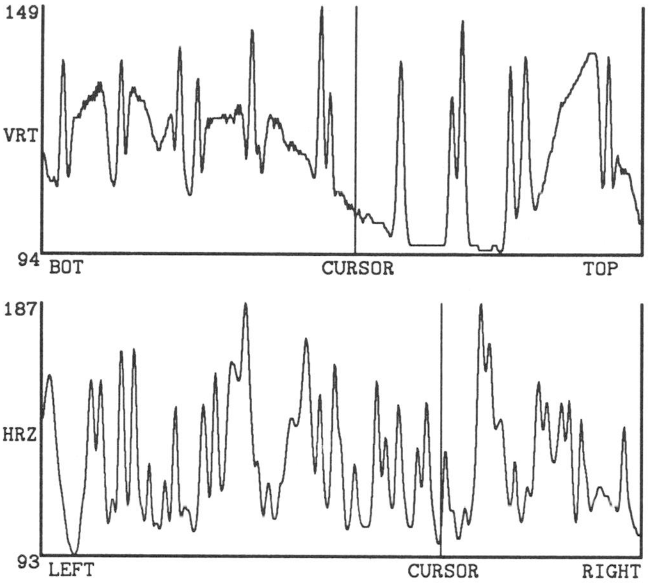

FIGURE 8

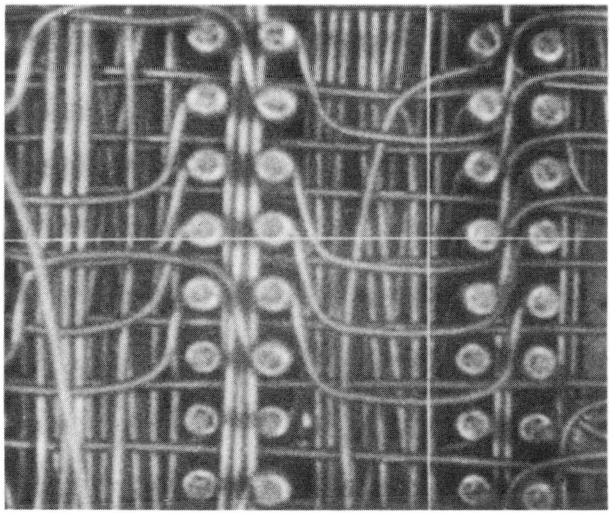

FIGURE 7

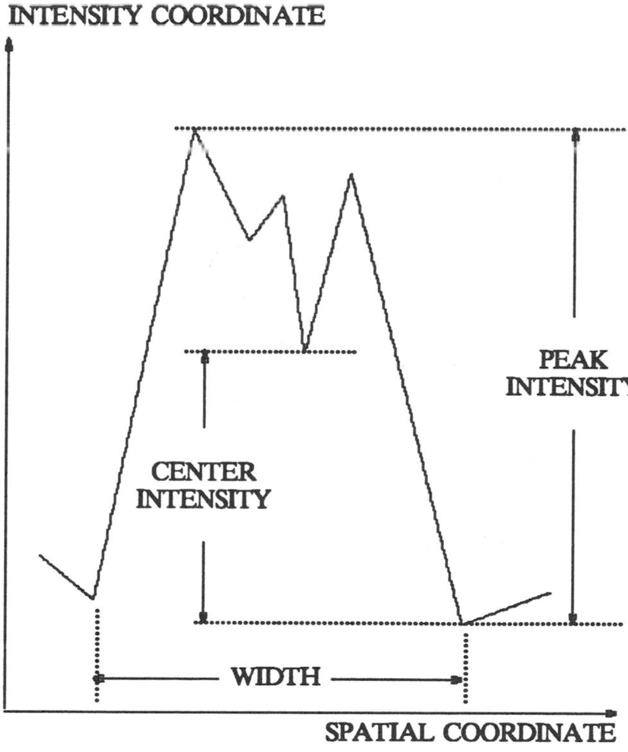

FIGURE 9

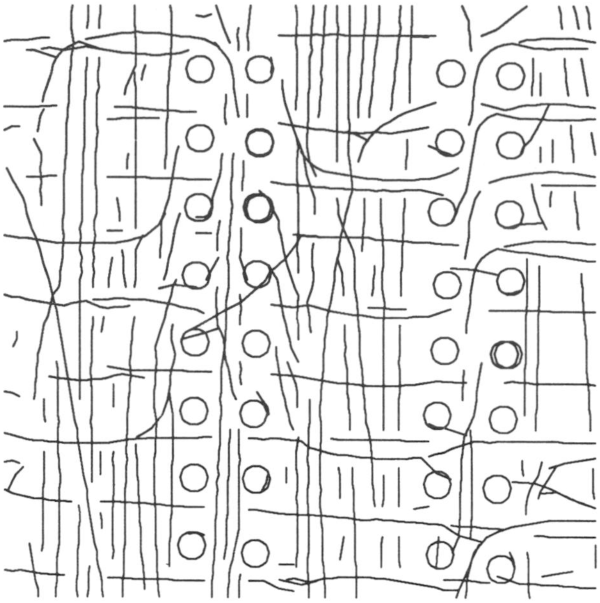

FIGURE 10

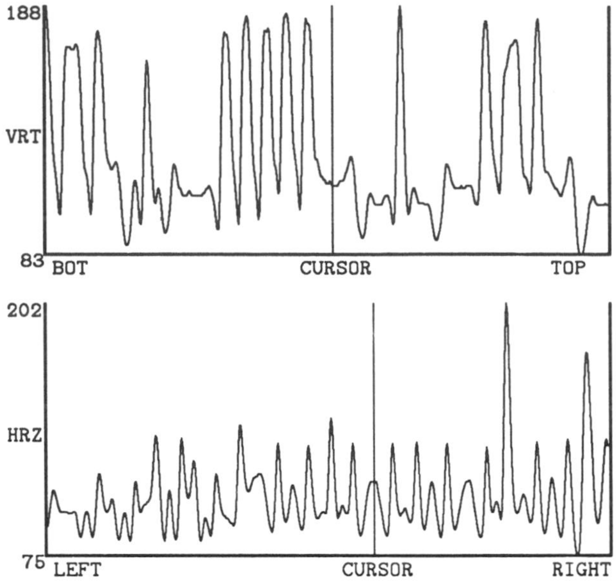

FIGURE 12

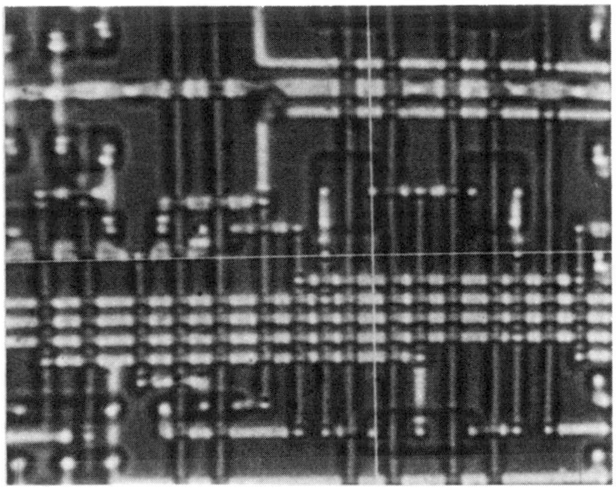

FIGURE 11

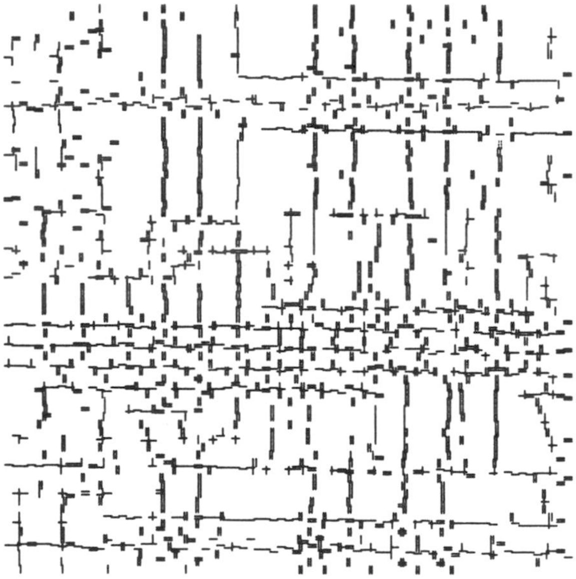

FIGURE 13

Converging Disparate Sensory Data *

Ruzena Bajcsy and Peter Allen

Department of Computer and Information Science
University of Pennsylvania
Philadelphia, PA 19104

Object recognition systems using single sensors (typically vision) are still limited in their ability to correctly recognize different three dimensional objects. By utilizing multiple sensors (in particular, vision and touch) more information is available to the system. This paper is an attempt to show the utility of multiple sensors and explore the problems and possible solutions to converging disparate sensory data for object recognition.

1. Introduction

Humans are able to make use of multiple sensory input to perform such tasks as object recognition very easily. In trying to recognize an object, we are able to integrate color, motion, touch, shape and language. The disparate kinds of information supplied by these sensors is somehow able to converge into a coherent understanding of the objects perceived in a scene. Robotic systems will eventually have to incorporate this multi-sensor capability [1]. Single robotic sensors (e.g. vision) are yet to be well understood and utilized on anything approaching a human scale. Multiple sensors can provide information that is difficult to extract from single sensor systems. Further, multiple sensors can complement each other to provide better understanding of a scene. The additional complexity posed by multiple sensor environments is tempered by the great rewards that more than one sensor can bring.

The utilization of multiple sensors forces us to confront five important issues for object recognition. They are:

- Representations for object models
- Organization of the database of models
- Accessing the database of models
- Strategies for using sensors
- Convergence of sensory data

This paper is an exploration of these issues involved in converging multiple sensor data for object recognition. Recent work by Henderson and Fai [11] and Shapiro and Haralick [5] has also dealt with these issues. Our discussion will focus on possible solutions to these problems and will provide an example from the limited domain of the kitchen.

* This work was supported by NSF grant MCS-820729, Air Force contract 82-NM-299, and grants from IBM Venture Fund, Lord Corporation and Digital Equipment Corporation.

2. Representations for Object Models

In model based object recognition, the sensed data must be related to the object models at hand. If we are to postulate a multiple sensor environment, we need to have multiple representations of objects. The nature of the data sensed from vision and touch is quite different and suggests different representational models at work [2][3]. Many different object model representations have been used in the past including generalized cylinders or cones [8][9], polyhedra [13] and curved surface patches [15]. These systems in general try to compute this primitive alone from the sensed data. A major difference between systems is the richness of the models. Systems that contain large amounts of information about object structure and relationships reduce the number of false recognitions. All these systems are discrimination systems that attempt to find evidence consistent with a hypothesized model and for which there is no contradictory evidence [4]. While our approach is similar it is not based upon a single primitive but upon multiple features and surface properties that our sensors can derive. Our model will contain geometric, topological and relational information about the objects to be recognized. Semantic discrimination is also an important candidate for inclusion in such a multiple representation system but is beyond the scope of this paper.

In human perception this discrimination is done in many different ways. We might perceive a unique feature, shape, or topology that will start us down a path of recognition. It is not clear apriori what the path will be. For this reason we cannot rely on a single representation from a single sensor as the mechanism for recognition. Rather, we must leave our system open and available to follow any representational avenue presented to it from the multiply sensed data. It is important that we try not to impose arbitrary hierarchies on these representations that will limit the strategies that we can use with the sensors. We want to be as aggressive and opportunistic as possible in exploring multiple paths towards recognition.

2.1. Sensor Environment

Multiple sensors provide us with the opportunity to discriminate between objects based on features that are derived from different sources. The sensing environment we are concerned with consists of a stereo pair of CCD cameras along with a robot manipulator containing a tactile sensor. Recognizing the strengths and weaknesses of each sensor system is necessary in order to effectively utilize them. The cameras are capable of extracting sparse 3-D data from the scene. The robot manipulator receives feedback from the touch sensor allowing it to trace surfaces subject to varying sets of constraints. The vision is passive in nature and fast, with large bandwidth while the touch sensor is slow, has low bandwidth and must be actively controlled. Vision, however is subject to the vagaries of lighting, reflectance and occlusion. Touch can feel occluded surfaces and report back 3-D world coordinates as well as surface normals.

2.2. Features for Discrimination

Given this sensing environment, we wish to be able to derive features for discriminating among objects. The features we wish to have in our model are:

- Gross shape descriptors
- Surface properties
- Topology

Gross shape descriptors are important because they limit the search space within the database [6]. The most important gross feature to be distinguished is the planarity of an object. If an object appears to be planar there are different representations and modeling techniques available for recognition than if it is three dimensional. Determining if an object is planar is difficult with vision alone, but if we trace across the object and analyze the 3-D data we can easily determine planarity. A tactile trace across the contour of the object in two orthogonal directions will allow us to interpolate a surface and test for planarity. In the kitchen domain that we are concerned with planarity is important in distinguishing flatware and plates from three dimensional objects. We would like to further extend gross shape descriptors to three dimensional objects by computing volumes, bounding parallelpipeds, and orthogonal slices across the object. While these descriptors are by themselves not sufficient for recognition their use with other sensed features will allow us to be able to further discriminate among competing models. Failure to find a gross shape description will cause a greater space to be searched but will not prevent recognition since multiple pathways of sensory recognition are available.

Surface properties are an extremely useful discriminator and are especially important with touch sensing. By modeling the objects as collections of surfaces, we can perform matching on a rich set of surface descriptions. The surface characteristics that we want to compute are area, curvature (including surface cavities) and 3-D moments(if a closed surface). Area is a weak discriminator but will add support to hypotheses. The other measures are much stronger surface characferistics and will narrow the range of possibilities greatly.

Holes are distinguishable features that can be sensed with both vision and touch. Vision processing can hypothesize holes and touch sensing can be used to verify their existence. Further, touch sensing can quantify the holes to aid in matching.

This approach emphasizes computing as many features as possible from the different sources to come up with a consistent set of interpretations of the data. The features range from weak descriptors like gross shape and area to specific descriptors such as surface curvature, holes and cavities. The conjunction of this sensed data will lead to a correct interpretation. It is important to note that we are using three dimensional measures. This allows us to utilize 3-D features of objects rather than projective features.

3. Organization of the Model Database

If we use multiple representations as stated above, we need to organize these representations in a coherent way for access to the model information. The important points to consider here are the relationships between different representations and allowing these different representations to converge (as discussed below). The database of object models consists of object records. Each object record contains a vector of features that can be sensed. An object record contains the following information:

- Object name
- Gross shape
- List of surface descriptions
- List of boundary curves
- List of holes
- List of cavities

3.1. Gross Shape

Gross shape properties in the object record include the volume of the object, a measure of its planarity, and a description of its bounding rectangular parallelpiped. These properties allow a coarse filtering of the objects to be recognized.

3.2. Surface Descriptions

The objects in the database are modeled as collections of surfaces. The surface descriptions may be planar, quadric or bicubic in nature allowing a wide variety of surface models to be used (as from CAM/CAD systems). Besides a parameterized description of the surface, we include the surface's area and locations of curvature maximum and minimum. If the surface is a closed surface that contains a volume, we also include a three-dimensional moment set for the surface. An example of this would be the handle of a cup. This is a very powerful feature because it provides us with the center of mass of the enclosed volume of the surface and the moments of inertia which form an orthogonal basis [10]. The center of mass allows us to find the translational parameters that take us from world to model coordinates and the inertial axes can be rotated to conform to the model's axes and determine the rotational parameters of the transform.

Surface descriptions are a good choice of primitive since we can interpolate surfaces from the combined visual and tactile data [7] [14]. Once these surfaces are built from the data, we can begin the matching against these descriptions.

3.3. Boundary Curves

The boundary curves represent the joining of surfaces. The relational information in the model is embedded in these curves. Whenever two surfaces join, a boundary curve exists with pointers to each of its constituent surfaces. They are important in that they may be sensed visually and by touch. A curve discovered by vision may be nothing more than a lighting artifact and touch sensing can verify or contradict the ambiguous visual data. Finding a boundary curve will help in ascertaining relations between surfaces as modeled in the database. They may be modeled by segments or space curves.

3.4. Holes

Holes are modeled as having a center, axis and diameter. The description of holes is useful for matching and determining the transform parameters from the model coordinates to sensed object coordinates. If we assume a canonical upright position for objects we need only find three translational and one rotation parameter to affect the transform. If we assume arbitrary position then we will need to find 2 extra rotational parameters. (we assume no scaling of objects). Holes are especially powerful in that they can be hypothesized by vision and explored by touch to determine their extent.

3.5. Cavities

Cavities are modeled as having a bottom point, depth and diameter. In our domain the size of a cavity can distinguish between a glass, cup or bowl. This can be done with a measure of the cavities depth versus diameter, all of which can be sensed by touch. This discriminator is especially useful in visually occluded parts of the scene.

4. Accessing the Database

With multiple representation schemes the intractability of search becomes important. We will not address this issue in detail here. We only mention the limited domain we work in since it will not be overly burdensome to multiply represent and index these objects. In the future, as larger sets of objects become candidates for recognition, this problem becomes more important. If we postulate parallel or multiple processors involved in this recognition process, the utility of this approach becomes apparent.

In accessing the database, we can index on the features that are found from the sensing. The object record is a rich data structure that tries to capture as much three dimensional information about the object as possible. It is necessarily broader than spatial data structures in which the multisensor data is indexed on a common thread, the thread being the three dimensional coordinates of some type of data. This is clearly too limiting a data structure. Point data is too small to achieve the kinds of higher level recognition we need. Primitives that we need are surface descriptions (with a spatial extent much greater than a few points), areas, moments, curvatures, holes and cavities. Further, we need relationships that are more complex than nearest 3-D point neighbors as has also been proposed. What this means is that our representations are disparate kinds of data linked back to the common thread of the object itself.

This indexing mechanism we are proposing contains pointers to all objects with commonality in terms of a particular feature. Indices will be built for any access method available from the sensed data. There will be access available through the attributes of surfaces, holes, cavities and boundary curves as well as through gross descriptors in the object record.

5. Strategies

Given the multiple representations and the organization of the data base above, how do we strategically employ these sensors? Here we will be dealing with vision and touch as our sensors. We must obviously begin with a bottom up approach to recognition. The stereo algorithm we are using [12] supplies us with sparse sets of 3-D points that reflect changes in image intensity due to reflectance, lighting and geometry. If we attempt to segment this image we will have regions that are surfaces, holes or background. Tactile inspection of these regions will help us determine their true nature. If we can define a closed contour of a region from vision, this will allow us to trace across the interior of the surface and create a bicubic surface description [7]. This description can be analyzed for curvature and area and finding the location of possible cavities. This analysis can then generate search paths into the database. If a hole is seen from the vision sensing, the tactile sensor can quantify it and further index into the database. Edges that form surface boundaries can be seen, verified by tactile and again used to index into the database. It is important to note that the sensing is providing true three-dimensional data which is less prone to multiple interpretation than projective data. We can also perform orthogonal slice tracing across the whole of the object to infer bounding volumes and planarity as discriminators. The meet of these different pathways into the database will give rise to candidate objects. If the meet is small we can proceed to verify the objects with appropriate sensors by following the relational pointers between parts of the objects under consideration. The idea is to have small amounts of bottom up search invoke high level knowledge to guide the remaining search. The high level knowledge is useful as a guide and important because it is three dimensional in nature and allows us to ignore the many to one problems of visual projection and can suggest what to look for with touch sensing in occluded parts of the scene.

Another useful strategy is to detect *outliers*. Outliers are regions detected by vision that are largely surrounded either by background or holes (e.g. the handle of a cup when imaged). This is a candidate for being a closed surface that encompasses a volume. By tracing both the visible and non-visible sides of the outlier, a closed surface can be interpolated and from this surface three dimensional moments computed. This moment set can then be matched against the database for correspondence. Finding a match will allow transform parameters to be calculated from object to world coordinates.

If this initial sensing is fruitless or confusing, we can suggest another view of the object. This can be done by moving the cameras or having the tactile sensor perform a search of the occluded part of the scene.

6. Convergence of Sensory Data

Given the multiple sensor data, how do we converge on an object? Since we are able to access the database from many sensory avenues, we eventually hope to yield a unique or possibly small number of interpretations of that data. A unique interpretation implies that we have achieved convergence with respect to the features sensed. It is entirely possible that an object with the same set of sensed features (but unknown to our database) has been sensed. We can only report convergence at this granularity of knowledge. This also implies a granularity in sensing. There are geometric features that are small enough to escape our sensors detection. We can only converge on an object space that is within a neighborhood of the sensory resolution of the feature.

How then do we measure convergence? We can measure a unique convergence based upon the number of features found and also upon the number of visual views and tactile probes performed. If the measure is less than a predetermined threshold then we can use the object record to guide us in a further search to verify the existence or absence of other features. We cannot say with certainty that the object being sensed is the modeled object without a lengthy and painful verification of all modeled features. Therefore, convergence is defined to be a measure based upon number of features found, granularity of the sensors and completeness of the model. If we constrain our environment to already modeled objects, with exact object models then unique convergence of a feature set is 100% convergence. As we relax the constraints, then the measure decreases.

If we have a small number of candidates then we can check each one for properties predicted by the model database. It is our feeling that sensing will soon arrive at a single candidate that can then be verified. If we in fact end up with a large set of models, then this will tell us that our view is lacking in discernable features and perhaps a new view is needed to converge the database access mechanisms. This will prevent us from wasting time on views that are not rich in feature data.

Convergence will be complicated by sensory errors. If we find a non-convergence of sensory data we can choose the largest uniquely converged subset of the feature data to try to eliminate the poor data. However if convergence still is not possible we can resort to new views/recomputation of sensory information to try to find the errors. In this case non-convergence is useful in isolating error sensing.

If we assume a world where objects other than our modeled objects exist, then we have a mechanism for partial matching. The largest uniquely converged subset of the features will be an indicator of object similarity and will allow us to proceed with partial recognition of similar objects.

7. Example Object

Figure 1 contains an example object record for an object in our domain. The record contains the gross shape characteristics of the cup as well as a detailed analysis of its surfaces. The cup is modeled as 3 surfaces joined together; the bowl of the cup, the handle and the bottom. Each surface is described by a parametric equations that model the surfaces by a spline technique [16]. The area, curvature analysis and moment set if applicable are part of each surface description. The finger hole in the cup is modeled by its center point, axis and diameter and the cavity where the coffee goes is modeled by its bottom point, depth and diameter. The relational information in the model is contained in the boundary curve descriptions. Where the surfaces are joined, boundary curves are defined. In this example, there is a boundary curve between the bottom of the cup and the bowl, and between the two handle joins and the bowl. These curves are parametric space curves, which can be compared to sensed boundary curves for matching. Recognizing a boundary curve will also allow the relational knowledge in the model to be used to verify an adjoining surface's existence.

We do not know what view we will initially be presented with when imaging this cup. We may have a view that nicely isolates the handle and hole allowing us to start down a recognition path by quantifying these features. However, we may have an initial view that occludes the handle. The relatively featureless cylindrical bowl is our only visible surface. Here, a series of orthogonal traces across the imaged object with the tactile sensor may allow us to discover the cup's cavity which can then start us down the path of recognition. If we can only see the bottom surface, we may be able to interpolate this planar surface and index into the database on the surface patch's planarity and computed area. Once discrimination proceeds, candidate objects are found and further sensing may be model driven. The multiple three dimensional features and representations in the model make the method robust.

8. Summary

As more and better robotic sensors become available, the richness of object models which contain multiple representations and features becomes important. Recognition can be done in many ways, utilizing different kinds of sensed data and access paths in the model database. Once a rich model description is built, control strategies must be developed to allow the sensed data to be matched against the model. Finally, the multiple access paths into the database can be used to measure convergence and determine to what granularity discrimination has occurred between competing models.

9. References

[1] Shneier, M., S.Nagalia, J. Albus, and R. Haar. "Visual feedback for Robot Control," in *IEEE Workshop on Industrial Applications of Industrial Vision,* (May 1982) pp. 232-236.

[2] Cooper, Lynn A., "Flexibility in Recognition Systems," in *Human and Machine Vision,* J. Beck, B.hope, and A. Rosenfeld eds., Academic Press, 1983.

[3] Posner, M., and Henik, A. "Isolating Representational Systems," in *Human and Machine Vision,* J. Beck, B.hope, and A. Rosenfeld eds., Academic Press, 1983.

[4] Fisher, R.B. "Using Surfaces and Object Models to Recognize Partially Obscured Objects," Proc. IJCAI 83 (Karlsruhe, August 1983) pp. 989-995.

[5] Shapiro, L. and Haralick, R. "A Hierarchical Relational Model for Automated Inspection Tasks," Proc. IEEE International Conference on Robotics (Atlanta, March 1984) pp. 70-77.

[6] Grimson, W. E. L. and Lozano-Perez, T. "Model based recognition and localization from sparse three-dimensional sensory data," A.I. memo 738, M.I.T. A.I. Laboratory, Cambridge, , August 1983.

[7] Allen, P. "Surface descriptions from vision and touch," in *Proc. International Robotics Conference,* (Atlanta, March 1984), pp. 394-397.

[8] Brooks, R. "Symbolic reasoning among 3-D models and 2-D images," *Artificial Intelligence* 17 (1981), 285-349.

[9] Nevatia, R. and Binford, T. "Description and recognition of curved objects," *Artificial Intelligence* 8 (1977), 77-98.

[10] Reeves, A. P., and Wittner, B. S. "Shape Analysis of three dimensional objects using the method of moments," *Proceedings of the IEEE conference on Computer Vision and Pattern Recognition,* (Washington, D.C., June 1983) pp. 20-26.

[11] Henderson, T. and Fai, W. S. "Pattern Recognition in a Multi-Sensor Environment," UUCS technical report 83-001, Department of Computer Science, University of Utah, Salt Lake City, UT, July 1983.

[12] Smitley, David and Bajcsy, Ruzena, "Stereo Processing of Aerial Images," International Conference on Pattern Recognition (Montreal, August 1984).

[13] Roberts, L., "Machine perception of three-dimensional solids", in *Optical and Electro-optical Information Processing,* J. Tippitt ed., MIT Press, Cambridge, MA, 1965, pp. 159-197.

[14] Brady, M., "Criteria for Representations of Shape," in *Human and Machine Vision,* J. Beck, B.hope, and A. Rosenfeld eds., Academic Press, 1983.

[15] Potmesil, M. "Generating Three dimensional surface models of solid objects from multiple projections," IPL technical report 033, Image Processing Laboratory, R.P.I., Rensselaer, N.Y., October 1982.

[16] Faux, I.D., and Pratt, M.J. *Computational Geometry for Design and Manufacture,* John Wiley, New York, 1979.

OBJECT NAME: COFFEE CUP

GROSS SHAPE

VOLUME
NONPLANAR
BOUNDING VOLUME

SURFACE S1: BOWL OF CUP

SURFACE EQUATION
AREA
CURVATURE
3-D MOMENT SET

SURFACE S2: BOTTOM OF CUP

SURFACE EQUATION
AREA
CURVATURE
3-D MOMENT SET: NONE

SURFACE S3: HANDLE OF CUP

SURFACE EQUATION
AREA
CURVATURE
3-D MOMENT SET

HOLE H1: FINGER HOLE

CENTER LOCATION
AXIS
DIAMETER

CAVITY C1: WELL OF CUP

BOTTOM POINT
DEPTH
DIAMETER

BOUNDARY CURVE B1: BOTTOM RIM

PTR TO SURFACE S1
PTR TO SURFACE S2

BOUNDARY CURVE B2: BOTTOM OF HANDLE

PTR TO SURFACE S1
PTR TO SURFACE S3

BOUNDARY CURVE B3: TOP OF HANDLE

PTR TO SURFACE S1

PTR TO SURFACE S3

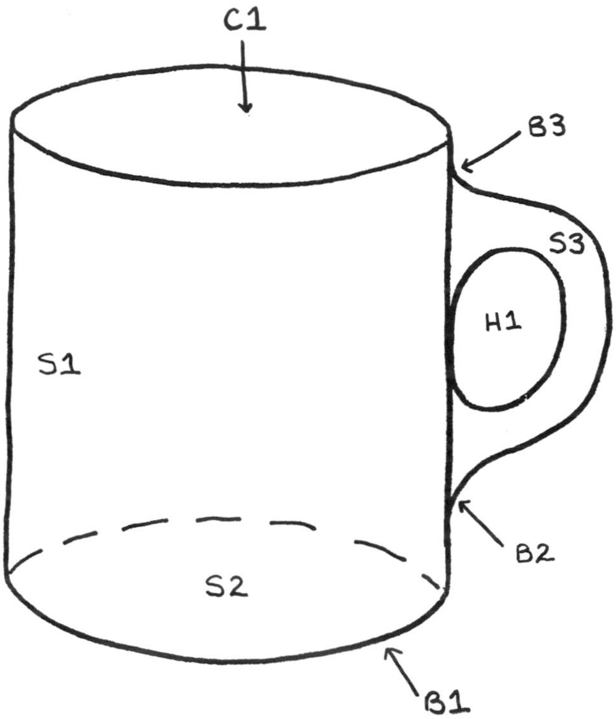

FIGURE 1: OBJECT RECORD FOR COFFEE CUP

SHAPE RECOGNITION BY HUMAN-LIKE TRIAL AND ERROR RANDOM PROCESSES

Makoto Nagao

Department of Electrical Engineering
Kyoto University
Yoshidahon-machi, Sakyo-ku, Kyoto 606 Japan

Pattern recognition and object detection systems so far developed required the procedural description of every detail for the objects to be recognized, and yet recognition has been a very rigid process. To overcome this problem and to give human-like flexibility to the machine recognition process, we developed a new system, which has non-algorithmic feature detection functions, and which does not require the procedural description for the object detection. The system only requires the declarative description (model) of an object structure. It uses a variable size slit which is applied to the most plausible parts in an image by a top-down command from an object model, and obtains the characteristic features of the object parts. This slit application is realized mostly in hardware, and has some autonomic ability to detect the best features by a sort of random search. The system has some other hardware functions such as mutual correlation of one and two dimensions, which are also flexible according to the variable size slit. The system interprets the user's declarative description of objects, and activates the slit application functions to obtain the characteristic features of the description. If the user gives many alternative descriptions of the whole/parts of an object, the system can choose a description which is easily satisfiable, and obtains the final whole description of an object in an image by a trial-and-error or search method. This new flexible approach to object detection can be used as a robot eye to recognize many simple two-dimensional shapes.

1. Reflections on Past Image Processing Algorithms

Research into image processing has made great strides in the past 20 years, and it is now fairly easy to design recognition procedures even for complex objects. However, in the author's opinion the following problems remain to be solved in present image processing technology.

1.1 From rigid algorithms to flexible ones

When analysing the object image, the processing algorithm must, of course, be written as a detailed program. There is little which leads us to believe that human recognition processes involve analysis and reasoning as rigid and detailed as computer programs. It seems, rather, that human recognition involves random trial and error processes to a great extent. Human recognition of pattern features is not so accurate, but still as a whole gets surprisingly reliable final recognition results. Therefore it seems necessary to incorporate a function which allows the system's peripheral feature detectors to seek the pattern features and feed the answer back autonomously when activated by a higher level instruction in the computer program. Feature detectors based on this type of function, which we call half autonomous feature detectors, will greatly clarify and simplify image processing software, so that we can write pattern recognition algorithms very easily without going into the detailed description of the low level processing.

1.2 From hardware realization of low level processing to that of high level processing

Efforts are being made to increase processing speed by developing special image processing hardwares since the work involved in image processing is tremendous. But the hardwares developed up to now are practically all for low level uniform two-dimensional processing such as noise elimination, differentiation and thresholding. A disadvantage here is that these processes occupy an extremely small part of the overall recognition process, and this expensive hardware section does not contribute to overall recognition in the same ratio as the cost of hardware. Much complex work is necessary by present-day recognition systems when attempting to improve the recognition process or to add new recognition objects. The breakthrough in these difficulties will be to couple the low level processing dynamically with high level structural descriptions of standard objects to be recognized, and to incorporate a top-down process which drives the low level processing, and gets back the feature parameters supported by hardware.

1.3 Needs for a higher level shape description language

In programming, separation of the algorithm and data sections strengthens the toughness of an overall program by allowing changes and additions to the data section. This type of programming methodology should be introduced into image processing and pattern recognition processes. This method will enable recognition of multiple objects within a single system by adding standard object descriptions without modifying the interpretation process and recognition algorithm.

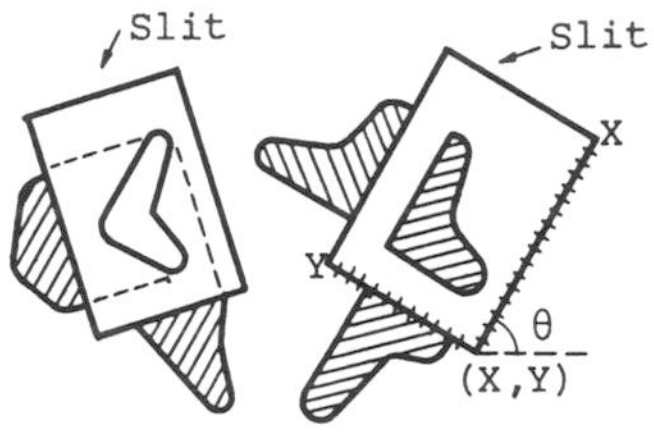

Fig. 1

A general outline of a system currently being developed to solve these three problems is given in this paper. A recognition system which can cope with comparatively simple binary object shapes is planned as the first step. The recognition process will be extended to combined binary images including occlusion. The future directions include expansion of the number of recognizable objects and recognition of gray density images.

2. Fundamental Feature Extraction Mechanism

2.1 Flexible slit method

As is widely known from computer tomography, much can be learned about the actual shape of an object by examining two-dimensional projection curves of the object. Here we place a rectangular slit at an arbitrary position on a binary graphic image as shown in Fig. 1, and project the graphic image in both the X and Y directions. The slit position (x, y), slit direction (θ), slit size and slit spacing are to be freely settable. Various predictions can be made about the object by analyzing the projection curves in the X and Y directions from this slit. Several slit applications can be performed semi-randomly to obtain significant projection curves which can suggest the existence of special shape features. The new position of the slit is calculated from the information of the past projection curves. The projection curves are also analyzed to confirm whether the expected shape is in fact correct. Recognition of the projection curves obtained from the slit is therefore necessary for many typical image shapes.

2.2 Feature extraction by the slit method

There are the following three objectives for the analysis of the projection curves:

(1) Estimation of a better location for a new slit in relation to the object by a rough classification of the projection curves

(2) Feature extraction and pattern recognition of the projection curves

(3) Correlation of a projection curve with a reference curve to identify the class of the curve

Process (1) enables the consistent extraction of features in steps (2) and (3) by positioning the slit for optimum extraction. Correlation with a standard projection curve in (3) is the most direct method for discrimination of complex curves that cannot be identified by step (2). One advantage here is that various different curves can be identified by using a single standard curve because the projection curves can be adjusted by varying the slit parameters and by setting the slit in a more appropriate position. For example, if we apply a slit in an appropriate position, angle and sample slit spacings for the different angular shapes shown in Fig. 2, the projected curve obtained will be approximately the same and matching can be carried out using a single standard curve. After getting a good match for an input angle with a standard angular curve, actual angle size and orientation of the input angular shapes can be calculated from slit parameters such as sample spacing and direction.

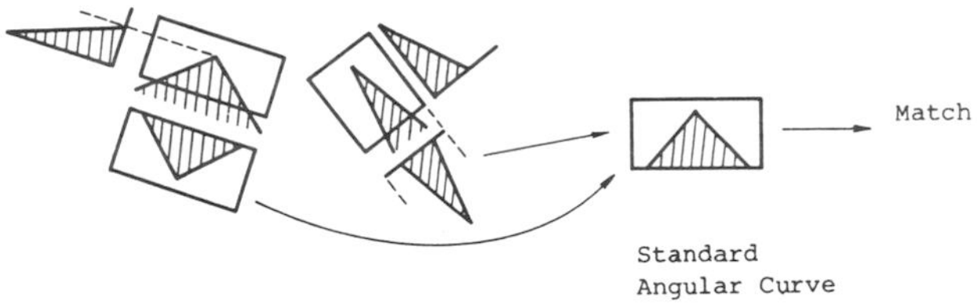

Fig. 2

The problem here is how to place the slit in an appropriate place. The slit is first placed at random at the position where the shape is assumed to be. The projection curve obtained here is analyzed by method (1), as will be explained later in detail, to give estimated parameters which allow the slit to be repositioned and the orientation and size changed appropriately. The best matching of the projection curve is obtained by repeating this trial and error process three or four times until the optimum slit position is found.

Let us look at an example of detecting a sharp angle. As shown in Fig. 3 the first slit is placed arbitrarily. From the projection curves of the slit, rotation through a certain angle and a new slit size is suggested. This process is repeated several times to obtain finally the best position and size for the angle, which is symmetrical about the center axis of the slit as shown in Fig. 4. This position is called the "normal position".

When the pair of projection curves are as shown in Fig. 5, the two-dimensional image is estimated as shown in Fig. 6. Then the next slit should be extended in the Y direction, and also extended in the X direction to get a better slit position as shown in Fig. 7.

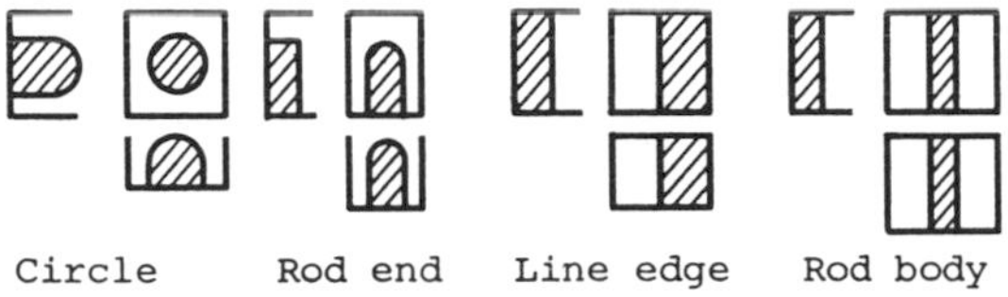

Fig. 8

The normal position for a circle, rod end, line edge and rod body are shown in Fig. 8.

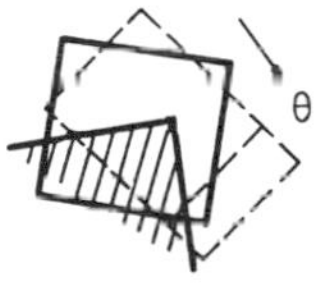

Fig. 3

Fig. 4

Fig. 5

Fig. 6

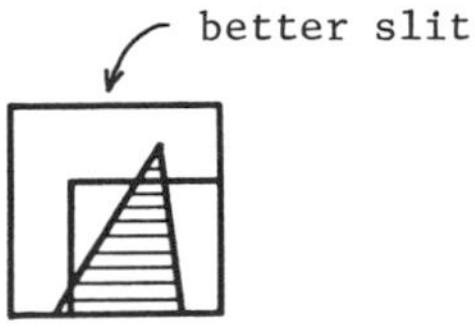

Fig. 7

If the projection curve and the standard curve cannot be satisfactorily matched regardless of the number of times the slit position is changed, the object shape is considered to be different from the predicted one (or a shape that cannot be detected by this method) and the test is regarded as unsuccessful.

2.3 Feature parameters of a projection curve

The feature parameters are to be calculated for projection curves in case (2) to predict the general shape of the projection curve. The following parameters are calculated:

Parameters to be calculated for a projection curve.

Definition of symbols (See Fig. 9)

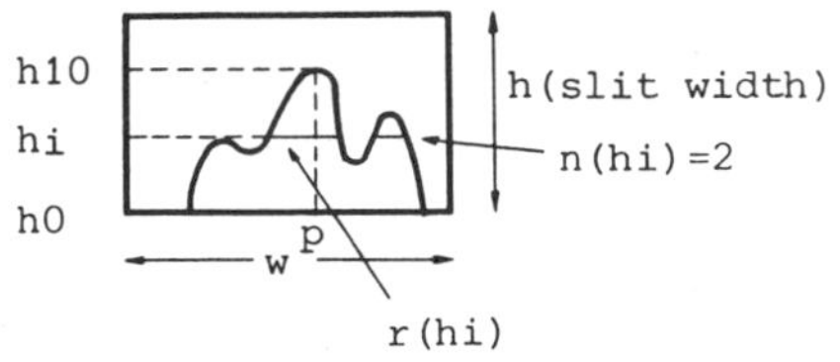

Fig. 9

Slit size (w steps x h steps)

h_{10} : maximum value of projection curve.
h_i : 10 x i% of h_{10}.
$r(h_i)$: maximum width of curve at height h_i
$n(h_i)$: number of crossing on the curve at height h_i
Le, Re : Logical value for the curve determining whether it touches the left side or right side (See Fig. 10)

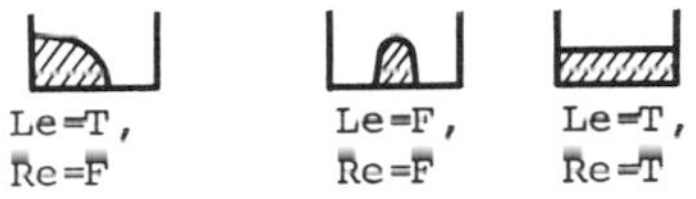

Fig. 10

Parameters obtained by hardware

(1) h_{10} and its position P.
(2) Whether h_{10} = h or not (Cd)
(3) Area of the projection curve (S)
(4) $r(h_i)$ and $n(h_i)$ for i=0,1, ..., 9
(5) Le, and Re
(6) $n(h_o)$

Parameters calculated by microprogram.

(7) mean of heights $\bar{h} = S/r(h_o)$
(8) variance of heights $\sigma_{\bar{h}}^2$
(9) mean of curve positions $\bar{x}$
(10) variance of curve positions $\sigma_{\bar{x}}^2$
(11) minimum height in the projection curve.

Parameters from the differentiated projection curve

(12) Position of the maximum
(13) Positions of local maximums

2.4 Trial and error process for feature extraction by the slit method

A variety of shapes can be estimated to exist from the parameters introduced in 2.3. For example, when the orientation of the slit (A) in Fig. 11 is approximately in line with the longer side of the L-shaped rod as shown in the figure, the variance of the projection height values will be a near minimum.

Therefore, when it is detected that the projection width at 80% of the height is almost the same as the width at 60%, a rod shape may be predicted. It is also possible to predict the orientation, width and length of the predicted rod. If we place slit B as shown in Fig. 11 from the calculated parameters of the slit projection curves of A, it just covers the rod exactly. Recognition of the rod shape is thus confirmed.

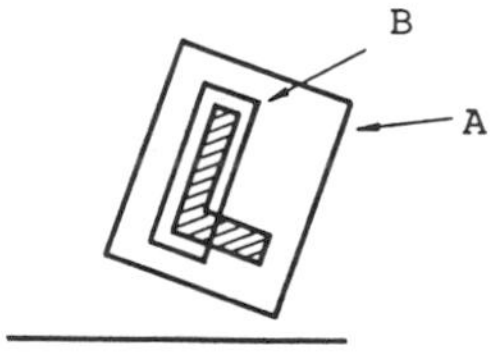

Fig. 11

When placing the slit based on accurate information such as with slit B in Fig. 11, analysis can be put forward with a fairly high reliability. This is an advanced stage of analysis. When there is little information about the shape of the projection, there is no alternative to placing the slit at random. As the projection curve obtained from the slit will contain various uncertainty factors due to this nature of randomness, it becomes pointless at this stage to make accurate calculation of complex components such as the projection curve parameters.

The first step necessary is to determine where the next slit should be placed from the information obtained by the parameters of the projection curves of the previous slit. We have the following results.

range of existence of projection curves

→ Rotate -45°, extend the width of Y.

→ Rotate +45°, extend the width of Y.

→ Rotate +45°, extend the width of Y.

→ Rotate -45°, extend the width of Y.

→ Rotate so that the position of Ymax comes to the center of the projection curve.

→ Extend the width of Y.

→ isolated object. rotate so that σ^2 for the projection curve becomes a minimum.

→ If the height of the curve is relatively small, rotate randomly to see if a different situation occurs.

→ Divide into two slits.

We have to check the possibilities of the combinations of the following projection curves (Fig. 12).

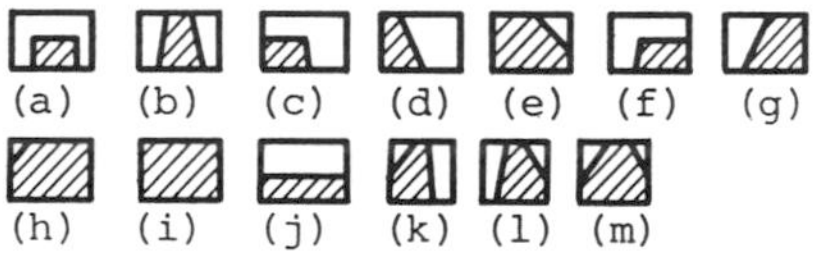

Fig. 12

Physically possible combinations of these as X and Y projection curves are surprisingly small. Meaningful combinations are the following (Fig. 13). The figures are two-dimensional shapes, which produce the projection curves written under each shape.

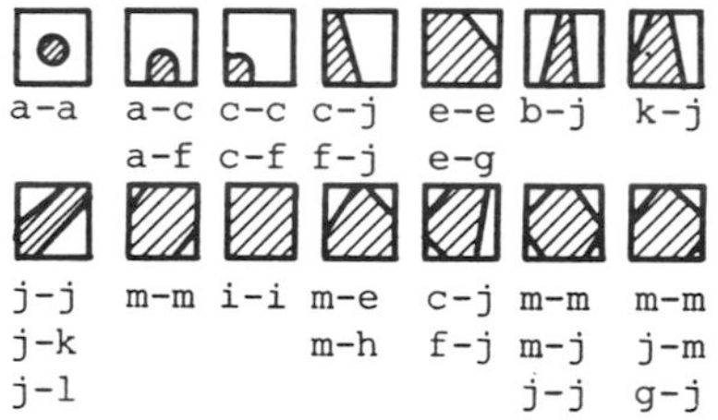

Fig. 13

For all these curve combinations we can estimate the positions and the size of the next slit. Next actions for the slit placement are the following, for example:

c-c, c-f } . rotate

c-j, f-j } . get vertical edge. . extend in the edge direction.

e-e, e-g } . rotate and extend in the edge direction.

b-j . extend in the rod direction.

k-j } . rotate and get b-j projection
j-j }   combination.
j-k } . extend in the rod direction.
j-l }
m-m }
i-i }
c-j } . enlarge the slit.
j-j }
etc.

Most typical projection curves will be obtained by repeating this process. Typical ones are the angle, rod end, half circle, rod body, and line edge as shown already in Fig. 8.

3. Two-Dimensional Pattern Matching Function

Although various methods have been described here for identification for the projection curves of the object shapes in the X and Y directions through a slit, there is a limit to the recognition of complex shapes with these methods based on the projection curves. Many objects are difficult to describe using simple projection curve information. The two-dimensional input image will have to be compared with two-dimensional standard pattern for recognition by two-dimensional matching. The method of two-dimensional matching is divided into two categories, one for isolated single objects, and the other for complex objects which are composed of two or more partial figures, each of which is to be matched two-dimensionally with a standard pattern.

3.1 Pattern matching of a single isolated shape

The method of two-dimensional matching when a single isolated object to be recognized is at an arbitrary position is as follows:

(1) Place the slit of a size which adequately covers the single object in any orientation at random, and obtain the X, Y projection curves. Using the parameters of these curves, determine the principal axis of inertia. The next slit is placed along this axis of inertia. An alternative method is to find out the longest direction of the object by applying the slit several times by rotating the direction. Then the next placement of a slit is along this axis in the longest direction.

(2) Place the slit parallel to the principal axis of inertia and adjust the slit so that the object is centered in the slit. Centering in the slit means a slit width of 1.1 x, 1.1 y, when the dimensions of the object in the X, Y directions are assumed to be x, and y.

The processes in (1) and (2) above are illustrated in Fig. 14.

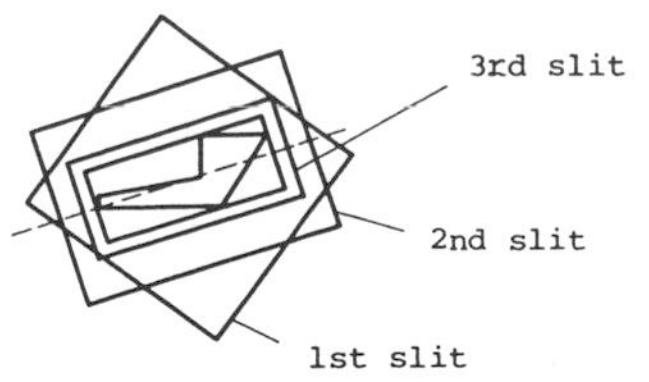

Fig. 14

(3) Construction of a two-dimensional standard template is exactly the same as (1) and (2) above, that is the recognition of an object shape. One example is the 3rd slit in Fig. 14. Irregularities in the input shape should be absorbed to a certain extent in this instance, and a don't care zone is introduced. A two-dimensional standard pattern obtained in this way is shown in Fig. 15. Although the best matching position is not sharply obtained by this matching method with don't care zones, the characteristics are very effective against noise components at the edges, and for the matching of a part of a complex shape.

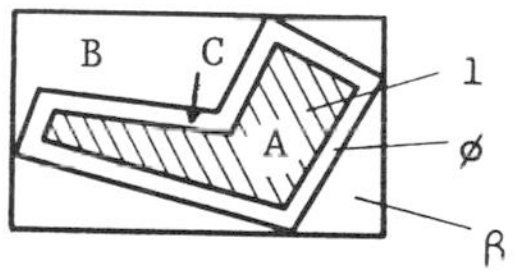

Fig. 15

A: The object shape area which has the value 1
B: The background area
C: Don't care zone

$$\sum_A 1 = \sum_B \beta, \quad \sum_C \phi \simeq 0.1 \sum_A 1$$

(4) Matching of the object and the standard pattern obtained in this manner is carried out at the 3rd slit position in Fig. 14 and the best match is obtained in this 3rd slit after shifting laterally a certain number of degrees from the principal axis of inertia.

3.2 Partial pattern matching in complex shapes

This two-dimensional pattern matching can also be used for partial pattern matching as follows:

(1) If a large slit in Fig. 16 is placed at various angles, it may be predicted from the projection curves that the object has a rod in the R_1 direction.

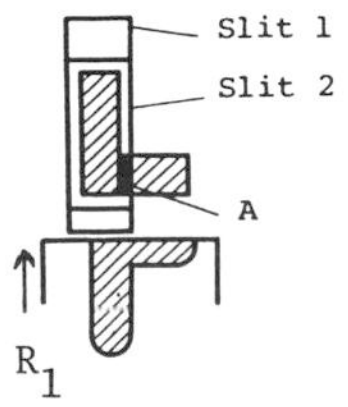

Fig. 16

(2) A long narrow slit (slit 1) is then placed at this position and slit 2 is determined by the length of the rod from the Y projection of slit 1.

(3) Two-dimensional matching is then carried out by the pattern of slit 2 against a standard rod pattern. Although area A in the diagram tends to interfere with the matching function, the effect will be minimal because it falls in the "don't care" area.

(4) Next, if steps (1), (2) and (3) are carried out for the remaining area after temporarily masking the already identified parts, the remaining area can be identified as a short rod. In this way the angle formed by the two rods can be obtained. Although the 2nd slit is used as an erase mask when carrying out recognition of the remaining area, if this erase mask is used in stage (1) only, and is not used in the remaining stages, the recognition will become as shown in Fig. 17.

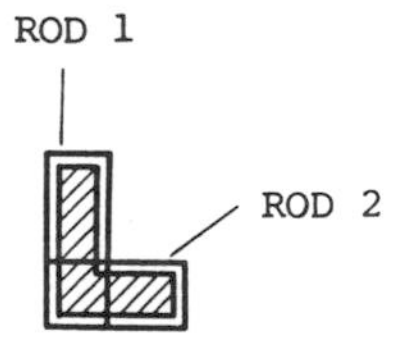

Fig. 17

There is another possibility for recognition process in cases such as the shape placed as shown in Fig. 18, and the primary features detected as shown by circles. That is, from the output curve of the slit of Fig. 18, the extreme corners can be detected easily as the crossing points of the end points a, b, a', b' of the projection curves. Then at these points the angle detection routine is activated and the angle directions, angle values and some other information are obtained. Then the connecting edge lines are obtained by the edge detection routine activated by the information of the angle edge directions. In this way the contour figure of the object can be obtained with the new findings of the two corners which were not detected at first. Therefore the object description must be not only a component sub-region description, but also include contour and some other descriptions. Even by the sub-region description, a complex object can be decomposed into different sub-region combinations, and all these must be accepted by the recognition system. This is very important for the recognition of occluded objects.

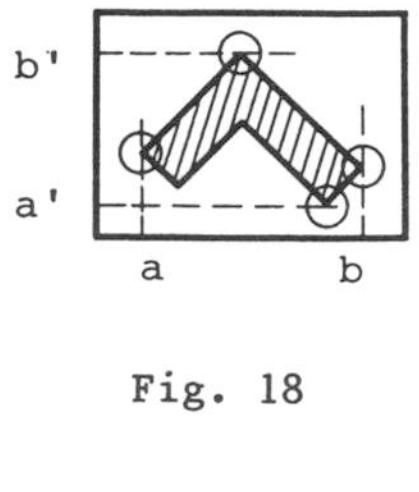

Fig. 18

4. Image Description System

4.1 Requirement for an image description system

Although image analysis and recognition are carried out using fundamental feature extraction functions as explained here, the best approach is one in which a structural description of the object is pre-prepared and in which the object description and the feature extraction function are coupled in an interpretive routine which carries out overall recognition. Since this interpretive routine will be a general process, it must be capable of operating even if a new object description is given. Other functions that it should incorporate are: (1) a hierarchical structural description of shapes, (2) Capability of holding multiple descriptions of the same graphic portion, (3) trial and error processes included as part of the interpretation routine and a function allowing decisions to be made for only those parts of the given input figure that can be confirmed from the image descriptions, (4) the function to decide by relative comparisons which object, out of a group of objects, is to be recognized, by using the smallest number of obtained features, rather than proceeding with overall indiscriminate recognition.

Generally speaking, recognition of shapes should not be too rigorous or strict. The general features should be extracted and the interpretation made within that range. If there is no match with the final target, recognition should proceed by finding other detailed features. If two input objects cannot be separated from the description and interpretation of a figure, object descriptions must be enriched, that is, much more detailed descriptions must be given which enable discrimination of the two objects. Such descriptions must be given in hierarchical order from global to local and exact for the interpretation system to be able to go top-down step by step to get the recognition result by the earliest stage of analysis.

4.2 Shape description system structure

A tentative description system of shapes is as follows.

(1) Object
(2) Name of component parts
(3) Description of the relationship of component parts
(4) Output parameters of the object

An example of the description of an L-structure such as in Fig. 17 is as follows:

(1) L-STRUCTURE
(2) A, B; rod
(3) A. DIR $\perp$ B. DIR
A. END $\simeq$ B. END

Another description of the same L-structure:

L-STRUCTURE
SIZE = max A. LENGTH, B. LENGTH
WIDTH = min A. LENGTH, B. LENGTH

In the first description we have two items which are partial components of the L-structure denoted as A and B; this line indicates that the objects A and B are "rod". The next line describes the relation between A and B. It shows that A. DIR (direction of A) and B. DIR are at right angles to each other and that A. END (end position of A) is at the same position as B. END. Matching of angles and position will always be approximate. In other words, a tolerance of ±10% for angles, and ±W (W is width of rod) for position will be permitted. A. END and B. END both have 2 values and the system checks for a match between any of the 4 combinations.

An example of a complex object is given in the following.

FLYPAN
A: rod
B: circle

A.END + [B.R*cos(A.DIR),B.R*sin(A.DIR)] ≈ B.CENTER

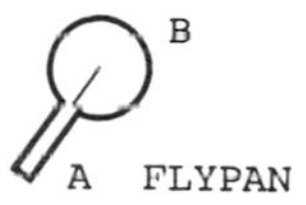

Fig. 19

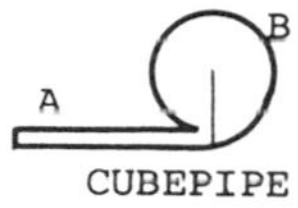

Fig. 20

CUBEPIPE
A: rod
B: circle

A.END + [B.R*cos(A.DIR + 90),0] ≈ B.CENTER

5. System Implementation

Hardware and software are being developed to incorporate the above algorithm in a single system. A general outline of this system is shown in Fig. 21.

Preprocessing, such as removal of noise, is carried out by the general image processing hardware (B) at the speed of memory cycles per pixel of the image memory (A). The image is then properly thresholded and sent to binary memory (C). The data in (C) and sometimes in (A) are sent to (D) where the processings explained earlier are executed by hardware. As the slit is replaced a number of times in the slit method, the memory readout time makes up a large portion of the processing time. Algorithms for placing optional size slits in optional positions and of getting values from grid points of a slit are all built into the hardware and are controlled by commands from (E).

The major part of the processes explained in 2. is supported by hardware, including two-dimensional correlation. Complex processes such as the calculation of variances are computed by the microprocessor in (D). For example, the time required to obtain the main results from a single positioning of a 32 x 32 slit is 32 x 32 x 0.2 μsec + 32 x 0.1 μsec + α = 210 μsec (approx.) if the cycle time of the binary memory is taken as 0.2 μsec. All calculations such as rotation of coordinate axes and density values by linear approximation at required grid points are processed by hardware within one cycle of binary memory. This means that one feature can be fetched in about 2 msec even if the slit is replaced 10 times to get it. Although this is not exceptionally fast, we believe this is sufficient compensation when we consider the advantage of not having to write a program in detail to fetch each of the features.

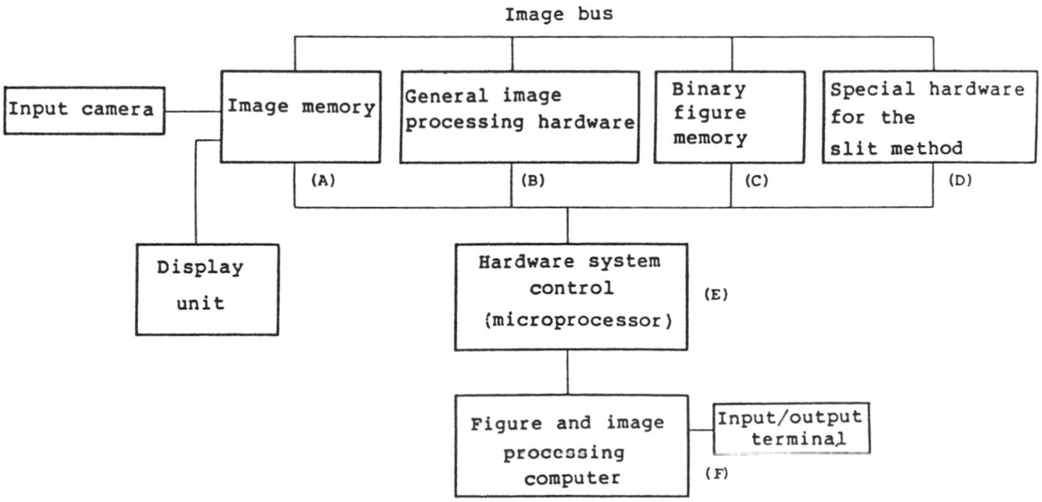

Fig. 21

6. Conclusion

This system is programmed to recognize comparatively simple two-dimensional shapes existing in isolation. Although the use of this system for recognition of objects which overlap each other to a certain extent will be a subject for the future, we believe that this will not be an excessively difficult problem. This is because it will simply be a question of detecting the features of partial figures and registering that these features possibly represent separate objects. A certain amount of additional study will no doubt be necessary in expanding this system to the recognition of variable density images, and this will hinge on how well the general image processing section (B) in the block diagram can construct the binary figure. Although, a binary image memory is used in this system mainly because of the problem of cost, we believe that the same system concept can be used for the analysis of variable density images with the same basic slit method by modifying memory (C) to store gray density images, and also by modifying the hardware (D) for multi-value data processing.

Reference

(1) M. Nagao: Control Strategies in Pattern Analysis, Pattern Recognition, Vol. 17, No. 1, pp.45-56, 1984.

A FLEXIBLE MULTI WINDOW VISION SYSTEM FOR ROBOTS

Hirochika Inoue and Hiroshi Mizoguchi

Department of Mechanical Engineering
The University of Tokyo
Hongo, Bunkyo-ku, Tokyo, JAPAN

This paper describes a flexible multi window robot vision system, which is designed and implemented to facilitate various real time interaction between vision and action. The prototype has sixteen local window memories. Location, shape and resolution of each window can be controlled independently. As we plan to process color image, four window memories are interfaced to a Motorola 68000 microcomputer. Four processor units of such configuration are connected to host through a communication processor. It provides a flexible hardware for robot vision. The hardware organization, software primitives, and experiments of visual attention control are described.

1. Introduction

The role of robot vision is manifold. It can be classified into four problem domains such as scene analysis, visual monitoring, visual feedback, and visual verification.

Scene analysis is employed at the beginning of the planning phase of robot control. Before making an action plan for a given goal, robot must recognize the initial state of environment. Vision system is requested to find objects and their locations, analyse the structural relationship among them.

Visual monitoring is used to trigger an appropriate action on a condition of some prescribed situation changes. In order to accomplish this kind of interaction, vision system must observe the environment all the time. In most cases, use of low resolution image is enough to notice the occurrence of expected situation changes.

Visual feedback is used to correct a robot motion by vision. For example, when a robot is requested to put a rope into a ring, visual feedback is essential to succeed the task. Visual attention is kept on a rope as well as a ring, so that the rope can be guided into the ring.

It is often necessary to verify specific preconditions or postconditions of a task to proceed the job successfully. For instance, before screwing, robot must verify that a screw is indeed held at the end of screwdriver. In this case, a glance at the end of screwdriver is needed.

Visual monitoring, visual feedback, and visual verification are employed in execution phase of action plan. They accomplish various interaction between vision and action in real time. In most cases, above mentioned vision program can be constructed so as to focus its attention to local regions in which the existence of key features are expected. Usually, points of attention should be multiple, although contents of each attention is simple. As the processing time is critical, those multiple attentions should run in parallel.

In order to realize such kind of visual interaction in real time, we designed and implemented a versatile multi window vision system. The window is a rectangular local region to be processed. It is not fixed on the screen. Location, shape, and resolution of each window can be controlled independently. Current version of our prototype has sixteen flexible local window memories. As our system is designed to process color image, four window memories are interfaced to a Motorola 68000 microcomputer. Four processor units of such configuration are connected to host through one communication processor. The hardware organization, software primitives, and experiments are described in this paper.

2. Multi Window Vision System

There are many approaches for designing fast vision processor. Use of pipeline architecture or array processor increases the throughput very much. Its performance is well proved for the tasks that require the same homogeneous preprocessing over the whole image. However, it may not be effective when many different attention programs must be applied to the scattered local areas, because too many unnecessary calculations are wasted. Parallel processor architecture seems suitable to our approach. But, one problem is an organization of image memory. If one common memory is accessed by a number of processing units, the memory access would face a serious bottleneck. To avoid the access bottleneck, we introduced a concept of transmitter/receiver organization for image data transfer. In our design principle, the data which would not be processed is never put into memory. Instead, the control of window is reinforced to make the shape, location, and resolution of the window programmable. In our configuration, a transmitter broadcasts all the pixel data. Each receiver unit samples only the necessary pixel data and stores them into local window memory. There is no access problem during such data acquisition. Hundreds of receivers are also able to sample their own data and process them simultaneously.

The block diagram of the multi window vision system is shown in Fig.1. As shown in the figure, the video bus connects a transmitter to receivers. It is a high speed uni-directional bus. The data width is 32bit, where red, green, blue and brightness data has 8 bit width, respectively. The display bus connects receivers to a display monitor. It is also high speed uni-directional bus, and has 8 bit data width. In current prototype, as mentioned above, there are four window processors, and each one has four window memories. Through a communication processor, these four processors are connected to the host which has hard disk based file system. Programs for window processor and communication processor are developed on the host and down loaded.

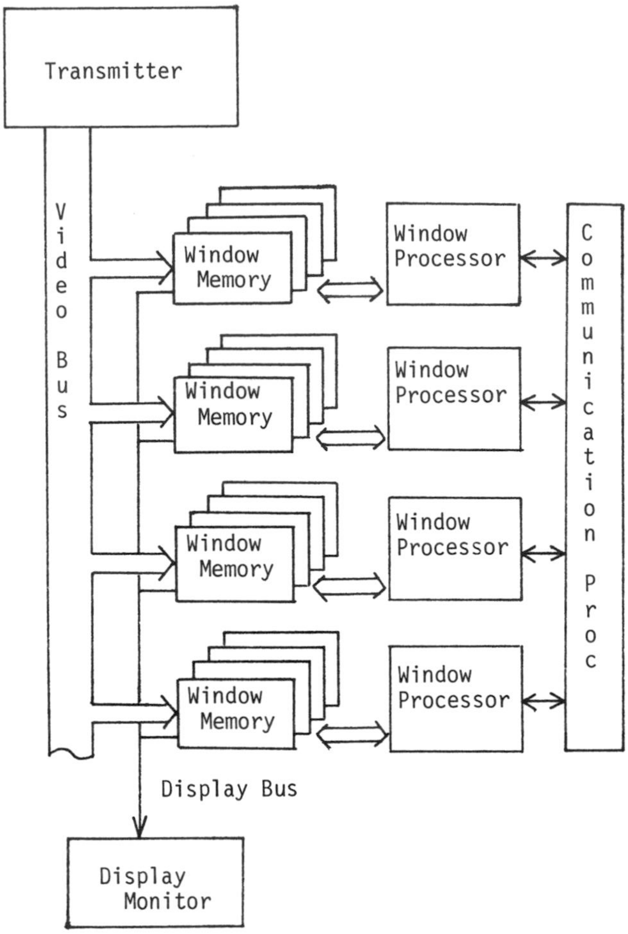

Figure 1. The prototype of a multi window robot vision system.

3. Hardware Description

The prototype is constructed of a transmitter, multiple receivers and a display monitor. The transmitter generates video bus signals, and broadcasts them through the bus. The display monitor superimposes the contents of window memories upon raw video scene, and reconstructs NTSC signal for monitor TV. In the following description, parenthesized symbols in capital letter denote signal names.

3.1 Transmitter

As shown in Fig.2, the transmitter is divided into following five blocks. They are master clock, decoder, sync pulse separator, H/V counter and A/D converter.

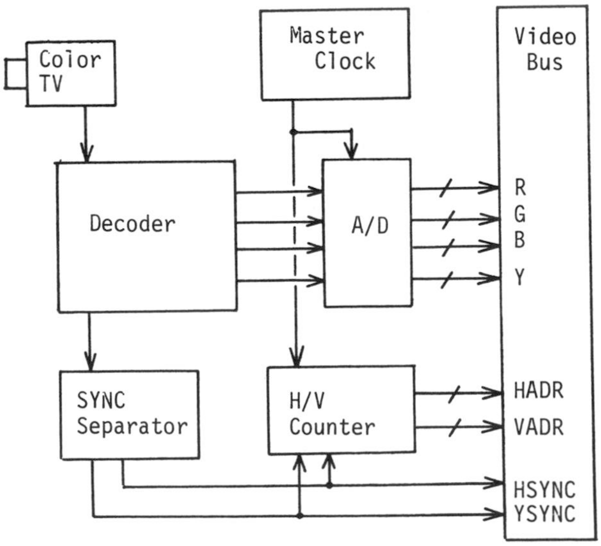

Figure 2. The block diagram of a transmitter.

Master Clock: Current implementation works in non-interlace mode. So, vertical resolution of image is 262.5 raster/frame. About 240 raster/frame is in visible area. As a ratio of horizontal size to vertical size of the screen is 4:3, horizontal resolution is about 320 pixel/raster. This resolution corresponds to 6.2 MHz pixel clock. In our design, master clock of 12.4 MHz is chosen as twice of pixel clock to improve TV jitter.

Decoder: The NTSC composite color signal is decoded into analog red(R), green(G), blue(B), brightness(Y) signals and SYNC pulse.

Sync Pulse Separator: It separates horizontal

sync pulse(HSYNC) and vertical sync pulse(VSYNC) from SYNC pulse output of decoder.

H/V Counters: This block generates horizontal address(HADR) and vertical address(VADR) of raster spot on the screen and puts them onto video bus. H counter counts pixel clock and V counter counts HSYNC pulse. The contents of H and V counters give horizontal and vertical addresses, respectively. Every HSYNC pulse initializes H counter. Every VSYNC pulse initializes V counter. Thus, the top left corner of the scene is defined as (0,0), and the bottom right corner is (319,239).

A/D Converter: The analog R,G,B,Y signals are digitized by 6 bit high speed A/D converters and the results are put onto video bus.

3.2 Receiver

A receiver consists of a window processor and one or more window controller/memory units. Block diagram of the controller/memory unit is shown in Fig.3.

Window controller performs DMA data transfer from video bus to window memory, in pixel clock rate (6.2MByte/sec). Window controller is built up from the following six blocks. They are window flag generator, sampling rate selector, input source selector, memory address counter, address multiplexer and window memory. Window flag generator, sampling rate selector and input source selector are programmable, while others are not.

Window Flag Generator: This block determines whether the current raster spot is included in a specified rectangular area or not. The area is specified by four parameters (h1, v1) and (h2, v2), where (h1, v1) denotes the location of upper left corner and (h2, v2) does the lower right. Comparing the current HADR and VADR with those parameters, it can be decided whether the current pixel belongs to the specified area or not. The condition is $(h1<HADR<h2)\wedge(v1<VADR<v2)$.

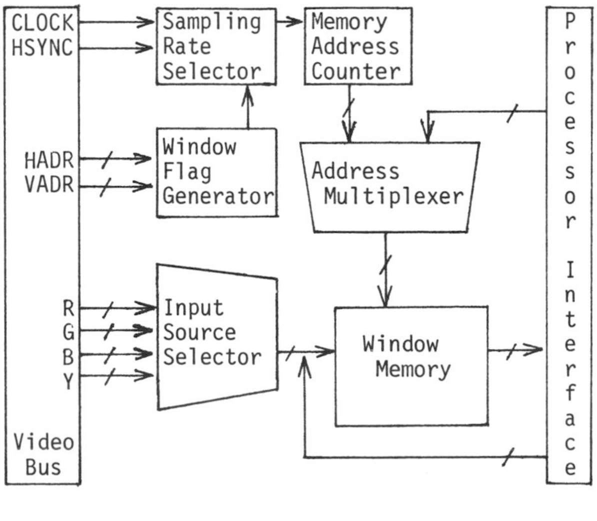

Figure 3. Window controller/memory

Sampling Rate Selector: This block has one parameter which determines the spacial sampling rate for window data. The value may be 1, 2, 4 or 8. The value 1 means the highest resolution, while 8 does the lowest. If we choose 1, every pixel data in the specified window are acquired. If we choose 2, one pixel is sampled from every 2x2 neighbors. In this circuit, pixel clock and HSYNC are divided by the sampling rate parameter. Conjunction of the above results and window flag is fed to the memory address counter.

Memory Address Counter: It counts the output pulse of the sampling rate selector. The counter value is used as DMA address for window memory.

Input Source Selector: This block has one parameter which selects one source signal out of R, G, B, and Y.

Window Memory: As the transfer rate on the video bus is relatively fast, high speed static RAM is used. In current implementation, the size of window memory is 4 KByte. If it is used as square window, it can store 64x64 pixel data. If we use a rectangular window of 256 width, then memory covers 256x16 pixels.

3.3 Display monitor

It seems very convenient for us to observe the contents of window memories. Display of window memories in real time help us to understand what is going on. Also, it would help our program debugging very much. For such purpose, we prepared the display bus. All the window memories are connected to the bus in order to display them on monitor TV. However, in case of multi window system, we must avoid a jamming of many windows. Display priority solves this problem. In current implementation, the priority chain is hard wired. Of course, we plan to make it programmable by software.

4. Software Description

Resident software on window processor are primitive functions and command interpreter. Primitive functions are closely related to the window hardware and handle the window oriented data structure described below. Command interpreter receives a command message, interprets it and calls a corresponding function.

4.1 Window Parameters

As mentioned above, a window unit has several parameters, such as window size, window location, spacial sampling rate, input signal selection, and so on. They are all programmable. Those parameters as well as pixel data must be organized in proper data structure. Parameters to be held are following : a flag to represent whether or not this window is area or line, a flag to designate direction of linear window, position of the upper left corner of the window, horizontal and vertical size, spacial sampling rate, input signal selection, and a pointer to window memory. All primitive functions described below handle this structure. Fig.4 illustrates the window oriented data structure.

4.2 Primitive functions

There are three major groups of functions, as listed in Table 1. The first concerns to the control of window hardware. They are used to set the location of the window, to specify its shape, to fetch image, to open or close it, or to select spacial sampling rate. The second concerns to data transfer. They are used to copy or move data between the window oriented data structures. In data transfer, not only the pixel data but also all of window parameters are copied or moved properly. The third concerns to process window memories. They are used to perform various numerical calculations over the window memories, to find the center of a figure, to make image binary, to find object edges on a scan line, and so on.

Photographs of basic features of the prototype are shown in Fig.7. In Photo.1, multiple windows are displayed on monitor screen. Up to sixteen windows can be used in current prototype system. Depending on the priority chain, overlapped areas are exclusively displayed. A window of higher priority inhibits to display those of lower priority exclusively.

As listed in Table 1, there are four primitive functions to control window. They are SET, FETCH, OPEN and CLOSE. SET specifies the location and the shape of the window. FETCH reads window data into memory and displays them. Functions OPEN and CLOSE control whether the window may be displayed or not. OPEN allows to display, while CLOSE inhibits. If FETCH is issued after CLOSE, window data are read into, while the data is never displayed.

Photo.2 shows square window, where the size is 64x64, spacial sampling rate is 1, and input source is Y (brightness). With holding the fetched data, the window position can be moved by another SET function. Thus, the window is displayed at different position as Photo.3. Window size is not fixed. Its horizontal and vertical sizes are programmable. Photo.4 shows a window of 128x32. Photo.5 shows a window of 32x128. The thinnest window is line. Photo.6 shows horizontal line, and Photo.7 shows vertical line. They can be used as "line sensor" for some kind of monitoring.

Not only the size of window but also spacial sampling rate is selectable. Photo.8 shows the 128x128 window whose resolution is 2. When the spacial sampling rate is 2, one pixel data is sampled from every 2x2 neighbors. Therefore 64x64 pixel data are stored into actual memory. In other words, the actual window memory hold a shrunk image, although the large and low resolution image is displayed on the screen. By changing window size to 64x64 and resolution to 1, the contents of the actual memory is displayed, as shown in Photo.9. Moreover, the window whose resolution is 4 and size is 240x200 is shown in Photo.10. And its reduced image is also shown in Photo.11. This feature of resolution control provides a quite efficient

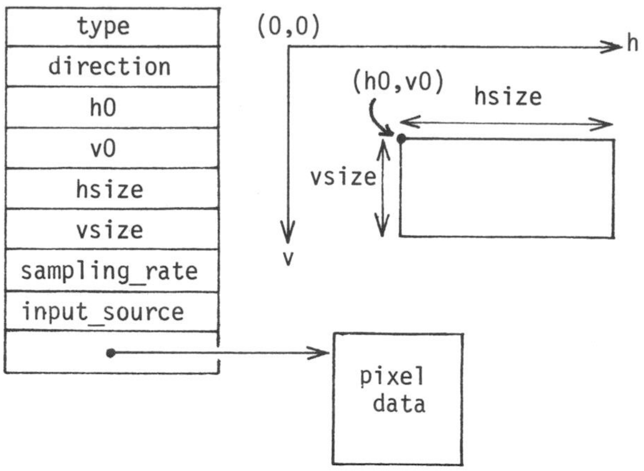

Figure 4. Window oriented data structure.

Group1: Window Control

SET	window,h0,v0,hsize,vsize
FETCH	window
OPEN	window
CLOSE	window
SOURCE	window,color
SAMPLE	window,s_rate

Group2: Data Transfer (A:Area,L:Line)

TRANS_AA	p_src,p_dst,h0,v0,hsize,vsize,s_rate
TRANS_AL	p_src,p_dst,h0,v0,size,s_rate,dir
TRANS_LL	p_src,p_dst,x0,size,s_rate
TRANS_LA	p_src,p_dst

Group3: Data Processing

ADD_K	p_src,const,p_dst
ADD_3	p_src1,p_src2,p_src3,p_dst
SUB_K	p_src,const,p_dst
SUB_2	p_src1,p_src2,p_dst
MUL_k	p_src,const,p_dst
DIV_K	p_src,const,p_dst
SQR	p_src,p_dst
SQRT	p_src,p_dst
MEAN	p_src,ret_val
MAX	p_src,ret_val
MIN	p_src,ret_val
VARI	p_src,ret_val
BINARY	p_src,p_dst
MASK	p_src,masktyp,p_dst
HISTO	p_src,rank,p_dst
CENTER	p_src,hc,vc
ASSIGN	p_src,const
CLIP	p_src

Table 1. Primitive Functions.

p_src : pointer to source window data
p_dst : pointer to destination window data
const : integer constant
s_rate: sampling rate

means to implement visual monitoring demon that uses rough global image. On the contrary, enlarged image can be gained by setting large size and large sampling rate. An example of such an enlarged image is shown in Photo.12. The original window is fetched at size of 64x64 and resolution of 1, and displayed window is size of 128x128 and resolution of 2.

4.3 Parallel Processing

As mentioned above, the control of each window is quite flexible. All windows can be controlled independently without any interference each other. This flexibility enables us to program wide variety of configuration in distributed processing.

The first is a pandemonium configuration. Pandemonium is a system in which a number of specialized demons are working on their own jobs. Using a number of window processing units, we can program this model straight on the multi window vision system. For instance, a demon is observing the whole scene through a large window of low resolution, and many demons focus their attention to distributed local regions of interests. Some demons use small square window, some other demons use linear window, and so on. The activity of each demon is programmed on each window processing unit. They work in parallel.

The second is an array configuration. Arranging many rectangular windows in array, we can process whole scene in parallel. In this configuration, the speed of processing depends on the number of employed processor.

The third is a pseudo pipeline configuration. It suit to applications which require a time consuming data processing for a real time image stream. In this configuration, all the windows are placed at the same position in the scene. Window units are connected together in a ring structure. Video image on the bus is updated every 1/60 seconds. Suppose that the processing of an image takes N/60 seconds. In this case, a ring of (N+1) window units suffice for processing all the image stream. As shown in the time chart of Fig.5, window #1 starts to read the data at time slot 0, it starts processing at 1 and finishes processing at N. Window #2 starts reading at 1 and finishes processing at N+1. Window #(N+1) starts at N and finishes at 2N. In such a way, all the image stream can be processed, although it has a time delay of (N+1)/60 seconds. Strictly speaking, this configuration is not a pipeline, because the processing procedure is not divided into many stages. However, it works like a pipeline system. Window units which are arranged in ring structure are employed in round robin fashion. The cycle time of output is same to that of input, although each output is obtained after a constant time delay. Provided with enough numbers of window units, all the image stream can be processed in real time.

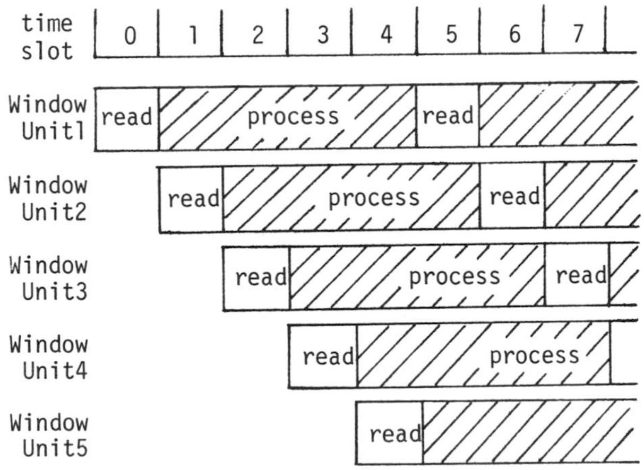

Figure 5. Time chart of a psudo pipeline application.

5. Experiment

A simple demonstration program, which searches and tracks an object, is described. Fig.6 shows state transition diagram of the program. It consist of three states. In the state "GLANCE", the program gives a glance to the entire scene and tries to find something. If an object is found, state changes to "TRACK". If nothing is found, state changes to "WIPER".
In the state "TRACK", the program continues to place small square window at the center of the object. So, if the object moves, the window follows. When the tracking fails, the state changes to GLANCE.
In the state "WIPER", a linear window continues to sweep the whole scene up and down, until it catches something. If something is caught, the state changes to "TRACK". Details of each processing are described below.

5.1 GLANCE

The purpose of this state is to examine whether or not something exists in the scene. If something is found, an approximate position of the object is calculated. In this case, precision is not required, but processing must be done quickly. Rough global image processing would suffice for this purpose. In the experiment, a 320x240 window with resolution value 8 is employed. So, the whole scene is shrunk to 40x30 window memory. After thresholding, the remaining bright pixels are counted. If the count is greater than 1, an object is considered to exist. The center of the figure is calculated and used for the initial position of TRACK. If nothing exists, the state changes to WIPER.

5.2 TRACK

In this state, a small square window is kept on the object unless the tracking fails. A window of size 64x64 and resolution 1 is employed. At first, the window is placed at the approximate initial position that is informed by either GLANCE or WIPER. Then, the program scans pixel data along the horizontal and vertical center lines within the window. The center of the object that is cut by horizontal scan gives the estimation of horizontal position of the object. Similarly, vertical position is estimated. According to the result, the window is moved to new position. When the object moves fast, above mentioned scan line may fail to cut the object. In such case, the program tries to cut the object by the border line of the window. If the object moves too fast, the program fails to track the object. In such case, the state changes to "GLANCE" to begin the global search again.

5.3 WIPER

In this state, a horizontal linear window is employed. Such linear window is moved up and down repeatedly. If the scan line succeeds to cut the object, the center of the cut gives the horizontal position of object. And the current position of wiper gives the vertical position. Bringing this results, the state changes to TRACK. If the window does not cut the object, the linear window keeps moving up and down like a window wiper of the car.

6. Concluding Remarks

A flexible multi window robot vision system is presented. It is designed and implemented to carry out various real time interaction such as visual monitoring, visual feedback, and visual verification. In such applications, it seems important to control wide variety of visual attentions on local regions of interests. Furthermore, those attentions must work in parallel. Multi window vision system satisfies this requirement.

Our current prototype system is equipped with sixteen window memories. Location, shape, and resolution of each window can be controlled independently. In order to process color image, four window memories are interfaced to a Motorola 68000 microcomputer. Four window units of such configuration are connected to the host computer through a communication processor. It provides a flexible hardware for robot vision study.

As the control of each window is quite flexible, we can program this system into several attractive configuration such as pandemonium, array, and pseudo pipeline. Those experiments need a lot of window units. If a hundred windows run in parallel, the performance of the multi window vision will be improved very much.

The prototype that is described in this paper is a step toward a large pandemonium in which hundreds of visual demons work in parallel. In fact, we are preparing the development of next version hardware by using semi-custom LSI.

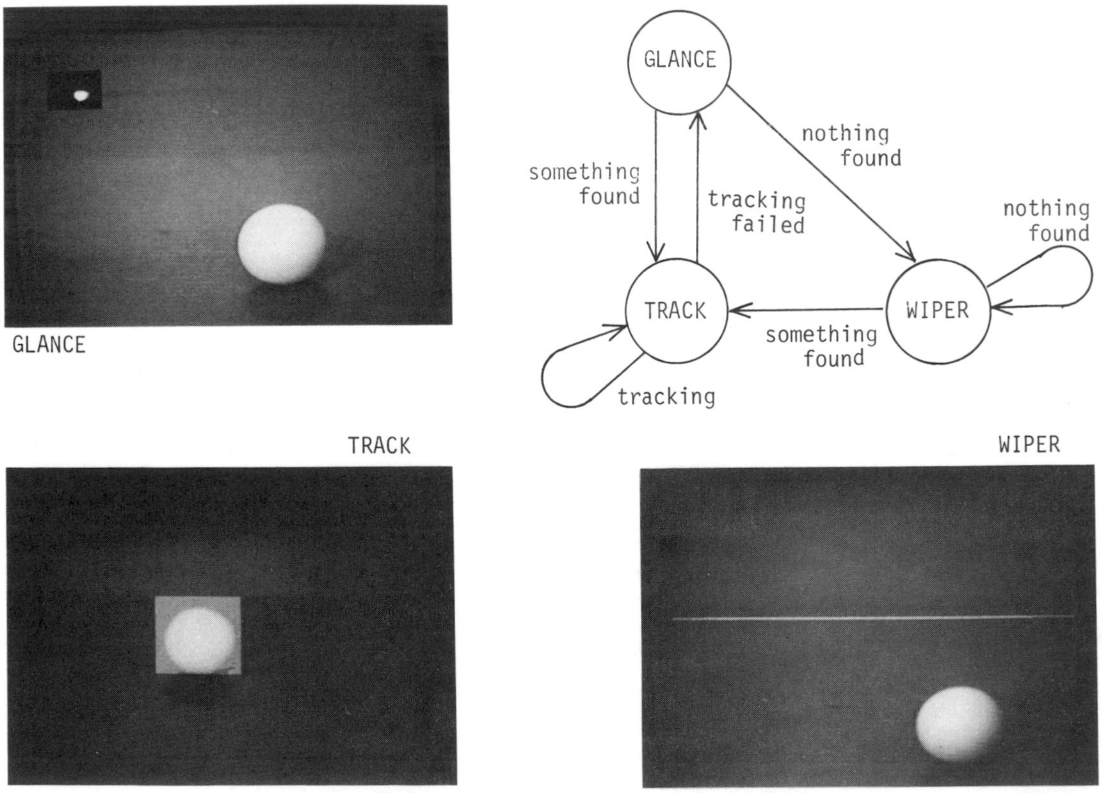

Figure 6. State transition diagram of the experiment.

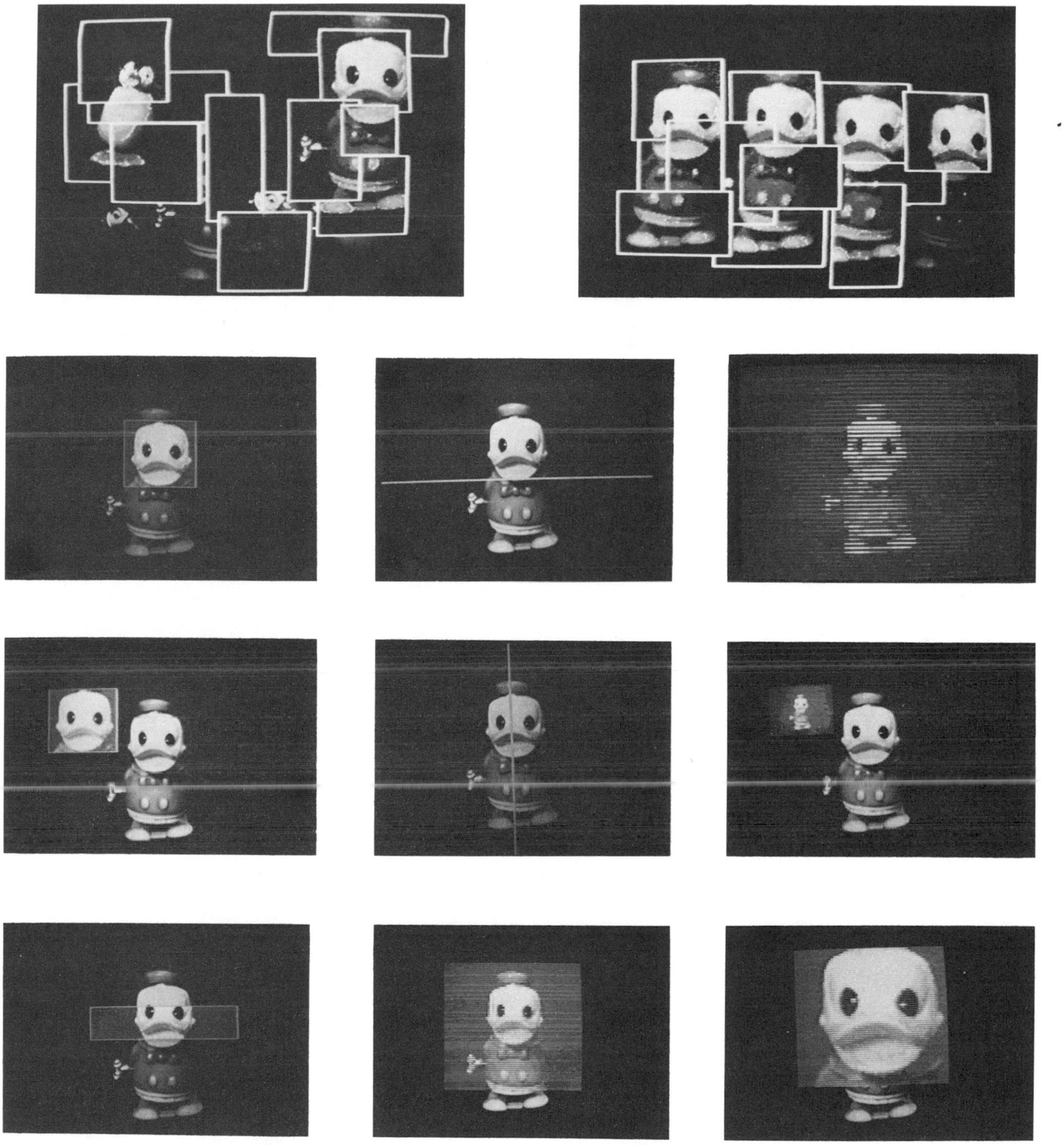

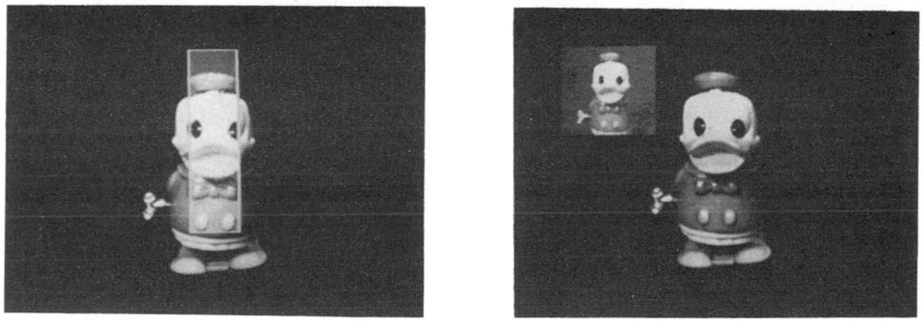

Figure 7.
Photographs of experiments

Photo. 1A		Photo. 1B
Photo.2	Photo.6	Photo.10
Photo.3	Photo.7	Photo.11
Photo.4	Photo.8	Photo.12
Photo.5	Photo.9	

Acknowledgement

The authors express their gratitude to Yoshio Murata and Toshihiko Morita for their contributions in the development of the system. They also thank Akira Tagawa for his help in hardware implementation.

References

Inoue, H. and Inaba, M. 1983, August, Hand Eye Coordination in Rope Handling, Proceedings of 1st ISRR, Bretton Woods, NH.

Lyndsay, P. H. and Norman D. A. 1977. Human Information Processing, Academic Press, New York.

Mizoguchi, H. and Inoue, H. 1984, July, Multiwindow Robot Vision System: Part1 The Design Concept, Proceedings of 23rd Annual Conf. of Society of Instrument and Control Engineers, Tokyo (in Japanese).

Mizoguchi, H. and Inoue, H. 1984. Multiwindow Robot Vision System: Part2 Hardware Description, ibid.

Mizoguchi, H., Morita, T. and Inoue, H. 1984. Multiwindow Robot Vision System: Part3 Basic Software, ibid.

COMPUTER VISION FOR FUTURE ROBOTS/TOWARDS REAL TIME SENSORY FEED BACK

Jean-Louis LACOMBE

SA MATRA - SPACE BRANCH - EPT/DT/068
BP 1 78146 VELIZY CEDEX FRANCE

Performance and effectiveness of vision system currently demonstrated remain too limited in many cases, particularly for real time sensory feed back applications (for example mobile robot navigation and manipulator motion and task control).

Major steps in performance requirements are
- 2D to 3D vision
- static to Dynamic Scene analysis (or in other words off-line to on-line (Real Time) image processing).

The system performance appears to be limited principally by the data processing capabilities. Improvement of algorithms efficiency is probably unable to solve the problem, development of processors able to process on-line the visual flow is of prime importance for the evolution of Robot eyes.
A second important field of research should concern the modification of data flow rate at the process input. New compression techniques like pixel grouping allows to have different spatial resolution for different image zones (location of which could be programmed). Such a technique could be used for reducing data flow rate without significant loss of information if the partition of the image is itself programmed after adequat image analysis.

1- CLASSIFICATION OF THE APPLICATIONS

The applications of computer vision to robot control can be classified on the basis of :
- the major characteristics of the imaging system configuration
  . static scene versus changeable scene
  . static imaging system versus mobile imaging system
  . steady lighting conditions versus unsteady lighting conditions
- the type of model enabling the description, the interpretation and the synthesis of the scene :
  . deterministic model versus heuristic model
  . geometrical model/movement model/physical model (colour, spectrum, etc.)
- the type of relation between the vision system and the human operator
  . supervised learning versus self learning
  . telepresence (image display) versus symbolic high level communication langage.

At the time being only the simplest applications are fully demonstrated e.g. robot vision is used for defining the location of parts involved in the assembly process in the case when :
- scene is static (or cinematics is known and predicted)
- the model of the local universe is very simple :
  . limited number of well defined, rigid (shape is not variable) elements
  . scene backround is adapted
- the scene is not disturbed by mechanical effects or by unsteady lighting conditions.

Many potential applications are clearly out of the reach of the state of the art, e.g. using computer vision for the control of a manipulator for cherry picking is difficult because :
- scene is changing, the wing disturb the tree
- lighting conditions are unsteady due to changing shadow.
- the model of the scene could be based only on heuristic approach.

The table 1 summarizes the major feature of typical applications.

2- VISION SYSTEM REQUIREMENTS

The performance requirements of the computer vision system are relating with :
- type of image element
  . segment/surface/volume/hypervolume
- physical characteristics of image element
  . monospectral versus multispectral (color)
  . binary versus multi level
- principle of imaging sensor
  . camera/radar/lidar
  . analogic versus digital sensor
  . line scan/2D/2D + range finder/ stereo vision/ etc
- performance of the sensing element
  . distorsion of optical image
  . sensing/noise ratio
  . sensitivity
  . linearity
  . spatial resolution

FEATURES \ APPLICATIONS	Assembly robot picking parts on a table	Mobile Robot for servicing a manufacturing cell	On-orbit servicing robot for satellite maintenance	Mobile Robot for planet exploration (e.g. Mars Rover)	Robot for apple or cherry picking	Vision for traffic control	Vision for automated car drive
0 Static scene / 1 changeable scene	0	1	0	1	1	1	1
0 Static camera / 1 mobile camera	0	1	1	1	1	0	1
0 steady lighting conditions / 1 unsteady lighting conditions	0	1	1	1	1	1	1
0 deterministic scene model / 1 heuristic scene model	0	0/(1)	0	1	1	0	0/1
0 geometrical model / 1 movement model physical model	0	0/(1)	0/(1)	1	1	0/(1)	0/1
0 supervised learning / 1 self learning	0	0	0	1	0/1	0	0/1
0 scene adapted to vision constraint (e.g. adapted background) / 1 scene could not be prepared and adapted	0	0/(1)	0	1	1	1	0/1
0 no disturbance / 1 highly disturbed environment	0	0	0	0/(1)	1	0/(1)	1

TABLE 1 : CHARACTERISTICS OF REPRESENTATIVE APPLICATIONS OF COMPUTER VISION FOR PROCESS CONTROL.

- performance of data processing system
  . image sampling rate
  . data processing duration time
  . level of confidence on sensor outputs data.

The performances required for robot vision are depending on :
- kinematical and dynamical characteristics of the robot enabling task execution
- characteristics of other sensors used for very short range operations (force/torque sensor, artificial skin, etc.)
- characteristics of robot environment.

Major steps in evolution of computer vision system should be :
- from 2D vision to 3D vision
- from off line data processing to on line data processing.

Both these evolutions are limited by data processing capabilities
- increased data volume per image
- more complex usefull data extraction
- increased data rate.

The figure 1 illustrates the evolution of data processing requirements based on existing research and development.

The number of picture element per image (for robot vision) is typically from 10^5 to 10^6 for 2D image ; 10^5 to 10^8 for 3D image.

The required image sampling rate is typically from 1 to 5 sec for off line analysis of static scene ; 5 to 20 images per second for on line analysis of variable scene (data processing shall be performed during the sampling period).

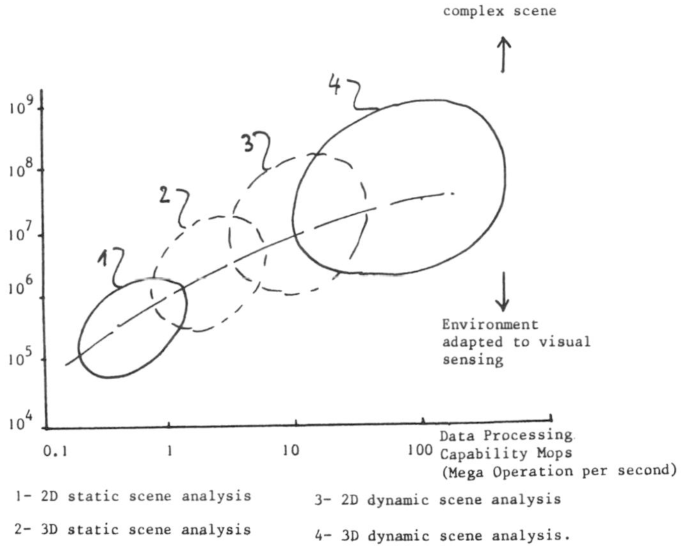

FIGURE 1 : REQUIREMENTS FOR DATA PROCESSING CAPABILITIES IN TYPICAL ROBOT VISION APPLICATIONS

The number of operation per pixel is very depending on the complexity of the model of the scene, it is typically from 5 to 20 for environment which may be described using deterministic model. It may reach 100 for complex images. One may notice that analysis of static scene each 5 sec with 2D image requires a data processing capability in the range of 0.2 to 1 Mops (Million of operation per second).

Analysis of dynamic (changing) scene with a 3 vision system with 10 images per seconds requires a data processing capability of 10 to 100 Mops depending on 3D system principle and configuration.

It appears that the major problems is to increase the data rate capability of the image processor system by at least a factor of 10.

Improvement of algorithms efficiency may not generate a suffisant decrease of computational loading.

3- VISION SYSTEM ARCHITECTURE

Typical architecture of computer vision system are well illustrated by two systems which are currently developped :
- visiomat
- high speed programmable processor.

3-1 Visiomat

The first system (visiomat) is a specialized system usable for robot control and inspection. The configuration is given in the figure 2.

The system is able to analyse a static scene with 2D vision at a frequency of 10Hz if the scene is simple (cooperative) and at a frequency of about 1Hz if the scene is "complex".

The data processing capability is mainly provided by integrated operators (edge extraction, convolution, mathematical morphology). The microprocessor ensures no more than 5% of the operations and it has a capability of 0.5 Mops. Nevertheless the microprocessor has a major contribution to the image processing time.

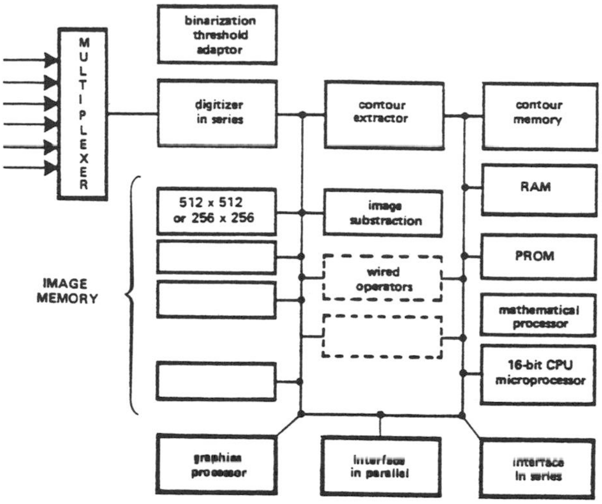

FIGURE 2 : ARCHITECTURE OF VISIOMAT SYSTEM.

		Model 1 Basic	Model 1 Optional	Model 2 Basic	Model 2 Optional
IMAGES	• Image size	256 x 256	-	512 x 512	-
	• Image memory volume (K bytes)	8 K	64 K	224 K	448 K
	• Grey level	16	64	64	-
	• Number of image plans	4	8	7	14
	[64 binary levels	ou { 1(16) / 4	et { 1 / 2	et { 1 / 1	et { 2 / 2
	• VLSI contour extractor	X	-	X	-
	• Image substraction processor	-	X	-	X
	• Dynamic threshold adapter processor	-	X	-	X
	• Graphics processor (256 × 256)	X	-	X	-
	• Reading/writing in image memory				
	• Number of cameras	6	-	X	-
PRINCIPAL PROCESSOR	• PROM memory (K bytes)	128	-	128	256
	• RAM memory (K bytes)	128	256	128	384
	• Fast mathematical processor	-	X	-	X
	• RS 232 series lines	2	10	2	10
	• Series lines processor	-	X	-	X
	• I/O in parallel	24	120	24	120
	• Parallel I/O processor	-	X	-	X
	• High-speed series line	-	X	-	X
	• High-speed series line coupler by fiber optics	-	X	-	X
	• Floppy discs	1	2	1	2
MAN-MACHINE DIALOG	• Teaching and programming console with graphic display	X		X	
	• Independent monitors		X		X
	• Programming and maintenance desk		X		X
	• Independent programming console with floppy discs		X		X
	• Servo control pcb's (2 interpolated axes)		X		X

	Model 1 & 2 Basic	Model 1 & 2 Optional
. Real-time multitask monitor	X	
. Shape-recognition and image-processing primaries		
- histogram	X	
- binarization threshold adapter	X	
- filtering		X
- gradient		X
- convolution		
- determination of parameters (CG, area)	X	
- determination of relations between contours	X	
- structural description of shapes	X	
- inspection by adaptive luminance check		X
- shape recognition	X	
- object localization, orientation	X	
- scene analysis, image substraction		X
- tracking moving objects		X
- dimensional check		X
- recognition of standardized characters		X
- digital meter reading		X
- pointer meter reading		X
. High-level programming language	X	
. Compiler, real-time interpreter	X	
. Teaching program	X	
. Maintenance and diagnostic programs	X	

TECHNICAL DESCRIPTION OF VISIOMAT (hardware and software characteristics)

3-2 High Speed Programmable Processor (HSPP)

This system was initially considered for on-board satellite image processing.

The configuration is given in the figure 3 and the design feature are summarized in the table 2.

The system with a capability of 600 Mops is usable for very demanding application like :
- traffic control
- visual flow processing for Eye-In-Hand, high resolution robot vision.

These limited comparison between VISIOMAT and HSPP well illustrate the gap existing between the architecture of a dedicated system applicable to simple cases and the architecture of a powerful system designed in the goal of having very high speed processing.

We emphasize the strong importance of development of very integrated operators which are the key components of future powerful vision systems.

Key Design Features

. MIMD-type parallel processor
. Processing elements (PE) :
  - bit slice processors, with monochip multipliers
  - specially designed for image or signal processing algorithms
. DMA-type mechanism to allow concurrent tasks execution and interprocessor communication.
. Ring bus with separate address and data paths, and decentralized control.
. Basic configuration : two uncommitted busses
. Possible extensions towards application oriented multiple bus configurations.

Technical features

. PE cycle time : 200 ns
. Performance per PE : 10 Madd/s + 5 M Mult/s
. Bus cycle time : 50 ns
. Throughput : 20 Mbytes/s per bus
. Address range : 16 Mwords per bus
. Word length : 16 bits
. 16 bit fixed point arithmetic
. Power concumption : 20 W per PE

Applications

. Mono and multispectral image compression
. Synthetic Aperture radar processing
. Geometric compensation (resampling)
. Image thematic classification
. Cloudy areas detection
. Pattern recognition : objects, landmarks
. Target tracking
. Robotics, ...

TABLE 2 : HSPP DESIGN FEATURES

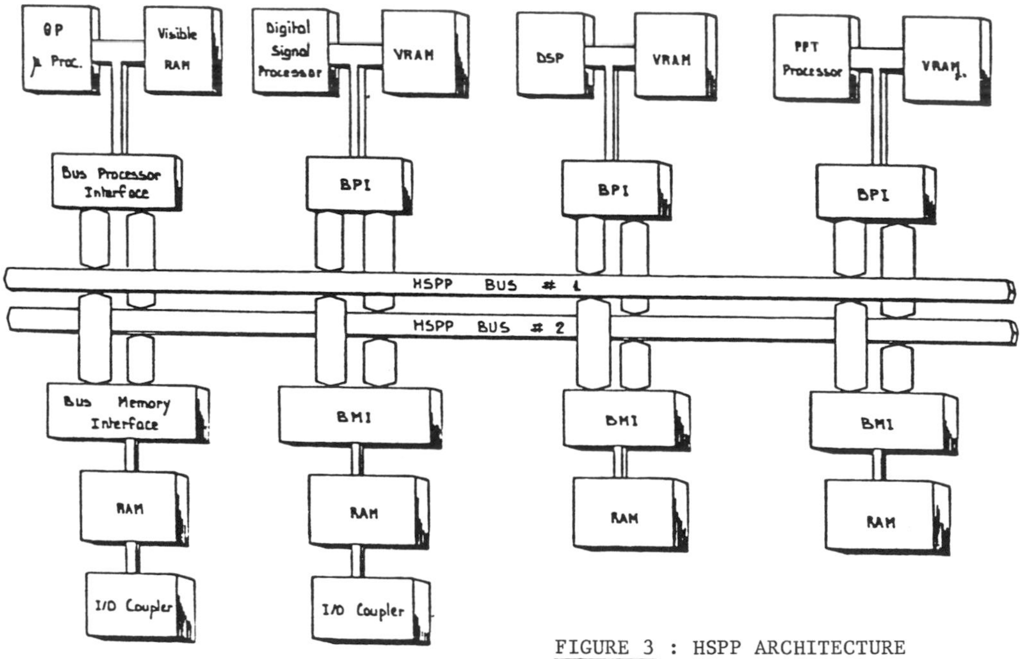

FIGURE 3 : HSPP ARCHITECTURE

4- LIMITATION OF DATA FLOW RATE

Imaging sensor improvement in order to reduce the data flow rate with respect to image processor limitation could be envisaged. Let us consider a 2D imaging sensor (typically a CCD or CID matrix) having a high resolution (typically 400 x 400).

Pixel grouping may be used for having lower image resolution outside selected zone in the image (inside which full resolution is selected) (figure 4).

Such a process enable a significant decrease of visual flow rate. The loss of information is limited if the full resolution windows are correctly placed.

The visual flow for a 2D image of N x N pixels each τ seconds is N^2/τ bytes/sec.

If 10% of the image is with full resolution and 90% of the image is composed with pixel grouping by 3 x 3 packet the visual flow is only 0.2 N^2/τ. The compression ratio is 5.

However, many theoritical problems shall be solved:
- what is the better image partition high between high and low resolution zones for a given limited visual flow ?

  In other words what is the minimum loss of information ?
- how to initialize the process and what kind of image analysis may be used for image partition ?

Least programmable pixel grouping is feasible but it may be difficult except if new sensing elements will be developped for this special purpose.

An other improvement could consist in having an image partition in 2 types of zones :
- high sampling rate zone
- divided sampling rate zone.

In this case only a (or many) part of the image is read at nominal sampling rate the other part is read at divided rate. (e.g. 10 times slower).

5- CONCLUSION

Computer vision will have an increasing role for robot control if 3D techniques and Real Time image processing techniques (at high rate, ~ 10 image per second) are developped successfully.

It is assumed that technical difficulties are more in the field of High Speed integrated operators, design processor architecture concepts, data flow optimisation methods than in the field of algorithms for data extraction and image analysis.

REFERENCES

G. GAILLAT - 1983
The design of parallel processor for image processing on board satellites ; 10th Annual Symposium on computer architecture, Stockholm.

G. GAILLAT - 1984
The Capitan parallel processor : 600 MIPS for use in real time imagery ; Premier colloque image, Biarritz - mai 1984.

J.L. LACOMBE et al. - 1984
Study of Service Manipulator System for in-orbit Servicing ; ESA contract.

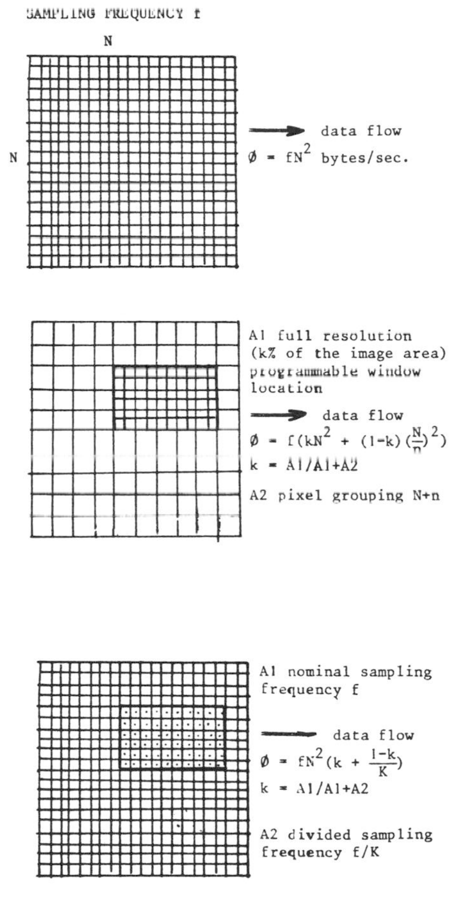

FIGURE 4 : PRINCIPLE OF VISUAL FLOW COMPRESSION USING PIXEL GROUPING TECHNIQUE (a) OR DIVIDED SAMPLING FREQUENCY TECHNIQUE (b).

HARDWARE IMPLEMENTATION FOR ROBOT VISION

Masatsugu Kidode, Hiroshi Hoshino and Youkio Shiraogawa

Information Systems Laboratory
TOSHIBA Research and Development Center
1, Komukai-Toshiba cho, Saiwai, Kawasaki 210, JAPAN

A high-performance image processor has been newly developed for robot vision. Several basic functions have been implemented into a simple hardware, which are efficiently used in object identification, position detection and inspection. Not only this vision processor can execute basic. functions at video-rate speed for 512 x 512 images, but also has technical features in image data access for more complex programming and in common bus structure for more flexible system.

Introduction

Several image processing machines have been implemented, which are mainly optimized for basic two dimensional signal processing, or low-level processing. Main efforts have concentrated on developing special hardware circuits for high speed image-to-image operations. Some interactive image processing machines of this kind are already commercially available with modest price, incorporating advanced digital technologies. Remote sensing, medical diagnosis and laboratory study are current application fields that benefit from the use of these machines. A newer, farther reaching aspect of image processing and pattern recognition devices is the development of machines, vision processors, for industrial applications such as visual inspection, assembly work, etc.

Most conventional vision processors have been designed to only process binary images, or preprocess gray-scale images even if possible. When realizing a more flexible vision system, it should be sufficiently free from rigid environmental conditions to obtain a good binary image, and have more basic functions not only for binary images but also gray-scale images. A more attractive alternative is to have more flexible interaction between low-level and high-level processings. In short, a vision processor should have the capability to accomplish low-level functions at high speed; image-to-image transform and feature detection from image, and to efficiently make use of these imagery and feature data in high-level programs. It is becoming possible to implement such vision processors at modest cost with modern digital technologies in memory chips, arithmetic and control circuits. The problem now to be solved is to determine what vision processor architecture is superior in terms of cost-effectiveness, or cost-performance ratio. Based on trade-off studies in speed, physical size, economy and generality, a programmable vision processor, TOSPIX-II TM , has been newly developed to improve the performance of another machine TOSPIX-I TM [Kidode, 1983].

In the second section, major design concetps of TOSPIX-II are discussed. In the third section, the detail of hardware implementation and its performance are described.

Design Concepts of Vision Processor TOSPIX-II

TOSPIX-I was developed using the same hardware architecture as two kinds of local parallel image processors, PPP [Mori, 1978] and IPU [Kidode, 1981]. These image processors employed the following characteristic concepts in their design so as to improve image processing cost-effectiveness.

Image Memory Centered System: An image memory is placed at the pivot of the image processor, which plays an important role in a large amount of image data transfer. This system configuration minimizes "idle" data transfer among hierarchical levels of the memory. The time for those data transfers generally shares a large fraction of the total throughput time by conventional computer configurations, which are not necessary for the essential calculations in image processing.

Select Image Processing Functions in Hardware: There are several kinds of computation that are frequently used in image processing. Most of such operations take a large amount of time. TOSPIX-II has implemented several basic functions, which can be executed with improvement in the cost performance ratio.

Local Parallel Processor: There are two kinds of hardware implementation to achieve parallelism in image processing: locally parallel and fully parallel. The most intuitive idea is a parallel array of identical processing elements corresponding to each pixel which works simultaneously on all of the image data. Image processors of this fully parallel category, however, face several problems in hardware realization and processing capability. This has led to our image processor design, which carries out image processings on a locally parallel basis. Specially designed circuits accomplish the local parallel operations (parallel data access and computation in the local window) which sequentially scan the entire image in the raster mode. The combination of locally parallel operations and sequential scanning fits the serial data transfer characteristic of an image memory and also reduces hardware cost and complexity.

In addition to these design concepts, TOSPIX-II has adopted more practical ideas described below.

More Powerful Functions for Feature Detection: Robot vision requires high-speed feature detection functions as well as image-to-image transform functions. Especially, feature parameters and their positional information are expected to be detected at high speed.

High-Speed Data Access by Program: Even with high-speed functions realized in special purpose modules, it is still necessary to perform more global and complex operations by programs. For this purpose, TOSPIX-II has a flexible control architecture capable of accessing image data pixel by pixel as well as detected feature parameters directly from programs.

Modular Structure and High Cost-Performance: TOSPIX-II has been designed on the basis of a standard common bus (IEEE 796 or Multi Bus) structure. This allows us to easily build up application oriented vision systems in combination with some of basic functional modules and other specially designed hardware. These flexibility and expandability in system construction optimizes the trade-off between cost and user's requirements.

TOSPIX-II Implementation and Performance: An overall blockdiagram of TOSPIX-II is depected in Figure 1. Two sets of common buses, the standard IEEE 796 bus and an image bus, transmit the internal parameter data and the high speed image data, respectively. The IEEE 796 bus, or the Multi-Bus, is mainly used for transferring command execution parameters, detected feature parameters, etc. between the system controller and hardware modules connected to the common bus. The image bus consisting of four sets of 8-bit image data, is dedicated to transmit the image data between the image memory and functional modules. The system controller is the TOSBAC-Super $\mu 7$ microcomputer with 512 KB main memory. The system controller controls the operational modes of all the hardware units connected to the common bus. When TOSPIX-II works as program development tools, it has several peripherals interfaced to the system controller; keyboards, a tablet, a mouse, disc file, etc. Application programs can be written in FORTRAN and C programming languages. An interactive image processing and analysis study can be done in TOSPIX-II with the aid of a command language. In order to access the image data efficiently by the system controller, a set of special machine instructions are prepared; for example, pixelwise 8-bit, 16-bit and 32-bit data access instructions.

Table I lists a repertoire of high speed image processing and feature detection functions. They are grouped in three categories: pixelwise functions, local parallel (neighbourhood) operations and feature measurements. Figure 2 shows the complete TOSPIX-II vision processing system.

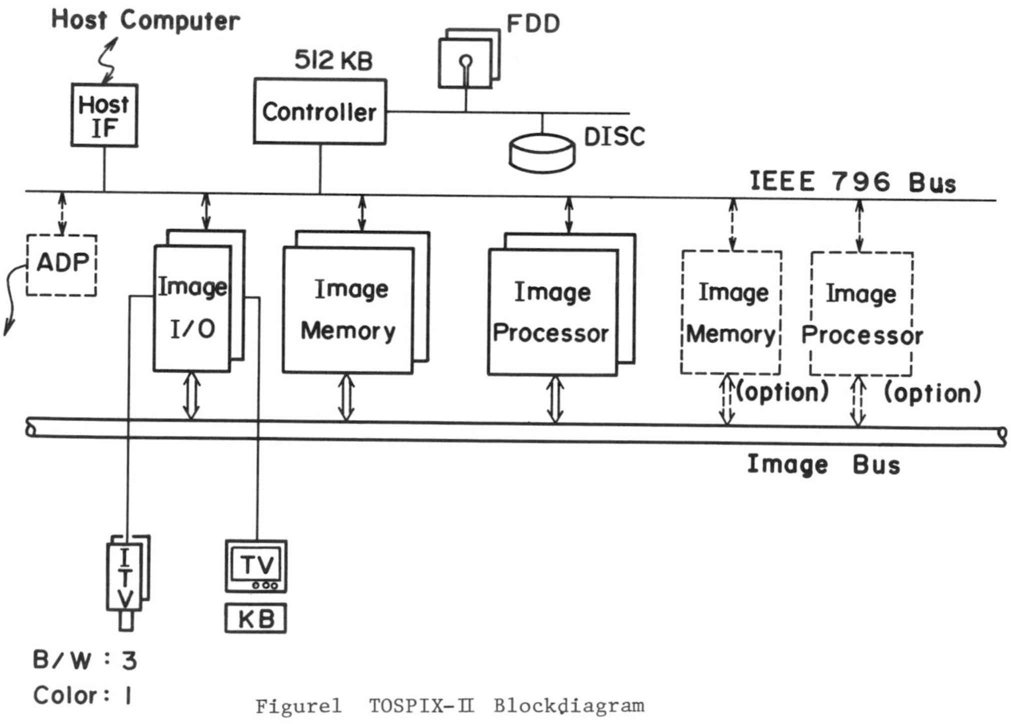

Figure1 TOSPIX-II Blockdiagram

Table I Repertoire of TOSPIX-II functions

Pixelwise ALU Operation	Add, Subtract, Absolute Difference, AND, OR, EXOR, Linear Combination
Point Mapping	Data Conversion
Affine Transform	Rotation, Scaling, Shift
2-D Convolution	Spatial Filtering
Logical Filtering	Noise Elimination, Thinning
Region Labeling	(up to 4,094 regions)
Histogramming	Gray Level Frequency Counting
Area / Length Counting	(binary image)
Projection	(x and y directions)
Measurement	Window Parameter, Run Length

Figure 2 TOSPIX-II Vision Processing System

Image Processing and Feature Detection Modules: Three hardware modules are included in TOSPIX-II. The first module contains the ALU for pixelwise ALU functions between two images, and the table memory for point mapping, histogramming, area counting and X-Y projection. A sum-of-products circuit with line image data buffers in the second module is provided for two dimensional convolution and pixelwise linear combination operation of three images. The last hardware module operates on binary image data, which can accomplish logical filtering by a 3 x 3 local mask and region labeling with a 3 x 2 connectivity test mask. This module also contains the buffer memory for storing a list of detected feature points and window information of a certain labeled region as illustrated in Figure 3.

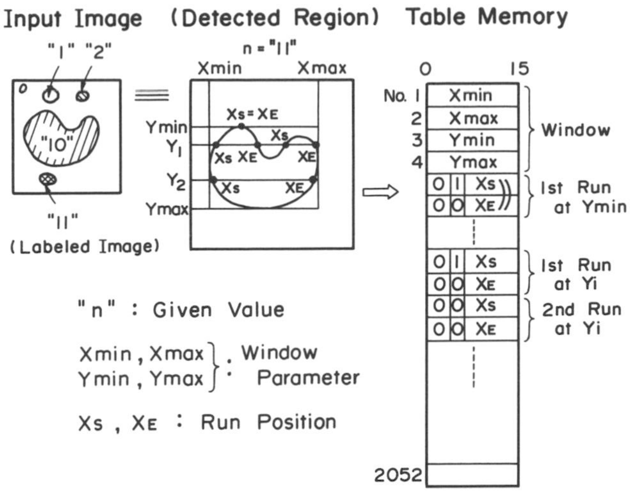

Figure 3 Featuse Measurement for Region

The following control operations are implemented in TOSPIX-II to perform more efficient and flexible algorithms. A programmable thresholding function is prepared to virtually produce a binary image, which allows a gray scale image to be an input with a threshold value and comparison condition. A mask control operation works on all the hardwised functions by assigning a certain image memory to mask plane, where the above programmable threshold control is also available. Figure 4 indicates these two control operation in histogram computation. A gray level histogram within a given labeled object can be obtained only by issueing the corresponding function.

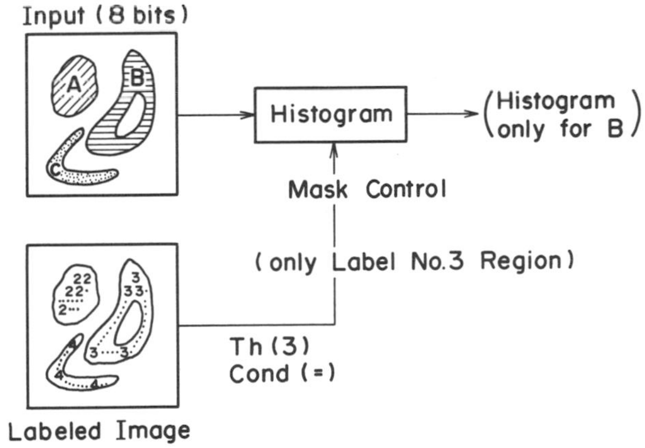

Figure 4 Histogramming with Programmable threshold Mask Control

Image Memory: The image memory consists of at most eight layers of 512 x 512 pixels with 8 bits per pixel. 1,024 x 1,024 image memory is optionally available. Each image memory unit includes a set of address controllers which can calculate the two dimensional addresses at high speed, and transfers image data to and/or from any functional module through the image bus. Since any image memory can be connected to one of four sets of the image bus under program control, different kinds of image processings can be performed in parallel as shown in Figure 5. The address controller is capable of calculating next image memory addresses automatically, and checking the window boundary of image data to be accessed.

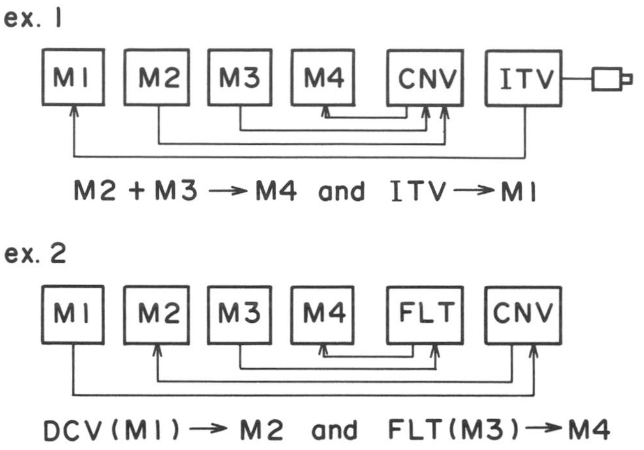

Figure 5 Examples of Parallel Operations

Video Image I/O: The standard analog video signal can be input from TV cameras and video tape recorders. Up to 3 video interfaces can be connected to TOSPIX-II. As depicted in Figure 6, each video interface has two video input ports, which converts one of the composite analog signals into 8-bit digital image under program control. The standard NTSC color video signal is also available by a color video interface. Two video signals from color TV cameras and/or color VTRs can be connected to the interface, one of which is input as three color component images (R, G and B). The size of input image is 512 x 512 or 256 x 256. In the case of 256 x 256 image input, a certain period of dynamic images can be automatically stored in the image memory; four 256 x 256 images per an image memory unit.

For the purpose of interactively developing image processing and analysis algorithms, a display monitor with key boards is provided. As illustrated in Figure 7, there can be seen 512 x 512 image data, 80 x 32 characters and two cursors on the monitor screen. The cursor is interactively controlled by a mouse or tablet.

Software: TOSPIX-II has been specially designed to perform basic functions for robot vision at high speed. For developing a variety of application programs, an easy-to-use programming system to operate TOSPIX-II is prepared. The ability to easily program data transfer and function execution allows efficient and flexible vision algorithms. Several application studies have proved that TOSPIX is a powerful and economical tool for notonly research studies but also field experiments in robot vison. It should be emphasized that TOSPIX has the gray scale image processing ability as well as binary image processing ability.

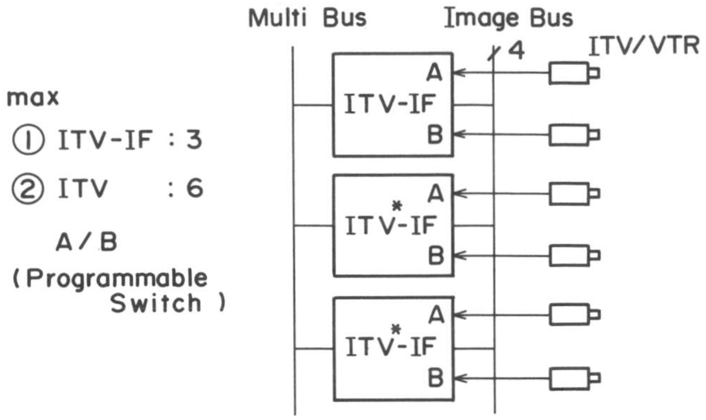

Figuer 6 Video Interfaces for B/W Images

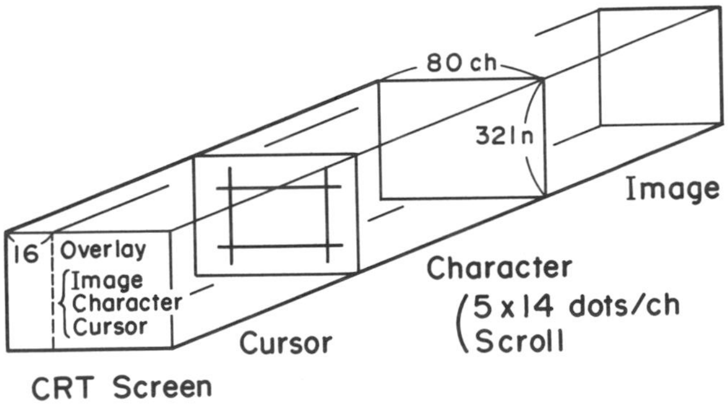

Figure 7 Display Data

A number of subprograms and application programs using TOSPIX have already been developed for industrial applications; for example, non-destructive testing by X-ray for carry-in baggage inspection and inner defect detection in moulding parts, thermometer gauge inspection [Nakamura, et al., 1984], electric parts inspection [Kuno, 1983], and so on. Programming methods to combine basic functions are listed below for simple applications.

Shape Recognition: Shape recognition is one primitive technique assigned to automated assembly work. For example, a pick and place operation is carried out after the location and orientation of an object are recognized. Logical filtering and feature measurement are used for detecting geometrical feature points and its counting; for instance, perimeter length, hole number, area etc.. When a more sophisticated vision algorithm is needed to recognize complicated shapes, edge detection and correlation techniques are used by two dimensional convolution function and associated programs.

Particle Measurement: Particle measurement techniques have been urgently needed in industrial inspection. The particles area measurement with their distribution is one example of applications in this category, which shows an assortment of basic TOSPIX functions. First, an input image is thresholded into a binary image by point mapping. The threshold value could be automaticakky derived from the histogram of an input image. By using region labeling function, particles are separated into disjoint ones that have distinct labels. The number of disconnected regions is consequently obtained and their area counting is done. Statistical parameters of particle's area distribution can be calculated.

Image Enhancement: The enhancement of poor quality images, taken in the non-destructive inspection, is another example of image processing applications. Many algorithms for the image enhancement have been proposed, some of which can be performed in TOSPIX at high speed. Histogram equalization technique can enhance an image which occupies a small portion of the available dynamic range. It can be performed by histogramming and point mapping functions. Spatial filtering is carried out by means of two dimensional convolution function.

Performance: Table II shows some examples of execution time for image data of 512 x 512 pixels. Each basic function can be carried out in 120 nsec or so per pixel.

Table II Execution Time by TOSPIX-II

Pixelwise ALU Operation	1/30 ~ 2/30 sec
Point Mapping	1/30 sec
Affine Transform	1/3 sec
2-D Convolution	1/10 sec
Logical Filtering	1/30 sec
Region Labeling	1/15 sec
Histogramming	1/30 sec
Area/Length Counting	1/30 sec
Projection	1/15 sec
Measurement	1/30 sec

Conclusions

A high-speed vision processor TOSPIX-II has been realized with capabilities of image processing and feature detection. TOSPIX-II has improved the cost-effectiveness of high-speed vision processings. The processing time is 1/30 second for 512 x 512 image, which is a real-time or video-frame processing. While basic vision functions are performed at high speed, more complex and global functions can be programmed in combination with these hardwared functions and flexible data accesses. TOSPIX-II is not only an efficient tool for exploring novel applications in industrial automation, but also a practical machine at real application fields.

References

Kidode, M. 1983. Image processing machines in Japan. IEEE Computer, 16, pp.68-80.

Mori, K., et al. 1978. Design of local parallel pattern processor for image processing. AFIPS, 47, pp.1025-1031.

Kidode, M., et al., 1981. Image processing unit hardware implementation. Real-Time Parallel Computing Image Analysis, ed. M. Onoe, et al., Plenum Publishing Corp., pp.279-295.

Nakamura, Y., et al., 1984. Automatic thermometer inspection system by high-speed image processor. Proceedings IECON, Tokyo (to be published).

Kuno, Y., et al., Robot vision implementation by high-speed image processor TOSPIX. Proceedings ICAR, Tokyo, pp.163-170.

II ACTION CONTROL

3 Control Theory

ON THE DEVELOPMENT OF HIGH PERFORMANCE ADAPTIVE CONTROL ALGORITHMS FOR ROBOTIC MANIPULATORS

Steven Dubowsky, Professor
Roy Kornbluh, Graduate Research Assistant
Department of Mechanical Engineering
Massachusetts Institute of Technology
Cambridge, MA 02139
U.S.A.

Complex industrial applications of robotic manipulators are beyond the capabilities of the relatively simple constant-gain linear control systems commonly used for current industrial manipulators. They compensate poorly for the nonlinear dynamic characteristics of manipulators and environmental changes. This paper presents the development of an adaptive control algorithm which adjusts, in real time, the control system parameters to compensate for manipulator nonlinear characteristics and changes in its environment and payload. Experimental results are also presented for two devices which show that the algorithm is practical and capable of producing significantly improved systems dynamic performance.

Introduction

Current commercial manipulators use relatively simple constant gain linear feedback control systems. While such control systems are reliable and easy to implement and design, their performance is rather limited. They compensate poorly for the nonlinear manipulator character and are sensitive to environmental changes, mechanical flexibility and actuator limitations. Hence, many complex industrial applications are beyond the capabilities of current industrial robotic manipulators [National Reseach Council].

A key to improved manipulator performance is the development of better control algorithms. In recent years, researchers have proposed a number of control methods that may substantially improve system performance. However, their value is almost always demonstrated analytically or by simulation, and only for idealized systems that may fail to consider important system factors which limit and degrade control system performance. These factors include manipulator friction, sensor noise, unknown system parameters and disturbances. In this paper an adaptive control algorithm for the motion control of robotic manipulators is presented which has been shown by simulation to signficantly improve system performance. Experimental results are presented which demonstrate the value of the algorithm on a laboratory robotic device and a commercial manipulator system.

The Literature

Many of the approaches suggested for improved motion control are based on explicit representations of the manipulator's nonlinear dynamics used in a feedforward manner [Raibert and Horn,1978].Linear feedback is provided to compensate for model errors and disturbances. Nonlinear feedback control laws have also been proposed [Freund, 1982; Luh, Walker and Paul 1980]. Optimal control theory has been applied linearized manipulator models [Kahn and Roth,1971], and more recently to manipulators with full nonlinear dynamics [Bobrow, Dubowsky and Gibson, 1983]. An important aspect of the above control approaches is that they require accurate dynamic models of the manipulator which are often difficult to obtain. A minipulator's dynamic behavior will vary over time due to such factors as varaiable joint friction and payload mass.

Adaptive control techniques have been proposed which attempt to adjust control system characteristics to compensate for changing dynamic properties based on measured performance rather than a detailed knowledge of the manipulator dynamics. Within adaptive control there are two fundamental approaches. The first is Learning Model Adaptive Control (LMAC), in which an improved model of the manipulator is obtained by on-line parameter identification techniques [Koivo and Guo,1983), and is then used in the feedback control of manipulators. The second approach is called Model Referenced Adaptive Control (MRAC). The controller is adjusted so that the closed loop behavior of a system matches that of a preselected model according to some criterion [Landau, 1974]. It is possible to have adaptation schemes which employ aspects of both approaches [LeBorgne, Ibarra, and Espiau 1981].

The manipulator model assumed in an adaptive control approach may range from a relatively simple linear uncoupled differential equation [Dubowsky and DesForges, 1979; Koivo, 1983] to more complex models of the manipulator dynamics [Vukobratovic and Kiracanski, 1982]. For high speed manipulator motion or control in task space there may be significant dynamic coupling between the joints which suggest mult-input-multi-output (MIMO) approaches [Takegaki and Arimoto, 1981]. However, studies have found that uncoupled single-input-single-output (SISO) algorithms can handle dynamic interaction without significant performance degradation [Koivo and Guo, 1983; LeBorgne, Ibarra and Espiau, 1981]. Adaptive algorithms have been proposed for manipulator control which employ non-adaptive nonlinear control in addition to adaptation [Lee, Ching and Lee, 1984].

MRAC algorithms can be developed in several ways. One common approach relies on a global stability theorem, such as Popov's Hyperstability Theorem. [Horowitz and Tomizuka, 1980]. Some MRAC algorithms, based on this approach, are unstable in practical applications due to unmodelled higher order dynamics and sensor noise [Rhors, 1983]. In this work MIMO algorithms are developed by applying the method of Steepest Descent to minimizing a cost function of the error between the model and the system.

Analytical Development

The manipulator dynamics, including its control, can be described by the nonlinear differential equation;

$$\dot{\underline{x}} = \underline{f}_s(\underline{x}, \underline{\alpha}, \underline{r}, \underline{d}) \qquad (1)$$

where $\underline{x}$ is the system state vector$(x_1,\ldots x_n)$,
$\underline{\alpha}$ is a system parameter vector$(\alpha_1,\ldots\alpha_m)$,
$\underline{r}$ is the input vector$(r_1,\ldots r_p)$, and
$\underline{d}$ is a disturbance vector$(d_1,\ldots d_q)$.

The $\underline{\alpha}$ vector is a function of x, and the control matrix, K(t), which is adjusted by the adaptive algorithm. The model state equation for the system to track is written as:

$$\dot{\underline{y}} = \underline{f}_m(\underline{y}, \underline{a}, \underline{r}) \qquad (2)$$

where $\underline{y}$ is the model state vector$(y_1,\ldots y_n)$ and
$\underline{a}$ is a model parameter vector$(a_1,\ldots a_m)$.

The error between the response of the model and the system is defined by the vector:

$$\underline{e}(t) = \underline{y}(t) - \underline{x}(t) \qquad (3)$$

The objective of the algorithm is to manipulate K(t), and hence $\underline{\alpha}$, in such a way as to drive $\underline{e}(t)$ to zero, and thereby match the system response to that of the model (i.e. $\underline{\alpha} = \underline{a}$), neglecting unmodelled disturbances. The development uses the method of Sensitivity-Steepest Descent [Donalson and Leondes, 1963; Brogan, 1974]. This method uses the parameters of the model rather than the system. Hence, it is computationally less burdensome than methods which evaluate complex, nonlinear models. It has also been shown to have very good noise rejection properties [Papadopoulos, 1983].

In this method, a scalar cost function is formulated as:

$$V(\underline{e}) = 1/2\ \underline{e}^T Q \underline{e} \qquad (4)$$

where Q is called the adaptive gain matirx. The change of $\underline{\alpha}$ in time, such that $V(\underline{e})$ moves along the steepest descent path to a minimum is given by:

$$\dot{\underline{\alpha}} = -k \frac{\partial V}{\partial \underline{\alpha}} = -k \frac{\partial \underline{e}}{\partial \underline{\alpha}}^T Q\, \underline{e} \qquad (5)$$

where $\partial \underline{e}/\partial \underline{\alpha}$ is an n by m matrix whose i,j element is $\partial e_i/\partial \alpha_j$. Q is an n by n symmetric matrix, and k is a positive scalar quantity. However, the partial derivative $\partial \underline{e}/\partial \underline{\alpha}$ in equation (5) cannot in general be calculated [Donalson, 1963; Dubowsky and DesForges, 1979]. It is approximated as follows:

$$\frac{\partial \underline{e}}{\partial \underline{\alpha}} = \frac{\partial(\underline{y}-\underline{x})}{\partial \underline{\alpha}} = \frac{-\partial \underline{x}}{\partial \underline{\alpha}} \simeq \frac{\partial \underline{y}}{\partial \underline{a}} \equiv \Lambda \qquad (6)$$

The n by m matrix Λ, called the sensitivity matarix, can be obtained from the partial derivative of equation (2) with respect to a as follows:

$$\frac{\partial \underline{y}}{\partial \underline{a}} = \frac{\partial \underline{f}_m}{\partial \underline{y}} \frac{\partial \underline{y}}{\partial \underline{a}} + \frac{\partial \underline{f}_m}{\partial \underline{a}} \qquad (7)$$

Assuming that $\partial \underline{y}/\partial \underline{a} = d[\partial \underline{y}/\partial \underline{a}]/dt$ and substituting the definition of Λ from equation (6) into equation (7) yields the matrix sensitivity equation:

$$\dot{\Lambda} = \frac{\partial \underline{f}_m}{\partial \underline{y}} \Lambda + \frac{\partial \underline{f}_m}{\partial \underline{a}} \qquad (8)$$

The adaption law, equation (5), can be written:

$$\dot{\underline{\alpha}} = -k\, \Lambda^T Q \underline{e}(t) \qquad (9)$$

$V(\underline{e})$ has the appearance of a Lyapunov function and [Papdopoulos, 1983; Brogan 1974] have suggested that this fact can be used to show that the method leads to a stable design. The stability of the method has been investigated for the continuous time case [Dubowsky and DesForges, 1979] and the discrete time case, including the effects of computational delays [Dubowsky, 1981].

Given $\dot{\underline{\alpha}}$, from equation (9), and assuming that the unknown parameters of the system change slowly, it is possilbe to solve for the time rate of change of the control gains required to satisfy equation (9), as seen in the following applicaion. A block diagram, Fig. 1, illustrates the above algorithm.

Consider the two degree-of-freedom robotic positioning device shown in Fig. 2. The closed loop system state equation,(1), for this device can be written as:

$$\dot{\underline{x}} = A(\underline{x})\underline{x} + B(\underline{x})\underline{r} + c(\underline{x})\underline{d} \qquad (10)$$

where

$$A = \begin{bmatrix} 0 & 1 & 0 & 0 \\ -k_{x11}\alpha_1' + k_{x21}\alpha_2' & -k_{x12}\alpha_1' + k_{x22}\alpha_2' + \alpha_3' & -k_{x13}\alpha_1' + K_{x23}\alpha_2' & -k_{x14}\alpha_1' + k_{x24}\alpha_2' + \alpha_4' \\ 0 & 0 & 0 & 1 \\ k_{x11}\alpha_5' - k_{x21}\alpha_6' & k_{x12}\alpha_5' - k_{x22}\alpha_G + \alpha_7' & k_{x13}\alpha_5' - k_{x23}\alpha_6' & k_{x14}\alpha_5' - k_{x24}\alpha_6' + \alpha_8' \end{bmatrix}$$

$$B = \begin{bmatrix} 0 & 0 \\ k_{r11}\alpha_1' - k_{r21}\alpha_2' & k_{r12}\alpha_1' - k_{r22}\alpha_2' \\ -k_{r11}\alpha_5' + k_{r21}\alpha_6' & -k_{r12}\alpha_5' + k_{r22}\alpha_6' \end{bmatrix} \quad C = \begin{bmatrix} 0 & 0 \\ \alpha_1' & -\alpha_2' \\ 0 & 0 \\ 0 & 0 \\ -\alpha_5' & \alpha_6' \end{bmatrix}$$

and x_1, x_2, x_3 and x_4 are equal to $\emptyset_1, \dot{\emptyset}_1, \emptyset_2$ and $\dot{\emptyset}_2$ respectively. The $\alpha_1(\underline{x})$ to $\alpha_8(\underline{x})$ terms are nonlinear functions of the state of the system and the payload it carries. Among other factors, they model the effects of the inter-axis dynamic coupling joint friction and changing inertia due to payload and system geometry. K_r is a two by two matrix with elements k_{rij} and K_x is a two by four control gain matrix with elements k_{xij} To provide unity position feedback k_{r11} was set equal to k_{x11} and k_{r22} equal to k_{x23}. The unknown parameter vector for the system becomes:

$$\underline{\alpha}(\underline{x},K_x,K_r)=[-k_{x11}\alpha_1'+k_{x21}\alpha_2',\ -k_{x12}\alpha_2+k_{x22}\alpha_2',$$
$$-k_{x13}\alpha_1'+k_{x23}\alpha_2',-k_{x14}\alpha_1'+k_{x24}\alpha_2'+\alpha_4',\ k_{x11}\alpha_5'-k_{x21}\alpha_6', \qquad (11)$$
$$k_{x12}\alpha_5'-k_{x22}\alpha_6'+\alpha_7',\ k_{x13}\alpha_5'-k_{x23}\alpha_6',\ k_{x14}\alpha_5'-k_{x24}\alpha_6'+\alpha_8']$$

The model selected is that of a linear constant coefficient dynamic system, or:

$$\begin{bmatrix} y_1 \\ y_2 \\ y_3 \\ y_4 \end{bmatrix} = \begin{bmatrix} 0 & 1 & 0 & 0 \\ a_1 & a_2 & a_3 & a_4 \\ 0 & 0 & 0 & 1 \\ a_5 & a_6 & a_7 & a_8 \end{bmatrix} \begin{bmatrix} y_1 \\ y_2 \\ y_3 \\ y_4 \end{bmatrix} + \begin{bmatrix} 0 & 0 \\ -a_1 & 0 \\ 0 & 0 \\ 0 & -a_7 \end{bmatrix} \begin{bmatrix} r_1 \\ r_2 \end{bmatrix} \qquad (12)$$

Choosing a_3, a_4, a_5 and a_6 to be zero, the model becomes uncoupled. The model has zero elements in locations where the system does not, due to its assumed decoupled structure. One of the tasks of the adaptive algorithm is to change the k_x's and k_r's as a function of time so as to make these terms approach zero, while making the other terms approximate the selected model constants.

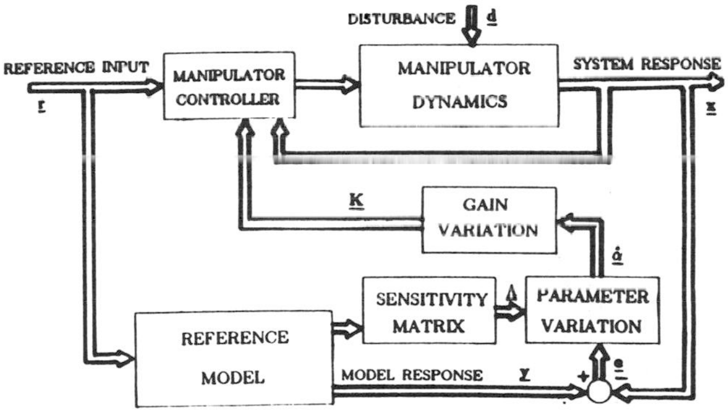

Fig. 1. MIMO Adaptive Algorithm.

It is not always possible to do this exactly, but only in a manner in which $V(\underline{e})$ will be minimized. The vector of selected model parameters is

$$\underline{a} = [\underline{a}_1, \underline{a}_2, \underline{a}_3, \underline{a}_4, \underline{a}_5, \underline{a}_6, \underline{a}_7, \underline{a}_8]^T \qquad (13)$$

Using equation (12) to evaluate equation (8) results in the following matrix sensitivity equation:

$$\dot{\Lambda} = \begin{bmatrix} 0 & 1 & 0 & 0 \\ a_1 & a_2 & 0 & 0 \\ 0 & 0 & 0 & 1 \\ 0 & 0 & a_6 & a_7 \end{bmatrix} \Lambda + \begin{bmatrix} 0 & 0 & 0 & 0 & 0 & 0 & 0 & 0 \\ y_1-r_1 & y_2 & y_3-r_2 & y_4 & 0 & 0 & 0 & 0 \\ 0 & 0 & 0 & 0 & 0 & 0 & 0 & 0 \\ 0 & 0 & 0 & 0 & y_1-r_1 & y_2 & y_3-y_2 & y_4 \end{bmatrix} \qquad (14)$$

The response of the model from the solution of equation (12), to any input becomes the forcing terms in equation (14). The solution of equation (14) yields $\Lambda(t)$ which can be used in equation (9) with the measured errors to find $\dot{\underline{\alpha}}(t)$. The final task in the application of the algorithm is to calculate the $\dot{K}_x(t)$ which will produce the desired $\dot{\underline{\alpha}}(t)$.

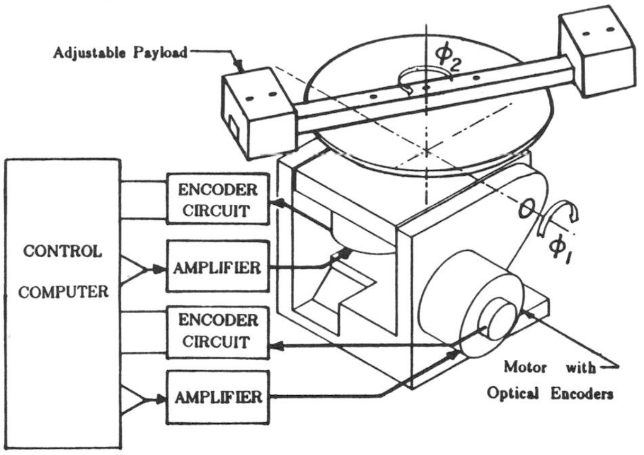

Fig. 2. Two Degree of Freedom Robotic Positioning Device.

Following [Donalson and Leondes, 1963], it is assumed that the parameters of the system, the $\underline{\alpha}$'s', change slowly as compared to the adaption process. It has been shown that while this assumtption is useful in developing this form of adaptive algorithm, in practice, it is not necessary for adequate performance of the algorithm [Dubowsky and Desforges, 1979]. With this assumption and the assumption that the adaptive algorithm causes the system parameters to remain close to the model, differentiating (11) yields:

$$\dot{k}_{x11} \approx \frac{k_{x13}\dot{\alpha}_5}{a_7} + \frac{k_{x11}\dot{\alpha}_1}{a_1} \qquad \dot{k}_{x21} \approx \frac{k_{x23}\dot{\alpha}_5}{a_7} + \frac{k_{x21}\dot{\alpha}_1}{a_1}$$

$$\dot{k}_{x12} \approx \frac{k_{x13}\dot{\alpha}_6}{a_7} + \frac{k_{x11}\dot{\alpha}_2}{a_1} \qquad \dot{k}_{x22} \approx \frac{k_{x23}\dot{\alpha}_6}{a_7} + \frac{k_{x21}\dot{\alpha}_2}{a_1}$$

$$\dot{k}_{x13} \approx \frac{k_{x13}\dot{\alpha}_7}{a_7} + \frac{k_{x11}\dot{\alpha}_3}{a_1} \qquad \dot{k}_{x23} \approx \frac{k_{x23}\dot{\alpha}_7}{a_7} + \frac{k_{x21}\dot{\alpha}_3}{a_1}$$

$$\dot{k}_{x14} \approx \frac{k_{x13}\dot{\alpha}_8}{a_7} + \frac{k_{x11}\dot{\alpha}_4}{a_1} \qquad \dot{k}_{x24} \approx \frac{k_{x23}\dot{\alpha}_8}{a_7} + \frac{k_{x21}\dot{\alpha}_4}{a_1}$$

These equations can be integrated forward in time to obtain the time varying feedback gains for the system which allows it to follow the behavior of the selected model.

The algorithm equations were put in discrete form for digital computer implementation as described in [Dubowsky, 1981]. Additional simplificiations to the algorithm were made for use in the experimental studies. The dynamic coupling between joints was neglected and simple viscous damping was assumed as each joint. The controller at each joint provides Proportional plus Derivative (PD) control. Following the same procedure a Proportional Integral Derivative (PID) MRAC was also developed. The PID structure used was the "PDF" type [Phelan, 1977]. In the experimental algorithms Q was chosen so that there were no coupled terms in V(e) and hence only two adaptive gains needed to be considered for each joint. These gains were qpi and qvi. The elements of Q can be written as combinations of these two.

Experiments and Simulations

The algorithms were tested on two different devices. One was a two degree-of freedom rotary positioning device (see Fig. 2). The other was a PUMA 500 robotic manipulator (manufactured by Unimation Inc.; see Fig. 3). The two systems are quite similar. Both have geared revolute joints driven by DC servo-motors which are powered by current source analog amplifiers. The dynamic properties of both systems were determined from dynamic tests. Also, both use optical encoders mounted on the motor shafts to provide position and velocity information. The encoder outputs are passed to a circuit which converts the encoder pulses to a sixteen-bit positon count for the control computer. The amplifiers are commanded using an eight-bit digital signal through a D/A converter. A PDP-11/23 minicomputer is used to control the two DOF positioning device. The PUMA was controlled with an Intel 8086 micorprocessor with an 8087 floating point processor, in conjuction with an Intel ICE 80 development system.

The control software for the positioning device was programmed in MACRO-11 assembly language for fast execution. The sampling times for the experiments were 5ms for the PD MRAC and 7ms for the PID MRAC algorithms. For tests in which the two axes were run simultaneously, the sampling times were twice as long. The PUMA algorithms were programmed in PLM86 and then assembled into 8086 assembly language. The PD MRAC algorithm required 2.3ms for execution, and the PID form required 4.4ms. Both systems used reference models with a bandwidth of 10 rad/sec for PD control. The model bandwidth was selected to eliminate any performance degradations due to sampling time and actuator amplifier saturation. The PID model was third order and was chosen to have 1% overshoot and the same saturation step size as the PD model.

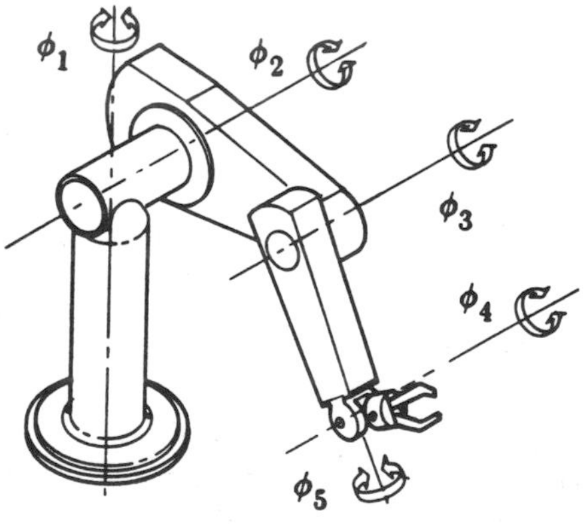

Fig. 3. PUMA Robotic Manipulator.

Simulations of both the table and the robot under adaptive control were run in conjunction with the experimental work. The dynamic model of both the table and the robot were derived assuming rigid links using Lagrange's formulation.

Experimental and Simulation Results

The gains used for the adaptation mechanism, the Q matrix, were bounded by stability analysis. This analysis was also helpful in selecting the values for good performance. Then simulations and the experimental system itself were used to optimize the algorithm's performance.

Fig. 4 shows experimentally measured feedback gains adapting for several sets of adaptive gains. Initially the value of the position feedback gain, for $\emptyset_2$, (k_{x22}) is 5 times lower than that required to match the model. Even for the relatively wide range of Q values, the adaptation can be seen to be quite well behaved. In all three cases k_{x22} is close to its final adapted value before the second corner of the profile occurs. The position and velocity errors were reduced by an order of magnitude after the first cycle. The gains in Fig. 4 do not converge to precisely the same value and oscillate about the average value. This effect is due to the nonlinearities in the physical system, such as friction.

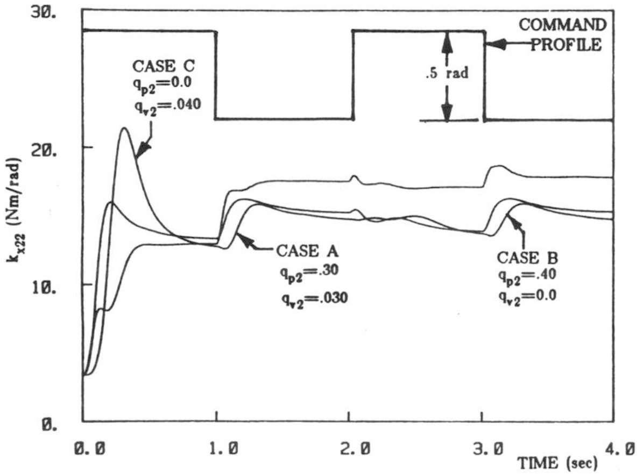

Fig. 4. Effect of adaptive gain selection on the adaptation of joint-2.

As with nearly all adaptive algorithms, the dynamics of the adaptive mechanism are functions of the initial parameter errors and the input. This algorithm is not very sensitive to the intial parameter error as can be seen in Fig. 5. Here, widely differing initial gains are used resulting in very different initial dynamic parameters. The adaptation of the position gain appears uniform in shape and speed.

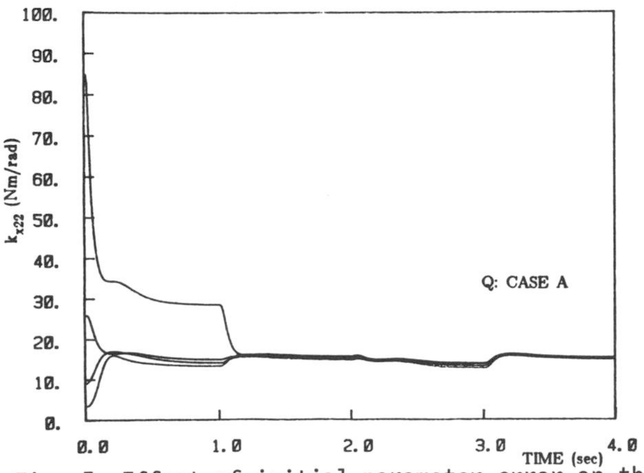

Fig. 5. Effect of initial parameter error on the adaptation of joint-2 for a step input command profile.

The adaptation sensitivity of the system to the input's form and magnitude was also investigated. The magnitude of the input can have a substantial effect on the adaptation performance. As shown in Fig. 6, decreasing the input step size, H, by a factor of two slows adaptation significantly. This effect can be elminated by normalizing Q to the magnitude of the input. Our experimental and simulation results also confirm that the gains can be normalized for a ramp input as well. The sensitivity to the form of the input is more of a problem. This is fundamental to adaptive control. To overcome this problem the use of special learning signals has been suggested [Dubowsky and Desforges,1979]. Since many trajectory planners use low order polynomials and ramps for position reference inputs, it may also be possible to normalize Q for these functions.

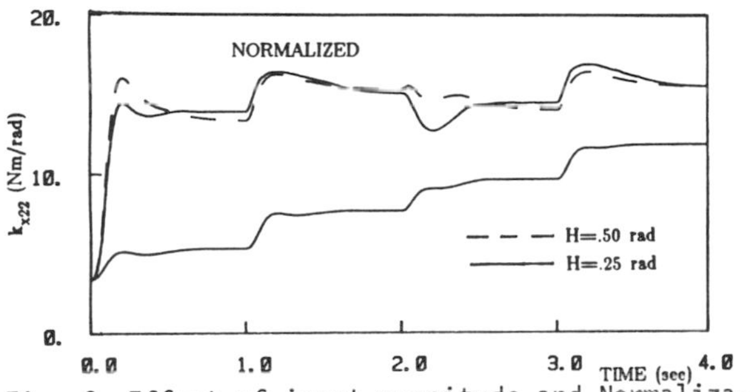

Fig. 6. Effect of input magnitude and Normalization on the adaptation of joint-2 with step command profile.

After selecting the values for Q, the experimental system was used to test the performance of the device under rather extreme conditions. Fig.7 shows an example of the performance of the ϕ_1 axis when a large payload was added causing the effective inertia of the axis to quadruple. Using feedback gains set for the device with no payload, a large overshoot in the system response results. This response is quite different from the reference model which has been selected to be criticially damped. The system response has been clearly degraded. The adaptive control enables the system to conform to the model by the end of the first step. A similar case for a ramp input is shown in Fig. 8. Here the performance of the system with adaptation is corrected before the first dwell is reached.

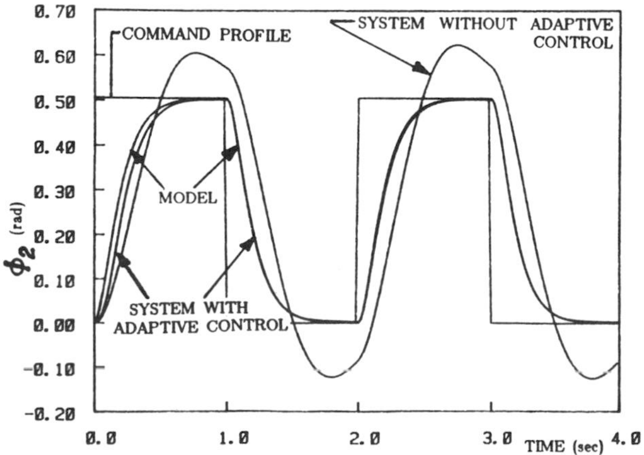

Fig. 7. PD control for joint-2 (with an added payload).

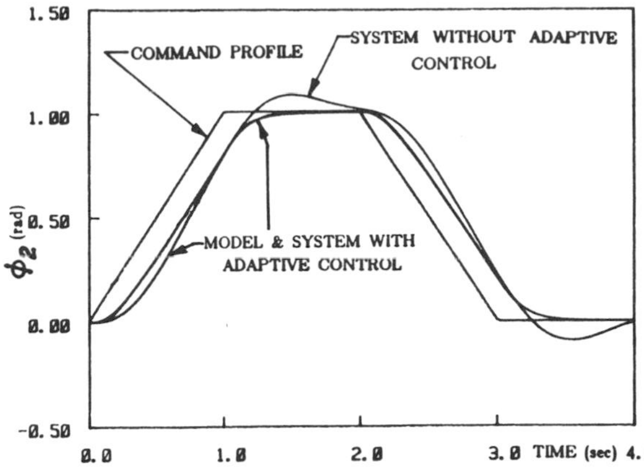

Fig. 8. PD control for joint-2 (ramp command profile) with a payload added.

Fig.'s 8 and 9 are for the motion of a single axis. For many robotic systems (cartesian designs being a notable exception) the dynamics of each axis are highly coupled. This fact is true even for the relatively simple two DOF system used in these tests. To experimentally investigate the adaptive control algorithm's ability to tolerate and compensate for this coupling, a test case was run in which axis 1 was mounted vertically and a payload bar with weights at each end was mounted on to axis 2; with the bar initally vertical (the minimum inertia configuration for joint 1). Joint 2 was commanded to move the payload bar to a horizontal position (the maximum inertia configuration for joint 1) with a ramp profile. At the same time joint 1 was commanded to follow a ramp profile with an amplitude of .5rad at .5rad/s. During this maneuver the effective inertia varies from a minimum to a maximum sinusoidally. Fig. 9 shows the performance for this axis. Without adaptation significant overshoot can be seen while the response with adaption closely follows the model. The maximum position error between the system and the model is 2 1/2 times larger for the nonadaptive case. At the same time the ϕ_1 axis is adapting, the ϕ_2 axis is adapting for the added payload. The response for this axis is nearly identical to the single axis result shown in Fig. 8. The error between the system and the model for the ϕ_2 axis is shown in Fig. 10. Fig. 11 shows simulation results for this case. Comparing these results Fig. 9 clearly shows the ability of the simulation to predict the

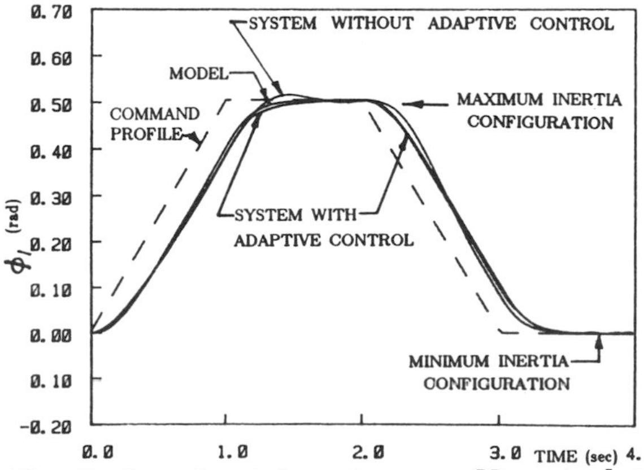

Fig. 9. Experimental performance PD control of joint-2 for multi-axis test case.

experimental results when it is based on accurately measured data.

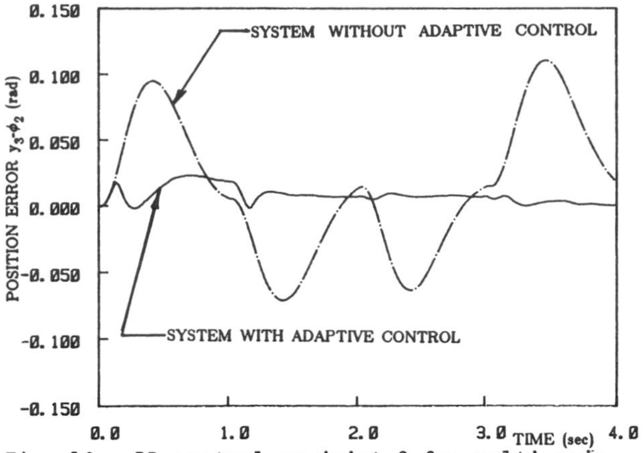

Fig. 10. PD control on joint-2 for multi-axis test case.

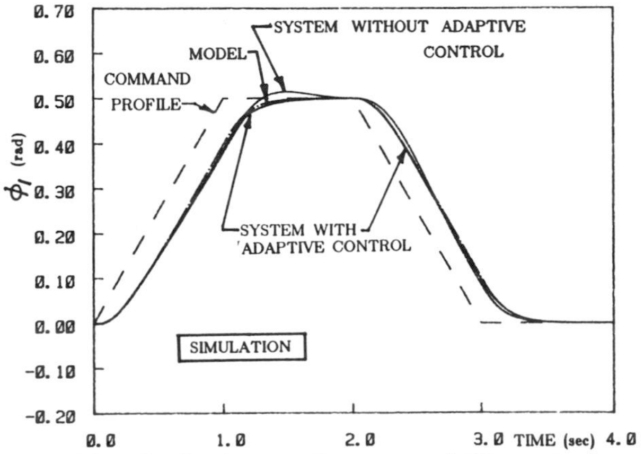

Fig. 11. Simulation performance of PD control on joint-1 for multi-axis test case.

Unmodelled disturbances, such as gravity and joint friction, can degrade manipulator performance. In the above experimental results the joint friction was modelled and used as a dynamic feedforward signal. However, it is not always possible to accurately compensate for joint friction. Integral adaptive control, the PID algorithm, was investigated as an alternative to the feedfoward approach. Fig 12 shows the performance of the PD MRAC without friction compensation as it is used to adapt to a payload change. A large steady state error results. Fig. 13 shows the same case with PID control. This performance closely matches the model, having no steady state error as well as a faster settling time. It would appear that this form of adaptive control offers significant advantages in cases where joint friction is difficult to model.

Fig. 14 shows the result of gravitational disturbances. Here a very large unbalanced payload was attached to axis 2 and axis 1 was tilted so that gravity applied a large varying disturbance to axis 2. Joint 2 was then commanded to move from bottom dead center with a step input. This performance shows serious degradation caused by the disturbance for both the adapting and nonadapting cases. In Fig. 15 the same test is performed with the adaptive PID controller and the error is dramaticaly reduced.

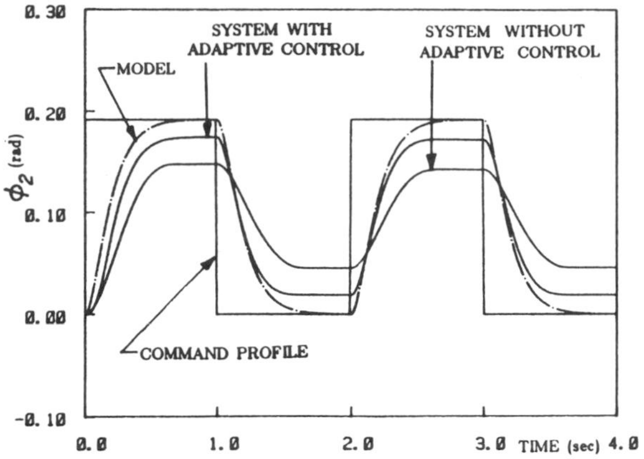

Fig. 12. PD control on joint-2 without Friction compensation.

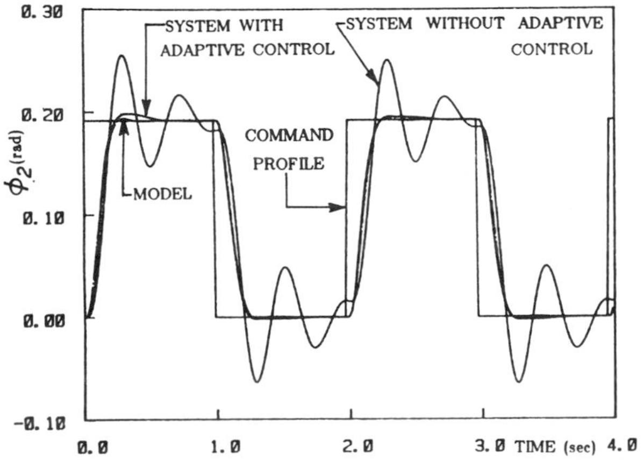

Fig. 13. PDF control on joint-2 without Friction Compensation

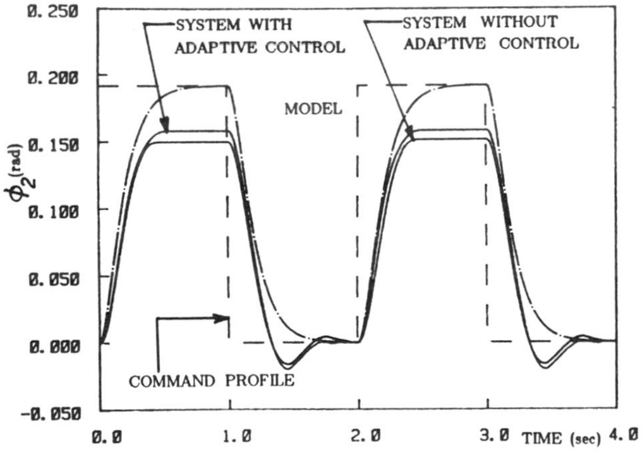

Fig. 14. PD control of joint-2 with unbalanced weight.

The MRAC algorithm was also implemented on the PUMA robotic manipulator. This work was done with the technical cooperation and support of the Westinghouse Corporation, Defense Systems Center, Baltimore, Maryland. The objective was to determine if the properties of commercial quality systems, such as gear train backlash, would degrade the performance of the MRAC algorithm. Many of the tests performed on the two DOF device were repeated using the PUMA with very similar results. The motors of the PUMA operate through very high gear ratios and therefore the effects of friction were relatively small. Hence, no friction compensation was needed.

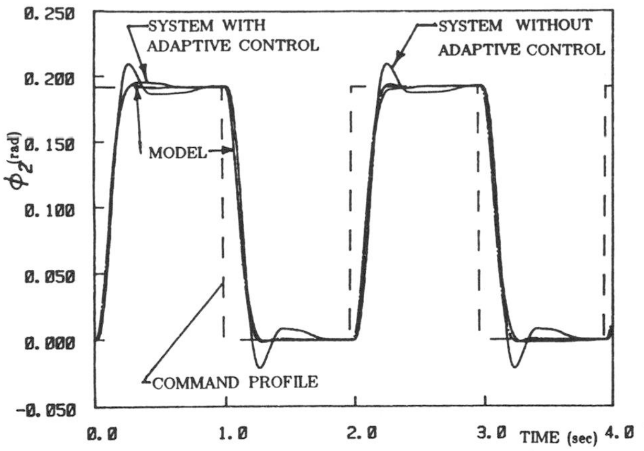

Fig. 15. PDF control of joint-2 with unbalance weight.

Fig. 16a shows the response of the PUMA $\emptyset_1$ axis when it matches a .707 of critically damped reference model. Fig. 16b shows the axis response to a step command profile without adaptive control, when the feedback gains are set low. For this straight out and horizontal configuration of the manipulator, the response is quite underdamped and does not match the model well. In Fig. 16c the adaptive control is enabled and the response converges to that of the model. In this case the adaptation gains, Q, have been intentionally set quite low so that the changing system response could be observed. The adapting position gain is shown in Fig. 17. The adaptive gains could easily be adjusted so that virtually no differences between the system and the model can be seen , even on the first step. Fig. 18 shows the adapting gains for such a case. Here the initial position gain is lowered by a factor of nearly 6. By the first dwell both gains are nearly at their steady state values. Similar results have been demonstrated for cases where the initial feedback gains were set too high. The gains were reduced smoothly and quickly. Other cases were done in which the manipulator adapted for changes in its configuration and payload. Payloads of up to 10kg were used which drastically degraded the performance of the system without adaptive control. The feedback gains were lowered and raised by the adaptive algorithm, as required to match the system performance to its model.

Conclusions

This paper has shown that an adaptive control algorithm can signficantly improve the performance of robotic manipulators over that obtained using conventional control. The experimental results demonstrate that the algorithm is practical for the control of commercial quality manipulators with relatively modest control computers. It has also been shown that disturbances such as joint friction and gravity, can degraded the performance of manipulator systems and should be considered in the development of their control systems. Results have been shown which demonstrate that these disturbances can be effectively compensated for using an integral adaptive control algorithm. It has also shown that simulations can be an effective aid in the design of manipulator

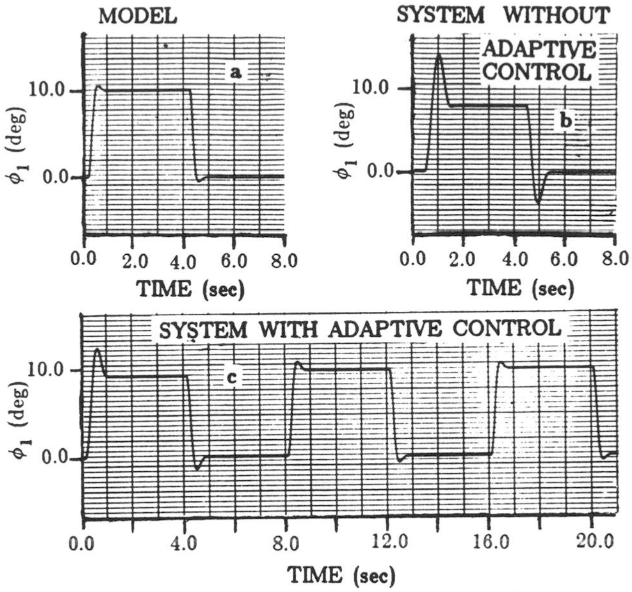

Fig. 16. PUMA response under adaptive and non-adaptive control.

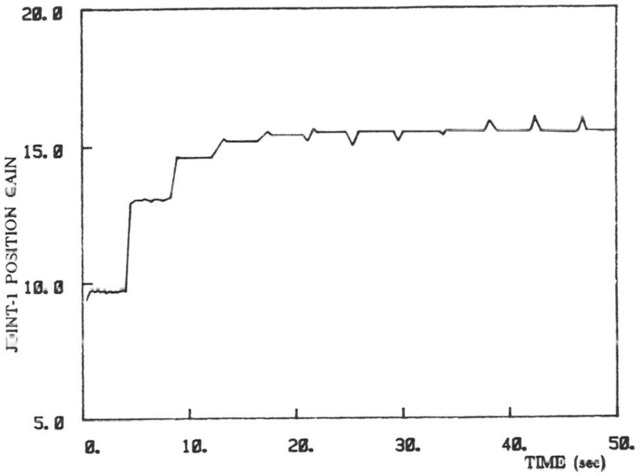

Fig. 17. PUMA slow gain adaptation.

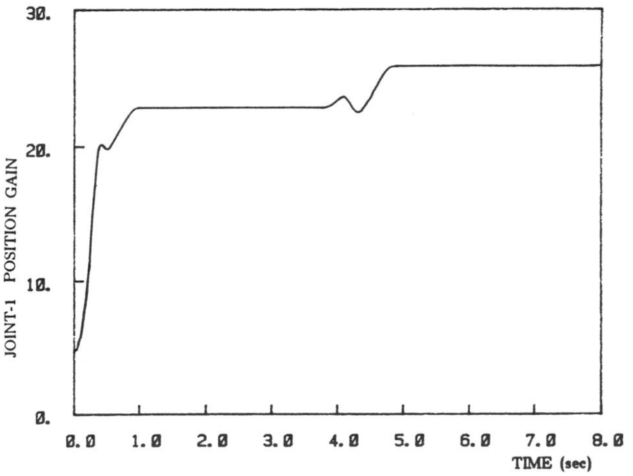

Fig. 18. PUMA fast gain adaptation.

controls when they are used in concert with experimental studies and based on accurately measured system parameters.

Acknowledgements

The authors would like to acknowledge the technical cooperation and support for this study from the Digital Equipment Corp and the Westinghouse Electric Corp. The technical contribution of J. Whalely, of M.I.T., was also invaluable.

References

Bobrow, J.E., Dubowsky, S., and Gibson, J.S., 1983. On the Optimal Control of Robotic Manipulators with Actuator Constraints, Proc. American Cont. Conf., San Francisco, CA

Brogan, W.L., 1974. Modern Control Theory, Quantum Pub., New York,NY.

Donalson, D.D. and Leondes, C.T. 1963. A Model Referenced Parameter Tracking Technique for Adaptive Control Systems, IEEE Trans. on Applications and Industry, 82;68, pp. 241-262.

Dubowsky, S. 1981. On the Adaptive Control of Robotic Manipulators: The Discrete Time Case, Proc.1981 Joint Auto Cont. Conf., Charlottesville, VA.

Dubowsky, S. 1981. On the Dynamics of Computer Controlled Robotic Manipulators, Proc.IV CISM-IFTOMM Sym. On the Theory and Practice of Robots and Manupulators, Warsaw, Poland.

Dubowsky, S., and DesForges, D.T. 1979. The Application of Model Referenced Adaptive Control to Robotic Manipulators, J of Dynamic Sytems, Measurement, and Control, 101:3, pp. 193-200.

Dubowsky, S., and Shiller, Z. 1984. Optimal Dynamic Trajectories for Robotic Manipulators, Proc.V CISM-IFToMM Sym. On the Theory and Practice of Robots and Manipulators, Udine, Italy.

Freund, E. 1982. Fast Nonlinear Control with Arbitrary Pole Placement for Industrial Robots and Manipulators, Intern'l J. of Robotics Research, 1:1, pp.65-78.

Horowitz, R., and Tomizuka, M. 1980. An Adaptive Control Scheme for Mechanical Manipulators - Compensation of Nonlinearity and Decoupling Control, ASME Paper No. 80-Wa/DSC-6.

Kahn, M.E., and Roth, B. 1971. The Near-Minimum-Time Control of Open-Loop Articulated Kinematic Chains, J. of Dyn Systems, Measurement, and Cont, 93:3 pp. 164-171.

Koivo, A.J., and Guo, T.H. 1983. Adaptive Linear Controller for Robotic Manipulators, IEEE Trans. on Auto Cont, AC-28:2, pp. 162-170.

Landau, I.D. 1974. A Survey of Model Reference Adaptive Techniques--Theory and Applications, Automatica, 10, pp.353-379.

LeBorgne, M, Ibarra, J.M. Espiau, B. 1981. Adaptive Control of High Velocity Manipulators, Proc. 11th ISIR, Tokyo, Japan.

Lee, C.S.G., and Lee, B.H. 1984. Resolved Motion Adaptive Control for Mechanical Manipulators, Proc. 1984 ACC, San Diego, CA

Luh, J.Y.S., Walker, M. W., and Paul, R.P.C. Resolved Acceleration Control of Mechanical Manipulators, IEEE Trans. on Automatic Control, AC-25:3, pp. 468-474.

National Research Council 1983. Applications of Robotics and Artificial Intelligence to Reduce Risk and Improve Effectiveness: A Study for the United States Army, National Academy Press, Washington, D.C.

Papadopoulos, E.G., 1983. An Investigation of Model Reference Adaptive Control Algorithms for Manufacturing Processes, MS thesis, M.I.T., Dept. of Mech. Engr. , Cambridge, MA

Phelan, R.M., 1977. Automatic Control Systems, Cornell University Press, Ithaca, NY

Raibert, M.H. and Horn, B.K.P., 1978. Manipulator Control Using Configuration Space Method, The Industrial Robot, 5:2, pp. 69-73

Rhors, C.E., Valvani, L., Athans, M., and Stein, G. 1982. Robustness of Adaptive Control Algorithm in the Presence of Unmodelled Dynamics, Proc. 21st IEEE Conf. on Decision and Control, Orlando, Florida.

Takegaki, M., and Arimoto, S. 1981. An Adaptive Trajectory Control of Manipulators, Inter Jour of Control, 34:2, pp. 219-230.

Vukobratovic, M., and Kircanski, N. 1982. An Engineering Concept of Adaptive Control for Manipulation Robots via Parametric Sensitivity Analysis, Bulletin T. LXXXI de l'Academie Serbe des Sciences et des Arts, Classe des Sciences Techniques, 20, pp. 24-39.

CAN MECHANICAL ROBOTS LEARN BY THEMSELVES ?

Suguru Arimoto, Sadao Kawamura,
and Fumio Miyazaki

Department of Mechanical Engineering
Faculty of Engineering Science
Osaka University
Toyonaka, Osaka, 560 Japan

In response to this question, an affirmative answer is given by proposing a betterment process for a motion control of mechanical robots. The process has a function of self learning through an iterative structure such that the input to joint actuators at the next (k+1)th operation consists of the present (k)th input plus an error modification term composed of the derivative difference between the motion trajectory at the (k)th operation and the given desired motion trajectory. It is shown that the betterment process betters the next operation of a robot in a certain sense and the motion trajectory converges eventually the given desired one through automatically repeated operations. To take a sight of learning abilities of the robot, numerical results by computer simulation are given, together with some results on the experiment carried out by employing a three-link mechanical arm.

1. Introduction

It has been widely believed that human beings have the ability to learn much from experience but mechanical robots do not. For that matter, the control of present industrial robots is subject to the scheme of so called "teaching and playback". Without being taught by human operators, industrial robots can not work fully at a prescribed task. However, are mechanical robots really unable to learn by themselves anything from the past operation data ?

In response to this question, we present an affirmative answer in case of motion control of robots. We propose a fundamental principle of self-learning for motion control, called "betterment process", which makes mechanical manipulators learn without help of human operators a prescribed form of motion through self training or automatically repeated operations. In general, a betterment process for a given dynamic system is composed of an iterative learning structure as depicted in Fig.1. A desired output $\mathbf{y}_d(t)$ which in case of manipulators may correspond to a prescribed motion trajectory is given in advance as a vector-valued function in time over a finite time interval $t\varepsilon[0, T]$ and stored in LSI RAM's as a set of densely sampled digital data. Given a control input $\mathbf{u}_k(t)$ that excites the system at the (k)th operation and eventuates in an output response $\mathbf{y}_k(t)$, then it may arise a difference from the desired output $\mathbf{y}_d(t)$ as defined by

$$\mathbf{e}_k(t) = \mathbf{y}_d(t) - \mathbf{y}_k(t), \qquad t\varepsilon[0, T]$$

which is called the error at the (k)th operation. The essence of the proposed betterment process lies in a simple rule that forms the next (k+1)th input $\mathbf{u}_{k+1}(t)$ on the basis of updated data on previous inputs and errors, that is,

$$\mathbf{u}_{k+1}(t) = \mathbf{u}_k(t) + \Gamma \frac{d}{dt} \mathbf{e}_k(t)$$

where Γ is a constant matrix. The differentiation of the error plays an essential role in the process and the gain matrix Γ can be chosen arbitrarily to some extent and fixed constant without knowing the description of system dynamics equation. In case of linear time-invariant or time-varying systems, it has already been shown [Arimoto et al, 1984a] that the next input $\mathbf{u}_{k+1}$ betters the system performance in comparison with the previous input $\mathbf{u}_k(t)$. More detailedly, it is proved that, for a certain kind of function norm, $\|\dot{\mathbf{e}}_{k+1}\|$ becomes less than $\|\dot{\mathbf{e}}_k\|$ and hence $\mathbf{y}_k(t)$ approaches the desired output $\mathbf{y}_d(t)$ uniformly in $t\varepsilon[0, T]$ as $k \to \infty$ by repeating the operation. This result is further extended to a class of non-linear dynamical systems, whose motion is subject to the equation

$$\begin{cases} \dot{\mathbf{x}} = \mathbf{f}(\mathbf{x}) + B\mathbf{u}, \\ \mathbf{y} = C\mathbf{x}, \end{cases} \qquad (1)$$

under appropriate conditions on matrix BC and non-linear function $\mathbf{f}(\mathbf{x})$ [Arimoto et al, 1984b]. Unfortunately, the dynamics equation that governs the motion of robot manipulators can not be represented by the form of equation (1). Instead of this, robot dynamics may be expressed in a form

$$\begin{cases} \dot{\mathbf{x}} = \mathbf{f}(\mathbf{x}) + B\mathbf{u}, \\ \mathbf{y} = C(\mathbf{x})\mathbf{x}, \end{cases} \qquad (2)$$

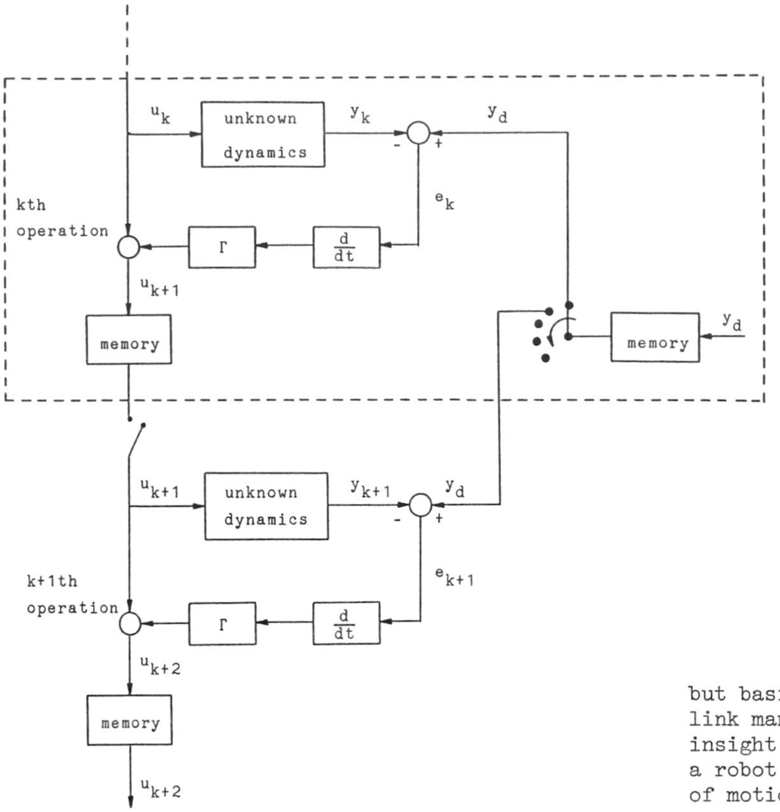

Fig. 1 Betterment process

or

$$\begin{cases} \dot{z} = g(z) + B(z)u, \\ y = Cz, \end{cases} \tag{3}$$

where $C(x)$ or $B(z)$ depends on state vector x or z, respectively.

In this paper we show that the betterment process designed for the control system of robot manipulators converges also in a similar sense to that explained above. It is then concluded that the motion trajectory $\theta_k(t)$ or $\dot{\theta}_k(t)$ described by the joint-angle coordinates or angular velocity coordinates approaches the prescribed desired trajectory $\theta_d(t)$ or $\dot{\theta}_d(t)$ as $k \to \infty$ by repeating the operation. Based on this result we discuss in Section 4 the ability for mechanical robots to acquire a prescribed motion form. To take a sight of such learning abilities, we show results of computer simulations on a three-link manipulator model, together with preliminary results on the experiments carried out by using a three-link mechanical robot arm. Further problems to be explored in relation to this learning control scheme will be discussed in a concluding section.

2. Betterment Process for Robot Manipulators

We consider generally a serial-link robot manipulator with n degrees of freedom. As a special

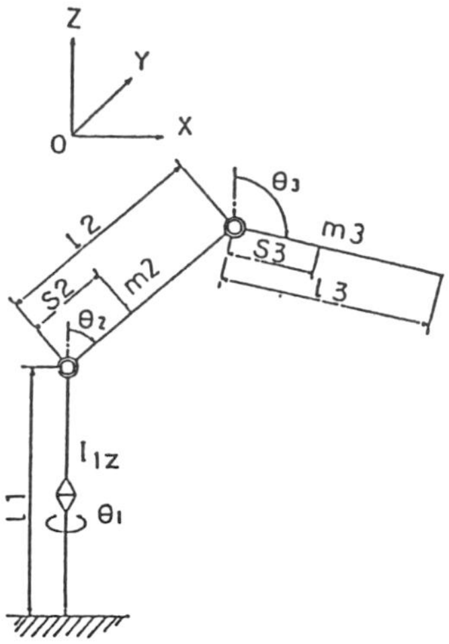

Fig.2 Three-link arm model

but basic example, we some time deal with a three link manipulator as shown in Fig.2, to gain an insight into the problem. The dynamics of such a robot system is described by a Lagrange equation of motion in the following form:

$$\frac{d}{dt}\frac{\partial L}{\partial \dot{\theta}} - \frac{\partial L}{\partial \theta} = u, \tag{4}$$

where L denotes the Lagrangian defined as $L = K-P$, the difference between the kinetic energy K and the potential energy P of the robot system, $\theta = (\theta_1, \ldots, \theta_n)$ denotes the joint-angle coordinates, $\dot{\theta} = d\theta/dt$ the angular velocity coordinates, and $u = (u_1, \ldots, u_n)$ the generalized torque coordinates. The kinetic energy K can be written in general as

$$K = \frac{1}{2}\dot{\theta}^T R(\theta)\dot{\theta} \tag{5}$$

where $R(\theta)$ is real symmetric and called an inertia matrix. In additional, it is well known [Greenwood, 1977] that each entry of $R(\theta)$ is a constant or a trigonometric function in $\theta_1, \ldots, \theta_n$ and $R(\theta)$ itself is positive definite for all θ for a wide class of serial-link manipulators. Hence it is possible to assume that

$$\alpha I_n \leqq R(\theta) \leqq \beta I_n, \tag{6}$$

where α and β are positive constants, I_n is the nxn identity matrix, and the inequality $X \leqq Y$ means the nonnegative definiteness of matrix Y-X. It should be also noted that the potential energy P is independent of $\dot{\theta}$ and in fact a simple combination of trigonometric functions in $\theta_1, \ldots, \theta_n$ only. Next, let $q = R(\theta)$ and call it the generalixed angular velocity coordinates. Then, equation (3) can be written in a form of state equation as

$$\begin{cases} \dot{\theta} = R^{-1}(\theta)q, \\ \dot{q} = -\frac{\partial \bar{K}}{\partial \theta} - \frac{\partial P}{\partial \theta} + u, \end{cases} \tag{7}$$

where

$$\overline{K} = \frac{1}{2} \underset{\sim}{q}^T R^{-1}(\underset{\sim}{\theta})\underset{\sim}{q}. \tag{8}$$

Now, suppose that a desired motion trajectory along which the manipulator must move is given in terms of a time evolution of the joint-angle coordinates as $\theta = \theta_d(t)$ for a finite time interval [0, T]. We assume that $\underset{\sim}{\theta}_d(t)$ is twice continuously differentiable, or else we assume that a continuously differentiable function $\dot{\theta}_d(t)$ is given, from which $\underset{\sim}{\theta}_d(t)$ can be produced through integration. If it is possible to excite each joint through the corresponding actuator by a control rule

$$\underset{\sim}{u} = \frac{\partial P}{\partial \underset{\sim}{\theta}} - A(\underset{\sim}{\theta} - \underset{\sim}{\theta}_d) - B(\dot{\underset{\sim}{\theta}} - \dot{\underset{\sim}{\theta}}_d) + \underset{\sim}{v}, \tag{9}$$

then the motion of the manipulator is subject to the state equation

$$\begin{cases} \dot{\underset{\sim}{\theta}} = R^{-1}(\underset{\sim}{\theta})\underset{\sim}{q}, \\ \dot{\underset{\sim}{q}} = -\dfrac{\partial \overline{K}}{\partial \underset{\sim}{\theta}} - A(\underset{\sim}{\theta} - \underset{\sim}{\theta}_d) - B(\dot{\underset{\sim}{\theta}} - \dot{\underset{\sim}{\theta}}_d) + \underset{\sim}{v}, \\ \quad = -\dfrac{\partial \overline{K}}{\partial \underset{\sim}{\theta}} - A(\underset{\sim}{\theta} - \underset{\sim}{\theta}_d) - B(R^{-1}(\underset{\sim}{\theta})\underset{\sim}{q} - \dot{\underset{\sim}{\theta}}_d) + \underset{\sim}{v}, \end{cases} \tag{10}$$

where A and B are positive definite constant matrices such as

$$A = \begin{bmatrix} a_1 & & 0 \\ & \ddots & \\ 0 & & a_n \end{bmatrix}, \quad B = \begin{bmatrix} b_1 & & 0 \\ & \ddots & \\ 0 & & b_n \end{bmatrix}.$$

The term $\partial P/\partial \underset{\sim}{\theta}$ in the right hand side of equation (9) means the compensation for the torque due to the gravity and the second and third terms mean the local position feedback and the local angular velocity feedback, respectively. As discussed in a previous paper [Takegaki and Arimoto, 1981 and Miyazaki and Arimoto, 1983], the control law of equation (9) is effective in tracking the prescribed motion trajectory given by $\underset{\sim}{\theta}_d(t)$ or $\dot{\underset{\sim}{\theta}}_d(t)$. However, if at the first operation of the manipulator the control input to the system is set as $\underset{\sim}{v}_1(t) \equiv 0$, the response $\underset{\sim}{\theta}_1(t)$ or $\dot{\underset{\sim}{\theta}}_1(t)$ which is a solution trajectory of the differential equation (7) with input $\underset{\sim}{v}_1(t) \equiv 0$ may differ from the desired trajectory $\underset{\sim}{\theta}_d(t)$ or $\dot{\underset{\sim}{\theta}}_d(t)$. Next we consider a problem to find a better input torque $\underset{\sim}{v}_2(t)$ that actuates the manipulator and achieves a better response $\underset{\sim}{\theta}_2(t)$ or $\dot{\underset{\sim}{\theta}}_2(t)$ in a certain sense. More generally, given an input torque $\underset{\sim}{v}_k(t)$ that excites the manipulator and makes it result in an error

$$\underset{\sim}{e}_k(t) = \dot{\underset{\sim}{\theta}}_d(t) - \dot{\underset{\sim}{\theta}}_k(t), \tag{11}$$

what is a simple rule that constructs a better (k+1)th input torque $\underset{\sim}{v}_{k+1}(t)$ on the basis of only updated data on $\underset{\sim}{v}_k(t)$ and $\underset{\sim}{e}_k(t)$? Here $\underset{\sim}{\theta}_k(t)$ is subject to the equation:

$$\begin{cases} \dot{\underset{\sim}{\theta}}_k = R^{-1}(\underset{\sim}{\theta}_k)\underset{\sim}{q}_k, \\ \dot{\underset{\sim}{q}}_k = -\dfrac{\partial \overline{K}}{\partial \underset{\sim}{\theta}_k} - A(\underset{\sim}{\theta}_k - \underset{\sim}{\theta}_d) - B(R^{-1}(\underset{\sim}{\theta}_k)\underset{\sim}{q}_k - \dot{\underset{\sim}{\theta}}_d) + \underset{\sim}{v}_k(t). \end{cases} \tag{12}$$

For candidates of such a simpler rule, let us consider a process

$$\underset{\sim}{v}_{k+1}(t) = \underset{\sim}{v}_k(t) + \Gamma \frac{d}{dt} \underset{\sim}{e}_k(t), \tag{13}$$

where Γ is an nxn appropriate constant matrix. This recursive relation is worth being called a betterment process as discussed in a previous paper [Arimoto et al, 1984a], if the (k+1)th response $\underset{\sim}{\theta}_{k+1}$ to the input $\underset{\sim}{v}_{k+1}(t)$ achieves a better performance than the previous response $\underset{\sim}{\theta}_k(t)$ in a certain sense.

In what follows, we regard the angular velocity coordinates $\dot{\underset{\sim}{\theta}}(t)$ as an output vector $\underset{\sim}{y}(t)$, provided that each component of $\dot{\underset{\sim}{\theta}}$ can be measured directly by a tacho-generator at the corresponding joint. This means

$$\underset{\sim}{y}_k(t) = R^{-1}(\underset{\sim}{\theta}_k(t))\underset{\sim}{q}_k(t) \tag{14}$$

and thereby equation (11) can be rewritten as

$$\underset{\sim}{e}_k(t) = \underset{\sim}{y}_d(t) - \underset{\sim}{y}_k(t), \tag{15}$$

where $\underset{\sim}{y}_d(t) = \dot{\underset{\sim}{\theta}}_d(t)$. The betterment process composed of iterative equations (12) to (15) is depicted in Fig.3.

3. Convergence of the Betterment Process for Robot Manipulators

Now we show the convergence of the iterative

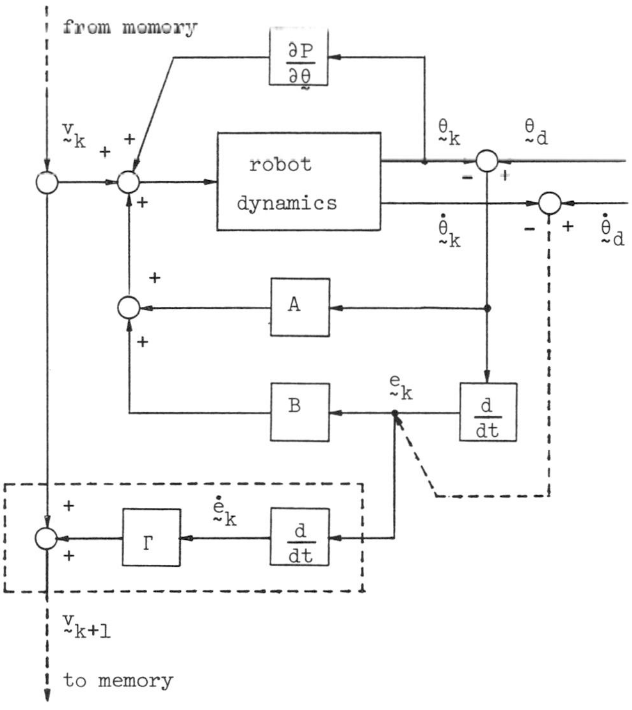

Fig.3 Betterment process for learning control of mechanical robots

betterment process, that is, the convergence of $\underset{\sim}{y}_k(t)$ $(=\dot{\underset{\sim}{\theta}}_k(t))$ and $\underset{\sim}{\theta}_k(t)$ to $\underset{\sim}{y}_d(t)$ $(=\dot{\underset{\sim}{\theta}}_d(t))$ and $\underset{\sim}{\theta}_d(t)$, respectively, with $k\to\infty$. To do this, we first note that equation (10) can be expressed in a form

$$\dot{\underset{\sim}{x}} = \underset{\sim}{f}(\underset{\sim}{x}) + c_1\underset{\sim}{\theta}_d + c_2\dot{\underset{\sim}{\theta}}_d + c_3\underset{\sim}{v} \tag{16}$$

by introducing a state vector $\underset{\sim}{x} = (\underset{\sim}{\theta}, \underset{\sim}{q})$. Second we note that $\underset{\sim}{f}(\underset{\sim}{x})$ is Lipschitz continuous in a certain domain $\tilde{X}\subseteq R^n x R^n$ such that

$$\|\underset{\sim}{f}(\underset{\sim}{x}) - \underset{\sim}{f}(\underset{\sim}{x}')\|_\infty \leqq \rho\|\underset{\sim}{x} - \underset{\sim}{x}'\|_\infty \tag{17}$$

for any $\underset{\sim}{x}, \underset{\sim}{x}'\varepsilon X$, where ρ is a positive constant, because the inertia matrix $R(\theta)$ is composed of trigonometric functions in θ and satisfies a good condition described by equation (6). Here the vector norm is defined as

$$\|\underset{\sim}{x}\|_\infty = \max_i |x_i|. \tag{18}$$

Now we are in a position to state the main result of this paper in the following way:

<u>Theorem</u> Assume that the difference state vector between the given desired state $\underset{\sim}{x}_d(t) = (\underset{\sim}{\theta}_d(t), R(\underset{\sim}{\theta}_d(t))\dot{\underset{\sim}{\theta}}_d(t))$ and the first response $\underset{\sim}{x}_1(t) = (\underset{\sim}{\theta}_1(t), \underset{\sim}{q}_1(t))$ to the input chosen as $\underset{\sim}{v}_1(t)\equiv 0$ in equation (12) remains in a subdomain $X'(\subseteq X)$. Then, the betterment process composed of equations (12)to (15) converges in a sense that

$$\underset{\sim}{y}_k(t)\longrightarrow \underset{\sim}{y}_d(t) \quad (\dot{\underset{\sim}{\theta}}_k(t)\longrightarrow \dot{\underset{\sim}{\theta}}_d(t)), \tag{19}$$

$$\underset{\sim}{\theta}_k(t)\longrightarrow \underset{\sim}{\theta}_d(t) \tag{20}$$

uniformly in $t\varepsilon[0, T]$ as $k\longrightarrow\infty$, provided that the initial condition

$$\underset{\sim}{\theta}_k(0) = \underset{\sim}{\theta}_d(0), \qquad \dot{\underset{\sim}{\theta}}_k(0) = \dot{\underset{\sim}{\theta}}_d(0) \tag{21}$$

is satisfied at every operation and the inequality

$$\|I_n - \Gamma R^{-1}(\theta)\|_\infty < 1 \tag{22}$$

holds for any $\underset{\sim}{\theta}$, where symbol $\|A\|_\infty$ for a square matrix A means the matrix norm induced by the vector norm $\|x\|_\infty$.

This result will be derived immediately from the use of the following basic relation:

<u>Proposition</u> Under the assumption of the theorem, there exist positive constants γ and λ such that it holds

$$\|R(\underset{\sim}{\theta}_{k+1})\dot{\underset{\sim}{e}}_{k+1}\|_\lambda \leqq \gamma\|R(\underset{\sim}{\theta}_k)\dot{\underset{\sim}{e}}_k\|_\lambda \quad \text{for } k=1,2,\ \ldots \tag{23}$$

and

$$0 \leqq \gamma < 1, \tag{24}$$

where symbol $\|\underset{\sim}{h}\|_\lambda$ means the norm for a vector-valued function $\underset{\sim}{h}(t)$ over $t\varepsilon[0, T]$ as defined

$$\|\underset{\sim}{h}\|_\lambda = \sup_{t\varepsilon[0,T]} \|e^{-\lambda t}\underset{\sim}{h}(t)\|_\infty. \tag{25}$$

This will be proved in Appendix. Recalling that the inertia matrix $R(\theta)$ satisfies equation (6), we have from equation (23)

$$\alpha\|\dot{\underset{\sim}{e}}_k\|_\lambda \leqq \|R(\underset{\sim}{\theta}_k)\dot{\underset{\sim}{e}}_k\|_\lambda \leqq \gamma^k\|R(\underset{\sim}{\theta}_1)\dot{\underset{\sim}{e}}_1\|_\lambda$$
$$\leqq \beta\gamma^k\|\dot{\underset{\sim}{e}}_1\|_\lambda \longrightarrow 0 \quad \text{as } k\longrightarrow\infty, \tag{26}$$

which implies

$$\sup_{t\varepsilon[0,T]} e^{-\lambda t}\|\dot{\underset{\sim}{\theta}}_d(t) - \dot{\underset{\sim}{\theta}}_k(t)\|_\infty \longrightarrow 0 \quad \text{as } k\longrightarrow\infty. \tag{27}$$

This proves equation (19). Finally, the convergence of equation (19) together with the condition of equation (21) implies the convergence of equation (20). Thus the theorem has been proved.

It should be noted that the condition of equation (22) is not so restricted, since it is possible to choose many Γ's owing to such a good property of $R(\underset{\sim}{\theta})$ as shown in inequality (6).

4. <u>Abilities to Acquire a Prescribed Motion Form</u>

It has been theoretically proved by using the proposed betterment process that even mechanical robots are able to acquire a prescribed motion form autonomously through repeated operations. However, for practical purposes of implementing this learning mechanism in robots, there are many important problems to be discussed and explored. The first is concerned with the condition that the initial state of a robot must satisfy at every beginning of operations. Fortunately,industrial robots manufactured recently have shown a remarkable repeating precision in positioning. In other words, the initial condition $\underset{\sim}{\theta}_k(0)=\underset{\sim}{\theta}_d(0)$ is realized usually with high precision. In additional, it is ordinarily possible to assume that the robot is still right before starting the maneuvering. This means $\dot{\underset{\sim}{\theta}}_k(0)=0$ for all k which satisfies automatically the remaining half of the initial condition in Theorem if a desired angular velocity is set at the initial time as $\dot{\underset{\sim}{\theta}}_d(0)=0$.

The second problem is the existence of unknown disturbances in the robot dynamics mainly due to frictional torques. However, even if there is an unknown disturbance $\underset{\sim}{f}(\underset{\sim}{\theta}, \underset{\sim}{q})$ in equation (10) or (12), the convergence of the betterment process is also assured, as far as term $\underset{\sim}{f}(\underset{\sim}{\theta}, \underset{\sim}{q})$ satisfies a Lipschitz condition such that

$$\|\underset{\sim}{f}(\underset{\sim}{\theta}, \underset{\sim}{q}) - \underset{\sim}{f}(\underset{\sim}{\theta}', \underset{\sim}{q}')\|_\infty \leqq \rho_1\|\underset{\sim}{\theta} - \underset{\sim}{\theta}'\|_\infty + \rho_2\|\underset{\sim}{q} - \underset{\sim}{q}'\|_\infty \tag{28}$$

with constants ρ_1 and ρ_2 for any pair $(\underset{\sim}{\theta}, \underset{\sim}{q})$ and $(\underset{\sim}{\theta}', \underset{\sim}{q}')$ in a domain $X(\subseteq R^n x R^n)$.

The third problem is concerned with servo-loops for joint-actuators. If a voltage-controlled servo-motor is used at one of actuators, then the torque generated is expressed as

$$T = \alpha_o\dot{\theta} + \beta_o v \tag{29}$$

Link No.	m[kg]	l[m]	s[m]	$I_x[kgm^2]$	$I_y[kgm^2]$	$I_z[kgm^2]$
1	——	0.63	——	——	——	0.022
2	5.4	0.40	0.13	0.062	0.052	0.013
3	3.6	0.40	0.17	0.046	0.041	0.0048

Table 1 Physical parameters of the arm model shown in Fig.2

with constants α_o and β_o, if the inductance in the armature circuit is negligibly small. In this equation, v is the input voltage and the term of $\dot{\theta}$ comes from a voltage-drop due to the inverse electromotive force. In this case, we can incorporate equation (29) with equation (10) by putting u=T and regard the voltage v as the control input, instead of u. Then it is possible to construct a betterment process in a similar way to Fig.3 and prove the convergency of the process. This proof of convergency can be extended to the case that the dynamics of servo-loops are taken into consideration when the armature inductance can not be ignored.

Finally we discuss a problem of implementation of the differential operator d/dt in a digital system. Formally the continuous-time operator of differentiation may be replaced with a difference operator as shown

$$\dot{x}_i = [x((i+1)\Delta t) - x(i\Delta t)]/\Delta t \tag{30}$$

in a micro-computer. However, the measurement signal on a physical variable is often contaminated by a random noise. In such a case, the continuous-time signal had better be passed through a low-pass filter with the best characteristics in linearity of phase. After sampling and quantizing this signal, it is then important to use a digital filter that well approximates the differentiation in respect of both amplitude and phase charateristics in frequency domain. However, it is quite interesting to see the fact that, according to an experimental result on a three-link mechanical arm to be shown later, a simple difference operator still works even for noisy measurement data on the output signal from tacho-generators and the betterment process converges eventually after repeated operations.

Now we show numerical results of computer simulation, where a three-link arm model shown in Fig.2 is employed with physical parameters listed in Table 1. To simulate the dynamics of equation (12) for this model, Runge-Kutta's method is used by setting the time increment as t=0.005 sec.. The model is set at an initial time as

$$\begin{cases} \theta_1(0)=0, \quad \theta_2(0)=\pi/2, \quad \theta_3(0)=\pi, \quad \text{(rad)} \\ \dot{\theta}_1(0)=0, \quad \dot{\theta}_2(0)=0, \quad \dot{\theta}_3(0)=0, \quad \text{(rad/sec)} \end{cases} \tag{31}$$

and a set of feedback gains defined in equation (9) is chosen as

$$\begin{cases} a_1 = a_2 = a_3 = 1.0, \\ b_1 = b_2 = b_3 = 1.0. \end{cases} \tag{32}$$

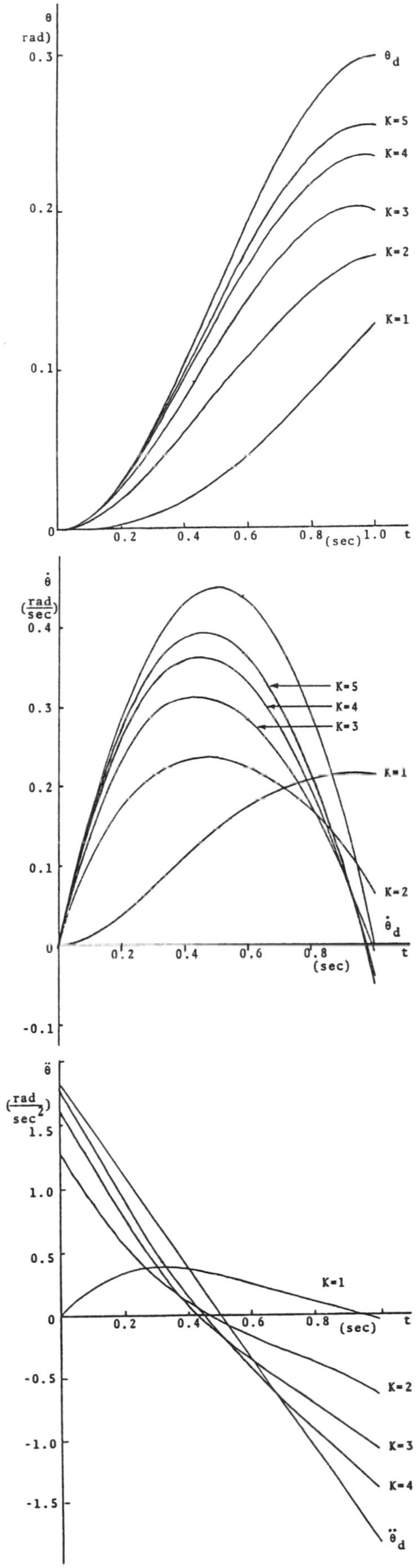

(a) (b) (c)

Fig.4 Plots of motion trajectories. In this simulation gain matrix Γ is set constant.

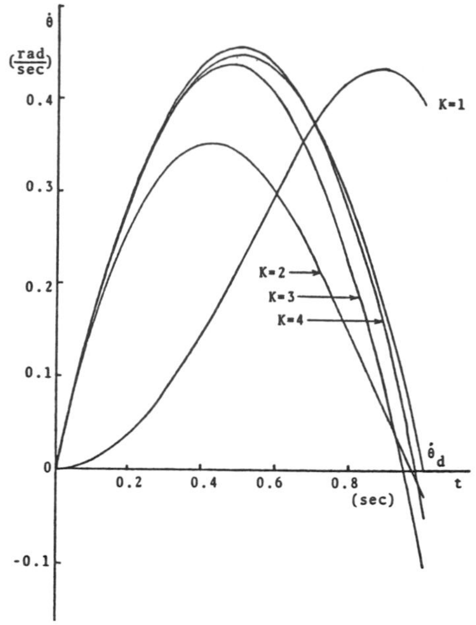

Fig.5 Plot of motion trajectories in case of $\Gamma = R(\underset{\sim}{\theta}_k(t))$

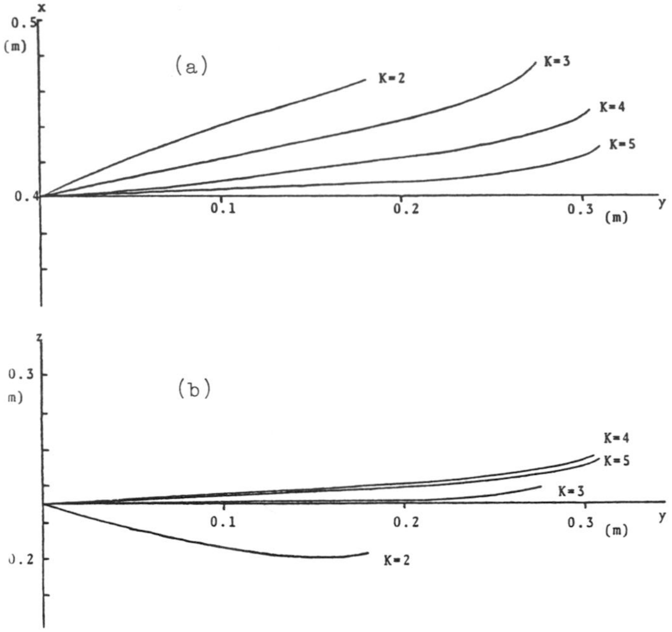

Fig.6(a),(b) Plots of motion trajectories in case that Γ is fixed

From now on we omit the indication of physical units, as all numerical values are expressed in the MKS system of units. A desired motion trajectory for each joint-angle θ_i is given as a quadratic function of time defined over a time interval $t\varepsilon[0, 1]$ and the final state is chosen as

$$\begin{cases} \theta_1(1) = 0.3, & \theta_2(1) = 1.27, & \theta_3(1) = 2.07, \\ \theta_1(1) = 0, & \dot{\theta}_2(1) = 0, & \dot{\theta}_3(1) = 0. \end{cases} \tag{33}$$

Figure 4(a), (b), and (c) show plots of the given desired trajectory of the first joint-angle θ_1, its angular velocity $\dot{\theta}_1$, and its angular acceleration $\ddot{\theta}_1$, respectively, and corresponding motion trajectories at repeated operation trials for k=1, 2, ..., and 5. In Fig.4, a gain matrix for the betterment process is chosen as

$$\Gamma = \begin{bmatrix} 0.5 & 0 & 0 \\ 0 & 0.5 & 0 \\ 0 & 0 & 1.0 \end{bmatrix} \tag{34}$$

and is fixed constant throughout the operation. It has been seen in this simulation that, around at the tenth operation trial, the motion trajectory for $\dot{\underset{\sim}{\theta}}_k(t)$ becomes almost coincident with the desired motion trajectory $\dot{\underset{\sim}{\theta}}_d(t)$. For the other joint-angles θ_2 and θ_3, the same tendency of convergence is observed, too.

In Fig.5 we show the convergence of the motion trajectories to the desired one under the same conditions except the gain matrix Γ for the betterment process. In this case we set

$$\Gamma = R(\underset{\sim}{\theta}_k(t)) \tag{35}$$

which satisfies the key condition of inequality

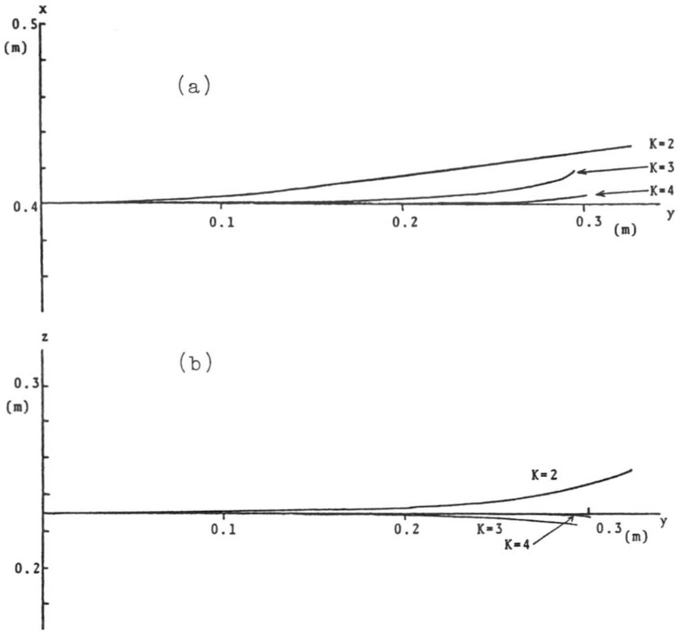

Fig.7(a),(b) Plots of motion trajectories in case that Γ is set as $\Gamma = R(\underset{\sim}{\theta}_k(t))J^{-1}(\underset{\sim}{\theta}_k(t))$

(22) in Theorem with allowing a broad margin. As predicted from the proof of Proposition given in Appendix, the motion trajectory $\dot{\underset{\sim}{\theta}}_k(t)$ for the case of Γ varying in accordance with $\underset{\sim}{\theta}_k(t)$ as given in equation (35) converges the desired one more rapidly than that for the case of constant Γ as in equation (34). As seen from Fig.5, around at the sixth or seventh operation, the motion

becomes almost coincident with the desired one.

In Figures 6 and 7 simulation results are given, when a desired motion trajectory is described in terms of the task-oriented coordinates (Cartesian coordinates $\underset{\sim}{x} = (x, y, z)$ in space), as follows:

$$\begin{cases} x_d(0) = 0.40, \quad y_d(0) = 0, \quad z_d(0) = 0.23 \\ \quad \text{(which corresponds to } \underset{\sim}{\theta}_d(0) = (0, \pi/2, \pi)) \\ \dot{x}_d(t) = \dot{z}_d(t) = 0, \quad \dot{y}_d(t) = 1.8\,t(1-t) \quad \text{for } t \in [0,1]. \end{cases} \tag{36}$$

In other words, the tip of the robot arm is ordered to move straight in the direction of y-axis on a xy-plane. In this case we use a feedback law

$$\underset{\sim}{u} = \frac{\partial P}{\partial \underset{\sim}{\theta}} - J^T[K_p(\underset{\sim}{x} - \underset{\sim}{x}_d) + K_v(\dot{\underset{\sim}{x}} - \dot{\underset{\sim}{x}}_d)] + \underset{\sim}{v} \tag{37}$$

instead of equation (9), where J denotes a Jacobian matrix defined as $\partial \underset{\sim}{x}/\partial \underset{\sim}{\theta}$ [Arimoto and Miyazaki; 1983]. Here, we chose

$$K_p = K_v = \begin{bmatrix} 1.0 & 0 & 0 \\ 0 & 1.0 & 0 \\ 0 & 0 & 1.0 \end{bmatrix}. \tag{38}$$

In additional, we use a betterment process described by

$$\begin{cases} \underset{\sim}{e}_k(t) = \dot{\underset{\sim}{x}}_d(t) - \dot{\underset{\sim}{x}}(t), \\ \underset{\sim}{v}_{k+1}(t) = \underset{\sim}{v}_k(t) + \Gamma \frac{d}{dt} \underset{\sim}{e}_k(t) \end{cases} \tag{39}$$

instead of equations (11) and (13). In Fig.6 Γ is kept constant as follows:

$$\Gamma = \begin{bmatrix} -1.0 & 1.5 & 0 \\ 0.2 & 0.1 & -1.8 \\ -0.3 & -0.2 & -0.1 \end{bmatrix}, \tag{40}$$

while in Fig.7 Γ is set as

$$\Gamma = R(\underset{\sim}{\theta}_k(t))J^{-1}(\underset{\sim}{\theta}_k(t)). \tag{41}$$

Comparing Fig.6 and Fig.7, we see that the tendency of convergence of the betterment process is more rapid for the latter case than for the former.

Finally we present an experimental result in Fig. 8. This experiment was carried out by using a three-link mechanical arm as modeled in Fig.2, under the following conditions:

Sampling period; $\Delta t = 6.025$ m sec,
Feedback gains; Λ, $B = \mathrm{diag}(6.0, 6.0, 6.0)$,
Initial condition; $\underset{\sim}{\theta}(0) = (0, 0, 0)$, $\dot{\underset{\sim}{\theta}}(0) = 0$,
Final condition; $\underset{\sim}{\theta}_d(T) = (67.5, 45, 67.5)$ deg,
Gain matrix of the betterment process; $\Gamma = \mathrm{diag}(0.102, 0.116, 0.0542)$ Kg m^2 .

Since physical parameters of the arm used in the experiment are not so much different from those in Table 1, each gain for the betterment process (each diagonal element of Γ) is too small, compared with Γ employed in the computer simulation. Therefore, the speed of convergence of the betterment process is not fast but even in this case

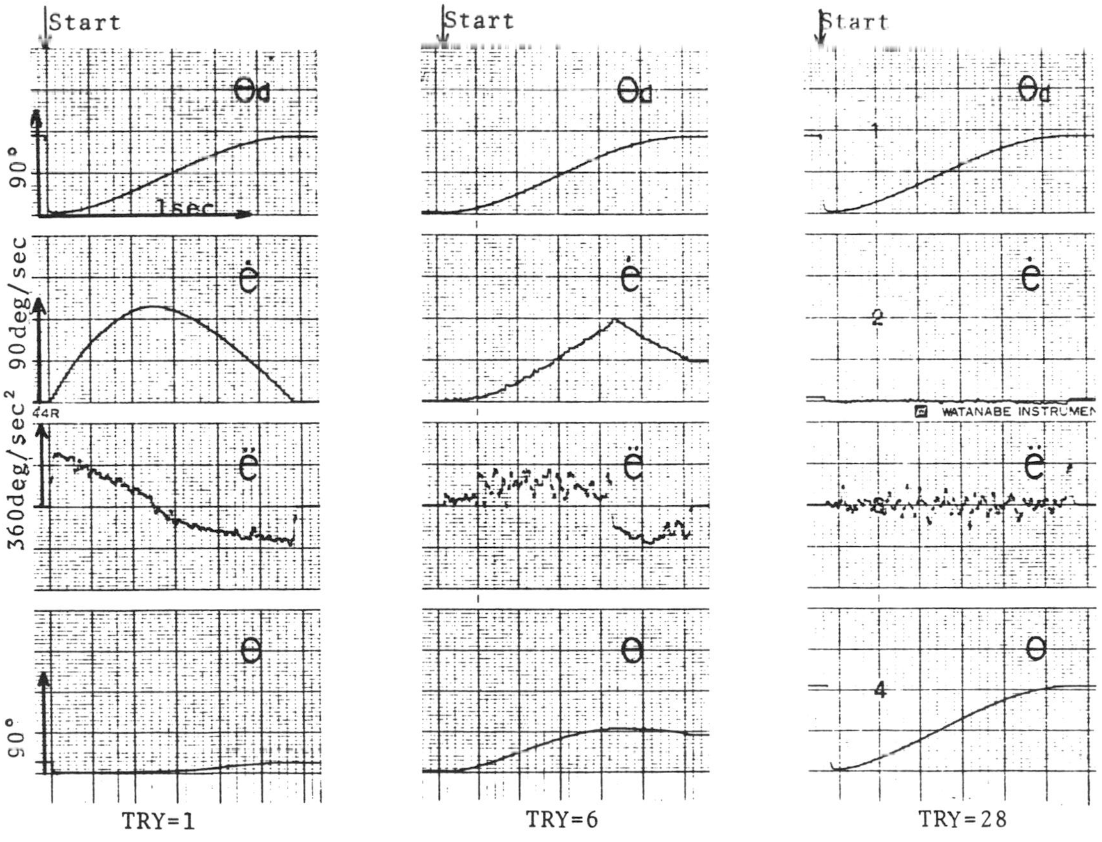

Fig.8 Experimental results obtained by using a three-link mechanical arm. In these records, $\theta = \theta_1$, $\theta_d = \theta_{d1}$, $e = \theta_{d1} - \theta_1$, $\dot{e} = de/dt$, $\ddot{e} = d\dot{e}/dt$

the convergence is eventually achieved aroud at the 20 30th operation trial. Further experimental results will be presented in our future work [Kawamura et al, 1984].

5. Concluding Remarks

We proposed a betterment process with a simple iterative rule for self-learning and demonstrated that it affords mechanical robots the ability to acquire a prescribed desired motion form through an automatic repetition of operation trials. Even in case that a desired motion trajectory is described in terms of the task-oriented coordinates, the betterment process is expected to converge as seen in an example of computer simulation (see Figs. 6 and 7). A theoretical treatment of this problem will be presented elsewhere in future.

Finally, we pose a further interesting and important problem for actualizing intelligent robots: Is it possible to make good use of the accumulation of experience and knowledge obtained by learning through the betterment process in a new and inexperienced task ?

Appendix

We will present a rough sketch of the proof of Proposition under the assumption that

$$\|\theta_k(t)\|_\infty < c_1, \qquad \|q_k(t)\|_\infty < c_2 \tag{A1}$$

for $t\varepsilon[0,T]$ and any k, since a rigorous proof may become too lengthy to describe within a limit of pages given to this paper. For simplicity, let

$$R_k = R_k(\theta_k(t)), \quad \dot{R}_k = dR_k/dt, \quad \dot{R}_k^{-1} = d(R_k^{-1})/dt.$$

From equations (12) to (15), it follows that

$$R_{k+1}\dot{e}_{k+1} - R_k\dot{e}_k = (R_{k+1} - R_k)\dot{y}_d + R_k\dot{y}_k - R_{k+1}\dot{y}_{k+1}$$
$$= (R_{k+1} - R_k)\dot{y}_d + (\dot{q}_k - \dot{q}_{k+1}) - \dot{R}_k y_k + \dot{R}_{k+1} y_{k+1}. \tag{A2}$$

By using equation (12), this can be rewritten as

$$R_{k+1}\dot{e}_{k+1} = (R_k - \Gamma)\dot{e}_k + r_k, \tag{A3}$$

where

$$r_k = -\frac{\partial\bar{K}}{\partial\theta_k} + \frac{\partial\bar{K}}{\partial\theta_{k+1}} - A(\theta_k - \theta_{k+1}) + (R_{k+1} - R_k)\dot{y}_d$$
$$- B(R_k^{-1}q_k - R_{k+1}^{-1}q_{k+1}) + \dot{R}_{k+1}(y_{k+1} - y_k)$$
$$+ (\dot{R}_{k+1} - \dot{R}_k)y_k. \tag{A4}$$

Note that every component of $\partial\bar{K}/\partial\theta_i$, R, R^{-1}, and $\partial R/\partial\theta_i$ is Lipschitz-continuous in $(\theta, q)\varepsilon X$ ($\subseteq R^n \times R^n$) and every component of R_k^{-1}, R_{k+1}, and $\dot{\theta}_k$ ($=R_k^{-1} q_k$) is bounded. Hence, it hold that

$$\|R_{k+1}\dot{e}_{k+1}\|_\lambda \leqq \max_{t\varepsilon[0,T]} \|I - \Gamma R_k^{-1}\|_\infty \|R_k\dot{e}_k\|_\lambda + \alpha_1\|x_{k+1} - x_k\|_\lambda \tag{A5}$$

where $x = (\theta, q)$. From now on we consider a general form of state equation

$$\dot{x}_k = f(x_k) + Dv_k, \tag{A6}$$

instead of equation (12), where f is assumed to satisfy the Lipschitz continuity. Then it holds

$$e^{-\lambda t}[x_k(t) - x_{k+1}(t)] = \int_0^t e^{-\lambda(t-\tau)} D e^{-\lambda\tau}\dot{e}_k(\tau)d\tau$$
$$+ \int_0^t e^{-\lambda(t-\tau)} e^{\lambda\tau}[f(x_k(\tau)) - f(x_{k+1}(\tau))]d\tau \tag{A7}$$

which leads to the inequality

$$z(t) \leqq c_0 \frac{1-e^{-\lambda T}}{\lambda} \|\dot{e}_k\|_\lambda + \int_0^t c_1 e^{-\lambda(t-\tau)} z(\tau)d\tau \tag{A8}$$

where we define

$$z(t) = e^{-\lambda t}\|x_k(t) - x_{k+1}(t)\|_\infty. \tag{A9}$$

According to Gronwall's lemma, equation (A8) means

$$z(t) \leqq c_0 \frac{1-e^{-\lambda T}}{\lambda} \|\dot{e}_k\|_\lambda \cdot \exp \int_0^t c_1 e^{-\lambda(t-\tau)} d\tau \tag{A10}$$

which yields

$$\|x_{k+1} - x_k\|_\lambda \leqq c_2(\lambda)\|\dot{e}_k\|_\lambda \leqq \beta^{-1} c_2(\lambda)\|R_k\dot{e}_k\|_\lambda. \tag{A11}$$

Since $c_2(\lambda)$ becomes arbitrarily small by increasing λ, we can conclude that

$$\|R_{k+1}\dot{e}_{k+1}\|_\lambda = [\max_{t\varepsilon[0,T]} \|I - \Gamma R_k^{-1}\|_\infty + \varepsilon(\lambda)]\|R_k\dot{e}_k\|_\lambda \tag{A12}$$

where $\varepsilon(\lambda) = c_2(\lambda)/\beta$. This proves equation (23) with condition (24).

Reference

Arimoto, S. and Miyazaki, F. 1983. Stability and robustness of PID feedback control for robot manipulators of sensory capabilities, Proc. of 1st International Symposium of Robotics Research, The MIT Press, Cambridge, Massachusetts.

Arimoto, S., Kawamura, S., and Miyazaki, F. 1984a. Bettering operation of robots by learning, Journal of Robotic Systems, 1-2, pp.

Arimoto, S., Kawamura, S., and Miyazaki, F. 1984b. Bettering operation of dynamic systems by learning: A new control theory for servomechanism or mechatronics systems, submitted to The 23rd IEEE Conference on Decision and Control, Las Vegas, Nevada. December 1984.

Greenwood, D.T. 1977. Classical Dynamics, Prentice-Hall, Englewood Cliffs, N.J., p.50.

Kawamura, S., Miyazaki, F., and Arimoto, S. 1984. Iterative learning control for robotic systems, Proc. of IECON'84, Tokyo, Japan, October 1984.

Miyazaki, F., Arimoto, S., Takegaki, M., and Maeda, Y. 1984. Sensory feedback based on the artificial potential for robot manipulators, Proc. of 9th IFAC, Budapest, Hungary, July 1984.

Takegaki, M. and Arimoto, S. 1981. A new feedback method for dynamic control of manipulators, Trans. of ASME, J. of Dynamic Systems, Measurement, and Control, 103, pp.119-125.

Collision Avoidance in Multi-Robot Systems

E. Freund, H. Hoyer

Chair of Automation and Information Processing
- A I T -
FernUniversität, Postfach 940, 5800 Hagen, West-Germany

In application of a new systematic design method for multi-robot systems including the hierarchical coordinator the collision avoidance problem is considered for three robots with a common collision space. In a new approach, the strategy for collision avoidance itself is based on analytically described avoidance trajectories which serve in the hierarchical coordinator for collision detection as well as avoidance. The derivation demonstrates the usefulness of this design method even for a larger number of robots involved.

1. Introduction

With increased automation and application of CAD/CAM methods in connection with automatically generated robot programs, e. g. in car manufacturing, an overall consideration of multi-robot systems becomes a basic requirement. This seems to be the only possibility to reduce the programming effort and the fault rate and to provide flexibility in manufacturing. In spite of the importance for future developments very few results are known in this field.

The design of multi-robot systems itself requires an overall approach where not only parts of the structure including the hierarchy is considered but a complete concept including the dynamics of the robots involved has to be developed. The performance of the basic control circuits are quite essential in this concept as these circuits have to react fast and accurately to the superimposed input signals of the hierarchy and must allow precise changes of their control dynamics by command of the hierarchy as well.

In [Freund 1983] the overall structure of a multi-robot system is developed and a hierarchical coordinator is introduced. Hereby the control of the variables of motion of the robots is based on the nonlinear control and decoupling method [Freund 1976, Freund and Syrbe 1976] where by a suitable partition of the dynamic equations directly applicable, explicit control laws for each drive are provided [Freund 1982]. The structure of the hierarchical coordinator with respect to the design of the multi-robot system is presented in [Freund 1984] where this design includes the change of the basic dynamics, the introduction of useful coupling and the change of the input gains by means of the hierarchical coordinator. The explicit equations of the resulting overall multi-robot system including the hierarchical coordinator are presented there as well.

A basic requirement in multi-robot systems are collision avoidance strategies which have to be superimposed on all coordinated operations of the robots. These strategies have to be guided by state-feedback to prevent collisions between the robots even in case of failure of certain control circuits. In the present treatment of the subject of collision avoidance there are simple realizations as well as complex theoretical approaches. In simple realizations the common working space is completely blocked for the other robot arm if the one robot arm enters [Dunne 1979, Tyridal 1980]. These methods lack flexibility of course. The more complex theoretical approaches, however, apply time-consuming optimization and search methods for the planning of a collision free path [Lozano-Peréz 1979, Hoel 1976] so that the practical use for industrial applications is limited. In [Freund 1983] the hierarchical coordinator is designed for collision avoidance of two robots and is based on an approach using various hierarchical strategies in connection with extremly time-efficient evaluation of decision tables [Freund and Hoyer 1983]. This method allows a simultaneous movement of both robots through the collision space and is based on a suitable description of this actual possible space. This collision avoidance strategy approach is very effective for two robots, however, it is quite complicated to handle for the design of collision avoidance in multi-robot systems with three or more robots.

A new approach for the solution of this problem is presented in this paper where the design method for multi-robot systems as derived in [Freund 1984] is used as the basis. The collision avoidance strategy itself applies analytically described avoidance trajectories (instead of decision tables as in [Freund and Hoyer 1983]) which are the basis for collision detection and collision avoidance in the hierarchical coordinator. For reasons of clearness the application is considered for a system of three robots in the paper. The resulting equations demonstrate the usefulness of the design method for multi-robot systems and provide a systematic approach to the solution of the collision avoidance problem even for a larger number of robots involved.

2. Basic equations

For the consideration of the collision avoidance problem for several robots, the general theory of multi-robot systems has to be treated first which is developed in [Freund 1983, Freund 1984]. In a system of r robots, the k-th robot (k=1,2,...,r) can be characterized by the state-space description

$$\dot{\underline{x}}_k(t) = \underline{A}_k(\underline{x}_k) + \underline{B}_k(\underline{x}_k)\underline{u}_k(t) \qquad (1)$$

$$\underline{y}_k(t) = \underline{C}_k(\underline{x}_k) \qquad k = 1,2,\ldots,r \qquad (2)$$

with $\underline{u}_k(t)$ and $\underline{y}_k(t)$ as the m_k-dimensional input and output vector, respectively. If the variables of motion of the k-th robot are denoted by $\underline{q}_{k,i}(t)$ and the corresponding velocities by $\dot{\underline{q}}_{k,i}(t)$, the state variable of (1), (2) are chosen as

$$\begin{aligned} x_{k,(2i-1)}(t) &= \underline{q}_{k,i}(t) \\ x_{k,2i}(t) &= \dot{\underline{q}}_{k,i}(t) \qquad i = 1,2,\ldots,m_k \end{aligned} \qquad (3)$$

Then, the state vector in the state space description (1), (2) has the dimension 2 m_k and is given by

$$\underline{x}_k(t) = \begin{bmatrix} x_{k1} \\ x_{k2} \\ \vdots \\ x_{k,2m_k} \end{bmatrix} \qquad (4)$$

where m_k is the number of axes or degrees of freedom of the k-th robot. The input vector $\underline{u}_k(t)$ consist of external forces and torques which drive the corresponding variable of motion $q_{k,i}(t)$. $\underline{y}_k(t)$ contains the outputs of the robot which are the variables of motion or combinations of them depending on the chosen coordinate system. For simplification it is assumed in the application considered there that the output variable of the robots are directly equal to certain state variables, i. e.

$$y_{k,i}(t) = x_{k,(2i-1)}(t) = \underline{q}_{k,i}(t) \qquad (5)$$

$$i = 1,2,\ldots,m_k$$
$$k = 1,2,\ldots,r$$

This means that in this case the general output equation (2) is reduced to (5). However, the theory of multi-robot systems holds for the general case, where the output variables are linear or nonlinear combinations of the state variables, as well [Freund 1983, Freund 1984].

On the basis of the state vector $\underline{x}_k(t)$ as given in (4) in connection with (3), $\underline{A}_k(\underline{x}_k)$ and $\underline{B}_k(\underline{x}_k)$ in (1) have a compatible order and the following form which is specific for robots and manipulators:

$$\underline{A}_k(\underline{x}_k) = \begin{bmatrix} x_{k2} \\ f_{k1}(\underline{x}_k) \\ \hline \vdots \\ \hline x_{k,2m_k} \\ f_{k,m_k}(\underline{x}_k) \end{bmatrix} \qquad (6)$$

$$\underline{B}_k(\underline{x}_k) = \begin{bmatrix} \underline{0} \\ \underline{B}_{k1}(\underline{x}_k) \\ \hline \vdots \\ \hline \underline{0} \\ \underline{B}_{k,m_k}(\underline{x}_k) \end{bmatrix} \qquad (7)$$

Each of the subsections in $\underline{A}_k$ and $\underline{B}_k$ corresponds to one variable of motion where the total number is m_k.

For the control of the robotic system as given by (1) and (2) or (5) in connection with (6) and (7), a feedback of the form

$$\underline{u}_k(t) = \underline{F}_k(\underline{x}_k) + \underline{G}_k(\underline{x}_k)\underline{w}_k(t) \qquad (8)$$

is applied to this system where $\underline{w}_k(t)$ is the new m_k-dimensional reference input vector and $\underline{F}_k(\underline{x}_k)$ and $\underline{G}_k(\underline{x}_k)$ are of compatible order. From these results the closed loop system

$$\dot{\underline{x}}_k(t) = \left[\underline{A}_k(\underline{x}_k)+\underline{B}_k(\underline{x}_k)\underline{F}_k(\underline{x}_k)\right] + \underline{B}_k(\underline{x}_k)\underline{G}_k(\underline{x}_k)\underline{w}_k(t) \qquad (9)$$

with the output equation (2) or (5), respectively. Applying the nonlinear control and decoupling method to the closed loop system (9) it is the goal to find $\underline{F}_k(\underline{x}_k)$ and $\underline{G}_k(\underline{x}_k)$ such that system (9) is decoupled from the inputs to the outputs and has arbitrarily designated poles. For the state space representation (1), (2) or (5) with $\underline{A}_k(\underline{x}_k)$, $\underline{B}_k(\underline{x}_k)$ from (6) and (7) these matrices are [Freund 1976, Freund and Syrbe 1976, Freund 1983]

$$\underline{F}_k(\underline{x}_k) = - \underline{D}_k^{*-1}(\underline{x}_k)\left[\underline{C}_k^*(\underline{x}_k) + \underline{M}_k^*(\underline{x}_k)\right] \tag{10}$$

$$\underline{G}_k(\underline{x}_k) = \underline{D}_k^{*-1}(\underline{x}_k)\underline{\Lambda}_k \tag{11}$$

where in (10) the term $- \underline{D}_k^{*-1}(\underline{x}_k)\underline{C}_k^*(\underline{x}_k)$ represents the part of the feedback that yields decoupling while $- \underline{D}_k^{*-1}(\underline{x}_k)\underline{M}_k^*(\underline{x}_k)$ performs the control part with arbitrary pole placement. $\underline{\Lambda}_k$ characterizes the desired input gains.

From substitution of (10) and (11) in system (9) with (5) results the following overall behavior of all input/output pairs $y_{k,i}(t)$, $w_{k,i}(t)$:

$$\ddot{y}_{k,i}(t) + \alpha^1_{k,i}\dot{y}_{k,i}(t) + \alpha^o_{k,i}y_{k,i}(t) = \lambda_{k,i}w_{k,i}(t) \qquad \text{for } i = 1,2,\ldots,m_k \tag{12}$$

In (12) $w_{k1}(t)$ to $w_{k,m_k}(t)$ are the reference inputs of the closed loop system (9) which are the components of the reference input vector $\underline{w}_k(t)$.

Equation (12) means that all input/output pairs $y_{k,i}(t)$, $w_{k,i}(t)$ for $i = 1,2,\ldots,m_k$ are completely decoupled from each other and have a dynamic that can be chosen arbitrarily via the coefficients $\alpha^1_{k,i}$ and $\alpha^o_{k,i}$ (with $\lambda_{k,i}$ as input gain). The matrix $\underline{M}_k^*(\underline{x}_k)$ in (10) contains the $\alpha^1_{k,i}$ and $\alpha^o_{k,i}$, the matrix $\underline{\Lambda}_k$ in (11) the $\lambda_{k,i}$. By the nonlinear control approach it is therefore possible to gain a decoupled overall behavior of the form (12) for each link of the robots by feeding back link-positions and velocities (eq. (8)). The design of multi-robot systems is presented in [Freund 1983, Freund 1984] so that only the results as needed in this context are repeated in the following.

3. Multi-robot system

The multi-robot system as considered here consists of r robots described by equation (1) and (5). Controlling these robots by corresponding nonlinear feedbacks of the type (8) leads to a robot system which consists of r equations of the form (9).

As the robots work in coordinated operation with a common working space, the reference inputs $\underline{w}_1(t),\ldots,\underline{w}_r(t)$ in (9) are not independent of each other anymore but have to be coordinated by hierarchical control.

This hierarchical coordinator can be set up in the following general form

$$\begin{bmatrix} \underline{w}_1(t) \\ \cdot \\ \cdot \\ \cdot \\ \underline{w}_r(t) \end{bmatrix} = \underline{H}(\underline{x}_1,\ldots,\underline{x}_r;\underline{v}_1,\ldots,\underline{v}_r) \tag{13}$$

where $\underline{v}_1(t),\ldots,\underline{v}_r(t)$ are the new external input vectors of dimension $m_1,\ldots,m_r$, respectively, referring to the robots 1...r. The hierarchical coordinator is provided with the actual information about the positions of all variables of motion of the robots as well as about the corresponding velocities by the state vectors $\underline{x}_1(t),\ldots,\underline{x}_r(t)$ which are also included in equation (13). Applying (13) to the system of r robots in the form of (9) leads to the general form of the hierarchical multi-robot system

$$\begin{bmatrix} \dot{\underline{x}}_1(t) \\ \cdot \\ \cdot \\ \cdot \\ \dot{\underline{x}}_r(t) \end{bmatrix} = \begin{bmatrix} \underline{A}_1(\underline{x}_1) + \underline{B}_1(\underline{x}_1)\underline{F}_1(\underline{x}_1) \\ \cdot \\ \cdot \\ \cdot \\ \underline{A}_r(\underline{x}_r) + \underline{B}_r(\underline{x}_r)\underline{F}_r(\underline{x}_r) \end{bmatrix} + \begin{bmatrix} \underline{B}_1(\underline{x}_1)\underline{G}_1(\underline{x}_1) & \cdots & \underline{0} \\ \vdots & \ddots & \\ \underline{0} & & \underline{B}_r(\underline{x}_r)\underline{G}_r(\underline{x}_r) \end{bmatrix} \cdot$$

$$\cdot\, \underline{H}(\underline{x}_1,\ldots,\underline{x}_r;\underline{v}_1,\ldots,\underline{v}_r) \tag{14}$$

where the output equations are given by (5). The structure of the multi-robot system is demonstrated in fig. 1.

Using the nonlinear control approach, the matrices $\underline{F}_k(\underline{x}_k)$ and $\underline{G}_k(\underline{x}_k)$ $(k = 1,2,\ldots,r)$ in (14) are substituted by (10) and (11). This yields in consideration of (12) the following explicit form of the hierarchical multi-robot system

$$\begin{bmatrix} \dot{\underline{x}}_1(t) \\ \cdot \\ \cdot \\ \cdot \\ \dot{\underline{x}}_r(t) \end{bmatrix} = \begin{bmatrix} \underline{A}_1^* & \cdots & \underline{0} \\ \vdots & \ddots & \\ \underline{0} & & \underline{A}_r^* \end{bmatrix} \begin{bmatrix} \underline{x}_1(t) \\ \cdot \\ \cdot \\ \cdot \\ \underline{x}_r(t) \end{bmatrix} + \underline{B}^* \cdot \underline{H}(\underline{x}_1,\ldots,\underline{x}_r;\underline{v}_1,\ldots,\underline{v}_r) \tag{15}$$

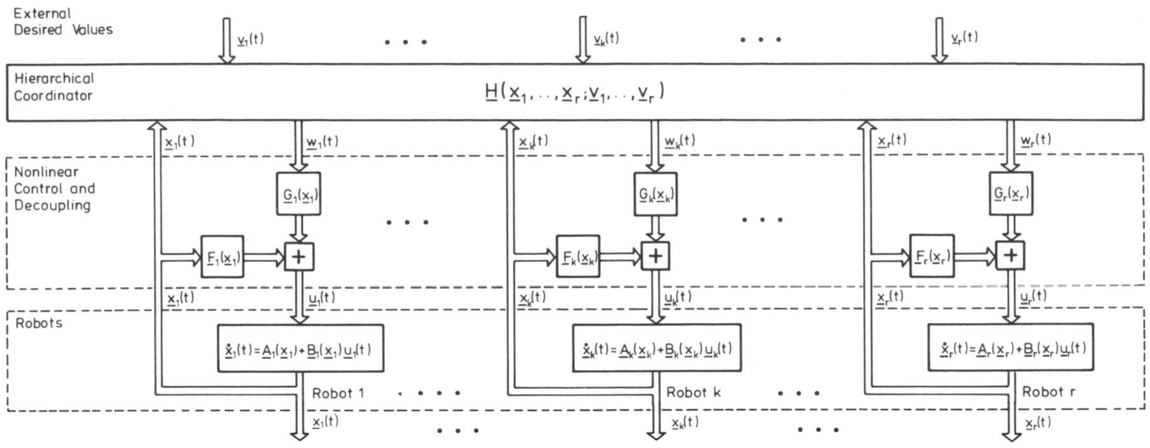

Figure 1. Multi-Robot System

with

$$y_{k,i}(t) = x_{k,(2i-1)}(t) \quad \text{for } k = 1,2,\ldots,r \quad i = 1,2,\ldots,m_k$$

where the matrices in (15) have the following form:

$$\underline{A}_k^* = \begin{bmatrix} \underline{A}_{k1}^* & & \underline{0} \\ & \ddots & \\ \underline{0} & & \underline{A}_{k,m_k}^* \end{bmatrix} \tag{16}$$

with

$$\underline{A}_{k,i}^* = \begin{bmatrix} 0 & 1 \\ -\alpha_{k,i}^0 & -\alpha_{k,i}^1 \end{bmatrix} \tag{17}$$

for $k = 1,2,\ldots,r$
and $i = 1,2,\ldots,m_k$

The $(2m\times m)$-matrix $\underline{B}^*$ is given by

$$\underline{B}^* = [\,\underline{b}_{11}^*,\ldots,\underline{b}_{1,m_1}^*;\ldots;\underline{b}_{r1}^*,\ldots,\underline{b}_{r,m_r}^*\,] \tag{18}$$

with $m = m_1 + \ldots + m_k$ and

$$\underline{b}_{k,i}^* = \begin{bmatrix} 0 \\ \vdots \\ 0 \\ \lambda_{k,i} \\ 0 \\ \vdots \\ 0 \end{bmatrix} \leftarrow \{2(m_1+\ldots+m_{k-1}+i)\}\text{- th-position}$$

$k = 1,2,\ldots,r$
$i = 1,2,\ldots,m_k$

The structure of the hierarchical overall system (15) in fig. 1, which is based on nonlinear control, shows that this system will in general not be decoupled anymore. This means that the external input $v_{k,i}(t)$ does not only effect the corresponding output $y_{k,i}(t)$ for $k = 1,\ldots,r$ and $i = 1,2,\ldots,m_k$ where $v_{k,i}(t)$ are the components of the external input vector $\underline{v}_k(t)$. This is due to the fact that the robots cooperate or interfere in coordinated operation so that these movements are in general not independent anymore.

In system (15), the dynamics of all variables of motion as represented by $\underline{A}_{k,i}^*$ seem to be independent combined with arbitrary pole placement. This is true if the hierarchical coordinator is of the type $\underline{H}(\underline{v}_1,\ldots,\underline{v}_r)$, i. e. if only the external inputs are coordinated with no comparison to the actual positions relying on the feedback systems of the basic controls. Including the state variables in the design of the hierarchical coordinator, i. e. $\underline{H}(\underline{x}_1,\ldots,\underline{x}_r;\underline{v}_1,\ldots,\underline{v}_r)$ implies that the hierarchical overall system has a second feedback system (fig. 1).

The hierarchical coordinator (13) itself can be structured and designed as follows [Freund 1984]:

$$\underline{H}(\underline{x}_1,\ldots,\underline{x}_r;\underline{v}_1,\ldots,\underline{v}_r) = \underline{H}^a \begin{bmatrix} \underline{x}_1(t) \\ \vdots \\ \underline{x}_r(t) \end{bmatrix} + \underline{H}^b(\underline{x}_1,\ldots,\underline{x}_r) + \underline{E} \begin{bmatrix} \underline{v}_1(t) \\ \vdots \\ \underline{v}_r(t) \end{bmatrix}, \tag{19}$$

where the control dynamics of the links can be changed by $\underline{H}^a$, useful couplings between the links of different robots are introduced by $\underline{H}^b(\underline{x}_1,\ldots,\underline{x}_r)$ and the input gains of the external inputs

$\underline{v}_1(t),\ldots,\underline{v}_r(t)$ are chosen by $\underline{E}$. The (m×2m)-matrix $\underline{H}^a$ is set up as follows:

$$\underline{H}^a = \begin{bmatrix} \underline{H}_1^a & \cdots & \underline{0} \\ \vdots & \ddots & \\ \underline{0} & & \underline{H}_r^a \end{bmatrix} \quad (20)$$

with

$$\underline{H}_k^a = \begin{bmatrix} \underline{H}_{k1}^a & \cdots & \underline{0} \\ \vdots & \ddots & \\ \underline{0} & & \underline{H}_{k,m_k}^a \end{bmatrix} \quad (21)$$

for k = 1,2,...,r

and

$$\underline{H}_{k,i}^a = \begin{bmatrix} \frac{\overset{o}{\alpha}_{k,i}}{\lambda_{k,i}} & \frac{\overset{1}{\alpha}_{k,i}}{\lambda_{k,i}} \end{bmatrix} \quad \text{for } k = 1,2,\ldots,r \text{ and } i = 1,2,\ldots,m_k \quad (22)$$

where the parameters $\overset{o}{\alpha}_{k,i}$ and $\overset{1}{\alpha}_{k,i}$ can be chosen arbitrarily.

The (m×1)-matrix $\underline{H}^b$ has in general the nonlinear form

$$\underline{H}^b(\underline{x}_1,\ldots,\underline{x}_r) = \begin{bmatrix} \underline{H}_1^b(\underline{x}_1,\ldots,\underline{x}_r) \\ \underline{H}_2^b(\underline{x}_1,\ldots,\underline{x}_r) \\ \vdots \\ \underline{H}_r^b(\underline{x}_1,\ldots,\underline{x}_r) \end{bmatrix} \quad (23)$$

with $\underline{H}_k^b(\underline{x}_1,\ldots,\underline{x}_r)$ as (m_k×1)-matrices for k = 1,2,...,r.

$\underline{E}$ is the following (m×m)-diagonal matrix with the parameters $\bar{\lambda}_{11}/\lambda_{11},\ldots,\bar{\lambda}_{1,m_1}/\lambda_{1,m_1},\ldots,\bar{\lambda}_{r_1}/\lambda_{r_1},\ldots,\bar{\lambda}_{r,m_r}/\lambda_{r,m_r}$ in its diagonal where the $\bar{\lambda}_{k,i}$ (k = 1,2,...,r; i = 1,2,...,m_k) can be chosen arbitrarily.

$$\underline{E} = \begin{bmatrix} \frac{\bar{\lambda}_{11}}{\lambda_{11}} & \cdots & 0 \\ \vdots & \ddots & \\ 0 & & \frac{\bar{\lambda}_{r,m_r}}{\lambda_{r,m_r}} \end{bmatrix} \quad (24)$$

The usefulness of this structure (19)-(24) for design procedures is demonstrated by the application to collision avoidance of several robots which is subject of the following paragraphs. This approach will use the proposed structure of the hierarchical coordinator directly and is quite different from the procedure for collision avoidance of two robots based on decision tables as presented in [Freund and Hoyer 1983, Freund 1983].

4. Design of the Hierarchical Coordinator

In application of equation (19) the hierarchical coordinator is designed for collision avoidance of three robots where the restriction to three robots is chosen for reasons of clearness. The derivation itself is of general character and is valid for a larger number of robots as well. Figure 2 shows the arrangement of these robots and the collision space in principle.

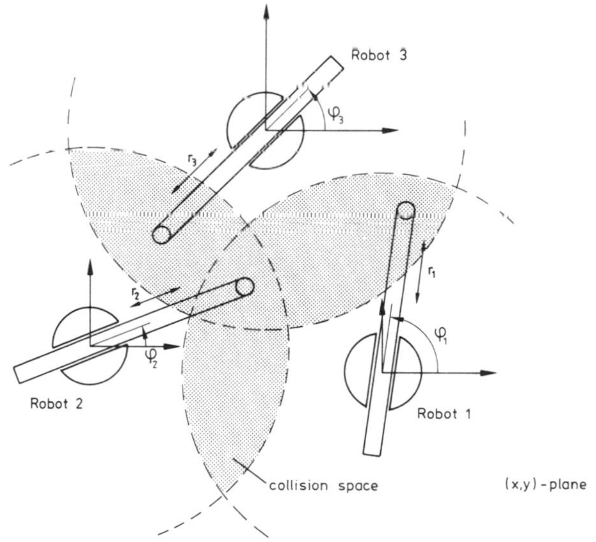

Figure 2. Robots in coordinated operation

It is assumed that the main axes of the robots involved have a cylindrical joint configuration, i. e. the k-th robot (k = 1,2,3) has a translational joint $r_k(t)$ and a rotational joint $\varphi_k(t)$ in the (x,y)-plane of the world coordinates system and another translational joint z(t) vertical to it. Therefore, the state vector has the form:

$$\underline{x}_k(t) = \begin{bmatrix} x_{k1}(t) \\ x_{k2}(t) \\ x_{k3}(t) \\ x_{k4}(t) \\ x_{k5}(t) \\ x_{k6}(t) \end{bmatrix} = \begin{bmatrix} r_k(t) \\ \dot{r}_k(t) \\ \varphi_k(t) \\ \dot{\varphi}_k(t) \\ z_k(t) \\ \dot{z}_k(t) \end{bmatrix} \qquad k = 1,2,3 \tag{25}$$

and the corresponding reference vector is

$$\underline{v}_k(t) = \begin{bmatrix} v_{k1}(t) \\ v_{k2}(t) \\ v_{k3}(t) \end{bmatrix} = \begin{bmatrix} v_{kr}(t) \\ v_{k\varphi}(t) \\ v_{kz}(t) \end{bmatrix} \qquad k = 1,2,3 \tag{26}$$

The cylindrical coordinates system is chosen as basic coordinates system for the hierarchical coordinator as well, because most robot coordinates can be easily transformed into this system. This allows a general applicability without changes of the algorithms for different types of robots. In the case considered here the robot system in fig. 2 has cylindrical coordinates so that no transformations are required.

In the configuration in fig. 2 the highest right-of-way precedence for collision avoidance is given to robot 2 and the lowest to robot 3. This means that robot 2 can follow its desired path, while robot 1 has to avoid a collision with robot 2 and at the same time robot 3 has to avoid a collision with robot 1 and robot 2.

As basis for the solution of the collision avoidance problem the hierarchical coordinator in (19) is used in a form extended by a dependency of $\underline{H}^b$ on the reference inputs. This is for three robots

$$\underline{H}(\underline{x}_1,\underline{x}_2,\underline{x}_3,\underline{v}_1,\underline{v}_2,\underline{v}_3) = \underline{H}^a \begin{bmatrix} \underline{x}_1(t) \\ \underline{x}_2(t) \\ \underline{x}_3(t) \end{bmatrix} + \begin{bmatrix} \underline{H}_1^b(\underline{x}_1,\underline{x}_2,\underline{x}_3,\underline{v}_1,\underline{v}_2,\underline{v}_3) \\ \underline{H}_2^b(\underline{x}_1,\underline{x}_2,\underline{x}_3,\underline{v}_1,\underline{v}_2,\underline{v}_3) \\ \underline{H}_3^b(\underline{x}_1,\underline{x}_2,\underline{x}_3,\underline{v}_1,\underline{v}_2,\underline{v}_3) \end{bmatrix} + \underline{E} \begin{bmatrix} \underline{v}_1(t) \\ \underline{v}_2(t) \\ \underline{v}_3(t) \end{bmatrix} \tag{27}$$

For the design of the collision avoidance strategy the term $H^b(\underline{x}_1,\ldots,\underline{v}_3)$ in (27) has a key position in collision detection as well as in collision avoidance as it represents useful couplings between the robots. Therefore, the structure and design of this vector is considered first where dependency on $\underline{v}_1$, $\underline{v}_2$ and $\underline{v}_3$ allows the introduction of switching conditions.

For the design of $\underline{H}^b$, two parameters q and p have to be introduced. These so-called collision parameters present a criterion for a possible collision where the parameter q is related to the rotational movement and the parameter p to the translational movement of the arms. In the following the parameters q and p are determined with respect to the robots 1 and 2. The procedure is the same for the parameters related to robots 1 and 3 as well to the robots 2 and 3.

For the determination of q and p the configuration of the two robots in fig. 3 is used where the length a_{21} is the shortest distance between the origins of the robot coordinates systems and the angles φ_{01} and φ_{02} denote the relative positions. The actual positions of both systems at the time t_ν are described in fig. 3 by $x_{11}(t_\nu)$, $x_{13}(t_\nu)$ and $x_{21}(t_\nu)$, $x_{23}(t_\nu)$ respectively. If the sampling-intervall of the basic robot control is denoted by Δt, the predicted positions of both robots for $t_{\nu+1} = t_\nu + \Delta t$ are $x_{11}(t_\nu) + x_{12}(t_\nu)\Delta t$, $x_{13}(t_\nu) + x_{14}(t_\nu)\Delta t$ and $x_{21}(t_\nu) + x_{22}(t_\nu)\Delta t$, $x_{23}(t_\nu) + x_{24}(t_\nu)\Delta t$, respectively. These positions are shown in fig. 3 by dotted lines.

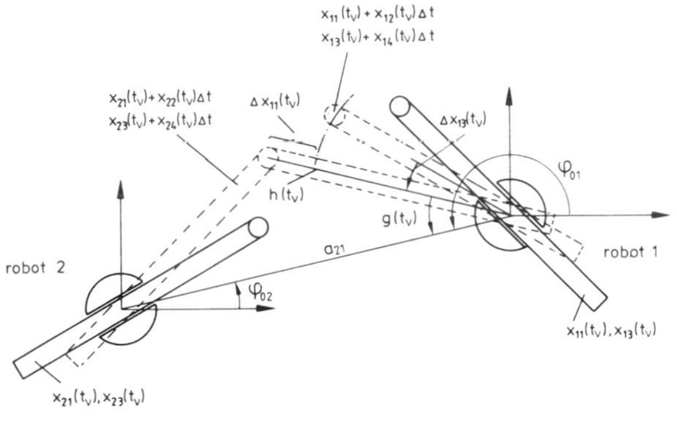

Figure 3. Geometrical Configuration of Robots 1 and 2

From fig. 3 follows for the length $h(t_\nu)$

$$h(t_\nu) = \sqrt{a_{21}^2 + [x_{21}(t_\nu) + x_{22}(t_\nu)\Delta t]^2 + - 2a_{21}[x_{21}(t_\nu)+x_{22}(t_\nu)\Delta t]\cos(x_{23}(t_\nu)+x_{24}(t_\nu)\Delta t-\varphi_{02})} \tag{28}$$

and for the angle $g(t_\nu)$

$$g(t_\nu) =$$

$$\arctan \frac{[x_{21}(t_\nu)+x_{22}(t_\nu)\Delta t]\sin(x_{23}(t_\nu)+x_{24}(t_\nu)\Delta t-\varphi_{02})}{a_{21}-[x_{21}(t_\nu)+x_{22}(t_\nu)\Delta t]\cos(x_{23}(t_\nu)+x_{24}(t_\nu)\Delta t-\varphi_{02})} \quad (29)$$

As a criterion for collision avoidance (which proved to be useful and is one amoung other possible ones), the length $\Delta x_{11}(t_\nu)$ defined by the difference

$$\Delta x_{11}(t_\nu) = [\, x_{11}(t_\nu) + x_{12}(t_\nu)\Delta t \,] - h(t_\nu) \quad (30)$$

is set in relation to the translational movement $\bar{x}_{12}\Delta t$ resulting from the nominal velocity $\bar{x}_{12}$ of the axis. This introduces the parameter $p(t_\nu)$ in form of

$$p(t_\nu) = \frac{\Delta x_{11}(t_\nu)}{\bar{x}_{12}\,\Delta t} \quad (31)$$

The parameter $p(t_\nu)$, therefore gives an indication how many time-intervalls Δt are required for the arm movement to assure a safe passing. For $p(t_\nu) > 0$, the arm has to draw back in order to avoid a collision, for $p(t_\nu) < 0$ the arm can still go forward, for collision it is $p(t_\nu) = 0$.

In the same way, the parameter $q(t_\nu)$ which corresponds to the angle $g(t_\nu)$ in (29) can be introduced as

$$q(t_\nu) = \frac{|\Delta x_{13}(t_\nu)|}{\tilde{x}_{14}(t_\nu)\Delta t} \quad (32)$$

with

$$\Delta x_{13}(t_\nu) = [\varphi_{01} - g(t_\nu)] - [\, x_{13}(t_\nu) + x_{14}(t_\nu)\Delta t] \quad (33)$$

and

$$\tilde{x}_{14}(t_\nu) = \begin{cases} \bar{x}_{14} & \text{for } \left| x_{14}(t_\nu) + \dfrac{g(t_{\nu-1})-g(t_\nu)}{\Delta t} \right| \le \bar{x}_{14} \\[2ex] \left| x_{14}(t_\nu) + \dfrac{g(t_{\nu-1})-g(t_\nu)}{\Delta t} \right| & \text{otherwise} \end{cases} \quad (34)$$

The angular velocity $\tilde{x}_{14}(t_\nu)$ consists of the nominal angular velocity $\bar{x}_{14}$ as well as of the actual angular velocity $x_{14}(t_\nu)$ of robot 1 and via $g(t_\nu)$ of $x_{24}(t_\nu)$ of robot 2. Based on this information, $q(t_\nu)$ indicates similar to $p(t_\nu)$ the number of time intervalls Δt before collision. The details of the derivation are given in [Hoyer 1984].

The variables $h(t_\nu)$, $g(t_\nu)$, $p(t_\nu)$ and $q(t_\nu)$ in (28), (29), (31) and (32) are the basic parameters for the description of the collision avoidance trajectory. Considering the translational movement of robot 1 which has to avoid collision with robot 2 (right-of-way precedence has robot 2) the following form of this trajectory can be derived

$$f_{11}(t_\nu) = [\, h(t_\nu) - r_1(t_\nu)] + q(t_\nu)\,[\,\bar{x}_{12}\Delta t + h(t_\nu) - h(t_{\nu-1})] \quad (35)$$

$f_{11}(t_\nu)$ represents for the translational movement the new reference value for robot 1 in case of danger of a collision and is permanently calculated in order to detect a collision. This trajectory consists of two parts: The first term on the right handside of eq. (35) describes the maximal length $h(t_\nu) - r_1(t_\nu)$ of the arm of robot 1 for the safe passing with respect to robot 2 (which has the right-of-way) where $r_1(t_\nu)$ is a safety factor. When the arm has this length in the passing position (fig. 3) then from (32) and (33) $q(t_\nu)$ is at the same time equal to zero. This means that the second term on the right handside of (35) is equal to zero while passing. The performance of the algorithm is improved by the second term on the right handside of (35) because it takes via $\bar{x}_{12}\Delta t$ the possible translational movement in Δt (based on the nominal velocity $\bar{x}_{12}$) as well as the difference between the distance vectors $h(t_\nu)$ at t_ν and $h(t_{\nu-1})$ at $t_{\nu-1}$ into account. As these terms are weighted by the parameter $q(t_\nu)$ in (32), this results in an extension of the allowed translational range of the arm as well as in faster reaction proportional to the distance for the predicted collision point.

In a similar way the rotational movement of robot 1 is guided by the trajectory in case of danger of a collision:

$$f_{12}(t_\nu) = [\,\varphi_{01} - g(t_\nu) + \gamma\varphi_1(t_\nu)\,] + \gamma p(t_\nu)\tilde{x}_{14}(t_\nu)\Delta t \quad (36)$$

This equation is based on the same principle as $f_{11}(t_\nu)$ and uses the parameter $p(t_\nu)$ in (31) instead of $q(t_\nu)$. In (36) φ_{01} is the angle, denoting the relative position of robot 1 to robot 2 (fig. 3). The angle $g(t_\nu)$ is given in (29) where $\varphi_1(t_\nu)$ is a variable safety factor. The angle $\tilde{x}_{14}(t_\nu)\Delta t$ takes via $\tilde{x}_{14}(t_\nu)$ in (34) the nominal angular velocity of robot 1 as well as the actual velocities of robot 1 and 2 into account and is weighted by the parameter $p(t_\nu)$. In (36) the predicted position of the arm of robot 1 in relation to the angle $(\varphi_{01}-g(t_\nu))$ of the distance vector in fig. 3 is regarded by the parameter

$$\gamma = \begin{cases} +1 & \text{for } [\varphi_{01}-g(t_\nu)] < [x_{13}(t_\nu) + x_{14}(t_\nu)\Delta t] \\ -1 & \text{for } [\varphi_{01}-g(t_\nu)] \geq [x_{13}(t_\nu) + x_{14}(t_\nu)\Delta t] \end{cases} \tag{37}$$

The trajectory $f_{12}(t_\nu)$ in (36), however, is only applied as new reference value for collision avoidance if

$$p(t_\nu) \leq q(t_\nu) + q_0 \tag{38}$$

with q_0 as safety factor. Otherwise a reaction of the translational movement with $f_{11}(t_\nu)$ in (35) as reference input is sufficient to avoid a collision. A detailed derivation can be found in [Hoyer 1984].

Studies have shown, that in most practical cases the vertical movement is restricted e. g. by conveyor belts, assembly stands etc. It is therefore not meaningful to use the vertical movement for collision avoidance. However, this axis can be involved in the avoidance strategies without principle difficulties.

It can be seen by (35) and (36) in connection with (37), that the collision detection is based on the state variables and not on the inputs. This has the advantage that the collision avoidance is based on the actual movement of the robots and still functions, if e. g. the control of the robot with right-of-way precedence is defective.

5. Hierarchical Coordinator for Collision Avoidance

Based on the principle of collision avoidance, which is considered in the foregoing paragraph, the design of the hierarchical coordinator for collision avoidance is continued for a system of three robots.

It follows from the theory of multi-robot systems, which was developed in paragraph 3, that the vector $\underline{H}_2^b$ in (27) is equal to zero because robot 2 has the highest right-of-way precedence. This means that the original reference vector $\underline{v}_2(t)$ is permanently used as input of the basic controls of robot 2. As the vertical movement of robot 1 and robot 3 are not involved in collision avoidance, the third row of the vectors $\underline{H}_1^b$ and $\underline{H}_3^b$ are equal to zero from the same reasons. This leads to the following structure of $\underline{H}_b$:

$$\underline{H}^b(\underline{x}_1,\underline{x}_2,\underline{x}_3,\underline{v}_1,\underline{v}_2,\underline{v}_3) = \begin{bmatrix} H_{11}^b(\underline{x}_1,\underline{x}_2,\underline{v}_1) \\ H_{12}^b(\underline{x}_1,\underline{x}_2,\underline{v}_1) \\ 0 \\ \hline 0 \\ 0 \\ 0 \\ \hline H_{31}^b(\underline{x}_1,\underline{x}_2,\underline{x}_3,\underline{v}_3) \\ H_{32}^b(\underline{x}_1,\underline{x}_2,\underline{x}_3,\underline{v}_3) \\ 0 \end{bmatrix} \tag{39}$$

Based on the results in paragraph 4, H_{11}^b in (39) is given by

$$H_{11}^b = \begin{cases} 0 & \text{for } v_{11}(t_{\nu+1}) \leq f_{11}(t_\nu) \\ f_{11}(t_\nu) & \text{for } v_{11}(t_{\nu+1}) > f_{11}(t_\nu) \end{cases} \tag{40}$$

This means that the trajectory $f_{11}(t_\nu)$ functions as a switching criterion. If the original reference input $v_{11}(t_{\nu+1})$ is smaller or equal to the trajectory for collision avoidance $f_{11}(t_\nu)$ in (35), then H_{11}^b is set equal to zero, i. e. the original reference input $v_{11}(t_{\nu+1})$ is applied. Otherwise it is replaced by the trajectory $f_{11}(t_\nu)$. For the rotational movement follows from $p(t_\nu)$ in (31), $q(t_\nu)$ in (32) and $f_{12}(t_\nu)$ in (36) in connection with γ in (37) in the same way:

$$
H^b_{12} = \begin{cases}
0 & \text{for } p(t_\nu) \le p(t_\nu)+q_o \\
 & \text{or for } p(t_\nu) > q(t_\nu)+q_o \\
 & \qquad \text{with } \gamma = -1 \text{ and } v_{12}(t_{\nu+1}) \le f_{12}(t_\nu) \\
 & \qquad \text{or with } \gamma = 1 \text{ and } v_{12}(t_{\nu+1}) \ge f_{12}(t_\nu) \\
f_{12}(t_\nu) & \text{for } p > q(t_\nu)+q_o \\
 & \qquad \text{with } \gamma = -1 \text{ and } v_{12}(t_{\nu+1}) > f_{12}(t_\nu) \\
 & \qquad \text{or with } \gamma = 1 \text{ and } v_{12}(t_{\nu+1}) < f_{12}(t_\nu)
\end{cases} \tag{41}
$$

In (39) H^b_{31} and H^b_{32} refer to robot 3 and have in principle the same basic form as H^b_{11} and H^b_{12} for robot 1, respectively.

From (19) with (20) - (24) the hierarchical coordinator for collision avoidance can be designed with $\underline{H}^b$ in (39), (40) and (41). This results in the form of the hierarchical coordinator which is given in (42).

It can be seen in (42) that the elements of the diagonal of $\underline{E}$ are equal to 1, if the elements of the same row of H^b are equal to zero. This is due to the fact that the original reference inputs are applied to the robot control wherever the hierarchical coordinator does not intervene. This is for example the case for robot 2 with $v_{21}(t)$ ... $v_{23}(t)$ because of its right-of-way precedence. The factor 1 follows from the choice of the input gains $\bar{\lambda}_{k,i}$ equal to $\lambda_{k,i}$. For those reference inputs, which are supervised by the hierarchical coordinator, the input gains are switched between 0 and 1 depending on $H^b_{k,i}$, i. e.

$$
e_{k,i}(H^b_{k,i}) = \frac{\bar{\lambda}_{k,i}(H^b_{k,i})}{\lambda_{k,i}} = \begin{cases} 0 & \text{for } H^b_{k,i} \ne 0 \\ 1 & \text{for } H^b_{k,i} = 0 \end{cases} \tag{43}
$$

This means that in case of danger of collision the reference input $v_{11}(t)$ for example is replaced by the new reference input $f_{11}(t_\nu)$ in $\underline{H}^b_{11}$.

The hierarchical coordinator as presented in paragraph 3 offers the possibility to change the dynamics of the resulting system matrix $\underline{A}^*_k$ with $\underline{A}^*_{k,i}$ in (16) and (17). This is done via $\underline{H}^a$ with $\underline{H}^a_k$ and $\underline{H}^a_{k,i}$ in (20) to (22). In the design of the hierarchical coordinator for collision avoidance this is used to change the dynamics of the control circuits in order to increase the fastness of reaction in case of danger of collision. Afterwards the control system can return to the original dynamics which guarantee accurate path control. Therefore, only the dynamics of those variables of motion are changed via $\underline{H}^a$ which are

$$
\underline{H} = \underbrace{\left[\begin{array}{c|c|c}
\begin{matrix} \underline{H}^a_{11} & \underline{0} & \underline{0} \\ \underline{0} & \underline{H}^a_{12} & \underline{0} \\ \underline{0} & \underline{0} & \underline{0} \end{matrix} & \underline{0} & \underline{0} \\ \hline
\underline{0} & \underline{0} & \underline{0} \\ \hline
\underline{0} & \underline{0} & \begin{matrix} \underline{H}^a_{31} & \underline{0} & \underline{0} \\ \underline{0} & \underline{H}^a_{32} & \underline{0} \\ \underline{0} & \underline{0} & \underline{0} \end{matrix}
\end{array}\right]}_{\underline{H}^a(\underline{H}^b)}
\left[\begin{array}{c} x_{11} \\ \vdots \\ x_{16} \\ \hline x_{21} \\ \vdots \\ x_{26} \\ \hline x_{31} \\ \vdots \\ x_{36} \end{array}\right]
+ \underbrace{\left[\begin{array}{c} H^b_{11} \\ H^b_{12} \\ 0 \\ \hline 0 \\ 0 \\ 0 \\ \hline H^b_{31} \\ H^b_{32} \\ 0 \end{array}\right]}_{\underline{H}^b}
+ \underbrace{\left[\begin{array}{c|c|c}
\begin{matrix} e_{11} & 0 & 0 \\ 0 & e_{12} & 0 \\ 0 & 0 & 1 \end{matrix} & \underline{0} & \underline{0} \\ \hline
\underline{0} & \begin{matrix} 1 & 0 & 0 \\ 0 & 1 & 0 \\ 0 & 0 & 1 \end{matrix} & \underline{0} \\ \hline
\underline{0} & \underline{0} & \begin{matrix} e_{31} & 0 & 0 \\ 0 & e_{32} & 0 \\ 0 & 0 & 1 \end{matrix}
\end{array}\right]}_{\underline{E}(\underline{H}^b)}
\left[\begin{array}{c} v_{11} \\ v_{12} \\ v_{13} \\ \hline v_{21} \\ v_{22} \\ v_{23} \\ \hline v_{31} \\ v_{32} \\ v_{33} \end{array}\right] \tag{42}
$$

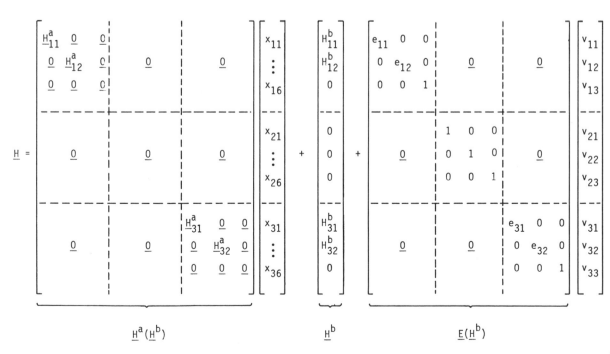

involved in the collision avoidance strategies. This results in the vectors $\underline{H}^a_{11}$, $\underline{H}^a_{12}$, $\underline{H}^a_{31}$, $\underline{H}^a_{32}$ in $\underline{H}^a$ which correspond to the elements H^b_{11}, H^b_{12}, H^b_{31}, H^b_{32} in (42). The other vectors in the diagonal of $\underline{H}^a$ are equal to zero, i. e. the original dynamics remain unchanged by the coordinator.

The change of the dynamics is realized on the basis of equations (20), (21) and (22) for $\underline{H}^a$, where $\underline{H}^a_{k,i}$ has the form

$$\underline{H}^a_{k,i} = \begin{bmatrix} \dfrac{\bar{\alpha}^0_{k,i}}{\lambda_{k,i}} & \dfrac{\bar{\alpha}^1_{k,i}}{\lambda_{k,i}} \end{bmatrix} \qquad (44)$$

The parameters $\bar{\alpha}^0_{k,i}$, $\bar{\alpha}^1_{k,i}$ can be chosen arbitrarily. One possibility is an aperiodic behavior of the axes of motion together with a dependency on the parameter $q(t_\nu)$ in (32), which is a criterion for the actual danger of collision. This leads to

$$\bar{\alpha}^1_{k,i} = 2\sqrt{\bar{\alpha}^0_{k,i}} \qquad (45)$$

and

$$\bar{\alpha}^0_{k,i}(t_\nu) = \begin{cases} 0 & \text{for } H^b_{k,i} = 0 \\ \dfrac{\alpha^0_{k,i\,max} - \alpha^0_{k,i}}{\mu q(t_\nu) + 1} & \text{for } H^b_{k,i} \neq 0 \end{cases}$$

$$(k = 1,3;\ i = 1,2) \qquad (46)$$

In (46) μ is a constant coefficient and $\alpha^0_{k,i\,max}$ denotes the maximal value of $\bar{\alpha}^0_{k,i}(t_\nu)$ with respect to technical limitations.

Equation (46) shows that the dynamics remain unchanged for $H^b_{k,i} = 0$, that means there is no danger of collision and the original inputs are applied to the robot controls. On the other hand in application of an avoidance strategy ($H^b_{k,i} \neq 0$) the dynamic will be changed via $q(t_\nu)$ depending on the actual danger of collision. This shows that similar to $E(\underline{H}^b)$ in (42) the matrix $\underline{H}^a$ depends on $\underline{H}^b$ as well, which is characteristic for the hierarchical coordinator (19) designed for collision avoidance. Corresponding to equation (42), fig. 4 demonstrates this structure of the hierarchical coordinator for collision avoidance which shows these interrelations.

The structure of equation (42) and of fig. 4 holds for a larger number of robots as well because the application to three robots (as demonstrated by the derivation) does not restrict the generality of this approach.

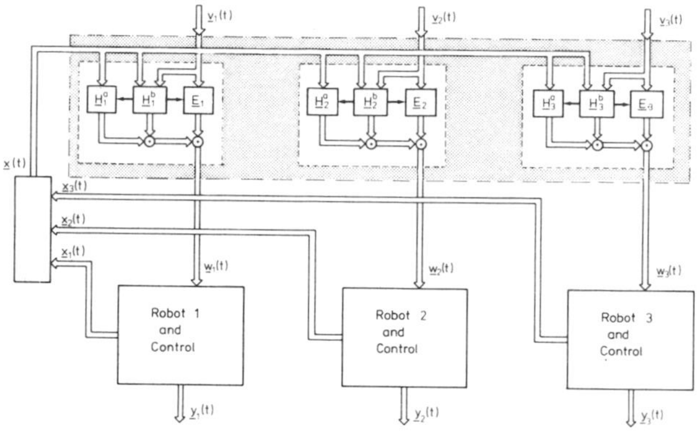

Figure 4. Structure of the hierarchical coordinator for collision avoidance

The performance of the hierarchical coordinator as presented in eq. (42) with (40), (41) and (43) to (46) is demonstrated by simulations in figs. 5 - 8 which are based on the configuration in fig. 2. For the simulation itself the block-orientated digital simulation language SIMAIT was used, which was developed at the Chair of Automation and Information Processing (AIT). Fig. 5 shows the trajectories of three robots which have a common collision space. Robot 1 collides with robot 3 after 4,8 time-units and with robot 2 after 5,3 time-units, while robot 2 collides with robot 3 after 6,5 time-units (after the collision with robot 1).

The hierarchical coordinator (eq. (42)) is designed for real-time collision avoidance where the highest right-of-way precedence has robot 2 and the lowest robot 3. This means that robot 2 can follow its desired path, while robot 1 has to avoid a collision with robot 2 and at the same time robot 3 has to avoid a collision with robot 1 and robot 2. Fig. 6 shows the resulting changes in application of the hierarchical coordinator (42) where all collisions are avoided: Robots 1 and 3 cannot pursue their original proposed paths but reach the target points. The deviations from the original paths can be influenced to some extend by the safety factors in eqs. (35), (36) but are of course mainly a function of the position of the collision points and the speeds of the robots. Figures 7 and 8 demonstrate the performance of the same hierarchical coordinator for different proposed trajectories and higher velocities of the three robots. The original trajectories are given in fig. 7 where three collisions occur. The collision-free trajectories provided by on-line path correction by the hierarchical coordinator are shown in fig. 8. The right-of-way precedences are the same as in the foregoing application. Based on these simulations the required amount of time for real-time processing of the collision detection and avoidance was estimated. It turned out that based on the hierarchical coordinator in form of eq. (42) the computation of the detection and avoidance strategies will require approximately 20 msec for three robots (3,5 to 7,3 msec per robot involved) on a microprocessor of the type Texas Instruments 9995. This computational time can be of course further reduced by parallel processing which can be realized according to the subdivision of the structure of the hierarchical coordinator in eq. (42) and fig. 4.

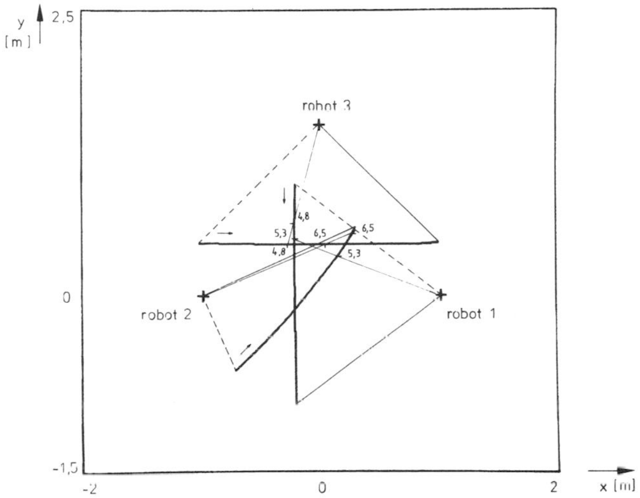

Figure 5. Collision of three robots
(application 1)

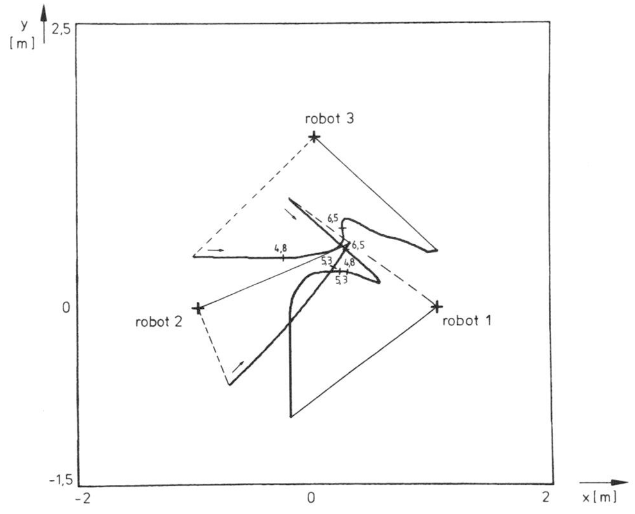

Figure 6. Automatic collision avoidance of three robots
(application 1)

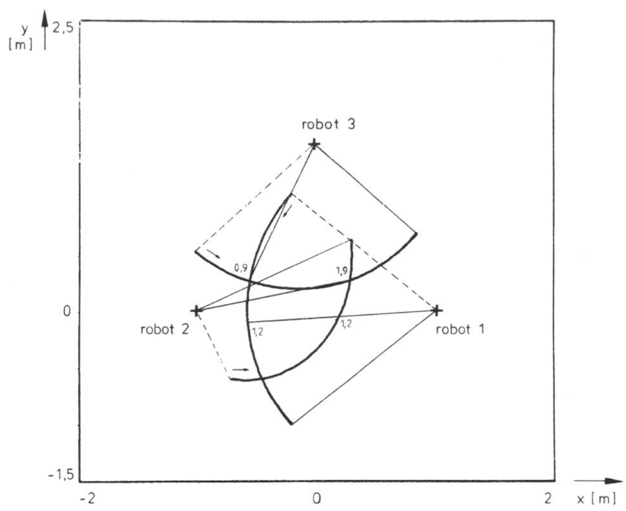

Figure 7. Collision of three robots
(application 2)

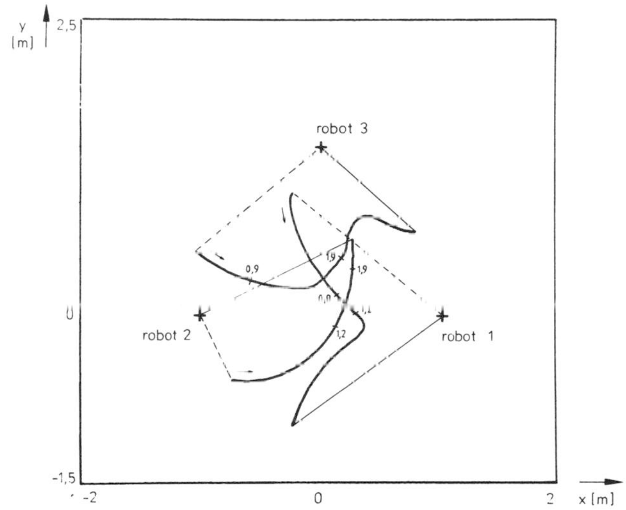

Figure 8. Automatic collision avoidance of three robots
(application 2)

Acknowledgement

This research was supported by the Minister für Wissenschaft und Forschung des Landes Nordrhein-Westfalen.

References

Dunne, M. 1979. An advanced assembly robot, Industrial Robots, Vol 2, Society of Manufacturing Engineers, Michigan, pp. 249-262.

Freund, E. 1976. Verfahren und Anordnung zur Regelung von Manipulatoren und industriellen Robotern. Deutsches Patentamt, Auslegeschrift 25 56 433. Method and arrangement for the control of manipulators and industrial robots. US Patent 4218172, Patent specification Japan Sho-53-75664.

Freund, E. and Syrbe, M. 1976. Control of industrial robots by means of microprocessors. Lecture notes in control and information sciences, New York: Springer-Verlag, pp. 167-185.

Freund, E. 1982. Fast nonlinear control with arbitrary pole-placement for industrial robots and manipulators, Int. Journal Robotic Research 1 (1), pp. 65-78.

Freund, E. 1983. Hierarchical nonlinear control for robots, Proc. First Int. Symp. Robotics Research, Bretton Woods, New Hampshire, pp. 12.1-12.14.

Freund, E. and Hoyer, H. 1983. Hierarchical control of guided collision avoidance for robots in automatic assembly, Proc. Int. Conf. on Assembly Automation, Tokyo, pp. 91-102.

Freund, E. 1983. On the design of multi-robot systems. Proc. IEEE Int. Conf. on Robotics, Atlanta, Georgia.

Hoel, J. 1976. Some variations of Lee's algorithm, IEEE Trans. on Computers 25 (1), pp. 19-24.

Hoyer, H. 1984. Verfahren zur automatischen Kollisionsvermeidung von Robotern im koordinierten Betrieb (Automatic collision avoidance for robots in coordinated cooperation), PhD dissertation, Fern-Universität Hagen, Electrotechnical Department.

Lozano-Perez, T. and Wesley, M. 1979. An algorithm for planning collision free paths among polyhedral obstacles, Communications ACM 22 (10), pp. 560-570.

Tyridal, P. 1980. New ideas in multi-task real-time control systems for industrial robots, Proc. 10th Int. Symp. Industrial Robots, Milan, pp. 659-670.

CLOSED LOOP CONTROL OF ROBOTS WITH LOCAL ENVIRONMENT SENSING : PRINCIPLES AND APPLICATIONS

Bernard ESPIAU

IRISA
Campus de Beaulieu
35042 Rennes Cédex - FRANCE

We present a study of the sensory-based control problem, using both local modelling relating sensors to elementary actions, and a global dynamic model in the adequate spaces. We give two methods (kinematics or dynamics) to synthetize the control loop, and present an example of real-time application to master/slave telemanipulation.

INTRODUCTION

In the classical control of robots and manipulators, two main levels may be considered : the first one is the most concerned with the point of view of automatic control, and involves the dynamic properties of the system. The used informations are then relative to intrinsic positions, velocities, acceleration, forces and torques, and are the basis of internal loops. The second level, which is the task's one, is related to the behaviour of a robot with regard to its environment. The information here are high-level, coming for example from 2D or 3D vision systems. In that case, they have an effect on the desired trajectory, but are not taken into account in the dynamic behaviour of the whole system : in fact the computing times resulting from high level processing and decision classically leads to distinguish the time-scales between basic loops (first level) and environment-based loops, thus to neglect the dynamic influence of the last ones.

However, there exists a kind of external informations which lie at the boundary of the two levels : these are tactile and force sensing. The related loops are either internal (for example in hybrid position/force control [Raibert, 1981]) or external. However, in most cases the related motions are local and slow, and the dynamic properties of the robot have not to be taken into account.

As a large extent of contact-based loops, this article discusses a more general point of view, mainly concerned with the concept of "remote touching", in which the requirements in modelling and control had been little investigated. The article is organized as follows : in section 1 we give the notion of local environment, and we propose a new description of sensory-based actions in the end effector, with a method of synthetizing a global action, either with dynamics or kinematics formulation. In section 2 we address the problem of controlling the whole system, using two kinds of dynamic models. In section 3, a typical application to telemanipulation is shortly described, and comments on this work are drawn in the conclusion.

1 - LOCAL ENVIRONMENT AND SYNTHESIS OF SENSORY-BASED ACTIONS

1.1 - Basic définitions

We consider a serial-link rigid robot with N degrees of freedom. A reference frame R_0 is fixed to the base of the robot. The frame linked to the end effector is R_N. The origins are respectively O_0 and O_N. As presented in figure 1, we define the *local environment* (LE) as a finite volume V_L surrounding the links of a robot at each time. This volume thus is mobile in the same way that the links, and constitutes the sensitive sheath which ensures remote touching. It is assumed that the related sensors, often called *proximity sensors*, do not provide any significative signal on the outside of V_L.

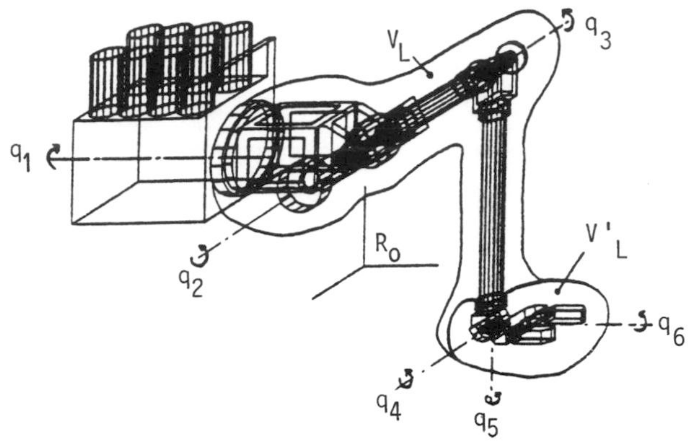

Figure 1 - Local environment

In a more general way, we define a proximity sensor as a sensor providing a scalar information, issued from LE, referring to the relative positions of the concerned link and an objet in LE, and directly suitable for control purposes. The practical interest of such sensors is underlined by many authors (see for example [Bejczy, 1980]). Obviously, this description of the local environment is here given from an intuitive point of view. A more formal definition, related to potential models of the environment may be stated (Fig.2) :

Let C_k be a simple geometric approximation of a link L_k. If $V_k(x,y,z)$ is a potential function associated to C_k, an equipotential surface $E_k(\varepsilon)=\{x,y,z : V_k=\varepsilon\}$ may define LE. The more useful case, related to obstacle avoidance problems, is the Newton model : $V_k(x,y,z) = \frac{\lambda}{d} + c$, where d is defined in figure 2.

The interest of a potential model for LE will be pointed out in the following.

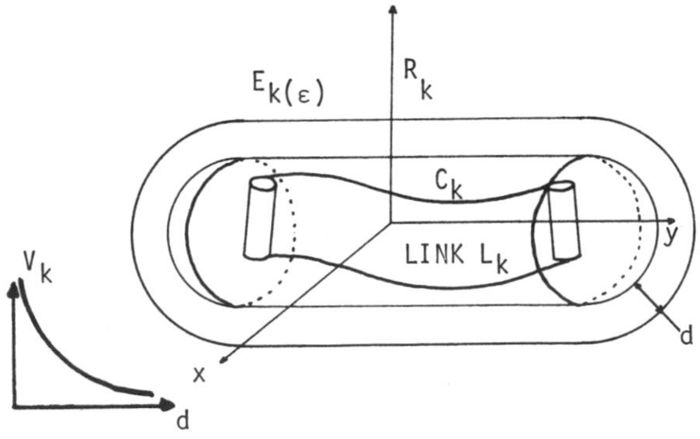

Figure 2 - Potential function for a link

For simplification, we consider in the following a reduction V'_L of V_L to the neighbouring of the end effector, assumed to be a rigid solid (S), with the associated frame R_n.

1.2 - Elementary actions

Let C be a set of elementary sensors $c_j (j=1...n_c)$ satisfying the previous requirements. Each sensor has fixed location and observation direction in R_n, and provides a scalar signal y_j. Associated to C, we define a set of n_v elementary actions, as follows :

an elementary action a_i includes in R_n :

-- an origin x_i

-- a vector v_i such as :

$$v_i = A_i d_i \tag{1}$$

with : $\|d_i\|=\|v_i\|=1$; dim $d_i=3$; dim $v_i \leq 3$, A_i is full rank.

-- a scalar parameter s_i depending on the measures provided by a given subset C_i of C, such as $V_i=s_i(..y_k..)v_i$.

Remarks

1 - The physical meaning associated to elementary actions is not here fixed. They may be understood as well as elementary displacements or velocities as forces and torques (see table 1 in section 1.4) ;

2 - A_i projects d_i onto a subspace of $\mathbb{R}^3$, for example to select the components of d_i remaining free of sensory-based actions. An example is given further : this is the "mixed mode" of section 3 ;

3 - Many kinds of sensors may be concerned with this description : force, proximity (infrared, inductive), range (ultrasonic), low level local vision.

1.3 - Primitives

As shown in [Espiau, 1984], sensors and actions may be gathered in a coherent way to build primitives. We thus may realize a partition of C in independant subsets C_k constituting such primitives. Defining these primitives provides a connection with the kinematic description of contacts between bodies [Salisbury, 1983] : a primitive realizes an artificial contact between (S) and the objects of LE. It is thus possible to describe a primitive by classical twist and wrench characteristics and to ensure a coherent behaviour with possible contact loops. Figure 3 gives a practical example of primitives integrated within a bidigital gripper. In the general case we distinguish three kinds of primitives :

-- a simple one : if all the actions have the same meaning (for example, all V_i are velocity translation vectors)

-- a mixed one : in the contrary case

-- an external primitive : a set of actions

not associated to or subset C_i : it is an important point, because this description allows to introduce an a priori modelling, or a nominal desired trajectory with the same formalism as LE - based actions.

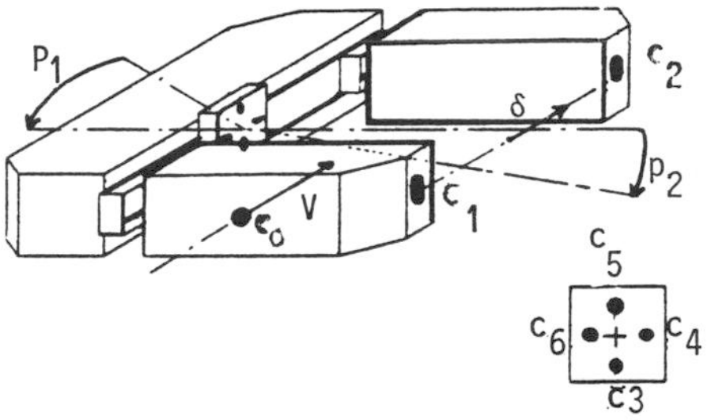

4 sensors (p_1,p_2) : surface following

2 sensors (δ) : centering

1 sensor (V) : collision advoidance

Figure 3 - Examples of primitives

1.4 - Synthesis of dynamics and kinematics actions

As shown in table 1, we may distinguish 8 cases according to the meaning of elementary actions :

Meaning of actions / rank of actions	$A_i = I_3\ \forall_i$	$\exists\ A_i$: rank(A_i) < 3
All actions forces	1.1	2.1
Forces and torques	1.2	2.2
All actions translation velocities	1.3	2.3
Translation and rotation velocities	1.4	2.4

List of possible cases

Table 1

Cases 1.1, 1.2, 2.1 and 2.2 give a dynamics meaning to the elementary actions. The most simple situation, 1.1, may be understood as the case of a rigid solid submitted to a finite set of external forces Vi. As for defining the local environment, this point of view may be related to a potential model of the environment, the gradient of which at point x_i would be the force V_i.

An other point of view (cases 1.3, 1.4, 2.3, 2.4) is to consider that the actions contribute to describe the trajectory of (S) in position and orientation. As absolute positions and orientations are not suitable values because local environment sensing is a *relative* concept, it is more convenient to specify the velocities. Case 1.3 is of special interest, as seen further.

In both points of view, the global effect is a vector $\phi \in \mathbb{R}^3 \times \mathbb{R}^3$.

1.4.1 - Dynamics

Let $A(x_A, y_A, Z_A)$ in $R_N \in (S)$ and $\delta_i = x_i - x_A\ \forall x_i \in R_N$. The antisymmetric matrix of the vector product $X\ \vec{Ax_i}$ is :

$$\Delta_i = \begin{bmatrix} 0 & \delta_i^{\ 3} & -\delta_i^{\ 2} \\ -\delta_i^{\ 3} & 0 & \delta_i^{\ 1} \\ \delta_i^{\ 2} & -\delta_i^{\ 1} & 0 \end{bmatrix} \tag{2}$$

Case 1.1 : In A, the synthetized dynamic vector is defined by

$$\phi_{11} = \begin{bmatrix} \sum_{i=1}^{n_V} V_i \\ \sum_{i=1}^{n_V} \Delta_i^T\ V_i \end{bmatrix} \tag{3}$$

Case 1.2 : Let $\{V_i\} = \{f_i\} \cup \{\tau_i\}$, where the $f_i(i=1...n_f)$ are the forces vectors and $\tau_i(i=1,...n_T)$ the torques. The resulting action then is :

$$\phi_{12} = \begin{bmatrix} \sum_{i=1}^{n_f} f_i \\ \sum_{i=1}^{n_f} \Delta_i\ f_i + \sum_{i=1}^{n_T} \tau_i \end{bmatrix} \tag{4}$$

Remark : Cases 2 may be treated by using pseudo-inverses of Ai, or, when possible, by direct sum of the subspaces defined by the Ai's (see [Espiau, 1984-1]).

1.4.2 - Kinematics

Case 1.3 : As (S) is a rigid solid, its velocity vector field W is completely defined by a six-components vector called T_c.

However, in general, given the set $\{V_1 ... V_{n_V}\}$ at points $\{x_1 ... x_{n_V}\}$, there is no reason to have at each time :

$$\exists\ W : W(x_i) = V_i \quad \forall i = 1...n_V$$

We thus set $\varepsilon_i = V_i - W(x_i)$, and try to find a field W which minimizes the cost function :

$$J = \sum_{i=1}^{n_v} \lambda_i \| \varepsilon_i \|^2 \qquad (5)$$

where λ_i is a weigthing parameter, with $\sum_{i=1}^{n_v} \lambda_i = 1$, and $\|.\|$ the Euclidean norm.

W is completely defined by ω and $s = W(A)$, for any choice of A. Thus, $\phi = \binom{s}{\omega}$, and we look for ϕ^* such as $J(\phi^*)$ be minimum.

It can easily be shown (proof in [Espiau, 1982-1]) that :

-- by choosing A as the origin of R_N and the mass center of (S') defined below, and taking R_N as a main inertia frame of (S')

-- with the condition (C) :

$\not\exists (D)$, straight line : $x_i \in (D)\ \forall i = 1, \ldots n_v$

then :

$$T_c^* : \phi^* = \begin{bmatrix} 1 \\ \bar{M}^{-1}\sigma \end{bmatrix} = \begin{pmatrix} f' \\ \tau' \end{pmatrix} \qquad (6)$$

where :

-- (S') is the ideal solid made with the n_v point masses λ_i, located in x_i and rigidly linked by massless bars

-- 1 and σ are the elements in A of T'_c, called "pseudo-kinetics torsor" of (S') :

$$T'_c = \begin{cases} 1 = \sum_{i=1}^{n_v} \lambda_i V_i & (7) \\ \sigma = \sum_{i=1}^{n_v} \lambda_i \Delta_i^T V_i & (8) \end{cases}$$

-- $\bar{M}$ is the non singular diagonal inertia matrix of (S') in R_N. Further, if (S') has a spherical inertia, $T_c^* = T'_c$.

Remark -
If (C) is not satisfied, and out of trivial cases $n_v = 0$ or 1, R has a one-dimensionnal undetermination.

Other cases -
As shown in [Espiau, 1982-1] they may be stated under the same form as previously, with different expressions for J. However, the previous result becomes invalid.

2 - GLOBAL CONTROL

Having got ϕ or T_c^*, we have now to examine how to insert them into a global control scheme.

2.1 - Modelling and control in operationnal coordinates

It is well known that the dynamic model of a rigid robot in joint space has the form :

$$A(q)\ddot{q} + H(q, \dot{q}) = \Gamma \qquad (9)$$

where A is the inertia matrix, q is the joint coordinates vector such as $q \in \mathfrak{D}_q$, dim q = N, and $H(q, \dot{q})$ has the form :

$$H(q,\dot{q}) = B(q,\dot{q}) + C(q) + D(\dot{q}) \qquad (10)$$

with C : gravity term, D : dissipative forces, B : vector of quadratic forms giving centrifugal and coriolis forces.

It is then easy to derive a model in operating coordinates :

By setting $\quad x = f(q) \qquad (16)$

and $\quad J(q) = \left\{\frac{\partial fi}{\partial qj}\right\} \qquad (17)$

and writing $Q(q,\dot{q}) = \frac{dJ}{dt}(q,\dot{q}) = \begin{bmatrix} \dot{q}^T W^1(q)\dot{q} \\ \vdots \\ \dot{q}^T W^N(q)\dot{q} \end{bmatrix} \qquad (18)$

where $W^i(q) = \left\{\frac{\partial Ji(q)}{\partial q}\right\}$ with $J^T = \begin{bmatrix} J_1^T \ldots J_N^T \end{bmatrix}$

we get the following dynamic model :

$$F = A'(x)\ddot{x} + H'(x,\dot{x}) \qquad (19)$$

$$\text{with} \quad \begin{cases} F = J^{-T}\Gamma \\ A' = J^{-T} A J^{-1} \\ H' = J^{-T}(N - MQ) \end{cases} \qquad (20)$$

where the inverse (or pseudo inverse) of J exists.

In that model, x includes the 3D position of O_N and a parametrization of the orientation of R_N in R_o (the Euler Angles, for example).

The general control vector has the following form:

$$F = \hat{A}'(x)\ u + \hat{H}'(x,\dot{x}) + \text{Fext} \qquad (21)$$

where $\hat{A}'$ and $\hat{H}'$ are the calculated or estimated counterparts of A' and H'. A firstway to close the loop with the final results of section 1 is thus to use eq(21):

2.1.1 - Dynamic case

The synthetised vectors ϕ_{11} or ϕ_{12} may constitute Fext, with the transformation :

$$\text{Fext} = P(q)\ \phi \qquad (22)$$

P(q) depending, as J(q), on the parametrization.

2.1.2 - Kinematic case

We have to insert the computed value T_c^* into the control (21). First, by using an appropriate Jacobian, T_c^* may be transformated in a set of desired inputs $\dot{x}_c$, which then may be introduced in a velocity control scheme. A most convenient way to realize this control is to use a so-called robust control method :

Following [Samson, 1983], an interesting form for u is :

$$u = -K_p \varepsilon - K_V \dot{\varepsilon} + \mu_2 \ ; \ Kp,Kv \text{ def} > 0 \qquad (23)$$

with $\varepsilon = x - x_r$ (24)

and $\ddot{x}_r = u_r$ (25) being and ideal reference model, the control of which is designed by the user.

It is obvious that, in the ideal case (A'=A,H'=H') the global error evolution equation is :

$$\ddot{\varepsilon} + K_v \dot{\varepsilon} + K_p \varepsilon = 0 \qquad (26)$$

However, in the general case, it may be shown by Samson's theorem ([Samson, 1983, 1984]) that it is possible to ensure the global stability of the system using non linear gains even if the choosen form of $\hat{A}'$ and $\hat{H}'$ is not close to A' and H'. It is not our purpose to further describe this class of control, but it is interesting to notice that, by this way, we may "forget" the dynamic contribution (A', H'), and only consider the ideal case, provided that the non linear control algorithm ensures a good behaviour of the actual global system. The interested reader will find all details and results in the cited references.

Coming back to the sensory-based control problem, we can see that $\dot{x}_c$ is an input of (25) such as, for example :

$$u_r = - L_v(x_r - \dot{x}_c) \qquad (27)$$

The interest of using a robust control is then obvious : analysis or simulation of sensory-based loops may be conducted with equations (25) and (27) only, when we are able to keep ε and $\dot{\varepsilon}$ small, which is possible with non linear gains.

2.2 - Modelling and control in operating space

The previous models are classical, but do not use directly the computed values T_C* and ϕ, because of the choice of x as a variable of the model. Further, the model in x present some other drawbacks :

-- The use of a parametrization adds singular points, in general different from the singular points due to the geometry of the robot.

-- Forces and torques acting on the effector have to be transformed into generalized (or joint) forces. As F depends on the parametrization, this transformation may hide the real behaviour of the manipulators and the goals of the control policy.

-- Specifying a trajectory in the used parametrization space may not lead to a good trajectory between two orientations.

Thus, it is better to use a parameter-free dynamic model of the end effector of the manipulator, and we propose in the following this new kind of model.

2.2.1 - Adequate dynamic model

The position of the origin of R_N with respect to R_o is completely specified by the vector x $\mathbb{R}^3$. The orientation of R_N with respect to R_o is the rotation r such as the vectorial basis associated to R_N be the image of the basis associated to R_o through r. *This means that we choose* $\mathbb{R}^3 \times SO_3(\mathbb{R})$ *as configuration space* (CS) to describe the evolution of R_N.

The velocity space is then the tangent space of (CS). The tangent space of $\mathbb{R}^3$ is $\mathbb{R}^3$ itself, and, due to the Lie group structure on $SO_3(\mathbb{R}^3)$, the tangent space of $SO_3(\mathbb{R})$ is $\mathbb{R}^3$ also.

The velocity of R_N is thus given by the couple $(\dot{x},\omega)$ where $\dot{x}$ is the velocity of O_N and ω the angular velocity. It is well known that the velocity of any point P linked to R_N is :

$$V(P) = \dot{x} + \omega \times \vec{O_N P} \qquad (28)$$

(28) shows that the vector field defined on each point as the velocity of the corresponding point linked to R_N is completely defined by (x,ω). Such a vector field is called a *"kinematic torsor"* and identified to (x,ω). This space is the velocity space (VS).

Since there is a duality between velocities and efforts through the virtual works principle, the efforts exerted on a rigid body linked to R_N are completely defined by the global torque in O_N, M, and the vector sum F of the different forces. Such as :

$$\forall P \quad R_N : M(P) = M + F \times \vec{O_N P} \qquad (29)$$

This torsor is called *"dynamic torsor"*, and we will use the space of dynamic torsors as *effort space.*

The last needed space is the *acceleration space.* It is simply $\mathbb{R}^3 \times \mathbb{R}^3$: An acceleration will be the couple $(\ddot{x}, \dot{\omega})$.

In [Leborgne, 1984] we show that, using these spaces, we may built a new dynamic model, with the following form :

$$\begin{pmatrix} F \\ \mathcal{M} \end{pmatrix} \; M\begin{pmatrix} \ddot{x} \\ \dot{\omega} \end{pmatrix} + \begin{pmatrix} \mu_T \\ \mu_R \end{pmatrix} + \begin{pmatrix} \nu_T \\ \nu_R \end{pmatrix} \qquad (30)$$

where : $$M = \begin{pmatrix} M_x & M_{xr} \\ M_{rx} & M_r \end{pmatrix} \quad (31)$$

with
$$M_x = J_T^{*T} A J_T^* \quad (32)$$
$$M_r = J_R^{*T} A J_R^* \quad (33)$$
$$M_{rx} = J_R^{*T} A J_T^* = M_{xr}^T \quad (34)$$

and :
$$\mu_T = J_T^{*T} B(q,\dot q) - M_{xr}\dot J_R \dot q - M_x \dot J_T \dot q \quad (35)$$
$$\mu_R = J_R^{*T} B(q,\dot q) - M_{rx}\dot J_T \dot q - M_r \dot J_R \dot q \quad (36)$$
$$\nu_T = J_T^{*T}(C+D) \quad (37)$$
$$\nu_R = J_R^{*T}(C+D) \quad (38)$$

where the Jacobians J_R and J_T are such as :

$$\dot x = J_T(q)\,\dot q \quad (39) \;;\; \omega = J_R(q)\,\dot q \quad (40)$$

Where J_R and J_T are non singular, the joint velocities space $\dot Q$ is the direct sum of Ker($\dot J_T$) and Ker($\dot J_R$). J_T^* and J_R^* are two applications from (VS) on to $\dot Q$, with the properties :

$$J_T^* J_T + J_R^* J_R = \mathrm{id}\,\dot Q \quad (41) \;;\; J_R J_T^* = J_T J_R^* = 0 \quad (42)$$

2.2.2 - Control

Starting with the dynamic model (30) the problem of decoupling and compensating for dynamical effects can be solved in a similar way as previously by taking :

$$\begin{pmatrix} F \\ M \end{pmatrix} = \hat M \begin{pmatrix} u_x \\ u_r \end{pmatrix} + \begin{pmatrix} \hat\mu_x \\ \mu_R \end{pmatrix} + \begin{pmatrix} \hat\nu_x \\ \nu_R \end{pmatrix} \quad (43)$$

as input torsor. u_x and u_r represent the control accelerations (linear and angular) of the end effector. Using (35) to (38), we get at the joint level, in the ideal case (no "$\wedge$") :

$$\Gamma = A(J_R^* u_r + J_T^* u_x) + B(q,\dot q) + C(q) + D(\dot q) - A(J_T^* \dot J_T + J_R^* \dot J_R)\,\dot q \quad (44)$$

-- Including sensory informations : dynamic synthesis

If the sensory informations are used to synthesize a dynamic torsor (ϕ), we get the new control torsor :

$$\begin{pmatrix} F \\ M \end{pmatrix} = M \begin{pmatrix} u_x \\ u_r \end{pmatrix} + \begin{pmatrix} \mu_x \\ \mu_R \end{pmatrix} + \begin{pmatrix} \nu_x \\ \nu_R \end{pmatrix} + \phi \quad (45)$$

By writing $\phi = \binom{1}{\sigma}$, this relation gives in the joint space :

$$\ddot q = (J_R^* u_r + J_T^* u_x) - (J_T^* \dot J_T + J_R^* \dot J_R)\,\dot q + A^{-1}(J_T^T 1 + J_R^T \sigma) \quad (46)$$

-- Including sensory informations : kinematic synthesis

In the case sensory informations are translated into a kinematic torsor T_c^* the velocities can be added to the velocities inputs in the closed loop control, i.e :

$$u'_x = u_x + K_v^x\,(1' - \dot x) \quad (47)$$
$$u'_r = u_r + K_v^r\,(\sigma' - \omega) \quad (48)$$

Thus, in both cases, the control loops do not depend on a parametrization of the orientation of R_n, and do not require a transformation of ϕ and T_c^*.

3 - AN EXAMPLE OF APPLICATION : THE MASTER/SLAVE TELEMANIPULATION

3.1 - About proximity Sensors

As stated in section 1, the local environment may be linked to a potential model of the environment. The importance of this point of view is emphasized when the elementary actions V_i may represent the gradient at x_i of such potential functions. This property is frequently encountered when using proximity sensors. For example, inductive systems generate a magnetic field, range finders may be related to an elastic potential. In the same way, optical sensors may provide in certain cases a signal close to the intensity of a local force field, gradient of a newtonian potential ([Espiau, 1984]) the form of which is $\frac{K}{d}$+c, d being the distance between an infrared reflectance sensor and a plane orthogonal to its axis. The experimental results presented below, taken from [André, 1983] [Espiau, 1984], [Vertut, 1984] use such sensors.

3.2 - Some experimental results

We have designed a set of sensors and various devices based upon the principles described in section 1. Primitives are of the kind given figure 3, and sensory outputs have either the form k d^{-2} or the linear one, k' d. The main realization is a bidigital gripper including up to 15 sensors. We have conducted two kinds of experimental works :

-- The first one was made with the help of a CAD system allowing the synthesis of iR signals among a 3D environment, and the design of control loops. Some examples may be found in [André, 1983] and [Leborgne, 1984].

-- The second kind of experimental work is in the field of Computer-Aided teleoperation, and uses force-based control in a master/slave system, with several sensor-referenced modes of control:

3.2.1 - Robot Mode and Unilateral Master/Slave (M/S) Mode

Here, proximity sensors allow to perform automatic subtasks, in the form of a sensor based compliance without contact. This fully automatic mode may be used everywhere an adaptive position control is required, like automatic guiding and grasping, surface following, tracking of moving targets, all allowing toincrease the slave's autonomy. If a passive copy is performed onto the master, this is the "Unilateral" M/S mode.

3.2.2 - Bilateral Master-Slave Modes

These modes are based on interactive (shared or traded) human-computer control, with fictive programmed constraints, actual force feedback, and sensor-referenced force feedback :

-- Mixed Mode

This mode implies that the operator is able to act in parallel with the computer. Futhermore, DOF sharing is essential for a lot of tasks. The Slave performs automatic functions which can be referenced to sensor data (dim n_1) (With or without passive feedback to the master). The other DOF (dim n_2) are driven by the operator in standard bilateral force reflecting mode.

For example, Sensor-referenced control is used to correct range, pitch and yaw errors relative to a surface ; translation is controlled by the operator.

-- Reflex mode

The proposed (so called "Reflex") mode realizes both classical force reflecting feedback and a supplementary sensor-referenced force feedback. This provides a efficient "shared control" between man and computer in such a way that the operator can feel, in master arm, artificial (sensor based) forces, like if objects (in the slave's work space) were magnets. However he keeps on line the priority of actions. This kinesthetic coupling results in a very impressive "remote touch" technique for obstacle avoidance, orientation of effectors, surface following (for inspection...).

Experimental Results and Conclusion

The experiments, shown in a videotape, have been performed with the IRISA Sensory System, implemted on a Master Slave MA 23 Telemanipulator and a minicomputer SOLAR. The sample rate is 100 H_z.

The typical useful operations are :

-- obstacle avoidance with proximity sensor based force feedback (=1à3 daN)

-- automatic tracking of moving object (30cm/s) and automatic grasping of a cylinder on a conveyor belt

-- automatic subtask, like tool grasping performed in 4 seconds

-- surface tracking with 5 DOF controlled, and 20cm/s velocity.

3 - CONCLUSION

Whe have proposed inthis article a coherent approach of the problem of controlling a robot in an operating space upon sensory informations. We have distinguished two kinds of control by using dynamics or kinematics torsors. The first one may easily be related to a potential model of the environment and is compatible with a dynamical analysis of the whole system. The second approach, which controls more finely the geometric trajectory, is velocity control, which is often the only possible control input for many existing robots. Finally, it is interesting to notice that dynamic torsor may be easily inserted in the Newton-Euler formalism for describing the dynamics equation of a robot. More, taking into account the whole local environment by creating force actions on each link is also easy in N-E algorithm. We have also proposed a new formalism for dynamic modelling, compatible with the description at sensory level, and allowing to analysis the behaviour of a manipulator under closed-loop sensory based control. The proposed approach is useful for a wide class of applications, as well in teleoperation as in navigation of 3D mobile robots, or in industrial problems like seam tracking in automatic arc welding.

However, this work has some limits at the present time : mainly, to derive a complete control scheme in the operation space, it is necessary to overcome some difficulties, including the study of the whole dynamic behaviour, T_c^* and ψ depending at each time of x and r. Two other problems are the building of a good reference model in the spac- $\mathbb{R}^3 \times SO_3$, and the overriding of singularities.

REFERENCES

André, G. 1983. Design and Modelling of Proximity Sensory Systems. Applications in Teleoperator control. Thesis, IRISA Rennes-University, France.

Bejczy, A.K. 1980. Smart Sensors for Smart hands, Progress in Astronautics and Aeronautics. Breckenbridge Editor, Vol.67, 1980.

Espiau, B. 1984-1. Use of External Sensory Feed back in the closed loop Control of Robots and Teleoperators. Internal report n°220, IRISA, Rennes, France.

Espiau, B. and André, G. 1984-2. Sensory Based Control of Robots and Teleoperators. 5th Symposium "Romansy", IFTOMM, Udine, Italia.

Leborgne, M. 1984. Geometric and Dynamic Modelling of Robots : an Unified Approach, Internal Report, IRISA, Rennes, France.

Leborgne, M. and Espiau, B. 1984. Modelling and Closed-loop control of robots in local operating space. Internal Paper, IRISA-Rennes, France, submitted to the 1984 IEEE conference on Decision and Control, Las Vegas.

Luh, J.S., Walker, M.W. and Paul R. 1980. Resolved Acceleration Control of Mechanical Manipulators. IEEE Trans. on Automatic Control, Vol.AC-25 n°3.

Raibert, M. and Craig, J. 1981. Hybrid Position/Force Control of Manipulators. Transactions of the ASME, Vol.102, Journal of Dynamic System, Measurement and Control.

Salisbury, J.K. 1983. Kinematic and Force Analysis of Articulated Hands. IBM Summer School in Robotics, Grassau, W. Germany.

Samson, C. 1983. Robust Non linear Control of Robotic Manipulators. IEEE Decision and Control Conference ; San Antonio, Texas, USA.

Samson, C. and Dumas, R. 1984. Robust Non linear Control of Robotic Manipulators : Implementation Aspects and Simulations. First World Conference on Robotics Research, Bethlehem, Penns. USA.

Vertut, J., Fournier, R., Espiau, B. and André, G. 1984. Sensor aided and/or computer aided bilateral teleoperator system. 5th Symposium "Romansy", IFTOMM, Udine, Italia.

AKNOWLEDGEMENTS

Thanks to Michel Leborgne and Guy André for their contribution to this paper.

TASK PRIORITY BASED REDUNDANCY CONTROL OF ROBOT MANIPULATORS

Yoshihiko Nakamura and Hideo Hanafusa

Automation Research Laboratory, Kyoto University
Uji, Kyoto 611, Japan

In this paper, the redundancy utilization of robot manipulators is discussed. We introduce the concept of task priority into the kinematic inverse problem and divide a required task into sub-tasks according to the order of priority. And then, we propose to resolve the joint motion of robot manipulators in such a way that the sub-tasks with lower priority should be performed utilizing the redundancy on the sub-tasks with higher priority. Two types of optimal redundancy control schemes are formulated using the null space of Jacobian matrix. One is the locally optimal control of redundancy, which is applicable to on-line redundancy control. And the other is the globally optimal control of redundancy, which is effective for off-line planning of redundancy utilization. Experiments and simulations are also shown to verify their effectiveness.

1. INTRODUCTION

Robot manipulators have usually been designed to have at most 6 degrees of freedom, which is the least degrees of freedom necessary for 3 dimensional tasks. Though it seems fit for the conventional sense of mechanism design, robot manipulators are inherently expected to be more flexible and adaptive like human arms. When a robot manipulator is required to trace a determined trajectory in a working space with obstacles, more degrees of freedom are necessary than the degrees of freedom necessary in a free working space. The additional degrees of freedom are not redundant, in the original sense of the word, for the robot manipulators to trace the trajectory avoiding obstacles.

The potential of redundant manipulators for singularity avoidance and obstacle avoidance has been pointed out [Whitney, 1972], [Uchiyama, 1979], [Freund, 1977]. Some anthropomorphic manipulators with 7 degrees of freedom have been developed and their kinematic inverse problem have been studied [Nakano, 1974], [Mizukawa et al., 1974], [Benati et al., 1982]. The redundancy utilization has been formulated for robot manipulators of general configuration using the pseudo-inverse of Jacobian matrix [Ligeois, 1977], [Hanafusa et al., 1978], [Konstantinov et al., 1981], [Klein et al., 1983]. However, the target of redundancy utilization was mostly focussed on the maximum availability, that is, on keeping the joint angles within their physical limitations.

The authors and a co-worker analyzed the redundancy and the manipulatability from the view point of linear mapping by Jacobian matrix. We introduced the concept of task priority, using which the problem of redundancy utilization was generally formulated as follows. The sub-tasks with lower priority should be performed by utilizing the redundancy on the sub-tasks with higher priority [Hanafusa et al., 1979(a), (b), 1981, 1983]. This formulation is also valid for non-redundant manipulators, for example, in the case that the position of end-effector is more significant than the orientation when they must pass the singular points on the trajectory.

As the method of redundancy control, the locally optimal control has been proposed so far, that is, the method optimizing some scalar functions instantaneously. However, the globally optimal control of redundancy is required, when the exact optimization is desired, for example, in case of the energy saving motion of space use manipulators and of the obstacle avoidance in a working space with complicated obstacles. In this paper, the globally optimal control of redundancy is discussed in the framework of task priority and is formulated based on Maximum Principle.

This paper is composed as follows. We give an outline of the redundancy analysis in the following section. In Section 3, the locally optimal control of redundancy is formulated in the framework of task priority. The globally optimal control of redundancy is discussed in Section 4. In Section 5, experimental results and simulated results are shown to indicate the effectiveness of proposed methods.

2. MANIPULATABILITY AND REDUNDANCY

2.1 Manipulatable Space and Degrees of Manipulatability

The variable describing the tasks of robot manipulators is called the manipulation variable and is expressed by a vector $r \in R^m$ (m dimensional Euclidian space). The manipulation variable and the joint variable $\theta \in R^n$ are related by

$$r = f(\theta) \qquad (1)$$

The above equation, in general, is of nonlinearity depending on the configuration of robot manipulators. Therefore, it was proposed to solve the kinematic inverse problem based on the following equation obtained by differentiating Eq. (1) with respect to time [Whitney, 1969].

$$\dot{r} = J(\theta)\dot{\theta} \qquad (2)$$

where $J(\theta) \triangleq \partial f/\partial \theta$ is the Jacobian matrix. Eq. (2) is significant not only for computational convenience' sake. If the dynamics of robot manipulators is governed by a differential equation of the higher order, its inverse problem considering dynamics is also represented by a linear equation with a coefficient of Jacobian matrix. Therefore, Eq. (2) can be regarded as a symbolic representation of the kinematic inverse problem of robot manipulators.

The manipulatability means the potential of robot manipulators in performing tasks at θ. From Eq. (2) it is obvious that the instantaneous task $\dot{r}$ can be performed if and only if $\dot{r}$ is an element of $\mathcal{R}(J)$, the range of $J(\theta)$. Hence, we define the manipulatable space and the degrees of manipulatability as follows:

DEFINITION 1.

$\mathcal{R}(J)$ and its dimension are called the manipulatable space and the degrees of manipulatability (d.o.m.) at θ respectively.

2.2 Redundant Space and Degrees of Redundancy

The redundancy means the arbitrarity of the solution $\dot{\theta}$, in the case that r is given in Eq. (2). Therefore, if r_d and $\dot{\theta}_d$ satisfy Eq. (2), the redundancy is represented by such $\dot{\theta}_a$ as

$$\dot{r}_d = J(\theta)(\dot{\theta}_d + \theta_a). \qquad (3)$$

It is obvious that $\dot{\theta}_a$ satisfies Eq. (3) if and only if $\dot{\theta}_a$ is an element of $\mathcal{N}(J)$, the null space of $J(\theta)$. Hence, we define the redundant space and the degrees of redundancy as follows:

DEFINITION 2.

$\mathcal{N}(J)$ and its dimension are called the redundant space and the degrees of redundancy (d.o.r.) at θ respectively.

Fig. 1 shows the relation between the manipulatable space and the redundant space from the view point of linear mapping by Jacobian matrix. It is well known in linear algebra that the range and the null space of matrix $M \in R^{m \times n}$ satisfy the following:

$$n = \dim \mathcal{R}(M) + \dim \mathcal{N}(M). \qquad (4)$$

Applying Eq. (4) to Jacobian matrix, we have the following proposition.

PROPOSITION

Between the d.o.m. and the d.o.r. of a robot manipulator with n degrees of freedom, the following relation holds regardless of θ:

$$\text{d.o.m.} + \text{d.o.r.} = n. \qquad (5)$$

The proposition indicates that the d.o.r. is calculated by subtracting m from n, unless the robot manipulator is on singular points or the tasks are not described by the independent manipulation variables.

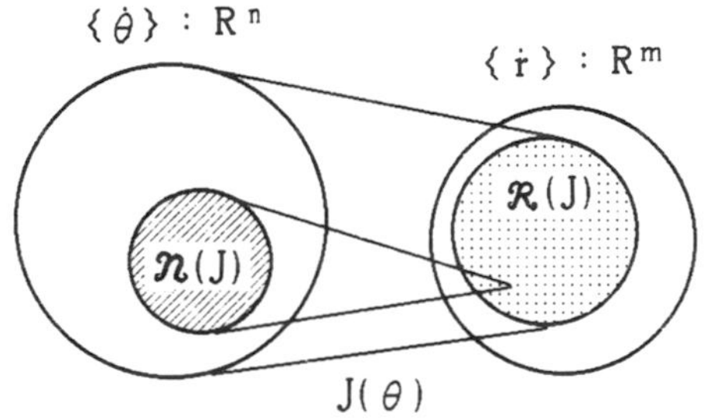

Fig. 1 Manipulatable space and redundant space

3. LOCALLY OPTIMAL CONTROL OF REDUNDANCY

3.1 Tasks with Priority

The specification on the position of end-effector is more significant than the orientation of end-effector in welding task as well as other many tasks. There are also the cases to the contrary, for example, painting task, directing task of a camera to objects and so on. When a task is composed of sub-tasks with different significance like the above cases, it is reasonable to perform the most significant sub-task firstly, and then perform the less significant sub-tasks to the possible extent using the remaining degrees of freedom, in the case that it is impossible to perform all of the sub-tasks completely because of the degeneracy or the shortage of degrees of freedom. In this section, we introduce the concept of task priority to formulate tasks like the above.

One of the important examples of tasks with priority is the utilization of redundancy for obstacle avoidance or singularity avoidance [Yoshikawa, 1983]. In this case, the position and the orientation of end-effector is given the higher priority, and the motion of manipulator for obstacle avoidance or singularity avoidance is given the lower priority.

3.2 Local Optimization in Framework of Task Priority

Let the sub-task with the first priority be specified by the first manipulation variable which is expressed by $r_1 \in R^{m_1}$. And let the sub-task with the second priority be specified by the second manipulation variable which is expressed by $r_2 \in R^{m_2}$. The following equations hold:

$$r_i = f_i(\theta), \qquad \text{for } i=1,2 \quad (6)$$

$$\dot{r}_i = J_i(\theta)\dot{\theta}. \qquad \text{for } i=1,2 \quad (7)$$

where $J_i \triangleq \partial f_i / \partial \theta$. The relation between the manipulatable spaces and the redundant spaces for the first and the second manipulation variables is shown in Fig. 2.

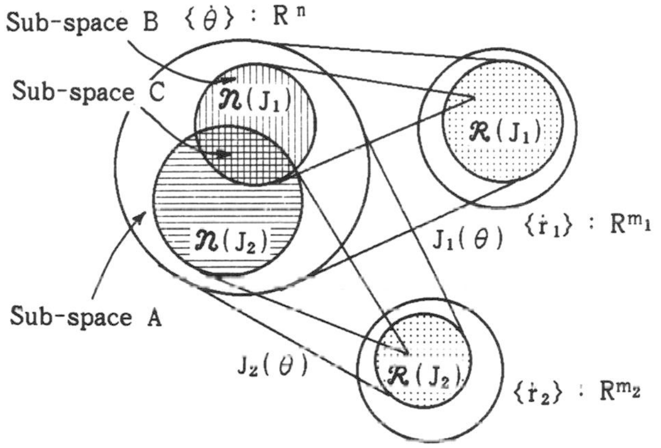

Fig. 2 Manipulatable spaces and redundant spaces for $\dot{r}_1$ and $\dot{r}_2$

In Fig. 2, Sub-space A is $\mathcal{N}(J_1)^{\perp}$, the orthogonal complement of $\mathcal{N}(J_1)$, which means the contributable $\dot{\theta}$ to the first manipulation variable. Sub-space B is the orthogonal complement of $\mathcal{N}(J_1) \cap \mathcal{N}(J_2)$ in $\mathcal{N}(J_1)$, which contributes to the second manipulation variable without disturbing the first manipulation variable. We propose to utilize Sub-space A for performing the first manipulation variable, and Sub-space B for performing the second manipulation variable. Sub-space C, $\mathcal{N}(J_1) \cap \mathcal{N}(J_2)$, means the remaining degrees of freedom which can be used for performing the third manipulation variable, if necessary. This idea is formulated as follows.

The general solution $\dot{\theta}$ of Eq. (7) for i=1 is obtained using the pseudo-inverse of $J_1(\theta)$.

$$\dot{\theta} = J_1^{+}\dot{r}_1 + (I - J_1^{+}J_1)y \quad (8)$$

where J_1^{+} is the pseudo-inverse of $J_1(\theta)$ and $y \in R^n$ is an arbitrary vector. If the exact solution does not exist, Eq. (8) means the optimal solution in the sense of minimizing $\| \dot{r}_1 - J_1(\theta)\dot{\theta} \|$ [Rao et al., 1971].

y minimizing $\| \dot{r}_2 - J_2(\theta)\dot{\theta} \|$, which yields the optimal solution $\dot{\theta}$ for $\dot{r}_2$ considering task priority, is obtained in the same way as Eq. (8) by substituting Eq. (8) into Eq. (7) for i=2

$$y = \tilde{J}_2^{+}(\dot{r}_2 - J_2 J_1^{+}\dot{r}_1) + (I - \tilde{J}_2^{+}\tilde{J}_2)z \quad (9)$$

where $\tilde{J}_2 \triangleq J_2(I - J_1^{+}J_1)$, and $z \in R^n$ is an arbitrary vector. After all, we have the following solution:

$$\dot{\theta} = J_1^{+}\dot{r}_1 + (I - J_1^{+}J_1)\tilde{J}_2^{+}(\dot{r}_2 - J_2 J_1^{+}\dot{r}_1) + (I - J_1^{+}J_1)(I - \tilde{J}_2^{+}\tilde{J}_2)z. \quad (10)$$

Using the basic character of pseudo-inverses, it is easily proved that $\mathcal{R}(J_1^{+})$, $\mathcal{R}((I - J_1^{+}J_1)\tilde{J}_2^{+})$ and $\mathcal{R}((I - J_1^{+}J_1)(I - \tilde{J}_2^{+}\tilde{J}_2))$, the ranges of the coefficient matrices of Eq. (10), are equal to Sub-space A, Sub-space B and Sub-space C, respectively. Now, we are permitted to omit the proof because of the limited pages.

In the case of $r_2 = \theta$, that is, $J_2(\theta) = I$, Eq. (10) results in simpler form as follows:

$$\dot{\theta} = J_1^{+}\dot{r}_1 + (I - J_1^{+}J_1)\dot{r}_2. \quad (11)$$

Eq. (11) will be applied to obstacle avoidance problem in Section 5.

The formulation above gives a solution of kinematic inverse problem considering task priority. However, it is the formulation making optimal use of the null spaces of Jacobian matrices instantaneously, in which sense it can be considered the locally optimal control of redundancy. It is not enough when the exact optimality covering the full working time is required. In the following section, the globally optimal control of redundancy is discussed.

4. GLOBALLY OPTIMAL CONTROL OF REDUNDANCY

4.1 Problem Formulation

The energy saving motion is required for robot manipulators of space use. The successful motion may not be always obtained for obstacle avoidance problem in the case of the working space with complicated obstacles, if we apply the locally optimal control of redundancy. It is also an interesting problem of redundancy utilization to find the optimal motion which maximizes the integral of measure of manipulatability for the interval of working time. In the cases like the above, the globally optimal control of redundancy is necessary.

We formulate the globally optimal control of redundancy in the framework of task priority, in such a way that the desired trajectory of end-effector is given the first priority and the process of minimizing a criterion index is given the second priority. That is,

$$r_1(t) = f_1(\theta), \tag{12}$$

$$r_2 = \int_{t_0}^{t_1} p(\theta, t)\, dt, \tag{13}$$

where t_0 and t_1 mean the initial and the final time. In Eq. (12) $r_1(t)$ is given. The problem is to find $\theta(t)$ which minimizes the criterion index of Eq. (13).

It should be pointed out that the above formulation includes finding the initial state, $\theta(t_0)$, which is optimal in the sense of Eq. (13). It is a distinctive feature of the globally optimal control of redundancy compared with the locally optimal control of redundancy.

4.2 Application of Maximum Principle

Using Eq. (8) which is equivalent to Eq. (12) and clarifies the degrees of redundancy, we can transform Eqs. (12) and (13) into

$$\dot{\theta} = J_1^{+} \dot{r}_1(t) + (I - J_1^{+} J_1)\, y$$
$$\triangleq g(\theta, t, y), \tag{14}$$

$$r_2 = \int_{t_0}^{t_1} p(\theta, t, y)\, dt. \tag{15}$$

Eq. (14) can be regarded as a system equation of a nonlinear dynamical system with a input vector y. We apply Maximum Principle to Eqs. (14) and (15), regarding them as a usual optimal control problem of a dynamical system.

Concerning boundary conditions, the left-hand endpoint $\theta(t_0)$ must satisfy $r_1(t_0)=f_1(\theta(t_0))$. On the other hand, the right-hand endpoint $\theta(t_1)$ is completely free because $\theta(t_1)$ necessarily satisfies $r_1(t_1)=f_1(\theta(t_1))$ if it is governed by Eq. (14) with the initial condition of $r_1(t_0)=f_1(\theta(t_0))$. Hence, this is an optimal control problem with a variable left-hand endpoint and a free right-hand endpoint.

From Maximum Principle [Pontryagin et al., 1962] Hamiltonian for a fixed time problem with a fixed left-hand endpoint and a free right-hand endpoint becomes as follows:

$$H(\psi, \theta, t, y) = -p + \psi^T g, \tag{16}$$

where $\psi \in R^n$ is an auxiliary variable vector. Now, the optimal trajectory $\theta(t)$ satisfies the following differential equations:

$$\dot{\theta} = (\partial H/\partial \psi)^T, \tag{17}$$
$$\dot{\psi} = -(\partial H/\partial \theta)^T, \tag{18}$$

where the optimal input y(t) must be chosen so that it should maximize $H(\psi, \theta, t, y)$ at every moment.

4.3 Boundary Conditions

Since Eqs. (17) and (18) have 2n differential equations, the boundary conditions of the same number are necessary. The self-evident boundary condition is $r_1(t_0)=f_1(\theta(t_0))$. And $\psi(t_1)=0$ is derived from the condition of free right-hand endpoint [Pontryagin et al., 1962]. The former has m_1 boundary conditions and the latter has n boundary conditions. The remaining $n-m_1$ boundary conditions are called the transversality condition. The transversality condition signifies in this case that $\psi(t_0)$ should be perpendicular to the tangential plane of the manifold, $r_1(t_0)=f_1(\theta(t_0))$, at $\theta(t_0)$.

The column vectors of $(\partial f_1/\partial \theta)^T$ mean the normal vectors of the manifold. Therefore, the transversality condition becomes that there must exist such vector $w \in R^{m_1}$ that satisfies

$$J_1(\theta(t_0))^T\, w = \psi(t_0). \tag{19}$$

The condition can be transformed equivalently into the following form, by using a pseudo-inverse [Rao et al., 1971]:

$$(I - J_1^{+}(\theta(t_0))J_1(\theta(t_0)))\, \psi(t_0) = 0. \tag{20}$$

Since the rank of coefficient matrix of Eq. (20) is $n-m_1$ if $J_1(\theta(t_0))$ is of full rank, Eq. (20) contains $n-m_1$ independent conditions. The transversality condition means that $\psi(t_0)$ should be an element of $\mathcal{R}(J_1)^{\perp}$ at $t=t_0$.

After all, the boundary conditions are summarized as follows:

$$\begin{aligned} &r_1(t_0) = f_1(\theta(t_0)), \\ &(I - J_1^{+}(\theta(t_0))J_1(\theta(t_0)))\, \psi(t_0) = 0, \quad \text{at } t = t_0 \\ &\psi(t_1) = 0. \quad \text{at } t = t_1 \end{aligned} \tag{21}$$

Eq. (21) shows that this is a two point boundary value problem with n conditions on each of the left-hand and the right-hand endpoints. On the computation of two point boundary value problems, the initial value adjusting method is proposed [for example, Ojika et al., 1979], where the left-hand endpoint values of the condition of which right-hand endpoint values are given are estimated at first, and then they are modified based on the resultant errors of the right-hand endpoint values. The adjustment process is repeated until they converge to the given values at the right-hand endpoint. In our problem, the adjustment for n conditions is necessary, which causes a large amount of computation.

The computational amount can be reduced considering the particularity of our optimal problem. If $\theta(t_0)$ satisfies $r_1(t_0)=f_1(\theta(t_0))$ and its dynamics is governed by Eq. (14), $\theta(t_1)$ necessarily reaches $r_1(t_1)=f_1(\theta(t_1))$. Therefore, we can equivalently transform Eq. (21) into

$$(I - J_1^+(\theta(t_0))J_1(\theta(t_0)))\ \psi(t_0) = 0, \quad \text{at } t = t_0$$
$$r_1(t_1) = f_1(\theta(t_1)),\quad \psi(t_1) = 0. \quad \text{at } t = t_1 \qquad (22)$$

Eq. (22) means that the left-hand endpoint has $n-m_1$ boundary conditions, and the right-hand endpoint has $n+m_1$ boundary conditions. It implies that in the case of one degree of redundancy the adjustment is required only for one condition if the differential equations, Eqs. (17) and (18), are integrated backward from t_1 to t_0. In this way, Eq. (22) can be used to reduce the number of adjustment condition by m_1.

4.4 Example of Criterion Index

In this sub-section, we show an example of criterion index, and derive the concrete form of Eqs. (17) and (18) for the example. The example is as follows:

$$r_2 = \int_{t_0}^{t_1} [k\ p_0(\theta) + \dot{\theta}^T \dot{\theta}]\ dt, \qquad (23)$$

where k is a scalar constant. If we consider the obstacle avoidance problem, $p_0(\theta)$ should be chosen as a function of the distance of robot manipulators from obstacles [Khatib et al., 1978]. If we consider the motion maximizing measure of manipulatability, $p_0(\theta)$ should be chosen as a function of measure of manipulatability. The second term of the integrand of Eq. (23) is included because it makes easy to find the input vector y(t) which maximizes Hamiltonian.

Hamiltonian becomes as follows:

$$H = -k\ p_0 - g^T g + \psi^T g$$
$$= -(g - 1/2\psi)^T (g - 1/2\psi) + 1/4\psi^T\psi - k\ p_0 \qquad (24)$$

From Eq. (24) it is clear that the optimal input vector y(t) which maximizes Hamiltonian is y(t) which minimizes $\| g - 1/2\psi \|$. Therefore, the optimal input vector becomes

$$y = 1/2(I - J_1^+ J_1)\psi, \qquad (25)$$

which can be easily derived from Eq. (14) by using the basic character of pseudo-inverses.

After all, it is clear from Eqs. (14),(17),(18) and (25) that the optimal trajectory is governed by the following differential equations:

$$\dot{\theta} = g, \qquad (26)$$

$$\dot{\psi} = (\partial g/\partial \theta)^T (2\ g - \psi) + k\ (\partial p_0/\partial \theta)^T, \qquad (27)$$

$$g = J_1^+ \dot{r}_1(t) + 1/2(I - J_1^+ J_1)\psi. \qquad (28)$$

In Section 5, we will show the results of numerical simulation of the globally optimal control problem with a criterion index of Eq. (23).

5. EXPERIMENTS AND SIMULATIONS

5.1 Experiments on Locally Optimal Control

We carried out experiments of trajectory control with obstacle avoidance, based on the locally optimal control discussed in Section 3. UJIBOT, a robot manipulator with 7 degrees of freedom, was used in the experiments. We chose the position of end-effector as the first manipulation variable, that is, $r_1 \in R^3$ which is expressed in Cartesian coordinate system. And we chose the arm posture θ as the second manipulation variable, that is $r_2 \in R^7$. The velocity commands of manipulation variables were calculated by

$$\dot{r}_1 = \dot{r}_1{}^0(t) - H_1(r_1 - r_1{}^0(t)), \qquad (29)$$

$$\dot{r}_2 = -H_2(r_2 - r_2{}^0(t)), \qquad (30)$$

where $r_1{}^0(t)$ and $r_2{}^0(t)$ are desired trajectories of the first and the second manipulation variables. $H_1 \in R^{3\times 3}$ and $H_2 \in R^{7\times 7}$ are constant matrices. Substituting $\dot{r}_1$ and $\dot{r}_2$ calculated by Eqs. (29) and (30) into Eq. (11) yielded the velocity command for joints, which was used as an input for the joint velocity control system constructed for UJIBOT. $\dot{r}_1{}^0(t)$ was a straight line of constant velocity, 0.1 m/s, and $r_2{}^0(t)$ was a constant angle θ_0.

Fig. 3 shows the result of experiment when we set H_1=3.0 I and H_2= 0.0 I, which can be regarded as 'Resolved Motion Rate Control' [Whitney, 1969]. UJIBOT came into collision with the obstacle.

Fig. 4 shows the constant angle θ_0, which was selected intuitively so as to give reference information for avoiding the obstacle. Fig. 5 shows the results of experiment when we set H_1=3.0 I and H_2= 0.3 I. UJIBOT successfully avoided the collision with the obstacle by utilizing redundancy so that the arm posture should approach the constant angle θ_0.

Figs. (4) and (5) clearly show the effectiveness of the locally optimal control of redundancy. The controller was composed of software and it took 47 ms of sampling time for the real-time computation including Eqs. (11), (29) and (30), using a minicomputer NOVA 03.

5.2 Simulations on Globally Optimal Control

We also carried out numerical simulations of globally optimal control of redundancy. Fig. 6 shows a numerical model of an anthropomorphic robot manipulator with 7 degrees of freedom, which was used for the simulations. We chose the position and the orientation of end-effector as the first manipulation variable, that is, $r_1 \in R^6$, where the position was expressed in Cartesian coordinate system and the orientation was expressed in Euler angles. Fig. 7 shows the desired motion of end-effector. The trajectory was a straight line of 0.5 m to be traced at a constant translational velocity of 0.5 m/s and with a constant orientation. Fig. 7 was computed based on 'Resolved Motion Rate Control' from an initial angle $\theta(t_0)$ which satisfies $r_1(t_0) = f_1(\theta(t_0))$.

Our optimal problem was to find the final angle $\theta(t_1)$ satisfying $r_1(t_1) = f_1(\theta(t_1))$ which should fulfill the transversality condition at $t=t_0$ after the backward integral computation of Eqs. (26), (27) and (28). Since $r_1 \in R^6$, the degree of redundancy on nonsingular points was equal to one, which was represented by the motion of the elbow around a line connecting the shoulder with the wrist. Therefore, we could uniquely indicate $\theta(t_1)$ satisfying $r_1(t_1) = f_1(\theta(t_1))$ by the rotational angle of elbow. We defined the following angle α as the rotational angle of elbow:

$$\alpha \triangleq \int_0^t \|\dot{\theta}_e(t)\| \, dt, \tag{31}$$

$$\dot{\theta}_e \triangleq (I - J_1^+(\theta_e)\, J_1(\theta_e))\, e$$

$$e \triangleq (0\ 0\ 1\ 0\ 0\ 0\ 0)^T$$

where the final angle $\theta(t_1)$ of Fig. 7 was chosen as the origin of α. It was found by computation that the elbow makes a round from $\alpha = 0°$ to $\alpha = 633°$.

Firstly, we used the following criterion index:

$$r_2 = \int_{t_0}^{t_1} \dot{\theta}^T \dot{\theta} \, dt, \tag{32}$$

which may be interpreted as an energy saving motion in a sense. Fig. 8 shows the graph of $\|(I - J_1^+(\theta(t_0))J_1(\theta(t_0)))\psi(t_0)\|$ versus α computed every 30° of α. From Fig. 8 it was found that there were four candidates of the optimal angle of α. Now, we have to remember that Maximum Principle gives us an necessary condition for optimal control. Therefore, we had to choose the optimal angle among the candidates considering the criterion index. Fig. 9 shows the graph of the criterion index versus α. The four curves respectively expresses the value of r_2 integrated from t=1.0 sec to t=0.75 sec, from t=1.0 sec to t=0.5 sec, from t=1.0 sec to t=0.25 sec and from t=1.0 sec to t=0.0 sec. From Fig. 9, it was clear that the optimal angle of α is around $\alpha = 120°$ or 390°. Searching for a local minimum around $\alpha = 120°$ and 390° by Newton method yielded $\alpha = 115.3°$ as the optimal angle. Fig. 10 shows the optimal motion for the criterion index of Eq. (32).

The above example tells us an important suggestion. The curve of Fig. 8 is steep for searching the local minimum, compared with the curves of Fig. 9. Furthermore, we have to consider the criterion index anyhow, in choosing the globally minimum. Therefore, the transversality condition is not needed from the view point of practical computation.

Secondly, Fig. 11 shows the optimal motion for the following criterion index:

$$r_2 = \int_{t_0}^{t_1} [\, 1/\sqrt{\det(J_1 J_1^T)} + \dot{\theta}^T \dot{\theta} \,] \, dt. \tag{33}$$

The criterion means that the trajectory far from singular points is desirable. The first term of the integrand of Eq. (33) evaluates the distance from singular points [Yoshikawa, 1983]. The optimal angle of elbow was $\alpha = 148°$.

These simulation results clearly shows the possibility and the effectiveness of the globally optimal control of redundancy. The computation in this sub-section was carried out in Kyoto University Data Processing Center.

6. CONCLUSION

The kinematic inverse problem of redundant manipulators has been studied in the framework of task priority. Two types of optimal redundancy control schemes have been formulated. One is the locally optimal control of redundancy formulated from the view point of linear mapping by Jacobian matrix. This is applicable to on-line redundancy control. The other is the globally optimal control of redundancy formulated based on Maximum Principle. This is effective for off-line planning of redundant robot manipulators. Results of experiments and simulations clearly shows the possibility and the effectiveness of proposed optimal redundancy control schemes.

This formulation based on Jacobian matrix should be regarded as a symbolic representation of the kinematic inverse problem of robot manipulators. It is easy to extend it to the kinematic inverse problem considering the dynamics of robot manipulators. In the same formulation of the globally optimal control, the energy saving motion in the strict sense can be considered only by extending the dimension of state variable.

REFERENCES

Benati, M., Morasso, P. and Tagliasco, V., 1982, "The Inverse Kinematic Problem for Anthropomorphic Manipulator Arms", Trans. ASME, vol. 104, pp. 110-113.

Freund, E., 1977, "Path Control for a Redundant Type of Industrial Robot", Proc. 7th Intern. Sympo. Industrial Robots, pp. 107-114.

Hanafusa, H., Yoshikawa, T. and Nakamura, Y., 1978, "Control of Multi-Articulated Robot Arms with Redundancy", Prep. 21st Joint Automatic Control Conference in Japan, pp. 237-238.

Hanafusa, H., Yoshikawa, T. and Nakamura, Y., 1979 (a), "Control of Multi-Articulated Robot Arms with Redundancy Part 1 Analysis and Determination of Input Considering Task Priority", Prep. 22nd Joint Automatic Control Conference in Japan, pp. 319-320.

Hanafusa, H., Yoshikawa, T. and Nakamura, Y., 1979 (b), "Control of Multi-Articulated Robot Arms with Redundancy Part 2 Application to Obstacle Avoidance Problem", Prep. 22nd Joint Automatic Control Conference in Japan, pp. 321-322.

Hanafusa, H., Yoshikawa, T. and Nakamura, Y., 1981,"Analysis and Control of Articulated Robot Arms with Redundancy", Prep. 8th IFAC World Congress, XIV 78-83.

Hanafusa, H., Yoshikawa, T. and Nakamura, Y., 1983, "Redundancy Analysis of Articulated Robot Arms and Its Utilization for Tasks with Priority", Trans. J. Soc. Instrum. & Control Eng., vol. 19, No. 5, pp. 421-426.

Ligeois, A., 1977, "Automatic Supervisory Control of the Configuration and Behavior of Multibody Mechanisms", IEEE Trans., vol. SMC-7, No. 12, pp. 868-871.

Mizukawa, M. et al., 1975, "Torque Position Control of Articulated Artificial Arm", Proc. 4th Biomechanism Sympo. in Japan, pp. 242-253.

Nakano, E. and Ozaki, S., 1974, "Cooperative Control of a Pair of Anthropomorphous Manipulators - MELARM", Proc. 4th Intern. Sympo. Industrial Robots, pp. 251-260.

Ojika, T. and Kasue, Y., 1979, "Initial-Value Adjusting Method for the Solution of Nonlinear Multipoint Boundary-Value Problems, J. Math. Anal. Appl., vol. 69, No. 2, pp. 359-371.

Pontryagin, L. S. et al., 1962, "The Mathematical Theory of Optimal Processes", New York, John Wiley & Sons. Inc.

Rao, C. R. and Mitra, S. K., 1971, "Generalized Inverse of Matrices and its Applications", New York, John Wiley & Sons. Inc.

Uchiyama, M., 1979, "Study on Dynamic Control of Artificial Arm Part 1", Trans. JSME, vol. 45, No. 391, pp.314-322.

Whitney, D. E., 1969, "Resolved Motion Rate Control of Manipulators and Humam Prostheses", IEEE Trans. Man-mach. Syst., vol. 10, pp. 47-53.

Whitney, D. E., 1972, "Mathematics of Coordinated Control of Prosthetic Arms and Manipulators", Trans. ASME J. Dynamic Systems, Measurement and Control, vol. 94, No. 4, pp. 303-309.

Yoshikawa, T., 1983, "Analysis and Control of Robot Manipulators with Redundancy", Prep. Intern. Sympo. Robotics Research, 13-4.

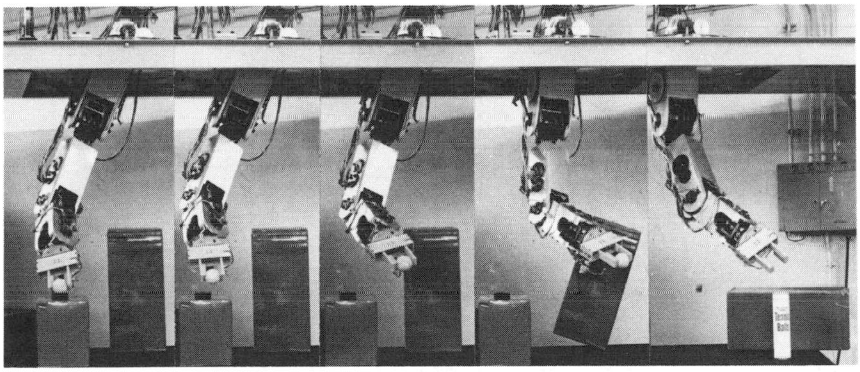

Fig. 3 Experimental result based on 'Resolved Motion Rate Control'

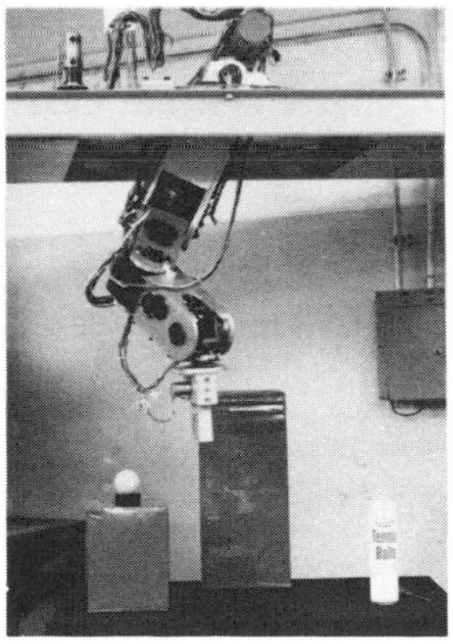

Fig. 4 Constant angle θ_0 selected intuitively so as to give reference information for avoiding obstacle

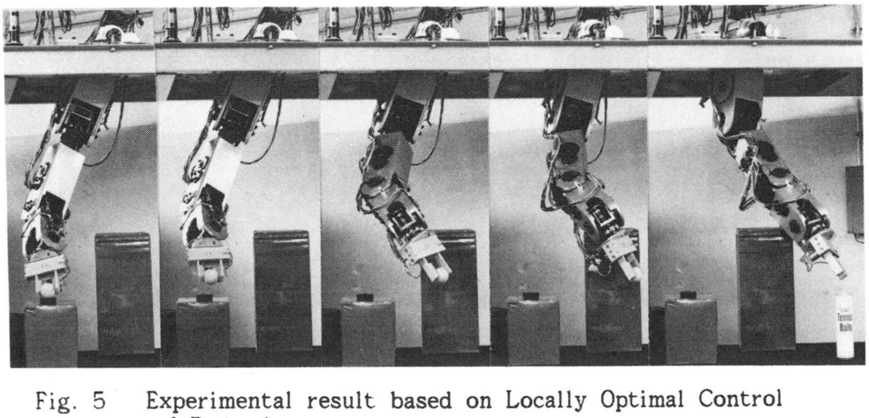

Fig. 5 Experimental result based on Locally Optimal Control of Redundancy

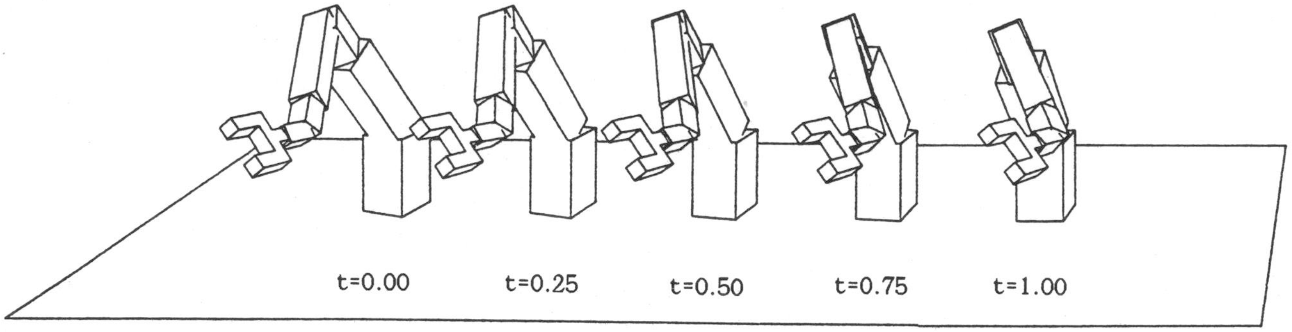

Fig. 7 Desired motion of end-effector (computed baced on 'Resolved Motion Rate Control')

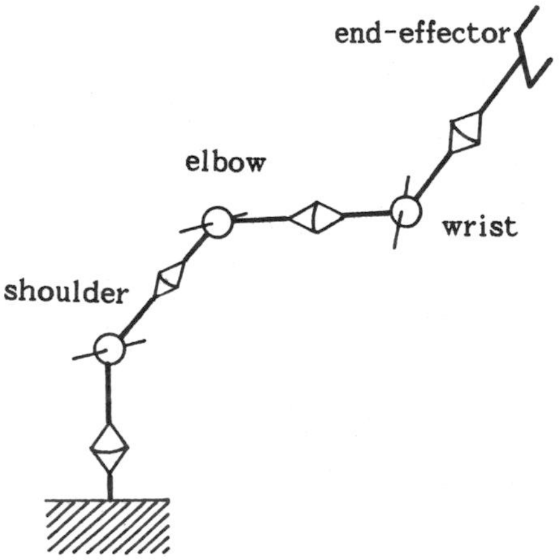

Fig. 6 An anthropomorphic robot manipulator with 7 degrees of freedom

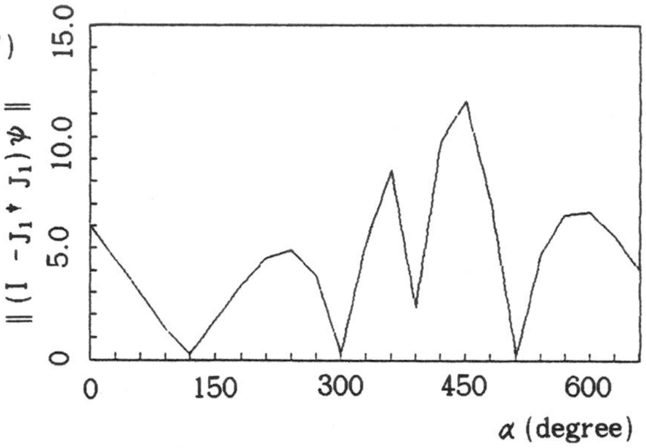

Fig. 8 Transversality condition versus rotational angle of elbow α

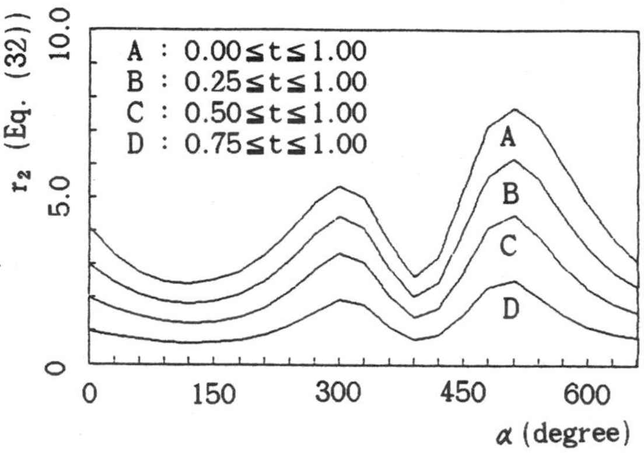

Fig. 9 Criterion Index versus rotational angle of elbow α

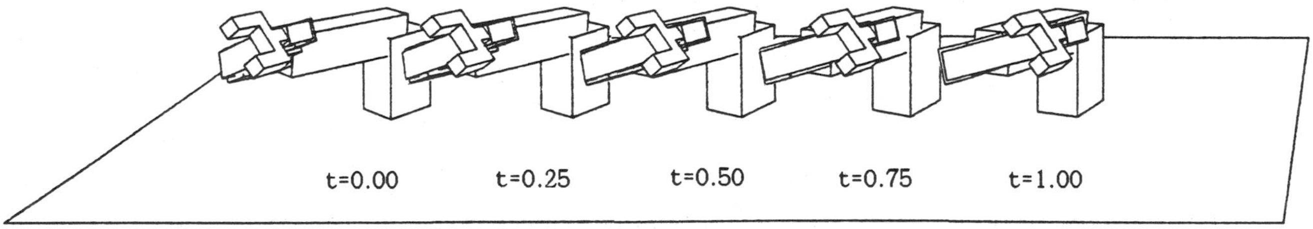

Fig. 10 Optimal motion for the criterion index of Eq. (32)

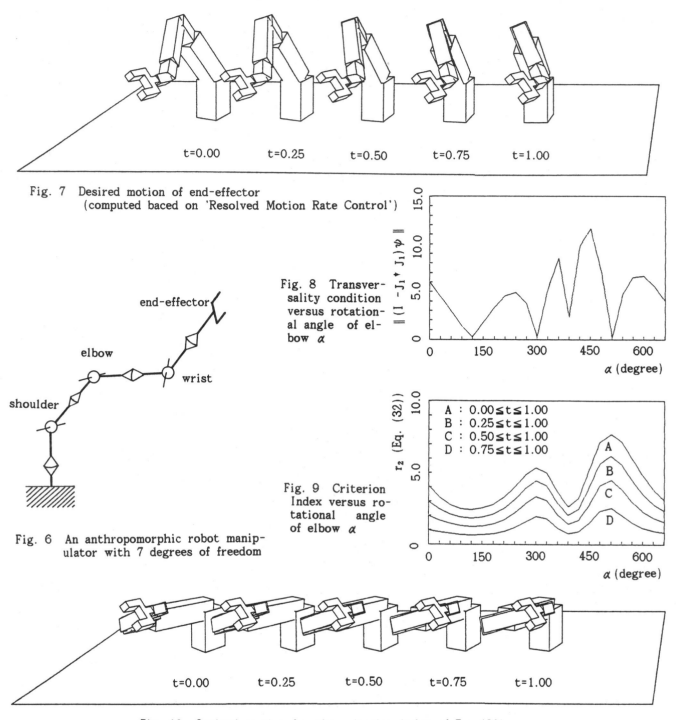

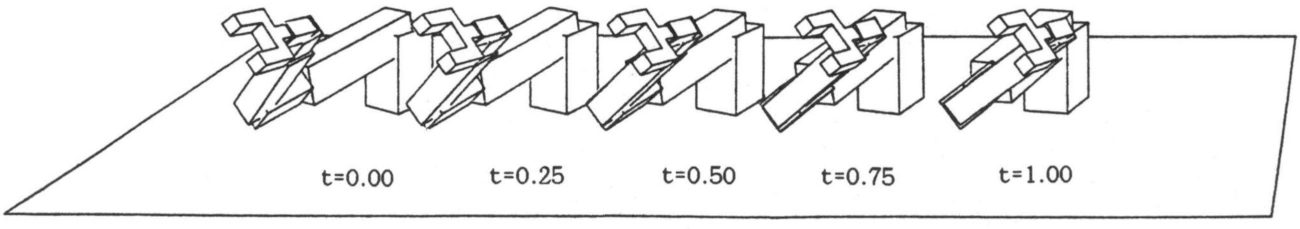

Fig. 11 Optimal motion for the criterion index of Eq. (33)

MODELING ROBOT CONTOUR PROCESSES*

Daniel E. Whitney and Alexander C. Edsall
The Charles Stark Draper Laboratory, Inc.
Cambridge, Massachusetts 02139

Robot contour processes include those with contact force like car body grinding or deburring of complex castings, as well as those with little or no contact force like inspection. This paper describes ways of characterizing, identifying, and estimating contours and robot trajectories. Contour and robot are modeled as stochastic processes in order to emphasize that both successive robot cycles and successive industrial workpieces are similar but not exactly the same. The stochastic models can be used to identify the state of a workpiece or process, or to design a linear or nonlinear filter to estimate workpiece shape and robot position from robot-based measurements.

Introduction

Robot contour processes are those processes which require continuous path motion rather than discrete positioning of the robot. The required and actual positions of the robot's end effector are dynamic processes which must have certain properties. Figure 1 is a simplified block diagram of a robot contour process. Processes that modify the contour (like grinding), as well as those that do not (inspecting), can be represented this way. The robot carries a sensor or sensors that measure either the surface shape or the deviation of that shape from a reference. The reference may be provided by the taught path of the robot, in which case either the displacement of the tool from the robot's endpoint or the force generated by that displacement can be used as the measurement. Alternatively, the measurement can be made independently of the robot, with a vision system, for example. Only robot endpoint and joint angle measurements will be considered here. The filter, informed of the commands to the robot and the measurements, as well as a priori information about the desired shape, estimates the actual shape. If the shape is supposed to be modified, the error is passed to a process model and control strategy so that new robot commands can be generated. The revised commands may be given to the robot in real time or they may be stored and used on the next pass over the contour.

This paper considers the characterization, estimation, and identification of workpiece contours and robot trajectories. Contours and trajectories are modeled as stochastic processes. This approach is justified for several reasons. Industrial workpiece contours may be thought of as belonging to families or ensembles in which all members are nominally identical but subject to slight random variations and jigging errors. The stochastic model is a convenient descriptor of the random components of contours. Robot trajectories are also subject to errors due to accuracy and resolution limitations and compliance of the robot arm. The stochastic model is again a convenient statistical descriptor of the robot's trajectory error.

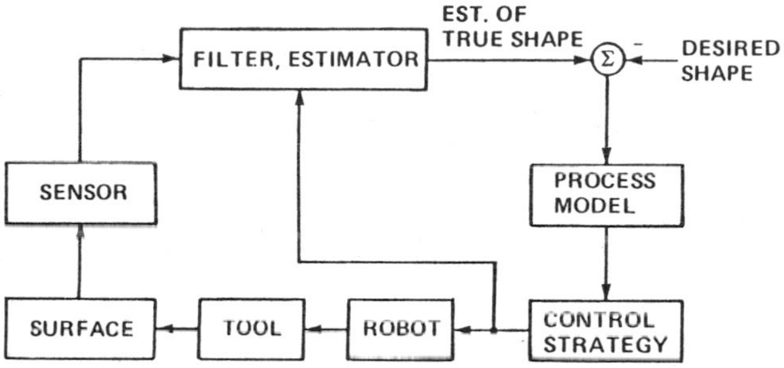

Figure 1.

Several applications of contour modeling are proposed. One area is characterization and identification of workpiece contours. The model parameters define a pattern space in which contours may be compared using conventional pattern-recognition techniques. The model may also be used as the basis for a contour following control system.

Another area is optimal filtering of robot wrist-mounted force or displacement sensor information. A fundamental problem in the use of wrist-mounted sensors is that the measurement reflects errors in the robot position as well as the process variables of interest. The robot is a noisy platform from which to make measurements. If the

*This work was supported by NSF Grant MEA 82-07167. The first author's contribution was performed while on a sabbatical supported by DFVLR, Oberpfaffenhofen, Federal Republic of Germany.

robot trajectory error can be modeled, optimal estimation techniques may be used to improve our estimates of the process variables by taking advantage of correlation in the robot's errors. Filter theory is applied to measurements from an Instrumented Remote Center Compliance (IRCC). The IRCC is a compliant tool mount at the robot's wrist. Its deflections under the load of contact forces are measured by optical sensors. The control algorithms can interpret these signals as either forces or displacements.[1]

The methods described here are based on techniques in signal processing, linear system theory, and optimal estimation. The autoregressive (AR) model is used for modeling trajectories and contours.

Autoregressive Processes

The autoregressive (AR) process[2,3] is a parametric model for the behavior of a signal. It is widely used in speech recognition and synthesis, signal detection, and data compression. The AR process is a discrete linear all-pole system driven by white noise. The parameters of the system are chosen to produce the desired statistics of the output. The virtues of the AR modeling technique are numerous.

1. It is a spectral matching method and an efficient method of high-resolution spectral estimation.[4]

2. Many methods exist for choosing its parameters to model stationary or slowly time-varying signals.

3. It can represent a complex waveform with only a few numbers. In speech synthesis, for example, one set of coefficients can represent a phoneme or about 30 to 40 ms of sound. Since speech typically has a bandwidth of 3 to 4 kHz, this represents a bandwidth reduction of about 100 in the amount of storage required to represent the phoneme compared with storing the waveform itself.

4. It is a stochastic model. For example, each utterance of the same word by the same person is a little different. The AR coefficients attempt to capture the statistical similarity between those utterances, and uncorrelated noise is assumed to be a good model of the differences.

5. It is a linear system excited by white noise -- a desirable formulation for optimal filtering.

6. It can be used to model multivariate processes[5] such as the vector description of a contour in space.

An AR process, s_n, is generated by the difference equation

$$s_n = \sum_{k=1}^{p} a_k s_{n-k} + u_n \tag{1}$$

where a_k are the model parameters and u_n is a purely random (white) sequence.

If u_n is zero mean, the optimal estimate of s_n from past values is

$$\hat{s}_n = \sum_{k=1}^{p} a_k s_{n-k} \tag{2}$$

which illustrates the use of the AR model as a linear predictor. The prediction error or residual is

$$e_n = s_n - \hat{s}_n = s_n - \sum_{k=1}^{p} a_k s_{n-k} \tag{3}$$

To model a given signal s_n, the optimal coefficients a_k can be found by imposing the orthogonality principle which says that for the optimal a_k, the residual e_n must be orthogonal to the data s_n

$$E[e_n s_n] = 0 \tag{4}$$

This leads to the normal equations

$$\sum_{k=1}^{p} a_k E[s_{n-j} s_{n-k}] = E[s_n s_{n-j}]; \; j = 1, \ldots, p \tag{5}$$

The AR process model (Eq. (1)) may conveniently be written in the vector form

$$\underline{s}_n = A \, \underline{s}_{n-1} + G \, \underline{u}_n \tag{6}$$

where $\underline{s}_n$ is a state vector of the past p values

$$\underline{s}_n = [s_{n-p+1} \; \ldots \; s_n]^T \tag{6a}$$

A is a "shift register matrix"

$$A = \begin{bmatrix} 0 & 1 & 0 & \ldots & 0 \\ 0 & 0 & 1 & \ldots & 0 \\ 0 & 0 & 0 & \ldots & 1 \\ a_p & a_{p-1} & a_{p-2} & \ldots & a_1 \end{bmatrix} \tag{6b}$$

and

$$G = [0 \; 0 \; \ldots \; 0 \; 1]^T \tag{6c}$$

These concepts may be extended to the multivariate case as in Ref. 5.

Modeling Contours

An autoregressive model for a contour can be written in the following form

$$x_n = \sum_{k=1}^{p} a_k x_{n-k} + u_n \tag{7}$$

where the x_k are positions of discrete points in the contour, as shown in Fig. 2. We are interested here in real physical contours that are supposed to be alike but are not identical. Furthermore, the contours will change during processing as we grind, smooth, or debur them. They will begin this process belonging to one statistical family or ensemble ("rough" or "raw") and will end up in another ("smooth" or "finished"), but in neither case will the ensemble members be identical, nor will they match a predefined ideal. So we have to be satisfied with some statistical measure that indicates whether the contour can be admitted to membership in the ensemble. For these reasons we are not going to use any of the many techniques that are suitable for representing a specific contour, such as Fourier coefficients, splines, orthogonal polynomials, etc. In the same spirit we may represent the robot's path as another correlated random sequence, indicating our assumption that the robot does not exactly follow the path it was taught and does not repeat itself exactly.

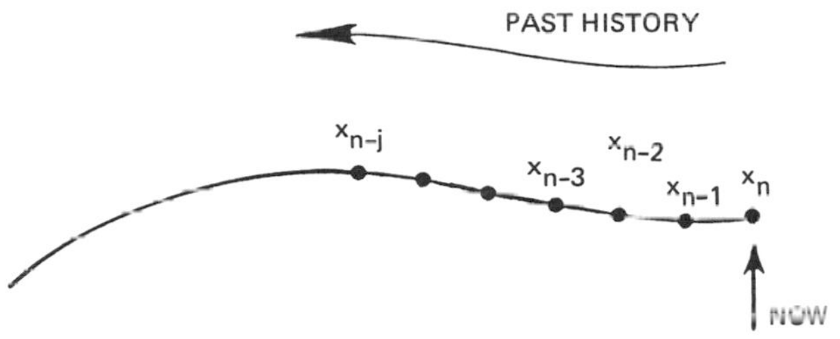

Figure 2.

We define the necessary coordinate systems and variables in Fig. 3. This shows schematically a contour and a robot. Most of the variables of interest are expressed in robot world coordinates, and all are vectors of appropriate dimension. These variables are:

- RR robot reference location in base coordinates
- WPR workpiece reference
- RS workpiece location in robot coordinates
- TP robot's taught path; also the shape we would like the contour to be
- RP position (and orientation) of the robot's endpoint or wrist, but not necessarily the position of a tool in contact with the workpiece
- WPS workpiece shape in workpiece coordinates

Assuming that robot paths belong to one ensemble, raw contours to another or others, finished contours to a third, and so on, we can write down several contour process problems:

1. Modify the raw contour until it is a member of the desired ensemble of finished contours. No physical process need be defined at this stage. Instead

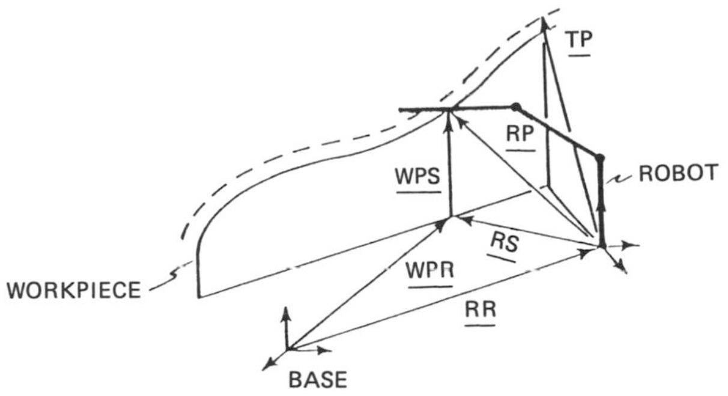

Figure 3.

we note that a "membership criterion" is needed so that we can decide when the contour is "finished".

2. Inspect the contour to determine which of several candidate ensembles (if any) it belongs to. Again, the membership criterion is the issue.

3. Monitor the process to detect possible errors such as robot failure, sensor error, jigging error, and drifts of various kinds.

4. Since we know that robots are imperfect followers of their taught paths, and since different contour processes or different contours make different demands on the robot's following capability, we would like a "suitability criterion" to allow us to match the robot to the job.

5. We also assume that contour processes require feedback, so we need to know what is observable and controllable depending on what measurements we make. Possible measuring means and their relation to the variables in Fig. 3 are:
   a. Vision sensor to observe (RS + WPS)
   b. Robot wrist displacement sensor (IRCC) to observe ((RS + WPS) - RP)
   c. Proximity sensor in place of IRCC
   d. Joint angle sensors on robot to read RP
   e. Force sensor to read K((RS + WPS) - RP) where K is a stiffness matrix.

6. The following estimation problems can be identified:
   a. Since the robot is compliant, its joint angle readings will not be enough to define RP. Additional knowledge in terms of gravity and applied endpoint forces will be needed.
   b. If the contour has been successfully processed, then we should be able to predict the next or next few values of ((RS + WPS) - RP)

using an AR model of $\underline{RP} - \underline{TP}$. That is, only measurement noise caused by the robot prevents us from exactly predicting the contour shape if it is the right shape.

c. In addition, we need an estimator for the contour shape itself or at least for the deviation of that shape from the desired shape. If we assume that $\underline{TP}$ represents the desired shape, then we need to estimate the "contour error", $((\underline{RS} + \underline{WPS}) - \underline{TP})$, which can be expressed as the problem of estimating $\underline{x}$ from a noisy measurement $\underline{z}$

$$\underline{z} = \underline{x} + \underline{v}$$

where

$$\underline{z} = (\underline{RS} + \underline{WPS}) - \underline{RP} + \underline{n}$$
$$\underline{x} = (\underline{RS} + \underline{WPS}) - \underline{TP}$$
$$\underline{v} = \underline{TP} - \underline{RP} + \underline{n}$$
$$\underline{n} = \text{uncorrelated noise}$$

The measurement $\underline{z}$ could come from an endpoint sensor like the IRCC or a force sensor.

d. If we assume that errors in $\underline{WPS}$ (the shape) are uncorrelated with errors in $\underline{RS}$ (jigging errors), can we design an estimator that will distinguish between them?

Some progress has been made in the estimation of contours from endpoint sensor measurements. This problem is more difficult than the typical estimation problem because the noise $\underline{v}$ (the robot's inability to follow a taught path) is correlated. Historically, two approaches have been suggested. Kalman[6] proposed adjoining the correlated noise process to the signal process and solving this augmented system in a conventional way. Bryson and Henrikson[7] suggested forming a linear combination of previous measurements such that only uncorrelated noise remained. Two other approaches are to design an observer or to design a non-recursive filter. This last approach and the Kalman filter are considered here.

Simplification to 1-dimensional problem

In many cases of interest, such as 2-dimensional contour following, a nominal contour will represent the ideal robot trajectory TP and the ideal workpiece geometry. For convenience, and without loss of generality, the true workpiece geometry and robot trajectory error may be defined to be normal to the nominal contour. In this case, all variables of interest and the measurement, z, become scalar quantities.

Filtering of Robot-based Measurements

Nonrecursive filter

The problem is diagrammed in Fig. 4. In Fig. 4a is shown a contour, a tool or sensor tip, and indications of present and several past measurements z at discrete points in time. In Fig. 4b this is specialized to the case of measurements

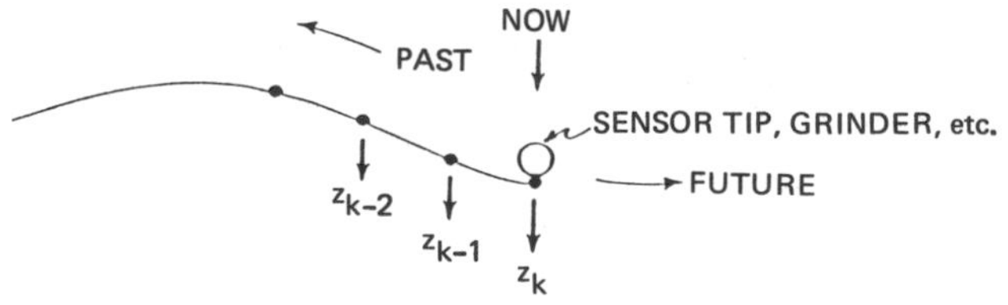

Figure 4a.

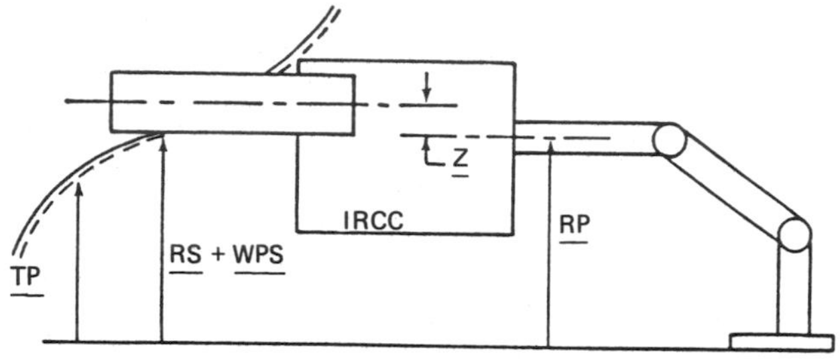

Figure 4b.

from an endpoint displacement sensor (IRCC). We teach the robot TP and hope it can follow. The correlated random variable we want to estimate is x, the deviation of the contour from the desired shape

$$x = (RS + WPS) - TP \tag{8}$$

The noise on this measurement is v, the inability of the robot to follow the taught path

$$v = TP - RP + n \tag{9}$$

The problem is then to estimate x from the measurement

$$z = x + v \tag{10}$$

Following Papoulis[8] we can write down the filter almost by inspection. We have a sequence of measurements z_k defined by Eq. (10). We seek constants a_j such that $\hat{x}_k$, defined as

$$\hat{x}_k = \sum_{j=0}^{n-1} a_j z_{k-j} \tag{11}$$

is the best mean square estimate of x_k given the measurements z_k. Following the procedure in Eq. (2) through (5), we can write n simultaneous equations for the a_j as

$$E[x_k x_{k-i}] = \sum_{j=0}^{n-1} a_j \left(E[x_{k-j} x_{k-i}] + E[v_{k-j} v_{k-i}]\right) \tag{12}$$

where $i = 0,1,\ldots,n-1$, on the assumption that

$$E[x_k v_j] = 0 \tag{13}$$

The mean square error is

$$E[e_k^2] = E[x_k^2] - \sum_{j=0}^{n-1} a_j E[x_k x_{k-j}] \tag{14}$$

Using Eq. (12) with i = 0 allows us to rewrite Eq. (14) as

$$E[e_k^2] = \sum_{j=0}^{n-1} a_j E[v_k v_{k-j}] \tag{15}$$

We may observe that if the surface shape approaches the desired shape TP, then the filter coefficients a_j will approach zero and the AR coefficients of the random sequence z_k will approach those of the process v_k. This may provide us with a membership criterion.

We will briefly pursue Bryson and Henrikson far enough to appreciate the calculations it requires. The problem is first written in state variable form as

$$\underline{x}_k = A\underline{x}_{k-1} + Bu_{k-1} \tag{16}$$

$$z_k = H(\underline{x}_k + \underline{v}_k)$$

$$\underline{v}_k = C\underline{v}_{k-1} + Dw_{k-1}$$

$$H = [0 \ldots 0 \; 1]$$

Both matrices A and C are shift register matrices where the superdiagonal consists of 1's and the bottom row consists of the AR coefficients of the respective processes. Variables u and w are zero mean uncorrelated noise. We need coefficients α_j such that a pseudomeasurement, p_k, defined as

$$p_k = z_k - \sum_{j=1}^{n} \alpha_j z_{k-j} \tag{17}$$

contains only white noise. In terms of Eq. (16), we can write Eq. (17) as

$$p = H\underline{x}_k - \sum_{j=1}^{n} \alpha_j H\underline{x}_{k-j} + H\Big[C\underline{v}_{k-1} - \sum_{j=1}^{n} \alpha_j \underline{v}_{k-j}\Big] + HDw_{k-1} \tag{18}$$

The pseudomeasurement noise will be uncorrelated if the term in square brackets equals zero. Because of the particular forms of H and C in our problem, this can be accomplished if we set

$$\alpha_j = a_{j-1} \; ; \; j = 1,\ldots,n \tag{19}$$

where the a_j are the AR coefficients of the noise process v_k. The spirit of the approach is thus the same as that given by Eq. (12): we must use the sum of the n previous measurements scaled by the AR coefficients of a relevant random process. In addition, much other computation is needed in order to express the $\underline{x}_{k-j}$ in terms of $\underline{x}_k$ and powers of matrix A.

In either approach, the result is a nonrecursive filter from the point of view of a single measurement. The directness of the Papoulis method makes it appealing for two reasons. First, one can easily write down predictors and smoothers that follow the same form. Only the indices on the sums in the equations for the a_j change:

A one-step predictor:

$$x_k = \sum_{j=1}^{n} a_j z_{k-j} \tag{20}$$

$$E[x_k x_{k-i}] = \sum_{j=1}^{n} a_j \big(E[x_{k-j} x_{k-i}] + E[v_{k-j} v_{k-i}]\big) \tag{21}$$

for i = 1,...,n

$$E[e_k^2] = E[x_k^2] - \sum_{j=1}^{n} a_j E[x_k x_{k-j}] \tag{22}$$

A one-step smoother:

$$x_{k-1} = \sum_{j=0}^{n-1} a_j z_{k-j} \tag{23}$$

$$E[x_k x_{k-i}] = \sum_{j=0}^{n-1} a_j \big(E[x_{k-j} x_{k-i}] + E[v_{k-j} v_{k-i}]\big) \tag{24}$$

for i = 0,...,n-1

$$E[e_k^2] = \sum_{j=0}^{n-1} a_j E[v_{k-1} v_{k-j}] \tag{25}$$

An estimator for the noise process:

$$v_k = \sum_{j=0}^{n-1} b_j z_{k-j} \tag{26}$$

$$E[v_k v_{k-i}] = \sum_{j=0}^{n-1} b_j \big(E[x_{k-j} x_{k-i}] + E[v_{k-j} v_{k-i}]\big) \tag{27}$$

for i = 0,...,n-1

$$E[e_k^2] = \sum_{j=0}^{n-1} b_j E[x_k x_{k-j}] \tag{28}$$

Second, the Papoulis method places clearly in evidence the statistical data needed to implement this type of filter. Two correlation functions, possibly more, are needed: the surface variation correlation(s), $E[x_i x_j]$, and the robot following error correlation, $E[v_i v_j]$. For the former we could require, for any specific case, data on how both raw and acceptable "finished" contours differ from some desired shape. For the latter we could obtain data by running the robot over many "finished" surfaces, while it tried to follow TP.

Kalman filter

The Kalman filter method is based on stochastic models for observed robot behavior and contour features and a deterministic model for robot compliance.[9] The contour error, x, is modeled as a random process as before. The robot trajectory error, (RP − TP), is assumed to consist of an AR component, s_k, given by Eq. (1) and a deflection component due to the robot arm's compliance. The force transmitted to the robot through the sensor causes a deflection

$$d_k = \beta x_k \tag{29}$$

where

$\beta = K_s/(K_s + K_R)$

K_s = the sensor stiffness

K_R = the robot stiffness

The total robot trajectory error is

$$y_k = RP - TP = \beta x_k + s_k \tag{30}$$

Using Eq. (1), the robot trajectory error model may be written

$$y_k = \sum_{j=1}^{p} a_j \left[y_{k-j} - \beta x_{k-j} \right] + \beta x_k + u_k \tag{31}$$

The measurement obtained from a wrist-mounted displacement sensor is

$$z_k = x_k - y_k + n_k \tag{32}$$

where n_k is uncorrelated measurement noise.

The robot trajectory error y_k and contour error x_k are to be estimated from the measurement z_k given by Eq. (32). Since y and x are indistinguishable from a measurement of their difference alone, the dynamic models, Eq. (31) and Eq. (16), must be used. The Kalman filter optimally combines the information contained in the measurement with the information implicit in the assumed model. The variables of interest are observable in this sense if the processes s_k and x_k are not spectrally identical. It is on the basis of spectral separation that the Kalman filter will be able to distinguish between y and x from a measurement only of their difference.

The Kalman filter is a linear dynamic system driven by the measurement, as shown in Fig. 5. Equations for the optimal filter gain may be found in Ref. 10.

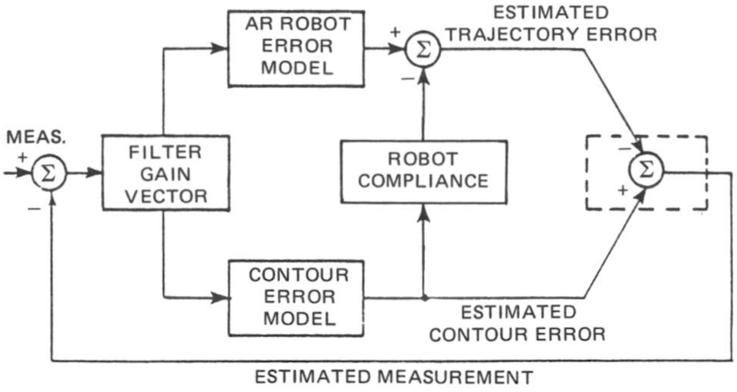

Figure 5.

Experimental Results

Experiments in optimal filtering of IRCC measurements were performed using a PUMA 560 robot and the Draper Laboratory model 4 IRCC. The PUMA robot was programmed to follow a straight surface with a normal contact force of 1.5 lb transmitted through a rolling bearing. Because the surface traced was straight and the robot was directly commanded to move in a straight line, the IRCC measurements obtained can be assumed to consist only of the robot trajectory error and measurement noise; the contour error is identically zero. An AR model fitted to this data was used in a Kalman filter for further experiments where the surface was intentionally altered without reprogramming the robot's path.

A typical time history of IRCC normal deflection while tracing a straight contour is shown in Fig. 6. The spectral density of this signal is shown in Fig. 7. The spectral density of a 5th order AR model of this signal is also shown in Fig. 7.

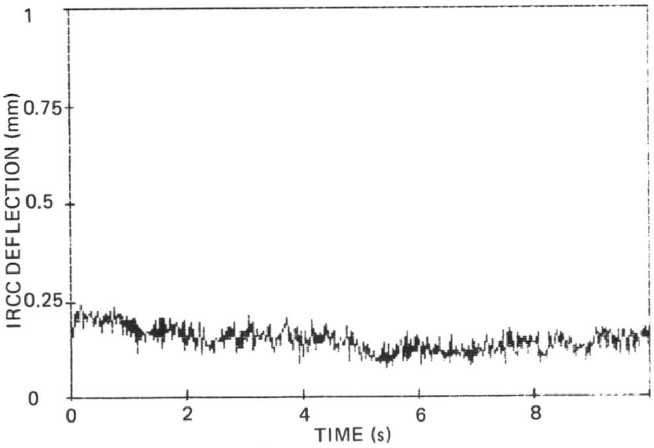

Figure 6.

The nominal straight contour was modified by the introduction of a 0.8 mm shim. The IRCC measurement obtained while tracing this contour is shown

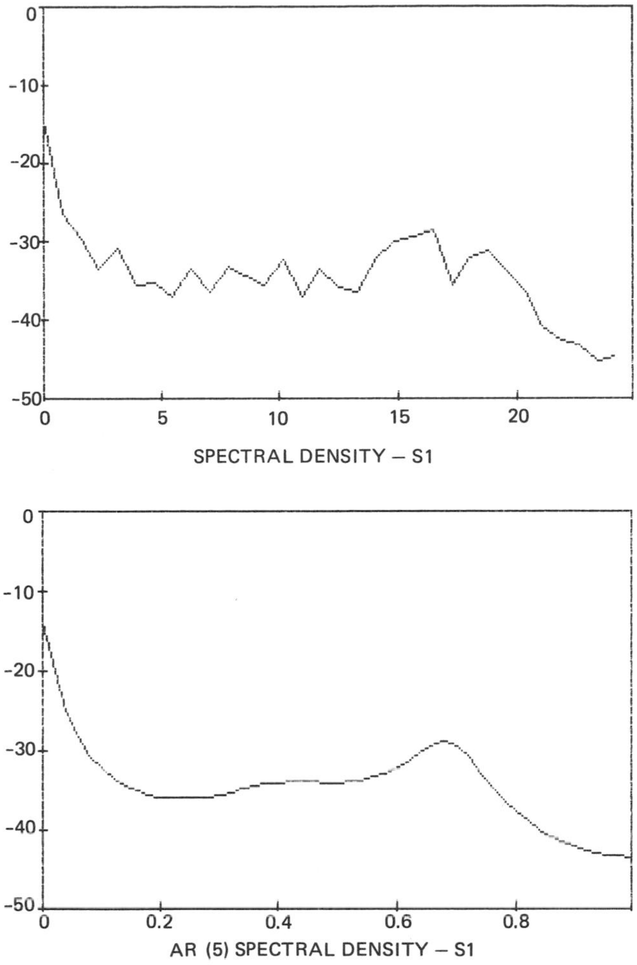

Figure 7.

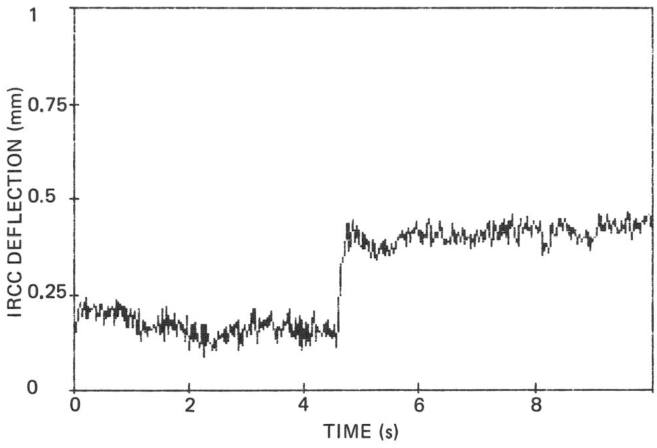

Figure 8.

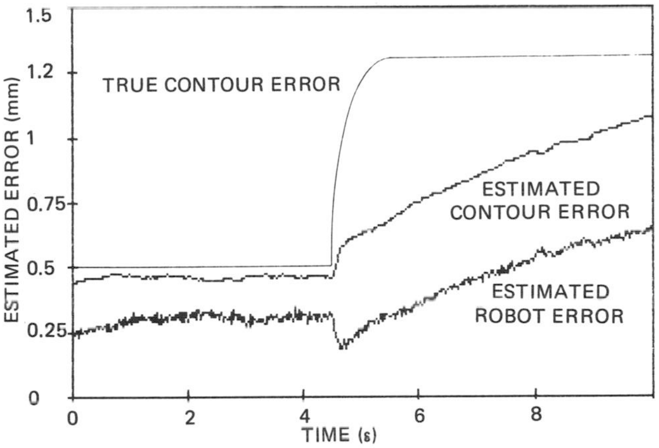

Figure 9.

in Fig. 8. Note that the measurement is biased because of the robot's compliance and noisy because of the random positioning error. To estimate the true contour from the measurement, a Kalman filter based on the 5th order AR robot error model and a random walk[10] model for the contour error was used. The random walk process

$$x_k = x_{k-1} + w_k \tag{33}$$

is frequently used in estimators for slowly varying random variables.[11] Using steady state Kalman filter gains computed for the assumed model, Eq. (31) through (33), the contour error and robot trajectory error were estimated as shown in Fig. 9. Note that the Kalman filter has attributed the low frequency energy in the measurement to the contour error and the high frequency energy to the robot error. This is a manifestation of the assumed models.

A nonlinear filter which will distinguish robot trajectory errors from contour errors on the basis of magnitude as well as frequency is illustrated in Figure 10. The nonlinear filter limits the estimated AR robot error to a predetermined magnitude and attributes large signals in the measurement to the contour error. The estimated robot error and contour error using the nonlinear

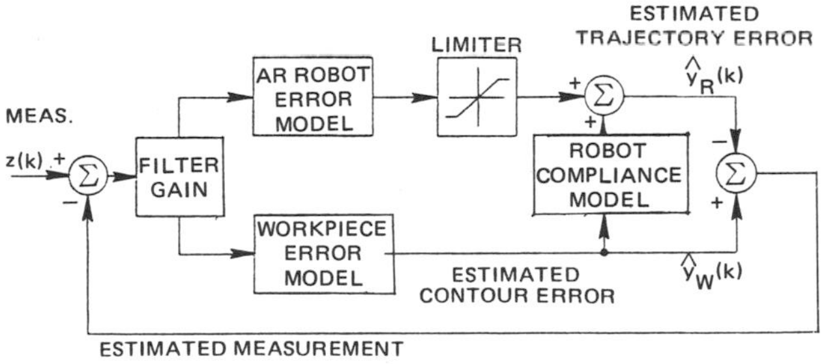

Figure 10.

filter are shown in Figure 11. In this experiment, the nonlinear filter achieved better results than the linear filter.

Conclusion

A technique for modeling continuous-path robot trajectories and workpiece contours has been presented. The contour model was proposed as a basis for identifying different contours or different states of similar contours with a minimum amount of stored information. The modeling method was also used to estimate robot location

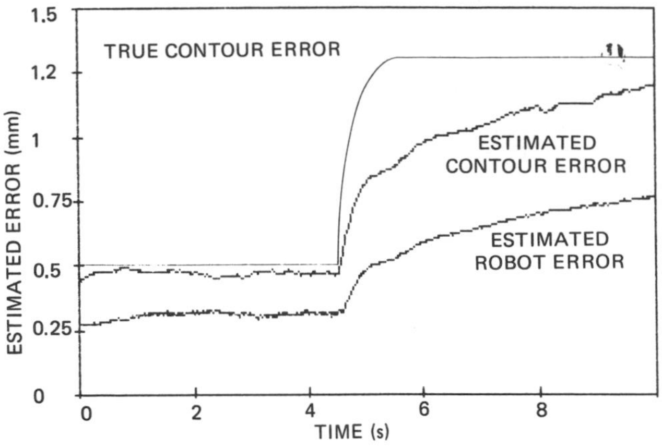

Figure 11.

and workpiece geometry from wrist-sensor measurements.

Experiments in estimation have shown that contour geometry may be measured with accuracy greater than the positioning accuracy of the robot itself.

References

1. Seltzer, D.S., "Tactile Sensory Feedback for Difficult Robot Tasks," presented at Robots VI Conference, March 1982.

2. Box, G.E.P., and G.M. Jenkins, Time Series Analysis, San Francisco, Holden-Day, 1976.

3. Makhoul, J., "Linear Prediction: A Tutorial Review," Proc. IEEE, Vol. 63, No. 4, April 1975.

4. Papoulis, A., "Maximum Entropy and Spectral Estimation: A Review," IEEE Trans. Acoustics, Speech, and Signal Processing, Vol. ASSP-29, No. 6, December 1981.

5. Kashyap, R.L., and R.E. Nasburg, "Parameter Estimation in Multivariate Stochastic Difference Equations," IEEE Trans. Automatic Control, Vol. AC-19, No. 6, December 1974.

6. Kalman, R.E., "New Methods in Wiener Filtering," Proc. First Symposium on Engineering Applications of Random Function Theory and Probability, ed. Bogdanoff and Kozin, J. Wiley, 1963, pp. 270-388.

7. Bryson, A.E., and L.J. Henrikson, "Estimation Using Sampled Data Containing Sequentially Correlated Noise," J. Spacecraft, Vol. 5, No. 6, June 1968, pp. 662-665.

8. Papoulis, A., Probability, Random Variables, and Stochastic Processes, New York, McGraw-Hill, 1965.

9. Edsall, A.C., "Optimal Filtering of Robot Sensory Feedback," Master of Science Thesis, MIT Department of Mechanical Engineering, June 1984.

10. Gelb, A., ed., Applied Optimal Estimation, Cambridge, MIT Press, 1974.

11. Kwakernaak, H., and R. Sivan, Linear Optimal Control Systems, New York, Wiley-Interscience, 1972.

Trajectory Control of Robot Manipulator based on the Preview Tracking Control Algorithm

Kenichi Yoshimoto and Hajime Sugiuchi

An application of the Preview Tracking Control Algorithm to trajectory control of robot manipulator was proposed at the 1st I.S.R.R. In this control algorithm, the ahead deviation is detected by comparing the predicted future position with the previewed trajectory and the control signal is generated by the integral action concerning the ahead deviation.

In this paper, firstly, the prediction by the fast-time model is adapted instead of the prediction by Taylor series to predict the future position. The effectiveness of the more accurate prediction is confirmed by the digital simulations. Secondly, the mathematical model of robot manipulator is improved to be more precise by introducing Coulomb's frictions and joint flexibilities to investigate the vibrations caused by them. Thirdly, the Preview Tracking Control Systems are analyzed theoretically to determine the concrete design policy of the P.T.C.S.

1. INTRODUCTION

The robot manipulator is usually designed to have high rigidity. The higher rigidity provides the more precise positioning. However, the highly rigid system increases its weight and it needs high-powered actuators. So, the dynamic characteristics and the energy consumption become worse. On the other hand, the flexible end-effector is employed to the rigid manipulator to reduce the system rigidity and realize the force control in the assembly works. If we can find the control scheme which can satisfy the accuracy of positioning and suppress the vibration caused by low rigidity, we can develop the low rigid and light weight manipulator which can achieve the good dynamic performance and energy saving.

In the trajectory control of robot manipulator, the desired trajectory has been given or has been generated beforehand. The control system is able to utilize the future information of the desired trajectory and correspond to the change of it earlier. Therefore the control accuracy without response lag will be expected.

Such a control system is called as a preview tracking control system and originally has been studied concerning to the driver's steering behavior. There have been proposed various preview tracking control algorithms. At first we would like to introduce them.

Kondo[1] has proposed the linear predictable correction model concerning the driver model, assuming that the driver can predict linearly the future position of the vehicle from the present position and the heading angle and that he handles the steering angle in proportion to the future deviation. The future deviation is predicted by comparing the previewed path with the linear extrapolation of the vehicle position. In this control model, the adequate proportional gain and the adequate preview span must be adjusted in accordance with each curved path and with each vehicle speed. It is difficult to satisfy the conditions for the stability and for the tracking accuracy simultaneously.

Ichikawa[2] has proposed a preview control algorithm in which the manipulating variable is computed by the inverse dynamics of the controlled element to coincide the controlled variable with the desired variable after τ second. He has confirmed that these preview control servo-mechanisms had more superior performance than conventional servo-mechanisms.

Ohno[3] has proposed the predetermined correction model concerning the driver's steering behavior, assuming that the driver can determine the programmed steerage beforehand based on the known characteristics of the vehicle and the pattern of the previewed path, and that he steers not only by the programmed signal but also by the feedback signals consisting with the lateral deviation and the heading deflection caused by the programmed steerage. This control algorithm is similar to that of trajectory control proposed by Paul.

Yoshimoto[4] has proposed the second order predictable correction model concerning the driver's steering behavior, assuming that the driver can predict circularly the future position of the vehicle from the present position, heading angle and lateral acceleration and that he corrects the steering force in proportion to the integrated future deviation. This control algorithm is insensitive to the unknown disturbances and follows up the desired path without response lag nor steady state deviation, because it employs the integral control action concerning the ahead deviation.

Sheridan[5] has proposed three models, one is the extended convolution model, another is the fast time trials with dynamic model of self and the other is the iterated determination of optimal trajectory over preview span. In the first model, the manipulating variable is determined by the following convolution-operation not only of the part error but also of the future input. It is given by

$$m(t)=\int e(t-\tau)W_m(\tau)d\tau+\int y(t+\tau)W_p(\tau)d\tau \qquad (1)$$

where $W_m(t)$ and $W_p(t)$ are the weighting function into the past error and the future input respectively. In the second model, introducing the importance function dictated by the environment of the desired path, the manipulating variable is determined by the convolution-operation into the predicted future error over preview span. In the third model, the optimal manipulating variable is determined iteratively by the method of dynamic programming according to the criterion function defined over preview span.

Hayase[6] has proposed the similar optimal control servo system model with Sheridan's making use of the method of the maximum principle.

Concerning the optimal finite preview control problem, Bender[7], Yamaura[8], Tomizuka[9] and Wada[10] have investigated the control algorithms and their effectiveness.

From the points of view as mentioned before, the trajectory control of robot manipulator is considered to be the preview tracking control. The authors applied the second order predictable model to the trajectory control of manipulator at the 1st I.S.R.R. last year. In this application, the virtual reference generated by nominal trajectory and integration of ahead servo-error, is provided to the position servo system closed around each joint actuator.

In this paper, firstly, the prediction by the fast-time model is adapted to predict the future position. The effectiveness of this prediction is confirmed by the digital simulations. Secondly, the mathematical model of robot manipulator is improved by introducing Coulomb's frictions and joint flexibilities to investigate the vibrations caused by them. Thirdly, the Preview Tracking Control Systems are analyzed theoretically to determine the concrete design policy of the P.T.C.S.

2. THE PREDICTION WITH THE FAST TIME MODEL

The block diagram of the P.T.C.S. for position servoed manipulator is shown in fig. 1. A closed loop including the P.T.C.A. is constructed around each joint servo actuator independently. The coupling forces of other links, Coulomb's friction, gravity and so on are considered to be the disturbances to this closed loop. This has the feedforward loops of the position and the velocity according to desired trajectory, $q_{ti}+T_{di}\dot{q}_{ti}$, and these loops compensate the response lag caused by the feedback loops, $q_{ai}+T_{di}\dot{q}_{ai}$,

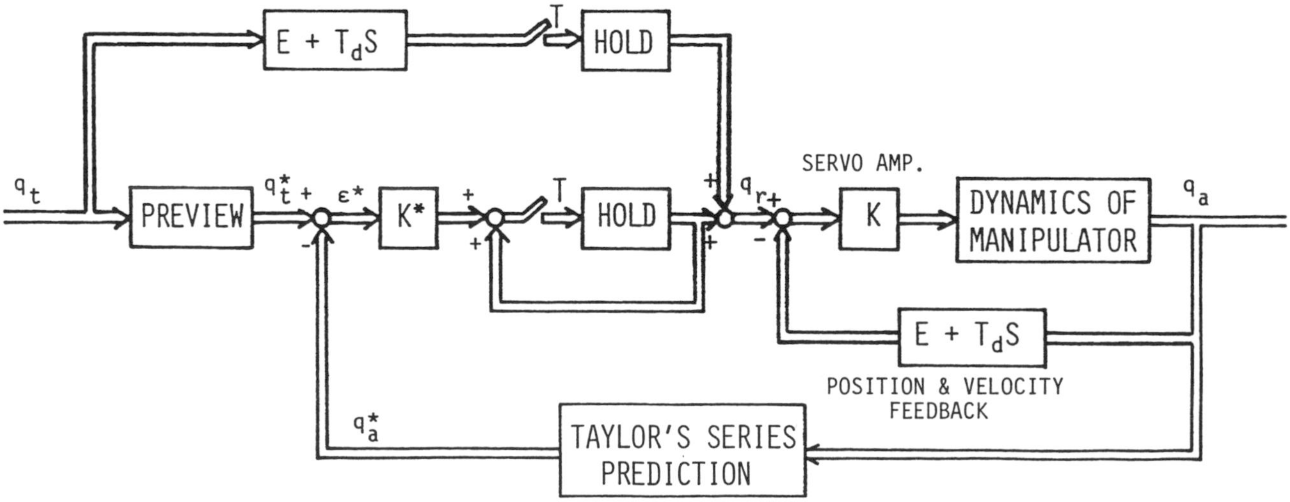

Fig.1 The block diagram of the P.T.C.S. with Taylor's series prediction.

of the position servoed system. So this type of P.T.C.S requires the velocity of the desired trajectory. Here, we propose a new control algorithm which doesn't require the velocity of the desired trajectory. The block diagram of the new P.T.C.A. is shown in fig. 2. In this control method, the possible future error is detected by the fast time model instead of the Taylor's series expansion.

The state equation of the position servoed system are followings,

$$\begin{bmatrix} \dot{q}_{ai} \\ \ddot{q}_{ai} \end{bmatrix} = \begin{bmatrix} 0 & 1 \\ -\frac{K_i}{I_i} & \frac{K_i T_{di}}{I_i} \end{bmatrix} \begin{bmatrix} q_{ai} \\ \dot{q}_{ai} \end{bmatrix} + \begin{bmatrix} 0 \\ \frac{K_i}{I_i} \end{bmatrix} q_{ri} \qquad (2)$$

where,

I_i : moment of inertia of i'th link
T_{di} : damping factor
K_i : gain of servo amplifier
q_{ai} : actual joint angle
q_{ri} : virtual reference angle

Solving the above equation, the predicted state values after seconds are given as follows.

$$\begin{bmatrix} q_{ai}(t+\tau) \\ \dot{q}_{ai}(t+\tau) \end{bmatrix} = A_i \begin{bmatrix} q_{ai}(t) \\ \dot{q}_{ai}(t) \end{bmatrix} + B_i q_{ri}(t)$$

$$A_i = \frac{1}{\beta-\alpha} \begin{bmatrix} (\beta e^{\alpha\tau} - \alpha e^{\beta\tau}) & (-c^{\alpha\tau} + e^{\alpha\tau}) \\ \alpha\beta(e^{\alpha\tau} - e^{\beta\tau}) & (-\alpha e^{\alpha\tau} + \beta e^{\beta\tau}) \end{bmatrix}$$

$$B_i - \frac{1}{\beta-\alpha} \begin{bmatrix} (-\beta e^{\alpha\tau} + \alpha e^{\beta\tau} + (\beta-\alpha)) \\ (-e^{\alpha\tau} + e^{\beta\tau}) \end{bmatrix} \qquad (3)$$

where α and β are the solution of the characteristic equation of the each joint servo system.

A_i and B_i are the coefficient matrix of the fast time model. The values of those matrix depend on the moment of inertia around each joint of manipulator, which alters in accordance with the configuration of manipulator. However, the moment of inertia around each joint is assumed to be the constant mean value of its maximum and minimum. To confirm the effectiveness of this control method, the simulation experiment is performed. Fig.3 shows the comparison between two types of the P.T.C.S, one of which has the Taylor series prediction, another has the fast time model. Table1 shows the values of the P.T.C.S. parameters which are employed in the simulation experiments. The new control method with the fast-time model, shows a little more error than previous one, which has the feedforward loops. But, this method has the good merit that it does not require the velocity of the desired trajectory.

3. MORE PRECISE SIMULATION MODEL

We simulate an articulated manipulator, each joint of which has analogue feedback loops of position and velocity. Fig.4 shows the general view of the simulated rigid body manipulator which is called D_Hand in our laboratory.

The usual Lagrange's formulation of the n'th degrees of freedom manipulator is given by

$$I(q)\ddot{q} + B(q,\dot{q}) + g(q) = F - V\dot{q} - f_r \qquad (4)$$

Joint no.	1	2	3	4	5	6
K^* (Nm/rad)	400	250	180	180	20	10
τ (ms)	50	50	50	50	25	5

(a) With fast time model.

Joint no.	1	2	3	4	5	6
K^* (Nm/rad)	50	60	30	300	40	20
τ (ms)	100	150	50	10	50	10

(b) With Taylor's series.
Table 1 The parameter of P.T.C.S.

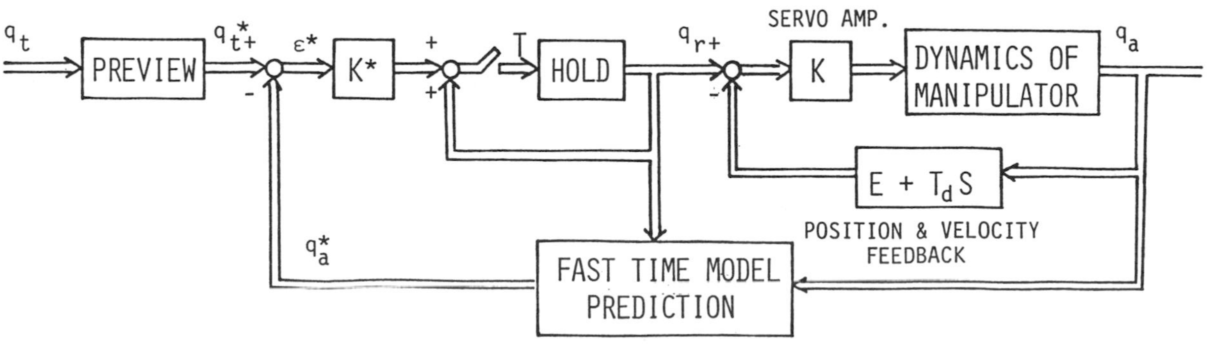

Fig.2 The block diagram of the P.T.C.S. with fast time model prediction.

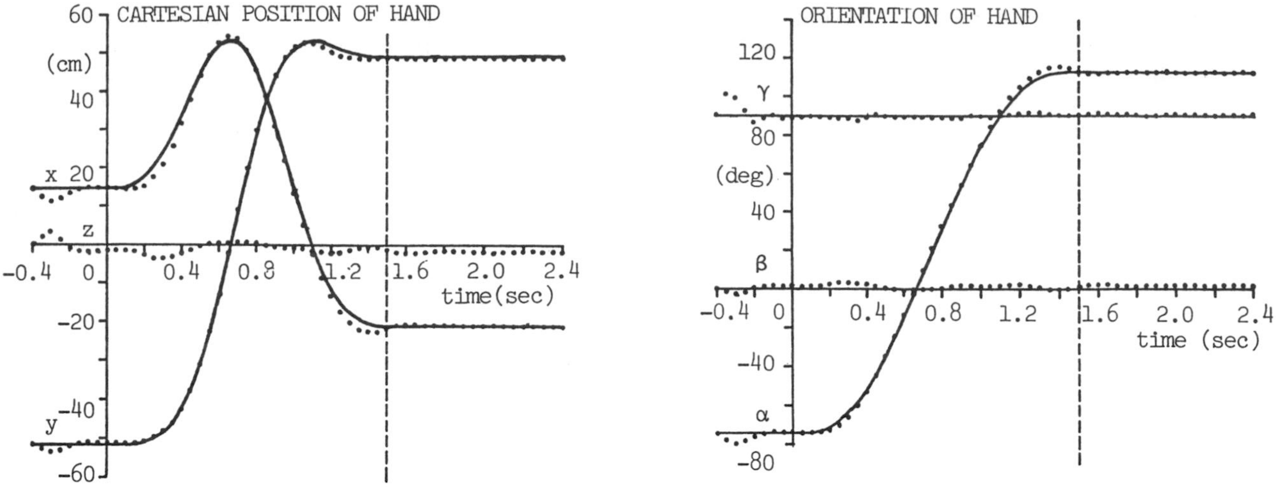

(a) With fast time model prediction.

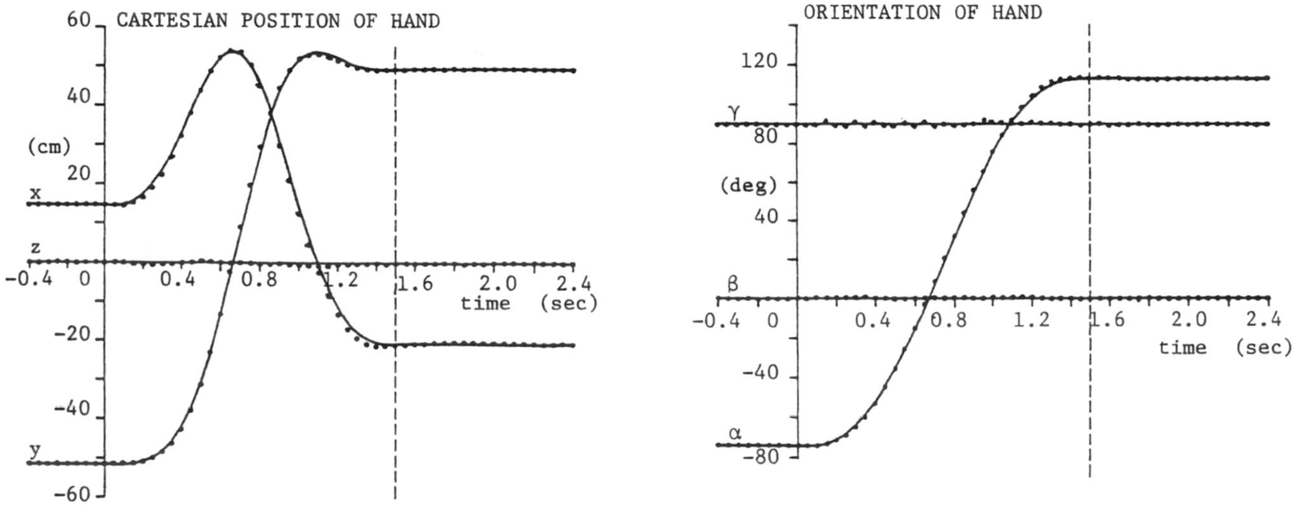

(b) With Taylor's series prediction.

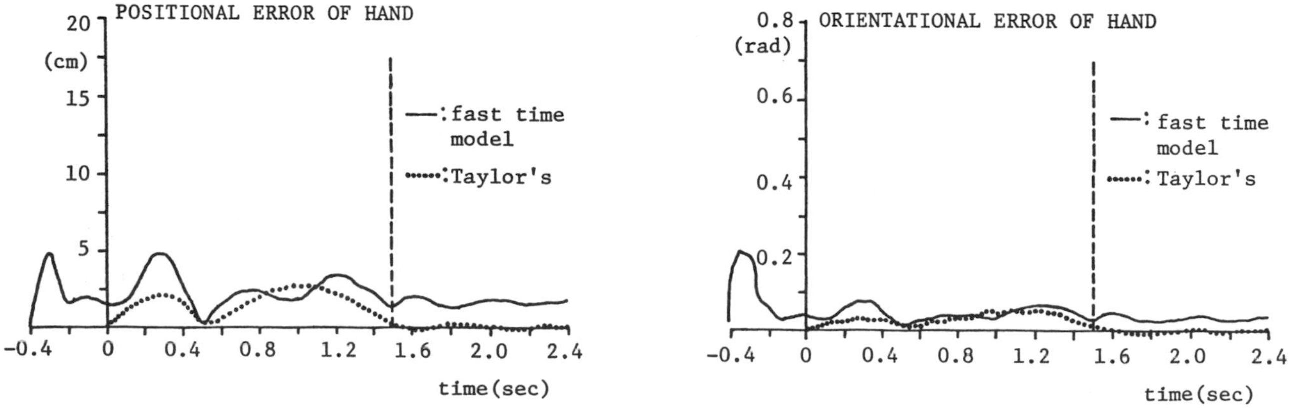

(c) The positional and orientational error of hand.

Fig.3 Comparison of the simulation result with the fast time model prediction and Taylor's series prediction.

where,

$I(q)$: inertia matrix

$B(q, \dot{q})$: centrifugal forces and Corioli's forces

$g(q)$: gravity

F : actuating forces of servo motors

$V\dot{q}$: viscous frictions

f_r : Coulomb's frictions

The terms of $I(q)$, $B(q,\dot{q})$ and $g(q)$ require much time to be calculated. However, we can obtain them numerically by means of the Recursive-Newton-Euler Formulation Method developed by Luh et. al. [11]. The terms of $V\dot{q}$ and f_r are difficult to be identified in real systems. But, all the terms are taken into account.

We obtain the equation of motion as follows;

$$\ddot{q}=I^{-1}(q)(F-V\dot{q}-f_r-B(q,\dot{q})-g(q)) \tag{5}$$

If F is given, all of the right hand side terms become numerically known. Then we can calculate it using the Runge-Kutta-Gill's numeric integration method.

We introduce two items as mentioned below, into the simulation program of the servo mechanism in order to analyze the servo system more precisely,

(1) More strict description of Coulomb's friction.

(2) The servo model includes the joint flexibility.

Coulomb's friction is supposed as shown in fig. 5 in the simulation program, where f_{rki} is kinetic friction and f_{rsi} is statical friction. The magnitude of f_{rsi} is supposed to be $1.5*f_{rki}$ at each joint. The result of the simulation experiment proved that this P.T.C.A. can remove the influence of such Coulomb's frictions.

Introducing the joint flexibility, the motion equations around each joint are derived as follows;

$$
\begin{aligned}
n_i^2 I_{mi}\ddot{q}_{si} &= K_{si}(q_{ri}-q_{si}+T_{di}\dot{q}_{si})-F_i \\
q_{vi} &= q_{si}-q_{ai} \\
F_i &= K_i q_{vi}
\end{aligned} \tag{6}
$$

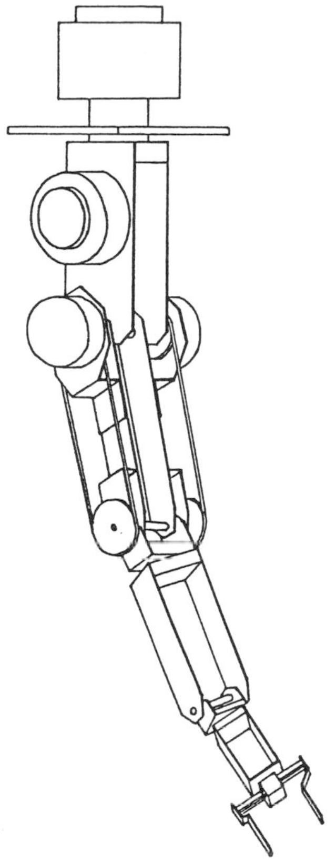

Fig.4 General view of the simulated manipulator.

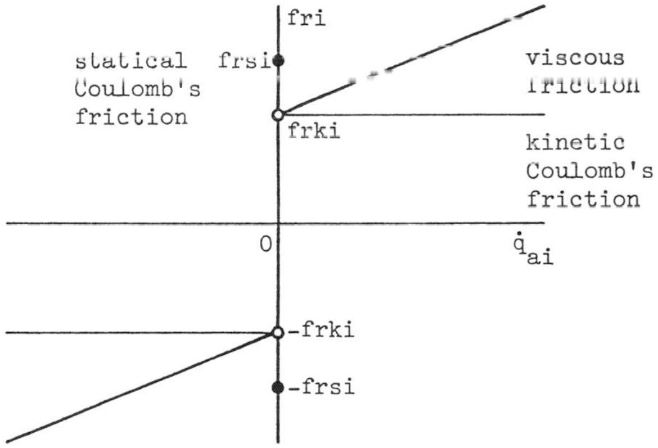

Fig.5 Coulomb's friction.

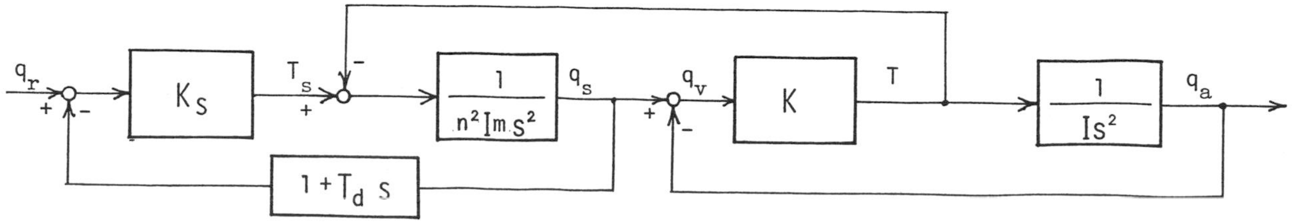

Fig.6 The block diagram of the position servoed system including the joint flexibility.

Joint no.	1	2	3	4	5	6
I (kgm^2)	0.96	1.16	0.20	0.16	0.16	0.0005
K (Nm/rad)	500	500	500	500	500	500
Td (sec)	0.23	0.20	0.16	0.16	0.13	0.05
Ks (Nm/rad)	183	159	40.6	40.6	27.1	4.8

Table 2 the system parameter of manipulator with joint flexibility.

Where;

n_i : gear ratio
I_{mi} : inertia of motor
K_{si} : gain of servo-amplifier
q_{vi} : twist angle of joint shaft
q_{si} : output angle of motor shaft
K_i : rigidity of joint shaft

Table2 shows these values of D-Hand as mentioned before.

The block diagram of the position servoed system including the joint flexibility is shown in fig.6, where I is the moment of inertia of link. There are two ways to detect feedback signal of position for the P.T.C.S. In the conventional way, the rotating angle of the motor shaft is detected. The other is the way in which the joint angle is detected directly. The latter way is better to the accurate control. In this simulation experiment , the joint angle is used as the feedback signal to the P.T.C.S. The results of the simulation is shown in fig.7. Figure(a) shows the joint angle. Figure(b) shows the deviation of the actual trajectory from the desired trajectory. Figure(c) shows the twist angle of joint shaft. In this simulation experiment, the influence of joint flexibility is not so serious. That is because the gain of servo-amplifier is low in comparison with the rigidity of joint shaft. If the rigidity of joint shaft are low enough, we must employ some means to suppress the torsion vibration.

4. DISCUSSION ON THIS CONTROL SYSTEM

In this control method, a closed loop including the P.T.C.A. is constructed around each joint servo actuator independently. The coupling forces of other links, gravity, Coulomb's frictions and so on are considered to be disturbanced to this closed loop. To investigate the concrete design policy of this control system, we derives the difference equation of each joint servo system.

By substituting the sampling time T into equation(3), the difference equation of the position servoed system is derived as follows;

$$\begin{bmatrix} q_{ai}((n+1)T) \\ \dot{q}_{ai}((n+1)T) \end{bmatrix} = A_i \begin{bmatrix} q_{ai}(nT) \\ \dot{q}_{ai}(nT) \end{bmatrix} + B_i q_{ri}(T) \tag{7}$$

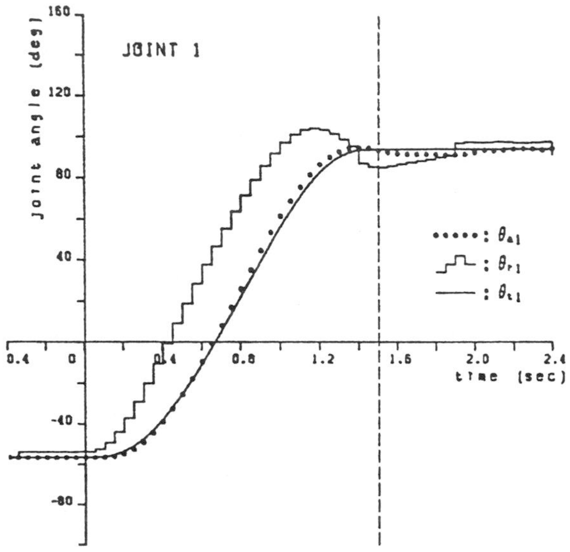

(a) The actual joint angle.

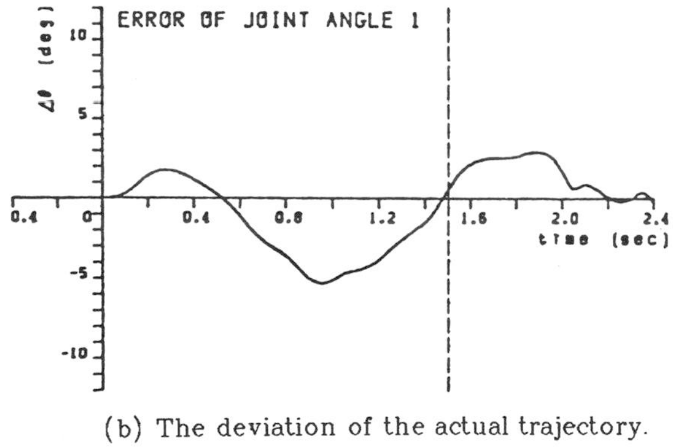

(b) The deviation of the actual trajectory.

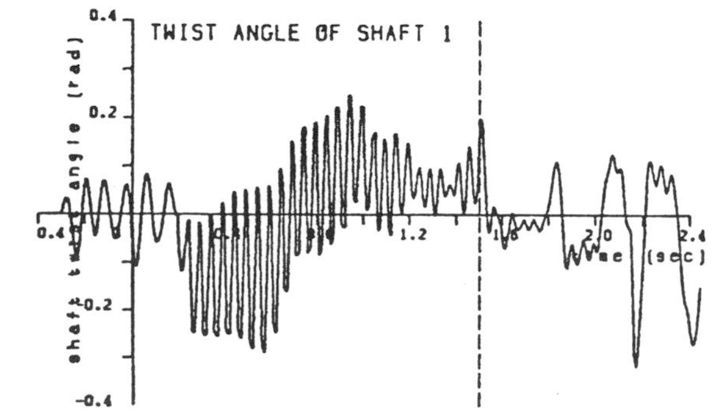

(c) The twist angle of the joint shaft.

Fig.7 The result of the simulation experiment with the joint flexibility.

where

$$A_i = \frac{1}{\beta-\alpha}\begin{bmatrix}(\beta e^{\alpha T}-\alpha e^{\beta T}) & (-e^{\alpha T}+e^{\beta T})\\ \alpha\beta(e^{\alpha T}-e^{\beta T}) & (-\alpha e^{\alpha T}+\beta e^{\beta T})\end{bmatrix}$$

$$B_i = \frac{1}{\beta-\alpha}\begin{bmatrix}-\beta e^{\alpha T}+\alpha e^{\beta T}+(\beta-\alpha)\\ -e^{\alpha T}+e^{\beta T}\end{bmatrix}$$

The virtual reference q_{ri}, which is generated by the integral control action of the P.T.C.A. and the feed-forward inputs as follows;

$$\begin{aligned} q_{ri}((n+1)T) = & -K^*_i q_{ai}(nT) - K^*_i \dot{q}_{ai}((n-1)T) \\ & + q_{ri}(nT) + q_{ti}((n+1)T) \\ & - \dot{q}_{ti}((n-1)T) + T_{di}(\dot{q}_{ti}((n+1)T) \\ & - \dot{q}_{ti}(nT)) + K^* q^*_{ti}((n-1)T) \end{aligned} \tag{8}$$

Then, the mathematical model of digital controlled joint servo system with the P.T.C.S. are given by the following equations:

$$\begin{bmatrix} q_{ai}((n+1)T) \\ \dot{q}_{ai}((n+1)T) \\ q_{ri}((n+1)T) \end{bmatrix} = \hat{A}_i \begin{bmatrix} q_{ai}(nT) \\ \dot{q}_{ai}(nT) \\ q_{ri}(nT) \end{bmatrix} + \hat{B}_i \hat{U}_i(nT) \tag{9}$$

Where, $\hat{A}_i$ and $\hat{B}_i$ are follows.

$$\hat{A}_i = \begin{bmatrix} A_i & B_i \\ -K^*_i, -K^*_i\tau & 1 \end{bmatrix}$$

$$\hat{B}_i = \begin{bmatrix} 0 \\ 1, -1, T_{di}, -T_{di}, K^*_i \end{bmatrix}$$

$$\begin{aligned} \hat{U}_i(nT) = & [q_{ti}(nT), q_{ti}((n-1)T), q_{ti}(nT) \\ & \dot{q}_{ti}((n-1)T), q^*_{ti}((n-1)T)]^t \end{aligned} \tag{9'}$$

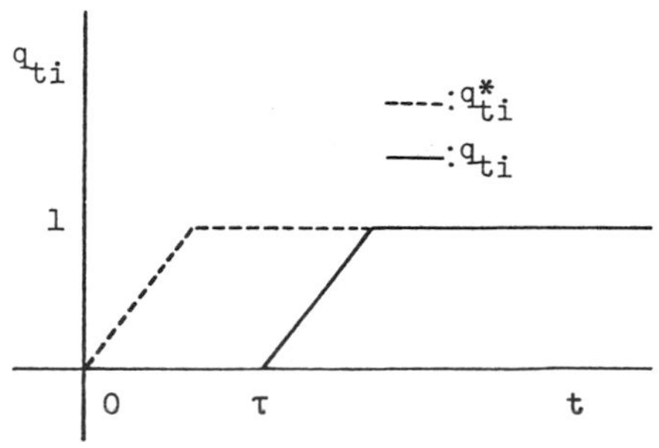

Fig.8 The trajectory function.

We can calculate the system response concerning to the given trajectory $q_{ti}(t)$, which is a simple ramp like function as shown in fig.8. The reason why we employed such a function instead of a step function is that $\dot{q}_{ti}$ must have a finite value. The value of performance index J_i is determined as follows:

$$J_i = \sum_{k=0}^{n} (q_{ai}(kT) - q_{ti}(kT)) \tag{10}$$

Fig.9 shows the distribution chart of the performance index value J_i in the control parameters plane (K_i, τ_i). This figure shows us the optimum parameter pair ($K^*opt._i$, $\tau opt._i$) when the sampling time is 50ms (as shown in table3). The P.T.C.S is stable in large range of K^* - τ plane, because the each joint has position and velocity analogue feedback loops. On the other hand, the torque servoed system which has no analogue feed-back loop requires short sampling time (in the case of our manipulator, about 5 ms). Moreover, the stable range is small.

Practical systems include the saturation of the amplifiers and Coulomb's frictions, but we leave them out of consideration in this parameter optimizing. The real optimal parameter must differ a little from ($K^*opt.$, $\tau opt.$). The results of a simulation experiment which includes Coulomb's frictions and saturations show that the parameter pair ($K^*opt.$, $\tau opt.$) gives satisfactory good tracking performance.

Consequently, in the application to the position servoed manipulator, the effectiveness of the P.T.C.A. is confirmed.

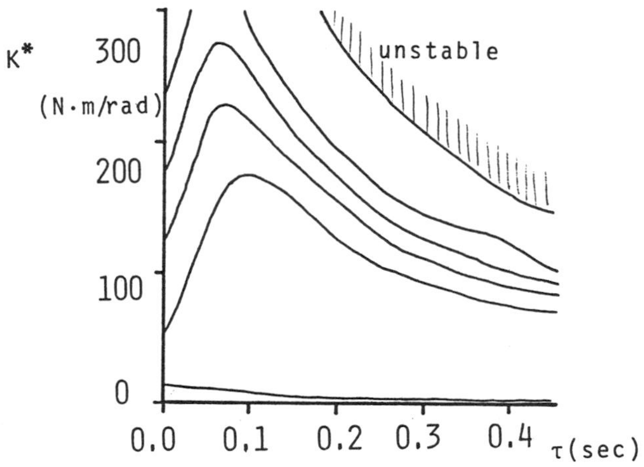

Fig.9 The distribution chart of the performance index.

Joint no.	1	2	3	4	5	6
K^* (Nm/rad)	95	72	50	53	16	4
τ (ms)	150	150	100	100	100	50

Table 3 The optimaized parameter of P.T.C.S.

References

[1] Kondo,M., 1958 "Fundamental Relation between the Steerage and the Behavior of Automobiles," Trans. of Japan Soc. Automobile Engineers. No.5. p.40. (in Japanese)

[2] Ichikawa,K., 1961, "Prediction Servomechanism and its Performance" Trans. of J.S.M.E., Vol.27, No.182, p.1652-1663. (in Japanese)

[3] Ohno,S., 1966, "The Driver's Steerage on Curved Paths" Journal of Japan Soc. Automobile Engineers. Vol.20, No.5, p.413-418, (in Japanese)

[4] Yoshimoto,K., 1969, "Simulation of Man-Automobile Systems by the Driver's Steering model with Predictability" Bull. of J.S.M.E. Vol.12, No.51, p.495-500.

[5] Sheridan,T.B. 1966, "Three Models of Preview Ccntrol," I.E.E.E. Trans. on H.F.E., H.F.E.-7-2, p.91-102.

[6] Hayase,M. and Ichikawa,K., 1969, "Optimal Servosystem Utilizing Future Value of Desired Function" Trans. Soc. of Instrument and Control Engineers. Vol.5, No.1, p.86-94. (in Japanese)

[7] Bender,E.K., 1968, "Optimum Linear Preview Control with Application to Vehicle Suspension" Trans. of A.S.M.E. Journal of Basic Eng. Vol.192, No.2, p.213-221.

[8] Yamaura,T. and Kobayashi,A., 1975, "Optimality of Sub-Optimal Tracking Control Locally Utilizing Future Value of the Desired Function" Trans. of S.I.C.E. Vol.11, No.2, p.229-233. (in Japanese)

[9] Tomizuka,M., 1977, "The Discrete Optimal Finite Preview Control Problem" Trans. S.I.C.E. Vol.11, No.6, p.663-668, (in Japanese)

[10] Wada,M., 1977, "The Optimal Finite Preview Control and Effect of Preview" Trans. S.I.C.E., Vol.13, No.6, p.547-552 (in Japanese)

[11] J.T.S.Luh, M.W.Walker and R.C.Paul, 1980, "On-line computational scheme of mechanical manipulators," ASME Trans. J. Dynamic Syst., Measurement and contr., Vol.10, No.11.

MANIPULATOR CONTROL USING AUTONOMOUS TRAJECTORY GENERATING SERVOMECHANISM

Kensuke Hasegawa and Takashi Mizutani

Department of Control Engineering
Tokyo Institute of Technology
2-12-1 Ookayama
Meguro-ku, Tokyo, JAPAN

The authors propose a novel method for the trajectory control of the end of manipulator based on the autonomous trajectory generating servomechanism technique (the ATGS Technique, in short). The ATGS is a multivariable servomechanism including a part of trajectory planner, in which, instead of giving nominal trajectories, the corresponding paths, the tangential motion rates and the algorithm of tracing the paths are prepared.
So that the ATGS is able to generate trajectories autonomously according to the practical requirements such as the execution of high precision trajectory controls, the avoidance of the pull-off from paths due to saturations in control signals, and the compliant motion for mechanical constraints.

1. Introduction

The paper deals with the novel method of trajectory control of the end of the manipulator.
The trajectory controls are the basic techniques concerning the manipulator controls and are imposed the practical requirements i.e.,

1) To keep the accuracy of trajectories even for the wide changes of parameters in manipulators.
2) To make it possible to introduce the flexibility in the trajectory control easilly.
3) To decrease the computation time for each sampled control signals.

The method proposed are especially suitable for (1) and (2).
The control system based on the method proposed contains a part of the trajectory planner in its control loop.
In the method, nominal trajectories are not given directly, but the corresponding paths and tangential motion rates are specified separately and also the algorithm of tracing the paths is prepared in the control system.
According to the practical requirements such as the execution of high precision trajectory controls, the avoidance of pull-off from the paths due to saturations in control signals and the compliant motion for mechanical constraints, the control system is arranged to be able to generate the corresponding trajectories autonomously. The authors call this technique the "Autonomous Trajectory Generating Servo Technique", in short, the ATGS Technique and the trajectory control using the ATGS Technique the ATGS Control.
In the paper, after the principle of the ATGS and its adoption to the trajectory control of the end of the manipulator are described, the features of the method satisfying the requirements mentioned above are discussed and verified by simulations.

2. Description of the Nominal Trajectory and the end of the manipulator

It is assumed that the path drawn by a nominal trajectory is able to be divided into segments of plane curves, e.g., the straight line, the circle,etc.
The coordinate systems, in which the curve is defined, is called the S-coordinates.
The coordinate frame of S-coordinates with respect to the base coordinates is described as

$$\underline{S} = \begin{bmatrix} \underline{L} & \underline{p}_s \\ 0\ 0\ 0 & 1 \end{bmatrix} \tag{2.1}$$

$$\underline{L} = [{}^s\underline{n}\ \ {}^s\underline{o}\ \ {}^s\underline{a}] \tag{2.2}$$

The curve is to be given on the x-y plane of S-coordinates as follows:

$$f(x',y') = 0 \tag{2.3}$$

$$z' = 0 \tag{2.4}$$

Where, x', y', and z', are values on the corresponding axis of the S-coordinates. Next the coordinate system on the curve is defined by the form of a coordinate frame $\underline{C}$ with respect to the S-coordinates as shown in Fig.1.

Let a point on the curve be point Q and the corresponding vector be $\underline{p}_c'$ in the S-coordinates.
Using the gradient of f(x' y') at point Q, i.e.,

$$\nabla f = (\ df/dx \quad df/dy\ ) = (\ f_x\ f_y\ ) \tag{2.5}$$

${}^c\underline{o}$, ${}^c\underline{n}$, ${}^c\underline{a}$ are given as

$${}^c\underline{o} = \begin{bmatrix} f_x/|\nabla f| \\ f_y/|\nabla f| \\ 0 \end{bmatrix}, {}^c\underline{n} = \begin{bmatrix} f_y/|\nabla f| \\ -f_x/|\nabla f| \\ 0 \end{bmatrix}, {}^c\underline{a} = \begin{bmatrix} 0 \\ 0 \\ 1 \end{bmatrix} \tag{2.6}$$

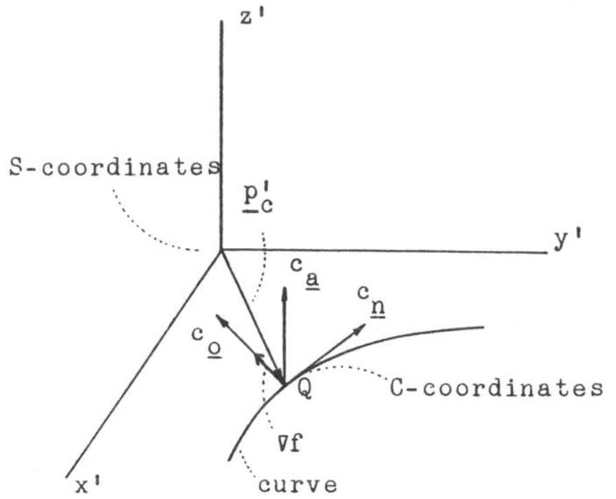

Fig.1 A Curve as Path and C-coordinate Frame

Then the coordinate frame $\underline{C}$ is defined as

$$\underline{C} = \begin{bmatrix} \underline{H} & \underline{p}_c' \\ 0\ 0\ 0 & 1 \end{bmatrix} \tag{2.7}$$

where

$$\underline{H} = \left[{}^c\underline{n}\ {}^c\underline{o}\ {}^c\underline{a} \right] = \begin{bmatrix} f_y/|\nabla f| & f_x/|\nabla f| & 0 \\ -f_x/|\nabla f| & f_y/|\nabla f| & 0 \\ 0 & 0 & 1 \end{bmatrix} \tag{2.8}$$

${}^c\underline{o}$, ${}^c\underline{n}$ are corresponding to the normal and the tangential unit vectors on the curve at point Q respectively. The vector ${}^c\underline{a}$ is a normal unit vector to the x-y plane at point Q.
If point Q moves on the curve in the direction of ${}^c\underline{n}$ with the motion rate V corresponding to the one on the original nominal trajectory, one segment of the nominal trajectory will be re-generated.

The coordinate frame of the end of the manipulator with respect to the base coordinates, the S-coordinates and the C-coordinates are given by $\underline{R}$, ${}^s\underline{R}$, ${}^c\underline{R}$ respectively as

$$\underline{R} = \begin{bmatrix} \underline{n}\ \underline{o}\ \underline{a}\ \underline{p} \\ 0\ 0\ 0\ 1 \end{bmatrix} \tag{2.9}$$

$${}^s\underline{R} = \begin{bmatrix} \underline{n}' & \underline{o}' & \underline{a}' & \underline{p}' \\ 0 & 0 & 0 & 1 \end{bmatrix} \tag{2.10}$$

$${}^c\underline{R} = \begin{bmatrix} \underline{n}'' & \underline{o}'' & \underline{a}'' & \underline{p}'' \\ 0 & 0 & 0 & 1 \end{bmatrix} \tag{2.11}$$

and they have next relations.

$$\underline{R} = \underline{S}\ {}^s\underline{R} \tag{2.12}$$

$${}^s\underline{R} = \underline{C}\ {}^c\underline{R} \tag{2.13}$$

or

$$[\ \underline{n}\ \underline{o}\ \underline{a}\ ] = \underline{L}[\ \underline{n}'\ \underline{o}'\ \underline{a}'] \tag{2.14}$$

$$\underline{p}' = \underline{L}^T(\underline{p}-\underline{p}_s) \tag{2.15}$$

$$[\ \underline{n}'\ \underline{o}'\ \underline{a}'\ ] = \underline{H}[\ \underline{n}'\ \underline{o}'\ \underline{a}'\ ] \tag{2.16}$$

$$\underline{p}'-\underline{p}_c' = \underline{H}\underline{p}'' \tag{2.17}$$

where $\underline{p}$, $\underline{p}'$, $\underline{p}''$ represent the vectors corresponding to a position of the end of the manipulator in the base, S-, C- coordinates respectively.

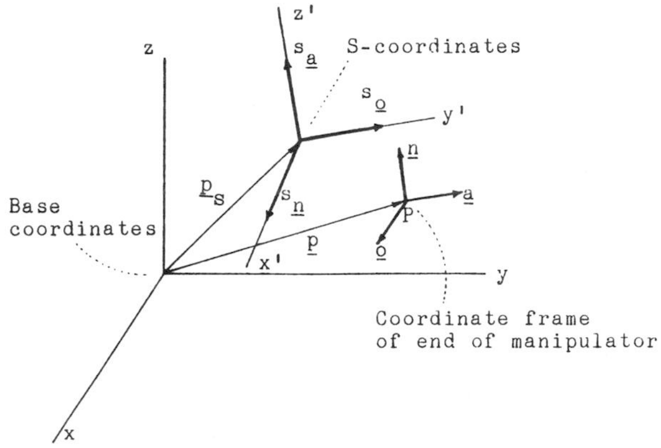

Fig.2 Configuration of S-coordinates and Coordinate Frame of End of Manipulator

In general, $\underline{R}$ is obtained from the joint position $\underline{q}$, therefore $\underline{R}$ is sometimes written as $\underline{R}(\underline{q})$.
Fig.2 shows the configurations of $\underline{R}$ and S-coordinates with respect to the base coordinates. In the figure, point P represents a position of the end of the manipulator.
The purpose of the trajectory control proposed here is to move the end of the manipulator along a curve with the reference motion rate keeping the orientation of the end of the manipulator to the reference orientation.

3. The principle of the trajectory control by the ATGS

It is assumed that the manipulator is compensated by the computed Joint Torque Servo Technigue (CJTS Tech. in short) (Paul,1972; Markiewicz,1973) in advance. Hereafter such a compenstion is called CJTS compensation.
Fig.3(a) shows the block diagram for explaining the CJTS compensation. It is considered that the CJTS compensation transforms the dynamics of arm to the six independent channels which consist of the cascade connection of two stages of integral as shown in Fig.3(b).

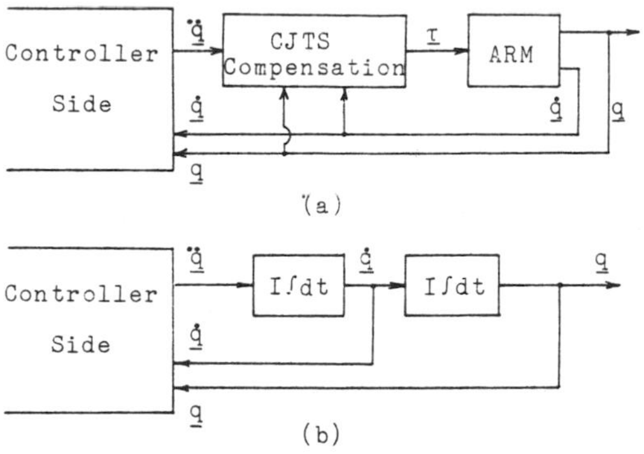

Fig.3 Compensation by CJTS Technique

Position control

In ATGS, the specified path will be given in the Cartesian Coordinate system as shown in Fig.1. Therefore it is natural way to describe the control algorithm in the cartesian coordinates and to transform the control signal to $\ddot{\underline{q}}$ in the joint coordinate later.
Assume that a position of the end of the manipulator is sufficiently near to the curve C, and let the nearest point on the curve C from point P be Q as shown in Fig.4.

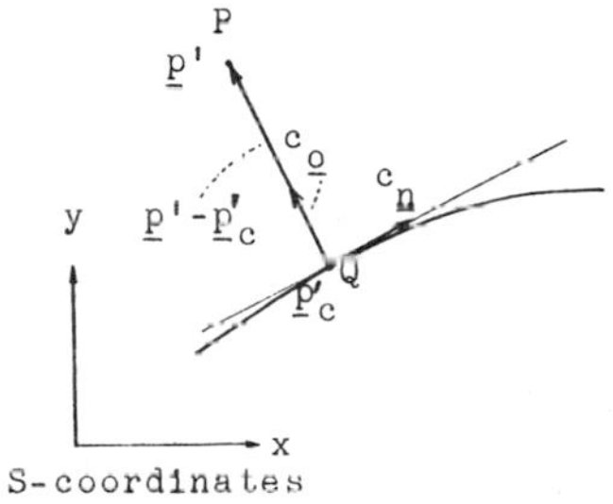

Fig.4 Position of the End of Manipulator, P and Corresponding C-coordinate frame with respect to S-coordinates (z-axis of S and C-coordinates are perpendicular to the sheet)

The vector from point Q to point P in the S-coordinates, i.e., $\underline{p}'-\underline{p}_c'$ can be considered as being on the y-z plane of the C-coordinates defined at point Q. The vector $\underline{p}''$ in the C-coordinates corresponding to $\underline{p}'-\underline{p}_c'$ can be given approximately by the next equation.

$$\underline{p}'' = [\,0\ \ y''\ \ z''\,]^T = [\,0\ \ f/|\nabla f|\ \ z''\,]^T \qquad (3.1)$$

By using (2.17), (3.1), $\underline{p}'-\underline{p}_c'$ is represented by the next equation.

$$\underline{p}'-\underline{p}_c' = \underline{H}\begin{bmatrix} 0 \\ f(x',y')/|\nabla f| \\ z'' \end{bmatrix} \qquad (3.2)$$

Point P is to be moved along the given curve C with the reference tangential rate v(t), and then the control law for this purpose is given as follows.

$$\ddot{\underline{p}}'-\ddot{\underline{p}}_r'+K_1(\dot{\underline{p}}'-\dot{\underline{p}}_r')+K_2(\underline{p}'-\underline{p}_c') = 0 \qquad (3.3)$$

where $\dot{\underline{p}}'_r$, $\ddot{\underline{p}}'_r$ are the reference translational velocity and acceleration of the end of the manipulator with respect to S-coordinates and the third term of the left side corresponds to the recovery acceleration orthogonal to the nominal specified curve.
It is noticed that $\underline{p}'-\underline{p}_c'$ is used in place of $\underline{p}'-\underline{p}_r'$, which appears in the conventional control in where $\underline{p}_r'$ is given as the moving reference position in the S-coordinates.
If (3.3) is stable, $\ddot{\underline{p}}'-\ddot{\underline{p}}'_r$, $\dot{\underline{p}}'-\dot{\underline{p}}'_r$, and $\underline{p}'-\underline{p}_c'$ will approach asymptotically to zero, then the required trajectory will be obtained with high accuracy.

The concrete control algorithm is deduced as follows. Multiply $\underline{H}^T$ to both side of (3.2).

$$\underline{H}^T(\ddot{\underline{p}}'-\ddot{\underline{p}}'_r)+K_1\underline{H}^T(\dot{\underline{p}}'-\dot{\underline{p}}'_r)+K_2\underline{H}^T(\underline{p}'-\underline{p}_c') = 0$$

$$\underline{H}^T\ddot{\underline{p}}'+K_1\underline{H}^T\dot{\underline{p}}'+K_2\underline{H}^T(\underline{p}'-\underline{p}_c')-\underline{H}^T\ddot{\underline{p}}'_r-K_1\underline{H}^T\dot{\underline{p}}'_r = 0 \qquad (3.4)$$

$\underline{H}^T\dot{\underline{p}}_r$ and $\underline{H}^T\ddot{\underline{p}}_r$ are obtained as follows.

$$\underline{H}^T\dot{\underline{p}}_r' = \begin{bmatrix} v(t) \\ 0 \\ 0 \end{bmatrix} \qquad (3.5)$$

$\underline{H}^T\ddot{\underline{p}}_r'$ is represented by the next equation using (3.5).

$$\underline{H}^T\ddot{\underline{p}}_r' = \begin{bmatrix} \dot{v}(t) \\ 0 \\ 0 \end{bmatrix} - \dot{\underline{H}}^T\underline{H}\begin{bmatrix} v(t) \\ 0 \\ 0 \end{bmatrix} \qquad (3.6)$$

$\dot{\underline{H}}^T\underline{H}$ in the above equation is transformed as follows.

$$\dot{\underline{H}}^T\underline{H} = \begin{bmatrix} 0 & \omega_z & 0 \\ -\omega_z & 0 & 0 \\ 0 & 0 & 0 \end{bmatrix} \qquad (3.7)$$

where

$$\omega_z = (f_y(f_{xx}\dot{x}+f_{xy}\dot{y})-f_x(f_{xy}\dot{x}+f_{yy}\dot{y}))/|\nabla f|^2 \qquad (3.8)$$

Substituting (3.2), (3.5), (3.6), (3.7) to (3.4) and multiplying $\underline{H}$, the following equation is obtained

$$\ddot{\underline{p}}' = -K_1\dot{\underline{p}}'+\underline{H}\begin{bmatrix} K_1v(t)+\dot{v}(t) \\ -K_2f/|\nabla f|+\omega_z v(t) \\ -K_2z' \end{bmatrix} \qquad (3.9)$$

where

$$\underline{\dot{p}}' = \begin{bmatrix} \dot{x}' \\ \dot{y}' \\ \dot{z}' \end{bmatrix} \tag{3.10}$$

Further, (3.9) can be transformed to the equation in the base coordinates by using the transformation Matrix $\underline{S}$ as follows.

$$\underline{\ddot{p}} = \underline{\ddot{p}}_s - \underline{K}_1(\underline{\dot{p}} - \underline{\dot{p}}_s) + \underline{r} \tag{3.11}$$

where

$$\underline{r} = \underline{L}\ \underline{H} \begin{bmatrix} K_1 v(t) + \dot{v}(t) \\ -K_2 f/|\nabla f| + \omega_z v(t) \\ -K_2 \dot{z}' \end{bmatrix} \tag{3.12}$$

In ordinary cases, $\underline{p}_s$ is constant, then

$$\underline{\ddot{p}} = -K_1\underline{\dot{p}} + \underline{r} \tag{3.13}$$

It is known that the system is stable if $K_1 > 0$, $K_2 > 0$ (Hasegawa and Mizutani, 1984).

Orientation control

For the orientation control of the end of the manipulator, the method presented by Paul (Paul, et.al, 1979) is used as follows.

The reference coordinate frame of the end of the manipulator is given in the base coordinates as

$$\begin{bmatrix} \underline{n}_r & \underline{o}_r & \underline{a}_r & \underline{p}_r \\ 0 & 0 & 0 & 1 \end{bmatrix} \tag{3.14}$$

where $\underline{p}_r$ is equal to the present position $\underline{p}$. The purpose of the orientation control is to have the present coordinate frame of the end of the manipulator to coincide with the reference coordinate frame shown by (3.14).

The control law for this purpose is obtained as follows.

Provided that $[\underline{n}\ \underline{o}\ \underline{a}]$ coincides with $[\underline{n}_r\ \underline{o}_r\ \underline{a}_r]$ by rotating the angle δ around the vector $\underline{h}$, the following relation is well-known:

$$\underline{h}\sin\delta = (\underline{n}\times\underline{n}_r + \underline{o}\times\underline{o}_r + \underline{a}_r\times\underline{a})/2 \tag{3.15}$$

This vector is defined as the orientation error. Then, the control law can be given by the next equation

$$\underline{\dot{\omega}} = \underline{\dot{\omega}}_r - K_1(\underline{\omega} - \underline{\omega}_r) - K_2\underline{h}\sin\delta$$

or

$$\underline{\dot{\omega}} = -K_1\underline{\omega} + \underline{s} \tag{3.16}$$

$$\underline{s} = \underline{\dot{\omega}}_r + K_1\underline{\omega}_r + K_2\underline{h}\sin\delta \tag{3.17}$$

Where $\underline{\omega}_r$, $\underline{\dot{\omega}}_r$ are their reference vectors. It is clear from (3.15) that the system is stable if K_1 and K_2 are positive.

If the orientation is to be kept constant in the base coordinates, $[{}^R\underline{n}_r\ {}^R\underline{o}_r\ {}^R\underline{a}_r]$ is chosen as constant according to the requirement, then ω_r and $\dot{\omega}_r$ are equal to zero.

If the orientation is to be kept constant with respect to the C-coordinates, $[\underline{n}_r\ \underline{o}_r\ \underline{a}_r]$, ω_r and $\dot{\omega}_r$ will be deduced from the reference orientation with respect to the C-coordinates, i.e., $[{}^C\underline{n}_r\ {}^C\underline{o}_r\ {}^C\underline{a}]$, ω_z, $\dot{\omega}_z$, and $\underline{L}$. That is,

$$[\underline{n}_r\ \underline{o}_r\ \underline{a}_r] = \underline{L}\ \underline{H}[{}^C\underline{n}_r\ {}^C\underline{o}_r\ {}^C\underline{a}_r] \tag{3.18}$$

$$\underline{\omega}_r = \underline{L}\begin{bmatrix} 0 \\ 0 \\ \omega_z \end{bmatrix} \tag{3.19}$$

$$\underline{\dot{\omega}}_r = \underline{L}\begin{bmatrix} 0 \\ 0 \\ \dot{\omega}_z \end{bmatrix} \tag{3.20}$$

Using new variables

$$\underline{u} = \begin{bmatrix} \underline{p} \\ \underline{\omega} \end{bmatrix} \tag{3.21}$$

$$\underline{w} = \begin{bmatrix} \underline{r} \\ \underline{s} \end{bmatrix} \tag{3.22}$$

The control laws for both the position and orientation control are represented by a vector equation:

$$\underline{\ddot{u}} = -K_1\underline{\dot{u}} + \underline{w} \tag{3.23}$$

The control signal in the Cartecian coordinates i.e., $\ddot{u}$ should be transformed to the control signal in the joint coordinates, i.e., $\underline{\ddot{q}}$ by using the next relationship.

$$\underline{\dot{u}} = \underline{J}(\underline{q})\ \underline{\dot{q}} \tag{3.24}$$

where $\underline{J}(\underline{q})(6\text{x}6)$ is the Jacobian deduced from $\underline{R}(\underline{q})$. By differenciating (3.24), the next equation is obtained.

$$\underline{\ddot{u}} = \underline{J}\underline{\ddot{q}} + \underline{\dot{J}}\underline{\dot{q}}$$

$$\therefore\ \underline{\ddot{q}} = \underline{J}^{-1}(\underline{\ddot{u}} - \underline{\dot{J}}\underline{\dot{q}}) \tag{3.25}$$

Then, (3.23) is transformed in the joint coordinates as follows

$$\underline{\ddot{q}} = -K_1\underline{\dot{q}} + \underline{J}^{-1}(\underline{w} - \underline{\dot{J}}\underline{\dot{q}}) \tag{3.26}$$

Fig.5 shows the control algorithm mentioned above.

Eq.(3.8) and ω_z for the concrete curves are shown as follows

(i) straight line

$$f(x,y) = y \tag{3.27}$$

$$\underline{H} = \underline{I} \quad : \text{unit matrix} \tag{3.28}$$

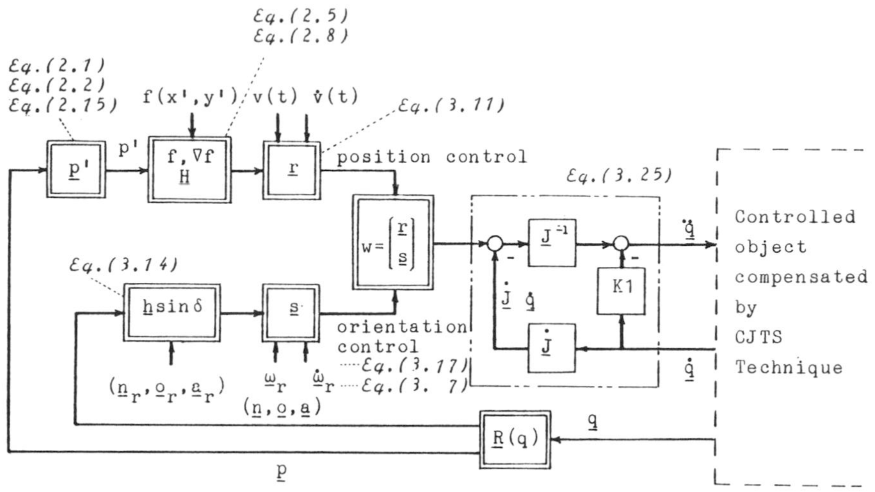

where ☐ means a computation algorithm.

Fig.5 Block Diagram for Control Algorithm

$$\ddot{\underline{p}} = -K_1\dot{\underline{p}} + \underline{LH}\begin{bmatrix} K_1 v(t)+\dot{v}(t) \\ -K_2 y'' \\ -K_2 z'' \end{bmatrix} \tag{3.29}$$

$$\omega_z = 0 \tag{3.30}$$

Where x", y", z" are values on each axis of the C-coordinates.
In this case the y and z components of S- and C-coordinates coincide each other.

(ii) circle

$$f(x,y) = (x^2+y^2-r^2)/2 \tag{3.31}$$

$$\nabla f = (x \quad y) \tag{3.32}$$

$$|\nabla f| = \sqrt{x^2+y^2} \fallingdotseq r \tag{3.33}$$

$$\underline{H} = \begin{bmatrix} y'/r & x'/r & 0 \\ -x'/r & y'/r & 0 \\ 0 & 0 & 1 \end{bmatrix} \tag{3.34}$$

$$\ddot{\underline{p}} = K_1\dot{\underline{p}}+\underline{LH}\begin{bmatrix} K_1 v(t)+\dot{v}(t) \\ -K_2\ ((x^2+y^2-r^2)\ /(2r))+\omega_z v(t) \\ -K_2 z' \end{bmatrix} \tag{3.35}$$

$$\omega_z = (y'\dot{x}'-\dot{y}x')/r^2 \tag{3.36}$$

4. The relationships between K_1, K_2 and trajectory generations

It should be noticed that trajectory generation in the ATGS technique are realized not by the "position" maneuvering for which the position reference is generated in the "off-loop" planner, but by the "velocity" maneuvering with the recovery acceleration proportional to the orthogonal deviation from the specified path.
Therefore, some features of the ATGS trajectory control will be expected for mechanical constraints and control limitations existing in the manipulator systems.
These features will come from the independency between the motion rate control and the trajectory recovery control.
In this section, the fundamental characteristics of the position control under the constraints and the limitations are analyzed and the relationships between coefficients K_1, K_2 and the system behavior will be discussed.
The path dealt with here is confined to a straight line described in 3.(i), the reference motion rate is constant V_r, and also the system is assumed to be in the steady state. Eventually, x',y' and x",y" are equal respectively as the incremental amounts in the discussion.

The effect of force disturbance

In general, the force disturbances can be transformed equivalently to the acceleration $\underline{r}_d$ in the base coordinates and added to the output side of the position control signal $\underline{r}$ in Fig.5.
Under the conditions mentioned so far, the following relationship can be deduced from (3.29).

$$K_1\underline{L}^T\dot{\underline{p}} = \begin{bmatrix} K_1 v_r \\ -K_2 y'' \\ -K_2 z'' \end{bmatrix} + \underline{L}^T\underline{r}_d \tag{4.1}$$

In the steady state, the y and z components of $\underline{L}^T\dot{\underline{p}}$ should be zero, therefore next equations will be obtained.

$$y'' = -{}^s\underline{o}\cdot\underline{r}_d/K_2 \qquad (4.2)$$

$$z'' = -{}^s\underline{a}\cdot\underline{r}_d/K_2 \qquad (4.3)$$

$$v = v_r - {}^s\underline{n}\cdot\underline{r}_d/K_1 \qquad (4.4)$$

where v is the real motion rate on the trajectory. (4.2), (4.3) represent the deviation from the path. For the conventional control, x-component of position error in the S-coordinate, i.e., x" is represented as

$$x'' = -{}^s\underline{n}\cdot\underline{r}_d/K^2 \qquad (4.5)$$

The effect of saturation of control outputs
The saturation of control outputs will be happened frequently in real systems in the case when the motion rate reference for a joint is beyond its control capacity. Here the effect of such a saturation to the ATGS will be analyzed.
For the simplicity, the saturation will be given at the control output $\underline{r}$. It corresponds to the case of the Cartesian coordinate type manipulator. Under the same conditions mentioned above, the next equation is deduced from (3.29).

$$\underline{L}\begin{bmatrix} K_1 v_r \\ -K_2 y'' \\ -K_2 z'' \end{bmatrix} = K_1\begin{bmatrix} \dot{x} \\ \dot{y} \\ \dot{z} \end{bmatrix} \qquad (4.6)$$

In the base coordinates, let output limits be given to each component of motion rate reference as follows

$$\left|{}^s n_x v_r\right| \leqq v_s \qquad (4.7)$$

$$\left|{}^s n_y v_r\right| \leqq v_s \qquad (4.8)$$

$$\left|{}^s n_z v_r\right| \leqq v_s \qquad (4.9)$$

Suppose that the x axis saturates as

$$\left|{}^s n_x v_r\right| \geqq v_s \qquad (4.10)$$

(4.6) can be rewritten as follows.

$$\underline{L}\begin{bmatrix} K_1 v_r \\ -K_2 y'' \\ -K_2 z'' \end{bmatrix} - \begin{bmatrix} K_1({}^s n_x v_r - v_s) \\ 0 \\ 0 \end{bmatrix} = K_1\dot{\underline{p}}$$

$$\therefore \begin{bmatrix} K_1 v_r \\ -K_2 y'' \\ -K_2 z'' \end{bmatrix} - K_1\underline{L}^T\begin{bmatrix} {}^s n_x v_r - v_s \\ 0 \\ 0 \end{bmatrix} = K_1\underline{L}^T\dot{\underline{p}} \qquad (4.11)$$

In the steady state, the velocity $\underline{L}^T\dot{\underline{p}}$ should be paralleled to x-axis in the S-coordinates. Then

$$\underline{L}^T\dot{\underline{p}} = \begin{bmatrix} \rho v_r \\ 0 \\ 0 \end{bmatrix} \qquad (4.12)$$

where ρ is the ratio of the real motion rate to the reference. By substituting (4.12) to (4.11) the next relation are obtained

$$y'' = -(K_1/K_2){}^s o_x({}^s n_x v_r - v_s) \qquad (4.13)$$

$$z'' = -(K_1/K_2){}^s a_x({}^s n_x v_r - v_s) \qquad (4.14)$$

$$\rho = 1-({}^s n_x)^2(1-v_s/({}^s n_x v_r)) \qquad (4.15)$$

(4.13), (4.14) represent the deviation from the specified path and (4.15) represents the regulation of motion rate. These equations mean that the saturated axis is not left behind from the specified path.
It is not the case when the conventional control is adopted.

The effect of mechanical constraints
Suppose that there exists a mechanical constraint in the base coordinates as

$$f_c(x,y,z) = a_1 x + a_2 y + a_3 z - 1 \geqq 0 \qquad (4.16)$$

The reaction from the constraint plane to the end of a manipulator is represented by $\lambda \nabla f_0$. Therefore, the motion of the end of the manipulator will halt as the following equation is satisfied.

$$-\lambda \nabla f_c = \underline{L}\begin{bmatrix} K_1 v_r \\ -K_2 y'' \\ -K_2 z'' \end{bmatrix} \qquad (4.17)$$

The amount of displacement $(x_0' \ y_0' \ z_0')$ in the S-coordinates after encountering the constraint is obtained by solving (4.17) as follows.

$$y_0' = -(K_1/K_2)v_r(\nabla f_c \cdot {}^s\underline{o})/(\nabla f_c \cdot {}^s\underline{n}) \qquad (4.18)$$

$$z_0' = -(K_1/K_2)v_r(\nabla f_c \cdot {}^s\underline{a})/(\nabla f_c \cdot {}^s\underline{n}) \qquad (4.19)$$

$$x_0' = -((\nabla f_c \cdot {}^s\underline{o})y_0' + (\nabla f_c \cdot {}^s\underline{a})z_0')/(\nabla f_c \cdot {}^s\underline{n}) \qquad (4.20)$$

The values of $K_1, K_2, K_1/K_2$ and the system behavior

Using the results obtain so far, it will be understood that coefficients K_1, K_2 and K_1/K_2 are related to the following features respectively.

K_1 in (4.4)   motion rate consistency

K_2 in (4.2), (4.3)   position consistency

K_2/K_1 in (4.13), (4.14) and (4.18), (4.19)

                                  path consistency

The more each value of coefficient is increased, the more strongly each consistancy will be executed. For example, whether the system halts at a constraint or continues to move along the constraint depends on whether the value of K_2/K_1 makes larger or smaller. In other word the path consistency is seen as a compromise between the position consistency and the motion rate consistency. How to decide the value of K_1 and K_2 is an interesting problem in practice.

5. Simulation

Two examples are analyzed by simulation and the effectiveness of the ATGS technique will be shown.

Example 1. The Influence of Saturation

The influence of saturation in the control signal is tested for the conventional control and the ATGS control.
The simulation is executed under the next condition.

Manipulator	Cartesian type
Path	circle
radius	0.5 m
reference motion rate	1.0 m/s
$\underline{L}$	unit matrix
controller	
K_2/K_1	40 1/s
K_1	33 1/s
max. static speed for each axis	0.6 m/s

The result of simulation shows the effectiveness of the ATGS technigue to the speed saturation as shown in Fig.6.

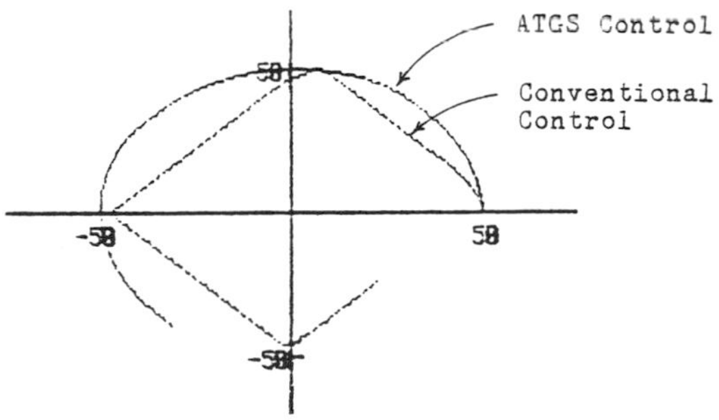

Fig.6 Comparison of ATGS Control with Conventional Control for the Effect of Saturation (60% Saturation)

Examle 2. Application of ATGS control to Articulated Manipulator without CJTS Compensation

In the simulation the ATGS controller is to be connected directly to the articulated manipulator without the CJTS compensation. Fig.7 depicts the manipulator used in the simulation. When the CJTS compensation is applied, the block diagram for one axis of the manipulator is shown as Fig.8(a). On the other hand, Fig.8(b) represents the dynamics for one axis without compenstion. In the figure, D and J mean the mechanical damping ratio and the moment of inertia. Interactions from other axis and the effect of gravity is represented by q_d. Comparing Fig.9(a) with Fig. 9(b), K_1 and K_2 should be modified to K'_1 and K'_2 according to the next equations.

$$K_2 = K'_2 J_o/J \tag{5.1}$$

$$K_1 = D/J + K'_1 J_o/J \tag{5.2}$$

where J_o is a value of J and its maximum value of J, 0.57 kgm is selected.
In general, D/J in (5.2) is considerably small comparing with $K'_1 J_o/J$, then

$$K_1 = K_1' J_o/J \tag{5.3}$$

Therefore

$$K_2/K_1 = K_2'/K_1' \tag{5.4}$$

That is, K_2/K_1 is considered as almost constant despite changing of J.
In the simulation, next conditions were selected;

case(1) K_2/K_1=130 1/s, $K_1'J_o$=18.5 kgm/s

case(2) K_2/K_1=130 1/s, $K_1'J_o$=157 kgm/s

case(3) K_2/K_1=130 1/s, $K_1'J_o$=157 Kgm/s

with 80% saturation of maximum rate during the rotation of R_1 axis in case(2).

The curve to be drawn is a circle with the radius 0.2m, the center (0.5m,0,z_o), and the reference motion rate is 0.8 m/s. As the result of simulation, errors in the radius and z, and regulations of the motion rate in each case were obtained as shown in Fig.9(a),(b).
The simulation results show that the features of the ATGS control are appeared in the articulated manipulater control without the CJTS compensation.

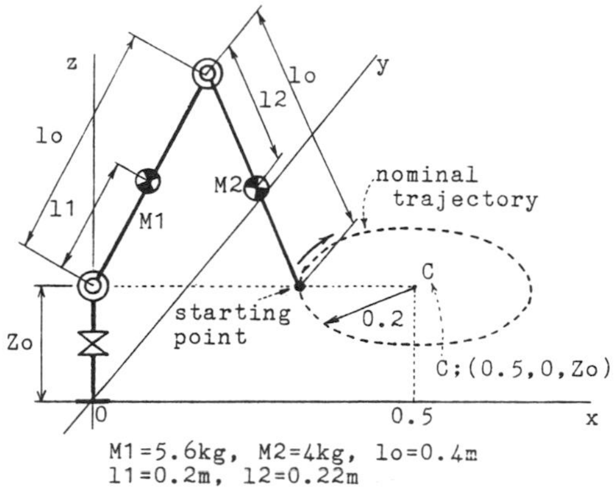

Fig.7 Manipulator and Nominal Trajectory

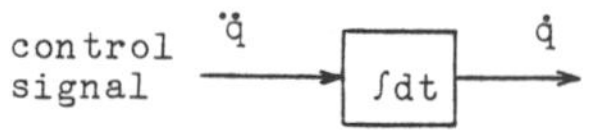

(a) with CJTS compensation

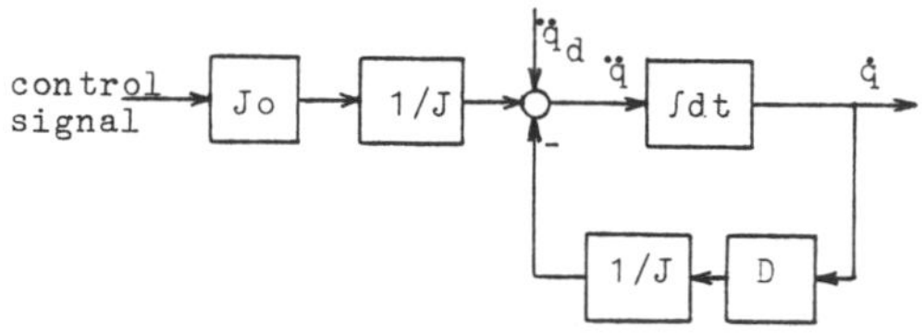

(b) without CJTS compensation

Fig.8 Block Diagrams of Controlled System (one axis only)

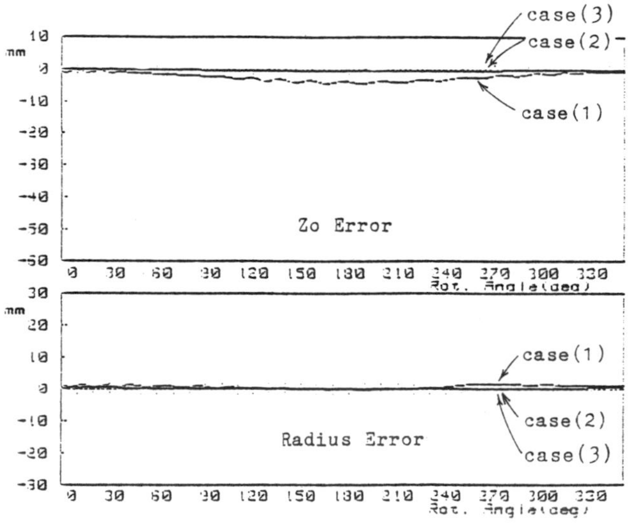

(a) errors in Zo and radius

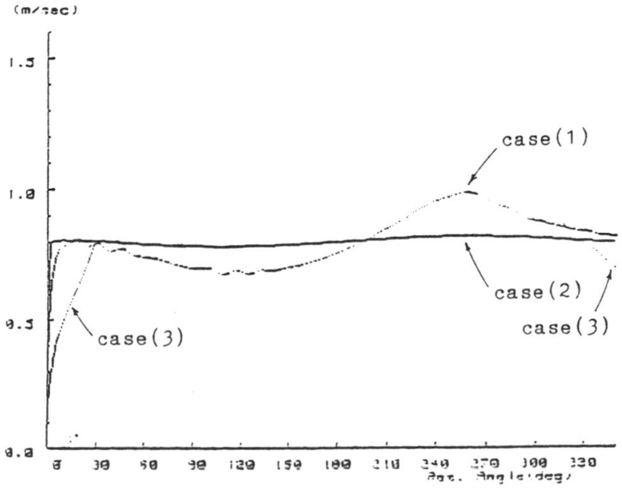

(b) regulation of the motion rate

Fig. 9 Simulation of ATGS control for Articulated Manipulator

Conclusion

The authors proposed the autonomous trajectory generating servomechanism as the practical method for the trajectory control of the end of the manipulators, and verified its effectiveness for practical requirements on the precision and the flexibility.

Total control system in which the acceleration at the source, the decceleration near the destination and smooth connections of segments in the trajectory are taken into consideration, will be completed in near future.

Reference

Hasegawa,K. and Mizutani,T. 1982 On the Multi Variable Servomechanism with Autonomous Trajectory Generating Function. Transactions of Society of Instrument and control Engineering in Japan (SICE), 18-8, pp.845-850

Hasegawa,K. and Mizutani,T. 1984 On the Analysis and Characteristic Improvement of Autonomous Trajectory Generating Servomechanism. Transactions of SICE, 20-1, pp.64-70

Markiewicz,B.R. 1973 Analysis of the Computed Torque Drive Method and Comparison with Conventional Position Servo for Computer-Controlled Manipulator. Technical Memorandom, 33-601 Jet Propulsion Laboratory, March

Paul,R.C. 1972 Modeling, Trajectory Calculation and Servoing of a Computer Controlled Arm. Ph.D Thesis, Stanford Univ.

Paul,R.C. et al 1979 Advanced Industrial Robot Control System. Second Report, Purdue Univ.

ROBOT MOTION TRAJECTORY SPECIFICATION AND GENERATION

Richard P. Paul
Hong Zhang

Purdue University
School of Electrical Engineering
West Lafayette, Indiana 47907
United States of America

This paper will discuss a consistent and efficient method of specifying and generating robot manipulator trajectories. We will classify manipulator motion specification into four basic categories: joint coordinate, orthogonal coordinate, procedural, and tabular. Joint coordinate motion is motion executed directly in the manipulator joint coordinates. It is the appropriate motion when time must be minimized or when the manipulator is to change kinematic configurations. Orthogonal or straight line motion is used when a well defined motion is important, when sensors are used, or when making motions of accommodation. Procedural motion is used when the trajectory is geometrically defined, for example, when describing circles or when making offset circular motions in using wrenches to tighten bolts. A tabular motion specification is used when direct teaching methods are employed in such activities as defining spray painting paths. All the above forms of motion may be defined in terms of moving coordinate systems: conveyors, floating objects, untethered robots, etc. We will present a method for the specification of all the above forms of trajectories in a dynamics free manner which is computationally efficient and which provides for transitions between all possible forms of trajectories in both fixed and moving coordinate systems.

INTRODUCTION

The fundamental description of a robot manipulator motion is of a sequence of positions through which the end of the manipulator is to pass. The description of the positions may be simple, as when manipulator joint coordinates are used, or complex, as for example when motion in orthogonal coordinates is referenced to some functionally defined coordinate frame. Motion between positions may be specified in detail or in general terms. When only the end-points of the motion are of importance, the motion may be specified as a coordinated, joint coordinate or orthogonal coordinate motion. When the intermediate positions are of importance then the motion may be specified by a procedure or by a table of coordinates.

Actions take place during motion between positions. Spray painting and the application of sealants might be specified by a table of coordinates through which the applicator must pass. Seam welding along complex geometric paths (such as along the joint between two cylinders) might be functionally defined. Straight line seam welds could be defined by a coordinated orthogonal motion to which is added a sinusoidal weaving pattern. Motions to bring parts together in assembly operations might be defined simply by orthogonal coordinate motions. End effector actions take place while the manipulator is at rest. The manipulator is brought to rest by the specification of a motion between two identical positions such that the manipulator remains stationary for the duration of the motion segment. When moving parts or tools, or when simply moving the manipulator to a new position no action takes place during the motion. These action free motions are frequently defined as coordinated joint coordinate motions which are most time efficient. Finally, any of the above activities might be performed on a work piece which is in motion, on a conveyor for example. A general purpose manipulator must be capable of performing any of the above types of motion.

We will separate kinematics from dynamics by first describing the kinematics of motion between positions parametrically in terms of relative path motion parameter h and then introduce dynamics by describing h as a function of time t.

$$\mathbf{x} = f(h) \tag{1}$$

The motion parameter h varies from 0 to 1 for each path segment. Motion along the path is then described by defining h as a function of time t.

$$h = g(t) \tag{2}$$

Segment time is reset to zero at the beginning of each path segment. In this paper, matrices will be represented by bold upper case letters, vectors will be represented by bold lower case letters, and scalars by italic letters. In Equation 1 $\mathbf{x}$ represents a vector of spatial coordinates while h and t represent scalars.

COORDINATE SYSTEMS

There are two fundamental coordinate systems in which to describe manipulator positions, joint coordinates and orthogonal coordinates. The position of a manipulator is uniquely specified by the joint coordinates and it is in joint coordinates that the manipulator is controlled. Joint coordinates are, however, generally non-orthogonal and do not provide a convenient set of coordinates in which to perform the coordinate transformations used in the specification of manipulation. Orthogonal coordinates are convenient for performing coordinate transformations; unfortunately, the mapping from orthogonal coordinates to joint coordinates is one-to-many. For most manipulators there is a small number of kinematically equivalent configurations all yielding the same end position. We solve this problem by specifying the desired configuration of the manipulator, thus reducing the mapping to one-to-one.

THE DESCRIPTION OF POSITION

The end of an n joint robot manipulator is specified by the joint coordinates $\boldsymbol{\theta}_n$ or by the homogeneous transformation $\mathbf{T}_n$ specifying the Cartesian position and orientation of the end of the manipulator with respect to its base. We will assume that a function "solve" exists that, once the configuration is specified, will map $\mathbf{T}_n$ into a unique set of joint coordinates $\boldsymbol{\theta}_n$ (Paul 1981).

A manipulator position may be specified by an equation which in its simplest form equates $\mathbf{T}_n$ to a transformation specifying the desired position. If this equation is labeled, then we may define a "move" statement, with the label as argument, as the instruction to move the manipulator in such a manner as to satisfy the equation. For example, to move the manipulator to a position described by the homogeneous transformation $\mathbf{A}$ we would first declare

$$\text{p1: } \mathbf{T}_n = \mathbf{A} \tag{3}$$

and then move the manipulator to $\mathbf{A}$ by the statement

```
move ( p1);
```

It is usually convenient to add more structure to the position equation. For example: if the manipulator is equipped with a tool described by a transformation **TOOL** with respect to $\mathbf{T}_n$, and the position $\mathbf{A}$ is one of many to be described with respect to an object **OBJ**, then the equation might become

$$\text{p1: } \mathbf{T}_n\ \mathbf{TOOL} = \mathbf{OBJ}\ \mathbf{A} \tag{4}$$

While the "move" statement remains the same, the equation must now be solved by the manipulation system in order to obtain $\mathbf{T}_n$. If the equations are specified as a doubly linked list, then the manipulation of the equation to obtain the solution is simple (Paul 1981).

Program execution continues after the execution of a move statement without waiting for the manipulator motion to be completed. If, however, another move statement is encountered before a prior motion is completed, program execution waits until the prior move statement is complete. It is by this mechanism that synchronization is maintained between program execution and manipulator motion.

The transforms in the above equation are of three types.

1) RO: in this case the transform $\mathbf{T}_n$ is read-only.

2) VAL: transforms of type VAL are passed to the motion process by value. Transforms such as **TOOL** and **A** might be assigned values which will not be changed after the "move" statement execution has commenced. When the "move" statement is to be executed a copy of the transform is passed to the motion process. Advantage is taken of the fact that the transforms will not change during the motion to premultiply pairs of these transforms together thus reducing the computational load during execution when the equation must be repeatedly evaluated (Hayward and Paul 1984). Another use of VAL transforms is demonstrated in the following program segment in which the manipulator is to move to a sequence of positions **A** to be read from a data file.

$$\text{p1: } \mathbf{T}_n\ \mathbf{TOOL} = \mathbf{OBJ}\ \mathbf{A}$$

```
read ( A );
while not eof do
   begin
      move ( p1 );
      read ( A )
   end;
```

When a new value for **A** is read, the current motion is unaffected as a copy of the transform is being used by the motion process. The synchronization mechanism provides for each motion to be completed before the next "move" and "read" statements are executed in the "while" loop.

3) REF: transforms of type REF are not copied as in the case of VAL transforms but the original transform is referenced whenever the equation is evaluated. These transforms are used to provide a mechanism to incorporate sensory feedback. Sensor information may

be used to modify such a transform to correct the position and orientation of the manipulator while it is in motion. The transform **OBJ**, in the above equation, could be of this type. A camera could, for example, monitor the approach of the manipulator to position **A** in the above equation. As errors in the approach were detected **OBJ** would be modified as shown in the following programming example.

```
move ( p1 );
while in_motion do
   begin
      read_camera ( ERROR );
      OBJ = OBJ *ERROR
   end;
```

Modifications of **OBJ** would have an immediate effect on the current manipulator motion as the "move" statement is outside the "while" loop.

Transforms of type REF may also be used to define procedural motions (Shimano, B, Geschke, C. and Spalding III, C.H. 1984). For example, to describe a circle with the manipulator we might use the following program segment to modify the x, y coordinated of **OBJ**.

```
OBJ.p.x = 100;
OBJ.p.y = 0;
move ( p1 );
while in_motion do
   begin
      OBJ.p.x = 100 cos(h*2*π);
      OBJ.p.y = 100 sin(h*2*π)
   end;
```

Note the use of the motion parameter h in the above example.

In many manipulation tasks, such as working with conveyors, moving coordinate frames are involved. These frames may be specified as homogeneous transformations which vary according to some external input. These transforms are of type MOV and return the current position of the moving frame every time they are accessed. The above task could be performed on a conveyor, specified by a transform **CONV**, of type MOV, by modifying the equation as follows:

$$\text{p1: } \mathbf{T}_n \ \mathbf{TOOL} = \mathbf{CONV\ OBJ\ A} \qquad (5)$$

In summary, manipulator positions may be specified by homogeneous transform equations comprised of transforms of types RD, VAL, REF, and MOV. One of these transforms is the RD transform $\mathbf{T}_n$ for which the transform equation is solved. A manipulator task can then be specified by a sequence of transform expressions specifying $\mathbf{T}_n$ through which the manipulator must be moved as follows:

$$\begin{aligned} \text{p1: } \mathbf{T}_n &= \mathbf{EXPR}_1 \\ \text{p2: } \mathbf{T}_n &= \mathbf{EXPR}_2 \\ &\vdots \\ \text{pi: } \mathbf{T}_n &= \mathbf{EXPR}_i \\ \text{pi+1: } \mathbf{T}_n &= \mathbf{EXPR}_{i+1} \end{aligned} \qquad (6)$$

DESCRIPTION OF MOTION

While we will specify manipulator positions in orthogonal coordinates we must be able to move the manipulator in joint coordinates as well as in orthogonal coordinates. The equivalent kinematic configurations of a manipulator are separated by kinematic degeneracies through which it is impossible to specify an orthogonal motion. A joint motion must be used to move the manipulator from one configuration to the another. It is also in joint coordinates that time optimal motions are naturally specified, as the motion limits are defined in joint coordinates.

The general motion scheme which we will employ is to move the manipulator at constant velocity, in either joint coordinates or orthogonal coordinates, from position to position. As each position is approached, the motion to the next position is determined in order to evaluate the change in velocity. Based on the maximum desired acceleration, a transition time is determined and a transition to the next path segment is initiated at one half the transition time before the end of the segment. The transition is concluded at one half the transition time into the next segment. We will label the position at the beginning of the transition to be A, the position to which we are currently heading to be position B, and the next position to be position C (see Figure 1).

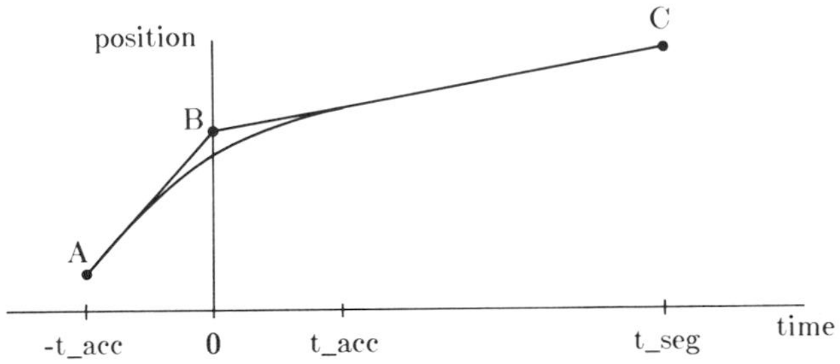

Figure 1. Manipulator Path Transition

Segment time will be initialized to $-t\_acc$ at the beginning of the transition, position A. Segment time will be t_acc at the end of the transition and will be t_seg at the end of the motion to position C. Of course we will never reach position C, as when we are approaching C we will initiate another transition on to the next position in the motion sequence, repeating the above cycle. At time $t = -t\_acc$, position A, we will start to generate a motion from position B to position C. The motion is parameterized in terms of h, the motion parameter, such that a constant velocity motion is directly proportional to h. We then define h as a function of time to provide a motion which starts from rest at $-t\_acc$ and accelerates until t_acc, at which time it moves at the specified constant velocity. The difference in position and velocity between the current motion to position B and the new motion will be compensated for by a second joint coordinate transition function which will match the two motions and will provide continuity.

We will begin by determining the linear motion from B to C. At time $t = -t\_acc$ we evaluate the values of $\mathbf{T}_n$ at positions of B and C.

$$\begin{aligned} \mathbf{B} &= \mathbf{EXPR}_i(-t\_acc) \\ \mathbf{C} &= \mathbf{EXPR}_{i+1}(-t\_acc) \end{aligned} \tag{7}$$

We have indicated by the argument $(-t\_acc)$ that both positions are to be evaluated at the current time.

JOINT COORDINATE MOTION

The motion from B to C may be defined in joint coordinates as a function of h by obtaining the joint coordinates corresponding to positions **B** and **C**, $\boldsymbol{\theta}_B$ and $\boldsymbol{\theta}_C$, as:

$$\boldsymbol{\theta} = r\boldsymbol{\theta}_{BC} + \text{solve}\ (\mathbf{EXPR}_{i+1}(t)); \tag{8}$$

where

$$\boldsymbol{\theta}_{BC} = \text{solve}\ (\mathbf{B}) - \text{solve}\ (\mathbf{C})$$

$$r = 1-h$$

The variable r changes from 1 to 0 as the motion is made. When $r = 1$ at the beginning of the motion $\boldsymbol{\theta} = \boldsymbol{\theta}_B$ the initial position. When $r = 0$ at the end of the motion $\boldsymbol{\theta} = \text{solve}\ (\mathbf{EXPR}_{i+1})$, the desired final position.

We will now define h to provide for continuity of motion. The motion parameter h is defined as a polynomial function of time to provide for continuity of position, velocity, acceleration, and jerk (the third derivative). The boundary conditions of h are shown in Table I.

Table I Boundary Conditions h

time	$-t\_acc$	t_acc	t_seg
h	0	t_acc/t_seg	1
$\dot{h}$	0	$1/t\_seg$	$1/t\_seg$
$\ddot{h}$	0	0	0
$\dddot{h}$	0	0	0

The function may be defined as follows:

$$\begin{aligned} &\text{if } (t \le t\_acc) \\ &\text{then} \\ &\quad p = (t + t\_acc)/(2t\_acc); \\ &\quad h = ((2p-6)p+5)p^4\ t\_acc/t\_seg; \\ &\text{else} \\ &\quad h = t/t\_seg; \end{aligned} \tag{9}$$

As noted above if we evaluate the motion by Equation 8 there will be a discontinuity at position A of $\boldsymbol{\theta}_A - \boldsymbol{\theta}_B$ in position and a discontinuity in velocity of $\dot{\boldsymbol{\theta}}_A - \dot{\boldsymbol{\theta}}_C$. In order to remove this discontinuity we will add to the set point $\boldsymbol{\theta}$, generated by Equation 8, a second matching polynomial to remove the discontinuities. This polynomial will be defined when $-t\_acc \le t < t\_acc$ and will reduce the errors to zero by t_acc. The initial acceleration and jerk of this matching polynomial are to be zero, as will be the final acceleration and jerk. We may assume that the position of the manipulator at position A is $\boldsymbol{\theta}_A$ and that its joint velocity is $\dot{\boldsymbol{\theta}}_A$. One sample period before the transition begins we will evaluate Equation 7 to obtain $\boldsymbol{\theta}_C(-t\_acc-\tau)$, where τ is the sample period of the control system. The velocity of position C, $\dot{\boldsymbol{\theta}}_C$ can then be approximated at time $-t\_acc$ by

$$\dot{\boldsymbol{\theta}}_C = (\boldsymbol{\theta}_C(-t\_acc) - \boldsymbol{\theta}_C(-t\_acc-\tau))/\tau \tag{10}$$

The boundary conditions of the matching polynomial are shown in Table II.

Table II Boundary Conditions $\boldsymbol{\theta}$

time	$-t\_acc$	t_acc
$\boldsymbol{\theta}$	$\boldsymbol{\theta}_A - \boldsymbol{\theta}_B$	0
$\dot{\boldsymbol{\theta}}$	$\dot{\boldsymbol{\theta}}_A - \dot{\boldsymbol{\theta}}_C$	0
$\ddot{\boldsymbol{\theta}}$	0	0
$\dddot{\boldsymbol{\theta}}$	0	0

The matching polynomial is of the following form:

$$\boldsymbol{\theta} = ((((\mathbf{a}_7 p + \mathbf{a}_6)p + \mathbf{a}_5)p + \mathbf{a}_4)p^3 + \mathbf{a}_1)p + \mathbf{a}_0 \tag{11}$$

where

$$\begin{aligned} p &= (t + t\_acc)/(2t\_acc); \\ \mathbf{a}_0 &= \boldsymbol{\theta}_A - \boldsymbol{\theta}_B \\ \dot{\boldsymbol{\theta}}_{AC} &= \dot{\boldsymbol{\theta}}_A - \dot{\boldsymbol{\theta}}_C \\ \mathbf{a}_1 &= 2t\_acc\,\dot{\boldsymbol{\theta}}_{AC} \\ \mathbf{a}_7 &= 10\mathbf{a}_1 + 20\mathbf{a}_0 \\ \mathbf{a}_6 &= -36\mathbf{a}_1 - 70\mathbf{a}_0 \\ \mathbf{a}_5 &= 45\mathbf{a}_1 + 84\mathbf{a}_0 \\ \mathbf{a}_4 &= -20\mathbf{a}_1 - 35\mathbf{a}_0 \end{aligned}$$

The joint motion between the two positions is defined by Equation 8, a function of r, which is a function of the path motion parameter h. The time dependence of the motion is specified by Equation 9, where h is defined. This motion, starts from rest, accelerates to the desired path velocity and then moves at constant velocity. The discontinuity in position and velocity between the two motions at the beginning of the path is removed by the addition of a second matching polynomial, defined by Equation 11, during the accelerating portion of the path segment.

ORTHOGONAL COORDINATE MOTION

If an orthogonal motion is desired from B to C then the position Equation 6 must be modified to include a drive transform $\mathbf{D}(r)$ (Paul 1981) in **EXPR**. The drive transform represents a translation **d** and rotation ψ about an axis **e** in space proportional to r, $1 < r \leq 0$. When the argument r is zero, representing the end of the motion, $\mathbf{D}(r)$ reduces to an identity transform. $\mathbf{D}(r)$ is of type RO. The position of the drive transform in the equation determines the frame in which the rotation is defined. We can rewrite Equation 6 with the drive transform included in the form

$$\text{pi: } \mathbf{T}_n = \mathbf{L}_i\ \mathbf{D}(0)\ \mathbf{R}_i \tag{12}$$

Here $\mathbf{L}_i$ represents the transform expression to the left of **D** and $\mathbf{R}_i$ represents the transform expression to the right. At the beginning of the motion from B to C position B is defined by Equation 7. This position is also defined with respect to position C

$$\mathbf{B} = \mathbf{L}_C(-t\_acc)\ \mathbf{D}(1)\ \mathbf{R}_C(-t\_acc) \tag{13}$$

which we may solve for $\mathbf{D}(1)$

$$\mathbf{D}(1) = \mathbf{L}_C^{-1}(-t\_acc)\ \mathbf{B}\ \mathbf{R}_C^{-1}(-t\_acc) \tag{14}$$

From $\mathbf{D}(1)$ we may obtain **d**,**e**, and ψ and the orthogonal motion from position B to position C may then be described by

$$\boldsymbol{\theta}_n = solve(\mathbf{L}_C(t)\ \mathbf{D}(r)\ \mathbf{R}_C(t)) \tag{15}$$

where

$$r = 1-h$$

as r varies from 1 to 0. The motion parameter h is defined in Equation 9. The transform $\mathbf{D}(r)$ represents a rotation about a unit vector **e** an angle $r\psi$ and a translation r**d**. The unit vector **e** is defined in terms of the first two Euler angles, ϕ and θ, and is:

$$\mathbf{e} = C_\phi S_\theta\, \mathbf{i} + S_\phi S_\theta\, \mathbf{j} + C_\theta\, \mathbf{k} \tag{16}$$

where $0 \leq \theta < \pi$. C_ϕ, S_ϕ, C_θ, etc. stand for $\cos(\phi)$, $\sin(\phi)$, $\cos(\theta)$, etc. The translation is defined to be $\mathbf{d} = rx\ \mathbf{i} + ry\ \mathbf{j} + rz\ \mathbf{k}$.

The transform $\mathbf{D}(r)$ is given by:

$$\mathbf{D}(r) = \begin{bmatrix} C_\phi^2 S_\theta^2 V_{r\psi} + C_{r\psi} & C_\phi S_\phi S_\theta^2 V_{r\psi} - C_\theta S_{r\psi} & C_\phi S_\theta C_\theta V_{r\psi} + S_\phi S_\theta S_{r\psi} & rx \\ C_\phi S_\phi S_\theta^2 V_{r\psi} + C_\theta S_{r\psi} & S_\phi^2 S_\theta^2 V_{r\psi} + C_{r\psi} & S_\phi S_\theta C_\theta V_{r\psi} - C_\phi S_\theta S_{r\psi} & ry \\ C_\phi S_\theta C_\theta V_{r\psi} - S_\phi S_\theta S_{r\psi} & S_\phi S_\theta C_\theta V_{r\psi} + C_\phi S_\theta S_{r\psi} & C_\theta^2 V_{r\psi} + C_{r\psi} & rz \\ 0 & 0 & 0 & 1 \end{bmatrix} \tag{17}$$

where $C_{r\psi}$, $S_{r\psi}$, and $V_{r\psi}$, stand for $\cos(r\psi)$, $\sin(r\psi)$, and $(1-\cos(r\psi))$, respectively.

We will now solve for the parameters x,y,z,ψ,ϕ,θ,. Defining the elements of $\mathbf{L}_C^{-1}(-t\_acc)\ \mathbf{B}\ \mathbf{R}_C^{-1}(-t\_acc)$ from Equation 13 to be

$$\mathbf{L}_C^{-1}(-t\_acc)\ \mathbf{B}\ \mathbf{R}_C^{-1}(-t\_acc) = \begin{bmatrix} n_x & o_x & a_x & p_x \\ n_y & o_y & a_y & p_y \\ n_z & o_z & a_z & p_z \\ 0 & 0 & 0 & 1 \end{bmatrix} \tag{18}$$

and equating $\mathbf{D}(1)$ with the elements of the right hand side of Equation 18 we obtain a matrix equation which may be solved directly for the parameters x,y,z,ψ,ϕ,θ,.

$$\begin{bmatrix} C_\phi^2 S_\theta^2 V_\psi + C_\psi & C_\phi S_\phi S_\theta^2 V_\psi - C_\theta S_\psi & C_\phi S_\theta C_\theta V_\psi + S_\phi S_\theta S_\psi & x \\ C_\phi S_\phi S_\theta^2 V_\psi + C_\theta S_\psi & S_\phi^2 S_\theta^2 V_\psi + C_\psi & S_\phi S_\theta C_\theta V_\psi - C_\phi S_\theta S_\psi & y \\ C_\phi S_\theta C_\theta V_\psi - S_\phi S_\theta S_\psi & S_\phi S_\theta C_\theta V_\psi + C_\phi S_\theta S_\psi & C_\theta^2 V_\psi + C_\psi & z \\ 0 & 0 & 0 & 1 \end{bmatrix} = \begin{bmatrix} n_x & o_x & a_x & p_x \\ n_y & o_y & a_y & p_y \\ n_z & o_z & a_z & p_z \\ 0 & 0 & 0 & 1 \end{bmatrix} \tag{19}$$

As matrix equality implies element-by-element equality we may obtain directly from Equation 19 that

$$x = p_x \qquad y = p_y \qquad z = p_z \tag{20}$$

Equating the sum of the diagonal elements from Equation 19 we obtain

$$1 + 2C_\psi = n_x + o_y + a_z \tag{21}$$

and thus

$$C_\psi = 1/2(n_x + o_y + a_z - 1) \tag{22}$$

Equating the difference of the off-diagonal pairs of the elements of Equation 19, we obtain

$$4S_\psi^2 = (n_y - o_x^2) + (a_x - n_z)^2 + (o_z - a_y)^2 \tag{23}$$

and as the rotation angle ψ is always less than π we obtain

$$S_\psi = +\frac{1}{2}\sqrt{(n_y-o_x)^2+(a_x-n_z)^2+(o_z-a_y)^2} \tag{24}$$

Finally, we obtain an expression for ψ from Equations 22 and 24 as.

$$\psi = \tan^{-1}\frac{+\sqrt{(n_y-o_x)^2+(a_x-n_z)^2+(o_z-a_y)^2}}{(n_x+o_y+a_z-1)} \tag{25}$$

Equating off-diagonal pairs from Equation 19 we obtain:

$$2C_\theta S_\psi = n_y-o_x \tag{26}$$

$$2S_\phi S_\theta S_\psi = a_x-n_z \tag{27}$$

$$2C_\phi S_\theta S_\psi = o_z-a_y \tag{28}$$

Squaring and adding Equations 27 and 28 we obtain

$$4S_\theta^2 S_\psi^2 = (a_x-n_z)^2+(o_z-a_y)^2 \tag{29}$$

As $0 \le \theta < \pi$ we obtain S_θ as

$$S_\theta = +\frac{1}{2S_\psi}\sqrt{(a_x-n_z)^2+(o_z-a_y)^2} \tag{30}$$

We may obtain directly from Equation 26 that

$$C_\theta = \frac{1}{2S_\psi}(n_y-o_x) \tag{31}$$

and thus

$$\theta = \tan^{-1}\frac{+\sqrt{(a_x-n_z)^2+(o_z-a_y)^2}}{(n_y-o_x)} \tag{32}$$

We may solve for ϕ from Equations 27 and 28

$$S_\phi = \frac{1}{2S_\theta S_\psi}(a_x-n_z) \tag{33}$$

$$C_\phi = \frac{1}{2S_\theta S_\psi}(o_z-a_y) \tag{34}$$

and as $0 \le \theta < \pi$ and $0 \le \psi < \pi$ we may obtain ϕ uniquely as

$$\phi = \tan^{-1}\frac{(a_x-n_z)}{(o_z-a_y)} \tag{35}$$

We thus complete the determination of all the drive parameters x, y, z, ψ, ϕ, θ. Note that the definitions for the angular drive parameters break down as the angle of rotation ψ approaches 180 °. This lack of stability of the solution reflects reality, as reorientations of approximately 180 ° are extremely unstable with the direction or rotation of the manipulator wrist reversing as the angle moves through 180 °. It is therefore reasonable to restrict reorientations to less than approximately 150 ° and then with this restriction the definitions of the drive parameters are valid. Rotations of greater than 150 ° can be executed by a sequence of rotations each of less than 150 °.

As in the case of joint motion Equation 15 represents a motion from position B to C only, and we need to add the matching polynomial given by Equation 11 to obtain a motion from position A through to C.

PROCEDURALLY DEFINED MOTION

If where the path is to be specified in detail a procedural motion is used in place of the orthogonal or coordinated joint motion. A procedural motion is obtained by including in the transform equation defining a position one or more of either, functionally defined transforms (type FUN), and/or tabular transforms (type TAB). A drive transform may also be included, in which case there will be a basic orthogonal motion superimposed on the procedural motion. Both function transforms and tabular transforms are evaluated as a function of h, the motion parameter, $0 \le h < 1$.

A functional transform of type FUN is defined, as a value of h, as h varies linearly from 0 to 1. The only continuity constraints are that the function and its first three derivatives are finite over the range of definition. The definition of the motion parameter h ensures continuity of velocity, acceleration, and jerk. A function is bound to the transform so that every time the transform is accessed the function is called to compute values of the transform. For example, a function to describe a circle, to be repeated one and one half times, of radius 100 in the xy plane, centered a $x=10$, $y=200$, would be:

$$\begin{aligned} p.x &= 10+100\cos(3\pi h); \\ p.y &= 200+100\sin(3\pi h); \end{aligned} \tag{36}$$

This function has a starting position of $x=110$, $y=200$ and it would be appropriate if the manipulator was moved to that position before the procedurally defined motion started. Notice once again the use of the motion parameter in the function definition.

A second type of procedurally defined motion is obtained when a transform is defined by a table of coordinates. In this case the transform is defined in a tabular manner. Values are obtained by a function which interpolates tabular entries in terms of the motion parameter h. Table entries correspond to the orthogonal position and orientation in the form of Euler angles and a position vector. Angles are stored in the form of rotations; i.e., 2π radians $=1$ rotation. The position and orientation are then scaled and integerized. Table entries correspond to the second difference of the position and orientation values. Included in the table header are the initial values of the position and orientation values, the table length, and the time increment values. Such a transform is of type TAB.

The generation of a path which is procedurally defined is the same as described above. The current state at position A is evaluated in joint coordinates. The position the manipulator is approaching is evaluated and the next position, which might be defined procedurally, is evaluated with $h=0$. If a drive transform is present in the equation then its parameters are evaluated as in the case of an orthogonal motion. The resulting motion is that described by the functionally defined position equation superimposed on a motion from the present position of the manipulator to the starting position of the function definition. All types of motion generation defined above are summarized in Table III.

CONCLUSIONS

We have presented a method of robot manipulator trajectory generation which separates kinematics from dynamics in terms of a motion parameter h. This parameter is available for the definition of functionally defined motions. Dynamics are included by specifying h as a function of time which maintains continuity of motion. While both joint coordinate and orthogonal motions are provided, path transitions are handled by a matching function defined in joint coordinates. This allows us to match all forms of motions without treating each as a special case. Joint coordinate motions are defined in such a manner as to provide tracking of moving coordinate frames. On average the control computer evaluates one position set point per sample period, and during path transitions the peak computational load becomes two position set points per sample period.

REFERENCES

Hayward, V. and Richard P. Paul. 1984. Introduction to RCCL: A Robot Control "C" Library. *Proc. IEEE International Conference on Robotics.* 293-297 Atlanta.

Paul, R. P. 1981. *Robot Manipulators: Mathematics, Programming, and Control,* Cambridge: MIT Press.

Shimano, B, Geschke, C. and Spalding III, C.H. 1984. VAL-II: A New Robot Control System for Automatic Manufacturing. *Proc. IEEE International Conference on Robotics.* 293-297 Atlanta.

ACKNOWLEDGEMENT

This material is based upon work supported by the National Science Foundation under Grant No. MEA-8119884. Any opinions, findings, conclusions or recommendations expressed in this publication are those of the authors and do not necessarily reflect the views of the National Science Foundation.

Table III. MOTION CONTROL SUMMARY

JOINT MOTION

$t < t\_seg - t\_acc - \tau$

$$\begin{aligned} h &= t/t\_seg; \\ r &= 1-h; \\ \boldsymbol{\theta} &= r\boldsymbol{\theta}_{BC} + \text{solve}\ (\mathbf{EXPR}_{i-1}(h,t)); \\ \dot{\boldsymbol{\theta}} &= d\boldsymbol{\theta}/dt; \end{aligned}$$

$t = t\_seg - t\_acc - \tau$

$$\begin{aligned} h &= t/t\_seg; \\ r &= 1-h; \\ \boldsymbol{\theta} &= r\boldsymbol{\theta}_{BC} + \text{solve}\ (\mathbf{EXPR}_{i-1}(h,t)); \\ \dot{\boldsymbol{\theta}} &= d\boldsymbol{\theta}/dt; \\ \boldsymbol{\theta}_{TMP} &= \text{solve}\ (\mathbf{EXPR}_{i}(0,t)); \end{aligned}$$

ORTHOGONAL MOTION

$t < t\_seg - t\_acc - \tau$

$$\begin{aligned} h &= t/t\_seg; \\ r &= 1-h; \\ \boldsymbol{\theta} &= \text{solve}\ (\mathbf{L}_{i-1}(h,t)\ \mathbf{D}(r)\ \mathbf{R}_{i-1}(h,t)); \\ \dot{\boldsymbol{\theta}} &= d\boldsymbol{\theta}/dt; \end{aligned}$$

$t = t\_seg - t\_acc - \tau$

$$\begin{aligned} h &= t/t\_seg; \\ r &= 1-h; \\ \boldsymbol{\theta} &= \text{solve}\ (\mathbf{L}_{i-1}(h,t)\ \mathbf{D}(r)\ \mathbf{R}_{i-1}(h,t)); \\ \dot{\boldsymbol{\theta}} &= d\boldsymbol{\theta}/dt; \\ \boldsymbol{\theta}_{TMP} &= \text{solve}\ (\mathbf{L}_{i}(0,t)\ \mathbf{R}_{i}(0,t)); \end{aligned}$$

IT IS POSSIBLE TO CHANGE FROM JOINT MOTION TO ORTHOGONAL MOTION HERE

JOINT MOTION

$t = t\_seg - t\_acc$

$$\begin{aligned} h &= t/t\_seg; \\ r &= 1-h; \\ \boldsymbol{\theta} &= \boldsymbol{\theta} + \dot{\boldsymbol{\theta}}\tau\ ; \text{ estimate position} \\ \boldsymbol{\theta}_B &= \text{solve}\ (\mathbf{EXPR}_{i-1}(1,t)); \\ \boldsymbol{\theta}_C &= \text{solve}\ (\mathbf{EXPR}_{i}(0,t)); \\ \mathbf{a}_0 &= \boldsymbol{\theta} - \boldsymbol{\theta}_B; \\ \boldsymbol{\theta}_{BC} &= \boldsymbol{\theta}_B - \boldsymbol{\theta}_C; \\ \dot{\boldsymbol{\theta}}_C &= (\boldsymbol{\theta}_C - \boldsymbol{\theta}_{TMP})/\tau\ ; \\ \dot{\boldsymbol{\theta}}_{AC} &= \dot{\boldsymbol{\theta}} - \dot{\boldsymbol{\theta}}_C; \\ \mathbf{a}_1 &= 2t\_acc\,\dot{\boldsymbol{\theta}}_{AC}; \\ \mathbf{a}_7 &= 10\mathbf{a}_1 + 20\mathbf{a}_0; \\ \mathbf{a}_6 &= -36\mathbf{a}_1 - 70\mathbf{a}_0; \\ \mathbf{a}_5 &= 45\mathbf{a}_1 + 84\mathbf{a}_0; \\ \mathbf{a}_4 &= -20\mathbf{a}_1 - 35\mathbf{a}_0; \\ t &= -t\_acc; \end{aligned}$$

$-t\_acc < t < t\_acc$

$$\begin{aligned} p &= (t + t\_acc)/(2t\_acc); \\ h &= ((2p-6)p+5)p^4 * t\_acc/t\_seg; \\ r &= 1-h; \\ \boldsymbol{\theta} &= r\boldsymbol{\theta}_{BC} + \text{solve}\ (\mathbf{EXPR}_{i}(h,t)) \\ &\quad + ((((\mathbf{a}_7 p + \mathbf{a}_6)p + \mathbf{a}_5)p + \mathbf{a}_4)p^3 + \mathbf{a}_1)p + \mathbf{a}_0; \\ \dot{\boldsymbol{\theta}} &= d\boldsymbol{\theta}/dt; \end{aligned}$$

$t\_acc \le t < t\_seg - t\_acc - \tau$

$$\begin{aligned} h &= t/t\_seg; \\ r &= 1-h; \\ \boldsymbol{\theta} &= r\boldsymbol{\theta}_{BC} + \text{solve}\ (\mathbf{EXPR}_{i}(h,t)); \\ \boldsymbol{\theta} &= r\boldsymbol{\theta}_{BC} + \boldsymbol{\theta}_B; \\ \dot{\boldsymbol{\theta}} &= d\boldsymbol{\theta}/dt; \end{aligned}$$

ORTHOGONAL MOTION

$t = t\_seg - t\_acc$

$$\begin{aligned} h &= t/t\_seg; \\ r &= 1-h; \\ \boldsymbol{\theta} &= \boldsymbol{\theta} + \dot{\boldsymbol{\theta}}\tau\ ; \text{ estimate position} \\ \mathbf{B} &= \mathbf{EXPR}_{i-1}(1,t); \\ \boldsymbol{\theta}_C &= \text{solve}\ (\mathbf{EXPR}_{i}(0,t)); \\ \mathbf{a}_0 &= \boldsymbol{\theta} - \text{solve}\ (\mathbf{B}); \end{aligned}$$

Solve for $x, y, z, \psi, \phi, \theta$ from

$$\begin{aligned} \mathbf{D}(1) &= \mathbf{L}_i^{-1}(0,t)\ \mathbf{B}\ \mathbf{R}_i^{-1}(0,t)); \\ \dot{\boldsymbol{\theta}}_C &= (\boldsymbol{\theta}_C - \boldsymbol{\theta}_{TMP})/\tau\ ; \\ \dot{\boldsymbol{\theta}}_{AC} &= \dot{\boldsymbol{\theta}} - \dot{\boldsymbol{\theta}}_C; \\ \mathbf{a}_1 &= 2t\_acc\,\dot{\boldsymbol{\theta}}_{AC}; \\ \mathbf{a}_7 &= 10\mathbf{a}_1 + 20\mathbf{a}_0; \\ \mathbf{a}_6 &= -36\mathbf{a}_1 - 70\mathbf{a}_0; \\ \mathbf{a}_5 &= 45\mathbf{a}_1 + 84\mathbf{a}_0; \\ \mathbf{a}_4 &= -20\mathbf{a}_1 - 35\mathbf{a}_0; \\ t &= -t\_acc; \end{aligned}$$

$-t\_acc < t < t\_acc$

$$\begin{aligned} p &= (t + t\_acc)/(2t\_acc); \\ h &= ((2p-6)p+5)p^4 * t\_acc/t\_seg; \\ r &= 1-h; \\ \boldsymbol{\theta} &= \text{solve}\ (\mathbf{L}_{i}(h,t)\ \mathbf{D}(r)\ \mathbf{R}_{i}(h,t)); \\ &\quad + ((((\mathbf{a}_7 p + \mathbf{a}_6)p + \mathbf{a}_5)p + \mathbf{a}_4)p^3 + \mathbf{a}_1)p + \mathbf{a}_0; \\ \dot{\boldsymbol{\theta}} &= d\boldsymbol{\theta}/dt; \end{aligned}$$

$t\_acc \le t < t\_seg - t\_acc - \tau$

$$\begin{aligned} h &= t/t\_seg; \\ r &= 1-h; \\ \boldsymbol{\theta} &= \text{solve}\ (\mathbf{L}_{i}(h,t)\ \mathbf{D}(r)\ \mathbf{R}_{i}(h,t)); \\ \boldsymbol{\theta} &= r\boldsymbol{\theta}_{BC} + \boldsymbol{\theta}_B; \\ \dot{\boldsymbol{\theta}} &= d\boldsymbol{\theta}/dt; \end{aligned}$$

4 Kinematics and Design

CONTROL AND MECHANICS OF SIMPLE MANIPULATOR SYSTEMS

Bernard Roth

Department of Mechanical Engineering
Stanford University
Stanford, CA 94305, USA

This paper describes several of the research problems which are now under investigation by our group at Stanford University. These problems involve the optimal design and placement, the robust control, the analysis of instantaneous kinematic properties and the description of the workspace of manipulators. In addition we are studying the mechanics of manipulation with multi-fingered dexterous hands.

The purpose of this paper is to briefly survey the major research problems currently being studied by my research group in the Design Division of Stanford University's Mechanical Engineering Department. I will discuss five separate problems:

1. The optimal design and placement of SCARA type systems.
2. Model-based controllers for manipulator systems.
3. The instantaneous kinematics of simple manipulator systems.
4. The workspace properties of closed chain systems.
5. The mechanics of dexterous hands.

These studies are in various stages of completion and it is expected that in each case much fuller separate descriptions will shortly be submitted for journal publication.

1. <u>The optimal design and placement of SCARA type systems</u>. This research deals with kinematics and dynamics of two-link planar manipulator systems (of the type shown in skeleton diagram in figure 1). There are three reasons for singling out such systems for study. Firstly, they are relatively simple to deal with analytically. Secondly, they model the important class of manipulators known collectively as SCARA type manipulators. Thirdly, such systems give insight into the behavior of more complex systems in which they are often present.

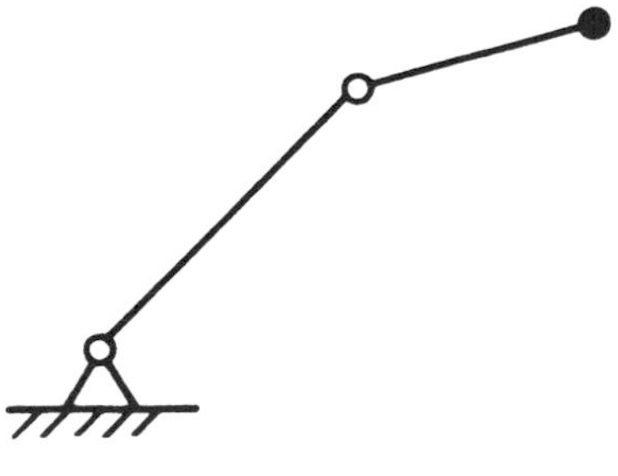

Figure 1. Planar Model of SCARA

Our objective in studying such systems is to determine how to choose design parameters so that the resulting manipulators will be able to perform in an optimum manner. The criteria we chose was shortest time, i.e., time optimal motions. In our work to date we have considered the following questions: (a) Given a specific 2-degree-of-freedom manipulator what is the best orientation relative to the workspace in order to obtain minimum time pick-and-place motions? (b) Given a specific pick-and-place task and specific actuators, what are the link lengths that result in a minimum execution time? To answer these questions we have developed a digital computer simulation of the planar two-link system. The links are modelled as idealized rigid bodies, secondary effects such as backlash are ignored. Starting with a specified initial configuration and velocity, and given the actuator torques, the simulator numerically integrates the equations of motion. Embedding this simulator within a gradient method iteration scheme we were able to study the two aforementioned questions. Our conclusions (which were presented at the RO.MAN.SY.-84 Symposium held two months ago [Scheinman, 1984]) are somewhat surprising:

We found that if we consider the chord length of the displacement of the free end of the two-link system, i.e., the length of the line between the initial and final position in a pick-and-place motion, then, under bang-bang control in a given time interval, the longest chord lengths occur for motions along radial rather than circumferential directions. This means that the best placement of such manipulators for time optimal motion occurs if the fixed pivot lies close to the line passing through the initial and final positions of the end point for the pick-and-place operation under consideration.

We also found that for time optimal motions (under bang-bang control for a given maximum acutator torque and pick-and-place task) the link connected to the fixed pivot should be shorter than the outer link. Interestingly most SCARA manipulators are not designed this way.

Finally, we have found that, for time optimal motions under bang-bang control, one of the endpoints of the pick-and-place motion should be near a maximum extension position of the manipulator. In other words, it is desirable to use the shortest manipulator the task requires.

The reader is cautioned that these preliminary results apply only to a rather restricted set of devices used in a particular manner [Scheinman, 1984]. Generalization to other devices or control modalities may not be warranted. We are now in the process of investigating the domain of validity and hope to soon be able to offer more general results on how to design a manipulator to best suit a given motion requirement and also how to orient a given manipulator relative to its work task.

2. Model-based Controllers. The purpose of this work is to develop a digital simulator for use in synthesizing control laws for manipulators and for studying the influence of manipulator design parameters on the performance of the control system. The method we have been developing depends on a state-space formulation which uses linear, robust servomechanism theory. The idea is to develop controllers which can deal effectively with the uncertainties inherent in many manipulator applications (e.g., modelling errors, non-linear effects, and changes in plant and controller parameters). Controllers which can operate well even with large uncertainties in the dynamic model are said to be robust. To accomplish the design of robust controllers for manipulator systems we start by following the standard approach [Vukobratovic, 1982] of separating the control problem into two parts: a nominal part which represents an idealized nonlinear system, and a linearized system to describe motion deviations from the nominal. In this way we obtain a vector of control inputs $\underline{\tau}$ composed of two parts:

$$\underline{\tau} = \underline{\tau}^* + \tilde{\underline{\tau}} \qquad (1)$$

where $\underline{\tau}^*$, the nominal torque, is obtained from the nonlinear plant model, and $\tilde{\underline{\tau}}$, the compensation torque, is obtained using linear, robust servomechanism theory in a manner which will be described below. The analytical model for the nonlinear plant is usually obtained by using one of the methods of dynamic analysis to derive equations of motion or by using analytical-experimental system-identification techniques. The nominal torque then follows from solving this model which is of the form:

$$\dot{\underline{x}} = \underline{f}\,(\underline{x},\underline{\tau}^*,t) \qquad (2)$$

$$\underline{y} = \underline{g}\,(\underline{x},t) \qquad (3)$$

where, $\underline{x}$ represents the desired state-space vector of the idealized motion variables (in joint-space or world-space or any other convenient space). $\underline{y}$ is the vector of actual joint-displacement variables (the joint angles, or for prismatic joints linear displacements). t is the time, and $\underline{f}$ and $\underline{g}$ represent nonlinear functions of these quantities.

The compensating torque, $\tilde{\underline{\tau}}$, is obtained from a linear time-invarient system of the form

$$\dot{\tilde{x}}(t) = F(t_i)\tilde{\underline{x}}(t) + G(t_i)\tilde{\underline{\tau}}(t) + G_1(t_i)\underline{w} \qquad (4)$$

$$\tilde{\underline{y}}(t) = H(t_i)\tilde{\underline{x}}(t) + J_1(t_i)\underline{w}\ , \quad t_i<t<t_{i+1}\ (i = 1,2,\ldots,m) \qquad (5)$$

where the time-invariance approximation is obtained by dividing the time for the motion into m intervals, and treating the functions F,G,H,J_1 and G_1 as constants whose values are fixed at the beginning of each time interval. Referring to (2) and (3), it can be shown [DeSa, 1984] that

$$F(t_i)= \frac{\partial \underline{f}}{\partial \underline{x}}\Big|_{t_i}\ ,\ G(t_i)= \frac{\partial \underline{f}}{\partial \underline{\tau}}\Big|_{t_i}\ \text{and}\ H(t_i)= \frac{\partial \underline{g}}{\partial \underline{x}}\Big|_{t_i}$$

$G_1(t_i)\underline{w}$ is a "disturbance", it is due to neglected higher order terms and errors in the system model; $J_1(t_i)\underline{w}$ is used to compensate for neglected nonlinear terms. $\underline{y}$ is the deviation of the joint vaiables from their desired ideal values. The desired ideal values are the ones these variables would have to take on to cause the manipulator to exactly follow a specified path as a specified function of time. This is known as "trajectory following." Hence in our application we would like $\tilde{\underline{y}}\,(t) \to 0$. In servomechanism jargon such problems are called "regulator problems."

If we apply the Internal Model Principle, and follow a method developed by Franklin and Emani-Naeini [Franklin, 1983], where we model the disturbance signal $\underline{w}$ as a pth order ordinary differential equation with constant coefficients:

$$\underline{w}^{(p)} = \sum_{i=1}^{p} \alpha_i \underline{w}^{(p-i)}\ , \qquad (6)$$

where $\underline{w}^{(k)} \equiv \dfrac{d^k \underline{w}}{dt^k}$, we obtain a control law for the system described by (4) and (5):

$$(\tilde{\underline{\tau}}+k_o\tilde{\underline{x}})^{(p)} = -\sum_{i=1}^{p} k_i \tilde{\underline{y}}^{(p-i)} + \sum_{i=1}^{p} \alpha_i (\tilde{\underline{\tau}}+k_o\tilde{\underline{x}})^{(p-i)} \qquad (7)$$

This control law can be shown [DeSa,1984; Franklin, 1983] to obey certain robustness criteria which make it insensitive to large uncertainties in the dynamic model of the plant. On the other hand if one ignored the effects of uncertainties and applied state-feedback one obtains the classical control law $\underline{\tau} = -k_o \underline{x}$ which, in general, does not have the property of robustness. In order to determine the (matrices of) control parameters k_i (i = 0,1,...,p) for the control law (7) we use a performance index, J, such that if the desired dynamic response of the system is $\dot{\tilde{y}} - A_m \tilde{y} = e(t)$ (where e is chosen to be as small as possible) we minimize

$$J = \int_0^\infty [\rho(\dot{\tilde{y}} - A_m \tilde{y})^T(\dot{\tilde{y}} - A_m \tilde{y}) + \mu^T \mu]dt, \qquad (8)$$

where $\underline{\mu} = \tilde{\tau}^{(p)} - \sum_{i=1}^{p} \alpha_i \tilde{\tau}^{(p-i)}$

and ρ is a scalar weighting function, subject to the constraint of the state-space equations for the linearized system. The result is that, for each weighting ρ, we obtain a unique set k_i and we avoid the difficulties inherent in choosing weighting matrices. This method is known as implicit model following [Kreindler, 1976].

We have implemented such a system and tested it on various spatial two-link revolute joint manipulator models. To date the results have been very encouraging, detailed numerical examples will be presented in [DeSa, 1984]. Our preliminary conclusions are: Robust servomechanism theory coupled with implicit model following provides a good approach to dealing with the nonlinear nature of the trajectory following control of manipulators. The resulting controllers yield very good performance in simulation of high speed, high precision applications. Because of the need for basing the computations on a well defined trajectory, the method is best applied to tasks where the kinematic and dynamic models can be generated before hand off-line.

3. <u>The instantaneous kinematics of simple manipulator systems</u>. The purpose of this study is to understand the basic capabilities of various simple manipulators, especially in regard to their so-called instantaneous kinematics. By instantaneous kinematic properties one means those properties which are functions of a single position and, if relevant an instant of time. So, for example, velocities, path tangents and curvatures, accelerations and all path derivatives are instantaneous properties, whereas the shapes of workspaces and the ranges of motion are not.

To better understand what we are studying let us look at a specific example. Figure 2 shows a

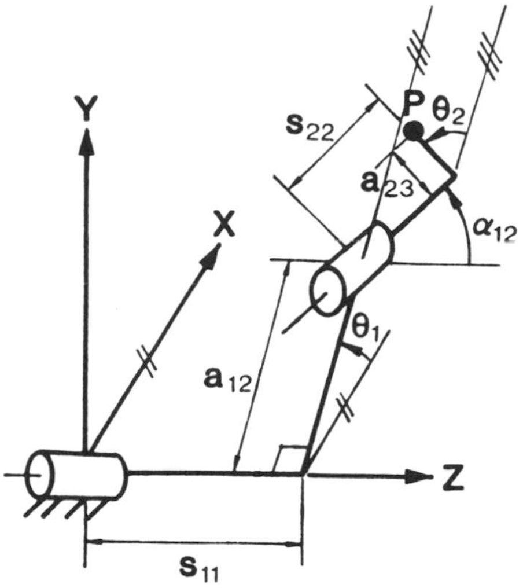

Figure 2. Spatial 2-link Manipulator

skeleton diagram of a two-link spatial manipulator with revolute joints. If $\underline{P}(\theta_1, \theta_2)$ is the position vector of point P as measured in the X,Y,Z coordinate system shown, then

$$\underline{x}_1 = \frac{\partial \underline{P}}{\partial \theta_1} = [-a_{12}s_1 + s_{22}c_1 s_{12} - a_{23}(s_1 c_2 + c_1 s_2 c_{12})],\ [a_{12}c_1 + s_{22}s_1 c_{12} + a_{23}(c_1 c_2 - s_1 s_2 c_{12})], 0$$

$$\underline{x}_2 = \frac{\partial \underline{P}}{\partial \theta_2} = a_{23}[-c_1 s_2 - s_1 c_2 c_{12}], a_{23}[-s_1 s_2 + c_1 c_2 c_{12}],\ a_{23}s_{12}c_2$$

where $c_i = \cos\theta_i$, $s_i = \sin\theta_i$, $c_{12} = \cos\alpha_{12}$, $s_{12} = \sin\alpha_{12}$, and all other quantities are defined on the figure. The velocity of P is given by $\dot{\underline{p}} = \underline{x}_1 \dot{\theta}_1 + \underline{x}_2 \dot{\theta}_2$ and it can easily be shown that at any instant the maximum and minimum velocities are along the directions

$$\underline{x}_1,\ \underline{x}_2 - \frac{\underline{x}_1 \cdot \underline{x}_2}{\underline{x}_1 \cdot \underline{x}_1}\underline{x}_1 \text{ and have magnitudes}$$

$$E[\dot{\theta}_1 + (F/E)\dot{\theta}_2],\ \left[\frac{Ea_{23}^2 - F^2}{E}\right]\dot{\theta}_2$$

$$\text{where } E = a_{12}^2 + s_{22}^2 s_{12}^2 + a_{23}^2(c_2^2 + s_2^2 c_{12}^2) + 2a_{23}a_{12}c_2 - 2s_{22}a_{23}c_{12}s_{12}s_2$$

$$\text{and } F = a_{23}(a_{12}c_2 c_{12} - s_{22}s_{12}s_2 + a_{23}c_{12})$$

Thus for example, if a manipulator moves so that

$$\theta_2 = 2\tan^{-1}\left(s_{22}s_{12} \pm \sqrt{(s_{22}s_{12})^2 - a_{23}^2 + a_{12}^2 c_{12}^2}\right)$$

then F = 0, and the maximum and minimum velocity directions coincide with $\underline{x_1}$ and $\underline{x_2}$. By studying the functions E and F we can determine how the velocity depends on the position (i.e., θ_1 and θ_2) and also the manipulator parameters (i.e., s_{22}, a_{12}, a_{23}, α_{12}). We are in the process of studying similar properties for higher derivatives and also for more complex manipulators. This work is at approximately its midway point, it will probably be completed in about one year [Ghosal, 1985].

4. The workspace properties of closed chain systems. At last year's Robotics Research Conference, Professor H. Asada spoke about his direct drive manipulator and J.P. Trevelyan spoke about his sheep shearing manipulator. Both manipulators have the same closed-loop chain, which is in effect a planar 5-bar mechanism. A skeleton diagram of a planar 5-bar mechanism is shown in figure 3. In these

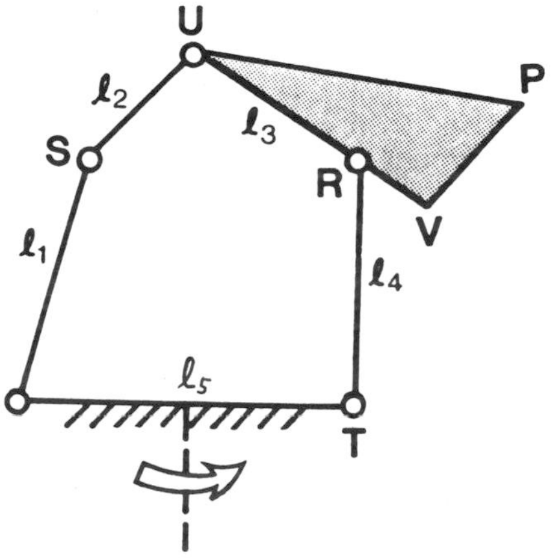

Figure 3. Planar 5-bar

manipulators, links ℓ_1 and ℓ_4 are driven by motors (or actuators) fixed to link ℓ_5, and the entire system is rotated about the dashed line perpendicular to ℓ_5. If a wrist is afixed to point P, the entire system then has 5 or 6 freedoms, depending upon if the wrist has 2 or 3 independent drives. In general, compactness and balance are improved if the motors which drive ℓ_1 and ℓ_4 are in-line, i.e., co-axial, and so one often finds that length $\ell_5 = 0$.

If we are interested in the workspace of such a system we can obtain some nice results by considering the planar 5-bar linkage and studying the coupler curves generated by point P, the wrist point. Ignoring the rotation about the dashed line causes no problems since all it accomplishes is to make a surface of revolution out of the coupler-curve planar workspace boundary. To study the planar 5-bar system it is useful to note the following:

1. For a fixed position of ℓ_4, the workspace of point P is a circle (or a portion of a circle) centered at point R and having radius RP.

2. For a fixed position of ℓ_1, the workspace of point P is a four-bar coupler curve (i.e., a tricircular trinodal sextic) generated by the four-bar which has S and T as fixed pivots and ℓ_2 and ℓ_4 as cranks. (Normally the workspace will only be a portion of the entire coupler curve.)

Since the properties of circles and four-bars are well known, it is quite easy for us to immediately obtain many useful results regarding the actual workspace of such systems and the dependence of the workspace on the linkage parameters. Simply applying Grashof's criteria for full crank rotation yields interesting results. For example, if $\ell_4 > \ell_2 > \ell_3$ where $\ell_3 = UR$, then we know that the link UVP can execute full 360° rotation provided $\overline{ST} + \ell_3 < \ell_2 + \ell_4$ when $\overline{ST} > \ell_4$ or $\ell_4 + \ell_3 < \overline{ST} + \ell_2$ when $\ell_4 > \overline{ST} > \ell_3$. Using this type of analysis it becomes fairly straight forward to determine the influence of the link lengths on workspace and to determine the various boundary and extreme cases. An extensive study of such results is just being completed and will shortly be available [Bajpai, 1984].

In closing, it is pointed out that the special case of PV = 0 in general does not change the results in any substantive way, and that there is no reason from the point of view of workspace to in fact make such a choice.

5. The mechanics of dexterous hands. We are also investigating articulated, multi-finger hands. Previous work in this area has been concerned with the analysis and design of a particular hand. This current work endeavors to generalize this previous work and develop additional techniques for the analysis of general multi-jointed, multi-fingered hands. Such hands will have the ability to manipulate objects as well as grasp them.

The classes of hands encompassed by this investigation include all hands made up of independent fingers, where each finger is considered to be an open kinematic chain of rigid links, connected by single degree of freedom joints. Contact with objects is restricted to a single contact at the most distal link of each finger. At each contact, however, a variety of contact constraint conditions with varying amounts of freedom are considered.

The areas of study include the analysis of grasping, the selection of internal grasping forces, the generation of both infinitesimal and finite motions of a grasped object, the determination of hand workspaces, and issues relating to the programming of hands. Much of the analysis is performed by considering the hand and object to be a closed kinematic chain. The analysis of grasping is then equivalent to the analysis of forces within the links of the mechanism and the forces or torques at the joints of the mechanism. The motion analysis is equivalent to determining the motions of the mechanism which will result in some desired motion of the grasped object.

Both the problems of grasping and imparting infintesimal motions or velocities to a grasped object can be examined with linear relationships analogous to the Jacobian matrix relationships used in the analysis of manipulators. For grasping, there is one linear relationship between the external forces applied to a grasped object, F_b, and the set of forces C, applied at each contact required to balance the external forces. This is written as the matrix equation $F_b = W\ C$. The matrix W is derived from the configuration of the contact points on the object. The set of contact forces is related to the finger joint torques, T, by a second linear equation, $T = J^t\ C$. J^t is the transpose of a Jacobian-like matrix, which is defined by the configuration of all of the fingers in the hand.

The problem of imparting velocities to the grasped object is also defined by the two matrices, W and J. The velocity associated with the object, V_b, is related to the set of velocities of the contact points, V_c, by the equation $V_c = W^t\ V_b$. The contact point velocities are related to the finger joint velocities, $\dot{\theta}$, by the equation $V_c = J\ \dot{\theta}$.

If both W and J are square and non-singular, they can be inverted to yield direct relationships between V_b and $\dot{\theta}$, and between F_b and T. Unfortunately, this is rarely the case with most grasping situations.

In most viable grasping situations, the W matrix will have greater width than height. This means that there will be some freedom in the choice of contact forces which will balance a given force, F_b, applied to the object. This freedom can be interpreted as freedom in choosing internal grasping forces. This work develops a method for choosing these internal forces so as to insure the satisfaction of friction, joint torque limit, and uniaxial contact constraints which must also be met to achieve a stable grasp. By linearizing the friction constraint, optimal internal forces can be chosen using the simplex method for linear optimization.

The fact that most hands do not have enough joints to manipulate objects with complete generality is manifested in the dimensions of the Jacobian matrix. Examination of the null space and range space of the Jacobian reveals the direction in which an object can or cannot be moved. The use of the pseudo-inverse provides useful results in these less than optimal situations.

Additionally, in situations where objects can be manipulated with complete generality, the eigenvectors and eigenvalues of combinations of these matrices determine preferred directions of motion or preferred directions in which to apply forces. This is useful when the hand is in a near singular configuration.

For large motions (when the fingertip surface and the object surface have finite curvatures), the surfaces will roll upon each other, and the point of contact will travel across each surface. Under these conditions, the joint angle trajectories required to produce a desired trajectory of the object are described by a set of coupled, nonlinear, time varying differential equations. In general, there will be no closed form solution to these equations. In this work, these equations are derived as a set of first order differential equations suitable for numerical integration.

In conjunction with the topic of finite motions we have the issue of hand workspaces, that is the range of motion possible by an object grasped in a hand. This problem is complicated by the fact that the size and shape of the workspace will vary with the choice of the grasp point configuration. A definition of the hand workspace using the grasp point configuration is developed, along with measures for ranges of possible orientations. A general description of hand workspaces has been developed, along with the generation of workspaces for the special case where each finger individually has a spherical workspace.

The relationship of the workspace size to the configuration of the grasp points has also been examined. For hands composed of fingers with the same workspaces, it has been shown that the configuration of grasp points which is identical to the configuration of the finger bases in the palm will produce the largest total workspace. This gives a general indication of the size of the objects best manipulated by a particular hand.

Lastly, issues in the programming of complex, articulated hands have been investigated. As with robotic arms, it is desirable to be able to specify motions of an object, or forces to be applied with it, without having to refer to the specific mechanism used for the task. A scheme for programming hands analogous to intermediate level manipulator programming is outlined. In this system grasp, point selection and internal grasp force selection are included. All of this work on multi-finger hands is described in the doctoral thesis of Jeffrey Kerr, which is in the final stage of completion [Kerr, 1984].

Acknowledgements

The financial support of the National Science Foundation and the Systems Development Foundation made this work possible.

References

Bajpai, A., 1984, The Workspace of a Closed-Loop Manipulator, Engineers Thesis, Mechanical Engineering Dept., Stanford University.

DeSa, S. and Roth, B., 1984, "Synthesis of Control Systems for Manipulators Using Robust Servomechanism Theory," manuscript in preparation.

Franklin, G. F. and Emani-Naeini, A., 1983, A New Formulation of the Multivariable Robust Servomechanism Problem, Internal report ISL, Stanford University.

Ghosal, A., 1985, Ph.D. Thesis, in progress, Mechanical Engineering Dept., Stanford University.

Kerr, J., 1984, The Analysis of Multi-fingered Hands, Ph.D. Thesis, Mechanical Engineering Dept., Stanford Unversity.

Kreindler, E., and Rothschild, D., 1976, "Model-Following in Linear-Quadratic Optimization," AIAA Journal, Vol. 14, No. 7, pp. 835-842.

Scheinman, V., and Roth, B., 1984, "On the Optimal Selection and Placement of Manipulators," Preprints Fifth CISM - IFToMM Symposium on Theory and Practice of Robots and Manipulators, Udine, Italy, pp. 25-32 (also to be published in final proceedings.)

Vukobratovic, M., and Stokic, D., 1982, Scientific Fundamentals of Robotics 2, Control of Manipulation Robots, Berlin, Springer-Verlag, 363 pp.

NEW CONCEPTS IN LIGHTWEIGHT ARMS

Wayne J. Book

School of Mechanical Engineering
Georgia Institute of Technology
Atlanta, Georgia 30332, U.S.A.

The conflict in designing a robot which is fast for large motions and small motions as well as accurate can be alleviated by strategies of operation such as the one described in this paper, called the bracing strategy. Large motions are assigned to joints which move the major links. When these motions are completed the arm is "braced" against the workpiece or a passive workbench. The small motions are assigned to other degrees of freedom which are referenced to the workpiece rather than the base of the robot. In this way lighter arms are possible without their disadvantages for fast, accurate small motions. The concept and issues of its implementation are discussed.

1 Introduction

A robot requires an effective and efficient combination of intelligence at various levels and a mechanical manipulator. Technology for implementing the intelligence, including lower level servo controls, is rapidly developing while the purely mechanical aspects are only slowly evolving. Various strategies must be employed to use intelligence in the form of controls and execution strategies to enhance the mechanical technologies and in improving the efficiency of an arm in manipulating a given payload weight. It is true in improving arm accuracy and dexterity as well. This paper discusses some ways of improving the ratio of payload weight to arm weight.

The rated payload of commercial robots today is 3% to 5% of the total arm weight. Current programs for heavily loaded arms allow about a second of settling time for arm oscillations to die out. These are facts indicative of a need to model and deal with arms as having compliant members both to deal with existing dynamics and to design more capable arms.

2 Lightweight Arms: Pros and Cons

Ultimately, one must have fast motion to have the highest performance for a robot arm. Most robot tasks consist of gross motion and fine motion phases. Gross motion involves large movements with a relatively predictable destination enabling trajectory planning. These motions require a high force to inertia ratio for rapid completion. Fine motion involves smaller, more precise movements which are less predictable. They are required after imprecise gross motions or could arise in response to disturbances, statistical variation in dimensions, or changes in the environment. To accomplish these motions quickly a high bandwidth servo system is required. Such bandwidth typically requires rigidity in the actuated structure, hence additional structural mass. The traditional approach accomplishes both gross and fine motions with the same actuators and linkage. Thus the structural mass required for the fine motion speed detracts from the gross motion speed. Correspondingly, a light and hence flexible arm will have low bandwidth when controlled by conventional means.

In addition to higher gross motion speed, other advantages exist. The advantages of lighter arms are summarized as follows:

1. Higher gross motion speeds can be obtained.
2. Cost of the mechanical subsystem can be reduced.
3. Energy efficiency is improved due to smaller actuators for the same cycle times.
4. Portability and mobility of arms is improved.
5. Safety is improved due to reduced moving mass.
6. Mounting requirements are reduced.

On the other hand problems arise due primarily to the greater flexibility of the arm. Strength of an arm is typically not the limiting constraint. Problems due to a lightweight arm include the following:

1. Bandwidth and hence fine motion speed are reduced, at least with conventional control schemes.

2. Vibrations (dynamic inaccuracies) may be excited by motions or external disturbances.

3. Static inaccuracies (droop) will occur in a gravitational force field.

4. Attempts to overcome the above disadvantages with improved controls will result in a more complicated control system.

5. The design and analysis of a flexible arm is much more complicated than for a rigid arm.

3 Limitations on the Control of Flexible Arms

The improved control of flexible, that is compliant, arms has been a research topic for a number of years. [Book, 1974] Recent studies show that the response of such an arm can be improved over conventional control algorithms intended for rigid arms. [Fukuda, 1984] [Truckenbrodt, 1981] These algorithms are limited with respect to their ability to respond to a disturbance on the arm. Their accuracy is inherently limited by the ability to detect the arm's deflection, as well as by joint sensors and their ability to totally eliminate vibrations. If one attempts to improve the speed of response of these algorithms without limit the robustness of the system may be compromised.

4 The Bracing Concept

The research underway seeks to eliminate the conflict between gross and fine motion speed. The configurations studied effectively reduce the distance from the end point to a "fixed" base during the fine motion phase by "**bracing**" it against a static structure or the work piece itself. This approach is especially relevant to long arms with light payloads. [Book, 1983] A wide range of tasks fall into this category including ultrasonic, visual, or other inspection of large objects, cleaning windows on multistory buildings, repairing transformers and insulators on utility poles, and assembly of space or underwater structures. A similar concept for teleoperator is being explored by the Canadian Electrical Association, and Robotic Systems International Ltd. and by Southwest Research Institute and EPRI for servicing power lines.

Bracing is analogous to the strategy of human workers who steady their hand for precise work by bracing their arm against a work bench as shown in Fig.1. It is also a variation of the strategy of extending the range of an arm by providing it with mobility. For mobile robots the strategy is typically to transport the arm to the vicinity of the work piece, deactivate the mobility subsystem, and activate the arm. Both cases are examples of allocation of the motion responsibilities to the most appropriate degrees of freedom. Similar approaches have been proposed by Moore and Hogan [Moore, 1983] and applied specifically to drilling.

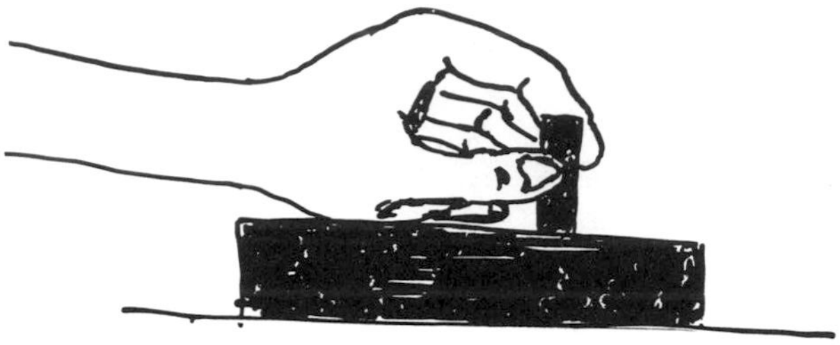

Fig. 1 Human employing bracing strategy.

Other examples of allocation of degrees of freedom to independent motions include:

- Conveyor belts and arms
- Arms and positioning tables
- Rockets, Lunar Landers, and Lunar Rovers
- Robot arms and positioning tables.

In these examples various means of effectively bracing one set of degrees of freedom from the remaining degrees of freedom are used. The means of bracing may inherently provide greater positioning accuracy relative to the workpiece than was previously available. Hence the Lunar Lander sitting on the surface of the Moon has a well defined height above the surface of the Moon. On the other hand, a positioning table which comes to rest has an accuracy only known as well as the sensors used in positioning it. Locating holes can be used in bracing an arm which accurately position an arm in several degrees of freedom relative to the workpiece. More versatile operation is possible if the accuracy of the position after bracing is obtained through end point sensing relative to the base, or better, relative to the workpiece.

Bracing requires supporting forces of the arm be developed in some manner. Consideration of several means of creating these forces have been considered. [Book, Le, Sangveraphunsiri, 1984] They include (1) a simple pressure contact, (2) mechanical clamping, (3) vacuum attachment, and (4) magnetic attachment. Multiple means may be appropriate in many cases.

The issues in controlling an arm to be braced are somewhat different than in controlling conventional robots. They can be broken down into issues of:

- Gross Motion

   1. Choosing a fast trajectory which does not unnecessarily excite vibrations

   2. Following the trajectory chosen with a controller that is accurate and stable over large changes in parameters

   3. Selecting a destination to allow best use of other degrees of freedom.

- Rendezvous and Inactive phases

   1. An accurate, gentle collision with bracing structure

   2. Passive damping of the high frequency dynamics

   3. Appropriate control of the statically indeterminate braced structure

- Fine Motion

   1. Sensing of position relative to target

   2. Fast, probably conventional control of fine motion degrees of freedom.

5 Conclusions

The bracing strategy holds promise for resolving design conflicts in achieving superior performance for certain types of applications. Economic questions of the value of the added complexity (increased number of degrees of freedom, more complex sensors and controls) can only be answered when research has made clearer what the payoff for this complexity will be in terms of performance.

Initial research in arm modeling, trajectory optimization, trajectory following, and terminal control is underway. [Book, 1984], [Sangveraphunsiri, 1984] This is now being tested on a single link arm experimentally. A two link large scale arm is planned for the near future.

Acknowledgements

This work was partially supported through the U.S. National Science Foundation, Grant MEA-8303539.

References

Book, W.J., Maizza-Neto, O., Whitney, D.E., "Feedback Control of Two Beam Two Joint Systems with Distributed Flexibility," Journal of Dynamic Systems, Measurement and Control, pp.424-431, Dec. 1975.

Book, W.J. and Majette, M., "Controller Design for Flexible Distributed Parameter Mechanical Arms Via Combined State Space and Frequency Domain Techniques," J. Dynamic Systems, Measurement, and Control, Dec. 1983.

Book, Wayne J., Le, S., and Sangveraphunsiri, V., "The Bracing Strategy for Robot Operation," CISM-IFToMM Symposium on Robots and Manipulators (RoManSy), 1984.

Book, W. J., "Recursive Lagrangian Dynamics of Flexible Manipulator Arms," to appear in The International J. of Robotics Research, MIT Press, 1984.

Fukuda, T. and Kuribayashi, Y., "Flexibility Control of Elastic Robotic Arms and its Application to Contouring Control," Proc., International Conference on Robotics, Atlanta, GA, March, 1984, IEEE Computer Soc. pp.540-545.

Moore, S.R. and Hogan, N., "Part Referenced Manipulation--A Strategy Applied to Robotic Drilling," in Control of Manufacturing Processes and Robotic Systems, D. Hardt and W.J. Book, eds. American Society of Mechanical Engineers, New York, pp. 183-191, 1983.

Sangveraphunsiri, V., "The Optimal Control and Design of a Flexible Manipulator Arm," Ph.D. Dissertation, School of Mechanical Engineering, Georgia Institute of Technology, 1984.

Truckenbrodt, A. "Modelling and Control of Flexible Manipulator Structures," Fourth CISM-IFToMM Symposium on the Theory of Machines and Mechanisms (RoManSy), 1981.

USE OF REDUNDANCY IN THE DESIGN OF ROBOTIC SYSTEMS

Charles A. Klein

The Ohio State University
Department of Electrical Engineering
205 Dreese Lab
2015 Neil Avenue
Columbus, OH 43210, USA

Most current industrial robots have no more than the minimum number of mechanical degrees of freedom necessary for a given task. By including kinematically redundant links, more flexible operation can be achieved. To solve these mathematically underdetermined systems, generalized inverses can be used to determine unique activator velocities, given end effector motion specifications. In addition, the set of homogenous solutions, which cause no end effector motion , can be used to satisfy secondary goals for the arm motion. One important use of the redundancy is in specifying that the arm avoid obstacles in the workspace. A technique will be described which automatically moves the arm away from obstacles while guiding the hand on the desired trajectory. An important element of this algorithm is the proper weighting of multiple constraints. Another use for the redundancy is in keeping the arm in a configuration which makes it as dexterous as possible. Several measures for this quantity will be examined.

INTRODUCTION

A robotics system can be termed redundant if it contains more than the minimum number of degrees of freedom needed to perform a class of tasks. Since the common task of arbitrarily locating and orienting a workpiece requires six degrees of freedom, a manipulator with seven or more degrees of freedom, not counting end-effector actuation, is kinematically redundant. In this case the space of redundant solutions can be used to either meet additional constraints or to optimize performance criteria.

A key mathematical tool for the solution of redundant problems is the pseudoinverse. An intuitive understanding can be obtained from the singular value decomposition theorem [Rao and Mitra, 1971] , which states that an arbitrary matrix A can be expressed as

$$A = \sum_{i=1}^{r} \mu_i \underline{e}_i \underline{f}_i^* \qquad (1)$$

where r is the rank, μ_i's are a set of real positive scalars, termed singular values, $\underline{e}_i$'s are a mutually orthonormal set of vectors termed output singular vectors, and $\underline{f}_i$'s are a mutually orthonormal set of vectors termed input singular vectors. In this form the pseudoinverse of A can be expressed as

$$A^+ = \sum_{i=1}^{r} (1/\mu_i) \underline{f}_i e_i^* \qquad (2)$$

For the solution of the system of linear equations

$$A\underline{x} = \underline{y} \qquad (3)$$

the general solution can be expressed as [Rao and Mitra, 1971]

$$\underline{x} = A^+\underline{y} + (I - A^+A)\underline{z} \qquad (4)$$

where $\underline{z}$ is an arbitrary vector. The first term represents the minimum-norm vector in the space of least-squares solutions to the right-hand side of (3); the second term uses a projection operator to select the component of $\underline{z}$ which is in the space of homogeneous solutions to (3) and therefore can be used for optimization.

In robotics the pseudoinverse techniques are applied through the Jacobian control method [Whitney, 1972]. In this technique the vector of end effector velocities and rotation rates is recognized as being the Jacobian matrix times the joint velocity vector,

$$J\dot{\underline{\theta}} = \dot{\underline{x}} \quad . \qquad (5)$$

For kinematically redundant manipulators J will not be square and cannot simply be solved by matrix inversion. Whitney [1969] described the use of the pseudoinverse as a means of minimizing joint velocity and therefore actuator power. Liegeois [1977] added the homogeneous solution term and demonstrated its use to optimize joint range availability. Further properties of this solution were described by Klein and Huang [1983]. A kinematically redundant robot has been built for sheep shearing [Trevelyan, Koresi, and Ong, 1983]. Use of the homogeneous solution to improve the dexterity and to avoid obstacles has been investigated by Yoshikawa [1983].

The goal of this paper is to discuss two aspects of the use of redundancy in robotic systems. The first aspect is obstacle avoidance as a criteria for the use of the homogeneous solutions of a kinematically redundant manipulator, and the second is an examination of several different quantities which have been proposed as a measure of dexterity for a manipulator.

OBSTACLE AVOIDANCE

Clearly one of the potential advantages of a kinematically redundant manipulator is the use of the extra degrees of freedom to maneuver in a cluttered workspace to avoid contact with tooling. The ability of human arms to work in such environments provide a model of this ability. What is needed is a plan for joint coordination to avoid obstacles while performing the desired task.

Previous work on obstacle avoidance [Udupa, 1977; Lozano-Perez, 1981; Loef and Soni, 1975; Khatib and LeMaitre, 1978; Brooks, 1983] has primarily been concerned with the planning of a trajectory between two given points of the end effector so as to avoid obstacles on the way. Other work [Yoshikawa, 1983] is directly suited to redundant manipulator control. In his work a nominal obstacle-free position is described in joint space and the homogeneous solution term of (4) becomes a velocity toward this position. The technique for obstacle avoidance described here differs in philosophy from both approaches. First the manipulator task specification will be given in terms of an end effector trajectory as would be required for jobs such as spray painting or arc welding [Paul, 1979]. Obstacle avoidance will be the goal of optimizing the redundant degrees of freedom to keep inboard links away from obstacles. Second, while the use of a desired joint position is well suited to manual training of a manipulator, the method described here is more suitable to design procedures with CAD/CAM databases and use of proximity sensors as direct sensors in dynamically changing environments. A third feature of this method is that it is conceptually simple and involves no future planning.

Pseudoinverse Formulation

The obstacle avoidance scheme involves both use of continuous pseudoinverse formulas and some decision making. For a given end effector velocity, the set of possible joint velocities is given applying (4) as

$$\dot{\underline{\theta}} = J_e^{+}\dot{\underline{x}} + P\,\underline{z} \quad , \tag{6}$$

$$P = I - J_e^{+}J_e \quad , \tag{7}$$

where is J_e is the Jacobian matrix for the end effector and $\underline{z}$ is an arbitrary vector. Next it is necessary to determine at any time which point of the manipulator is closest to an obstacle, termed the obstacle avoidance point, and to assign a velocity of this point directly away from the obstacle (See Fig. 1). Therefore the joint velocity should also satisfy

$$J_o\,\dot{\underline{\theta}} = \dot{\underline{x}}_o \tag{8}$$

where the right-hand side is the obstacle point velocity and J_o is the Jacobian for this point. One possible way to find a common solution to both (5) and (8) would be to adjoin the two matrices and the right-hand sides into a single matrix equation.

If the row space of J_o is same order as the redundancy of the manipulator, then mathematically the system has now been fully specified and is no longer redundant. If the matrix is not square or of full rank, then obviously its pseudoinverse could be applied to give a best approximate solution. However, for this application it is not desirable to treat end effector and obstacle velocities in the same way since the end effector trajectory must be followed but the obstacle velocity need not always be directly away from the obstacle.

Substituting (6) into (8) gives an equation for the redundant solution for joint velocities.

$$J_o\,P\,\underline{z} = \dot{\underline{x}}_o - J_oJ_e^{+}\dot{\underline{x}}_e \tag{9}$$

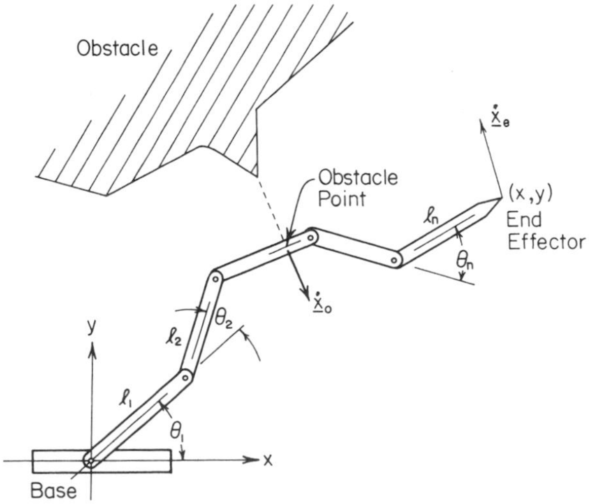

Fig. 1. Geometry of planar manipulator showing the point nearest the obstacle. Homogeneous solution term is used to maximize the distance to the obstacle.

Since the degree of redundancy may not be high enough to exactly match the desired obstacle velocity, a pseudoinverse is again applied to obtain a least-squares fit. This result is then substituted back into (6) to solve for joint velocity. Because the projection operator is Hermitian and idempotent, it is possible to simplify the answer to the following [Maciejewski, 1984]:

$$\dot{\theta} = J_e^{+}\dot{x}_e + [J_o P]^{+} (\dot{x}_o - J_o J_e^{+}\dot{x}_e) \quad . \qquad (10)$$

Decision Making

Although (10) is the basis of the obstacle avoidance scheme used here, proper decision making is equally as important to successful operation of the algorithm. The first type of decision is based on a fundamental nature of the pseudoinverse. One of the esthetic attractions of pseudoinverse formulations is that they are valid independently of the rank of the matrix. However, unlike nonsingular matrices, as two matrices approach each other, their pseudoinverse can diverge [Noble, 1975].

The main problem in a pseudoinverse formulation is not at a singularity when a zero component weights the missing degree of freedom but near a singularity where a very large component may be applied according to (2). The solution involves evaluating the effective rank of the matrix and treating it as singular whenever it would yield unacceptably large answers. Since this is used in a real-time controller for a physical system, limits must be based on physical speed limitations rather than on loss of significance as would apply in a numerical analysis situation. However, independent of the value of the threshold of rank, there will be a discontinuity when the change of rank is noted.

Proper decision making regarding rank is especially important since the system tends to move such that either the obstacle point cannot move any further without moving the end effector or else a new point becomes the obstacle point. Besides choosing the proper threshold, two methods can be applied to minimize rank change effects. The first is to only consider obstacle avoidance when sufficiently close to an obstacle, which would be compatible with limited range proximity sensors. In order not to introduce a discontinuity, obstacle avoidance velocity should be tapered as a function of distance. In order to effectively control the degree of influence which an obstacle has on the resultant manipulator motion, the solution for the joint angle rates has been modified to

$$\underline{\dot{\theta}} = J_e^{+}\dot{x}_e + \alpha_h [J_o P]^{+} (\alpha_o \dot{x}_o - J_o J_e^{+}\dot{x}_e) \qquad (11)$$

where the obstacle velocity itself is considered to be a unit vector specifying direction only. Fig. 2 shows how the distance to the obstacle, d, determines the gains α_o and α_h in four separate regions. For d less than d_{ta} there is imminent danger of a collision and the task should be aborted. The distance d_{ta} should include the thickness of manipulator

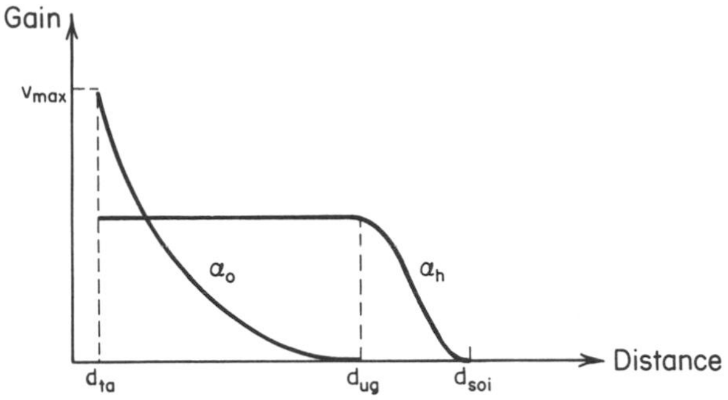

Fig. 2. Assignment of gains in the obstacle avoidance term as a function of obstacle distance.

arms. In the next region an obstacle velocity is inversely related to the distance. Further away the homogeneous term tapers off until for d greater than d_{soi}, it has no effect and the homogeneous solution may be used to optimize some other desirable criterion.

Using multiple secondary goals has been considered as a second way of minimizing switching of homogeneous solutions. In this implementation the two worst-case obstacles were considered. Thus the solution for the joint angles is expressed as

$$\underline{\dot{\theta}} = J_e^{+}\dot{x}_e + \alpha_1 (d_2/d_1)\underline{h_1} + \alpha_2 (d_2/d_1)\underline{h_2} \qquad (12)$$

where $\underline{h_i}$ is the ith homogeneous solution, α_i is its corresponding gain and d_i is the distance to the obstacle where the subscript 1 denotes the worst-case obstacle. The greater the disparity between d_1 and d_2, the closer α_1 comes to unity, with α_2 approaching zero. With d_1 approximately equal to d_2, $\alpha_1 = \alpha_2 = .5$ with the overall homogeneous solution split between the two goals. By blending the homogeneous solutions in this manner the manipulator has the capability to make smooth transitions to allow for the varying priorities of the secondary goals.

In implementation certain tradeoffs in performance must be recognized. Desirable, but contradictory, qualities are smoothness of motion, responsiveness, and automatic operation without planning. For example, including more multiple obstacle goals improves smoothness, but reduces the performance of the most critical one. By adding some specific information about link geometry, speed can be increased at the cost of generality .

RESULTS

The above obstacle avoidance scheme has been implemented in both two-dimensional and fully general three-dimensional computer graphics simulations on a PDP 11/70 computer provided with a Hewlett-Packard 1350 vector graphics display. The primary goal, a specified end effector trajectory, is entered either through a file or interactively with a joystick. The secondary goal information, the obstacle avoidance point and velocity, is determined from a mathematical description of the world. In a physical implementation, the secondary goal information would be obtained from sensory range finding devices [Espiau and Andre, 1984]. Details of the implementation can be obtained from [Maciejewski, 1984].

The Jacobian is efficiently computed by using the screw axis formulation [Waldron, 1981]. Since the end effector Jacobian is of full rank, unless the specified task is unachievable, its pseudoinverse need not be explicitly calculated and Gaussian elimination can be applied instead [Klein and Huang, 1983].

The pseudoinverse of the matrix in (10) must also be calculated. Since no assumption on the rank of this matrix can be made, the above approach cannot be applied. In this case the pseudoinverse is explicity calculated using the recursive method presented by Greville [1960]. Within this algorithm one implicitly makes decisions regarding the rank in terms of evaluating the linear independence of matrix columns. Therefore a sufficiently large threshold must be applied to limit high velocities near singularities. Although theoretically this technique works as well on a matrix as on its transpose, numerically it is very important to transpose this matrix so that the smaller dimension is the number of columns. Since this algorithm operates on columns, the correct decision for rank is much more easily applied to the smaller dimension.

The majority of the evaluation of the obstacle avoidance formulation was performed using the two-dimensional simulation due to the greater degree of redundancy available with respect to the task and the corresponding reduction in computation time which allows for real-time joystick specification of end effector trajectory. The cycle time for a seven degree-of-freedom, two-dimensional manipulator, including secondary goal calculation and graphic display time, was 47 msec. Fig. 3 depicts a typical simulation run illustrating the effectiveness of the formulation. The manipulator is commanded along a specified end effector trajectory which is required to complete the task. The triangle represents a moving obstacle. The secondary goal terms generated from environmental information serve to reorient the manipulator in such a manner as to conform to the obstacle surface thereby retaining maximum use of the redundant degrees of freedom in avoiding the obstacle. Note that the workpiece itself is seen as an obstacle by the inboard links. Results obtained from a somewhat more imposing obstacle (fig. 4) illustrate the effectiveness of the multiple secondary goal formulation. The close quarters present with the end effector investigating the interior of the obstacle result in multiple worst-case goals. The appropriate blending of homogeneous solutions however, keeps the manipulator close to the center of the opening maintaining an optimum orientation without oscillations.

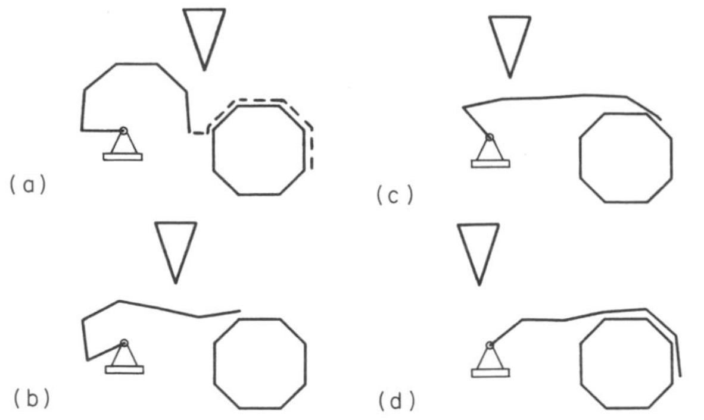

Fig. 3. Simulation results for redundant manipulator motion in the presence of moving triangular obstacle. End effector trajectory is shown in (a).

The three-dimensional simulation was evaluated for a nine degree-of-freedom manipulator design proposed by Waldron [1980]. A single frame from a simulation in which the manipulator was commanded to spray paint a car door illustrates the action of the homogeneous solution in preventing contact of inboard links with the car door while the end effector follows the required trajectory. (See Fig. 8.) The computation cycle time for the simulation, excluding graphics and secondary goal calculation, was 102 msec.

While originally planned for dynamically changing environments, for repetitive situations this technique can be used for an entirely different purpose. By using this technique in the simulation of a task and using a database for the obstacle description, the optimal joint

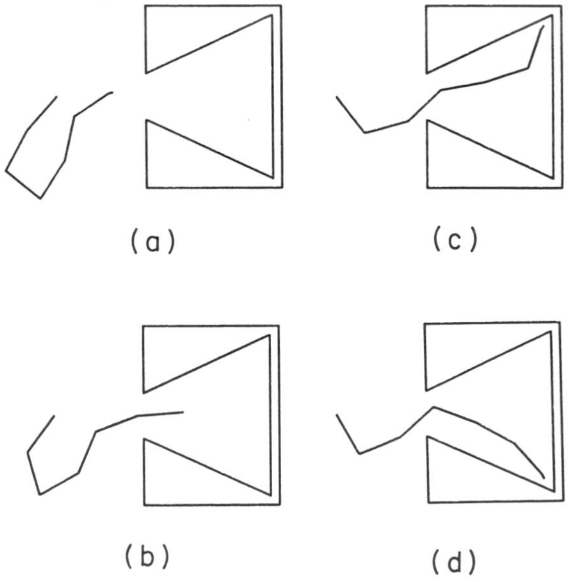

Fig. 4. Simulation results for a redundant manipulator working in a cavity with inboard links avoiding the throat.

angles can be saved and reused as the desired joint angle position in the homogeneous term [Yoshikawa, 1983]. This way an extremely detailed obstacle and arm description can be used without slowing the control. Probably only key-frame desired angles would be needed and spline interpolation could be used for intermediate points. This would be particularly advantageous when the arm's reach is long, or moving conveyers are employed, and one single desired joint state would not be sufficient.

DEXTERITY MEASURES

Since a kinematically redundant manipulator can operate its end effector in the same state using different joint configurations, a natural question is which joint angles constitute the most "dexterous" configuration. Clearly this question cannot be answered without more precisely defining dexterity and a number of researchers have suggested measures, for both redundant and nonredundant manipulators, which quantify this concept. This section will examine a number of these measures and examine their properties.

One of the oldest measures used to describe the "goodness" of a linear system is the determinant. For nonredundant manipulators the determinant has been used to evaluate wrist configurations [Paul and Stevenson, 1983]. For redundant manipulators Yoshikawa [1983] has defined manipulatibility as the square root of the determinant of $J_e J_e^T$ and used its gradient as the vector $\underline{z}$ in (6) for optimizing the dexterity of the configuration. While the determinant of a nonsquare matrix is not usually defined, the singular value decompositions (1) and (2) suggest a definition that is compatible with square matrices of full rank and with the use of the pseudoinverse for "inverting" problems.

$$\det (J_e) = \mu_1 \mu_2 \cdots \mu_r \tag{13}$$

Yoshikawa [1983] has shown a geometrical visualization of this measure. Alternatively this can be described as follows: The locus of all vectors in the row space of J_e with magnitude 0.5, when multipled by J_e, yields an ellipsoid. The volume of a box bounding this ellipsoid is the determinant of J_e.

While a determinant going to zero marks the presence of a singularity, the actual value of the determinant cannot be used as a practical measure of the degree of ill-conditioning [Forsythe and Moler, 1971]. Instead the matrix condition number has been recommended by numerical analysts [Isaacson and Keller, 1966], and has been used as a guide in formulating electromagnetic problems [Mittra and Klein, 1975]. The expression for the Euclidean condition number can be logically extended to nonsquare matrices used with the pseudoinverse as

$$\mathrm{Cond}_2 (J_e) = \mu_1/\mu_r \tag{14}$$

where μ_1 and μ_r are the largest and smallest singular values, respectively.

In robotics literature the condition number has been recommended as a dexterity measure for selecting the best working point for a nonredundant manipulator [Salisbury and Craig, 1982] because of the existence of quantitative accuracy estimates. While their description was in terms of forces and torques, in terms of velocities,

$$\|\delta\dot{x}\|/\|\dot{x}\| \leq \mathrm{Cond}\,(J_e)\ \|\delta\dot{\theta}\|/\|\dot{\theta}\| \tag{15}$$

Where $\delta\dot{x}$ and $\delta\dot{\theta}$ are errors in rectilinear and joint velocities, respectively, and double bars indicate the vector norm.

An intuitive notion of a dexterous configuration is one that has evenly distributed joint angles and has a "natural" appearance. Such a concept can be quantified by summing the squares of the deviation of the actuators displacments from their midpoint. This Joint Range Availability has been used by Liegeois [1977] for automatically reconfiguring redundant arms to minimize the possibility that a joint will reach a stop.

To compare these measures some numerical experiments were tried for the simple case of a planar manipulator with three links. First the properties of the homogeneous solution itself were examined. Relative joint angles shown in Figure 1 were used; the Jacobian can be found in [Klein and Huang, 1983]. Because there are three angles and one homogeneous solution, the homogeneous solution can be calculated in a straightforward way. Since the homogeneous solution is orthogonal to the row space of the Jacobian, the homogeneous solution is in the direction of the cross product of the two rows. Figure 5 shows the direction of the homogeneous solution as a function of the joint angles for equal length links.

Several properties of the homogeneous solution can be seen from Figure 5. First configuration space can be divided into two regions based on the arm's reach. Suppose that the length of each of the three links is ℓ. When the reach of the arm is between ℓ and 3ℓ from the base, the locus of possible joint configurations forms a closed loop in joint space. As the reach approaches 3ℓ, the loop arc length approaches zero which corresponds to the center of Figure 5 . For a reach between 0 and ℓ the locus of joint configurations forms a spiral which continues indefinitely in the θ_1 direction. In this region, unlike the first region, not all joint configurations for a given end effector position can be reached by travelling along the homogeneous velocity solution. For the end effector at the base itself ($\theta_2=\theta_3=2\pi/3$), this spiral becomes a vertical line and the configuration forms an equilateral triangle.

Next several dexterity measures were examined for different joint configurations for the same end effector position. To cover the possible joint configurations in a uniform way, the homogeneous solution was followed from a given starting point and the dexterity measures are plotted against the arc length of this path. The path itself is generated by a variation on Jacobian control. Suppose the end effector should be at (x_c, y_c) but due to approximation error from the previous cycle it is actually at (x_a, y_a). Let $\underline{h}$ be the cross-product of the two rows of J_e, normalized to unit length. Then Gaussian elimination can be applied to the following square system to get an increment in θ space to move in the direction of the homogeneous solution:

$$\begin{bmatrix} J_e \\ \hline \underline{h}^T \end{bmatrix} \Delta\underline{\theta} = \begin{bmatrix} x_c - x_a \\ y_c - y_a \\ \varepsilon \end{bmatrix} \qquad (16)$$

where ε is the desired arc length increment. While one could simply use $\varepsilon\,\underline{h}$ for $\Delta\underline{\theta}$, (16) corrects the drift in end effector motion due to finite $\Delta\underline{\theta}$ steps. The procedure starts with an initial set of angles placing the end effector at (x_c, y_c) and stops when either the path returns to the starting point or else any angle has changed by 2π.

Figures 6 and 7 show several dexterity measures plotted along the path of joint configurations comprising a constant end effector position. In both cases the total arc length has been scaled to a constant. The manipulator configuration itself is shown with the base on the bottom. For a second order system both the determinant of J_e and its condition number are determined from the two singular values, and so these too have been explicitly plotted. Including the Jacobian's output singular vectors permits plotting the ellipse of possible rectilinear velocity caused by constant magnitude joint velocities with pseudo-inverse Jacobian control. The norm of the joint angles is the measure of joint availability where zero is each angle's centerpoint and all angles' range are equal.

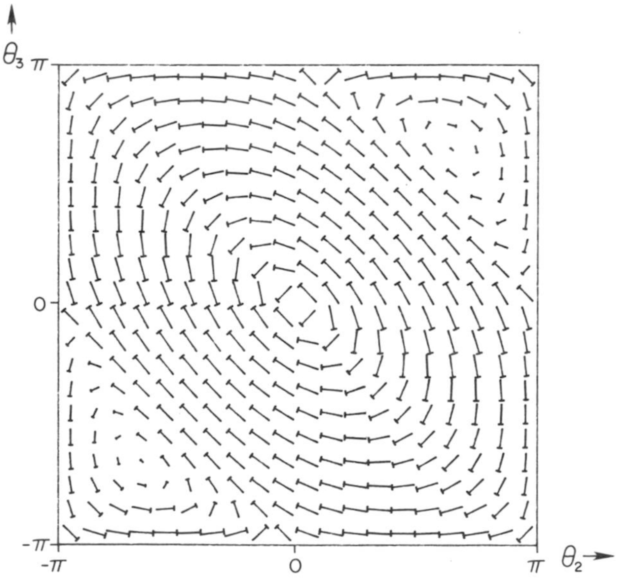

Fig. 5. Direction of the homogeneous solution for a planar, 3-link manipulator plotted against θ_2 and θ_3. Results are independent of θ_1. The length of the segments are constant and foreshortening indicates the component in the θ_1 direction. The bar on the segment marks the larger θ_1-valued end.

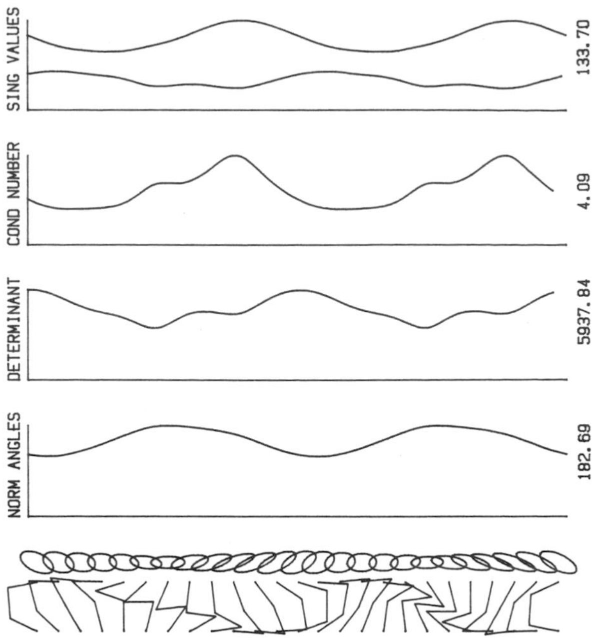

Fig. 6. Dexterity measures plotted along arc length of path of possible configurations in joint space for three, equal-length, links. Operating point is 1.6 times the link length from the base.

Figure 6 represents a reach further from the base than a link length. Each of the measures appears to go through two periods. The second period can be seen from the configurations as being due to each angle being reversed. The two singular values are close, relatively slowly changing, but never cross. As a consequence the condition number, their ratio, is moderate but never down to the optimal value of one and the determinant, their product, is slowly varying.

Figure 7 shows radically different behavior since some configurations are close to a singularity. For this case, the singular values appear to cross and at these points the ellipse becomes a circle and the condition number reaches its optimal value, one. The configuration of minimum joint angles is close to the configuration of lowest condition number but slightly displaced from the highest determinant. Near the singularities the ellipse is collapsed and the minor axis shows the direction for which motion is difficult. Comparing the best configuration of each figure, one can see that the condition number is better for the one with the closer reach.

Comparison of these different measures suggests a new measure. Since in this problem the deter-

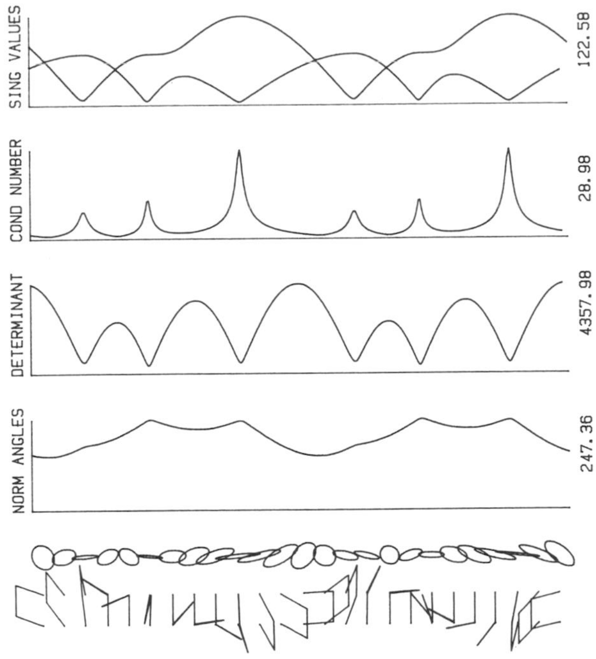

Fig. 7. Dexterity measures for the same manipulator as in Fig. 6, but operating at 1.01 times the link length from the base.

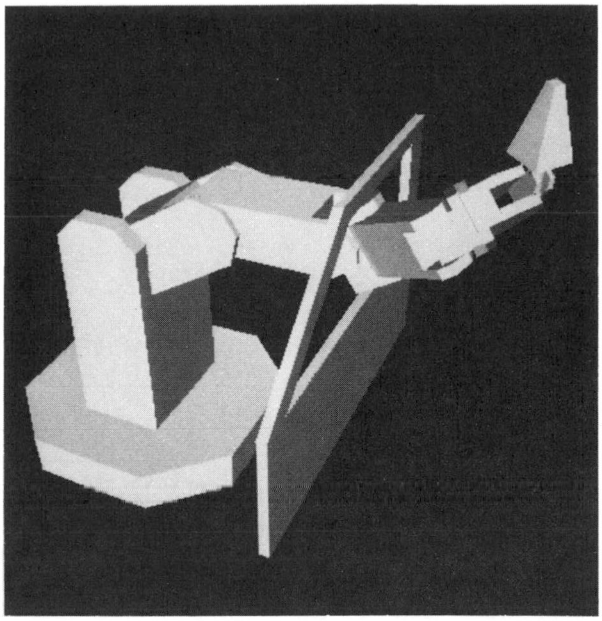

Fig. 8. Photo of simulation of 3-D redundant manipulator operating through the door of an automobile.

minant and the condition number differ only by factors of the minimum singular value, that quantity itself can be considered a useful measure. With pseudoinverse control it shows the minimum responsiveness in rectilinear space due to a unit change in joint space, or inversely, since its reciprocal is the norm of J_e^+, it indicates the maximum joint velocity needed for a unit rectilinear velocity.

The size of a manipulator affects the dexterity measures differently. If a manipulator is doubled in size, the condition number is unchanged since it represents relative sensitivity. The minimum singular value will double which properly indicates that the same joint velocity causes a rectilinear velocity twice as large. However, for the 2-D use, the determinant will be four times larger. This seems to indicate that some type of normalization for scale and dimension is needed before the value of the determinant can be used as an absolute, rather than relative, guide.

For more realistic 3-D cases it is clear that the measures may behave differently. A key difference is that intermediate values of the singular values are included in the determinant but not in the condition number. While it does not seem as if they should be completely ignored, typically it is the minimum singular value which determines singularities. As a basis for using (6) for optimizing dexterity, joint norms may be the only measure whose gradient can be calculated in real time. Simulation experiments with these measures for 3-D are currently underway.

CONCLUSIONS

When using kinematically redundant manipulators the homogeneous solution can be used to optimize performance criteria. One such criterion is obstacle avoidance which can be best described in Cartesion coordinates rather than in joint angles.

The real-time demands of obstacle avoidance in practical applications, particularly in dynamic environments, demands a computationally efficient algorithm. The above formulation, with a cycle time of 102 msec. on a timed-shared computer for a 9 link, 3-D manipulator, clearly demonstrates the potential for a viable system in a physical realization.

A second use of homogeneous velocity solutions is to move toward configurations of optimal dexterity. Several previously used measures have been compared. The minimum singular value is suggested as a new measure.

ACKNOWLEDGEMENT

This work was supported by the National Science Foundation through Grant ECS-8121519. Work reported here has included thesis results by A. Maciejewski and B. Blaho, whose help in preparing this paper is gratefully acknowledged.

REFERENCES

Brooks, R. A., 1983, Solving the Find-Path Problem by Good Representation of Free Space, IEEE Transactions on Systems, Man and Cybernetics, Vol. SMC-13(2):190-197.

Espiau, B. and Andre, A., 1984, June 26-29, "Sensory-Based Control for Robots and Teleoperators," 5th Romansy Symposium, Udine, Italy.

Forsythe, G. and C. B. Moler, 1967, Computer Solution of Linear Algebraic Systems, Englewood Cliffs, Prentice-Hall.

Greville, T. N. E., 1960, "Some Applications of the Pseudoinverse of a Matrix," SIAM Review, Vol. 2(1):15-22.

Isaacson, E. and Keller, H. B., 1966, Analysis of Numerical Methods, New York, Wiley.

Khatib, O. and Le Maitre, J.F., 1978, Sept. 12-15, "Dynamic Control of Manipulators Operating in a Complex Environment," 3rd Symposium on Theory and Practice of Robots and Manipulators, Udine, Italy.

Klein, C. A. and Huang, C. H., 1983, "Review of Pseudoinverse Control for Use with Kinematically Redundant Manipulators," IEEE Transactions on Systems, Man, and Cybernetics, Vol. SMC-13(2):245-250.

Liegeois, A., 1977, "Automatic Supervisory Control of the Configuration and Behavior of Multibody Mechanisms," IEEE Transactions on Systems, Man, and Cybernetics, Vol. SMC-7(12):868-871.

Loeff, L. A. and Soni, A. H., 1975, "An Algorithm for Computer Guidance of a Manipulator in Between Obstacles," Journal of Engineering for Industry, Vol. 97(3), Series B:836-842.

Lozano-Perez, T., 1981, "Automatic Planning of Manipulator Transfer Movements," IEEE Transactions on Systems, Man, and Cybernetics, Vol. SMC-11(10):681-698.

Maciejewski, A. A., 1984, "Obstacle Avoidance for Kinematically Redundant Manipulatiors," M.S. thesis, The Ohio State University, Department of Electrical Engineering.

Mittra, R. and Klein, C. A. 1975. "Stability and Convergence of Moment Method Solutions." Numerical and Asymptotic Techniques in Electromagnetics, R. Mittra ed., New York, Springer-Verlag, pp. 129-163.

Noble, B., 1975, "Methods for Computing the Moore-Penrose Generalized Inverse, and Related Matters,", Generalized Inverses and Applications, M. Z. Nashed ed., New York, Academic Press, pp. 245-301.

Paul, R., 1979, "Manipulator Cartesian Path Control," IEEE Transactions on Systems, Man, and Cybernetics, Vol. SMC-9(11):702-711.

Paul, R. P. and Stevenson, C. N., 1983, "Kinematics of Robot Wrists," The International Journal of Robotics Research, Vol. 2(1):31-38.

Rao, C. R., and Mitra, S. K., 1971, Generalized Inverse of Matrices and its Applications, New York, Wiley.

Salisbury, J. K. and Craig, J. J. 1982, "Articulated Hands: Force Control and Kinematic Issues," The International Journal of Robotics Research, Vol. 1(1):4-17.

Trevelyan, J. P., Kovesi, P. D. and Ong, M. C. H., 1983, Aug. 28-Sept. 2, "Motion Control for a Sheep Shearing Robot," International Symposium of Robotics Research, Bretton Woods, N.H.

Udupa, S., 1977, Aug 22-28, "Collision Detection and Avoidance in Computer Controlled Manipulators," 5th International Joint Conference on Artificial Intelligence, Massachusetts Institute of Technology, Cambridge, MA ., pp. 737-748.

Waldron, K. J., 1980, private communications.

Waldron, K. J., 1981, "Geometrically Based Manipulator Rate Control Algorithms," Seventh-Applied Mechanics Conference, Kansas City, MO.

Whitney, D. E., 1969, "Resolved Motion Rate Control of Manipulators and Human Prostheses," IEEE Transactions on Man-Machine Systems, Vol. MMS-10(2):47-53.

Whitney, D. E., 1972, "The Mathematics of Coordinated Control of Prostheses and Manipulators," Journal of Dynamic Systems, Measurement, and Control, Transactions ASME, Vol. 94, Series G:303-309.

Yoshikawa, T., 1983, Aug. 28-Sept. 2, "Analysis and Control of Robot Manipulators with Redundancy," International Symposium of Robotics Research, Bretton Woods, N.H..

OPTIMUM KINEMATIC DESIGN FOR A SEVEN DEGREE OF FREEDOM MANIPULATOR

John M. Hollerbach

MIT Artificial Intelligence Laboratory
545 Technology Square
Cambridge, MA 02139 USA

While today's general purpose manipulators contain six degrees of freedom, effective reduction in degrees of freedom occurs from singularity regions and from workspace obstacles. It is argued that the future general purpose manipulators will contain seven degrees of freedom, and that one particular kinematic design is superior to other possible 7 degree of freedom kinematic designs. Considerations of elimination of singularities, mechanical realizability, kinematic simplicity, and workspace shape are taken into account in arriving at this design.

Current robot manipulators invariably are kinematically nonredundant, that is, they have at most the 6 degrees of freedom necessary for general positioning. The nonredundancy is associated with two difficulties that are not readily overcome: singularities and obstructed workspaces. Singularities are manipulator configurations where the degrees of freedom of the manipulator are reduced below 6, and arise from certain kinematic alignments of rotary joint axes. For example, the rotary manipulator without offsets in Fig. 1 (henceforth referred to as the 6R manipulator after the notation of [Pieper, 1968]) has three kinds of singularities [Featherstone, 1982], designated here as shoulder, elbow, and wrist singularities. For the shoulder singularity (Fig. 1A), the wrist is above the shoulder, making movements of the wrist perpendicular to the forearm–upper arm plane impossible. The elbow singularity (Fig. 1B) prevents radial movement of the wrist, which lies at the outer boundary of the workspace. The wrist singularity (Fig. 1C) aligns the roll axes of the forearm and hand, reducing by one the degrees of freedom.

Singularities are manifested in inverse kinematic problems where it is desired to find joint velocities that correspond to desired hand velocities. Joint velocities $\dot{\underline{\theta}}$ and hand velocities $\dot{\mathbf{x}}$ are related by the Jacobian matrix $\mathbf{J}$:

$$\dot{\mathbf{x}} = \mathbf{J}\dot{\underline{\theta}}$$

where the 6-dimensional hand velocity $\dot{\mathbf{x}} = (\dot{\mathbf{p}}\ \underline{\omega})$ consists of a linear velocity vector $\dot{\mathbf{p}}$ of some hand reference point and an angular velocity vector $\underline{\omega}$, and where for an n degree of freedom manipulator $\dot{\underline{\theta}} = (\dot{\theta}_1, \ldots, \dot{\theta}_n)$. The Jacobian J is square for a 6 degree of freedom arm, but becomes noninvertible at a kinematic singularity. Desired Cartesian motions at the singular configuration become impossible to realize, manifested mathematically by the joint velocities evidently going to infinity. Near singularities the movements are also ill-conditioned, in the sense that while infinite joint velocities do not result, still very large joint velocities are required. Thus there are forbidden regions represented by cones of ill-conditioned joint angles centered at the singular joint values [Paul and Stevenson, 1983]. As these cones are swept through configuration space by the more proximal joints, a substantial fraction of the workspace is lost. For this reason Paul and Stevenson characterize a kinematic 6 degree of freedom manipulator as functionally a 5 degree of freedom manipulator.

Singularity problems for 6 degree of freedom manipulators have long been recognized, and two main approaches have evolved to deal with them. One approach is to avoid singularities and associated ill-conditioned regions entirely by planning trajectories that stay away from them. Unfortunately it is not always possible to keep away from singularity points, and even if it were, a considerable burden is placed on the trajectory planner given the difficulty of relating the hand Cartesian space and joint space [Lozano-Perez, 1982]. The second approach is to violate the Cartesian motion specification, in effect achieving some compromise between desired hand motion and possible joint motion. Near singularities, for example, one can switch from Cartesian trajectories to joint-interpolated motion [Taylor, 1979]. Another possibility is to use generalized inverses to compromise selectively one of the Cartesian velocity components [Hanafusa, Yoshikawa, and Nakamura, 1981; Yoshikawa, 1983].

A second difficulty with nonredundant arms is workspace obstacles. Reaching around objects and through holes restricts the range of motion of joints and may effectively reduce the degrees of freedom. Whole regions of the workspace may become unreachable if the manipulator

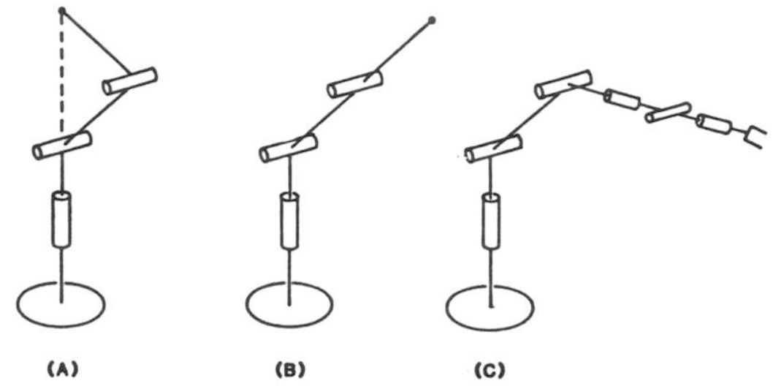

Figure 1. Singularities arising from a 6 degree of freedom rotary manipulator. (A) The wrist lies along the first shoulder rotary axis in the shoulder singularity. (B) The elbow is straight in the elbow singularity. (C) The wrist is straight in the wrist singularity.

degrees of freedom do not mesh with the task constraints. For example, the major motions of the upper arm and forearm for the 6R manipulator take place in a vertical plane. If an object obstructs primarily vertical plane movement, then it would not be possible for the manipulator to work behind the object.

The two difficulties of singularities and obstructed workspaces can be considerably ameliorated by adding degrees of freedom to a nonredundant manipulator. Internal singularities, which are inside the workspace boundary as for the shoulder and wrist singularities, could be virtually eliminated. Following Paul's dictum, a kinematic 7 degree of freedom manipulator would then function as a 6 degree of freedom manipulator, and hence would seldom manifest singularities.

Secondly, obstructions would be handled more easily. For example, the 7 degree of freedom manipulator with a spherical shoulder joint in Fig. 2, which is labeled manipulator 1 to distinguish it from alternative redundant designs considered later, has a self-motion describable by the rotation of the elbow point about a line joining the shoulder to wrist (Fig. 3). By a self-motion is meant an internal movement of the linkage that does not move the endpoint. For the 7 degree of freedom manipulator there is one degree of freedom in the self-motion, since six are constrained by the hand position; note that the self-motion requires movement in all the joints, though the relative joint motions are coupled. During the self-motion,

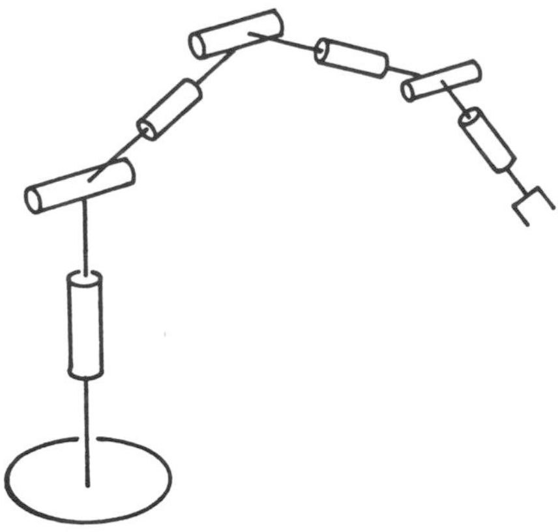

Figure 2. Manipulator 1: a 7 degree of freedom arm with a spherical shoulder joint, created by adding a roll motion in the upper arm link of the 6R manipulator.

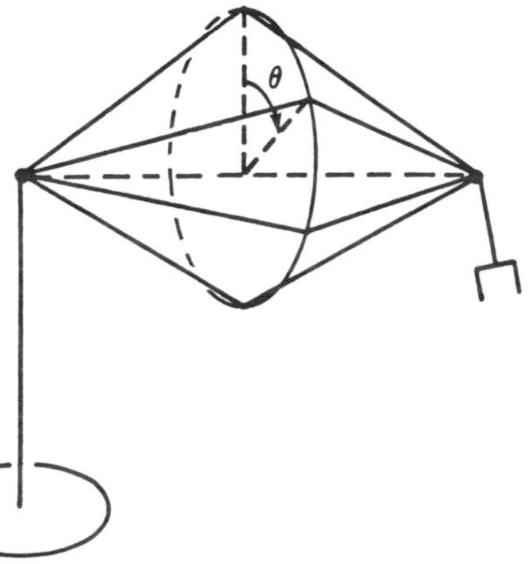

Figure 3. The self-motion of manipulator 1 corresponds to rotation of the elbow point about a line joining the shoulder to wrist. The angle θ between a normal line from the elbow to the shoulder-wrist line and this normal line when the elbow is straight up succinctly describes the redundancy.

the upper arm/forearm plane of motion is rotated about the shoulder/wrist line; thus the major plane of motion can be selected to avoid for example a predominantly vertical obstruction.

Lastly, as an added bonus the kinematic redundancy would allow the minimization of torque loading at a weak joint. Suppose the manipulator has to absorb a force directed along the hand axis (Fig. 4A). Manipulator wrists are notoriously weak, and the external force could easily overcome the wrist motors. With a redundant arm, however, the forearm could be positioned through a self-motion so as to reduce the torque at the weakest wrist motor (Fig. 4B). The external force would be more completely absorbed by the more powerful proximal joints.

Kinematic Criteria for Redundant Arms

In designing geometries for a redundant manipulator, several criteria were set forth.

(i) Elimination of internal singularities. It is taken here as an absolute prerequisite that the extra degrees of freedom eliminate the internal singularities at the shoulder and wrist. The external singularity at the elbow is of course inevitable because there is always an outer boundary of the workspace corresponding to maximum reach. If multiple degeneracies arise, it should be possible to exercise a self-motion of the redundant arm to find a configuration that avoids a singularity. In any case the redundancy should allow a planner to pass a trajectory through any point in the internal workspace without precondition.

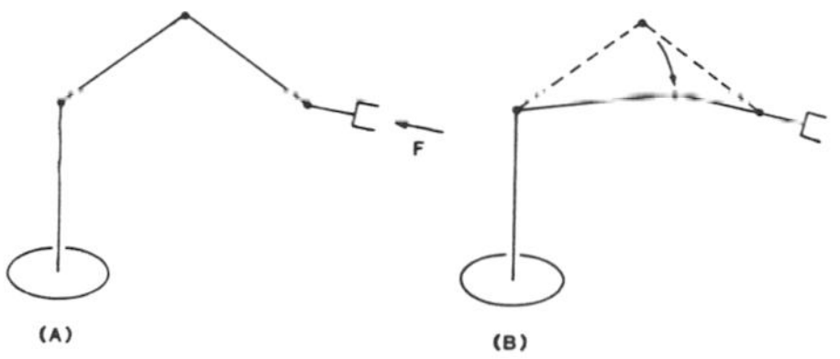

Figure 4. Torque loading at the wrist joint due to an external force along the hand can be minimized by selecting a self-motion that brings the forearm into an optimal alignment with the wrist.

(ii) Optimization of workspace. The extra joints should enhance as much as possible the ability to avoid obstacles and work in cluttered environments.

(iii) Kinematic simplicity. The ease of solving the kinematic equations aids path planning.

(iv) Mechanical constructability. The extra joint should lead to a facile mechanical design.

One of the most important geometries for 6 degree of freedom robot arms is the 6R manipulator of Fig. 1, which Roth [1980] argued as having a superior workspace relative to other geometries. The selection of a redundant arm is particularized here to the following design problem:

- *How is a rotary joint best added to the 6R manipulator to yield a 7 degree of freedom arm?*

The design goal is a 7 degree of freedom arm rather than an arm with 8 or more degrees of freedom, because as will be seen the 4 criteria above can be adequately matched by an arm with only one extra degree of freedom. As suggested above, multiple degeneracies lead to internal singularities in the optimum 7 degree of freedom arm that can be avoided, but adding more joints will never solve this problem (Appendix I). Hence the added complexity of even more degrees of freedom is not warranted.

The addition of a sliding joint rather than a rotary joint is ruled out because a sliding joint cannot eliminate the wrist singularity. Suppose the forearm is vertical, the wrist is straight, and θ_4 has been rotated so that $\mathbf{z}_4$ is parallel to $\mathbf{z}_1$ and $\mathbf{z}_2$ (Fig. 5). Then the $\mathbf{z}_3/\mathbf{z}_4$ plane is parallel to the $\mathbf{z}_0/\mathbf{z}_1$ plane, and since $\mathbf{z}_3$ and $\mathbf{z}_5$ are colinear all joint axes lie in the same plane. Thus this configuration represents a rotational singularity, because no component of hand angular velocity can lie normal to this plane. Adding a sliding joint can only change the hand linear velocity, not the hand angular velocity. Thus a sliding joint is incapable of eliminating this rotational singularity.

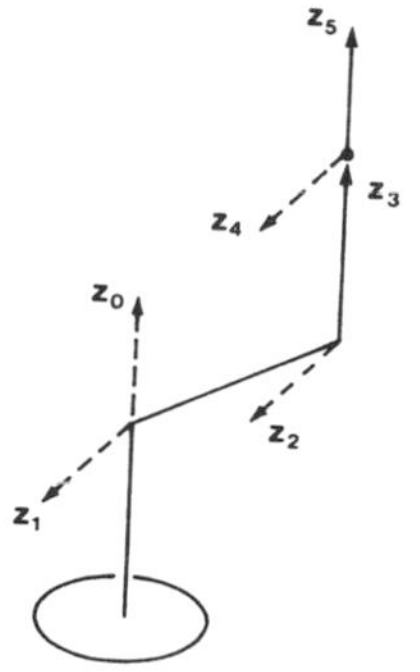

Figure 5. When θ_1 is set to 0, axes $\mathbf{x}_1$ and $\mathbf{x}_2$ are parallel and normal to the $\mathbf{z}_0/\mathbf{z}_1$ plane. Since $\mathbf{z}_2$ is also perpendicular to $\mathbf{x}_2$, it is also parallel to the $\mathbf{z}_0/\mathbf{z}_1$ plane.

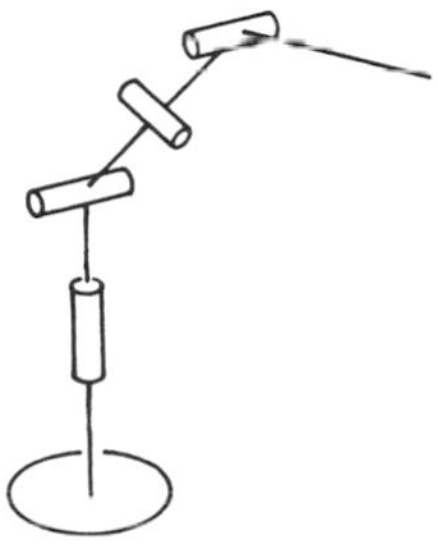

Figure 6. Creating a new link by adding a yaw motion within the upper arm link leads to a kinematically complex manipulator.

For generating possible arm geometries, the added joint is only allowed to increase the degrees of freedom at the shoulder, wrist, or elbow joint. Geometries that

Joint i	a_i	s_i	α_i
1	0	s_1	$\pi/2$
2	0	0	$\pi/2$
3	0	s_3	$-\pi/2$
4	0	0	$\pi/2$
5	0	s_5	$-\pi/2$
6	0	0	$\pi/2$
7	0	0	0

Table 1. Denavit-Hartenberg parameters for manipulator 1.

give rise to a totally new link of non-zero length and an associated spatially distinct joint, such as adding a yaw motion within the upper arm link (Fig. 6), are ruled out because of kinematic complexity [Pieper, 1968]. Three distinct possibilities that arise are analyzed below.

Manipulator 1: Spherical Shoulder Joint

By adding a roll motion in the upper arm link (Fig. 2), the 6R arm is given a spherical shoulder joint that makes it kinematically equivalent to the human arm (not counting shoulder movement, which adds several more degrees of freedom). An example of this manipulator appeared in [Takase, Inoue, and Sato, 1974]. The Denavit-Hartenberg parameters are listed in Table 1. Manipulator 1 has a regular kinematic structure of a roll axis on a link alternating with a pitch axis located at a joint; mechanically, this is an ideal configuration because consecutive motors are separated. The self-motions of this arm were analyzed in Fig. 3 and were shown to facilitate obstacle avoidance by selecting different planes of major motion. The criterion for kinematic simplicity is satisfied because the inverse kinematics is quite easily solved using wrist partitioning algorithms (Appendix II).

Both the shoulder and wrist singularities as they arise from single degeneracies are eliminated. If the wrist is above the shoulder, it is now possible to move the wrist perpendicular to the major plane of motion. If the wrist is straight, the loss of rotary motion direction is compensated by the new joint. A double degeneracy can arise when the wrist is straight and the upper arm is vertical (Fig. 7), leading to a singularity. By rotating the elbow about the shoulder-wrist line, a configuration can be found where the upper arm roll axis and the forearm roll axis are made non-parallel with the base and hand roll axes respectively. This is the only situation where a trajectory planner must take special steps; the Cartesian point remains in the usable portion of the workspace.

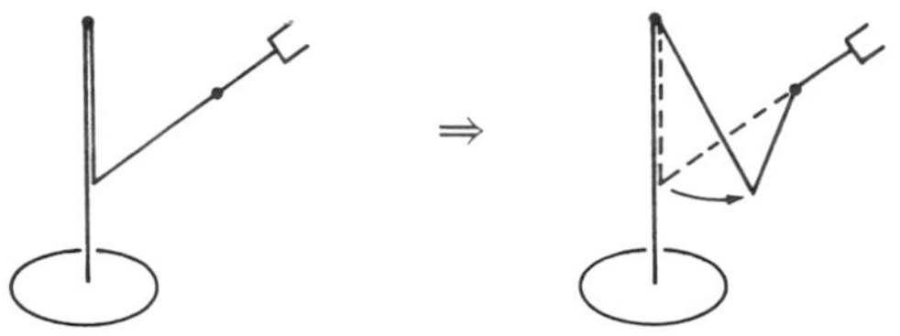

Figure 7. A double degeneracy for manipulator 1 arises when the wrist is straight and the upper arm is vertical. A self-motion brings the arm out of both degeneracies without moving the endpoint.

Manipulator 2: Two Degree of Freedom Elbow

In manipulator 1 a degree of freedom was added to the shoulder; for manipulator 2 a degree of freedom is added to the elbow. Essentially the only one way to add this degree of freedom without either duplicating the manipulator 1 kinematics or yielding a nonrational design is adding a yaw motion (Fig. 8); the Denavit-Hartenberg parameters are given in Table 2. First, it is a matter of viewpoint whether the shoulder in manipulator 1 is spherical or the elbow has two degrees of freedom, since the upper arm

Joint i	a_i	s_i	α_i
1	0	s_1	$\pi/2$
2	a_2	0	0
3	0	0	$-\pi/2$
4	0	0	$\pi/2$
5	0	s_5	$-\pi/2$
6	0	0	$\pi/2$
7	0	0	0

Table 2. Denavit-Hartenberg parameters for manipulator 2.

roll motion intersects the elbow as well; thus adding this roll motion does not give a distinct geometry. Second, adding a roll motion to the forearm duplicates the roll motion that is already there. This leaves a yaw motion acting after the pitch motion (the reverse is kinematically equivalent); a skew angle between these two rotary axes other than 90° is not considered a rational design.

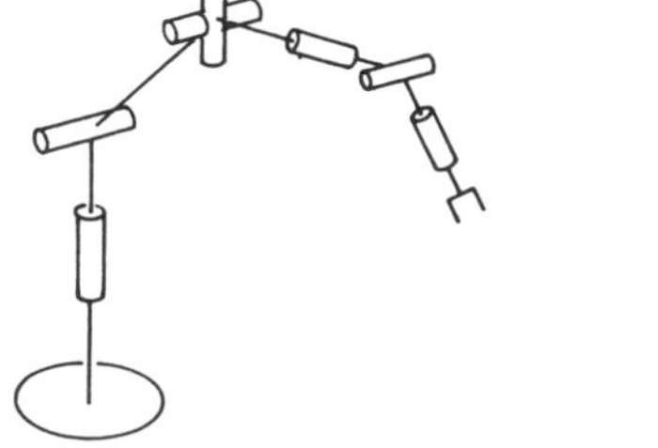

Figure 8. Manipulator 2: a two degree of freedom elbow joint created by adding a yaw motion to the elbow after the pitch motion.

Manipulator 2 has the same self-motion as manipulator 1, so the workspace is equivalent, modulo the shape of the links which are swept differently. The inverse kinematics are as readily solved using a similar algorithm (Appendix III). Both the wrist and shoulder singularities are eliminated, except for the situation where the pitch elbow angle is 0° and the yaw angle is 90° (Fig. 9). If the wrist is then also straight, a double degeneracy results since 3 roll motions coincide. This configuration is avoidable, however, because a self-motion can be used to unstraighten the wrist and pitch the elbow.

Mechanically, this type of joint is not a desirable design. The motors interfere with each other, and a rather bulky joint would result even with offsets. Tendon actuation might improve the joint compactness, but 2 degree of freedom tendon actuated joints have proven difficult to design. The motor mass is also more distal than in manipulator 1. The advantage of alternate motor placements in links and joints is apparent when examining the manipulator 2 design.

Manipulator 3: Four Degree of Freedom Wrist

The last joint in the 6R arm whose degrees of freedom can be increased is the wrist, from 3 to 4. This is a common solution to the gimble lock problem for gyroscopes. Again,

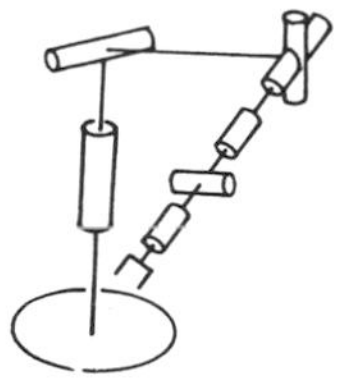

Figure 9. A double degeneracy arises for manipulator 2 when the elbow is at right angles due to a zero pitch angle and a 90 degree yaw angle coupled with a straight wrist. A self-motion can avoid this singularity.

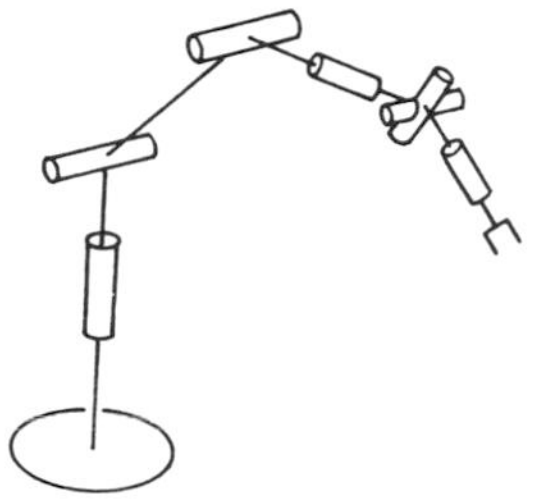

Figure 10. Manipulator 3: a yaw motion is added to the wrist after the pitch motion.

the only kinematically distinct way of increasing the wrist degrees of freedom is to add a yaw motion (Fig. 10); the Denavit-Hartenberg parameters are given in Table 3. While the wrist singularity is eliminated, the shoulder singularity remains. The self-motion moves no links, but merely changes the 4 wrist motor angles. Hence the workspace is not significantly improved; in general, a more proximal joint placement is required to improve workspace since greater volumes are swept out in configuration space. Mechanically this design suffers from the same problems as manipulator 2. The motor mass is moved even farther towards the distal end, significantly increasing the loading at the more proximal joints.

Conclusion

Joint i	a_i	s_i	α_i
1	0	s_1	$\pi/2$
2	a_2	0	0
3	0	0	$-\pi/2$
4	0	s_4	$\pi/2$
5	0	0	$-\pi/2$
6	0	0	$-\pi/2$
7	0	0	0

Table 3. Denavit-Hartenberg parameters for manipulator 3.

On balance manipulator 1 best satisfies the 4 criteria listed initially. Manipulator 2 suffers on the basis of mechanical design. Moreover, it could be argued that the double degeneracy of manipulator 2 is worse than the double degeneracy of manipulator 1, since it is more desirable to have bent elbows than upper arms straight up or down. Manipulator 3 must be rejected because it does not eliminate the shoulder singularity and it suffers from mechanical design difficulties.

Acknowledgments

This research was supported by the AFWAL/XRPM Defense Small Business Innovation Research Program under grant F33615-83-C-5115, awarded to Scientific Systems Inc., and in part by the Defense Advanced Research Projects Agency under Office of Naval Reserach contract N00014-80-C-0505, awarded to the MIT Artificial Intelligence Laboratory. The author wishes to acknowledge the many useful discussions concerning redundant arms with Roger Brockett and John Baillieul.

Appendix I: Persistence of Internal Singularities

It is proven in this appendix that for any rotary manipulator with arbitrary Denavit-Hartenberg [1955] parameters and numbers of joints, there will always exist multiple degeneracies that lead to internal singularities[1]. Thus a trajectory planner will always face avoiding singular configurations, and it is useless to add extra degrees of freedom in an attempt to completely eliminate internal singularities.

To proceed with the proof, the Denavit-Hartenberg link labeling is summarized first. Rotation axis $\mathbf{z}_{i-1}$ is located at joint i, which connects links $i-1$ and i;

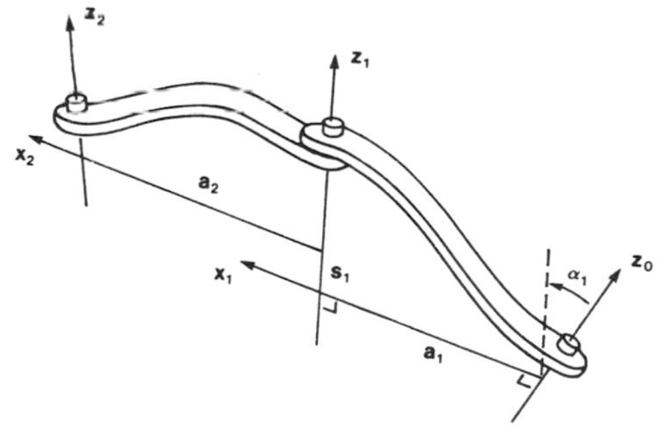

Figure 11. Joint angle θ_1 is set to zero, making $\mathbf{x}_2$ parallel to $\mathbf{x}_1$ and $\mathbf{z}_2$ parallel to the $\mathbf{z}_0/\mathbf{z}_1$ plane.

the angle at joint i is θ_i. The common normal between axes $\mathbf{z}_{i-1}$ and $\mathbf{z}_i$ defines $\mathbf{x}_i$, and the internal coordinate system for link i is located at the intersection of $\mathbf{z}_i$ and $\mathbf{x}_i$. Neighboring coordinate systems are related by three parameters:

a_i is the distance between $\mathbf{z}_{i-1}$ and $\mathbf{z}_i$ measured along $\mathbf{x}_i$,

s_i is the distance between $\mathbf{x}_{i-1}$ and $\mathbf{x}_i$ measured along $\mathbf{z}_{i-1}$, and

α_i is the angle between $\mathbf{z}_{i-1}$ and $\mathbf{z}_i$ measured in a righthand sense about $\mathbf{x}_i$.

The rotation matrix $\mathbf{A}_i$ which transforms from link i coordinates to link $i-1$ coordinates is given by:

$$\mathbf{A}_i = \begin{bmatrix} \cos\theta_i & -\sin\theta_i\cos\alpha_i & \sin\theta_i\sin\alpha_i \\ \sin\theta_i & \cos\theta_i\cos\alpha_i & -\cos\theta_i\sin\alpha_i \\ 0 & \sin\alpha_i & \cos\alpha_i \end{bmatrix}$$

The basis for demonstrating the persistence of singularities is provided by the following lemma.

Lemma: For any arbitrary n-joint manipulator, it is possible to orient all joint axes parallel to the same plane.

Proof: Assume $\mathbf{z}_0$ and $\mathbf{z}_1$ are not colinear (otherwise find the first $\mathbf{z}_i$ not colinear with $\mathbf{z}_0$). Note that $\mathbf{x}_1$ is normal to the plane defined by $\mathbf{z}_0/\mathbf{z}_1$. All subsequent $\mathbf{z}_i$, $i > 1$, can be placed in the $\mathbf{z}_0/\mathbf{z}_1$ plane by the following induction argument.

- Set θ_2 to 0 or π. Then $\mathbf{x}_2$ is parallel to $\mathbf{x}_1$, hence is normal to the $\mathbf{z}_0/\mathbf{z}_1$ plane. Since $\mathbf{z}_2$ is perpendicular to $\mathbf{x}_2$, then $\mathbf{z}_2$ is parallel to the $\mathbf{z}_0/\mathbf{z}_1$ plane (Fig. 11).
- Suppose all joint angles from θ_2 to θ_{i-1} have been set to 0 or π. If θ_i is set to 0 or π, then $\mathbf{x}_i$ is made parallel to $\mathbf{x}_{i-1}$ and hence by induction is normal to the $\mathbf{z}_0/\mathbf{z}_1$ plane. Hence $\mathbf{z}_i$ is parallel to the $\mathbf{z}_0/\mathbf{z}_1$ plane.

By induction, all joint axes can be made parallel to the same plane.

Definition: A rotational singularity is an arm configuration in which an arbitrary angular velocity of the hand cannot be specified.

From the Denavit-Hartenberg notation, the angular velocity $\underline{\omega}$ of the hand is given by:

$$\underline{\omega} = \sum_{i=1}^{n} \mathbf{z}_{i-1}\dot{\theta}_i$$

Theorem: For given orientations of the first two joint axes, there are 2^{n-2} rotational singularities.

Proof: By the Lemma, for each joint angle θ_i beyond the second, there are two angles 0 and π that align $\mathbf{z}_i$ with the $\mathbf{z}_0/\mathbf{z}_1$ plane. Thus for an n-joint manipulator, there are 2^{n-2} configurations in which all joint axes lie parallel to the same plane. Each such configuration leads to a rotational singularity since there can be no component of hand angular velocity normal to the $\mathbf{z}_0/\mathbf{z}_1$ plane.

Corollary: There are infinitely many internal rotational singularities.

Proof: Each value of θ_1 changes $\mathbf{z}_i$, hence the 2^{n-2} rotational singularities define a swept volume. Some of these singularities will be internal, corresponding to one or the other choice of 0 or π for each θ_i.

Appendix II: Inverse Kinematics for Manipulator 1

The solution of inverse kinematics for position is readily accomplished by modifying the wrist partitioning algorithm outlined in [Featherstone, 1983; Hollerbach and Sahar, 1983]. An alternative solution using a quadratic optimization rather than a specification of the self-motion is presented in [Benati, Morasso, and Tagliasco, 1982].

Suppose the redundancy is resolved by specification of the forearm-upper arm plane rotation θ about the shoulder/wrist line (Fig. 3).

Step 1: Find the wrist position. Given the position $\mathbf{p}$ of the hand reference point and the orientation matrix $\mathbf{R}$

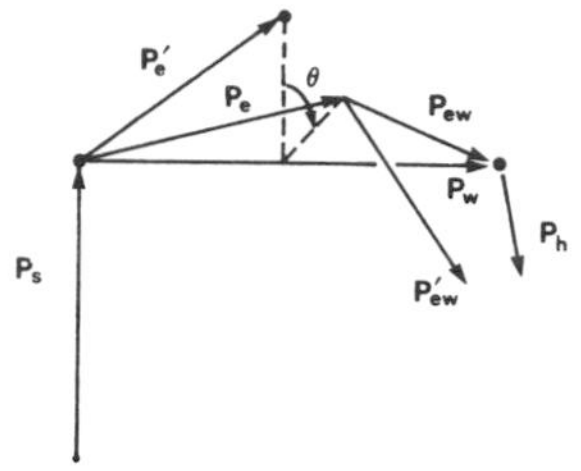

Figure 12. Inverse kinematic solution for Manipulator 1: Relative positions of the shoulder ($\mathbf{p}_s$), elbow ($\mathbf{p}_e$, with respect to the shoulder), wrist ($\mathbf{p}_w$, w.r.t. the shoulder, and $\mathbf{p}_{ew}$, w.r.t. the elbow), and hand ($\mathbf{p}_h$, w.r.t. the wrist). ($'$) denotes a quantity refered to $\theta = 0$.

of the hand, the wrist position $\mathbf{p}_w$ relative to the shoulder point is (Fig. 12):

$$\mathbf{p}_w = \mathbf{p} - \mathbf{R}\,^7\mathbf{p}_h - \mathbf{p}_s$$

where $^7\mathbf{p}_h$ is a vector from the wrist to the hand reference point specified in link 7 coordinates and $\mathbf{p}_s$ is a vector from the base to the shoulder.

Step 2a: Find the first 4 joint angles that would result if $\theta = 0$. This step is the same as in the 6R case, except with the new upper arm roll motion $\theta_3 = 0$. The results are modified directly from [Hollerbach and Sahar, 1983]:

$$\theta_1' = \tan^{-1}\left(\frac{p_{wy}}{p_{wx}}\right)$$

$$\sin\theta_4 = \frac{s_3^2 + s_5^2 - p_w^2}{2s_3s_5}$$

where the ($'$) denotes a quantity referred to $\theta = 0$. Note that the elbow angle θ_4 is independent of θ. Having found θ_1', $\mathbf{p}_w$ can now be expressed in terms of link 1 coordinates, $^1\mathbf{p}_w'$. The first six rotational transformations have the form:

$$\mathbf{A}_i = \begin{bmatrix} \cos\theta_i & 0 & \sin\theta_i \\ \sin\theta_i & 0 & -\cos\theta_i \\ 0 & 1 & 0 \end{bmatrix}$$

The shoulder pitch angle θ_2' is then found from ${}^1\mathbf{p}_w' = \mathbf{A}_1'^T \mathbf{p}_w$:

$$\sin\theta_2' = \frac{{}^1p_{wy}'(s_3 - s_5 \sin\theta_4) - {}^1p_{wx}' s_5 \cos\theta_4}{s_3^2 + s_5^2 - 2s_3 s_5 \sin\theta_4}$$

$$\cos\theta_2' = \frac{{}^1p_{wx}' + s_5 \cos\theta_4 \sin\theta_2'}{s_3 - s_5 \sin\theta_4}$$

$$\theta_2' = \tan^{-1}\left(\frac{\sin\theta_2'}{\cos\theta_2'}\right)$$

Step 2b: Find the elbow position by rotating the elbow point about $\mathbf{p}_w$ *by the angle* θ. The elbow position corresponding to $\theta = 0$ is given by:

$$\mathbf{p}_e' = \mathbf{A}_1'\mathbf{A}_2' \begin{bmatrix} 0 \\ 0 \\ 1 \end{bmatrix} = \begin{bmatrix} \cos\theta_1' \sin\theta_2' \\ \sin\theta_1' \sin\theta_2' \\ -\cos\theta_2' \end{bmatrix}$$

The Rodrigues formula can be used to find the new elbow position. Define $\mathbf{n} = \mathbf{p}_w / |\mathbf{p}_w|$. Then

$$\mathbf{p}_e = \mathbf{n}(\mathbf{n} \cdot \mathbf{p}_e')(1 - \cos\theta) + \mathbf{p}_e' \cos\theta + \mathbf{n} \times \mathbf{p}_e' \sin\theta$$

Step 2c: Find the first two joint angles from the elbow position. Note that the zero position of the upper arm is straight down.

$$\theta_1 = \tan^{-1}\left(\frac{p_{ey}}{p_{ex}}\right)$$

$$\theta_2 = \tan^{-1}\left(\frac{\sqrt{p_{ex}^2 + p_{ey}^2}}{-p_{ez}}\right)$$

Step 2d: Find the roll angle θ_3. Consider the wrist position that would be located if the arm were placed by the (unprimed) angles θ_1, θ_2, and θ_4, with $\theta_3 = 0$. The unit vector from the elbow point $\mathbf{p}_e$ to this wrist point $\mathbf{p}_{ew}'$ is given by $\mathbf{p}_{ew}' = \mathbf{A}_1\mathbf{A}_2\mathbf{A}_4 {}^4\mathbf{z}_4$. The actual forearm vector is given by $\mathbf{p}_{ew} = \mathbf{p}_w - \mathbf{p}_e$. Thus

$$\theta_3 = \tan^{-1}\frac{|\mathbf{p}_{ew}' \times \mathbf{p}_{ew}|}{\mathbf{p}_{ew}' \cdot \mathbf{p}_{ew}}$$

Step 3: Find the hand orientation relative to the forearm. The only difference from the 6R case is the added roll motion θ_3 which must be incorporated. Define $\mathbf{W}_j = \mathbf{A}_1 \ldots \mathbf{A}_j$ and ${}^i\mathbf{W}_j = \mathbf{A}_{i+1} \ldots \mathbf{A}_j$. Noting that $\mathbf{W}_7 = \mathbf{R}$ is the absolute orientation of the hand, then the relative hand orientation is given by:

$${}^4\mathbf{W}_7 = \mathbf{W}_4^T \mathbf{W}_7$$

Step 4: Find the wrist joint angles. This step is equivalent to that in [Hollerbach and Sahar, 1983] and is omitted.

Appendix III: Inverse Kinematics for Manipulator 2

The steps in the inverse kinematics for position is substantially the same as for manipulator 1. Where they differ, additional details are given.

Step 1: Find the wrist position.

Step 2a: Find the first 4 joint angles that would result if $\theta = 0$. Note that the pitch angle at the elbow is now θ_3, while the yaw angle $\theta_4 = 0$ when $\theta = 0$. Also θ_3 is now dependent on θ.

$$\sin\theta_3' = \frac{a_2^2 + s_5^2 - p_w^2}{2a_2 s_5}$$

Step 2b: Find the elbow position by rotating the elbow point about $\mathbf{p}_w$ *by the angle* θ.

Step 2c: Find the first two joint angles from the elbow position. Since the zero position of the upper arm is horizontal,

$$\theta_2 = \tan^{-1}\left(\frac{p_{ez}}{\sqrt{p_{ex}^2 + p_{ey}^2}}\right)$$

Step 2d: Find the roll angle θ_3. Express $\mathbf{p}_{ew} = \mathbf{p}_w - \mathbf{p}_e$ in link 2 coordinates, given θ_1 and θ_2. Thus

$${}^2\mathbf{p}_e = \mathbf{A}_3\mathbf{A}_4(s_5 {}^4\mathbf{z}_4) = s_5 \begin{bmatrix} \cos\theta_3 \sin\theta_4 \\ \sin\theta_3 \sin\theta_4 \\ -\cos\theta_4 \end{bmatrix}$$

Solving,

$$\theta_3 = \tan^{-1}\left(\frac{{}^2p_{ewy}}{{}^2p_{ewx}}\right)$$

$$\theta_4 = \tan^{-1}\left(\frac{{}^2p_{ewx}\cos\theta_3 + {}^2p_{ewy}\sin\theta_3}{-{}^2p_{ewz}}\right)$$

Step 3: Find the hand orientation relative to the forearm.
Step 4: Find the wrist joint angles.

Footnote

1. This is an alternative proof to a theorem originally derived by Roger Brockett.

References

Benati, M., Morasso, P., and Tagliasco, V., 1982, "The inverse kinematic problem for anthropomorphic manipulator arms," *ASME J. Dynamic Systems, Meas., Control*, **104**, pp. 110-113.

Denavit, J., and Hartenberg, R. S., 1955, "A kinematic notation for lower pair mechanisms based on matrices," *J. Applied Mechanics*, **22**, pp. 215-221.

Featherstone, R., 1983, "Position and velocity transformations between robot end-effector coordinates and joint angles," *Int. J. Robotics Research*, **2** no. 2, pp. 35-45.

Hanafusa, H., Yoshikawa, T., and Nakamura, Y., 1981, August, "Analysis and control of articulated robot arms with redundancy," *Prep. 8th IFAC World Congress* , pp. XIV-78-83.

Hollerbach, J. M., and Sahar, G., 1983, "Wrist-partitioned inverse kinematic accelerations and manipulator dynamics," *Int. J. Robotics Research* , 2 no. 4, pp. 61-76.

Lozano-Perez, T., 1982, "Task Planning," *Robot Motion: Planning and Control* , ed. J. M. Brady, J. M. Hollerbach, T. L. Johnson, T. Lozano-Perez, M. T. Mason, Cambridge, Mass., MIT Press, pp. 463-488.

Paul, R. P., and Stevenson, C. N., 1983, "Kinematics of robot wrists," *Int. J. Robotics Research* , 2 no. 1, pp. 31-38.
Pieper, D.L., 1968, The Kinematics of Manipulators under Computer Control, Ph.D. Thesis, Stanford University, Department of Computer Science.

Roth, B., 1980, April 15-17, "Kinematic design for manipulation," *NSF Workshop on Research Needed to Advance the State-of-Knowledge in Robotics* , U. Rhode Island, pp. 110-118.

Takase, K., Inoue, H., Sato, K., 1974, Nov. 19-21, "The design of an articulated manipulator with torque control ability," *Proc. 4th Int. Symp. Industrial Robots* , pp. 261-270.

Yoshikawa, T., 1983, August 28 – Sept. 2, "Analysis and control of robot manipulators with redundancy," *Proc. 1st Int. Symp. Robotics Research* , Bretton Woods, N. H.

DEVELOPMENT OF SIMULATION SYSTEM OF ROBOT MOTION AND ITS ROLE IN TASK PLANNING AND DESIGN SYSTEMS

Masaharu TAKANO

Faculty of Engineering, University of Tokyo
7-3-1, Hongo, Bunkyo-ku
Tokyo, 113, JAPAN

Computer simulation system of robot has been developed used for task planning and design of robot, and the roles of main system and external subsystems were clarified. Main system of robot simulation includes kinematics, inverse kinematics (synthesis), statics, dynamics, control system analysis, deflection and its compensation, and they are arbitrarily selected according to the demand. A new method to solve the synthesis problem was proposed for robot with six degrees of freedom, where position synthesis by first three joints (rotation and/or sliding) and orientation synthesis by the last three joints (rotation) are carried out analytically, and the solution is obtained by iteration of both synthesis procedures. Results showed that the calculation time by this new method is about one-tenth of that by 6×6 inverse Jacobian method. Examples of robot simulation of pick-and-place motion were shown.

I. INTRODUCTION

There are two purposes for the application of simulation system of robot motion; one is for the task planning and command data programming of robts used in workshop, another is for the design of robot. The system for the task planning purpose could be classified into two different levels; simple simulation system and that of general purpose.

Simple simulation system is adopted for a robot used in a simple environment, where it produces the command data of the robot, and operator evaluates its performance and time sequence by seeing the animation on CRT [Hanafusa,1981, Arai,1983, Sjolund,1983]. This system hardly needs dynamics analysis or more complicated calculations. One of the problems for practical use is that the programming data cannot be directly applied to robot control because of setting error of robot and deviation of position and orientation from ideal point due to arms and workpiece weights, or other unknown reasons.

The simulation system for general purpose of task planning is used for the evaluation of robot utilization in workshop and task programming, where the time efficiency, synchronization to other machines, sequential motion trajectories of workpiece etc. are calculated, considering the interference with machines and other environments. In this system not only the simulation of kinematics and inverse kinematics, but statics, dynamics, and other more complicated analyses are needed. It is useful for the decision of higher level such as the selection of robot with most adequate specifications, number of robots to be deployed in plant. Many simulation systems heading for general purpose are developed or under development [Heginbotham,1977, Weck,1981, Hazony,1982, Bonney,1983, Yang,1983, Okino,1983, Warnecke,1983, Dillman,1983, Pennington,1983]. The problem is that it needs large amount of environmental data. They are different in every plant and it takes much time and man power to input them in the system. This problem should be solved in the field of research of geometric modelling.

The simulation system for robot design is used as a part of CAD system [Liegeois,1980, Comstock,1981, Soroka,1982, Queromes,1982, Vukobratovic,1982, Imman,1982, Takano,1982]. There are also two different levels; simple system and that of general purpose. The latter would be used for the design of any type of robot where many calculation procedures such as determination of configuration, degrees of freedom, structure of joints, transmissions, actuators, etc. should be practicable. The development of this large scale system is very complicated and takes much time, however, once accomplished it would be very universal to any robot design. In order that this system might be in practical use, characteristics of machine elements such as efficiency, friction, compliances which are unknown at present must be clarified.

II. STRUCTURE OF SIMULATION SYSTEM

Simulation system is considered as a part of task planning system or computer aided design system. Fig.1 shows the system, where it is considered that interference check and design of devices is out of the main robot simulation system.

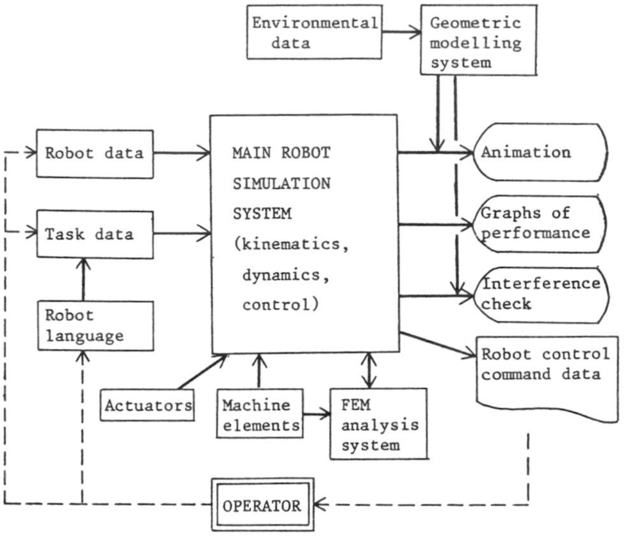

Fig. 1. Structure of task planning or robot design system

The main simulation system of robot should have the following analysis subsystems;

1) Kinematics: to obtain displacement, velocity, and acceleration from joint motion.
2) Inverse kinematics (snsthesis): to obtain joint displacement from robot position and orientation.
3) Statics: to calculate joint torque(force) due to gravitational force and external force and torque.
4) Dynamics(I): to calculate joint torque (force) due to dynamic force and moment.
5) Dynamics(II): to obtain the robot motion from joint torque(force) variation with time.
6) Deflection: to obtain the deflection due to static and dynamic force and moment.
7) Dynamics(III): to calculate the vibrations.
8) Control system analysis: to calculate the dynamic characteristics of control system with internal sensor feedback loop.
9) Path generation: to obtain the continuous path data from discrete points series.
10) Compliance analysis: to determine compliance matrices from arm and joint dimensions by FEM.
11) Inertia data: to determine mass, gravity center, inertia matrix of arms and workpiece from their dimensions.

The latter three analyses subsystems are considered as out of the main system.

The advanced robot will possess some external sensing devices, then the analysis subsystem of sensor feedback control should be added.

In the following chapter details of the simulation system of robot developed in our laboratory are described, where some of subsystems above mentioned are now being developed. The configuration of robot is restricted to serially connected joint type.

III SUBSYSTEMS OF SIMULATION

3.1 Kinematics

Fig.2 shows the general type of robot,where joints (rotation or sliding) is named $J_1,J_2,\ldots,J_n$ and arms $B_1,B_2,\ldots,B_n$. Using transformation matrix [Denavit,1955, Paul,1981], the coordinate system Σ_i on ith-arm origin of which is fixed at ith-joint is transformed to coordinate system Σ_{i-1} as shown in Fig.3 by

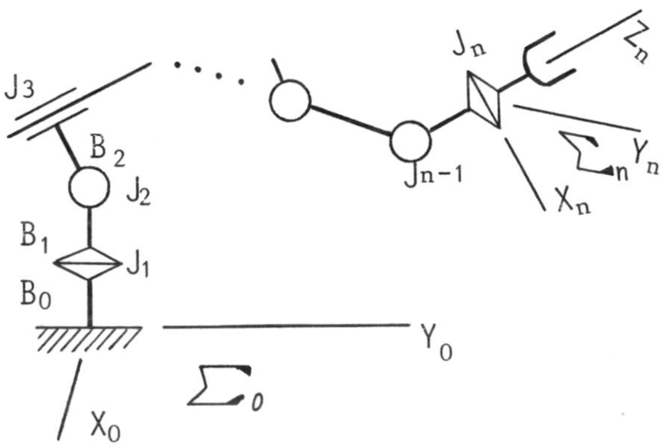

Fig. 2. General type of robot

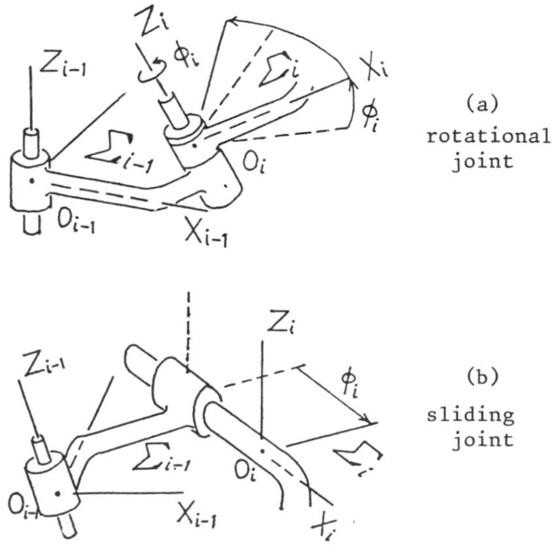

Fig. 3. Definition of coordinate system

$$A_i = A_{si}A_{di}, \tag{1*}$$

$$A_{si} = \begin{pmatrix} C_{si} & \mathbf{l}_i^{(i-1)} \\ 0\ 0\ 0 & 1 \end{pmatrix} = \begin{pmatrix} \mathbf{a}_{i1}, & \mathbf{a}_{i2}, & \mathbf{a}_{i3}, & \mathbf{a}_{i4} \\ 0 & 0 & 0 & 1 \end{pmatrix}, \tag{2}$$

$$A_{di} = \begin{pmatrix} \cos\phi_i, & -\sin\phi_i, & 0 & 0 \\ \sin\phi_i, & \cos\phi_i, & 0 & 0 \\ 0 & 0 & 1 & 0 \\ 0 & 0 & 0 & 1 \end{pmatrix}, \quad \text{(rotation)} \tag{3}$$

$$= \begin{pmatrix} 1 & 0 & 0 & \phi_i \\ 0 & 1 & 0 & 0 \\ 0 & 0 & 1 & 0 \\ 0 & 0 & 0 & 1 \end{pmatrix}. \quad \text{(sliding)} \tag{4}$$

A_{si} means the transformation $\Sigma_i \rightarrow \Sigma_{i-1}$ when $\phi_i=0$. The position of gravity center of ith-arm $\mathbf{r}_{Gi}$ expressed in Σ_i is transformed to Σ_0

$$\begin{pmatrix} \mathbf{r}_{Gi}^{(0)} \\ 1 \end{pmatrix} = A_1A_2\cdots A_i \begin{pmatrix} \mathbf{r}_{Gi}^{(i)} \\ 1 \end{pmatrix}, \tag{5}$$

and the position and orientation of workpiece are

$$\begin{pmatrix} \mathbf{r}_{W}^{(0)} \\ 1 \end{pmatrix} = A_1A_2\cdots A_n \begin{pmatrix} \mathbf{r}_{W}^{(n)} \\ 1 \end{pmatrix}, \tag{6}$$

$$E_W^{(0)} = C_1C_2\cdots C_n E_W^{(n)}. \tag{7}$$

$E_W = (\mathbf{e}_{wx}, \mathbf{e}_{wy}, \mathbf{e}_{wz})$ is a group of three orthogonal orientation vectors.

Velocity, acceleration, angular velocity and angular acceleration are expressed as follows,

$$\begin{pmatrix} \mathbf{v}_{Gi}^{(0)} \\ 0 \end{pmatrix} = \sum_{j=1}^{i} A_1A_2\cdots\dot{A}_j\cdots A_i \begin{pmatrix} \mathbf{r}_{Gi}^{(i)} \\ 1 \end{pmatrix}, \tag{8}$$

$$\begin{pmatrix} \mathbf{a}_{Gi}^{(0)} \\ 0 \end{pmatrix} = \sum_{j=1}^{i} A_1A_2\cdots\ddot{A}_j\cdots A_i \begin{pmatrix} \mathbf{r}_{Gi}^{(i)} \\ 1 \end{pmatrix} + 2\sum_{j=2}^{i}\sum_{k=1}^{j-1} A_1\cdot\cdot\dot{A}_k\cdot\cdot\dot{A}_j\cdot\cdot A_i \begin{pmatrix} \mathbf{r}_{Gi}^{(i)} \\ 1 \end{pmatrix}, \tag{9}$$

$$\boldsymbol{\omega}_i^{(i)} = C_i^T\boldsymbol{\omega}_{i-1}^{(i-1)} + \dot{\boldsymbol{\phi}}_i^{(i)}, \quad \text{(rotation)} \tag{10}$$

$$= C_i^T\boldsymbol{\omega}_{i-1}^{(i-1)}, \quad \text{(sliding)} \tag{10'}$$

$$\boldsymbol{\alpha}_i^{(i)} = C_i^T\boldsymbol{\alpha}_{i-1}^{(i-1)} + (C_i^T\boldsymbol{\omega}_{i-1}^{(i-1)})\times\boldsymbol{\omega}_i^{(i)} + \ddot{\boldsymbol{\phi}}_i^{(i)}, \quad \text{(rotation)} \tag{11}$$

$$= C_i^T\boldsymbol{\alpha}_{i-1}^{(i-1)}, \quad \text{(sliding)} \tag{11'}$$

where

$$\dot{\boldsymbol{\phi}}_i^{(i)} = (0,\ 0,\ \dot{\phi}_i)^T, \quad \ddot{\boldsymbol{\phi}}_i^{(i)} = (0,\ 0,\ \ddot{\phi}_i)^T, \tag{12}$$

$$\dot{A}_i = A_{si}\frac{dA_{di}}{dt} = A_{si}\frac{dA_{di}}{d\phi_i}\dot{\phi}_i, \tag{13}$$

$$\ddot{A}_i = A_{si}\frac{d^2A_{di}}{dt^2} = A_{si}\left(\frac{dA_{di}}{d\phi}\ddot{\phi} + \frac{d^2A_{di}}{d\phi^2}\dot{\phi}^2\right). \tag{14}$$

3.2. Statics and Dynamics (I)

For the analysis of robot dynamics, many people discuss about the calculation time by Newton-Euler formulation [Orin,1979, Walker,1982, Featherstone,1983, Kane,1983, Schwartz,1984], Lagrangian formulation [Mahil,1977, Hollerbach,1980, Vecchio,1980, Thomas,1982, Renaud,1983], or other method [Potkonjak,1979]. For the design of robot all three components of force and torque applied to joints are needed to know the strength of bearings, axis and other elements of the joint, therefore Lagrangian formulation cannot be adopted.

According to Newton-Euler formulation,

$$\mathbf{F}_{Ji}^{(i)} = C_{i+1}\mathbf{F}_{Ji+1}^{(i+1)} - m_i(\mathbf{a}_{Gi}^{(i)} + \mathbf{g}^{(i)}), \tag{15}$$

$$\mathbf{M}_{Ji}^{(i)} = C_{i+1}\mathbf{M}_{Ji+1}^{(i+1)} - (I_i\boldsymbol{\alpha}_i^{(i)} + \boldsymbol{\omega}_i^{(i)}\times I_i\boldsymbol{\omega}_i^{(i)}) + \mathbf{l}_{i+1}^{(i)}\times(C_{i+1}\mathbf{F}_{i+1}^{(i+1)}) - \mathbf{r}_{Gi}^{(i)}\times m_i(\mathbf{a}_{Gi}^{(i)}+\mathbf{g}^{(i)}), \tag{16}$$

and

$$\mathbf{F}_{Jn}^{(n)} = \mathbf{F}_{ex}^{(n)} - m_n(\mathbf{a}_{Gn}^{(n)}+\mathbf{g}^{(n)}) - m_w(\mathbf{a}_w^{(n)}+\mathbf{g}^{(n)}), \tag{17}$$

$$\mathbf{M}_{Jn}^{(n)} = \mathbf{M}_{ex}^{(n)} - \{(I_n+I_w)\boldsymbol{\alpha}_n^{(n)} + \boldsymbol{\omega}_n^{(n)}\times(I_n+I_w)\boldsymbol{\omega}_n^{(n)}\} + \mathbf{r}_{ex}^{(n)}\times\mathbf{F}_{ex}^{(n)} \tag{18}$$

$\mathbf{F}_{ex}$, $\mathbf{r}_{ex}$, $\mathbf{M}_{ex}$: external force, force acting point, and external torque,
m_i, I_i, m_w, I_w : mass and inertia tensor of ith-arm and workpiece,
$\mathbf{g}=(0,0,g)^T$: gravity acceleration vector.

3.3. Dynamics (II)

Joint motion and robot motion is calculated when joint torques(forces) are applied. The equation of motion can be obtained from eqs.(5) and (6), but it is easier to use Lagrangian equation for its formulation. Omitting all the calculations, we obtain the equation of motion

$$\ddot{\Phi} = D_1^{-1}(Q - \dot{\Phi}^T D_2\dot{\Phi} - D_3), \tag{19}$$

where $\mathbf{Q}=(Q_1,Q_2,\ldots,Q_n)^T$ is generalized joint driving force and $\Phi=(\phi_1,\phi_2,\ldots,\phi_n)^T$. When $\mathbf{Q}$ is given as the function of time t, joint displacement vector Φ is calculated by Runge-Kutta-Gill method, and the motion of workpiece is calculated by eq.(5).

---

* A_i is defined by 7 parameters, because origin is taken at joint and initial position can be taken as we wish.

3.4 Control System Analysis

Generally the driving torque(force) of ith-joint is given as

$$Q_i = K_{i1}V_i - K_{i2}\dot{\phi}_i - Q_{i\mu}\,\mathrm{sgn}(\dot{\phi}_i), \qquad (20)$$

where V_i is input value(volt) to actuator, K_{i1}, K_{i2} are torque(force) constant(Nm/volt,N/volt) and dampimg constant(Nm/(rad/s),N/(m/s)), respectively and $Q_{i\mu}$ is friction registance, in which characteristic of reduction, transmission mechanism and actuator driving circuit are included. When it has PID control system as is shown in Fig.4, the input V_i becomes

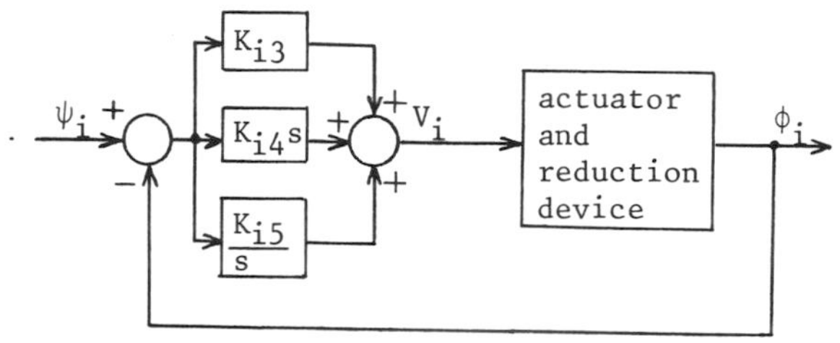

Fig. 4. Standard control system for joint drive

$$V_i = K_{i3}(\psi_i-\phi_i) + K_{i4}(\dot{\psi}_i-\dot{\phi}_i) + K_{i5}\int(\psi_i-\phi_i)dt \qquad (21)$$

where $\psi_i(t)$, $\dot{\psi}_i(t)$ are displacement and velocity command given to actuator driving circuit.
From eqs.(19), (20), and (21) response of robot motion to input $\psi_i(t)$ is obtained.

3.5 Inverse Kinematics (Synthesis)

Synthesis (calculation of joint displacements from workpiece position and orientation) is one of most important problem in robot simulation system. For the special type of robot in which adjacent joint axes intersect at right angles each other or are parallel synthesis can be solved analytically by the formulation proper to each case [Lee,1983, Paul,1983]. But in general type of robot it is solved only by iteration procedure, and methods to save the computing time are proposed [Gaglio,1981, Konstantinov,1982, Takano,1982, Melouah,1982, Milenkovic,13, Van Aken,1983].

A new method to solve the synthesis is proposed, where three displacements are synthesized analytically by workpiece position, and other three joint displacements analytically by orientation, and two syntheses are iteratively carried out until the solution reaches the value in sufficient accuracy. Fig.5 shows this procedure.

The problem is,
"Robot has six joints the last three of which are rotational. Obtain joint displacements ϕ_i's to put workpiece in robot hand to position $\mathbf{r}_w^{(0)}$ and orientation $E_w=(\mathbf{e}_{wx}^{(0)},\mathbf{e}_{wy}^{(0)},\mathbf{e}_{wz}^{(0)})$."

(a) Position synthesis by first three joint displacements

Equation to determine ϕ_1, ϕ_2, ϕ_3 is

$$\begin{pmatrix}\mathbf{r}_w^{(0)}\\1\end{pmatrix} = A_1(\phi_1)A_2(\phi_2)A_3(\phi_3)\begin{pmatrix}\mathbf{r}_w^{(3)}\\1\end{pmatrix}, \qquad (22)$$

$$\begin{pmatrix}\mathbf{r}_w^{(3)}\\1\end{pmatrix} = A_4A_5A_6\begin{pmatrix}\mathbf{r}_w^{(6)}\\1\end{pmatrix}. \qquad (23)$$

$\mathbf{r}_w^{(3)}$ is supposed constant. ϕ_1, ϕ_2, ϕ_3 can be obtained analytically but there are eight different kinds of configurations: $J_1J_2J_3$ = RRR, RRS, RSR, SRR, RSS, SRS, SSR and SSS. The formulae are different from each other and only those for the following case are described here.

In case of $J_1J_2J_3$ = SRR

$\cos\phi_i$, $\sin\phi_i$ are written as $c\phi_i$, $s\phi_i$.

$$B_{c2}c^2\phi_3 + B_{s2}s^2\phi_3 + 2B_{cs}c\phi_3 s\phi_3 + 2B_{c1}c\phi_3 + 2B_{s1}s\phi_3 + B_x = 0, \qquad (24)$$

$$\left\{\begin{aligned} c\phi_2 &= \frac{Q_{b1}R_1 + Q_{b2}R_2}{R_1^2 + R_2^2},\\ s\phi_2 &= \frac{Q_{b2}R_1 + Q_{b1}R_2}{R_1^2 + R_2^2}, \end{aligned}\right. \qquad (25)$$

$$\phi_1 = \frac{1}{b_{231}}(Q_3 - R_3), \qquad (26)$$

where

$$\left\{\begin{aligned} B_{c2} &= b_{21}^2R_{31}^2 - b_{231}^2(R_{11}^2+R_{21}^2+R_{31}^2),\\ B_{s2} &= b_{21}^2R_{32} - b_{231}^2(R_{12}^2+R_{22}^2+R_{32}^2),\\ B_{cs} &= b_{21}^2R_{31}R_{32} - b_{231}^2(R_{11}R_{12}+R_{21}R_{22}+R_{31}R_{32})\\ B_{c1} &= b_{21}^2R_{31}R_{33} - b_{231}^2(R_{11}R_{13}+R_{21}R_{23}+R_{31}R_{33})\\ &\quad + Q_{c1}R_{31},\\ B_{s1} &= b_{21}^2R_{32}R_{33} - b_{231}^2(R_{12}R_{13}+R_{22}R_{23}+R_{32}R_{33})\\ &\quad + Q_{c1}R_{32},\\ B_x &= b_{21}^2R_{33}^2 - b_{231}^2(R_{13}^2+R_{23}^2+R_{33}^2)\\ &\quad + 2Q_{c1}R_{33} + Q_{c0}, \end{aligned}\right. \qquad (27)$$

$$\begin{cases} R_{i1} = a_{3i1}r_{31} + a_{3i2}r_{32}, \\ R_{i2} = a_{3i2}r_{31} - a_{3i1}r_{32}, \\ R_{i3} = a_{3i3}r_{33} - a_{3i4}, \end{cases} \quad (28)$$

$$R_i = R_{i1}c\phi_3 + R_{i2}s\phi_3 + R_{i3}, \quad (29)$$

$$\begin{cases} Q_{c1} = b_{211}(b_{231}Q_1 - b_{211}Q_3) + b_{221}(b_{231}Q_2 - b_{221}Q_3), \\ Q_{c0} = (b_{231}Q_1 - b_{211}Q_3)^2 + (b_{231}Q_2 - b_{221}Q_3)^2, \end{cases} \quad (30)$$

$$\begin{cases} Q_{b1} = Q_1 - b_{211}(Q_3 - R_3)/b_{231}, \\ Q_{b2} = Q_2 - b_{221}(Q_3 - R_3)/b_{231}, \end{cases} \quad (31)$$

$$\begin{pmatrix} Q_1 \\ Q_2 \\ Q_3 \\ 1 \end{pmatrix} = A_{s2}^{-1}A_{s1}^{-1}\begin{pmatrix} \mathbf{r}_w^{(0)} \\ \\ 1 \end{pmatrix}, \quad (32)$$

$$\mathbf{r}_3 = (r_{31}, r_{32}, r_{33})^T = \mathbf{r}_w^{(3)}, \quad (33)$$

$$A_{s2}^{-1} = \begin{bmatrix} \mathbf{b}_{21}, & \mathbf{b}_{22}, & \mathbf{b}_{23}, & \mathbf{b}_{24} \\ 0 & 0 & 0 & 1 \end{bmatrix}, \quad (34)$$

$$\mathbf{b}_{2i} = (b_{21i}, b_{22i}, b_{23i})^T, \quad (35)$$

$$A_{s3} = \begin{bmatrix} \mathbf{a}_{31}, & \mathbf{a}_{32}, & \mathbf{a}_{33}, & \mathbf{a}_{34} \\ 0 & 0 & 0 & 1 \end{bmatrix}, \quad (36)$$

$$\mathbf{a}_{3i} = (a_{31i}, a_{32i}, a_{33i})^T. \quad (37)$$

Eq.(24) is 4th power polynomials of $c\phi_3$ or $s\phi_3$ and maximum four sets of roots of the equation can be obtained analytically by Ferrari's method.

In case of $J_1J_2J_3$ = SSS

$$\phi_1 = \frac{a_{331}(Q_2-S_2) - a_{321}(Q_3-S_3)}{b_{221}a_{331} - b_{231}a_{321}}, \quad (38)$$

$$\phi_3 = \frac{b_{221}(Q_3-S_3) - b_{231}(Q_2-S_2)}{b_{221}a_{331} - b_{231}a_{321}}, \quad (39)$$

$$\phi_2 = Q_1 - b_{211}\phi_1 - (S_1 + a_{311}\phi_3), \quad (40)$$

$$\begin{pmatrix} S_1 \\ S_2 \\ S_3 \\ 1 \end{pmatrix} = A_{s3}A_4A_5A_6\begin{pmatrix} \mathbf{r}_w^{(6)} \\ \\ 1 \end{pmatrix}. \quad (41)$$

(a_{321}, a_{331}), (b_{221}, b_{231}) and (Q_1, Q_2, Q_3) are expressed in eqs.(37), (35) and (32), respectively. In this case only a solution exists.

(b) Orientation synthesis by last three joint displacements

Equation which gives ϕ_4, ϕ_5, ϕ_6, is

$$(\mathbf{e}_{wx}^{(0)}, \mathbf{e}_{wy}^{(0)}, \mathbf{e}_{wz}^{(0)}) = C_1C_2C_3C_4(\phi_4)C_5(\phi_5)C_6(\phi_6)(\mathbf{e}_1^{(6)}, \mathbf{e}_2^{(6)}, \mathbf{e}_3^{(6)}). \quad (42)$$

For the simplicity, $(\mathbf{e}_1^{(6)}, \mathbf{e}_2^{(6)}, \mathbf{e}_3^{(6)})$ = unit matrix is supposed. ϕ_4, ϕ_5, ϕ_6 are given by the following equations:

$$\begin{cases} \cos\phi_4 = \dfrac{a_{513}e_{5z1} + a_{523}e_{5z2}}{a_{513}^2 + a_{523}^2}, \\ \sin\phi_4 = \dfrac{a_{513}e_{5z2} - a_{523}e_{5z1}}{a_{513}^2 + a_{523}^2}, \end{cases} \quad (43)$$

$$\begin{cases} \cos\phi_5 = \dfrac{a_{613}e_{6z1} - a_{623}e_{6z2}}{a_{613}^2 + a_{623}^2}, \\ \sin\phi_5 = \dfrac{a_{613}e_{6z2} - a_{623}e_{6z1}}{a_{613}^2 + a_{623}^2}, \end{cases} \quad (44)$$

$$(\cos\phi_6, \sin\phi_6) = (e_{6x1}, e_{6x2}), \quad (45)$$

$$A_{s5} = \begin{bmatrix} \mathbf{a}_{51}, & \mathbf{a}_{52}, & \mathbf{a}_{53}, & \mathbf{a}_{54} \\ 0 & 0 & 0 & 1 \end{bmatrix}, \quad (46)$$

$$\mathbf{a}_{53} = (a_{513}, a_{523}, a_{533}), \quad (47)$$

$$A_{s6} = \begin{bmatrix} \mathbf{a}_{61}, & \mathbf{a}_{62}, & \mathbf{a}_{63}, & \mathbf{a}_{64} \\ 0 & 0 & 0 & 1 \end{bmatrix}, \quad (48)$$

$$\mathbf{a}_{63} = (a_{613}, a_{623}, a_{633})^T, \quad (49)$$

$$(e_{5z1}, e_{5z2}, e_{5z3})^T = (C_1C_2C_3C_{s4})^{-1}\mathbf{e}_{5z}^{(0)}, \quad (50)$$

$$\mathbf{e}_{5z}^{(0)} = \mathbf{d}\cos\gamma + (\mathbf{d}\times\mathbf{f})\sin\gamma, \quad (51)$$

$$\mathbf{d} = \frac{\mathbf{e}_{4z}^{(0)} \times \mathbf{e}_{6z}^{(0)}}{|\mathbf{e}_{4z}^{(0)} \times \mathbf{e}_{6z}^{(0)}|}, \quad (52)$$

$$\mathbf{f} = \frac{a_{633}\mathbf{e}_{4z}^{(0)} - a_{533}\mathbf{e}_{6z}^{(0)}}{|a_{633}\mathbf{e}_{4z}^{(0)} - a_{533}\mathbf{e}_{6z}^{(0)}|}, \quad (53)$$

$$\sin\gamma = \left|\frac{|a_{633}\mathbf{e}_{4z}^{(0)} - a_{533}\mathbf{e}_{6z}^{(0)}|}{\mathbf{e}_{4z}^{(0)} \times \mathbf{e}_{6z}^{(0)}}\right|, \quad (54)$$

$$\mathbf{e}_{4z}^{(0)} = C_1C_2C_3(0, 0, 1)^T, \quad (55)$$

$$\mathbf{e}_{6z}^{(0)} = \mathbf{e}_{wz}^{(0)}. \quad (56)$$

Eq.(54) gives two values γ, π-γ, so two kinds of solution of ϕ_4, ϕ_5, ϕ_6 exist.

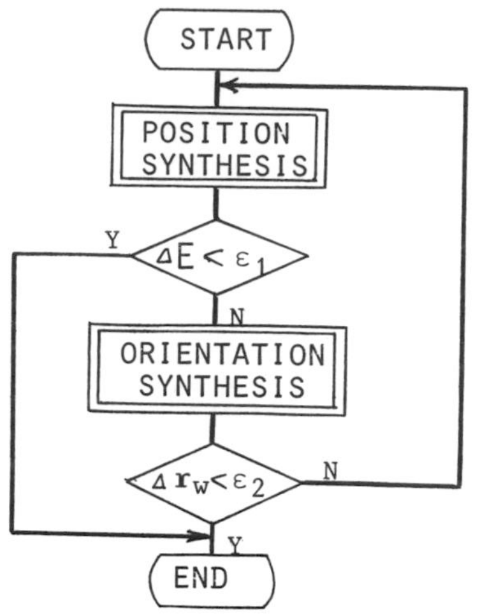

ΔE : orientation error

$\Delta \mathbf{r}_w$: position error

Fig. 5. A new method to solve synthesis problem

Fig.6 shows the comparison of the rapidity of convergence of a new method with conventional method. Calculation time was about one-tenth of that by 6×6 inverse Jacobian method.

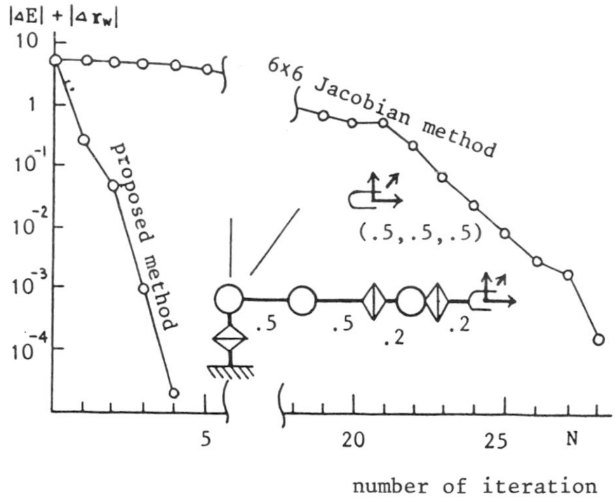

Fig. 6. Comparison of convergence for synthesis

3.6. Deflection Analysis and Its Compensation

Let compliance matrix of ith-arm and -joint S_i be the ratio of position and orientation variation to force and moment applied at (i+1) th joint, and let S_{Gi} be the ratio those to force and moment applied at gravity center. The deflection of (i+1)th joint shown in Fig.7 is expressed by

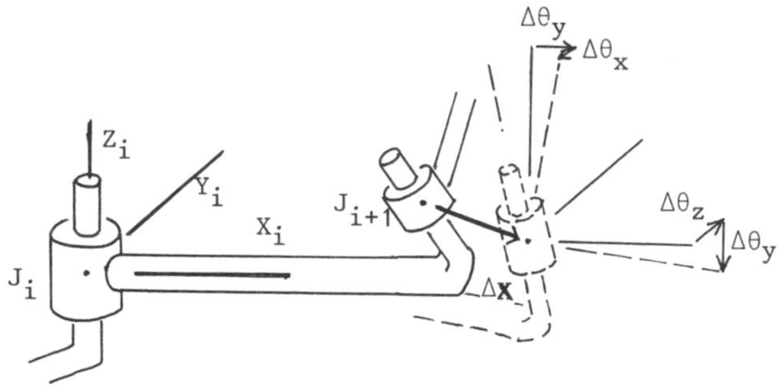

Fig. 7. Deflection of robot arm

$$\begin{pmatrix}\Delta \mathbf{X}_i^{(i)}\\ \Delta\boldsymbol{\theta}_i^{(i)}\end{pmatrix} = S_i \begin{pmatrix}\mathbf{F}_{i+1}^{(i)}\\ \mathbf{M}_{i+1}^{(i)}\end{pmatrix} + S_{Gi}\begin{pmatrix}\mathbf{F}_{Gi}^{(i)}\\ \mathbf{M}_{Gi}^{(i)}\end{pmatrix} . \qquad (57)$$

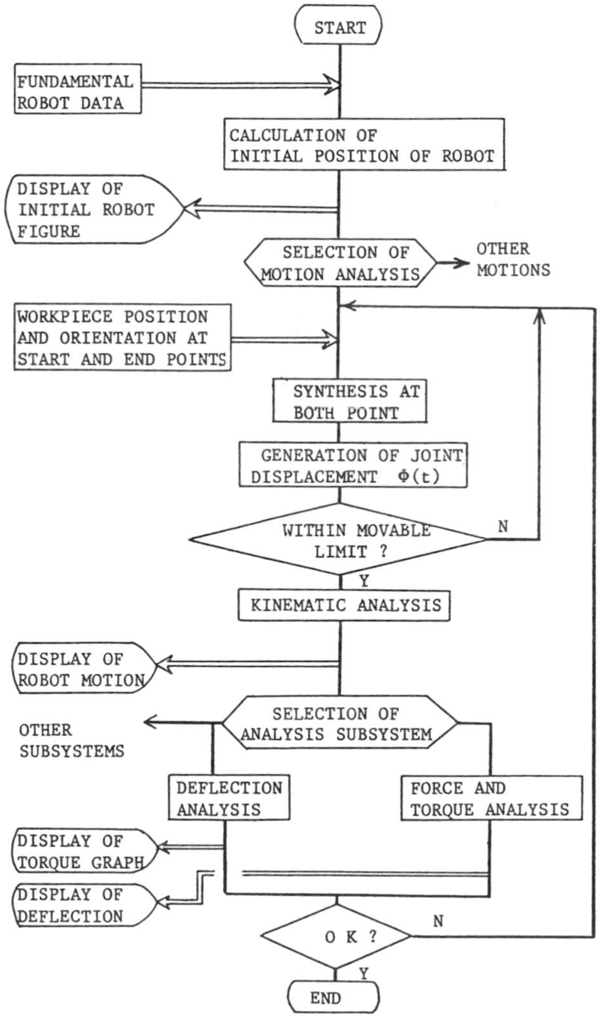

Fig. 8. An example of simulation of robot motion (pick-and place)

By this deflection transformation matrix A_{i+1} are changed to A_{i+1}.

$$A^{*}_{si+1} = \begin{bmatrix} C^{*}_{si+1} & l^{*(i)}_{i+1} \\ 0 \quad 0 \quad 0 & 1 \end{bmatrix} \tag{58}$$

where

$$C^{*}_{si+1} = \begin{bmatrix} 1 & -\Delta\theta_{iz}, & \Delta\theta_{iy} \\ \Delta\theta_{iz}, & 1 & \Delta\theta_{ix} \\ -\Delta\theta_{iy}, & \Delta\theta_{ix}, & 1 \end{bmatrix} C_{si+1} \tag{59}$$

$$\Delta\boldsymbol{\theta}_i = (\Delta\theta_{ix}, \Delta\theta_{iy}, \Delta\theta_{iz})^T \tag{60}$$

$$l^{*(i)}_{i+1} = l^{(i)}_{i+1} + \Delta x^{(i)}_i \tag{61}$$

and the position and orientation of workpiece are changed from $\mathbf{r}^{(0)}_w$ to $\mathbf{r}^{*(0)}_w$, as

$$\begin{pmatrix} \mathbf{r}^{*(0)}_w \\ 1 \end{pmatrix} = A^{*}_1 A^{*}_2 \cdots A^{*}_n \begin{pmatrix} \mathbf{r}^{(n)}_w \\ 1 \end{pmatrix}, \tag{62}$$

$$E^{*(0)}_w = C^{*}_1 C^{*}_1 \cdots C^{*}_n E^{(n)}_w . \tag{63}$$

$\phi_1, \phi_2, \ldots, \phi_6$ must be revised in order to put back to the original point. This compensation procedure can be done by synthesis procedure mentioned in 3.4.

IV EXAMPLES OF SIMULATION

In the simulation system developed here operator can select any analysis subsystems written in Chapter III. External subsystems are diffrent with the purpose of task planning and design. An example of simulation of pick-and-place motion is shown in Fig.8

Fundamental robot data (dimensions, transformation matrix, etc) and workpiece data, starting and end points, and motion time are input and animation of robot, graphs of $\phi_i(t)$, $Q_i(t)$, deflection, and other data are output. Fig.9 shows results of CRT display.

V. CONCLUSION

Simulation system of robot motion is utilized as a part of robot task planning and robot design systems, the roles of main simulation system and external systems have been made clear. The main system for general purpose was developed in which kinematics, inverse kinematics (synthesis), dynamics, control system analysis, deflection analysis and other subsystems are shown. A new method of synthesis for general type of robot are proposed, and the results showed that calculation time is about one-tenth of that by conventional method. An example of simulation of pick-and-place motion was presented.

REFERENCES

Hanafusa, H. 1981. Development of computer-aided teaching system for articulated robot. Proc. 24th. Auto. Cont. p199.

Arai, T. 1983. A robot language system with a color graphic simulator. Advanced Software in Robotics. p15.

Heginbotham, W. B. et al. 1977. Computer graphics simulation of industrial robot interactions. Proc. 7th ISIR. p169.

Okino, N. et al. 1983. Study on robot simulator. Proc. Japan Soc. Prec. Engg.(March). p191.

Warnecke, H. J. et al. 1983. Simulations of multi-machine service by industrial robots. Proc. 13th ISIR. p2-10.

Liegeois, A. et al. 1980. A system for computer aided design of robot and manipulators. Proc. 10th ISIR. p441.

Queromes, J. G. 1982. Computer aided design and robotics: A full of promise cooperation. Proc. 12th ISIR. p185.

Vukobratovic, M. et al. 1982. General software for manipulation robots. Mihailo Pupin Inst.

Takano, M. et al. 1982. Development of computer simulation system of kinematics and dynamics of robot. J. Fac. Engg., Univ. Tokyo(B). 36, 4. p677.

Paul, R. P. 1981. Robot manipulators. Cambridge MIT Press.

Kane, T. R. and Levinson, D. A. 1983. The use of Kane's dynamical equations in robotics. Int. J. Robotics Res. 2. 2. p13.

Featherstone, R. 1983. The calculation of robot dynamics using articulated-body inertias. Int. J. Robotics Res. 2. 1. p13.

Walker, M. W. and Orin, D. E. 1982. Efficient dynamic computer simulation of robotic mechanism. ASME J. Dyn. Sys. Meas. Cont. 104. p205

Thomas, M. and Tesar, D. 1982. Dynamic modelling of serial manipulator arms. ASME J. Dyn. Sys. Meas. Cont. 104. p218.

Renaud, M. and Megahed, S. 1983. Dynamic modelling of robot manipulators containing closed kinematic chains. Advanced Software in Robotics. p147.

Hollerbach, J. M. 1980. A recursive Lagrangian formulation of manipulator dynamics and a comparative study of dynamics formulation complexity. IEEE Sys. Man Cyber. SMC-10. 11. p730.

Konstantinov, M. S. and Patarinski, S. P. 1982. A contribution to the inverse kinematic problem for industrial robots. Proc. 12th ISIR. p459.

Melouah, H. and Andre, P. 1982. High speed computation of the inverse Jacobian matrix and of servo inputs for robot arm control. Proc. IEEE Conf Decis Cont Symp Adapt Processes. 21. p89.

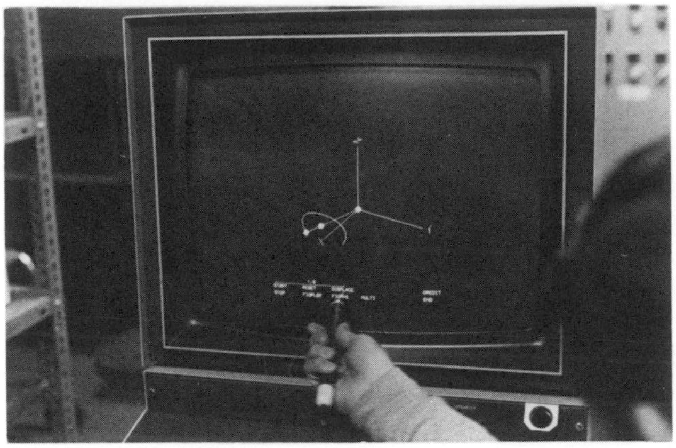

(a) Selection of subsystem of analysis

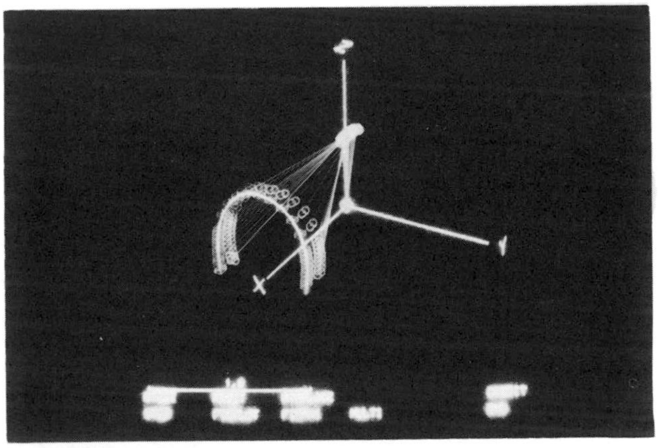

(b) Animation

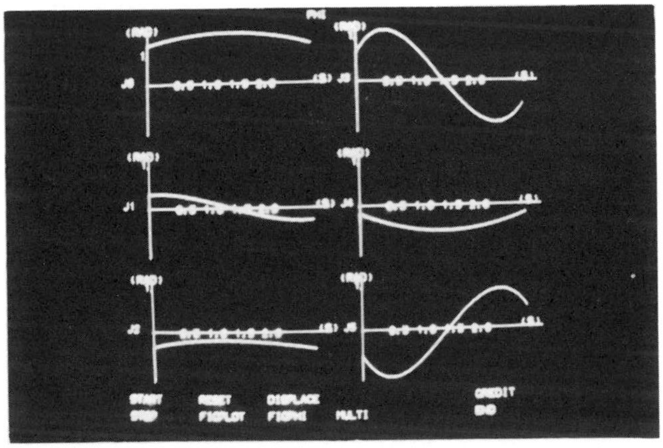

(c) Joint displacement

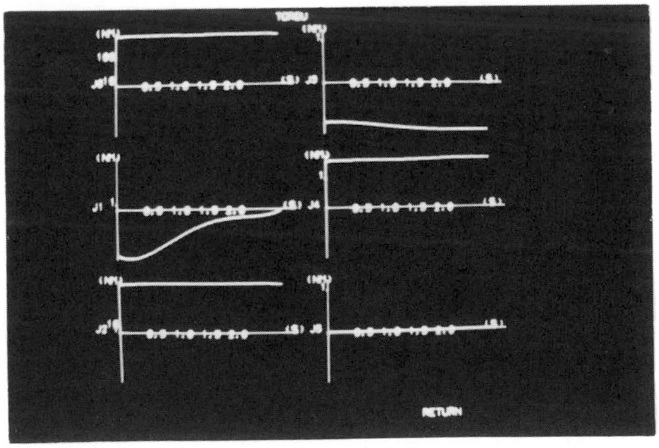

(d) Joint drive torque

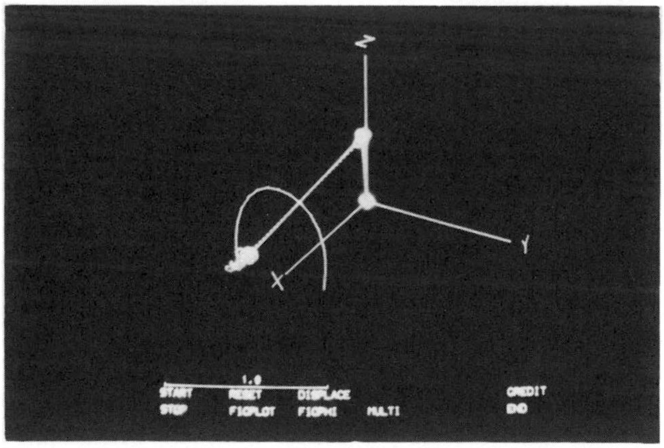

(e) Deflection (broken line)

Fig. 9. CRT display of motion and output data (articulated robot)

Compensation of Positioning Errors Caused by Geometric Deviations in Robot System

Koichi SUGIMOTO
Takushi OKADA

Production Engineering Research Laboratory, Hitachi, Ltd.
292 Yoshida-cho, Totsuka-ku, Yokohama 244, Japan

There esxist some geometric deviations such as dimensional errors in the mechanism of a robot and misalignments between the reference frame of a robot and the work area. This paper presents a method to estimate these deviations and to compensate positioning errors caused by them. The method for estimating the deviations has been derived by applying the least squares method to data obtained from positioning error measurements, and approximate inversed coordinate transformation using the estimated dimensional errors in the mechanism is discussed. It is also clarified by numerical examples that the positioning errors can be well compensated within a limitted work area by approximating the non-linear effects of the deviations on the positioning errors to a linear projective transformation.

1. Introduction

In robot control, movement of the robot hand is described by a fixed Cartesian coordinate system, the corresponding movements of kinematic pairs are calculated, and actuators that drive the kinematic pairs are controllled in accordance with these calculated results. The calculations that convert the motion of the robot hand in the Cartesian coordinate system into motion within a kinematic pair coordinate system is called inversed coordinate transformation. The variables used in inversed coordinate transformation are at once parameters that express motion of the hand, and also functions of the dimensions of a robot mechanism. In conventional industrial robot, inversed coordinate transformation is simplified to enable real-time computation during robot operation by setting the twist angles between the axes of adjacent kinematic pairs at 0 or 90 degrees, and setting both the lengthes of most links and the many offsets along the axes of kinematic pairs at zero. However, the actual dimensions of the robot mechanism do not agree with values set and include a certain degree of error. As a result, when a robot is controlled using simplified inversed coordinate transformation, actual movement by the robot deviates somewhat from the required robot movement. This is one of the largest factors detracting from the absolute positioning accuracy of a robot. A method for estimating the errors for a robot mechanism from the robot positioning errors has been proposed, but because of the complexity of inversed coordinate transformation, this method disregards the errors in the twist angles between the axes of adjacent kinematic pairs, making accurate correction for positioning errors difficult.

This paper describes a method for estimating the errors in a robot mechanism, including the twist angles between the axes of kinematic pairs and the setting error of the robot with respect to work area coordinates, by applying the least squares method to data obtained from error measurements taken during positioning. Approximate inversed coordinate transformation using the estimated mechanism errors is also discussed. The practical utility of this method is illustrated through the use of examples of numerical calculations.

2. Robot Coordinate System and Screw Notation

The robot mechanism treated in this paper is an open kinematic chain. Each of the kinematic pairs is assumed to have just single degree of freedom. The kinematic pairs are numbered consecutively 1,2,...,n from the fixed coordinates side. Fig. 1 illustrates the relationship between the j_{th} and k_{th} pairs. $\bar{a}_{jk}$ is a unit vector parallel to the common perpendicular to the axes of the j_{th} and k_{th} pairs, while $\bar{d}_j$ is a unit vector parallel to the axis of the j_{th} pair. the origin O_k of coordinates $X_kY_kZ_k$ fixed at the k_{th} pair is located at the intersection of link $\bar{a}_{jk}$ and pair axis $\bar{d}_k$; the Z_k axis is oriented in the $\bar{d}_k$ direction, and the X_k axis is oriented in the $\bar{a}_{jk}$ direction. Using vectors $\bar{d}_j$ and $\bar{a}_{jk}$, the relationship between the position $\bar{r}_j$ of the j_{th} coordinate origin and the position $\bar{r}_k$ of the k_{th} coordinate origin is expressed as

$$\bar{r}_k-\bar{r}_j=d_j\bar{d}_j+a_{jk}\bar{a}_{jk} \qquad (1)$$

Here, we shall call d_j the offset and a_{jk} the link length. Next, let us call the angle formed by the Z_j and Z_k axes α_{jk}, and the angle formed by the X_j and X_k axes θ_j. α_{jk} and θ_j shall be assumed to be positive with respect to $\bar{a}_{jk}$ and $\bar{d}_j$ in the clockwise direction.

The relationship between fixed coordinates

$X_0Y_0Z_0$ and coordinates $X_1Y_1Z_1$ of the first kinematic pair is shown in Fig. 2. The common perpendicular to axis Z_0 of the fixed coordinates and the pair axis $\bar{d}_1$ shall be called the axis X_1, and the intersection of this perpendicular with the $\bar{d}_1$ pair axis shall be called the origin O_1. Here, as in Eq. (1), the position vector $\bar{r}_1$ of origin O_1 in the fixed coordinates is expressed as

$$\bar{r}_1=d_0\bar{d}_0+a_{01}\bar{a}_{01} \tag{2}$$

Next, the coordinates $X_{n+1}Y_{n+1}Z_{n+1}$ are determined as shown in Fig. 3 as the reference for the displacement of the n_{th} pair. Letting the reference point of the hand be O_{n+1}, a perpendicular is dropped from here to pair axis $\bar{d}_n$. An axis X_{n+1} is located coaxially to this perpendicular and extended from pair axis $\bar{d}_n$ toward origin O_{n+1}. The unit vector parallel to this is called $\bar{a}_{n,n+1}$, and the length of perpendicular, $a_{n,n+1}$. The Y_{n+1} and Z_{n+1} axes can be determined arbitrarily.

When the robot coordinates are determined in this way, the axes at the j_{th} pair coordinates may be described as a screw with origin O_{n+1} serving as the reference point:

$$\bar{X}_j=\bar{a}_{ij}+\varepsilon(\bar{r}_j-\bar{r}_{n+1})x\bar{a}_{ij} \tag{3}$$

$$\bar{Y}_j=\bar{d}_jx\bar{a}_{ij}+\varepsilon(\bar{r}_j-\bar{r}_{n+1})x(\bar{d}_jx\bar{a}_{ij}) \tag{4}$$

$$\bar{Z}_j=\bar{d}_j+\varepsilon(\bar{r}_j-\bar{r}_{n+1})x\bar{d}_j \tag{5}$$

3. Estimating the Geometric Deviations of the Robot

The position vector $\bar{r}_{n+1}$ for the fixed coordinates of the refernce point of the hand is a function of 27 parameters: d_0, θ_0, a_{01}, d_1, expressed as follows:

$$\bar{r}_{n+1}=\bar{f}(d_0,\ \theta_0,\ \ldots,\ \theta_6,\ a_{67}) \tag{6}$$

These parameters include some errors. We shall assume the true parameter values to be:

$$\left.\begin{aligned} d_i' &= d_i+\Delta d_i \\ \theta_i' &= \theta_i+\Delta\theta_i \\ a_{ij}' &= a_{ij}+\Delta a_{ij} \\ \alpha_{ij}' &= \alpha_{ij}+\Delta\alpha_{ij} \end{aligned}\right] \tag{7}$$

Here, when the position of the robot hand is calculated from Eq. (6) as $\bar{r}_{n+1}$, an error of $\Delta\bar{r}_{n+1}$ results, and so we shall assume the position to be $\bar{r}_{n+1}'$.

$$\bar{r}_{n+1}'=\bar{r}_{n+1}+\Delta\bar{r} \tag{8}$$

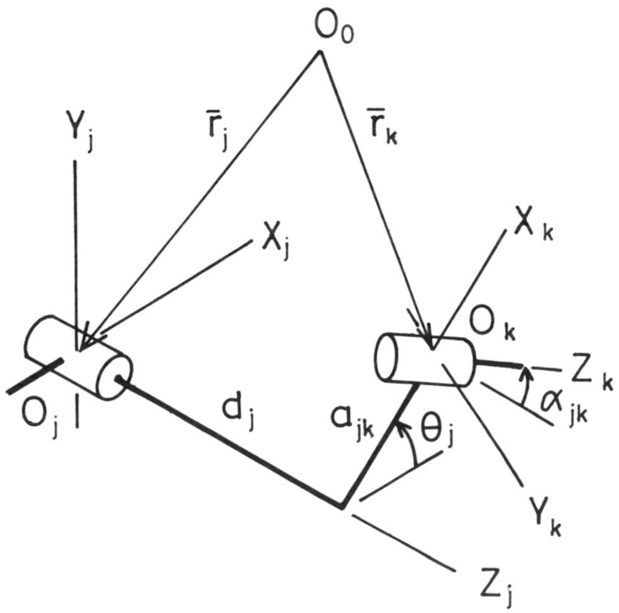

Fig.1 Relation between j_{th} and k_{th} Kinematic Pairs

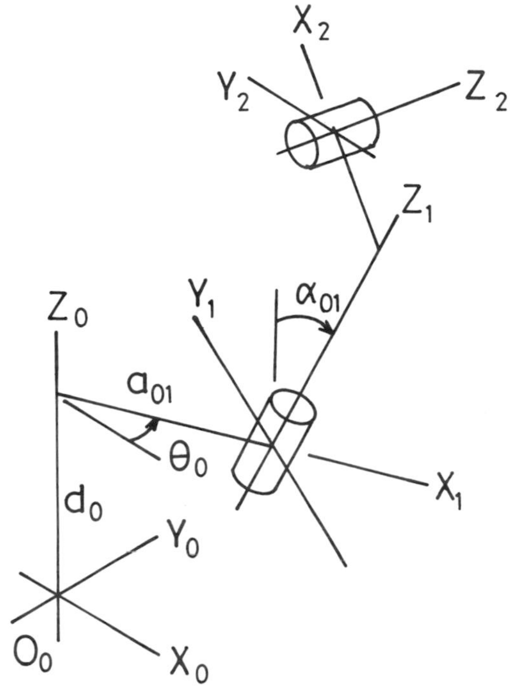

Fig. 2 Fixed Coordinates

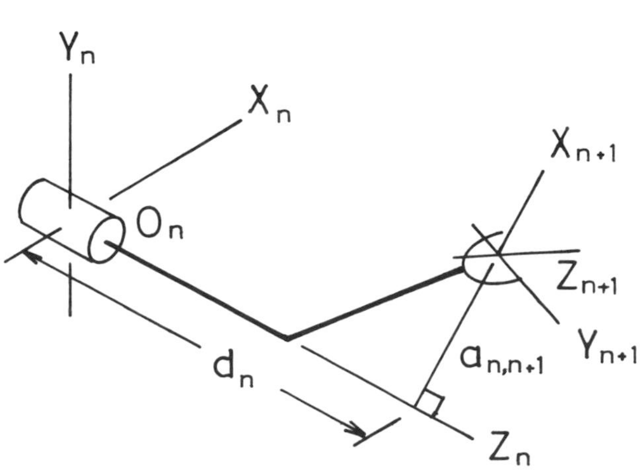

Fig. 3 Hand Coordinates

In this case, the relationship betwwen $\Delta\bar{r}$, Δd_i, $\Delta\theta_i$, Δa_{ij} and $\Delta\alpha_{ij}$, when these are sufficiently small, is as follows:

$$\Delta\bar{r}=\Sigma\frac{\partial\bar{f}}{\partial d_i}\Delta d_i+\Sigma\frac{\partial\bar{f}}{\partial\theta_i}\Delta\theta_i+$$

$$\Sigma\frac{\partial\bar{f}}{\partial a_{ij}}\Delta a_{ij}+\Sigma\frac{\partial\bar{f}}{\partial\alpha_{ij}}\Delta\alpha_{ij} \qquad (9)$$

where

$$\frac{\partial\bar{f}}{\partial d_i}=V(\bar{Z}_i) \qquad (10)$$

$$\frac{\partial\bar{f}}{\partial\theta_i}=D(\bar{Z}_i) \qquad (11)$$

$$\frac{\partial\bar{f}}{\partial a_{ij}}=V(\bar{X}_j) \qquad (12)$$

$$\frac{\partial\bar{f}}{\partial\alpha_{ij}}=D(\bar{X}_j) \qquad (13)$$

V designates the vector part of the screw and D designates the dual part.

However, when $\sin\alpha_{ij}=o$,

$$\frac{\partial\bar{f}}{\partial d_i}=\frac{\partial\bar{f}}{\partial d_j} \qquad (14)$$

and it becomes impossible to distinguish Δd_i from Δd_j. We shall therefore introduce β_i in Fig. 4 in place of d_i as a new parameter. β_i is the angle of rotation of Z_{i+1} about the Y_{i+1} axis. When there is no error, β_i eqauls zero degree. Replacing d_i with the parameter β_i gives the function:

$$\frac{\partial\bar{f}}{\partial\beta_i}=D(Y_j) \qquad (15)$$

Here, letting

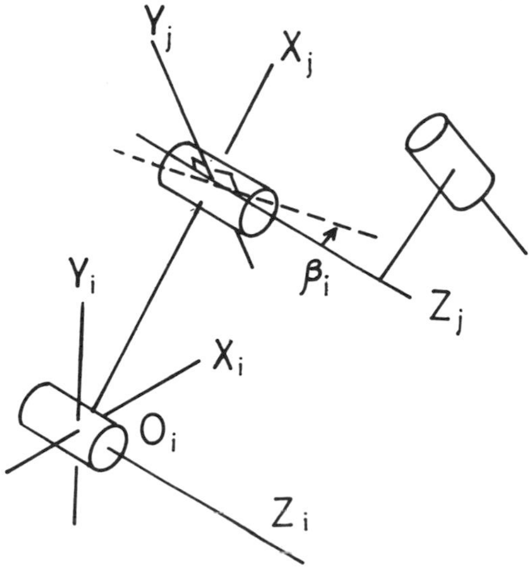

Fig. 4 New Parameter

$$\left.\begin{array}{l}\bar{x}=(d_o,\ \theta_0,\ \ldots,\ \theta_6,\ a_{67})^T\\ \Delta\bar{x}=(\Delta d_o,\ \Delta\theta_0,\ \ldots,\ \Delta\theta_6,\ \Delta a_{67})^T\end{array}\right] \qquad (16)$$

$$P=(\frac{\partial\bar{f}}{\partial d_0},\frac{\partial\bar{f}}{\partial\theta_0},\ \ldots,\ \frac{\partial\bar{f}}{\partial\theta_6},\ \frac{\partial\bar{f}}{\partial a_{67}}) \qquad (17)$$

,where T indicates a transposed matrix, then Eq. (9) becomes

$$\Delta\bar{r}=P\Delta\bar{x} \qquad (18)$$

From this relationship, we can estimate the geometric deviations as follows.

First, we assign m points $\bar{r}'^1$, $\bar{r}'^2$, ..., $\bar{r}'^m$ for which the positions with respect to the fixed coordinates $X_0Y_0Z_0$ are accurately known. Next, the reference point of the hand is positioned at these points. The orientation of the hand in this operation is arbitrary but shall be varied for each point. The displacements of the kinematic pairs when the hand is positioned at point $\bar{r}'^i$ are read off by detectors attached to actuators, and $\bar{r}^i$ and P_i are calculated from these and the mechanism constants, using Eq. (16) and Eq. (17), respectively. When the values selected as the constants for the robot mechanism include errors, $\bar{r}'^i$ and $\bar{r}^i$ do ont agree. Assuming this difference to be

$$\Delta\bar{r}_i=\bar{r}'^i-\bar{r}^i \qquad (19)$$

we get the relationship

$$\Delta\bar{r}_i=P_i\Delta\bar{x} \qquad (20)$$

Letting

$$\Delta\bar{r}_{all}=(\Delta\bar{r}_1^T,\ \Delta\bar{r}_2^T,\ \ldots,\ \Delta\bar{r}_m^T)^T \qquad (21)$$

$$P_{all}=(P_1^T,\ P_2^T,\ \ldots,\ P_m^T)^T \qquad (22)$$

we get

$$\Delta\bar{r}_{all}=P_{all}\Delta\bar{x} \qquad (23)$$

When the value of m is sufficiently large, we can estimate the value of $\Delta\bar{x}$ by the least squares method. The result becomes

$$\Delta\bar{x}=(P_{all}{}^TP_{all})^{-1}P_{all}{}^T\Delta\bar{r}_{all} \qquad (24)$$

4. Inversed Coordinate Transformation

When geometric deviations are estimated, the coordinate transformation equation must be revised accordingly. Let us consider here the case normally used in conventional robot control in which the hand position and orientation data is converted into displacements of kinematic pairs. When errors exist in all the dimensions of the robot mechanism, the coordinate transformation equation becomes identical to the equation used for displacement analysis of a seven-link single loop spatial mechanism that is an polynomial in up to the 32nd degree. Deriving an polynomial in the 32nd degree is in itself an extremely laborious process; computing its solutions in real time during robot operation presents great difficulties. The practical approaches to this problem consists of either carrying out an approximate coordinate transformation or driving the robot by rate control, the operation in which is equivalent to iterative computation of displacements of kinematic pairs.

When the robot mechanism include errors, from Eqs. (8) and (18), the position of the hand becomes

$$\bar{r}_{n+1}{}'=\bar{r}_{n+1}+P\Delta\bar{x} \tag{25}$$

Expressing deviations in the orientation of the hand in terms of the unit vector $\bar{e}$ of the axis of rotation and the angle of rotation $\Delta\phi$, we get

$$\Delta\phi\bar{e}=Q\Delta\bar{x} \tag{26}$$

where

$$Q=(\bar{q}_{d0}, \bar{q}_{\theta 0}, \ldots, \bar{q}_{\theta 6}, \bar{q}_{a67}) \tag{27}$$

$$\bar{q}_{di}=\bar{q}_{aij}=0 \tag{28}$$

$$\bar{q}_{\theta i}=V(\bar{Z}_i) \tag{29}$$

$$\bar{q}_{\alpha ij}=V(\bar{X}_j) \tag{30}$$

In the case of replacing d_i with β_i,

$$\bar{q}_{\beta i}=V(\bar{Y}_j) \tag{31}$$

Expressing the orientation of the hand as the set of unit vectors $\bar{f}$, $\bar{g}$ and $\bar{h}$, respectively parallel to the X_{n+1}, Y_{n+1} and Z_{n+1} axes of the hand coordinates, the relationship between the hand orientation $\bar{f}'$, $\bar{g}'$ and $\bar{h}'$ that include the influence of geometric deviations, and the hand orientation $\bar{f}$, $\bar{g}$ and $\bar{h}$ that does not, becomes

$$(\bar{f}', \bar{g}', \bar{h}')=R(\Delta\phi, \bar{e})(\bar{f}, \bar{g}, \bar{h}) \tag{32}$$

where

$$R(\Delta\phi, \bar{e}) = I\cos\Delta\phi+(1-\cos\Delta\phi)\bar{e}\bar{e}^T +\sin\Delta\phi\, E \tag{33}$$

$$E=\begin{pmatrix} 0 & -e_z & e_y \\ e_z & 0 & -e_x \\ -e_y & e_x & 0 \end{pmatrix} \tag{34}$$

e_x, e_y and e_z are elements of $\bar{e}$ and I is a unit matrix.

In Eqs. (25) and (32), P and R are respectively the functions of the position $\bar{r}_{n+1}$ and orientation $\bar{f}$, $\bar{g}$, $\bar{h}$ of the robot hand in the absence of geometric deviations. These can be regarded as fair approximations of the functions of $\bar{r}_{n+1}{}'$ and $\bar{f}'$, $\bar{g}'$, $\bar{h}'$. The approximate coordinate transformation in this case is carried out as follows.

First of all, when the position and orientation of the hand is given. these are assumed to be $\bar{r}_{n+1}{}'$ and $\bar{f}'$, $\bar{g}'$, $\bar{h}'$. Next, the displacements of kinematic pairs θ_1, θ_2, ..., θ_6 corresponding to $\bar{r}_{n+1}{}'$ and $\bar{f}'$, $\bar{g}'$, $\bar{h}'$ are taken to be a value of geometric deviations, and these used together with the selected values representing the dimensions of the robot mechanism, in accordance with Eq. (16), to define the vector $\bar{x}$. Vector $\bar{x}$ is then used to define functions P and R, from which, using the geometric deviations $\Delta\bar{x}$ estimated earlier, we can now calculate:

$$\bar{r}_{n+1}=\bar{r}_{n+1}{}'-P\Delta\bar{x} \tag{35}$$

$$(\bar{f}, \bar{g}, \bar{h})=R^{-1}(\bar{f}', \bar{g}', \bar{h}') \tag{360}$$

The results obtained by calculating the displacements of kinematic pairs for $\bar{r}_{n+1}$ and $\bar{f}$, $\bar{g}$, $\bar{h}$, which represent values free of geometric deviations, serve as an approximate solution of the actual displacements of kinematic pairs.

5. Error Compensation by Projective Transformation Approximation

The method described in the preceding section corrects for robot positioning error due to geometric deviations by performing inversed coordinate trsansformation. However, use of this method significantly increases the computing time required for inversed coordinate transformation. One possible way around this is a method that compensates for geometric deviations within a limited work area by means of a simple approximation using the projective transformation of homogeneous coordinates.

Let us first consider the fixed coordinates for the robot, the hand coordinates, and the coordinates of the work area. We shall assume that the work area coordinates are fixed in the fixed coordinetes for the robot. The position and orientation data for the hand to be located shall be given as $\bar{r}, \bar{f}, \bar{g}$ and $\bar{h}$ in the work area coordinates. These shall now be expressed together as a projective transformation matrix of homogeneous coordinates:

$$T_{data}=\begin{vmatrix} 1 & 0 & 0 & 0 \\ \bar{r} & \bar{f} & \bar{g} & \bar{h} \end{vmatrix} \tag{37}$$

In order to position the hand at T_{data}, the robot is driven such that the transformation matrix T_{hand} expressing the position of the hand coordinates in the fixed robot coordinates satisfies the following codition:

$$T_{hand}=T_w T_{data} \tag{38}$$

where T_w is a matrix expressing the position of the work area coordinates in the fixed robot coordinates. T_{hand} is defined as a fuction of both parameters of the robot mechanism and the displacements of kinematic pairs. We shall let $\bar{x}$ be the value selected for the parameters and the displacements, and assume that this includes an error $\Delta\bar{x}$. It follows that, by solving:

$$T_{hand}(\bar{x}+\Delta\bar{x})=T_w T_{data} \tag{39}$$

where T_{hand} is a function of $\bar{x}+\Delta\bar{x}$, we get the displacements of kinematic pairs when $\bar{x}$ includes the error. However, we shall assume here that we can make the following approximation:

$$T_{hand}(\bar{x}+\Delta\bar{x})=\{I+A(\Delta\bar{x})\}T_{hand}(\bar{x}) \tag{40}$$

Here, $A(\Delta\bar{x})$ is a 4x4 matrix that is the function of just the error $\Delta\bar{x}$. Matrix A is usually a function of $\bar{x}$ and $\Delta\bar{x}$. What this assumption means is that the effects of $\bar{x}$ on A within a given range is regarded as being constsnt.

If Eq. (40) holds, then

$$B=\{I+A(\Delta\bar{x})\}^{-1}T_w \tag{41}$$

is always constant regardless of $\bar{x}$. If the value of B can be estimated, then, using the T_{data} and B given, we can easily determine the displacements of kinematic pairs corresponding to T_{data} from

$$T_{hand}(\bar{x})=DT_{data} \tag{42}$$

Matrix B can be estimated as follows. First we set m points T^1_{data}, T^2_{data}, ..., T^m_{data} at which the robot can be positioned within the work area coordinates through teaching. Next, from the results of detections of the displacements of kinematic pairs obtained when the robot is positioned at these points, we can determine $\bar{x}_1$, $\bar{x}_2$,..., $\bar{x}_m$. Here, the value of $\bar{x}_i$ is taken to be a set value that excludes geometric deviations. Assuming here that

$$C=\{T_{hand}(\bar{x}_1),\ T_{hand}(\bar{x}_2),\ ...,\ T_{hand}(\bar{x}_m)\} \tag{43}$$

$$D=\{T^1_{data},\ T^2_{data},\ ...,\ T^m_{data}\} \tag{44}$$

and applying the least squares method, the estimated value of B becomes:

$$B=CD^T(DD^T)^{-1} \tag{45}$$

6. Numerical Examples

Examples of numerical analysis that illustrate the estimation of geometric deviations and error compensation are given below. The robot used in these examples is an articulated robot with six degrees of freedom comprised of six revolute kinematic pairs. The displacements of the kinematic pairs are represented by θ_1, θ_2, ..., θ_6. $\Delta\theta_1$, $\Delta\theta_2$, ..., $\Delta\theta_6$ accordingly represent the fixed errors for the position of the origin of the displacements.

Table 1 shows the results obtained by estimating the geometric deviations. In this example, since a_{01}=0 and α_{01}=0, then θ_0 and θ_1 represent the same item, making $\Delta\theta_0$ unnecessary. The maximum values of the estimated errors, in terms of length and angle, are 0.0188mm and 0.0068degree, respectively.

Iterative computations carried out for the deviations of the origins of the displacements of the kinematic pairs and the results are given in Table 2. In this case, estimated values for the deviations of the origin positions are used in the next computation. Iterative computations are not carried out other than for errors in the origin position. It is evident that even large deviations are estimated at high accuracy by means of iterative computation.

Table 3 gives the results obtained by calculating error compensation using projective transformation approximation.
The geometrical deviations in this case are the same as listed in Table 1. It is clear that error compensation has cut the error in positioning of the hand to about one-tenth of what it was previously.

7. Conclusion

The deviations in the robot system such as errors in the dimensions of a robot mechanism and misalignments between the robot coordinates and work area coordinates were estimated by the least squares method from displacement data of kinematic pairs when the robot is positioned at a number of preestablished points. Based on these results, we developed a method that compensates for positioning errors. Making use of the fact that α_{ij} equals 0 or 90 degrees in the inversed transformation equations used in normal robot control, we simplified this equations by setting several of the terms to zero. As a result, several of the estimeted dimensional errors in a robot mechanism can be fed back to the inversed coordinate transformation equations. However, the remainder are difficult to handle in these equations. Thus, in error compensation, one practical approach is to fed back to the equations the parameters used in it and compensate for the remaining errors by approximation. Error compensation by projective transformation approximation is especially effective when the work area of a robot is limited. By incorporating these functions in the robot controller, it becomes possible to easily estimate compensation parameters in the work place of a robot.

Table 1 Result of Estimation

	x	Δx	Result
θ_1	- degree	0.0	0.0000
θ_2	- degree	0.0	0.0003
θ_3	- degree	0.0	0.0004
θ_4	- degree	0.0	-0.0010
θ_5	- degree	0.0	0.0068
θ_6	- degree	0.0	-0.0001
d_0	0.0 mm	0.0	-0.0188
β_1	0.0 degree	0.0	-0.0001
β_2	0.0 degree	0.0	-0.0002
β_3	0.0 degree	0.0	0.0012
d_4	0.0 mm	0.0	0.0003
d_5	60.0 mm	0.5	0.4895
d_6	100.0 mm	0.0	-0.0019
a_{01}	0.0 mm	0.0	-0.0016
a_{12}	0.0 mm	0.0	0.0008
a_{23}	400.0 mm	0.5	0.4919
a_{34}	400.0 mm	-0.5	-0.5063
a_{45}	0.0 mm	0.0	0.0032
a_{56}	0.0 mm	0.0	-0.0111
a_{67}	50.0 mm	0.0	0.0053
α_{01}	0.0 degree	0.0	0.0025
α_{12}	90.0 degrees	0.1	0.0987
α_{23}	0.0 degree	0.1	0.1002
α_{34}	0.0 degree	0.0	-0.0025
α_{45}	90.0 degrees	0.0	0.0009
α_{56}	90.0 degrees	0.0	-0.0051

References

Kumar, A., and Waldron, K.J., 1981. Numerical Plotting of Positioning Accuracy of Manipulators. Mechanism and Machine Theory 16(4):361-368.

Wu, C., 1984. A Kinematic CAD Tool for the Design and Control of a Robot Manipulator. Robotics Research 3(1):58-67

Sugimoto, K., and Matsumoto, Y., 1983. Kinematic Analysis of Manipulators by Means of Projective Transformation of Screw Coordinates. Proceedings of the first ISRR.

Table 2 Results of Estimation by Iterative Computation

x		Δx	Results: Number of Times of Computation 1	2	3	4
θ_1	- degree	10.0	10.5412	9.9998	10.0001	10.0001
θ_2	- degree	-8.0	-7.9646	-8.0050	-7.9997	-7.9997
θ_3	- degree	-10.0	-9.6503	-9.9923	-9.9996	-9.9996
θ_4	- degree	5.0	6.2457	5.0002	4.9987	4.9988
θ_5	- degree	-7.0	-9.4143	-7.0542	-6.9944	-6.9939
θ_6	- degree	-4.0	-1.2050	-3.9658	-4.0000	-4.0003
d_0	0.0 mm	0.1				0.0802
β_1	0.0 degree	0.0				0.0000
β_2	0.0 degree	0.0				-0.0001
β_3	0.0 degree	0.0				0.0011
d_4	0.0 mm	-0.2				-0.2004
d_5	60.0 mm	0.5				0.4897
d_6	100.0 mm	0.0				-0.0023
a_{01}	0.0 mm	0.0				-0.0013
a_{12}	0.0 mm	0.3				0.3006
a_{23}	400.0 mm	0.5				0.4921
a_{34}	400.0 mm	-0.5				-0.5063
a_{45}	0.0 mm	-0.2				-0.1965
a_{56}	0.0 mm	0.25				0.2399
a_{67}	50.0 mm	-0.35				-0.3450
α_{01}	0.0 degree	0.0				0.0026
α_{12}	90.0 degrees	0.1				0.0985
α_{23}	0.0 degree	0.1				0.1002
α_{34}	0.0 degree	-0.05				-0.0525
α_{45}	90.0 degrees	0.07				0.0705
α_{56}	90.0 degrees	-0.03				-0.0350

Table 3 Compensation of Positioning Errors by Projective Transformation Approximation

Point Number	Errors: before Compensation	after Compensation
1	0.526 mm	0.037 mm
2	0.531 mm	0.014 mm
3	0.528 mm	0.038 mm
4	0.480 mm	0.025 mm
5	0.495 mm	0.048 mm
6	0.490 mm	0.023 mm
7	0.434 mm	0.047 mm
8	0.441 mm	0.013 mm
9	0.438 mm	0.042 mm

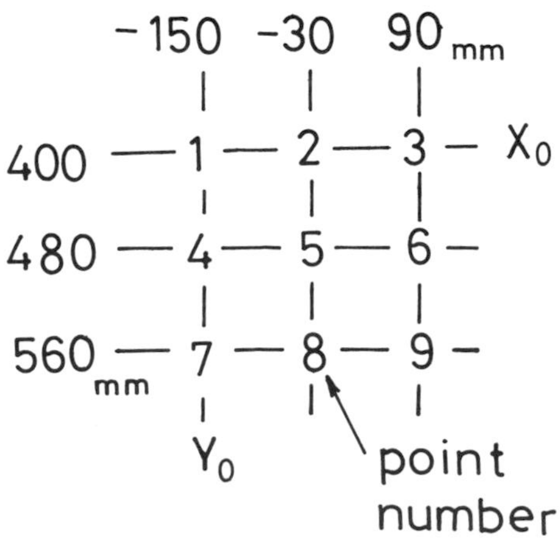

KINEMATIC ANALYSIS AND DESIGN FOR AUTOMATIC WORKPART FIXTURING IN FLEXIBLE ASSEMBLY

Haruhiko Asada and Andre B. By

Department of Mechanical Engineering
and
Laboratory for Manufacturing and Productivity

Massachusetts Institute of Technology
Cambridge, MA 02139 U.S.A.

An automatic fixturing system for computer-integrated advanced assembly is presented. The system employs reconfigurable fixture modules or elements that are used to locate and hold various workparts for assembly. The fixture configuration or layout can be changed automatically depending upon the workpart geometry and the assembly operations required. Based on a CAD database description of the assembly, the system determines the optimal layout for the reconfigurable fixture elements and builds the desired fixture automatically using a robot manipulator.

The basic concept of the reconfigurable fixturing system and its hardware implementation are first described. Analytic tools for automatic design of fixture layouts are next developed. Kinematic modeling, analysis and characterization of workpart fixturing are presented. Conditions for a fixture layout to locate a given workpart uniquely and to constrain its motion completely are derived. Desirable fixture layout characteristics to avoid jamming during the process of workpart positioning are discussed. The fixturing of a plastic cover of an electrical appliance with complex shape is used as an example to verify the analytic results and for demonstrating the concept.

1. Introduction

Important to any assembly operation or system is the issue of workpart positioning and constraint. For operations to be successful, workparts must in general be placed and oriented within specific tolerances appropriate to the particular assembly process. The workparts must also be constrained to remain in position and orientation when subjected to disturbance forces and inputs during the manufacturing process. In mating multiple workparts, one workpart must be first positioned and constrained so that subsequent workparts can be joined with the first.

Mechanical fixturing and tooling is traditionally employed in manual and automated assembly systems to provide the required workpart guiding, presentation, orientation and constraint functions. The jigs and fixtures used are typically single-purpose devices designed and manufactured for specific workparts and operations. A significant amount of manual effort is required for setting up and changing the jigs and fixtures when an assembly station operation is modified. Thus, the traditional approach is generally costly and time consuming for lower volume production applications. This severely limits the overall flexibility of the assembly system.

Recent research efforts have addressed alternatives to conventional fixturing. Sensory information can be used to compensate for tolerancing errors of workparts and assembly setups. Vision modules such as that developed at SRI can reduce tight requirements for accurate workpart positioning within a fixture [Nitzan, et al., 1979]. The well known Remote Center Compliance (RCC) wrist concept developed at Draper Laboratories enables a robot to perform precision insertion operations without using costly, high precision jigs and fixtures [Whitney, 1982]. Employing two manipulator arms, one for holding one workpart and the other for transferring and mating a second workpart, might also reduce requirements for fixturing devices [Takeyasu, et al., 1977].

Although such advances in sensory based compensation and other areas can greatly reduce fixturing requirements, it is nonetheless impractical or impossible to completely eliminate the need for some form of fixturing in assembly systems. Assembly operations still require a means for locating and holding workparts for these operations to be possible. However, conventional fixturing methods are a significant bottleneck to flexible assembly. In consequence, a central issue for achieving fully flexible assembly is to develop an alternative approach that would completely replace single-purpose jigs and fixtures.

This paper presents and describes a general-purpose fixturing system which eliminates single purpose hardware and reduces the human intervention required for assembly station fixture setup and change. This approach more fully exploits the advantages and features of robotic assembly. It will reduce the requirement for teach-mode programming of robots at manufacturing sites. Thus, overall system flexibility will be increased while reducing the cost and lead time associated with fixturing implementation.

2. Automatically Reconfigured Fixturing

2.1 Concepts

A major limitation to flexible assembly is that a significant amount of human intervention is still required for making jigs and fixtures and for setting up the assembly stations. The approach proposed in this paper is for fixture design and setup change to be performed automatically by a computer-integrated system that includes a robot manipulator. Namely, the robot would be used to configure the layout of a fixture, which is designed automatically on the basis of a CAD database description of the required assembly.

To achieve this, conventional single-purpose fixtures are replaced by a group of relocatable fixture elements that can be reconfigured for building different fixtures. The fixture elements are designed in such a way that various fixtures can be constructed using different combinations and layouts of these primitive elements. Each element is also designed so that a robot manipulator can handle the element easily and precisely to change the overall fixture configuration.

The controller of the robot manipulator is linked to a CAD system with which the fixture element layout is designed. This system is also used to generate the robot motion commands for implementing the layout. These commands are downloaded to the robot controller from the CAD system. Given the geometry of workparts and the assembly description, the system optimizes the fixture layout using the fixture elements available.

In this process, human intervention is greatly reduced. Empirical techniques of fixture design are replaced or reduced by a systematic method. The hardware fabrication effort is minimized and its management is computerized. Another significant reduction of human intervention is possible since manual teaching of robots for overall assembly operations can be reduced or eliminated. A human operator does not need to teach the location of the fixture and the environment since the fixture layout data, workpart geometric data, and assembly description are all known to the system. Thus, the CAD-CAM-Robot integration greatly reduces lead times for setting up and changing the assembly station.

2.2 Hardware Implementation

Photograph 1 shows a prototype system developed at MIT for demonstrating our basic concept of reconfigurable fixturing. The robot manipulator used is an IBM RS-1 robot, a hydraulically driven cartesian type of robot with 6 degrees of freedom. This robot employs an IBM Series 1 mini-computer with AML as the robot control language. Key components of this system are a fixture base and the fixture elements. The fixture base is a flat horizontal table with magnetic chucking capability. As the fixture elements are positioned on the table by the robot, the magnetic chuck is activated as required to secure the elements.

Photograph 2 shows the fixture elements as positioned in a storage magazine. Four fixture element types are employed in the prototype system; vertical clamps, horizontal clamps, horizontal guides and vertical supports. These were designed so that various fixtures could be constructed for the assembly of electrical appliances and mechanical systems that employ an exterior case as the reference workpart [Steines, 1984]. The support and guiding elements provide constraint and guiding in horizontal and vertical or near vertical planes. The clamping elements are actuated to provide final constraint in these planes after the workpart is positioned in the fixture.

Figure 1 shows a particular example of the plastic case of an electric hand drill. This representative workpart is approximately a half shell in shape, and can be fixed completely by a combination of the four primitive fixture elements presented above. Note, however, that it is essential that the fixture element layout be optimally designed such that a given workpart is completely constrained at a desired location. This location must be reliably accessed by the robot without jamming in the positioning process.

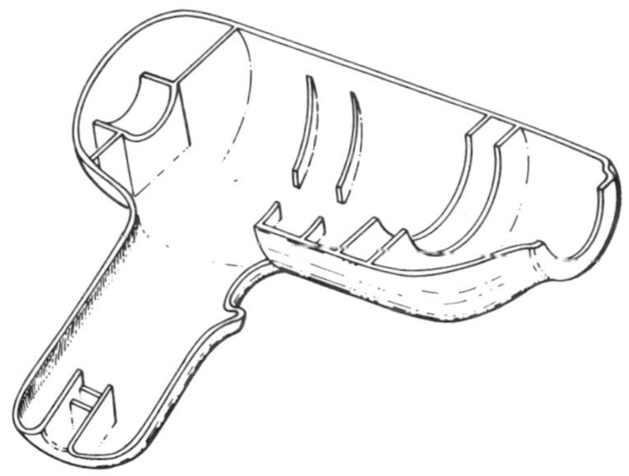

Figure 1 - Electric Hand Drill Case

The fixturing of the electric hand drill case has been implemented on our demonstration system as shown in Photographs 3 through 6. In this sequence, the fixture elements are first laid out, the workpart is transferred to the fixture and guided by the fixture elements to its final position, then the clamping fixtures are actuated. The clamping elements provide the final securing constraints on the workpart.

Photograph 3 shows the first few fixture elements as placed on the magnetic chuck. This includes vertical support clamps that will, with gravity, hold the workpart at a certain elevation. A horizontal guide and horizontal clamp has also been positioned at this stage of the fixture layout sequence. Photograph 4 shows the complete fixture element layout, which includes the addition of two vertical clamps and two more horizontal guides.

Photograph 5 shows the workpart as positioned within the fixture by the robot. In this case, the fixture layout has been designed such that the workpart need only be positioned approximately within the fixture. In combination with gravity, the vertical supports constrain the motion of the workpart to the horizontal plane. This feature of the fixture design is important since a moderate positioning inaccuracy of the workpart is tolerated by the system.

Actuation of the horizontal clamp, as shown in Photograph 6, positions the workpart uniquely in the horizontal plane. The vertical clamps are next actuated to augment the limited vertical constraint provided by gravity. With all clamps actuated, the workpart is now completely constrained and the assembly operation can proceed.

3. Kinematic Analysis

3.1 Modeling

For the adaptable fixturing approach described in the previous section a workpart is first transferred to a fixturing station, guided by fixture elements to a desired location, then clamped into the fixture firmly. In this process, the fixture elements must locate the workpart uniquely at the desired position and orientation. The fixture layout design must also be such that the workpart can be mated with the fixture properly without jamming during the positioning. After the clamping fixture elements are positioned and actuated, the workpart must be totally constrained from motion. In this section, we develop analytical tools for designing fixture layouts from a kinematic standpoint. The conditions necessary for a fixture layout to provide deterministic positioning and jam-free positioning are derived.

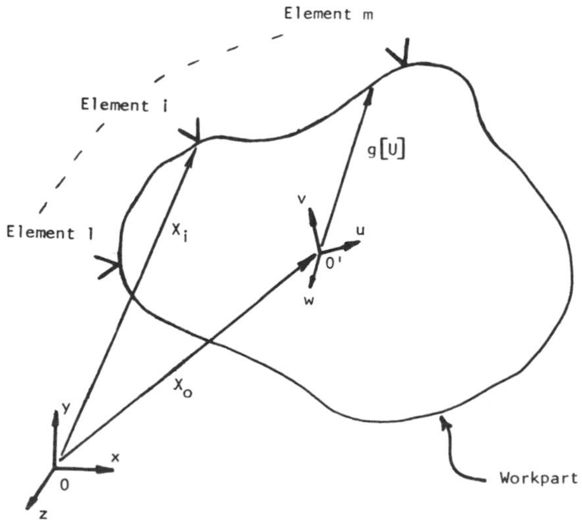

Figure 2 - Fixturing System Model

Figure 2 shows a kinematic model of a fixturing system. Coordinate system O-xyz is fixed to the assembly station while O'-uvw is fixed to the workpart. We assume the workpart to be a rigid body with a surface that can be represented by a piecewise differentiable function in terms of coordinates U = col. [u, v, w],

$$g[U] = 0 \qquad (1)$$

It is also assumed that this function is defined such that the points outside of the workpart surface are represented by

$$g[U] > 0 \qquad (2)$$

Similarly, points within the workpart surface result in a negative value of the function.

Let X_o = col. $[x_o, y_o, z_o]$ be the origin of the coordinate system O'-uvw and Θ = col. $[\theta, \psi, \phi]$ be three independent angles representing the orientation of O'-uvw relative to O-xyz. Then the coordinate transformation from U to X = col. [x, y, z] is given by

$$X = A(\Theta)\, U + X_o \qquad (3)$$

Where A is a 3 x 3 rotation matrix in terms of the three angles. Solving eq. (3) for U and substituting it into eq. (1), one obtains the workpart surface representation in O-xyx.

$$g[\, A(\Theta)^t \{ X - X_o \} \,] = 0 \qquad (4)$$

Consider a system of fixture elements numbered 1 through m as shown in Figure 2. We assume that each element is in point contact with the workpart surface and that the contact is modeled as a point whose coordinates are X_i = col. $[x_i, y_i, z_i]$. When the i-th element is in contact with the workpart surface, the following is satisfied:

$$g[\, A(\Theta)^t \{ X_i - X_o \} \,] = 0 \qquad (5)$$

To simplify this expression, let us combine the position and orientation vectors and define

$$q = \text{col.}\, [x_o, y_o, z_o, \theta_o, \psi_o, \phi_o]$$

$$g_i[q] = g[\, A(\Theta)^t \{ X_i - X_o \} \,] \qquad (6)$$

When the fixture elements lie outside of the workpart surface and are thus not in contact with it, the following inequality holds:

$$g_i[q] > 0 \qquad (7)$$

Note that the only possible fixture element positions are those which lie outside of the workpart or on its surface. Thus, when the fixture element position is fixed with respect to the assembly station frame, all possible workpart positions and orientations are represented by eqs. (5) and (7).

3.2 Deterministic Positioning

One of the fundamental roles of a fixture is to locate a workpart to a specific location and orientation that is unique. Let us now derive the condition for unique workpart positioning with a given fixture element layout.

Let q^* be the desired location at which a workpart is to be positioned. A system of fixture elements, $X_i \ldots X_m$ are located so that they are in contact with the surface of the workpart at the desired location q^*. Namely,

$$g_i [q^*] = 0 \qquad 1 < i < m \qquad (8)$$

In positioning a workpart, the goal is to mate the workpart surface with the fixture elements when the workpart is at the desired location q^*. The positioning is <u>deterministic</u> when the workpart location is unique when all fixture elements are made to contact the workpart surface. This condition is equivalent to requiring the following set of simultaneous equations to have a unique solution:

$$g_i [q] = 0 \qquad 1 < i < m \qquad (9)$$

Assuming that the workpart can be reliably placed by the robot within the vicinity of the desired location q^*, uniqueness of the solution in the vicinity of q^* need only be considered. Let Δq be a small deviation of the workpart position from the desired location. At this alternate position, eqs. (9) can be expressed as follows:

$$g_i[q^* + \Delta q] = g_i[q^*] + \nabla g_i \Delta q = 0 \quad 1 < i < m \quad (10)$$

Here, eqs. (9) have been linearized using the m x 6 Jacobian matrix G. The term ∇g_i in eq. (10) corresponds to the partial derivatives of g_i with respect to q and is the i-th row vector of the Jacobian matrix G defined below:

$$G = \begin{matrix} \frac{\partial g_1}{\partial x}, & \ldots, & \frac{\partial g_1}{\partial \phi} \\ \vdots & & \\ \frac{\partial g_m}{\partial x}, & \ldots, & \frac{\partial g_m}{\partial \phi} \end{matrix} \qquad (11)$$

The first part of the right hand side of eq. (10) is equivalent to eq. (8), thus it is possible to rewrite eq. (10) as follows:

$$G \Delta q = 0 \qquad (12)$$

For the fixturing layout to support deterministic positioning, q^* must be the only solution to eq. (10). This requires that there must exist only one solution for eq. (12), the solution where $\Delta q = 0$. In order for this to be true, the Jacobian matrix of eq. (11) must have full rank.

$$\text{rank } G = 6; \qquad \text{full rank} \qquad (13)$$

When the above is satisfied, there will be only one position and orientation of the workpart such that its surface contacts all of the fixture elements. Therefore, the process of placing the workpart in contact with the fixture is deterministic.

Consider cases of planar motion of a rectangular workpart as shown in Figure 3. Here, the fixture elements are depicted as circular surfaces. Layout A does not determine the workpart location uniquely since the workpart can rotate while in contact with the two fixture elements. The rank of the Jacobian matrix for this system is two, whereas the full rank for planar motions is three. The matrix rank for layouts B and C is also not full. While maintaining contact with these fixture element layouts, the workpart is free to rotate and slide respectively. For layouts D through F, the workpart cannot move without loosing contact with the fixture element surfaces. The matrix ranks for these cases is three, thus the positioning is deterministic.

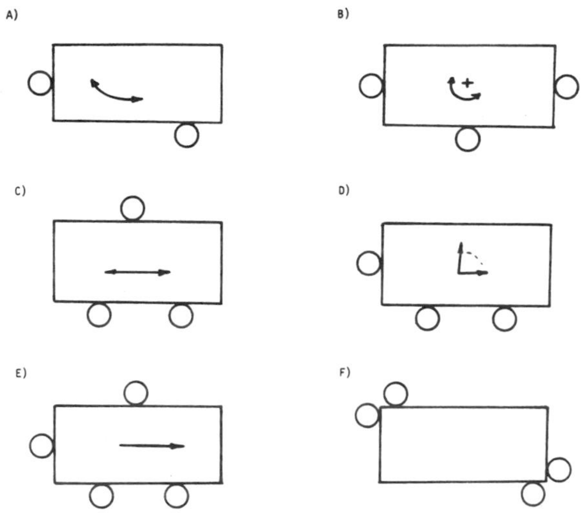

Figure 3 - Planar Motion Constraint Examples

3.3 Accesibility

In this section we derive the condition for an accessible fixture layout. Layout F in Figure 3, for example, is not accessible when workpart trajectories are limited to planar motion only. On the other hand, for layouts D and E one can move the workpart to the desired locations from an initial position outside of the fixture. In general, a fixture layout is considered to be accessible when there exists at least one non-conflicting mating trajectory between the desired final workpart location and an outside position.

Let us consider the local behavior of a workpart in the vicinity of the desired final location to derive a local condition for accessibility assuming that the workpart can be successfully placed in this vicinity from an outside location. As defined previously, let Δq be a small displacement of the workpart from the desired final location q^*. The linear approximation of the left hand side of eq. (9) is again employed as below:

$$g_i[q^* + \Delta q] = g_i[q^*] + \nabla g_i \Delta q \qquad 1 < i < m \qquad (14)$$

If the i-th fixture element position is outside of the workpart surface, the left hand side of eq. (14) is positive, as defined previously. Note that by eq. (8) the first term of the right hand side of eq. (14) is zero. Thus, the small workpart displacement Δq will cause the workpart to move away from the i-th fixture element when the following condition is held:

$$\nabla g_i \Delta q \;>\; 0 \qquad (15)$$

A similar expression results when this condition is expressed in terms of screw theory [Ohwovoriole and Roth, 1981]. The resulting workpart motion is referred to as REPELLING to the fixture element when the above condition is held.

When the workpart maintains contact with the i-th fixture element for a given Δq, eq. (14) has a value of zero. As before, by substitution of eq. (8) into eq. (14) it can be seen that the small workpart motion Δq will cause the workpart to slide along the i-th fixture element when the following condition is held:

$$\nabla g_i \Delta q \;=\; 0 \qquad (16)$$

The resulting workpart motion is referred to as RECIPROCAL to the fixture element when the above condition is held.

Since fixture element positions must always lie either on or outside of the workpart surface, the only possible workpart motions are those that are either reciprocal to or repelling to the fixture elements. Thus, all admissible small motions of a workpart must satisfy either eqs. (15) or (16).

In order for a fixture element layout to be accessible in the vicinity of the desired final location, there must exist at least one admissible displacement Δq such that the workpart will dettach from the fixture elements to a position outside of the fixture. The desired final location q^* is thus accessible from this position $q^* + \Delta q$ by moving the workpart in the opposite direction to Δq. A fixture layout is defined as either <u>weakly</u> or <u>nominally</u> accessible when there exists a non-zero solution to the following,

$$G \, \Delta q \;\geq\; 0 \qquad (17)$$

where G is again the Jacobian matrix representing the set of m fixture elements. Note that this Jacobian is full rank as required for the fixture layout to support deterministic positioning. Because there exists no non-zero solution to eq. (12) when G is full rank, all the non-zero displacements that satisfy eq. (17) are repelling to at least one fixture element. Therefore, a non-zero solution to eq. (17) moves the workpart away from at least one fixture element. Note, however, that the workpart can still be in contact with other fixture elements in this case.

A fixture layout is defined as <u>strongly</u> or <u>robustly</u> accessible in the vicinity of the desired final location q^* when there exists a non-zero solution Δq to the following,

$$G \, \Delta q \;>\; 0 \qquad (18)$$

where G is again full rank. Any admissible displacement Δq that satisfies eq. (18) moves the workpart away from all the fixture elements at once. Namely, the workpart motion is repelling to all the fixture elements. Thus, the opposite motion could be applied to mate the workpart and fixture such that the workpart contacts the fixture elements only at the final position q^*.

Let us discuss the significant differences between the two conditions. In actual assembly operations, tolerancing errors in workpart dimension and positioning trajectories must be taken into account. A nominally accessible fixture layout is not adequate in this sense. Namely, it can be shown that if a layout is not strongly accessible but simply nominally accessible, there exists at least one direction in which there is no tolerance or margin for the workpart positioning motion. Therefore, either the workpart positioning operation would not be possible or the robot would jam the workpart between the opposing fixture elements. Thus, the strongly accessible condition is significant in that it characterizes fixturing layouts that are more robust against tolerancing errors and more resilient to workpart jamming during the positioning process.

Let us return again to a discussion of the examples presented in Figure 3. Layout F satisfies neither eq. (17) or eq. (18). This layout is not accessible. Layout E, on the other hand, satisfies the nominally accessible condition, that is, eq. (17). The workpart can be moved without conflict to the right. Here the workpart looses contact with one fixture element yet still remains in contact with the others. Thus, in the positioning trajectory, the workpart might either collide with the fixture elements are jam between them due to tolerancing errors.

Layout D satisfies the strongly or robustly accessible condition of eq. (18). Here, there exists an admissible displacement that detaches the workpart from all the fixture elements at once, as shown in the figure. Significant advantages of this type of fixture layout are that the workpart positioning can be performed despite tolerancing errors and that friction between the fixture and workpart can be avoided in removing or positioning the workpart. This is advantageous for avoiding workpart jamming in these operations.

3.4 Workpart Constraint

In this section we derive the condition for the fixture layout to totally constrain the workpart from motion. This is the condition required of the final fixture layout when the clamping fixtures are actuated. Layout F, for example, is the only fixture layout in Figure 3 where the workpart is constrained from any planar motion.

A fixture layout is considered to provide total constraint when there exists no admissible workpart trajectory from the desired final position q*. No repelling or reciprocal motion from this position must thus exist for the fixture layout. Using the results from the previous sections, this implies that there must not exist any non-zero solution Δq to the following,

$$G_f \Delta q \geq 0 \qquad (19)$$

where G_f is the full rank Jacobian matrix representing the final fixturing layout (the clamped configuration). The above condition requires that no Δq exists that is either repelling to or reciprocal to each of the fixture elements in the clamped configuration. Thus, all Δq will be CONTRARY to at least one of the fixture elements as below:

$$\nabla g_i \Delta q < 0 \qquad (20)$$

This implies that the i-th fixture element will move within the surface of the workpart. Since this violates our definition of the workpart, no possible Δq exists if there does not exist any non-zero solution Δq to eq. (19). The above result is equivalent to the screw theory definition of total constraint established in the literature [Ohwovoriole and Roth, 1981].

4. Numerical Example

An example application of the above analysis tools is now presented for the fixturing of the electric drill case. As illustrated in Figure 4, the constraints provided by the fixture elements are represented by normal vectors 1 through 9. These normal vectors face inward to the surface and correspond to the rows of the Jacobian matrix G defined in eq. (11) above. Normal vectors 1 through 3 represent the vertical support elements while normals 5, 8 and 9 represent the horizontal guides. The horizontal clamp corresponds to normal vector 5 with the vertical clamps modeled by normals 6 and 7. Normal vector 10 represents the gravity constraint on the workpart and is aligned with the gravity force.

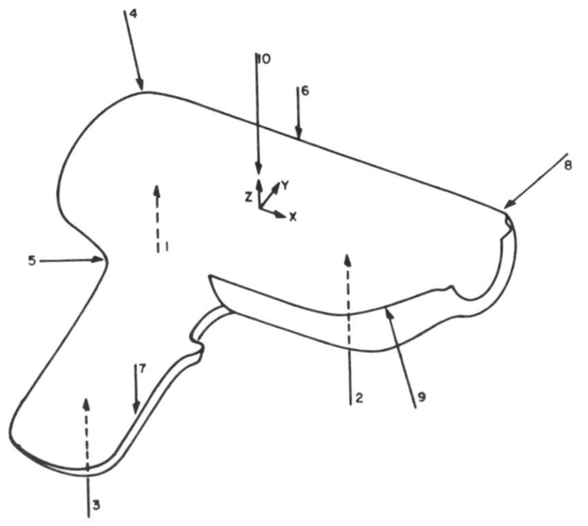

Figure 4 - Drill Case Fixture Element Normals

Table 1 includes the values of the Jacobian G_f for the workpart and the clamped fixture layout. Each row of this table is associated with the corresponding normal vector. The first three columns represent the direction cosines (L, M, and N) of the normals in the o′-xyz frame defined in Figure 4. The last three columns correspond to the moments of the normals about the coordinate frame (P, Q, and R). The values presented in Table 1 have not been normalized.

Table 1

Fixture Layout Jacobian for Drill Case Example

Normal Vector	Jacobian Elements					
	$\frac{\partial g}{\partial x}$	$\frac{\partial g}{\partial y}$	$\frac{\partial g}{\partial z}$	$\frac{\partial g}{\partial \theta}$	$\frac{\partial g}{\partial \psi}$	$\frac{\partial g}{\partial \phi}$
1	.25	-.3	1.0	.4	1.25	.275
2	-.2	-.3	1.0	.6	-2.6	-.66
3	.05	.1	.6	-1.56	.48	.05
4	.2	-.4	.0	.0	.0	.74
5	.3	.4	.0	.0	.0	-.32
6	.0	.0	-1.0	-2.2	.4	.0
7	.0	.0	-1.0	3.2	.0	.0
8	-.1	-.7	.0	.0	.0	-2.18
9	-.2	.2	.0	.0	.0	.58
10	.0	.0	-1.0	.0	.0	.0

Using this Jacobian, let us now demonstrate some of the fixture layout conditions previously defined. First consider the Jacobian G for the unclamped fixture configuration. Here, we eliminate the rows corresponding to the vertical clamps, gravity and the horizontal clamp (rows 6, 7, 10, and 5, respectively). Ideally, this Jacobian must be such that the fixture layout is both deterministic and robustly accessible. From eq. (13), the unclamped (intermediate) fixture layout is determinstic if the Jacobian has full rank. For the example fixturing layout, the determinant of this Jacobian is non-zero, and the layout is indeed deterministic.

The intermediate fixture layout is robustly accessible only if there exists a displacement Δq that satisfies eq. (18). The displacement Δq = [-1.2, -1, 1, 0, 0, 0] clearly satisfies this requirement. If normal 5 (the horizontal clamp) is included in the intermediate Jacobian, the intermediate fixture layout is only weakly accessible since all admissible displacements are in the vertical direction and are reciprocal to normals 4, 5, 8 and 9.

When all fixture element normals are included in the Jacobian, there should exist no Δq that satisfies eq. (19) if the workpart is to be totally constrained. This is true for the example fixture layout as can be verified using established mathematical approaches for the analysis of simultaneous linear inequalities [Ohwovoriole and Roth, 1981].

Closure

This paper has introduced the concept of adaptable fixturing for robotic reconfiguration as part of an advanced robotic assembly approach. A geometric formulation has been employed to define the necessary condition for a workpart to be totally constrained by point contacts kinematically. The conditions for an intermediate fixture layout to provide deterministic orientation and jam-resilient accessibility can be summarized as follows:

1. The condition for determinstic positioning represented in eq. (13) characterizes fixture element layouts where the positioning of the workpart is unique in the fixture. From this unique position, no non-zero displacement exists which is reciprocal to the fixture layout constraint Jacobian.

2. The conditions for nominal and robust accessibility presented in eqs. (17) and (18) characterize fixture layouts where the workpart is locally accessible to the fixture. For the layout to be nominally accessible, there must exist a displacement repelling or reciprocal to the fixture layout constraint Jacobian. For robust accessibility, there must exist a displacement which is repelling to this Jacobian in order to provide resilience to tolerancing errors.

These conditions were derived using a geometric formulation rather than a formulation based on screw theory as previously employed [Asada and By, 1984]. The use of a geometric formulation allows more potential in extending the analysis to additional issues that must be addressed in dealing with more general applications. This includes fixturing applications where workparts and fixtures can not be assumed rigid.

Appendix A - Screw Theory Equivalence

Screw theory is based on the principle that finite or infinitesimal three-dimensional rigid body displacements can be characterized by a rotation and translation about a unique axis (called a twist). The concept of the wrench in statics similarly is based on the characterization of a set of forces and couples on a body as a combination of a couple along a unique axis and a force along this same axis. The twist and wrench can be represented as screws in a uniform manner based on Plucker line coordinates.

The geometric conditions derived in this paper have equivalent representations using the established definitions of screw pairs. The following conditions are used to define contrary, reciprocal, and repelling motion between two bodies:

$$W_{F_i\alpha} < 0 \qquad 1 < i < m \tag{A1}$$

$$W_{F_i\alpha} = 0 \qquad 1 < i < m \tag{A2}$$

$$W_{F_i\alpha} > 0 \qquad 1 < i < m \tag{A3}$$

Here, $W_{F\alpha}$ represents the virtual coefficient between a force (wrench) F and a displacement (twist) α. In applying the above to describing fixturing constraint, the wrenches characterize the m normal forces exerted by a fixturing system on a workpart. The α can characterize the possible motions of the workpart. Significantly, the three screw pair types are the <u>only</u> ones possible when two bodies are in contact.

A twist α that satisfies eq. (A1) is contrary to the fixturing system. Similarly, those twists that satisfy eq. (A2) are reciprocal to the system while twists satisfying eq. (A3) are repelling. These three equations are essentially parallel to eqs. (20), (16) and (15) presented above. Although the choice of coordinate systems is different, for the assumption of pure force constraints the formulations are identical.

The rows of the Jacobian matrix G represent the normal vectors pointing inward into the workpart at the points of contact with the fixture elements. This is identical to the definition of the wrenches used to define the fixture constraints when employing the screw theory formulation. The interpretation of the displacement Δq is also equivalent to the twist α.

References

Asada, A. and By, A. B., 1984. Implementing Automatic Setup Change Via Robots to Achieve Adaptable Assembly. <u>Proceedings of the 1984 American Control Conference</u>, San Diego, California.

Nitzan, D. et al., 1979. Ninth Report on Machine Intelligence Research Applied to Industrial Automation. Menlo Park, California. SRI International.

Ohwovoriole, M.S. and Roth, B., 1981. An Extension of Screw Theory. <u>Journal of Mechanical Design</u>, vol. 103, October.

Steines, R. C., 1984. Design of Reconfigurable Fixtures for Robotic Assembly. SB Thesis, MIT Department of Mechanical Engineering.

Takeyasu, K., et al., 1977. An Approach to the Integrated Intelligent Robot with Multiple Sensory Feedback: Construction and Control Functions. <u>Proceedings of the Seventh International Symposium on Industrial Robots</u>, Tokyo, Japan.

Whitney, D. E. 1982, Quasi-static Assembly of Compliantly Supported Rigid Parts. <u>Journal of Dynamic Systems, Measurement, and Control</u>, vol. 104. March.

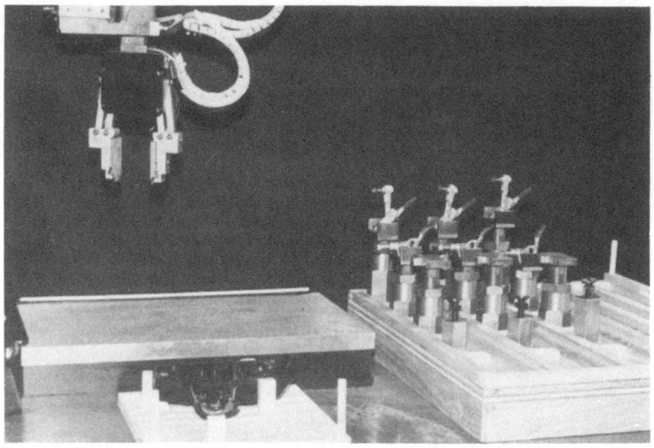

Photo 1 - Prototype Reconfigurable Fixturing System

Photo 2 - Fixture Elements in Storage Magazine

Photo 3 - Early Stage of Fixture Element Layout

Photo 4 - Completed Fixture Element Layout

Photo 5 - Approximately Positioned Drill Case

Photo 6 - Actuation of Horizontal Clamp for Unique Positioning

OPTIMIZATION OF MECHANISMS FOR FORCE GENERATION BY USING PULLEYS AND SPRING

Tokuji Okada
Electrotechnical Laboratory
1-1-4 Umezono, Sakura-mura
305 JAPAN

We propose link mechanisms for force generation by using pulleys and spring (FGPS). The mechanisms are based on a scissors structure having two arms and are effective in realizing energy saving, simplification, and miniaturization of a total system of the force generation. We analyze the relationship between the motion of the mechanism and its output force to optimize structure and dimensions of the mechanisms. In the optimization of the shape of the pulleys, we discuss analytical and approximate methods. Experimental results show the eccentric non-circular pulleys make accurate force satisfying conditional relations between the force and displacement of mechanisms than the circular pulleys. The mechanism is useful in various kinds of requirements for the characteristics of the force versus displacement.

1. Introduction

In order to obtain the force of stretch or pull, coil springs are useful. In fact, it contributes to a system directly when the force proportional to the displacement of the ends of a spring is required since the spring operates on the Hook's law. However, it is required to modify mechanisms of force generation to make force which is not proportional to the displacement of the ends of the spring. If the force is required to become constant in a wide range of distance between two points at which ends of the spring attach, ropes connecting the spring is servo controlled to keep the length of the spring adequate. Evidently, the servo control makes the force generation system complex and troublesome. To solve these problems, we consider the *Force Generation by Using Pulleys and Spring* which we call *FGPS* .

We devise link mechanisms for the FGPS to drive the pulleys automatically by making use of the motion of arms in a force transmitting system. Right and left parts of the mechanisms are symetrical in this study. In the optimization of the mechanism of the FGPS, force members are analyzed to find out the most adequate structure and dimension. We consider two types of shape for the pulleys. One is circular and the other is eccentric non-circular. In the latter case, we discriminate flat pulleys from fusees. Shapes of the non-circular pulleys are determined under such condition that the radii of the pulleys are expressed by a linear function with respect to the angular displacement. Analytical and approximate methods are described for determining the shape of these pulleys. Results of the two methods are compared to find the most appropriate one for practical use. We fabricate circular pulleys and flat pulleys of non-circular-shaped to compare delicacy of the force generation.

2. Basic Mechanism for Force Generation

Figure 1 shows the force generation mechanism which is the origin of this study. Two arms AB

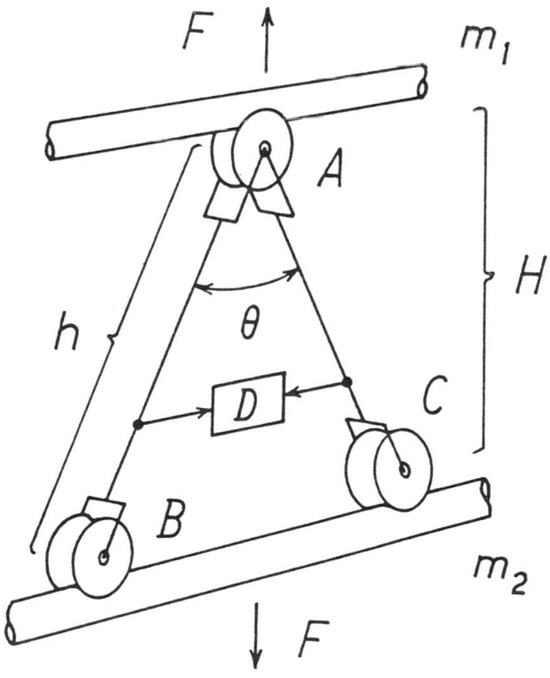

Fig.1 Basic mechanism for obtaining the stretch force.

and AC are the same in length h and have free wheels on their ends. One ends of the two arms put together to have three wheels totally. Symbols θ, F, D and H stand for the angle between two arms, pressing force against ropes m_1 and m_2 existing in one plane, device for pull and distance of A from the line connecting two points B and C, respectively. Three wheels have their rotational axes perpendicular to the plane in which the arms exist, and rest between the two ropes. Points A, B, C form an appropriate isosceles triangle by changing the angle θ according to the distance between two ropes since the spring always makes the two arms put together. Under these conditions, we treat the problem of keeping the magnitude of F constant in a wide range of H. Gravity is not taken into consideration for the simplicity of the study in this paper. For the solution of this problem, such six types of mechanism as shown in Fig.2 are considered when the extension spring S is available. Dots in the figure show pivot joints which rotate freely. All of the mechanisms are symmetric with respect to the line bisecting the angle θ.

To begin with the calculation of the relation between the angle θ and force F, let suppose that two ends of each spring connect directly to free joints. Also, let k stand for the elasticity of a spring and L_0 stand for the length of the spring in no-load condition. Notice the mechanism is in equilibrium when the sum of moment about any point in the system is zero. Then the relation between the angle θ and force F of each mechanism is obtained by using the partial length r_0 of the two arms and the lengths a, b and c of subsidiary links in Fig.2.

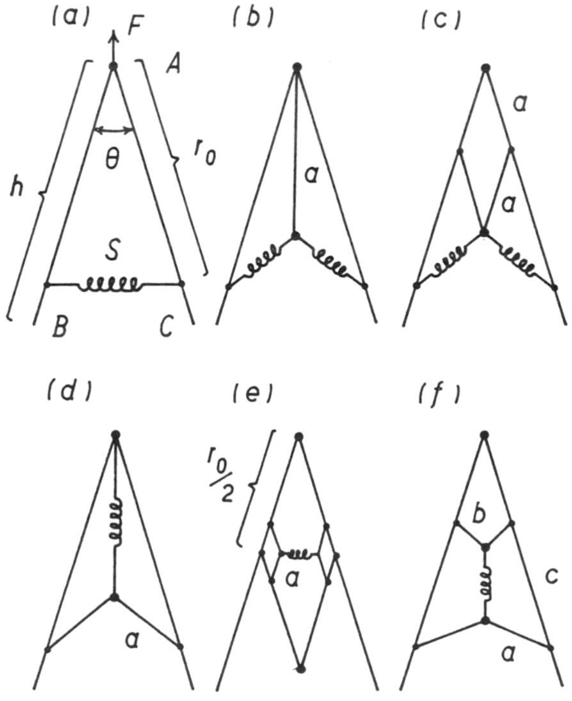

Fig.2 Various kinds of mechanisms for generating the force.

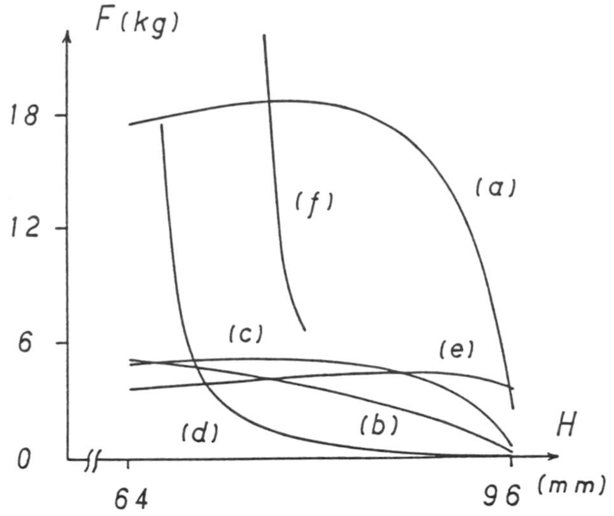

Fig.3 Calculated results of the relation between H and F under such conditions that $h=r_0$ =100mm, k=0.1Kg/mm and $30° \leq θ \leq 100°$. The value of a in (b),(c),(d),(e) and (f) are $3/5r_0$, $2/5r_0$, $3/4r_0$, $1/6r_0$ and $2/3r_0$, respectively. Parameters b and c are $1/3r_0$ and $3/4r_0$.

Figure 3 shows the calculated results of the relation between the distance H (=hcos(θ/2)) and force F of the types in Fig.1 when the springs are all the same in elasticity. It is observed, from the figure, that most structures have such characteristics that the force F increases as the distance H becomes small. However, in the curves (a), (c) and (e), the force tends to decrease as the distance becomes small. Remarkable change of the value of F is observed in the curves (a), (d) and (f). Partial expressions of the curves (d) and (f) are caused by motional limitation of the linkages of the mechanism. We can see that there is no linear curve in the six curves. The curve (e) is rather linear in the six and thus the mechanism in Fig.2 (e) is considered to be the most appropriate to make constant force without the affect of the angle θ. However, the mechanism is too complex to use actually. Further, we can extract such important remarks that the spring stretches too much to keep the force F constant, in general. This is caused by the fact that the ends of the spring are connected to the linkages by points. We notice that the ends of the spring should be connected to a certain body which is adjustable in its position or length, instead of a fixed body. Therefore, we consider the modified mechanisms in the following Section.

3. Force Generation by Pulleys and Spring

Based on the consideration in Section 2, we devise the link mechanisms for the FGPS. We explain how it works, and then analyze the force members of the mechanisms to know relation between the angle between two arms and the stretch force. We show the relation actually. Shape of the pulley is circular in this Section.

3.1 Link Mechanism

Figure 4 shows a link mechanism for the force

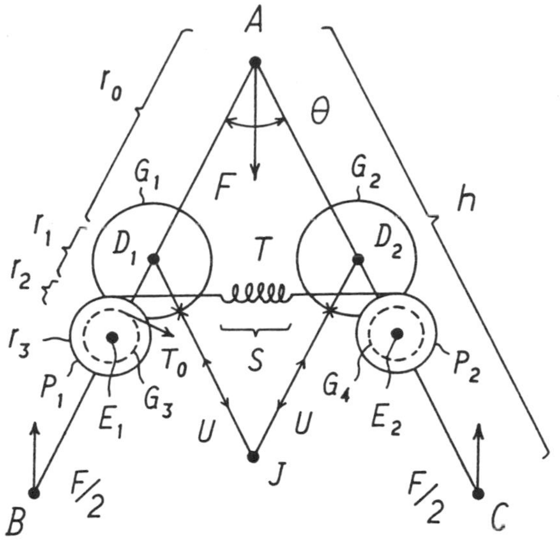

Fig.4 Proposed mechanism for the force generation.

generation. Two arms AB and AC connect the ends of two subsidiary links at points D_1 and D_2 at a distance r_0 from the point A. The other ends of the links put together to make a joint J. Partial links AD_1, AD_2 and subsidiary links D_1J, D_2J are connected with each other by using pivot joints having rotational axes perpendicular to the plane in which the two arms locate. Therefore, the links compose a four-bar linkage mechanism A-D_1-J-D_2. Since the four links are the same in length, four points A, D_1, J and D_2 make a rhombus. The gear G_1 locating at the point D_1 is combined with the link D_1J firmly but free from the link AB. Similarly, the gear G_2 locating at the point D_2 is combined with the link D_2J firmly but free from the link AC. Therefore, two gears G_1 and G_2 rotate about the axes at points D_1 and D_2 with the links D_1J and D_2J, respectively. The gears G_1 and G_2 drive the pulleys P_1 and P_2 through the gears G_3 and G_4. Extension spring S connects one ends of two ropes. The other ends of the ropes are wounded around the pulleys P_1 and P_2. Rotational shifts of the pulleys enable the spring to adjust its length so that it can give the most appropriate force of pull.

If it is required to attach the pulleys P_1 and P_2 on the links D_1J and D_2J, the gears G_1 and G_2 would be fixed to the links AD_1 and AD_2, respectively. Depending on the conditional relation between the distance H and force F, we can omit the gears G_3 and G_4 and replace the gears G_1 and G_2 by the pulleys P_1 and P_2, respectively. That is, centers of a couple of pulleys are attached to the points D_1 and D_2. We call *simple mechanism* for this case, and *complex mechanism* for the case as shown in Fig.4. The major difference of the mechanism in Fig.4 from the mechanism in Fig.2 is that the ends of the spring are wounded around pulleys by using flexible ropes. Two links of the four-bar linkages are parts of the two arms. No other links are required to the mechanisms in Fig.4 for simplicity.

3.2 Analyses of Motion and Force Members of the Mechanism

The mechanism in Fig.4 is valid only when the spring extends as the angle θ increases. However, it is not still explained whether the spring extends or not when the two arms open. Therefore, we clarify the relation between the angle θ and the length of the spring. Let the radii of the gears G_1 and G_2 be r_1, and those of gears G_3 and G_4 be r_2. Also, let the radii of the pulleys P_1 and P_2 be r_3. Now let M be the minimum length of the rope connecting the pulley with the end of the spring, and let W be the length of the rope around a pulley. The length W depends on the number of turn around the pulley. Then, the total length between the two points where the ends of the ropes fix to the pulleys is $2M+L$, where L is the variable length of the spring. Subtract the length ($=2(r_0+r_1+r_2)\sin(\theta/2)$) between the centers of the two pulleys from the total length $2M+L$ to calculate the length of the rope which is wounded around the pulleys P_1 and P_2. Then we have

$$2M+L=2(r_0+r_1+r_2)\sin(\theta/2)+2(2\pi-\theta)r_1\cdot r_3/r_2 +2r_3(2\pi-\theta/2)+2W. \qquad (1)$$

Differentiate L in eq.(1) by θ to yield

$$dL/d\theta=(r_0+r_1+r_2)\cos(\theta/2)-r_3(2r_1/r_2+1). \qquad (2)$$

The equation implies that the value of L becomes large as the angle θ increases when the value of $dL/d\theta$ is positive. In most cases, the value is positive since the values of r_1, r_2 and r_3 are smaller than that of r_0. The spring must extend to give large force when the two arms open. Thus, the mechanism is reasonable in motion and is proved to be valid for the force generation.

We analyze the relation between the angle θ and force F on referring to Fig.4 illustrating force members exerting on each links of the mechanism. Let T denote the output force of the spring S, then the gear G_1 is driven by the force T_0

$$T_0=r_3/r_2 T. \qquad (3)$$

The compression force U exerting on the link D_1J is obtained by making the moment about the point D_1 zero concerning the link D_1J.

$$U=2r_1/r_0 T_0/\sin\theta. \qquad (4)$$

Consider the moment about the point A concerning the arm AB to obtain

$$(r_0+r_1+r_2)T\cos(\theta/2)=hF/2\sin(\theta/2) +r_0U\sin\theta. \qquad (5)$$

Eqns.(3), (4) and (5) are used to have the form

$$F=2T\{(r_0+r_1+r_2)\cos(\theta/2)-r_3(1+2r_1/r_2)\} /h/\sin(\theta/2). \qquad (6)$$

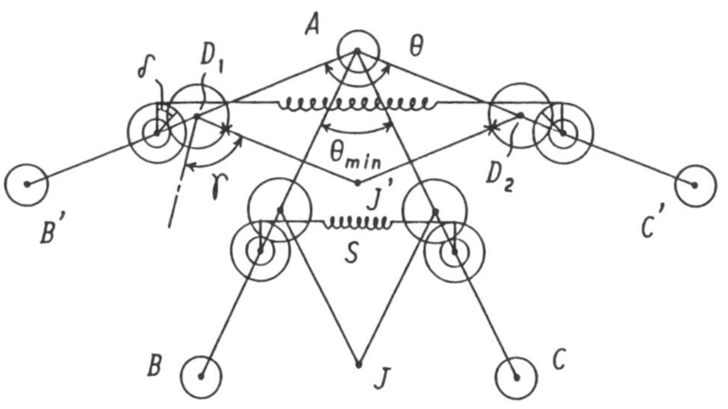

Fig.5 Geometrical illustration for analyzing equilibrium of the mechanism in force.

Figure 5 shows a geometrical illustration of the mechanism having two different values of θ. The symbol θ_{min} denotes the minimum value of θ. In the configuration of the links having the angle θ, link D_1J inclines with the amount $\gamma(=\theta - \theta_{min})$ and the pulley rotates $\delta(=(\theta-\theta_{min})/2)$ by itself, from the configuration of the links having the angle θ_{min}. Let ϕ be the angular shift of the pulley P_1 between these two situations, i.e. total angular shift of the pulley from the condition $\theta = \theta_{min}$, to express

$$\phi = \delta + r_1 / r_2 \gamma ;$$
$$= (0.5 + r_1/r_2)(\theta - \theta_{min}) . \quad (7)$$

Suppose L_{min} express the length of the spring when $\theta = \theta_{min}$. Then we have

$$L=2(r_0+r_1+r_2)\sin(\theta/2)-\xi-\eta_1-\eta_2 , \quad (8)$$

where

$$\xi = 2(r_0+r_1+r_2)\sin(\theta_{min}/2) - L_{min} , \quad (9)$$
$$\eta_1 = \phi r_3 , \quad (10)$$
$$\eta_2 = \eta_1 . \quad (11)$$

ξ is the length of the rope connecting the spring and two pulleys when $\theta = \theta_{min}$. η_1 and η_2 are the lengths of the rope which are unfastened from the pulleys P_1 and P_2, respectively. When two arms intersect with the angle θ_{min}, we can express the length L_{min} by $\varepsilon_0 L_0$, where ε_0 is a constant greater than 1. The force T is written as

$$T = k(L - L_0) ;$$
$$= k[2(r_0+r_1+r_2)\{\sin(\theta/2)-\sin(\theta_{min}/2)\} + L_0(\varepsilon_0-1)-2r_3\phi] . \quad (12)$$

We have the final form by inserting T in eq.(12) to eq.(6)

$$F = 2k[2(r_0+r_1+r_2)\{\sin(\theta/2)-\sin(\theta_{min}/2)\}+L_0(\varepsilon_0-1)-2r_3\phi] \times [(r_0+r_1+r_2)\cos(\theta/2)-r_3(1+2r_1/r_2)]/h/\sin(\theta/2) . \quad (13)$$

3.3 Relationship between Force and Deformation of the Mechanism

By using the eq.(13), we obtain the realtion between the distance H and force F since the value of ε_0 can be given to make the force F equal to ideal force Q when θ is θ_{min}. At first, we consider the simple mechanism which uses only the pulleys. In this case, r_1 and r_2 are zero. Therefore, eq.(13) is simplified as

$$F = 2k[2r_0\{\sin(\theta/2)-\sin(\theta_{min}/2)\}+L_0(\varepsilon_0-1)-2r_3\phi] \times [r_0\cos(\theta/2)-r_3]/h/\sin(\theta/2) , \quad (14)$$

where

$$\phi = (\theta - \theta_{min})/2 . \quad (15)$$

In the second, we consider complex mechanism combining pulleys with gears as shown in Fig.4. In this case, eq.(13) is available. Figure 6 shows the results of the relation between H and F in the mechanism. For instance, the curve c_3 is obtained when $r_3 = 6$mm. By comparing the results of the relation betweeen H and F of the complex mechanism with those of the simple mechanism which are not shown here, it is evident that the value of r_3 is smaller than that of the simple mechanism to make the same amount of force in general. Also, shape of the curve is more smooth as compared with that of the simple mechanism. Based on these facts, combination of pulleys and gears are desirable. The curves in Fig.6 imply that it is difficult

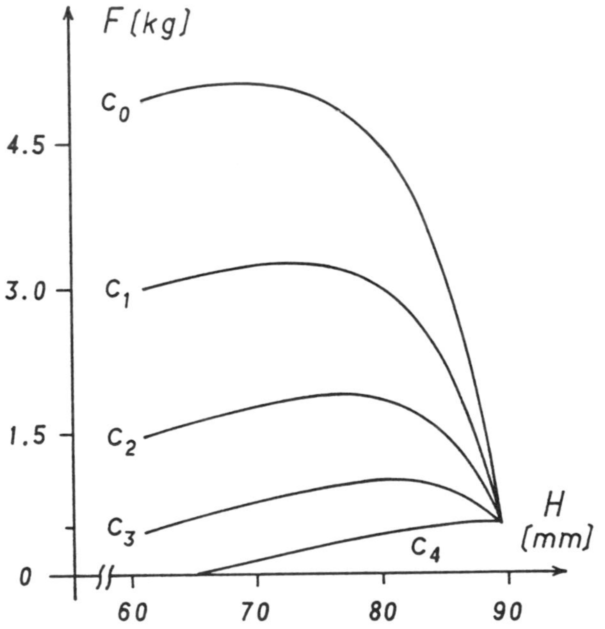

Fig.6 Calculated relation between H and F when circular pulleys are used in the complex mechanism under such conditions that h=95mm, r_0=35mm, r_1=7.5mm, r_2=5mm, L_0=19.05mm, k=0.14Kg/mm, Q=0.5Kg and $40° \le \theta \le 100°$. The curve c_0 is obtained under r_3=0. The curves c_1 to c_4 increase r_3 with the increment 2mm in this order.

to make the force F constant in a wide range of the distance H. However, we can find out intuitively that there is an appropriate curve between the curves c_3 and c_4 to make the force which is roughly equal to the ideal force Q. We discuss about optimization methods in the following Section to have dimensions of the pulleys which give the appropriate curve.

4. Optimization of Force Generation Mechanism

The force generation mechanism, specifically the dimension of the pulleys, should be exactly determined since the mechanism has a flexibility to adjust the length of the spring for bringing about the force we wish. We consider two types of pulleys: One is circular pulleys which are generally used. The other is eccentric non-circular pulleys which are classified into flat pulleys and fusees. In the complex mechanism, the parameters r_1 and r_2 affect to the characteristics of the force generation, however, these are supposed to be given in this paper. In determination of the dimension of pulleys, we propose analytical and approximate methods. Optimization of an elasticity of the spring is also discussed under the condition that the parameters of the pulleys are given.

4.1 Analytical Method

Note the force F is calculated from eq. (13). At this point, we express the radius r_3 by the term $r(\rho)$ defining the relation between the radius of the pulley and its angular shift ρ. The force F is given by

$$F = 2k[2(r_0+r_1+r_2)\{\sin(\theta/2)-\sin(\theta_{min}/2)\}+L_0(\varepsilon_0-1) - 2G]$$
$$\times[(r_0+r_1+r_2)\cos(\theta/2)-r(\rho)(1+2r_1/r_2)]/h/\sin(\theta/2), \quad (16)$$

where G stands for the term expressing the circumference of the pulley which is unfastened when θ changes from θ_{min}. In this paper, we treat the pulley of which the relation between the pulley radius r and angular shift ρ is linearly expressed as

$$r(\rho) = 2a + b . \quad (17)$$

Such parameters as a and b are constants to figure out the shape of the pulley. Evidently, the value of b is positive and that of a is zero when the pulley is circular. In such a case that the pulley radius is expressed by eq. (17), we have the following relations

$$G = \int_0^{\phi} r(\rho)\, d\rho ;$$
$$= a\phi^2 + b\phi , \quad (18)$$

and

$$r(\rho) = 2a\phi + b , \quad (19)$$

where ϕ is determined from eq. (7). Therefore, eq. (16) is written by the expression

$$F = 2k[2(r_0+r_1+r_2)\{\sin(\theta/2)-\sin(\theta_{min}/2)\}+L_0(\varepsilon_0-1)-2(a\phi^2+b\phi)]$$
$$\times[(r_0+r_1+r_2)\cos(\theta/2)-(2a\phi+b)(1+2r_1/r_2)]/h/\sin(\theta/2) \quad (20)$$

Now suppose a function giving the ideal value Q for F such that

$$Q = f(\theta) . \quad (21)$$

Then, we define the error function E by the relation

$$E = \{ F - Q \}^2 . \quad (22)$$

The values of a and b are determined by making the value of E minimum in the range of θ. That is to minimize the value calculated by

$$Z = \int_{\theta_{min}}^{\theta} E\, d\theta . \quad (23)$$

Since contents of E are decomposed into the terms $\theta^p \sin^m\theta \cos^n\theta$ (p, m, n are positive integers), the integration in eq. (23) is performed and expressed by the terms of a and b. We consider the equations obtained by differentiating the function Z with respect to a and b. Thus, we have two equations with unknown parameters a and b. The order of the unknown parameters is three. It is difficult to solve the simultaneous equations in general. At this point, we notice that we can assign the value of the parameter b. Also, the parameter ε_0 should be given by considering the initial condition $\theta=\theta_{min}$ ($\rho = 0$, $\phi = 0$), where the value of F is Q_0 ($=f(\theta_{min})$). Therefore, from eq. (20)

$$\varepsilon_0 = hQ_0\sin(\theta_{min}/2)/[2kL_0\{(r_0+r_1+r_2)\cos(\theta_{min}/2)$$
$$- b(1+2r_1/r_2)\}] + 1 . \quad (24)$$

Then, we can determine the value of a by solving the cubic equation.

When the shape of the pulley is circular, the calculation process is simple since the value of a is zero and we can determine the value of b by solving the equation obtained by differentiating the function Z in eq. (23) with respect to b, however, the order of the unknown parameter b is three. The result of b is useful in the calculation of a. We can recommend that we should find the optimum radius of the circular pulley at first. Then we can calculate the parameter a for the non-circular pulley by using the value of b efficiently.

4.2 Approximate Method

We can determine the optimum dimension of the pulley also by using the Least Square Method (LSM), when the change of the radius of the pulley to the angular displacement is supposed to be smooth. Let Q_j denote the ideal value of F when $\theta = \theta_j$. Then we have the following expression from eq. (20) since the eqns. (19) and (24) are valid

$$F_j = 2k[2(r_0+r_1+r_2)\{\sin(\theta_j/2)-\sin(\theta_{min}/2)\}+J-2(a\phi_j^2+b\phi_j)]$$
$$\times [(r_0+r_1+r_2)\cos(\theta_j/2)-(2a\phi_j+b)(1+2r_1/r_2)]/h/\sin(\theta_j/2) , \quad (25)$$

where J is the term of $L_0(\varepsilon_0-1)$ which is written as

$$J = hQ_0\sin(\theta_{min}/2)/[2k\{(r_0+r_1+r_2)\cos(\theta_{min}/2)-b(1+2r_1/r_2)\}] , \quad (26)$$

and

$$\phi_j = (0.5+r_1/r_2)(\theta_j - \theta_{min}) . \quad (27)$$

Subtract F_j from the ideal value Q_j and square the result to have the absolute error Z.

$$Z = \sum_j (F_j - Q_j)^2 \quad (28)$$

Several sets of data are used to make the force close to the ideal force as far as possible. After summing the terms obtained by using these actual data, differentiate the summation Z with the parameter a and b. Since similar procedures are performed in the same fashion described in Section 4.1, we can determine the values of a and b , by equating the results of the differentiation zero to make the error minimum. When the pulley is circular, the value of a equals to zero and we can solve the unknown parameter b.

When the pulley is eccentric non-circular, we can assign a certain value for b. Mostly, it is recommended to use the solution of the circular pulley for the assignment. Then, the value of a is obtained by solving a cubic equation.

As far as the shape of the pulley is smooth (i.e. $a \fallingdotseq 0$), the spring coils or decoils by making a spiral winding of the rope around the pulley. If it occurs that the effective angular range exceeds 2π(rad), the rope can turn many times around the pulley by changing the groove continuously like a fusee. The shift of the groove along the axis of the fusee will be negligible small. When the effective angular range is less than 2π(rad), we can make flat pulleys of non-circular-shaped by interpolating radii of non-effective area of the pulley so that the groove make a single smooth loop.

Figure 7 shows the rope connecting two non-circular pulleys P_1 and P_2. Thick curve is the effective groove and broken curve is for the non-effective. When the pulley is a fusee, the rope detatches from points u_1 and u_2 since the groove is not in one plane, however, the rope in flat pulleys detatch at points v_1 and v_2. The length between two points v_1 and v_2 is not equal to the length between two rotational centers (i.e. E_1 and E_2) of the pulleys. The distance r_3 from the center to the rope is larger than that (i.e. distance between two points u_1 and E_1) of the fusee, in regardless to the sign of the parameter a . Since the eq.(25) is not useful

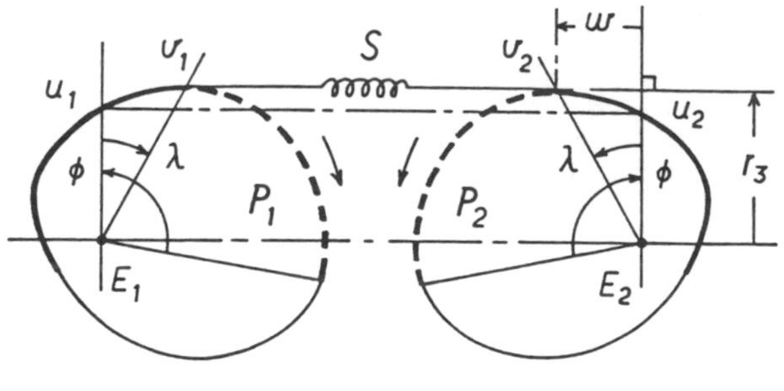

Fig. 7 Connection of a couple of non-circular pulleys by ropes through a spring.

now, we consider a form to determine dimensions of the flat pulleys in the following.

Let λ denote the angle between the line connecting points E_1 and u_1 and the line connecting points E_1 and v_1 to find the form for the calculation of the force F. Suppose that the value of a in eq.(19) is small enough to be neglected, we can approximate that

$$\lambda = \tan^{-1}\left(\frac{-2a}{2a\phi + b}\right) , \quad (29)$$

$$r_3 = \sqrt{4a^2 + (2a\phi + b)^2} . \quad (30)$$

In such the initial condition that $\phi = 0$, it is evident that r_3 is equal to b when a is less than or equal to zero. But eq.(30) is valid when a is positive. Then, we define r_{30} for the value of r_3 in the initial condition.

$$r_{30} = \begin{cases} b , & a \le 0 \\ \sqrt{4a^2 + b^2} , & a > 0 \end{cases} \quad (31)$$

It follows that

$$w = r_3 \tan\lambda \quad (32)$$

The values of λ and w are positive when a is positive, and vice versa. In the same manner as we have the eq.(25), we obtain the following expression for the force F.

$$F_j = 2k[2(r_0+r_1+r_2)\{\sin(\theta_j/2) - \sin(\theta_{min}/2)\}$$
$$+ J - 2\{a(\phi_j - \lambda_j)^2 + b(\phi_j - \lambda_j)\} - 2w_j]$$
$$\times [(r_0+r_1+r_2)\cos(\theta_j/2)-r_{30}(1+2r_1/r_2)]/h/\sin(\theta_j/2), \quad (33)$$

where

$$J = h\,Q_0 \sin(\theta_{min}/2)$$
$$/[2k\{(r_0+r_1+r_2)\cos(\theta_{min}/2)-r_{30}(1+2r_1/r_2)\}] . \quad (34)$$

By assigning an appropriate value to b, the

value of r_{30} is given from eq.(31). Then, by assuming a small value to a, we can obtain the force F_j from eq.(33) and have the error Z by evaluating the eq.(28). The form of Z is too complicated to differentiate with respect to a and b. So it is difficult to have the value of unknown parameters a and b, uniquely. In order to find out the most appropriate value of a for making the value of Z minimum, we can check the value of Z by adding or subtracting a little to zero. This process is exhaustive, however, we can obtain the optimum value.

In such a case that the dimension of the pulleys are given, we can optimize the force generation mechanism by selecting an appropriate elasticity of the spring. It is easy to extract the form to determine the elasticity since the eqns.(25) and (33) expressing the force F include only the term k. That is to subtract eq.(25) or (33) from the ideal value Q_j and square the result to have the absolute error Z in eq.(28). Several sets of data are used to make the force close to the ideal force as far as possible. After summing the terms which are obtained by using actual data, differentiate the summation with the parameter k. By equating the results of the differentiation zero so that the error becomes minimum, we can determine the elasticity k of the spring.

5. Design of Pulleys and Experimental results

Dimensions of the pulleys are now calculated by using either of the analytical and approximate methods. We design optimum shapes for circular pulleys and eccentric non-circular pulleys in the simple and complex mechanisms under such conditions that the value of Q is constant and eqns.(17) and (24) are valid. We compare the results of the optimization to know which one is accurate. We show experimental results about the relation between the distance H and force F to verify the validity of the optimization.

5.1 Circular Pulley

We take the condition in eq.(24) into consideration to use the eq.(25). When the shape of the pulley has a circular form, the value of a is zero and the radius b is obtained by solving a cubic equation. Figure 8 shows the results of the relation between the distance H and force F when Q = 0.5 Kg. Results of the circular pulleys in simple and complex mechanisms are discriminated by the curves (a) and (b). We can observe that the force from the complex mechanism becomes closer to the ideal force Q than that from the simple mechanism.

5.2 Fusee

Circular pulleys are useful to make the force F which is nearly equal to the indicated force Q . However, in the strictly sense, the shape of curve expressing the relation between the distance H and force F is not similar to the indicated curve by the function (21). Actually, the curves (a) and (b) in Fig. 8 are not satisfactory to bring about constant force in the wide ranges of θ. Therefore, we can

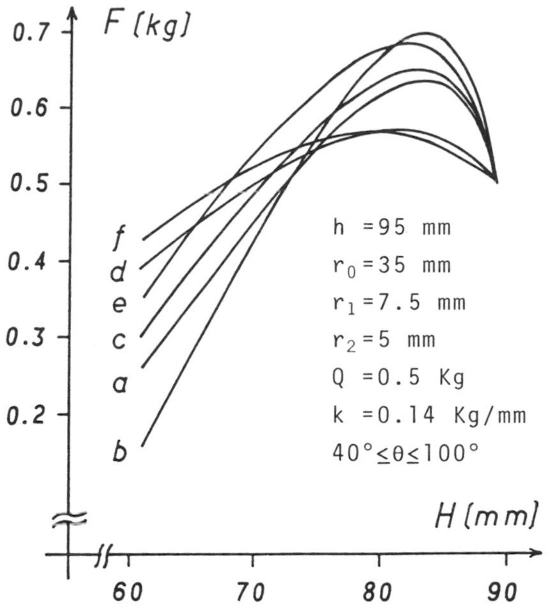

Fig. 8 Optimized relation between H and F. The curves (a) and (b) are the results of circular pulleys for the simple and complex mechanisms. The values of b are 18 mm and 6.9 mm, respectively. The curves (c) and (d) are the results of fusees of non-circular-shaped for the simple and complex mechanisms. The values (a,b) are (-0.69,18) and (-0.60,8.5), respectively. The curves (e) and (f) are the results of flat pulleys of non-circular-shaped for the simple and complex mechanisms. The values (a,b) are (-0.60,17.25) and (-0.66,8.5), respectively.

consider the pulleys of non-circular-shaped. The dimension of the fusees are determined by finding the parameters a and b which make the value of Z in eq.(28) minimum. We suppose that the displacement of the groove along the axis of the pulley is small enough to be neglected. Fig.8 (c) shows the result of the relation between the distance H and force F of the pulley for the simple mechanism. Fig.8 (d) shows the result of that for the complex mechanism. It is evident that not only the force but also the shape of the curve becomes similar to that of the indicated curve by the function Q ; the curve (d) is almost parallel to the horizontal axis.

5.3 Flat Pulleys of Non-circular-shaped

We design flat pulleys having eccentric non-circular shapes by using the exhaustive method which is discussed in the latter half of Section 4.2. The curve in Fig.8 (e) shows the results of the relation between the distance H and force F for the simple mechanism. Fig.8 (f) shows the result of that for the complex mechanism. The shapes of these curves are found to be similar in those of the fusees.

5.4 Experimental Results

In the actual design, the size of the pulley is an important factor. Since the size of the

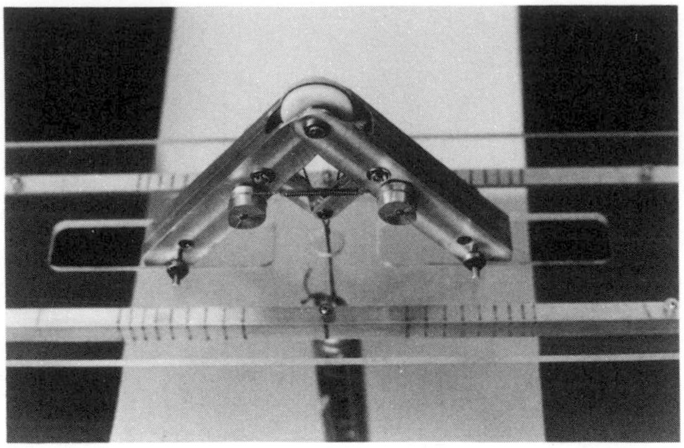

Fig. 9 Overview of the fabricated mechanism.

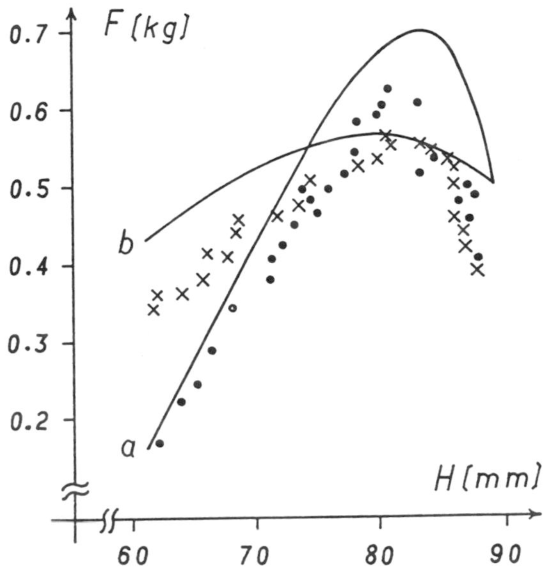

Fig.10 Relationships between F versus H of the complex mechanism. Curves (a) and (b) are the calculated results relating to the circular and non-circular pulleys. Dots and cross marks are the experimental results relating to those pulleys, respectively.

pulley in the simple mechanism tends to become large, complex mechanism is recommended to make the force generation mechanism compact. Also, such a mechanism is recommended that has greater value of $r_1 + r_2$ and smaller value of r_1/r_2 for obtaining great force F. However, smallness of r_1/r_2 makes r_3 large and prevents us from fabricating compact device for the force generation. In this point of view, we adopted the complex mechanism and made the equipment as shown in Figure 9. Physical conditions of the mechanism are k=0.14 Kg/mm, h=95 mm, r_0=35 mm, r_1=7.5 mm, r_2=5 mm, Q_j=0.5 Kg, $40° \leq \theta \leq 100°$. Under these conditions, we made circular pulleys and flat pulleys of non-circular-shaped.

With respect to the circular pulleys, we have b=6.9 mm. The curve (a) in Figure 10 shows the calculated relations between H and F, and dots show the experimental relations of the pulley.

Concerning the optimized parameters of the flat pulley of non-circular-shaped, we have a= -0.66 and b=8.5 mm. These values are obtained exactly, by considering the position where the rope detatches from the groove of the flat pulley. The curve (b) in Fig.10 shows the calculated result and the cross marks show the measured result . The fact that the calculated and measured results are almost close proves that the analyses for calculating the force F are valid. We can confirm that the eccentric non-circular shape in the flat pulley makes it possible to generate the force close to the designated force Q than the pulley of circular shape.

We could confirm that the profile of the groove and the characteristics of the ρ versus G relating to the fusees are almost the same to those of the flat pulleys. It is comprehensible that the result of the approximate method is almost the same as that of the analytical method when the function $f(\theta)$ is simply expressed by Q_0. Thus, the approximate method is shown to be effective in practical use.

6. Conclusion

Force generation mechanism and its optimization have been discussed. We have proposed the link mechanism for obtaining force of stretch. This mechanism is characterized by the fact that it uses pulleys and spring. The ends of the spring are connected to the flexible ropes wounded around the pulleys. By taking advantage of the motion of the linkages in the mechanism, the pulleys are rotated to adjust the length of the spring so as to bring about the force we wish. Two methods to optimize the dimension of the pulleys have been proposed and eccentric non-circular pulley has been proved to be useful to keep the relation between the displacement and force of the mechanism accurate. It has become evident that the approximate method is useful for determining the shape of the pulley when the change of the relation is smooth. The major advantage of the proposed FGPS is that the servo control is no longer needed, in addition to simplicity of the mechanism. Complex mechanism has been recommended to a reasonable pulley in size since the size of the pulley in the simple mechanism is greater than that of the complex mechanism. We are now designing three-wheeled self-adjusting vehicle in pipe. The vehicle would be able to rest and travel smoothly in pipe by making use of the FGPS.

Acknowledgement

Most of this work was carried at the Robotics Institute of the Carnegie-Mellon University while the author was staying there. The author thanks to Mr. S. Wakamatsu, head of his division and Dr. H. Akahori, chief of his section of the Electrotechnical Laboratory for giving him the opportunity, and also thanks to Prof. R. Reddy and Prof. T. Kanade of the Robotics Institute for encouraging him to do this research.

III ROBOT MECHANISMS

5 Manipulators and End Effectors

A MANIPULATION SYSTEM BASED ON DIRECT-COMPUTATIONAL TASK-COORDINATE SERVOING

TAKASHI SUEHIRO and KUNIKATSU TAKASE

Automatic Control Division
Electrotechnical Laboratory
1-1-4 Umezono, Sakura-mura
Ibaraki, JAPAN

This paper describes the implementation of a task-coordinate servoing system by a direct computational approach, the application of the servoing method to a direct-drive manipulator, and the incorporation of a motion control system into a LISP system. All these systems are integrated into a manipulation system. In this manipulation system, the position, velocity, compliance and damping in a task coordinate frame can be controlled by a program written in the LISP language, and even dexterous manual operations can be easily described. A servoing routine including the computation of dynamics and coordinate transformations is executed every 0.0025 second. A high speed micro-computer and fast computation techniques such as the fixed point arithmetic support the real-time processing.

1. INTRODUCTION

In order to perform delicate tasks such as parts assembly , it is indispensable that arbitrary components of position, force, and subsidiarily compliance and damping of manipulators are controllable in the task space. And, to realize smooth and fast motions, the dynamic control is necessary. In addition, in order to make the characteristics of the servo control independent of the arm configuration, adaptive adjustments of the servo gains are needed. [Paul, 1972] The task-coordinate servoing method [Takase, 1979] enables all these controls in a unified way. In this method, the servo control processes as follows. First, joint angles are measured, and the position and velocity of the hand (end effector) are computed in the task coordinate frame. Then, by applying control laws to these variables, the needed values of the acceleration and force are determined in the task space. And then, the joint torques which will produce the acceleration and force are computed on the basis of dynamics. Finally joint actuators output the torques to form a servo loop.

In this paper, a direct-computational, task-coordinate servo system which relies on a high-speed micro computer and fast computation techniques, and a manipulation system which utilizes the servo system are described. In the manipulation system, the direct-drive manipulator ETA-2 is used, and the joint torques are presicely controllable based on the current control of d.c. torque motors [Takase, 1983]. Motion control functions for manipulations are incorporated into a Lisp system, and a program for describing motions can be written in the Lisp language.

There are previous works related to this study, as follows. The primary concept of the force vector generation, stiffness control and partially constrained motion control was proposed in [Takase, 1974]. The concept of the generalized compliance and damper was discussed in [Nevins, 1974]. A proposal for the task-coordinate servoing method and an implementation of the servo system by a table look-up approach were presented in [Takase, 1977]. The motion control problem, by manipulating the acceleration in the task space, was also dealt with in [Luh, 1980]. Methods for the path control in the task space, based on the feedback of task-coordinate position and rate, were presented in [Takegaki, 1981; Hanafusa, 1983] . The mixed control of the position and force was discussed in [Paul, 1976; Raibert, 1981], however, the force of inertia was ignored and the control was static. The spatial distribution problem of the position control and the force control in compliance with the environmental constraint was dicussed in [Mason, 1981].

2. OUTLINE OF MANIPULATION SYSTEM

2.1 Hardware

The hardware system consists of the ETA-2 manipulator, a micro computer for servoing (MIPROC-16, hereafter referred to as the servo-computer), and a mini computer for the motion control and the system development (VAX11/780, hereafter referred to as the control computer). Fig. 1 shows the hardware setup. The ETA-2 is a direct-drive manipulator whose joint torques are precisely controllable. Input signals to the PWM current amplifiers are motor drive levels, and the motor torques proportional to the input signals are generated. Joint angles of the manipulator are detected by pulse encoders. Opening distance of the gripper is detected by a potentiometer.

Performances of the servo-computer are: instruction time- 250 nano second, progran memory- 10 k words, data memory- 8 k words, ROM- 32 k words (for sin, arctan, and square root function tables).

Input/output functions are: analog output- 8 ch, analog input- 16 ch, digital output- 1 ch, digital output- 8 ch. In addition, the computer is equipped with a multiplier whose execution time is 250 nano second.

The control computer is a host computer on which the program development and the execution monitoring of the manipulator are carried out. While controlling motions, the parameters for servoing and the trajectory data are generated by this computer and transmitted to the servo-computer through a DMA channel. A serial transmission line is used for starting the system.

2.2 Control Software

The control software consists of a servoing system and a motion control system, as shown in Fig. 2. The motion control system interpretes motion programs, generates the servoing parameters and trajectory data, and then, sends them to the servoing system. It also examine the result of motion and decides the next motion. The servoing system inputs the parameters and trajectory data, and performs servoing actions. Fig. 3 shows the general flow of the servoing loop. The servoing cycle which consists of reading of the joint angles, evaluation of the task variables , application of the control laws, determination of the torques and driving the motors is processed in 0.0025 second.

2.3 Software for System Development

All program developments are done on the control computer. The servoing program is, in principle, written in MIPROC assembly language. In addition, some arithmetic forms such as

A <- operation(B, C)

can be jointly used. A, B and C may be scalar, vector or matrix variables. The servoing program including these arithmetic forms are expanded into the program written in the assembly language alone by an arithmetic macro processing routine. The mneumonic program is further translated into machine codes by the cross assembler. The "Monitor" system facilitates the downline loading to the servo-computer, memory dumping and debugging (ODT) of the servo-computer. A Lisp system is mainly used for making up the motion control system. Data transmission is conducted by the DMA transmission module.

3. COMPUTATION ALGORITHM FOR TASK COORDINATE SERVOING

3.1 Notation

The meanings of symbols are described here. In principle, vectors in the fixed reference frame are denoted by lower case, boldface characters, for example, $\mathbf{v}$. Vectors in a frame other than the fixed reference frame are marked with ~ , for example , $\tilde{\mathbf{v}}$. Time derivatives of a variable, say s, are denoted as $\dot{s}$ (ds/dt), $\ddot{s}$ ($d^2 s/dt^2$). A row of vectors enclosed with parenthesises, for example, ($\mathbf{v}1$,$\mathbf{v}2$) composes a matrix.

[$\mathbf{x}_i$,$\mathbf{y}_i$,$\mathbf{z}_i$,$\mathbf{p}_i$]: $\mathbf{x}_i$,$\mathbf{y}_i$,$\mathbf{z}_i$ are unit vectors along x, y and z axes of the frame fixed on the i-th link, respectively. $\mathbf{p}_i$ is a position vector of the origin of the frame. The position and posture of the frame is expressed by the combination of these vectors.

[$\mathbf{x}_i$,$\mathbf{y}_i$,$\mathbf{z}_i$,$\mathbf{p}_i$]: Position and posture of the controlled frame fixed on the hand (hand frame).

[$\mathbf{x}_c$,$\mathbf{y}_c$,$\mathbf{z}_c$,$\mathbf{p}_c$]: Position and posture of the task-coordinate frame, properly located in the robot environment.

[$\hat{\mathbf{a}}_{7x}$,$\hat{\mathbf{a}}_{7y}$,$\hat{\mathbf{a}}_{7z}$,$\tilde{\mathbf{d}}_7$]: Position and posture of the hand frame with respect to the 6-th link frame.

[$\tilde{\mathbf{b}}_{ix}$,$\hat{\mathbf{b}}_{iy}$,$\hat{\mathbf{b}}_{iz}$,$\tilde{\mathbf{c}}_i$]: 3 unit vectors along principal axes of inertia, and a position vector of the center of gravity of the i-th

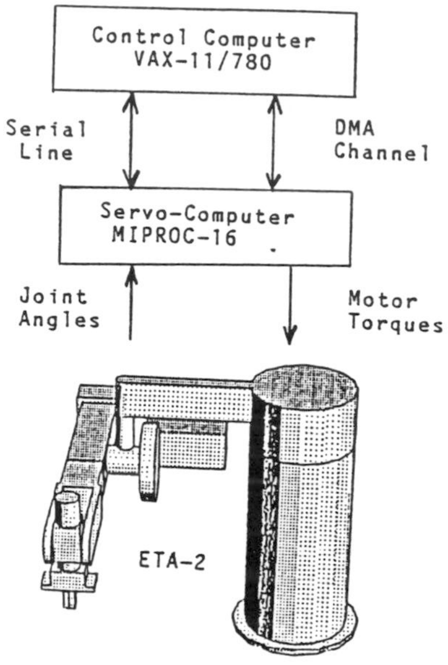

Fig. 1 Hardware Setup of Manipulation System (Graphics is by Dr. Ogasawara at ETL)

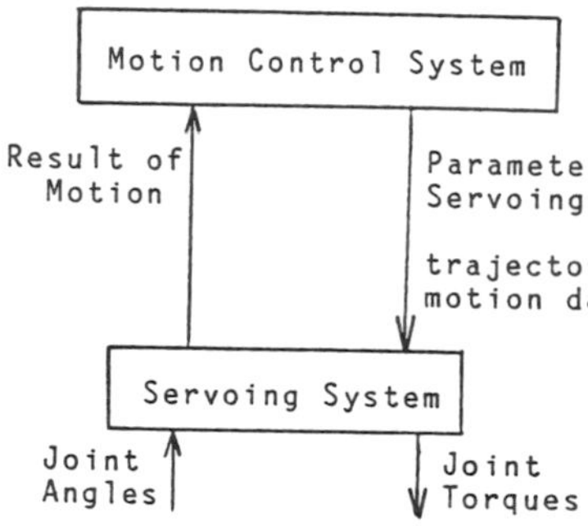

Fig. 2 Control Software

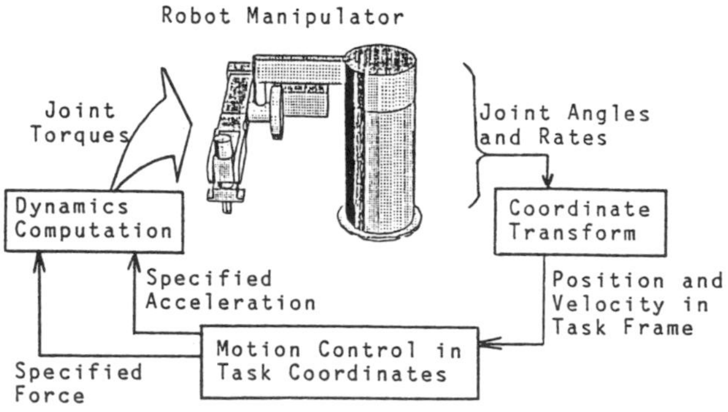

Fig. 3 Task-Coordinate Servo Control Loop

link, with respect to the frame fixed on the i-th link. In case i=7, the notation represents those of an grasped object with respect to the hand frame.

c_i: Representation of $\tilde{c}_i$ in the fixed reference frame.
θ_i: Angle of rotation of the i-th joint. Fig. 4 shows the case of θi = 0 (i=1..6).
ω_i: Angular velocity (a vector) of the i-th link.
${}^i p_j$: Distance vector between the origins of the i-th and j-th link frame.
v_i : Velocity of the origin of the i-th link frame.
v_7: Velocity of the origin of the hand frame.
g : Gravitational acceleration vector.
f_i, m_i : Force and moment of force that is applied to the i-th link by the (i-1)-th link.
f_7, m_7: Force and moment of force exerted by the hand.
f_8, m_8: Force and moment of force for controlling the force, compliance and damping properties.
$mass_i$: Mass of inertia of the i-th link.
$mass_7$: Mass of inertia of an object.
I_{ix}, I_{iy}, I_{iz} :Mass moment of inertia of the i-th link.
I_{7x}, I_{7y}, I_{7z} :Mass moment of inertia of an object.

$v \times v$: Cross product. $v \cdot v$: Dot product.

Fig. 4 shows the coordinate frames for the six-joint ETA-2 manipulator.

3.2 Coordinate Transformation of Position and Velocity

3.2.1 Position and posture

Position and posture of the links can be easily computed based on kinematics and the computation algorithm is not described here.

3.2.2 Velocity

Angular velocity of the 6-th links is

$$\omega_6 = \dot{\theta}_1 z_1 + \dot{\theta}_2 z_2 + \dot{\theta}_3 x_3 + \dot{\theta}_4 y_4 + \dot{\theta}_5 x_5 + \dot{\theta}_6 y_6 \quad (1)$$

Velocity of the origin of the hand frame is

$$v_7 = \omega_1 \times p_2 + \omega_2 \times {}^2p_3 + \omega_3 \times {}^3p_4 + \omega_6 \times {}^6p_7 \quad (2)$$

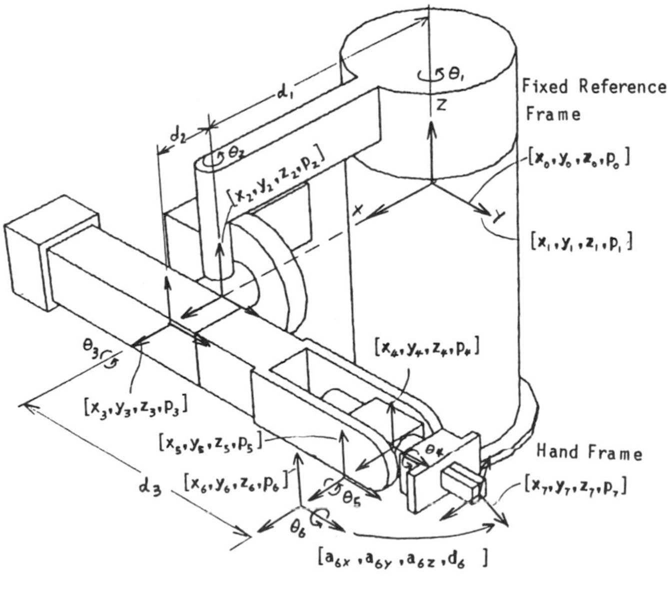

Fig.4 Coordinate Frames for the ETA-2 Manipulator

3.2.3 Position and Posture of Hand Frame with respect to Task Frame

Fig. 5 shows the relationship between the hand frame and the task frame. Catesian coordinates of the origin of the hand frame are

$$X = (p_7 - p_c) \cdot x_c,\ Y = (p_7 - p_c) \cdot y_c,\ Z = (p_7 - p_c) \cdot z_c \quad (3)$$

Euler angles representing the posture are

$$\gamma = \arctan(-x_c \cdot y_7 / x_c \cdot x_7)$$

$$\beta = \arctan(x_c \cdot z_7 / x_c \cdot x_s) \quad (4)$$

$$\alpha = \arctan(-z_s \cdot y_c / z_s \cdot z_c)$$

where $x_s = \cos\gamma \cdot x_7 - \sin\gamma\, y_7$, $z_s = -\sin\beta\, x_s + \cos\beta\, z_7$

3.3 Application of Control Laws in Task Space

Accelerations to diminish the position and rate errors are determined by the control laws. The acceleration can be set in the generalized form as

$$\ddot{q} = \ddot{q}_{ref} + k_v(\dot{q}_{ref} - \dot{q}) + k_e(q_{ref} - q) \quad (5)$$

where q is one of the [X, Y, Z, α, β, γ], and $\dot{q}$ is the rate of it. q_{ref} is a desired position. k_e and k_v is the position feedback gain and the rate feedback gain, respectively. In case of trajectory control, let q_{ref}=f(t), $\dot{q}_{ref}$= df(t)/dt and $\ddot{q}_{ref}$ = $d^2f(t)/dt^2$. When keeping q at a constant position, q_{ref}= const, $\dot{q}_{ref}$ = $\ddot{q}_{ref}$= 0. In case, force, compliance or damping is to be controlled, the force component is set as

$$f = f_o, \quad f = k_c(q_{ref} - q), \quad f = k_d(\dot{q}_{ref} - \dot{q}) \quad (6)$$

,respectively. f is one of the [$f_x, f_y, f_z, m_x, m_y, m_z$].

3.4 Dynamics Calculation for Determining Joint Torques

3.4.1 Accelerations and Forces in Fixed Reference Frame

The acceleration in the fixed reference frame becomes

$$\dot{v}_7 = \ddot{X}\, x_c + \ddot{Y}\, y_c + \ddot{Z}\, z_c \quad (7)$$

$$\dot{\omega}_6 = \ddot{\alpha}\, x_c + \ddot{\beta}\, y_c + \ddot{\gamma}\, z_c + \dot{\alpha}\dot{\beta}\, z_s - \dot{\gamma}\dot{\alpha}\, y_s + \dot{\beta}\dot{\gamma}\, x_s$$

THe force with respect to the fixed reference frame is

$$f_8 = f_x\, x_c + f_y\, y_c + f_z\, z_c \quad (8)$$

$$m_8 = m_x\, x_c + m_y\, y_c + m_z\, z_c$$

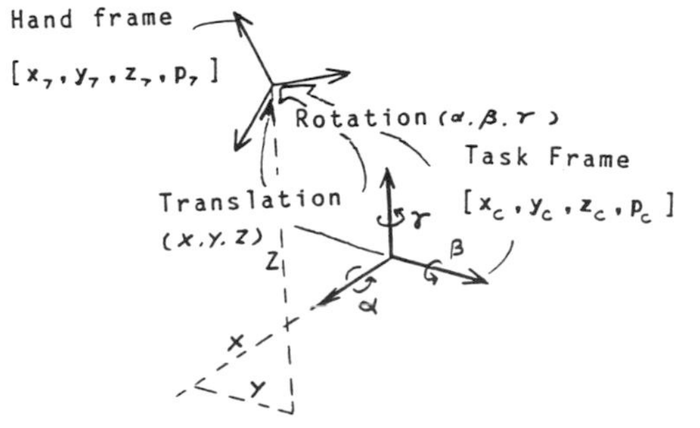

Fig. 5 Position and posture of Hand Frame with respect to Task Frame

3.4.2 Angular Accelerations of Joints

By differentiating the equations (1) and (2), we have

$$\dot{\omega}_6 = \ddot{\theta}_1 z_1 + \ddot{\theta}_2 z_2 + \ddot{\theta}_3 x_3 + \ddot{\theta}_4 y_4 + \ddot{\theta}_5 x_5 + \ddot{\theta}_6 y_6 + \dot{\theta}_3(\omega_2 \times x_3) + \dot{\theta}_4(\omega_3 \times y_4)$$
$$+ \dot{\theta}_5(\omega_4 \times x_5) + \dot{\theta}_6(\omega_5 \times y_6)$$

$$\dot{v}_7 = \ddot{\theta}_1(z_1 \times p_7) + \ddot{\theta}_2(z_1 \times {}^2p_7) + \ddot{\theta}_3(x_3 \times {}^3p_7) + (\ddot{\theta}_4 y_4 + \ddot{\theta}_5 x_5 + \ddot{\theta}_6 y_6) \times {}^4p_7$$
$$+ (\dot{\theta}_3(\omega_2 \times x_3) + \dot{\theta}_4(\omega_3 \times y_4) + \dot{\theta}_5(\omega_4 \times x_5) + \dot{\theta}_6(\omega_5 \times y_6)) \times {}^4p_7$$
$$+ \omega_1 \times (\omega_1 \times p_2) + \omega_2 \times (\omega_2 \times {}^2p_3) + \omega_3 \times (\omega_3 \times {}^3p_4) + \omega_6 \times (\omega_6 \times {}^4p_7)$$
$$+ \dot{\theta}_2(\omega_2 \times x_5) \times {}^3p_4 \qquad (9)$$

These equations can be solved for $\ddot{\theta}_1 \sim \ddot{\theta}_6$, and $\dot{\omega}_i$, $\dot{v}_i$ can be easily determined

3.4.3 Equations of Motion

The vector equation of the translational motion of the i-th link is

$$\mathbf{f}_i = \mathbf{f}_{i+1} + \mathrm{mass}_i(\dot{\mathbf{v}}_i + \dot{\boldsymbol{\omega}}_i \times \mathbf{c}_i + \boldsymbol{\omega}_i \times (\boldsymbol{\omega}_i \times \mathbf{c}_i) + \mathbf{g}) \qquad (10)$$

$$(i=7..2)$$

The vector equation of the rotational motion of the i-th link is

$$\mathbf{m}_i = \mathbf{m}_{i+1} + {}^ip_{i+1} \times \mathbf{f}_{i+1} + \mathbf{c}_i \times (\mathbf{f}_i - \mathbf{f}_{i+1})$$
$$+ (I_{ix}(\dot{\omega}_i \cdot x_i) + (I_{iz} - I_{iy})(\omega_i \cdot y_i)(\omega_i \cdot z_i))x_i$$
$$+ (I_{iy}(\dot{\omega}_i \cdot y_i) + (I_{ix} - I_{iz})(\omega_i \cdot z_i)(\omega_i \cdot x_i))y_i$$
$$+ (I_{iz}(\dot{\omega}_i \cdot z_i) + (I_{iy} - I_{ix})(\omega_i \cdot x_i)(\omega_i \cdot y_i))z_i \qquad (11)$$

$$(i=7..1),$$

$\mathbf{f}_i$ and $\mathbf{m}_i$ can be recursively computed from the hand (i=7) to the base (i=1).

The joint torques are determined by

$$T_1 = z_1 \cdot m_1, \quad T_2 = z_2 \cdot m_2, \quad T_3 = x_3 \cdot m_3 \qquad (12)$$
$$T_4 = y_4 \cdot m_4, \quad T_5 = x_5 \cdot m_5, \quad T_6 = y_6 \cdot m_6$$

4. SERVOING PROGRAM

4.1 Dimensions

Servoing process involves fairly large amount of real-time computation. Hence, in order to speed up the processing, the fixed point arithmetic is mainly used, instead of the floating point arithmetic. The mechanism of the fixed point multiplication is illustrated in Fig. 6. The product of two single-precision integers N_1, N_2 is a double precision integer $N_1 * N_2$. In case of the fixed point arithmetic, the product of two numbers N_1, N_2 is a single precision number $N_1 * N_2 / 32768$, that is the enclosed part with doted line in Fig. 6. Accordingly, the decimal point is regarded as being placed between the MSB and the bit next to the MSB. The MSB is a sign bit and the range of the single-precision fixed point number is -32767/32768 ~ 32767/32768.

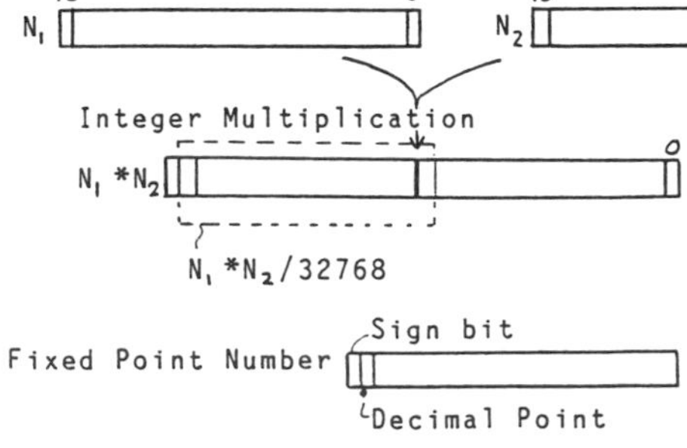

Fig. 6 Fixed Point Multiplication

Dimensions of the physical quantities for servoing are listed in Table 1. With this dimension system, we can use the fixed point arithmetic without worrying about the scaling, in the same way as the floating point arithmetic. In case, a multiplicand is a physical quantity marked with **, the product must be multiplied by 32 (by shifting 5 bit left) to adjust the dimension. For example,

(force) = (mass) * (acceleration) * 32

The resolution of distance is 0.05 mm, and the maximum error involved in a multiplication is 0.025 mm

4.2 Arithmetic Macros

Dominant part of the servoing routine is arithmetic calculation such as vector additions or matrix multiplications. If arithmetic macros are available, number of lines of the servoing program will be drastically reduced. So, we prepared simple text macro facilities which expand arithmetic forms into the MIPROC assembler codes. A line starting with "%" is treated as an arithmetic macro statement. The format

Table 2 Arithmetic Macros

Arithemetic macro statement	Operations
%DS page s1, s2, s3, ...	declaration of scalar variables and memory page assignment
%DV page v1, v2, v3, ...	declaration of vector variables
%DM page m1, m2 ,m3, ...	declaration of matrix variables
%VADD v1 v2 v3	v1 ← v2 + v3 (addition)
%SVPR v1 s v2	v1 ← s·v2 (extension)
%INPR s v1 v2	s ← v1•v2 (dot product)
%EXPR v1 v2 v3	v1 ← v2 x v3 (cross product)
%MPR m1 m2 m3	m1 ← m2·m3 (matrix multiplication)

Table 1 Dimensions of Physical Quantities for Servoing

Physical quantities	Dimensions corresponding to the fixed point number 32767/32768
sin, cos	0.999969
angle *	π rad
angular rate	4 π rad/sec
angular acceleration	157.9136 rad/sec²
distance	1.6384 m
speed	20.5887 m/sec
acceleration	258.726 m/sec²
torque	401.408 N.m
force	245 N
mass of inertia**	30.3024 kg
mass moment of inertia	2.54194 kg.m²
position feedback gain**	5053.24 1/sec²
rate feedabck gain**	402.124 1/sec

* Consistent dimension for angle is 1 rad, but to cover the motion range, it is set to π rad.

of macro`is
macro_id parameters
where macro_id is the name of the macro. Macro_body, that is the text to be substituted whenever the macro_id is encountered in the program, is predefined.

The basic functions of the macros are
(1) Handling of the types of data
The datatypes of variables can be declared and handled.
(2) Page management of the data memory
(3) Scalar,vector and matrix arithmetic
Table 2 shows some examples of the arithmetic macro statements.

4.3 Servoing Routine

Fig. 7 shows a flow chart of the servoing routine.

4.3.1 Angles, Angular Rates and Trigonometric Functions

Joint angles θ_1, θ_2 and θ_3 are measured by encoders with the resolution of 16384 pulse/revolution. The output of the encoder is zero when θ_i=-180 degree, and 16383 when θ_i =180 degree. Hence, the transformation formula from the encoder output(DIN) to the angle is
θ_i=DIN*4 - 32767

θ_4, θ_5 and θ_6 can be also obtained in the same way.

The angular rate is able to be estimated from the angular change in 0.0025 second as
$=((\theta_n - \theta_{n-1})/0.0025) * (\pi/4\pi) = (\theta_n - \theta_{n-1}) * 100$

The trigonometric function is evaluated by looking up a sin function table. Fig. 8 shows the computation algorithm and Table 3 is the sin function table. Besides the sin table, an arctan and a square root table are prepared.

4.3.2 Digital Filter

In order to stabilize the servo control around the resonance frequency, a first-order lag element is inserted into the velocity feedback loop. For the purpose, the deviation of rate $d\dot{q} = \dot{q}_{ref} - \dot{q}$ is transformed into y which is determined by the following difference equation.
$T(y_i - y_{i-1})/L + y_i = d\dot{q}_i$

where y_i is a value of the present sampling time, and y_{i-1} is that of the last sampling time. T is a time constant of the first-order lag, L is a sampling period. Solving the equation for y , yield
$y_i = ((T/L)/(1 + T/L))y_{i-1} + (1/(1 + T/L)d\dot{q}_i$

In the actual system, L = 0.0025 second, and T = 0.05 second for translation and 0.01 second for rotation.

5. CONTROL OF MOTION

5.1 Organization of Control System

As shown in Fig. 9, the control system is consists of
(1) Servoing routine
(2) Command interpreter on the servo-computer
(3) Motion control subroutines
(4) PETL system

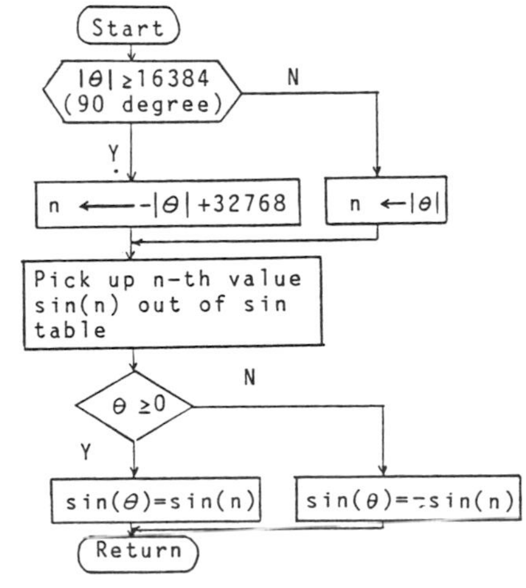

Fig. 8 Evaluation of Sin Function by Table Look-up Method

Table 3 Sin Function Table

Angle	Function value
0	0
1	-
2	-
-	-
-	-
-	-
n	32767*sin(n·π/32766)
-	-
-	-
-	-
16383 (90 degrees)	32767 (0.999969)

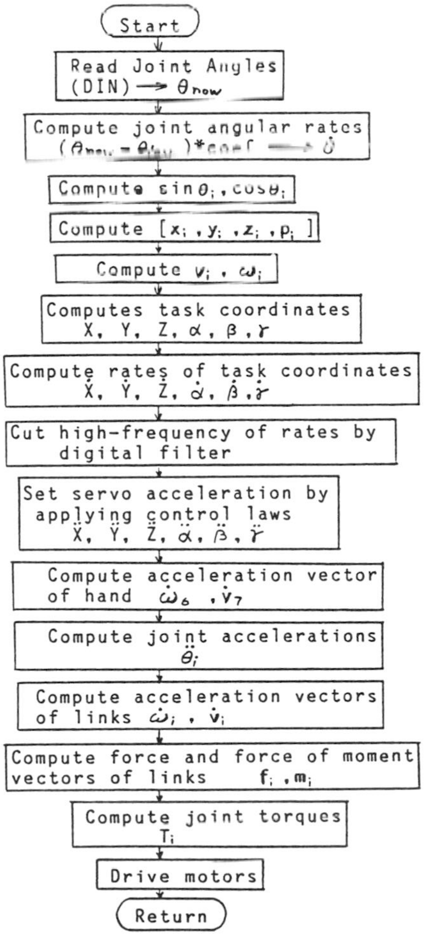

Fig. 7 Flow Chart of Servoing Routine

The command interpreter interpretes the control commands issued by the motion control subroutines, and performs required actions such as setting the parameters for servoing, or sending the states of the manipulator to the subroutines. The command interpreter combined with the servoing routine forms a single control loop that is repeatedly run around every 0.0025 second. Fig. 10 shows a flow chart of the control loop.

The motion control subroutines get original data for motions from the PETL program, and generate command codes and accompanying data, and send them to the command interpreter. The subroutines also receive data from the command interpreter and hand them to the PETL program.

The PETL is a kind of Lisp interpreter and able to call any of these subroutines. Hence, the program for the motion control can be developed and directly executed under the PETL programming environment. Hereafter, the PETL including the motion control subroutines will be referred to as the PETL system.

5.2 Parameters for Servoing

Table 4 lists the servoing parameters that are classified into 4 groups. Desired values of control variables belong to the first group (parameter 0). By temporally changing the values of these parameters, the manipulator is moved. The position is designated by the Cartesian coordinates X, Y and Z of the origin of the hand frame, and the posture by the Euler angles α (yaw), β (pitch) and γ (roll) of the hand frame with respect to the task frame. The rate and acceleration are the first and second derivatives of them, respectively.

Feedback gains belong to the second group (parameter 1). These parameters determine passive characteristics of the servo control.

Frames, transformations and miscellaneous parameters belong to the third group (parameter 2). The task frame is often altered so as to be suited for the task structure, and represented by a homogeneous transformation with respect to the fixed reference frame. The hand transformation is a homogeneous transformation from the 6-th link frame to the hand frame.

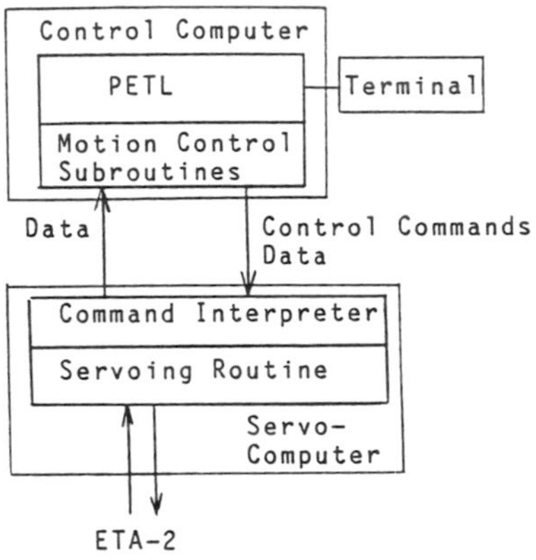

Fig. 9 Organization of Motion Control System

Table 4 Parameters for Servoing

Parameter 0: Desired value of control variables	
position and posture	q_{ref}
velocity and angular velocity	$\dot{q}_{ref}$
acceleration and angular acceleration	$\ddot{q}_{ref}$
force and moment of force	$[f_x, f_y, f_z, m_x, m_y, m_z]$
etc.	
Parameter 1: Feedback gains	
position feedback gain	k_e
rate feedback gain	k_v
compliance coefficient	k_c
damping coefficient	k_d
Parameter 2: Frames, transformations and mass	
hand transformation	$[a_{7x}, a_{7y}, a_{7z}, d_7]$
task frame	$[x_c, y_c, z_c, p_c]$
mass of inertia	$mass_7$
mass of moment of inertia	I_{7x}, I_{7y}, I_{7z}
Parameter 3: Limits	
See Table 5	

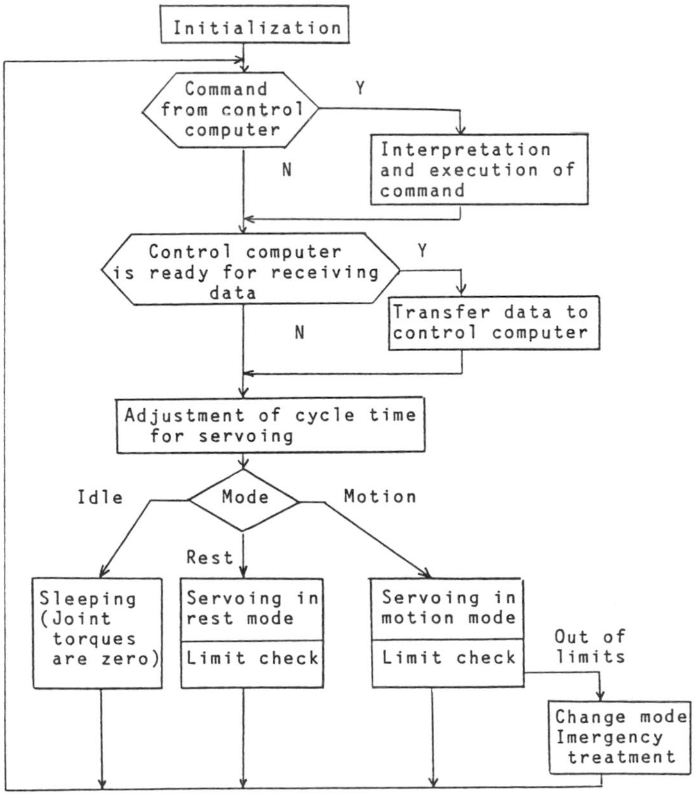

Fig. 10 Flow Chart of Control Loop

5.3 Control Modes

There are following three control modes.

(1) idle mode
(2) rest mode
(3) motion mode

In the idle mode, all motor torques are set at zeroes. The system is put into this mode, directly after the system is started, and in case some serious errors have occured.

In the rest mode, the servoing is in operation, and the manipulator stands still. When jumping into this mode, the desired position of the servoing is set at the current position. Other parameters are set at the preset values. These parameters are not changed as long as the system stays in this mode.

In the motion mode, the manipulator is moved by setting and/or changing the desired values of control variables. In case some motion errors are detected, the system is put into the rest mode. When serious errors such as DMA transfer errors happen, the system is put into the idle mode.

The rest mode and the motion mode have their several buffer of parameters listed in Table 4.

5.4 Limit Check

For the sake of safety securing and condition monitoring, variables listed in Table 5 are checked whether the present values of them are within limits or not. Currently the limit check is mainly used for detecting abnormal states. In case, some variable is out of limits, the mode is shifted from the motion to the rest, or from the rest to the idle. And the imergency information is sent to the PETL system via a motion control subroutine.

5.5 Control Commands

Control commands include mode changing, parameter setting, parameter sending and states sending commands, as shown in Table 6. The "sleep" command changes the mode to the idle, "stop" and "settle" command to the rest. Difference between "stop" and "settle" is that "stop" changes the desired position to the current position, while "settle" uses the current desired position continuously.

"get_prX" gets parameter X (X = 0..3) from the PETL system and puts them into the rest mode buffer of the parameter. "get_pmX" does the same thing except that it puts into the motion buffer. "get_move" is a command to set dynamically changing parameters when the manipulator is moving.

"put_prX" and "put_pmX" are commands for sending parameters to the PETL. "put_status" and "put_current" send the current mode and position to the PETL, respectively. Fig. 11 shows the format of these commands. At the end of data, a checksum for checking sum errors is appended.

5.6 Motion Control by Control Commands

By combining these control commands, the motion of the manipulator can be controlled. Two examples out of a variety of PETL functions prepared for controlling motions are described here.

Table 5 Variables to be Limit-Checked

Joint variables	World variables
joint angle θ_i joint angular rate $\dot{\theta}_i$ joint torque τ_i etc.	position and posture $[X, Y, Z, \alpha, \beta, \gamma]$ velocity $[\dot{X}, \dot{Y}, \dot{Z}, \dot{\alpha}, \dot{\beta}, \dot{\gamma}]$ error of position and posture error of velocity etc.

Table 6 Control Command

Command	Operation
 sleep stop move settle	change mode to idle to rest to motion to rest
get_prX (X=0..3) get_pmX	set parameter X in rest mode buffer in motion mode buffer of servoing routine.
put_prX put_pmX	send parameter X to PETL system from rest mode buffer from motion mode buffer
put_status put_current	send current mode current position to PETL system

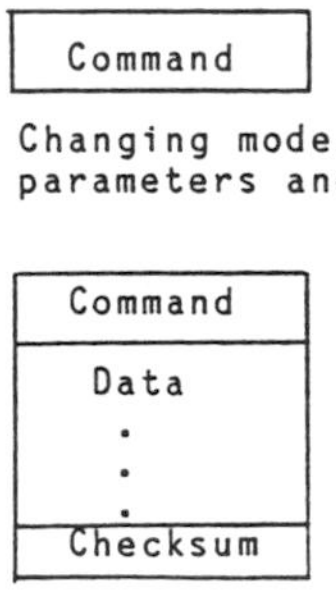

(1) Changing mode, sending parameters and status

(2) Setting parameters

Fig.11 Format of Control Command

(1) Control of trajectory motion
The motion to move in a straight line to a destination from the present position is specified by
(ETA 'MV_STR destination)

The move command is executed in the following procedures.
(a) Read in the desired position of the rest mode.
(b) Put it into the desired position of the motion mode.
(c) Change mode to the motion mode.
(d) Set the trajectory data every 0.0025 second.
(e) Change mode to the rest mode.

(2) Control of force and damping, resulting in motion.
This example demonstrates control of the motion that is caused by the zero position-feedback-gain, constant rate-feedback-gain and constant force in z direction. The motion is terminated, when the speed becomes zero. The following PETL command designate the motion.

```
(POINT_MOVE_ETA (POS @)
  (WITH (Z (FORCE force) (GPOS 0))))
(WAIT_STOP)
```

(POS @) means that position parameters are unchanged. (GPOS 0) means that the position feedback gain is zero. The procedures to execute the move command is
(a) Read the desired position of the rest mode.
(b) Put it into the desired position of the motion mode and set the desired force at a constant value (force).
(c) Set the position feedback gain at zero
(d) Change mode to the motion mode.
(e,f) Read the current position and stop when the speed becomes zero.

Fig. 12 shows the corresponding control commands.

6. CONCLUSION

A manipulation system which consists of a direct-drive manipulator with torque control ability, a task coordinate servoing system, and a Lisp system has been developed. This is the first system, in which, the position, force, compliance and damping in the task frame can be generally and reliably controlled, by a program written in a high level language. Consequently, the system provides us with powerful tools for describing and executing dexterous robot motions.

Future development of the system will include
(1) Higher speed, 32 bit servo-computer to improve the resolution and the processing speed.
(2) More flexible, and quickly responsive motion control system.
(3) Lighter and preciser manipulator with torque control ability.

The system will be incorporated with robotic skills in order to perform delicate operations, and with a high level intelligence for the task planning. The scheme of the manipulation system is also suited for developing a man-robot interactive system such as a computer-aided teleoperator or a man-aided robot.

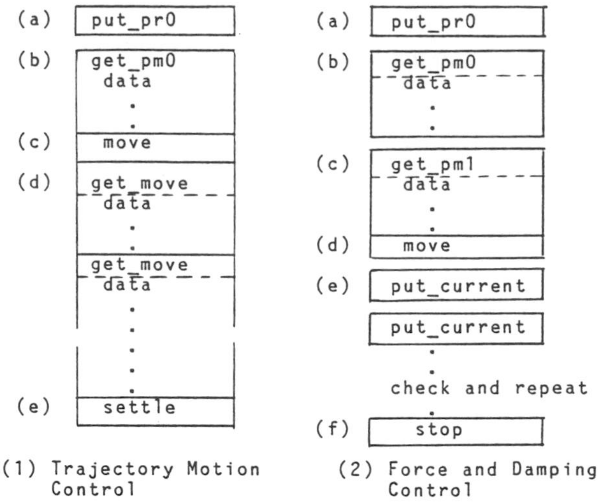

Fig. 12 Motion Control by Control Commands

REFERENCES

Hanafusa, H. and Nakamura, Y.,1983, Autonomous Trajectory Control of Robot Manipulators, Proc. First ISRR

Luh, L.Y.S. and Walker, M.W. and Paul, R.P.C., 1980, Resoluved Acceleration Control of Mechanical Manipulators, IEEE Trans. Automat. Contr.,AC-25, 3, pp 468-474

Mason, M.T., 1981, Compliance and Force Control for Computer Controlled Manipulators, 1981, IEEE Trans. Sys., Man, Cyber., SMC-11, 6, pp 418-432

Nevins, J.L. and Whitney, D.E.,1974, The Force Vector Assembler Concept, Proc. First IFToMM Symp. Theory, Practice of Robots, Manipulators

Paul, R.,1972, Modelling, Trajectory Calculation and Servoing of a Computer Controlled Arm, Stanford Univ. A.I. Lab. AIM-177

Paul, R. and Shimano, B., 1976, Compliance and Control, Proc. 1976 Joint Automat. Cotr. Conf.

Raibert, M.H. and Craig, J.J., 1981, Hybrid Position/Force Control of Manipulators, Tran. ASME, J. of D.S.M.C., 103, pp 126-133

Takase, K., 1977, Task-Oriented Variable Control of Manipulator and Its Software Servoing System, Proc. IFAC Int. Symp., pp 139-145, Tokyo

Takase, K., 1979, Skill of Intelligent robot, Proc. IJCAI-79, pp 1095-1099

Takase, K., 1983, Design of Torque Controlled Manipulators Composed of Direct and Low Reduction-Ratio Drive Joints, Proc. First ISRR

Takase, K. and Inoue, H. and Sato, K., 1974, The Design of an Articulated Manipulator with Torque Control Ability, Proc. 4th ISIR, pp 261-270

Takegaki, M. and Arimoto, S., 1981, A New Feedback Method for Dynamic Control of Manipulators, Trans. ASME, J. of D.S.M.C., 103, pp 119-125

Fine Motion Control for a Small Articulated Robot

Takashi Uchiyama Tadashi Akita Makoto Araki

FUJITSU LABORATORIES LTD.

1015, Kamikodanaka Nakahara-ku Kawasaki, 211 JAPAN

This paper describes development of a small articulated robot with six degrees of freedom. The robot is intended for use in precision applications. It features high positioning resolution, smooth travel under new tracking velocity control, and fast trajectory calculation. The least significant bit (LSB) of a position command from a CPU corresponds to 2 µm anywhere in the operating area. So, actual positioning resolution of 4 µm (±1 LSB) has been achieved with an accurate servo control designed on the state space method. As a result, this robot is satisfactory for precision applications, as has been demonstrated in the assembly of optical fiber devices.

1. INTRODUCTION

Typical applications for industrial robots are material handling, arc and spot welding, and spraying. But, as robots become more popular, new application areas are constantly being evaluated. It is now considered that to automate assembly with flexibility is an important subject in flexible manufacturing system. So, one of the strong demands is to use robots in precision applications, such as the assembly of electronics parts, optical devices, semiconductor devices. However, the major difficulties involved in a precision application is high positioning resolution and good repeatability, which are not available in robots up to now. For example, to assemble optical fiber devices, it needs to travel incrementally in steps on the order of 1 um. The positioning repeatability is ± 50 um at best in today's robot. In order to achieve accurate positioning, mechanical rigidity of an arm, to eliminate backlash in an actuator mechanism, and the accurate servo system which can overcome friction are required. Further, to apply a robot to precision tasks, compactness and dexterity of an arm, smoothness of motion, and safety monitoring functions are required.

This paper discusses the development of an articulated robot (MICROARM 150) which has high positioning resolution for such precision applications. Arm configuration, an accurate and stable servo system by a reference generator and a state observer , new trajectory control algorithm, and tested capability are described.

2. ROBOT SYSTEM CONFIGURATION

2.1 Arm construction

For precision applications dealing with small electronic parts, payload and working volume need not be as large as for many material handling and welding tasks. The arm is an articulated type with six degrees of freedom and has smaller dimensions than a human arm as shown in Figure 1. The length of the upper arm and the forearm are 150 mm each, and the distance from wrist center to the mounting plate is 111 mm. So, the horizontal reach from the center of the base to the mounting plate is 411 mm. The working volume is shown in Figure 2 and the arrangement of joints is shown in Figure 3. Each axis is driven by a DC servo motor through a reduction mechanism. An optical rotary encoder is used to generate a position feedback signal. A feature of the drive mechanism is that the motor, reduction mechanism, encoder, and brake (for θ_2 axis) are attached to a common shaft, whose axis coincides with that of arm rotation. This unified actuator is built in each joint. This joint design makes the robot compact and rugged. The drive mechanism is shown in Figure 4. All joints are sealed to prevent contaminations for use in a clean room.

2.2 Controller

The controller is made up of a multi-microcomputer system and servo control circuits. The microcomputer system consists of a 16 bit microprocessor, four arithmetic data processors, 32 KW RAM, floppy disk unit, CRT terminal console, and digital I/O ports. A force sensor is used to control the grasping force. The configuration of the controller is shown in Figure 5.

2.3 Teaching

This robot is a teaching playback type robot. There are three teaching modes: single axis, Cartesian coordinate, and offset center mode. The teaching method can be selected either by remote teach pendant or by CRT terminal. Furthermore, the function which generates point data for lined objects is implemented. By interactive operation utilizing a menu, initial set of various parameters and teaching of tasks can be done easily.

3. HIGH POSITIONING RESOLUTION

The MICROARM 150 is intended for use in precision work , such as assembly of small electronics parts. So, one of the most important features is high positioning resolution. The rotary encoders as a position sensor provide 5400 pulses per revolution for θ_1 axis and 1024 P/R for the other axes. The two phased encoder signals are quadrupled in digital process. By means of this quadruplication and the reduction mechanisms, one rotation of θ_1 axis is divided into about 2×10^6 pulses. Therefore, the least significant bit (LSB) of the position command from CPU corresponds to 2 μm anywhere in the operating area. Each joint has a DC servo motor, harmonic drive gears as a reduction mechanism and an optical rotary encoder encoder, attached to the common shaft. A newly contrived double harmonic drive gear mechanism eliminates backlash and contributes to high resolution.

Rotation of each joint is controlled by velocity and position commands from CPU. The arm travels according to velocity data supplied after every sampling and calculation. Approaching the target, the servo system is switched to position control to achieve accurate positioning.

The servo system consists of two major blocks: a reference function generator, and feedback loop with a state observer. Figure 6 shows the servo control system.

The reference function generator generates the reference position X_R , velocity V_a and acceleration signal α_R in response to changes in the velocity command. The reference acceleration signal α_R is the feedforward signal which provides the current required to accelerate a motor. It is effective to improve the response of the servo control system. The basic profile or the reference velocity V_a , which is generated by OSC and ROM, is trapezoidal to get smooth motion of the robot arm. The velocity input V_c and position input are commands from the CPU. By use of the reference function generator, not only the position but also the velocity and acceleration can be controlled simultaneously. It means that the velocity of the arm can be changed at any moment of travel. So, this function makes it possible to control the trajectory by the velocity input without start/stop motion.

The state observer is added to the feedback loop to suppress mechanical resonance, making it possible to use higher servo gain and wider bandwidth. It can reconstruct unobserved state variables. In this case, the velocity error is generated by the observer. Therefore, it needs no velocity sensor such as a tachometer. The feedback gain K_1 , K_2 , K_3 are optimally designed to minimize the position error and the input energy.

The integrator is inserted to cancel the offset error caused by weight of the arm itself and also to overcome the friction torque of the drive mechanism. It responds satisfactorily to the torque change related to arm attitude or object weight. Furthermore, the smoother is devised to smooth the position error signal, which is the output of the D/A converter. It combines the digitized error signal from the D/A converter and the analog source signal from the encoder. By the smoother, the limit cycle caused by the feedback of non-linear error signal is prevented.

4. TRACKING RATE CONTROL BY VELOCITY VECTOR

Various technical contributions have been made to the trajectory control problem. But, to take the exact path, it needs to compensate both the position and velocity offset dynamically. Another feature of the MICROARM 150 is dynamic path control by velocity vector, which is calculated based on the current position and forecasted target at next sampling. It is very effective in getting smooth travel, specially in the cartesian coordinate mode. The velocity vector supplied to the servo system is calculated by the following equations.

$$(1)\quad \mathbf{X}(t_K) = f(\Theta_S(t_K))$$

$$(2)\quad \mathbf{X}(t_{K+1}) = \mathbf{X}(t_K) + \dot{\mathbf{X}}\cdot\Delta T$$

$$(3)\quad \Theta_C(t_{K+1}) = g(\mathbf{X}(t_{K+1}))$$

$$(4)\quad \dot{\Theta}(t_K) = (\Theta_C(t_{K+1}) - \Theta_S(t_K))/\Delta T$$

where

Sampled data of joint angle;

$$\Theta_S = [\Theta_{S1}, \Theta_{S2}, \Theta_{S3}, \Theta_{S4}, \Theta_{S5}, \Theta_{S6}]$$

Calculated data of joint angle;

$$\Theta_C = [\Theta_{C1}, \Theta_{C2}, \Theta_{C3}, \Theta_{C4}, \Theta_{C5}, \Theta_{C6}]$$

Velocity vector;

$$\dot{\Theta} = [\dot{\theta}_1, \dot{\theta}_2, \dot{\theta}_3, \dot{\theta}_4, \dot{\theta}_5, \dot{\theta}_6]$$

Position and Euler angle;

$$\mathbf{X} = [X, Y, Z, B, S, R]$$

Desired velocity;

$$\dot{\mathbf{X}} = [\dot{X}, \dot{Y}, \dot{Z}, \dot{B}, \dot{S}, \dot{R}]$$

Sampling interval;

$$\Delta T = t_{K+1} - t_K$$

Coordinate transformation function;

$$g = f^{-1}$$

Figure 7 shows the principle of the tracking rate control method.

By the use of velocity vector, smooth straight-line travel in the cartesian coordinate system is obtained. Further, by sampling the current position, trajectory error caused by friction is also corrected in real-time. The robot has the capability changing the velocity in the Cartesian mode while traveling, and it is useful in case of cooperation with another systems and adaptive control using sensors.

High resolution requires a wide range of the position data. For example, one revolution of θ1-axis is divided into 2×10^6 pulses. So, to achieve high precision and high speed processing, 4 floating-point arithmetic processors are used. These processors operate in parallel to be supervised by the host microcomputer through DMA channel. As a result, all processings including trajectory calculation and I/O operations are executed in 60 ms.

5. RESULTS AND APPLICATION

Figure 8 shows the effect of the smoother. Figure 8(a) shows the position signal and the motor current in absence of the smoother, and Figure 8 (b) Fig.8(b), the spike noise is reduced by use of the smoother. Multistep response measured by a non-contact position sensor is plotted in Fig.9. It was measured with the mounting plate driven in 4 μm steps. The robot responds to commands for increments of 4 μm, and further changes direction in response to a single step. Positioning repeatability for steps of 200 mm are shown in Fig.10. Repeatability for a long stroke is ± 6 μm. A little irregularity of multistep response and the difference of the repeatabilities are caused by non-linearity of a reduction mechanism, and it is the theme in future. Figure 11 shows an example of application. The robot can align optical fibers with the accuracy of ± 7 μm in the X,Y, and Z direction by monitoring the light output. Figure 12 shows the configuration of the fiber alignment system.

6. CONCLUSION

A small articulated robot with six degrees of freedom has been developed. Extremely high positioning resolution of 4 μm has been achieved by the application of a new control system including a reference function generator and a state observer with an integrator. Further, positioning repeatability has been much improved. Also, smoothness of travel has been obtained owing to a tracking rate control and fast trajectory calculation. The overall performance of the robot has been demonstrated by its ability to assemble optical fiber devices .

ACKNOWLEDGEMENT

The authors wish to express their gratitude to Mr. S. Kawakami of FUJITSU LABORATORIES LTD. for his invaluable advice.

REFERENCES

1) Nishimoto K., T. Uchiyama, K. Tamamushi, and T. Akita "Small-sized Robot with High Positioning Accuracy". Proceedings of 4th CISM-IFToMM Symposium on Theory and Practice of Robots and Manipulators, pp.170-179 (Warsaw 1981)

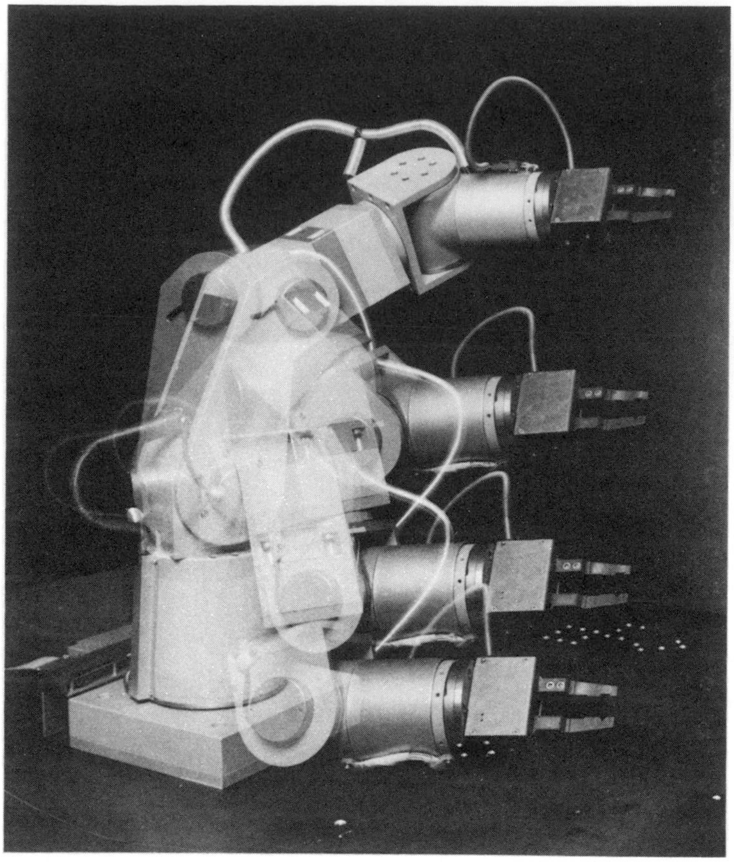

Figure 1 The robot (MICROARM 150)

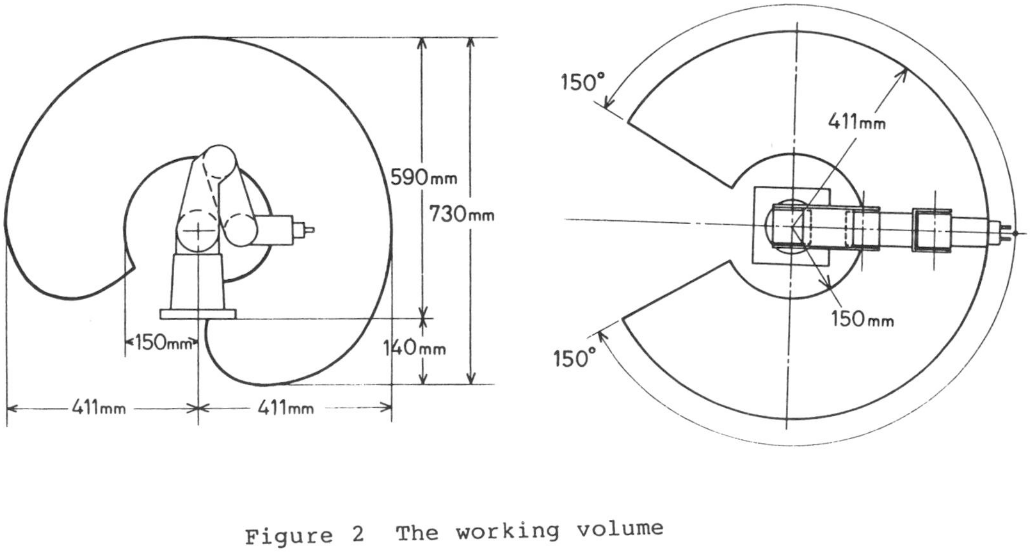

Figure 2 The working volume

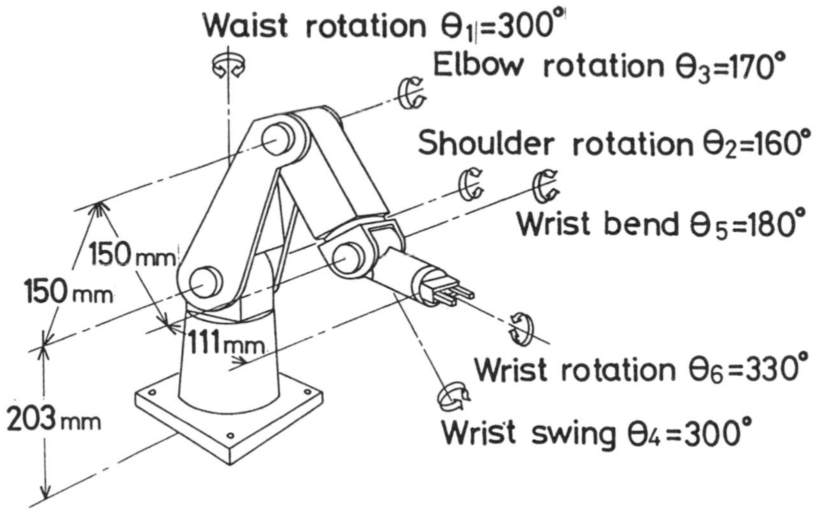

Figure 3 Arrangement of joints

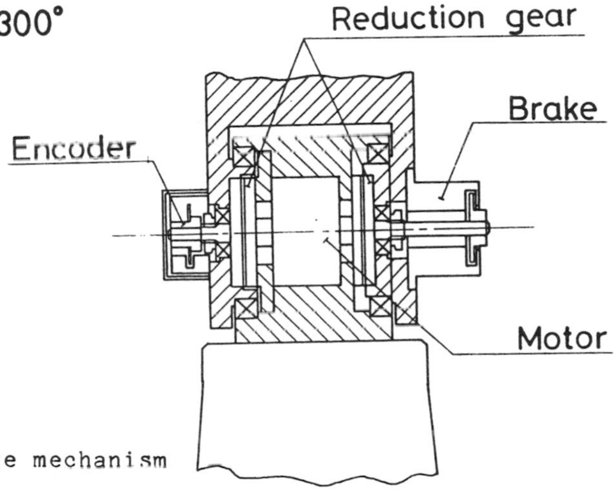

Figure 4 The configuration of drive mechanism

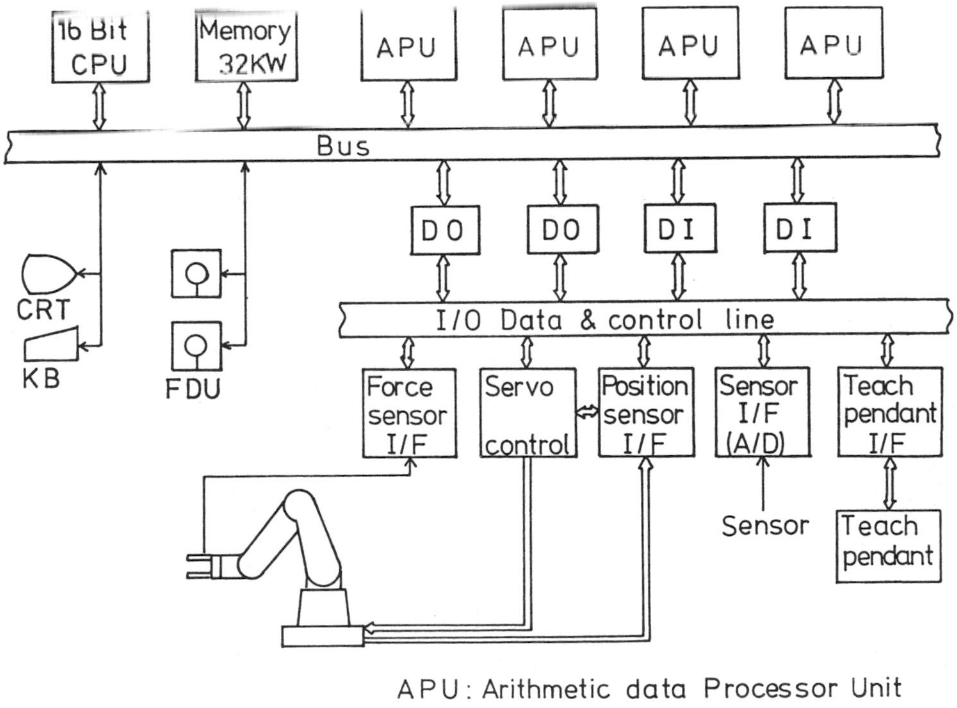

Figure 5 System configuration

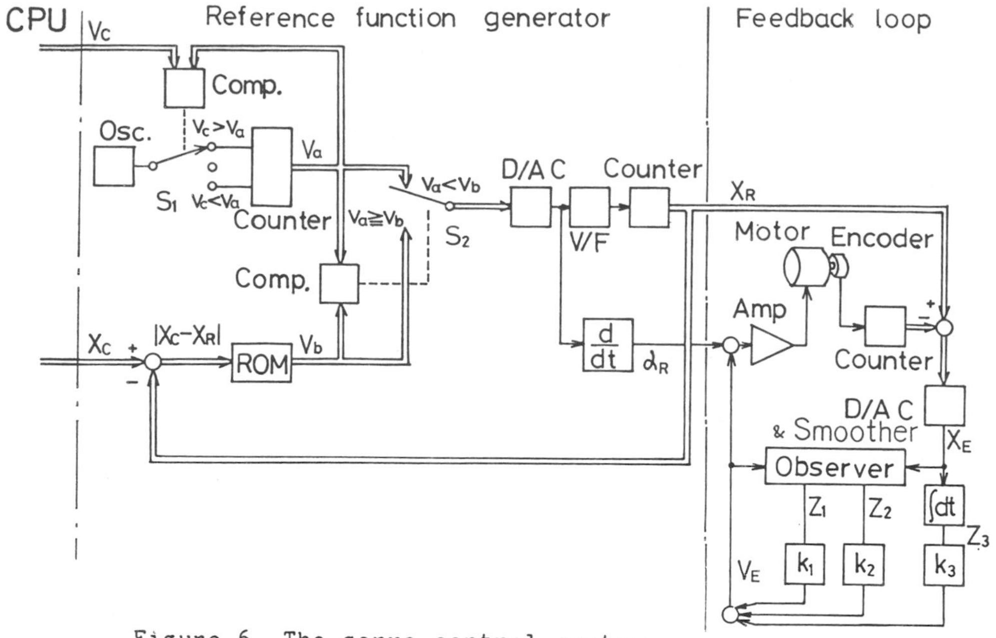

Figure 6 The servo control system

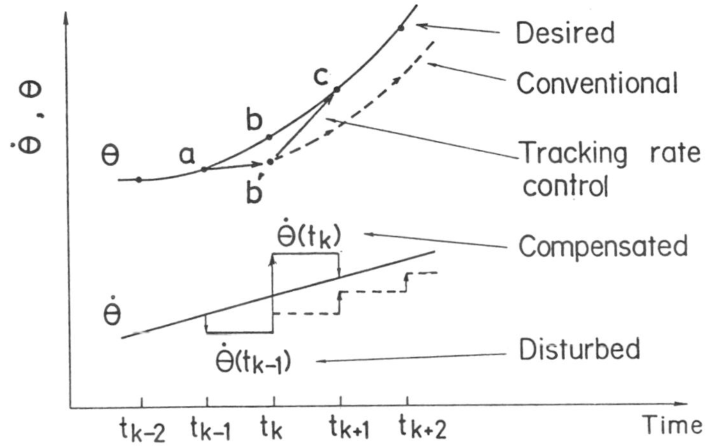

Figure 7 Principle of tracking rate control method

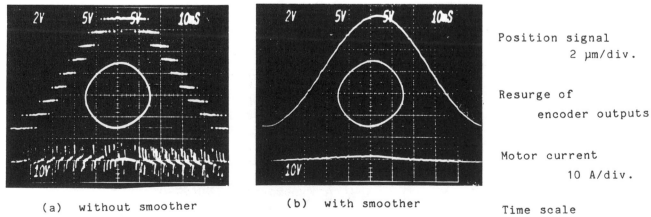

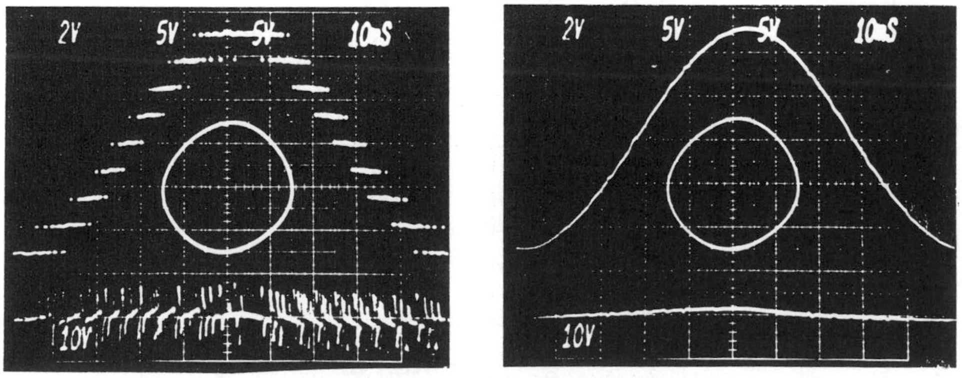

(a) without smoother

(b) with smoother

Position signal 2 μm/div.

Resurge of encoder outputs

Motor current 10 A/div.

Time scale 10 ms/div.

Figure 8 Effect of smoother

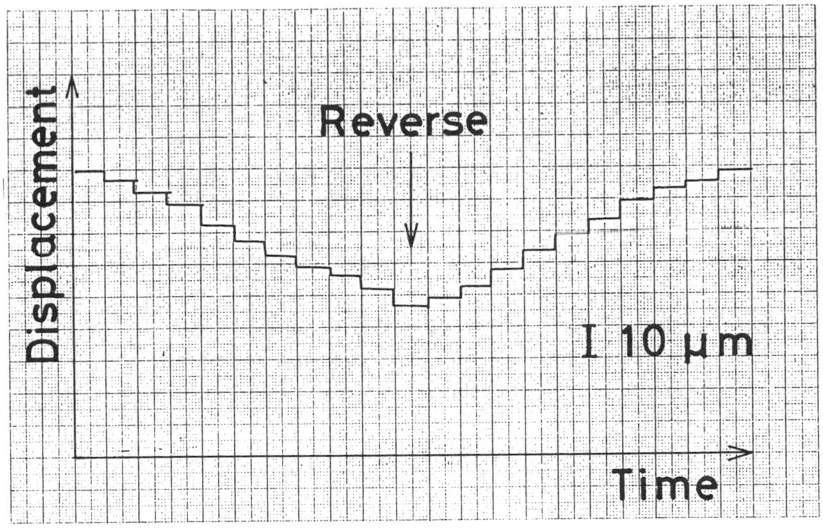

Figure 9 Multistep response in Cartesian mode (4 μm)

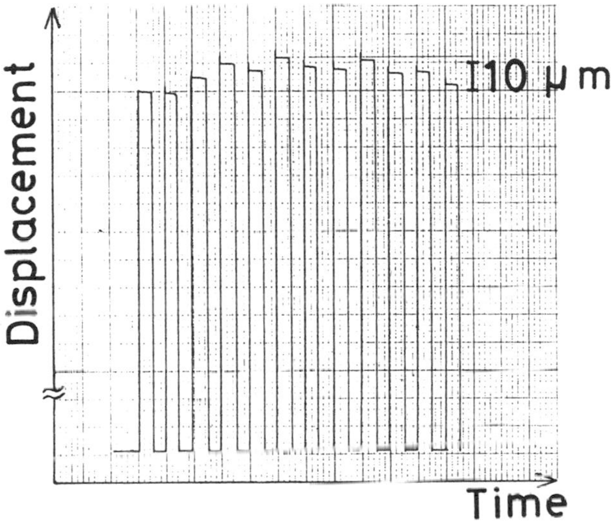

Figure 10 Positioning repeatability (200 mm)

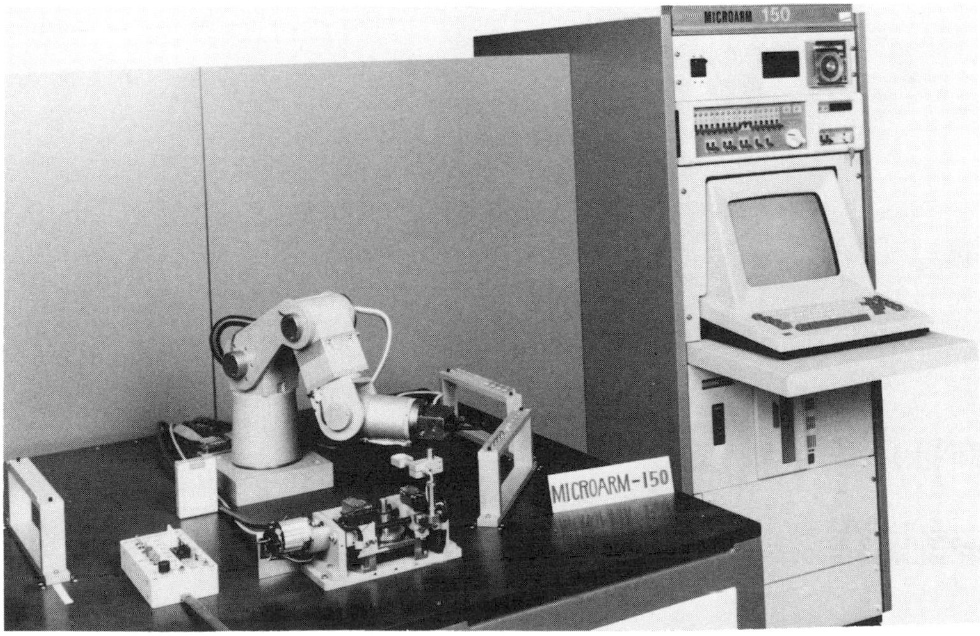

Figure 11 Assembling optical fiber devices

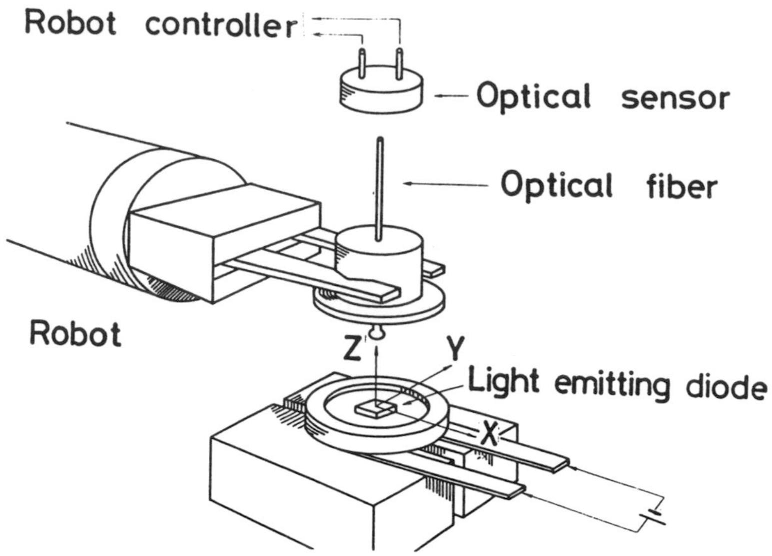

Figure 12 Configuration of fiber alignment system

SKILLS FOR A SHEARING ROBOT: DEXTERITY AND SENSING

JAMES P. TREVELYAN

Continuing research into the application of robotics to shearing sheep has focussed on sensing, shearing technique, programming and dexterity. Important skills learned from expert human shearers have been transformed into improved sensing techniques and new programming techniques. Automatic 'emergency' handling programs temporarily override the normal sequence of programmed operations. Studies for a new robot have highlighted the problem of dexterity, which is limited principally by the design of the wrist mechanism. Factors such as degeneracy, angular ranges of joints and mechanical arrangement affect the usable workspace, and additional factors such as drive stiffness and size affect dynamic performance. Some progress has been made in devising a novel kinematic arrangement for a wrist which has a large workspace without degenerate configurations.

Research in automated sheep shearing was concentrated initially on shearing experiments [Trevelyan and Leslie, 1981] and then on sheep restraint and manipulation [Elford and Key, 1983]. Recently the emphasis has moved to the consideration of a practical robotic shearing system and has focussed initially on the design of a shearing robot arm for eventual field use.

The original experimental robot (ORACLE) has been used for shearing experiments since July 1979. While it has demonstrated the technical feasibility of automated shearing it has suffered from major restrictions on its usable workspace [Trevelyan et al, 1983]. It is also large and heavy, and with all the hydraulic services and wiring exposed it looks complicated. Design studies for a new robot to be called SM commenced in 1983, and have focussed on the requirements for simplicity, dexterity, potential for low cost, and speed. These requirements have now been met and construction is expected to be complete in 1985.

This paper looks at two skills required for such a shearing robot: dexterity and sensing. Dexterity has been the most difficult to achieve, and a new wrist mechanism has been devised to meet the requirements of shearing. Sensing skills have been devised for ORACLE and can be transferred in a modified form for SM, as can the movement skills learned from manual shearing.

DEXTERITY

Figure 1 illustrates the usable workspace of the traversing linkage arm of ORACLE. The location of the sheep results from the experimental nature of ORACLE and the manipulator, and is not optimal. The SM robot requirement was for access to the entire exposed section of sheep in three principal manipulation positions illustrated in figure 2. This removes the need for rotation and translation of the manipulator, greatly simplifying the design of sheep restraint mechanisms. An overhead mounting for the robot was chosen. Figure 3 illustrates an artist's conception of a mobile shearing installation from which it can be seen that an overhead robot mounting provides efficient utilisation of space and free access for sheep transfer mechanisms, wool handling and operators.

The major restriction on dexterity has been imposed by the wrist mechanism which must provide the necessary freedom of movement for the cutter mechanism in all the possible shearing areas. Figure 4 illustrates the ORACLE wrist mechanism, and the first candidate mechanism for SM. The major difference between them is the relocation of the rapid response follower actuator to the end of the wrist mechanism. This is possible because the actual range of follower movement required for shearing is much less than expected when ORACLE was designed; the range has been reduced from 200mm to 50mm. The original requirement for wrist rotation axes to pass through the cutter centre point was largely associated with dynamic response requirements on rotations of the cutter, and computational limitations. Both requirements have been relaxed; the first because the rotational response required for shearing is less than originally anticipated and the second because faster computers are now relatively inexpensive.

The cones of degeneracy [Paul and Stephenson, 1983] of both wrists shown in the diagram show that ORACLE has no degeneracies within its

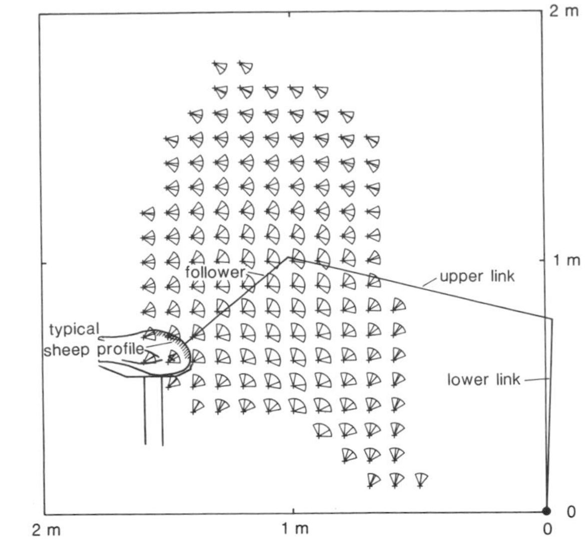

Fig 1 Workspace of ORACLE robot
Each point marked + can be reached and the arc at each point shows the range of wrist orientations achievable.

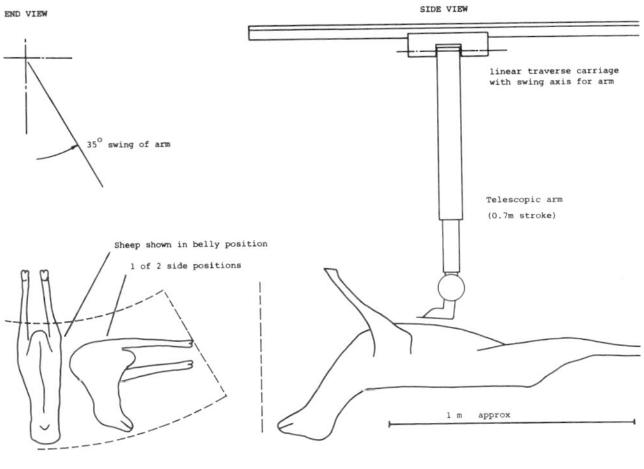

Fig 2 Approximate workspace required for SM

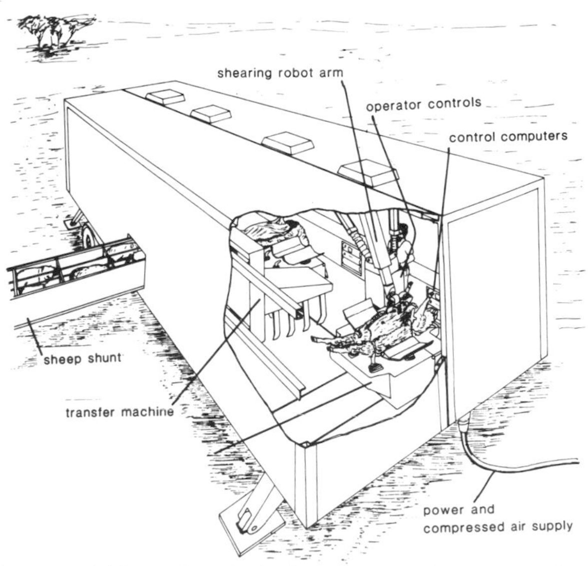

Fig 3 Mobile automated shearing system concept

mechanical limits, but that the candidate wrist for SM has one.

Figure 5 shows a re-arrangement of the cutter relative to the wrist axes resulting in changes in the nature of degeneracies within the context of shearing. In the case of figure 4b, shearing is possible in any direction provided the normal vector of the surface lies outside the degeneracy cone. The re-arrangement in figure 5 can shear the entire exposed sheep surface, but not in the direction of the degeneracy cones. Thus in the one case, the shearable area is restricted, and in the other case the direction of shearing is restricted. Neither alternative could meet the dexterity requirements without additional robot joints.

So far, however, the only effect of degeneracies which has been considered is the effect on dynamic performance; when operating within the degeneracy cones, actuator rates may rise to unacceptable values and stability of the robot sensing system may be affected. Tests with models have shown that limits to actuator movements interact with degeneracies in a more complex manner, and that shearing paths which avoid degenerate wrist positions may still be impossible as a result of this interaction!

In the idealised diagram of figure 4b, joints W1 and W3 may be rotated indefinitely. However, in a practical robot, services such as electrical connections, power for the cutter drive and hydraulic connections for the follower actuator must be provided for the cutter assembly and an umbilical cable connection is required for this. Even the Cincinnatti Millacron three roll wrist mechanism [Stackhouse, 1979] is subject to these limitations. Thus wrist rotations must be mechanically limited and in practice a total rotation of 400 degrees represents a reasonable compromise value for joint W1.

The interaction of this limitation with degenerate wrist positions is shown by considering the shearing path illustrated in figure 6. Although the wrist configuration of figure 4b has been used as an example, the alternative configuration exhibits the same properties. The shearing path avoids the zones of the surface where the surface normal lies in the degeneracy cone; however the locus of the surface normal vector plotted on a unit sphere travels round the degeneracy cone in a complete revolution. This requires a complete revolution of joints W1 and W3 (in opposite directions) which in general is impossible unless both joints just happen to be at the appropriate ends of their operating ranges at the start of the path. This is rather unlikely; and in the general case the path described is impossible to execute in a single operation even though the degeneracy cones have been avoided.

Sheep surfaces are neither simple nor predictable enough to avoid these complications. Unexpected surface irregularities and sheep movements detected by sensors can cause the locus of the surface normal to pass round a degeneracy even if the planned path would not. This effect can be overcome in some applications with a temporary

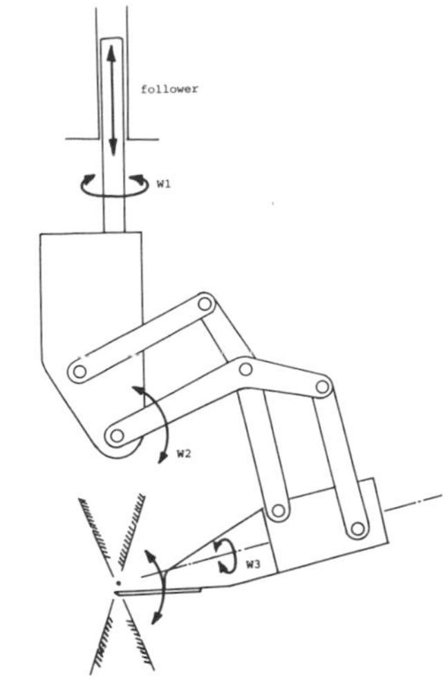

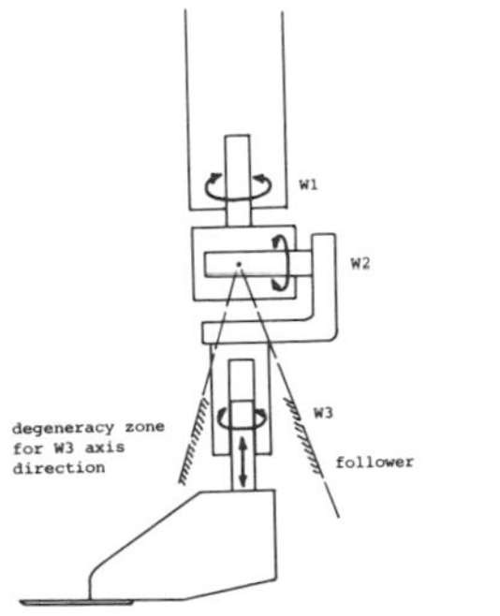

Fig 4a ORACLE wrist (type 3Ra)

Fig 4b Proposed SM wrist (type 3R)

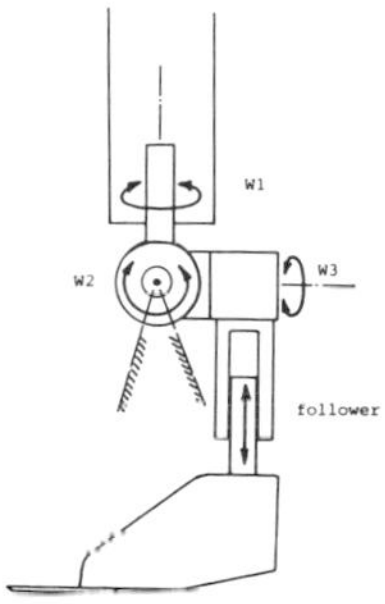

Fig 5 Alternate wrist for SM (type 3Ra)

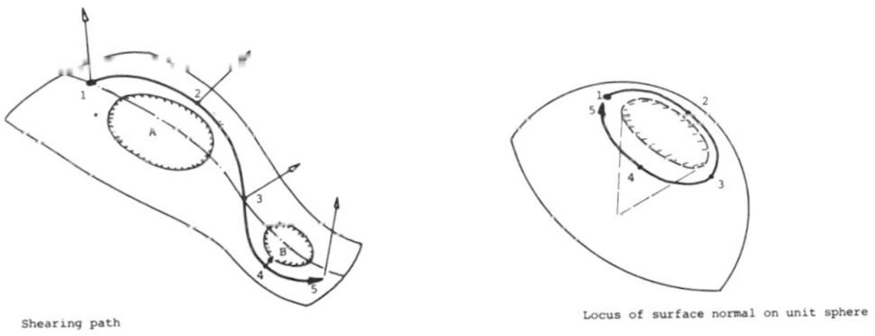

Fig 6 Interaction between degeneracy and limits
The shearing path avoids regions A and B where a degenerate configuration would be required. The locus of the surface normal encloses the degeneracy, requiring complete wrist revolutions.

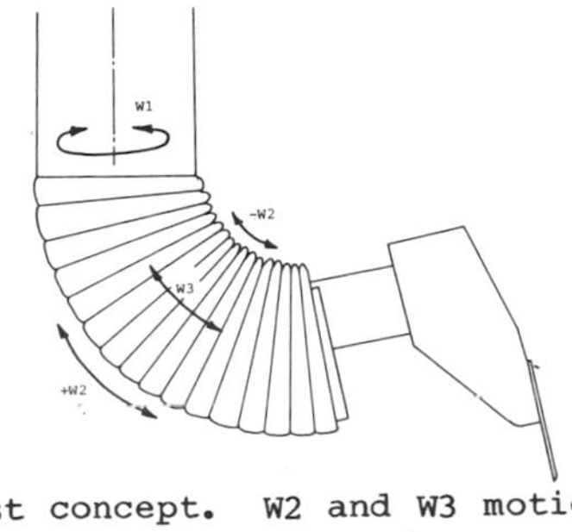

Fig 7 ET wrist concept. W2 and W3 motions consist of symmetrical expansion/contraction on opposite sides of the trunk.

deviation from the planned path to 'unwind' the wrist actuators (sometimes known as a 'flip'). However, interrupting a shearing blow is not easy, and represents a major penalty on performance. Full rotation of joints W1 and W3 requires two complete rotations of the umbilical around the wrist assembly. The mechanical implications of this requirement, and of providing 400° of rotation at joint W3, were sufficient to motivate a search for a better wrist arrangement.

ET Wrist

Figure 7 illustrates the concept which represented a starting point for a new wrist design. The cutter is mounted on the end of a flexing element which can be flexed in two directions, and rotated, to provide the necessary freedom of motion for the cutter. This arrangement has no degenerate configurations within its mechanical limits. Because of its similarity to the trunk of an elephant, this arrangement has been known as the 'Elephant Trunk Wrist' (ET).

Two Hooke joints (universal couplings) can be arranged to provide a comparable mechanical arrangement of the concept. The movements of the joints need to be synchronised to reduce the number of actuators required to three. Figure 8 illustrates a mechanical arrangement for synchronisation, and figure 9 is a photograph of a model of the wrist for the SM robot.

Kinematic analysis [Kovesi, 1984] has resulted in the map shown in figure 10 which shows the peak actuator velocity required for a unit cutter angular velocity in the most unfavourable direction. The only degenerate configuration for the wrist requires a 90° rotation of both joints which is well beyond the mechanical limits.

Thus the ET wrist exhibits none of the undesirable kinematic properties of the other wrist arrangements. It will provide the necessary dexterity for the SM robot arm to access all of the exposed sheep surface in each of the three principal sheep positions in the range of shearing directions considered necessary. The ET wrist in particular and the use of linear hydraulic actuators to power the W2 and W3 movements, has resulted in large weight savings in the SM design. Umbilical problems have been greatly reduced since there is sufficient space with the W1 joint for internal rotary connections; services to the cutter pass down the sides of the wrist.

While there are more mechanical elements than in a conventional wrist, the kinematic control equations, using motion rate control methods, are relatively simple because of the symmetrical arrangement and placement of axes. Only marginally more computations are involved than for a more conventional wrist.

The mechanical arrangement is relatively simple but not easy to design; the model shown in the photograph represents an interim design stage which was required to overcome the limitations of

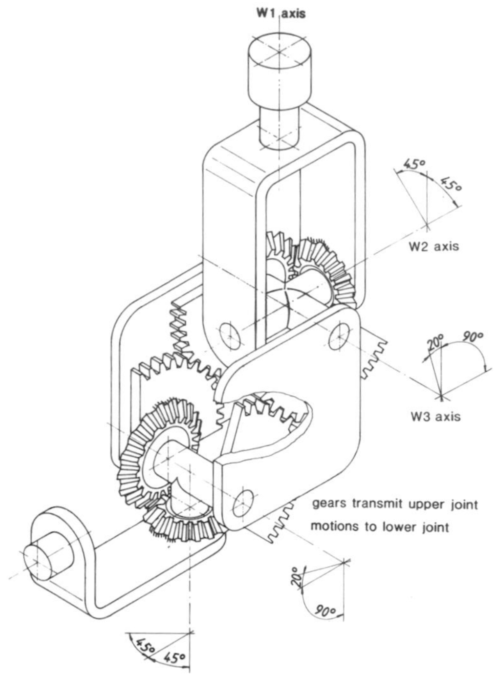

Fig 8 ET wrist mechanism

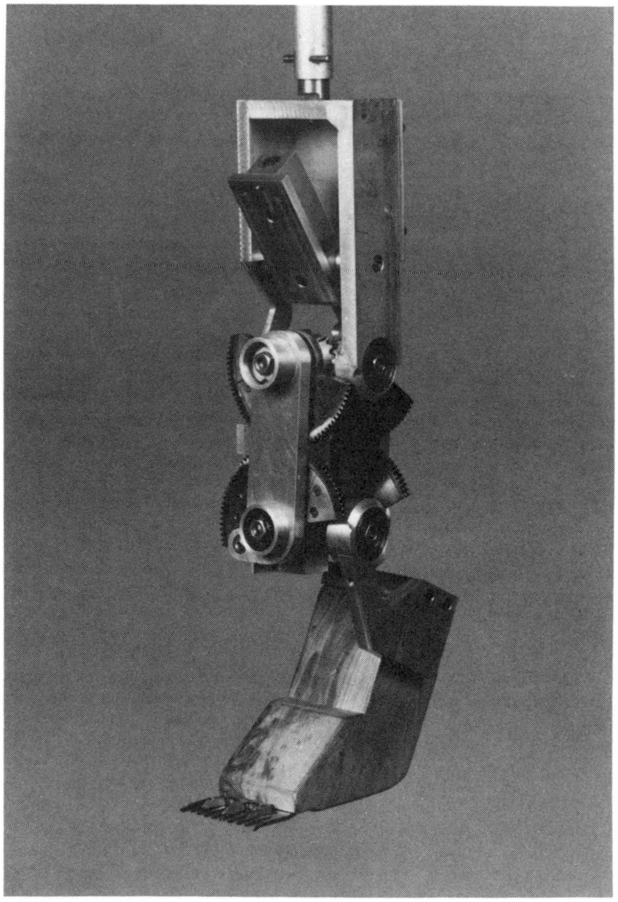

Fig 9 Prototype ET wrist for SM robot

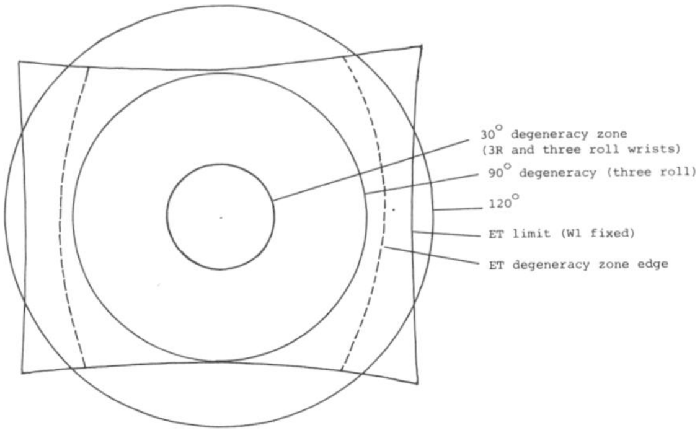

Fig 10 Approximate polar map of degeneracy zones. The map shows the range of allowable cutter directions relative to the W1 axis direction.

normal two dimensional drawings. For the SM robot, the wrist had to be designed for both kinematic and dynamic requirements [Ong, 1984].

Protection for the wrist mechanism from dirt and wool fibres is required, and will take the form of a flexible boot with rigid reinforcing members. This is still being designed.

Sensing

Several different sensors have been used for experimental shearing by robot. The most successful have been:

- resistance contact sensing (figure 11); current flows between the tips of the metal shearing comb and the skin of the sheep in response to an applied potential difference. Although other parts of the cutter assembly can be in contact with the sheep, the wool stubble which remains after the fleece is shorn off provides effective insulation between other metal components and the skin. The contact resistance decreases with increasing mechanical force. As the skin has some compliance, though it is extremely variable, it is possible to estimate a deformation of the skin for a given value of contact resistance [Trevelyan, 1981]. which is used to modify the comb position.

- capacitance sensing (figure 12); the capacitance between three reference electrodes on the underside of the comb and the sheep is measured electrically. [Crooke, 1982]. The capacitance depends on the distance between the respective electrodes and the skin of the animal and therefore the distance may be estimated. Variations in wool properties and in the shape of the sheep surface significantly affect the relationship between distance and capacitance.

- inductance sensing (figure 13); high frequency (VHF) eddy currents can be induced in the sheep skin, modifying the apparent impedance of radiating coils placed under the comb. The effect is dependent on distance and is less

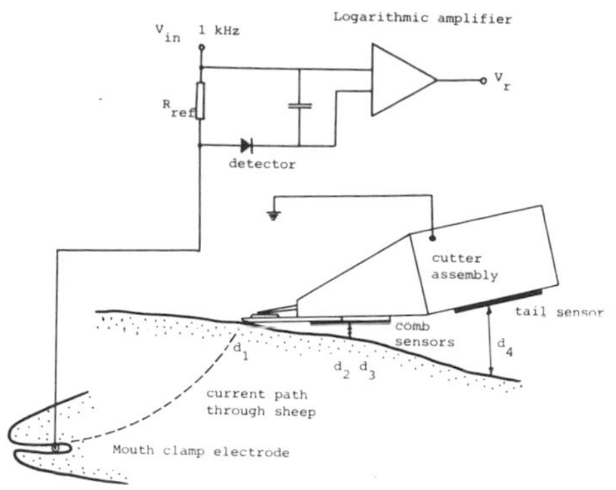

Fig 11 Resistance contact sensing
The location of other sensors has been shown.

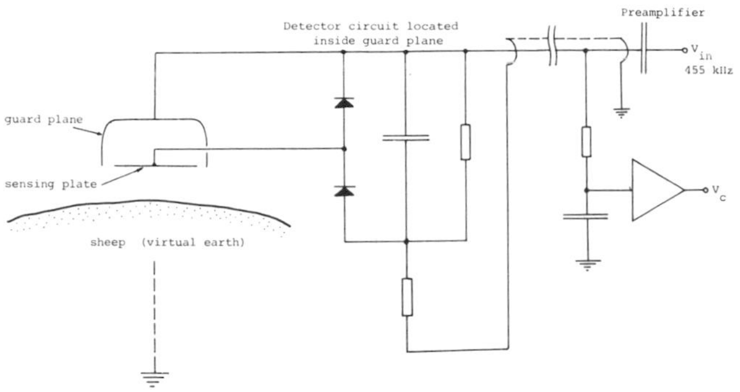

Fig 12 Capacitance sensing

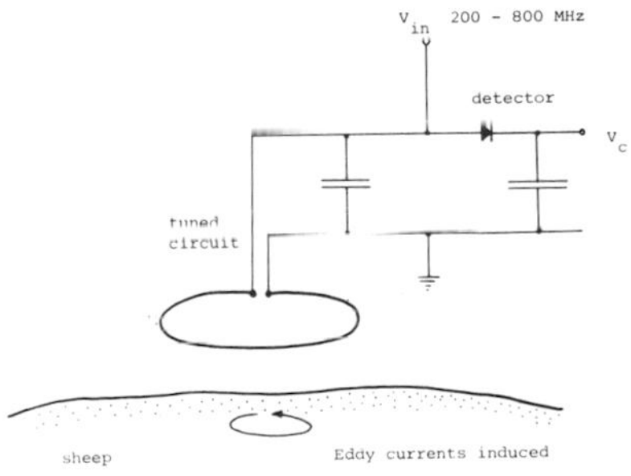

Fig 13 Inductance sensing

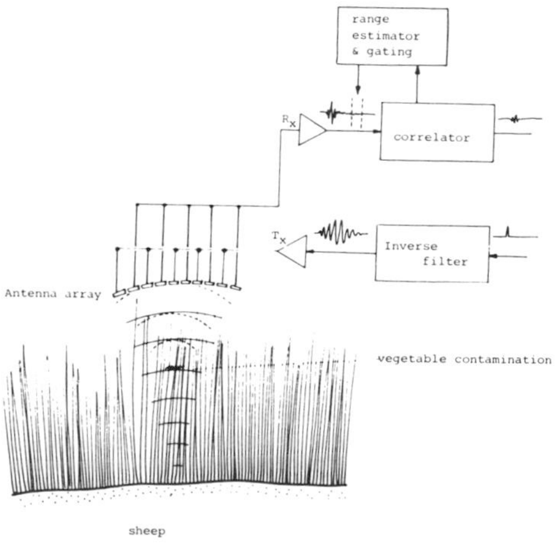

Fig 14 Ultrasonic sensing

susceptible to wool properties, but more difficult to implement than the capacitance sensors. [Dell, 1979].

- ultrasonic distance measurement (figure 14); an array of ultrasonic transducers is used to focus a beam on the sheep surface ahead of the comb. Suitable signal processing electronics can be used to detect the echo of a transmitted pulse in spite of attenuation through the fleece of up to 80dB. [Bognor and Bryant, 1984].

- sonic contact measurement; vibrations from the reciprocating mechanism of the cutter are transmitted to the sheep's body when the comb touches the skin. These vibrations may be detected and used to sense contact pressure [Crooke, 1982].

- force sensing; the contact force between the comb and the skin may be used as a regulated variable instead of position, and sensors to measure forces in various directions have been used to control an experimental shearing robot [Baxter, 1984].

All the sensing devices described have significant deficiencies and more than one type of sensing device is required for shearing. Resistance contact sensing yields a useful signal only when the comb is in electrical contact with the sheep skin. Even when the comb is pressing on the skin, electrical contact is interrupted by dirt and grease, dead skin particles and wool fibres. The variation of resistance with contact force is highly erratic, and varies with sheep position, ambient temperature and humidity, wool characteristics and contaminants such as salt or urine. However, the sensing points are at the tips of the comb and this is the only sensing device which provides an indication from this position. If the skin is penetrated by one or more comb teeth, a sudden and sustained drop in resistance is observed, and this signal is used to initiate recovery action.

Capacitance and inductance sensing of the proximity of the skin requires either coils or sensing electrodes of a significant area relatively close to the skin. Therefore, they can only be used effectively when they are located under the comb appoximately 70mm or more behind the comb tips. These comb sensors provide a continuous indication while the skin is within 30 mm.

Ultrasonic sensing provides an indication of the sheep surface profile ahead of the cutter. However, it can yield erroneous results in the presence of severe contamination of the wool, and embedded vegetable matter. Because reflection from the sheep skin is primarily specular, the attenuation of the transmitted pulse rapidly increases with increasing curvature of the surface, to the point where separation of the signal from background noise is impracticable.

An experimental prototype sensor has only been used in conjunction with the robot for a limited

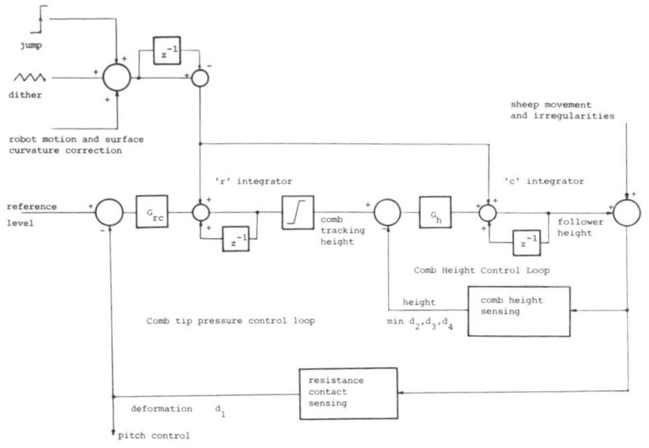

Fig 15 Follower height control algorithm

series of tests, and further experimentation is required before reliable algorithms can be developed.

Force sensing has been used by a commercial research and development group in Adelaide, South Australia and the first shearing tests in late 1983 have shown encouraging results. However, considerable further testing is required before one can have confidence in the performance of force sensing on soft parts of the sheep. The implementation of force sensing considerably complicates the mechanical design of the cutter head.

Signal Processing

Signals from the sensors used for shearing are sampled by an analogue to digital convertor and multiplexor at intervals of 4 milliseconds. Each signal is converted to a distance estimate based on previously measured calibration data. In the case of resistance sensing, the resistance signal is measured in the form of a voltage (V_r) proportional to the logarithm of the current flowing between the comb teeth and the skin. It is assumed that this corresponds to a deformation of the skin d_1 given by:

$$d_1 = - R_k (V_r - V_{ro})$$

where R_k is a constant
V_{ro} is the measured voltage when the comb is away from the sheep.

The capacitance sensors produce a voltage output V_c proportional to capacitance which is assumed to be inversely proportional to distance. The distance d_i for each sensor is computed from:

$$d_i = \frac{C_k}{(V_c - V_{co})} \qquad i = 2,3,4$$

where C_k is a constant determined by calibration for each sensor,
V_{co} is the voltage measured when the sensor is away from the sheep, for each sensor.

A similar relationship has also been used for inductance sensors.

Signal processing for the ultrasonic sensor is relatively complex and is performed by a specially designed correlator. The resulting range value is passed in digital form to the robot control computer where it is used to define a path deviation profile in front of the present cutter position. It is also proposed to use the ultrasonic sensing device to directly adapt the surface model in which the planned trajectory of the robot is defined. Some of the techniques used for surface adaptation have been reported earlier [Trevelyan et al, 1982].

Adaptive Control System

The wrist arrangements of ORACLE and SM were devised to meet the requirements of adaptive control [Trevelyan et al, 1983]. The follower and wrist orientation actuators are used to respond to rapid variations in the skin relative to the comb as the comb is moved forward over a moving sheep with skin wrinkles, folds and other irregularities. As the follower actuator moves from its nominal centre position, the trajectory of the robot is given an additional correcting component in the follower direction such that the follower will be forced to return towards its centre position to keep the comb at the correct distance from the skin. The dynamic separation of the wrist action from the normal robot movement is the principal design feature which makes shearing feasible at speeds of up to 0.35 m/sec.

Follower Position and Wrist Orientation Control

The follower actuator is moved in response to the sensed position errors. If only one sensor was used, then the control of the follower motion would be simple. However, several sensors are used to control both the follower position and the attitude of the comb through the follower and wrist actuators. The requirements which have been set for this control scheme include the following:-

- to maintain the comb teeth as close to the skin as possible, while exerting only a nominal force on the sheep. It is assumed that the depth of wool stubble is to be controlled by the comb thickness, so that the underside of the comb should be in contact with the skin while shearing.

- to effect a smooth transition between repositioning and shearing movements.

- to provide as much safety for the sheep as possible in situations where sensors provide conflicting data.

- to detect penetration of the skin by the comb teeth and to automatically select a suitable alternative control strategy.

- to control the orientation of the comb such that the leading edge conforms to the skin surface in the required way and the angle of the comb centreline to the skin surface is at a minimum consistent with control stability.

Various schemes have been tested since experimental shearing began in 1979. The presently favoured scheme is also the simplest of those tested so far (figure 15).

Although the resistance contact sensing provides the only direct sensing of contact between the comb and the skin, it is highly variable, intermittent, and not useful when the comb is not in contact with the skin. Therefore, the comb sensors have been used as the primary feedback signal for height control and the resistance contact signal is used to modify the tracking height. Neglecting orientation control, the safest strategy for height control is to select the minimum of the distances measured by the two comb sensors d_2 and d_3 as the feedback signal. Therefore, the behaviour will not depend on both sensors being able to operate when shearing on legs and other sharply curved parts of the sheep. In the absence of any indication from the resistance contact sensor, the 'r' integrator decreases the set height for the inner capacitance loop until a preset limit is reached, representing the minimum safe height for comb sensing. If the resistance contact sensor is the only one operating then the arrangement appears to be unstable because the two integrators are in series in the absence of comb sensing feedback. However, additional logic causes the 'r' integrator to be reset to the detection distance measured by the two comb sensors (which is the distance assumed when no contact is detected) whenever the state of resistance contact changes from 'no contact' to 'contact' and vice versa. This results in a small limit cycle oscillation of acceptable amplitude for shearing.

While the control laws used are by no means optimal, the conditions under which they operate are highly variable, with several non-linearities, some of which are deliberately imposed and others not. Satisfactory performance is required in all conditions, so some performance is sacrificed to achieve sufficient stability under marginal conditions.

Two refinements to the basic strategy are the 'jump' and 'height perturbation'. A jump is programmed automatically when the level of resistance contact voltage rises to a level which suggests that skin penetration is about to take place, or has already started. This often arises when a fold of skin is encountered. The jump consists of a single step increase in height above the skin after which further jumps are suppressed for a period of time. In most instances the comb successfully jumps over the skinfold. If penetration has occurred, the jump will not succeed because the skin will be lifted by the cutter. Simply raising the cutter will not extricate the comb tooth; instead, the cutter must be withdrawn backwards. As this can only be done by modifying the robot trajectory, an "emergency" motion procedure is invoked to do this, and further lifting of the cutter is suppressed until it is safe to do so. Manual shearing normally results in many small nicks and cuts, and occasionally larger ones requiring some attention. The control strategy described has been demonstrated to cause only occasional small nicks and is considerably less injurious to the animal than manual shearing.

The second refinement is 'height dither'; a height variation of preset amplitude and frequency is programmed by adding a suitable signal at the 'r' integrator. This has the effect of reducing the drag force when shearing very dense wool such as on the back and head of the sheep.

Both the jump and height perturbation are introduced by a feed forward by-pass to the 'c' integrator.

The effect of altering the robot's trajectory to return the follower actuator to its central point is resolved into a robot motion correction which is also differentiated and added to the 'r' integrator as shown.

Wrist Orientation Control

Orientation is controlled fundamentally by using the difference in distances measured by the two comb sensors to correct roll and between the comb sensors and resistance contact sensor to control pitch. Early experiments showed, however, that using a surface model to predict the correct orientation greatly improved performance and so a combination of the two methods is used.

Roll correction is computed from the difference between the left and right comb sensor distances, multiplied by a gain parameter . Pitch correction is computed only from the resistance contact error signal (see figure 15). While this seems to ignore comb sensor data, the resistance contact signal is not a very reliable signal and is effectively filtered in the height control loop. Therefore over the time interval in which a resistance contact error can be confidently averaged, the comb distance error will have been reduced to zero by the height control loop. In practice, most rapid changes in comb height error are caused by sheep movements which result in large position changes but only small orientation changes and this simplified approach has worked well.

Curvature Correction

The comb sensors are aproximately 70 mm behind the leading edge and so surface torsion and normal curvature along the shearing path require offsets to be applied to the sensor signals to avoid significant comb attitude errors. Surface curvature and torsion are computed from the surface normal derivative.

Robot Trajectory Modification

The difference between the planned and actual extension of the follower actuator is used to modify the calculation of each incremental robot position change.

Requirements for Difficult Shearing

Shearing plain parts of the sheep such as the belly requires that the comb be oriented as parallel to the skin as possible. However, when shearing more difficult parts of the sheep quite different strategies are required. As the sheep surface becomes more sharply curved the comb sensors change their distance to voltage relationship. Also, on legs and other narrow parts of the sheep, it is no longer practical to try to align the comb with the surface being shorn; instead, the aim is first to reduce the width of each shearing blow so that only part of the comb is used, and second to orient the comb so that the edge which is deepest into unshorn wool is as close to the skin as possible. The distribution of the comb sensors makes it impractical to attempt this by sensing alone so increasing use is made of surface model data. This can be done through moding or gain factor variation. In the former method, all sensed attitude corrections changes in either roll or pitch or both are suppressed. For example, when shearing along a leg, it is desirable to suppress sensed roll corrections but to retain pitch corrections. On certain very soft parts of the sheep both roll and pitch corrections should be suppressed.

It has also been found necessary to include offset values for roll and pitch which introduce an intentional roll or pitch orientation offset. Certain types of wool require shearing to be performed with a steeper or flatter pitch angle than the normal 5-8°.

In devising the control algorithms it has been assumed that there is only limited interaction between the comb tip height and the gap measured by the comb sensors. However, when shearing a stiff part of the sheep such as a leg, comb tip pressure deflects a large section of the leg - not just the skin adjacent to the comb tips. Therefore, if a particularly dry section of leg skin is encountered heavier comb pressure is exerted as the cutter pitches forward. However, this causes the whole leg to be deflected and therefore to move away from the comb sensors. This leads to a more rapid downward movement, because the comb sensor gap is increased, resulting in still higher comb tip pressure, large follower movements and possible injury to the animal. A simple measure was introduced to guard against this. The outward excursion of the follower and the amount of downward adaptation of the robot trajectory (relative to the surface model) are kept within programmable limit values.

Acknowledgement

The author acknowledges the financial support of the Wool Research Trust Fund administered by the Australian Wool Corporation for the work described in this paper.

The author would also like to thank Peter Kovesi and Michael Ong for their contributions in the analysis and synthesis of the wrist concept, and David Elford and Dan Pitic for the mechanical design and drafting of the wrist mechanisms.

REFERENCES

Baxter, J.R. 1984. Progress report. Merino Wool Harvesting Pty. Ltd.

Bognor, R.E. and Bryant, R. 1984. Ultrasonic surface imaging in adverse environments. IEEE Transactions on Sonics and Ultrasonics, Special Issue on Digital Ultrasonic Imaging.

Crooke, M.D. 1982. Investigation of sensing techniques and development of sonic sensing. Technical Report 420/504-R-82, Department of Mechanical Engineering, University of Western Australia.

Dell, J. 1979. Remote Sensing of Objects B.Eng. Thesis, Department of Electrical and Electronic Engineering, University of Western Australia.

Elford, D. and Key, S.J. 1983. Animal positioning, manipulation and restraint for a sheep shearing robot. International Conference on Robotics and Intelligent Machines in Agriculture, Florida.

Kovesi, P. 1984. Kinematics of ET wrist. Technical Report 115/081-R-84, Department of Mechanical Engineering, University of Western Australia.

Ong. M.C. 1984. Dynamics of ET wrist. Technical Report 115/082-R-84, Department of Mechanical Engineering, University of Western Australia.

Paul, R.P. and Stephenson, C.N., 1983. Kinematics of robot wrists. The International Journal of Robotics Research. Vol.2. No.1., pp 31-38.

Stackhouse, E. 1979. A new concept in wrist flexibility. Proceedings of 9th International Symposium on Industrial Robots, Washington D.C.

Trevelyan, J.P. and Leslie R.A. 1981. Automated Shearing Experiments. Proceedings of 2nd National Conference on Wool Harvesting Research and Development, Sydney, N.S.W.

Trevelyan, J.P. 1981. Report on sensing developments. Technical Report 420/503-R-81 Department of Mechanical Engineering, University of Western Australia.

Trevelyan, J.P., Key, S.J. and Owens, R. 1982. Surface representation and adaptation for automated sheep shearing. Proceedings of 12th International Symposium on Industrial Robots, Paris, France.

Trevelyan, J.P., Kovesi, P.D. and Ong, M.C. 1983. Motion control for a sheep shearing robot. Proceedings of 1st International Symposium on Robotics Research, MIT, Cambridge, Massachusetts, USA.

APPLICATION OF ELECTROMAGNETIC IMPULSIVE FORCE TO PRECISE POSITIONING TOOLS IN ROBOT SYSTEM

Toshiro Higuchi

Institute of Industrial Science
University of Tokyo
7-22-1, Roppongi, Minatoku, Tokyo, Japan

It is not easy for a common robot to position works by its hand onto a given place with an accuracy under 0.1 mm. The method presented in this paper has possibility to provide a tool which aids robots to adjust the position and attitude of objects placed on a flat surface. The principle of the positioning method is based on the following well known kinematic phenomenon. When a small but impulsive force is given on an end of a solid body placed on a plane surface, the solid body is moved to the direction of the force with a very small displacement. This phenomenon is often used when a man wants to move slightly something placed on a table. However, it has scarcely been applied in industrial use, since such an apparatus that can supply an appropriately controlled impact has not been obtained. In the micro-positioning method, electromagnetic force which is produced between a coil and a conductive plate is used as the source of the impact. This electromagnetic impulsive force can be controlled its waveform by the electric circuit. The micro-positionig method is utilized in two kinds of applications. The first case is that the conductive plate is fixed to the object and the coil is attached to a hand of a robot. The second case is that both coil and conductive plate are loaded on the object. In either case, the object can move step by step. Experiments show that a rigid mass of 3 kg can be moved from 0.1 μm to 200 μm by one shot of electric discharge according to the charged energy.

Introduction: In this paper a method of micro-positioning in which electromagnetic impulsive force is applied as a source of driving impact is described. Since we sometimes make a fillip in order to adjust the position and attitude of an solid object, it is known from experience that we can move an object placed on a plane surface by giving an impulsive force to its end with a very small distance. A method of micro-positioning which is based on the kinematic phenomenon is studied in this report.

In servomechanism also in robot dynamics, friction in the mechanism usually gives undesirable influences to the accuracy of movement and positoning. And impulsive force always causes vibrations in servomechanism. Regarding to the micro-positioning method introduced here, however, the friction between an object and a surface and the impulsive force play important roles. In other words, friction and impact are utilized positively for precise positoning control.

In the field of robotics this method seems to have possibilities to provide robots a tool which can adjust the position and attitude of workpieces or robot itself. In the present report the principle of the micro-positioning method is introduced first with explanations about the mechanism of movement and how to produce electromagnetic impulsive force. Then fundamental experiment which was performed to examine the realizability of the idea of the micro-positioning method is reported with some results to confirm its effectiveness.

Micro-positioning method: When an impact is given to an end of an solid object placed on a plane surface as shown in Fig. 1, the object can move with a certain displacement according to the impulse of the applied impact in its direction. To analyze theoretically the mechanism of this kinematic phenomenon with mathematical accuracy is not easy. Because it involves complicated problems of frictional phenomenon and propagation and dissipation of stress waves in the solid body. Therefore, the explanation described here may be rather inaccurate, but it represents the conception of the micro-positioning method.

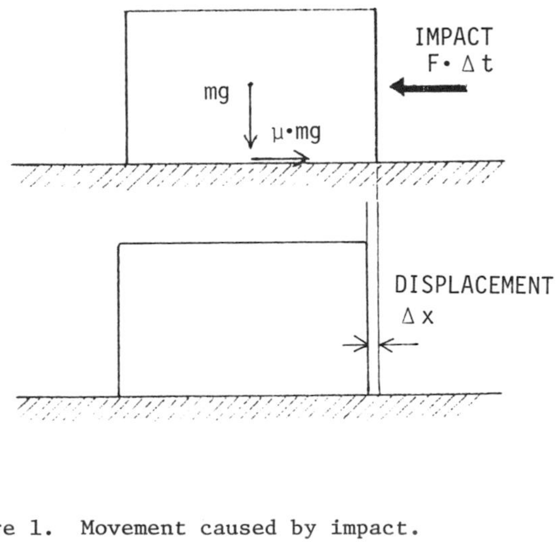

Figure 1. Movement caused by impact.

Since the static friction exists between the object and the surface, the peak of the impulsive force must be no less than the friction so as to move it. The impulse of the impact is transmitted to the increase of the momentum of the object. The more the impulse is given, the more the movement is obtained. The aim of the micro-positioning method developed here, however, is to obtain microscopical movement of several microns and submicron. In oder to move the object with as small distance as possible, the shape of the impact is desirable to be sharp. And regarding to the source of the impact, it is necessary that the impulse and the shape of the impact can be controlled easily. Considering these requirements electromagnetic impulsive force is utilized as the impact.

The electromagnetic impulsive force has been used in the field of high speed metal forming known by the name of electromagnetic forming. This electromagnetic force is generated between a coil and a conductive plate. Its brief explanation is as follows. When an impulsive current flows in the coil in a moment impulsive magnetic field is produced. And in the same instant eddy current is induced in the conductive plate placed close to the coil. Repulsive force is obtained between the current of the coil and the eddy current. The electromagnetic repulsive force F is represented by the equation.

$$F = \frac{1}{2}\frac{\delta L}{\delta x} I^2$$

where L is effective inductance of the coil including the influence of the conductive plate, x is distance between the coil and plate in the direction of the force, I is current in the coil. As shown in Fig. 2, the impulsive current can be generated by using a discharge circuit which consists of condenser banks, high voltage supply and a discharge switch. Since the shape of the discharged current is controllable by the charged voltage and capacitance of the condenser banks and the inductance of the coil, the waveform of the impact can be controlled. The electromagnetic impulsive force has another advantage for the micro-positioning method that it is generated without mechanical contact nor collision.

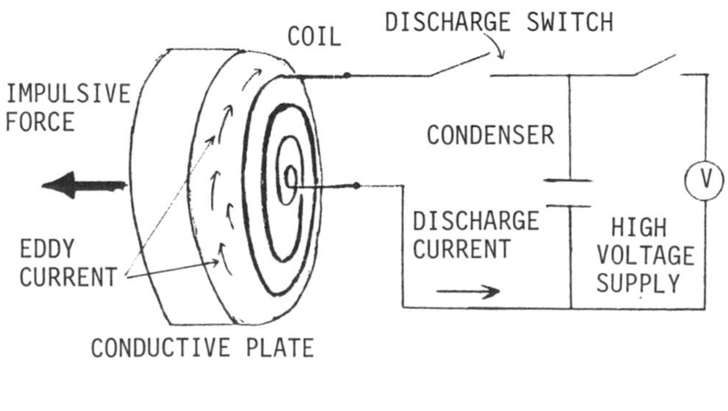

Figure 2. Generation of electromagnetic impulsive force.

The micro-positioning method is able to be used in two different ways. The first case is that the conductive plate is attached to the object and the coil is fixed to the base as shown in Fig 3. In this type the range or the movement of the object is limited for the reason that the electromagnetic force is reduced with distance between the coil and the conductive plate.

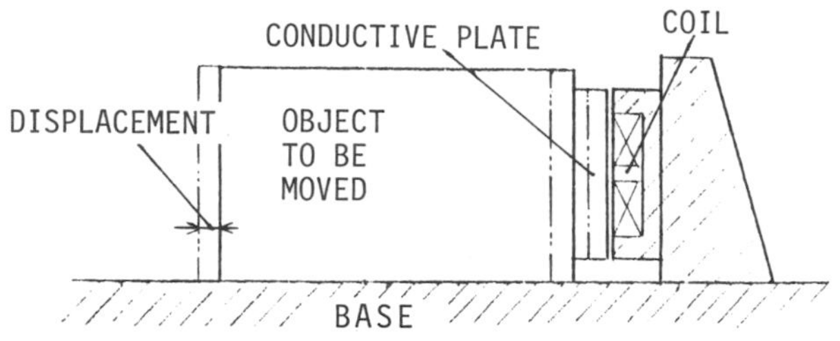

Figure 3. Micro-positioning method type I. (It shows for movement of a direction)

The second case is that both the coil and conductive plate is loaded onto the object to be moved as shown in Fig. 4. The conductive plate is fixed rigidly to the end of the object like in type I. On the other hand the coil is connected to the object by inserting a buffer like a spring or a damper between them. By using the buffer to hold the coil the object can move step by step with each discharge without limitaion of distance. An impact acting on the conductive plate makes the object move instantly. Simultaneously the mass of the coil part is accelerated by the reactive force. Then the mass of the coil part is decelerated gradually by the buffer. The force in the buffer is much smaller than the force of the impact. And if the peak of the force in the buffer is not larger than the friction between the object and the surface, the object does not move back during the deceleration of the coil. Even if the force is bigger than the friction, the movement is small in comparison with the one caused directly by the impact. This micro-positioning method type II provides us a means for a self-micro-moving vehicle.

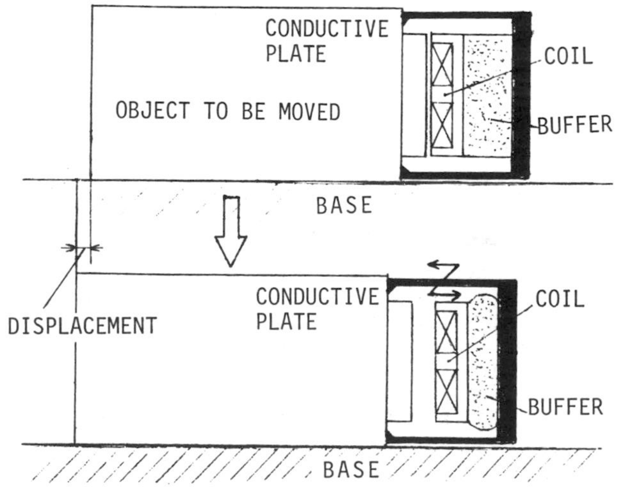

Figure 4. Micro-positioning method type II.

Experiments: In oder to examine the effectiveness of the idea described in the last section, fundamental experiments were performed. Experimental equipment was made so as to study both type I and type II of the micro-positioning method.

The experimental setup for the type I is shown in Fig. 5. The table is guided on the base to be able to slide along a straight horizontal line. Impact is produced by means of the electromagnetic impulsive force between the coil and the conductive plate. The coil has no iron core, since the core prevent the generation of impulsive magnetic flux due to is magnetic saturation. The coil is fixed to the base and its number to turns is 58. The inductance of the coil itself is 64 µH. As the conductive plate a disk of aluminum with 38 mm diameter and 10 mm thikness is fixed to the end of the moving table. The displacement of the table is measured by means of noncontact position detector. The mass of the table is 0.63 kg. To vary the total mass of the moving part 1.5 kg weights are loaded on the table. The coefficient of static friction was measured to be about 0.34.

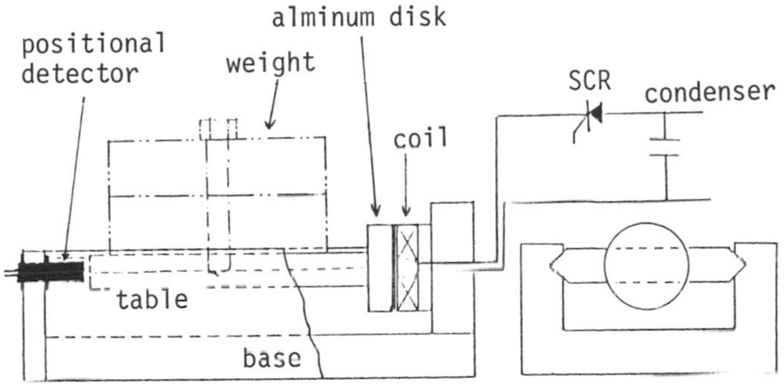

Figure 5. Experimental setup for type I.

The electrical circuit for impulsive current is basically the same as shown in Fig. 2. The capacitance of the discharge circuit is setted from 10 µF to 50 µF. SCR thyristor is used for the main switch of the circuit. An example of the wave form of discharge current is shown in Fig. 6. As SCR allow electric current to flow in one direction the discharge current has only one peak. Therefore as for the force a single clear impact can be produced by a discharge.

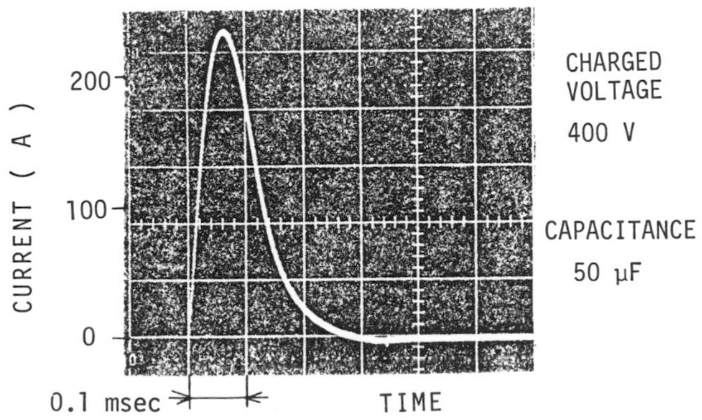

Figure 6. Example of discharge current.

The relationships between the amount of displacement obtained by one discharge and the charged energy of the condenser are presented in Fig. 7. The total mass of the moving part in (a) of Fig. 7 is 0.63 kg, in (b) is 2.28 kg , and in (c) is 3.82 kg, respectively. As for the capacitance of the condenser experiments were done with 10 µF, 30 µF, and 50 µF.

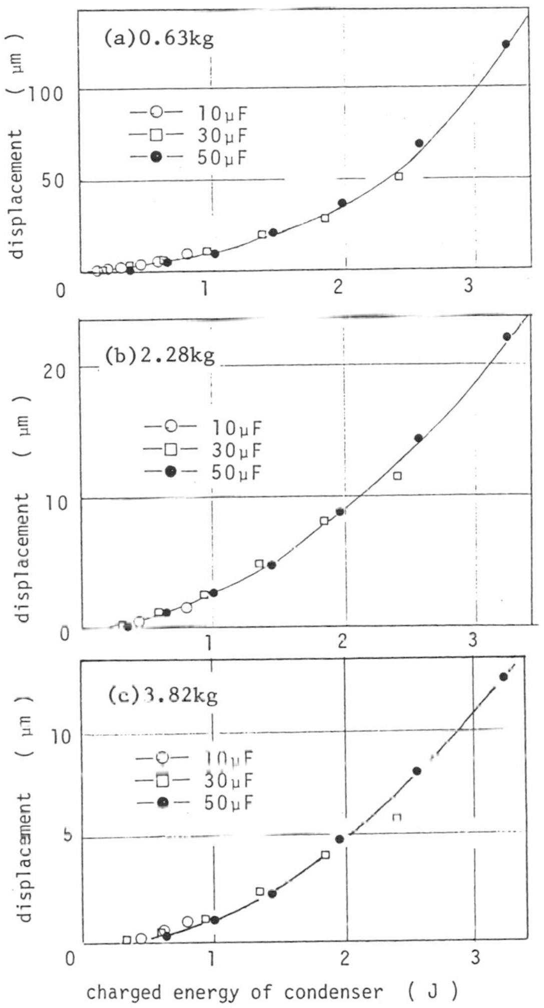

Figure 7. Relationship between displacement and charged energy of condenser.

Form the experimental results it is known that the displacement of the movement by an elecromagnetic impulse depends on the charged energy of condenser $\frac{1}{2}CV^2$ (where C is capacitance and V is charge voltage), and that it does not directly influenced by the value of capacitance itself. The movement for a certain impact decreases prominently by increasing the mass of the moving part. Therefore it indicates that microscopic momement of the oder of 0.1 µm can be given to an solid object by adjusting the discharge enegy accoding to its mass.

Experiments were also done as to the type II of the positioning method. The experimental setup for the type II is shown in Fig. 8. The coil is not fixed to the base but loaded on the table. And the coil is supported by means of a spring as shown in Fig. 8. The other experimental conditions are same as in the case for type I. The relationship between the displacement for one discharge and the charged energy of condenser banks is shown in Fig. 9 with regard to the effect of the mass of moving part and the capacitance of condenser.

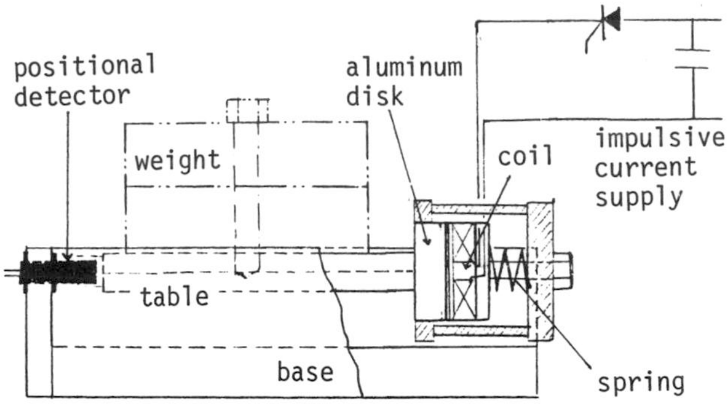

Figure 8. Experimental setup for type II.

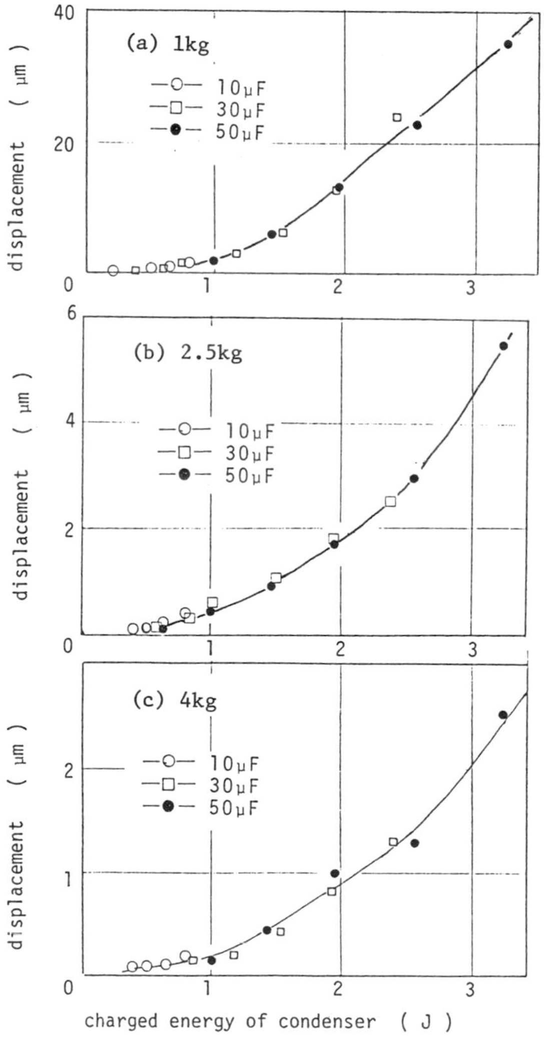

Figure 9. Relationship between displacement and charges energy in case of type II.

The exprimental results prove the concept of the self-moving method of micro-positioning. The tendency of the performance is almost the same as in type I. To comper in the same condition of the stored energy, however, displacement obtained by type II is smaller than that of type I, because of energy disspation in accelerating the mass of the coil. The repeat acuuracy is fairly good especially in the case of type II.

Applications in robotics: Based on the experiment performed as to the movement of only one guided direction, the micro-positioning method using an electromagnetic impulsive force seems to have practicability in many applications in verious fields. In this section some possible applications concerning robots are presented. Two kinds of applications can be thought of corresponding to the two types of the micro-positioning method described before. Applying the type I such a tool that can aid robots in adjusting the position and attitude of something placed on a table would be developed. The tool consists of the coil in which impulsive current flows and it is held by the hand of a robot as ahown in Fig. 10. The robot positions the tool close to the object so as to give an impact in appropriate direction. This tool is effective when the surface of the object is made of cunductive material. For a nonconducting object a few conductive thin plates are necessary and fixed on its surface with appropriate location. The influence of the reactive force of the impact on the robot can be reduced by the aid of buffer.

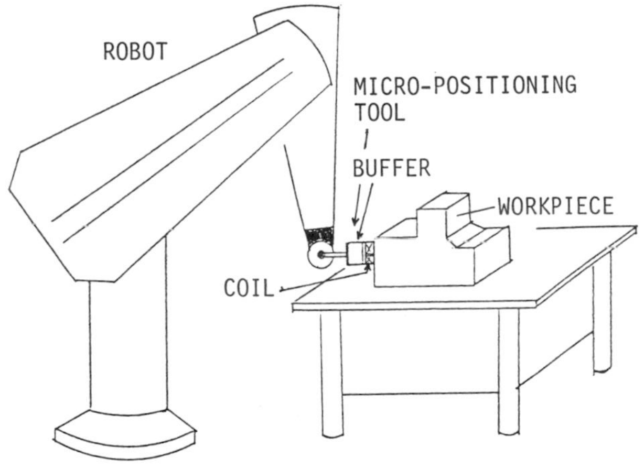

Figure 10. Micro-positioning tool for robots.

Related to the micro-positioning method of type II one of the promising applications is micro-moving vehicle. Eight or six equipments for impact of type II are attached to a block as shown in Fig. 11. Microscopic movement of both translations and rotations can be obtained in the manner as follows. Actuating simultaneously the impact equipment a-1 and equipment a-2 the block plased on a plane surface can be moved in the direction A as shown in Fig. 12. By discharge the coils simultaneously of d-1 and d-2 the block can be moved in the direction of D. When impacts are given in the same instant by a-1 and b-1 or by c-1 and d-1 the block can be made a very small rotation as shown in Fig. 12. Thus selecting the impact equipments micro-positioning as to every direction guided on a flat can be achieved. Since the structure of the micro-positioning vehicle is very simle it can be made easily on a reduced scale. Therefore it has a possibility to be used such apparatuses as micro-positioning stage of a microscope and micro-positionig vehicle for micro robots.

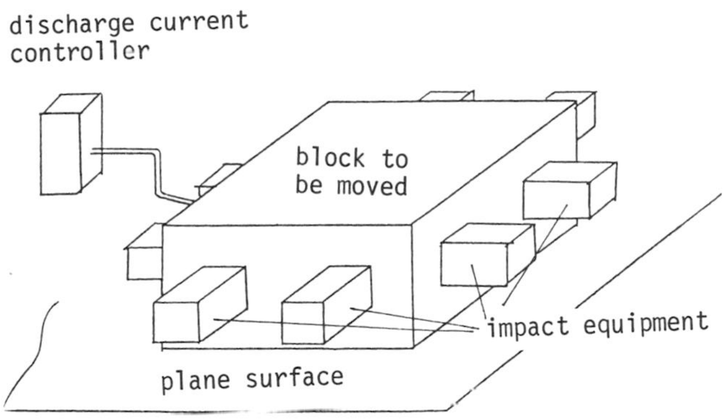

Fig. 11 Micro-moving vehicle.

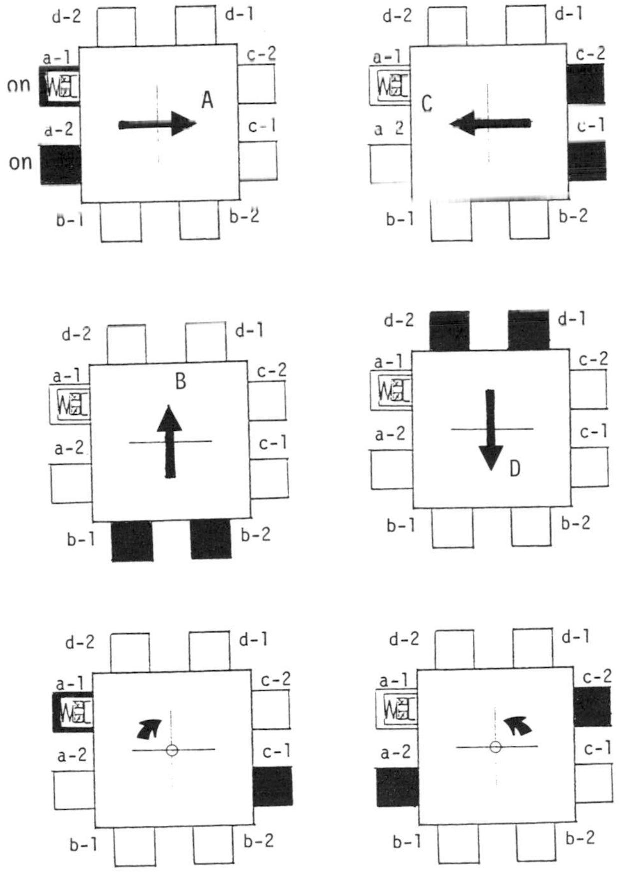

Fig. 12 Movement of translations and rotations.

Conclusions: A new method of adjusting position and attitude of an object placed on a plane surface could be developed by using electromagnetic impulsive force. The fundamental experiments confirms effectiveness of the idea of micro-positioning method as to both type I and type II with the result that displacement of 0.1 μm oder could be obtained. The method has possibility to be applied in robotics and the other various fields where microscopical positioning is demanded.

Studies are continued in order to analyse the mechanism of the movement by an impact. And an experimental apparatus as to the micro-positioning vehicle as ahown in Fig. 11 is to be constructed in the immediate future.

Acknowledgement: The author wish to thank Mr. T. Setoguchi for his help in experimental study.

MECHANICAL ANALYSIS OF A GRIPPER-MANIPULATOR

GUINOT J.C., BIDAUD P., LALLEMAND J.P.

Université Pierre et Marie Curie
Laboratoire de Mécanique et Robotique
4, place Jussieu - T. 66
75230 PARIS CEDEX 05 - FRANCE -

Université de Poitiers
Laboratoire de Mécanique des Solides
40, avenue du Recteur Pineau
86022 POITIERS CEDEX - FRANCE -

CNRS - Programme ARA

A general analysis of a gripper - manipulator is presented. The apparatus, without gripping object, is an arborescent mechanism with 3 sub-structure, both of them has 3 ddl. During the grasping process, the prototype is a closed loops mechanism, with an isostatic condition with compatible displacements in the ponctual contacts between object and fingers. The kinematic equations give the control system and the conditions for no parasite mobilities. The static equations after treatment, give the stress screw applied to object. Elastic transmissions are necessary to have a high resolution in force control, and so, in displacements. All actuators are c.c. motors with optical sensors; specific sensors are implanted on the fingers for a high contact detection. If we are fixing a given attitude to different kinematic variables, the gripper - manipulator is so acting as a passive compliant system. In general cases, the method of differents objects displacements control under unknowed external stresses prescribes the simultaneous resolution of control equations and static equations.

Introduction

After an antropomorphic approach of the gripper [1][2][3][4][5], giving us more or less complicated mechanism, which usually have weak static stresses, we enter upon mechanical studies in order to ensure the stability of grip and to control stresses which are developped between object and gripper [6][7]. More usually, the mechanical analysis can give some stability conditions for the grip in the case of a gripper allowing movements, whether in plan [8] or in space [9][10].

A study of a plane case for a gripper having three free fingers with deformable elements, leads us to specify a method for the control of movements, being acquainted with stresses, developped between object and fingers, stresses which are expressed in terms of elastic potential of deformable elements. Yet, it is necessary to get some stresses (others beside grip ones) to make the control of the object position sure. So, this appliance can only be applied for assembly workings. This analysis has been developped in order

- to define a complex mecanism able to secure the stable grip of the piece with a minimum of contact hyperstatic unknowns.
- to animate the gripped object with 6 mobilities, giving fine, more different, controled movements with high resolution
- to know, at every time, stresses which are exerted during an assembly (closed kinematic chain)
- to define an assembly strategy by getting movements and stresses under control.

This objective leads us to an other possibility for the architecture of an assembly robot different from the complient wrist which stays effective but also too limited in its versatility.

So the problem consists in defining the better mechanism, for a gripper-manipulator, to produce fine movements with high resolution, and to accept a load, which would be consistent with one supported by a light rapid carrier, but with a specific precision usually at variance with the precision in an industrial assembling working.

Besides, this gripper-manipulator can work in a passive way like a compliant wrist.

1 - Structure and mechanical analysis of the gripper-manipulator.

In the case of a gripper securing the stable grip of the piece, without giving it any movement, the full study of the grip stability whatever the shape of object may be, is written in [7]. To this analysis, we add the following condition :
Such are mobilities of fingers that they most secure six fine independant movements of the object, while preserving a normal character for the assembly so realised (no parasitic redundant

mobilities).

We admit the hypothesis that the gripper is tridigital according to the following diagram (see fig. 1)

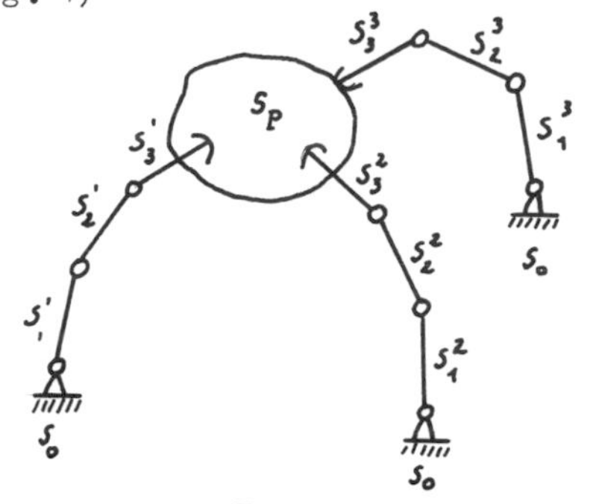

Fig. 1.

The object, S_p, is bounded to the last element of carrier, S_0, by mean of 3 fingers, themselves constitued with solids, S_i^d , connected among themselves by binary joints. By realising the structural graph of this assembly (see fig. 2),

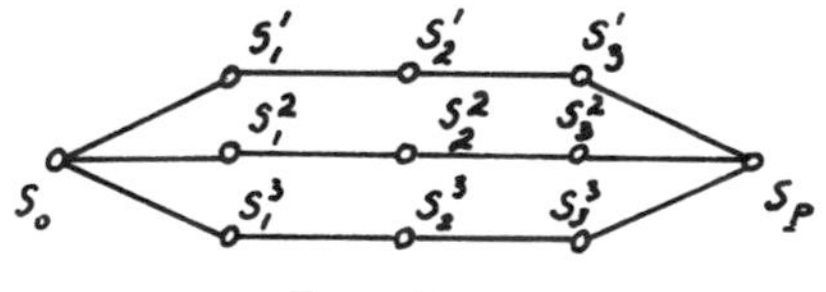

Fig. 2.

we are immediately identifying 2 independant circuits in the graph. For instance

$S_0 - S_1^1 - S_2^1 - S_3^1 - S_p - S_3^2 - S_2^2 - S_1^2 - S_0$

and

$S_0 - S_1^1 - S_2^1 - S_3^1 - S_p - S_3^3 - S_2^3 - S_1^3 - S_0$

We are making the new hypothesis (for obvious reasons of technology) that joints, others beside representing contacts S_3^i / S_p , are in class one (that's to say : just one mobility).

Enumeration of b summits and n sides (b solids, n binary joints), leads immediately to calculate the number of kinematic equations, translating the closing of both independant circuits.

$$E_c = 6(n - b + 1) = 12$$

As general mobility of assembly must be equal to six, the number of kinematic unknowns I_c is equal to 18, and according to the previous remark, such is the class of contacts S_3^i / S_p that the sum is 9. So this condition leads us to choose 3 contacts on class C_3, representing punctual contacts with friction , easy to realise.

A necessary condition of normality of assembly, represented by a homogeneous system with E_c = 12 equations and I_c = 18 unknowns, is that rank of system is strictly equal to $r_c = E_c = 12$.

So, as soon as equations are written, we must **verify** this condition and identify geometrical configurations when $r_c < 12$.

Putting in kinematic equations make use of the dual formalism of screws. By respectively noting $\hat{\omega}$ et $\hat{a}$ the coordinates of principal screw of the relative movement of two consecutive solids according to the principal axis $\hat{a}$ of the joining, general equations of closing of both kinematic chains are :

$$(1)\ \hat{\omega}_{S_0/S_1^1}\,\hat{a}_{S_0/S_1^1} + \hat{\omega}_{S_1^1/S_2^1}\,\hat{a}_{S_1^1/S_2^1} + \hat{\omega}_{S_2^1/S_3^1}\,\hat{a}_{S_2^1/S_3^1} + \hat{\omega}_{S_3^1/S_p}\,\hat{a}_{S_3^1/S_p} + \hat{\omega}_{S_p/S_3^2}\,\hat{a}_{S_p/S_3^2} + \hat{\omega}_{S_3^2/S_2^2}\,\hat{a}_{S_3^2/S_2^2} + \hat{\omega}_{S_2^2/S_1^2}\,\hat{a}_{S_2^2/S_1^2} + \hat{\omega}_{S_1^2/S_0}\,\hat{a}_{S_1^2/S_0} = 0$$

$$(2)\ \hat{\omega}_{S_0/S_1^1}\,\hat{a}_{S_0/S_1^1} + \hat{\omega}_{S_1^1/S_2^1}\,\hat{a}_{S_1^1/S_2^1} + \hat{\omega}_{S_2^1/S_3^1}\,\hat{a}_{S_2^1/S_3^1} + \hat{\omega}_{S_3^1/S_p}\,\hat{a}_{S_3^1/S_p} + \hat{\omega}_{S_p/S_3^3}\,\hat{a}_{S_p/S_3^3} + \hat{\omega}_{S_3^3/S_2^3}\,\hat{a}_{S_3^3/S_2^3} + \hat{\omega}_{S_2^3/S_1^3}\,\hat{a}_{S_2^3/S_1^3} + \hat{\omega}_{S_1^3/S_0}\,\hat{a}_{S_1^3/S_0} = 0$$

Both general equations lead, on the whole, to 12 scalar equations we must make clear by specifying the geometrical configuration of assembly.

Yet, those equations describing every kinematical properties of gripper, don't make relations interpose, relations between the six variables for the control of movements of object S_p, represented by vector $[\theta] = [\theta_1 , \ldots, \theta_6]^t$ and expressed for exemple by parameters

$\omega_{S_1^i/S_2^i}$, $\omega_{S_2^i/S_3^i}$, $i \in [1, \ldots 3]$

and kinematics parameters of this movement, noted in the axis which is bounded to S_0, that's to say, for exemple, six scalar components of distributor of speeds of S_p/S_0, in one given referring point and in one bounded to S_0 reference :

$$(3)\ [X] = [X_1, \ldots X_6]^t = [V_x, V_y, V_z, \Omega_x, \Omega_y, \Omega_z]$$

The additional relations, to define the control of gripper-manipulator, can be got by making clear the movement of S_p/S_0 in one of three arborescent parts of graph, for exemple :

$$(4)\ \hat{\omega}_{S_p/S_0}\,\hat{a}_{S_p/S_0} = \hat{\omega}_{S_p/S_3^1}\,\hat{a}_{S_p/S_3^1} + \hat{\omega}_{S_3^1/S_2^1}\,\hat{a}_{S_3^1/S_2^1} + \hat{\omega}_{S_2^1/S_1^1}\,\hat{a}_{S_2^1/S_1^1} +$$

$\hat{\omega}_{S_1^1/S_0}$ $\hat{a}_{S_1^1/S_0}$

On this way, we are constructing a system with 18 equations and 24 unknowns and we directly write :

$$(5) \qquad [A] = [M]\,[X]$$

In this line, $[X]$ is defined by (3), and (A) is one vector with 9 components representing on the one hand, the six active components $[\theta]$ and on the other hand the three passive supplementary components $[P]$.

So we can notice that to write the relation (5), we have proceed to the elimination between (1), (2) and (4) of 9 scalar components which represent joints S_3^i/S_p, $i \in [1,3]$

So, a new elimination of variables can lead to :

$$[\theta] = [N]^{-1}\,[X]$$

it represents a system 6 - 6, bounding active parameters to kinematic parameters of displacement of object.

By a direct calculation, we can express :

$$[X] = [N]\,[\theta]$$

and $[N]\,[N]^{-1} = I$ leads to a checking of previous equations.

We give, in Annexe, the value of $[N]^{-1}$ for a geometrical configuration defined in next section.

2 - Gripper-manipulator design.

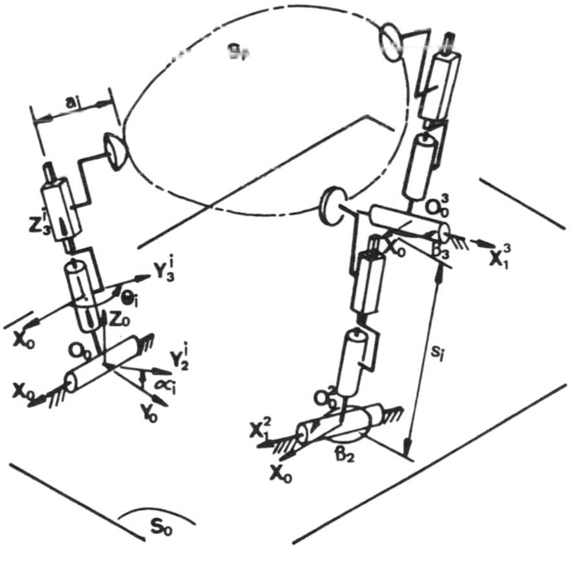

Fig. 3

Previous general equations are expressed if geometry of gripper-manipulator is according to previous figure 3.

For technological reasons, three identical modules are forming mechanism.

A first important analysis consists in displaying fact that rank of kinematic equations system is equal to 12, to be sure of getting $m = m_c = m_s = 6$, according to hypothesis.

This calculation, if we want to lead it in an analytic way, is very difficult on account of coefficients appearing in determinants 12 x 12.

Yet, we can just reduce it by noting control variables $[\theta]$ haven't effect upon parasite local mobilities and only passive variables ensure isostatism of the mechanism when actuator variables are locked in any position.

More, only geometric properties, make rank of equations system reduce. We are deliberately choosing this unfavorable case, if axis of joints C_1 are parallel.

So, we are just getting analysis of an easier assembly represented below, itself isostatic $m = m_c = m_s = 0$ (Fig. 4).

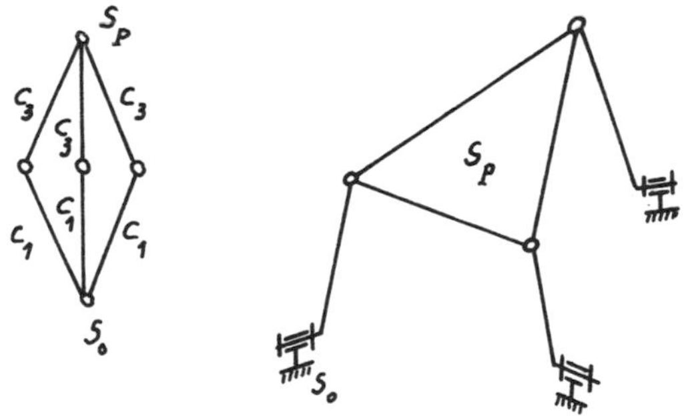

Fig. 4.

Its analysis displays two simple cases for ordering of principal axis of joint and give some parasite mobilities to assembly :

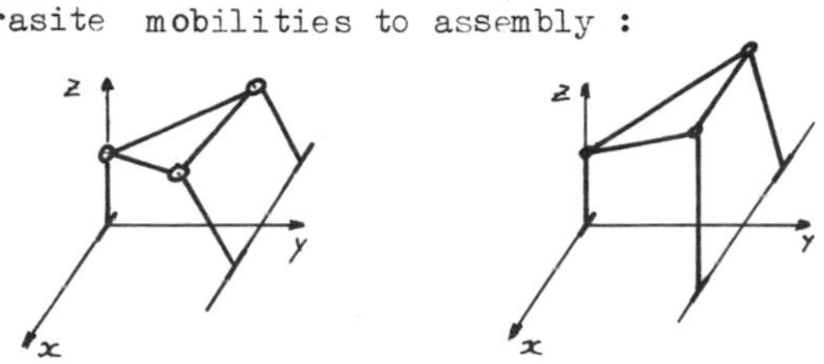

* Contacts points are in a parallel plane with (x,y); joint axis C_1 are parallel, both of them being on the same line.

* Two contact points M_2 and M_3 are on parallel straight line with x; joint axis C_1 are parallel, both of them being on the same line.

These two simple cases are dismissed into practice.

Résolution.

From control equations $[\theta] = [N]^{-1}[X]$, we are defining elementary movements to give to object: translation respectively according to three coordinate axis, rotation respectively according to three axis, parallel with coordinates axis, and which pass on a arbitrary point of object.

Curves, below, give us evolution of actuator variables for elementary movements and allow define resolution of control variables, by taking variables of movements imposed to object into account. ($\sim 10^{-2}$mm for displacements, 10^{-2} for rotations).

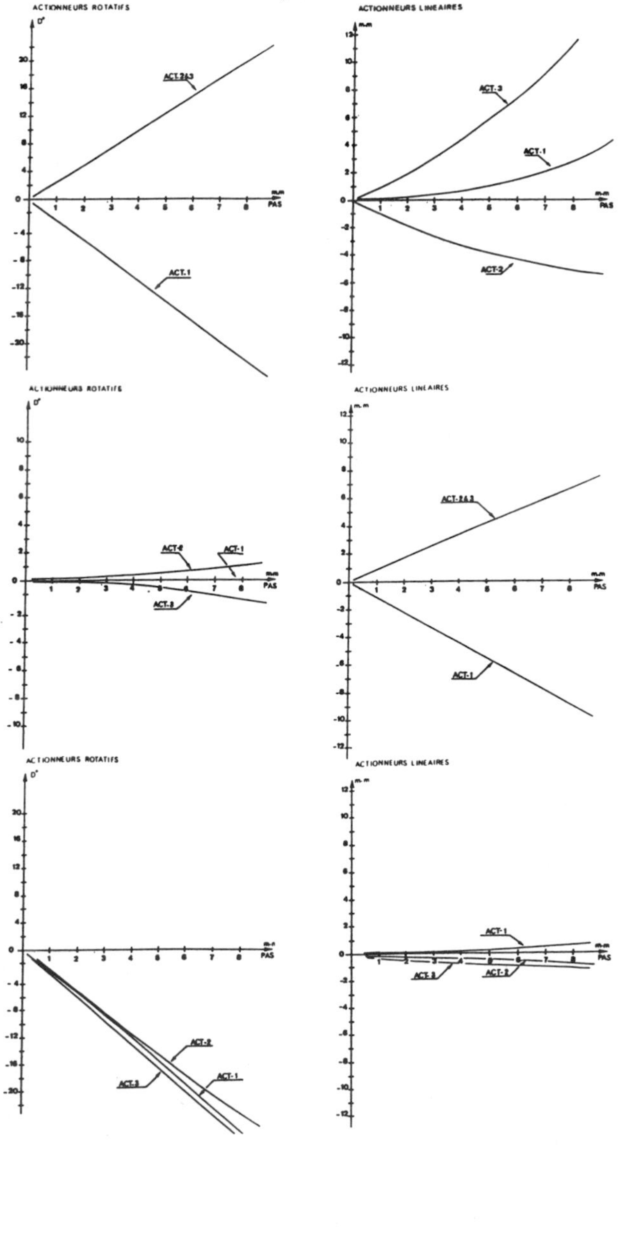

3 - Realization of prototype.

From the kinematic schéma, realization of prototype enforces respect of practical conditions, principal of which are :

- static load to contact : 10 daN
- movements amplitude : $\pm$ 10 mm in translation
  : $\pm$ 25° in rotation
- resolution of these movements: 10^{-2} mm, 10^{-2}°.
- Mesure of stresses developped on the object with a resolution of 10^{-1} N for detection of contact finger-object.
- Acquaintance, at every moment, of attitude of gripper- manipulator, owing to resolution of control equations
- clearance and friction minimum
- weight as light as possible.

Nature of contact joints between object and gripper was described in [7].

To worry about reduction, every finger is constitute with similar modules successively including :

- actuator for opening and grip
- " for rotation
- " for prismatic joint (translation C_1).

Our choice of actuator turned to torque motor associated with a reducer like a harmonic - drive (ratio 1/100).

The grip motor is producing a maximal output torque equal to 35 cmN, when motors, associated to mobilities, are only producing a maximal couple equal to 8,7 cmN.
The contact detection between finger and object is realized with the help of sensor with high sensibility giving a binary information, distinct from sensors giving value of stresses screw applied to object, and implanted on extremety of every finger.

From a equivalent contact equal to 10^{-1} N, control is stopping the advance of finger while three contacts aren't established. This grip strategy, practised with success in [12], allow us to grip an object without moving it.

Acquaintance of instantaneous attitude of mechnism and stresses mesure, is obtained, for every module, owing to 2 optical sensors, connected by an elastic torsion element, acting as transmission.

We chose absolute encoder (1024 points), on the side of driven parts giving us a digital information according to Gray code, easily manageable by microcomputer, and incremental generator (250 pts x 100), answering to a double function.

On the one hand, the control in position is asking for a secundary loop, appreciably improving static and dynamic performances.

On the other hand, differential reading of informations owed to 2 encoders, connected by an elastic element, allows us to go, after writing static equations [13] back the global compliance matrix of assembly, the coefficients of which are determined to reach an adequate resolution (about 1 N for grip actuator, and 0,1 N for active mobilities), this with acquaintance of stresses which are applied to object.

Yet, we can notice this resolution isn't consistent with the resolution of contact detection (10^{-2} N at most); reason for which we must have implanted specific contact detectors.

In the meantime, only one module $[C_1 - C_1 - C_1 - C_3]$ is realized, and control of its attitude on constant stresses which are applied on the top of finger, and for a given displacement of object, or at fixed attitude on variable stresses, is on experimentation.

Of course, these different control methods , in the real case where external stresses are unknown, impose simultaneous resolution of control equations and static equations of mechanism.

Let's notice if we are fixing a given attitude to different kinematic variables, for variations of external stresses which are c nsistent with elastic deformations of flexible elements, the gripper-manipulator is so acting as a passive compliant system with 6 mobilities.
Acquaintance of external stresses from mechanism, and of the position of every actuator variable, allow to impose to object, the most general movement, and consequently, to correct, in active mode, object displacements according to the work to realise (for instance : no elementary assembly).

Annexe :

For the geometrical configuration defined in section 2, coefficients of matrix N^{-1} are given by :

$$[\theta] = [N]^{-1}\,[X]$$

or

$$\begin{vmatrix} V_1 \\ V_2 \\ V_3 \\ \omega_1 \\ \omega_2 \\ \omega_3 \end{vmatrix} = [a_{ij}] \begin{vmatrix} V_x \\ V_y \\ V_z \\ \Omega_x \\ \Omega_y \\ \Omega_z \end{vmatrix}$$

with :

$$a_{11} = \frac{a_1}{s_1}\, c\theta_1 \;;\; a_{12} = -\, s\alpha_1 + \frac{a_1}{s_1}\, s\theta_1 c\alpha_1 \;;$$

$$a_{12} = c\alpha_1 + \frac{a_1}{s_1}\, s\theta_1 s\alpha_1 \;;$$

$$a_{14} = (-y_P c\alpha_1 - z_P s\alpha_1) + \frac{a_1}{s_1}\, s\theta_1\, (z_P c\alpha_1 - y_P s\alpha_1) \;;$$

$$a_{15} = x_P c\alpha_1 + \frac{a_1}{s_1}\, s\theta_1\, (-\, z_P \frac{c\theta_1}{s\theta_1} + x_P s\alpha_1) \;;$$

$$a_{16} = x_P s\alpha_1 + \frac{a_1}{s_1}\, s\theta_1\, (y_P \frac{c\theta_1}{s\theta_1} - x_P c\alpha_1)$$

$$a_{21} = \frac{a_2\, c\theta_2}{s_2} \;;\; a_{22} = \frac{a_2}{s_2}\, s\theta_2 c\alpha_2 - s\alpha_2 \;;$$

$$a_{23} = \frac{a_2}{s_2}\, s\theta_2 s\alpha_2 + c\alpha_2 \;;$$

$$a_{24} = c\alpha_2 (y_{12} + y_P) - S\alpha_2 (z_{12} + z_P) + \frac{a_2}{s_2}\, s\theta_2$$
$$(s\alpha_2\, (y_{21} - y_P) + c\alpha_2\, (z_{12} + z_P)) \;;$$

$$a_{25} = (x_{12} + x_P)\, c\alpha_2 + \frac{a_2}{s_2}\, (c\theta_2 (z_{21} - z_P) +$$
$$s\theta_2 s\alpha_2\, (x_{12} + x_P)) \;;$$

$$a_{26} = s\alpha_2 (x_P - x_{21}) + \frac{a_2}{s_2}\, (c\theta_2 (y_{12} + y_P) +$$
$$s\theta_2 c\alpha_2\, (x_{21} - x_P)) \;;$$

$$a_{31} = \frac{a_3\, c\theta_3}{s_3} \;;\; a_{32} = \frac{a_3}{s_3}\, s\theta_3 c\alpha_3 - s\alpha_3 \;;$$

$$a_{33} = \frac{a_3}{s_3}\, s\theta_3 s\alpha_3 + c\alpha_3 \;;$$

$$a_{34} = c\alpha_3\, (y_{13} - y_P) - s\alpha_3\, (z_{13} + z_P) + \frac{a_3}{s_3\, s\theta_3}$$
$$(s\alpha_3 (y_{31} - y_P) + c\alpha_3\, (z_{13} + z_P)) \;;$$

$$a_{35} = (x_{13} + x_P)\, c\alpha_3 + \frac{a_3}{s_3}\, (c\theta_3 (z_{31} - z_P) +$$
$$s\theta_3 s\alpha_3\, (x_{13} + x_P)) \;;$$

$$a_{36} = s\alpha_3\, (x_P - x_{31}) + \frac{a_3}{s_3}\, (c\theta_3\, (y_{13} + y_P) +$$
$$s\theta_3\, c\alpha_3\, (x_{31} - x_P)) \;;$$

$$a_{41} = -\, \frac{1}{a_1\, s\theta_1} \;;\; a_{42} = a_{43} = a_{44} = 0 \;;$$

$$a_{45} = \frac{z_P}{a_1\, s\theta_1} \;;\; a_{46} = -\, \frac{y_P}{a_1\, s\theta_1} \;;$$

$$a_{51} = \frac{z_2\, c\theta_2\, s\beta_2}{a_2\, s_2\, s\theta_2\, (c\alpha_2 c\theta_2 s\beta_2 - s\theta_2 c\beta_2)} - \frac{1}{a_2\, s\theta_2} \;;$$

$$a_{52} = \frac{s\beta_2 c\alpha_2 z_2}{a_2 s_2 \,(c\alpha_2 c\theta_2 s\beta_2 - s\theta_2 c\beta_2)} \;;$$

$$a_{53} = \frac{s\beta_2 s\alpha_2 z_2}{a_2 s_2 \,(c\alpha_2 c\theta_2 s\beta_2 - s\theta_2 c\beta_2)} \;;$$

$$a_{54} = \frac{s\beta_2 z_2}{a_2 s_2 \,(c\alpha_2 c\theta_2 s\beta_2 - s\theta_2 c\beta_2)} \times [c\alpha_2 \,(z_{12} + z_P)$$

$$+ s\alpha_2 \,(y_{21} - y_P)] \;;$$

$$a_{55} = \frac{s\beta_2 z_2 \,[s\theta_2 \,(x_{12} + x_P)\, s\alpha_2 + c\theta_2 \,(z_{21} - z_P)]}{a_2 s_2 s\theta_2 \,[c\alpha_2 c\theta_2 s\beta_2 - s\theta_2 c\beta_2]}$$

$$+ \frac{1}{a_2 \, s\theta_2} \,(z_P - z_{21}) \;;$$

$$a_{56} = \frac{s\beta_2 z_2 \,[s\theta_2 c\alpha_2 \,(x_{21} - x_P) + c\theta_2 \,(y_{12} + y_P)]}{a_2 s\theta_2 s_2 \,(c\alpha_2 c\theta_2 s\beta_2 - s\theta_2 c\beta_2)}$$

$$- \frac{1}{a_2 \, s\theta_2} \,(y_{21} + y_P) \;;$$

for a_{61} to a_{66}, transpose index 2 to 3 in a_{51} to a_{56}.

References :

[1] OKADA T. 1979 - "Computer control of multi-joint finger system" 6th Int. Joint Conference on artificial Intelligence - Tokyo -

[2] ERSKINE CROSSLEY F.R., UMHOLTZ F.G. 1977 - "Design for a three-fingers hand" Mechanism and machine theory, Vol. 12

[3] KONOSHITA G. "Pattern classification of the grasped object by the artificial hand" Proc. 3rd conf. on Artificial Intelligence.

[4] VON MULDAU H. 1972 - "Automatische arbeitsh hande" Technische Rundschau - N° 22 - May.

[5] SKINNER F. 1975 Sept. - "Multiple prehension hands for assembly robots" Proc. Mech. Eng.

[6] GUINOT J.C. ESPIAU B. 1982, juin 2, 3, 4 - "Optimisation de la prehension avec perception de la proximétrie et des forces de contact". 1er Workshop NSF-CNRS Ministère de la Recherche.

[7] GUINOT J.C., LALLEMAND J.P., ZEGHLOUL S. 1983, December 15-20 - "Etude d'un prehenseur tridigital avec sens tactile pour une opération d'assemblage" Proc. 6th Congress of T.M.M., New-Delhi.

[8] BIANCHI G., ROVETTA A. 1978 - "On grasping process for objects of irregular shape" Proc. 3rd CISM Symp., Udine.

[9] ROTH B. 1982, juin 2, 3, 4 - Kinematics - Workshop NSF-CNRS. MIR Paris.

[10] SALISBURY J.K., CRAIG J.J. 1982 - "Articulated hands : Force control and kinematic issues" Int. Journal of Robotics Research, Vol 1.

[11] ANAFUSA H., ASADA H., 1978 - "Adaptive control of a robot hand with elastic fingers" Proc. 3rd Int. Symp. on Industrial Robots - Udine.

[12] ZEGHLOUL S. 1983, Octobre 25 - "Analyse de la préhension. Application à un préhenseur tridigital dote de sens tactile". Thèse de 3ème cycle. Université de Poitiers.

[13] BIDAUD P. Thèse de 3ème cycle à soutenir. "Préhenseur manipulateur à haute résolution".

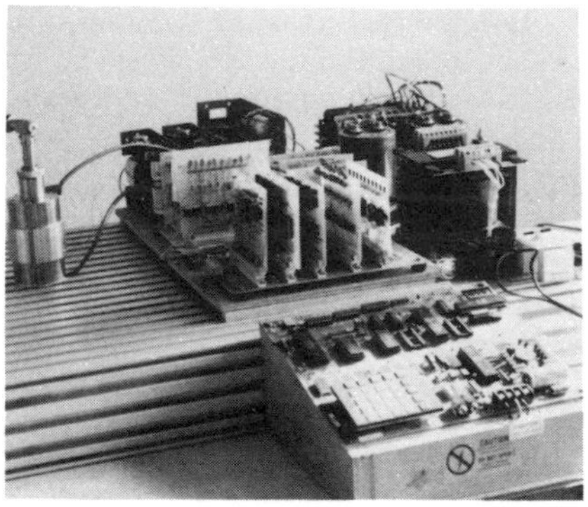

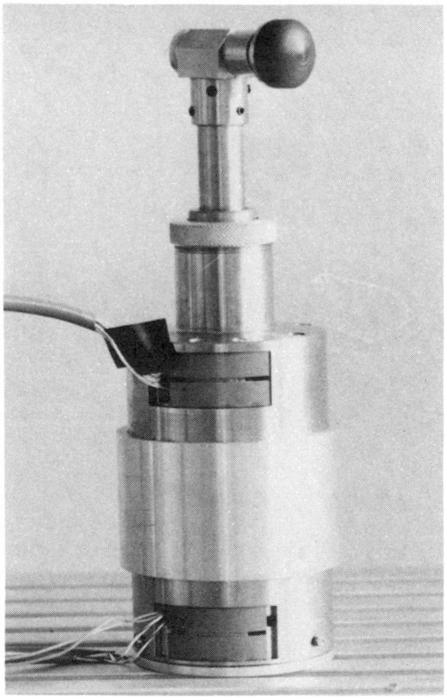

ON THE ARTICULATED HANDS

HIROAKI KOBAYASHI

Precision Engineering, Meiji University

Tama, Kawasaki 214, Japan

Kinematic problems are discussed for articulated hands. Necessary condistions to grasp an object securely and handle it freely are obtained. Handling force and grasping force are also obtained by using the principle of virtual work. Then grasping postures are discussed. The most suitable posture is selected for a task by taking account of expected external force while working. Finally, these results are applied to an articulated hand with three fingers and twelve joints. A control system with a force feedback loop is developed for the hand. Several experimental results are shown.

1. INTRODUCTION

Articulated hands can grasp and handle objects of various forms flexiblly. Furthermore they can grasp them with a suitable posture for a required task. Thus articulated hands are flexible, versatile and adaptable end effectors.

There have been several papers about articulated hands so far. For example, T. Okada[1980] has succeeded to handle balls and small boards with a hand which has three fingers and eleven joints. J. K. Salisburg and J. J. Craig[1982] have investigated the basic properties of articulated hands. They used the concept of the mobility and the connectivity to obtain the conditions for grasping and handling of objects. Then they designed a hand with three fingers and nine joints and developed a tendon control system. H. Hanafusa, H. Kobayashi and K. Terasaki[1983] gave algebraic solutions of basic kinematic problems for articulated hands. For a grasping posture, T. Yoshikawa[1984] has proposed to use the posture for which the determinant of the Jacobi matrix is maximum, while J. K. Salisburg and J. J. Craig[1982] recommanded the posture for the minimum condition munber of the matrix.

Now let's consider an assembly task. Then it is practical that, at first, a robot arm carries a grasped object near the parts to be assembled and then a hand handles the object to set them together. The situation will be reasonable for many other tasks which require the help of hands. For these cases, it will be enough for hands to move objects locally in fine motion. Therefore the kinematic problems for the fine motion control of objects by articulated hands are discussed in this paper.

The grasping posture is also considered. A hand is a part where various external force affects directly. Therefore how to cope with such force is an important problem. For example, when a hand is required to put a brittle glass on a desk, the hand must grasp it softly enough not to break it by contact shock. On the other hand, the hand should grasp it stiffly in order to insert a pin into a rather narrow hole. Of course, different grasping posture is used for each task. Thus the grasping posture is selected by taking account of the external force and the required task in this paper.

The paper organized as follows. In section 2, imaginary joints are introduced in order to describe the degrees of freedom left at the contact location of an object with a finger tip. Then kinematic problems are discussed in section 3. These sections describe the results given in H. Hanafusa, et. al.[1983] briefly. In section 4, grasping force and handling force are obtained and a grasping posture is discussed. Section 5 shows the experiments. Results obtained in this paper are applied to a hand with three fingers and twelve joints. A control system with a force feedback loop is developed.

2. ACTIVE JOINTS AND PASSIVE JOINTS

Suppose that one of fingers of a hand touches an object at one point and the object can roll on the surface of the finger tip without slipping (see Fig. 1). Then the object has three degrees of freedom with respect to the finger tip [Salisburg 1982]. Therefore three additional variables must be introduced in order to specify the position and the orientation of the object with respect to the finger tip. To do this, we introduce imaginary joints and call them passive joints. Joints which have no drive units and move according to the movement of other joints are also called passive joints. On the other hand, usual joints which are connected to drive units are called active joints. In Fig. 1, θ_5, θ_6 and θ_7 are passive joints and the others are active joints. This paper considers kinematic problems for an articulated hand with N fingers and M active joints. It is assumed that each active joint can move independently one another.

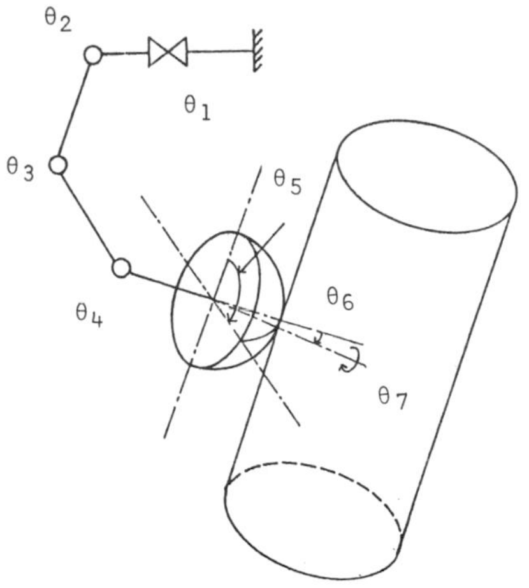

Fig. 1 Active Joints and Passive Joints

The vector of joint variables of active joints of the i-th finger is denoted by θ_{ia}, while the one for the passive joints is expressed by θ_{ip}. For Fig. 1 we have

$$\theta_{ia} = (\theta_1, \theta_2, \theta_3, \theta_4)^t,$$
$$\theta_{ip} = (\theta_5, \theta_6, \theta_7)^t ,$$

where v^t denotes the transposed vector of v.

3. KINEMATICS

Fig. 2 shows an object grasped by a hand, where F_o is a coordinate frame fixed at the bottom of the object to express the position and the orientation of it and F_h is the base coordinate frame fixed at the center of the palm of the hand.

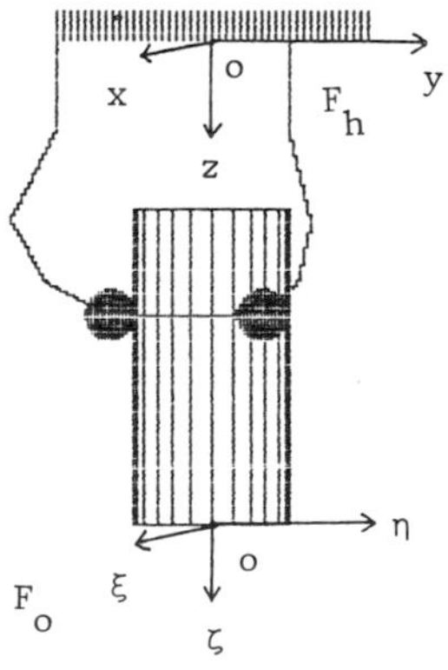

Fig. 2 Hand and Object

Then the coordinate transformation matrix T_i from F_o to F_h is obtained by using θ_{ia} and θ_{ip} [R. Paul 1981]. If joints of the finger move a little from θ_{ia} and θ_{ip} to $\theta_{ia} + \delta\theta_{ia}$ and $\theta_{ip} + \delta\theta_{ip}$, then coordinate frame F_o also move to F_o' and T_i changes to $T_i \delta T_i$ where δT_i is the coordinate transformation matrix from F_o' to F_o and given as follows.

$$\delta T_i = \begin{pmatrix} 1 & -\delta\gamma & \delta\beta & \delta\xi \\ \delta\gamma & 1 & -\delta\alpha & \delta\eta \\ -\delta\beta & \delta\alpha & 1 & \delta\zeta \\ 0 & 0 & 0 & 1 \end{pmatrix}.$$

Then we have

$$\delta\underline{\xi} = J_{ai}\delta\theta_{ia} + J_{pi}\delta\theta_{ip} . \qquad (1)$$

where

$$\delta\underline{\xi} = (\delta\xi, \delta\eta, \delta\zeta, \delta\alpha, \delta\beta, \delta\gamma)^t.$$

Now define following subspaces from Eq. (1).

$$S_m = \bigcap_{i=1}^{N} R\{[J_{ai} : J_{pi}]\} , \qquad (2)$$

$$S_f = \bigcap_{i=1}^{N} R\{J_{pi}\}, \qquad (3)$$

where R{A} is the range space of matrix A. Then it is shown that $S_m = R^6$ is necessary for handling the object freely around this posture in the three dimensional space and $S_f = \{0\}$ is necessary to grasp it securely. That is, the following simultaneous equations have a set of solutions $\delta\theta_{ia}$ and $\delta\theta_{ip}$ (i= 1, 2, ..., N) for any $\delta\underline{\xi}$ if $S_m = R^6$;

$$\delta\underline{\xi} = J_{ai}\delta\theta_{ia} + J_{pi}\delta\theta_{ip}, \quad i= 1, 2, \ldots, N.$$

Furthermore $S_f = \{0\}$ implies $\delta\underline{\xi}$ is determined uniquely only by $\delta\theta_{ia}$ (i= 1, 2, ..., N) as follows;

$$\begin{pmatrix} \delta\underline{\xi} \\ 0 \end{pmatrix} = \begin{pmatrix} J_p^{\#} J_a \\ J_p^{\perp} J_a \end{pmatrix} \delta\theta_a , \qquad (4)$$

where

$$\delta\theta_a = (\delta\theta_{1a}{}^t, \delta\theta_{2a}{}^t, \ldots, \delta\theta_{Na}{}^t)^t,$$

and matrices $J_p^{\#}$, $J_p^{\perp}$ and J_a are given in Appendix.

The degrees of redundancy of the hand is defined as follows.

$$r = M - \operatorname{rank} \begin{pmatrix} J_p^{\#} \\ J_p^{\perp} \end{pmatrix} J_a \qquad (5)$$

If the hand has r degrees of redundancy, then r other additional conditions are required to determine $\delta\theta_a$ from Eq. (4) such that

$$J_r \delta\theta_a = 0,$$

and

$$\operatorname{rank}\begin{pmatrix} J_p^{\#}J_a \\ J_p^{\perp}J_a \\ J_r \end{pmatrix} = M.$$

Then $\delta\theta_a$ is determined uniquely by

$$\delta\theta_a = \hat{H}\ \delta\underline{\xi}\ , \qquad (6)$$

where

$$H = \begin{pmatrix} J_p^{\#}J_a \\ J_p^{\perp}J_a \\ J_r \end{pmatrix},\ H^{\#} = (H^tH)^{-1}H^t = [\ \hat{H} : \tilde{H}\ ],$$

and $\hat{H}$ is an M×6 sub-matrix of $H^{\#}$.

4. HANDLING FORCE, GRASPING FORCE AND GRASPING POSTURE

To handle an object with an articulated hand, three kinds of force must be considered, i. e. handling force, grasping force and the force for the redundancy.

Let f_o be the external force applied to the origin of F_o, i. e.,

$$f_o = (\ f_\xi,\ f_\eta,\ f_\zeta,\ m_\xi,\ m_\eta,\ m_\zeta\ )^t,$$

where f_ξ, f_η and f_ζ are the force along the axes of F_o and m_ξ, m_η and m_ζ are the torque about them. Then t_a, the torque (force) vector of active joints, must balance with f_o. t_a is obtained by applying the principle of virtual work to the system and assuming that the constraint force does no work;

$$t_a = -(J_p^{\#}J_a)^t f_o + (J_p^{\perp}J_a)^t r_1 + J_r^t r_2, \qquad (7)$$

where r_1 and r_2 are appropriate vectors with compatible dimensions, and they correspond to Lagrange's indeterminate coefficients. The first term of the right hand side is the handling force, the second the grasping force and the last the force for the redundancy.

Now we consider a grasping posture. As mentioned in the introduction, a robot hand is a part where various external force directly. Therefore the most suitable posture for the task should be selected. To consider this problem, define an index ρ for expected external force f as follows.

$$\rho(f) = \sqrt{f^t(J_p^{\#}J_a)(J_p^{\#}J_a)^t f}. \qquad (8)$$

Namely ρ(f) is the norm of the handling force for f. ρ(f) varies with grasping postures. If we have

$$\rho_I(f) > \rho_{II}(f)$$

for two grasping postures, then it implies that posture I is influenced more significantly by the force than posture II, so posture I is more flexible than posture II for f.

Fig. 3 illustrates an example. In this case, ρ was calculated for the force applied upwards at the bottom of the object. The distance from the palm to the object is kept constant, while the contact angle is varied. Posture I shown in Fig. 3 (a) gives the maximum of ρ(f) and posture II (Fig. 3 (b)) gives the minimum. That is, posture I is the most flexible posture, so it would be suitable when the hand puts an object on a table softly. On the other hand, posture II is useful for inserting a pin into a hole or push an object onto a table. This observation agrees with our experience. Experimental results will be shown in the following section.

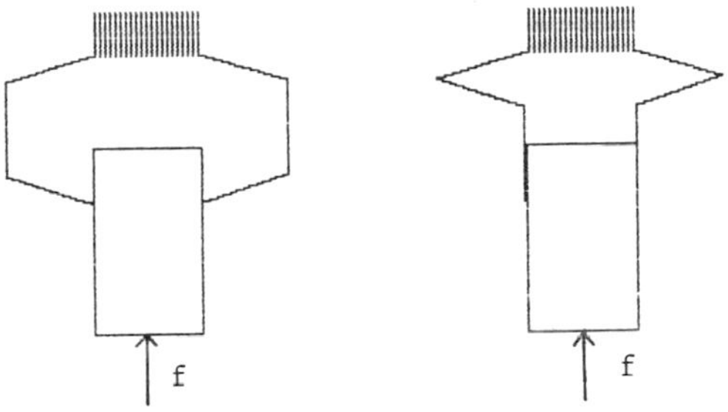

Fig. 3 Grasping Postures

5. EXPERIMENTS

5 - 1 Kinematics

Photo. 1 shows the articulated hand and the object used in the experiments. It has three fingers and each finger has four joints. The structure of a finger is shown in Fig.4. Joints are connected to dc-servo motors placed apart from the hand with tension cables through several idle pulleies. Potentio-meters are mounted at all the joint axes.

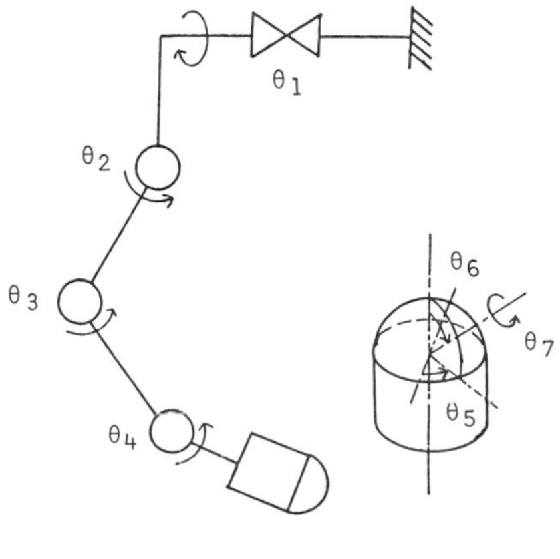

Fig. 4 Structure of Finger

The configulation of the hand and the cylindrical object (diameter: 7.5 cm, length: 14.5 cm and mass: 85g) is shown in Fig. 5 along with coordinate frames F_h and F_o. Round finger tips contact with the object and there exists friction. Therefore there are three passive joints at each contact point: θ_1, θ_2, θ_3 and θ_4 are active joints and θ_5, θ_6 and θ_7 are passive joints (see Fig. 4).

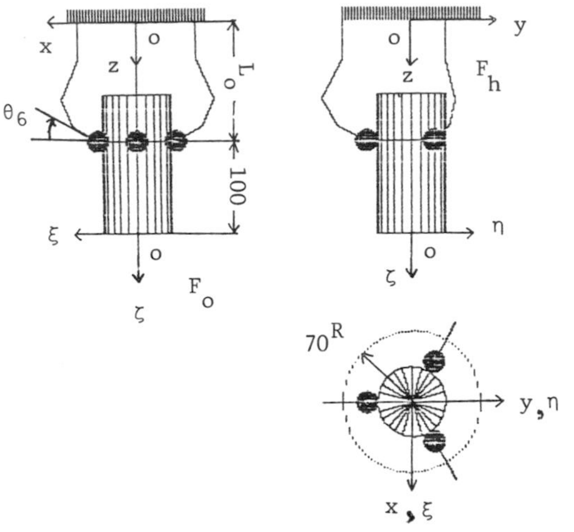

Fig. 5 Hand and Object [mm]

It is shown that this hand has three degrees of redundancy for the grasping posture shown in Fig. 5. For robot arms, the redundancy is used in order to minimize the system kinetic energy during the motion [Whitney 1969]. T. Yoshikawa [1983] used it to optimize the manipulatability or to avoid obstacles in the motion. For articulated hands, another consideration is necessary. Hands must grasp objects by pushing flat or round finger tips against objects so that those objects do not slip out from fingers. It is very difficult to grasp and handle round objects by articulated hands with no redundancy. If the hand has some degrees of redundance, we can control fingers to keep it among fingers safely while working.

For this system, additional three conditions are chosen as follows;

$$J_r \delta\theta_a = 0,$$

where

$$J_r = \begin{pmatrix} 0\,1\,1\,1 & 0\,0\,0\,0 & 0\,0\,0\,0 \\ 0\,0\,0\,0 & 0\,1\,1\,1 & 0\,0\,0\,0 \\ 0\,0\,0\,0 & 0\,0\,0\,0 & 0\,1\,1\,1 \end{pmatrix}.$$

Above condition implies that $\theta_2 + \theta_3 + \theta_4$ is kept constant during the handling. Especially, the contact points do not change when the object is moved upwards or downwards.

Next we consider the grasping posture for the external force applied upwards at the bottom of the object. The posture is specified by the pair (L_o, θ_6) where L_o is the distance from the palm of the hand to the contact point and θ_6 is the contact angle (see Figs. 4 and 5). Fig. 6 - (a) shows $\rho(f)$ for the admissble pair (L_o, θ_6) for this hand. If it is desired for the hand to move the object upwards or downwards about 1 cm from the initial position, L_o= 12 cm and θ_6=15° (posture I) would be prefer for a soft task and L_o= 14 cm and θ_6=55° (posture II) is useful for a stiff task. Fig. 6 - (b) and (c) shows these postures.

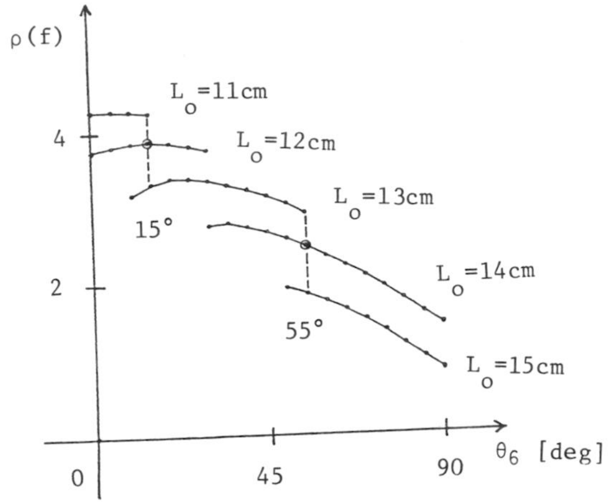

(a) $\rho(f)$ - (L_o, θ_6)

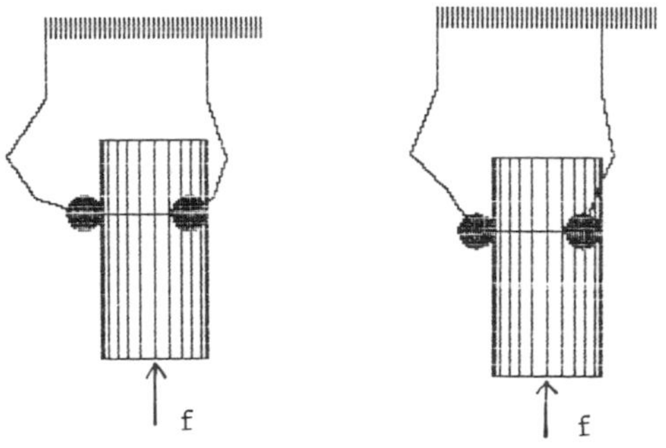

(b) posture I (c) posture II

Fig. 6 Grasping Posture

5-2 Control System

Hands are exposed to various external force. The ability will be very improved if a feedback loop of the force is closed. For example, the information is used in order to set the center of compliance at the center of the bottom of the object (the origin of F_o) just like as RCC hand, then assembly tasks become very easy [Whitney, 1983]. In the following such control system is developed.

Since the gear ratios of this system are very large as shown in the followings, small external force can not move the object. So the measurement of the force is used to move the object to the same direction as the force. Then the object moves as if it is supported by a spring. The input voltage to dc-motors are generated as follows;

$$v = W^{-1}[K_p\{\hat{H}(\delta\underline{\xi}_d + K_f f\ ) - \delta\theta_a\} - K_v\dot{\theta}_a] + W^t(J_p^{\perp}J_a)^t r. \qquad (9)$$

where $\delta\underline{\xi}_d$ is the desired displacement of the object and K_p, K_f and K_v are diagonal matrices with non-negative elements. W is the transmission matrix from dc-motors to active joints and is given as follows;

$$W = \begin{pmatrix} \hat{W} & 0 & 0 \\ 0 & \hat{W} & 0 \\ 0 & 0 & \hat{W} \end{pmatrix},$$

where

$$\hat{W} = \frac{2}{369}\begin{pmatrix} 1 & 0 & 0 & 0 \\ 1 & 5/6 & 0 & 0 \\ 0 & -1 & 1 & 0 \\ 0 & 0 & -1 & 1 \end{pmatrix}.$$

Note that the last term of the right hand side of Eq. (9) generates the grasping force. The block diagram is shown in Fig. 7 where G(s) expresses the dynamics of dc-motors. The other dynamics is ignored. f is measrured with strain gauges attached to a work table. If this system is stable, we have

$$\delta\underline{\xi}_d - \delta\underline{\xi} = -K_f f,$$

in the steady state, where

$$\delta\underline{\xi} = \hat{H}\delta\theta_a.$$

This means that the object is moved from $\delta\underline{\xi}_d$ to $\delta\underline{\xi}_d + K_f f$ by the external force f.

The main controller is a 16-bit micro computer and the program is written in Fortran with machine language I/O subroutines. The cycle time is about 30 msec.

Using this system, the cylindrical object shown Photo. 1 has been placed on a table with two different postures I and II given in Fig. 6 (a) and (6). $\delta\xi_d$ is set 1 cm under the table and matrices K_p, K_f and K_v and vector r are determined by experiments. The contact force is measured by a strain gauge attached to the table. The typical results are shown in Fig. 8. Fig. 8 - (a) is for posture I and (b) for posture II. The maximum value of the contact force is 0.71 N and 1.02 N for posture I and II, respectively. Therefore the contact force for posture II is about one and half larger than that for posture I. These results verify the discussion in section 4.

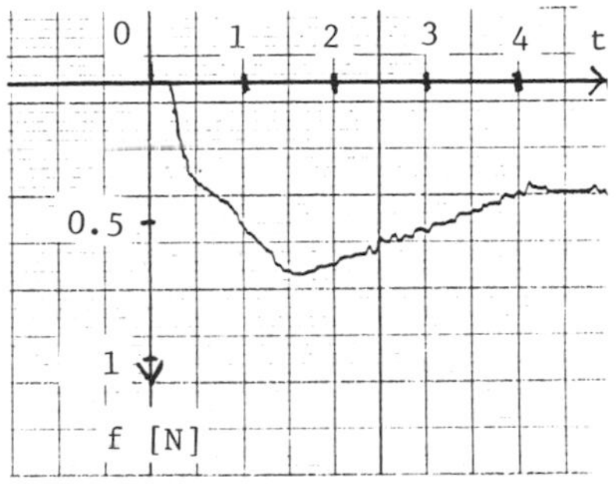

(a) posture I

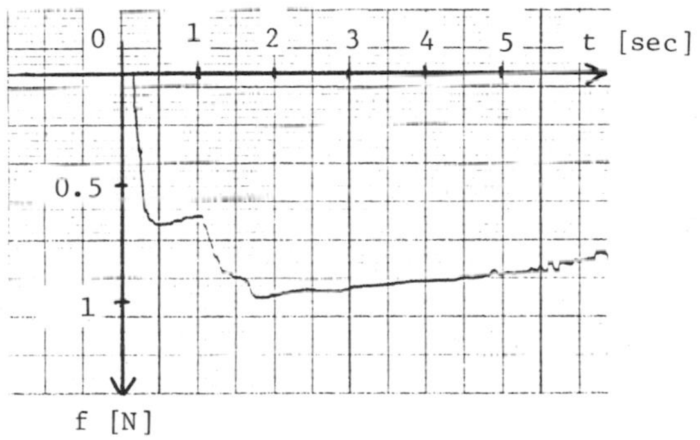

(b) posture II

Fig. 8 Measure of Contact Force

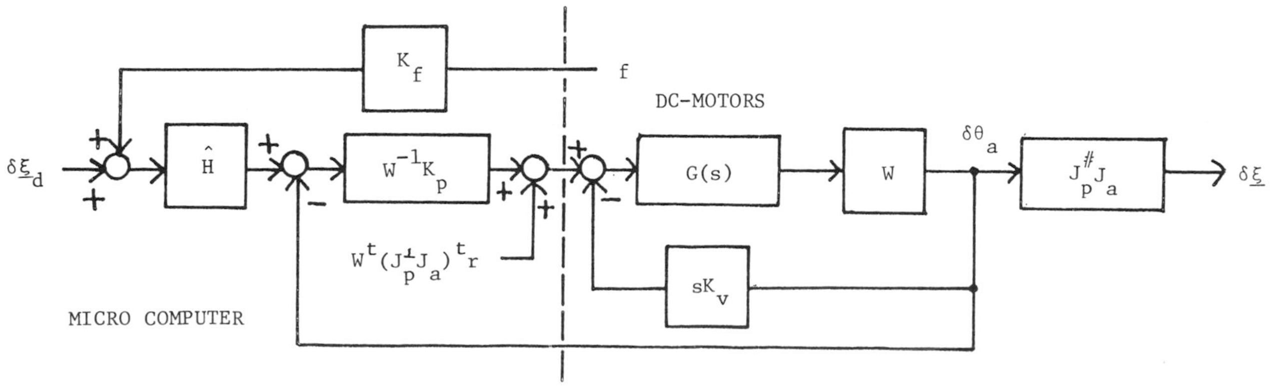

Fig. 7 Block Diagram of System

Next, a ball pen was attached to the center of the bottom of the object and simple figures were drawn. Posture II in Fig. 6 - (b) was used and the pen was pushed down on a sheet of paper by setting $\delta\underline{\xi}_d$ 0.5 cm under the table. The figures written by the hand are shown in Fig. 9. Fig. 9 - (a), (b) and (c) are a circle with the diameter of 2 cm, a cross of lines with the length of 2 cm and an isoceles triangle, respectively. Straight lines are written fairly well.

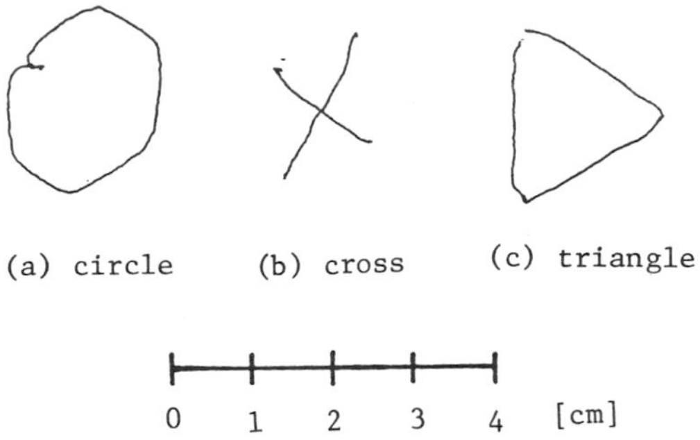

Fig. 9 Simple figures

A tennis ball also grasped and handled by this system successfully. The ball was grasped not with finger tips, but with finger pads and the same conditions for the redundancy as the one given above was used.

6. CONCLUSIONS

In this paper, kinematic problems for articulated hands were discussed briefly, and grasping force and handling force were obtained. Using the grasping force, grasping postures were considered. These results were applied to an articulated hand with three fingers and twelve joints. A control system where contact force is closed was developed. Finally, several experimental results were shown.

ACKNOWLEGEMENTS

I would like to thank Prof. H. Hanafusa, Kyoto university for his kind and vluable advice.

APPENDIX

Here, Eq. (4), i. e.

$$\begin{pmatrix}\delta\underline{\xi}\\ 0\end{pmatrix} = \begin{pmatrix} J_p^{\#}J_a \\ J_p^{\perp}J_a\end{pmatrix}\delta\theta_a , \qquad (4)$$

is reduced from simultaneous equations

$$\delta\underline{\xi} = J_{ai}\delta\theta_{ia} + J_{pi}\delta\theta_{ip}, \quad i=1, 2, \dots, N.$$

Now we can assume that J_{ip}'s have full rank without loss of generality. Then the following equation are obtained from the simultaneous equations described above;

$$J_p\delta\underline{\xi} = J_a\delta\theta_a, \qquad (A-1)$$

where

$$\delta\theta_a = (\delta\theta_{1a}^t, \delta\theta_{2a}^t, \dots , \delta\theta_{Na}^t)^t,$$

$$J_{pi}^{\perp} = I_6 - J_{pi}(J_{pi}^t J_{pi})^{-1} J_{pi}^t,$$

$$J_p = [J_{p1}^{\perp} : J_{p2}^{\perp} : \dots : J_{Na}^{\perp}]^t,$$

and

$$J_a = \begin{bmatrix} J_{p1}^{\perp}J_{a1} & 0 & \cdots\cdots & 0 \\ 0 & J_{p2}^{\perp}J_{a2} & \cdots\cdots & 0 \\ \vdots & \vdots & \ddots & \vdots \\ 0 & 0 & \cdots\cdots & J_{pN}^{\perp}J_{aN} \end{bmatrix}.$$

Then we have

$$N\{J_{pi}^{\perp}\} = R\{J_{pi}\},$$

therefore

$$N\{J_p\} = \bigcap_{i=1}^{N} N\{J_{pi}^{\perp}\} = S_f = \{0\} ,$$

where N{A} denotes the null space of matrix A. Thus $S_f = \{0\}$ implies that J_p is a full rank matrix and $\delta\underline{\xi}$ is determined from Eq. (A-1) by $\delta\theta_a$ uniquely. By defining following matrices Eq. (4) is reduced;

$$J_p^{\#} = (J_p^t J_p)^{-1} J_p^t,$$

and

$$J_p^{\perp} = I_{6N} - J_p J_p^{\#}.$$

Furthermore $\delta\theta_{pi}$ is given as follows;

$$\delta\theta_{ip} = (J_{pi}^t J_{pi})^{-1} J_{pi}^t (\delta\underline{\xi} - J_{ai}\delta\theta_{ia}).$$

Note that matrices $J_p^{\#}J_a$ and $J_p^{\perp}J_a$ can be obtained more easily as follows;

$$J_p^{\#}J_a = (\sum_{i=1}^{N} J_{pi}^{\perp})^{-1} [J_{p1}^{\perp}J_{a1} : J_{p2}^{\perp}J_{a2} : \dots$$
$$\dots : J_{pN}^{\perp}J_{aN}]$$

and

$$J_p^{\perp}J_a = J_a - J_p(J_p^{\#}J_a).$$

REFERENCES

Hanafusa, H., Kobayashi, H. and Terasaki, K. 1983. Fine control of the object with multi-finger robot hands, Proceedings of 83' International Conference on Advanced Robotics, 245-252.

Okada, T. 1980. Analysis of finger tip motion for precise object-handling, Trans. SICE, vol. 16, no. 4, 597-602.

Paul, R. P. 1981. Robot manipulators, the MIT Press.

Salisburg, J. K. and Craig, J. J. 1982. Articulated hands: Force control and kinematic issues, the International J. of Robotics Research, vol. 1, no. 1, 4-17.

Whitney, D. E. 1969. Resolved motion rate control of manipulators and human prosthese, Trans. IEEE, vol. MMS-10, no. 2, 47-53.

Whitney, D. E. 1982. Quasi-static assembly of compliantly supported rigid parts. Trans. ASME, J. of DSMC, 65-77.

Yoshikawa, T. 1983. Analysis and control of robot manipulators with redundancy, the 1st International Symposium of Robot Research.

Yoshikawa, T. 1984. Measure of manipulatability of robot manipulators, J. of the Robot Society of Japan, vol. 2, no. 2, 63-67.

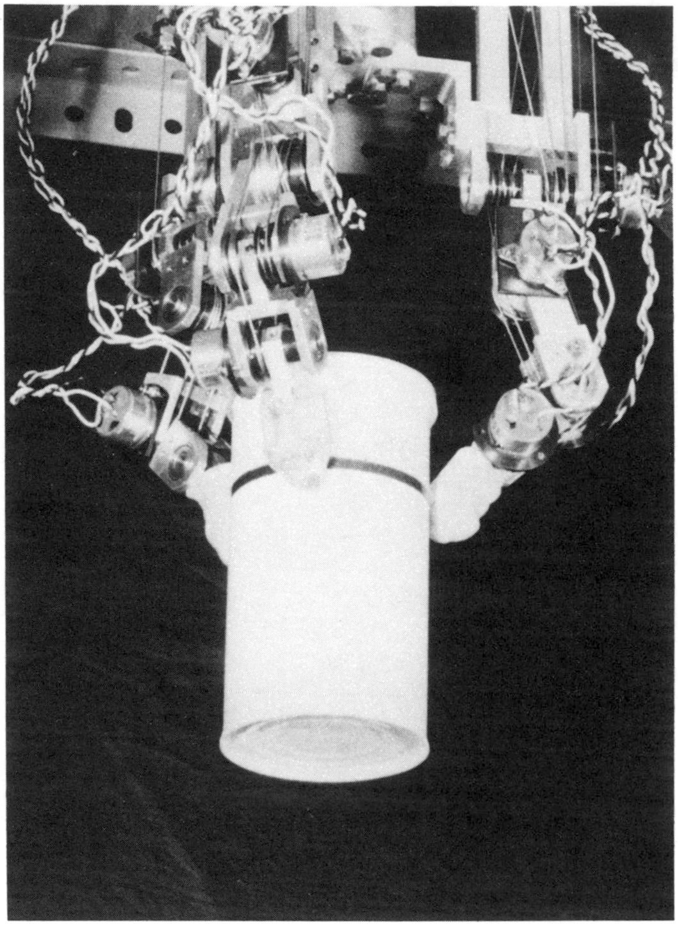

Photo. 1 Hand and Object

THE VERSION I UTAH/MIT DEXTROUS HAND

S.C. JACOBSEN, J.E. WOOD, D.F. KNUTTI, K.B. BIGGERS, E.K. IVERSEN
CENTER FOR BIOMEDICAL DESIGN, DEPARTMENT OF MECHANICAL AND INDUSTRIAL ENGINEERING
AND DEPARTMENT OF BIOENGINEERING, UNIVERSITY OF UTAH

It is intended that the Utah/MIT Dextrous Hand (DH) be used first as a research tool for the investigation of various issues related to artificial manipulation where a high degree of dexterity is required. At a later time the system will be simplified for specific applications in areas of robotics, teleoperation, prosthetics and others. Since the system is intended to be a research tool, it has been designed to maximize the two characteristics, 1) generality of operation, and 2) high performance. At the present time an entire hand is not available, therefore, only the performance of an individual 4DOF (4 degree-of-freedom) finger will be presented. Initial evaluations have been conducted to characterize system performance in terms of factors such as frequency response, step response, strength, output impedance, stability, stiction, power consumption, and others. More comprehensive tests, aimed at evaluating complete hand performance will be undertaken when an entire hand is available. Additional understanding of the manipulation process will probably be necessary in order to systematically formulate performance criteria for a dextrous hand. In parallel with hand development activities, subcontrol systems which supervise internal components of the DH and higher control systems which provide overall systems management are being defined.

1. INTRODUCTION

1.1 COMMENTS ON DESIGN PHILOSOPHY

In any development activity, especially one as multi-faceted as the dextrous hand project, it is important to have a number of guiding attitudes which govern design decisions as various activities evolve. A design strategy guides the decision making process so that when design compromises are made, unintentional limitations are not imposed on the future system. At the core of our project have been three attitudes which have produced success in this and other endeavors. Firstly, systems such as artificial limbs and robots may be successfully developed only in the presence of exhaustive interaction between researchers involved in theory, experiment and application. The development of dextrous hand machinery and its controllers must evolve in synchrony so that positive and negative aspects of system configuration or performance are recognized clearly as they emerge. In most cases, hope is the designer's enemy and it is always true that faulty thinking applied to the design of physical systems will be later manifest by poor performance. The goal is to recognize flaws and correct them before irreversible positions are taken. Secondly, each element of the system must be examined in a very general way in order to identify individual performance characteristics as well as how that element interacts with other parts of the system. The use of off-the-shelf componentry typically gives the illusion of time and cost savings, however, in radically new systems a more desirable approach is to first achieve success and then pursue the optimization of component acquisition at a later time. Thirdly, it is our opinion that high performance systems are possible only if individual components have suitable intrinsic behavior. In contrast to much current practice, feedback control loops should be used for prudent supervision of a system rather than attempting gross modification of its dynamics.

It is interesting to note that the graceful behavior of musculoskeletal components in biological systems is not a superfluous quality added later via neural control systems to enhance aesthetics, but rather it is a byproduct of appropriate component behavior. Similarly, high performance manipulation systems, if properly designed, will be well behaved and graceful without resorting to extravagent and complicated networks of transducers and controllers.

1.2 OUTLINE OF THE PAPER

The DH project actually consists of a number of subprojects. Only three of those projects will be discussed in this paper. They are: 1) the hand structures project which includes the design of mechanical components; 2) the tendon systems project which includes the design of tendons and systems for their routing; and 3) the actuation system project which includes the investigation and design of hydraulic, electric and pneumatic actuators.

Later papers will discuss subprojects devoted to the development of: 1) lower and higher control systems; 2) internal and tactile sensor systems; 3) microprocessor based computation systems; and 4) a 7DOF tendon operated arm for spatial positioning of the DH.

2. DEXTROUS HAND (DH) CONFIGURATION

2.1 DESIGN GOALS

As discussed in Reference [3], the Version I dextrous hand is to be anthropomorphic. Our reasons for this choice are: 1) the natural human hand provides an existence proof that a hand with anthropomorphic geometry, properly controlled, can be a powerful tool for the execution of various manipulative tasks; 2) we all have extensive experience with our own natural hands and, therefore, during the learning/research process investigators will certainly be able to correlate dextrous hand performance with their own human hands; 3) it is our opinion that the system being developed can have near term application as a slave member in teleoperation systems. Therefore, the choice of an anthropomorphic configuration can eliminate later development stages prior to application. However, we note that the system is actually a series of modules which can be easily reconfigured to provide alternate nonanthropomorphic geometries when desired.

As a result of certain realities, it has not been possible to achieve an exact anthropomorphic configuration. In fact, two significant deviations are present in the Version I DH. They are: 1) elimination of the small finger was necessary in order to decrease system complexity while maintaining acceptable redundancy in order to permit flexibility in grasping tasks and to minimize reliance on friction during certain manipulations; 2) the separation of Joints 0 and 1 was necessary due to the limits imposed by our decision to use rectangular cross-section tendons as shown in Figures 1 and 5. Note that it would certainly be better to route tendons as they are in biological systems [4]. However, a variety of desirable characteristics demonstrated by biological tendons cannot be achieved by artificial tendons, thus limiting routing options.

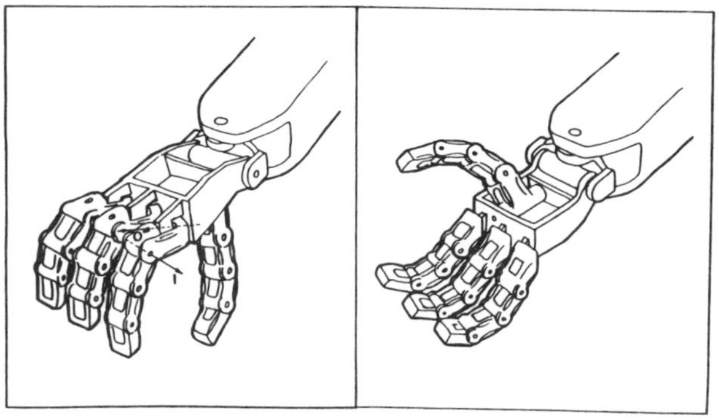

FIGURE 1. Utah/MIT DH. Note the separation between the 0 and 1 joint axes of each digit.

Once Joints 0 and 1 are separated, the optimization procedure then reduces to one of determining the orientation of the axes of the 0 Joints of each finger relative to the palm so that acceptable operational flexibility of the finger tips is possible. Our goal is to produce a well behaved system of fingers, especially in the work space above the palm where the thumb and fingers interact for manipulative tasks.

In order to determine the orientation of the 0 axes, two procedures were undertaken: 1) a number of adjustable geometric prototypes were manually evaluated. The orientations of the 0 axes were adjusted to permit desired finger/thumb interactions via a systematic, nonanalytic procedure; 2) analytical procedures were undertaken to investigate various kinematic issues as per Reference [5].

Eventually an acceptable configuration was generated that represents a compromise between functional issues and the limitations imposed by tendon routing complexity.

As shown in Figure 2, orientation of the 0 joint axes is defined relative to the palm base plane. The palm base plane is fixed by the two vectors which originate at the 3DOF wrist joint and project out to the center point of the 0 axes of the index and middle finger. The center point is defined by the intersection on the 0 axis of the mutual perpendicular between the 0 Joint axis and the Joint 1 axis as indicated in Figure 2.

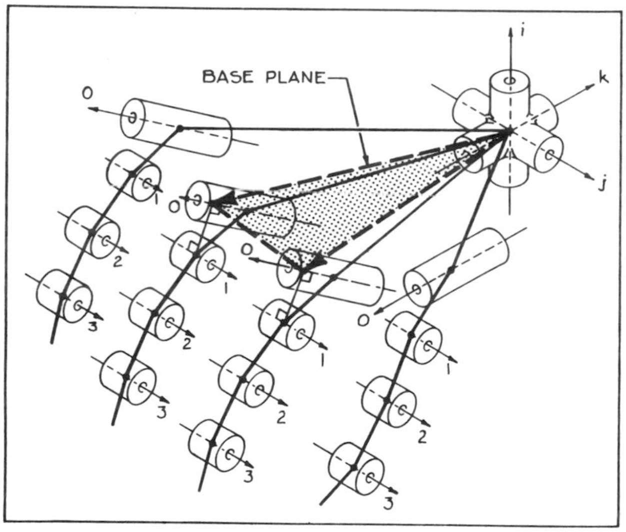

FIGURE 2. Geometry of the DH. Note also the coordinate system axes i, j, k.

2.2 THE HAND

Figure 1 illustrates details of the intended Version I hand. Each DH includes three 4DOF fingers, one 4DOF thumb, and one 3DOF wrist, which results in a total of 19 degrees-of-freedom. Since a 2N tendon routing approach is used, the system requires 38 independent tendons and actuators.

Figure 3 photographically illustrates the current Version I hand prototype which includes one active finger, two passive fingers and a passive thumb. The figure also illustrates the actuator package which currently includes 8 valve and cylinder sets. It is intended that later this package will contain 32 of the modular actuation systems shown in Figure 4.

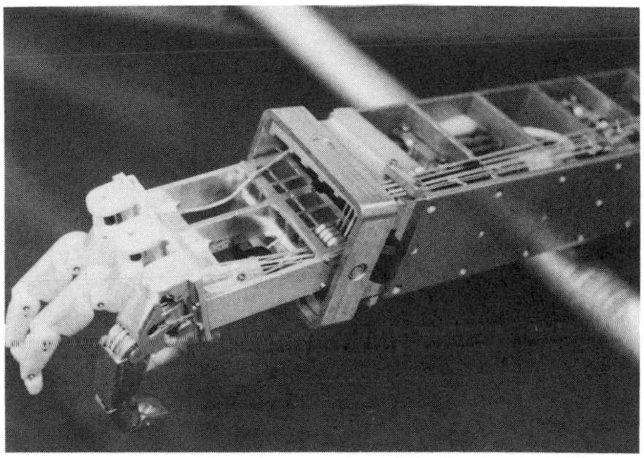

FIGURE 3. The prototype Version I DH.

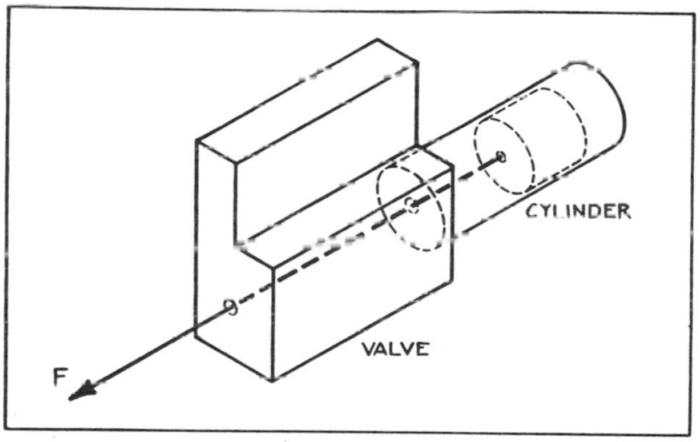

FIGURE 4. The pneumatic actuator includes pressure controlling valve and cylinder.

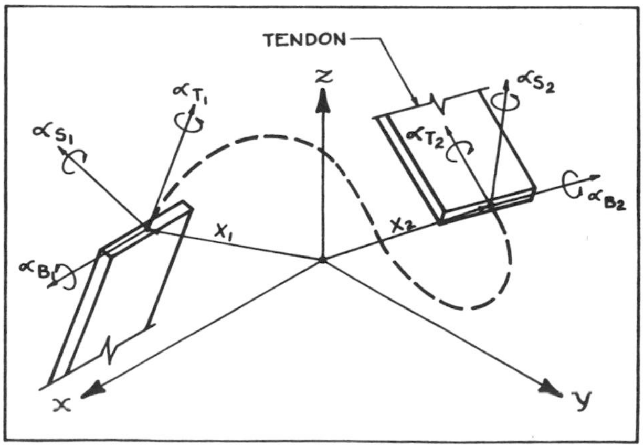

FIGURE 5. Tendon location and orientation transformation.

Note that the tendon routing components and structures, required to operate the system and yet leave sufficient room for subsequent inclusion of tactile and other sensors, are quite complex. Also note that in Figure 3 the Version I finger joint angles are measured by small electric potentiometers. Later systems will include more reliable, optical fiber based, non-absolute digital position encoders.

3. TENDON SYSTEMS

3.1 JUSTIFICATION OF THE APPROACH

The use of tendons permits the remote location of actuators which: 1) minimizes distal weight on the manipulator arm; 2) enhances flexibility of design for both actuators and hand structures in multi-degree-of-freedom grippers; and 3) opens up space within hand structures for integration of various sensor systems.

Two major problems exist which inhibit the successful use of tendons in gripper systems. Firstly, suitable tendons don't exist and must, therefore, be developed. Secondly, the routing of tendons over moving joints and through complex stuctures presents difficult conceptual and practical problems.

During the DH project we have investigated a number of commercially available elements which might serve as tendons including: 1) urethane covered woven metal ropes and belts; 2) monolithic metal tapes; 3) monolithic polymer rods and bands; and 4) various woven plastic belts and ropes.

As a result of various problems, we finally elected to develop our own tendons which include composite fibrous structures with rectangular cross sections. A more detailed discussion of tendon design will be deferred to a later paper.

3.2 TENDON ROUTING

The routing of tendons is a mildly complex design problem for one finger. It is substantially more difficult for a single finger and wrist, and the exercise becomes an overwhelming geometric challenge when the thumb and additional fingers are added. The routing problem is further complicated by packaging considerations which exist at the proximal end of tendons where the actuators are located.

Tendon routing within the existing Version I hand has been accomplished by conventional design techniques, however, it is clear that the design of multiple tendon systems can be enhanced if more systematic approaches for routing synthesis can be developed. We are, therefore, involved in the development of such a methodology which addresses the following issues: 1) tendons must be efficiently transferred through a spatial labyrinth within the structure between actuators and actuated joints; 2) the tendons must traverse joints which move, and they must avoid other tendons (38 in this case); 3) they must be compact, low in friction, and the tendon transfer must be accomplished in typically overconstrained volumes.

Probably the most desirable way to approach the generation of a synthesis methodology is to think in "tendon coordinates". In this approach, location of the proximal end of the tendon is defined by vector X_1 and its orientation indicated by the attached coordinate system, defined by orthogonal unit vectors U_1, U_2, and U_3, shown in Figures 5 and 6. Changes in orientation are defined by angles. α_B (bend), α_T (twist) and α_S (scuff), and position changes by variations in the vector X. The problem then involves transferring the tendon to another location and orientation in space via a sequence of bending and twisting deformations defined by changes in α_B and α_T. Furthermore, a distal location, as defined by X_2, may change its position and orientation, relative to X_1, due to articulation of the structure.

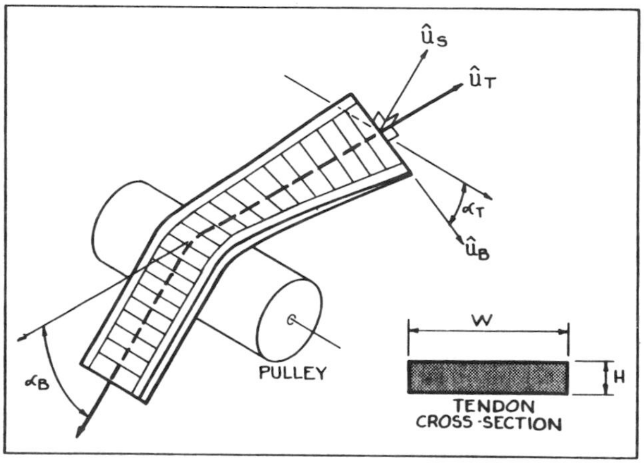

FIGURE 6: Twisting and bending of the tendon.

The synthesis technique involves determining the number of pulley interactions required to make the transition, simultaneously considering that tendon loading limitations further constrain design flexibility. It can be seen that special orientations of the proximal and distal vectors yield cases which require the use of only one pulley, however, the general transition typically requires more pulleys.

Each set of transitions in space produce internal stresses on the tendon. The goal of the design process is to configure the tendon such that it supports desired longitudinal loads while minimizing internal stresses which produce frictional losses and reduce the life of the system. Specifically, wrapping the tendon over a pulley produces bending and contact stresses which depend on the pulley radius and the total wrapping angle. Twisting of the tendon produces longitudinal shear stresses, variable fiber tensions and transverse compressive stresses as a function of the rate of twist and width of the tendon. Improper tendon routing, caused by misaligned pulleys, produces asymmetrical axial stresses over the tendon cross section and side tracking, which produces scuffing loads as the hand operates.

Presently, tendons are available which are acceptable for our work, however, current efforts are focused on the development of more suitable tendons which avoid internal stresses and maximize life. As demonstrated in the biological case, a desirable tendon configuration would be a loose bundle of longitudinal fibers, well lubricated, adaptively self tensioning and able to reconfigure their cross sections depending on the twisting and bending requirements of the particular geometry. For a number of reasons these approaches are presently impossible and our current tendon development project will, therefore, pursue more limited approaches.

4. ACTUATORS

4.1 JUSTIFICATION OF THE APPROACH

Obviously there exists no "best" actuator. Actuators are complex devices defined by a large number of parameters. The real issue is "which set of actuator characteristics best suit the specific actuation problem". At the beginning of our project we examined hydraulic, electric and pneumatic systems as candidates for the dextrous hand. Hydraulic systems were quickly discarded, however, at a later time we intend to re-examine hydraulic valve design issues with a specific goal of developing water-based hydraulic tendon actuators.

We actually constructed electrical tendon pullers and conducted extensive analytical and experimental evaluations of these systems. They exhibited reasonable performance, however, weight, cost, complexity and bandwidth considerations encouraged the search for an alternate system. Finally, we elected to attempt the design of a pneumatic actuator which would possess advantageous characteristics such as low weight, high force generation, rapid operation, high power to weight ratio and high power to size ratio.

The rationale for selecting the pneumatic approach is reviewed by the following comments: 1) Pneumatic cylinders have the potential for desirable intrinsic properties. They are fast, generate large forces and, with properly designed seals, can operate with extremely low friction. 2) Pneumatic actuators, however, exhibit undesirable characteristics due to the compressibility of the working gas which results in springy actuation if flow control valves are used [1]. We, therefore, elected to incorporate a pressure control valve which essentially negates the effects of compressibility provided that the valve is sufficiently fast to dominate natural system dynamics generated by the masses of the structures and the compressibility of the operating fluid. It is interesting to note that these considerations determine the minimal intrinsic speed of the dextrous hand. That is, it must be at least as fast as the fundamental frequencies which result from compressibility and mass effects. 3) The resulting valve/cylinder system is then a mechanical force source which produces a force in response to an input current. The force source behaves with no spring constant, very low mass and low damping. 4) Placing two cylinder/valve systems together as antagonists over a pulley produces a torque source as shown in Figure 7.

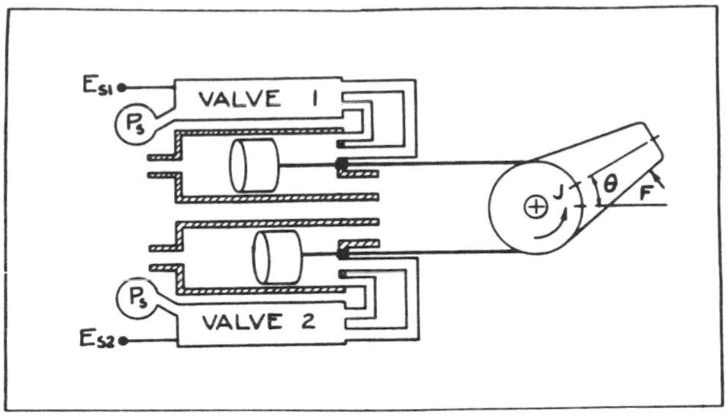

FIGURE 7. The antagonist actuators (from Reference [2]).

Adding joint-angle feedback converts the system into a position servo with low mass, low damping and an adjustable spring constant within the limits of stabililty. In the actual system, inherent tendon damping aids system stability and, as will be shown, the resulting system acts as a very fast position servo. Later activities will include the development of more complex damping schemes to further enhance system performance [3].

4.2 THE ACTUATOR SYSTEM

The actuator cylinder consists of a glass tube and a graphite piston. This combination results in a well lubricated system with compatible thermal expansion characteristics so that close tolerances may be maintained. This slightly leaky system exhibits low mass and low damping characteristics and operates at pressures up to 689.5 kilopascals (100 psi).

The pressure controlling valve is essentially a two stage pressure divider. This particular approach is unfortunately leaky, and therefore, consumes significant power. The valve, as shown in Figure 8, includes first and second stages implemented via jet pipes with the second stage using a pressure feedback pathway.

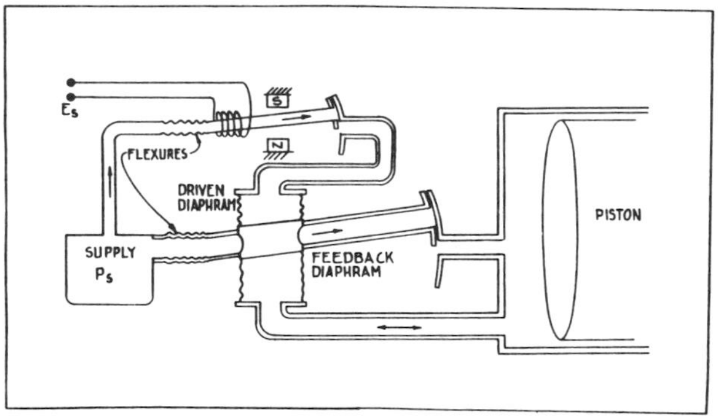

FIGURE 8. The two stage pneumatic pressure controlling valve (from Reference [2]).

The valve/cylinder combination can be packaged in a number of configurations to permit the generation of a compact and light weight system of actuators immediately proximal to the hand.

5. PERFORMANCE OF A SINGLE FINGER

5.1 COMMENTS

Ultimately, only the comprehensive evaluation of a complete hand can indicate the actual utility of the DH. For the present time, however, less comprehensive experiments must suffice to examine performance. Specifically, the response of single and multiple joints of a single finger, to step and harmonic inputs, have been examined. The following section illustrates performance of the finger executing various tasks. The controller used in these experiments includes simple proportional control of joint angle with linearization of the valve included to soften and stabilize its behavior. Also, the tendon decoupling matrix (TM in Reference [3]) has been included to separate actuator effects on joints. The use of other controller enhancements such as smart damping, proximal stiffening, distal curling, co-contraction, and modification of performance via integration of touch information, will be deferred.

5.2 EXPERIMENTAL RESULTS

This section briefly reviews seven experimental procedures utilized to evaluate the finger. Spatial tracking activities and force interactive surface tracking experiments will be deferred for future publications. The seven experiments identified below are discussed via each figure's caption:

1) Joint step responses.
2) Grabbing motion.
3) Extend/Retract motion.
4) Run forward.
5) Run backward.
6) Circling motion.
7) Disturbance response.

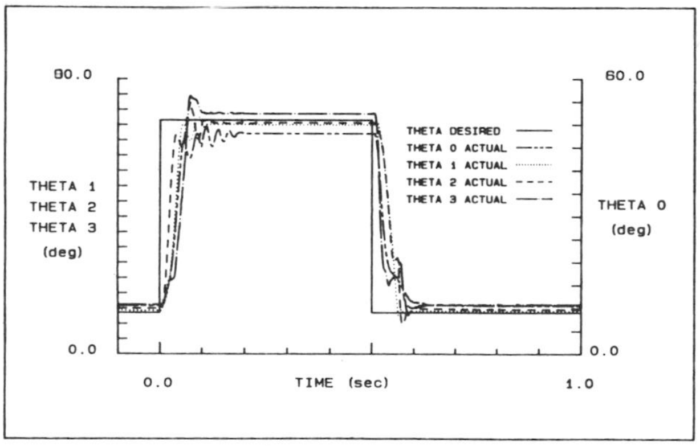

Figure 9. Step response of joints 0, 1, 2 and 3, executed simultaneously. Joint 0 was abducted then adducted, while Joints 1, 2 and 3 were flexed then extended. Note the similarities in rise times. Note the oscillation of Joint 0 with the finger flexed. These become less pronounced when the finger is extended. This attenuation is due to an increased effective inertia as seen by Joint 0.

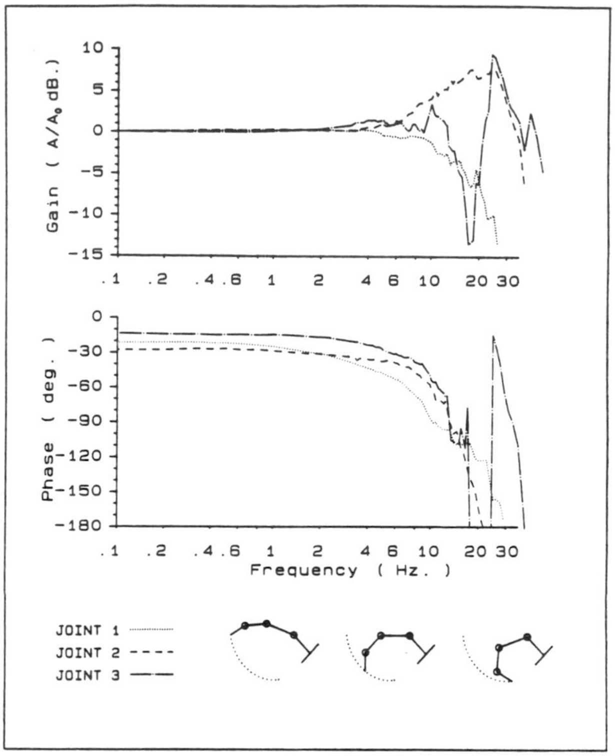

Figure 10. Gain and phase plot for joints 1, 2 and 3 executing an oscillating grabbing motion. Joints 1, 2 and 3 are commanded by A_o sin ωt. The ± 3 db point, for the worst joint, occurs at about 8 hz. Note the coupling, due to both dynamic and kinematic effects, principally effecting joint 3. Dynamically, the distal joints are applying tendon moments about the proximal joints. These effects are partially -- compensated for by terms b, c and f of matrix TM [3]. Kinematically, the actuators of the distal joints have their displacements affected by the movement of the proximal joints. Thus, for this experiment, the distal actuators must undergo larger displacements for simultaneous joint-angle displacements. These effects are partially compensated for by terms d, g and h of matrix TM [3].

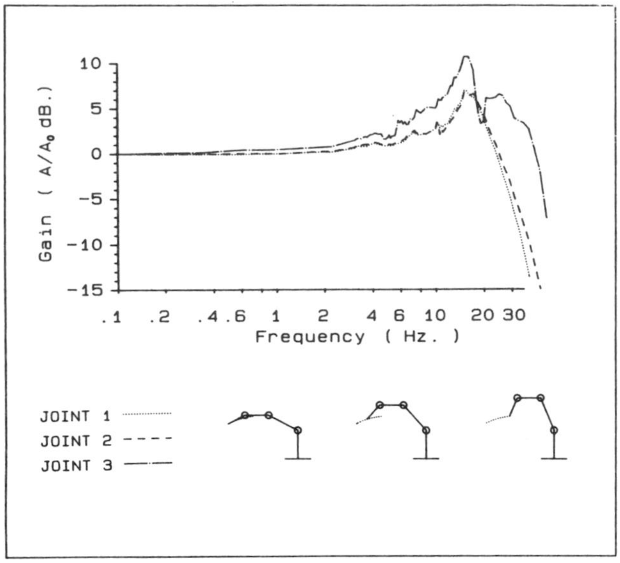

Figure 11. Gain plot for oscillating retract/extend motions (phase plot excluded). Joint 1 is driven by A_o sin ωt, while joints 2 and 3 are driven by A_o sin (ωt - π). Note that the dynamic and kinematic coupling effects are less than for the case of Figure 10. This is partially due to offsetting tendonesis coupling.

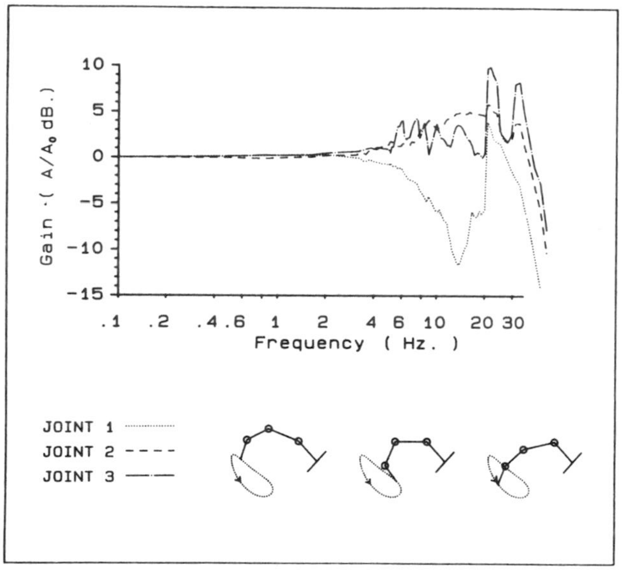

Figure 12. Gain plot for forward running motion. Joint 1 is driven by A_o sin ωt, while Joints 2 and 3 are driven by A_o sin (ωt - π/2). Again note strong coupling effects above 6 Hz.

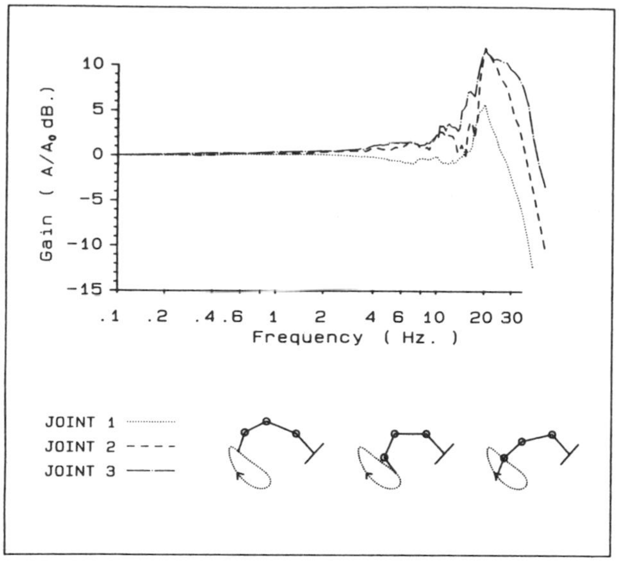

Figure 13. Gain plot for backward running motion. Note that the planar trajectory of the finger tip is identical to that of Figure 12, except that the motion is reversed. Thus, the kinematic coupling effects should be the same for both cases. Here, however, joint 1 is driven by A_0 sin ωt, while joints 2 and 3 are driven by A_0 sin (ωt + π/2). Note that the dynamic coupling effects are different than those of "forward" running, with the finger following the commands accurately to 10 Hz.

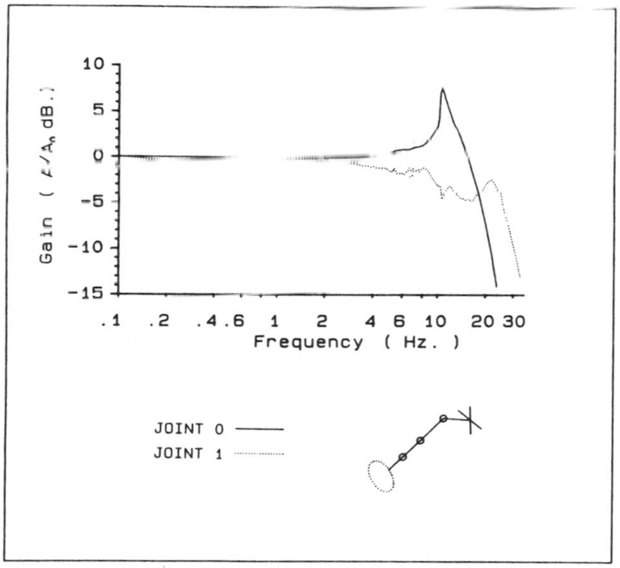

Figure 14. Gain plot for the finger executing a two-joint finger tip circling motion. Joint 0 was driven by A_0 sin ωt while joint 1 was driven by A_0 sin (ωt−π/2). Joints 2 and 3 were fixed. Note resonant spike in joint 0 at 10 Hz. There were no TM decoupling terms between joints 0 and 1.

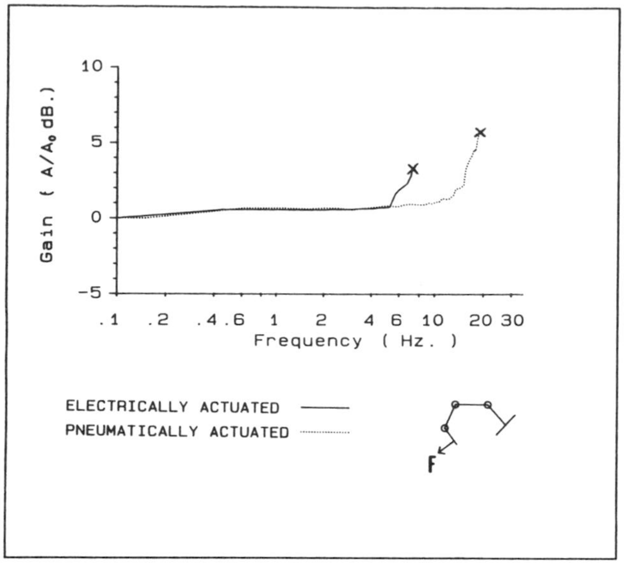

Figure 15. Gain plot of contact force between the finger and a disturbance device during cyclic loading. Note that the electric system is able to behave in a compliant manner for disturbances up to approximately 5 Hz, but above that frequency the disturbance exceeds the bandwidth of the actuation system and therefore the electric finger system becomes extremely stiff. However, the pneumatic system is inherently compliant, even above the bandwidth of the actuator, due to the compressability of the fluid, and therefore operates compliantly up to disturbance frequencies of 12 Hz. The x's denote the point at which tendon slack begins to occur.

6. CONCLUSIONS

The paper illustrates that the single finger of the Version I DH performs very well. The finger is 5 to 8 times faster than the human finger and generates approximately the same force levels as its natural counterpart. Its joint impedences are adjustable over a wide range and the system is well behaved, even with the use of only a simple control system. Structures of the finger possess adequate room for the addition of sensor systems. Most importantly, it appears that this DH can become an important tool for the investigation of complex artificial manipulation.

The project will continue with: 1) the finalization of the Version I hand design including sensor systems, 2) the construction of prototypes for functional evaluation by staff at the Artificial Intelligence Laboratory at MIT and the Center for Biomedical Design at the University of Utah, and 3) work on subcontrol systems and investigation of higher controller issues as prototype capabilities improve. Finally, efforts will be devoted to the construction of additional systems using advanced production techniques so that a number of hands will be available for other investigators working in this area.

ACKNOWLEDGEMENTS

This work was supported by: The Aritificial Intelligence Laboratory at the Massachusetts Institute of Technology (contract #GC-A-290956-02), the Systems Development Foundation, the Defense Advanced Research Projects Agency (contract #F33615-82-K-5125), and the Office of Naval Research (contract #N00014-82-K-0367).

Also, we would like to thank Dr. John Hollerbach (at the Massachussetts Institute of Technology) for facilitating the day-to-day collaborative details between the M.I.T. Artificial Intelligence Laboratory and the Center for Biomedical Design (at the University of Utah).

REFERENCES

[1] Andersen, B.W. (1976); "The Analysis and Design of Pneumatic Systems," Robert E. Kreiger Publishing Co., New York.

[2] Jacobsen, S.C., Knutti, D.F., Biggers, K.B., Iversen, E.K., Wood, J.E. (1984); "An Electropneumatic Actuation System for the Utah/MIT Dextrous Hand," Presented at the Vth CISM-IFToMM (International Federation for the Theory of Machines and Mechanisms) Symposium, Udine, Italy.

[3] Jacobsen, S.C., Wood, J.E., Knutti, D.F. and Biggers, K.B. (1983); "The Utah/MIT Dextrous Hand: Work in Progress," SDF/MIT First International Symposium of Robotics Research, Bretton Woods, NH (28 August - 2 September 1983). Also to appear in International Journal of Robotics Research 3(4).

[4] Kapandji, S.A. (1970); "The Physiology of the Joints: Upper Limb," Vol. 1, E & S Liverstone, London.

[5] Salisbury, J.K.(1982); "Kinematic and Force Analysis of Articulated Hands," Ph.D. Dissertaion, Stanford University. Also, Stanford Computer Sciences Department Report No. STAN-CS-82-921.

6 Mobile Robots

Four-Legged Running with One-Legged Algorithms

Marc H. Raibert

Department of Computer Science
and The Robotics Institute
Carnegie-Mellon University
Pittsburgh, PA., USA

1. Abstract

Previous work resulted in a set of simple algorithms that control one-legged systems that balance as they hop on one leg. This paper explores the generalization of the one-leg algorithms for the control of systems with several legs. The generalization is simple for the *one-foot*, a class of running gaits that sequences the support legs one at a time. Sutherland's idea of a *virtual leg* is used to reduce the gaits that employ the legs in pairs, the trot, the pace, and the bound, into virtual biped one-foot gaits. The symmetry of stepping is used to understand more complicated gaits like the gallop and canter.

2. Introduction

During the past several years we have explored the control of legged systems that hop on one springy leg (Raibert, 1981, Murthy and Raibert, 1983, Raibert and Brown, 1984, Raibert et al., 1984). This work has focussed on the role of balance in legged locomotion, with an emphasis on the dynamic aspects of the problem. Actively balanced legged systems with just one leg are easier to study and understand than those with many legs, and we have argued that the lessons learned from the study of such one-legged systems can be generalized to multi-legged systems. The discussion that follows is a first attempt to make such generalizations.

The approach is to decompose the behavior commonly observed in biped and quadruped locomotion, into components that we understand from work with one leg. We do not address the problem of gait selection, focussing instead on methods of maintaining balance and forward speed once a gait is chosen.

A first step in generalizing understanding of systems with one leg to systems with many legs, is to avoid focussing on the legs themselves, and to concentrate, instead, on the influence the legs have upon motion of the body. The legs must provide support and they must propel the system forward. (See Fig. 1.) If we can understand what the body needs in terms of forces and torques to obtain support and propulsion, and if we can find ways to make the legs work together to provide support and propulsion, then we should be able to formulate effective control algorithms. Presumably, a control algorithm of this kind might apply to the locomotion of systems with one leg, two legs . . . N legs. A theory that could explain dynamic behavior in all sorts of legged creatures, and that could guide the design of man-made vehicles is a primary goal of this research.

3. One Leg at a Time

For the purpose of this discussion, let us take for granted that the previous work on 2D and 3D one-legged systems provides effective algorithms for controlling devices that have a leg, a body, and a suitable collection of actuators and sensors. The algorithms we explored decompose the control problem into three parts; a vertical hopping part, a forward velocity part, and a body attitude part. These algorithms provide leg thrust to maintain vertical hopping, place the leg during flight to control the forward running velocity, and torque the body during stance to control attitude. With this starting point, it is not hard to propose a mechanism that would work for humans and other bipeds running on two legs.

Despite a number of real differences[1], running on one and two legs is remarkably similar. Rather than use one leg over and over again as a system with only one leg must, a biped alternates in the use of two separate legs. The thrust each leg delivers, the placement of the legs, and the torque generated between the hip and leg during stance can be identical to the corresponding values generated for systems with one leg. While one-legged systems use the same leg over and over to achieve these functions, the human biped uses two legs alternately. The basic characteristics as seen from the body are not much different in the two cases -- alternation of springy support and ballistic flight.

We characterize running by one- and two-legged systems in the following terms:

- Only one leg provides support at a time.
- Support phases and flight phases proceed in strict alternation.

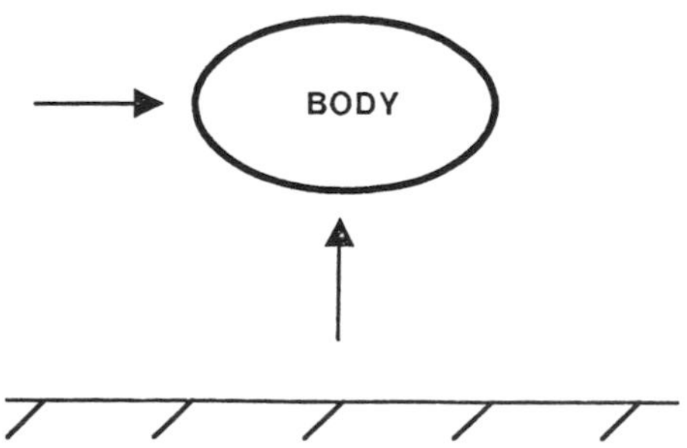

Figure 1: The purpose of the legs in a legged system is to provide support for the body and to propel it forward.

We call this class of running gait the *one-foot*. All the legs are kept off the ground, except for the one whose turn it is to provide support. The human biped runs in this manner, as do the one-legged machines we have built. I know of no example of a natural quadruped that employs a one-foot gate.

In principle, the control algorithm used for the one-legged system will permit a systems with any number of legs to run using a one-foot gait. A quadruped performing the one-foot gait would cycle through use of the legs in some regular order. Each would deliver a vertical thrust to maintain hopping and correct body attitude during stance when providing support, while the next leg moved to a forward position appropriate for landing. It would be like a Gatling gun with legs in place of barrels.

A practical problem with this sort of running is the difficulty of locating the legs close enough to the center of the body to permit the feet to reach the points that would provide balance. The foot must be placed so that the average point of support during stance is under the center of mass. It is not hard to attach one or two legs near the center of mass, but the design problem becomes more difficult with more legs. It is also hard to keep many legs from interfering with each other in their motions, when they are mounted close together.

To summarize, the one-foot is a class of running gaits in which only one leg provides support at a time and a flight phase occurs between each support phase. Control of each leg in a system executing a one-foot could be like that used in our one-legged systems.

4. Pairs of Legs in Unison

The next step in generalizing from one leg to several legs is to consider pairs of legs that act together. The quadruped gaits that might be understood and produced in this way are the trot, the pace, and the bound. In each of these gaits, two legs strike the ground in unison, and they leave the ground in unison. While one pair of legs is providing support, the other pair swings forward in preparation for the next step.

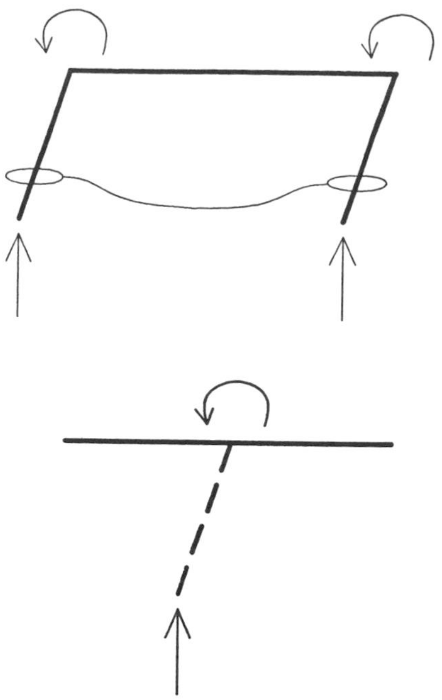

Figure 2: A pair of legs that act in unison can be replaced by an equivalent *virtual* leg that exerts equivalent forces and moments on the body. This is a simple form of Sutherland's (1984) more general concept.

Suppose for the moment that when a pair of legs provides support, both members of the pair are controlled to act like an equivalent single leg. This is a simple form of Sutherland's idea of a virtual leg (Sutherland, 1984). One might suppose that the effective point of support is determined by the position of each foot and the force each delivers to the ground. The sum of torques delivered by the pair of hip actuators would contribute to the hip torque, but the difference in thrust of the legs would also influence the effective torque. The height of a hop would be determined by the sum of thrusts. Murphy and Raibert (1984) explored the problem of controlling pairs of legs to make them act together in these ways.

Thinking in terms of pairs of legs, the trot, the pace and the bound are very much like a biped one-foot, in which each biped leg is replaced with a pair of legs. Given that pairs of legs can be controlled to act like single virtual legs, then these gaits reduce to that of the running biped, which we have already discussed and reduced further. The kangaroo ricochet reduces to a one-legged system directly.

When pairs of legs act together during support, the effective point of support can be located near the center of mass, even though the physical legs are located a substantial distance from the center of the body. The one-foot running gaits are difficult to realize in a quadruped because it is difficult to locate the legs close enough to the system's center of mass. When two legs provide support simultaneously, the effective point of support lies somewhere on the line that connects the two feet. In the trot, the gait involving diagonal support pairs, the lines containing the effective points of support for both leg pairs pass under the center of the body. In the pace, the gait involving lateral support pairs, the lines connecting the feet may pass under the center of mass if the legs are angled inward during stance, or they may pass quite close to the center of the body if the body is narrow.

In the bound the virtual legs do not necessarily provide support under the center of mass. Therefore, the analysis does not

---

[1] There are three primary differences between the behavior of systems with one and two legs:

- Two legs permit running without pitching motions of the body. A one-legged system must move its leg forward and backward at different times. When a one-legged system swings its leg forward during flight, the body must pitch forward so that angular momentum is conserved. In a biped it is possible to overlap in time the backward motion of the supporting leg with the forward motion of the other leg. If the legs move forward and backward in this complementary fashion, then conservation of angular momentum during flight can occur without pitching motions of the body, and without a tail.

- Since forward and backward motions of the legs can occur simultaneously in the biped, the time available for the recovery motion of the swing leg is not uniquely determined by the duration of flight. Therefore, if the recovery motion of one leg is overlapped with the stance motion of the other leg, then a biped will run faster than a one-legged system if both can move a leg back and forth at the same rate.

- It is desirable for a biped to recover one leg to a forward position while the other leg supports weight. The recovery leg must be substantially shorter than the support leg, if it is to clear the ground without stubbing. In the one-legged systems we have explored, the leg was always at maximum length during recovery, but the forward recovery motion occurred when the body achieved peak height during flight. A biped should have a mechanism that will permit the swing leg to shorten substantially during recovery, and to lengthen again in time for landing.

completely account for stability in that case, and a rocking motion in the pitch direction results. Actually, the pace often has the same characteristic, with rocking in the roll direction. Additional mechanisms that take pairs of steps into account, can be used to provide stability for the pace and the bound.

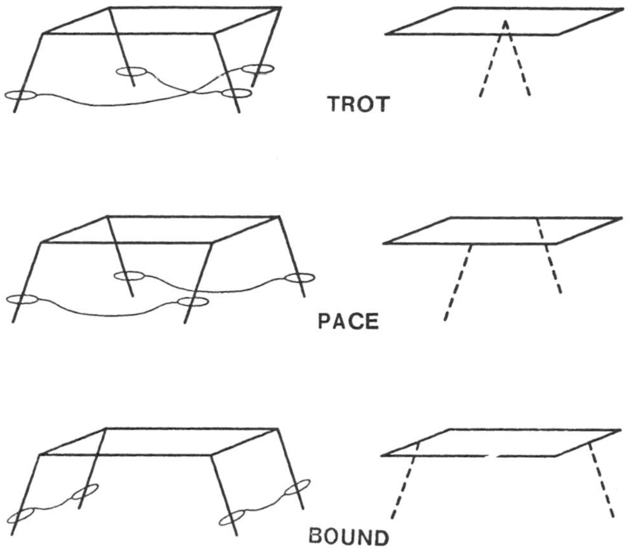

Figure 3: There are three quadruped gaits that use pairs of legs in unison. In the trot (TOP), diagonal pairs of legs strike the ground at the same time, they leave the ground at the same time, and they swing forward at the same time. In the pace (MIDDLE), lateral pairs of legs act in unison. In the bound (BOTTOM), the front legs act in unison, as do the rear. Using the virtual leg idea, each of these gaits can be reduced to biped one-foot gaits.

5. Pairs of Legs in Sequence

A basic tenant of dynamic stability is that the legs need not provide a base of support continuously, but only over time. The stability we have described so far in this discussion relies on finding a foot placement that will result in symmetric behavior during each support interval, for each leg or pair of legs. If the motion of the body is symmetrical about the effective point of support provided by the feet, then there is no net acceleration of the system (Raibert, 1984). We now consider the case where each support interval causes the system to accelerate, but successive pairs of support intervals are matched to generate equal and opposite accelerations. See Fig. 4. Such anti-symmetric pairs of steps generate no net acceleration.

Suppose we modify the control algorithm for the one-legged system, so that on every even hop the algorithm that calculates desired foot placement adds a factor, Δx, and on every odd hop it adds an extra factor, $-\Delta x$. For some suitably small range of Δx, the system would hop side to side, with no net horizontal acceleration. Figure 5 plots data from just such an experiment, performed with the 3D one-legged hopping machine.

The system continues to balance provided that the accelerations caused by the offset of the foot do not cause the system to tip over entirely before the next step. On the next step there will be an opportunity to accelerate the system in the other direction, with no net acceleration over the pair. This analysis becomes relevant when we think of Δx as representing the distance from the hip to the center of the body. For the pace, Δx may be small. For the bound in a quadruped with a rigid body, Δx is about half the length of the body.

6. Pairs of Legs Overlapped in Time

The most complicated quadruped running gaits, the canter, the gallop and the half bound, do not yet fit into this framework. These gaits are characterized by partially overlapping periods of support between pairs of legs and larger numbers of legs. For instance, in the gallop the following sequence for the front feet is typical: place front right, place front left, lift front right, lift front left. Similar overlapping support periods occur for other pairs of legs.

So far we only have a vague idea of how to decompose and understand these sorts of gaits. To simplify the analysis, consider a biped running with overlapping support periods for each leg. Humans can gallop in this way. See Fig. 7. Assume that both legs have equal support periods, and therefore, the CG-print associated with both legs are of equal length. We see that in steady state running, the biped with overlapped support still has a symmetrical support pattern. The single support phases at the beginning and end of the stance interval have symmetry about the center of the stance interval. The configuration of the body and legs during the double support phase is also symmetrical.

7. Independent Legs

So far we have concentrated on representing the behavior of entire multi-legged systems in terms of the equivalent behavior of one-legged systems. Another way to generalize the results from the one-legged case to the multi-legged case, is to think in terms of the behavior of several one-legged systems that are loosely constrained to operate together. The idea is that each leg of a multi-legged system, along with part of the body behaves like the one-legged systems we have described. Perhaps during a gallop, the vertical bouncing motion of the front half of a horse might be controlled separately from the vertical bouncing motion of the back half. This approach is explored more fully in chapters 3 and 5 of Raibert et al. (1983).

A primary motivation for our work on systems with one leg was to provide simple ideas about legged locomotion that we could generalize to more complicated configurations with more legs. Actually, we would like to find concepts that are not tied to particular locomotion systems, but that apply to whole classes of legged systems. We would like to transform the question of how many legs a legged system has, from a central determinant of behavior to a mere implementation detail.

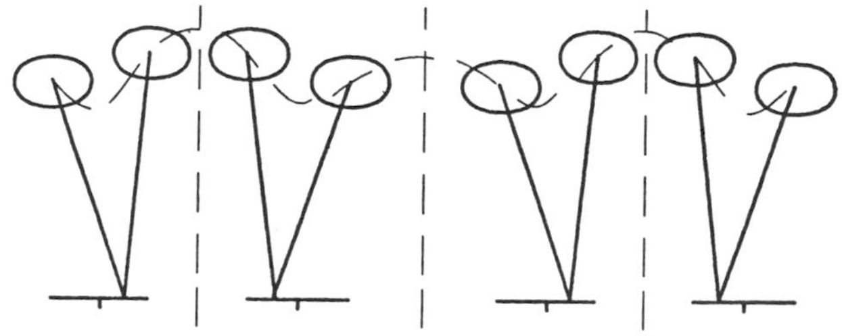

Figure 4: Sequence in which body and leg are shown at each touch-down and lift-off, for pairs of steps that are symmetrical. If the foot is positioned behind the center of the CG-print on one step, and in front of the center on the next step, then there can be a symmetrical pattern that produces zero net acceleration over the pair of steps. The strides will be of different sizes because the speed during the flight phase of each step is different. The dashed lines indicate symmetry.

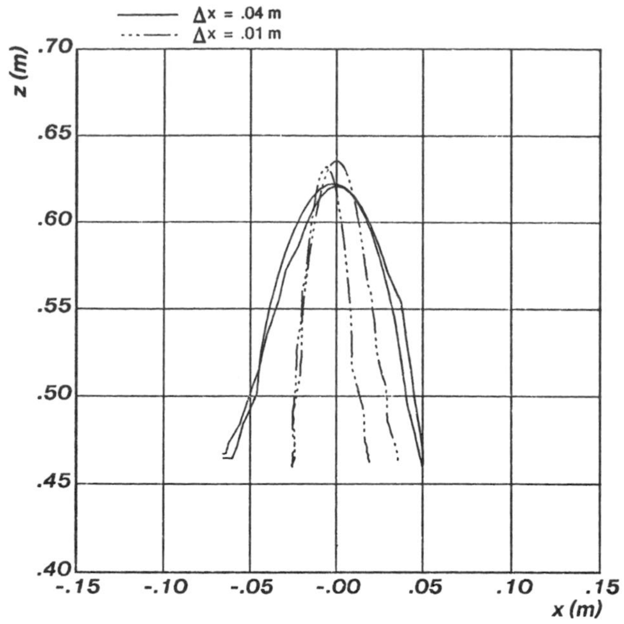

Figure 5: Position of center of mass of physical 3D hopping machine using pairs of balanced steps. The control algorithms were those described by Raibert, Brown, and Chepponis (1984), but an offset, Δx, was added to the foot position on even hops, and subtracted on odd hops. The magnitude of Δx was set to two different values, shown separately in the two curves. The body moved back and forth on alternate hops. The system was not stable during a single hop, but only over a pair of hops. This experiment is relevant to running gaits that do not place the effective point of support under the body, such as the pace and bound. The displacements of the foot, $\pm\Delta x$, correspond to the displacement of the hip from the center of the body. The trot and kangaroo hop do not involve such offsets.

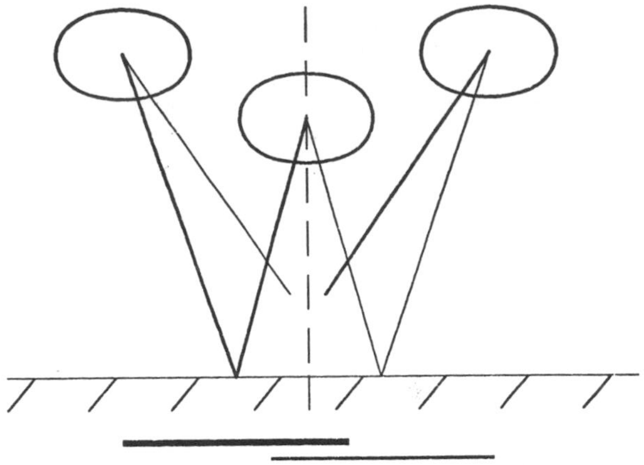

Figure 6: Symmetry that exists about the center of the stance phase in a gallop, for a pair of legs. The bars underneath the figure indicate the CG-prints for each leg.

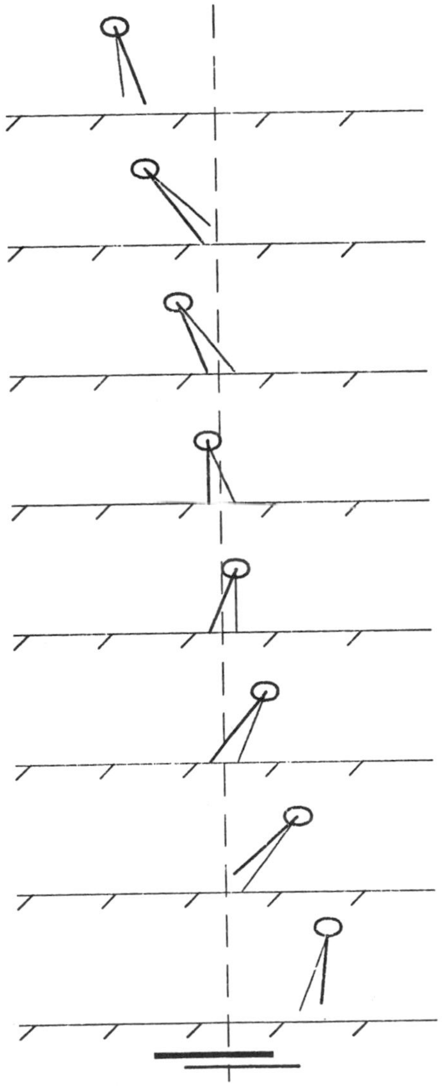

Figure 7: Galloping with two legs. In a gallop the two legs are just slightly out of phase. One leg touches down and lifts off just ahead of the other. There can be symmetry in a gallop, about both the center of stance, when both legs are touching the ground and equally compressed, and about the half way point in flight. The dashed line indicate the first symmetry plane. The horizontal bars at the bottom indicate the CG-prints for each leg. See also, Fig. 6

To summarize briefly the main points of this section:

- Existing algorithms are effective in controlling systems with a body and one springy leg. They decompose control into a hopping part, a forward velocity part, and a body attitude part.

- Bipedal running is very much like running on one leg, except that two legs are used in alternation. The same control algorithms apply.

- There is a special class of gaits we call the one-foot, for which only one leg touches the ground at a time. The same control algorithm applies to all one-foot gaits, independent of the number of legs.

- When pairs of legs acting in unison are controlled to behave like single virtual legs, then the trot and pace of a quadruped are like the biped run.

- The quadruped bound is also like a biped run, but with an alternating offset in the point of support.

- We do not yet understand the canter, gallop, or half bound, though there is symmetry in the pattern of stepping for these multi-legged gaits.

8. Acknowledgements

This research was sponsored by a grant from the System Development Foundation, and by the Systems Science Office of the Defense Advanced Research Projects Agency.

9. References

Murphy, K., Raibert, M.H. Trotting and Bounding in a Planar Two-Legged Model. In *Fifth Symposium on Theory and Practice of Robots and Manipulators*, A. Morecki, G. Bianchi, K. Kedzior, Eds., Elsevier Scientific Publishing Co., Amsterdam, 1984.

Murthy, S.S., Raibert, M.H. 3D Balance in Legged Locomotion: Modeling and Simulation for the One-Legged Case. Inter-Disciplinary Workshop on Motion: Representation and Perception, ACM, June, 1983.

Raibert, M.H. Dynamic stability and resonance in a one legged hopping machine. In *Fourth Symposium on Theory and Practice of Robots and Manipulators*, A. Morecki, G. Bianchi, K. Kedzior, Eds., Elsevier Scientific Publishing Co., Amsterdam, 1981.

Raibert, M.H. "Hopping in legged systems -- Modelling and simulation for the 2D one-legged case." *IEEE Tran. Systems, Man, and Cybernetics 14*, 3 (1984), In Press.

Raibert, M.H., Brown, H.B.,Jr. "Experiments in balance with a 2D one-legged hopping machine." *ASME J. Dynamic Systems, Measurement, and Control 106*, 1 (1984), 75-81.

Raibert, M.H., Brown, H.B.,Jr., Chepponis, M., Hastings, E., Koechling, J., Murphy, K., Murthy, S.S., Stentz, A. Dynamically Stable Legged Locomotion -- Third Annual Report. Tech. Rept. CMU-RI-TR-83-20, Robotics Institute, Carnegie-Mellon University, 1983.

Raibert, M.H., Brown, H.B.,Jr., Chepponis, M. "Experiments in balance with a 3D one-legged hopping machine." *International Journal of Robotics Research 3*, 2 (1984), 75-92.

Sutherland, I.E. "Footprints in the Asphalt." *International Journal of Robotics Research 3*, 2 (1984), 29-36.

DYNAMICAL WALK OF QUADRUPED ROBOT (COLLIE-1)

Hirofumi Miura, Isao Shimoyama,
Mamoru Mitsuishi and Hiroshi Kimura

Department of Mechanical Engineering
Faculty of Engineering
The University of Tokyo
7-3-1, Hongo, Bunkyo-ku
Tokyo 113, Japan

Dynamical walk of the quadruped robot (COLLIE-1) is discussed. COLLIE-1 is the advanced type of the BIPERs (the biped robots developed by the authors). COLLIE-1 has 12 actuators (4 legs x 3 DC motors) and 24 sensors (4 x 5 potentiometers for joint angles and 4 touch-sensors for contact detection of the leg to the floor). Special high level language "COL" (Control Oriented Language) is being developed for multitasking system ---- for instance, COLLIE-1 control system.

1. Introduction

The interest to the locomotion of robots is rising up recently. Conventional locomotive robots with wheels have been developed and discussed by many researchers. Today, lots of researchers are conducting researches on legged locomotive robots.

Many kinds of legged locomotive robots ---- one legged, biped, tri-legged, quadruped, six-legged and so on ---- have been developed and investigated experimentally and theoretically. Many papers on construction and control theory of them have been and are being contributed in many countries. The authors started the research on biped locomotive robots several years ago. They have already developed five robots and called these robots "BIPER-1, ..., -5".

BIPER-3 and BIPER-4 were reported at the first International Symposium of Robotics Research in the United States. BIPER-3 with no ankle joints performs three dimensional stilts-like walk. BIPER-4 with ankle joints performs three dimensional humans-like walk. These BIPER's walk is dynamical walk which differs from statical walk in the case of which the center of gravity remains always upon the sole of the supporting leg. The first main goal of development of BIPERs was to realize dynamical walk on the smooth and flat floor. After the upper goal was completed successfully, the next goal was settled to the realization of dynamical walk of robot on the non-flat configuration ---- for instance the rough, bumpy or stepped floor. To complete this second goal, the authors are intending to develop such a robot that can recognize the configuration and environment where it is walking, deciding the gait by itself. BIPERs are considered not to be suitable for this goal. Because, the computer is so busy for dynamical balance that it doesn't have enough time for looking around and recognizing the environment. This is the main reason why the quadruped robot "COLLIE-1" is being developed. COLLIE-1 can stand still stably and can do anything during standing.

In this paper, the construction and the design concept of COLLIE-1 are described first and secondly the software system for controller of walk is explained precisely. Of the software system, the managing system for multitasks is mainly explained. On COLLIE-1, 12 actuators and 24 sensors are mounted. Consequently, skillful managing of multitasks ---- obtaining data from sensors and supplying control values to actuators ---- is indispensable for dynamical walk of COLLIE-1. Experiment of COLLIE-1 has just started. As the first stage of dynamical walk, COLLIE-1 is being controlled to walk similarly to BIPER-4.

2. Construction of COLLIE-1

The former machine has been controlled by mechanical or simple electric signal. Four bar linkage and cam are examples of that. But now, we can easily attach the computer to the machine. As this kind of machine is controlled by the software, we can construct the robot with simple mechanism but performing the complicated motion.

In COLLIE-1 design, it is the important problem that what is done by mechanism and what is done by software. If the mechanism becomes simpler, the load imposed on the software is heavier. On the other hand, the robot controlled by the mechanism lacks the adaptability and flexibility on walking (e.g. walking on the rough road). Which course the designer selects depends on himself. COLLIE-1 in this paper is designed to be the quadruped robot having necessary and minimum mechanism for walk and controlled by the software. Such a kind of robot was considered nonsense ten years ago. But now, as computer is getting better and cheaper, it is valuable to construct such one and to conduct reseach on the adaptability and the effectiveness of the software for it.

In such a case, the heaviest load for the computer is to execute the task that makes the robot dynamically stable. No analog circuits for feedback control are included in this robot system, that is, COLLIE-1 is controlled only by the software. Taking all conditions into consideration, the sampling time should not exceed 15 ms for stable walk. In other words, the feedback/feedforward control should be waked up within 15 ms interval and terminate by next waked up. If the computer executes only this task, the software design is easy. But the computer may execute tasks concurrently when several tasks are added. Furthermore, when we want to add the functions that COLLIE-1 decides its motion by recognizing the environment with vision, the multitasking system should be introduced for convenience. This is the reason why we need the tool that can describe the concurrent tasks. This software system is discussed in detail at 3.

Outline of COLLIE-1 is shown in Fig.1-4. COLLIE-1 is regarded as the combination of two BIPER-4s each of which is located in front and rear side respectively. COLLIE-1 has 12 actuated joints and 8 nonactuated joints (at the feet). These actuators are 12 DC motors and gear reduction ratio is as small as possible to avoid the effect of the friction. The COLLIE-1's state is measured with potentiometers at the joints and contact sensors on the soles. The potentiometers at the joints measure the ralative angles between the segments. Therefore the potentiometers at the feet measure the relative angles between the legs and the floor. The contact sensors are conductive plastic attached to the soles of feet. Anyway, COLLIE-1 is simple enough in mechanism that the software should be designed considering the future extended system.

3. Software system "COL" for COLLIE-1

3.1 Outline of COL

Execution of control program of the robot is triggered by the satisfactory value of sensors (for instance, visual-sensor, touch-sensor, force-sensor, auditory-sensor and so on) or by manual operation, and control process starts. For describing such kind of control program, ordinary programming language is not so useful. Because, the program described in ordinary language is basically executed sequentially from top to bottom. If the ordinary language is used, very skillful and tricky technique is necessary to describe such a control program, by which one of some branches of execution is selected depending on external conditions (e.g. outputs of sensors) or on the scheduled (predefined) time. Unexpected error probably occurs during execution of program. Therefore, it is indispensable to provide the special programming language in which control program of the robot can be described easily and clearly. The programming language for the robot control must have functions describing the following, adding the functions to the ordinary language.

1) Concurrent processing
2) Status control processing of processes
3) Priority processing
4) Shared variable processing
5) Real time processing
6) I/O processing
7) Feedback/Feedforward processing

The authors are developing the language "COL" (Control Oriented Language) which has the above mentioned functions. COL consists of two parts. The first part is the compiler which generates P-code. The second part is the assembler-interpreter which executes P-code. The compiler and the assembler-interpreter are described in Pascal for portability. The basic part of grammer of COL is the same as that of Pascal and some extended rules are added.

3.2 Explanation of COL

3.2.1 Concurrent Processing

In the robot control, there are various kinds of processes. They are the sensor managing process, the trajectory planning process, the control process to make the robot follow the planned trajectory (so called feedback/feedforward process) and so on. These processes must be executed concurrently. Using COL, concurrent processes can be described independently and compiled separately. Separate compilation makes genaration and modification of each process easy. But it must be noticed that "link" is necessary. The authors are trying to complete such system that the users of COL need not operate "link" explicitly in it.

3.2.2 Status control processing of processes

One process sends the event to other processes to trigger them. Declaration of the event can be done by the following manner in COL.

var e : event;

When the following built-in procedure has been executed, the process is put in the queue of the event "e".

await(e);

If some process executes the following built-in procedure, the process which was put in the queue formerly becomes the executable status.

cause(e);

3.2.3 Priority processing

The process is executed according to its priority. Declaration of the priority can be done by the following.

setpri n;

"n" is called the priority number. The smaller priority number, the higher priority. For the highest priority, n=0. In the present

COL, the fixed priority is being used. In future, dynamic priority shall be introduced.

3.2.4 Shared variable processing

In order that only one process may substitute or refer at one moment the shared variable which is possibly substituted or refered by many processes, "mutual exclusion" would be useful. Declaration of the shared variable is the following.

```
program task1(input,output);
  var a : integer; global;
      :
program task2(input,output);
  var a : integer; external;
      :
```

Critical region for mutual exclusion is described in the following manner.

region a do statement;

Providing critical region, access error concerning the variable or the resource which needs mutual exclusion can be detected during compilation.

3.2.5 Real time processing

In the robot control, some process ---- e.g. the feedback control, the feedforward control and so on ---- is triggered at the scheduled time. In many cases, the process is triggered periodically. The periodicity of the process is declared in the following manner in COL.

periodic p;

"p" is called the periodic number. In the case that the declaration of p is not found or p=0, the process is triggered only once. Otherwise the process is triggered at every the following time:

(unit time) x *(periodic number)*

where unit time is 1 ms, for instance.

3.2.6 I/O processing

Input_to/Output_from the port is executed by ordinal read/write. The assignment of the port can be done in the same manner as file assignment.

3.2.7 Feedback/Feedforward processing

In COL, basic function of feedback/feedforward control is built in the interpreter. Some messages are transmitted to it. Built-in procedure "feedback" is provided for transmitting the message concerning feedback/feedforward.

feedback(sptime,$x^*,\dot{x}^*,u^*$*,f,g);*

Receiving this message, the interpreter performs the following control:

$$(\text{sampling time}) = (\text{unit time}) \times (\text{sptime})$$

$$u = u^* + \Delta u, \quad \Delta u = f.(x-x^*) + g.(\dot{x}-\dot{x}^*)$$

where * means planned trajectory.

3.3 COL machine (interpreter)

COL compiler generates instruction codes for the virtual machine so that emulation may be performed on various computers. COL machine of stack type executes these instruction codes. In this section COL machine is described.

3.3.1 Memory allocation

COL machine consists of the interpreter segment which executes virtual instuction codes of each process, the process i segment which memorizes instruction codes and data of each process, the shared variable segment and the interpreter work space segment (Fig.5). Precise description of the process i segment is shown in Fig.6. The process i segment consists of the region for memorizing instruction codes, the region for memorizing constants, the stack and the heap region.

3.3.2 Registration of process

One process of COL is registered in the interpreter as one task by generating task control block (Fig.7). Status of the task is "Run", "Ready", "Dormant", "Wait on Semaphore", "Wait for Event" or "Wait for Command".

3.3.3 Mutual exclusion

Mutual exclusion of the shared variable is realized by p-operation and v-operation to semaphore s in the following manner.

```
initialize    s := 1;
p-operation   s := s - 1;
              if s < 0 then the running
              task is put into the
              queue of s;
v-operation   s := s + 1;
              if s <= 0 then a task is
              picked out from the
              queue of s and is made
              "Ready".
```

When the access to the shared variable occurrs firstly, semaphore control block for that variable is created (Fig.8).

3.3.4 Event

The event is registered in the interpreter by the event control block (Fig.9). When the event occurred, all tasks which are in the queue of that event become "Ready".

3.3.5 Status transition of the task

The task of the higher priority is executed the earlier. Status transition of the task occurrs in the following cases (Fig.10).

1) When the trigger at scheduled time happens.
2) When the operation concerning semaphore is executed.
3) When the operation concerning event is executed.
4) When the command is given.
5) When the execution of process terminates.

3.3.6 Garbage collection

The garbage collection of queue control blocks is executed (Fig.11).

3.4 Summary

COL compiler and COL machine were presented. In appendix, COL description of control program for 3 DOF arm is presented as an example. COL has the following excellent characteristics.

1) Concurrent processes can be described easily and clearly.
2) Management software of control program (concerning the shared variable, interpreting and so on) does not trouble the programmer. That means that the program gets clear and easy understanding (readability) on the whole.
3) Transmission of the messages to other processes is easy.

The authors dare say that COL is being developed not only for describing the robot control program but also for describing the environment for development of robot control system. This environment for development (named COLLEAGUE) supports the following functions.

1) The user can develop his software in dialogue mode with the system, using the display, the keyboard and the pointing device (the mouse).
2) Even during the robot is being operated, new functions can be added.
3) Performance of the software can be ascertained by simulation.
4) The capability of debugging can be improved by tracing and displaying the status of concurrent processes.

4. Experiment

By now, the parallel dynamical walk has been realized by using the commercial OS at a market that can manage multitasking. The parallel dynamical walk means that the motion of two front legs is identical with that of the rear ones. Sequence of the parallel dynamical walk is as follows: 2 legs supporting phase -- 4 legs supporting phase(supporting legs exchanging phase) -- 2 legs supporting phase. There is no 3 legs supporting phase.

For COLLIE-1's dynamical walk, the dynamics (equations of motion) is obtained first. These equations of motion are represented as the nonlinear differencial equations including the variables corresponding to the joints. And they vary with the number of contacting feet. The treatments of these equations are the same as BIPER's. This means that we adopt the following assumptions. (1) The equations of motion can be decomposed into the independent motion about the roll and pitch axis. (2) The motion of front and rear legs are controlled identically (parallel walk). Under these conditions, the motion of COLLIE-1 is equivalent to that of BIPER-4.

BIPER-4, the biped locomotion with knees, is shown in Fig.12. In order to achieve BIPER-4's walk, feedback/feedforward control is utilized. By computing the required actuator torque (Fig.13) from the equations of motion, the feedforward control produces the planned ideal motion. The feedback control makes BIPER-4 stable around the planned trajectories. COLLIE-1 parallel dynamical walk is realized by feedback/feedforward control as same manner as that of BIPER-4.

Conccurrent tasks for COLLIE-1 are executed using commercial real time multitasking operating system. The feedback/feedforward task and man-machine interface task have been implemented. (As the feedforward actuator torques cannot be calculated at walk time, they are calculated before starting walk and stored in memory.) Feedback/feedforward task is waked up every 15 ms. Then 24 sensor outputs are sampled and 12 actuator torques are decided. Man-machine interface task transfers the messages among man and tasks trough the shared variables.

5. Future work

Only parallel dynamical walk has been realized on COLLIE-1 and a few tasks are implemented. The authors are intending to implement the following functions.

1) Realizing the complicated walk.
2) Adding the various sensors including vision.
3) Improving the man-machine interface process.

The basic idea to implement them is as follows. All functions are executed as concurrent tasks. COL, a high level language introduced at 3, is a tool to describe them. Using COL, the programmer need not be conscious of the operating system. The goal of our project is to develop the programming environment for control (Fig.14). In this environment, the programmer can easily use the software products that have been completed.

References

Miura,H. and Shimoyama,I.1983. Dynamical Walk of Biped Locomotion, Proceedings of ISRR, New Hampshire.

Hansen,P.B. 1973. Operating System Principles, Prentice-Hall Inc., Englewood Cliffs, NJ.

Hansen,P.B. 1975. The Programming Language Concurrent Pascal,IEEE Trans. on Software Engineering, SE-1, 2, pp.199-207.

Hansen,P.B. 1977. The Architecture of Concurrent Programs, Prentice-Hall Inc., Englewood Cliffs, NJ.

Wirth,N. 1976. Algorithms + Data Structures = Programs,Prentice-Hall Inc., Englewood Cliffs, NJ.

Wirth,N. 1983. Programming in Modula-2,Springer-Verlag, New York, NY.

Pemberton,S. and Daniels,M.C. 1982. Pascal Implementation:The P4 Compiler, EllisHorwood Ltd, Market Cross House, England.

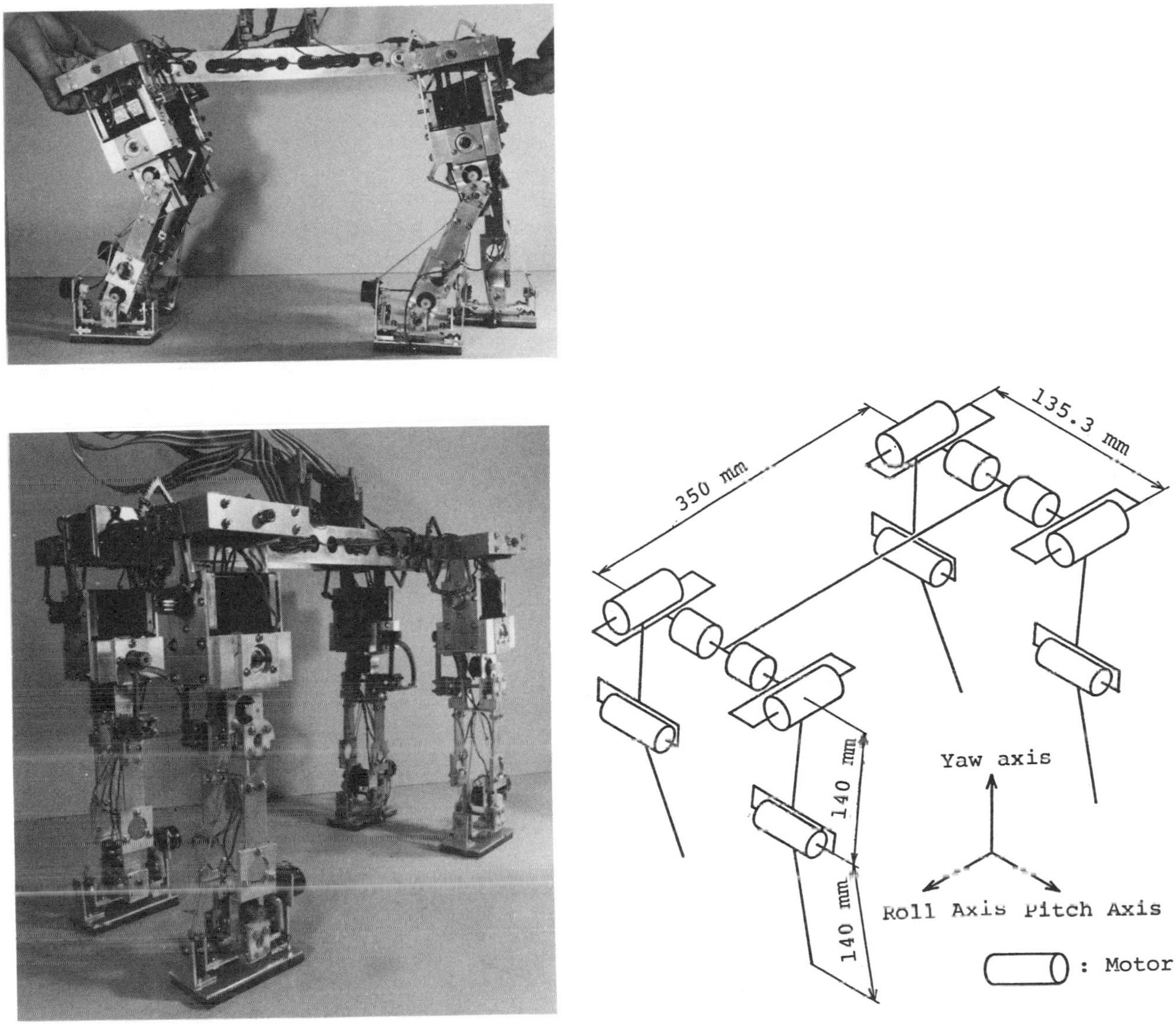

Fig. 1 Construction of COLLIE-1

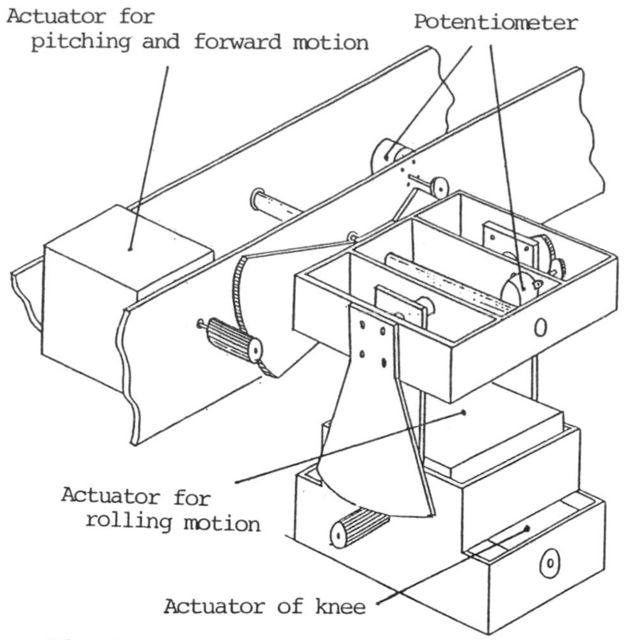

Fig. 2 Shoulder/Hip Joint

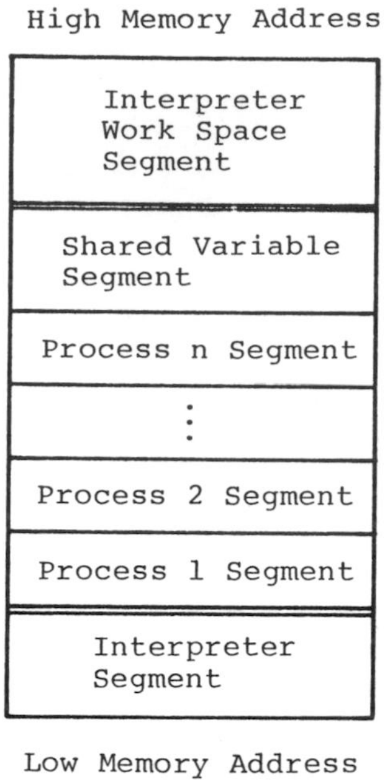

Fig. 5 Overview of COL Machine's Memory Allocation

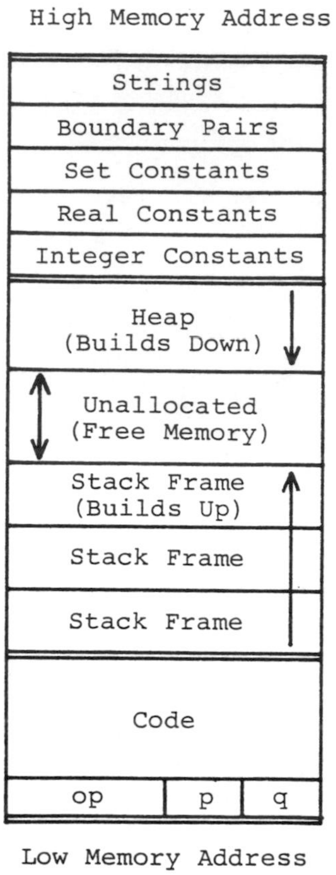

Fig. 6 Detail of Process i Segment

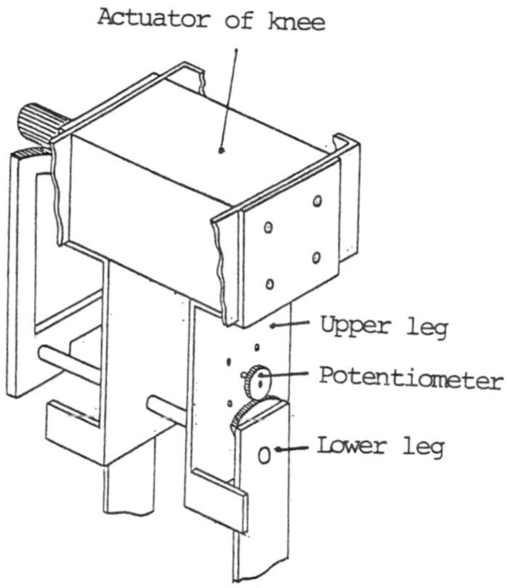

Fig. 3 Knee Joint

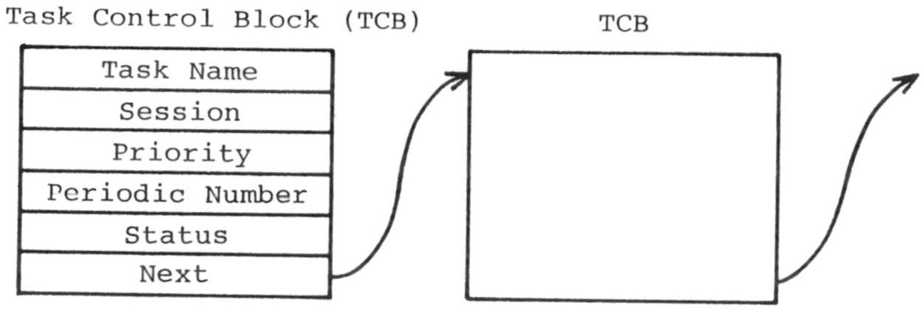

Fig. 7 Task Control Block

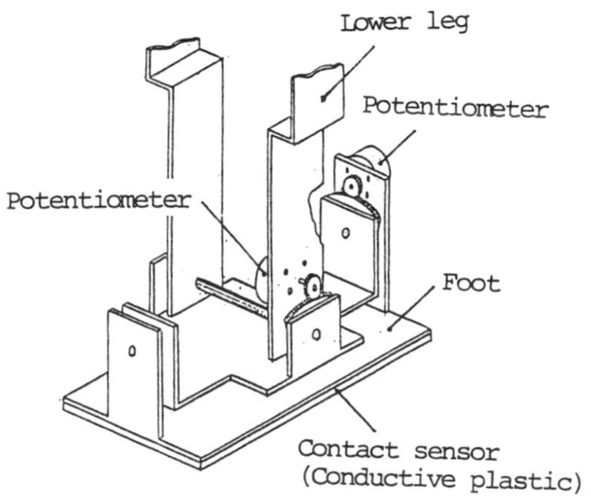

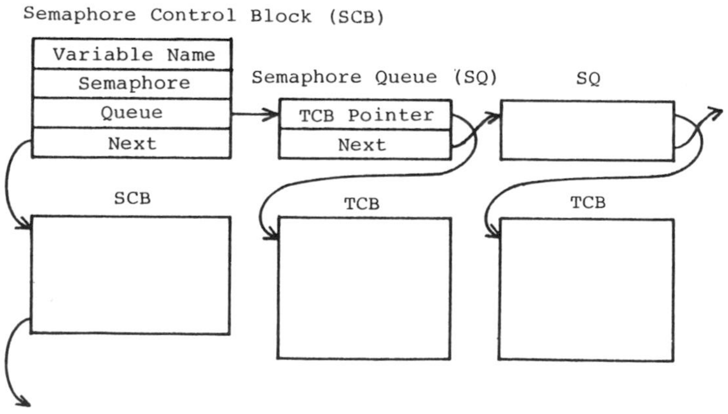

Fig. 8 Semaphore Control Block

Fig. 4 Foot Joint

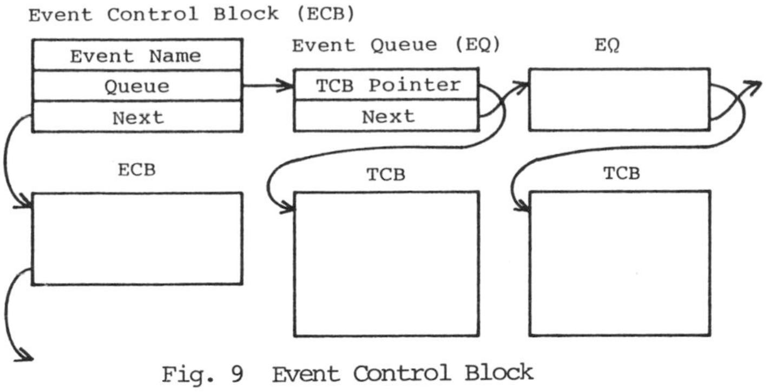

Fig. 9 Event Control Block

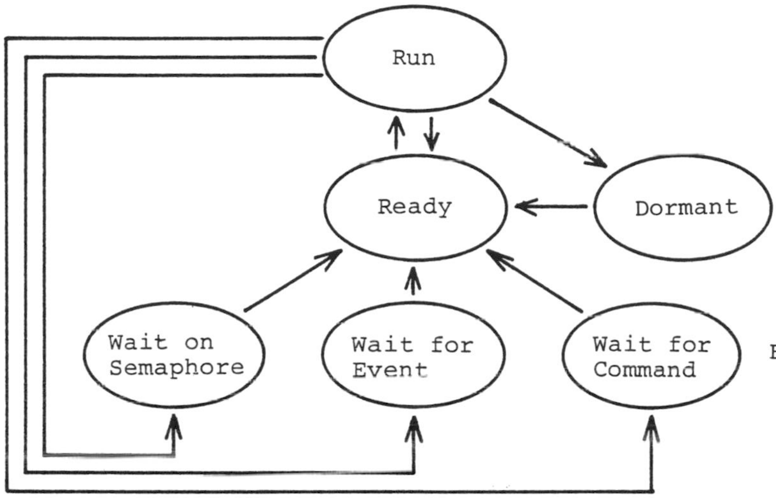

Fig. 10 Task Status Transition

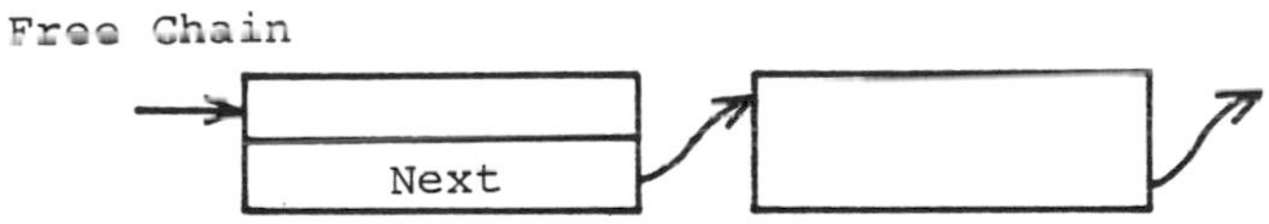

Fig. 11 Garbage Collection

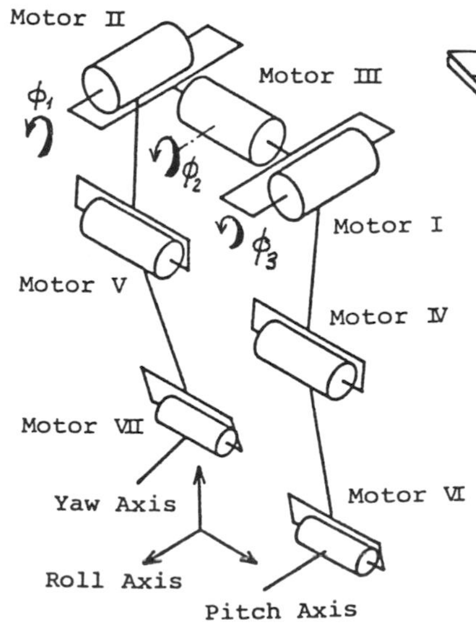

Fig. 12 Construction of BIPER-4

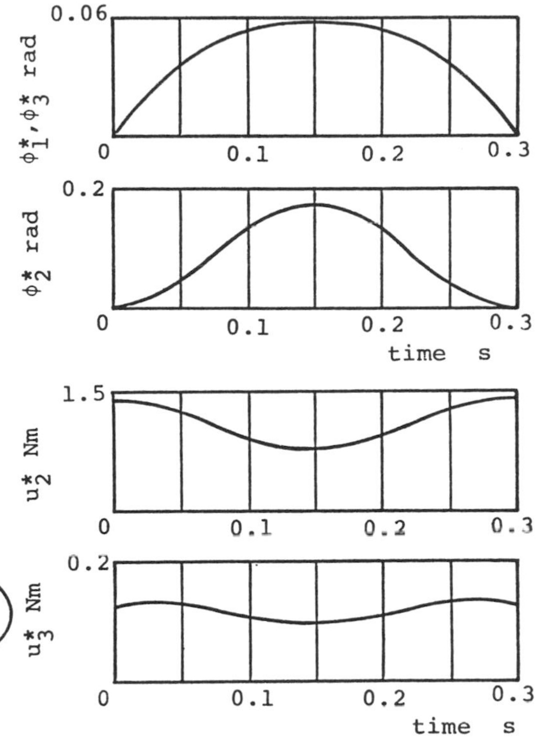

Fig. 13 Planned Trajectories and Required Torques (about Roll Axis)

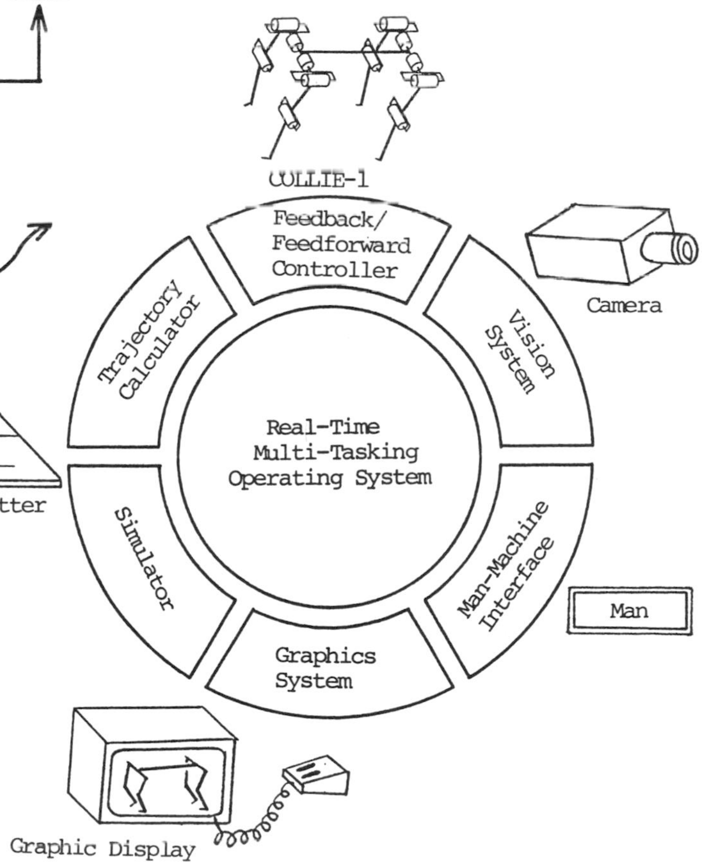

Fig. 14 Control Software System for COLLIE-1

Appendix

The example of control program for 3 DOF arm.

Process 5

Giving the desired value in orthogonal coordinates.

Process 4

Transforming the above desired value into relative angles between links.

Process 3

Giving velocity and torque with interpolation.

Process 2

Sending messages to "feedback".

Process 1

Initializing.

```
(* --- process 1 --- *)
program initialize(input,output);
setpri     1;
periodic   0;
begin
  (* initialization of variables *)
end.

(* --- process 2 --- *)
program feedbk(input,output);
setpri     2;
periodic   30;
const
  dof = 3; (* degrees of freedom *)
  sptime = 5; (* sampling time (ms) *)
type
  r_angle = array [1..dof] of real;
  i_angle = array [1..dof] of integer;
var
  pos, vel, trq : r_angle; global;
  xcalib, ucalib : r_angle;
  x, v, u, f, g : i_angle;
  j : integer;
begin
  (* calibration *)
  region pos, xcalib do
    for j := 1 to dof do
      x[j] := round(pos[j] * xcalib[j]);
  region vel, xcalib do
    for j := 1 to dof do
      v[j] := round(vel[j] * xcalib[j]);
  region trq, ucalib do
    for j := 1 to dof do
      u[j] := round(trq[j] * ucalib[j]);
  (* send message to feedback *)
  feedback(sptime,x,u,v,f,g);
end.

(* --- process 3 --- *)
program trajplan(input,output);
setpri     3;
periodic   30;
const
  dof = 3; (* degrees of freedom *)
  divpnt = 10;
type
  r_angle = array [1..dof] of real;
  i_angle = array [1..dof] of integer;
var
  theta : r_angle : global;
  pos, vel, trq : r_angle; external;
  finish : event;
  count : integer;
procedure interpolation;
  var j : integer;
  begin
    ...
    region pos do begin
      pos[j] := ...; end;
    region vel do begin
      vel[j] := ...; end;
    region trq do begin
      trq[j] := ...; end;
  end;
begin
  count := ( count + 1 ) mod divpnt;
  if count = 0 then begin
    ...
    await(finish);
    interpolation;
  end
  else interpolation;
end.

(* --- process 4 --- *)
program coordtrasform(input,output);
setpri     4;
periodic   300;
const
  dof = 3; (* degrees of freedom *)
type
  space = record x, y, z : real; end;
  r_angle = array [1..dof] of real;
var
  point : space; global;
  theta : r_angle; external;
  refer, finish : event;
procedure relativeangle;
  var j : integer;
  begin
    ...
    region theta do
      begin theta[j] := ...; end;
  end;
begin
  await(refer);
  relativeangle;
  cause(finish);
end.

(* --- process 5 --- *)
program destination(input,output);
setpri     5;
periodic   300;
type
  space = record x, y, z : real; end;
var
  point : space; external;
  refer : event;
begin
  region point do
    with point do begin
      x := 50; y := 100; z := 150;
    end;
  cause(refer);
end.
```

TITAN III: A QUADRUPED WALKING VEHICLE

-- Its Structure and Basic Characteristics --

Shigeo Hirose*, Tomoyuki Masui**, Hidekazu Kikuchi*

Yasushi Fukuda*, Yoji Umetani*

* Tokyo Institute of Technology
2-12-1, Ōokayama, Meguro-ku, Tokyo, JAPAN

** Production Engineering Research Laboratory, Hitachi, Ltd.
292 Yoshidachō, Totsuka-ku, Yokohama, JAPAN

In the first part of this study, the positioning and evaluation of the walking machine as a moving vehicle capable of travelling over uneven ground, and consideration of the number of legs and morphology of legs in relation to the moving efficiency are presented. In the second part, the report on the mechanism, control system and basic actions of the quadruped walking vehicle TITAN III, produced on a trial basis, and experimentally demonstrated are presented.

1. Preface

In the near future, robots will quickly make their way out of the factory and other prepared environments, and find their way to the wild environment of nature as their work site. When this happens, the guadruped walking vehicle will be used as one practical mount to move about on uneven surfaces. The authors have been conducting research on such a vehicle by constructing model. We have succeeded in developing a third model, the TITAN III (third model constructed at the Tokyo Institute of Technology). In this paper, we would like to state the principles of its design and report on the basic characteristics of its function, which have been obtained from the experimental operations of the model itself.

2. Design of the Walking Machine

We will state the basic principles of TITAN III's design first, then we will give our comments on various concrete problems related to the design.

2-1 Basic Principles of Design and Characteristics of Walking Movement

The purpose of designing this walking machine is not to develop a walking machine per se. It is to develop a "machine that can move about freely on the uneven ground of the natural environment (rugged and irregular surfaces and/or soft soil texture) with high energy efficiency and high adaptability to surface topography."

For this purpose, all available mechanical and engineering methods must be surveyed and evaluated. As for the system of travelling on land surfaces, nothing seems to be better than wheeled vehicles and their derivatives such as the endless track crawler. If we are to develop an alternative walking machine, there must be a convincing reason. Therefore, in this paper, we will present our position regarding the walking machine vis-a-vis the transport machines using wheels.

Wheeled vehicles are ideal for operation on level and hard surfaces. But when the surface is rough and has projections and depressions whose dimensions are greater than the diameter of the wheel, or when the surface is soft, resistance to movement increases drastically and their function as transport machines is almost completely lost. The track-laying crawler transport machine, which was developed to overcome these difficulties, has better maneuvability on the surface of unreclaimed land. Yet, the following problems still exist: 1) maneuvability on uneven ground is still poor; 2) the body sways excessively when travelling on uneven ground; and 3) its energy efficiency is reduced when operating on soil of soft texture.

In contrast, walking vehicles have such characteristics as: 1) ability to maneuver over very rugged and uneven surfaces due to the "active," as it were, suspension function of its legs; 2) ability to move around over the land of any topography without swaying, due to the active functioning of its legs; and 3) ability to keep on going without a large reduction in energy efficiency even on soft ground.

Points 1) and 2) above have been discussed extensively, and they have been confirmed in our experiments in which we used our own experimental models. As to point 3), it will be appropriate to think of the difficulty one experiences when trying to ride a bicycle through mud. In that case, the front wheel must be able to move against strong resistance because it has to remove the mud as it proceeds leaving a deep rut in its wake. In the case of walking, however, this resistance is kept to a minimum. Indeed, the legs sink into the mud, but the amount of mud displaced is small because the displacements take place at discontinuous points. Thus, the energy consumption involved is far less than that of forming ruts. Moreover, a walking vehicle can take advantage of the legs' sinking because legs can thereby "catch" the ground to support forward movement. [Bekker, 1969] If we can develop a leg design which reduces the resistance which it receives when it is pulled our of the mud, we would be able to develop a vehicle of high energy efficiency.

Also, the area of sole can be made fairly large compared to the narrowness of a wheel's effective support area (though it cannot be made as wide as that of a track-laying crawler), and thereby eliminate the drawback of the leg's sinking too deep into the mud. And the body can be maintained in a stable posture even when the vehicle is travelling on soft ground, owing to the active functions of the legs. These two points may be raised here as the merits of walking vehicles.

In addition to these, we would like to make special mention of the fact that the energy efficiency of walking vehicle, which is generally considered to be very low, can be improved significantly by restructuring the driving mechanism. We have already pointed out that the major part of loss of potential energy at the time of the walking operation can be eliminated by the introduction of the GDA system, which we will talk about in Section 2-3, below. [Hirose, 1980a], [Hirose, 1983a]

We also believe it possible to reduce other losses of kinetic energy by structuring the driving mechanism of the legs in such a way that the kinetic energy of the leg can be converted temporarily to torsion energy of an elastic body.

The authors believe that the reasons given above warrant the development of a walking machine. But, in view of the fact that, in the present-day level of technology, wheeled vehicles perform far better than the walking vehicles do on hard and even surfaces, we decided to develop a vehicle which is equipped with both wheels and legs.

2-2 Number of Legs

The first thing we have to decide upon is the number of legs for developing an efficient walking machine. In this section, we will discuss the problem from various points of view to arrive at the optimum number of legs.

a) Maintenance of Stable Posture while the Vehicle is at a Standstill

In terms of the practical use of the vehicle, walking is not the only function of the walking vehicle. It must eventually stop walking and remain stationary in order to perform some of the assigned works. The walking vehicle, therefore, must have the function of remaining stationary at a place of any topography while maintaining a stable posture. One way to achieve this function is to attach a very large sole to each leg and let the soles support the stationary posture. But this system is not feasible in view of the rugged terrain over which the vehicle must operate. Thus, the vehicle must have three or more legs. A tripod walking vehicle, in the shape of camera's tripod, is structurally simple and it seems to have a high degree of controllability in performing a dynamic walk, as is discussed below. Serious consideration must be given to this tripod walking system in the future.

b) Practicability of Static Walk

In order to perform static and statically stable walk, the body of the vehicle must be supported by at least three legs at all times. Therefore, the walking vehicle must have four or more legs. If we are to measure the practicability of static walk by the "stability margin S," [McGhee, 1968] the stability margin S increases sharply as the number of legs increases from four to five and to six, but it tends to level off when the number of legs becomes greater than seven.

c) Raising the Speed of Static Walk

Let the notation V represent the maximum structural velocity of the leg's swing. The maximum travelling velocity of the walking vehicle is determined by V. Let K denote the number of the legs of the walking vehicle. When $K \geq 4$, and when the vehicle is performing static and stable walk functions, ratio (ρ) of the time duration in which a leg is in the swing against the time duration in which the leg is in contact with the ground is given by the following equation, $\rho=(1-\beta)/\beta$ where β is the duty factor [McGree, 1968] and $\beta=3/K$.

Thus, if we can neglect the time spent by the legs in vertical movement, and thus take the average returning velocity of the leg as V, the travelling velocity of the machine is given by V/3 when K=4, by 2/3V; when K=5, and by V when $K \geq 6$. When K=6 the two sets of tripods are alternately in swing and support of the body in the performance of the static walk function. When $K \geq 7$, the returning velocity of the legs can be reduced, but the travelling velocity of the vehicle cannot exceed V. When $K \leq 5$, it is necessary to adopt a dynamic walking function, in order to achieve maximum travelling velocity, V.

d) Practicability and Stability of the Dynamic Walk Function

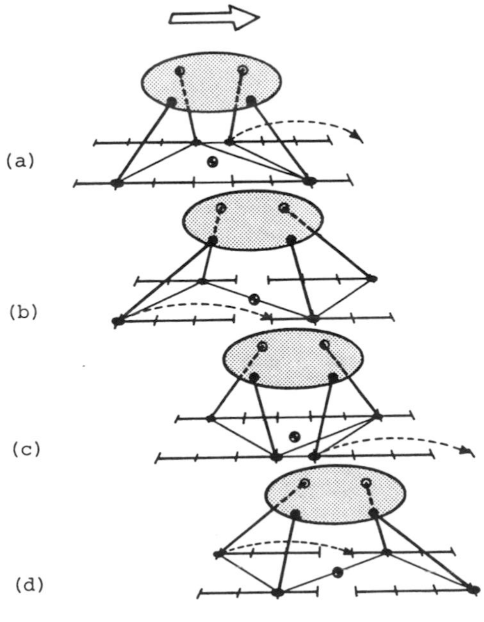

Fig. 1. The Pattern of Crawl Gait. Fundamental Sequence of Operation.

Here, we would like to discuss the dynamic walk function of a walking machine with three or more legs, which, as far as we know, has not been discussed very often. To state our conclusion first, the authors believe that, when a walking machine has three or more legs, the feasibility of the dynamic walk function is high in terms of both controllability and practicability. In order to see this, let us look at the Fig. 1, which illustrates the crawl gait of a quadruped walking machine. Instead of shifting into mode (b), dynamic walking can be achieved by putting leg No. 3 into swing before leg No. 1 touches the ground, letting the two legs of Nos. 2 and 4 support the entire body. In this case, the following two points can be theoretically made. 1) The dynamic and stable movement of the body can be treated as the inverse pendulum in a plane which is perpendicular to the straight line connecting legs Nos. 2 and 4. This means that freedom of control can be greatly reduced. 2) Even when the machine loses balance and falls to the ground due to poor control, the swinging legs will be being restored to the normal positions at a very close level to the ground. Therefore, the movement of the vehicle may be disturbed temporarily, but normal walking can be restored immediately. The details of these characteristics will be discussed at a later date.

e) Reduction of Freedom

The weight of the actuators in the total weight of the walking machine and the pressure it exerts on the net loading capacity of the vehicle may both be reduced in the future by new designs of power transmission systems and other improvements. But if we are to construct a walking machine using the kind of technology that is available today, it is highly desirable to restrict the freedom in the system of the walking machine to the lowest possible degree, because the weight of the actuator system is excessive when compared to the power output of the actuator. It is better to keep the number of legs as few as possible.

f) Overall Evaluations

Table 1 summarizes our discussions so far. At the present state of technology, the static walk function is far more practical than the dynamic walk function regarding the structure of the control system, efficiency of the motor drive system, etc. In our project, we decided to design a static walking machine. We will set the number of legs at four because the number of freedoms can be reduced to the lowest possible level. Also, a quadruped system can easily be adjusted to the dynamic walk function when we will have to introduce it in order to raise the travelling velocity of the vehicle. In a sense, a quadruped system forms a connecting link between the static and dynamic walking systems. Therefore, it has the possibility of an interesting evolution.

2-3 Morphology of Legs

a) Introduction of the Gravitationally Decoupled Actuator (GDA)

We will use the system of the gravitationally Decoupled Actuator, which we have proposed before, [Hirose, 1980a], [Hirose 1983a] as the actuator of the legs. In this system, the actuator's function is divided into two separate directions, one for support of the body against gravitational pull, and the other for horizental movement. The energy efficiency of the walking machine can be improved by the use of this system. Since the major part of the loss of potential energy, which was inevitable when ordinary type leg-joints were used, can be eliminated by it.

b) Choice of the Linear Actuator

Employment of the GDA system has been decided, yet there remains another question of whether to use the linear type actuator or rotating type. Generally speaking, it has been maintained thus far that one should use rotating joints as much as possible when he designs any component of the machine and that it is better not use sliding elements of linear movement because of the strength, low friction, and reliability of ball bearings. And a few examples of walking machine design which combined the GDA system will the linking system by the use of rotating joints alone [Waldron 1981], [Abe, 1983] have been advanced. Yet, in our opinion, the rotational drive mechanism in the structure of the GDA legs is not an absolute requirement for two reasons: 1) even though quasi-linear movement is realized in terms of translation movement, acceleration in the vertical direction will become unignorable during high-speed operation, causing body vibration during operation; 2) In order to increase the freedom in choosing the spot at which a leg comes into contact with the ground, the addition of the linear drive system will eventually become inevitable.

On the other hand, the technological improvements in recent years of linear sliding machine elements have been so remarkable that many elements with high reliability, low friction, and high load capacity have already been put into use. In our project, we decided, therefore, to choose a system in which GDA's are used with the linear movement system.

Evaluations \ Number of legs	1	2	3	4	5	6	7	8
Capacity of Maintaining Static Posture	●	●	○	◎	◎	◎	◎	◎
Capacity of Performing Statically Stable Walking	●	●	●	○	◎	◎	◎	◎
Capacity of Performing High Speed Statically Stable Walking	●	●	●	△	○	◎	◎	◎
Capacity of Performing Dynamically Stable Walking	△	△	◎	◎	◎	○	○	○
Mechanical Simplicity in terms of Limited Degrees of Freedom of Motion	◎	◎	○	○	○	△	△	△

Table 1 Number of Legs and Walk Function

In the near future, when a large-scale, automatic walking machine is developed, it is likely that hydraulic cylinders will be used in the structure of the walking machine as in the case of a new walking machine already experimented with at Ohio State University. In that case, the back and forth movement of the hydraulic cylinders can be transferred directly to the driving movement of legs. This, we believe, is one of the merits of the linear movement system.

c) Adoption of a Three Dimensional Pantographic Mechanism (PANTOMEC)

As we have done before, [Hirose, 1980b] we will use the three dimensional pantographic mechanism (PANTOMEC) in order to implement the linear drive type GDA. The designed structure of PANTOMEC is shown in Fig. 2. The reasons why we chose this mechanism are: 1) PANTOMEC allows to drive legs following the principle of GDA 2) PANTOMEC can secure a wide range of the legs' range because the legs consist of a joint-type structure 3) The movement of the legs' feet are easily controlled in cartesian coordinates 4) The weight of the legs, which must perform back and forth movements, can be kept low because the actuators can be installed in the main body of the vehicle.

d) Insect Type or Mammal Type?

The authors have classified the types of legs of the walking machine into the insect type and mammal type, and discussed the characteristics, advantages and disadvatages of each type. [Hirose, 1980a] Of course, if both types are practical for the construction of a walking machine, we have nothing else to hope for needless to say. In our design, we decided to leave this choice open because our objective is to develop a highly flexible system.

2-4 Structure of Leg-Wheel Hybrid System

When we think of the hybrid system of legs and wheels, the choice which we have before us is where to put the driving wheels; at the tip of each leg or on the body? We opted to put the wheels on the body because our goals were: 1) To make the weight of legs as light as possible in order to facilitate the high-speed swinging movement of the legs; and 2) To increase the range of gait control when the vehicle is operating on land of irregular topography or to minimize resistance to movement when the vehicle is operating on land of soft texture by taking advantage of the mode of movement in which the vehicle comes into contact with the ground over which it operates at discontinuous locations. Thus, the vehicle will take the walking mode of movement only over unreclaimed land surfaces. That is, the legs will be folded up and put into storage when the vehicle travels over highway; but the legs will be deployed when the vehicle proceeds into unreclaimed land or when the vehicle must change its orientation by rotating the body in one location.

3. Design of TITAN III

In the following, we will describe the details of

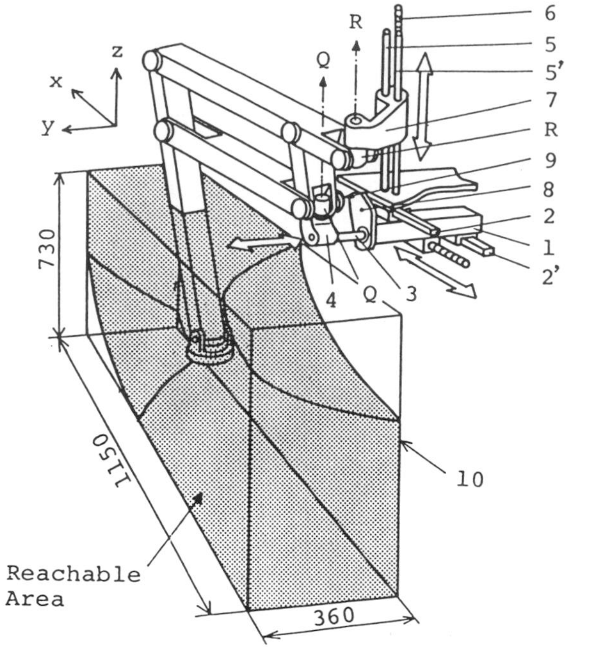

Fig. 2. Driving Mechanism of a Three Dimensional PANTOMEC with Enlarged Range

TITAN III, the quadruped walking machine constructed according to the design principles stated above.

3-1 Structure of Legs and Driving Mechanism

PANTOMEC is used as the structure of legs, and Carbon FRP is used as material in order to provide a high level rigidity to the legs and to make them as light as possible at the same time. The lengths of the thigh and shank are both 600mm with a combined length of 1200mm. The total weight of one leg is 3.4kg, and the pantograph's magnifying ratio is set at 1 : 3.

In order to expand the leg's scope and in order for the legs to take both insect and mammal-type shapes, we designed the driving mechanism illustrated in Fig. 2. Here, the y-axis actuator unit 1 is supported by the roller linear guides 2 and 2', thus it can drive along the x-axis. At the same time, the movement of the y-axis actuator unit along the y-axis is guided by ball spline 3 to the side of vehicle body. And ball spline 3 is connected to joint Q of the pantograph mechanism by eccentric block 4 in such a way that linkage can turn freely around the vertical axis. Thus the foot of the leg are made to move in the two directions along the x-and y- axes. The movement in the direction along the z-axis is given to the leg by the drive of U-shaped block 7 which is connected to joint R of the pantographic mechanism, and supported by ball splines 5 and 5', to which up-and-down movement is given by ball screw 6. The U-shaped block is connected to joint R in such a way that the linkage can turn freely around vertical axis R, also.

In this new model, the driving mechanism along the

y-axis, which was located under point Q in the previous models, [Hirose, 1980b] is installed in the lower part of the main body, and the leg is driven from one end of the spline. Thus, even when the leg is extended straightly downward and is formed into a mammal-type leg, the driving mechanism along the y-axis will not interfere with the leg's y-axis movement. As a result, the range has been extended as is shown in Fig. 2. Incidentally, the reason why blocks 4 and 7 are shaped the way they are is because interference with the motion of the legs can be eliminated, and the range of the legs can be extended.

The overhanging structure used to support the driving mechanism along the y-axis may be judged as structurally weak. Yet, we have to notice that the support system of the body weight by legs can always be regarded as essentially an overhanging beam structure. Needless to say, the leg mechanism is designed in such a way that the legs can bear the total weight of 120kg at one time with two legs.

The range of TITAN III's legs has the form as is shown in Fig. 2 in which a long cube from which two spherical portions are carved off can be seen. We believe that extensive research in the processes of gait control is called for in order to utilize the entire range.

As actuators for the x-, y-, and z-axes, DC motors of 30w, 20w, 30w, respectively, coupled with the servo systems, using potentio-meters are used. Maximum speed components of the tip of the leg along the three axes, were, in actual measurements, 560mm/sec, 100mm/sec, and 65mm/sec, respectively. Maximum power delivered along the three axes, was approximately 100N, 100N and 800N, respectively.

3-2 Introduction of a Freedom Limiting Board

If we adopt the PANTOMEC design as is shown in Fig. 2 so that the leg can be deployed in the shape of a mammal type, one serious difficulty arises. When the vertical axes Q and R come into alignment, that is, at the singular point, the position of PANTOMEC around axis R cannot be fixed uniformly. Although PANTOMEC has several meritorious points, this one difficulty must never be forgotten.

In the design of TITAN III, we arrived at a partial solution to this difficulty by installing what we call the "freedom limiting board" at the end of the linear bearing of the y-axis spline as is shown in Fig. 2 by 8. In this system, when the vehicle is proceeding straight forward, which takes up a major part of the operating time under normal circumstances, the projection along the y-axis is set at the shortest limit so that the leg is swung in inside plane 10 of the leg's range, and, the inner panel 9 of the leg at joint R is in contact with the freedom limiting board at all times. Thus, even when axes Q and R come into alignment, if the leg is confined in sagittal plane 10, the posture of the vehicle can be definitely fixed. Thus, the difficulty of fixing the posture is solved.

Though a slight complexity develops concerning the gait control at the time when the vehicle shifts from the mode of travelling straight forward to other modes of operation because of the shortening of the y-axis spline, it also has positive effects. Since the legs repeat the back and forth movement in the sagittal plane alone, and therefore do not swing sideways, kinetic energy losses are kept at a minimum and the vehicle can operate in narrow land areas. If we are to provide movement along the y-axis to the leg, utilizing freedom in that direction, the only thing we must do is to arrange the process to that effect. The introduction of the freedom limiting board is in no way detrimental to the essentail functions of PANTOMEC.

3-3 Tactile Sensors

The feet of the walking machine are the junctures at which most of the interactions between the walking machine and its external enviornment take place. The sensing functions of the feet are of great significance. The feet of TITAN III are equipped with tactile sensors as is shown in Fig. 3. They have four functions. 1) One is an ON-OFF sole switch which monitors the sole's contact with the ground. (cf. fig. 3, (4))

The other tactile sensors are new inventions of ours. They are whisker sensors which utilize extremely high elasticity of shape memory alloy. These whisker sensors are of an arc shape, and a pair of electodes sandwich them from above

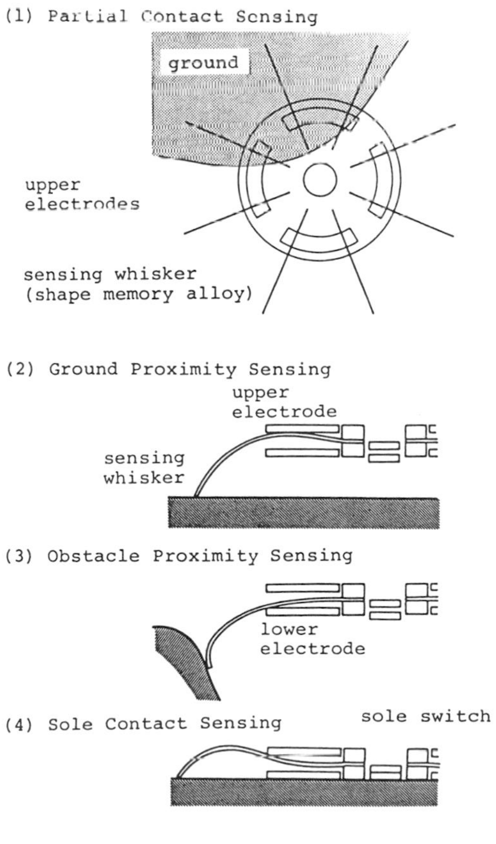

Fig. 3. Four Functions of Foot Tactile Sensors.

and below near the fulcrum. The principle of the whisker sensor can be explained as when the whisker contacts an object and bends, its base is also bent to contact the electrode, and this contact signal is electrically picked up. These whisker sensors fulfill three functions. 2) When the whiskers touch an obstacle, they come into contact with the lower electrode and signal action to avoid contact with the obstacle (cf. Fig. 3, (3)). 3) When a foot is being lowered, the whiskers will touch the ground first, and they come into contact with the upper elctrode, thus signalizing an appropriate action to slow down the speed of lowering the foot (cf. Fig. 3, (2)). 4) The upper electrode is divided into four equal parts so that it can pick up signals from different directions independently. This device can detect partial contact of sole with rugged and irregular ground surfaces (cf. Fig. 3, (1)).

We used shape memory alloy because it has a very high elastic limit of 6%, which is more than ten times as high as that of piano strings (SWP) and other generally used materials. Since those whiskers come repeatedly into rough contact with ground surfaces, it is the best material we have today to use as sensing equipment of the feet. The whisker sensor is believed to become a proximity sensor with high durability against soil stains, in comparison to the proximity sensor utilizing the supersonic light beam system, should the base of the whisker sensor be covered by materials such as silicone rubber.

3-4 Posture Sensor

We used two of servo accelerometer posture sensors. They were installed in two directions to detect rolling and pitching. The sensor has a relatively high characteristic frequency of 250Hz, so it proved to be suitable high-speed posture sensor if a low-pass filter is coupled with it.

3-5 Control System

A 16 bit microcomputer (CPU 8086 with 8087) PC 9801 is used as the control computer of TITAN III. It is located on the outside of the walking machine. The computer and the walking machine are linked together by DA with twelve channels (for command of servo-machinisms), AD with 14 channels (for signals of potentiometers plus two channels for posture sensors), and digital IO which handles the signals from 24 bits tactile sensors. All of the control systems use C compiler (CIC 86 on CP/M 86). The entire control system of the present model uses a memory storage capacity of about thirty kilo bytes. The sample time to start up control system levels C and D discussed in [Hirose, 1980c] is 50m sec at the present.

4..Characteristics of TITAN III's Basic Actions

The experiments we have conducted using our model of the walking machine TITAN III are the operation of wheels with legs in reserve (photo 2), walking sideways, rotation around a randomly chosen axis (photo 5 shows the rotation around the axis which goes through the center of gravity), walking on rugged and irregular surfaces, and climbing up and down staircases (photo 4). In photo 6, the motion of the body and foot are shown by the trajectories of small lamps. The maximum walking velocity at present was 50mm/sec. The details of the experiments will be reported in another paper together with their controlling algorithms.

BIBLIOGRAPHY

Abe, M., Kaneko, M., Nishizawa, S., "A study on a Hexapod Walking Machine Using Quasi-Linear Mechanism -- Development of Experimental Models MELWALK Mark I and II," Proc. of 1st Annual Conf. of Robotics Society of Japan, 125-128, 1983. (In Japanese)

Bekker, M. G., Introduction to Terrain-Vehicle Systems, Univ. of Michigan Press, Ann Arbov, Michigan, 1969

Hirose, S., Umetani, Y., 1980a, Some considerations on leg configuration and locomotion properties of walking vehicles (In Japanese), Biomechanism 5, University of Tokyo Press, pp. 242-250.

Hirose, S. and Umetani, Y. 1980b, The synthesis of basic motion regulator systems for quadruped walking vehicle and its experiments, (in Japanese) Trans. of the Society of Instrument and Control Engineers, 16 (5), pp. 747-753

Hirose, S. and Umetani, Y. 1980c, The basic motion regulation system for a quadruped walking vehicle, Trans. of ASME, 80-DET-34.

Hirose, S., Nose, M., Kikuchi, H., Umetani, Y., "Adaptive Gait Control of a Quadruped Walking Vehicle," Proc. of the 1st Int'l Symp. of Robotics Research, MIT Press, 1983. a.

Hirose, S., Kikuchi, H., Umetani, Y., "A study on a Sophisticated Gait Control System of Quadruped Walking Machine, No. 5 the Height Control of the Center of Gravity," 1983b, Proc. of 1st Annual Conf. of Robotics Society of Japan, 117-118, (in Japanese)

McGhee, R. B., Frank, A. A., "On the Stability Properties of Quadruped Creeping Gait," Mathematical Biosciences, 3(3), pp. 331-351, 1968.

Waldron, K. J., Kinzel, G. L., "The Relationship between Actuator Geometry and Mechanical Efficiency in Robots," Proc. of the 4th ROMANCY Symp., Zaborow, Poland, pp. 366-374, 1981.

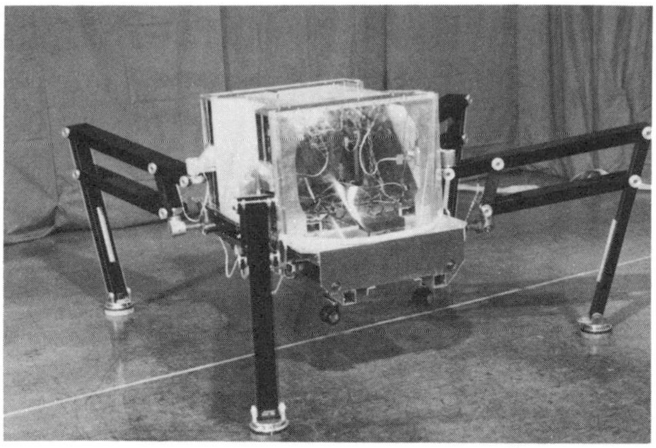

Photo 1 Total View of Our Model TITAN III (picture shows a position in which legs are extended sideways in the y-direction,)

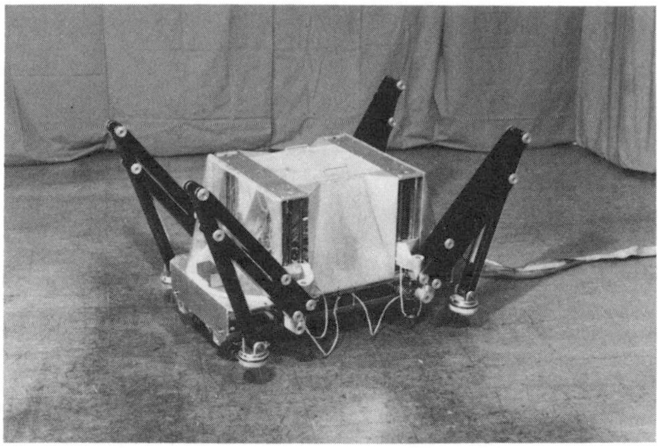

Photo 2 TITAN III in the Wheel Mode of Operation

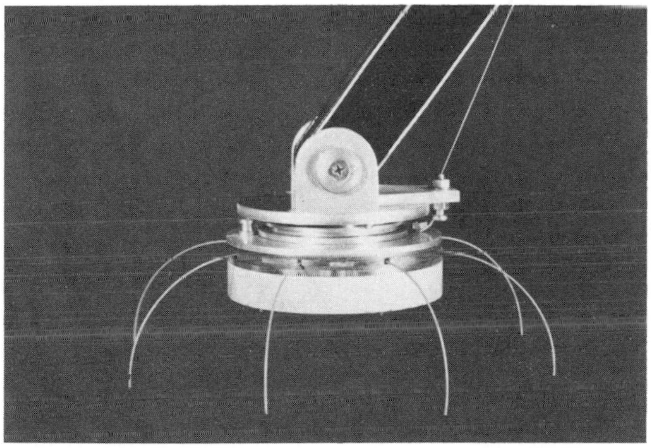

Photo 3 Mechanism of Foot and Sensing Equipemnt (shape memory alloy is used as material of the whisker sensors.)

Photo 4 Driving Mechanism of the Leg (designed to reduce interference between moving parts.)

Photo 5 TITAN III Performing Stationary Rotating Operation (lights attached to the front and back of the body indicate the rotation movement of the body.)

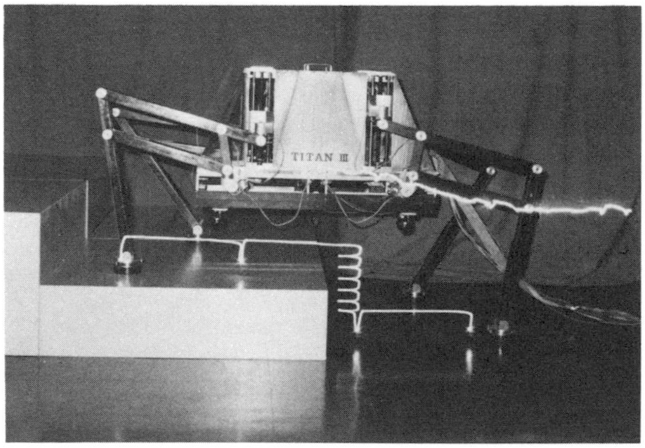

Photo 6 TITAN III Climbing Steps (light attached to the foot shows the probe motion of the leg at each step. Also, the light attached to the center of the body shows the way in which the smooth translation movement of the body is carried out by forming a revolving plane for shifting the center of gravity.)

GUIDE DOG ROBOT

Susumu Tachi and Kiyoshi Komoriya

Mechanical Engineering Laboratory, MITI
Tsukuba Science City
Ibaraki, 305 Japan

The Guide Dog Robot Project started in the 1977 fiscal year at MEL. The project's goal is to enhance mobility aids for the blind by providing them with the functions of guide dogs, i.e., obedience in navigating or guiding a blind master, intelligent disobedience in detecting and avoiding obstacles in his/her path, and well-organized man-machine communication which does not interfere with his/her remaining senses. In this paper the design concept of the Guide Dog Robot MELDOG is described first. Next, the navigation method using an organized map and landmarks, obstacle detection/avoidance system based on the ultrasonic environment measurement and man-machine communication via electrocutaneous stimulation system are presented. The results of the feasibility studies using MELDOG MARK I, II, III and IV test hardwares are discussed. Future problems are also elucidated.

INTRODUCTION

Independent travel is one of the strongest desires of about three hundred and forty thousand blind or severely visually impaired individuals in Japan. Since the concept of technological assistance for the blind is of recent origin (after World War II), they have been largely on their own, depending upon more sensitive and subtle utilization of their remaining senses, and extending them through the use of the cane, or relying upon human or dog guides.

Ideal mobility aids for the blind should support the three necessay functions for mobility; i.e., (1) the blind person's next step, (2) his/her directional orientation, and (3) his/her navigation along reasonably long travel path on both familiar and unfamiliar terrain [Mann, 1974]. However, existing mobilty devices; e.g., the Pathsounder [Russell, 1971], the Sonic Glasses [Kay, 1973], the Laser Cane [Farmer et al., 1975], the Mowat Sensor [Morrissette et al., 1981] and the Nottingham Obstacle Detector [Dodds et al., 1981], have only functions (1) and (2). The information processing system employed by the existing devices is very simple and crude so that the blind user must concentrate on the devices, resulting in the fatigue of the user or loss of other information which otherwise might be obtained through the remaining senses.

It is quite desirable to design more intelligent mobility aids for the blind which combine the above three functions with the enhancement of functions (1) and (2) by increasing the information processed by the device or the machine. These devices should warn only if the blind persons are in danger, thereby not distracting the attention of the blind traveler from other potential cues through their remaining senses. This design concept is very similar to traveling with a guide dog (Seeing-eye).

The purpose of the Guide Dog Robot Project (dubbed MELDOG) which started in 1977 is to enhance mobility aids for the blind by providing them with the functions of guide dogs; i.e., obedience in navigating a blind master, intelligent disobedience in detecting and avoiding obstacles in his/her path, and well-organized man-machine communication which does not interfere with his/her remaining senses.

In this paper the design concept of MELDOG is first described. Next, the navigation using an organized map and landmarks, obstacle detection/avoidance system based on the ultrasonic environment measurement and man-machine communication via an electrocutaneous stimulation system are presented. While theoretical consideration has been done for the realization of these functions by machines, feasibility studies of the proposed methods have been conducted both by computer simulation and field tests using the test hardwares.

The results of the feasibility experiments using MELDOG MARK I, II, III and IV test hardwares are discussed and the future problems are elucidated.

GUIDE DOG ROBOT

In order to realize a robot that can assist a blind master's mobility, the following three fundamental control and communication problems of man-machine systems must be solved.

(a) How a robot guides itself by using an organized map of the environment and registered landmarks in the environment.

(b) How the robot finds obstacles which are not registered on the map and avoids them.

(c) How the robot informs its blind master about the route and the obstacles detected.

Two main functions of real guide dogs are obedience and intelligent disobedience, which corresponds to the navigation and obstacle detection, respectively. Adding to these is the necessary communication between the blind master and the dog is necessary. In order to realize these main functions by solving the above three problems we have set the following specifications for the guide dog robot:

(1) In principle, the master takes the initiative. The master commands the robot by control switches connected by a wired link. The robot precedes the master and stops at each intersection, waits for the master's next order (right, left,straight, or stop) and obeys it. If the master does not know the area and wants full automatic guidance, all he has to do is assign the starting code and the destination code. The robot determines whether there is a route to the destination. If more than one route exists, it chooses the optimal route and guides the master accordingly. The robot stops at each intersection as a safety precaution (See Landmark Sensor Subsystem of Fig. 1).

(2) When the robot detects a dangerous situation on the road, it no longer obeys the master's command but gives him a warning. If the obstacle is moving toward the master, it stops and alerts the moving object and the master. If the obstacle is moving in the same direction but slower than the master, it asks the master to reduce his/her speed to follow the preceding object, probably a human traveler. If something is crossing in front of the robot, the robot waits till it passes. If it detects an obstacle which does not move, it tries to determine if it is possible to find space that will permit the safe transport of the master around the obstacle. If space exists, it safely guides the master around the obstacle. If not, it tries to find a new route to the destination without using an undesirable path (See Obstacle Detection Subsystem of Fig. 1).

(3) In general , the speed of the robot is controlled so that it coincides with that of the blind master's gait. Thus, if the master walks slowly or rapidly, the robot moves accordingly, keeping the distance between them almost constant. As long as the master is considered to be safe by the robot he is not warned, so that (s)he may concentrate on his/her remaining senses and his/her own decisions. Only when (s)he fails to detect an obstacle or is out of the safety zones, is (s)he warned by the robot (See Man-Machine Communication Subsysytem of Fig. 1).

NAVIGATION

The fundamental data base of the robot is its navigation map stored in the auxiliary memory; e.g., cassette tapes, and transferred into the main memory of the robot when in use. The navigation map consists of information about intersections, i.e., names and types of intersections, distance between two adjacent intersections, and orientation to the adjacent intersections. Information on the landmarks to identify the intersections and other essential points of navigation are also included in the navigation map. This map is represented as an automaton as shown in Fig. 2.

The next step the robot should take is to identify the real intersection as specified on the map and correct its position and orientation so that it can travel farther. In order to do so, specific landmarks are chosen for each intersection or other essential points of navigation. In the initial phase (from 1977 to 1982) white painted lines on the streets with a length of about 2m and a width of 0.15m were adopted as the landmarks. These marks had to be set at every crossing at this stage of development. The automaton represention map for the robot could be automatically produced by an off-line computer from an ordinary map using picture processing techniques. Landmark laying

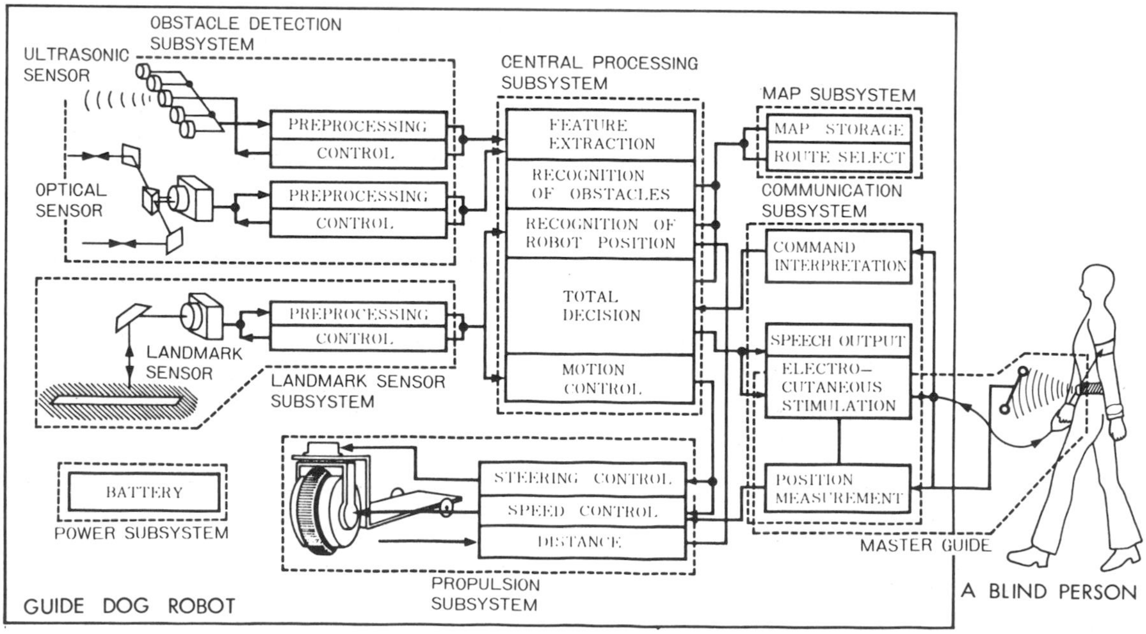

Fig. 1 Schematic diagram of the guide dog robot system (MELDOG).

instructions which would be used to place the landmarks on the streets could be provided at the same time [Kaneko et al., 1983].

At the second stage (from 1983 to the present) registered natural landmarks such as poles and walls are being used as markers for the correction of the robot's position and orientation. However, the navigation method is fundamentally the same.

Navigation Map

Figure 2 shows an example of landmarks set on the streets and the automaton representation of the map of landmarks in the memory. Landmark codes which contain information on intersection identification number, intersection type, i.e., crossings, forked roads, straight roads, etc., and stop information, i.e., it should stop at the landmark or not, correspond to the states of the automaton. Commands from the blind traveler (or Central Processing Subsystem (CPS) in automatic guidance mode) such as turn to the left, right, or go straight correspond to the input of the automaton, while information to the CPS and/or the blind master such as the steering angle to be used to reach the next landmark, the distance between two landmarks, and intersection attributes correspond to the automaton outputs.

The same map can be interpreted as the tree-structure shown in Fig. 3. In this representation landmark codes correspond to the nodes of the tree and commands from the user correspond to the branches. Each branch has an attribute represented as the output in the automaton representation. If the user assigns a starting landmark code and a destination code, the robot can find whether there is a route to reach the destination or not, by using the tree-structure representation of the map and searching techniques commonly used in artificial intelligence study, and can find an optimal route if plural routes exist.

Once an optimal route is determined the robot can determine the command sequence such as turn to the left, go 30 m, then turn to the right etc., by following the tree-structure. This sequence is used as the input sequence to the aforementioned automaton, resulting in the fully automatic guidance of the traveler. Photo 1 shows a general view of the outdoor experiments of the test MELDOG MARK II using landmarks and the navigation map.

Figure 4 shows an example of the navigation map and some results of the route search. In the figure, s indicates the total length of the route in meters. In this example the area is 500 m x 500 m with 276 landmarks, which requires 2 K byte memories.

The search area of the optimal route can be extended by connecting the above sub-maps. Figure 5 shows an example of an extended map. By applying the dynamic programming method an optimal route can be found that minimizes the total length of the route. Any criteria can be chosen arbitrarily, e.g., the total length of the route, minimum number of intersections encountered, etc., or a combination of these [Tachi et al., 1980].

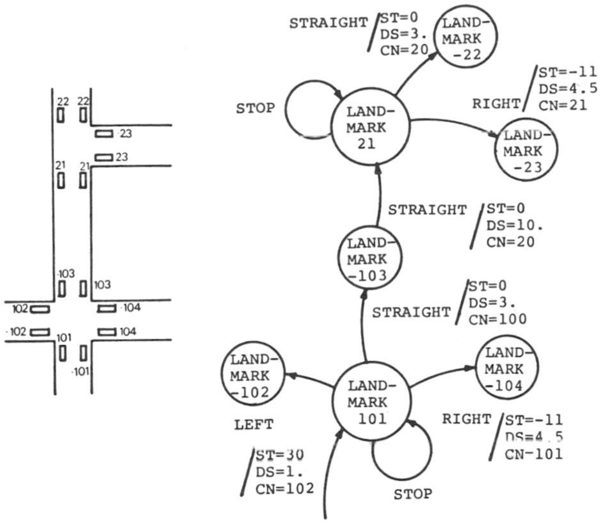

Fig. 2 An example of the landmarks and the automaton representation of the navigation map.

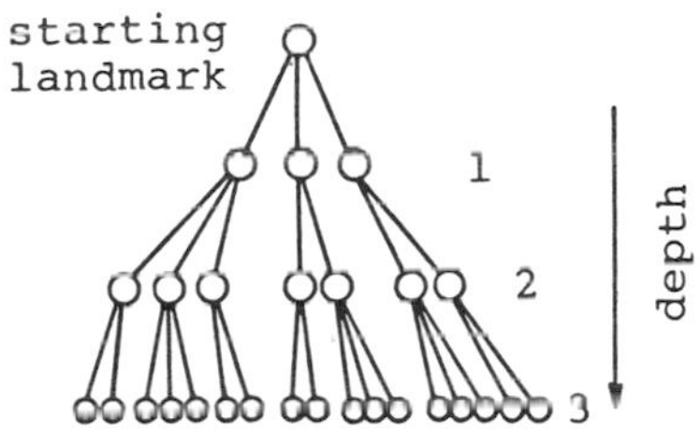

Fig. 3 Tree-structure representation of the navigation map.

Photo. 1 Navigation experiment with MELDOG MARK II using landmarks and navigation map.

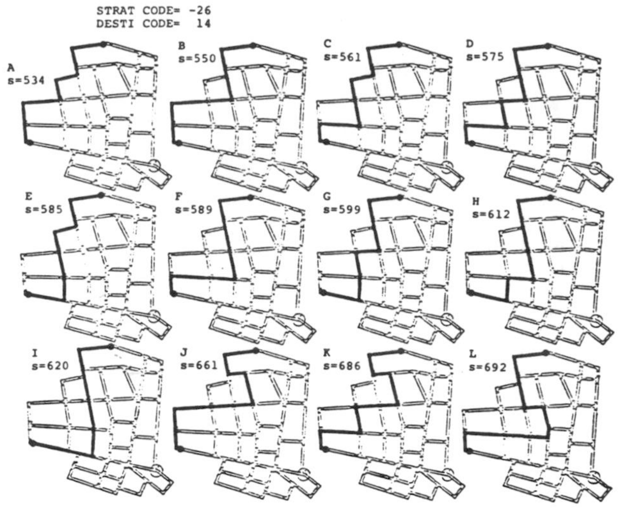

Fig. 4 Results of the route search.

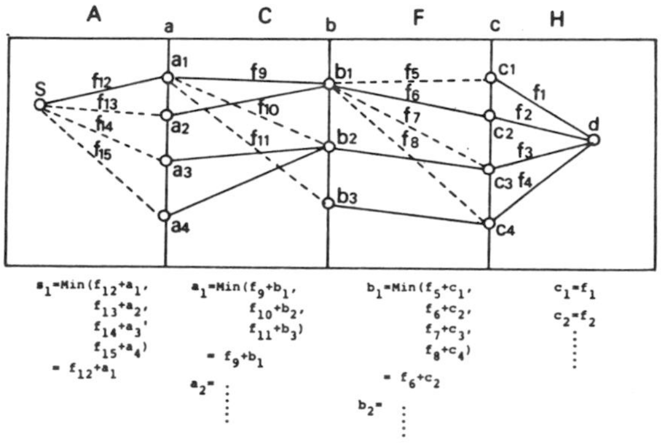

Fig. 5 Optimal route searching by connecting sub-maps.

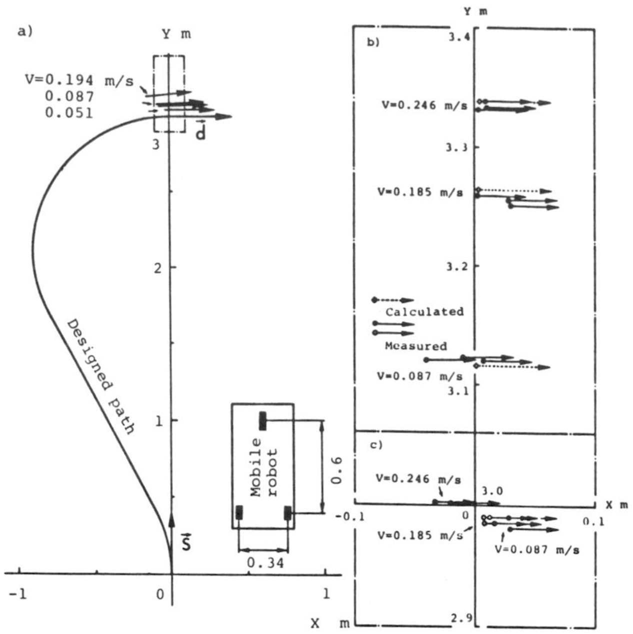

Fig. 6 Path generation and the result of the path following experiments.

Navigation between Landmarks

The robot travels from one landmark to another using landmark information in the navigation map to generate a desirable path.

Figure 6 shows an example of path generation when the starting vector and the destination vector are assigned. The designed path, which connects the current position with an arbitary intermediate destination, consists of two arcs and their common tangent. After determining a path the robot travels along it using the encoders of the steering shaft and the rear wheels. Each arrow of Fig.6 indicates the final experimental position of the robot after following the path. In the figure, b) and c) show better navigation results through controlled steering compensation [Komoriya et al., 1984].

In navigation using internal sensors, accumulation of error from a course is inevitable. In order to guide the robot along the path accurately it is necessary to compensate for this. Three methods are studied to solve this problem.

i) landmark tracking method

In the first method landmarks are used to compensate for course error. When the robot reaches a landmark, it adjusts its orientation and position by moving along the landmark (See Fig.7). The robot has two landmark sensors, one at its front and one at its rear end, which optically detect landmark edges. After lateral course error Δy and orientational error $\Delta\phi$ are measured, equation (1) gives the steering angle which enables the robot to follow the landmark [Komoriya et al., 1983, Tachi et al., 1980].

$$\theta = K_1 \cdot \Delta y + K_2 \cdot \Delta\phi \qquad \ldots.(1)$$

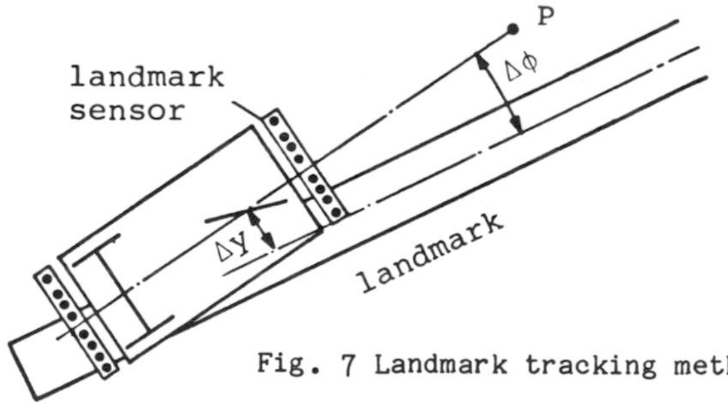

Fig. 7 Landmark tracking method.

ii) Utilization of road edges

A landmark tracking method is effective if the deviation from the course can be within the detection area of landmark sensors when the robot reaches a landmark. This condition restricts the distance between landmarks. Using the road edges as an auxiliary method, supports landmark tracking, and enables the distance between landmarks to be longer.

Fig.8 shows a general view of this method. The robot detects the road edge, shown as the x-coordinate axis, from the points where the road edge crosses the CCD camera's field of view by processing the visual data using the road edge attributes of the navigation map. After calculating ϕ_R robot's orientation to the road edge, and y_R distance from its course by equations (2), the steering angle is given by equation (3).

$$\phi_R = \tan^{-1}\frac{X_2 - X_1}{Y_1 - Y_2}$$
$$y_R = X_1 \cos\phi_R + Y_1 \sin\phi_R \qquad \text{....(2)}$$

$$\theta(t+\tau) = K_1\,\phi_R(t) - K_2\,(y_R(t) - y_s) \qquad \text{....(3)}$$

where τ is sampling time.

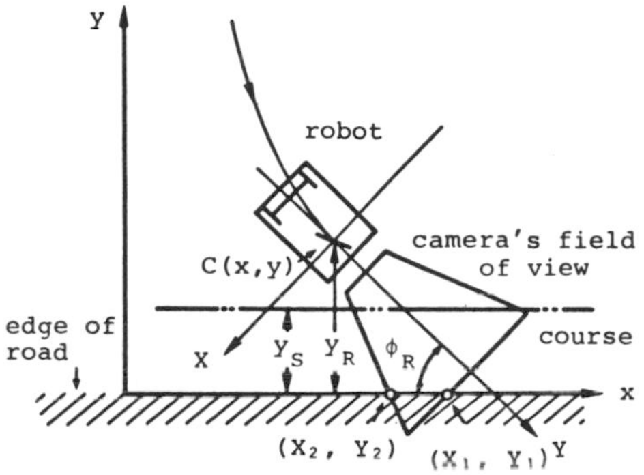

Fig. 8 Utilization of road edges.

Photo. 2 MELDOG MARK IIb with CCD visual sensor for detection of road edge.

Photo.2 shows the CCD camera assembled for this purpose and installed on MELDOG MARK IIb. Its field of view can be changed to the front, right and left side of the robot by turning the table which supports the camera and far and near by tilting the mirror which alters the vision line. One micro-computer is mounted on board the robot to control these operation and to process visual data exclusively [Tachi et al., 1982 a].

iii) Utilization of natural landmarks

Instead of artificial landmarks such as painted lines, natural landmarks such as poles and walls which have rather simple shapes so that the sensor on board the robot can measure their position easily are more desirable for navigation.

From the view point of signal processing in real-time, ultrasonic sensors are preferable. The construction of the ultrasonic sensor used here and the position measurement algorithm is described in the next section.

Landmark position using this kind of ultrasonic sensor is measured as shown in Fig.9. In this figure the robot is assumed to move along the x-axis and to measure the position of a cylinder-like shaped object from the plural points Pi. In order to increase accuracy, only distance data si is used. Using the radius of the object, relative position of the object (xm, ym) can be calculated by equations (4). However this information is not sufficient to decide the absolute position of the robot because of the lack of directional data.

$$x_m = \frac{1}{2n(n+1)d}\left\{\sum_{i=1}^{n} s^2_{-i} - \sum_{i=1}^{n} s_i^2 - 2r\sum_{i=1}^{n}(s_i - s_{-i})\right\}$$
$$y_m = \sqrt{\frac{1}{2n}\left\{\sum_{i=1}^{n}(s_i+r)^2 + \sum_{i=1}^{n}(s_{-i}+r)^2\right\} - \frac{1}{6}(n+1)(2n+1)d^2 - x_m^2} \qquad \text{....(4)}$$

Among several methods to solve this problem such as utilization of a rate gyro sensor and two landmarks at one time, the use of flat surfaces

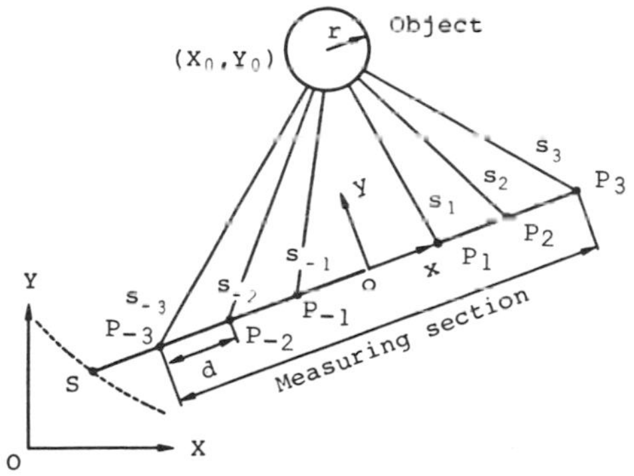

Fig. 9 A method to measure an object as a landmark.

Photo .3 MELDOG MARK IV used to demonstrate the navigation using walls as landmarks.

such as walls is practical if the navigation is inside buildings. Photo.3 shows the test hardware MELDOG MARK IV which has this ability to use walls as landmarks and with ultrasonic sensors at both sides of its body [Komoriya et al., 1984].

Obstacle Detection

It is important for the robot to find various obstacles while it guides the master, which appear in front of it, such as obstacles which block its path, objects and humans that come toward the robot and the master, steps or uneven streets, overhanging objects like awnings, etc.

In order to detect these obstacles, an ultrasonic sensor, which can determine not only the distance from the obstacle but also its direction by the traveling time measurement of ultrasound was developed.

Fig.10. shows its construction with one transmitter and plural receivers arranged in a array d distance apart from each other. A tone burst of frequency 40KHz and duration time 25msec is sent by the transmitter. Each of the receivers detects the reflected signal by obstacles ti seconds later from the transmission, which corresponds to the distance Si from T to Ri through the obstacle surface. Detected signals are amplified, processed by band-pass-filters and compared with the appropriate threshold so as to make stop-pulses for the counters which measure ti in order to get the aforementioned Si.

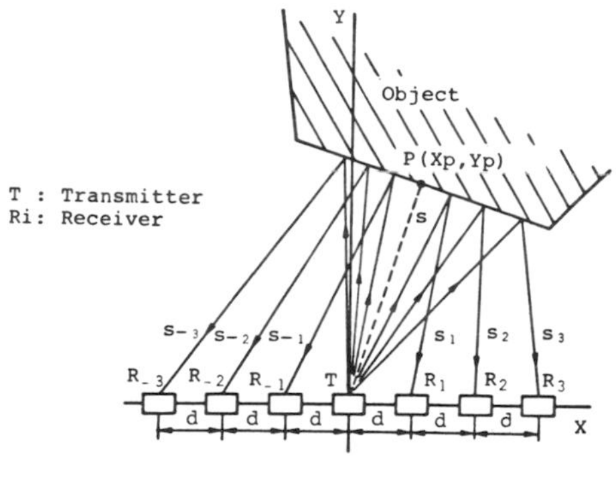

Fig. 10 Construction of ultrasonic sensor.

Location of the object can be calculated from Si by equations (5), which assumes that the ultrasound is reflected at a flat surface as shown in the figure. According to the numerical calculation this algorithm gives almost correct position and direction with less than two percent error if the obstacle has a cylindrical surface or is a circle in a two dimensional figure [Komoriya et al., 1984].

$$s = \sqrt{\frac{1}{2n}\left(\sum_{i=-n}^{n} s_i^2 - \sum_{i=-n}^{n} i^2 d^2\right)} \qquad \ldots .(5)$$

$$x_p = \frac{1}{2n(n+1)}\left(\sum_{i=-1}^{-n} s_i^2 - \sum_{i=1}^{n} s_i^2\right) \qquad y_p = \sqrt{s^2 - x_p^2}$$

When the robot detects an object in its sensing area, it can determine the relative speed V of the object by measuring distance at more than two instances. If V is positive, it means that the object is moving away from the robot and it will not bother the robot. Therefore the robot needs not take any action.

If V is negative, the robot behaves as follows. If the absolute value of V is larger than the speed of the robot Vr, i.e. the object is coming towards the robot, the robot quickly stops and warns the master and the object in order to avoid a collision.

If the absolute value of V is smaller than Vr, i.e. the object is moving in the same direction of the robot and the master at a slower speed, the robot asks the master to slow down and tries to follow the object keeping a safe distance between them (See Photo.4).

If the absolute value of V is equal to Vr, i.e. the object is standing still, the robot modifies its path to avoid the obstacle. Fig.11 shows the path to avoid an obstacle in front of it. At the

Photo. 4 MELDOG MARK III in the experiment to demonstrate an obstacle detection.

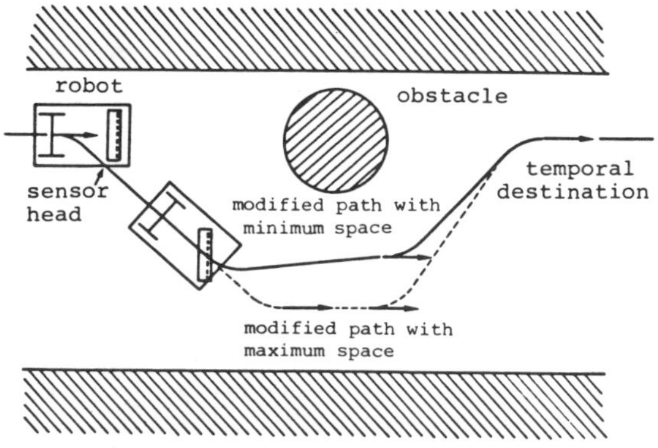

Fig. 11 Example showing the avoidance of an obstacle by modifying the robot's path.

time the robot detects a stationary obstacle, it generates a path with maximum space between the obstacle and the robot as shown by the dotted line.

While it moves along this modified path, the ultrasonic sensor continues to detect obstacles along the road by turning the sensor head. If the obstacle leaves the detection area of the sensor and the robot has open space in front of it, the robot generates its path again to return to the initial path with minimum space as shown by the solid line after avoiding the obstacle.

When the robot doesnot have open space along the path with maxmum space, i.e. the road is blocked, the robot turns back generating a new path to its final destination.

COMMUNICATION

In order to guide a blind individual in accordance with the information acquired, an information communication channel between the master and the robot must be established.

When a robot which directs or guides a blind individual has somehow acquired information about the direction of, and width of, an unobstructed path along which it should lead the blind individual, the problem is the choice of sensory path display and its safe margins appropriate for presentation to the remaining exterior receptive senses of the blind individual. Quantitative comparison method of display scheme has been proposed and an optimal auditory display scheme has been sought [Tachi, et al., 1983].

In the MELDOG system the location of the master is measured by the robot in real-time by the triangulation of the ultrasonic oscillator put on the belt of the master and the two receivers on board the robot (See Fig.12). The result of the measurement is used to control the robot's speed to coincide with that of the blind master.

A safety zone is set behind the robot in which the master is supposed to walk (See Fig.13). The triangulation is also used to transmit warning signals from the robot to the master. When he is outside the zone he is warned by the robot, while he receives no feedback when he is safe. When the orientation of the master within the safety zone is not appropriate, the Master Guide detects the condition and informs the master. These signals are transmitted through a wired link and presented to the master in the form of electrocutaneous stimulation. One set of Ag-AgCl wet electrodes is placed on the skin of each brachium. The signals used are pulse trains with a pulse width of about 100 μs, the energy of which is controlled by a constant energy circuit [Tachi, et al., 1982 b].

In the test hardware MELDOG MARK I (See Photo.5) the repetition rate of the pulse train was set at 100 pps for normal warning stimuli that the master was outside the safety zone and 10 pps for warning that the master's orientation was inappropriate. For example, the signal presented to the right arm with 100 pps means the master should step to the right to come back to the safety zone and with 10 pps means (s)he should turn his/her body counterclockwise to correct his/her orientation [Tachi, et al., 1978 and 1981a].

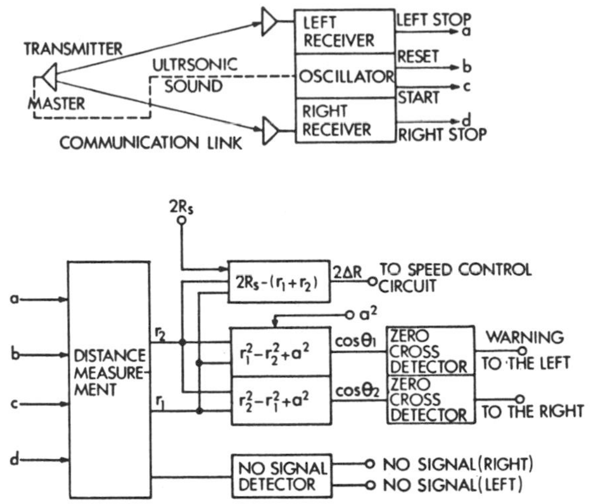

Fig. 12 Block diagram of measurement system of the master location using ultrasounds.

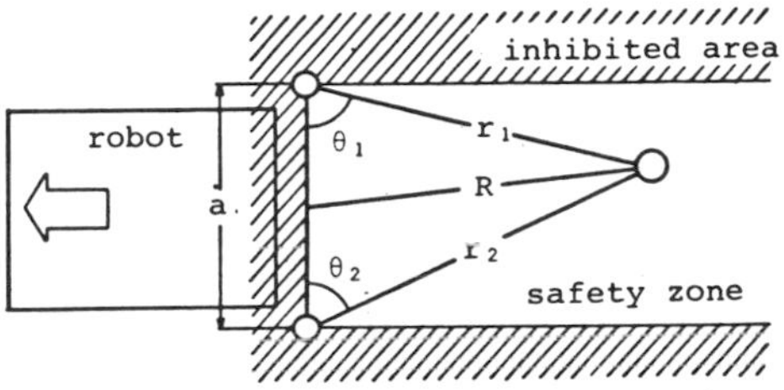

Fig. 13 Safety zone set behind the robot.

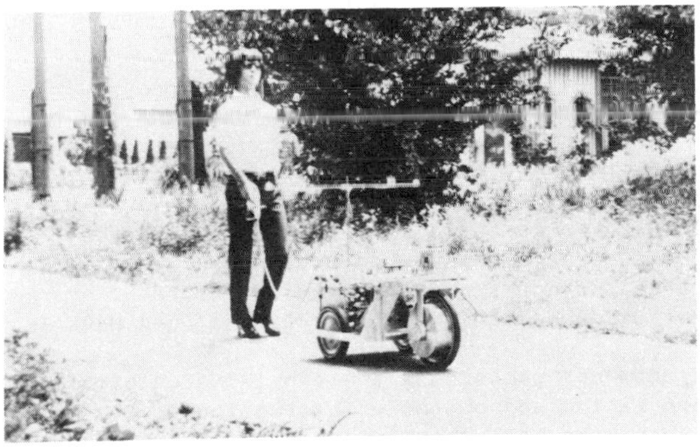

Photo. 5 Communication experiment with MELDOG MARK I.

CONCLUSIONS

The idea of guiding a blind person using an autonomous robot and a method for the realization of the idea were proposed (Photo.6). The robot processes both the information stored in the memory of the robot and environmental information acquired by the sensors on board the robot and passes the processed information to the blind master.

Photo. 6 General view of the guidance by MELDOG (MARK IV).

A navigation map is given to the robot prior to guidance. The robot travels according to the information on the navigation map. The error between the internal representaion of the environment (navigation map) and the real world is compensated by detecting landmarks in the real environment and correcting the robot's position and orientation according to the landmark location measurement. The landmark location data is already stored on the navigation map.

The feasibility of the navigation method was demonstrated both by computer simulation and outdoor experiments using the test hardware called MELDOG MARK II and MARK IV.

Some of the obstacle detection and avoidance functions were considered theoretically and the feasibility of the method was demonstrated by the test hardware called MELDOG MARK III and MARK IV.

Experiments concerning the transmission of course information and obstacle information via electrocutaneous stimulation were conducted using the test hardware called MELDOG MARK I and MARK IV.

The remaining problems include:

(1) The selection of general criteria for environmental objects as navigation landmarks, the detection method of the landmarks, and organization and utilization method of the navigation map with the information of the selected landmarks.

(2) Finding a more general obstacle detection and avoidance method.

(3) Finding an optimal choice of sensory display method of the navigation information acquired by the robot appropriate for presentation to the remaining exterior receptive senses of the blind individual.

ACKNOWLEDGEMENTS

The authors would like to express their thanks to the members of the Mechanical Engineering Laboratory who are concerned with this project for their kind support and valuable advice.

REFERENCES

Dodds, A.G., Armstrong J.D. and Shingledecker, C.A. 1982. The Nottingham Obstacle Detector: Development and evaluation, J. Visual Impairment & Blindness, 75, pp. 203-209.

Farmer, L.W., Benjamin, J.M. Jr., Cooper, D.C., Ekstrom, W.R., and Whitehead, J.J. 1975. A teaching guide for the C-5 laser cane: An electronic mobility aid for the blind, Kalamazoo: College of Education, Western Michigan University.

Kaneko, M., Tachi, S., and Komoriya, K. 1983. A constructing method of data base for mobile robot navigation, J. of Mechanical Engineering Laboratory, 37, pp. 160-170.

Kay, L. 1973. Sonic glasses for the blind - Presentation of evaluation data, Research Bulletin of the American Foundation for the Blind, 26.

Komoriya, K., Tachi, S., Tanie, K., Ohno, T., and Abe, M. 1983. A method for guiding a mobile robot using discretely placed landmarks, J. Mechanical Engineering Laboratory, 37, pp. 1-10.

Komoriya, K., Tachi, S., and Tanie, K. 1984. A method for autonomous locomotion of mobile robots, J. Robotics Society of Japan, 2, pp. 223-232.

Mann, R.W. 1974. Technology and human rehabilitation: Prostheses for sensory rehabilitation and/or sensory substitution, Advances in Biomedical Engineering, 4, pp. 209-353.

Morrissette, D.L., Goodrich, G.L. and Hennessey, J.J. 1981. A follow-up study of the Mowat Sensor's applications, frequency of use, and maintenance reliability, J. Visual Impairment & Blindness, 75, pp. 244-247.

Russell, L. 1971. Evaluation of mobility aids for the blind, Pathsounder travel aid evaluation, National Acad. Eng., Washington, D.C.

Tachi, S., Komoriya, K, Tanie, K., Ohno, T., Abe, M., Hosoda, Y., Fujimura, S., Nakajima, H., and Kato, I. 1978. A control method of a mobile robot that keeps a constant distance from a walking individual, Biomechanisms, 4, pp. 208-219.

Tachi, S., Komoriya, K., Tanie, K., Ohno, T., Abe, M., Shimizu, T., Matsuda, K. 1980. Guidance of a mobile robot using a map and landmarks, Biomechanisms, 5, pp. 208-219.

Tachi, S., Tanie, K., Komoriya, K., Hosoda, Y., and Abe, M. 1981 a. Guide Dog Robot - Its basic plan and some experiments with MELDOG MARK I, Mechanisms and Machine Theory, 16, pp. 21-29.

Tachi, S., Komoriya, K., Tanie, K., Ohno, T., and Abe, M. 1981 b. Guide Dog Robot - Feasibility experiments wit MELDOG MARK III, Proceeding of the 11th International Symposium on Industrial Robots, Tokyo, Japan, pp. 95-102.

Tachi, S., Komoriya, K., Tanie, K., Ohno, T., Abe, M., Hosoda, Y. 1982 a. Course control of an autonomous travel robot with a direction-controlled visual sensor, Biomechanisms, 6, pp. 242-251.

Tachi, S., Tanie, K., Komoriya, K., and Abe, M. 1982 b. Electrocutaneous communication in Seeing-eye Robot (MELDOG), Proceedings of IEEE/EMBS Frontiers of Engineering in Health Care, pp. 356-361.

Tachi, S., Mann, R.W., and Rowell, D. 1983. Quantitative comparison of alternative sensory displays for mobility aids for the blind, IEEE Trans. on Biomedical Engineering, BME-30, pp. 571-577.

INTELLIGENT ROBOT SYSTEM II

A. Ooka, K. Ogi, Y. Wada, Y. Kida, A. Takemoto, K. Okamoto, and K. Yoshida

Sumitomo Electric Industries, Ltd.
1-3, Shimaya 1-chome, Konohana, Osaka Japan, 554

The prototype vision system and four-legged vehicle for intelligent robot-II, which is one approarch to intelligent robot system, was described. The vision system has special circuits which can extract the edge lines from a grey level image within 200 milli-seconds, and it can recognize the shapes of objects and measure the distance from it to the object with a laser scanner.
The locomotion system is a four-legged vehicle and can walk statically stably at a speed of 8 cm/s. Each leg, which is similar to scalar type manipulator, has three degrees of freedom.

1. Introduction

Robots are indispensable today for improved process efficiencies and labor savings in the industry. The importance of robots has also been recognized in work in critical environments such as outer space, the ocean bottom, nuclear power plants, etc. as well in the fields of clinical medicine, hazard prevention, etc., with the result that a variety of robots tailored to special applications have been proposed and built on a trial basis. However, the overwhelming majority of such robots do nothing but repeat the predetermined maneuvering and even if the layout is changed just a little, one must expend much time and labor to teach them new patterns of movement. Awaited, therefore, is the development of "intelligent robots" which would recognize the environment and behave autonomically.

In our research laboratory, too, researches have been conducted for equipping robots with the functions of "knowing, thinking and acting intellectually". Following the development of the first robot system [1] which proved capable of acting intelligently in some measure, a further research work for developing a second robot system with improved functional capabilities in various behavioral aspects has been underway. A schematic diagram of the second system is presented in Figure 1. As a device for environment recognition, a vision system comprising a gray level image pre-processor consisting of two TV cameras and a laser distance measuring unit has been contemplated. As a behavioral device, a coordinated manipulation system comprising two arms with 7 degrees of freedom and a locomotion system comprising a four-legged vehicle have been proposed and

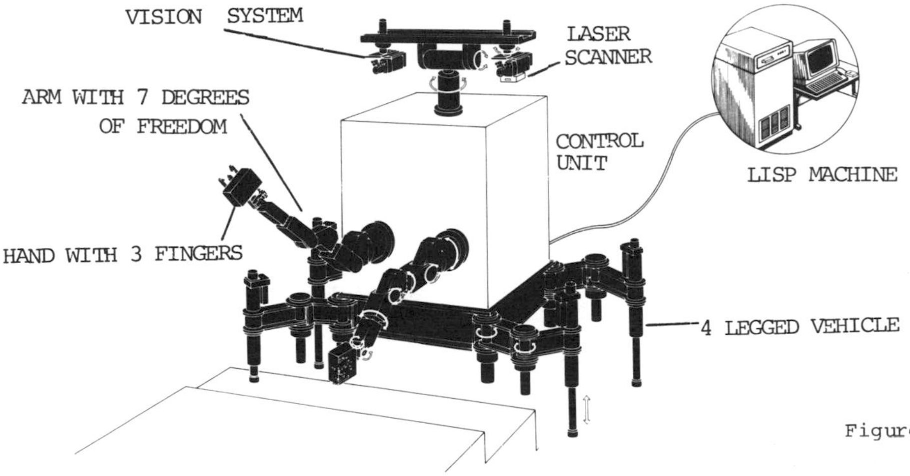

Figure 1 Schematic diagram of the Intelligent Robot II

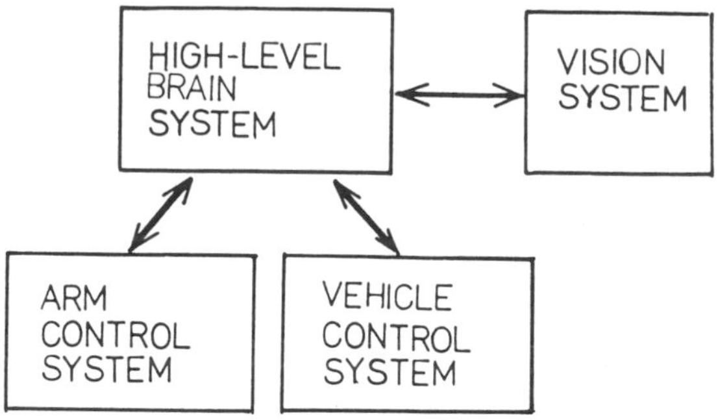

Figure 2 Archtecture of the Intelligent Robot II.

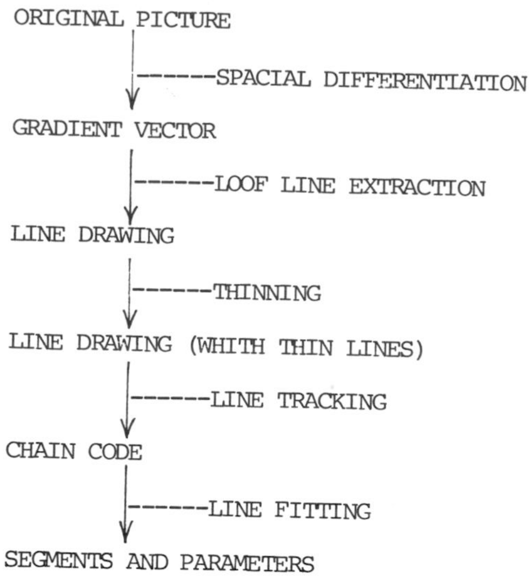

Figure 3 The flow of line extraction.

tested. As a brain system for superintending these actions, an artificial intelligence system using an LISP machine has been proposed. The architecture of the whole system is shown in Figure 2. Based on video information, a search for the optimum route to the destination, detection and avoidance of obstacles, and recognition of work at the destination are performed and the corresponding functional systems are driven by hierarchical control utilizing a microprocessor operations.

The level of implementation to date is such that these various functional systems are already functioning well on an individual basis. This paper deals with the vision system and four-legged vehicle system of the intelligent robot II.

2. Vision System [2]

In order that such functions as a search for the route to the destination and recognition of the target work may be discharged by way of visionary faculty, three-dimensional information is an essential requisite. The binary level image technique which is generally employed today cannot generate three-dimensional information obviously, such information can only be obtained by gray level image processing. However, any system using a universal computer is unsuited for robot-mounted systems in terms of processing time required, size of device, etc. Therefore, a gray level image preprocessor comprising a distance measuring device consisting of two TV cameras and a laser unit was designed and constructed on a trial basis.

This prototype system extracts a line drawing from the gray level image as a pre-processing procedure for analysis. The algorithm for this pre-processor was evaluated by software processing with a frame memory and a mini-computer. However, since the speed of operation and ease of implementation at the software level are generally different from those at the hardware level, due consideration was given to the ease of hardware implementation.

The flow of line extraction is shown in Figure 3. In view of the objectives of the present system, the differentiation process was given a smoothing function using a fairly coarse mask (5 x 5) so as not to pick up too fine structural details with computations being carried out without involving multiplications. While line tracking usually involves complicated calculations and judgements, simple logic processing is being used instead through a contour line extraction utilizing local gradients and fine line processing. The actual landscape is rich in floor and wall boundaries and these provide clues to analyses. Therefore, the extracted line is approximated as a bent straight line to compress the data and permit searches in terms of gradient and other parameters.

Software processing has resulted in a remarkable compression of information at the line image level but the amount of information is still enormous in general landscapes and it was judged that such a straight line approximation should impose too great a load on a vehicle-mounted microcomputer. It was, therefore, decided to perform processing up to bent line approximation at pre-processor level.

The construction of the prototype gray level image pre-processor is shown in Figure 4. It is a hierarchical control system in which various blocks such as the video interface serving as the entrance and exit for video signals, video memory (8 bits, 256 x 256, 3 frames), gray image processor for processing of video images, binary image processor, etc. are all caused to function under the integral control of a system controller. These blocks are connected to a system higher level processor via the inter-board level buslines

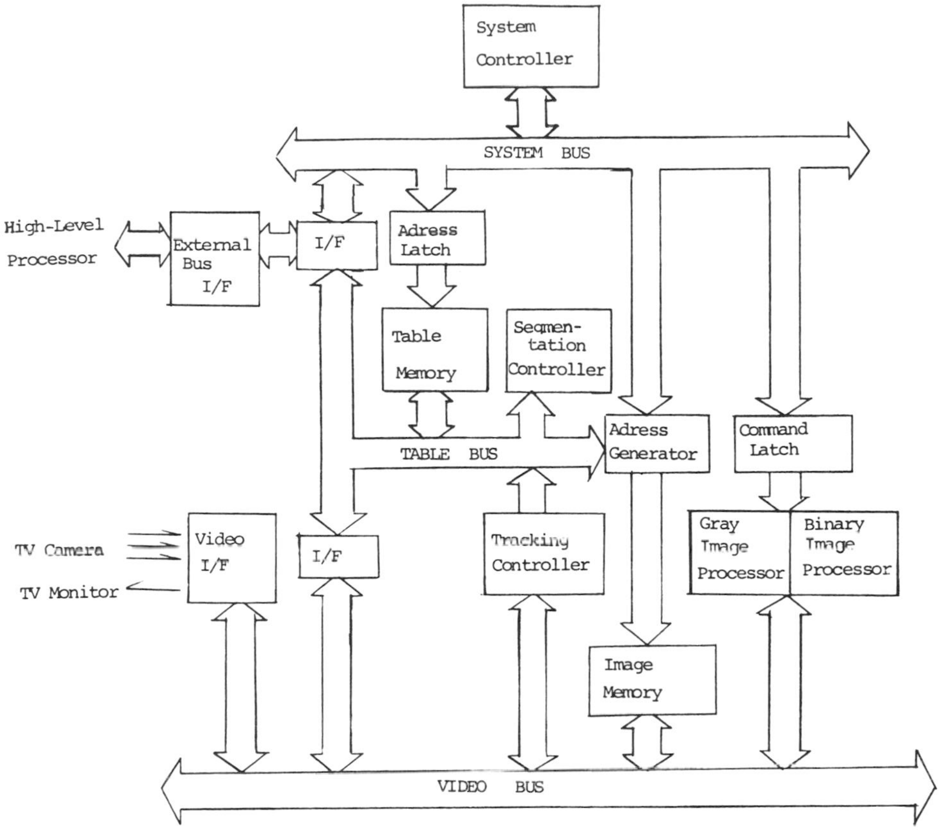

Figure 4 Construction of the image pre-processor.

and share the table memory for an exchange of results of processing and parameters.

The prototype vision sensor unit built for walking robots is shown in Photo 1. This vision sensor unit consists of two TV cameras and a laser pointer secured to one of the TV cameras. In Photo 2, (a) is the original image (no special illumination is provided) and (b) is the extracted contour line drawing. While the processing speed depends on the complexity of images, it is about 200 milli-seconds on the average.

3. Four-legged Vehicle

3.1 Structure

To ensure the maximum adaptability to rough terrains, a multi-legged system for locomotion was selected in the construction of the proto-type robot. Specifically, a four-legged system was adopted in view of its greater maneuvera-bility.

Photo 3 shows an exterior view of the proto-type system and Figure 5 is a schematic view of the same system. SCARA type manipulators with 2 degrees of freedom for rotation and 1 degree of freedom for sliding motion were disposed at the corners of a square frame. This structure was adopted partly because it permits stating the position of the extreme end (tip) of the leg on two independent cordinates, i.e. horizontal cordinates and vertical cordi-nates, and, hence, simplifying cordinate trans-formation calculations and partly because it permits savings in power for the support of dead weight. The total of 12 joints are driven by DC motors and their angles are sensed by optical rotary encoders. The whole mechanism was constructed of carbon fiber reinforced plastic (CFRP) for weight-reducing purposes. The prototype system shown in Figure 1 weighs 60 kilograms, inclusive of the control circuitry. The link length for the legs is uniform at 20 cm, the sides of the square frame are 60 cm long each, and the telescoping length of the sliding mechanism is 20 cm. The stride of each leg is variable and 60 cm at the maximum.

3.2 Construction of the Control System

Figure 6 is a control block diagram of the four-legged vehicle. It is a hierarchical structure with the brain and vision system at the top. The B system prepares drive instructions for respective joints in accordance with commands from the superior brain system. The C system forms an internal servo loop with the leg drive system and controls the four-legged vehicle by servo control. In locomotion on a rough terrain, the position of contact of each leg

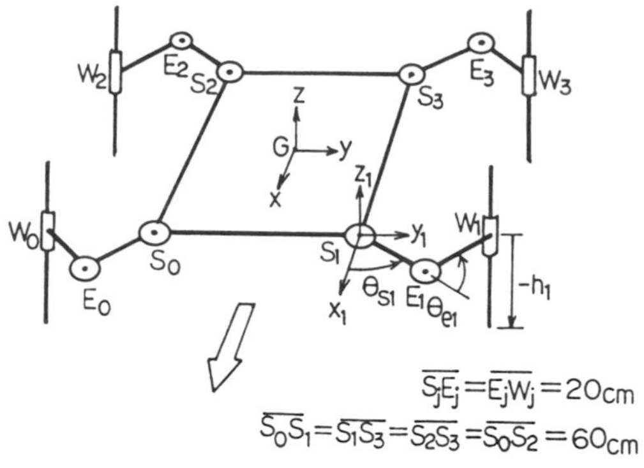

Figure 5 Schematic view of the four-legged vehicle.

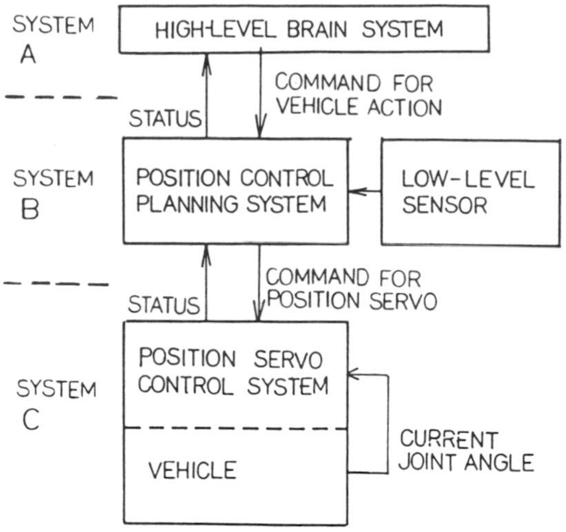

Figure 6 Block diagram of control system of the four-legged vehicle.

with the ground must be decided for each step based on information from the vision system. However, it is undesirable from the standpoint of speedy locomotion to employ such a control scheme for locomotion on a flat terrain. Therefore, the B system was provided not only with the mode of positioning the leg in accordance with the x y z cordinates for the tip of the leg from the brain system but also the high-speed locomotion mode in which the locomotion sequence stored as a table memory is executed. The table currently available is useful for forward and reverse movements only but it is being contemplated to implement a complete system incorporating in site turning motions and thus permitting free movements through a combination of such fundamental gait elements.

The B and C systems were constructed using one "8086" microprocessor each. The microprocessor in the C system forms a servo loop with a motor driver which was developed so that it could be used for all the servo systems in Intelligent Robot System II, and all the continuous path control functions are performed by software servo. Figure 7 is a structural block diagram of the C system. The software has been stated in C language.

The gait given in the data table in the B memory is what is known as crawl gait. [3][4] The crawl gait can be implemented by imparting to each leg the motions shown in Figures 8 and 9 (of course, the reverse of actions shown in Figures 8 and 9 applies to the two hind legs) in suitable phases. One cycle of this leg motion is assumed to be T, and the phases of legs 1, 2 and 3 with respect to leg 0 (see Figure 5) are assigned as T/2, T/4 and 3T/4, respectively. Figure 10 shows an example of crawl gait based on the above assumptions. In order to implement a

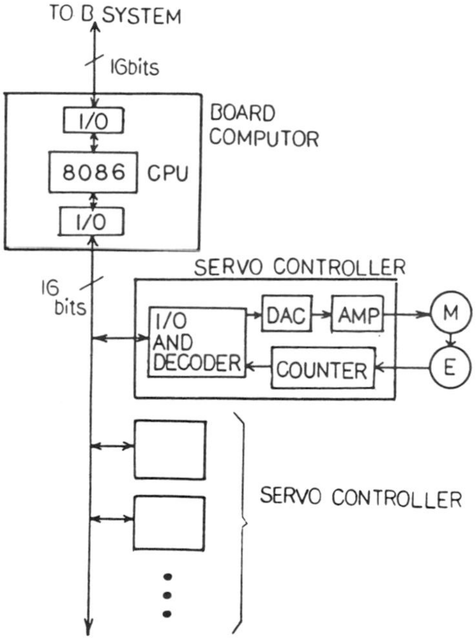

Figure 7 Structual block diagram of the servo system.

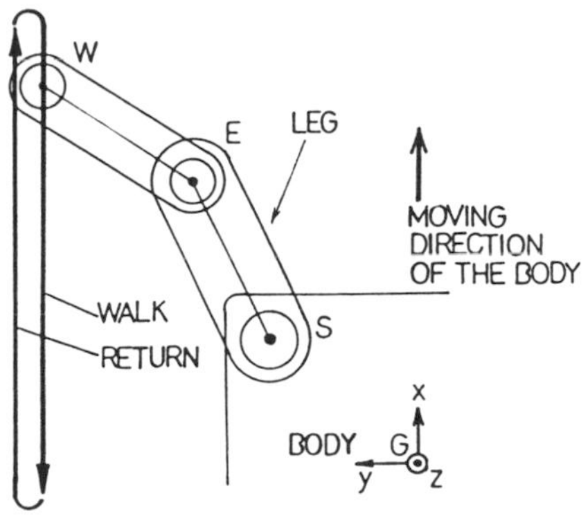

Figure 8 A leg movement in X-Y plane.

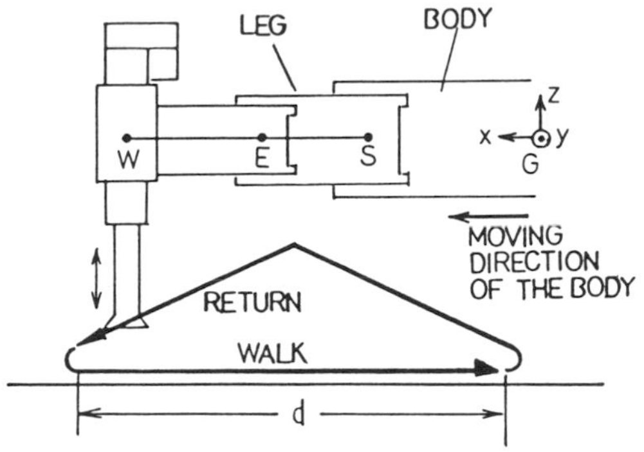

Figure 9 A leg movement in X-Z plane.

stable locomotion, it is necessary to satisfy the condition: $0.75<\beta = t/T<1.0$ where t is the ground-contact locomotion time of a leg. The parameter β is called "duty factor". A greater latitude of stability is available when the stride d and the parameter β are larger but if $\beta = 1$, the leg return time becomes 0 so that no locomotion can be executed. Therefore, in consideration of the leg return speed that can be realized from the structure of legs, the range of $\beta = 0.85$ to 0.9 was selected.

If the parameters d, β, and T (or t) and the initial position of the point cordinates for the vertical movement of a given leg joint are fixed, the movements of all legs for crawl gait are determined. By adding the x direction motion of Figure 6 to the above movements, the position of the leg tip for each sampling interval Δt of servo control in C system is determined. Such values were transformed into data at the joint drive level by simple inverse trigonometric function calculations and stored in the table memory.

In C system, this table is used sequentially to perform servo control. The algorithm for this control is

$$i = g_f\ (\theta_I - \theta c) + g_v\ (\dot{\theta}_I - \dot{\theta} c))$$

where i is the motor driving current, θ_I and θc are the target instruction value and current value, respectively, of joint angle; $\dot{\theta}_I$ and $\dot{\theta} c$ are the respective time differentials; and g_f and g_v are the gains. For g_f and g_v, optimal values were experimentally determined by trials using 1 leg or 4 legs. With the program stated in C language, Δt was 12 ms. Therefore, the table data in B were also prepared with $\Delta t = 12$ ms.

3.3 Locomotion Experiment

In the above setup, a locomotion experiment was performed with the prototype four-legged vehicle robot. Since the brain system was yet to be completed, a simple command interpretation function was given to B system, and human inputs from a terminal unit were used in lieu of the brain system. With t being fixed at 5s, β and d were varied within the settable ranges. In this experiment, the leg return speed could not catch up at $\beta > 0.9$, with the result that the robot dragged its legs. At

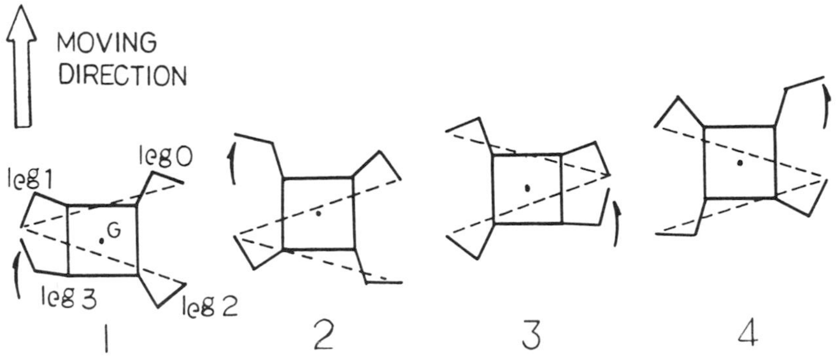

Figure 10 An example of crawl gait.

the stride of d < 25 cm, the vibrations of the body were very great. The most stable locomotion was obtained at d = 40 ∿ 45 cm and β = 0.85 ∿ 0.88, and the locomotion speed of 8 cm/s could be realized. Photo 4 shows the sequential shots of the robot behavior.

4. Conclusion

Of the functional components to be built into the Intelligent Robot II, the prototype vision and locomotion systems have been described. As the vision system, a prototype gray level image pre-processor for mounting on the robot was constructed on a trial basis and a high-speed line drawing processing at 200 ms was realized. As regards locomotion faculty, a prototype four-legged vehicle was constructed and a forward-reverse locomotion function at the speed of 8 cm/s was thereby implemented.

This four-legged system will be upgraded by adding a rough terrain locomotion function utilizing gradient sensors and a spinning function. It is also our major goal to develop a brain system incorporating vision functions.

References

[1] K. Yoshida, K. Sato, A. Ooka, Y. Wada and T. Takemoto; Development of Intelligent Robot System, Sumitomo Electric Tech. Rev. 23, 147 (1984).

[2] Y. Kida, Y. Wada and K. Yoshida; Image Processor for Intelligent Robot, Proc. 1st National Conf. of Robotics Soc. Jpn., Dec. 1983, Tokyo, paper 1305 (in Japanese).

[3] R. B.McGhee, A. A. Frank; On the Stability Properties of Quadruped Creeping Gaits, Math. Biosciences, 3, 331 (1968).

[4] A. P. Bessonov, N. V. Umnov; The Analysis of Gaits in Six-legged Vehicles According to Their Static Stability, Proc. 1st Int. CISMIFTOMM Symposium, 1 (1974).

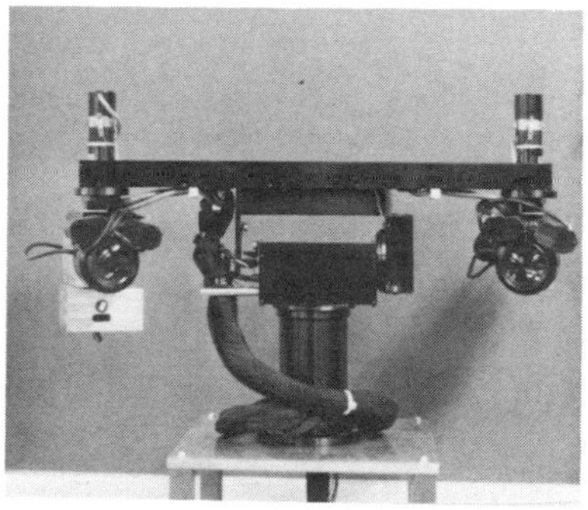

Photo. 1 Vision sensor unit with laser scanner

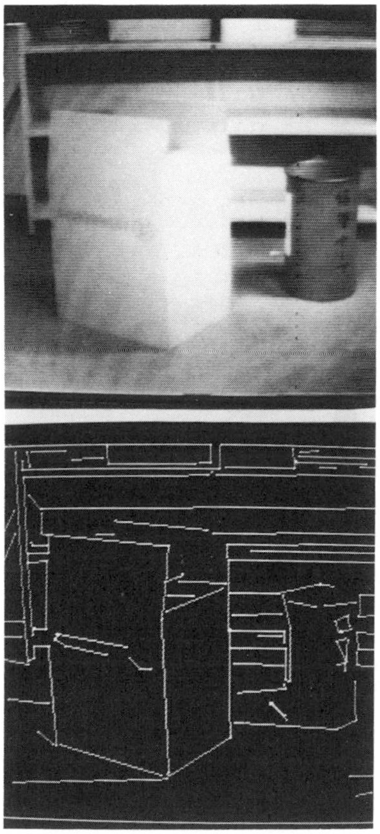

(a)

(b)

Photo. 2 An example of the image processing (a) before and (b) after of the processing.

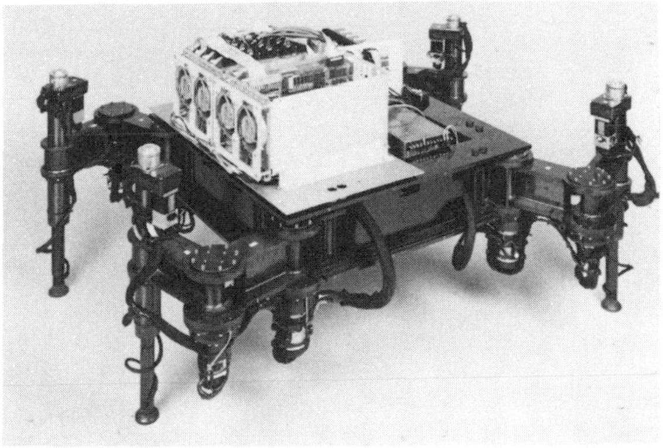

Photo. 3 The four-legged vehicle.

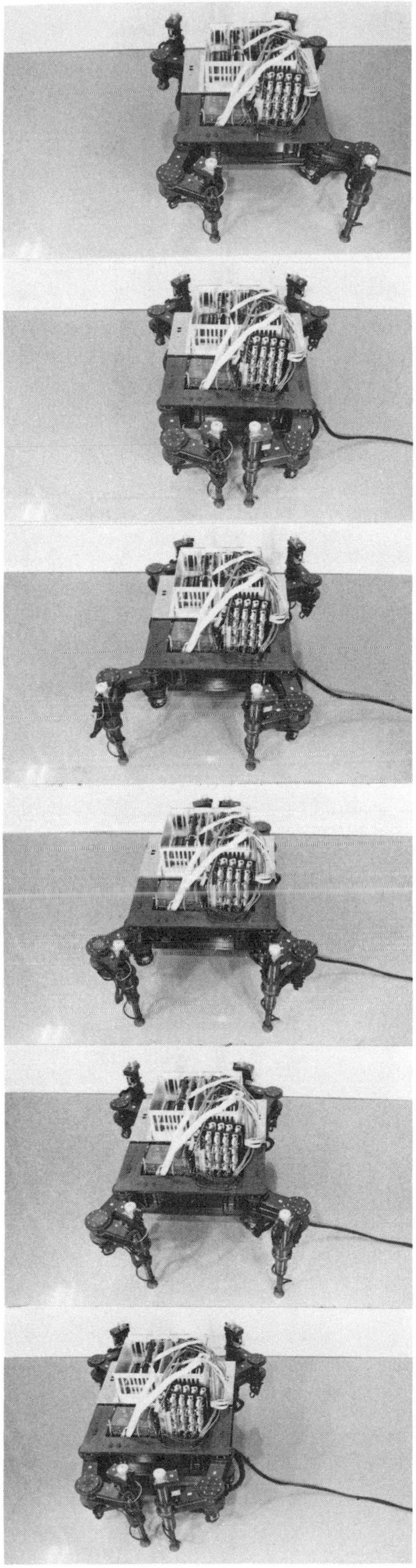

Photo. 4 Sequential shots of the robot behavior.

MONITORING OF A BUILDING ENVIRONMENT BY A MOBILE ROBOT

Saburo Tsuji

Department of Control Engineering
Osaka University
Toyonaka, Osaka 560, Japan

This paper describes model-guided monitoring of a building environment by a mobile robot. The prior knowledge on the environment is used as an a priori world model and constraints for image analysis. The world model is arranged in a hierarchy with three levels so as to provide coarse to fine structures of environment; 1-D route, 3-D work space and 2-D patterns of specified objects. In the preliminary experiments, a mobile platform with a TV camera is driven around passages of a building via a given route and reports changes there to a human operator. It stops every a few meters, takes pictures and finds correspondences between line features detected in the image and those in the image model generated from the work space model. Mismatched lines are further examined to detect changes in the scenes. The drawbacks in the system design are discussed, and a brief overview of hardware and software systems of a new mobile robot is described.

1. INTRODUCTION

Mobile robots need much intelligence for performing their tasks in unstructured environments, and many research groups have studied autonomous vehicles as a challenge in Artificial Intelligence research [Nilsson 69; Giralt 79; Moravec 83]. These robot plan routs to the specified destination and navigate in the real world using visual, ultrasonic and proximity sensors. Most groups assume the environments are indoor but unknown, and their efforts have been concentrated on the problem of building the world model by the robot from sensory data with little prior knowledge on the environment.

The author's group in Osaka University has been also studying an intelligent mobile robot, but from a slightly different view point. Monitoring of a large man-made area, such as plants, buildings and factories, is the task of the robot, therefore its sensory system needs not only to find the pathway and obstacles there for navigation but also to examine the scene in detail for monitoring. We select the vision as the main sensor of our robot, because it is considered as most effective for the monitoring.

This work is supported by Grand-In-Aid No.58420031 from Ministry of Education, Science and Culture, Japanese Government.

One important feature of our research is the robot's utilization of prior knowledge on the environment for both navigation and monitoring. Since much information on the environment, such as the structure and geometry of building or plant, is available, we arrange it into an a priori world model for guiding the process of image understanding and change detection. We can use another type of knowledge, constraints which are valid in most indoor environments; for example, "Scenes are rich in vertical and horizontal edges." or "The robot navigates on an almost flat floor." The knowledge is used as uniform or structured rules for inference or as procedural knowledge embedded in image processing and navigation modules.

The first phase of our research is the preliminary study of the knowledge utilization by the mobile robot [Yachida 83]. A simple mobile platform with a TV camera was used to collect data in a building environment for testing the feasibility of model-guided monitoring. The world model is arranged in a hierarchy with three levels so as to provide coarse to fine structures of environment; 1-D route, 3-D work space and 2-D patterns of specified objects.

The robot is initially parked at a standard position and is then driven around passages of the building via a given route. While moving around, it stops every a few meters, takes pictures and analyzes the images to find obstacles and changes in the scene. It first extracts vertical edges in the image, reliable features in the building scene, by the Hough-like method, and then determines camera parameters by matching the extracted features to the building model. Using these camera parameters, it generates an image model from the building model and detects changes in the scene by comparing the input image with the generated image model. If there are important changes in the scene, it reports them to a human operater.

The preliminary study proves that the model-guided approach is effective for monitoring of the building environment, however the robot is sometimes difficult to interpret the complex images because of the limited capabilities of its hardware and software systems. The major drawback in the system design is its simple control flow; procedures for observing scenes are predestinated and inflexible. The robot neither changes its camera parameters nor select expert modules suitable for the scene to cope with the dynamic environment. As a result, the robot fails after wasting long time to analyze images containing insufficient information. We need to provide our robot with the active sensing capability, a prominent feature of the robot vision; it makes a plan, based on the incomplete world model, to acquire better views and choose experts for the images.

The knowledge on the environment such that the floor is almost flat provides very useful constraints for the image interpretation, however some parts of it are not always true. Difficulties arise when they happen to be invalid by unpredictable disturbances. Therefore, monitoring of preconditions for applying expert modules is useful for the planner to modify the observation plan.

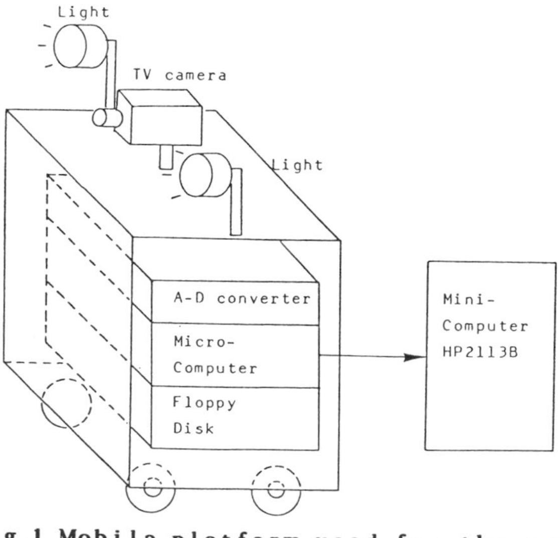

Fig.1 Mobile platform used for the preliminary study.

Another drawback in the image analysis is that the scene observed at each stop is independently analyzed. Integration of information available in consecutive images taken while the robot is moving will make the image interpretation easy and provide more useful information for understanding the environment.

To permit the above-mentioned high-level control and processing, an integrated mobile system is being designed and built. A brief overview of its hardware and software systems is described in Section 3.

2. PRELIMINARY STUDY

2.1 SYSTEM DESCRIPTION

Fig.1 shows hardware configuration of a mobile robot used for the preliminary experiments, which is a mobile platform with a control unit and a micro-computer. The image from a camera fixed on the platform is converted into a 256 by 256 4bit digital picture and is sent to a mini-computer via a communication line.

The robot is initially parked at a standard position in front of a known object. It views the object and calibrates seven camera parameters; its position (x,y,z), viewing angles (α,β,γ) and focal length (f). Then the robot moves around passages of the building via a given route; however, as an initial step, it is driven manually. While moving around, it stops every a few meters (currently 1 meter) and takes pictures to find obstacles and changes in the scene. Since we assume the floor is flat, variables in the camera parameters are x, y and α; the x, y, position and the panning angle of the camera. Changes of these parameters ($\Delta x,\Delta y,\Delta\alpha$) from the last stop are estimated from outputs of internal sensors of robot; the number of wheel rotations and the steering angle. The estimates, however, usually have a considerable amount of error, and therefore we utilizes the viewed image to determine more precise values of these camera parameters. Then, the image is analyzed to detect obstacles and changes in the scene. Fig.2 shows image analysis modules and its processing flow used at this stage. If any important changes are found in the scene, they are reported to an operater. If not, the robot is driven a few meters and observes the scene. This process is iterated until all the scenes along the given route have been examined.

2.2 WORLD MODEL

A hierarchical model shown in Fig.3 is used for guiding the navigation and image interpretation. At the top level,

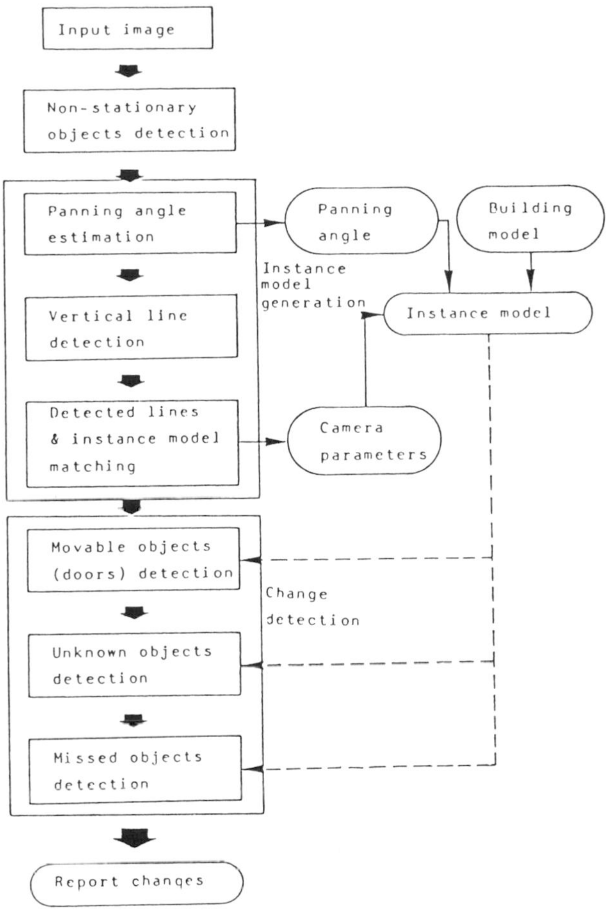

Fig.2 Flow of image interpretation.

a 1-D route model represents the robot's route and the record of its past stops in the current navigation.

At each stop, the information on a rather small area in which the robot exists and works is important. The model of this area, the work space model, is transferred from the data base and is used for the image interpretation. Thus, the work space model does not contain the objects far from the robot, because we cannot obtain their detailed shapes in image. Important global features of a distant view such as vanishing points, however, can be computed from the work space model.

As shown in Fig.3, the work space model consists of the camera model and a map of the current and next a few blocks viewed from the vertical direction, but the attributes such as height are attached to each object and we can access 3-D information. Movable objects such as doors have additional attributes of motion constraints, the range of rotation and the location of rotation axis. Utilizing the robot model in terms of its position and panning angle, we can generate the model of image taken by the camera as shown in Fig.4 from the work space model. This image is generated as all doors are at the standard positions (closed). Since the distance from the robot to the end of the current passage is known, we can generate an approximate distant view of both side walls beyond the current work space as the dotted lines in Fig.4 display.

At the lowest level, the object models provide more detailed information on

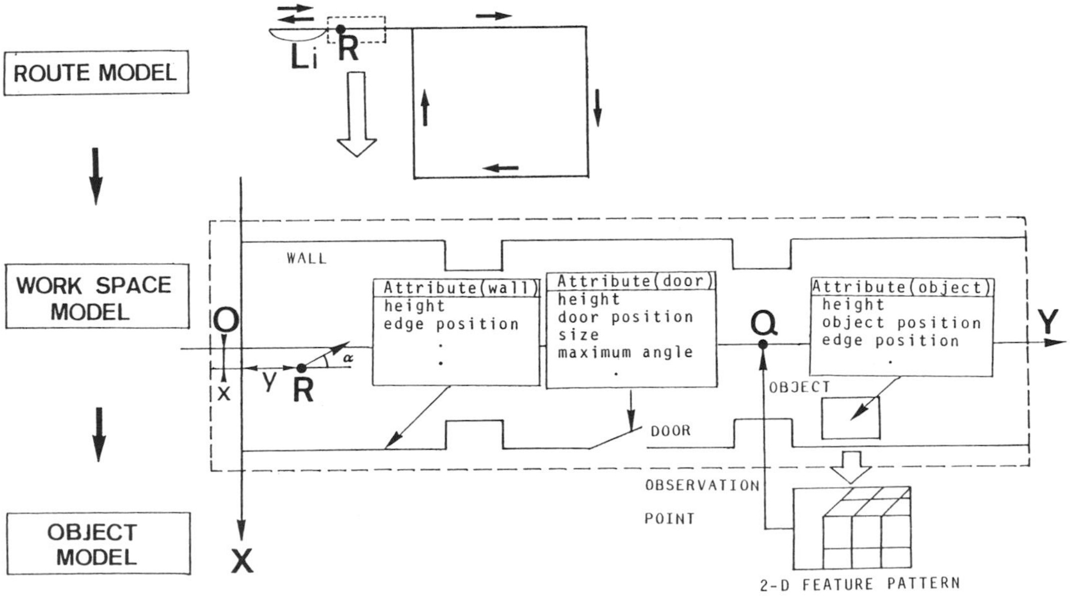

Fig.3 World model.

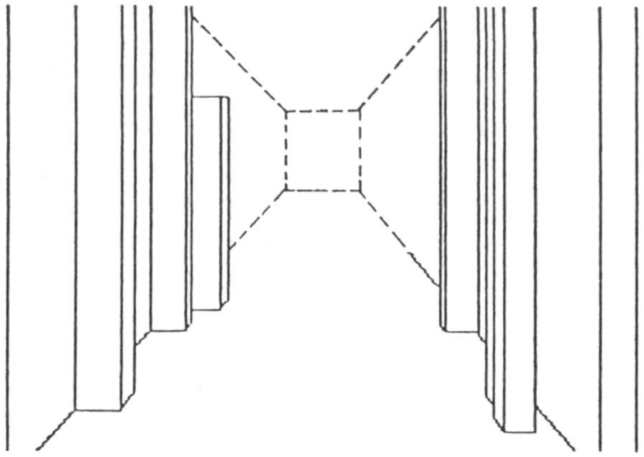

Fig.4 Image model generated from the work space model.

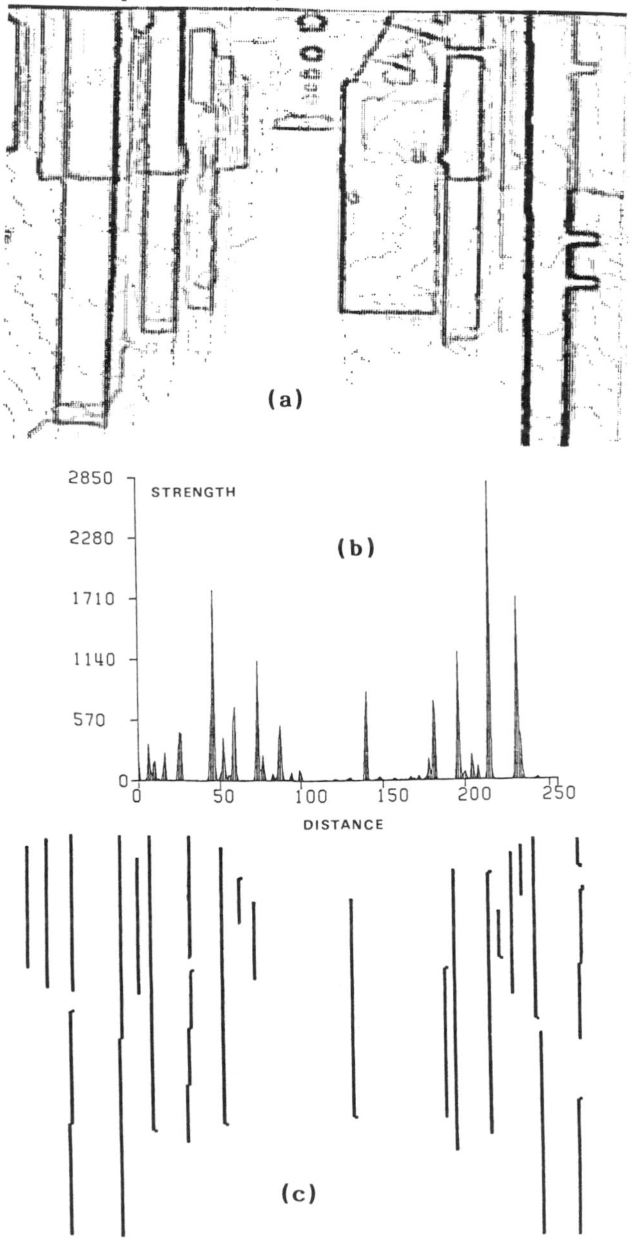

Fig.5 Detection of vertical edges,
(a) edge picture,
(b) histogram of vertical edge points,
(c) detected vertical edges.

important objects or complex-shaped objects. At present, the model is simple; it specifies the observation point for the robot and a 2-D template of the object's view. The robot moves to the observation point and takes a picture to find the object by the simple pattern matching method.

2.3 IMAGE ANALYSIS

Moving object detection

When the robot stops to view a scene, it first examines if there are non-stationary objects in the scene. It takes several pictures and detects non-stationary objects (usually man) by a systematic difference method [Yachida 81]. The size of each non-stationary region is then calculated in order to know whether the moving object is coming closer to or going away from the robot. If the size becomes larger, the object is considered as coming closer, and the robot stays there until the moving object passes by the robot so as to avoid collision. If not, the image is further analyzed to find changes in the scene, but the non-stationary regions are left as "don't care" regions in the rest of the image analysis.

Vertical edge detection

After eliminating noise in the input image by an edge preserving smoothing operation [Nagao 79], we apply a 5 by 5 gradient operator to find edge points and their directions. The edge image is sought for vertical lines because they are reliable features in the building scene. To find vertical lines, we make a histogram of vertical edge points versus their horizontal positions in image. Finding each peak in the histogram which corresponds to a vertical line in the image, we trace the line in the edge picture. Fig.5 shows results of this process. After erasing all vertical lines in the edge picture, we find other lines by the Hough method.

Now we try to determine precise camera parameters. Since the approximate changes of three camera parameters are estimated from outputs of internal sensors, we can generate an image model from the work space model. If the matching of the vertical lines found in the image to the generated image model is in success, the estimation of precise camera parameters is possible. However, a problem here is that even a small error in the estimate of panning angle causes significant differences in the image model, thus finding of correspondence between the detected vertical lines and the image model is often not easy. Therefore, a more precise estimate of the panning angle helps to simplify the matching process.

Panning angle estimation

If the vanishing point of floor is known,

it is easy to determine the panning angle of camera. Since the light illuminated by the robot is almost parallel to the floor, the floor appears in the image as a dark triangle whose vertex is the vanishing point. We can generate this triangle model from the work space model, and estimate its average darkness (G) from a small window around the center of the triangle. Since the change in panning angle causes the horizontal translation of the vanishing point in the image, we move the triangle model horizontally in the image. Then, at each position of translation, the difference between the G and the average gray level in the triangle is calculated. The triangle with the minimum difference specifies the location of vanishing point in the input image, and the panning angle of the camera is determined.

Matching vertical lines to image model
Since the rather precise estimate of panning angle has been obtained, we generate an image model from the work space model. Then this image model is compared with the vertical lines obtained from the input image as follows.

We first set a search region around each vertical line in the image model. The size of search region is determined from the errors in the estimates from the internal sensors. Then we examine if a vertical line of similar length exists in each search region. From the positions of matched lines, we can determine more precise camera parameters by the hill climbing method.

Change detection
We have obtained the precise camera parameters. Then we generate the more precise image model using them, and detect changes in the scene by finding the correspondence between the image model and the input image.

Each line in the generated image model is examined whether it actually exists in the input images. For the line shorter than a thereshold (the object is far from the robot), we do not mind if the line is missed in the input image, because the robot can get a better view when it comes closer to the object. If two or more lines in the model are very close to each other and at least one of them is matched to the input image, then miss of the other lines is also allowed.

For the vertical lines of the movable objects (doors), we compute their allowable positions and lengths from the geometry and movable angle of each door. We examine whether the unmatched lines in input image are qualified as the candidates for the vertical edges of any door in the work space model. If so, the instance model of the door is generated, and we search the input image for the upper and lower edges of the door model. If the finding of these two edges is in success, the vertical line is verified as the side edge of the door.

After comparing all the lines in the generated image model, we classify the uninterpretable lines in the model into two cases: they are (1) hidden by other objects, or (2) the object containing the lines has been missed. The first case that the lines are hidden by either the moving objects detected earlier or the open doors is easily distinguished by checking whether the lines are contained in the regions corresponding to these objects. For the rest of lines, we classify them into the second case and the robot reports the disappearance of the object.

After all the lines in the generated image model have been examined, we check whether all the lines in the input image have been matched to some part of the image model. If the unmatched vertical lines are in the distant view of side walls beyond the current work space, they are interpreted as patterns in the walls. The robot considers that the other unmatched lines belong to some

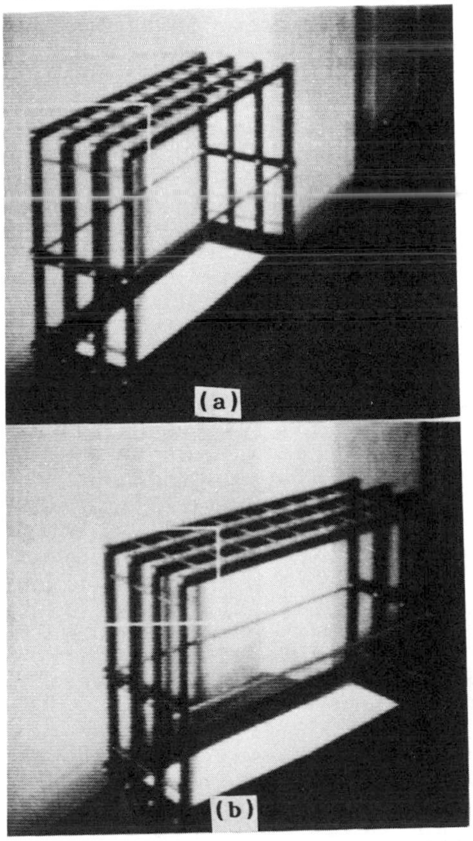

Fig.6 Monitoring of an object utilizing the object model,
(a) an object's view from its observation point and the template,
(b) the movement detection of the object by matching the template.

unknown objects and reports them to an human operator.

If the work space model contains the object model which specifies the observation point and template, the robot makes and executes a simple plan to stop there and monitor the object by the pattern matching. Fig.6 (a) is a picture of an object and its template in its object model, and Fig.6 (b) shows the detected position of the object when the robot monitors the building. From this information, the movement of the object is reported.

3. NEW ROBOT SYSTEM

3.1 PROBLEMS OF THE PRELIMINARY SYSTEM

The preliminary study proves the model-guided approach is useful for analyzing the building scenes and detecting changes there. The image interpretation is efficient and reliable while the environment is not so unstructured that key features, vertical edges of both side walls, are visible. Input images, however, do not always satisfy the above condition, and the robot cannot cope with such cases because it lacks planning capabilities.

A serious problem in its hardware performance is that control of camera's view angle is strictly limited, because the camera is fixed on the platform. Since most objects are aligned with the side walls, they are always viewed from oblique directions. As a result, their vertical edges appear in image as distributed densly along the horizontal direction and are sometimes difficult to discriminate. Interpretation of their front views is much easier, but it takes much time to drive the platform so as to face the object.

Thus, the major drawback in the design of the preliminary system is its simple control flow restricted by the limited capabilities of the hardware and software. The procedures for observing scenes are predestinated and inflexible. We, therefore, need to provide our robot with the active sensing capabilities, a prominent feature of robot vision, such that the robot plans, based on the incomplete world model, to acquire better views and choose suitable expert modules to analyze them.

We utilize the knowledge on the world as constraints for image analysis. For example, the flatness of the floor on which the robot moves constrain the pitch and roll angles of the camera to be almost zero. However, it is not always true, because of small obstacles on the floor. Monitoring of these angles will help the system to modify the camera model when they are larger than a threshold. Our new robot continuously observes the scene while it is moving, but it suddenly bounces over a small obstacle and the input image is moved and blurred significantly. Monitoring of such case is easy and useful to discard such less important pictures. We extend this idea to monitor preconditions for applying each expert monitor and send message to the planner to modify the observation plan.

Another drawback in the image interpretation is that the scene observed at each stop is analyzed independently. Since the movement of the robot between two successive stops is small, we could efficiently analyze the scene at the next stop by utilizing the result of the current scene. We can use many theories developed in the study on the dynamic scene analysis for interpreting the consecutive views taken while the robot is navigating.

3.2 SYSTEM DESIGN OF NEW ROBOT

A new integrated robot system, of which hardware configuration is shown in Fig.7, is being designed and built. A Heathkit HERO ROBOT [Heath Company 82], an autonomous vehicle with an ultrasonic range detector, a simple light sensor and a sound sensor, is used as a computer controlled vehicle. A TV camera is installed instead of its arm, thus we can control its panning and tilt angles by rotating its head and shoulder joint. An internal sensor, an encoded disk of the front wheel, provides an estimate of distance it moved. However, any good estimate of its yaw angle from outputs of internal sensors is not available, because the robot cannot move straight but along a circular arc even if the front wheel is set at its center position.

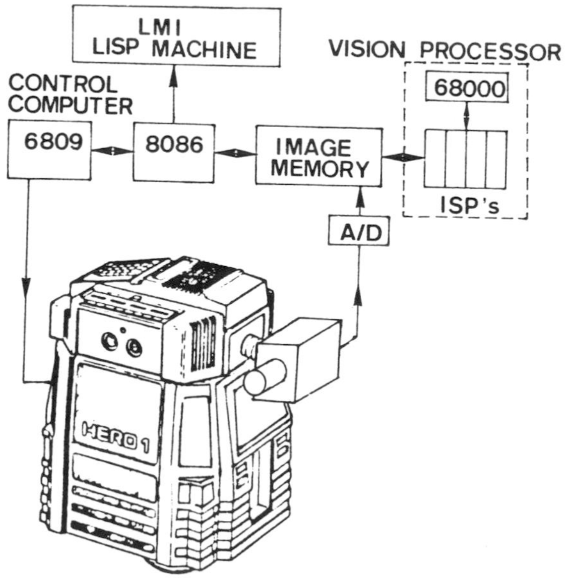

Fig.7 Hardware configuration of a new monitoring robot.

Since a microprocessor 6808 mounted on the robot is too weak for our purpose, we connect the TV camera and the 6808 with a remote computer system. The input image is converted into a 256 by 256 8bit digital picture and analyzed by a microprocessor 6808 augumented by an image processor, a 68000 plus four LSI image processing chips (Hitachi ISP's) [Fukushima 83], which can compute correlation of digital image with a 4 by 4 mask at the video rate. An LMI Lambda Machine is used for high-level processing such as manipulating of the world model and planning. A microprocessor 6809 is used as a control computer; it interprets each macro command from the planner into a sequence of instructions to control the motors or access the ultrasonic range detector, and send them to the 6808.

3.3 MONITORING OF ENVIRONMENT

Most vision systems of autonomous vehicles do not continuously view the environment but analyze images taken at each stop. A small number of exceptions are equipped with real-time vision systems to accept consecutive images sent from the TV cameras, however their capabilities are limited to perform a fixed task such as finding of obstacles in a specified range [Tsugawa 79].

We investigate continuous monitoring of scene while the robot navigates by analyzing the input images as the time-varying scene. Theorics of computing the camera's motion from the optical flow, the instantaneous velocity of brightness pattern, have been developed [Prazdney 81; Bruss 83]. Examples of applying these theories to real dynamic scenes, however, are very few, because determining of the precise optic flow in the time-varying imagery of real scenes is difficult and, therefore, estimates of as many as six motion parameters are unreliable.

We utilize the knowledge on the building scene as constraints on determining the robot's movements. Two motion parameters, roll and pitch, are easily determined from the vanishing points of lines corresponding to vertical edges in scene. The height z of the camera is also computed from the rotation of shoulder joint. At present. the tilt is set at zero while it navigates, then z is almost invarient.

The robot moves slowly, currently at a speed of 0.3m/sec, and 10 images are taken and analyzed in a second. Therefore, the movements of edges between consecutive frames are very small and, as a result, finding of correspondence of the edges between frames is easy. We can estimate the yaw angle from the horizontal displacements of edge points between the two frames if they are located around the center of image and are known as distant objects.

From these estimates, we can compute more precise camera parameters by finding correspondence between edges in the image and those in the image model, as described in Section 2. Much simpler analysis, however, is possible utilizing the following idea. If the correspondence between the image and the model is established for the current frame, then most lines in the next frame are already interpreted as edges in the scene because the interframe correspondence has been found. Thus, the estimation of camera movement between two frames is easy. We only need to examine whether the matching of the distant objects to the model is possible or not, as each frame.

The above-mentioned method for navigating and monitoring is not always applicable, and the robot must cope with such cases. For this purpose, we are now implementing several expert modules, such as floor edge detector, motion detector, object matcher and navigator, and a planner to select suitable experts, based on the world model and the preconditions for applying the experts, on the computer system.

4. CONCLUSION

Model-guided monitoring of a building environment is presented and discussed. The preliminary system proves the method is effective while key features are visible, but its inflexibility in control flow is the major drawback. A new robot system is being designed and built for more intelligent monitoring.

ACKNOWLEDGEMENT

This paper describes the cooperative research by M. Yachida, M. Asada, T. Hayase, T. Ichinose, Y. Yagi, M. Tazumi and the author.

REFERENCES

Bruss, A.R. and Horn, B.K.P., 1983. Passive navigation, **Computer Vision, Graphics and Image Processing**, Vol.21, no.1, pp.3-20.

Elfes, A. and Talukdar, S.N., 1983. A distributed control system for the CMU Rover, **Proc. 8th Int. Joint Conf. Artificial Intell.**, Munich, pp.830-833.

Fukushima, T. et al., 1983. An image signal processor, **IEEE Intn'l Solid-States Circuit Conf. Digest of Tech. Papers**, pp.258-259.

Giralt, G., Sobek, R. and Chatila, R., 1979. A multi-level planning and navigation system for a mobile robot, **Proc. 6th Int. Joint Conf. Artificial Intell.**, Tokyo, pp.335-337.

Heath Company, 1983. **Heathkit user's manual for the HERO ROBOT.**

Iijima, J., Kanayama, Y. and Yuta, S., 1981. A location control system for mobile robots, **Proc. 7th Int. Joint Conf. Artificial Intell.**, Vancouber, pp.779-784.

Laumond, J.P., 1983. Model structuring and concept recognition: two aspects of learning for a mobile robot, **Proc. 8th Int. Joint Conf. Artificial Intell.**, Munich, pp.839-841.

Moravec, H.P., 1983. The Stanford Cart and The CMU Rover, **Proc. IEEE**, Vol.71, no.7, pp.872-884.

Nagao, M. and Matsuyama, T., 1979. Edge preserving smoothing, **Computer Graphics and Image Processing**, Vol.9, no.4, pp.394-407.

Nillson, N.G., 1969. A mobile automaton, **Proc. 1st Int. Joint Conf. Artificial Intell.**, pp.509-520.

Prazdney, K., 1981. Determining instantaneous direction of motion from optical flow generated by a curvilinearly moving observer, **Computer Graphics and Image Processing,** Vol.17, pp.238-248.

Tsugawa, S. et al., 1979. An automobile with artificial intelligence, **Proc. 6th Int. Joint Conf. Artificial Intell.**, Tokyo, pp.893-895.

Yachida, M., Asada, M. and Tsuji, S., 1981. Automatic analysis of moving images, **IEEE Trans. Pattern Anal. Mach. Intell.**, Vol.PAMI-3, no.1, pp.12-20.

Yachida, M., Ichinose, T. and Tsuji, S., 1983. Model-guided monitoring of a building environment by a mobile robot, **Proc. 8th Int. Joint Conf. Artificial Intell.**, Munich, pp.1125-1127.

IV TASK LEVEL STUDIES

7 Modelling, Programming, and Monitoring

ROBOTICS AND SOLID MODELLING: A DISCUSSION OF THE REQUIREMENTS ROBOTIC APPLICATIONS PUT ON SOLID MODELLING SYSTEMS

A.P.Ambler
Department of Artificial Intelligence
University of Edinburgh
Forrest Hill
Edinburgh EH1 2QL, Scotland

Conventional solid modelling systems are concerned with single, static objects. The essence of robotics is moving things around, and bringing objects into contact with each other. Robotic applications, and in particular, robot programming systems are therefore likely to require additional information from the solid modelling system. In programming a robot system we shall be interested in questions of stability of structures, freedom to move in particular directions and restrictions in others. We also need to take account of uncertainty, both in shape and in position. As well as the ability to represent this uncertainty in a usable way, coping with it could imply the use of sensors. Predicting and interpreting the information gathered from sensors involves novel use of solid modellers. Movement itself not only raises interesting questions in dynamics, but also involves the necessity to plan movements which avoid unintentional collisions.

1. Introduction

An intelligent robot system which has some degree of understanding of the task that it is required to do is going to need descriptions of the parts involved in the task. It has to be capable of reasoning about the task, possibly planning how to do it, checking the likelihood of success of a given plan, deciding when to use sensors, and knowing how to interpret the data obtained from them. It therefore needs to ask specialised questions of the system concerned with the parts descriptions. Computer Aided Drafting (CAD) is a traditional method of producing parts descriptions and more recently solid modelling systems have come into use. However, these systems have not been developed with robotic applications in mind. It is the purpose of this paper to discuss what is required from a parts description system for robotic applications, and whether existing CAD or solid modelling systems can be expected to meet them.

As the name implies, Computer Aided Drafting systems have been developed to help people to produce drawings of parts they wish manufactured, and the emphasis has been on the production of drawings of individual parts which other people can interpret as solid objects. Other systems, such as APT, have been developed whose purpose is to produce descriptions which can be easily converted into programs for numerically controlled machine tools. Recently, solid modelling systems have been developed in which individual parts can be represented as solid objects, and applications packages provided for such things as drafting, NC tape production, mass property calculations, stress analysis etc. Robotics applications differ from the above in three major ways:

- robotics is typically about collections of objects related to each other in specific ways, and not about individual objects. We are therefore going to need a system which allows us to specify and reason about how objects relate to each other.

- robotics is about moving objects around. This means that we need to represent movement, plan how to achieve it, and consider dynamic effects of movement.

- robotics is about doing things with actual objects in the real world. This means that not only do we need to represent tolerances on the dimensions of objects, but we also need to be able to reason about the effects of uncertainties on the probablities of success of plans, and in some cases we need to use sensors to obtain information about the actual objects we have.

This paper only considers the assembly of rigid bodies. While we are aware that restriction to rigid bodies is unrealistic, it should be noted that some flexible bodies can usefully be represented as assemblies of rigid bodies connected by springs.

2. The robot task

The problem of achieving a task in robotics can be broken down into three main areas:

- specification of the task
- planning how to do it
- actually doing it.

While these three all impinge on each other (specifying the task can to some extent be couched in terms of the actions necessary to do it, and it may sometimes be necessary to plan actions after the start of execution of the task), it is convenient to use these three categories for discussion. It should be noted that "task" is here used at many different levels, from the overall assembly task, down to simple sub-tasks. It should also be noted that when using the terms "planning" and "description" we are not making any assumptions about whether this is done by humans or by the system. Thus we can talk about the description of a task without making any assumption about who produced the description or whether planning the achievement of that task is to be performed by the system or by a person.

The concepts with which the reasoning will be done are similar whether it is done by man or by machine, and the need for validation and verification will be the same. The need for simulation arises in both cases - if a plan has been automatically produced then people will want to be able to run the task in simulation just to see what has been chosen.

There are various levels at which a task will be described at some stage in the programming process. These include:

- function of the product
- final assembly configuration
- intermediate configuration
- graspin, placing and insertion
- path description
- trajectory description

and some of the problems to be considered are:

- stability of the structures
- bringing objects into contact with each other
- uncertainty
- use of sense data
- monitoring the task execution

3. Task description at the level of function

While one can conceive of a robot task being described in terms of the function of the object being assembled - for example that the given set of parts should be put together so that they form a pump, where a pump is a device which has an inlet and an outlet and actuation of the device causes an equal quantity of fluid to be drawn into the inlet and pushed out from the outlet - the production of a system capable of doing this is some way into the future. However, one can imagine a system which would be required to check whether a given set of parts in a given configuration would indeed perform the function required of it. This is a problem which would certainly require the parts descriptions to include solid models and which would require the calculation of the residual degrees of freedom in the assembled parts. This is a question which is addressed in the next section.

One can also imagine a system which would generate plans in which the functions of some operations are stated - for example the function of some grasping operation is to hold an object firmly while some other operation is performed on it. This question is addressed in the section on stability.

4. Task description at the level of the final assembly configuration

4.1 Describing the configuration

At this level an overall robot assembly task is defined in terms of the configuration of the parts that make up the final assembly. The way in which this is specified will depend to some extent on the richness of the descriptions of the individual parts. Thus in a system which represented parts merely as collections of co-ordinate frames, the configuration could be specified in terms of the relative positions of the frames. However, since an assembly is a set of objects in contact with each other, and with particular surface features in particular relationships with each other a sensible and useful way of specifying the final configuration of the parts is to specify how surface features relate to each other. This means that it is desirable to have parts modelled in such a way that descriptions of surface features are easily accessible. The type of surface feature needed certainly includes vertices, edges, plane faces, cylindrical shafts and holes, spherical and conical faces and possibly some other more complex shapes. One can then specify the desired configuration in terms of the spatial relationships that hold between such features. Thus two plane faces might be described as being against each other or co-planar, and two cylindrical shafts might be specified as being aligned, and so on. It will be necessary to define the meaning of the terms used - for example what it means in terms of spatial constraints to say that two plane surfaces are against each other, and it will also be necessary to have some inference system which converts this type of specification to a more compact form - such as relative positions of body co-ordinate frames. The RAPT system developed at Edinburgh (Corner, Ambler & Popplestone 1983) provides such definitions, and such an inference system.

In defining an assembly configuration it is sometimes useful to be able to refer to surface features which do not contribute to the shape of the part concerned - for example points and lines on a surface. Thus one might partially define a grasp position by specifying that a point on a surface of a body is coincident with a point on the surface of the palm of the gripper. Similarly, one might want to say that an actual edge of one body is to be brought against a reflectance edge on the surface of another body.

The point to be made here is that the demands that such a method of specification puts on the parts description system include:

- *** Easy access to surface feature descriptions

- *** Ability to specify surface features which do not contribute to the shape of the body concerned

The method of specifying a configuration by means of specifying spatial relationships holding between features of bodies also implies that there is some means of indicating the features concerned - thus the task definition system might refer to some feature of a part as "face1" and this needs to be mapped on to a particular surface feature in the body model. This mapping needs to be stable under spatial transformations of the part in question. A further requirement on the modelling system is therefore

- *** establishment of a reference system for surface features which is stable under spatial transformations

A refinement of this requirement is that the reference system needs to be stable under small changes to the parts definition. This is because one of the important features of an intelligent robot system is the ability to specify generic tasks - ie a specification of an assembly task (and a plan for achieving that task) should be applicable to a whole family of similar assemblies which only differ in dimensions. Changing the dimensions of a part may change its topology. Consider the simple example of a part which is described as the union of two blocks

block(10,10,10)+block(10,10,Z)to(a,0,0)

then the topology varies with Z and a. It can take the shapes shown below.

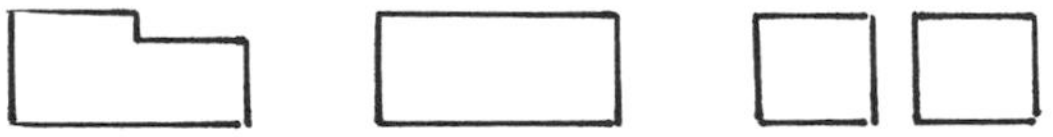

(a) (b) (c)

It would be useful if the modelling system were to be able to check that two similar parts descriptions described objects with the same topology. This should ensure that the feature reference system actually referred to the "same" features. A desirable feature of a modelling system is therefore:

- *** ability to check the topological similarity of parts descriptions

4.2 Interpreting the configuration

Once the description of the final assembly configuration has been completed and the inference system has been used to compute the relative positions of the parts in the assembly then the system should check the results. There may be several outcomes to this ranging from an unsatisfiable set of constraints through to an incompletely specified set of positions.

1. It may be impossible to satisfy all the specified spatial constraints simultaneously. In this case the task definition must be faulty and will have to be changed.

2. The relative positions of all parts involved are fully defined. While this means that it is possible to satisfy all the spatial constraints on features simultaneously it does not necessarily mean that it is physically possible for the parts concerned to take up this configuration - there may be interference between the parts. Therefore reference has to be made to the solid models of the parts to decide whether interference occurs or not. Now it should be noted that the whole point of the assembly is to have parts in contact with one another, and the difference between two objects being in contact and one object violating the space of the other object is very small. Therefore another desirable feature of the modelling system is:

    - *** the ability to do robust and efficient interference detection over a set of bodies some of which may be in contact.

3. There are a finite number of configurations in which the constraints can be satisfied - for example a given specification may have two solutions, one of which is "elbow up" and the other "elbow down". In this case the solid modelling system might be used to reduce the number of solutions by eliminating those which involve interference - in the example above the elbow down solution can be discarded because it implies interference between the table top and the arm.

4. The relative positions of all the parts are not fully defined. This means that it is possible to satisfy all the spatial constraints simultaneously, but even when they are satisfied, some parts still have degrees of freedom relative to the system as a whole. Here the solid modelling system might be used to restrict the range of the solutions in a variety of ways.

    a. If the assembly is symmetrical with respect to a degree of freedom, then an arbitrary choice can be made for the relevant position. An example of this would be the orientation of a pin in a hole. A desirable feature of a solid modelling system would therefore be

        - *** capability to detect symmetries about features

    b. There may be constraints on the range imposed by space occupancy considerations. This state of affairs can be thought of as movement of the relevant part of the assembly about its degree(s) of freedom, and restrictions on the range of configurations as restrictions on the movement - ie detections of collision points in moving objects. The movements will be limited - eg a rotation or a linear movement, and the techniques of producing solids of revolution or sweeping bodies along paths should be useful. Another desirable feature is therefore:

        - capability of defining solids of revolution and swept volumes

4.3 Tolerances on the dimensions of the parts

We are eventually concerned about the assembly of real parts, and there will be discrepancies between the actual dimensions of the parts used and their nominal dimensions. These discrepancies could prevent the assembly from fitting together. We therefore need a modelling system which will allow us to make statements about the tolerances to be expected on the dimensions of the parts, and, furthermore, we shall need a system which will allow us to analyse how the tolerances build up in the static assembly, so that we can determine the tolerances on features of the assembly as a whole. A requirement on the parts description system is therefore:

- *** Representation of tolerances on dimensions of parts in a way which allows us to reason about the build up of tolerances over the whole assembly when this is specified as spatial relationships between surface features.

5. Task description at the level of intermediate configurations

While task description at the level of intermdeiate configurations has much similarity to that at the final level, there is the difference that constraints in one sub-task may affect constraints in another, and therrefore sub-task configurations are unlikely to be fully specified. Some of the parts involved will have relative degrees of freedom, at any rate as far as the individual sub-task is concerned. Never-the-less it will still be important to eliminate solutions which are impossible even given these degrees of freedom, and to restrict the degrees of freedom where possible. So here again we need to be able to use the solid modelling system to find collision points between bodies which have relative movement.

6. Stability of structures

If we describe an intermediate configuration of parts one of the things that we need to know is whether the parts will stay where they have been put, or whether they will move as a result of the forces to which they are exposed - be this gravity or other. When inserting a pin in a hole one might wish the object with the hole to be able to move slightly in a direction perpendicular to the hole, but to be fixed in the direction parallel to the hole.

Let us consider first of all the simple case of stability of an assembly of perfect objects under the influence of gravity. This has been considered by Fahlmann in his BUILD program(Fahlmann 1973). We need to know where the centres of gravity of individual parts are, and how they contact each other. While calculating the centre of gravity of a modelled part is fairly routine for a solid modelling system, the question of how two parts in a given configuration contact each other is not. Questions about area of contact are two dimensional ones, whereas solid modelling systems are expert at three dimensional questions. What can be done is to make a small perturbation in the position of one of the parts in a suitable direction, and then to determine the intersection and use this to determine the contacting area. However, the direction of the perturbation has to be decided. An alternative might be to increase the size of one object in the assembly slightly. However, increasing the size of a single object in a set of objects is not necessarily a facility which is provided by a solid modelling system. The conclusions to be drawn are that useful features of a solid modelling system would be:

- *** ability to determine areas and points of contact of assemblies of objects

- ***ability to make small adjustments to the size of modelled objects

We need information about contacting features not only for considering stability under gravity but also for considering stability under the effect of other forces.

7. Movement and bringing objects into contact

An assembly is a collection of objects which have been moved into contact with each other by the use of manipulators or other such devices. Whereas the first part of this paper dealt with static configurations of bodies, this part considers the implications of movement. The object of the movement is ultimately to bring surface features of objects into particular relationships - this may be as in grasping when, for example, features of the hand are brought up against features of an object, or in placing, when the grasped object is moved to take up the specified relationship with the rest of the assembly. In these operations one has to plan how to achieve the desired situation and it is here that the effect of the uncertainty about the actual positions of the objects becomes particularly apparent (Lozano-Perez 1983, Brooks 1982).

Let us imagine using a two-fingered gripper to pick up a square block from the worktop. In planning how to do this without considering uncertainties, a gripping position has to be chosen in which the block will be firmly held and for which there is a collision free path. Much work has been done on choosing gripping positions (eg Wingham 1977,Laugier 1981)) and useful techniques include the projection onto selected surfaces of the contents of boxes of space around the surfaces in order to locate possible obstructions. Thus another useful feature of a modelling system would be:

- *** the ability to specify volumes to the modelling system within which some computations need to be done. The position of these volumes may well be specified with reference to features of objects.

Now let us assume that it has been decided to pick up the block by grasping two parallel sides, and so the gripper will be moved above the block, the fingers aligned with the relevant sides, the gripper opened, lowered and then closed against the object. If the block and gripper positions were to be perfectly known, the situation before the gripper closed would look like this in plan.

1

However, if the position of the block and/or the gripper is uncertain, then the actual situation may look like any of these:

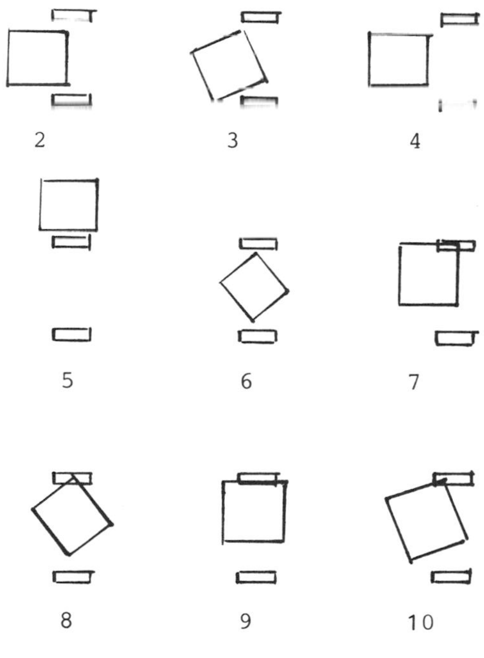

In case 1 the planned motions should succeed. In cases 2 and 3 the planned motions should succeed though the block might not be grasped firmly enough. In 4 and 5 the planned motions will succeed but the end product will not be the desired one because the block will be entirely missed. In 6 the motion will succeed, but whether the planned situation will come about will depend on whether the block will slide round as the fingers close. In 7,8,9,and 10 however, the first motion will fail because of interference between the block and the tips of the fingers.

Having decided on some particular motion, if uncertainty in position (and dimension) has to be taken into consideration then the problem is to determine what the set of possible initial contacts is, so that the likelihood of success of the planned action can be decided. In the example above, if only situations 1,2 or 3 can occur, then the action should succeed. In all the other cases steps will have to be taken to reduce the uncertainty, or the plan will have to be modified in some way.

Again in trying to decide what the initial contacts are likely to be we shall be looking for collision points for a body moving along a specified trajectory. Since we have to consider uncertainty it will be useful to be able to calculate the minimum distances between objects in a given configuration, and also distances between pairs of features. Contacts are likely to occur when the distance between features becomes less than the relative uncertainty in the relevant direction.A useful modelling system should therefore have:

- *** the capability to compute the minimum distances between objects

In some cases the uncertainty will be sufficiently great that sensory information will be needed to compensate for it.

8. Uncertainty and sense data

If the uncertainty is sufficiently great, then we shall need to make use of sense data to compensate for it. Sensory devices might be used to reduce the uncertainty before beginning a sub-task, or they might be used during the execution of the subtask to distinguish between the possible actual situations that arise.

In the first case, a vision system might be used to reduce the uncertainty in the position of a part by looking for the image of specific features of that part. In this case when the plan is made it will be useful to predict the appearance of the scene from the chosen camera so that it can be confirmed that images of the selected features do occur within the camera's field of view and are not obscured by other objects and are not likely to be confused with similar images of other features. In order to do this properly one would need a parts description system which contained a lot of extra vison-specific information such as details of surface reflectance, and illumination conditions. Conventional modelling systems do have good graphics packages, and if it is a person who is checking then the standard graphics facilities should be adequate, but if it is to be done automatically then the output will have to be more structured - for instance one might need a list of the edge images that could occur in a particular area of the picture irrespective of what object produced them.

Once the sensory device device to be used has been selected then the system will need some way of interpreting the data it will acquire during the task execution. This requires an understanding of the process which produced the data.

In the second case, sensory information is used during the execution of a task to distinguish between the possible actual configurations that can arise. Thus when inserting a peg in a hole there may be a number of possible initial contacts. These should have been predicted when the action was planned. As the task is executed the sensory data obtained should be used to eliminate some of the possible situations from the set, and so reduce the uncertainty and so allow a suitable next step to be chosen.

9. Path description

Objects have to be moved from one part of the robot's world to another and this involves avoiding obstacles. Much work has been done on planning collision free paths, particularly at MIT (Brooks 1983, Lozano-Perez & Brooks 1983), and solid models of the objects are obviously of the first importance here. In this paper we briefly mention methods of describing paths rather than their automatic planning.

It is common to need to make movements relative to features of parts - thus one might move a pin along its axis, or rotate it, and one might move a part perpendicular to the worktop when lifting it. The only requirement from the modelling system here is to obtain geometrical information about the named features. However, in describing paths which avoid obstructions it may be necessary to make statements about them - for example "move partA perpendicular to the worktop until it is clear of partB". In this case one would need to find the lower extreme point of partA in the direction perpendicular to the worktop, and the upper extreme point of partB.

In general for making path descriptions it would be useful to be able to fit convex hulls and bounding spheres to objects, and to assemblies of objects.

10. Conclusions

In this brief overview of some aspects of the requirements of robot systems from solid modelling systems it has been shown that modelling systems as they exist today do not provide all the facilities that are needed. The major limitations are the lack of usuable representations of tolerances, the inability to provide information about contacts between objects and the poor facilities for representing relative movement.

11. Acknowledgements

This work has been supported by the Science Research Council.

12. References

Brooks, R.A. 1982. Symbolic error analysis and robot planning. Int. J. Robotics Res.1 No 4.

Brooks, R.A. 1983. Planning collision free motions for pick and place operations. Proceedings Int Symp of Robotics Research Bretton Woods, N.H.

Corner,D.F., Ambler,A.P. and Popplestone, R.J. 1983. Reasoning about the spatial relationships derived from a RAPT program for describing assembly by robot. proceedings IJCAI-83 Karlsruhe

Fahlmann,S.E. 1973. A planning system for robot construction tasks. Ou(MIT Art. Int. Lab Technical report 283).

Laugier,C. 1981. A program for automatic grasping of objects with a robot arm. Proceedings 11th ISIR(Tokyo)

Lozano-Perez,T., Mason,M.T. & Taylor,R.H. 1984. Automatic synthesis of fine-motion strategies for robots. Ou(Int. J. Robotics Res.) 3 pp.3-25

Lozano-Perez,T. & Brooks,R.A. (1983) A subdivision algorithm in configuration space for findpath with rotation. Proceedings IJCAI-83 Karlsruhe

Wingham,M. 1977. Planning how to grasp objects in a cluttered environment. M. Phil Thesis, University of Edinburgh.

Aspects of Mobile Robot Visual Map Making

Rodney A. Brooks
Computer Science Department
Stanford University

Mobile robots sense their environment and receive error laden readings. They try to move a certain distance and direction, and do so only approximately. Rather than try to engineer these problems away it may be possible, and may be necessary, to develop map making and navigation algorithms which explicitly represent these uncertainties, but still provide robust performance. This paper combines and extends two threads of previous work: the freeway representation for free space, and explicit symbolic reasoning about uncertain quantities. A plausible new design for a mobile robot map making and navigation system is developed. The key idea is to use a relational map, which is rubbery and stretchy, rather than try to place observations in a 2-d coordinate system.

1. Introduction

In this paper we examine some problems which must be solved by a mobile robot which explores an unknown environment, building a map from visual observations. In particular we introduce a symbolic map representation whose primitives are suited to the task of navigation, and which is explicitly grounded on the assumption that observations of the world are inaccurate and control of the robot is inaccurate.

The problems are far from solved. The ideas in this paper play two roles. First, we clearly state some of the problems involved and give formal definitions of their mathematical properties. Second, we suggest some approaches to solving the problems, but much remains to be done to produce complete solutions.

1.1 *Levels of competence*

One approach to the goal of eventually building autonomous robots with human level intelligence is to try to recapitulate the successful path of evolution. Since we know in some sense where we want to end up it may be possible to search the development space using a much smaller branching factor than did biological evolution in building us.

We can define a number of levels of competence for a robot, each one requiring significant advances in one or more of (a) perceptual abilities, (b) action abilities, (c) internal representations of the world and reasoning about them, or (d) goals.

Consider, for example, the following levels of competence for a mobile robot which lives indoors, in an office building or a house, in an otherwise unstructured environent. Suppose at first that the environment is static.

1. Wander aimlessly around without hitting things.
2. Build a map of the environment and plan routes from one place to another.
3. Notice changes in the "static" environment.
4. Reason about the world in terms of identifiable objects and perform tasks related to certain objects.
5. Formulate and execute plans which involve changing the state of the world in some desirable way.
6. Reason about the behavior of objects in the world and modify plans accordingly.

A housecat might perform at about level 4 on this scale.

An evolutionary approach to intelligent mobile robots would solve each of these problems in turn, and incorporate the solution to the last problem in the next, as a complete, operational, robust, fall-back module. In addition, inputs and outputs of the modules from the previous levels of competence might be used by a higher level. When the module operating at level j is unable to cope with the situation it can fall back to module $j-1$ to provide control in a less intelligent but hopefully robust manner.

1.2 *Our task*

We are currently interested in competence level 2. We want to use vision to build reliable maps of the world which are suitable for navigating about the world. We plan on using a system of [Khatib 1983] to provide a robust lower level control system maintaining level 1 competence through acoustic sensing.

Figure 8 shows the target robot, known as MOBY. It is based on a three wheeled omni-directional platform built by Unimation, with an LSI-11 running VAL. David Kriegman, Sathya Narayanan, Sandy Wells and Elmer Moots have extended it significantly. An MC68000 interfaces to the LSI-11, and 12 acoustic sensors. A 600 baud link to a VAX-11/780 provides control communication. Two TV cameras are multiplexed to a TV transmitter. A receiver feeds video signals to a Grinell image processing system which makes digitized images available to the controlling VAX-11/780.

The only assumptions made about the robot in the rest of this paper are that it is omni-directional and it uses stereo vision to provide a sparse depth map (in particular we consider the use of a [Moravec 1983] style feature point depth map). No consideration is given to the use of acoustic sensors.

The algorithms described in this paper have not been implemented and therefore have not been tested on real data. In some cases only a computational problem has been formulated and no algorithm is given here.

1.3 *Other approaches*

There have been a number of projects with mobile robots whose goals correspond roughly to our competence level 2. We briefly review the two best known and successful projects.

[Moravec 1983] describes work carried out at Stanford and CMU. He took account of uncertainty in all his robot's observations. In particular feature points were represented by their uncertainty ellipses. However he then placed them in a 2-d map, and used camera solving techniques to get a best guess representation of the world, trying to minimize summed squared errors. Between motions of the robot he used a visual feature memory in order to match subsequent observations to an existing map. Path planning is based on a visibility graph of tangents to grown obstacles.

The Hilare project [Giralt et al 1983] tries to build a more complete map of the world using a laser range finder. A fairly controlled environment is used so that the perception modules can detect planar surfaces and build them into a 2-d map. Best fit techniques are used to handle observational errors. In addition, beacons are used to provide continual updates on the robots achieved motions. The map is decomposed into convex regions to structure path planning. An additional level of abstraction [Laumond 1983] provides hierarchical path planning.

2. Major Issues

A visually guided mobile robot inhabits a mental world somewhat different from the real world. Its observations do not exactly match the real world. Its physical actions do not occur exactly as intended. The task of navigating around the world can be eased by having the world map based on primitives suitable for navigation. The map should also be constructable from visual observations.

2.1 *Uncertainty*

Observations of the world are uncertain in two senses, providing two sources of uncertainty. Action in the world is also uncertain leading to a third source of uncertainty.

(a) There is inherent error due to measuring physical quantities. In particular, a pixel raster as used in computer vision enforces a minimal spatial resolution at the sensor beyond which there is no direct information. Physical constraints, such as continuity of surfaces in the world or averaging an identified event over a number of pixels, can be used to obtain sub-pixel accuracy of certain measurements, but the finite amount of information present ultimately can not be escaped. For the purposes of this paper we will only consider single pixel accuracy at best. For stereo vision this discretizes the possible depth measurements into a small number of possibilities, based on the maximum disparity considered by the algorithm. The error in depth measurements, increases with the distance from the cameras and the possible nominal values become more sparse.

(b) There may be errors in stereo matching. Thus a depth point may be completely wrong.

(c) When a robot is commanded to turn or go forward it does not carry out the action completely accurately. If drive shaft encoders are used then the best possible accuracy is to within on encoder count. If this were the only source of error it could almost be ignored as shaft encoders can be built with many thousands of marks resulting in very small physical errors. The real source of error is wheel slippage on the ground surface. This can be reduced somewhat with very accurate dynamic models, and accurate knowledge of the ground surface and wheel characteristics.

Our approach is to take explicit account of the first source of observational uncertainty in the design of all algorithms and to use the principle of least commitment to handle it in a precise and correct manner. The second source is handled more heuristically, by making the algorithms somewhat fault tolerant.

2.2 *Map primitives*

[Brooks 1983a] introduced a new representation for free space, useful for solving the find-path problem for a convex polygon. (See [Brooks 1983b] for an extension to the case of a manipulator with revolute joints.) The key idea is to represent free space as *freeways*, elongated regions of free space which naturally describe a large class of collision-free straight line motions of the object to be moved. Additionally there is a simple computation for determining the legal orientations (i.e. those where the moving object stays completely within the freeway) of the object while it is moved along a freeway.

Using freeways as a map representation for a mobile robot has a number of positive aspects. These are:

1. Visual observations provide natural freeway descriptions. If the robot can see some point in the distance, then it must be the case that there are no obstacles along the line of sight from the robot to that observed point. We will call this the *Visibility Constraint*.

2. For a simple circular robot, such as MOBY, navigability of a freeway depends only on its minimum width.

3. Freeway descriptions of free space do not rely on having each point of free space represented uniquely. Freeway representations are naturally overlapping. It is not necessary to know that two descriptions of pieces of free space are refering to the same place; the map can still be useful for navigation tasks.

It should be noted however that not all of free space is best described by elongated primitives. Some places are best described as convex regions. We will include such regions in our map, and refer to them as *meadows*. (David Kriegman has suggested they be called parking lots, to augment the freeways, and then it could be called the Los Angeles spatial representation.)

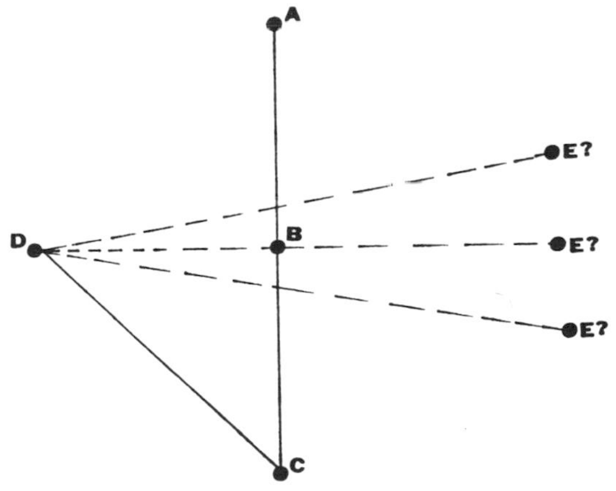

Figure 1. Metric information leads to incorrect represenatations when the information contains uncertainty.

2.3 *Combining these ideas*

These ideas can be combined in a map representation by avoiding the use of a 2-d coordinate system. Instead, only relationships between parts of the map are stored, in a graph representation. The relationships include estimates on their associated uncertainties.

Consider figure 1. It is one aspect of a map built by a mobile robot as it has moved from some place A, to place B, and so on to place E. It tried to travel in straight lines between places. The representation uses a 2-d coordinate system, so that straight lines in the map correspond to straight line paths in the world. It did not know the places beforehand but has been labelling them as it goes. Suppose it has been using nominal distances travelled and nominal angles turned, to give nominal 2-d coordinates for A, B, etc. Given that these values include errors there may be three physical positions for E, that give rise to the same measurements mad by the robot in moving from D. Any coordinates chosen for E implicitly add unsupported conclusions to the map. It can not be known whether the path from D to E crossed the path from A to B, went via place B, or crossed the path from B to C.

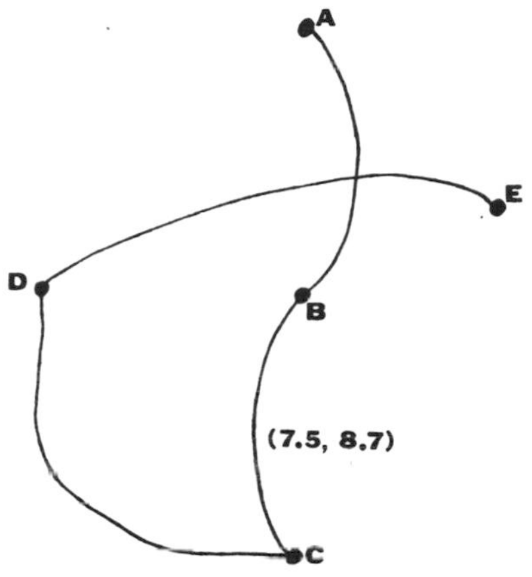

Figure 2. A better representation. The graph is not embedded in the 2-d plane, except for the purpose of drawing this diagram.

A better approach then is to use an abstract graph as in figure 2 where the arcs, which represent straight line motions in the real world, are not represented as straight lines in the model, but are simply arcs with labels. For instance, arc BC is labelled with the robot's estimate of the distance it travelled. Intersections of arcs in this representation are purely an artifact of our attempt to draw the graph on paper. It will be possible however, to determine from the arc labels that the path represented by arc DE somewhere crossed the path followed by the robot from A to C.

In the next two sections we consider in more detail what class of labels should be used to decorate the map graph, what entities should be represented in the graph.

3. Dealing with Uncertainty

If a mobile robot is moving in a flat two dimensional world, and if it has a labelled direction as forward then its space of possible locations and orientations is a three dimensional *configuration space* [Lozano-Pérez 1983]. We

x–y plane by a circle with radius

$$\frac{(d_1+d_2)^2}{4\cos^2\alpha} - d_1 d_2$$

centered distance

$$\frac{d_1+d_2}{2\cos\alpha}$$

from the start of the motion. We can then bound the complete manifold in configuration space by a cylinder sitting above the bounding circle with have constructed, and ranging from $\eta_0 - \alpha$ to $\eta_0 + \alpha$ in height.

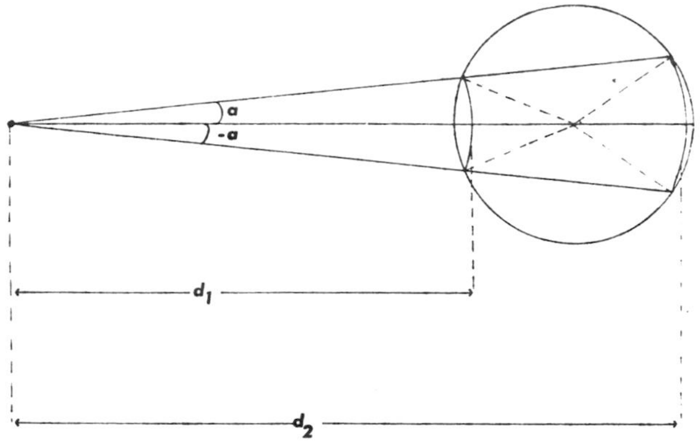

Figure 4. Bounding the projection of the uncertainty manifold.

It is simple now to propagate bounds on the uncertainty. The vector sum of two cylinders is again a cylinder, whose radius is the sum of the two cylinder's radii, and whose height is the sum of the two cylinder's heights.

Figure 5 shows the projection of uncertainty manifolds produced by four successive motions into the x–y plane. After the last, the am-I-there-yet question has an affirmative answer, i.e. "maybe", relative to the point of origin.

In figure 6 we see an example of backward reasoning. Suppose we have used forward reasoning to determine that it is plausible that the robot is in the same circular meadow from which the journey commenced. It might be plausible that the robot is in other meadows too. In any case the plausibility condition cuts down the number of possible meadows the robot might be in. If there are some visual landmarks associated with the meadow then perhaps one of the hypotheses can be verified (if a similar landmark is visible in another meadow then the forward reasoning will sometimes provide the disambiguation). So suppose such reasoning does indeed determine that the robot is in the original meadow. The intersection of the uncertainty cylinder cross section and the meadow determines a smaller region where the robot really might be. We bound that with a circle to produce a new uncertainty cylinder. If orientation information was gleaned from the landmark observation then that can be used to cut down the cylinder's range in the θ direction. This projection of this cylinder is illustrate in figure 6.

Now we can use backward reasoning, and ask "What are all the points I could have been at, before the last motion and gotten into this new uncertainty cylinder?". This does not involve shrinking the cylinder by subtracting the uncertainly cylinder of the last motion, rather it involves adding its inversion through the origin of configuration space. The resulting uncertainty cylinder, is shown in figure 6. Since the robot got to the third observation point by travelling forward around the path, it must have been in the intersection of the two cylinders before the fourth motion. Now a new uncertainty cylinder can be constructed to bound that intersection. It specifies an uncertainty relationship between the start of the journey, and any observations which were made after the third stop. Thus it ties down some of the rubbery map just a little bit better, and the effects of this additional constraint will be able to be used in later references to the map. Notice that the backward reasoning can continue from the last uncertainty cylinder we constructed. Soon however the uncertainties will become so large that no new information will be gained.

4. Map Representation and Reasoning

There are some desirable properties for a map representation.

1. It should be stable. Small variations in observations should almost everywhere lead to structurally isomorphic representations.

2. It should be mostly monotonic. Usually when additional observations are made the representation of the world should be augmented rather than being restructured. This need not always be the case.

The challenge then is to find primitive representations for freeways and meadows which can be derived from visual observations in a manner which satisfies the above conditions. A multiple scale representation could be useful to make the representation insensitive to variations below the threshold where they might effect navigability through a region.

We will represent freeways by a length and minimum width, and meadows by circles. Note that these shapes are **not meant to describe free space exactly**. Instead they are used to represent topological properties of free space and to summarize navigability conditions. They have metric properties to help with disambiguation and for path planning purposes.

This same representational problem was tackled from a slightly different viewpoint by [Laumond 1983]. The convex decomposition representation and description extraction method used by [Giralt et al 1983] suffers from gross instability. Laumond tried to put an abstract layer above the convex region level by analyzing the connectivity graph.

Figure 7 shows a map consisting of freeways and meadows.

can label its axes x, y, and θ. When the robot is at two dimensional coordinates (x_0, y_0) with orientation θ_0, its configuration corresponds to point (x_0, y_0, θ_0) in configuration space. For now lets refer to such a configuration as P_0.

Suppose the robot has configuration P_0, and it re-orients by angle η then travels distance d. Its new configuration would be:

$$P_1 = (x_0 + d\cos(\theta_0 + \eta), y_0 + d\sin(\theta_0 + \eta), \theta_0 + \eta).$$

However there is always error associated with the robot's motion. Typical errors might be $\pm 5°$ angular error and $\pm(5 + 0.05d)$ centimeters, in distance error, as a function of the distance travelled.

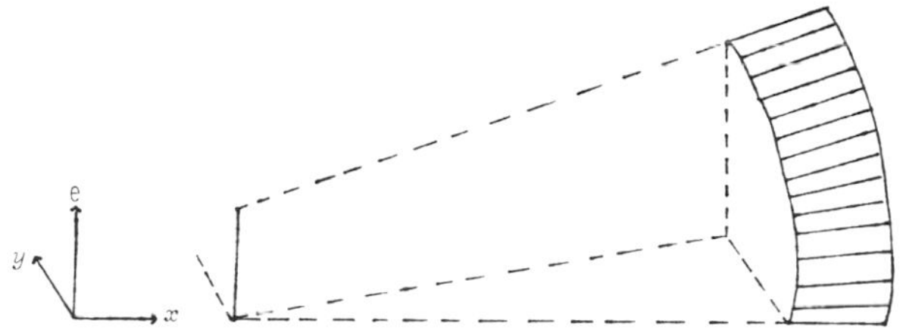

Figure 3. An uncertainty manifold arising from an uncertain motion in an uncertain direction.

3.1 *Uncertainty manifolds*

We have shown that P_1 can not be uniquely identified. Instead P_1 can range over an *uncertainty manifold* (see figure 3) in configuration space. If the range of possible values for d is $[d_1, d_2]$ and for η is $[\eta_0 - \alpha, \eta_0 + \alpha]$ then the uncertainty manifold is:

$$\begin{aligned} &M_1(x_0, y_0, \theta_0) = \qquad (1)\\ &\{\,(x_0 + d\cos(\theta_0 + \eta), y_0 + d\sin(\theta_0 + \eta), \theta_0 + \eta)\\ &\qquad \mid d \in [d_1, d_2], \eta \in [\eta_0 - \alpha, \eta_0 + \alpha]\,\}. \end{aligned}$$

Notice that this is a two dimensional manifold in three dimensional space.

A simple question, but nevertheless a useful one to ask while exploring the world, is "Am I back some place I've already been?", which, without loss of generality, can be simplified to "Am I back where I started?". Given that each individual motion is uncertain, it will be necessary to take into account the cumulative uncertainty, and in fact, without further sensing, the toughest question that can be answered is "Is it plausible that I am back where I started?". We will call this the *am-I-there-yet* question.

The uncertainty manifold resulting from two motions can be written as

$$M_1(x_0, y_0, \theta_0) + M_2(0, 0, 0) \qquad (2)$$

where the sum of two sets means, as usual, the set of points which are the vector sum of two points, one in each set. This manifold is three dimensional and "solid"; i.e., it has a non-empty interior. The surfaces of this manifold become progressively harder to express as the number of motions increase.

One approach to answering the am-I-there-yet question is to introduce three more variables for each motion (besides nominal angles and distances and bounds on errors in each), and write explicit symbolic inequalities of the form

$$P_1 \in M_1(x_0, y_0, \theta_0),$$

$$P_2 \in M_1(x_0, y_0, \theta_0) + M_2(0, 0, 0),$$

etc. Note that each P_i introduces three more variables. Then we can add the constraints

$$(x_0, y_0, \theta_0) \in M_1(x_0, y_0, \theta_0) + \sum_{i=2}^{n} M_i(0, 0, 0), \qquad (3)$$

and, using the methods of [Brooks 1983] ask whether all the constraints are together satisfiable. This is *forward reasoning* with constraints. Additionally one would like to be able to use auxiliary information, such as from landmarks, to be able to assert inequalities such as (3). Then one would use the symbolic bounding algorithms from the above paper to determine the implications in terms of constraints on the actual physical values of angles of re-orientation and distances travelled. This is *backward reasoning* with constraints.

Unfortunately this approach doesn't work well because of the presence of so many trigonometric terms.

3.2 *Approximating uncertainty manifolds*

A second approach, used more successfully in reasoning about uncertainties in assembly processes, is to use bounds on trigonometric functions, such as

$$\sin\alpha \le \sin(\eta - \eta_0) \le \eta - \eta_0$$

for $\eta \ge \eta_0$ and

$$1 - \frac{1}{2}(\eta - \eta_0)^2 \le \cos(\eta - \eta_0) \le 1$$

This has the effect of making an individual 2-d manifold M_i a little fuzzy, giving it some three dimensional volume. This makes the resulting manifolds (e.g. equation (2)) a little nicer in form. Unfortunately, again the constraint propagation methods fail because of the large number of cascading variables.

Broader bounding volumes for the uncertainty manifolds, with fewer parameters, and with simpler interactions, are needed if we are to make use of them in either forward or backward reasoning.

3.3 *Cylinders in configuration space*

The projection of the uncertainty manifold (1) into the x–y plane is shown in figure 4. It can be bounded in the

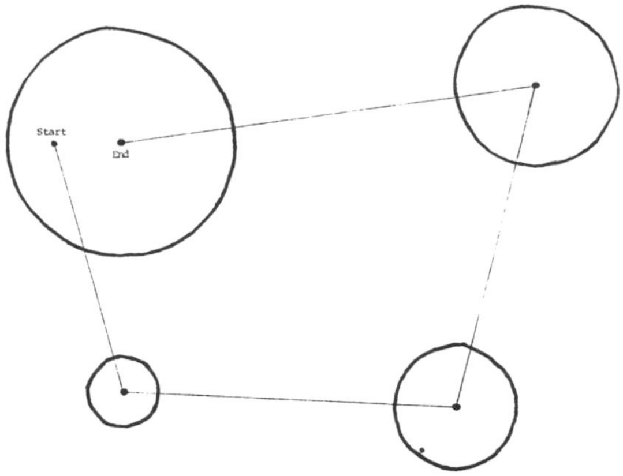

Figure 5. An example of forward reasoning, deciding that it is plausible that the robot is back where it started.

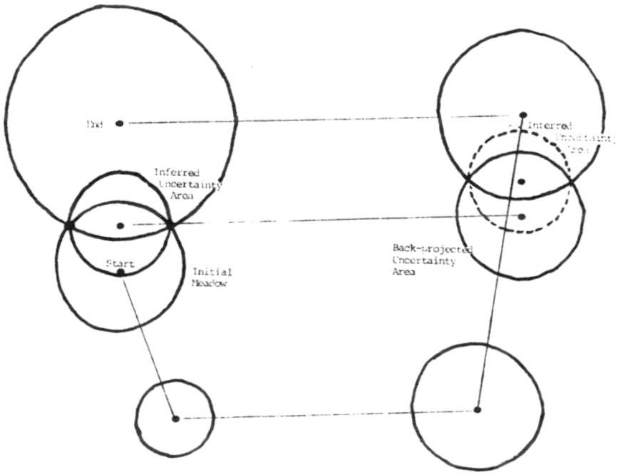

Figure 6. Backward reasoning. Additional information indicated the robot was in the meadow. The dashed circle shows bounds where the robot really must have been before.

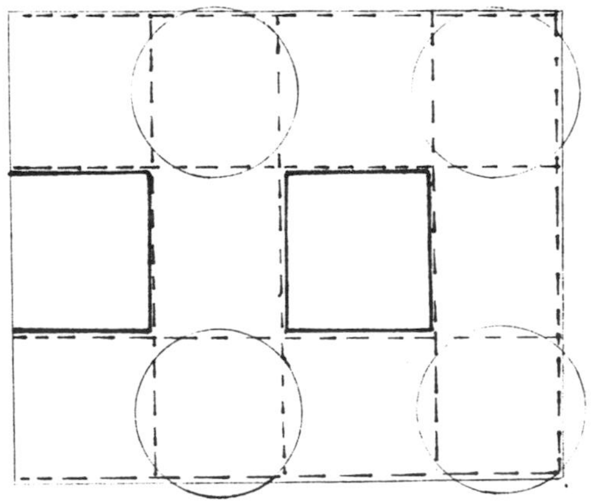

Figure 7. Freeways and meadows inside a building.

Freeways represent elongated pieces of free space, while meadows represent convex, and relatively compact regions of free space. Neither primitive is intended to exactly describe a region of free space. Rather they summarize the navigability properties of regions of free space. Freeways and meadows may overlap, and any given point in free space my be part of many instances of each primitive.

The map is represented as a graph. Nodes of the graph are meadows. Arcs of the graph are freeways. Meadows and freeways are further described with metric and relative position and orientation properties. There are degenerate meadows where colinear freeways meet. There are degenerate freeways where meadows overlap.

4.1 *Visual Observations*

When a feature is observed, using a [Moravec 1983] style stereo system, its distance and direction are not exactly known. Exactly the same type of bounding circle can be used as illustrated in figure 4. The problem now is how to extract meadow and freeway descriptions from sets of feature points represented as uncertainty circles realtive to the observer.

One possibility for meadows, which are themselves circles, is to look around in all directions. The meadow is the maximum radius circle which includes the point of observation and does not contain any uncertainty circle wholly in its interior. There may be more than one local maximum of such circles in which case the observation point is within more than one meadow. The radius for the meadow may be too large and this can be taken into account in matching meadow descriptions.

Freeway descriptions can be extracted by using the Visibility Constraint. If a point in can be seen in the distance, and if it is bounded left and right in the field of view by closer points, then there is a channel (no matter how small) running between those bounding points from the observer to the distant point.

4.2 *Augmenting the Map*

As the robot wanders around it records its motions as uncertainty cylinders. It observes the world and records freeway and meadow descriptions relative to its stopping places. When a new freeway or meadow is seen it can ask the am-I-there-yet question to see if it has candidates already in its map to match it to.

If it can determine surfaces patches then it can use the visibility constraint to decide that a newly observed spatial feature can not be distinct from those already in its map.

As the robot wanders around it does not matter too much if it fails to recognize that it is back to some place it has already been. It can build up its map and have different parts of the graph referring to he same physical parts of space. As more landmarks are recognized and forward and backward reasoning constraints become stronger it may be able to identify nodes or arcs of the graph and collapse them together, folding the graph in on itself and combining observations from multiple traversals of the same area.

5. Conclusion

In this paper we examined some problems which must be solved by a mobile robot which explores an unknown environment, building a map from visual observations. In particular we introduced a symbolic map representation whose primitives are suited to the task of navigation, and which is explicitly grounded on the assumption that observations of the world are inaccurate and control of the robot is inaccurate.

The problems are far from solved. The ideas in this paper play two roles. First, we clearly stated some of the problems involved and give formal definitions of their mathematical properties. Second, we suggested some approaches to solving the problems, but much remains to be done to produce complete solutions.

Acknowledgements

This research was partially supported by the Air Force Office of Scientific Research under contract no: F49620-82-C0092. Ana Haunga cheerfully drew the figures.

Figure 8. MOBY the robot.

References

[**Brooks 1982**] Rodney A. Brooks, *Symbolic Error Analysis and Robot Planning* in **International Journal of Robotics Research**, vol 1, no. 4, 29-68.

[**Brooks 1983a**] Rodney A. Brooks, *Solving the Find-Path Problem by Good Representation of Free Space* in **IEEE Systems, Man and Cybernetics**, SMC-13, 190–197.

[**Brooks 1983b**] Rodney A. Brooks, *Planning Collision Free Motions for Pick and Place Operations* in **International Journal of Robotics Research**, vol 2, no. 4, 19-44.

[**Giralt et al 1983**] Georges Giralt, Raja Chatila and Marc Vaisset, *An Integrated Navigation and Motion Control System for Autonomous Multisensory Mobile Robots* in **Proceedings of the First International Symposium on Robotics Research**, Bretton Woods, New Hampshire, to be published by MIT press.

[**Khatib 1983**] Oussama Khatib, *Dynamic Control of Manipulators in Operational Space* in **Sixth IFT-OMM Congress on the Theory of Machines and Mechanisms**, New Delhi.

[**Laumond 1983**] Jean-Paul Laumond, *Model Structuring and Concept Recognition: Two Aspects of Learning for a Mobile Robot* in **Proceedings IJCAI-83**, Karlsruhe, West Germany, 839–841.

[**Lozano-Pérez 1983**] Tomás Lozano-Pérez, *Spatial Planning: A Configuration Space Approach* in **IEEE Transactions on Computers**, (C-32):108-120.

[**Moravec 1983**] Hans P. Moravec, *The Stanford Cart and the CMU Rover* in **Proceedings of the IEEE**, (71)872–884.

The LM Robot Programming System

by

J.C.Latombe, C.Laugier, J.M.Lefebvre, E.Mazer
Laboratoire LIFIA, BP 68, 38402 Saint Martin d'Hères Cédex, France

and J.F.Miribel
ITMI s.a., Chemin des Clos, ZIRST, 38240 Meylan, France

Abstract:
In 1977 the Artificial Intelligence Group of the LIFIA Laboratory (previously IMAG) has started a Robotics project, with the long-term goal of automating the programming of assembly robots. Simultaneously it was decided to develop a manipulator-level programming language (LM) as the target language for this research.
Since then this language not only has been defined and implemented; it also has grown into a complete robot programming system providing support for developing and debugging programs. This system includes a textual programming language, in both compile and interactive modes, augmented by program-by-showing utilities. It also incorporates a graphic simulator, which can be used both to debug and assess existing programs and to develop new ones. An extension to the programming language makes it possible what we call geometric programming of robots, using a CAD data base. Finally, a motion planner is available for computing complex trajectories described by symbolic equations.
This paper gives an overall description of the LM system. It is organized according to the main functions provided and includes brief sections presenting design philosophy, implementation, and experimentation.

1. INTRODUCTION

1.1. Robot programming

A robot manipulator can perform a certain variety of tasks without major hardware modification. Such versatility implies that for each new task the robot must be reprogrammed. This requires determining which actions must be executed, which sensing is necessary, and how actions and sensing are to interact.

Robot programming interweaves several more basic problems. Two are particularly important:

1) Specifying safe positions
A manipulator is a positioning device: it can move a part or a tool from one position to another. The core of robot programming is to define the sequence of positions through which the robot must pass during execution of the task. This includes specifying positions at which parts are to be grasped and ungrasped, positions at which special-purpose end-effectors are to be operated, trajectories to be followed by the robot, etc... Each position should be reachable without collision at the time it must be attained.

2) Dealing with uncertainty
Both the environment and the actions of the robot are not exactly predictable. Uncertainty is not important as long as it is lower than the precision required by the task, for instance the clearance between two parts to be mated. But this is directly achieved only in carefully engineered environments. Often sensing is a more appropriate way to deal with uncertainty. Then the robot program must implement a strategy in which action and sensing interact for reducing uncertainty below task requirement.

In addition to being a solution to these two problems, as well as to some others (for instance: parts must remain in stable positions during manipulation), a robot program must also be acceptable with respect to both economic and reliability considerations.

1.2. Robot programming systems

The goal of a robot programming system is to provide a language for specifying how action and sensing functionalities of one or several robots are to be applied, and to interpret this language. Its definition faces apparently conflicting requirements. On the one hand, the system must be easy to use so that it is accessible to the least sophisticated users. On the other hand, it should be expressive enough so that experienced users can describe the most complex tasks. These requirements have motivated the development of

several classes of robot programming systems based on different approaches:
- Program-by-showing versus textual programming,
- Manipulator-level versus task-level.

Program-by-showing systems record and play back robot actions produced by the programmer using an interactive guiding device. They are attractive both because of their immediacy and because they require almost no specialized knowledge from the user. However, they give access only to a few functionalities of the robot. In particular they lack expressiveness when sensing is needed or when several robots are to be used concurrently.

Systems based on textual programming, such as AL [Finkel et al. 74], VAL-II [Shimano, Geschke and Spalding 84], LM [Latombe and Mazer 81], AML [Taylor, Summers and Meyer 82], and RCCL [Hayward and Paul 84], provide larger access to robot functionalities. Although they have entered industry, they still are often considered to be only accessible to expert users. In fact, they can be used for implementing program-by-showing utilities to be operated by less sophisticated users; however these utilities alone suffer the same limitations than the pure program-by-showing systems. Planning sensory interaction and orchestrating several robots actually requires programming expertise.

Both program-by-showing systems and the textual programming systems introduced above are called manipulator-level systems because they require explicitly specifying the actions of the robots. In contrast, task-level systems are based on an approach aimed at automating programming. Their function is to convert a robot-independent task description input as a sequence of goal situations into an executable robot program. For instance, the description of an assembly task may include both the CAD models of the parts and the specification of the assembly relations.

Task-level systems potentially make it possible describing complex tasks without needing expert programmers. Although no complete prototype system has been implemented so far, research on this topic is very active (see for example [Lozano-Perez 76] [Lieberman and Wesley 77] [Lozano-Perez 81] [Brooks 84] [Laugier and Pertin 84] [Latombe 83] [Dufay and Latombe 84] [Lozano-Perez, Mason and Taylor 84] [Gouzènes 84] [Lozano-Perez and Brooks 84]), and it is likely that useful tools and systems will emerge from it soon.

1.3. Purpose of the paper

The Artificial Intelligence Group of the LIFIA Laboratory (previously IMAG) has started a Robotics project in 1977. The motivation was to develop an experimental support for AI research on topics such as planning, interaction of perception and action, learning, and spatial reasoning [Mazer 81]. The main tangible goal of this project was automation of robot programming [Latombe 82].

This project needed a manipulator-level programming language as the target language for automatic programming. None was available to us at that time, so we decided to develop our own. We thought that, drawing upon the concepts developed in the AL language, a few men-months were sufficient to make this language (named LM) operational.

Since 1978, not only we have designed and implemented the LM language, but this language also has grown into a complete system providing support for developing and debugging programs. Although it has never become the main research focus of our group, about 30 men-years have been "consumed" into the development of this system. This also led us to work with multiple French companies, both robot users and manufacturers, and a major US computer manufacturer. In August 1982, several researchers, including one of the authors, left the group and started a company, which now markets a subset of the LM system.

The discrepancy between our early previsions and the actual investment in the LM system has been the consequence of several initial misjudgements:

1) We underestimate the difficulty of implementing a reliable robot programming system.

2) We overestimated our understanding of robot programming. This led us to shift the purpose of LM from just being the target language of our work on automatic programming to being also a programming system for ourselves, with which we could directly experiment.

3) We underestimated the maintenance problem. As a tool for long-term research, LM, once developed, had to remain operational. This led us to get companies involved in the development and the marketing of the system. Then, needs other than ours had to be taken into account.

Because of our initial misjudgements, the design of the LM system has always been an evolving design guided by both research and application needs. To-day, it turns out that we have got one of the most complete robot programming systems ever developed. It includes a textual programming language, in both compile and interactive modes, augmented by program-by-showing utilities. It also incorporates a graphic simulator, which can be used both to debug and assess existing programs and to develop new ones. An extension to the programming language makes it possible what we call geometric programming of robots, using a CAD data base. Finally, an off-line motion planner is available for computing complex trajectories described by symbolic equations and kinematical constraints.

The system has been experimented on several application tasks, some rather unconventional, e.g.: assembly of a windscreen-wiper, assembly of a shock-absorber, insertion of non-standard electronic components on a card, tuning of the electronic controller of a display terminal.

This paper gives an overall description of the LM system. It is organized according to the main functions provided and includes brief sections presenting design philosophy, implementation, and experimentation.

2. LM SYSTEM FUNCTIONS

a. Textual programming

The core of the system is the LM textual programming language. It combines conventional general-purpose algorithmic constructs with robot-specific facilities for modelling the robot world, for communicating with the environment (including sensing), for specifying manipulator motions and tool operations, and for process control.

The interpreter of the language can be used either in interactive mode -- statements input on the terminal are executed upon request -- or in compile mode -- full programs are compiled into an intermediate code and linked together before execution.

b. Programming by showing

The LM language has been used for developing several program-by-showing utilities. One of them, LM-EX, is intended to assist the programmers of complex assembly tasks. It generates LM textual code in a file, which can later be edited and combined with other LM programs.

c. Graphic simulation

The interpreter of the LM language can control either actual robots or simulated ones. The simulator includes functions for simulating properties of the real world (unpredictability and collisions) and for simulating sensors. It can be used either for assessing existing programs or for generating new ones using the program-by-showing utilities.

d. Geometric programming

Using the LM language, one has to model the world by cartesian frames. LM-GEO is an extension of this language, which makes use of CAD geometric models of objects. It permits the programmer to specify location of objects by explicit geometric relations. Statements in LM-GEO are converted into LM code by a program inferring frame positions from these relations.

e. Motion planning

The interpreter of the LM language computes straight and circular motions in real time. A separate module plans more complex trajectories, described by symbolic equations. It generates tables of points in cartesian coordinates, in a format directly usable by LM programs.

Typically one develops a new program using the interpreter in the interactive mode, and tools like program-by-showing utilities, the graphic simulator, the LM-GEO interface, and the trajectory planner. Once created and hopefully debugged, the program is compiled and later executed using the interpreter in the compile mode.

3. LM LANGUAGE

3.1. Presentation

There are two basic approaches to the design of a textual robot programming language: one consists in extending an existing language by a library of procedures (e.g.: [Hayward and Paul 84]); the other is to develop a new language (e.g.: [Finkel et al. 74], [Taylor, Summers and Meyer 82]).

In LM, we have chosen the second approach. One potential advantage is to make programs more easily understandable thanks to an appropriate syntax. An other one is to make it possible detecting more programming errors during syntactical analysis, thus leading to improved experimental safety.

In order to make these advantages a reality, we have built the LM language upon a rather limited number of basic concepts, which can be combined in many different ways through simple syntactical constructs (Section 3.2). This contrasts LM against languages like AML and VAL-II, which tend to provide many concepts embedded into a uniform syntax. The architecture of the interpreter of the language (Section 3.3) reflects this philosophy: a rather small number of modules running asynchronously interact in many ways.

The need to implement the language on several types of equipment led us to design the interpreter so as to maximize the portability. As a result, the language is now available on several computers and robots.

The initial specifications of the language were aimed at being implementable on the kind of equipment commercially available at the beginning of the 80's. More recently, extensions of the language, requiring extensive parallel computing, have been defined, and are now being implemented (Section 3.4).

3.2. Language functionalities

The presentation below is limited to main concepts. [Miribel and Mazer 84] gives a complete description of the language.

a. General-purpose algorithmic facilities

In general a robot program is far from being just a sequence of MOVE statements. Often it also has to perform complex robot-independent information processing. For example, in some application tasks presented in Section 8, 80 per cent of the programs are dedicated to computations and algorithmic control. One application -- insertion of non-standard electronic components on a card using a 3D vision sensor -- requires extensive geometrical computations. The other application -- tuning the electronic controller of a display terminal by analyzing test-pattern images using a black-and-white vision system -- makes use of a diagnostic procedure implemented in the LM language for determining which corrective actions (for example rotating a potentiometer) should be taken in reaction to image defaults.

The LM language makes use of algorithmic constructs drawn from the PASCAL language. Thus it favors structured programming, making programs easier both to write and to understand. These constructs include data types (boolean, integer, real,...) and declarations of symbolic variables, control statements (IF-THEN-ELSE, WHILE-DO, CASE,...), and procedure and function calls with value and address parameters.

In order to keep the language portable from one computer to an other, LM includes only simple file manipulation statements, like READ, WRITE and REWIND, and no facility for invoking functions of the operating system. However, programs written in languages other than LM can be linked with the interpreter and called from LM programs as procedures in order to extend these facilities when needed.

b. World modelling

The aim of modelling the world is to provide the robot program an interface through which different statements can interact. Typically motion statements read part positions in the model, while both sensing and computation statements update the model.

Like many other robot languages, LM uses cartesian frames to model the world. They permit the representation of the locations of both objects, including end-effectors, and features on the objects.

LM directly provides frames, transforms and vectors as data types. Transforms are used to define the locations of frames, and vectors to generate transforms. Some frames are predefined in the language, e.g.: ROBOT(i) is a frame attached to the extremity of manipulator number i (several manipulators can be controlled by a single program); STATION is the reference frame known from both the language interpreter and the user.

LM includes the AFFIX/UNFIX statements for creating/destructing rigid relationships among frames. Two affixed frames remain in the same relative position in the model of the world. If the position of one frame is modified, for instance by a motion statement, then the position of the other frame is automatically updated by the language interpreter. If a frame f is affixed to ROBOT(i), then it becomes movable. This means that frame f can directly appear in a motion statement. For example:

```
AFFIX f TO ROBOT(2); MOVE f TO location_1;
```

will cause a motion of robot number 2 bringing f onto frame location_1. The interpreter verifies that f is affixed to a ROBOT frame, but it does not check that the part represented by f is physically grasped by the robot.

World modelling with cartesian frames makes it possible an implementation characterized by both conciseness of representation and simplicity of algorithms [Paul 81]. It also has some drawbacks:

- Frames are not always easy for humans to reason about, both for writing and for reading a program. This difficulty has motivated the development of the LM-GEO interface.

- Frames sometimes lead to overspecify locations, in particular when dealing with symmetric objects. Partially constrained locations require symbolic computation facilities not present in current robot languages because of their cost.

- Frames are only appropriate for modelling worlds made of rigid objects. However this is also the case of most available geometric modelling paradigms.

Because of their computational advantages, cartesian frames are likely to remain in use for a long time. Meanwhile they could be usefully extended both by constructs for representing uncertainty on their locations, and algorithms for propagating changes on uncertainty. Indeed, explicit knowledge about uncertainty is often needed in a program for deciding whether to use sensing. Currently, such a decision is based on the programmer's intuition and/or on previous experimentations with the program.

c. Communication with the environment

More and more, robot applications require both sensing and communication with other devices. Two main constructs are available in the language to that purpose: state variables and sensory functions. At first approximation, state variables are sensory functions with no parameter.

A sensory function (or a state variable) evaluates itself to an elementary piece of information (a boolean, an integer, a real, a vector, or a transform), which is not under the direct control of the programmer. For example, it can be a sensory datum (torque about a vector, location of a part measured by a vision system,...), a piece of information sent by another device (e.g. status of this device), the elapsed time since the beginning of the last motion, etc... It may appear in any expression; for instance, VISION(obj-num) evaluates to the transform defining the position of object identified by number obj-num; then

```
grasp:=VISION(obj-num)*TRANSLAT(VZ,50);
```

may define the grasping position of this object.

State variables differ from sensory functions mainly because they can be passed as "state parameters" to a procedure (or a function). The corresponding formal parameters in the procedure definition are then considered as state variables when the procedure is executed. This makes it possible writing a procedure using sensory data of unknown kinds. For instance, if FX(i), FY(i), and FZ(i) are elements of array state variables representing the three components of the force exerted by robot i, then an insertion procedure can use three state parameters, let say f1, f2 and f3, each representing any one of the state variables.

Two additional statements:

```
   WRITE v ON CHANNEL z;
   READ v ON CHANNEL z;
```

are available to send (resp. receive) pieces of information to (resp. from) the environment.

d. Motions

In LM, motions are controlled by MOVE statements combining three different notions: path geometry, kinematics, and interaction with sensors (other than internal position sensors).

- Geometry of the path:

The most natural way to describe a path in LM is to specify the displacement of a movable frame. Then the path consists of one or several segments, each being either a free segment (the default type of segment) -- only the terminal position is given, and the joints will be coordinated so that they start and arrive together --, or a cartesian (straight) segment -- which includes a possible rotation about a fixed vector --, or a circular segment, or a predefined segment -- using a precomputed table of cartesian positions, such as those generated by the planner of Section 7.

Example:

```
   MOVE object VIA frame1 CARTESIAN,
                   frame2 FREE
               TO goal CARTESIAN;
```

The interpreter generates short transition paths between two consecutive segments.

Path description using cartesian frames suffers from some drawbacks:

* It does not explicitly handle configuration changes during motions.
* The internal representation (e.g. homogeneous transforms) does not completely specify how rotations should be executed. For example:
  `MOVE f BY ROT(VZ,3*PI/4) CARTESIAN;`
  suggests rotating f about its Z axis by 3*PI/4; however the actual rotation, due to the convention taken in the interpreter, will be about Z axis by -PI/4.

Experience has shown that these drawbacks can be partly avoided by providing the programmer a construct for describing displacements of individual joints, e.g.:

```
   MOVE AXES 1,2,4 OF ROBOT 2 TO 3.,6.2,.7;
```

This construct also turns out very useful for controlling simple mechanical devices with 2 and 3 degrees of freedom.

- Kinematics:

The programmer can set a speed factor between 0 and 1 for each manipulator. Let T1 be the minimum time for executing a motion along a path given the maximum speed and acceleration known by the interpreter. Let TC be the time for executing a motion along the same path with a speed factor equal to C. The interpreter computes the speed profiles along the path so that TC=T1/C.

Despite its simplicity, the speed factor allows the user to have reasonable control over the velocity during motion. More control and accuracy can be obtained by using predefined motions computed by a planner.

- Interaction with sensors:

With respect to sensory interaction, three types of motions can be considered: free motions, guarded motions, and compliant motions.

Free motions are purely position-controlled motions. They involve no interaction with sensors other than internal position sensors.

Guarded motions are position-controlled, but they are to be stopped before completion if a sensory-based condition becomes true. They are described in LM using the UNTIL clause, e.g.:

```
   MOVE f BY TRANSLAT(v,dist)  UNTIL  FZ(1)>2.5*N;
   MOVE f TO goal UNTIL MOVE-TIME>10*S;
```

The condition is evaluated at a rate which can be set by the programmer (otherwise it has a default value), e.g.:

```
   MOVE f ... UNTIL FX(1)+FY(1)>5.0 FREQUENCY 50;
```

The interpreter reports any failure in evaluating the condition at the right frequency.

Compliant motions may be position-controlled along some axes; but along perpendicular axes, their control makes use of other sensors, typically force and proximity sensors. Until now compliant motions required specific hardware, and LM currently includes no construct for specifying them directly. In theory it is possible to generate compliant motions using several guarded motions with the NOWAIT and IMMEDIATELY options defined in Section f below; in practice this possibility leads to motions with slow adaptation to the environment. New constructs are under preparation (see Section 3.4.a).

e. Tool operations

The potential variety of end-effectors which may be operated by a robot led us to include two different kinds of statements in the language.

A general-purpose instruction is intended for operating any type of end-effector:

```
   OPERATE TOOL j OF ROBOT i WITH x1,...,xn;
```

where x1,...,xn are parameters such as speed, distance,... Their meaning depend on the type of end-effector which is used.

A specific, but more readable instruction is available for describing operations of classical two-jaw grippers:

```
   WIDEN GRIPPER OF ROBOT i TO/BY y;
```

Additional specific instructions can be added to the language thanks to its easily modifiable syntax (see Section 3.3.a).

The UNTIL clause can be used in all these statements, e.g.:

```
WIDEN GRIPPER ... TO 0. UNTIL PRESSURE>2.5;
```

f. Process control

Many application tasks require the coordination of several devices. Although LM is not a general-purpose concurrent programming language, it offers simple but powerful constructs for coordinating parallel operations. The two main ones are the NOWAIT and IMMEDIATELY options which may appear in both MOVE statements and tool operation statements:

- The NOWAIT option permits continuing the execution of the program without the completion of a motion or a tool operation.
  Example:
  ```
  MOVE ROBOT(1) TO somewhere NOWAIT;
  CLOSE GRIPPER OF ROBOT 2;
  ```
  Comment: The gripper of robot 2 will be closed immediately after the robot 1 starts moving. Execution of the program will then be suspended until the gripper is closed.

- The IMMEDIATELY option makes it possible starting a motion (or a tool operation) without waiting for the completion of the previous one.
  Example:
  ```
  MOVE ROBOT(2) BY TRANSLAT(v1,d1) NOWAIT;
  ...
  MOVE IMMEDIATELY ROBOT(2) BY TRANSLAT(v2,d2);
  ```
  Comment: If the second MOVE statement is executed while robot 2 is still moving along vector v1, then the trajectory is modified on the fly to become a translation along vector v2. The interpreter generates a transition path between the two paths.

The IMMEDIATELY clause can also appear in a statement setting the speed factor of a robot in order to modify the speed of the robot while it is moving.

In addition, a PAUSE instruction, consisting of a list of condition-action pairs, is available for expressing coordination among parallel operations. Conditions are evaluated until one becomes true; then the corresponding action is executed.

3.3. Language implementation

a. Overview of the interpreter

The interpreter of the LM language is made of three parts: the compiler, the linker and the LM machine.

The compiler checks syntax and produces an intermediate code using tables automatically produced from a BNF description of the language. This makes the compiler easy to modify.

The linker operates as in a conventional programming environment.

The LM machine is a virtual machine which interprets the code produced after compilation and link editing. It is described in the next section.

The control structure permits the interpreter to run either in the compile mode or in the interactive mode:

- In the compile mode the user has to go through the edit-compile-link-run sequence. The main advantage is to get rid of the syntactical analysis during execution, and consequently to speed up interpretation.

- In the interactive mode, the user can type one or several statements and ask for their execution by typing a special character. He can also ask for execution of statements contained in a file. This is made possible by calling alternatively the compiler and the LM machine; the linker is called once at the beginning of the session. The interpreter compiles all the statements before passing code to the LM machine; this makes the execution by the LM machine respond exactly as in the compile mode.

In the interactive mode the user can also select among the input statements those which have to be saved into a file. This permits him both writing and debugging programs at the same time.

The interactive mode is now being extended in order to make it possible reverse execution of statements [Grossman 77].

b. LM machine

The LM machine is a virtual stack machine with virtual registers. It is split into three main modules: the virtual processor, the motion interpreter, and the input-output interface.

- The virtual processor:
  It decodes the numerical code produced by the compiler and generates the corresponding function calls. It executes all robot-independent statements and it handles parallel execution required by guarded motions and tool operations.

- The motion interpreter:
  The syntax of the MOVE statement results in a large number of possible motion situations. As a consequence, the motion interpreter is made of several interacting modules operating concurrently, including on-line trajectory planning, computation of inverse kinematics and servo control.

  In principle any cut through these modules defines a level of interfacing the LM interpreter with preexisting equipment. However we usually consider a low-level cut which corresponds to an interface, called RACCORD, handling three types of query only: joint initialization query, joint status query, and joint motion query. For instance the joint motion query specifies the following parameters:

an interval of time T, the goal location and speed at the end of this interval, and the generalized forces to be applied by the joint during the next interval of time. This interface level is very convenient because the format of the exchanged messages is easily defined. Often it also corresponds to a natural partition in the robot controller architecture.

On-line trajectory planning makes use of methods similar to those described in [Paul 81].

The motion interpreter runs asynchronously with the virtual processor, and is duplicated for each robot controlled by the LM interpreter.

- Input-output interface:
  It is the software interface in charge of all the input-output operations of the LM machine: evaluation of state variables and sensory functions, read-write operations on files and terminals.

c. Portability

Both the compiler and the linker are written in Fortran and are hardware independent.

The LM machine is also written in Fortran. Transporting the virtual processor requires only minor software changes. Transporting the motion interpreter requires using the particular facilities of the new operating system for creating parallel processes and defining communication channels among them; with respect to robot hardware, it turned out to be easily adaptable. Transportation of the input-output interface requires limited modification to fit the particular hardware configuration.

The portability of LM is demonstrated by the number of currently existing implementations. Indeed, LM is running on several robots (SCEMI, MATRA, CITROEN, DISTRIBEL, AUTOMATA, GDA, RENAULT V80 and TH8, AKR,...) and multiple computers (DEC LSI 11/23, VAX 750, INTEL 8086, MOTOROLA 68000, HP-1000, GOULD SEL-32,...). Some of these implementations can be classified into industrial implementations. Others are laboratory ones.

3.4. Current development

Two new constructs, guarded commands and parallel blocks, have been added to the language [Lefebvre 82], and are now being implemented.

a. Guarded commands

One goal is to extend the current facilities for specifying sensor-based motions. The other goal is to permit the user to orchestrate reactions to asynchronous events, typically external interrupts.

Guarded commands of the form <guard> => <command>, are the basic construct for attaining these two goals. <guard> is a boolean condition, and <command> a LM statement. Whenever the interpreter meets a guarded command, it instantiates all the variables in the guard by their current values, except state variables. The instantiated guard is then periodically evaluated, in parallel with the execution of the rest of the program. If the guard becomes true, then <command> is executed.

Guarded commands may appear as part of MOVE statements, or as stand-alone statements:

- A guarded command in a motion statement becomes active when the motion is started. It is deactivated when the motion has physically been executed. It permits the programmer to describe the modification of the trajectory in response to sensory inputs. Nested guarded commands make it possible implementing compliant motions based on different models of compliance [Lefebvre 82].

- A guarded command appearing as a statement in a program may be used to handle interrupts. It can be labelled, and ACTIVATE and DEACTIVATE statements make it possible defining non-interruptible subprograms (for example, a manipulator should not be interrupted for unloading a mobile robot while it is executing a part-mating operation).

b. Parallel blocks

The goal is to extend the current facilities for coordinating several robots. The implemented version of the language can handle parallel execution by several robots using the NOWAIT option. This facility is adequate for close interaction among robots. In principle, it also allows the programmer to define separate sections of code to be executed by different robots, but is is not truly suitable to this purpose.

We have defined a new statement of the form:

```
COBEGIN
  [label-1] <block-1>
  [label-2] <block-2>
  ...
  [label-N] <block-N>
COEND;
```

specifying that N blocks of program are to be executed concurrently. Typically (but not necessarily) each block corresponds to a distinct robot. Two other statements:

```
SEND <message> TO <block-label>;
RECEIVE <message> FROM <block-label>;
```

are used for communicating among blocks. A message may be a value; then it is stored in a queue by the SEND statement. It can also be the reserved word SIGNAL; then each of the two blocks will proceed to next statements only after the exchange is terminated.

The version of the language including these extensions is now being implemented on the CESAR/CLEOPATRE system (a multi-68000 architecture) developed by the CERT/DERA laboratory.

4. PROGRAMMING BY SHOWING

Programming by showing is often opposed to textual programming. The former is considered to favor simplicity, and the latter expressiveness. In fact, this is only part of the truth. Indeed consider the following LM program:

```
PROGRAM utility;
  BOOLEAN more; FRAME pos; FILE prog;
  BEGIN
    WRITE "POGRAM play-back;" IN prog;
    WRITE "BEGIN;" IN prog;
    more := TRUE;
    WHILE more DO
      pos := ROBOT;
      TEACH;
      IF DISTANCE(ROBOT,pos) /= 0
         OR ANGLE(ROBOT,pos) /= 0
         THEN WRITE "MOVE ROBOT TO (", ROBOT, ");"
                    IN prog;
         ELSE more := FALSE;
      ENDIF;
      WRITE "END;" IN prog;
    ENDDO;
  END;
```

This program can be operated by a user ignoring all of LM, as a program-by-showing utility. It iteratively gives control on the teach pendant (statement TEACH). When control is returned back to the program, the new position and orientation of the robot end-effector (frame ROBOT) are compared to the old ones (recorded by frame pos). If one value at least has changed, then the current location of ROBOT is used to generate a MOVE statement into a program file.

A simplification of this program consists in recording just the successive locations of ROBOT into a file and in running a play-back program using this file. However, an interesting point in explicitly generating a LM program is that this program is easily editable: it can later be augmented by both control and sensor-based statements. In addition, once compiled, it can behave more efficiently than the play-back program.

This illustrative example, although very simple, shows that a textual language like LM is a powerful tool for developing utilities. This property can be exploited in two ways:

- For implementing interfaces to be operated by users with no computer programming experience: it is relatively easy to create special-purpose program-by-showing utilities adapted to various types of tasks such as pick-and-place, palettizing, and point-to-point welding.

- For implementing program development tools to be used by experienced programmers: even for such users, program-by-showing utilities are very helpful for describing robot environments using the robot as a measuring device, or for creating simple pieces of programs, or for building skeletons of programs to be edited later.

This complementarity of textual programming and programming by showing has also been recognized and exploited in a few other systems, e.g.: POINTY in the AL system [Grossman and Taylor 78], and XPROBE in the AML system [Summers and Grossman 84].

Several program-by-showing utilities have been implemented using the LM language. Most of them are fairly simple (in fact several were created by students at the undergraduate level as exercises in robot programming). One of them, named LM-EX [Bansard 83], which has been developed for assisting the programmer of complex assembly tasks, is particularly sophisticated. It stands both as a programming environment and as an execution environment:

- As a programming environment, it combines programming commands and editing commands.

  Programming commands include interactive guiding from the teach pendant augmented by the terminal keyboard; for example, gross motions can be generated from the teach pendant and refined by small motions incrementally controlled from the keyboard. Programming commands also include a subset of the facilities of the LM language built around a small number of predefined cartesian frames. This subset provides both computational facilities and access to predefined procedures.

  Each programming commands can be stored into files using editing commands, or forgotten. Before it is stored a command is converted into LM textual code.

- As an execution environment, LM-EX permits the user to execute a program generated using LM-EX in either step-by-step or automatic mode. The program being executed can be interrupted and its context is automatically saved in order to resume execution later. Interruptions may be used for modifying the program by returning into the programming environment.

LM-EX has been applied to generate the complete program for assembling a windscreen-wiper. Experience drawn from LM-EX has been used by the ITMI company to develop a general-purpose teach pendant with programmable functional keys connected to its robot controller.

5. GRAPHIC SIMULATION

5.1. Main features

During the last five years, graphic simulation has emerged as a valuable tool for robot programming when CAD facilities are available [Meyer 81] [Dooner, Taylor and Bonney 82] [Sata, Kimura and Amano 81] [Arai 83] [Liégeois, Borrel and Dombre 84].

The main features of the LM simulator are the following:

1) It can be used either for executing existing application programs in order to assess them,

or for executing program-by-showing utilities in order to create new application programs.

2) It includes functions for simulating both unpredictability of the real-world and sensors.

3) In order to provide the user a realistic feeling of the three-dimensional world, it can visualize scenes as shaded color pictures.

The simulator interacts with both the interpreter and the user. It can receive three types of commands as input:

- Program commands:
  They are sent by the interpreter in response to the program being executed, e.g. robot motions, sensing.

- Simulation commands:
  They are sent either by the interpreter or by the user. They concern time emulation, tuning of visualization parameters, simulation interrupt, etc.

- User commands:
  They are input by the user. They concern interactive guiding during execution of program-by-showing utilities.

The interpreter of the LM language is used without modification, in both compile and interactive modes, to control actual robots and to interact with the simulator. The same LM program can be executed in both situations. Program commands are emitted by the RACCORD interface of the interpreter (see Section 3.3.b) just as if it were commands sent to a robot controller. Simulation commands are sent by the interpreter in response to the execution of standard LM WRITE statements of the form:

WRITE <simulation command> IN SIMUL;

where SIMUL is a channel reserved for communicating with the simulator.

The user interacts with the simulator through an interactive graphic device, menus and keyboard.

5.2. Components of the simulator

a. Manipulator simulation

This component simulates the execution of both the robot motion and the tool operation statements in the LM program. Its input is the sequence of servo points in joint coordinates which are emitted by the interpreter. Its output consists of requests to the world modelling module for updating the world model. Several robots can be handled simultaneously.

The simulator makes use of a purely kinematical model of the manipulators; it ignores dynamics.

b. World modelling

This component is in charge of updating a geometric model of the world. Its inputs are:

- Simulation commands for positioning objects, (e.g. setting the initial arrangement of the world), and for linking objects (e.g. representing physical attachments),

- Requests sent by the module simulating manipulators, specifying new positions of the robots,

- Requests sent by the module simulating real world, which generates perturbations on positions of objects.

The world model is a graph of solid objects connected by relations. These can be either articulated or rigid relations. Articulated ones [Laugier and Pertin-Troccaz 84] are used to represent manipulators and end-effectors. Rigid relations are temporary or permanent ones. Temporary relations are created and destroyed by ATTACH and DETACH simulation commands.

c. Graphic interface

This component is in charge of both displaying robot scenes and handling interaction with the user.

Scenes are presented either as line drawings or shaded pictures. In both cases, the scene is displayed as if it was watched by a virtual camera. This camera is positioned on a "vision sphere" so that the center of the sphere projects itself on the center of the image. The location of the center and the radius of the sphere, the position of the camera on the sphere (latitude and longitude), and the focal length of the camera are all tunable parameters set by simulation commands. The center of the sphere can be located on a moving object to be tracked by the camera.

Simulation commands concerning the graphic interface also provide the following facilities: make some objects invisible, superpose several successive images, move the source of light (when scenes are displayed as shaded pictures), perform traveling and zooming on a fixed scene, ...

d. Time emulation

This component sets sampling rates both for updating the world model and for displaying robot scenes on the screen according to simulation commands. It orchestrates the operations of the simulator according to these rates.

The sampling rate f0 of the generation of servo points by the LM interpreter is defined by the internal clock of the interpreter. During the execution of either a robot motion or tool operation statement the simulator updates the world model at a rate $f1=f0/n$, where n is a tunable positive integer. It displays a new image at a rate $f2=f1/p$, where p is another tunable integer.

At any moment, simulation can be interrupted (this means: time is suspended) and resumed later by simulation commands. When simulation is interrupted, the world model is updated according to the last servo command sent by the LM interpreter, and the corresponding image is displayed.

A simulation command PAUSE permits the user to set the minimal duration of the same image on the screen.

Servo points sent by the interpreter are stored in a buffer. When this buffer is full, the simulator interrupts the interpreter until simulation has progressed further.

e. Real-world simulation

This component simulates two aspects of the real world: unpredictability and collisions.

- One function brings random modifications to the positions of some objects in the world model. It is evaluated in response to simulation commands, each specifying an object name and the maximum perturbation, and it sends a request to the world modelling module.

  This function is applicable both to parts of the robots environment and to the segments of the manipulators. The position of attached objects are updated accordingly.

- An other function is used for detecting collision. Each evaluation of this function activates a new virtual touch sensor, gives it a name, and passes it a list of objects to watch for. Then, whenever the world model is updated, possible interferences among these objects are computed. Several virtual sensors can be active simultaneously. They can be deactivated separately at any time by simulation commands.

  When an interference among objects is detected, simulation is interrupted. In case of true collision, the user can stop the motion and resume simulation. In case of compliant contact, he can deactivate the corresponding touch sensor and resume simulation (motion is not stopped).

  Interference computation makes use of polyhedral approximations of objects.

These facilities greatly extend the applicability of simulation as a tool for debugging robot programs. Nevertheless they still present obvious shortcomings. In particular, the simulator has no model of friction, and it ignores the gravity law.

f. Sensor simulation

This component is in charge of simulating sensors. Whenever a state variable or a sensory functions has to be evaluated in the application program, a program command is sent to this component, which invokes the appropriate function.

Some functions simulating sensors are autonomous functions needing no interaction with the user. For example, a 2D vision sensor for locating parts is simulated by extracting the location of a part from the simulator´s world model and by slightly modifying it in order to take into account imprecision of the actual sensor.

Other functions require limited user intervention. These functions make use of data contained in reserved areas of the computer memory, which may be updated by the user when simulation is interrupted. For instance, the function simulating force sensing reads data representing force and torque components in a given frame. Typically these data may be initialized to 0.0; when a collision is detected, simulation is interrupted (see Section e), and the user can input new values.

The primary advantage of this. simulation is simplicity. However, the response times of a simulated sensor and of an actual sensor may be different.

g. Teach-pendant simulation

The goal of this component is to permit the user to teleoperate a simulated robot, just like a teach-pendant makes it possible the interactive guiding of an actual robot. It is activated by a program command whenever the TEACH statement is executed.

The actual teach-pendant or functional keys on the terminal could be used to this purpose. However, guiding a robot on a graphical display is much harder than guiding an actual robot, so that we have chosen rather to implement an interactive module based on concepts developed at the LAM laboratory [Liégeois, Borrel and Dombre 84]. Using an interactive device like a light-pen, the user shows two points (or two lines,...), one belonging to a movable object, the other to a fixed one, and asks for their superposition (or their alignment,...). Combining such commands makes it possible defining any robot configuration in space.

Although guiding methods are different, the same program-by-showing utility can be used whether the robot is an actual one, or a simulated one.

5.3. Implementation of the simulator

The LM simulator is implemented in Lisp. It displays images on the HELIOS terminal developed at the IMAG laboratory [Martinez 82]. This terminal includes several hardware functions for generating and manipulating color shaded images. One function makes it possible moving the virtual source of light in real time. Figure 1 shows images generated by the simulator using this terminal.

Object models are input using SMGR, a modelling system developed by our group [Pertin-Troccaz 84].

6. GEOMETRIC PROGRAMMING

6.1 Objective

Defining the locations of cartesian frames by transforms combining translations and rotations, as in the LM language, is often tedious. It may also lead to programs which are difficult to understand.

Most of the time the programmer makes use of program-by-showing utilities. This solves the input problem, but does not improve the readability of the resulting programs. In addition, modification of locations requires reentering the program-by-showing session, or editing files produced by the utilities.

We have developed an extension of the LM language, named LM-GEO, which make it possible defining object locations by explicit geometric relations among objects [Mazer 83]. LM-GEO is intended to replace the on-line input of locations using program-by-showing techniques by an off-line, easily readable textual description. This basic idea is inspired from the RAPT language [Popplestone, Ambler and Bellos 80].

Although LM-GEO has the flavor of a task-level language, it definitively is a manipulator-level one. Indeed, it requires the programmer to specify all manipulator motions and tool operations, and sensory interaction.

6.2. LM-GEO language

LM-GEO is an extension of the LM language; all the constructs available in LM are also available in LM-GEO. However the primary advantage of LM-GEO is to avoid the explicit use of both cartesian frames and transforms among them. This is made possible by the introduction of a new construct called geometric situation.

For example, in LM, in order to make a robot grasp an object, one has to write statements such as:

```
t:=TRANSLAT(VECT(-3.,2.,5.),8.)*ROT(VZ,PI/2);
MOVE ROBOT(1) TO box*t;
```

In LM-GEO this can be expressed by a single statement, for instance:

```
MOVE ROBOT 1 TO ACHIEVE grasp-box;
```

where grasp-box is a geometric situation.

A geometric situation is defined by symbolic relations among features of the objects. For example, grasp-box may be defined by:

```
top OF gripper IS-AGAINST (50) f1 OF box;
jaw1 OF gripper IS-AGAINST (0) f2 OF box;
jaw2 OF gripper IS-AGAINST (0) f3 OF box;
side1  OF  gripper IS-PARALLEL-TO (25) f4 OF box;
```

In this definition, gripper and box are names given to two objects; top, jaw1, jaw2, and side1 denote faces of the object gripper.

Relations for describing geometric situations are currently limited to the following ones:

- <plan> IS-AGAINST (d) <plan>, where d is the distance between the two plans,
- <plan> IS-PARALLEL-TO (d) <plan>, which means that the two plans have the same external normal vector,
- <line> IS-ALIGNED-WITH <line>,
- <line> IS-PARALLEL-TO <line>,
- <point> IS-ON <point>.

Each geometric situation involves an ordered pair of objects, e.g. (gripper,box), and is intended to define the position of the first object of the pair with respect to the second. Each of the two objects can be either an elementary object or a situation (i.e. a compound object).

Each elementary object must be described in a model data base. A cartesian frame must be attached to each object model (this frame is used by the interpreter of LM-GEO). Each object feature to be used in a geometric situation is given a name. Its equation(s) or coordinates are defined with respect to the corresponding cartesian frame.

The initial location of an object may be defined by a geometric situation, for example:

```
CURRENT SITUATION IS start-prism-1;
```

which may involve objects with a priori known positions (e.g. the working table of the robot). It may also not be defined if it is to be provided at execution time, for instance by a vision system.

6.3. LM-GEO interpretation

The interpreter of LM-GEO is basically a rewrite program generating LM code. It operates in three steps.

The first step consists in computing the transform between the two frames attached to the objects in each geometric situation [Mazer 82]. Relations in the situation are converted into vector equations, which are then transformed into a set of linear equations and one non-linear equation; this set is solved by conventional means. Unlike the RAPT method based on symbolic calculus, this analytical method finds a transform value whenever it exists and is unique; otherwise it reports failure (the situation is not constrained enough, or it is inconsistent).

The second step consists in generating LM code declaring frame variables, Object(i), for all elementary objects used in the LM-GEO program and transform variables, Situation(j), for all geometric situations. The transform values computed at the first step are assigned to these transform variables.

The third step consists in transforming LM-GEO constructs into LM constructs. For instance:

```
CURRENT SITUATION IS start-prism-1;
```

is translated into something like:

```
Object(5):=Object(3)*Situation(1);
```

Similarly:

```
MOVE prism-1 TO ACHIEVE approach-prism-2;
```

may be translated into:

```
MOVE Object(5) TO Object(6)*Situation(4);
```

etc... [Mazer 83].

The LM-GEO interpreter is implemented in Lisp. It has been experimented on simple assembly tasks [Mazer 83].

7. MOTION PLANNING

The motion interpreter of the LM machine (see Section 3.3.b) plans and executes in real time motions along sequences of straight and circular segments. The speed along a segment is constant, except along short transition paths between segments.

There are several application tasks which require very precise control of position and speed along complex paths. These include seam tracking for arc welding and glue deposit. The off-line motion planner presented in this section is intended to be a tool for this class of tasks.

A motion is described to the planner as a set of symbolic equations specifying the geometry of the path and the speed along the path. The output is a table of cartesian positions and speed values uniformly distributed along the time axis according to a given sampling period. This table is stored into a file and is used by LM statements of the form:

```
MOVE f ALONG TRAJECTORY table;
```

During execution of the motion, the LM interpreter transforms all the positions in the table by applying the transform which brings the first position in the table onto the initial position of frame f. Because of this transform, the planner does not check limits on joint speed and acceleration. This is the task of the LM interpreter at run time.

The motion planner was first developed for motions with fixed orientation. Then a motion is specified by four symbolic equations defining the path of the center of the frame to be moved and the speed along this path:

```
X=X(C)  Y=Y(C)  Z=Z(C)  V=V(C)
```

where C is a parameter linking the four equations. Such a definition makes it possible specifying path geometry and speed separately. The planner automatically computes the relation between C and the time.

More recently, the planner has been extended to permit the description of motions involving rotations of the moving frame. The rotation is specified by three equations defining Euler angles as functions of C. The rotational speed is imposed by the linear speed.

Finally the motion planner allows the user to describe a motion as a sequence of several segments. Each segment is defined as above. The planner computes short transition paths from one segment to the next.

The planner is implemented in Fortran. It has been experimented on several tasks including glue deposit along the contour of an electrical iron.

8. EXPERIMENTATION

We present shortly three experimentations conducted using the LM system (or part of it). Each makes use of a single SCEMI robot with six degrees of freedom. Cooperation among robots has also been experimented on simpler application tasks.

a. Assembly of a shock absorber

The task consists in assembling a shock absorber of a Peugeot 505 automobile [Crébassa, Salmon and Schmitt 84]. Most assembly operations are vertical insertions, but the parts have multiple shapes, sizes, and matters. In addition, tolerances between some pairs of parts are very tight.

The assembly has been performed using the SCEMI robot equipped with a force sensing wrist, a 2D black-and-white vision system, and a 3D vision system. The latter makes use of a laser-light strip [Borianne 84]. Figure 2 shows some stages of the assembly process.

The 2D vision system is used for determining the initial location of some parts. Force sensing appears in guarded motions to face uncertainty on part locations during difficult insertions. The 3D vision sensor makes possible the accurate alignment of the rod axis with the cylinder axis in order to initialize the most delicate insertion of the task.

Use of sensors has resulted in a crude arrangement of the robot environment. In particular, fixtures are simple combination of modular components. Nevertheless the time spent in defining this arrangement was still unexpectedly long with respect to the time spent in writing programs.

b. Insertion of electronic components

The task consists in inserting non-standard electronic components such as resistors and capacitors on a card [Caloud and Durand 84]. The SCEMI robot is equipped with the same 3D vision sensor as above. Experiments have been conducted with components with two legs of different lengths. The card is in a known position with respect to the 3D sensor. Figure 3 shows several stages of the insertion of a capacitor.

Vision is used for locating legs in space. A first guarded motion brings the extremity of the longest leg on the light plane. Then a free motion provides the LM program a second point along the leg, which is now approximated by the LM program as a straight line. Additional free motions rotate the leg in order to make it vertical, translate it above the hole, and perform insertion. Insertion of the second leg is achieved in the same way; it may require bending the first leg slightly.

The method turned out reliable, if calibration was executed carefully, allowing large variations on the relative position and orientation of the two legs. It is also potentially quicker than methods based on force sensing.

c. Tuning a display terminal

The task consists in tuning the TV controller of a CII-HB alphanumeric display terminal [Mondot 84]. It requires analyzing test-pattern images and executing corrective actions such as rotating potentiometers, and positioning magnets. The terminal is equipped with a processor which generates the test-pattern images.

Most of the task has been automated using a SCEMI robot augmented by a vision system with the CAIMAN software. Figure 4 illustrates the operations executed by the overall system.

The robot is used both for pushing functional keys in order to display test-pattern images and for executing corrective actions. The LM program not only controls these operations, it also determines the corrective actions from the image defaults detected by the vision system (for example: the image is tilted with respect to the screen axes).

This experimentation illustrates the need for general-purpose algorithmic and computing facilities in a robot programming language. Although the overall system is still quite slow (this is mainly due to the vision system which is too general), it also demonstrates the feasability of automating the task using a robot.

9. CONCLUSION

During the last three years, the LM system (or part of it) has been intensively experimented:

- As a stand-alone system, for developing robot programs on application tasks such as those presented in Section 8, both by ourselves and by engineers in several companies,

- As the target language of our research on automatic programming: grasp planning [Laugier and Pertin 84], part-mating planning [Dufay and Latombe 84], and path planning [Germain 84].

Several general conclusions have emerged from these experiments:

1) Automatic programming of robots is a real need.

   Indeed, the difficulty of programming robots increases much more quickly than the apparent complexity of the application tasks. While a simple toy assembly may take only a few hours or less to be programmed, several weeks are necessary for a device like a shock absorber.

   Although automatic robot programming techniques have recently made impressive progress [Latombe 83], a complete industrial system is still far away. Nevertheless, interactive tools based on these techniques could contribute to dramatically simplifying the task of programming robots.

2) Design is an important ingredient of robot programming.

   Programming robots not only consists in planning action and sensing; it also requires designing the environment of the robots (e.g. fixtures). Although sensing undoubtly reduces the amount of engineering required to operate robots, the design of the environment remains a large part of the task of programming robots.

   Until now, work on automatic programming has only addressed the problem of planning action and sensing, considering the description of the environment an input. We now think that the design of the environment should also be considered an important part of the full problem. In that perspective our group has started a research work on fixture design [Ingrand 84].

3) Automating programming should operate on-line.

   A major difficulty of programming a robot derives from the need to foresee all the classes of situations requiring different processing. The number of these classes increases with the complexity of the tasks.

   Operating automatic programming techniques on-line would avoid the need of identifying all the relevant situations, thus leading to a simplification of the techniques themselves. In addition it could significantly reduce the amount of engineering required to run the robots, because the number of different situations could then augment arbitrarily. Inductive learning techniques [Dufay and Latombe 84] could then be very useful to increase efficiency of the overall system by limiting the calls to automatic programming routines.

Interestingly these conclusions concern automatic programming, not the LM system itself. In fact, we feel that in the short and medium terms there are more potential results to draw from research on automatic programming than from the redesign of a manipulator-level system.

Acknowledgments:

Development of the LM system has been funded by various government organizations and industrial companies: ARA Project, Agence de l'Informatique, DIELI, DRET, CERCI, SCEMI, ITMI, MATRA, and PSA.

REFERENCES

- Arai T. 1983: "A robot language system with a color graphic simulator", Proc. Advanced

Software in Robotics, Liège, p215-226.
- Bansard J.P. 1983: "The LM-EX system" (in French), Internal Report, LIFIA Laboratory, 116p.
- Borianne P.L. 1984: "Contributions to three-dimensional computer vision" (in French), Thesis Diss., National Polytechnic Institute of Grenoble, 153p.
- Brooks R.A. 1984: "Planning collision free motions for pick and place operations", Robotics Research, The First International Symposium, edited by Brady M. and Paul R., MIT Press, p5-37.
- Caloud P. and Durand P. 1984: "Automatic programming of robots: application to the insertion of non standard electronic components on a card" (in French), DEA Report, LIFIA Laboratory, 128p.
- Crébassa M., Salmon F. and Schmitt P. 1984: "Assembly of a shock absorber by a robot" (in French), Internal Report, LIFIA Laboratory.
- Dooner M., Taylor N.K., and Bonney M.C. 1982: "Planning robot installations by CAD", CAD Conference, Brighton.
- Dufay B. and Latombe J.C. 1984: "An approach to automatic robot programming based on inductive learning", International Journal on Robotics Research, vol.3, no.4.
- Finkel R.A. et al. 1974: "AL, a programming system for automation", Memo AIM 243, Artificial Intelligence Laboratory, Stanford University.
- Germain F. 1984: "Automatic generation of collision-free trajectories" (in French), DEA Report, LIFIA Laboratory, 67p.
- Gouzènes L. 1984: "Collision avoidance for robots in an experimental flexible assembly cell", Proc. IEEE International Conference on Robotics, Atlanta, p474-476.
- Grossman D.D. 1977: "Programming a computer controlled manipulator by guiding through the motions", IBM T.J.Watson Research Center, Report RC 6393.
- Grossman D.D. and Taylor R.H. 1978: "Interactive generation of object models with a manipulator", IEEE Trans. Systems, Man, Cybernetics SMC-8,9, p667-679.
- Hayward V. and Paul R.P. 1984: "Introduction to RCCL: a robot control ´C´ library", Proc. IEEE International Conference on Robotics, Atlanta, p293-297.
- Ingrand F. and Latombe J.C. 1984: "Functional reasoning for automatic fixtures design", CAM-I´s 13th Annual Meeting and Technical Conference, Clearwater Beach, Florida.
- Latombe J.C. 1982: "Artificial Intelligence and Robotics: group status report" (in French), IMAG Report, no.291, 211p.
- Latombe J.C. 1983: "Automatic synthesis of robot programs from CAD specifications", NATO Advanced Study Institute on Robotics and Artificial Intelligence.
- Latombe J.C. and Mazer E. 1981: "LM: a high-level programming language for controlling manipulators", 11th International Symposium on Industrial Robots, Tokyo, p683-690.
- Laugier C. and Pertin J. 1984: "Automatic grasping: a case study in accessibility analysis", in "Advanced Software in Robotics", edited by Danthine A. and, p201-214 Géradin M., North-Holland, p201-214.
- Laugier C. and Pertin-Troccaz J. 1984: "Graphic simulation as a tool for debugging robot control programs", 1st Intenational Symposium on Design and Synthesis, Tokyo, p685-690.
- Lefebvre J.M. 1982: "New definition of the MOVE statement in the LM language" (in French), DEA Report, LIFIA Laboratory.
- Lieberman L.I. and Wesley M.A. 1977: "AUTOPASS: an automatic programming system for computer controlled mechanical assembly", IBM Journal of Research and Development 21,4, p321-333.
- Liégeois A., Borrel P. and Dombre E. 1984: "Programming, simulating and evaluating robot actions", Proc. of 2nd Int. Symposium on Robotics Research, Kyoto, p309-316.
- Lozano-Perez T. 1976: "The design of a mechanical assembly system", Artificial Intelligence Laboratory, Massachusetts Institute of Technology, AI TR 397.
- Lozano-Perez T. 1981: "Automatic planning of manipulator transfer movements", IEEE Trans. Systems, Man, Cybernetics SMC-11,10, p681-689.
- Lozano-Perez T. and Brooks R.A. 1984: "An approach to automatic robot programming", in "Solid modelling by computers: from theory to applications", edited by Boyse J.W. and Pickett M.S., Plenum Press, New York.
- Lozano-Perez T., Mason M.T. and Taylor R.H. 1984: "Automatic synthesis of fine-motion strategies for robots", The International Journal of Robotics Research, MIT Press, Vol.3, No.1, p3-24.
- Martinez F. 1982: "Toward a systematic approach to image synthesis. Software and hardware aspects", Thesis Diss., National Polytechnic Institute of Grenoble, 378p.
- Mazer E. 1981: "Realization of an experimental Robotics research support. Design and implementation of the LM language" (in French), Thesis Diss., National Polytechnic Institute of Grenoble, 191p.
- Mazer E. 1982: "An algorithm for computing the relative position between two objects from symbolical specifications", IMAG Report, no.297.
- Mazer E. 1984: "Geometric programming of assembly robots", in "Advanced Software in Robotics", edited by Danthine A. and Géradin M., North-Holland, p99-110.
- Meyer J. 1981: "An emulation system for programmable sensory robots", IBM Journal of Research and Development, vol.25, no.6.
- Miribel J.F. and Mazer E. 1984: "LM V2.1. Reference Manual" (in French), Société ITMI, Meylan.
- Mondot T. 1984: "Automatic tuning of TV monitors", DEA Report, LIFIA Laboratory, 78p.
- Paul R. 1981: "Robot manipulators: mathematics, programming and control", MIT Press, Cambridge, Massachusetts.
- Pertin-Troccaz J. 1984: "SMGR: a geometric and relational modelling system for Robotics" (in French), IMAG Report, no.422.
- Popplestone R.J., Ambler A.P and Bellos I. 1980: "An interpreter for a language for describing assemblies", Artificial Intelligence 14,1, p79-107.
- Sata T., Kimura F. and Amano A. 1981: "Robot simulation system as a task programming tool", 11th International Symposium on Industrial Robots, Tokyo.
- Shimano B.E., Geschke C.C. and Spalding C.H. 1984: "VAL-II: a new robot control system for automatic manufacturing", Proc. IEEE International Conference on Robotics, Atlanta.

- Summers P.D. and Grossman D.D. 1984: "XPROBE: an experimental system for programming robots by examples", The International Journal of Robotics Research, Vol.3, No.1, p25-39.
- Taylor R.H., Summers P.D. and Meyer J.M. 82: "AML: a manufacturing language", The International Journal of Robotics Research, vol.1, no.3.

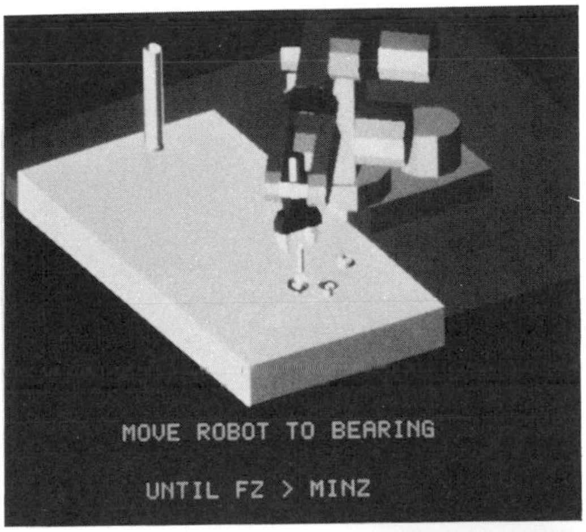

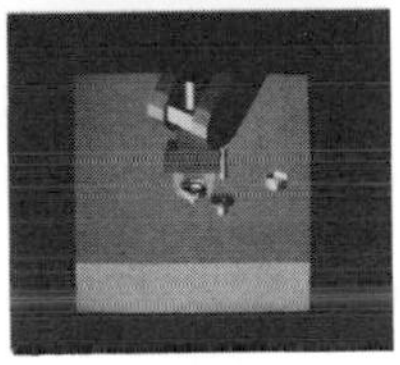

Figure 1:

Images generated by the LM simulator

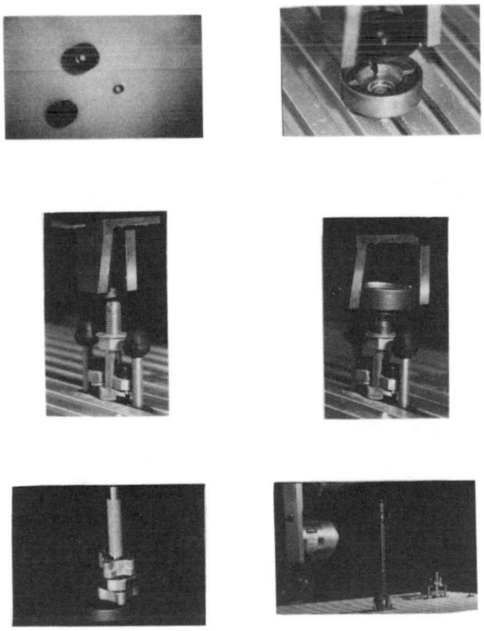

Figure 2: Assembly of a shock absorber

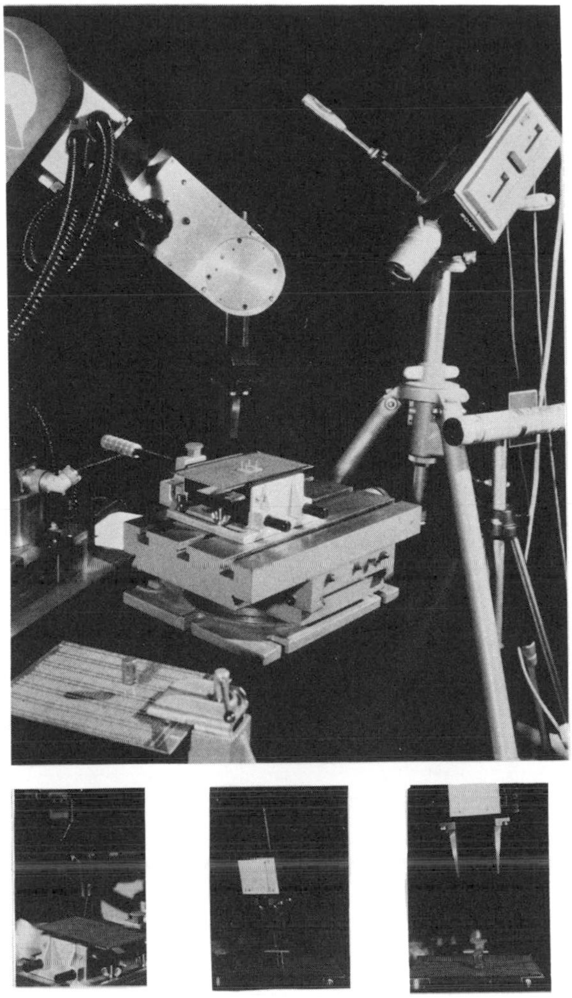

Figure 3: Inserting a capacitor

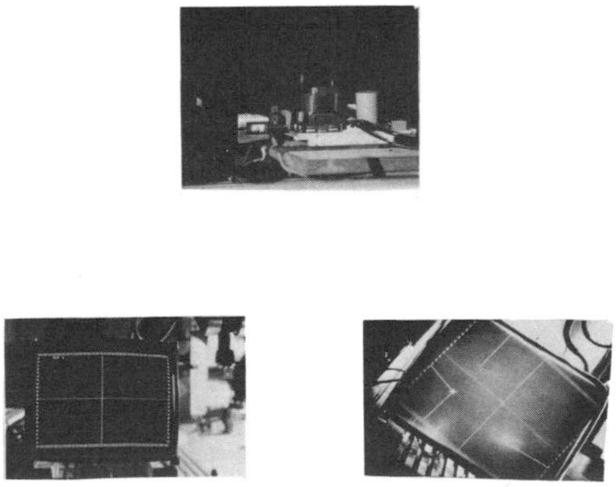

Figure 4: Tuning a display terminal

TASK EXECUTION MONITORING BY COMPILED PRODUCTION RULES IN AN ADVANCED MULTI-SENSOR ROBOT

Malik Ghallab

Laboratoire d'Automatique et d'Analyse des Sytèmes du CNRS
7, Avenue du Colonel Roche
31400, Toulouse
France

The execution of a task by an advanced multi-sensor robot must be carefully monitored in order to take into account unexpected changes in the environment, uncertainties in the world model, and inaccuracies in the sensors and effectors. The Execution Monitor must have two apparently conflicting features: 1) a real time response to stimuli from its sensors reporting particular events; and 2) a decision making capability: what information to acquire in order to find the relevant differences between the current state of the system and the planned one, and what to do accordingly to achieve the specified task.
Rule-based Pattern Directed Inference Systems are known for complying with the last feature, but they are also well known for their computing inefficiency which makes them inadequate in a real-time environment. The present paper reports on the design of a robot execution monitor using a rule-based system, together with a compiler which transforms the costly procedure of rule evaluation and chaining into a single traversal of a decision network. From an initial set of production rules whose antecedents are a conjunction of propositions, the proposed compiler suppresses the rules with only a "deduction" consequents and transforms the remaining rules into a set of complete decision rules, which is subsequenbtly translated into an optimized decision network.

Section 1

1.1. Introduction

Intelligent robots are those with decision making capabilities, able to perceive through a multi-sensory perception system and analyse their environment, to model and represent this environment for efficient reasoning, to generate plans for carrying out a specified task and to monitor the execution of the plans, to learn from past experiences and improve their behavior and performances, and to communicate with a human operator in natural language. In order to provide these decisionnal skills in future robots, new or significantly improved formalisms and methods for representing and manipulating knowledge must be developed. This is the case for a decision task with real-time constraints (like execution monitoring) mainly because of the inefficiency and high computational complexity of known representation formalisms such as formal logic, Production Systems, frames, semantic networks (i.e. Pattern-Directed Inference Systems [Waterman]).

The focus of this paper will be on a robot **Execution Monitor (EM)** and on **Production Systems (PSs)**. Its aims is to show that, using a rule compiler for a sub-class of **PSs**, it is possible to design an efficient **EM**, while keeping all advantages of this knowldge representation formalism.

1.2. Execution Monitor

During the execution of a task by a robot significant differences between planned and real states of the robot and its environment will always happen and must be expected: the robot **Plan Generator (PG)** has an abstract model of the world with uncertainties and missing details, unforseen changes will take place in the environment, the robot sensors and effectors are prone to inaccuracies and errors, partial failures will have to be by passed. For all these reasons the task execution must be carefully monitored. The function of an **EM** is to coordinate the various robot sub-systems, to monitor through them the robot's current state and find the relevant differences with the planned state, and to take the corrective actions needed to achieve the specified task.

Usually the literature on robot plan execution stresses the ability of replanning [Fikes], [Farreny], [Lanusse]. Here we advocate the fact that while replanning is not fundamentally distinct from planning and can be done with the same tools, execution monitoring is quite different and has to be done much more efficiently. It is important to separate and have **both** a **PG** and an **EM** such that, if needed, the corrective action of the **EM** could be a request for a new plan.

Section 2 of this paper will report on an **EM** using **PSs** currently under design for an autonomous mobile robot. The proposed rule compiler is dealt with in section 3. For readers unfamiliar with **PS** terminology and main definitions we briefly introduce this formalism in the remainder of this section.

1.3. Production Systems

PSs arosed in the 40's as sets of rewrite rules in formal grammars, and are now a knowledge representation scheme very popular in the Artificial Intelligence community, and widely used (see surveys in [Davis] or [Waterman]). In the usual definition a **PS** is a triple (Working Memory, Production Memory, Interpreter):

-the **Working Memory** (**WM**) is a set of data elements that discribe in some formalism a situation (what is explicitly known in the initial or current state), and eventually a goal (state aimed at, or properties desired in such a state);
-the **Production Memory** (**PM**) is a set of operators which transforme **WMs**. Each operator is a conditional statement, called production rule, of the form: **If (antecedent)** Then **(consequent)**. The antecedent is a logical expression on "conditions" specifying the subset of **WM** to which the rule apply. The consequent is an ordered set of "actions" describing mainly the **WM** transformations associated with the rule.
-the **Interpreter** is a control structure which, starting from the initial **WM**, repeatedly 1) evaluates the antecedent of the **PM** rules relative to the data in the current **WM**, and finds the "valid" rules; 2) choses one or several valid rules; 3) executes the chosen rules, i.e. carries out the actions specified in their consequents and defines the resulting **WMs**; and 4) decides either to continue and it choses the current **WM** among known ones, or to stop. The whole interpreter computation will be called a **Decision Process** (**DP**).

PS proponents usually stress their various qualities and advantages: the declarative aspect of the rules which separate clearly the knowledge from its use and frees the rule programmer from worrying about how the rules must be sequenced and when they must be executed (control information); the (relative) rule independance and knowledge modularity which simplifies the design and the addition deletion and modification of rules; the uniform knowledge structure and coding which eases rule understanding. **PS** proponents insist on their disadvantages like the difficulty to express algorithmic knowledge or follow the flow of control (e.g. for debugging purposes). All **PS** users agree on their computing inefficiency.

Section 2

The proposed **EM** will be defined and exemplified in the the context of Hilare, a multi-sensor general-purpose autonomous mobile robot (a vehicle with 1 free and 2 independantly powered wheels, camera, laser range finder, ultrasonic sensors, and infrared triangulation beams; see [Giralt 83] or [Chatila] for a detailed description of the robot and its navigation and motion control system). Hilare is a distributed system. At the functionnal level, it is composed of various subsytems, called modules, which interact through the **EM**. The system decomposition obeys the following principles:
-each robot effector or sensor is managed at the lowest level by its own module;
-a module deals with only one task, using for that its own specific algorithms and (eventually shared) world models;
-modules are independant from each others with no master-slave relation, they exchange information and requests through messages ; the sender module informs the **EM** if the receiver does not acknowledge normal reception of the message (see [Vaisset] for the exchange procedure used);
-each module computes and maintains the current value of some features (about that part of the robot state it is concerned with), these data are given on request to the **EM**; eventually a module checks out and notifies the **EM** if some particular condition on this data arises. Such messages to the **EM** will be called **Interruptions** (**IT**)

2.1. System structure & interactions

Let us illustrate the interactions managed by the **EM** through a discription of the main functions of the various modules of the navigation and motion control part of Hilare, which is of interest to us. These modules will be characterized functionnally, as they are seen from the **EM** (not all are actually running as discribed bellow, for Hilare's actual implementation state see [Giralt 83]):

M1. The sonar range monitor: checks out in turn all or part of the robot 14 ultrasonic sensors and stops robot motion if any range data is less than its corresponding threshold (unexpected obstacle). It receives as input: activate or inhibit the monitoring; threshold parameter for each sensor (constant or dependant on robot speed); and signals from the sensors. In case of an unexpected obstacle it sends a message to the wheel control module for deceleration until a final stop.

When activated, M1 checks out the normal functioning of each sensor and in case of one or several failures sends an **IT** with a diagnosis to the **EM**. If an unexpected obstacle is met an **IT** with the range data pattern is sent **after** full stop of the robot. Examples of **EM** (simplified and informal) rules which involve M1 are:
R1: **If** (plan step= docking) **Then** (Proceed to (inhibit M1));
R2: **If** (M1 inhibited) & (plan step= navigation using vision) **Then** (Proceed to (activate M1 with threshold= Close-value));
R3: **If** (M1 inhibited) & (plan step= navigation without vision) & (local obstacle avoidance permitted) **Then** (Proceed to (activate M1 with threshold= Far-value)).

M2. Local obstacle avoidance (LOA) or wall following: is done by controlling a closed loop on the wheel motors using the ultrasonic sensors feedback. One or several normal stopping conditions (on distance covered, robot orientation, wall discontinuity, crossing a previously computed trajectory, etc.) are used together with default and failure stopping conditions. Input data are: closed-loop paramaters (robot side, sensors, distance to surface); stopping conditions (normal and failure); and signals from the sonars. M2 output is the motor control signal. No world model is used.

When requested by the **EM** to follow a wall or avoid an obstacle M2 first checks the sensors involved in the closed-loop, and in case of failure sends an **IT** with a diagnosis. Otherwise the task is carried out, and when the robot is stopped an **IT** identifying the stopping condition (normal, default, failure) is sent to the **EM**. Rules which concern this module are for example:
R4: **If** (**IT** from M1= unexpected obstacle) & (plan step= trajectory following) & (LOA permitted) **Then** (proceed to (a LOA with stopping condition= crossing trajectory));
R5: **If** (plan step = follow wall on side ?s) & (M1 range data on side ?s does not show a close wall pattern) **Then** (proceed to (navigate to meet stopping condition));

R6: **If** (**IT** from M2= wall following stopped on failure condition) then (proceed to (navigate to meet normale stopping condition));
R7: **If** (**IT** from M2= LOA stopped on failure) then (proceed to (navigate with vision till goal of current step).

M3. Wheel motors control: controls the wheel motors with optical shaft encoders feedback along a given sampled trajectory. The code which specifies this trajectory may contain between 2 control samples particular instructions to be forwarded to the **EM** (e.g. at this point set the threshold monitor for the right side sonars to Close-value; at this other point aim the laser in such a relative orientation; now read the laser range). M3 does not deal itself with this instructions, it has just to send them at the right time to the **EM** without stopping or altering the robot motion control. M3 input are: the coded trajectory with its instructions, and eventually a message (from M1 or the **EM** for example) requesting a deceleration until full stop. It may send the following **ITs** to the **EM**: instructions read in the trajectory; control failure and its diagnosis (e.g. too large difference between actual control parameters and trajectory values, a blocked motor); robot stopped at the normal end of followed trajectory; or robot stopped to comply with an external request.

When robot motion, controlled either by M2 or M3 is externally stopped, and if the robot does not move, then the normal trajectory or surface following can be properly resumed at the **EM** request by the concerned module.

M4. Absolute position referencing: uses an infrared triangulation system for measuring the robot's absolute position, when in a room equipped with fixed beacons whose positions in the frame of reference are known. M4, when requested to measure the absolute position, returns back to the **EM** one of the following **ITs**: done (with the position found); or error (with a diagnosis: failure of the triangulation system, missing beacon, robot in an eccentric position to beacons). A possible **EM** rule affecting M4 is:
R8: **If** (robot position belongs to room with beacons)& (M4 is operating) **Then** (note (triangulation is possible)).

M5. Odometry: takes as input the wheels optical-encoder signals; gives the current robot position and orientation in some reference frame, its motion state (moving or stopped), and an estimate of the drift error since last absolute position reference. The value of this estimate is monitored relatively to some thresholds. When a triangulation is successfully completed, M4 reinitializes M5. The **EM** deals (partially) with M5 according to the following rules:
R9: **If** (robot motion state= idle) & (drift error estimate > Low-error) & (triangulation is possible) **Then** (proceed to (beacon));
R10: **If** (**IT** from M5= drift error estimate > High-error) & (triangulation is possible) & (motion state= moving) then (proceed to (stop robot)(triangulate)(resume motion));

Note that while in R9 the **EM** asks for the information on the drift error, in R10 this information is volunteered by M4.

M6. Low level vision: gives the vertices and edges of the planar projection of obstacles (assumed polyhedral) seen with laser and camera in some relative angled sector.

M7. Navigation: deals with a topological space model which relies on known empty polygonal cells (free space), partially unknown cells and their connectivity graph. M7 takes as input: the initial robot position, the desired final position (given explicitly or as a geometrical condition) and the location of seen obstacles (M6 output). It outputs a path, in the topological graph model, given as a sequence of cell vertices to be traversed from the robot initial position to the final position or to an intermediate vision position, and when a vision is required it also outputs the angular sector (M6 input) to be probed (see [Chatila] for details).

In the general case the navigation module proceeds repeatedly by: computing a path lying in the known part of the universe which will bring the robot closer to the specified goal; requesting the execution of this path; requesting when this is achieved a vision in some sector; analysing its results, and extending and updating the space model accordingly. In the case of a travel entirely in the known part of the universe no vision is necessary. Two navigation modes are possible: normal or cautious (e.g. in case of a large drift error or a sonar failure).

When the robot knowledge of the universe grows, the topological graph is decomposed (by the space learning module M15) into subgraphs labelled as rooms connected with corridors and doors. The path computation is then done hierarchically: routing , i.e. finding the sequence of rooms doors and corridors to be traversed, and then specifying the path along this route (further simplification can be added by precomputing once and for all the different pathes which traverses each room). Examples of **EM** rules which refer to this module are: R2, R3, R5, R6, and R7.

M8. Trajectory generation: takes as input the topological path computed by M7, and relys on the low-level geometrical model of the universe together with the dynamic model of the robot and the estimate of the odometry drift error; it computes and outputs the geometrical trajectory which corresponds to the given path and the control parameters (speed, acceleration) needed by M3 to carry it. Instructions such as those which involves M1 thresholds are added to this trajectory. M8 informs the **EM** if the requested trajectory cannot meet the normal safety conditions (e.g. path in between too close obstacles given the current drift error). In which case either an immediate triangulation is carried out if possible, or Navigation is asked to compute a new path farther from obstacles (cautious mode) and/or through a room with fixed beacons.

M9. Relative referencing: computes the robot position relative to known obstacles using the camera and laser.

M10. Docking: manages a closed-loop control on ultrasonic sensors for the last phase of docking or maneuvers in known frames (working stations). It is also able to hook up or unhook the robot to a cart for towing purposes.
M11. Battery charging: monitors the charge level

of the batteries relative to thresholds, is involved in **EM** rules such as:
R11: **If** (motion state= idle) & (batteries level < Safe) **Then** (Proceed to (navigate to closest reloading socket)(dock into socket frame)).

M12. Space exploration: takes as input a mass plan of the universe or some other partial information (its frontiers, beacon positions, etc.). This module drives the robot into various places with the only aim to discover and build a complete topological space model. It uses for that goal the Navigation module and the other perception and control modules. Exploration can be requested explicitly by the operator (e.g. initially) or the plan generator. The **EM** can also start an exploration (e.g. robot idle in a partially known part of the universe) or interrupt it (e.g. when a new task is submitted by the operator, a partial failure which need repair).

M13. Space learning: deals with the topological graph decompositon and labelling mentioned in M7. This is done on the basis of the graph connexity properties (biconnected or triconnected components are potential "rooms", articulation nodes or pairs are potential "doors"), and using some heuristic criteria on space geometrical features and frequencies of robot paths and presence of obstacles (see [Laumond] for details). M13's output is the "room-graph", each node of which is a labelled topological subgraph, used in M7 for the hierarchical path computation.

M14. Plan Generator: has knowledge of the different space models, of current relative locations of the various objects in the universe, and of the abilities of the system modules. It takes as input a task submitted by the operator, or a request from the **EM** to replan for the current task. It produces as output a sequence of actions to be affected to the various modules, with eventually instructions to the **EM** between 2 consecutive actions (see a complementary presentation in [Giralt 84]). For example the task: "fetch tool cart TC2 and convey it to the work station WS1" could produce the following plan:
(EM: LOA permitted)
step1. (M7: go to door D1)
step2. (M9: line-up on the right side along wall)
(EM: check closeness Condition-1 to wall surface on the right side)
step3. (M2: follow wall to door D2)
step4. (M7: go to position (x1, y1, θ1))
step5. (M9: compute relative position to TC2)
(EM: check closeness Condition-2 with TC2)
step6. (M10: hook up to TC2)
step7. (M7: convey to position (x2,y2,θ2))
(EM: check closeness Condition-1 to WS2 surface on left side)
step8. (M2: follow wall to WS2)
step9. (M10: unhook TC2)

The correct execution of a plan rests on the **EM**. The transition between 2 plan steps is the crucial part and is done in the following way:
i) upon receiving a report of a step completion, the **EM** checks out some default conditions to test the success of this step; it also carries out and checks what is explicitly specified in the **PG** instructions (noted here "EM:"). In our example that involves checking the robot's correct position (relatively to: door D1 after completion of step1, door D2 after step3, position (x1,y1,θ1) after step4,...), the normal result of the other actions (e.g. hooking up after step6), and the instructions relative to closeness conditions 1 and 2 after step 2, 5 and 7. This is mainly how the difference between planned and current robot states is computed and monitored.
ii) when a step is successfully concluded and checked, the **EM** analyses the next one (considered now to be the current plan step) and takes some default actions, according to rules like for example:
R12: **If** (next step= conveying) **Then** (set (M1 front sensors threshold to Far-value)(LOA not permitted));

This rule is used before step7. Note that R12 turns off the first instruction to **EM** (before step1), which says that if needed in the forthcoming wall or trajectory following a LOA procedure could be used.

If a step is not successfully concluded, the **EM** tries to find a rule or a sequence of rules which specify a corrective action (e.g. rule R6 if step 3 fails); if none is found or if the corrective action does not succeed to bring back the robot to the planned state, then the **EM** requests a new plan from the current state to the current goal.

2.2. EM organization & functioning

The **EM** organization relies first on a particular description of the state of the system. The robot and its environment are seen by the **EM** as a state vector in a discrete finite state-space representation. Some components of this representation characterize locally a robot subsystem, as for example:
*sonar system (in one of the following):
- -monitoring,
- -on closed feedback for surface following,
- -on closed feedback for docking,
- -inhibited.

Other components are global features of the robot, like for example:
*robot motion state:
- -idle (ready for motion),
- -stopped: .computing/decision making/planning,
  - .seeing (image/range data acquisition processing),
  - .triangulating,
  - .battery charging,
  - .failure
- -in motion: .trajectory following
  - .wall following
  - .obstacle avoiding
  - .docking/hooking up
- -conveying a cart ...

*robot activity:
- -idle,
- -pursuing a goal: .planning/replanning,
  - .executing a plan step,
  - .in transition phase between 2 plan steps,
- -exploring/structuring the universe ...

*plan step:
- -navigation with vision:
  - .computing a path and trajectory (mode normal/cautious),
  - .moving (trajectory following, surface following, ...),
  - .stopped (seeing, ...),
- -navigation without vision: .computing ...

-triangulating,...
*robot operational state:
-fully operational,
-1st degradation level:
.drift error estimate > High-error,
.battery level < Low-error,
.a side or back sonar sensor failed,
-2nd degradation level:
.a front sonar sensor failed,
.odometry system failed, ...
-3rd degradation level: .camera/laser system failed, ...
-broken.

Not all state components values are at each moment explicitly known by the **EM**, nor are they all needed. In fact the **EM** stays informed by the various modules of the current values and changes intervening in most of these state components. However, some components have to be evaluated, either by a specific request to the concerned module (e.g. to M4: what is the robot position? what is the drift error estimate? to M7: is the robot in a room equipped with fixed beacons?), or internally as a result of one or several rules evalution and execution (e.g. rule R8).

This vector state may change either because of unvoluntary events (e.g. an order from the operator, a failure) or because of actions performed by the system as a result of a rule execution. There are 3 different types of actions in **EM** rule antecedent.
-"external actions" to be physically carried out by the robot; in our rules syntax they are given as an ordered sequence after the label "Proceed to" (e.g. R1, R2, R3);
-"internal actions" involving changes in the **EM** and/or modules settings and parameters; they are preceeded by the label "Set" (e.g. R12)
-"deductions": implicit informations (state vector components) are explicited by a rule antecedent; the label used is "Note" (e.g. R8, R15 and R16 bellow).

Execution of rules which contain only deductions in their antecedent does not change the state vector. In fact such rules express only a dependancy relation between the various components of the state space. In R8 for example the conclusion (triangulation is possible) is a redundant information resulting from the knowledge of the robot position, the topological graph node labels (with/without fixed beacons) and the operational state of the infrared triangulation subsystem. This redundancy is very convenient for the **PS** rule programmer (modularity, grannularity), but is one of the reasons for **PS**s inefficiency; it can be supressed by the proposed rule compiler.

The vector state changes which result from the execution of a rule with internal actions can be either explicit or implicit but they are always immediate in that sense that they do not require from the **EM** any wait or monitoring. This is not the case for the various state changes involved by external actions. Let us analyse them through the example of rule R10 antecedent: (Proceed to (stop the robot)(triangulate)(resume motion)).

In order to know what to do if some of these actions does not succeed, or if some unexpected event happens during the sequence execution, the **EM** memorizes the causes which lead to this sequence (i.e. the rule R10). It then sends the stop request to module M3, stacks the whole sequence on top of the current execution list, and waits for completion of the requested action. This is the first state change. If the **IT** returned from M3 informs that the robot has been correctly stopped (another state change), the **EM** removes the first action from the current sequence, checks if there is a continuation subsequence and proceeds with its next action: it requests M4 for an absolute position measurement and enters again the wait mode. A normal return will lead to the last action: remove R10 and the rest of the sequence from the execution list, check and resume the previously interrupted sequence. But, if M3 returns a failure **IT**, a rule like the following one will be applied:
R13: **If** (**IT** from M3= failure) & (**EM** sequence= R10) & (diagnosis= a missing beacon) & (plan step= Navigation) **Then** (Set (failure label for current room beacons)(delete **EM** current sequence))(Proceed to (navigate to current goal in cautious mode)).

As this example illustrates, the main part of the **EM** corresponds to an asynchronous processing system. It reacts to a particular sollicitation (an **IT**), tests some components of the state vector, finds out if according to its set of rules any external and/or internal actions have to be undertaken, sends orders to carry out parts of these actions, and waits for the next sollicitation, which is normally the report on the order execution results.

Eventual time conflicts between sollicitations are processed according to a predefined priority order and on the basis of a FIFO policy in case of equal priority. When the processing of a sollicitation IT1 is interrupted by a higher priority level **IT**2, not only the current **EM** computations are definitely ignored, but also all other sollicitations waiting to be processed (necessarily of a priority level lower than **IT**2) are disregarded. This is due to the fact that **IT**2 is reporting an unexpected event which changed the vector state and made the causes of **IT**1 and other waiting **IT**s obsolete. Actually, we need only 2 priority levels: normal and emergency; with the only **IT**s at the emergency level being: a stop request message to M3 not acknowledged, and M3 reporting a failure to comply normally with a stop request.

There is however an important part of the **EM** task which cannot be dealt with asynchronously as described here: it is the state monitor itself. For a distributed system our idea is to have a distributed monitor. Each local condition which can be evaluated locally by one module is monitored by this particular module. There will be conditions which are permanently monitored by a module and give rise to an **IT** (subsection 2.1 examples are in this case), and other local conditions whose monitor can be set or inhibited by the **EM**. There may be however some general conditions to monitor which are out of the scope of any single module (e.g. a task, submitted by the operator, to be carried out only at some specific time and/or robot state), or conditions on the normal functioning of a module which cannot be monitored, for safety reasons, by this same module (e.g. after acknowledgement by a module of an **EM** order, a time out is set for receiving back a report either of normal execution or of failure). Monitoring such time-outs and other global conditions is realized by a part of the **EM** which will be called the Surveyor.

The Surveyor task is to run an infinite loop checking out in turn a set of conditions on the system state. When a condition is found to be true an **IT** wakes up the asynchronous part of the **EM** which reacts according to its set of rules and may either inhibit this condition or leave it. New conditions needing monitoring can be added in the Surveyor's loop. The evalution of a condition may need information requests and messages exchanges with the various modules, but it has to be fast enough as to make the check frequency of each condition high in comparison with its frequency of changes. Otherwise, a more structured Surveyor must be implemented with a number of nested loops corresponding to the different frequency ranges, with most quickly changing conditions put at the deepest loop.

Let us now see an important characteristic of the **EM** organisation: how the set of rules is structured. Indeed, the set **PM** is not seen by the **EM** as an untructured body of rules but as a collection of specialized and partly overlapping subsets. There is a particular subset of rules dealing with the transition phase between 2 plan steps and mainly analysing and setting the correct execution context of the next step (e.g. rule R13 belongs to this subset). There is another subset specialized in processing the orders received (through an interface) from the operator: submitted to planning immediately carried out, postponed, etc.

Some subsets are specialized each in processing a particular **IT**. A given module may issue several possible **IT**s and at least 2: a failure to acknowledge a message (an "Acknowledgement defect" **IT**, sent by the system messages manager) and a failure to comply with a request (Failure **IT**). Each **IT** which corresponds to a condition permanently monitored by a module is associated to a specialized subset of rules. Let us close this section by some examples of this type:

*Unexpected obstacle **IT** from M1 (sent after full stop of the robot): processed by R1 and the following rule (the **IT** identification test is implicit):

R14: **If** (plan step= wall following) **Then** (navigate with vision to meet stopping condition)

*Failure IT from M1:

R15: **If** (diagnosis= sensor ?y failed) & (?y is a side or back sensor) **Then** (note (operational state= 1st degradation level))

R16: **If** (diagnosis= sensor y? failed) & (y? is a front sensor) **Then** (note (operational state= 2nd degradation level))

R17: **If** (operational state= 1st degradation level) & (plan step= navigation without vision) **Then** (Proceed to (stop robot)(inform operator about failure)(navigate without vision to current goal in cautious mode))

R18: **If** (operational state= 2nd degradation level) & (plan step= navigation without vision) **Then** (Proceed to (stop robot)(navigate with vision to current goal))

*Report on normal execution IT from M2:

R19: **If** (plan step= wall following) **Then** (proceed to (compare robot position to step goal)(resume plan execution))

R20: **If** (**EM** sequence= R4) **Then** (Proceed to (resume trajectory following))

*Acknowledgement defect **IT** for a stop request sent to M3 (emergency **IT**):

R21: **If** (motion state= moving) **Then** (proceed to (emergency power cut off)(warning signal).

Section 3

Here we will deal explicitly with Decision Processes (**DPs**), and show how their complexity can be reduced through the use of a rule compiler. The presentation of **PSs** given in (1.2) is a too broad definition which covers various possible formalisms. There is fact no precisely defined and generally agreed upon **PS** formalism but instead a rich abundance of related systems. Nor is there to our knowledge a taxonomy of the existing formalisms which compares their expressive powers (for representing knowledge) versus the complexity of the decision process involved. Section 3.1 will attempt to sketch an approach toward such a taxonomy for our restricted purpose of defining subclasses of **PSs** with various compiling levels. Two types will be considered: "closed" DPs and "open" **DPs**.

3.1. Closed and Open Decision Processes

Let E being some particular set such that at the current time $\mathbf{e} \in E$ is the state of the dynamic system we are interested in. This system is modelled by a finite set of functions called predicates: $X = \{X_1, X_2, \ldots, X_p\}$; each X_i mapping E into a discrete set Z_i

$X_i : \forall e \in E \longrightarrow X_i(\mathbf{e}) \in Z_i$

The Cartesien product $Z = Z_1 x Z_2 x \ldots x Z_p$ is the system state space representation; the current state **e** can be known only through the projection $X(e) = (X_1(e), X_2(e), \ldots, X_p(e))$ into Z, called the state vector.

Let us define a **PS** on this representation by a set of rules: **PM** = $\{R_1, R_2, \ldots, R_m\}$; each R_j being of the form:

R_j: **If** $(X_{j1}(e)=a_{j1})$ & .. & $(X_{jr}(e)=a_{jr})$ **Then** (A_j)

-1) the consequent A_j is either

a) of the "deduction type": it fixes the value $X_i(e)$ of some X_i, not previously known in the current **DP**, as a result of the known values $X_{j1}(e), \ldots, X_{jr}(e)$; or

b) of the "action type": it modifies the system state **e**, and in this case R_j is a terminal rule which stops the **DP**, and

-2) each X_i in R_j antecedent is either

a) directly evaluable (e.g. we have a program for computing the current value $X_i(e)$), or

b) results from the previous execution of some other rule R_k which consequent fixes the value $X_i(e)$.

Rule R_j is said to be valid if each X_i in its antecedent is either evaluable or has a known value, and $X_i(e)$ corresponds to the value specified in R_j.

When a decision has to be taken on this system, the **PS** interpreter starts with an empty **WM**, repeatedly looks for any valid rule and carries out its consequent, putting in the **WM** evaluated or infered X_is, and this until a terminal rule is reached.

Such **DP** will be called a **Closed Decison Process** (**CDP**) iff:

H1) the state space representation Z is an explicitly defined finite set; and

H2) the state vector X(e) does not change during the decision process.

Let us comment on this definition, and illustrate why the **PS** used in the proposed **EM** is of the **CDP** type. Condition H2 is the restrictive hypothesis. Note first that the system's state may change either intensionnaly (as a result of an action), or randomly (an external event). Because of the definition of terminal rules which stop the **DP**, H2 is concerned only with the last case. Moreover, it is not the real state **e** which is assumed to remain unchanged during a **CDP**, but its projection on Z. Figuratively speaking, the state e is supposed to stay locally in the same area in E in order to give the same projection in Z. For example the (x,y,θ) coordinate of the mobile robot may change, but not the fact that its current position does or does not belong to a room with fixed beacons. This of course cannot be guarranteed unless the system is frozen in its current state until the end of the **DP** (not very convenient for monitoring a dynamic system), but the assumption can be reasonably justified in many cases if:

-the dynamics of the system is slow comparatively to the **DP** computing time (would be true in our case if we use an efficient rules compiler);

-the rules programmmer takes conservative measures (e.g. adding **EM** rules to stop the robot motion before going into further tests and actions when a critical situation is recognised; not considering the robot when it is moving out of an area with fixed beacons and close to its border as beeing inside a triangulation area); and mainly if

-the system is controlled in a global closed-loop: an important state change will make the **DP** terminal action impossible to be effectively carried out, and give rise to a new **DP** (e.g. an order of triangulation outside a proper area produces a failure **IT**); or this state change if monitored may stop the current **DP** and start another one (e.g. an emergency **IT**).

Another important aspect of **CDPs** is the interpreter's **determinism:** no choice of a particular rule among valid rules, or backtracking on this choice is involved. For a given state **e**, there may be various possible rule sequences (chainings) leading to the same terminal rule and action, but since the computed or deduced value of an X_i does not change during a **DP**, the only difference between these sequences can be on the order of deduction, or eventually the deduction of redundant X_is (not needed for the terminal rule reached). However, if no particular care is taken in programming and testing a set of rules, we can have for the same state 2 rules sequences leading to 2 different and conflicting actions. Thus we will say that a **PS** of the **CDP** type is:

a) consistent iff to any state **e** corresponds at most one action (i.e. one terminal rule or several specifying the same action); and

b) complete iff to each state **e** corresponds a terminal rule.

Consistency and completeness checks are part of the compiling process and will be considered in the next subsection.

For sake of simplicity, the proposed description of **CDPs** has been intentionally restricted. Various extensions can be easily added, for example:

-relations such as inequality, less than, belonging to, ..., on the values of the X_is;

-conjunctions, disjunctions, and negations in rule antecedents.

Other less obvious extensions can be added like using predicates with non quantified variables: to comply with H2 such variable can be instantiated only once during a **DP**, and according to H1 the possible values of this variable must be known in advance (e.g. in rule R5 variable ?s can have only one value at a time, either left or right).

Finally, let us remark that a **CDP** can be started with a non empty **WM:** any initial knowledge on the actual state of the system can be used. Note that in general this initial **WM** has nothing to do with the **WM** reached at the end of the previous decision process. As it is clear now, and to summurize, our definition sees the state of the system at 3 different levels:

-1) the real state **e** (all what is happening in the robot and its environment);

-2) its projection X(e) in a representation space (the only thing of concen to the **DP**); and

-3) the **DP** current knowledge of X(e), which is the **WM**; because of assumption H2, the **WM** can only grow monotonically during a **CDP**.

Note that the state **e**, and thus X(e), evolve along some time axis, whereas the DP is seen to be instantaneous for this axis and takes place along an orthogonal one.

Let us now more briefly introduce a second type of **PS** for which hypothesis H1 and/or H2 are not valid. Such **PSs** are said to involve an **Open Decision Process** (**ODP**). Their rules are expressed in a more general formalism than for **CDPs**, mainly through the use of quantified variables (i.e. an infinite representation space), and matching mechanisms for evaluating antecedent conditions (called "patterns").

If H2 is valid and only H1 is false, we have an **ODP** in which again the **WM** can only grow monotonically. A theorem prover in 1st order logic is of this type; e is the interpretation basis and does not change during a proof; any fact established along the **DP** cannot be refuted later. This simplifies considerably the rules chaining (control of the **ODP**) in comparison to the next case (see "commutative" **PSs** in [Nilsson]).

If H2 is also missing (with or without H1) we have a non monotonous **ODP**. In general state changes can be either intentional (as a result of an action rule, here not considered to be terminal), or random. A **PG**, an interesting example of this type of **PS**, considers only the first case of state changes: during the planning process the system is supposed to stay in the same state. The **ODP** starts with the representation of this state in the initial **WM**, and relying on the description of the effects of actions specified in rules antecedents, it tries in simulation to find a sequence of state changes bringing to some desired state. Usually no distinction is made between augmenting the knowledge on some current state (inference making) and simulating a state change; so the **WM** data represent the state vector and several **WMs** are managed by this simulation process.

There are cases however where planning involves actions for which no model is available or none can be given (e.g. the possible outcomes of a robot vision in an unstructured environment). Such actions are once again terminal for the **ODP**; they must be considered as side goals, introduced only when needed and explicitely planned for.

The more difficult case is to take into account (part of) state changes while planning, i.e. to monitor in the evolution of the system what is relevant for the plan currently under generation.

We know of no work or proposition for using on line an **ODP** on a dynamic process.

3.2. PS compiling

On the light of the previous classification, the two following results give the possible compiling levels of a **PS** (see [Ghallab 82]):

i) **PS** rules of the **CDP** type can be compiled entirely into optimized decision networks, which supresses completely the costly process of rule chaining and reduces the multiple interpreter iterations with their various steps to a single traversal of this network; and

ii) an **ODP** is a sequence of **CDPs**, thus the first and most costly interpreter step (i.e. defining the set of valid rules) can be entirely compiled and reduced to traversal of a "matching-network" and propagating the found matchings through a "join-network", both networks being optimized by the compiling process (see [Ghallab 81] and [Dufresne]).

This last result is of great importance for the design of a **PG**, but with regard to **EMs** what is of interest to us here is the first one. Indeed, the proposed design of an **EM** with **PSs** has been conceived solely because of this result: compiling is mandatory to comply with real-time constraints. For all known implementations, one cannot assume that the computing time of an interpreted **DP** would be short enough to make assumption H2 reasonable. To use interpreted **PSs**, one would have to resort to an on-line **ODP**.

Let us now give the main characteristics of the rule compiling process. As we have seen there are two types of predicates: evaluable X_is and deduced X_is. This last type is recognized when found in the consequent part of a rule. Such deduction rules are dependancy relations between evaluable and deduced predicates making the last ones completely redundant in the **DP**. The first compiler step consists in supressing such redundancy. This is done by:

-duplication of deduction rules in order to have only one deduction per rule (e.g. a rule like **If** (a)&(b)&(c) **Then** (Note (d)(f)) is replaced by the 2 rules **If** (a)&(b)&(c) **Then** (Note (d)) and **If** (a)&(b)&(c) **Then** (Note (f)));

-replacement, in each terminal rule which has a deduced X_i in its antecedent, of this predicate X_i by the antecedent of the deduction rule setting it to the proper value (e.g. continuing the above example, a rule like **If** (f)&(g)&(h) **Then** (A_j) is replaced by **If** (a)&(b)&(c)&(g)&(h) **Then** (A_j)). Duplication is done if more than one deduction rule apply; it must be checked however that each antecedent replacing X_i is compatible with the rest of the terminal rule antecedent (i.e. the result does not specify 2 conflicting values for the same predicate).

This leads to a set of terminal rules each one, called a complete decision rule, having only evaluable predicates in its antecedent. Let **PM'** be this set of decision rules and Z' the Cartesien product of the evaluable predicate ranges $Z'=Z'_1 x \ldots xZ'_n$ (unless given as input, the range of X_i is considered to be the set of values it has explicitly in these rules, plus an "else" value). The next compiler step is to check the consistency and completeness of **PM'**. Consistency requires an $O(n|\mathbf{PM'}|^2)$ computation. Completeness is much more complex: in $O(|Z'|)$, unless one assumes that no pairs of rules in **PM'** overlap (i.e. there are no predicate values for which both rules are valid).

An interactive software at this step is a very useful tool for the rules programmer. It enables him to write his rules worrying about those which specify different actions for the same situation. When this is recognized by the compiler the programmer is asked:

-if it is an error, and a correction has to be made; or

-if the overlapping situation has to be transformed into one rule performing all the different actions, and the actions ordering is requested; or

-the overlapping situation is a dependancy relation of the predicates (i.e. there is no state e giving these predicates values), and it is exploited as such.

Any other dependancy relations between evaluable predicates known to the programmer can also be given: their knowledge will simplify the compiling process and enable it to find out a more efficient decision network. If the size of Z' is manageable enough (or if the non-overlapping hypothesis holds) the completeness can be checked: for any situation in which no rule applies the programmer is requested either to specify that it is a dependancy relation or to give the corresponding action. If no completeness checking is required an "else" rule is added (whose action in our case would be to stop the robot and to send a message to the operator).

The last compiler step is the generation of the decision network equivalent to the set **PM'** of decision rules. For that the compiler needs to know the following:

i) If there are any constraints on the predicates evaluation order. Such constraints can be given in the same formalism as the rules; they express the fact that the domain of a predicate is not the entire set E but only a subset of it specified by the values of some other predicates. If no sequencing constraint is given predicates are assumed to be evaluable in any order.

ii) If there are any known parameters, such as the frequency distribution of the states (or at least most frequent and unfrequent states), and the computer time needed for evaluation of the features (or information such as the list of predicates permanently updated free of cost).

iii) Desired optimization criteria and eventually an approximation level parameter (saying how far at most from the exact optimum solution can be the decision network generated by the compiler).

The set **PM'** is translated into a near-optimal decision tree (as close to the optimum as specified by the given parameter). Each node in this tree is an evaluable predicate, the values of which are labels on the branches issued from the node; tree leaves are labelled by terminal actions.

We use for that translation an algorithm called AO_ε for the heuristic search of And/Or graphs (AO_ε is a near-admissible algorithm which generalizes the AO* algorithm proposed by [Martelli]). Its worst case complexity is of $O(\prod_{1\leq i\leq n}(1+2|Z'_i|))$ for an exact optimal solution; but according to our experiments on a system with binary predicates (i.e.

$|Z'_i|=2$ $\forall i$), an average complexity of $O(1.3^n)$ can be expected (see [Ghallab 82] for details on the AO_ε algorithm, and for more information on this compiling and optimisation process).

Note that when the set **PM** is structured, as in our case, into specialized subsets of rules, each subset is independantly translated into a decision tree, thus reducing considerably the compiling complexity

Finally, in order to reduce coding space, this decision tree can be, if needed, transformed into a smaller decision network by finding and merging common subtrees. Note that deduction features correspond to possible labellings of some subtrees and can be retreived if convenient for I/O with the operator.

In a simplified analysis, the difference in complexity between an interpreted and a compiled **DP** is in O(p-n), i.e. corresponds to the removing of deduced predicates; but in fact the gain is much more important. The suppressed redundancy in the compiled **DP** does not correspond only to the (p-n) predicates, because not all evaluable predicates are needed and effectively evaluated in each **DP**: an optimized decision tree will lead to evaluate in the average a minimum number of predicates (or spend a minimum of computing time). Furthermore the compiled **DP** has not to worry, as does the interpreted **DP**, about reading a rule, checking the status of a predicate (evaluable, value known in **WM**,...), and eventually leaving out this rule, checking some other rules, deducing information, and going to the 1st rule checking again. So the significant reduction in complexity has to be measured experimentally in each particular application.

The author and his colleagues in the robotics group at LAAS ([Dufresne] and [Sobek]) have implemented several **PS** compilers, both for **CDPs** and **ODPs** in several programming languages and with various properties. No comparison results on performance of interpreted versus compiled **PSs**, with a significant set of rules, are available to us now. However, for a system like the **EM** currently under implemention we can expect a gain similar to the one obtained on the Prospector expert system whose **PS** part of (the **CDP** type) was initially interpreted, and later on compiled. According to measures on a set of 105 rules [Konolidge], the compiled system runs 4 orders of magnitude faster than the interpreted one (from an average **DP** of 3.1 millisecond to 30 seconds). Similar results were obtained by [Forgy].

Conclusion

One of the important aspects of current research on intelligent robots lies at the crossroads of decision making and on-line processing in dynamic systems. A prototype of such a conflicting intersection is the execution monitor of an advanced multi-sensor robot.

For decision making, rule-based Production Systems are one of the most popular knowledge representaion formalisms, but their computing inefficiency seems to rule out their on-line use in dynamic processes.

This paper has defined a sub-class of **PSs**, said to involve Closed Decison Processes for which the deduction phase or rule chaining, whose sole function is to make explicit certain information, can be in a preprocessing step completely supressed, thus reducing the whole decision process to a single traversal of an optimized decision network.

Further it was shown, on the basis of the detailled analysis of the various interactions dealt with, and of the structure and functionning of the execution monitor currently under development for the mobile robot Hilare, that the production rules used in the design of such an **EM** are of the **CDP** type and thus can profit from the compiling algorithms and tools developped by the author.

References

Chatila R. 1982. Path planning and environment learning in a mobile robot system. Proc. 1st European Conference on Artificial Intelligence, Orsay.

Davis R. and King J. 1976. An overview of production systems. Machine Intelligence 8, Wiley, New York, pp. 300-332.

Dufresne P. 1984. Contribution algorithmique à l'inférence par régles de production. Thèse de Docteur-Ingénieur, Univ. P. Sabatier, Toulouse

Farreny H. 1980. Un système pour l'expression et la résolution de problèmes orienté vers le controle de robots. Thèse de Doctorat d'Etat, Univ. P. Sabatier, Toulouse.

Fikes R.E., Hart P.E. and Nilsson N.J. 1972. Learning and executing generalized robot plans. Tech. note 70, AI Center, SRI.

Forgy C.L. 1979. On the efficient implementation of production systems. Ph.D. thesis, Dep. of Computer Science, Carnegie Mellon Univ., Pittsburgh.

Ghallab M. 1981. Decision trees for optimizing pattern matching algorithms in production systems. Proc. 7th IJCAI, Vancouver.

Ghallab M. 1982. Optimisation de processus décisionnels pour la robotique. Thèse de Doctorat d'Etat, Univ. P. Sabatier, Toulouse.

Giralt G., Chatila R. and Vaisset M. 1983. An integrated navigation and motion control system for autonomous multisensory mobile robots. Proc. 1st ISRR, Bretton Woods.

Giralt G. 1984. Research trends in decisional and mmultisensory aspects of third generation robots. Proc. 2nd ISRR, Kyoto.

Konolidge K. 1979. An inference net compiler for the Prospector rule-based consultation system. Proc. 6th IJCAI, Tokyo.

Lanusse A. 1983. Contribution à la conception et à la réalisation du système de conduite d'un automate reconfigurable. Thèse de Docteur-Ingénieur, Univ. P. Sabatier, Toulouse.

Laumond J.P. 1983. Model structuring and concept recognition: two aspect of learning for a mobile robot. Proc. 8th IJCAI, Karlsruhe.

Martelli M. and Montanari U. 1978. Optimizing decision trees through heuristically guided search. Com. ACM, 21, 12, pp. 258-282.

Sobek R.P. 1984. Compiling patterns for a production system: implementation considerations. Tech. note LAAS, Toulouse (to be published).

Vaisset M. 1983. Intégration des structures décisionnelle et informatique pour le robot mobile Hilare. Thèse de Docteur-Ingénieur, Univ. P. Sabatier, Toulouse.

Waterman D.A. and Hayes-Roth F. 1978. An overview of pattern-directed inference systems. In Pattern-Directed Inference Systems, Waterman and Hayes-Roth ed., Academic Press.

PROJECTION DERIVED SPACE CUBE SCENE MODELS FOR ROBOTIC VISION AND COLLISION-FREE TRAJECTORY PLANNING

R.A. Jarvis
Department of Computer Science
Australian National University
GPO Box 4, CANBERRA ACT 2601
Australia

A semantic-free low level approach to scene modelling for robotic vision and collision-free trajectory planning is described in the context of research being carried out in the Computer Vision and Robotics Laboratory at the Australian National University. Multiple silhouette and colour image projections are used to create a space occupancy and surface coloured model in a 3D voxel array. 3D connectivity analysis separates the distinct object groups in the scene. For each group, intensity/colour based segmentation needs only to contend with local variations to isolate individually discernable objects, each of which is as yet unrecognised.

3D distance transforms propagated from single or multiple goal points through unoccupied space (diminished by obstacle growth corresponding to vehicle extent) provide a distance 'potential field' where down-hill from a nominated starting point leads to the nearest goal by the shortest collision-free path.

Extension of other well known binary image analysis algorithms (smoothing, shrinking, high order moments, skeletonizing, boundary tracking, logical operations, etc.) into 3D can provide a rich set of shape related parameters supporting object description and recognition.

This approach to robotic vision represents a consistent attempt to provide a robust base upon which to build higher level structures with increasing semantic and goal driven content.

1. Preamble

That, for sighted humans, vision dominates the sensory mechanisms by which the world of solid objects is appreciated, manipulated and navigated through, is hardly a coincidence of nature. Evolution, the slave of the forces of survival, has clearly favoured, for good reason, this means by which data about the world can be gathered prior to physically negotiating parts of it. In this fashion, the remote sensing that is vision permits planning before action, a keystone of intelligent behaviour. It is no wonder, then, that computer vision, which aims primarily at replicating the function of biological vision on a computing device, promises to become a major component of sensory-based robotics in the attempt to expand the sphere of applicability of automation towards less structured environments where adaptive adjustments are crucial to the success of completing some given task. Often the motivation behind such goals of automation is related to the hostility of the environment which poses a threat to the safety of humans, or that the task is tedious and below the dignity of human labour, or simply that economic factors dictate such an approach to maintain the competitiveness of a product or indeed the survival of an entire industry.

The best known work done in computer vision at M.I.T. in the late 1960's and early 1970's has been collectively called the 'blocks world' experiments since it was concerned mainly with the simplistic visual world of plane faced objects with trihedral vertices. For this domain, [Guzman, 1968] and then [Waltz, 1975] were able to use the ways in which the vertices might appear in a single view perfect line drawing to constrain 3D interpretation to, ideally, only one case. Attempts have been made to extend the work to include curvature [Turner, 1974] but the complexity of the problem rises sharply. The 'blocks world' experiments were and are still perhaps the most impressive examples of semantically driven interpretation in the computer vision field. More recently, however, there has been increasing interest in data driven approaches to computer vision, at least at the low level stages of interpretation. Such approaches generally promise wider applicability and, in any case, seem to be a natural prerequisite for more structured analysis at higher levels.

The views of [Gibson, 1966] have had a powerful influence on the manner in which data driven computer vision has been developed. Gibson's central thesis concerning the psychology of vision was that the proper analysis of time sequence visual phenomena as it entered the human visual system as retinal stimulus involving image flow was sufficient to the task of making correct 3D interpretations of the natural world and that semantically dominant interpretations were fallen back to only when active data was lacking or where some unnatural visual circumstance was to be accommodated. The extension to this thesis was that the world is essentially made up of planes which meet at edges, the horisontal support plane being the most important of these, particularly since it is the one with which the gravity vector is associated. The physical laws of optics and those principles governing the reflectance of visible radiant energy off these surfaces were considered by Gibson to hold the keys to correct interpretation.

From the practical stance of computer vision for robotics support, neither the semantically driven nor the data driven Gibsonian approach can be ignored. A well balanced combination would seem the best approach, the former narrowing interpretation to those consistent with constraining knowledge of the domain and the latter promising not only wider scope but also considerable data reduction at the early stages of analysis.

2. Robotic Vision

Robotic vision should be considered in the context of the complete 'hand/eye' manipulation cycle such as depicted in Figure 1.

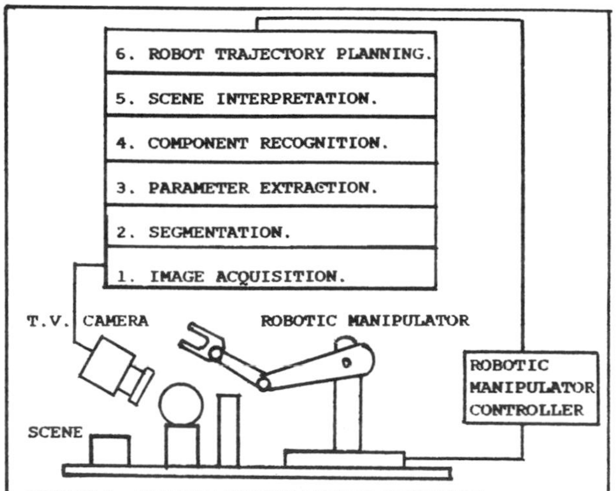

FIGURE 1. ROBOTIC VISION SYSTEM HIERARCHY.

Image acquisition not only includes the transduction of light patterns into computer readable form but also the control of lighting conditions and camera optical settings necessary for quality data retrieval. In some cases, direct range data collection might also be included. By segmentation is meant the process of breaking up scene image data into the components which will hopefully prove to correspond to the semantically distinct objects and backgrounds in the scene. Parameter extraction deals with the process of specifying the placement, orientation, shape, colour and texture of segmented components sufficient to support both the pattern classification of the objects present and subsequent manipulator trajectory planning (including actual gripper/object interaction).

The recognition stage is responsible for the placement of samples represented by feature vectors into predetermined object classes by the application of decision rules based on prototypical models and/or labelled samples. Scene interpretation refers to the process of describing the set of objects in terms of their identities, positions, orientations, juxtapositions, structural relationships and semantic associations in a coherent and consistent way. This consistency should extend beyond treating the scene merely as a subject of scrutiny, towards supporting some goal directed manipulative tasks in that domain, the details of which are dealt with at the robot trajectory planning stage. Even in known environments (complete and correct parameter extraction, recognition and interpretation), the problem of planning robotic manipulation strategies, collision-free trajectories and object grip contact and removal is by no means trivial. A scene description data structure which simplifies these tasks is invaluable in rendering the task tractable in terms of applicability to real-time robotic manipulation. The successful execution of a planned robotic action is a most apt method of testing the correctness of the scene interpretation and appropriate action hypotheses provided by the anlaysis chain. The scene is modified by robotic action and may need to be submitted once more to visual scrutiny unless updates to a world model of the robotic environment are sufficient to guarantee the correctness of subsequent planned action. In some situations it may prove valuable if the interactions of the manipulator with the scene (including 'eye-in-hand' analysis) are used in disambiguating interpretation. One example might be the testing of a support relationship by lifting the supported object indirectly.

3. Scene Analysis Problem Classes

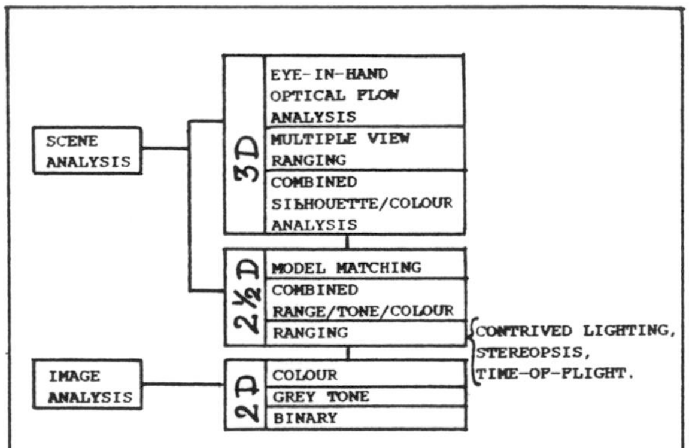

FIGURE 2. SCENE ANALYSIS PROBLEM CLASSES.

Consider Figure 2 which shows a complexity ordering on problem classes in the scene analysis domain. The majority of industrial vision systems currently available in the marketplace fit into the lowest (binary vision) class; some have the potential to extend into grey tone and/or colour. However, beyond the purely 2D level one is in research laboratory territory where a number of results are exciting to report but where widespread industrial application will have to wait for considerable improvements either in reliability or cost effectiveness. The maturation process from laboratory demonstration to industrial viability is usually a long and expensive one.

The ½D increment to take image analysis into the lower scene analysis block is essentially that of adding range data (either directly acquired or inferred from multiple image analysis) relative to a single general view point. Hidden objects or fragments, including surfaces turned away from the viewing position cannot be specified.

Correct and complete 3D analysis is something of a myth in practical terms. To obtain an accurate volumetric model of complex object assemblages via remote sensing (non-contact imaging and ranging in this context) is almost impossible due to various forms of inaccessibility.

4. Research Stance

This paper is mainly concerned with scene analysis and collision-free trajectory planning at the second level up in the 3D class of scene analysis. The work presented here clings tenaciously to the principle that as much as possible should be done in a semantic-free mode of analysis as this promises generality, simplicity and considerable data compression which will eventually 'pay off' when high level semantically guided phases of analysis are invoked. This is not a universally supportable approach but one which, in respect of the work done in the Computer Vision and Robotics Laboratory at the Australian National University, has proven fruitful in the past and promises to be useful in a wide range of industrial applications in the future. Another general principle adhered to in the research approach described here is that methods capable of providing the kind of scene analysis results necessary for robotic support over a computational cycle not in excess of several minutes on a medium scale machine should be concentrated on in the not particularly outlandish hope that such algorithms, when executed on specially architectured, but not too expensive machines, will run at cycles of seconds or tenths of seconds in the near future, thus complying with the real-time needs of many robotic manipulation applications. These restrictions do severely narrow the field of applicable analysis tools but the advantage of being able to complete an eye/hand coordination experiment in the laboratory within a tolerable time span should not be overlooked. In terms of a productive research environment, this situation is not unlike that of interactive terminal computing versus batch submissions for overnight computation runs for unbugged programs continually in development.

5. Space Cube Constructions from Multiple Image Projections

Consider a space cube, M, of N x N x N cells, each being addressed by three indices. Let there be three 2D image arrays F, S and P, each N x N, to represent front elevation, side elevation and plan views, respectively, of the 3D scene, each element being addressed by two indices. Two types of images are acquired for each viewing direction, the first being a binary image obtained from scene silhouettes using contrast enhancing back lighting, the second being a full colour image with red, green and blue components separately digitised.

Figure 3 shows a scene example and the set of six images used for its analysis. Three silhouette views and the three corresponding colour views are acquired. The colour views and the silhouette views are not needed at the same time in the analysis stages to follow.

Figure 4 shows the experimental set-up used to acquire silhouette and colour image data, whilst Figure 5 shows the overall equipment configuration in the laboratory.

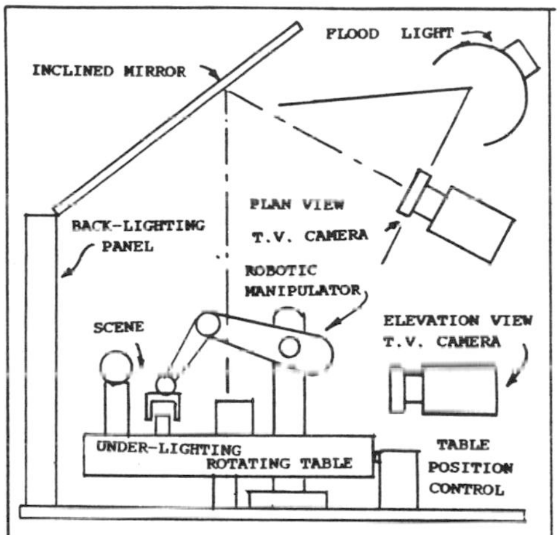

FIGURE 4. IMAGE BASED 3D VOLUMETRIC MODELLING: EXPERIMENTAL SET-UP.

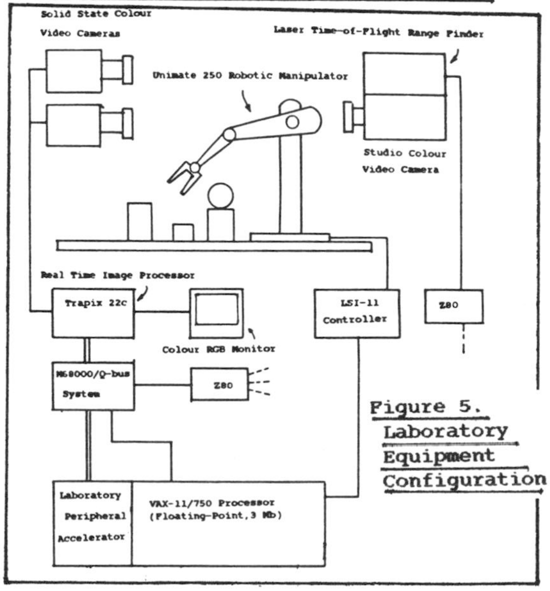

Figure 5. Laboratory Equipment Configuration.

An under-lit table can rotate in front of a back-lit panel to present elevation and plan silhouette views to a colour TV camera several metres away, the plan being viewed via the inclined mirror shown. The camera is tilted upward to acquire the plan view via the mirror, zoom lens adjustments being used to compensate for the extra viewing distance introduced by the mirror. The use of three TV cameras would obviate the need for movement and permit more accurate registration. Note that the under-lit table not only provides the silhouette lighting for the plan view but also serves to render the scene support bright for the elevation silhouette views so that the support plane appears as part of the background. The significance of this will become clearer in the next section when 3D connectivity analysis is discussed. An auto-iris adjustment on the camera compensates for the brightening of the scene. The table and backdrop lighting is maintained whilst colour imagery is acquired as this tends to minimise shadow effects. One advantage of placing the TV camera some distance away is that parallel projection geometry can be assumed without significant error.

The silhouette data is used to determine 3D scene space occupancy in the space cube by simply marking as occupied space cube cells which are at intersections of orthogonal rays from occupied elements of the three binary image 2D arrays. This process is computationally trivial though a large number of tests are required. Obviously, for $N > 64$ a large amount of memory is required, but this is no longer seen as a serious disadvantage given the trends in the marketplace. Even at this first stage of processing a fairly robust base for obstacle avoidance analysis is imbedded in the space cube. This will be taken up later.

Although it is true that by using Oct-tree [Tanimoto, 1980] representations of the space cube considerable memory savings could be achieved, the complexity of manipulating such data structures for subsequent stages of processing was judged to be prohibitive. A closer investigation of this alternative data structure would, however, be valuable.

Of course, with only a small number of views, space modelling of some obscured portions of the scene will not be possible; however it is conceptually straightforward to include a larger number of views in this approach and such might be necessary for cluttered scenes containing complexly shaped objects.

For non-touching, free standing, basically convex objects, the plan silhouette view projection through the cube will be a powerful means of distinguishing solids (used in this paper to mean distinct volumes occupied by material, each of which may consist of one or more objects in contact) not so easily separated by either elevation silhouette view.

For collision-free robotic manipulation trajectory planning [Lozano-Perez, 1979], [Udupa, 1977], [Jarvis, 1983] the space occupancy result provided by the space cube will always be an upper limit of space actually occupied by the solids in the scene. The swept volume of a hypothesised robotic arm movement can be directly tested for logical intersection with the occupied space cube elements; these intersections could be used as the basis for modifying a proposed trajectory until a collision-free path could be assured.

6. 3D Connected Component Analysis

Rosenfeld's binary connectivity analysis algorithm [Rosenfeld, 1966] has been used extensively for 2D binary image analysis, and run length encoded modifications of the algorithm are utilised in several industrial binary vision systems available on the market [Reinhold, 1980], [Gleason, 1979], [Holland, 1979].

The intent of such algorithms is to assign to each element a label indicating its membership to a connected component in the binary image with different labels indicating distinct components.

It is straightforward to extend Rosenfeld's algorithm into 3D for labelling connected occupied cell components in the space cube introduced in Section 5. If the sequence of testing proceeds from left to right, top to bottom, front to back, then, except for some edge effects (which can be avoided using a false empty cell shell around the cube), the connectivity decision for any one cell is made in the context of its 3 x 3 x 3 spatial neighbourhood instead of the 3 x 3 2D neighbourhood of the original algorithm [See Fig. 6]. Instead of the four already labelled neighbours of the 2D case, an entire 3 x 3 block in front of the current layer plus the four already labelled cells at the same depth of the cell in question need be tested in the algorithm given.

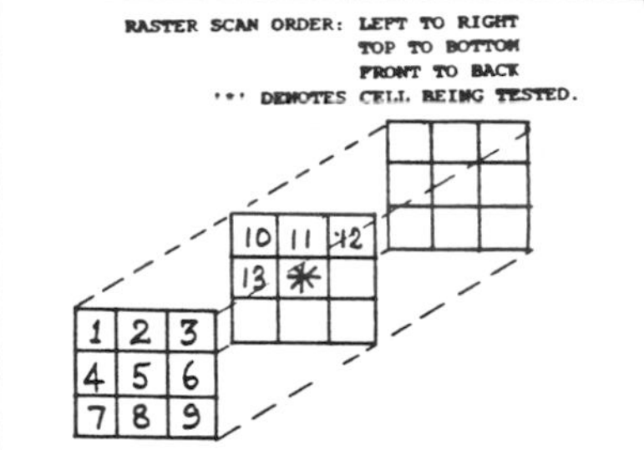

FIGURE 6. THREE DIMENSIONAL BINARY CONNECTIVITY, 3x3x3 NEIGHBOURHOOD.

The complexity for examining each cell goes up by a factor 13/4 and the number of cells requiring examination is N^3 instead of N^2. However, in general, the proportion of the space cube which is occupied is usually much smaller than the proportion of a 2D image which is not background so that a large proportion of the space cube cells examined do not require tests to be implemented. No doubt the run length encoding modifications of the original algorithm could also be extended into the 3D case.

The result of this phase of analysis is that each separate chunk of occupied space in the space cube is distinguished by label. The lighting for the silhouette image data collection can easily be arranged so as to avoid the problem of the supporting plane linking all objects together. Alternatively, some bottom levels of the space cube could be voided before connectivity analysis.

After this processing phase, each connected piece of occupied space in the cube can be dealt with in isolation, considerably simplifying further segmentation refinement. It is trivial to extract parameters such as enclosing rectangular prism, centre of volume, principal axes and various shape measures from this representation. Further, by extending various binary image analysis tools into 3D, such operations as outlining, shrinking, skeletonisation, distance transforms etc. can be applied to the entire cube structure or each connected component separately. Figure 7 shows some views of isolated solids for the scene example introduced in Figure 3. Cross sections of isolated solids can also be easily extracted.

7. Painting the Solids

The second set of images mentioned in Section 5 are now used to complete the third analysis phase. These images are full colour views, one corresponding to each of the silhouette images. Red, green and blue components of each are acquired using a colour TV camera. The colours are 'painted' back onto the outside cells of solids in the space cube from each of the three view directions. This is done for all three views, resulting in a coloured shell layer on three sides (front, side, top) of each solid except where occlusions occur. Obscured portions, insides and non-viewed sides (back, other side, bottom) are not 'painted' and remain 'black', but 'black' is not the same as empty since labelling information still distinguishes solids from void. This computation is both simple and fast.

After this third processing stage, 3D viewing transformations can be carried out by simple geometric rotation calculations on the positions of occupied cells and mapping the appropriate colours into a viewing frame. A depth array is kept for the viewing direction so that the colours displayed are those of the front most cells with respect to that selected viewing point. During the processing sequence (raster) any occupied cell closer to the viewing point than the closest one so far represented in the depth array is over painted and that depth array value updated. All depth array values are initially very large. These operations can be applied to the entire space cube or to selected subsets of solids. If the viewing transformations give a view which would expose unpainted portions these parts show up as black and can be distinguished from the background void which is conveniently considered to be white. For example, a bottom view would show a coloured border along only two sides, the remainder of each solid appearing as black. Back and other side colour images could be added to paint the solids as well but a bottom colour view could be impractical to acquire.

A view of the painted solids in combination (example scene) is shown in Figure 8 (20° rotation, 20° tilt). Note that quantisation effects in applying the rotation transformation equations can cause small holes in the viewed image; these are of no critical importance in the context of this analysis since the transformations are only applied for viewing the results of painting the solids and do not affect the space cube itself.

8. Segmenting the Solids into Objects

After the third processing stage, the space cube contains a number of painted solids distinguished by labels in a space occupancy connected component sense. However, each painted solid can be made up of only one or perhaps several objects in contact. Segmenting each solid into objects is a much easier task than segmenting any of the complete coloured views, since fewer decisions are involved, 3D spatial segmentations having reduced a considerable amount of interpretation ambiguity. One simple approach to segmenting the solids into objects would be to once again apply connectivity analysis, this time based on colour intensity variation. For brightly coloured objects, this would give quite reliable results except where two objects in contact are the same colour [Jarvis, 1982, 1983] or where occlusion has left the solid with parts 'unpainted' (black). But at least there is some indication that the 'unpainted' portions do exist as material which occupies space. However, there is no guarantee that 'unpainted' portions actually represent parts of occupied space, since certain object configurations can give rise to false space occupancy volumes in the space cube, the total space cube occupancy volume always enveloping the actual space occupied by the scene if it were imbedded in the space cube. In some complex situations it may be necessary to robotically remove some of the objects so that obscured objects might be more completely examined via another analysis cycle. Thus, a reasonable, somewhat simplistic strategy might be to pass over the segmentation stage for solids with large 'unpainted' patches when viewed from any of the originally determined directions. The more completely visible solids can be segmented and their object components robotically removed, at which stage a new analysis cycle can begin. Hopefully a small number of such cycles would suffice to complete the analysis. This phase has not yet been specifically implemented for space cube data but typical results of the colour intensity based segmentation approach are shown in the earlier papers cited above.

9. Collision-Free Trajectory Planning

Even after complete and correct scene interpretation remains the task of collision-free trajectory planning for the robotic vehicle or manipulator to approach its goal point efficiently from some starting position. In many situations the simplistic approach of removing objects in order of accessibility may not be acceptable and more complex procedures need to be examined. Two basic approaches to obstacle avoidance dominate the literature. The 'swept volume' approach [Boyse, 1979], [Udupa, 1979] consists of proposing robotic movement, calculating the volume that would be swept out by that movement and using the intersection with obstacle occupied space volumes (if any) in refining the trajectory towards an acceptable non-collision path. Fulfilling some optimality criterion along with achieving non-collision is not easily approached using this method. The 'grown obstacle' approach [Lozaño-Perez,1979], [Jarvis, 1983] ingeniously simplifies the problem by shrinking the robotic vehicle to a point and growing each obstacle to account for the original extent of the robotic vehicle (vehicle and obstacles each represented by one or several (possibly overlapping) convex polyhedra). The problem becomes one of finding a (piece-wise linear) shortest distance path from the start point to a goal, which solution can be found using Nilsson's A* search strategy [Nilsson, 1971]. When the vehicle is permitted to rotate as well as translate the complexity increases to that of searching through families of grown obstacle fields, each one associated with a given rotation position. In the three-dimensional, translation/rotation case, a 6-dimensional search space is involved and the method becomes computationally expensive to apply.

An entirely different approach using the concept of 'distance transforms' [Rosenfeld, 1968] in the quantised 3D space represented in the space cube approach to solid geometry modelling presented in earlier sections can be applied in a robust and computationally trivial manner [Jarvis, 1984]. The method is not restricted by any convexity assumptions on the shape of the robotic vehicle or obstacles and is capable of solving complex maze problems with multiple goals without modification.

Consider the translation only case for a specified rigid robotic vehicle in 3 space. The 'outsides' of the obstacles can easily be extended to account for the vehicle extent by simple cell filling relative to a reference point on the vehicle. In this transformed domain the problem becomes one of finding the shortest succession of unoccupied cells to a goal point. The solution is simply to propagate distance from the set of goal points (whether isolated or clumped in any fashion) through all of free space enveloping the grown obstacles and move from the nominated start point down hill in this distance 'potential field' to a goal. Details are given in [Jarvis, 1984]. The computational complexity depends on the shapes of the grown obstacles but the algorithm itself is trivial to develop and entirely robust. Figure 10 shows the trajectory of a 4 x 4 x 4 cube vehicle from a nominated start point to a goal point for the scene shown in Figure 9. The rotating and translating vehicle case can be dealt with by providing a set of 3D distance potential field results, one for each rotation position, and simply jumping between rotationally adjacent members of this family in a sequence which most rapidly diminishes distance to zero. A path, if it exists, will be found in this way. The optimality requirement needs further analysis. To extend the method to multi-jointed robotic manipulators is a much harder undertaking in the general case, but simplifying assumptions may ease the computational burden somewhat.

10. Other 3D Binary Analysis Algorithms

The simplicity and lack of ambiguity of the occupied cell solid geometry scene modelling approach suggested in this paper has much to recommend it as a basis for more complex binary analysis which can begin as extensions of well known 2D algorithms [Jarvis, 1970] into 3D by trivial modification and then be developed into more specialised functions. Some examples are suggested below:

(a) Smoothing.
In the 2D binary image case, smoothing can be achieved by testing the occupancy of cells in the 3 x 3 neighbourhood of each candidate cell and emptying the control cell if some simple test is failed (e.g. less than 3 occupied neighbours) or filling that cell if unoccupied when the test succeeds. The same type of process in the 3 x 3 x 3 neighbourhood of a 3D binary cell can achieve similar smoothing results.

(b) Outsides and Insides.
An occupied cell with insufficient occupied neighbours can be considered an outside cell whether in the 2D or 3D case. Otherwise the cell is inside. A count of outside cells of an object in the 3D case is analogous to the perimeter in the 2D case. In the 3D case, surface area is extracted.

(c) High Order Moments.
Various moments of area can be used in the 2D case to determine centre of area, principal axes and other parameters useful for shape analysis. Moments of volume can be applied in a similar fashion in the 3D case.

(d) Intersections and Removals.
Logically AND-ing two binary areas or volumes will give the area or volume of intersection, respectively. Exclusive OR operations between an object and a scene containing that object will remove that object.

(e) Skeletons.
The local maxima of distance transforms into objects from their outsides provide important skeletal shape information [Rosenfeld, 1968]. Furthermore, fragments of the skeleton can be used to grow back components of the original objects. The 2D algorithms extend simply into the 3D case. An alternative skeletonising algorithm can be found in [Saraga, 1968].

(f) Elongation.
One can describe 'elongation' as the measure of what proportion of an object is near its outside. Iterative stripping away of outsides of objects can give an appropriate shape measurement of this type.

(g) Shrinking.
Levialdi's shrinking algorithm [Levialdi, 1972] can be used to quickly count and specify the bounding rectangular frame of isolated objects in the 2D case. Extensions into 3D would provide count and containment data.

(h) Similarity.
Hamming distance, which is a count of the number of dissimilar bits between two binary words, can be easily applied to both 2D and 3D binary data. Counting the filled cells after the exclusive OR operation between the two binary constructs which are to be compared is all that is required.

(i) Normalising.
In the 2D binary case, image normalisation for size, skew and distortion correction using affine transforms based on high order moments [Hu Ming, 1962] can be used on 3D data as a useful preprocessing operation before applying pattern recognition decision rules.

(j) Diffusion.
A diffusion operation based on a modified version of heat flow analysis [Bell, 1968] which can be used to grow image fragments resulting from flawed digitisation or poor quality image source into reasonably complete objects could be extended into 3D to correct some fragmentation

caused by misalignment of multiple camera views in the space cube modelling process.

11. Discussion, Further Work and Conclusions

The robotic manipulation implications of this approach to 3D scene modelling are relatively clear. The results of this analysis provide information on the location, size and juxtaposition of distinct objects in a scene without semantic guidance. Each stage of analysis is computationally simple and the entire analysis sequence could probably be completed on a dedicated supermicro or supermini computer system in an acceptable time frame provided that the scene is fairly brightly coloured and not too complex, the space cube and image resolutions are relatively coarse, and assembly code is used. Although a relatively large amount of memory is required this is not a prohibitive factor at this time. Following stages of analysis could include object recognition in terms of 3D geometry and colour attributes, robot trajectory planning with obstacle avoidance and means/ends analysis [Nilsson, 1975] for construction tasks. Although the semantic content of such analysis could be high, the 3D data structure provided by the space cube construction would appear to be very supportive of all these extensions. Placing a colour camera in the 'hand' of the robotic device in what is called the 'eye-in-the-hand' configuration for robotic vision would allow further levels of sophistication to be applied to the space cube modelling approach because of the variety of viewing positions made available by such a mode of operation.

In conclusion, this paper has presented an easily realisable semantic-free approach to modelling 3D scenes using colour and silhouette multiple view imagery for the construction of a space cube data structure which can be conveniently used for various kinds of analysis. These include space occupancy, 3D connectivity, object segmentation, 3D shape parameter extraction, juxtaposition analysis and collision-free trajectory planning. The method shows promise as the basis of a robotic vision system with a wide scope of application.

This unified 3D space cube modelling approach has become more practical in recent times, partly due to the steep downturn in solid-state memory price and partly because of the improving technical feasibility and economic viability of custom chip design and fabrication. The computations involved are intrinsically simple and many of the algorithmic components could be 'cast in silicon' using VLSI technology, taking advantage of the regularity of the calculations in designing massively parallel or pipelined architectures leading to high speed processing for real-time robotic application.

12. Acknowledgements

This work was carried out with the support of ARGS grant No. F 7815776 and on a special equipment grant from the Australian National University in 1983.

13. References

Bell, D.A. 1968. Computer Aided Design of Image Processing Techniques, IEE NPL Conference on Pattern Recognition.

Boyse, J.W. 1979. Interference Detection among Solids and Surfaces. Commun. ACM, 22, 1, 3-9.

Gibson, J.J. 1966. The Senses Considered as Perceptual Systems, Houghton-Mifflin, Boston.

Gleason, G.J. & Agin, G.J. 1979. A Modular Vision System for Sensor-Controlled Manipulation and Inspection, Proc. 9th International Symposium on Industrial Robots, Washington, D.C., 57-70.

Guzman, A. 1968. Computer Recognition of Three Dimensional Objects in a Visual Scene, Ph.D. Thesis, MAC-TR-59, Project MAC, M.I.T., Mass..

Holland, S.W., Rossol, L. & Ward, M.R. 1979. Consight-I: A Vision-Controlled Robot System for Transferring Parts from Belt Conveyors, in Computer Vision and Sensor-Based Robotics edited by Dodd, G.G. & Rossol, L., Plenum Press, 81-100.

Hu Ming, K. 1962. Visual Pattern Recognition by Moment Invariants, IRE Trans. on Information Theory.

Jarvis, R.A. & Patrick, E.A. 1970. Interactive Binary Picture Manipulation, Proc. UMR - Mervin J. Kelly Communications Conference, University of Missouri-Rolla, 20-1-1 to 20-1-8.

Jarvis, R.A. 1982. Vision Driven Robotics in a Partially Structured Environment, Proc. 9th Aust. Comp. Conf.,Tasmania, 526-548.

Jarvis, R.A. 1983. Expedient Range Enhanced 3-D Robot Colour Vision, Robotica, 1, 25-31.

Jarvis, R.A. 1984. Collision-Free Trajectory Planning Using Distance Transforms, submitted for presentation at National Conference and Exhibition on Robotics, Melbourne, Australia.

Levialdi, S. 1972. On Shrinking Binary Picture Patterns, Commun. ACM, 15, 1, 7-10.

Lozano-Perez, L. & Wesley, M.A. 1979. An Algorithm for Planning Collision-Free Paths among Polyhedral Obstacles, Commun. ACM, 22, 10, 560-570.

Nilsson, N.J. 1971. Problem-Solving Methods in Artificial Intelligence, Mc-Graw Hill.

Nilsson, N.J. 1975. Some Examples of AI Mechanisms for Goal-Seeking, Planning and Reasoning, AI Centre, Stanford Research Institute, Technical Note 130.

Reinhold, A.G. & Vanderbrug, G. 1980. Robot Vision for Industry: The Autovision System, Robotics Age, 2, 3, 22-28.

Rosenfeld, A. & Pfaltz, J.L. 1966. Sequential Operations in Digital Picture Processing, Journal ACM, 13, 4, 471-494.

Rosenfeld, A. & Pfaltz, J.L. 1968. Distance Functions on Digital Pictures, Pattern Recognition, 1, 33-61.

Saraga, P. & Woolons, D.J. 1968. The Design of Operators for Pattern Recognition, IEE NPL Conf. on Pattern Recognition.

Tanimoto, S.L. 1980. Geometric Modelling with Oct-Trees, Proc. Workshop on Picture Data Description and Management, Asilomar, California, 117-123.

Turner, K.J. 1974. Computer Perception of Curved Objects using a Television Camera, Ph.D. Thesis, Dept. Machine Intelligence, University of Edinburgh, Scotland.

Udupa, S.M. 1977. Collision Detection and Avoidance in Computer Controlled Manipulators, Proc. 5th Int. Joint Conf. on A.I., M.I.T., 737-748.

Waltz, D. 1972. Generating Semantic Descriptions from Drawings of Scenes with Shadows, Ph.D. Thesis, M.I.T., Mass. (Also Ch.2 of The Psychology of Computer Vision, Winston, P.H. (Ed), McGraw Hill, New York, 1975).

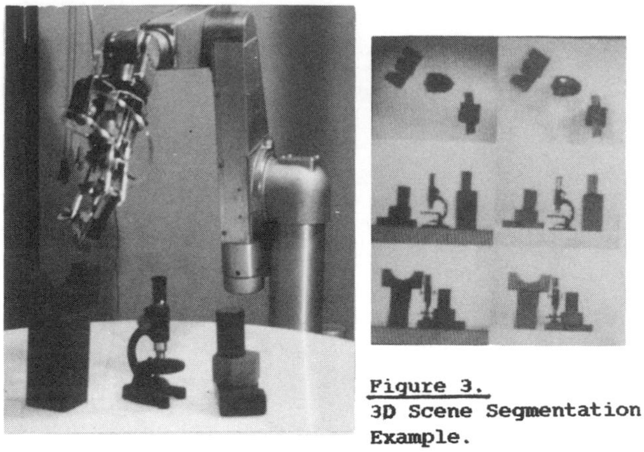

Figure 3.
3D Scene Segmentation Example.

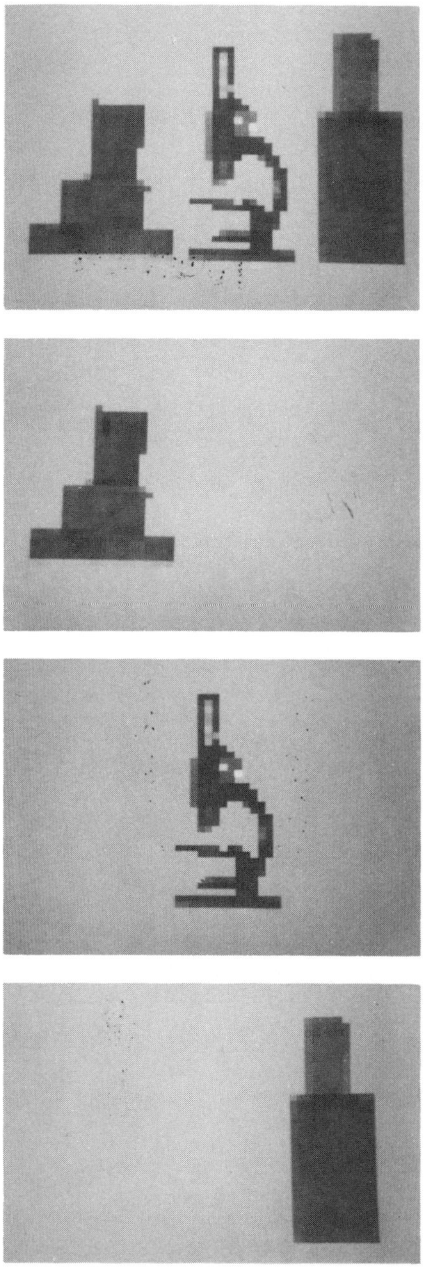

Figure 7.
Segmented Solids for Example Scene.

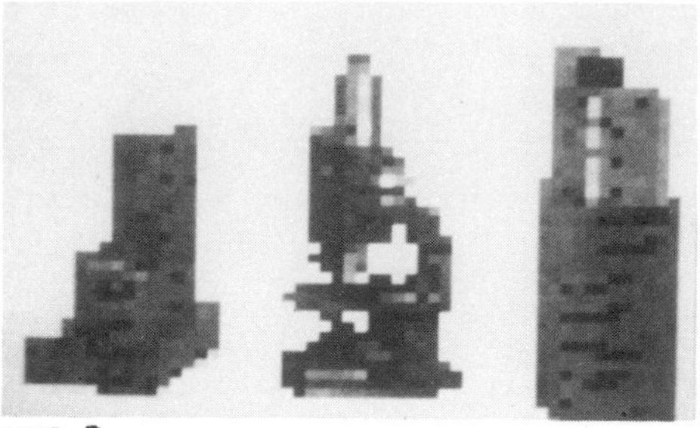

Figure 8.
Rotated View of Solid Geometry Scene Model.

Figure 9.
Scene for Obstacle Avoidance Example.

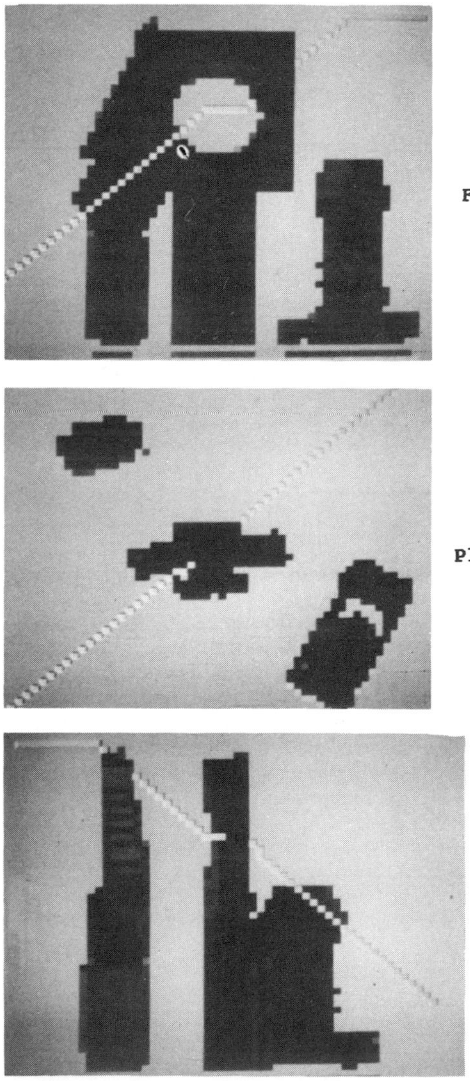

Figure 10.
Collision-Free Trajectory for Figure 9 Example.

PROGRAMMING, SIMULATING AND EVALUATING ROBOT ACTIONS

A. LIEGEOIS, P. BORREL, E. DOMBRE

Laboratoire d'Automatique et de Microélectronique
de Montpellier
France

In this paper, methodologies and software developped for analyzing robot performances are presented.
This work makes use of a CAD-CAM System, which allows the designers and the users of robots to evaluate:

- the geometric capabilities: workspace, interferences with environmental objects,
- the static and dynamic forces/torques required to perform a given task,
- the robot's behaviour in the course of a continuous path or a point-to-point motion.

The three-dimensional models of the mechanisms, the environment and the tasks are entered interactively into the data-base by means of a light pen and a keyboard. The mathematical models required for the applications are automatically generated. The system allows easy communication with the geometric data-base of parts to be handled, welded, machined, etc., and is able to generate inputs for robot programs.

INTRODUCTION

The essential goal of a robotic mechanism is to modify the relationships between its own mechanical parts in order to change the states of the other components of the environment. Therefore a robot is programmed to change the spatial and the force relationships between physical objects. Traditionnaly, industrial robots were programmed "manually" by means of a teach-box or a master arm, then their repectitive operations were tested in the workplace, and the program adjusted if necessary. Such a process is time-consuming, requires the stopping of the production line, and lacks flexibility. Current robots, with sophisticated sensors, must do their work with a high reliability despite the growth of environmental complexity and variability. For these reasons, off-line programming and emulating of robot actions is necessary to improve their operational quality and reliability. Futhermore, the display of a robot moving in an environment containing the three-dimensional C.A.D. models of parts to be machined, assembled, etc.. is expected to greatly facilitate the design of a production unit and the tuning of robot programs /BOR.83/, /DOM.84/, /HEGIM.77/, /LIEB78/, /LAT.84/, /QUER.82/, /SORO.80/.

Most of the systems that model robots in a geometric data-base developped so far, are able to check the geometric capabilities and the possible collisions, for given robots. However, such systems require that the geometric and kinematic equations be entered into the system. In addition to the development of such facilities, the work of the Robotic Group of the L.A.M.M. to provide the designers and users with general tools has led to the following original features discussed in this paper:

- automatic determination of any robot range of operation, including the multiple solutions,
- evaluation of the near-optimal cycle time in point-to-point motions with intermediary passing points,
- computation of the torques or forces at the joints,
- determination of the envelope of any part moving continously, in order to check for interferences.

The results are implemented in the C.A.T.I.A. (Trade Mark of Dassault-Systèmes) interactive system.

1. GEOMETRIC CAPABILITIES

1.1. General

The CATIA data base consists of tables, representing geometric elements (points, polygons, curves, patches, surfaces, polyhedra, triedra, etc) and sets. The relationships between elements and/or sets is kept using a system of pointers.

For robotic applications the data base has been extended to include two specific types of geometric elements.

i) Joint element: a manipulator is considered as a kinematic chain of rigid bodies connected by joints. A joint element contains the type of joint (revolute, prismatic, or "coupled revolute") and its angular or linear limits. The linkage of joint elements form a robot.

ii) Task element: This element is used to describe the succession of relationships between the various geometric elements of the universe which make up a "task": point-to-point or continuous path.

A geometric set table may contain several robot sets and several task sets has been constructed to represent the assembly cell designed in Toulouse for the A.R.A. Project experiments.

The task function allows the user to specify the links between robot elements and environment elements, to grasp and release objects, to track a curve (fig. 2) with or without additional orientation constraints, etc.

1.2 Workspace determination

The goal of this study is to provide the designer, the programmer and finally the robot itself with a geometric model of the range of action. As a robot is defined in CATIA only by topoligical and geometric data, with no reference to the kinematic or dynamic equations, the workspace definition program has limited information with which to function.

Consider then the following common geometric and variational models:

$$\underline{X} = \underline{f}\ (\underline{q}) \qquad (1)$$

$$\dot{\underline{X}} = J\ (\underline{q})\ \dot{\underline{q}} \qquad (2)$$

where:

$\underline{X}$ is the vector defining the present state of the end-effector (the so-called task or operational coordinates),

$\underline{q} = q_1, q_2, \ldots, q_N$ is the vector of the joint coordinates,

$\underline{f}$ is the function vector which defines the direct coordinate transformation,

$J\ (\underline{q})$ is the instantaneous Jacobian matrix related to $\underline{f}$.

It is well known that equations such as (1) and (2) may have zero, a finite number , or an infinite number of solutions ($\underline{q}$).

Consider also that there exists an N-dimensional configuration domain in joint coordinate space, where:

$$q_i \text{ min} \leqslant q_i \leqslant q_i \text{ max} \qquad i = 1, 2, \ldots, N \qquad (3)$$

This domain is bounded by hyperlanes such as

$$q_i = q_i \text{ min}, \quad q_i = q_i \text{ max} \quad i = 1, 2, \ldots, N \qquad (4)$$

whose vertices and edges are defined as combinations of other similar constraints.

There exist hypersurfaces that divide this domain into a finite number of connected hypervolumes called "aspects"/BOR.84/, /TAN. 84/. These surfaces represent where the determinants of certain m-order minors of the Jacobian matrix are zero (m being the number of independant coordinates related to the task X, i.e. the dimension of the operational space). Each resulting aspect corresponds to one of the various solutions or sets of solutions of equation (1).

A program has been written that:

i) finds the aspects in the configuration domain
ii) maps each aspect into the cartesian space
iii) produces a representation in a data base which can be viewed and manipulated interractively.

The methodology developped acts at three levels:

1) the numerical level for tracking the boundaries of the aspects defined above,

2) the topological level for generating and reducing the connected graph describing the aspects,

3) the geometric level for obtaining the surface and volume representation of the image of the aspects in three dimensional space.

Figure 3 and 4 are examples of robot aspects.

The results can be used for many purposes:

- one can optimize the range of a planned mechanism by selecting a proper choice of joints, of joint limits and segment lengths.

- the work area of a given robot can be obtained by merging the aspect volumes and then used for optimally locating the robot with respect to its environment.

- finally, knowledge of the aspect volumes gives the robot programmer, and later the control program, information required for choosing trajectories within the work area that avoid joint limits and losses of mobility when the robot must move from one aspect to another (such as the move from the "upper arm" posture to the "lower arm" posture by an anthropomorphic robot).

1.3 Modeling the volume swept by a robot part /SEGU. 84/

The volume swept by a robot is a union of several envelopes corresponding to motions of mechanical objects including the end effector of the robot and the part grasped by it. Detecting possible interferences between the robot and other objects off-line, is convenient for programming a task and for automatically generating collision-free movements.

The problem is solved by using polyhedral approximations of the considered robot part(s) and convex hulls.

The computation of the convex hull of a polyhedron starts with the data defining the set of its vertices and gives the following data which define the convex envelope:

- vertices,
- edges,
- faces, with normals and distances to a reference point,
- maximal lengths in three mutually perpendicular reference directions.

Such a representation has been used to determine the equilibrium positions and grasping strategies of an isolated part. Here it is used to model the volume swept by a moving polyhedron.

When a polyhedron is convex, the volume swept by it when a translation is applied is again a convex polyhedron, although this is not necessarily the case when a rotation is applied. A similar conclusion can be made for volumes swept by a nonconvex polyhedron.

The computations are simplified by considering mainly convex polygons and by introducing the following approxmations:

- "small" parts are approximated by their convex hulls,
- larger nonconvex parts are divided into convex ones,
- a general motion is discretized such that the swpet volume results in the concatenation of smaller convex ones, each corresponding to an elementary motion.

Figures 5 and 6 illustrate the results as displayed on a graphics terminal.

2. MOTION GENERATION

Another feature which has been added to an experimental robotic version of CATIA, implemented in Montpellier, is the evaluation of the time duration of a point-to-point motion. The user can specify auxiliary intermediate points, so as to avoid obstacles for example. Although studies of algorithms and computer programs have concentrated on the problem in both cartesian and joint spaces, only the former has been implemented in the interactive system.

2.1. Motion generation in the cartesian space

In the case of motion generation in cartesian space, a starting and a final point where the velocities are zero are given, in addition to a number of intermediate points near which the reference point of a robot must pass. The problem is to find an evaluation of the minimum time, given the following constraints :

. velocity limitation,
. acceleration limitation,
. error bounds at intermediate points (the tracking of the definition polygon).

The formalization to this problem has been stated by R. Paul et al/PAUL.78/, /PAUL 79/. It is a non-linear programming one which has been solved /LUH.81/ by using a converging sequence of linear-programming problems. In the method referenced above, distance constraints at intermediate points are introduced through the use of a parameter k which is more or less meaningful to most users. For this reason, the method has been modified slightly in order to deal explicitely with the euclidian errors at the passing points /TONDU.84/. The optimal motion still consists in phases of constant velocity and of constant acceleration, or deceleration, which are visualized as shown in figure 7 and the corresponding travelling time is computed and displayed.

2.2. Motion generation in the joint space

The problems of generating and/or identifying control laws which govern optimal motions in the joint space are studies, while taking into account constraints on velocities, accelerations, synchronization of the joint motions and errors. Depending also on additional constraints relative to jerks, the solution to the problem is found numerically to provide accelerations which are either discontinuous (piecewise constant) or polynomial /LIE.84a/.

The results obtained in sections 2.1 and 2.2 can be used to compute, by using the robot coordinate transformations generated automatically:

i) the trajectories of the parts of the robot, for studying collisions (see section 1.3).

ii)the time evolutions of the joint variables, velocities, and accelerations, for evaluating the dynamic forces or torques at the joints, as explained in the following section.

3. STATIC AND DYNAMIC TORQUES/FORSES AT THE JOINTS

Despite the criticisms currently voiced by many industrial robot designers and users, few people have the convicton that mechanical models will improve the design, location and operation of such machines. Such models relate the geometric (dimensions), kinematic (assembly), kinetic (masses and inertias) parameters, the motion characteristics (generalized coordinates, velocities and accelerations) and the torque and force vectors at the hinges of a mechanism. Commonly, the 'direct model' is used for simulations. The inputs are the internal and external forces, the output is the state (for example joint positions and velocities) of the mechanical system. This model has been widely used in aerospace design and control.

On the other hand the 'inverse model' has the motion and external forces as inputs, and calculates the forces/torques at the highes. The components of these vectors constitute the set of reaction forces and of the so-called 'generalized forces' in the Lagrangian sense. The lattercomprises all the non conservative forces such as friction and motor actions.

Of the two models, the latter is of interest for designers, as well as for users and is more appropriate for the self-adaptative behaviour of the robot itself. In some circumstances or fields of application the knowledge of stresses, loads on shafts, and generalized forces simplifies the design of the mechanism, the workplace, and the choice of optimal motions (in the sense of minimizing wear) eiher by a human programmer or by future intelligent robots, the higher-level problems discussed in the previous paragraphs having been solved.

An 'inverse model' has been successfully implemented in CATIA /LIE.84b/. Figure 8 shows the graphics display of static requirements or the joint actuators, while figure 9 represents the time-history of a generalized force in the development of a particular movement. The treatment of complex (non-planar) closed kinematic loops will be included later, depending on the requirements of future applications. It is presently operational as a batch process /TOU.84/ /ALD.85/.

4. CONCLUSION

The links between computer modeling and robotics has several facets, and still require much work both in software and hardware. Advances will be made with optimal use of the state-of-the-art in research and technology having in mind the particular constraints of complexity, flexibility, speed, and ease of operation of a robotic system. Future improvements in the field will come with new developments in both the software and hardware domains. Such work has the effect of filling the gaps between Artificial Intelligence, Computer Science, Control Engineering and Mechanics.

At the slave level, CAD can help make the robots more perfect generators of positions, motions ad forces. Using graphics as a tool for programming and emulating robot grograms on-site will provide the users with 3-D displays and gestual commands which complement textual or voice interaction.

At a higher level, large facilities could link the robot simulation with process control facilities, knowledge of the part and assembly techniques, resulting in a more fully integrated flexible manufacturing and control system.

ACKNOWLEGEMENTS

The authors are greatly indebted to M.J. ALDON, A. FOURNIER, P. TANNER, B.TONDU, P. TOURON and S.SEGURA for contributing to the studies presented here. The financial support of C.N.R.S., D.R.E.T., and the cooperation with the Dassault Company have been a significant help in their work.

REFERENCES

/ALD.85/ M.J. Aldon, A. Liegeois, B. Tondu, P. Touron: A Software for Computer-Aided Design of Industrial Robots. Proc. CAD-CAM, Robotics and Automation Conf., Tucson, Arizona, 11-15 Feb.1985.

/BOR.83/ P. Rorrel, et al: The Robotics facilities in the CAD-CAM CATIA System. Developments in Robotics 1983, Brian Rooks ed., pp. 245-256.

/BOR.84/ P. Borrel. P. Tanner, A. Lié-geois: Determination of the workarea of a robot arm using a decomposition of the joint space. To be published 1984.

/DOM.84/ E. Dombre, P. Borrel, A. Lié-geois: A CAD System for Programming and Simulating Robot Actions. Digital Systems for Industrial Automation, vol.2, number 2, 1984, pp 201-226.

/HEGIN.77/ W. B. Heginbotham, M. Dooner, D. N. Kennedy: Computer Graphics Simulation of Industrial Robot Interactions, Proc. 7th ISIR, Tokyo, 1977, pp. 169-176.

/LAT.84/ J. C. Latombe, et al: Design and

implementation of a Robot Programming System combining textual and graphical facilities. Proc. 2nd ISRR, Kyoto, Aug. 1984.

/LIEB.78/ L. I. Lieberman et al: Three Dimensional modeling For Automated Mechanical Assembly. RC7089 IBM Research Report, Yorktown Heights, 1978.

/LIE.84a/ A. Liégeois, B. Tondu: Etude de I'dentification et de la commande des robots. Progress Reports. Contrat LAMM-DRET 83-1455, 1984.

/LIE.84b/ A. Liegeois, B. Tondu, p. Touron: Simulation de tra-jectoires et contrôle automatique des efforts aux articulations d'un robot, Proc-ASME Congress, Modeling and Simulation, Minneapolis, Aug. 84.

/LUH.81/ J. Y. S. Luh, C. S. Lin: Optimal Path Planning for Mechanical Manipulators. Transactions of the ASME. Vol. 102, June 1981.

/PAUL.78/ R. Paul et al: Advanced Industrial Robot Systems, Purdue University Report TR-EE 78-25, May 1978.

/PAUL.79/ R. Paul: Manipulator Cartesian Path Control, IEEE Trans. on Systems, Man, and Cybernetics, SMC-9, n°11, Nov. 1979.

/QUER.82/ J. Queromes: Computer-Aided-Design and Robotics. A full of promise cooperation. Proc. 12 th ISIR, Paris, June 1982, pp. 185 195.

/SEGU.84/ S. Segura: Contribution aux problèmes de la détection de collisions et de la saisie automatique en Robotique. Rapport de D.E.A., U.S.T.L., Montpellier, France, July 1984.

/SORO.80/ B. I. Soroka: Debugging Robot Programs with a simulator. Proc. CADAM-8 Conf. Anaheim, CA, Nov. 1980.

/TAN.84/ P. Tanner, P. Borrel, A. Liégeois: Automatic Generation and representation of the work area of a robot arm in a CAD.CAM System. To be published 1984.

/TONDU.84/ B. Tondu: Thesis (in preparation) U.S.T.L., Montpellier, Fall 1984.

/TOU.84/ P. Touron: Modélisation de la Dynamique des mécanismes polyarticulés. Application à la C.A.O. et à la simulation de robots. Thesis U.S.T.L., Montpellier, July 1984.

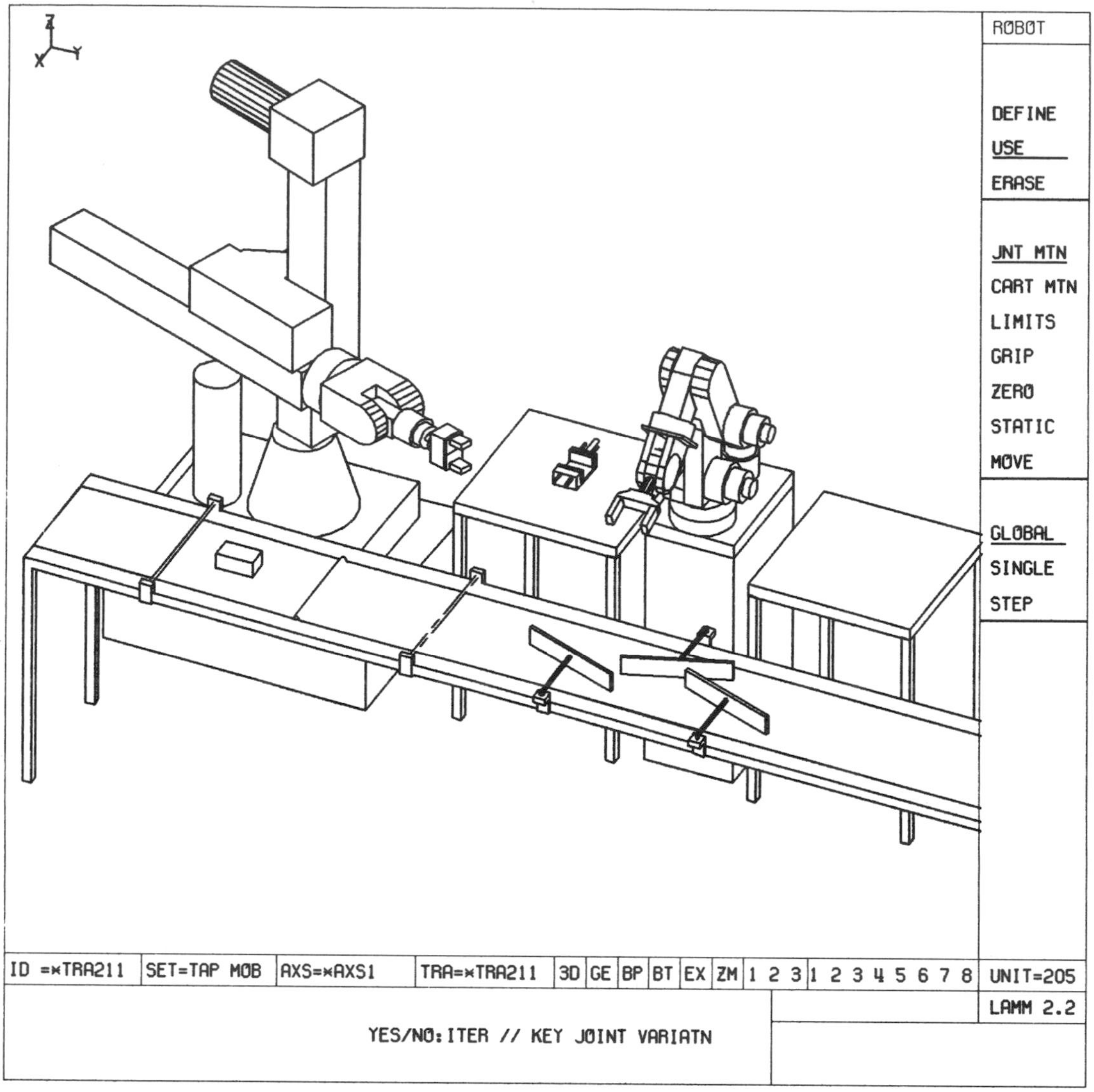

Figure 1 : Model of the assembly workstation

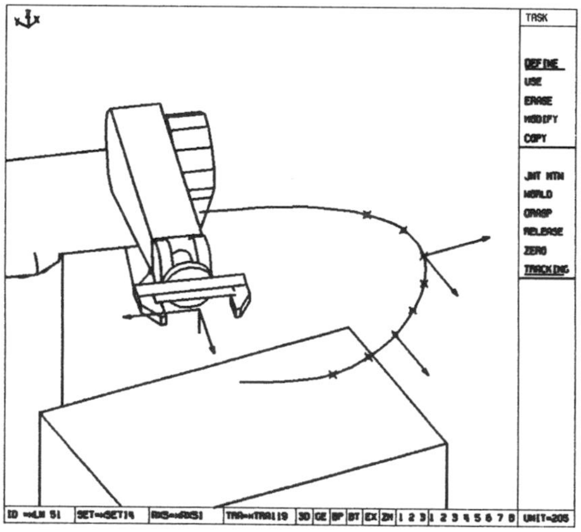

Figure 2 : Curve tracking

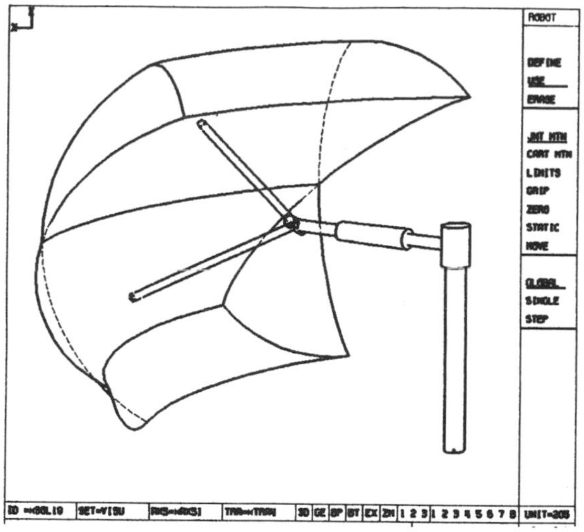

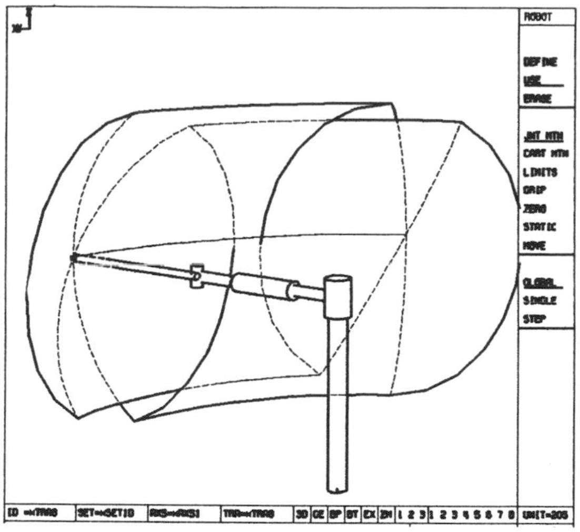

Figures 3 and 4 : The four "aspects" of a 3R robot

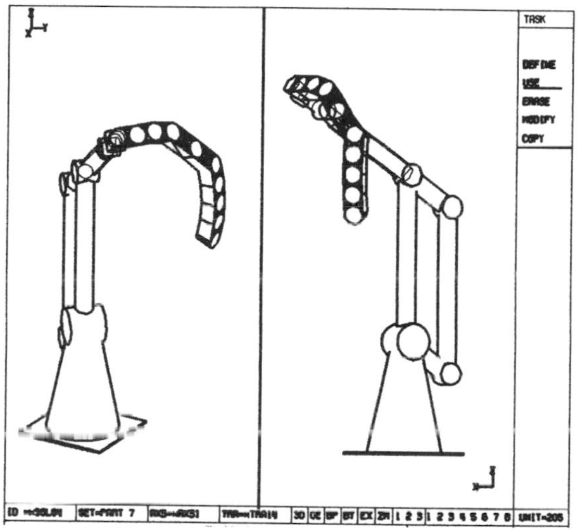

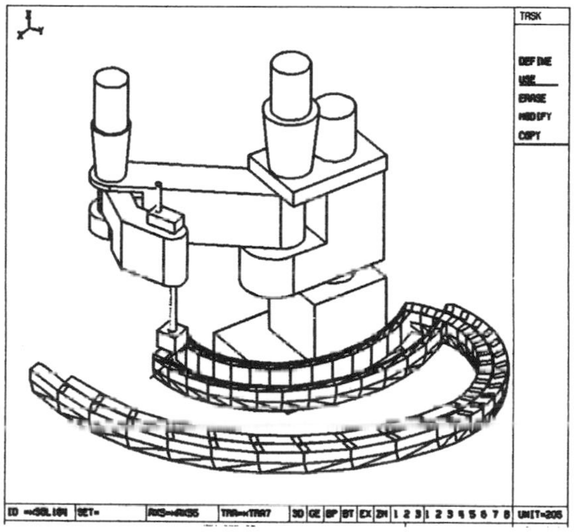

Figures 5 and 6 : Volumes swept by robot parts

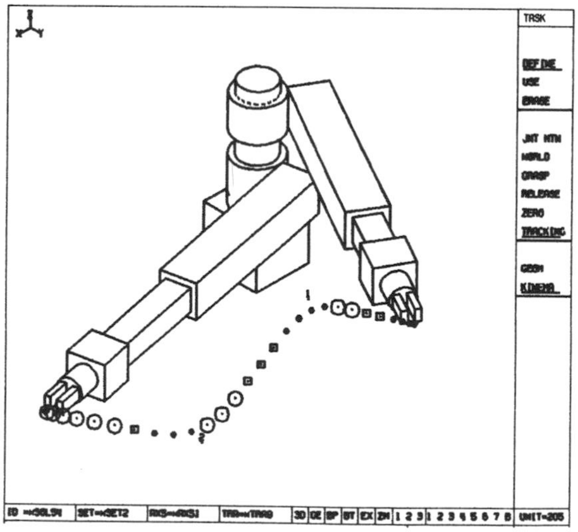

Figure 7 : Motion generation

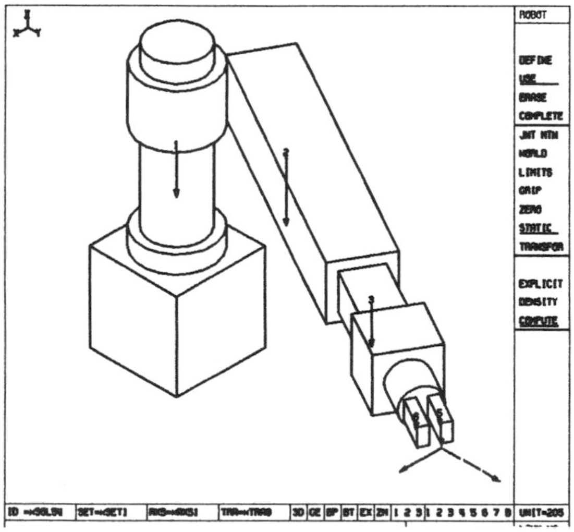

Figure 8 : Static analysis

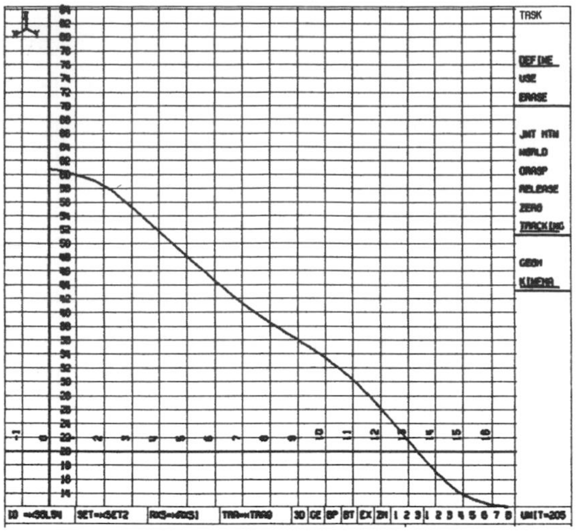

a - joint coordinate

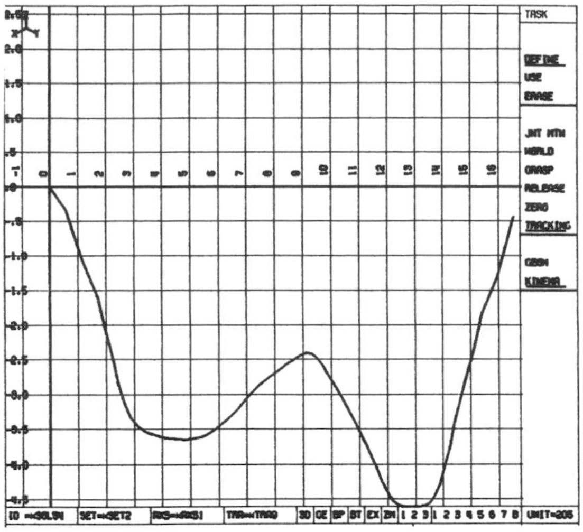

b - joint velocity

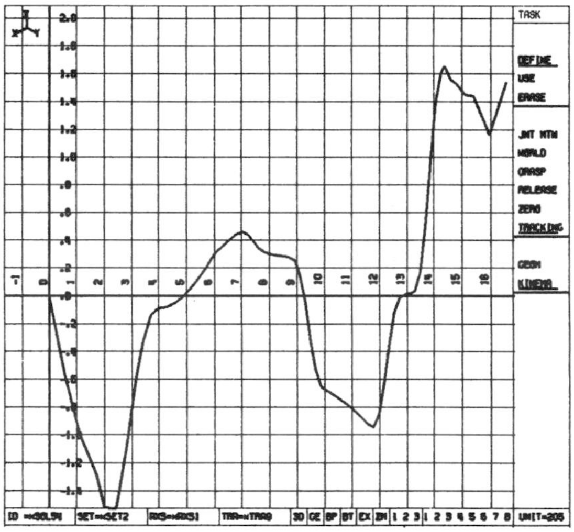

c - joint acceleration

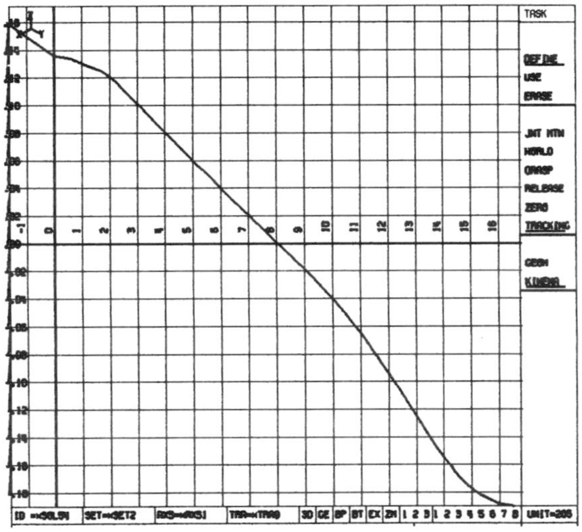

d - torque at the joint

Figures 9 : Dynamic analysis : time evolutions

8 Theory of Manipulation

MECHANICS OF PUSHING

Matthew T. Mason

Computer Science Department and Robotics Institute
Carnegie-Mellon University, Pittsburgh, PA 15213

Pushing is an essential component of many manipulator operations. This paper presents a theoretical exploration of the mechanics of pushing, and demonstrates application of the theory to analysis and synthesis of manipulator operations.

I. INTRODUCTION

Effective robotic manipulation requires an understanding of the underlying physical processes. We need to know how the different elements of a manipulator operation combine to give a desired effect, under what circumstances an operation is appropriate, and how to select and tailor an operation to fit the present task.

This paper describes the mechanics of *pushing*, which is an important element of some manipulator operations, such as grasping, but which is also an operation in its own right, as when rearranging the furniture in your living room. Pushing is a complex process, whose outcome is unpredictable in most practical situations. Nonetheless, the results presented in this paper provide a theoretical basis sufficient for analyzing and planning pushing operations.

Section I of this paper is self-contained—section I.A demonstrates analysis of a pushing operation, and section I.B previews the theory. Section II derives the primary elements of the physics of pushing.

A. Analysis of hinge-plate grasping.

The operation shown in figure 1 was devised by R. P. Paul [Pingle, Paul, and Bolles 1974] to grasp a hinge-plate prior to assembling a hinge. This operation achieves the seemingly impossible: it eliminates translational and rotational uncertainty without any sensory feedback. The hand will grasp the hinge-plate with the leading edge of each finger contacting an inside corner formed by the

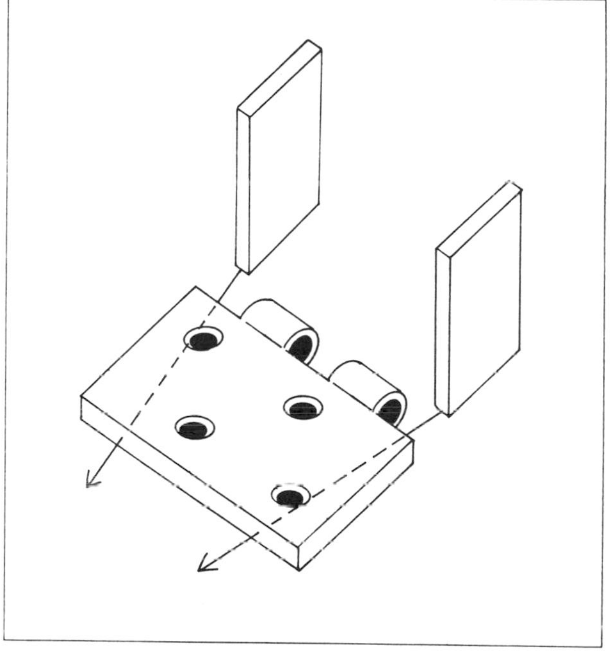

Figure 1. Hinge grasping. Each finger performs a uniform translation, without sensory feedback. Ultimately the hinge-plate will be aligned with the leading edges of the fingers, and centered between the fingers, eliminating all uncertainty in the position of the hinge-plate with respect to the fingers.

hinge-sleeves. The hand moves at a fixed rate in a straight line while the fingers close at a fixed rate. The hand deliberately moves past the range of possible positions of the hinge-plate. At some point in its trajectory it strikes the hinge and pushes it forward as the fingers close. The motion is designed so that the hinge will align itself with the fingers, eliminating uncertainty in orientation. The remaining uncertainty in position is eliminated by a self-centering action which occurs as the hinge-sleeves are squeezed between the closing fingers.

The progress of the grasping operation through stages is shown in figure 2, showing the fingers and hinge-plate in cross-section. Beginning with no contact, the fingers proceed in the direction shown (stage 0). When one of the fingers strikes the hinge-plate, the hinge-plate will begin to move on the table, rotating with respect to the fingers

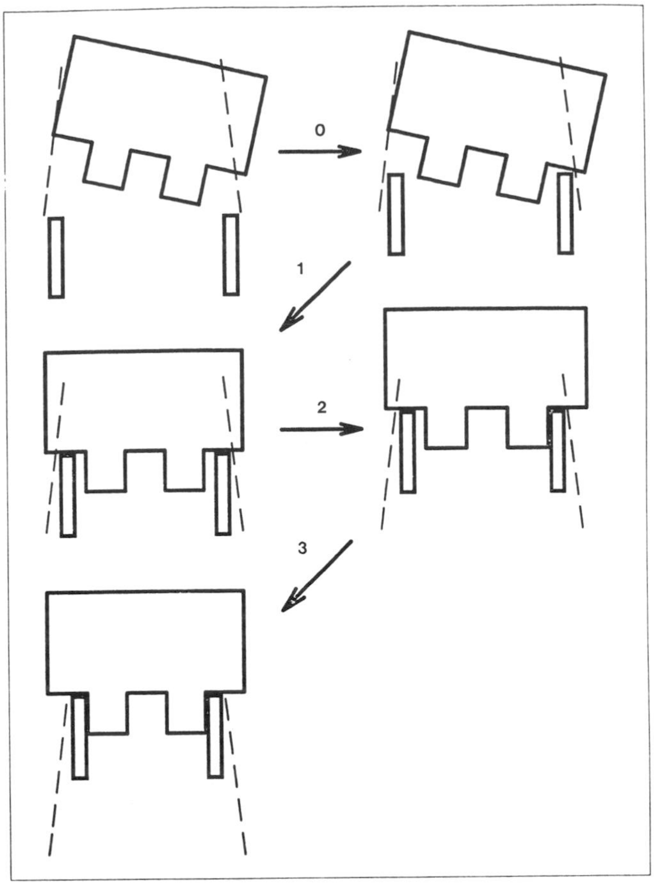

Figure 2. The hinge-plate grasping operation progresses in stages.

(stage 1). Eventually the hinge-plate rotates to contact the second finger, which initiates stage 2. In stage 2, the hinge-plate translates, while one or both of the fingers slides towards the sleeves. Stage 3 occurs with one sleeve in contact with a finger, and complete prehension occurs when the second finger contacts its sleeve.

That is what is *supposed* to happen. The problem is to guarantee that this sequence of events actually takes place. [Mason 1982] verifies the action of all four stages. In this paper we will consider only stage 1.

When stage 1 commences, one finger is in contact with the appropriate edge of the hinge-plate. We wish to ensure that the hinge-plate will rotate in the proper direction until contact with the second finger occurs. Without loss of generality, we assume the initial contact is between the hinge-plate and the finger on the right. From the contact we construct the normal to the hinge-plate edge (figure 3), and also rays at an angle from the normal equal to the arc-tangent of the coefficient of friction. The area between these two rays is the *cone of friction*. We also indicate the center of gravity of the hinge. A simple result from section II says that the hinge will rotate counter-clockwise if the friction cone passes entirely to the right of the center of gravity. With the center of

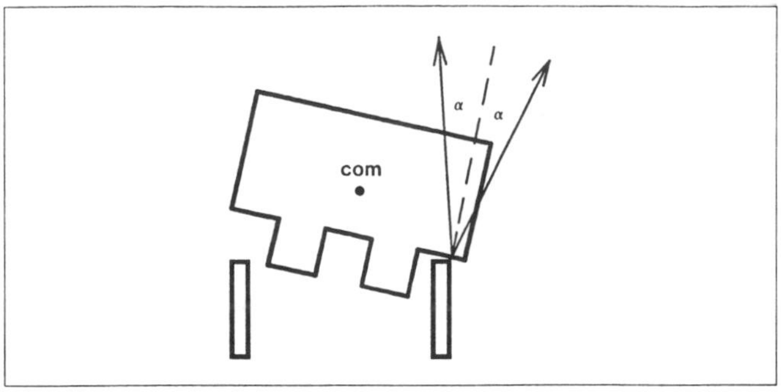

Figure 3. Analysis of stage 1. Counter-clockwise rotation occurs regardless of the initial orientation, for any contact between right finger and corresponding edge of hinge-plate.

gravity as shown, the proper rotation will occur no matter where the finger touches the edge, and no matter the initial orientation.

To guarantee that stage 2 is attained, we would have to address two other problems. It is easy to check that the finger cannot slip off the edge. To check that the rotation is completed before the fingers close too far is more difficult, but see [Mason 1982].

Implicit in this verification are two important assumptions. First, it is assumed that the frictional forces obey Coulomb's law. Second, it is assumed that frictional forces dominate the inertial forces arising from acceleration of the hinge-plate. For the case at hand, the results should be very accurate at a finger speed of 20 cm/sec or less [Mason 1982].

A similar analysis of the other stages of the operation results in the following initial conditions:

1) The initial position/orientation must ensure initial contact between one finger and the corresponding hinge-plate edge.

2) A condition relating the initial finger separation to the finger closing speed.

3) The friction cone, drawn from any point on the hinge-plate edge, must not include the center of gravity of the hinge-plate. This condition is independent of the hinge-plate orientation.

4) The *ray of pushing*, drawn parallel to the finger velocity from the junction of the hinge-sleeve and the hinge-plate edge, must pass outside the center of gravity of the hinge-plate.

This verification demonstrates a deep understanding of the hinge-plate grasping operation. We know why it works, and can find conditions which guarantee success of the program.

The hinge-grasping maneuver can readily be generalized to work with other object shapes. It would seem that

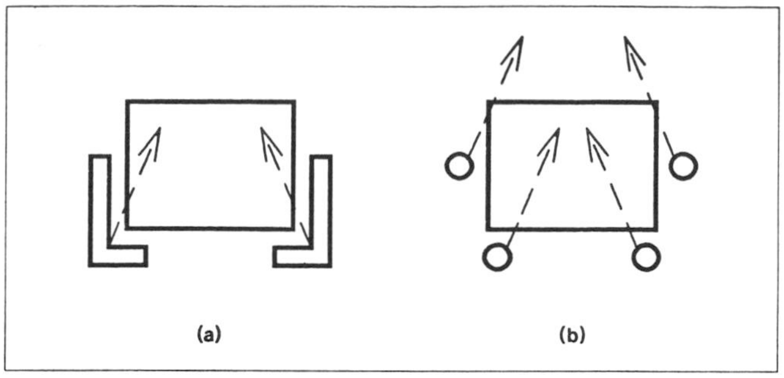

Figure 4. Generalizing the hinge-plate grasping operation to other shapes. (a) suggests a special gripper shape for gripping the box. (b) suggests an approach using a multi-fingered hand.

the tabs on the hinge-plate are necessary to the success of the operation, and indeed they are, unless we tailor the gripper shape to suit the object. Figure 4 shows how the maneuver can be applied to a simple block, without tabs. Changing the shape of the gripper might be accomplished simply by reconfiguring the fingers of a four-fingered hand.

B. Overview of paper

So far, we have briefly considered the role of pushing in manipulation, and looked at an example grasping operation in some detail. Two other example applications are shown in figures 14 and 15. Section II develops a few key results in the mechanics of pushing, providing a foundation for the analysis and synthesis of pushing operations. The basic problem is formulated as follows:

1) A rigid *object* is in planar motion on a horizontal *support*. The object has a single point contact with a *pusher*. The pusher velocity is given.

2) The support forces and the pushing force are assumed to obey Coulomb's law. The only other force applied to the object is gravity. The object's center of mass is given.

3) Inertial forces are assumed to be negligible.

4) The locations and magnitudes of the support forces are indeterminate.

Point 4 is an important one: the results would have little practical value if they required detailed knowledge of the support forces. In many practical situations the support forces are very sensitive to small variations in the shape of the object, and cannot be predicted accurately.

Two problems will be considered:

1) What is the motion of the object?

2) Does the object rotate? If so, is the rotation clockwise or counter-clockwise?

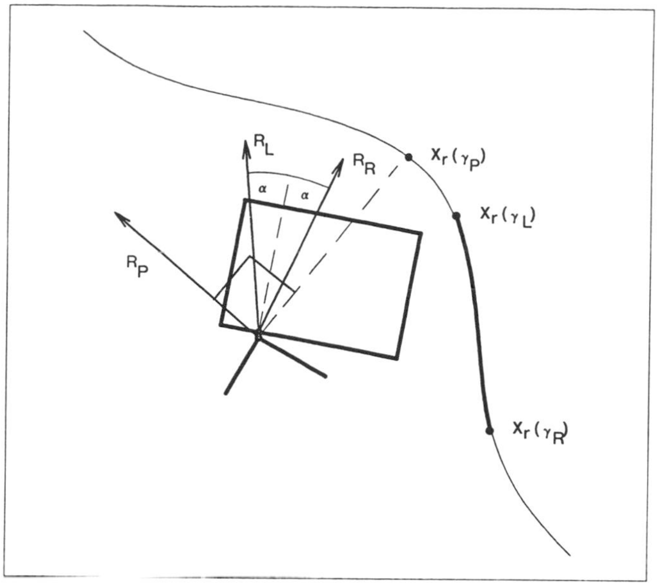

Figure 5. Finding the motion of the object, given the distribution of support forces. First a plot of rotation centers is constructed by numerical means, parameterized by the angle of force γ. The feasible rotation centers must lie in the subplot delimited by $\underline{x}_r(\gamma_R)$ and $\underline{x}_r(\gamma_L)$. A line perpendicular to the ray of pushing is constructed. If this line strikes the plot within the delimited region, the intersection is the rotation center. Otherwise the nearest of $\underline{x}_r(\gamma_R), \underline{x}_r(\gamma_L)$ is the rotation center.

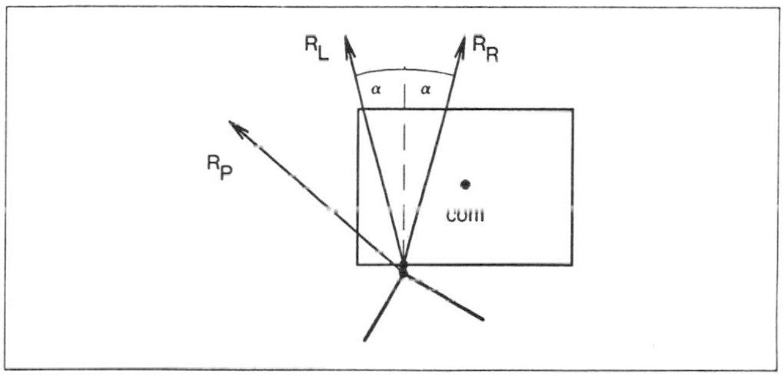

Figure 6. Finding the direction of rotation. $\alpha = \tan^{-1}\mu$. Three rays, comprising the edges of the friction cone R_R and R_L, and the velocity of the pusher R_P, vote on the direction of the object's rotation. Ties result in pure translation. Each vote is determined by the relation of the ray to the object's center of mass. In this case the vote is unanimous for clockwise rotation.

The answer to problem 1 is indeterminate. The object's motion depends on the distribution of support forces, which is assumed indeterminate. If we assume the support forces to be given, deleting assumption 4, then a numerical procedure, illustrated in figure 5, can readily determine the object's instaneous rotation center.

The answer to problem 2 is determined, and in fact is quite easily found. We construct three rays (see figure 6): the two edges of the friction cone, and a ray parallel to the pusher velocity. The rays vote on the direction of rotation, with ties resulting in a pure translation. For instance, if two rays pass to the left of the center of mass, then the object will rotate clockwise.

C. Previous work.

This paper closely follows [Mason 1982]. Some of the results have been omitted for brevity. The statement of primary results and proofs is improved.

Previous work on the mechanics of pushing is surprisingly limited. Most studies of friction-related topics focus on the fundamental sources of friction, on lubrication, and on the effect of friction in the operation of machines. The only studies relevant to the mechanics of pushing are due to Jellett [1872], Prescott [1923], and MacMillan [1936]. Jellett notes some conditions for which the problem reduces to a one-dimensional problem or to the problem of a point in a plane.

Both Prescott and MacMillan find expressions for the total force and moment of friction during planar sliding. Prescott assumes a constant distribution of support forces, and MacMillan assumes a linear distribution. Prescott alone addresses the problem of finding the motion of an object being pushed, for which he assumes known support forces at a few points.

The most important contribution of this paper is that *no* assumption is necessary to predict the object's sense of rotation. This paper also extends Prescott's work by the application of numerical techniques, and by addressing frictional forces arising at the pushing contact as well as at the support contact.

II. MECHANICS OF PUSHING

This section presents a theoretical development of the mechanics of pushing, providing the foundation for analysis and synthesis of manipulator pushing operations. We will focus on the two problems described previously: which way does an object being pushed rotate? and where is the object's instantaneous rotation center? First, though, we will develop some useful expressions for the total frictional force and the moment of frictional force arising from general planar motion.

A. Force and moment of friction

Any planar motion is either a simple translation or a rotation about some instantaneously motionless point. Translation and rotation are handled separately. For translation, we find that the system of frictional forces reduces to a single force through a point whose position is independent of the direction of translation. This point is the *center of friction*. No analogous reduction occurs for rotation.

To find useful expressions for the force and moment of sliding friction some nomenclature is required.

R	region of contact between object and support surface.
dA	differential element of area of R.
$\underline{x}$	position of dA.
$p(\underline{x})$	pressure at $\underline{x}$.
$\underline{v}_x$	velocity of object relative to support at $\underline{x}$.
$\underline{f}_f$	total frictional force.
m_f	total moment of frictional force.

We will assume Coulomb friction, with coefficient of friction μ. The normal force at $\underline{x}$ is given by

$$p(\underline{x})\, dA$$

so the application of Coulomb's law gives for the tangential force at $\underline{x}$

$$-\mu \frac{\underline{v}_x}{|\underline{v}_x|} p(\underline{x})\, dA\,.$$

The total frictional force $\underline{f}_f$ is obtained by integrating over the support contact region R:

$$\underline{f}_f = \int_R -\mu \frac{\underline{v}_x}{|\underline{v}_x|} p(\underline{x})\, dA\,. \tag{1}$$

The total frictional moment m_f is obtained by similar means.

$$m_f = \int_R \underline{x} \otimes -\mu \frac{\underline{v}_x}{|\underline{v}_x|} p(\underline{x})\, dA \tag{2}$$

where by $(a,b)^{\mathrm{T}} \otimes (c,d)^{\mathrm{T}}$ we mean $ad-bc$, i.e. $\hat{k}\cdot(a,b,0)^{\mathrm{T}} \times (c,d,0)^{\mathrm{T}}$.

Translation

During a pure translation, all points in the object move in the same direction $\underline{v}_x/|\underline{v}_x|$. Hence this term may be factored out of the integral, along with the coefficient of friction:

$$\underline{f}_f = -\mu \frac{\underline{v}_x}{|\underline{v}_x|} \int_R p(\underline{x})\, dA \tag{3}$$

$$m_f = -\mu \int_R \underline{x}\, p(\underline{x})\, dA \otimes \frac{\underline{v}_x}{|\underline{v}_x|}. \tag{4}$$

Let f_0 be the total normal contact force, and let $\underline{x}_0$ be the centroid of the pressure distribution $p(\underline{x})$:

$$f_0 = \int_R p(\underline{x})\, dA$$

$$\underline{x}_0 = \frac{\int_R \underline{x}\, p(\underline{x})\, dA}{f_0}.$$

Substituting into equations 3 and 4 we obtain

$$\underline{f}_f = -\mu \frac{\underline{v}_x}{|\underline{v}_x|} \underline{f}_0$$

$$m_f = \underline{x}_0 \otimes \underline{f}_f.$$

Inspection of these equations shows that the system of frictional forces reduces to a single force applied at $\underline{x}_0$. This result is the basis upon which all other results rest.

Theorem 1. *The system of frictional forces of a translating object reduces to a single force, applied at the centroid of the pressure distribution, whose direction is opposite the direction of translation. Proof:* given above.

When the system of frictional forces reduces to a single force applied at a particular point, whose location is independent of the direction and velocity of motion, and whose direction is opposite the direction of motion, we say that that point is the *center of friction* [MacMillan 1936]. Theorem 1 says that during translation a center of friction exists, and it is the centroid of the pressure distribution. We also know that the magnitude of the frictional force is the product of the applied normal force with the coefficient of friction, and hence that the problem reduces to the problem of a point in a plane with the same coefficient of friction, but that is less important for our purposes.

This result may appear to be useless in those cases where the pressure distribution is indeterminate. In many practical situations, the pressure distribution is not known. Microscopic variations in the contact surfaces may drastically alter the pressure distribution. Fortunately, the contact pressure and moment must balance certain components of the applied forces, fixing the position of the centroid in the process. For example, if gravity alone acts on the object, the centroid of the pressure distribution lies directly beneath the center of mass. This gives us a practical method for finding the center of friction without concern for indeterminate details of the pressure distribution.

Rotation

Let $\underline{x}_r$ be the instantaneous center of rotation, and let $\underline{\omega}$ be the angular velocity vector. The velocity at $\underline{x}$ is given by

$$\underline{v}_x = \underline{\omega} \times (\underline{x} - \underline{x}_r)\,.$$

Let $\hat{k}$ be the unit vector normal to the x–y plane. Then $\underline{\omega} = \mathring{\theta}\hat{k}$, so

$$\underline{v}_x = \mathring{\theta}\left(\hat{k} \times (\underline{x} - \underline{x}_r)\right).$$

The direction of the motion at $\underline{x}$ is given by

$$\frac{\underline{v}_x}{|\underline{v}_x|} = \operatorname{sgn}(\mathring{\theta})\,\hat{k} \times \frac{\underline{x} - \underline{x}_r}{|\underline{x} - \underline{x}_r|}.$$

Substituting into equations 1 and 2, we obtain after simplification:

$$\underline{f}_f = -\mu \operatorname{sgn}(\mathring{\theta})\,\hat{k} \times \int_R \frac{\underline{x} - \underline{x}_r}{|\underline{x} - \underline{x}_r|} p(\underline{x})\, dA\,; \qquad (5)$$

$$m_f = -\mu \operatorname{sgn}(\mathring{\theta}) \int_R \underline{x} \cdot \frac{\underline{x} - \underline{x}_r}{|\underline{x} - \underline{x}_r|} p(\underline{x})\, dA\,. \qquad (6)$$

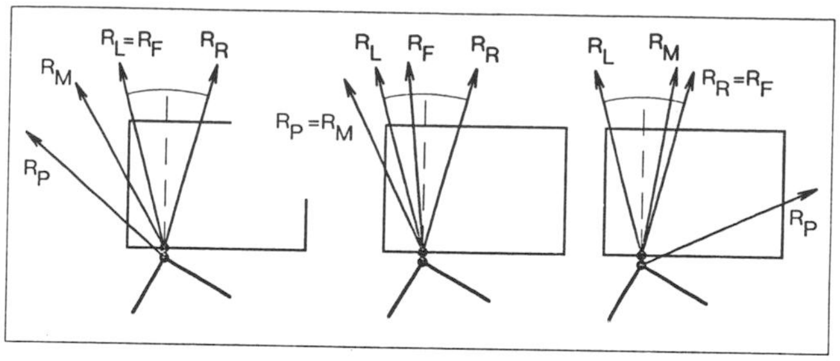

Figure 7. Rays. The rays of motion and of pushing, R_M and R_P respectively, are parallel to the velocities of the two points in contact. The ray of motion refers to the motion of the contact point in the object; the ray of pushing refers to the motion of the contact point in the pusher. The rays R_R and R_L delimit the friction cone. The ray of force R_F is parallel to the force applied to the object at the pushing contact. The three cases illustrated exhaust the possibilities: either $R_F = R_R$ and R_M is to the left of R_P; $R_F = R_L$ and R_M is to the right of R_P; or R_F lies in the friction cone and $R_M = R_P$.

Comparing with equations 3 and 4, we see that the simplification obtained for the case of translation does not apply to rotation. The center of friction plays no apparent role during rotation of an object.

It is sometimes useful to consider a translation to be a rotation about an infinitely distant rotation center. Henceforth we will allow the range of $\underline{x}_r$ to include points at infinity, so that equations 5 and 6 may be used for both rotation and translation.

B. Which way does it turn?

In this section we derive the method for determining the sense of rotation of an object being pushed.

The arguments often depend on comparing various rays with the center of friction. When we say that a ray R *dictates* the sense of rotation, we mean that if the center of friction lies to the left of R, counter-clockwise rotation occurs, and if the center of friction lies to the right of R, clockwise rotation occurs. If the center of friction lies on R, translation occurs.

The rays of interest and their inter-relationships are shown in figure 7. The rays of force and of motion directly dictate the sense of rotation, but those rays are often indeterminate. The primary result, stated in theorem 4, says that the rays R_R, R_L, and R_P vote on the sense of rotation. However, the argument is indirect. First we will prove that the ray of motion R_M dictates the sense of rotation (theorem 2), and that the ray of force R_F dictates the sense of rotation (theorem 3).

Theorem 2. *The ray of motion dictates the sense of rotation.*

Proof: First, we construct an x-y coordinate system with the origin at the contact point and with the y-axis

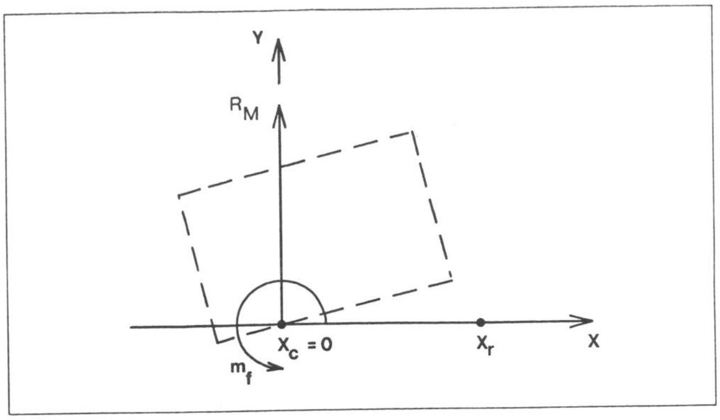

Figure 8. Coordinate conventions for the proof of theorem 2. The origin coincides with the contact point, and the y-axis coincides with the ray of motion. Consequently, the instantaneous rotation center lies on the x-axis.

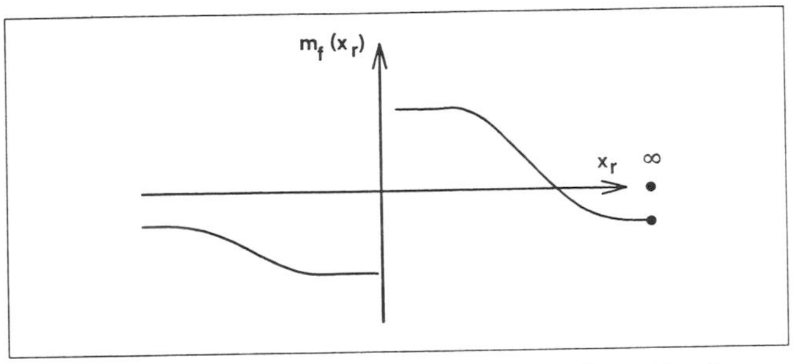

Figure 9. A typical plot of $m_f(x_r)$. Analysis of equation 6 shows that $m_f(x_r)$, where $\underline{x}_r = (x_r, 0)^T$, is continuous and strictly decreasing. There is a unique root, whose sign is dictated by the ray of motion.

parallel to the ray of motion (see figure 8). The instantaneous rotation center must lie on a line perpendicular to the velocity at the contact point, i.e. it must lie on the x-axis. Let $\underline{x}_r = (x_r, 0)^T$ be the rotation center.

Define $m_f(x_r)$ giving the total frictional moment as a function of the directed distance to the rotation center. The domain of this function includes infinity, but not zero. We consider the high, positive, x-axis to be connected to the low, negative, x-axis at infinity. Since the pushing force is applied at the contact point, it exhibits no moment about the origin. Hence a rotation center giving sliding equilibrium would be a root of $m_f(x_r)$.

Straightforward analysis shows that $m_f(x_r)$ is continuous and non-increasing. As x_r approaches zero from above, $m_f(x_r)$ approaches $\mu \int_R |\underline{x}|\, p(\underline{x})\, dA$, which is positive. As x_r approaches zero from below, $m_f(x_r)$ approaches $-\mu \int_R |\underline{x}|\, p(\underline{x})\, dA$, which is negative. Hence as x_r increases from small positive values, through infinity, and on up to low negative values, m_f passes continuously from positive values to negative values. A typical plot is shown in figure 9.

The result is obtained by considering the moment during translation $m_f(\infty)$. During translation, the moment is easily found by theorem 1. For instance, assume

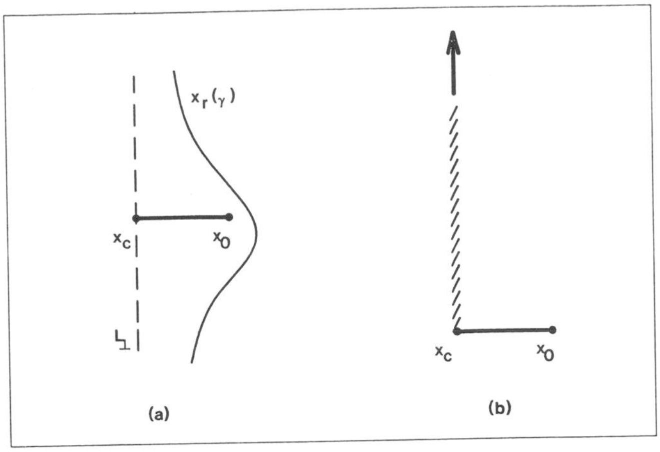

Figure 10. (a) shows a plot of $\underline{x}_r(\gamma)$, for $\gamma \in (0, \pi)$. The plot lies entirely to one side of $L_\perp$. (b) shows the case of $\gamma = \pi/2$. This case shows that the plot in (a) must lie to the right of $L_\perp$, which implies clockwise rotation.

that the center of friction lies in the right half-plane. We know that the tangential support forces reduce to a single force acting through the center of friction. This will give a negative moment, i.e. $m_f(\infty) < 0$. We conclude that the root of $m_f(x_r)$ lies in the positive x-axis, and therefore that clockwise rotation occurs. We can likewise show that if the center of friction is in the left half-plane, counter-clockwise rotation occurs. If the center of friction is on the y-axis, the root is at infinity, so translation occurs. ∎

If we could determine the ray of motion, we could determine the sense of rotation. However, the ray of motion is often indeterminate, so theorem 2 doesn't solve the problem by itself. The next step is to prove a similar result for the ray of force R_F.

Theorem 3. *The ray of force dictates the sense of rotation.*

Proof: Let γ be the angle of the ray of force relative to $\overline{\underline{x}_c \underline{x}_0}$, and let $\underline{x}_r(\gamma)$ be the rotation center as a function of the force angle. It can be shown that $\underline{x}_r(\gamma)$ exists and is continuous. Theorem 1 says that for $\gamma \in \{0, \pi\}, |\underline{x}_r| = \infty$, and that for all other γ, $|\underline{x}_r|$ is finite.

Consider the interval $\Gamma_{CW} = (0, \pi)$. We will prove that all force angles in this interval lead to clockwise rotation. Since $\underline{x}_r(\gamma)$ is continuous, it maps Γ_{CW} into a connected set, which does not intersect the line at infinity. Nor does it intersect $L_\perp$ (see figure 10a): such a point would give a ray of motion passing through $\underline{x}_0$, which would imply $|\underline{x}_r| = \infty$.

Thus all of $\underline{x}_r(\Gamma_{CW})$ is confined either to the right of $L_\perp$ or to the left of $L_\perp$. We can determine which of these two alternatives holds by considering the case shown in figure 10b, where $\gamma = \pi/2$. This case corresponds to pulling the object by a rope running upward in the figure.

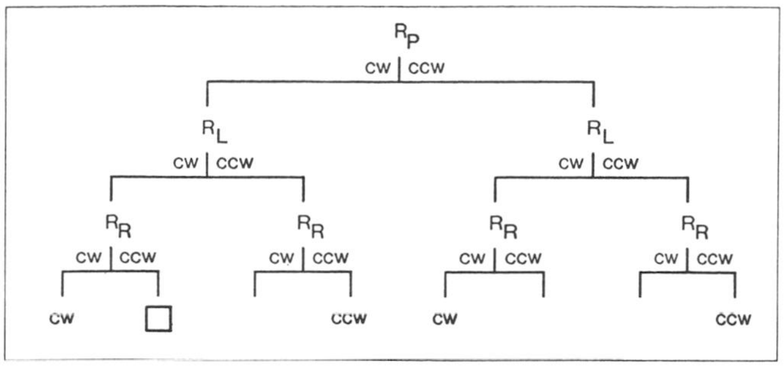

Figure 11. A tree showing the possible results of polling R_P, R_L, and R_R. The four cases where R_L and R_R agree are easily verified. The remaining four cases are similar to the case marked by the square, which is analyzed in figure 12.

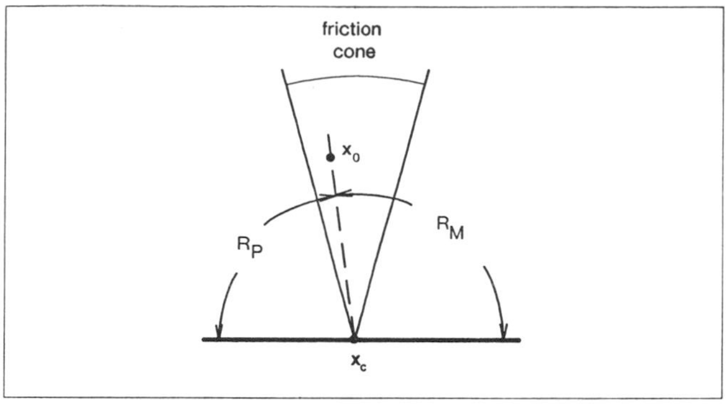

Figure 12. For the case marked with a square in figure 11, assume the outcome of the vote to be incorrect. The center of friction $\underline{x}_0$ is constrained to lie in the friction cone above the pushing constraint, and the rays of pushing and of motion are constrained as shown. But a ray of pushing to the left of the ray of motion would imply that $R_F = R_L$, contrary to assumption.

Clearly the ray of motion must have a positive vertical component—the rope is performing work to overcome the frictional forces. Hence the ray of motion passes $\underline{x}_0$ on the left, dictating a clockwise rotation. We conclude that $\underline{x}_r(\Gamma_{CW})$ lies entirely to the right of $L_\perp$, as shown in figure 10a, giving a clockwise rotation in every case. The proof for $\gamma \in \Gamma_{CCW}$ is similar. ▮

The proofs of theorems 2 and 3 are valid for finite $p(\underline{x})$. If we allow the support pressure to be infinite, so that the support may be confined to a few points or to a line, some revision of the theory is necessary. In most instances, no problems arise, but in some cases the sense of rotation may be indeterminate. The only change necessary is that where translation is predicted, a rotation might also occur. Predictions of clockwise or counter-clockwise rotation are always valid.

Theorem 3 can be applied directly to the problem of pulling an object with a rope, but usually the ray of force is indeterminate. However, we now have the ammunition to prove the primary result, which gives the sense of rotation using easily observed data.

Theorem 4. *The rays R_L, R_R, and R_P vote to determine the sense of rotation.*

Proof: The vote can be represented by the tree shown in figure 11. First, consider the situation if the votes of R_L and R_R agree. The ray of force R_F must lie in the friction cone, so we can invoke theorem 3 to show that the vote is correct. That takes care of four of the eight possible outcomes of the poll, as indicated in the figure. Of the remaining four cases we will consider just one, where the votes cast by R_P, R_L, and R_R are CW, CW, CCW, respectively. Given such an outcome, there are three possibilities:

1) $R_F = R_L$. By theorem 3, this implies clockwise rotation.

2) $R_M = R_P$. By theorem 2, this implies clockwise rotation.

3) $R_F = R_R$. By theorem 3, this implies counter-clockwise rotation.

For cases (1) and (2) the outcome of the vote is correct. We will complete the proof by proving that case (3) cannot happen. Figure 12 shows the situation arising from case (3). The votes of R_L and R_R imply that the center of friction is in the friction cone. A typical choice is shown in the figure. Now R_P voted CW, so the center of friction is on its right. Counter-clockwise rotation implies that the center of friction is to the left of the ray of motion R_M. The possible directions of R_P and R_M are shown by arcs in the figure. Note that both R_P and R_M must be above the pushing constraint—otherwise the pusher would not be pushing. Now it is obvious from the figure that the ray of motion must lie to the right of the ray of pushing, which according to Coulomb's law would give us $R_F = R_L$, a contradiction. We conclude that either case (1) or case (2) must apply, and hence that the outcome of the vote is correct. ▮

C. Where is the instantaneous rotation center?

In this section we will investigate the circumstances under which the trajectory of the pushed object may be completely determined. The simplest characterization of a planar motion is in terms of instantaneous rotation centers. In our case, this is especially convenient, since, once the rotation center is determined, the remaining variable (the speed of rotation) is a simple function of the speed of the pusher.

The motion of an object being pushed generally depends on the distribution of support forces. The basic approach of this section is the use of the *plot of rotation centers*, which is compiled from the support forces and the pushing contact location. Once the plot is con-

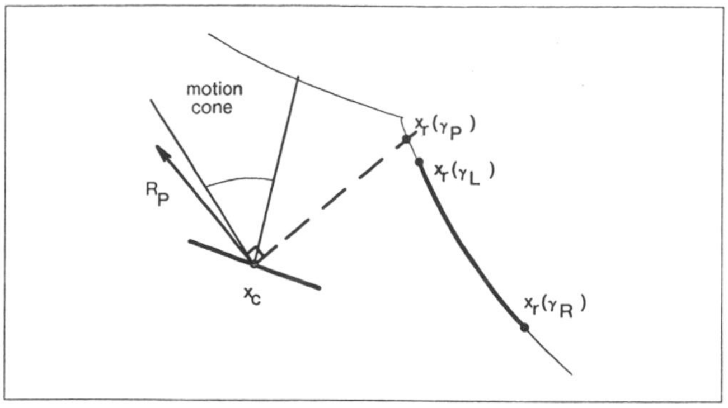

Figure 13. Construction of the motion cone. If $\underline{x}_r(\gamma_P)$ is above $\underline{x}_r([\gamma_R, \gamma_L])$, then the ray of pushing is to the left of the motion cone, and γ_L is the true force angle. The other cases follow similarly.

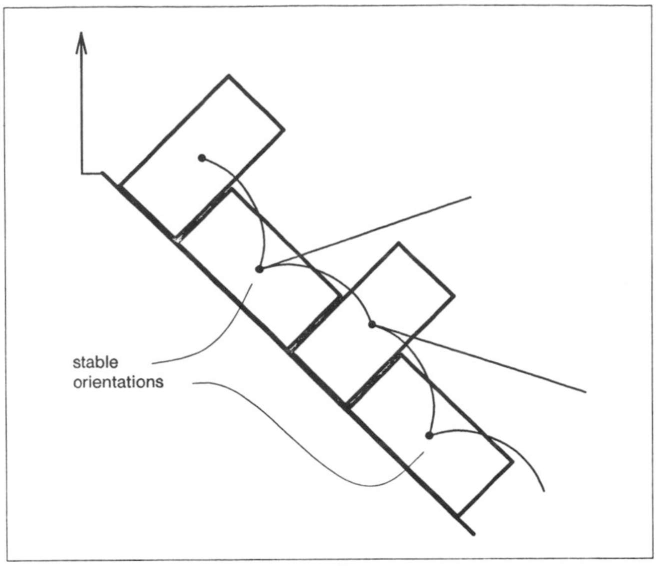

Figure 14. Pushing to orient boxes. A fence over a conveyor is a simple method of orienting boxes. The operation is most easily analyzed by drawing the path of the center of friction as the box tumbles along the fence. The orientation of the box is stable at every minimum. (See [Mason 1982] for details.)

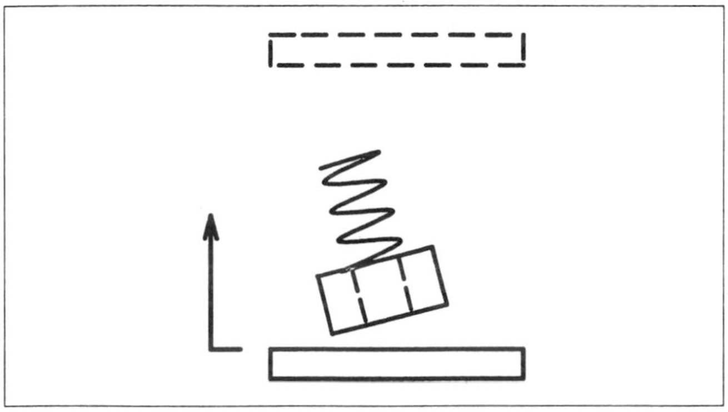

Figure 15. Automatic planning of *push-grasp* operations has been implemented, using the results of the paper. The first finger pushes the object long enough to correct any initial misalignment, then the second finger closes. The hand orientation, approach direction, and duration of the push are tailored to the object and the initial conditions. (See [Mason 1982] for details.)

structed, the instantaneous rotation center may readily be obtained for a variety of problems. If the ray of force or the ray of motion is given, the instantaneous rotation center is determined directly. If the friction cone and ray of pushing are given, the procedure illustrated in figure 5 is applicable. The plot of rotation centers also provides some useful insights into pushing.

Theorem 5. *The procedure described in figure 5 for finding the instantaneous rotation center is correct.*

Proof: Refer to figure 13. The first step is to define and construct a *motion cone*, which plays the same role for the ray of motion that the friction cone plays for the contact force. The construction is simple: since the contact force must lie in the friction cone, the angle of force γ must lie in the interval $[\gamma_R, \gamma_L]$. Define $\theta(\gamma)$ to be the angle of $\overline{\underline{x}_c\underline{x}_r}$ with respect to $\overline{\underline{x}_c\underline{x}_0}$. Since $\underline{x}_r(\gamma)$ is continuous, with $\underline{x}_r \neq \underline{x}_c$, $\theta(\gamma)$ is continuous. It can also be shown that $\theta(\gamma)$ is strictly increasing. Hence the feasible rotation centers form a segment of the plot, delimited by $\underline{x}_r(\gamma_R)$ and $\underline{x}_r(\gamma_L)$. A feasible ray of motion must be perpendicular to a ray through a feasible $\underline{x}_r$, so the direction of motion must lie in the interval $[\theta(\gamma_R) + \frac{\pi}{2}, \theta(\gamma_L) + \frac{\pi}{2}]$. This interval of directions defines a cone, the *motion cone*, within which the ray of motion must lie.

The rest of the proof is simple. Suppose the ray of pushing lies to the left of the motion cone. Then the object must slide rightward along the pusher, and the ray of force is equal to R_L. The rotation center is $\underline{x}_r(\gamma_L)$. Similarly, if the ray of pushing lies within the motion cone, the rotation center is $\underline{x}_r(\gamma_P)$, and if the ray of pushing lies to the right of the motion cone, the rotation center is $\underline{x}_r(\gamma_R)$. ∎

REFERENCES

Jellett, J. H., *A Treatise on the Theory of Friction*, MacMillan, London, 1872.

MacMillan. W. D., *Dynamics of Rigid Bodies*, Dover, 1936.

Mason, M. T., *Manipulator Grasping and Pushing Operations*, MIT Artificial Intelligence Laboratory, TR-690, October 1982.

Pingle, K., Paul, R., Bolles, R., *Programmable Assembly, Three Short Examples*, Film, Stanford Artificial Intelligence Laboratory, October 1974.

Prescott, J., *Mechanics of Particles and Rigid Bodies*, Longmans, Green, and Co., London, 1923.

ON THE MOTION OF OBJECTS IN CONTACT[1]

John Hopcroft and Gordon Wilfong
Department of Computer Science
Cornell University
Ithaca, N.Y. 14853

There is an increasing use of computers in the design, manufacture and manipulation of physical objects. An important aspect of reasoning about such actions concerns the motion of objects in contact. The study of problems of this nature requires not only the ability to represent physical objects but the development of a framework or theory in which to reason about them. In this paper such a development is investigated and a fundamental theorem concerning the motion of objects in contact is proved. The simplest form of this theorem states that if two objects in contact can be moved to another configuration in which they are in contact, then there is a way to move them from the first configuration to the second configuration such that the objects remain in contact throughout the motion. This result is proved when translation and rotation of objects are allowed. The problem dealing with more generalized types of motion is also discussed. This study has obvious applications in compliant motion and in motion planning.

Keywords: compliant motion, motion planning, solid modelling, robotics, complexity theory

Introduction

The increasing use of computers in the design, manufacture and manipulation of physical objects underscores the need for a theory to provide a framework for reasoning about transformations of objects. In this paper we take a first step towards developing such a theory.

One may define an object such as a shaft or connecting rod without instantiating its position or orientation. More generally one can define a rectangular solid without specifying its dimensions. In fact one can define an object without instantiating its shape. For example, the shape of an ellipsoid parameterized by the ratio of its axes is determined only when the parameter is fixed. To obtain a specific instance of the ellipsoid one provides the ratio of major to minor axis, the length of the major axis and its orientation with respect to some coordinate system along with the position in 3-space of the center of the ellipsoid. In this framework an object is the image of an instance of a parameterized homeomorphism from a canonical region in $\mathbb{R}^3$ to $\mathbb{R}^3$. Thus all instances of an object are homeomorphic and therefore topologically equivalent. A sphere and an ellipsoid can be instances of the same object but a sphere and a torus cannot. A sphere might be given by the parameterized mapping

$$f(x,y,z)=(xr+a,\ yr+b,\ zr+c)$$

from a unit sphere centered at the origin in $\mathbb{R}^3$ where a,b and c give the coordinates of the center and r is the radius. Corresponding to a particular instantiation of the sphere is a point in the four dimensional parameter space.

In this generalized setting a motion is a continuous mapping from [0,1] into the appropriate parameter space. Thus a motion is a path in the parameter space. A motion can be a combination of translation, rotation, growth or more complicated continuous deformation of shape. It is our hope that this view will be useful in defining and manipulating generic objects as well as deformable or nonrigid objects. For our purposes we limit ourselves to motions where the transformation can be parameterized by a finite number of parameters.

Although it is traditional to think of objects in terms of their shape and dimension and then to deduce functionality from the shape, it is enticing to think of representing objects by functionality and then deducing shape. In designing for automatic assembly one is normally free to modify objects for ease of assembly. Thus designing for functionality and allowing the functionality and assembly process to determine shape and size is a desirable goal. Furthermore, parameterized design provides additional advantages. For example, instead of designing a drive shaft for a particular torque, it would be preferable to design the drive shaft with torque as a parameter. This allows changes in design specification without necessitating redesign of components. The study of problems of this nature will require substantial advances in the representation of physical objects and in our ability to reason about them. In this paper we begin with a modest step by establishing a fundamental theorem concerning the motion of objects in contact.

In the special case where motion is restricted to rotations and translations the theorem states that if there is a way to move a set of objects from an initial configuration where the objects form a connected component to a final configuration where the objects form a connected component then there is a way to move the objects from the initial to the final configuration such that at all times the objects form a connected component. To understand the theorem in a more general setting consider the motion of two objects A and B relative to one another. Normally one would consider A fixed and that B moves relative to A. For ordinary motions such as translations or rotations there is of course no loss in generality in fixing A. However, the fact that A may be changing shape makes it more desirable to view both objects as moving. A point in configuration space represents the values for the parameters of A and B. Certain points correspond to positions and orientations where B overlaps A. In the situation where configuration space is contractible to a point the theorem states that the existence of a path, P_1 in Figure 1, from initial configuration to final configuration where A and B always intersect and of a path, P_2 in Figure 1, where A and B do not overlap implies the existence of a path, P_3 in Figure 1, where A and B touch at all times but are not overlapping. One should observe that the point of contact need not be a continuous function even though motion is continuous.

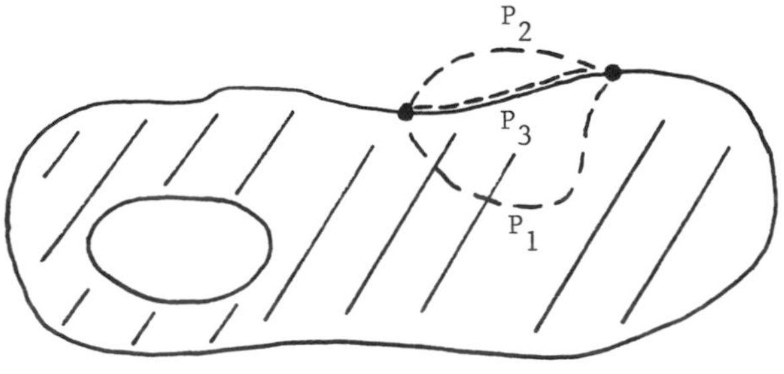

Figure 1. Configuration Space.

Care must be exercised in applying the theorem. For example, in Figure 2 there are two objects A and B, A is fixed and B is permitted only to rotate about x. Rotating B $2\pi-\alpha$ in the clockwise direction results in the same apparent configuration as rotating B α radians in the counterclockwise direction. However, these two configurations are the same in configuration space only if we identify points that differ by a rotation of 2π. This results in a cylindrical shaped space that is not contractible to a point and hence the hypothesis of our theorem is not valid. Observe that in the above example the only motion from $\theta=0$ to $\theta=2\pi-\alpha$ is a motion where the objects do not overlap and thus there is no motion that keeps the objects intersecting.

In addition to the obvious applications in compliant motion, the theorem has potential applications in motion planning and in complexity theory. In planning of coordinated motion not only must trajectories be determined but also the relative timing of objects as they move on their individual trajectories. A path in configuration space contains this information about relative timing. Thus searching the paths in configuration space conceptually simplifies the problem. In general, configuration space is of very high

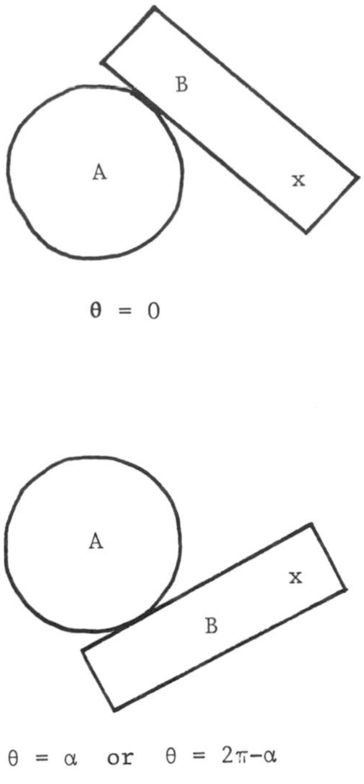

Figure 2. Restriction to rotational motion

dimension. The above theorem reduces the search from this high dimensional space to that of a lower dimensional surface in the space. The surface can be thought of as composed of faces that intersect in lower dimensional faces that in turn intersect in still lower dimensional faces. Under suitable restrictions, the surface of contact in configuration space will have vertices that are edge connected. In order to move a set of objects from one configuration to another we first push the objects together in both the initial and final configurations. Then we move the objects along faces until they reach lower dimensional faces. We continue this process until the initial and final configurations have been converted to vertices of the surface in configuration space at which the objects are in contact. This reduces the problem to a graph searching problem. In general the number of vertices of the graph will be astronomical. We need not construct the entire graph but only generate vertices and edges as the search progresses. With a suitable heuristic it may be possible, in practical situations, to find the desired path having only generated a tiny fraction of the graph. The knowledge of such a path could be used in constructing a path where the objects do not touch one another.

In complexity theory it is often important to show that if a certain motion exists, then a canonical motion exists. In the case of linkages [Hopcroft, Joseph and Whitesides, 1982], for example, it is important from a complexity point of view that various joints need not be moved to locations that are algebraically independent in order for a motion to take place. Our theorem establishes that if a motion exists, then one that follows features of the surface exists and hence a canonical motion exists.

The paper consists of four sections. In the first section, some general properties of the space of all configurations are developed. These properties are used in the second section to show that certain regions of the space of all configurations are path connected or contractible to a point. From this it is shown in the second section that if there is a motion between configurations in which two objects touch then there is a motion between them such that at all times two objects touch. In the third section an inductive argument is developed to show the main result. That is, it is shown that if there is a motion of rotations and translations between two configurations in which the objects form a connected component then there is a motion which keeps the objects in a connected component. In the fourth section we discuss the case where more general motions are allowed.

1. Basic Properties of Configuration Space

Let A be a set in $\mathbb{R}^n$. The interior of A, denoted int(A), is the union of all open sets of $\mathbb{R}^n$ contained in A. A point x is a limit point of A if there exists a sequence $\{x_i\}$ of points in A such that

$$\lim_{i\to\infty} x_i = x.$$

The closure of A, denoted by cl(A), is the set of all limit points of A.

An object is a convex, compact region of $\mathbb{R}^n$ that is the closure of its interior and is bounded by a finite number of algebraic surfaces. (The limitation of convexity will be removed later by introducing composite objects.) Each object contains a designated point, called the origin, at which the origin of a coordinate system, affixed to the object, is located. The position and orientation of an object are specified by the location of the origin of the object in $\mathbb{R}^n$ and orientation of the affixed coordinate system relative to the coordinate system of $\mathbb{R}^n$. Given a set of objects, a configuration is a vector whose components specify the position and orientation of each object. The space of all such vectors is called configuration space. Given a set of objects and a point x in the corresponding configuration space we let B(x) denote the region in $\mathbb{R}^n$ occupied by object B in the given configuration. If b is a point on object B then let b(x) be the point in $\mathbb{R}^n$ occupied by b when B is in the position and orientation specified by x.

Objects B_i and B_j intersect in configuration x if $B_i(x) \cap B_j(x) \neq \emptyset$. The objects overlap if their interiors intersect. If the objects intersect but do not overlap then we say that they touch in configuration x.

It is convenient to partition the set of objects into subsets called composite objects. A composite object is intended to be a single object made up of smaller objects. With each composite object associate a graph whose vertices are the objects and whose edges are pairs of objects that intersect. A composite object is connected if the associated graph is connected. A configuration is proper if each composite object is connected. A configuration is valid if in addition to being proper the interiors of each pair of objects in a composite object do not intersect. Let VALID denote the set of valid configurations.

Composite objects are used in an inductive argument in Section 3. By considering two or more objects to be a single composite object we are able to establish a motion for n objects from a motion for n-1 objects, one of which is a composite object. We introduce the notion of valid so that individual objects in a composite object will touch but not overlap throughout the motion.

Let OVERLAP denote the set of valid configurations in which two or more composite objects overlap. Let TOUCH denote the set of valid configurations in which two or more composite objects touch and no two composite objects overlap. Let NONOVERLAP be the complement of OVERLAP with respect to the set of valid configurations.

Figure 3 shows two objects, B_1 and B_2. Object B_2 is stationary and object B_1 is allowed only translational motion. Given two configurations in which the two objects are touching and a motion between the configurations in which the objects do not overlap, we wish to show that there is a motion where the objects are always in contact. The graphic representation of configuration space of Figure 1 suggests that the boundary of the region where the objects intersect corresponds to the configurations where the objects touch. Figure 3 shows that this is not exactly the case. The configurations where B_1 is in the opening of B_2 are not in the boundary of the space of configurations where the objects intersect. The first goal of this section is to show that the configurations where at least two composite objects touch is exactly

$$\mathrm{cl(OVERLAP)} - \mathrm{OVERLAP}$$

That is, TOUCH = cl(OVERLAP) $\cap$ NONOVERLAP.

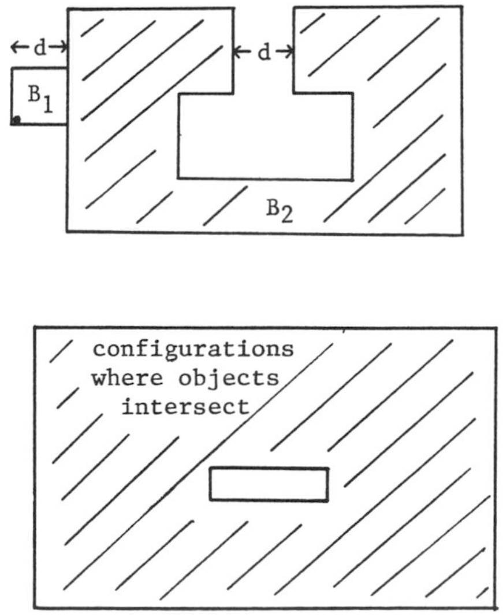

Configuration Space

Figure 3. Two objects and corresponding configuration space

The second aim of this section is to prove a lemma concerning TOUCH that will aid us in the next section in proving that certain motions in TOUCH exist. Towards this end, we designate one object in each composite object as the <u>base</u> object. We will call the origin of the base object the origin of the composite object. Let <u>BASE</u> be the set of proper configurations in which the base object of some composite object intersects the base object of the nth composite object. Let

$$FILL = cl(OVERLAP) \cup BASE \ .$$

In Section 2 we will need the fact that FILL $\cup$ NONOVERLAP is contractible to a point. Suppose we had not included BASE in FILL. Consider the example shown in Figure 4. Here we have three circles that are allowed to move along a line. Object B is fixed and objects A and B form one composite object in which B is the base object. In this case NONOVERLAP is four rays and cl(OVERLAP) $\cup$ NONOVERLAP is two parallel lines. Thus not only is cl(OVERLAP) $\cup$ NONOVERLAP not contractible to a point it is not path connected. However when we include BASE, the set FILL $\cup$ NONOVERLAP becomes contractible to a point. Thus the points of FILL fill in the holes of NONOVERLAP so that the union of FILL and NONOVERLAP is contractible to a point. We will show that

$$TOUCH = FILL \cap NONOVERLAP \ .$$

This will be used in the next section to show that if there is a path in NONOVERLAP between two configurations in TOUCH then there is a path in TOUCH between them. Throughout this section B_i will denote an object and A_i will denote a composite object.

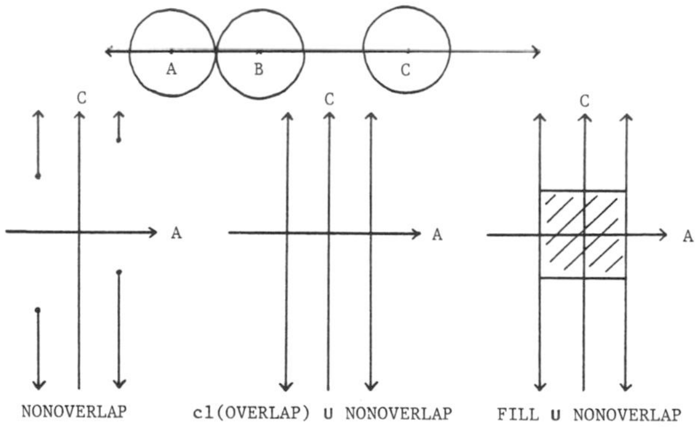

Figure 4. Three circles constrained to horizontal motion, B is fixed. A and B form a composite object with B as base.

We now proceed with a series of lemmas. Lemmas 1.1 through 1.4 are used to establish in Theorem 1.5 that TOUCH = cl(OVERLAP) $\cap$ NONOVERLAP and in Theorem 1.6 that TOUCH = FILL $\cap$ NONOVERLAP. This latter theorem is used in the next section to prove that certain motions in TOUCH exist.

First we show that for any configuration in which two objects intersect there is an arbitrarily close configuration in which the two objects overlap.

<u>Lemma 1.1</u>: Let $S = \{x \mid int(B_i(x)) \cap int(B_j(x)) \neq \emptyset\}$. Then $\{x \mid B_i(x) \cap B_j(x) \neq \emptyset\} \subseteq cl(S)$.

<u>Proof</u>: Let x be a configuration such that $B_i(x) \cap B_j(x) \neq \emptyset$. Let y be a point on $B_i(x)$ and z be a point on $B_j(x)$ such that y and z occupy the same point b in $\mathbb{R}^n$. Since an object is the closure of its interior there are sequences of points $\{y_\alpha\}$ of $int(B_i(x))$ and $\{z_\alpha\}$ of $int(B_j(x))$ such that $\lim_{\alpha\to\infty} y_\alpha = y$ and $\lim_{\alpha\to\infty} z_\alpha = z$. Let $\{x_\alpha\}$ be the sequence of configurations in S such that all objects except B_i and B_j have the same position and orientation as in configuration x and $B_i(x_\alpha)$ and $B_j(x_\alpha)$ have the same orientation as in configuration x but y_α and z_α are at position b in $\mathbb{R}^n$. Thus $\lim_{\alpha\to\infty} x_\alpha = x$ and so x is in cl(S). □

Next we show that the closure of the set of configurations in which two objects overlap is contained within the set of configurations where the two objects intersect. This result combined with the previous lemma establishes that these two sets are equal.

<u>Lemma 1.2</u>: $cl(\{x \mid int(B_i(x)) \cap int(B_j(x)) \neq \emptyset\}) \subset \{x \mid B_i(x) \cap B_j(x) \neq \emptyset\}$.

<u>Proof</u>: Let $S = \{x \mid int(B_i(x)) \cap int(B_j(x)) \neq \emptyset\}$. Let x be in cl(S). Then there exists a sequence of configurations $\{x_\alpha\}$ in S such that $\lim_{\alpha\to\infty} x_\alpha = x$. Corresponding to $\{x_\alpha\}$ is a sequence $\{\langle y_\alpha, z_\alpha \rangle\}$ where y_α and z_α are points of $B_i(x_\alpha)$ and $B_j(x_\alpha)$ that occupy the same location in $\mathbb{R}^n$. Since the objects are compact the cross product space is compact and so there is a subsequence $\{\langle \hat{y}_\alpha, \hat{z}_\alpha \rangle\}$ that converges to some pair of points $\langle y, z \rangle$. Since objects are closed, y and z are in B_i and B_j. Define the usual distance metric d. Since $d(y_\alpha, z_\alpha) = 0$ for all α, clearly $\lim_{\alpha\to\infty} d(\hat{y}_\alpha, \hat{z}_\alpha) = 0$. Since d is continuous we can move the limit inside and get $d(y,z) = 0$. Thus $B_i(x) \cap B_j(x) \neq \emptyset$. □

We now conclude from Lemmas 1.1 and 1.2 that the set of configurations in which two given objects intersect is equal to the closure of the set of configurations in which the interiors of the two objects intersect. Since a composite object is some union of objects we get that two composite objects intersect in a configuration if and only if there is an object in each composite object that intersect in the configuration. Thus, the set of configurations where the two composite objects intersect is some union of sets of configurations where two objects intersect. Similarly the set of configurations where the interiors of two given composite objects intersect is some union of sets of configurations in which the interiors of two objects intersect. Since the closure of the union is the union of the closure, the closure of the set of configurations in which the interiors of two given composite objects intersect is some union of the closure of sets of configurations in which the interiors of two objects intersect. Thus we can conclude that the set of configurations in which two given composite objects intersect is equal to the closure of the set of configurations in which the interiors of the two composite objects intersect. By the same argument we can show that the set of configurations in which there are at least two composite objects which intersect is equal to the closure of the set of configurations where the interiors of at least two composite objects intersect.

The next step is to show that a composite object also has the property that it is the closure of its interior. Note that interior points of a composite object may not be interior points of any object.

<u>Lemma 1.3</u>: For composite object A, A=cl(int(A)).

<u>Proof</u>: Let $A=\bigcup_i B_i$. Suppose $y \in A$. Then $y \in B_i$ for some i. Since $B_i = cl(int(B_i))$ there is a sequence $\{y_\alpha\}$ in $int(B_i)$ such that $\lim_\alpha y_\alpha = y$. But each $y_\alpha \in int(B_i)$ implies each $y_\alpha \in int(A)$. Thus $y \in cl(int(A))$ and so $A \subseteq cl(int(A))$.

Suppose $y \in cl(int(A))$. Then y is the limit point of a sequence in int(A) and hence the limit point of a sequence in A. Since A is closed y must be in A. Thus $cl(int(A)) \subseteq A$. □

Since VALID is a closed set we can compute the closure of OVERLAP by taking the closure of all configurations where two composite objects overlap and then intersecting with VALID.

<u>Lemma 1.4</u>: $cl(OVERLAP) = cl(\{x \mid \exists i,j \;\; i \neq j \;\; int(A_i(x)) \cap int(A_j(x)) \neq \emptyset\} \cap VALID) = \{x \mid \exists i,j \;\; i \neq j \;\; A_i(x) \cap A_j(x) \neq \emptyset\} \cap VALID$.

<u>Proof</u>: Let $F = \{x \mid \exists i,j \;\; i \neq j \;\; int(A_i(x)) \cap int(A_j(x)) \neq \emptyset\}$. Then $cl(OVERLAP) = cl(F \cap VALID) \subseteq cl(F) \cap cl(VALID) = cl(F) \cap VALID$ because VALID is closed.

Let $x \in cl(F) \cap VALID$. We want to show $x \in cl(OVERLAP)$. Since $x \in cl(F)$ we know by the remark after Lemma 1.2 that for some i and j, $i \neq j$, $A_i(x) \cap A_j(x) \neq \emptyset$. By a construction similar to that in Lemma 1.3 we create a sequence $\{x_\alpha\}$ with limit point x such that $int(A_i(x_\alpha)) \cap int(A_j(x_\alpha)) \neq \emptyset$ and $x_\alpha \in VALID$. Thus $x \in cl(F \cap VALID) = cl(OVERLAP)$. □

We can now establish the result that TOUCH = cl(OVERLAP) ∩ NONOVERLAP.

<u>Theorem 1.5</u>: TOUCH = cl(OVERLAP) ∩ NONOVERLAP

<u>Proof</u>: By definition $TOUCH = \{x \mid \exists i,j \;\; i \neq j \;\; A_i(x) \cap A_j(x) \neq \emptyset\} \cap \{x \mid \forall i,j \;\; i \neq j \;\; int(A_i(x)) \cap int(A_j(x)) = \emptyset\} \cap VALID$. Therefore, $TOUCH = NONOVERLAP \cap \{x \mid \exists i,j \;\; i \neq j \;\; A_i(x) \cap A_j(x) \neq \emptyset\} = NONOVERLAP \cap cl(OVERLAP)$ by Lemma 1.4. □

<u>Theorem 1.6</u>: TOUCH = FILL ∩ NONOVERLAP

<u>Proof</u>: By definition FILL = cl(OVERLAP) ∪ BASE. Since TOUCH = cl(OVERLAP)∩NONOVERLAP by Theorem 1.5 we get that $TOUCH \subseteq cl(OVERLAP) \subseteq FILL \subseteq FILL \cap NONOVERLAP$.

Let $x \in FILL \cap NONOVERLAP$. If $x \in cl(OVERLAP)$ then $x \in TOUCH$. Suppose $x \in BASE$. Since $x \in NONOVERLAP$ we have $x \in VALID$. Also $x \in BASE$ implies two composite objects intersect and so $x \in cl(OVERLAP)$. Thus $x \in TOUCH$. Therefore, $FILL \cap NONOVERLAP \subseteq TOUCH$. □

2. Requiring Two Objects To Touch Throughout A Motion

In this section we show the following intermediate result. Given two configurations x and y with n objects, at least two of which are touching in each configuration, if it is possible to move the objects from configuration x to configuration y, then it is possible to do so by a motion such that two objects are always touching. To do this, we make use of the Mayer-Vietoris theorem from algebraic topology to show that the path connected components of TOUCH are in one to one correspondence with the path connected components of NONOVERLAP.

Notice that if TOUCH was a retract of NONOVERLAP then if there was a motion in NONOVERLAP between two configurations in TOUCH then we could conclude that there was a motion in TOUCH between these configurations. This is because there must be a continuous function f:NONOVERLAP→TOUCH such that f(t)=t ∀ t∈TOUCH and so if m is a motion in NONOVERLAP between $t_1, t_2 \in TOUCH$ then f(m(t)) is a continuous path in TOUCH between t_1 and t_2.

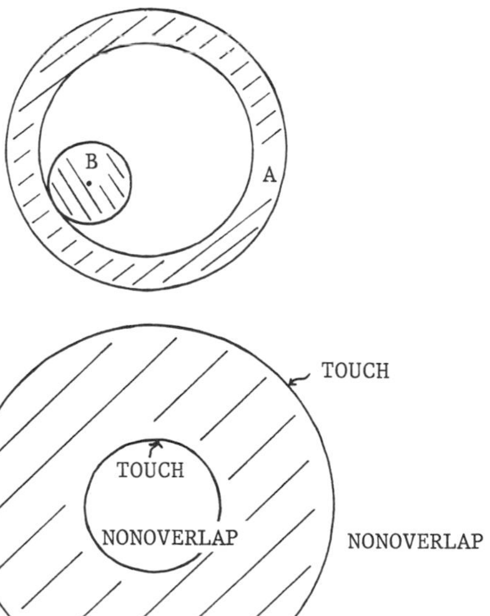

Configuration Space

Figure 5. TOUCH not a retract of NONOVERLAP

However we cannot guarantee that TOUCH will be a retract of NONOVERLAP. Consider Figure 5 where there is one stationary object A and another object B which is free to move about. Configuration space is just $\mathbb{R}^2$ where a configuration consists of the position of the center of the disk. NONOVERLAP is the unshaded region in the figure. Thus in this case NONOVERLAP is not retractible to TOUCH, the boundaries of NONOVERLAP in configuration space.

We begin by defining a motion. A movement of the objects corresponds in an obvious manner to a path in configuration space. Thus a <u>motion</u> is a continuous function from [0,1] to configuration space. If m is a motion then the <u>reversal</u> of the motion m^r is defined as $m^r(t) = m(1-t)$. If m_1 and m_2 are motions where $m_1(1) = m_2(0)$ then the composition $m = m_1||m_2$ is a motion defined by

$$m(t) = \begin{cases} m_1(2t) & 0 \le t \le 1/2 \\ m_2(2t-1) & 1/2 \le t \le 1. \end{cases}$$

At certain times we shall be concerned with motions where the orientation of each object is maintained while each object is moving along a straight line at a constant rate. Thus in configuration x(t) the location of point b of an object is given by

$$b(x_t) = b(x_0) + [b(x_1) - b(x_0)]t.$$

When we talk about a motion in which objects move in a straight line we are referring to a motion of the above type. When we talk about moving a composite object in a straight line, the objects making up the composite object maintain their relative spacing.

In many of the following results a straight line motion is used. In Lemma 2.1 we show that a straight line motion of two objects keeps the objects intersecting if they intersect at the beginning and at the end of the straight line motion.

<u>Lemma 2.1</u>: Let x and y be configurations and B_1 and B_2 be objects. Suppose that b_1 and c_1 are points of B_1 and b_2 and c_2 are points of B_2 such that $b_1(x)=b_2(x)$ and $c_1(y)=c_2(y)$. Then moving B_1 and B_2 along straight lines so that c_1 and c_2 are positioned at $c_1(y)$ keeps the objects intersecting. See Figure 6.

<u>Proof</u>: At time t during the motion, the point of B_1 on the line between b_1 and c_1 given by $b_t=b_1+(c_1-b_1)t$ occupies the same point as the point of B_2 on the line between b_2 and c_2 given by $b_t=b_2+(c_2-b_2)t$. □

Now it is shown that there is a motion between any two configurations in PROPER in which the base object of some composite object intersects the base object of the nth composite object such that during the motion all configurations have that property. This is done by showing that there is some fixed configuration with the pro-

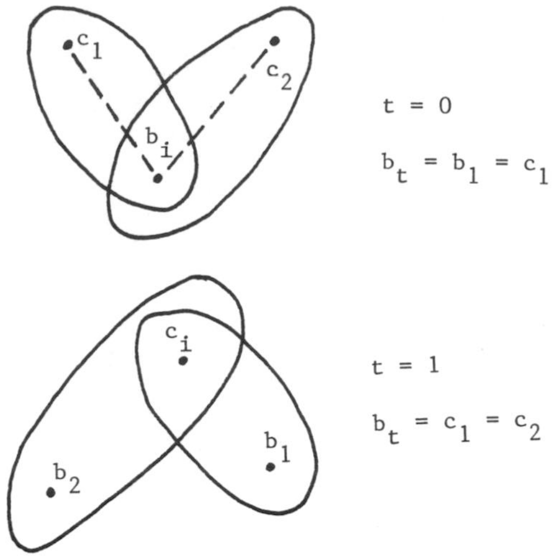

Figure 6. Straight line motion

perty such that there is a motion, which keeps the property true, between any configuration with the property and the fixed configuration.

<u>Lemma 2.2</u>: BASE is path connected.

<u>Proof</u>: Fix some configuration y in BASE such that in y, the origin of every object has the same location. Let $x \in$BASE. Move the objects in a straight line from configuration x to the configuration z that has the same orientations as x but the location in z of the origins of the objects are as in y. By Lemma 2.1 any objects that intersect in x will intersect throughout the motion. Now rotate the objects about their origins to the orientations given by y. Thus there is a path in BASE from any $x \in$BASE to y. Since motions are reversible there is a path in BASE from y to any $x \in$BASE and so BASE is path connected. □

The following theorem shows that FILL is path connected by constructing a motion from any configuration in FILL to some configuration in BASE. BASE is path connected, by the previous result, and since BASE is contained in FILL we conclude that FILL is path connected.

<u>Theorem 2.3</u>: FILL is path connected.

<u>Proof</u>: Let $x \in$FILL. We will show that there is a path in FILL from x to some configuration in BASE and since BASE is path connected and motions are reversible we will conclude that FILL is path connected.

By definition FILL = cl(OVERLAP) ∪ BASE. If $x \in$BASE then we are done. Suppose $x \in$cl(OVERLAP). Then $A_i(x) \cap A_j(x) \neq \emptyset$ for some i and j, $i \neq j$ and $x \in$VALID. Let b be the origin of the base object of A_i and b' the origin of the base object of the nth composite object. Move A_i and A_j in a straight line (considering A_i and A_j as one composite object) to the configuration where the location of b is b'(x). All other objects remain stationary. Thus the motion is in cl(OVERLAP) and hence in FILL and the resulting configuration is in BASE. Therefore FILL is path connected. □

The next lemma will be used when we show that FILL ∪ NONOVERLAP is contractible to a point. We show that there is a path in VALID from any configuration in VALID to a configuration in BASE in which the origins of all the composite objects have the same location. The same construction can be used to construct a path in BASE from any configuration in BASE to some configuration in BASE in which the origins of all the composite objects have the same location.

Lemma 2.4: From every configuration in VALID (BASE) there is a path in VALID (BASE) to some configuration in BASE in which the origins of the composite objects coincide.

Proof: Let $x \in$ VALID (BASE). Move the composite objects in a straight line from x to the configuration where all the origins have location equal to the location in x of the origin of the nth composite object. The resulting configuration is in BASE and the motion described is as desired by Lemma 2.1. □

We now use the motions constructed in Lemmas 2.2 and 2.4 to show that FILL ∪ NONOVERLAP is contractible to a point. That is, we show that there is a configuration $y \in S=$FILL ∪ NONOVERLAP and a continuous function $f: S \times [0,1] \to S$ such that

$$\left.\begin{array}{l} f(x,0) = x \\ f(x,1) = y \end{array}\right\} \forall x \in S$$

$$f(y,t) = y \quad \forall t \in [0,1] .$$

In order that FILL∪NONOVERLAP be contractible to a point we cannot identify a rotation of 2π with no rotation at all as is done in [Schwartz and Sharir, 1982]. Thus in configuration space a dimension corresponding to a rotation is infinite even though every 2π radians the object returns to its apparent initial position.

Theorem 2.5: FILL ∪ NONOVERLAP is contractible to a point.

Proof: Let S=FILL ∪ NONOVERLAP. Then S=BASE ∪ VALID. Let y be the fixed configuration in BASE as in Lemma 2.2. Define $f: S \times [0,1] \to S$

$$f(x,t) = \begin{cases} m_1(2t) & 0 \le t \le 1/2 \text{ where } m_1 \text{ is the motion described in Lemma 2.4 and } m_1(0)=x \\ m_2(2t-1) & 1/2 \le t \le 1 \text{ where } m_2 \text{ is the motion described in Lemma 2.2 and } m_2(0)=m_1(1) \end{cases}$$

Then

$$\left.\begin{array}{l} f(x,0) = x \\ f(x,1) = y \end{array}\right\} x \in S$$

$$f(y,t) = y \quad t \in [0,1]$$

By the construction of m_1 and m_2, f is continuous. Thus f is a homotopy between the retraction $r: S \to \{y\}$ and the identity $i: S \to S$. That is {y} is a deformation retract of S and so S is contractible to a point. □

The above construction gives a motion in S=FILL∪NONOVERLAP from any configuration in S to the fixed configuration $y \in S$. Thus if x_1 and x_2 are two configurations in S and m_i is the motion constructed from x_i to y in S then $m_1 || m_2^r$ is a motion in S from x_1 to x_2 and so S is path connected.

Corollary 2.6: FILL∪NONOVERLAP is path connected.

If configuration space is restricted so that each parameter that corresponds to an orientation is only allowed to range within some closed and bounded interval then the portion of FILL in this restricted space is clearly still path connected. Also FILL∪NONOVERLAP is still contractible to a point in this restricted configuration space. For the rest of this section we will be considering such a restricted configuration space. Thus when we speak of some set such as NONOVERLAP then we will mean the part of the set which is in the restricted configuration space.

Theorem 2.7: NONOVERLAP consists of a finite number of path connected components.

Proof: As in [Schwartz and Sharir, 1982] we divided configuration space into finitely many cells such that the set of polynomials that describe the relative positions of the objects are sign invariant within each cell. Then NONOVERLAP is the finite union of some of these cells and for any two points x,y in a cell there is a path within the cell between them. Thus there must be finitely many path connected components in NONOVERLAP. □

Theorem 2.8 (Mayer-Victoria): The sequence

$$H_1(A \cup B) \to H_0(A \cap B) \to H_0(A) \oplus H_0(B) \to H_0(A \cup B) \to \{0\}$$

is an exact sequence when A and B are closed.

Proof: See [Massey, 1978]. □

In the following we will use the Mayer-Vietoris sequence with A = FILL and B = NONOVERLAP to show that in our restricted configuration space TOUCH and NONOVERLAP have the same number of path connected components.

Theorem 2.9: H_0(NONOVERLAP) $\cong$ H_0(FILL∩NONOVERLAP) = H_0(TOUCH).

Proof: By Theorem 2.5, S=FILL∪NONOVERLAP is contractible to a point and so $\Pi_1(S)=\{0\}$ (see [Massey, 1967]). Since $\Pi_1(S)$ is abelian $H_1(S)=\Pi_1(S)=\{0\}$. Also we have that $H_0(S)=\mathbf{Z}$ because by Corollary 2.6, S is path connected. By Theorem 2.3 FILL is path connected so $H_0(\text{FILL})=\mathbf{Z}$. Therefore the sequence in Theorem 2.8 is as follows:

$$\{0\} \xrightarrow{h_1} H_0(\text{TOUCH}) \xrightarrow{h_2} \mathbf{Z} \oplus H_0(\text{NONOVERLAP}) \xrightarrow{h_3} \mathbf{Z} \xrightarrow{h_4} \{0\}.$$

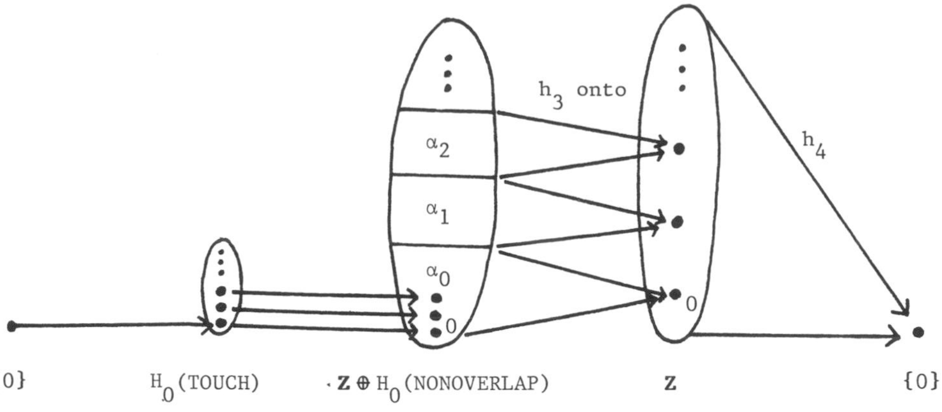

Figure 7. Mayer-Vietoris sequence

Since the sequence is exact, $Im(h_3)=ker(h_4)=\mathbf{Z}$ and so h_3 is onto. Also $ker(h_2)=Im(h_1)=\{0\}$ and so h_2 is one-to-one. Thus we have the situation shown in Figure 7.

Therefore $H_0(\text{TOUCH}) \simeq IM(h_2)$. The α_i's are the cosets of $Im(h_2)$ and so there is a one-to-one correspondence between any α_i and $Im(h_2)$. Hence $\mathbf{Z} \oplus H_0(\text{NONOVERLAP}) \simeq \mathbf{Z} \oplus Im(h_2) \simeq \mathbf{Z} \oplus H_0(\text{TOUCH})$. Then since $H_0(\text{NONOVERLAP}) \simeq \mathbf{Z} \oplus \ldots \oplus \mathbf{Z}$ (n copies of **Z**) and $H_0(\text{TOUCH}) \simeq \mathbf{Z} \oplus \ldots \oplus \mathbf{Z}$ (m copies of **Z**) by Theorem 2.7 it must be that m=n and so $H_0(\text{NONOVERLAP}) \simeq H_0(\text{TOUCH})$. □

Thus it has been shown that the number of path connected components of NONOVERLAP, denoted by #NONOVERLAP, equals the number of path connected components of TOUCH, denoted by #TOUCH. Let m=#TOUCH=#NONOVERLAP and let $t_1,\ldots,t_m$ be the path connected components of TOUCH and $n_1,\ldots,n_m$ be the path connected components of NONOVERLAP.

<u>Lemma 2.10</u>: Each t_i intersects at most one n_k.

<u>Proof</u>: Suppose there is a t_i such that $t_i \cap n_k \neq \emptyset$ and $t_i \cap n_j \neq \emptyset$. Let $x_1 \in n_j$, $x_2 \in n_k$, $x_3 \in t_i \cap n_j$ and $x_4 \in t_i \cap n_k$. Then since n_j is path connected there is a path P_1 in n_j from x_1 to x_3. Similarly there is a path P_2 in n_k from x_4 to x_2 and a path P_3 from x_3 to x_4 in t_i. Since TOUCH=FILL∩NONOVERLAP by Theorem 1.6 we get TOUCH⊆NONOVERLAP and so a path in t_i is a path in NONOVERLAP. Thus $P_1||P_3||P_2$ is a path from x_1 in n_j to x_2 in n_k and the path is in NONOVERLAP. Hence n_j and n_k must be the same path connected component of NONOVERLAP. □

Thus for each i, $t_i \cap n_k \neq \emptyset$ for at most one k and since TOUCH⊆NONOVERLAP we know that for every t_i there is one n_k such that $t_i \subseteq n_k$. Now it will be shown that each n_k contains at most one t_i and so each n_k contains exactly one t_i.

<u>Lemma 2.11</u>: For each n_k there is a t_j such that $t_j \subseteq n_k$.

<u>Proof</u>: We must show that for any x∈NONOVERLAP there is motion in NONOVERLAP from x to some configuration y∈TOUCH. Let x∈NONOVERLAP and suppose x∉TOUCH. Let a_1 and a_2 be the origins of A_1 and A_2 respectively and let $s(t)=ta_2(x)+(1-t)a_1(x)$. Let m(t) be the motion such that $a_1(m(t))=s(t)$ and everything else stays constant. Let $t_0=\min_t\{m(t) \notin \text{NONOVERLAP-TOUCH}\}$. Thus $\exists$ij such that $A_i(m(t_0)) \cap A_j(m(t_0)) \neq \emptyset$. If $a \in A_i(m(t_0)) \cap A_j(m(t_0))$ then $a \in A_i(m(t_0))-int(A_i(m(t_0)))$ and $a \in A_j(m(t_0))-int(A_j(m(t_0)))$ otherwise we would contradict the definition of t_0. Therefore $m(t_0)$∈TOUCH as required. □

<u>Theorem 2.12</u>: For each n_k there is exactly one t_j such that $t_j \subseteq n_k$.

<u>Proof</u>: By Lemma 2.11 we know there is at least one $t_i \subseteq n_k$. By Lemma 2.10 each t_i is contained in at most one n_k. Since #NONOVERLAP = #TOUCH we conclude that there is exactly one t_j contained in each n_k. □

We call a motion m of n objects a <u>k-component motion</u> if for all t in the closed interval [0,1], m(t) has at most k connected components. A configuration x is said to be a <u>k-component</u> configuration if x has at most k connected components. We will call a 1-component configuration a <u>connected configuration</u>.

Thus Theorem 2.12 can be restated: If there is an n-component motion from x to y (i.e. $x,y \in n_k$) and x and y are (n-1)-component configurations, then there is an (n-1)-component motion from x to y (i.e. $x,y \in t_j$).

3. <u>The Existence of a Motion in Contact</u>

In this section we establish our main result. Suppose we have n objects and that x and y are two configurations in which the n objects form a connected composite object. Suppose further that there is a motion from configuration x to configuration y such that no two objects overlap. Then there is a motion such that all configurations throughout the motion are also connected.

For the remainder of the section, all configurations will be in NONOVERLAP. Thus if it is said that a configuration x has k components then we mean that x is in NONOVERLAP and x has k components.

Let $P_1, P_2, \ldots P_p$ be the partitionings of the n objects into k+1 or fewer connected components. We say that a configuration x satisfies P_i if the connected component of P_i are contained in the connected components of x. Let x_1 and x_2 be configurations of n composite objects both of which have k, $1 \le k \le n$, or less connected components and let m be a (k+1)-component motion from x_1 to x_2. Partition NONOVERLAP into regions so that all x satisfying a given P_i are in one region. Further partition NONOVERLAP into path connected components. Without loss of generality we assume that m never returns to a path connected component satisfying P_i once it has left it. Let $T_i = \{t \mid m(t) \text{ satisfies } P_i\}$, $1 \le i \le p$. Since m(t) is a continuous function and T_i is the set of all t such that m(t) is a closed region of configuration space, each T_i is a closed set. Furthermore, each T_i is a finite union of closed intervals. Partition the interval [0,1] into a finite number of closed subintervals $J_i = [a_i, a_{i+1}]$, $1 \le i \le t$, such that for each J_i there are k+1 sets of composite objects where each set remains as a connected composite object during the motion m on interval J_i. We can assume that the J_i's are maximal with respect to the above conditions. Thus $m(a_i)$, $1 \le i \le t+1$, is a k-component configuration and the motion m_i, which is m on J_i, is a (k+1)-component motion. Notice that during m_i the composite objects in each of the k+1 sets that define J_i remain as a connected composite object and so we can think of m_i as a motion of k+1 composite objects rather than a motion of n composite objects.

We will use such a partitioning of the interval [0,1] in the following result where we show that it is possible to reduce the number of components during a motion to the number of components in the initial and final configurations if there is a motion during which there is one more component.

<u>Lemma 3.1</u>: Let n be the number of composite objects and let k be such that $1 \le k < n$. If there is a (k+1)-component motion between two k-component configurations then there is a k-component motion between them.

<u>Proof</u>: The proof is by induction n, the number of composite objects.

> <u>Base Step</u>: If n=2 then k=n-1 and the result follows from Theorem 2.12.
>
> <u>Induction Step</u>: Assume the result holds when there are less than n composite objects. Suppose we have n composite objects. For k=n-1 the lemma is true by Theorem 2.12.

Let k be such that $1 \le k < n-1$. Partition [0,1] into $J_1, \ldots, J_t$ as above. Then m_i is a (k+1)-component motion of k+1 composite objects between k-component configurations a_i and a_{i+1}. Since k+1<n the induction hypothesis holds for each m_i and so there is a k-component motion m'_i between a_i and a_{i+1}. Thus $m' = m'_1 \| m'_2 \| \ldots \| m'_t$ is a k-component motion between the given k-component configurations. □

Now an immediate corollary to Lemma 3.1 for the case of connected configurations is stated.

<u>Corollary 3.2</u>: If there is a (k+1)-component motion between two connected configurations of composite objects ($1 \le k < n$) then there is a k-component motion between them.

It is now possible to prove the major aim of this paper. Thus we now show that if there is any motion between two connected configurations such that during the motion no two composite objects overlap then there is a motion between the configurations such that all configurations during the motion are connected and no two composite objects overlap.

<u>Theorem 3.3</u>: If there is any motion between two connected configurations x and y then there is a motion between them such that throughout the motion the configurations are connected.

<u>Proof</u>: Suppose there is a (k+1)-component motion between x and y for $k \ge 1$. Then by Corollary 3.2 there is a k-component motion between x and y. Thus by induction there is a 1-component motion between x and y. □

4. <u>Generalizations</u>

In the previous sections we restricted motion to be translation and rotation. There it was shown that if there was a motion between two connected configurations such that throughout the motion no two objects overlapped, then there was a motion between the configurations such that throughout the motion the objects formed a connected configuration. This result depended on the fact that certain subsets of configuration space were path connected and that one subset, namely FILL ∪ NONOVERLAP was contractible to a point. These facts used translational motions in their proofs. Notice that the results hold if the only motions allowed are translations. However as noted earlier if only rotations are permitted then the result does not hold as stated.

For more general motion that allows continuous deformation of the objects such as stretching or radial growth about some point of an object, we must make sure that FILL and FILL ∪ NONOVERLAP are again path connected and FILL ∪ NONOVERLAP is contractible to a point. If so, we can again conclude that if there is a generalized motion, that keeps the objects from overlapping one another, between two connected configurations then there is a generalized motion between these configurations that keeps the configurations connected throughout.

Suppose motions consist of translations and any kind of continuous deformation of objects such that the objects remain convex and the deformation has a fixed point. The motions described in Theorem 2.3 and Theorem 2.5 can be extended in the obvious way to include the type of motion described above. Thus FILL ∪ NONOVERLAP is contractible to a point and FILL is path connected for these motions and hence we can conclude that if there is a motion in NONOVERLAP between two connected configurations then there is a motion that keeps the objects connected throughout.

For some types of generalized motions FILL will not be path connected. Suppose FILL is not path connected but it is the case that the set consisting of all the configurations of one path connected component of FILL and all the configurations in a path connected component of NONOVERLAP which intersects the path connected component of FILL is contractible to a point. Then by taking A to be the path connected component of FILL and B to be the path connected component of NONOVERLAP in the Mayer-Vietoris sequence of section 2 we can conclude that for two configurations which are in both the path connected component of FILL and the path connected component of NONOVERLAP and hence in TOUCH, there is a motion in TOUCH between these configurations.

If we strengthen the definition of VALID such that VALID remains a closed set in configuration space then the results of the previous sections still hold. For example instead of just requiring that a composite object be connected we could insist that the objects of the composite object touch each other in a specific manner. In this way we could have nonconvex objects by dividing them into convex pieces and then defining VALID so that a configuration is in VALID only if the convex pieces form the nonconvex object that is required. An example of this is shown in Figure 8 where the four rectangular objects form a nonconvex composite object and a configuration must have these objects touching in this way for it to be in VALID.

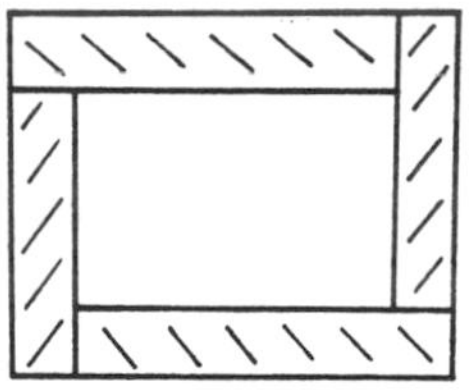

Figure 8. A nonconvex object

Acknowledgements

The authors would like to thank Peter Kahn for pointing out the use of the Mayer-Vietoris sequence.

Footnotes

This work was supported in part by NSF grant ECS-8312096 and an NSERC graduate scholarship.

References

Croom, F. H., 1978, "Basic Concepts of Algebraic Topology", New York, Springer-Verlag.

Goldberg, R. R., 1976, "Methods of Real Analysis", New York, John Wiley & Sons, Inc.

Hopcroft, J. E., Schwartz, J. T. and Sharir, M., 1984, Robotics Research Technical Report No. 14, "On the Complexity of Motion Planning for Multiple Independent Objects; PSpace Hardness of the 'Warehouseman's Problem'", New York, New York University, Computer Science Division.

Hopcroft, J. E., Joseph, D., and Whitesides, S., 1982, Technical Report No. TR82-515, "Movements Problems for 2-Dimensional Linkages", Ithaca, Cornell University, Dept. of Computer Science. (To appear in the SIAM J. on Computing.)

Massey, W. S., 1978, "Homology and Cohomology Theory", New York, Marcel Dekker, Inc.

Massey, W. S., 1967, "Algebraic Topology: An Introduction", New York, Springer-Verlag.

Schwartz, J. T., and Sharir, M., 1982, Technical Report No. 41, "On The Piano Mover's Problem II: General Techniques for Computing Topological Properties of Real Algebraic Manifolds", New York, New York University, Computer Science Department.

Willard, S., 1970, "General Topology", Reading, Addison-Wesley.

MANIPULABILITY OF ROBOTIC MECHANISMS

Tsuneo Yoshikawa
Automation Research Laboratory
Kyoto University
Uji, Kyoto 611, Japan

The concept of manipulability measure of robotic mechanisms is discussed. This is a measure of manipulating ability of robotic mechanisms in positioning and orienting the end-effectors. Some properties of this measure are obtained and the best postures of various types of manipulators and a four degrees-of-freedom finger from the viewpoint of this measure are given. It is found that these postures have some resemblance with those taken by human arms and fingers. A four-joint wrist mechanism is also analyzed with respect to its ability of orienting the end-effector, and a control algorithm for this redundant mechanism is developed.

1. INTRODUCTION

Determination of the mechanism and size of a robot manipulator at the design stage, and determination of the posture of the manipulator in the workspace [Gupta and Roth, 1982] for performing a given task at the operation stage, have largely been done on the basis of experience and intuition. One of various measures used for these determinations, seems to be the easiness of changing arbitrarily the position and orientation of the end-effector at the tip of the manipulator. It will be beneficial for design and control of robots and for task planning if we have a quantitative measure of manipulating ability of robot arms in positioning and orienting the end-effectors. The concept "manipulability measure" has been proposed in a previous paper [Yoshikawa, 1983] as one such measure.

Manipulability measure is a generalized concept of the determinant of Jacobian matrix, the latter having been used in [Paul and Stevenson, 1983] as a measure of degeneracy for the analysis of robot wrists. They have shown that any three-joint orienting system (wrist) has two cone regions of degeneracy in which its ability to orient the end-effector is poor. One way to overcome this difficulty is to use a 4 or more degrees-of-freedom (d.o.f.) wrist mechanism.

In the present paper, some properties of the manipulability measure and its utilization for determining the best postures of various types of manipulators and an articulated robot finger, will be discussed. A four-joint wrist mechanism will also be analyzed from the viewpoint of the manipulability measure, and a control algorithm for this redundant mechanism will be given.

2. MANIPULABILITY MEASURE

In this section the definition of manipulability measure is given, and some properties of this measure are discussed.

We consider a manipulator with n d.o.f. whose joint variables are denoted by θ_i, i=1, 2, ..., n. We assume that a class of tasks we are interested in can be described by m variables r_j, j=1, 2, ..., m ($m \leq n$), and that the relation between θ_i and r_j is given by

$$r = f(\theta) \tag{1}$$

where $\theta = [\theta_1, \theta_2, \ldots, \theta_n]^T$ is the joint vector, $r = [r_1, r_2, \ldots, r_m]^T$ is the manipulation vector and the superscript ^{T} denotes the transpose. Differentiating (1) with respect to time yields

$$\dot{r} = J(\theta)\dot{\theta} \tag{2}$$

where $\dot{r} = dr/dt \in R^m$ (m dimensional Euclidian space), $\dot{\theta} = d\theta/dt \in R^n$, and $J(\theta) = df(\theta)/d\theta \in R^{m \times n}$ (the set of all m×n real matrices). The matrix $J(\theta)$ is called the Jacobian.

We assume that the following condition is satisfied.

$$\max_{\theta} \ \text{rank}\, J(\theta) = m \tag{3}$$

Failing to satisfy this condition usually means that the selection of manipulation variables is redundant and the number of these variables m can be reduced. When condition (3) is satisfied, we say that the degree of redundancy of this manipulator is (n-m). More detailed discussion on the degree of redundancy and a related concept of redundant space can be found in [Hanafusa et al., 1981].

If for some θ^*,

$$\text{rank } J(\theta^*) < m \tag{4}$$

then we say that the manipulator is in a singular state. This state θ^* is not desirable since the manipulation vector r cannot move in a certain direction, meaning that the manipulability is seriously deteriorated.

In order to analyze this singularity problem we proposed the following quantitative measure of manipulability in the previous paper [Yoshikawa, 1983].

Definition: A scalar value w given by

$$w = \sqrt{\det J(\theta)J^T(\theta)} \tag{5}$$

is called the manipulability measure at state θ with respect to manipulation vector r.

The following three facts have been established in [Yoshikawa, 1983].

(i) Let the singular value decomposition [Klema and Laub, 1980] of J be

$$J = U\Sigma V^T \tag{6}$$

where $U \in R^{m \times m}$ and $V \in R^{n \times n}$ are orthogonal matrices and

$$\Sigma = \left[\begin{array}{cccc|c} \sigma_1 & & & 0 & \\ & \sigma_2 & & & \\ & & \cdot & & 0 \\ & & & \cdot & \\ 0 & & & \sigma_m & \end{array}\right] \in R^{m \times n} \tag{7}$$

with

$$\sigma_1 \geq \sigma_2 \geq \ldots \geq \sigma_m \geq 0. \tag{8}$$

Then the measure w can be expressed as the product of the singular values $\sigma_1, \sigma_2, \ldots, \sigma_m$:

$$w = \sigma_1 \sigma_2 \cdots \sigma_m \tag{9}$$

(ii) We can show that the subset S_v of the realizable velocity $\dot{r}$ in the space R^m using joint velocity $\dot{\theta}$ such that $\| \dot{\theta} \|^2 = \dot{\theta}_1^2 + \dot{\theta}_2^2 + \cdots + \dot{\theta}_n^2 \leq 1$ is an ellipsoid with principal axes $\sigma_1 u_1, \sigma_2 u_2, \ldots, \sigma_m u_m$, where $u_i \in R^m$ is the i-th column vector of U, i.e., $[u_1 \; u_2 \cdots u_m] = U$. This ellipsoid can be called the manipulability ellipsoid and could be a good means for the analysis, design and control of robot manipulators. The volume v_e of this ellipsoid is given by

$$v_e = d\, w \tag{10a}$$
$$d = \{\pi^{m/2} / \Gamma[(m/2)+1]\} \tag{10b}$$

where $\Gamma(\cdot)$ is the gamma function. Therefore, w is equal to the volume of the manipulability ellipsoid except for the constant coefficient d. The manipulability ellipsoid can be expresed by

$$\{\dot{r} \mid \dot{r}^T (JJ^T)^{-1} \dot{r} \leq 1, \text{ and } \dot{r} \in \text{Im}(J)\} \tag{11a}$$

Except at the singular states where the volume of the ellipsoid becomes zero, the ellipsoid can be defined by

$$\dot{r}^T (JJ^T)^{-1} \dot{r} \leq 1 \tag{11b}$$

instead of (11a). The measure can also be regarded as a distance from the singular states since at singular states w takes the minimum value 0.

(iii) When m=n, i.e., when we consider nonredundant manipulators, the measure w reduces to

$$w = |\det J(\theta)| \tag{12}$$

This type of measure has been used in [Paul and Stevenson, 1983] for analysis of robot wrists.

Now we will make clear several new properties of the measure.

(iv) When m = n, the measure has the following physical interpretation as well as that of (ii). The subset of the realizable velocity $\dot{r}$ using $\dot{\theta}$ such that

$$|\dot{\theta}_i| \leq 1, \quad i = 1,2,\ldots,m \tag{13}$$

is a parallelepiped in R^m, and its volume is $2^m w$. In other words, the measure w is proportional to the volume of the parallelepiped. This result can easily be obtained from a property of determinants.

(v) Next we discuss the relation between the measure w and the maximum velocities of joints. So far, we have implicitly assumed that the maximum velocities of all joints are the same. When this assumption does not hold, the velocities of joints should be normalized. After fixing a set of units for distance, angle, and time (for example, m, rad, sec), we denote the maximum (angular) velocity of joint i by $\dot{\theta}_{io}$. We also select the desirable maximum (angular) velocity of each manipulation variable $\dot{r}_{jo}$ taking into consideration the class of tasks which the manipulator is supposed to perform. Then letting

$$\hat{\dot{\theta}} = [\hat{\dot{\theta}}_1, \hat{\dot{\theta}}_2, \ldots, \hat{\dot{\theta}}_n]^T, \quad \hat{\dot{\theta}}_i = \dot{\theta}_i / \dot{\theta}_{io} \tag{14}$$

$$\hat{\dot{r}} = [\hat{\dot{r}}_1, \hat{\dot{r}}_2, \ldots, \hat{\dot{r}}_m]^T, \quad \hat{\dot{r}}_j = \dot{r}_j / \dot{r}_{jo} \tag{15}$$

we obtain

$$\hat{\dot{r}} = \hat{J}(\theta)\hat{\dot{\theta}} \tag{16}$$

where

$$\hat{J}(\theta) = T_r J(\theta) T_\theta^{-1} \tag{17}$$

$$T_r = \text{diag}[1/\dot{r}_{jo}] \in R^{m \times m} \tag{18}$$

$$T_\theta = \text{diag}[1/\dot{\theta}_{io}] \in R^{n \times n} \tag{19}$$

Since $|\hat{\dot{\theta}}_i| \leq 1$ and $|\hat{\dot{r}}_j| \leq 1$, we can define the manipulability measure w using the normalized Jacobian $\hat{J}(\theta)$.

Defining the measure w for $J(\theta) T_\theta^{-1}$ as $\hat{w}_\theta$, and that for $\hat{J}(\theta) = T_r J(\theta) T_\theta^{-1}$ as

$\hat{w}$, we have

$$\hat{w} = [\prod_{j=1}^{m} (1/\dot{r}_{j0})]\,\hat{w}_\theta \qquad (20)$$

and especially when n=m, we have

$$\hat{w} = [\prod_{i=1}^{n} (\dot{\theta}_{i0}/\dot{r}_{i0})]\,w \qquad (21)$$

Hence the transformation T_r has only the effect of multiplying the scalar value $\prod_{j=1}^{m} (1/\dot{r}_{j0})$. The relative shape of w as a function of θ is independent of the transformation T_r. Furthermore, when n=m, the relative shape of w is independent of both T_r and T_θ.

(vi) Letting h denote the force (and moment) applied to an object by the end-effector and letting τ denote the necessary joint driving force (and torque), we have [Paul, 1981]

$$\tau = J^T h \qquad (22)$$

Hence the set of manipulating force h which is realizable by a joint driving force τ such that $\|\tau\| \leq 1$, is given by (except for the singular states)

$$h^T J J^T h \leq 1 \qquad (23)$$

This set is an ellipsoid that can be called the manipulating force ellipsoid. Its principal axes are given by $(1/\sigma_1)u_1$, $(1/\sigma_2)u_2, \ldots, (1/\sigma_m)u_m$, and its volume is d/w. In other words, the volume of the manipulating force elipsoid is in the inverse proporton to that of the manipulability ellipsoid. Also the length of each principal axis of the manipulability ellipsoid is in inverse proportion to the magnitude of realizable manipulating force in the direction of this axis. This means that the direction in which a large manipulating force can be generated is the one in which the manipulability is poor and vice versa.

The force elipsoid defined in [Asada, 1983] is equivalent to the above manipulating force ellipsoid when the motor constants of all motors are the same.

3. BEST POSTURES OF VARIOUS ROBOTIC MECHANISMS FROM THE VIEWPOINT OF MANIPULABILITY

3.1 Two-Joint Link Mechanism

In this section, the manipulability measure is calculated for various robotic mechanisms, and the best postures and the best points in the workspace of these mechanisms from the viewpoint of manipulability are determined.

First of all, a two-joint link mechanism shown in Fig. 1, which is the simplest case of multi-joint manipulators, will be considered. When the hand position $[x, y]^T$ is taken as the manipulation vector r, the Jacobian matrix is given by

$$J(\theta) = \begin{bmatrix} \ell_1 c_1 + \ell_2 c_{12} & \ell_2 c_{12} \\ -\ell_1 s_1 - \ell_2 s_{12} & -\ell_2 s_{12} \end{bmatrix} \qquad (24)$$

where $c_1 = \cos\theta_1$, $c_{12} = \cos(\theta_1 + \theta_2)$, $s_1 = \sin\theta_1$, $s_{12} = \sin(\theta_1 + \theta_2)$. Hence the manipulability measure w is

$$w = |\det J(\theta)| = \ell_1 \ell_2 |s_2| \qquad (25)$$

Therefore, the manipulator takes its best posture when $\theta_2 = \pm 90°$, for any given values of ℓ_1, ℓ_2, and θ_1. If the lengths ℓ_1 and ℓ_2 can be specified under the condition of constant total length, i.e., $\ell_1 + \ell_2 =$ const., the manipulability measure attains its maximum when $\ell_1 = \ell_2$ for any given θ_1 and θ_2.

Fig. 2(a), (b), and (c) show the manipulability ellipsoid, the manipulability measure, and the manipulating force ellipsoid, respectively, for the case $\ell_1 = \ell_2 = 1$, taking ℓ_a, the distance between the first joint and the hand, as a parameter. The magnitude and direction of the realizable tip velocity and manipulating force can be easily understood from the figure.

When the human arm is regarded as a two-joint link mechanism by neglecting the d.o.f. of sideward direction at the shoulder and the d.o.f. of the wrist, it approximately satisfies the relation $\ell_1 = \ell_2$. Moreover, when we handle some object by our hands, the elbow angle is usually in the neighborhood of 90°. Hence it could be said that people are unconsciously taking the best arm posture from the viewpoint of manipulability.

3.2 SCARA Type Robot Manipulators

Consider the SCARA type manipulators with four d.o.f. shown in Fig. 3. Let $r = [x, y, z, \alpha]^T$, where $[x, y, z]^T$ is the hand position and α is the rotational angle of the hand about z axis. The Jacobian matrix for this case is given by

$$J(\theta) = \begin{bmatrix} \ell_1 c_1 + \ell_2 c_{12} & \ell_2 c_{12} & 0 & 0 \\ -\ell_1 s_1 - \ell_2 s_{12} & -\ell_2 s_{12} & 0 & 0 \\ 0 & 0 & -1 & 0 \\ 1 & 1 & 0 & 1 \end{bmatrix} \qquad (26)$$

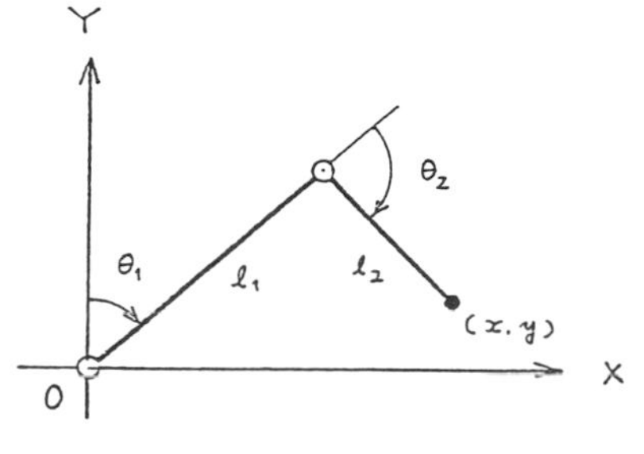

Fig. 1 Two-joint link mechanism

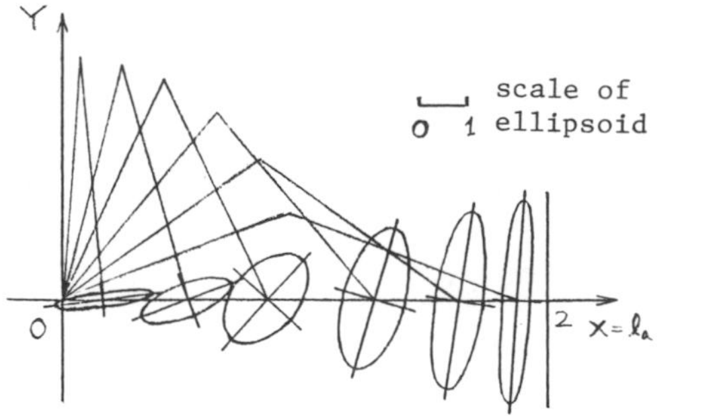

(a) Manipulability ellipsoid

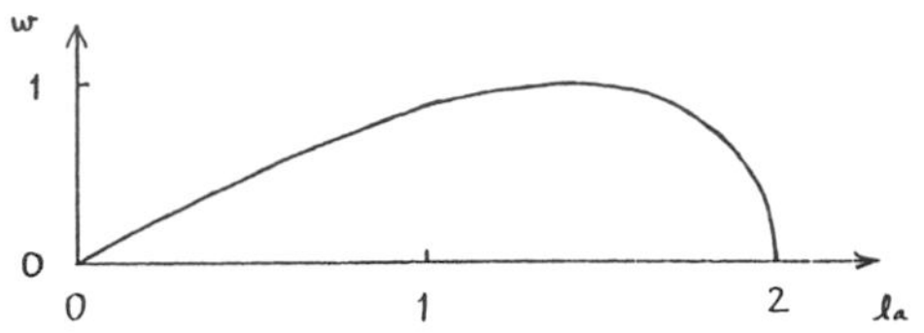

(b) Manipulability measure

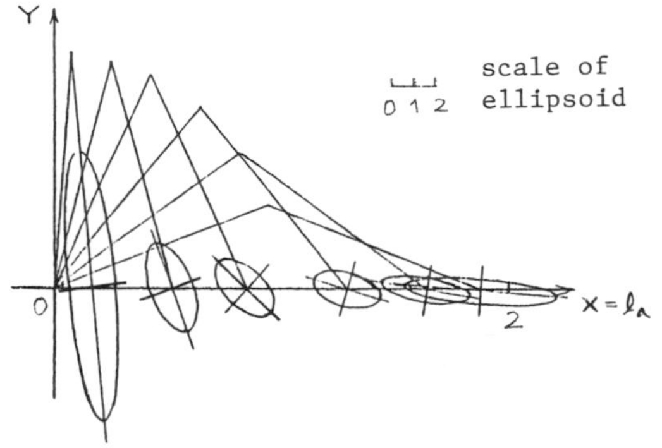

(c) Manipulating force ellipsoid

Fig.2 Manipulability ellipsoid, manipulability measure, and manipulating force ellipsoid of two-joint link mechanism

Hence

$$w = \ell_1 \ell_2 |s_2|$$

Therefore as in the case of two-joint link mechanism of Fig. 1, the best posture is given by $\theta_2 = \pm 90°$, for any given values of ℓ_1, ℓ_2, θ_1, θ_3, and θ_4. Also under the constraint of $\ell_1 + \ell_2 =$ const., the manipulability measure attains its maximum when $\ell_1 = \ell_2$, $\theta_2 = \pm 90°$. Notice that there are many commercial SCARA type manipulators satisfying $\ell_1 = \ell_2$.

3.3 PUMA Type Robot Manipulators

Most of the PUMA type robot manipulators commercially available today have five or six d.o.f.. Many of them have links with some displacements in the direction of joint axes. However, we consider only the main 3 joints shown in Fig. 4 neglecting the d.o.f. placed at the wrist and neglecting the displacements in the direction of joint axes. The joint vector is $\theta = [\theta_1, \theta_2, \theta_3]^T$. The manipulation vector is taken to be $r = [x, y, z]^T$. Then the Jacobian matrix is

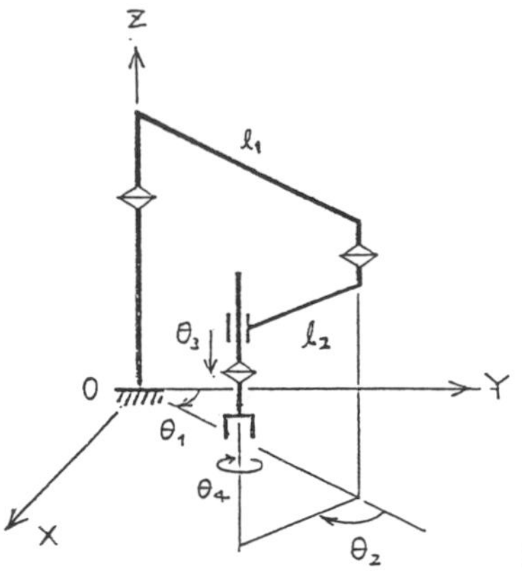

Fig.3 SCARA type robot

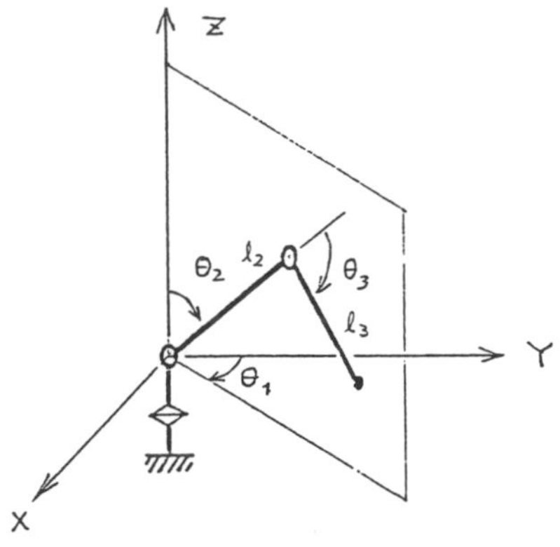

Fig.4 PUMA type robot

$$J(\theta) = \begin{bmatrix} -s_1(\ell_2 s_2 + \ell_3 s_{23}) & c_1(\ell_2 c_2 + \ell_3 c_{23}) & c_1 \ell_3 c_{23} \\ c_1(\ell_2 s_2 + \ell_3 s_{23}) & s_1(\ell_2 c_2 + \ell_3 c_{23}) & s_1 \ell_3 c_{23} \\ 0 & -(\ell_2 s_2 + \ell_3 s_{23}) & -\ell_3 s_{23} \end{bmatrix} \quad (27)$$

and the manipulability measure is

$$w = \ell_2 \ell_3 |(\ell_2 s_2 + \ell_3 s_{23}) s_3| \quad (28)$$

The best posture for given ℓ_2 and ℓ_3 is obtained as follows. First, θ_1 is not related to w and can take any value. Second, from $\partial w / \partial \theta_2 = 0$ we have

$$\tan\theta_2 = \frac{\ell_2 + \ell_3 c_3}{\ell_2 s_3} \quad (29)$$

This means that the tip of arm should be on the xy plane, i.e., at the same height as the second joint. This can further be interpreted as making maximum the contribution of the angular velocity of the first joint to the manipulability measure.

Substituting (29) into (28) yields

$$w = \ell_2 \ell_3 \sqrt{\ell_2^2 + \ell_3^2 + 2\ell_2 \ell_3 c_3}\, |s_3| \quad (30)$$

The value of θ_3 which maximizes w is given by

$$c_3 = c_3^* = \{ \sqrt{(\ell_2^2 + \ell_3^2)^2 + 12\ell_2^2 \ell_3^2} - (\ell_2^2 + \ell_3^2) \} / 6\ell_2 \ell_3 \quad (31)$$

Fig. 5 shows the best postures for the cases $\ell_3 = \gamma \ell_2$, $\gamma = 0.5, 1, 2$ (only those satisfying $0° \leq \theta_2 \leq 90°$ are shown in the figure). If the manipulator is regarded as a

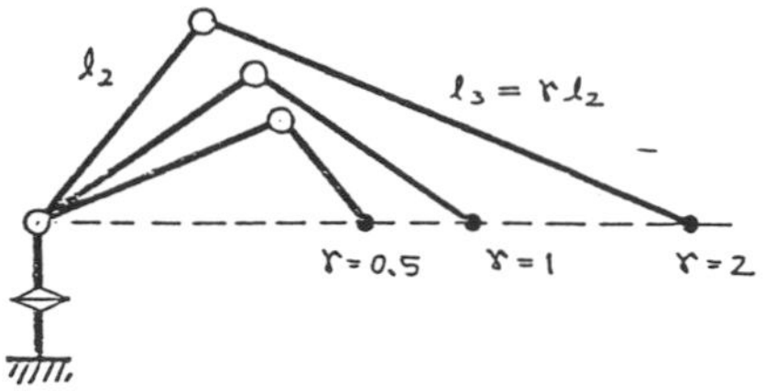

Fig.5 Best arm posture for PUMA type robot

two-joint mechanism consisting of θ_2 and θ_3, the optimal angle for θ_3 is 90° from the discussion in 3.1. In the present case, however, the optimal θ_3 is smaller than 90°. The reason for this is that the contribution of $\dot{\theta}_1$ to w can be made larger by placing the tip of arm farther away from the first joint axis.

For $c_3{}^*$ given by (31), w is calculated as

$$w = (\ell_2 \ell_3)^{3/2} (1 - c_3{}^{*2}) \mid c_3{}^* \mid^{1/2}$$

Hence unde the constraint $\ell_2 + \ell_3 =$ const., the best ratio of ℓ_2 and ℓ_3 is again 1 to 1.

3.4 Four-Joint Robotic Finger

Various robotic hands with multi-articulated fingers have been developed, for example in [Okada, 1979], [Salisbury and Craig, 1982] and [Hanafusa et al., 1983] to realize the dexterity and flexibility of human hands in handling and assembling jobs. In this section a four-joint finger shown in F ig. 6 will be considered from the viewpoint of manipulability measure.

The Jacobian matrix relating $\theta = [\theta_1, \theta_2, \theta_3, \theta_4]^T$ to $r = [x, y, z]^T$ is

$$J(\theta) = \begin{bmatrix} 0 & -a_1 & -a_2 & -a_3 \\ c_1 a_1 & s_1 b_1 & s_1 b_2 & s_1 b_3 \\ s_1 a_1 & -c_1 b_1 & -c_1 b_2 & -c_1 b_3 \end{bmatrix} \quad (32)$$

where

$$a_1 = \ell_2 s_2 + \ell_3 s_{23} + \ell_4 s_{234}$$
$$a_2 = \ell_3 s_{23} + \ell_4 s_{234}$$
$$a_3 = \ell_4 s_{234}$$
$$b_1 = \ell_2 c_2 + \ell_3 c_{23} + \ell_4 c_{234}$$
$$b_2 = \ell_3 c_{23} + \ell_4 c_{234}$$
$$b_3 = \ell_4 c_{234}$$

The manipulability measure is calculated as

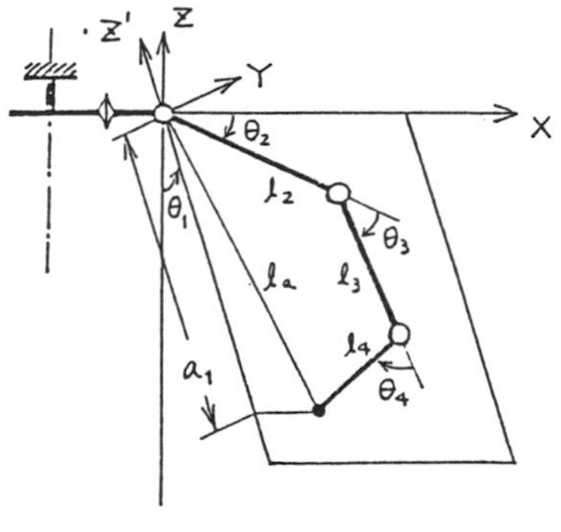

Fig.6 Finger with four d.o.f.

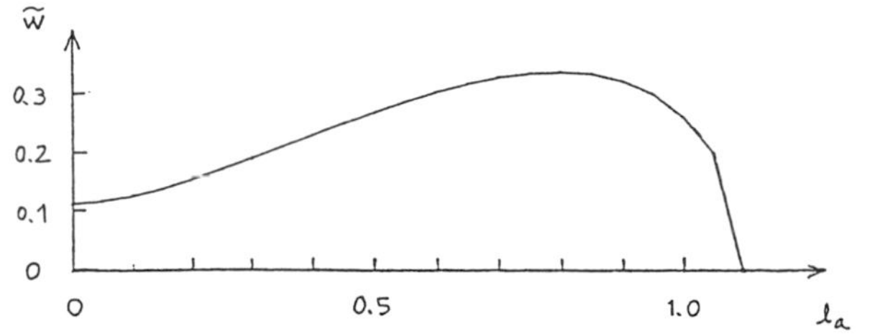

Fig.7 Maximum value of $\tilde{w}$ as a function of ℓ_a

$$w = \mid a_1 \mid \tilde{w}(\theta_2, \theta_3, \theta_4) \quad (33)$$

where

$$\tilde{w}(\theta_2, \theta_3, \theta_4) = \sqrt{\det \mathcal{J} \mathcal{J}^T} \quad (34)$$

$$\mathcal{J} = \begin{bmatrix} a_1 & a_2 & a_3 \\ b_1 & b_2 & b_3 \end{bmatrix} \quad (35)$$

The maximum value of $\tilde{w}(\theta_2, \theta_3, \theta_4)$ for a given distance ℓ_a between joint two and the tip of the finger (see Fig. 6), is shown in Fig. 7 for the case $\ell_2 = \ell_3 = 0.4$, $\ell_4 = 0.3$. The corresponding finger posture is shown in Fig. 8. Notice that these postures are independent of the angle θ_2. Fig. 9 shows the maximum value of w as a function of the finger tip position in the xz'-plane (only the lower half portion is shown since the value in the upper half is symmetric with respect to the x axis). The best finger posture is also shown in the figure by a broken line.

Notice that the finger postures given in Fig. 8 are quite similar to those taken by human fingers during the manipulation of small objects. Hence we can expect that these postures would be useful in determining the grasping posture of a robotic hand with several four d.o.f. fingers.

The condition number $c(J^T(\theta))$ of the transpose of the Jacobian matrix $J(\theta)$ has been used in [Salisbury and Craig, 1982] as a measure of workspace quality. This is a measure of the accuracy with which forces can be exerted. Hence the meanings of the manipulability measure w discussed in this paper and the dondition number are quite different. For example, Fig. 10 compares the best postures of a simple two-joint link mechanism for these two measures. The figure clearly shows the difference between these two measures.

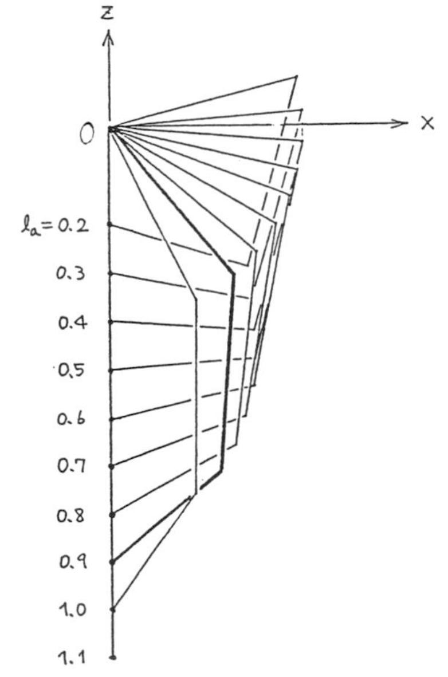

Fig.8 Best finger posture

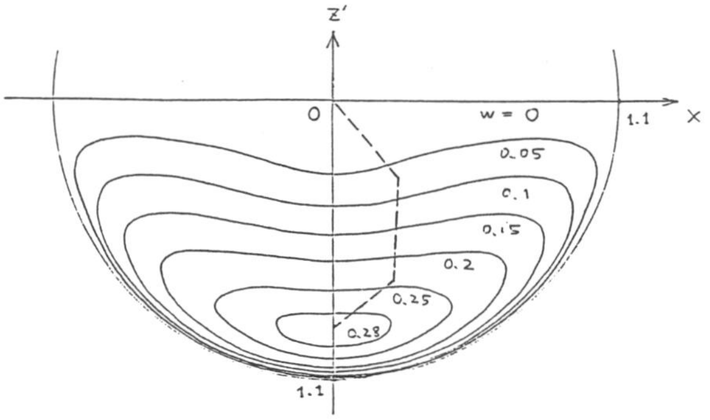

Fig.9 Maximum value of w as a function of the finger tip position

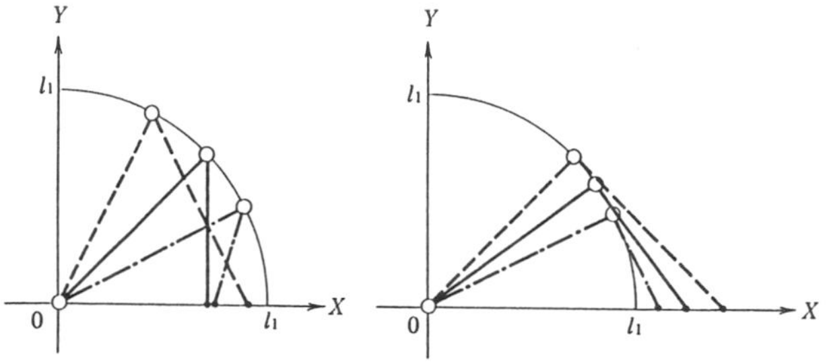

(a) $c(J^T)$ (b) w

Fig.10 Comparison of the best postures of two-link mechanism
—·—·: $\ell_2 = 0.5\,\ell_1$
———: $\ell_2 = 0.707\,\ell_1$
— — —: $\ell_2 = \ell_1$

3.5 Four-Joint Redundant Wrist Mechanism

In [Hanafusa et al., 1982] a wrist mechanism, called AWM (Additional Wrist Mechanism), has been proposed. When attached to the tip of a manipulator, the AWM changes only the hand orientation without giving any effect on the hand position. It has also been mentioned that this AWM is capable of arbitrary orientational motion except for the case when the wrist configuration is such that the approach directions of hand and arm are the same. The degradation of the orienting ability at this configuration is, however, not desirable since this configulation is usually around the center of the workspace for orientation. As mentioned in Introduction, It has been shown in [Paul and Stevenson, 1983] that any three-joint orienting system (wrist) has two cone regions of degeneracy in which its ability to orient the end-effector is poor. One way to overcome this difficulty wiil be to use a 4 or more d.o.f. wrist mechanism. One such wrist has already been developed by Itoh [1982], but without detailed study of manipulating ability or control algorithm.

In this section, a four-joint wrist mechanism whose basic structure is shown in Fig. 11(a), is proposed and analyzed from the viewpoint of manipulability measure. This mechanism can be regarded as a universal joint with two rotational joints at its both ends. The unique figures of this structure are that the hand position is determined uniquely when the hand orientation is given, and that the universal joint part can be rotated freely without changing the hand orientation and position at all. The change of the hand position caused by the change of the hand orientation can usually be compensated by the control of arm to which the wrist is attached. Hence, in the following, we assume that the purpose of the wrist mechanism is only to control the orientation of the hand.

By attaching the coordinate frame Σ_i to link i and taking the configuration shown in Fig. 11(b) as the standard state where the joint vector $\theta=[\theta_1, \theta_2, \theta_3, \theta_4]^T=0$, the Jacobian matrix relating the joint velocity $\dot{\theta}$ and the angular velocity $\dot{\phi}=[\dot{\phi}_x, \dot{\phi}_y, \dot{\phi}_z]^T$ around the coordinate axes of hand coordinate frame Σ_4, is given by

$$J(\theta)=\begin{bmatrix} c_2s_3s_4-s_2c_4 & c_3s_4 & c_4 & 0 \\ c_2s_3c_4-s_2s_4 & c_3c_4 & -s_4 & 0 \\ c_2c_3 & -s_3 & 0 & 1 \end{bmatrix} \tag{36}$$

The manipulability measure for this case is

$$w = \sqrt{2(1-s_2{}^2 s_3{}^2)} \tag{37}$$

For any given hand orientation, we define the angle β to be the angle between the z_4 and z_0 axes as shown in Fig. 12. Then we have

$$\cos\beta = c_2 c_3 \tag{38}$$

Using this angle β, we obtain

$$\sqrt{2} \geq w \geq \sqrt{2\{1-(1-|\cos\beta|)^2} \tag{39}$$

The maximum value of w, $w_{max}=\sqrt{2}$, is attained when $s_2=0$ or $s_3=0$, and the minimum value $w_{min}=\sqrt{2\{1-(1-|\cos\beta|)^2}$ is attained when $c_2{}^2=c_3{}^2=|\cos\beta|$. Fig. 13 shows the values w_{max} and w_{min} as functions of β in a polar coordinate form. From the figure, it is understood that when $\beta=90°$, the manipulability measure can vary very much depending on the joint angles. But since the maximum value of the measure is $\sqrt{2}$ for any β, the wrist has the possibility of avoiding degradation of manipulability by properly selecting the joint angles.

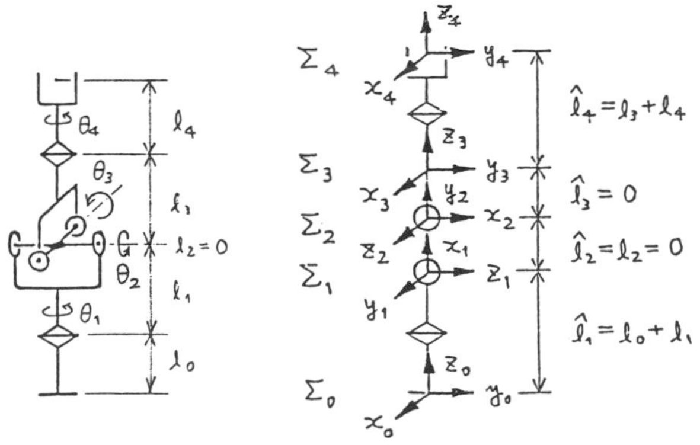

(a) Basic structure (b) Coordinate frames

Fig.11 Four-joint wrist mechanism

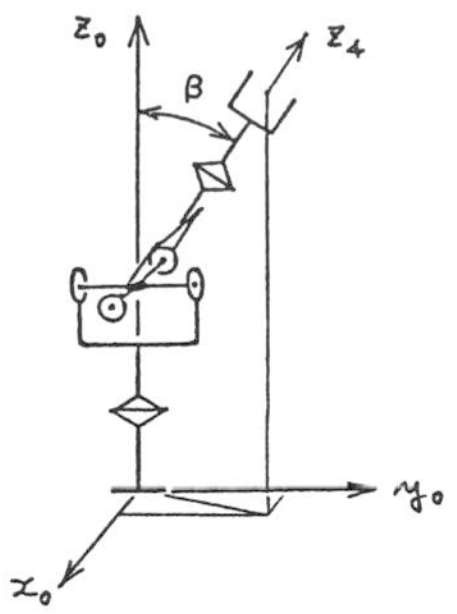

Fig. 12 Angle β

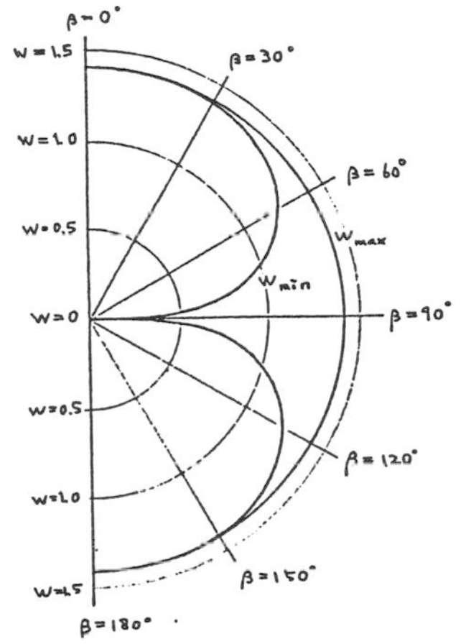

Fig. 13 Maximum and minimum values of manipulability measure

In designing a wrist with above basic structure, we tried to make the angle limit for θ_2 large in the plus side. This is for enlarging the workspace. When it is necessary to move θ_2 into the minus direction, we can change this motion to that in the θ_2 plus direction by rotating θ_1 for 180°.

Now the control problem of this wrist mechanism will be discussed. We specify the task of the wrist as consisting of two subtasks. The subtask with the first priority is to realize the given desirable trajectory of hand orientation. The second subtask, which should be performed using the ability left to the wrist after achieving the first subtask, is to maximize a given performance criterion which implies a compromise of three objectives; (a) to keep the manipulability measure large, (b) to bring the joint angle θ_2 to the plus side, and (c) to keep all joints within their hardware limits.

The general solution of (2) for a given desired velocity $\dot{\phi}_d$ is given by

$$\dot{\theta}=J^{+}(\theta)\dot{\phi}_d+[I-J^{+}(\theta)J(\theta)]k \qquad (40)$$

where $J^{+}(\theta)$ is the pseudo inverse of $J(\theta)$, and k is an arbitrary vector. It is known that, after realizing the desired velocity $\dot{\phi}_d$, one way of making the given performance criterion $q(\theta)$ large is to select the vector k as follows [Ligeois, 1977], [Yoshikawa, 1983]

$$k=\xi k_1, \quad \xi=dq(\theta)/d\theta \qquad (41)$$

where k_1 is a constant to be determined.

The following criterion has been chosen for the wrist mechanism.

$$q(\theta)=k_a w(\theta)+k_b\theta_2 + \sum_{i=1}^{4} k_{ci}\{(\theta_i-\bar{\theta}_i)^{-2}+(\theta_i-\underline{\theta}_i)^{-2}\}/2 \qquad (42)$$

where k_a, k_b, and k_{ci} are constants to be determined, and $\bar{\theta}_i$, $\underline{\theta}_i$ are upper and lower limits for θ_i.

To verify the effectiveness of the control algorithm given by (40), (41), and (42), computer simulation has been done. For simplicity the dynamics of the wrist has been neglected, and the joint velocity $\dot{\theta}$ calculated by (40) has been assumed to be realized exactly. The sampling period is 0.05 sec, and

$$\bar{\theta}_2=140, \quad \underline{\theta}_2=-110$$

$$\bar{\theta}_3=-\underline{\theta}_3=\begin{cases}180, & 90\le\theta_2\le140\\ (3(\theta_2-90)/8+100), & -110\le\theta_2\le90\end{cases}$$

$$k_1=1,\ k_a=3,\ k_b=20,\ k_{c2}=k_{c3}=1,\ k_{c1}=k_{c4}=0$$

The desired trajectory for the hand orientation has been specified by the Euler angles with respect to the base coordinate frame Σ_0. The solid line in Fig. 14(a) shows the time trajectory of the manipulability measure for the case where the wrist is rotated around the z_0 axis with $\dot{\alpha}=30$ (deg/sec) from the initial state $\theta=[0, 90, 45, 0]^T$ shownin Fig. 14(b). The broken line in the figure is for the algorithm (40) with k=0. It can be seen from the figure that the algorithm (40) with (41) and (42) keeps the wrist away from the singular state.

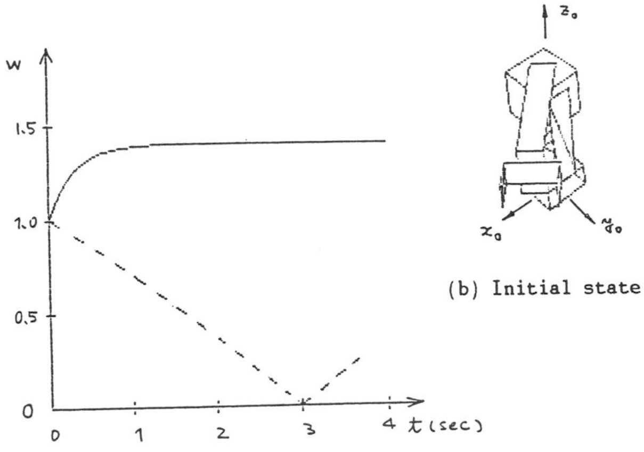

(b) Initial state

(a) Manipulability measure
——— : control algorithm (40) with (41) and (42)
– – – : control algorithm (40) with k=0

Fig. 14 Comparison of control algorithms

Fig. 15 shows the simulated motion of the wrist for the command $\dot{\beta}$=15 (deg/sec) from the initial state θ=[0, -10, 5, 0] ^{T}. Although the command is the motion in the direction of minus θ_2, it is seen that the second joint rotates about 180°, resulting in a motion in the plus θ_2 direction.

From these simulation results, it is expected that the four-joint wrist mechanism will be controlled satisfactorily by the pseudo inverse control algorithm (40) with (41) and (42).

4 CONCLUSION

Properties of the manipulability measure, which was proposed in a previous paper as a measure of manipulating ability of robot arms in positioning and orienting the end-effectors, have been studied. Its utilization for determining the best postures of various types of manipulators and an articulated robot finger has been discussed. The obtained best postures have some resemblance to those taken by human arms and fingers. As an application of the manipulability measure, a four-joint wrist mechanism has been analyzed with respect to its ability of orienting the end-effector, and a control algoritm has been developed. A simulation study shows the effectivness of the algorithm in controling this wrist mechanism.

The author would like to thank Mr. S. Kiriyama for his help in computer simulation.

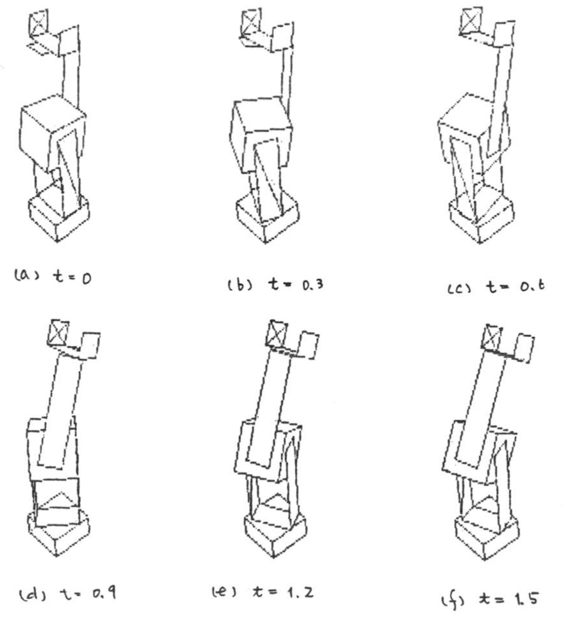

Fig.15 Simulation result of motion in the direction of minus θ_2

REFERENCES

Asada, H. 1983. Development of a direct-drive arm using high torque brushless motors. Preprints of the 1st International Symposium of Robotics Research. New Hampshire, USA.

Gupta, K.C., and Roth, B. 1982. Design considerations for manipulator workspace. Trans. ASME, J. Mechanical Design 104: 704-711.

Hanafusa, H., Kobayashi, H., and Terasaki, N. 1983. Fine control of the object with articulated multi-finger robot hands. Proc. of the 1983 International Conference on Advanced Robotics: 245-252.

Hanafusa, H., Yoshikawa, T., and Nakamura, Y. 1981. Analysis and control of articulated robot arms with redundancy. Prep. 8th IFAC World Congress XIV: 78-83.

Hanafusa, H., Yoshikawa, T., and Nakamura, Y. 1982. Design and control of additional wrist mechanism fr fine motion control of manipulatos. Prep. IFAC Sympo. Components and Instruments for Distributed Contol Systems: 133-139.

Itoh,H. 1982. Development of adaptive manipulator. Tech. Rep. Mechanical Engineering Laboratory,No. 120 (Japanese)

Klema, V.C. and Laub, A.T. 1980. The singular value decomposition: its computation and some applications. IEEE Trans. on Automatic Control AC-25(2): 164-176.

Liégeois,A. 1977. Automatic supervisory control of the configulatin and behavior of multibody mechanisms. IEEE Trans. on System, Man ad Cybenetics SMC-7(12): 868-871.

Okada, T. 1979. Computer control of multi-jointed finger system. Sixth Int. Joint Conf. on Artificial Intell., Tokyo, Japan.

Paul, R.P. 1981. Robot manipulators. Cambridge Mass.: MIT Press.

Paul, R.P. and Stevenson, C.N. 1983. Kinematics of robot wrists. Int. J. of Robotics Research 1(2): 31-38.

Salisbury, J.K. and Craig, J.T. 1982. Articulated hands: force control and kinematic issues. Int. J. of Robotics Research 1(1): 4-17.

Yoshikawa, T. 1983. Analysis and control of robot manipulators with redundancy. Preprints of the 1st International Symposium of Robotics Research. New Hampshire, USA.

PERFORMANCE EVALUATION OF MANIPULATORS USING THE JACOBIAN AND ITS APPLICATION TO TRAJECTORY PLANNING

Masaru Uchiyama, Kunitoshi Shimizu* and Kyojiro Hakomori

Department of Precision Engineering, Tohoku University
Aoba, Aramaki, Sendai 980, JAPAN

The use of the Jacobian as a performance index of manipulators is discussed from the kinematic and static standpoint of view. The Jacobian is an index for the evaluation of manipulator dexterity at a point in the workspace. The index takes the least value at singular points at which the manipulator loses capability of moving in a certain direction and is least dexterous. The distribution of the index value in the whole workspace which is visualized on a color graphics display gives an overall understanding of the manipulator performance. This is illustrated by numerical examples for two different types of robotic manipulators with six revolute joints. As an example of application of this performance index, optimal trajectory planning using the index is presented. The trajectories obtained for several cases such as turning a crank show that the method generates a kinematically reasonable trajectory.

1. INTRODUCTION

In recent years, expanding developments of robotic devices in the industry have made it essential that the design and control of the robotic devices be made on the scientific basis. What is crucial for doing this is to establish a standard on which performance of the devices can be evaluated. As to robotic arms concerning this problem, the manipulation performance has to be evaluated first of all. Of various factors in manipulator characteristics which determine the performance, the mechanical factor is most fundamental.

An index for the evaluation of the mechanical performance which is most commonly used is the workspace volume. However, due to different distributions of singular points in the workspace, arms with the same workspace volume have different mechanical performance. The mechanical performance is deteriorated at and near the singular point [Uchiyama, 1979]. A more elaborate index for the evaluation of the mechanical performance than the workspace volume is required in order for the manipulation performance at each point in the workspace including the singular point to be evaluated quantitatively.

Most recently, some researchers [Salisbury and Craig, 1982; Yoshikawa, 1983; Uchiyama et al., 1983] have proposed to use the Jacobian matrix in some way, which was used for the analysis of the singular point [Uchiyama, 1979], for the evaluation of the manipulation performance. [Salisbury and Craig, 1982] argue the use of the condition number of the Jacobian matrix for the evaluation of error propagation in force control of robotic fingers. [Yoshikawa, 1983] has proposed to use the product of the singular values of the Jacobian matrix as a measure of maniputability. The same index has been proposed independently by [Uchiyama et al., 1983], where they have proposed to use the Jacobian (determinant) as a performance index of manipulator arms.

* He is now with Atsugi Plant, Sony Corporation
4-14-1, Asahicho, Atsugi 243, JAPAN

In this paper, the use of the Jacobian as an index for the evaluation of manipulation performance of robotic mechanisms is discussed from the kinematic and static standpoint of view. Allowing for its application to the CAD of robotic mechanisms, color graphics display of the distribution of the values the Jacobian takes in the whole workspace is presented, with numerical examples provided for two different types of robotic arms with six revolute joints.

Optimal trajectory planning using the index is also discussed in this paper. The trajectory planning problem is formulated as that of calculus of variations with constraint conditions and approximate numerical solutions for some cases are presented. The results show that kinematically reasonable trajectories are obtained using the index.

The balance of this paper is divided into four parts. Mathematical background for the Jacobian as a performance index is described in Section 2, with color graphics display of the distribution of the Jacobian for some cases provided in Section 3. Application of the index to optimal trajectory planning is described in Section 4. Brief comments and conclutions are presented in Section 5.

2. PERFORMANCE EVALUATION OF ROBOTIC MECHANISMS USING THE JACOBIAN

The robotic arm is a spatial actuation system

which positions an end effector such as a hand or a specially designed tool and applies force and moment to a work through the end effector. Generally speaking, the joint coordinates, i.e. the rotations and slides of the joints determine the workspace coordinates, i.e. the position and orientation of the end effector in the workspace, and the joint torques and forces determine the applying force and moment. In programming robot tasks, it is helpful for the position and orientation of the end effector and the applying force and moment to the work to be able to be described in the workspace coordinates.

Let the position vectors described in the joint coordinates and the workspace coordinates be denoted as

$$\theta = (\theta_1, \theta_2, \cdots, \theta_n)' \tag{1}$$

and

$$p = (p_1, p_2, \cdots, p_m)', \tag{2}$$

respectively. Let also the corresponding force vectors in the joint coordinates and the workspace coordinates be denoted as

$$\tau = (\tau_1, \tau_2, \cdots, \tau_n)' \tag{3}$$

and

$$q = (q_1, q_2, \cdots, q_m)', \tag{4}$$

respectively. m and n are the dimensions of the workspace coordinates and the joint coordinates, respectively.

The transformation from θ to p is nonlinear. The Jacobian matrix J of the robotic mechanism is the locally linearized transformation matrix which is defined by the equation:

$$dp = Jd\theta. \tag{5}$$

The principle of duality between velocity and force in mechanics leads to the equation:

$$\tau = J'q \tag{6}$$

which describes the transformation from q to τ. Easiness in controlling dp and q is an important factor which influences the manipulation performance. As is clear from (5) and (6), dp and q are determined by $d\theta$ and τ, respectively, using the Jacobian matrix J, which, therefore, reflects the kinematic and static performance of the arm.

Because the robotic arm is a general purpose spatial actuation system as was mentioned above, the degree of homogeneity of the transformation by J is essential in evaluating its manipulation performance. The more homogeneous the transformation is, the more easily fine motion and fine force control can be implemented in the workspace coordinates. In order for the manipulation skill to be achieved successfully, the transformation has to be as homogeneous as possible.

The range of dp when $d\theta$ takes values satisfying

$$|d\theta| \leq 1 \tag{7}$$

is an ellipsoid which is called a maniputability ellipsoid [Yoshikawa, 1983]. The homogeneity of the transformation can be measured by the shape of the ellipsoid; the homogeneity is high when the shape is near to a sphere. The shape of the ellipsoid can be studied by the singular value decomposition [Iri et al., 1982]. The condition number is an index for the measurement of the homogeneity of the ellipsoid.

Let the singular values of J be denoted by $\sigma_1 \geq \sigma_2 \geq \cdots \geq \sigma_m \geq 0$. The maximum singular value σ_1 have an upper limit σ_u and a lower limit σ_l which are determined by the link proportion, i.e.

$$\sigma_u \geq \sigma_1 \geq \sigma_l. \tag{8}$$

This means that the ellipsoid apsis is in the region between two concentric spheres of which radii are σ_u and σ_l. This is illustrated in Figure 1. Under the circumstances, the shape of the ellipsoid becomes round when its volume is large. Therefore, the volume can be an index of the manipulation performance.

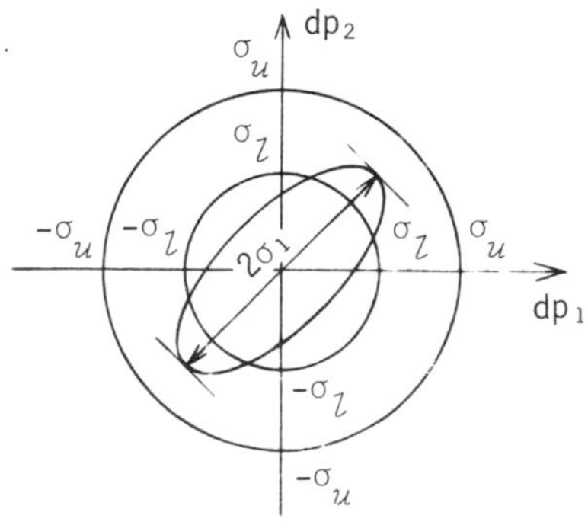

Figure 1. Relationship between the shape and the volume of the maniputability ellipsoid.

For non-redundant manipulators, i.e. for the case that m=n, the volume of the ellipsoid is directly proportional to $|\det J|$, which is shown as follows:

Squaring each side of inequality (7) and substituting

$$d\theta = J^{-1}dp \tag{9}$$

which is from (5), we obtain

$$dp'J^{-1\prime}J^{-1}dp \leq 1 \tag{10}$$

where $J^{-1\prime}J^{-1}$ is positive definite and symmetric. It is calculated at any other point than singular points. By an appropriate orthogonal transformation:

$$d\tilde{p} = Udp, \tag{11}$$

(10) is transformed to

$$\sum_{i=1}^{m} \lambda_i \tilde{p}_i^{\,2} \leq 1 \tag{12}$$

where λ_i is the ith eigenvalue of $J^{-1\prime}J^{-1}$ and $\lambda_i = 1/\sigma_i^{\,2} > 0$. The transformation by (11) does not change the ellipsoid volume which is calculated as

$$V_m = \frac{\sqrt{\pi}^{\,m}}{\Gamma(\frac{m}{2}+1)} \prod_{i=1}^{m} \frac{1}{\sqrt{\lambda_i}} . \tag{13}$$

Because λ_i is the eigenvalue of $J^{-1\prime}J^{-1}$,

$$\prod_{i=1}^{m} \lambda_i = \det(J^{-1\prime}J^{-1}) = (\det J)^{-2}. \tag{14}$$

From (13) and (14), we obtain

$$V_m = \frac{\sqrt{\pi}^{\,m}}{\Gamma(\frac{m}{2}+1)} |\det J| , \tag{15}$$

which takes the minimum value at singular points which are excluded in the above derivation.

Now, it has been shown that the Jacobian can be an index for the evaluation of manipulation performance; the performance is evaluated high where $|\det J|$ takes large value.

3. DISTRIBUTION OF THE JACOBIAN IN THE WORKSPACE

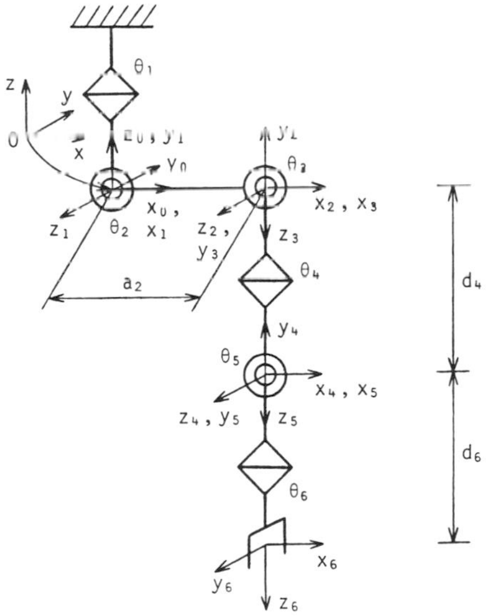

Figure 2. Link mechanism of D-HAND.

Table 1. Link parameters for D-HAND.

i	a_i	d_i	α_i	Variable
1	0 mm	0 mm	90°	θ_1
2	300 mm	0 mm	0°	θ_2
3	0 mm	0 mm	90°	θ_3
4	0 mm	300 mm	-90°	θ_4
5	0 mm	0 mm	90°	θ_5
6	0 mm	d_6	0°	θ_6

The Jacobian evaluates the manipulation performance of a robotic arm at each point in the workspace, and the distribution of its value in the whole workspace gives an overall understanding of the mechanical characteristics of the arm. Therefore, in order to utilize the Jacobian for the design and control of the arm, it is essential that its distribution be calculated and displayed. However, it is difficult to display the distribution over the whole workspace in an intuitively intelligible way because the Jacobian is a function of the vector p of which dimension is usually 6. One way to display the distribution is to do it on a cutting plane of the workspace. Color graphics display, three-dimensional display [Uchiyama et al., 1983], etc. may be utilized for visualizing the distribution on the plane. The color graphics display is an excellent way as man-machine interface for such application as the CAD of robotic mechanisms.

In the following of this section, numerical examples of the color graphics display are presented for two different types of articulated robotic arms, with some comments and comparison of two arms based on the results also presented at the end. The arms for numerical examples are the Tokico ET-101 electric manipulator and the Hitachi A6030 assembly robot. The former has been developed for research use [Uchiyama, 1979], and is called D-HAND. The link mechanisms of D-HAND and A6030 are shown in Figure 2 and Figure 3, respectively. The link parameters by Denavit-Hartenberg notation [Paul, 1981] are also listed in Table 1 and Table 2, respectively.

For both arms, the position vector in the joint coordinates is

$$\theta = (\theta_1, \theta_2, \cdots, \theta_6)' \tag{16}$$

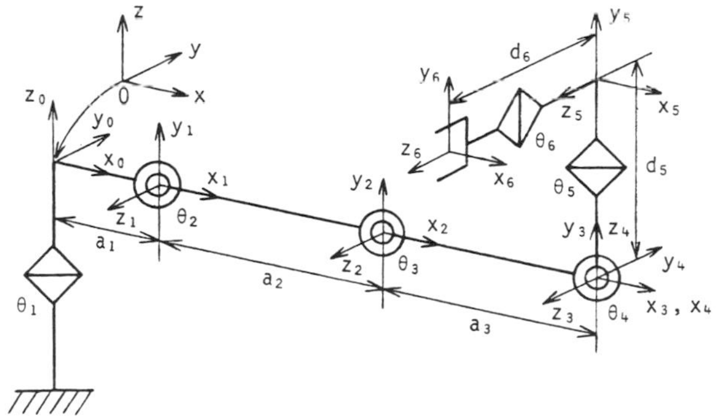

Figure 3. Link mechanism of A6030.

Table 2. Link parameters for A6030.

i	a_i	d_i	α_i	Variable
1	45 mm	0 mm	90°	θ_1
2	400 mm	0 mm	0°	θ_2
3	400 mm	0 mm	0°	θ_3
4	0 mm	0 mm	-90°	θ_4
5	0 mm	130 mm	90°	θ_5
6	0 mm	100 mm	0°	θ_6

We assume $\theta_1, \theta_2, \cdots, \theta_6$ have no limit in their ranges. The workspace coordinates are the position and orientation of the hand in the Cartesian coordinates O-xyz which is shown in Figure 2 and Figure 3, respectively. The position vector in the workspace coordinates is

$$p = (x, y, z, \alpha, \beta, \gamma)' \tag{17}$$

where x, y, and z are the position coordinates of the origin of $O_6\text{-}x_6y_6z_6$ described in O-xyz, and α, β, and γ are the orientation angles of $O_6\text{-}x_6y_6z_6$ against O-xyz as shown in Figure 4 (a). Changes of the position and orientation of the O-xyz frame do not change the value of the Jacobian. Therefore, analysis using the Jacobian based on the workspace coordinates has generality. The differential changes $d\alpha$, $d\beta$, and $d\gamma$ are defined as shown in Figure 4 (b): they are small rotations around each axis. The difinition is not faithful to the mathematical definition of the differential, but is preferable because it makes the duality relation between velocity and force clear as represented in (5) and (6).

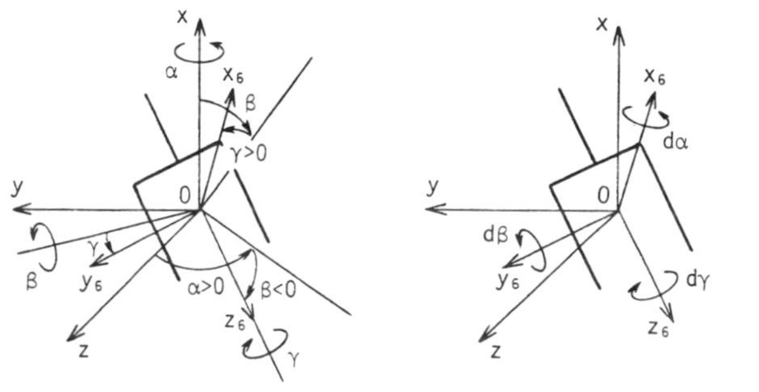

(a) Orientation angles (b) Differential changes

Figure 4. Definition of the hand orientation angles and their differential changes.

Based upon the above definition of the workspace coordinates and their differential changes, the Jacobian is calculated analytically for each arm: for D-HAND

$$\det J = a_2 d_4 (a_2 c_2 + d_4 s_{23}) c_3 s_5 \tag{18}$$

and for A6030

$$\det J = a_2 a_3 (a_1 + a_2 c_2 + a_3 c_{23} - d_5 s_{234}) s_3 s_5 \tag{19}$$

where $c_i = \cos\theta_i$, $s_i = \sin\theta_i$, $c_{23} = \cos(\theta_2+\theta_3)$, $s_{23} = \sin(\theta_2+\theta_3)$, and $s_{234} = \sin(\theta_2+\theta_3+\theta_4)$. It is known from equations (18) and (19) that, for both arms, the distribution of the detJ value is symmetric with respect to the z axis and does not depend on the orientation angle γ. The distribution is a function of x, z, α, and β.

In addition, detJ for the same p takes different values because there are several ways of the arm solution θ for the same p. For both arms, there are eight ways of the solution which are numbered systematically by

$$\Delta = (1-\delta_1)2 + (1-\delta_2) + (1-\delta_3)2^{-1} + 1 \tag{20}$$

from 1 through 8, where δ_1, δ_2, and δ_3 are defined as, for D-HAND

$$\delta_1 = \mathrm{sgn}(a_2 c_2 + d_4 s_{23}) \tag{21a}$$
$$\delta_2 = \mathrm{sgn}(c_3) \tag{21b}$$
$$\delta_3 = \mathrm{sgn}(s_5) \tag{21c}$$

and for A6030

$$\delta_1 = \mathrm{sgn}(a_1 + a_2 c_2 + a_3 c_{23} - d_5 s_{234}) \tag{22a}$$
$$\delta_2 = \mathrm{sgn}(s_3) \tag{22b}$$
$$\delta_3 = \mathrm{sgn}(s_5) \tag{22c}$$

Consequently, the $|\det J|$ distribution is displayed on the (x,z) plane or on the (α,β) plane where Δ and the other variable pair are parameters. Examples are shown in Figure 5 and Figure 6 for D-HAND and A6030, respectively. In both cases, four examples: two on the (x,z) plane and two on the (α,β) plane are presented. The value of $|\det J|$ is normalized by its maximum value and represented by the color codes shown at the right-hand side of each picture. The number at the upper left corner are the solution numbers calculated by equation (20).

The position and orientation which are advantageous to manipulation tasks are known by the figures. By comparing (a) and (b) of the figures, it is noted that, for A6030, the advantageous region of the hand position is divided into only two parts, i.e. both sides of the z axis, whilst the region for D-HAND is further divided into two parts on both sides of the z axis. It is known from this observation that A6030 is more advantageous than D-HAND to moving on the (x,z) plane with constant hand orientation. It is also noted that the advantageous region and the disadvantageous region are complementary for different ways of the arm solution. The selection of an appropriate way of the arm solution in programming robot tasks is very important to improving manipulation performance.

4. APPLICATION TO TRAJECTORY PLANNING

In planning robot tasks, the trajectory of arm motion has to be set as far as possible in the region where high manipulation performance is achieved. The manipulation performance is measured by $|\det J|$ as has been shown in the foregoing, and it is high where $|\det J|$ takes large value. Consequently, the trajectory has to be planned so as for $|\det J|$ along it to take as large value as possible. Allowing for it, the performance index:

$$\text{I.P.} = \int_{P_0}^{P_1} \frac{ds}{|\det J|} \tag{23}$$

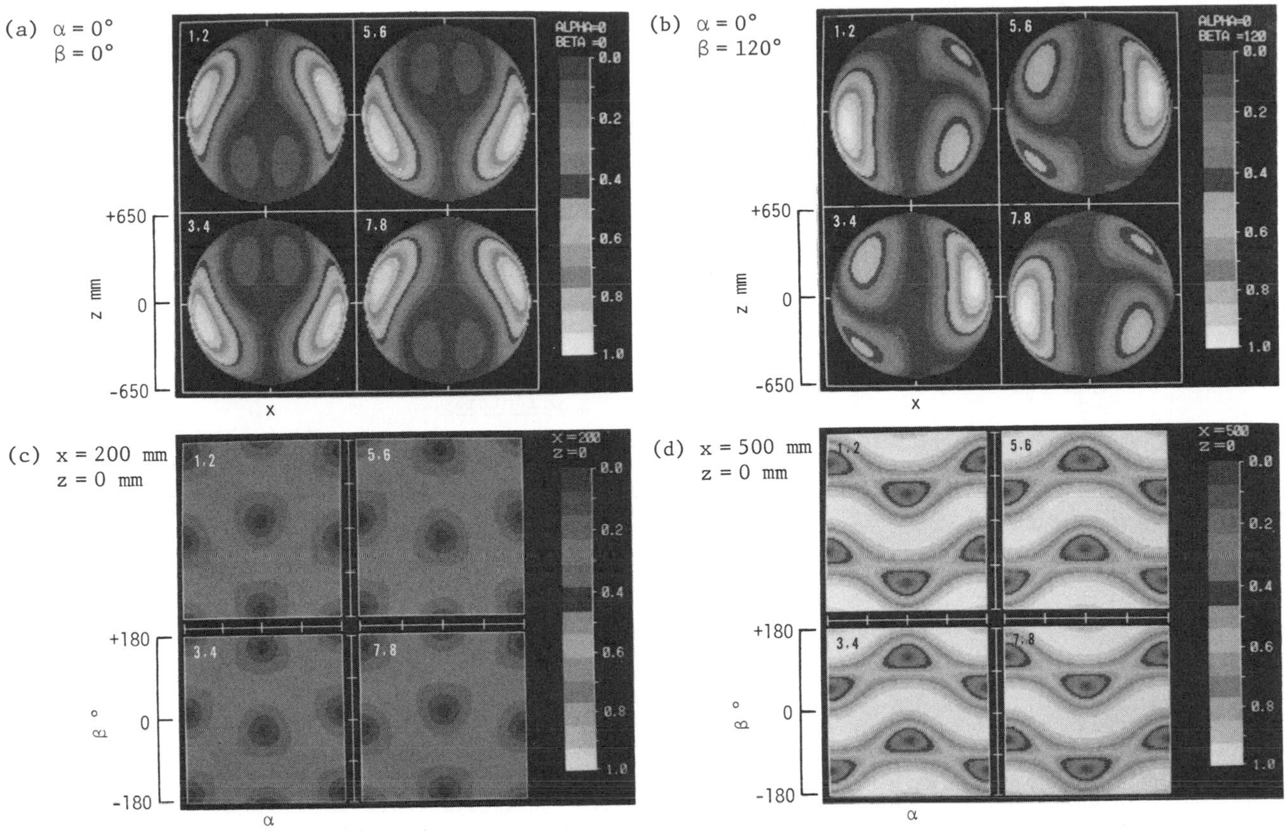

Figure 5. Color graphics display of the |det J| distribution for D-HAND.

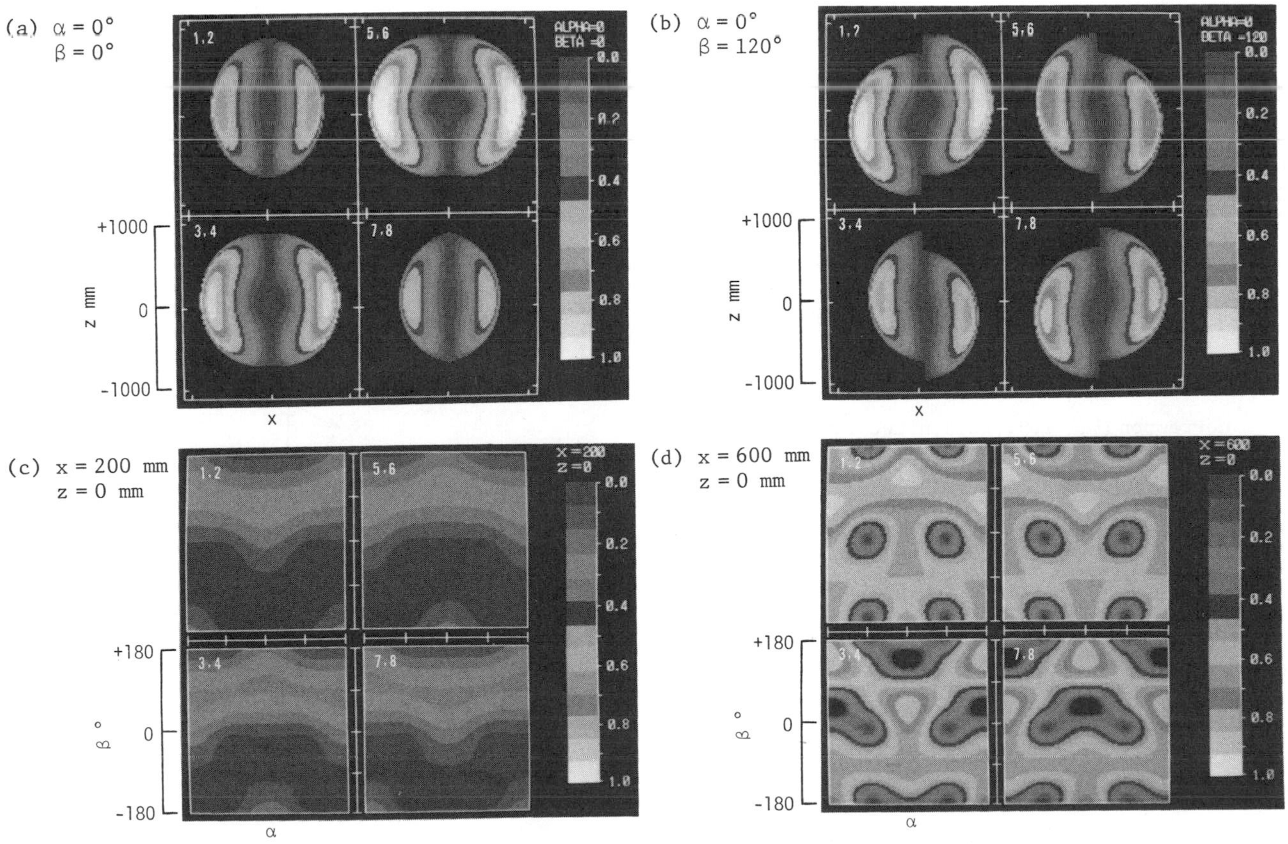

Figure 6. Color graphics display of the |det J| distribution for A6030.

is constructed using $|\det J|$, where P_0 and P_1 are a start point and a terminal point, respectively, and ds is the differential distance along the trajectory. The optimal trajectory is calculated so that I.P. may take the minimum value.

In robot tasks, the position and orientation of the end effector are often constrained, e.g. in carrying a glass filled with water without spilling the water, the hand orientation has to be kept constant during the task. Let write the constraints imposed generally as

$$\left.\begin{array}{l} f_1(p_1, p_2, \cdots, p_m) = 0 \\ f_2(p_1, p_2, \cdots, p_m) = 0 \\ \vdots \\ f_\ell(p_1, p_2, \cdots, p_m) = 0 \end{array}\right\} . \qquad (24)$$

Under the above constraints, the $(m-\ell)$ independent workspace coordinates are determined so that I.P. may take the minimum value. The procedure generates a kinematically resonable trajectory which satisfies the constraints imposed by the task.

The problem formulated above is that of calculus of variations with constraint conditions. To obtain the exact solution for the problem is difficult even by numerical methods. Therefore, in this paper, an approximate solution is calculated by a random search method.

The $(m-\ell)$ independent workspace coordinates are described by polynomials of a parameter t which does not necessarily represent time. Let the workspace coordinates be denoted by p_i $(i=1,2,\cdots,m-\ell)$ and the polynomials be written as

$$p_i(t) = \sum_{j=1}^{N} a_{ij} t^j . \qquad (25)$$

I.P. is a function of the coefficients a_{ij}. The optimal solution of a_{ij} is searched by the following algorithm [Nair, 1978]:

(1) Assume initial values of a_{ij} and evaluate I.P. for them. Let the initial values and the corresponding I.P. be denoted by $a_{ij}^{(0)}$ and $\mathrm{I.P.}^{(0)}$, respectively.

(2) Compute search points by $a_{ij}^{(k)} = a_{ij}^{(0)} + bx_{ij}^{(k)}$ $(k=1,2,\cdots,K)$ where b is the radius of search range, $x_{ij}^{(k)}$ is a random number between -0.5 and +0.5, and K is the number of search points.

(3) Evaluate I.P. for each set of $a_{ij}^{(k)}$ and let it be denoted $\mathrm{I.P.}^{(k)}$.

(4) Let $\mathrm{I.P.}^{(m)} = \min_k(\mathrm{I.P.}^{(k)})$ and go to (6) if $\mathrm{I.P.}^{(0)} > \mathrm{I.P.}^{(m)}$. Otherwise, go to the next step.

(5) Let b=0.6b and go to (2).

(6) If $|\mathrm{I.P.}^{(0)} - \mathrm{I.P.}^{(m)}| < \varepsilon$, terminate. Otherwise, let $a_{ij}^{(0)} = a_{ij}^{(m)}$ and $\mathrm{I.P.}^{(0)} = \mathrm{I.P.}^{(m)}$, and go to (2). ε is a small positive quantity for stopping the search.

Two numerical examples of trajectory planning by the above algorithm using I.P. is presented below. The robotic manipulator for the examples is A6030 of which joints are supposed to have no limit of range. The solution number defined by (20) is given a priori for both cases.

A. Moving Between Two Points With Constant Hand Orientation

The motion of this example is illustrated in Figure 7. The hand moves from P_0 to P_1 with holding its orientation constant. Glass-carrying is an example of this sort of motion. The position vectors at P_0 and P_1 in the workspace coordinates are

$$(-400\text{mm}, -300\text{mm}, 300\text{mm}, 180°, 0°, 0°)' \qquad (26)$$

and

$$(400\text{mm}, 300\text{mm}, 100\text{mm}, 180°, 0°, 0°)', \qquad (27)$$

respectively. There is a singular point on the straight line connecting P_0 and P_1. The constraint conditions are

$$\alpha = 180° \qquad (28a)$$

$$\beta = 0° \qquad (28b)$$

$$\gamma = 0° . \qquad (28c)$$

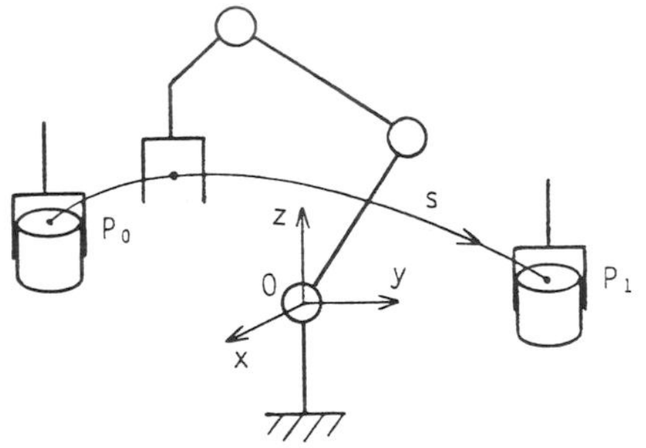

Figure 7. Moving between two points with constant hand orientation.

x, y, and z are approximated by the polynomials of 6th degree:

$$x(t) = \sum_{i=0}^{6} a_i t^i \qquad (29a)$$

$$y(t) = \sum_{i=0}^{6} b_i t^i \quad (29b)$$

$$z(t) = \sum_{i=0}^{6} c_i t^i \quad (29c)$$

where $0 \le t \le 1$. $x(t)$, $y(t)$, and $z(t)$ satisfy the boundary conditions (26) and (27) at $t=0$ and 1, respectively. The trajectory obtained is illustrated in Figure 8 which was drawn by a computer. The solution number Δ for this case is 3. It is noted that the singular point is successfully avoided.

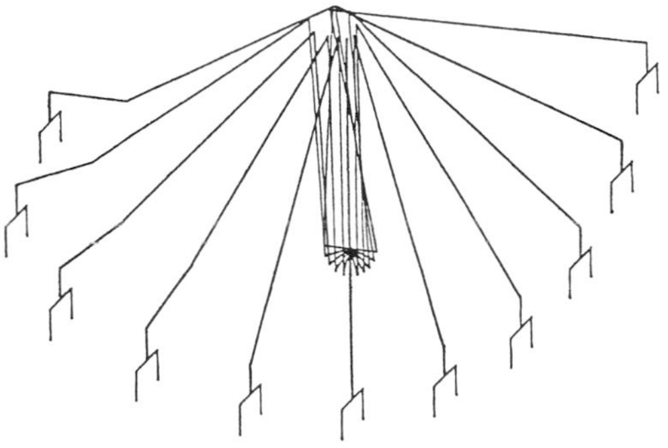

Figure 8. Optimal trajectory for the motion of Figure 7.

B. Turning a Crank

In this example, the hand position and orientation are constrained by those of the crank grip. The crank is placed in the workspace horizontally as shown in Figure 9. The position vector of the crank origin is

$$(x_0, y_0, z_0)' = (500\text{mm}, 0\text{mm}, 0\text{mm})', \quad (30)$$

and the crank radius is

$$r = 200 \text{ mm}. \quad (31)$$

The crank trajectory is written as

$$x = x_0 + r\cos 2\pi t \quad (32a)$$

$$y = y_0 + r\sin 2\pi t \quad (32b)$$

$$z = z_0 \quad (32c)$$

where $0 \le t \le 1$. The above equations are the constraint conditions imposed on the hand position. The other constraint conditions are on the hand orientation. Two of the three orientation angles of the hand against the crank grip, i.e. α_c and β_c in Figure 10, are chosen independently on the grip orientation. The other one γ_c which is also shown in Figure 10 is determined uniquely by the grip orientation. The angle β_c cannot be changed during the task, whilst α_c can be changed freely. Consequently, the constraint conditions on the hand orientation are

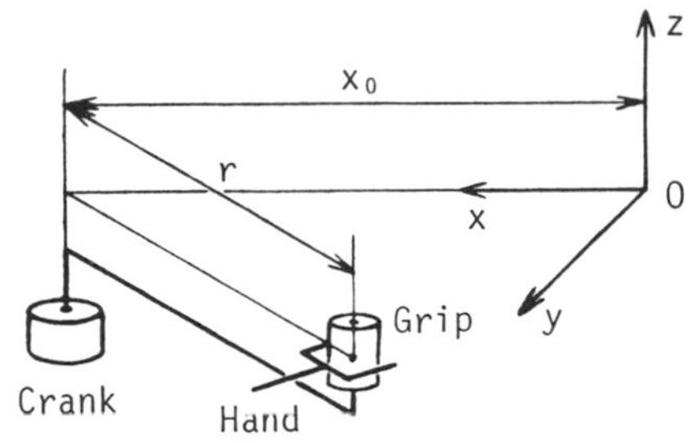

Figure 9. Crank position and orientation.

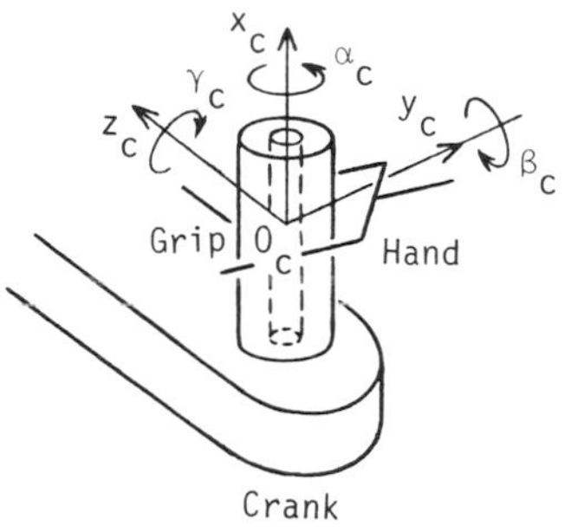

Figure 10. Hand orientation against a grip.

$$\beta_c = \beta_0 \quad (33a)$$

$$\gamma_c = 0° \quad (33b)$$

where β_0 is an arbitrary constant value.

Under the constraint conditions (32) and (33), the hand orientation are calculated for two different cases: one is for the case that the hand orientation against the base frame is held constant during the task, and the other is for the case that α_c is moved freely. For the former case, the optimal set of values of α and β is determined using I.P. and γ is calculated from the values determined, where α, β, and γ are the hand orientation angles as has been defined in Figure 4 (a). For the latter case, α_c is approximated by the polynomial of 7th degree:

$$\alpha_c(t) = \sum_{i=0}^{7} a_i t^i \quad (34)$$

where $0 \le t \le 1$. The boundary conditions for $\alpha_c(t)$ are

$$\alpha_c(0) = \alpha_c(1), \ \dot{\alpha}_c(0) = \dot{\alpha}_c(1) \text{ and } \ddot{\alpha}_c(0) = \ddot{\alpha}_c(1). \quad (35)$$

The coefficients a_i and the value of β_0 are determined using I.P. and the above boundary conditions. The results for both cases are shown in Figure 11. The solution number Δ for both cases is 2. The change of $|\det J|$ along the obtained trajectories are also shown in Figure 12. It is seen that, on average, $|\det J|$ for the latter case

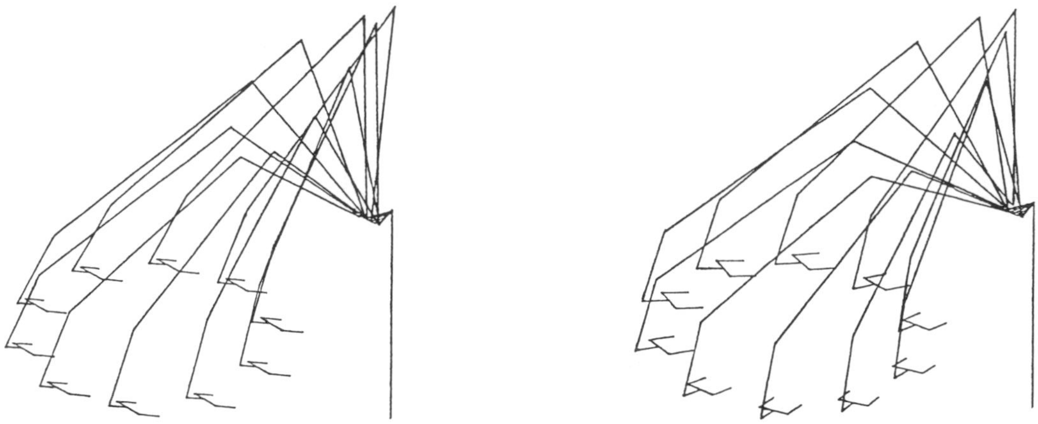

(a) α, β, γ: constant (b) α_c: free

Figure 11. Optimal trajectories for crank turning.

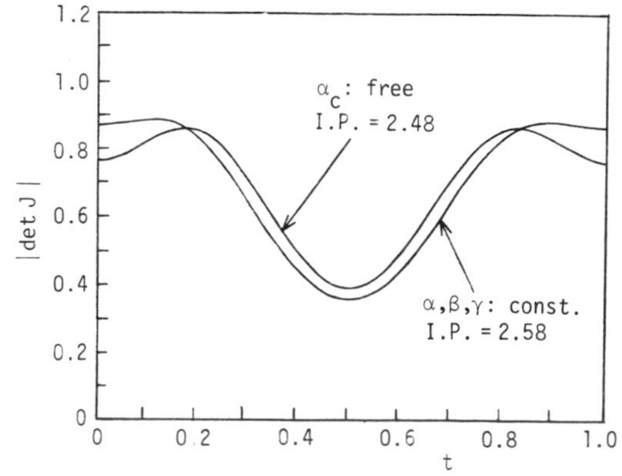

Figure 12. Change of $|\det J|$ along crank-turning trajectories.

is larger than that for the former case, which means that the trajectory for the latter case is kinematically more reasonable.

5. CONCLUDING REMARKS

The use of the Jacobian as an index for the quantitative evaluation of manipulator performance at a point in the workspace has been proposed, and its mathematical background, means to display the distribution of the values the index takes in the workspace, and application to trajectory planning have been presented.

Numerical results of the distribution which are visualized on a color graphics display have illustrated that the index is a proper measure to evaluate mechanical characteristics of manipulators within the workspace and also have suggested the future application of the display method as man-machine interface to the CAD of manipulators.

Through the application to trajectory planning, it has been shown that, using the index, automatic singular point avoidance or determination of the working orientation of a hand can be implemented. The method generates kinematically reasonable trajectories.

Future research will be directed to selection of ways of the arm solution or determination of the working position of a locomotive manipulator using the index. Integration of the index with other performance indices will also be studied to provide a basis on which intelligent robotic systems are constructed.

REFERENCES

Iri, M., Kodama, S. and Suda, N. 1982. Singular Value Decomposition and Its Applications to Control System Theory. Journal of the Society of Instrument and Control Engineers, Vol. 21, No. 8, pp. 763-772.

Nair, G. G. 1978. Suboptimal Control of Nonlinear Systems. Automatica, Vol. 14, No. 5, pp. 517-519.

Paul, R. P. 1981. Robot Manipulators: Mathematics, Programming, and Control. Cambridge, Massachusetts, The MIT Press, pp. 50-55.

Salisbury, J. K. and Craig, J. J. 1982. Articulated Hands: Force Control and Kinematic Issues. Int. J. of Robotics Research, Vol. 1, No. 1, pp. 4-17.

Uchiyama, M. 1979. A Study of Computer Control of Motion of a Mechanical Arm (1st-3rd Reports). Bulletin of the JSME, Vol. 22, No. 173, pp. 1640-1664.

Uchiyama, M., Hakomori, K. and Shimizu, K. 1983 Nov. 10-12. Performance Evaluation of Robotic Arm Mechanisms Using the Jacobian. Prepr. of the 26th Joint Conference of Automatic Control, Tokyo, Japan, pp. 231-232.

Yoshikawa, T. 1983 Aug.28-Sept.2. Analysis and Control of Robot Manipulators with Redundancy. 1st Int. Symp. of Robotics Research, Bretton Woods, New Hampshire, USA.

V PANEL DISCUSSIONS

9 Robotics for Future Industry

Design Concept of Factory Automation Systems

Minoru Morita
Matsushita Electric Industrial Co., Ltd.
Corporate Production Engineering Division
2-7, Matsuba-cho, Kadoma, Osaka 571, Japan

Predicting what automated production lines will be like several years from now is difficult. Moreover, insisting upon one specific production line system may result in serious problem. When considering factory automation of the future, therefore, the way we formulate the system's concept will be the key. This paper describes some of my views concerning the design concepts of factory automation systems.

1. Introduction

Phenomenal changes have occurred since around 1980. It is commonly understood now that, as one of such changes, the rapid market expansion of the '70s was checked and the market is now in a more stable growth period.

The production system must fit these circumstances. If production doubles every year as was seen in the high growth period, an automated production system that matches the growth can be adapted to improve efficiency. In a stable, or more precisely, low growth period, the size of the market remains almost unchanged. Even if a company could increase its production capacity, the increase would result only from gaining a larger share of the limited market. This inevitably limits the growth rate to around 10 percent at best.

Consequently, the ability of coping effectively with production variations of less than 10 percent will become more important. In terms of "production equipment," this translates into improving the operating rate of the fixed costs.

Viewing the market as simply one entity is not harmful to businesses in a high growth period. But such a view is out of place today. Scrutinizing the market -- the market's composition in detail -- provides important insights.

In addition to the quantitative aspects of change, we must not overlook equally important changes in the qualitative aspects due to technological innovations. Recently, pronounced growth has been recorded in certain fields such as semiconductors and VTRs where man's ingenuity and proficiency fail. In other words, these are fields made possible by automated machines developed from new technology. In this situation, the qualities required for the operator change. That is, the importance shifts from the proficiency of skill to the ability of controlling such automatic machines so that they will perform well.

Another important thing to mention is "timing." It is frequently said that any business can flow with the tide when the economy is expanding rapidly. But in a low growth period, it is difficult or risky to construct new plants, for example, every year. If a development in the production process is initiated behind schedule, the introduction of the process in a new plant will be postponed no matter how magnificient the process is. The increasingly longer intervals between new plant constructions may cause some production processes to be obsolete before they are instituted. This will cause the money and labor invested in the development of production processes to be wasted. We must admit that we face some definite hardships in this low growth period.

2. Requirements for Factory Automation

Factory automation has long been a means of reducing costs and increasing quality. By considering factory automation in the context described above, it is obvious that we must assume a fresh approach to factory automation to meet the needs of the times. In other words, factory automation systems must meet the following three requirements.

1) Production know-how should be implemented in the automatic production system.
2) The automatic production system should be flexible to meet changes.
3) The automatic production system should harmonize with human activity so that human resources can be fully utilized.

3. Design Concept of Factory Automation Systems

The term "Flexible Manufacturing System (FMS)" (in which robots will play the major role) is frequently used in these days. This tendency sounds good because we have to meet today's needs. However, it seems to us that those who advocate such systems satisfy themselves simply by mentioning the term FMS.

In my childhood, I did not imagine that man could go to the moon. The moon was a beautiful satellite which was frequently mentioned in fairy tales. Children of today, however, never doubt that humans can go to the moon. Since the times are changing in this way, predicting what automated production lines will be like several years from now is difficult. Moreover, insisting on one specific production line system may result in serious problems. Therefore, how to define the system design concept of the factory automation system (FAS) is a very important problem when we consider the factory automation system.

At present, much effort is being exerted in the development of new fundamental and original technology on which FAS is based on. If the concept is not properly determined, the technology cannot be fully utilized.

- FAS should be constituted so that it can accept rapidly-advancing technology without making many changes.
- Automatic machines in a system should function properly when they are used independently and when they are incorporated in a production line without disturbing the line.
- It seems to us that FAS has some basic problems in terms of concept, particularly in regard to the basic functions of machine modules, control network, data communication, interface, and the relationship between the "intelligent" devices, sensors and control systems.

4. Closing

Any production system should be kept up-to-date by daily maintenance. Therefore, the factory automation system or flexible manufacturing system should be flexible so that the system can accept new technology. We believe that this is the basic problem to be solved.

VIEWS ON ROBOTICS FOR FUTURE INDUSTRY

Masakazu EJIRI

Central Research Laboratory,
Hitachi Ltd.,
Kokubunji, Tokyo 185, Japan

A few personal views on future directions for pursuing robotic research more realistically and fruitfully are discussed from the viewpoints of three essential robot capabilities; task-understanding, vision, and decision-making. Especially in vision, it is suggested that more research should be directed to inspection problems, in conjunction with the efforts to realize new sensors and powerful image processors for gray/color images by the use of VLSI/ULSI techniques. Investigation of how to integrate CAD data with robot systems may be another key problem in future robotics.

INTRODUCTION

As suggested in my earlier paper on the prototype intelligent robot [Ejiri et al, 1972], three types of functions seem to be essential for realizing intelligent machines. One is a "task understanding" function to enable the robot to determine the task objectives as communicated by the instruction of the human operator. The second is a "recognition" function that allows the robot to determine the outside world through vision or other sensors. The third is a "decision-making" function that enables the robot to work on the outside world, based on the objectives and conditions recognized through the first and second functions, respectively. The relations between these functions are summarized in Fig. 1.

In this article, my personal view on future robotics in industry are described in relation to these three functions. Since my research effort for the past 20 years has been focused on vision and its application, more stress is placed on the second capability than on the other two functions. The current state of the art for robotics is also described, together with certain recent achievements.

TASK UNDERSTANDING

In general, the man-machine interface is difficult, regardless of what the machine is. As the machine becomes more intelligent, the easier and more efficient communication is expected to be between man and machine. In early robots, and even in today's robot, each instruction the human gave had one-to-one correspondence with machine movement, such as in the case of direct teaching or machine-code programming. Since robot movement is usually sequential, these sequential instruction methods have an intrinsic advantage. However, from the viewpoint of adaptability to a new task with minimum overhead in production changeover, a more efficient scheme is desirable. Robot programming languages are the result of such demand, and are finding wide use in today's industrial robots.

These rather low-level languages, however, do not significantly lessen the burden on the robot programmer or operator. A higher-level language, one that does not normally depend on one-to-one correspondence to machine motion, will be expected of future robotics. With such a language approach, the ultimate goal is always the recognition and understanding of natural language, which is the highest and most familiar language to the human.

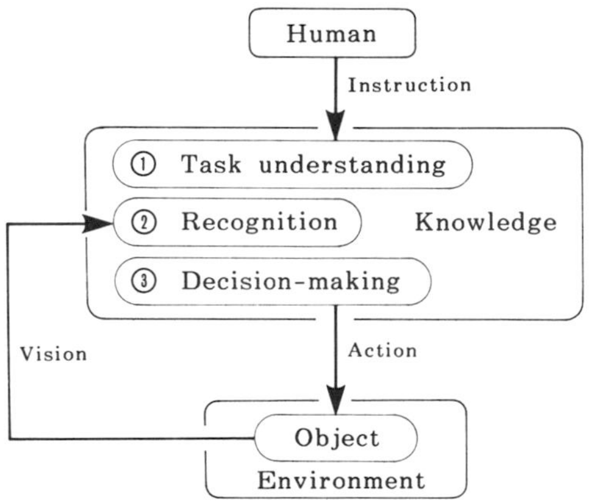

Fig. 1 Basic functions of an intelligent machine.

The ideal goal in instructing robots is to only give the objective of the task the human wants the robot to do, rather than giving a precise description of the task. The sequential motion to achieve the given objective should be automatically analized, and the best sequence of motion to achieve the task should be generated by the robots. However, the higher the instruction level becomes, the more ambiguity is apt to be encountered in the instruction. Therefore, we have to very carefully determine the limitations of the language approach.

To describe the objective in a macroscopic way, a pictorial method, such as that shown in Fig. 2, may be an alternative. It can be utilized in conjunction with a language. This pictorial method was first suggested in my previous paper, in which the assembly of simple blocks by means of assembly drawings was attempted. Recently, the recognition of drawings is again receiving attention, and automatic digitizers for engineering drawings are being developed as initial input devices for CAD [Kakumoto et al, 1983], [Ejiri et al, 1984]. A schematic of one such digitizer is shown in Fig. 3. This device utilizes line and contour tracking methods to yield coded data for further processing in a subsequent CAD process. An example of coding by automatic digitizer is shown in Fig. 4.

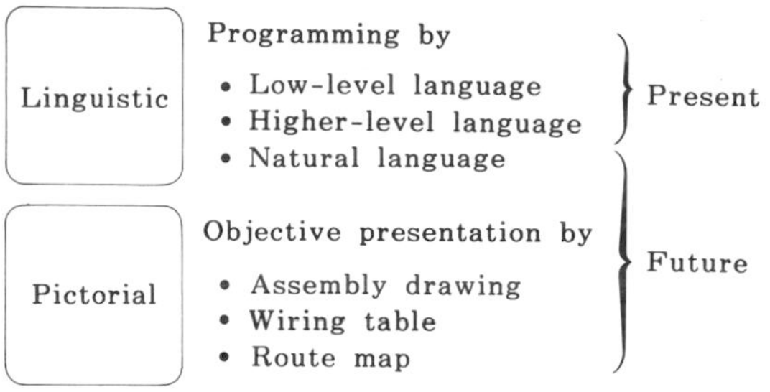

Fig. 2 Instruction methods for robots.

These approaches may make it possible to realize the intelligent manufacturing systems conceived in the above-mentioned paper, with the CAD data directly connected to the manufacturing process. Therefore, the effort to integrate CAD-processed data directly with robot systems may be most fruitful in future robotics. If this can be realized, a true FMS may be within our reach.

VISUAL RECOGNITION

The second function that a future intelligent machine should have is recognition of the outside world in order to adapt itself to changes in object position and orientation, as well as to changes in other environmental conditions.

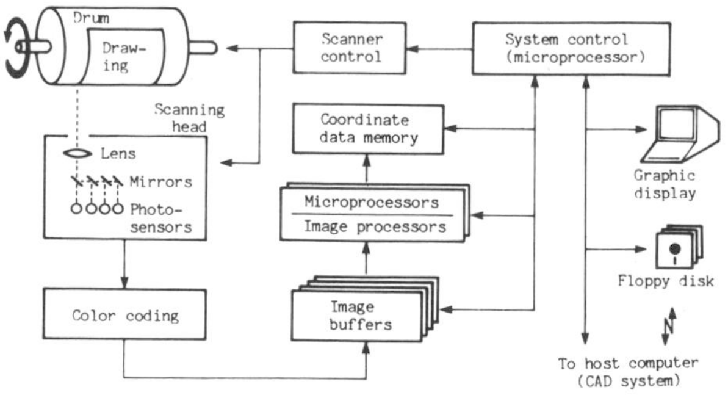

Fig. 3 Schematic of an automatic digitizer for color drawings.

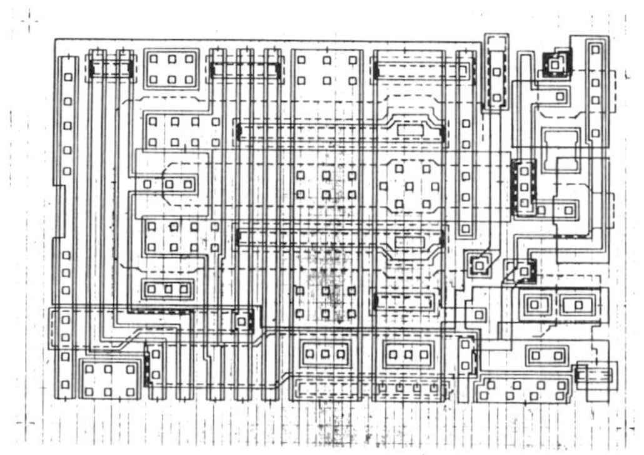

(a) Input drawing (LSI cell diagram): original;color.

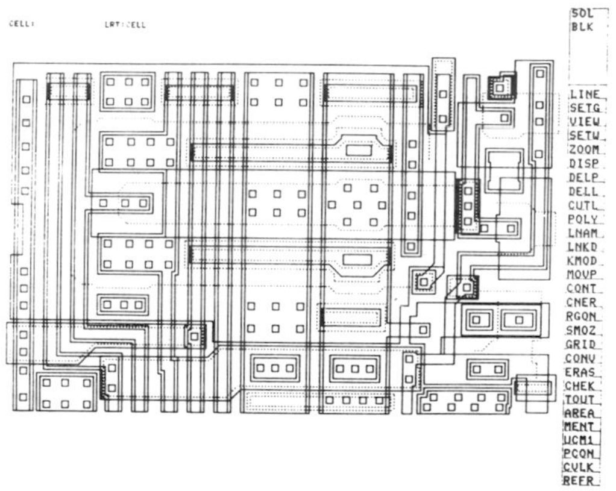

(b) Result of coding: printed CRT image.

Fig. 4 An example of coding by the automatic digitizer.

State of the art of vision

Similar to the way eyesight plays an important role in human life, there is no doubt that a vision system will be a requisite for sophisticated robot systems in the future. A tremendous amount of research and development has been conducted to date along these lines. Such vision techniques are now being well-developed, especially in the semiconductor field, and many fruitful achievements can be seen in automating the production processes. One typical example is the wire-bonding process in LSI manufacturing. However, these are rather special-purpose vision applications dedicated to specific missions. No concrete and clear way to realize general-purpose vision systems, such as for industrial robots, has been reported in the past 20 years of robotics research.

The purpose of vision is to observe the external world and to recognize objects. Objects are three-dimensional, and usually have three aspects of features to be recognized. These are summarized in Table 1. As shown in that table, recognition of these features is regarded as key technologies in such essential production processes as classification, assembly and inspection. Numerous efforts have been devoted to this area, and a few typical vision techniques are now finding use in some of the application fields indicated in the table.

In general, vision in robotics necessitates a tremendous amount of image processing to yield a final result. Therefore, to realize useful vision device, high-speed image processing is an important key. One method of obtaining high-speed processing capability is to reduce the processing to a two-dimensional problem by limiting the attitude of the three-dimensional objects. In this case, the vision from one direction can be used to find all information required for subsequent tasks.

If we adopt this concept extensively from the beggining of product design, there is a possibility that we can even eliminate the vision requirement from complicated assembly tasks, thus obtaining low-cost automation systems. Assembly of VTRs is a typical example of what can be designed from the beginning to make one-directional assembly possible. Here, every component can be assembled from the vertical direction, thus more than 85 per cent of the total assembly can be automated by simple SCARA-type pick-and-place robots without using vision. This is one positive solution to the problem of the present costly vision systems. A fairly large number of products can make use of such vertical assembly, if we analyze the product function and consider possible assembly sequences.

Another method of obtaining high-speed capability is to threshold the image data into binary form in an early stage of processing. This can convert the image processing scheme from one including arithmetic calculations into one consisting mainly of logical operations. Using this method, special-purpose logical circuits can be utilized as the image processor. Thus, both high-speed processing and cost effectiveness can be achieved.

Along these lines, many floating-type thresholding techniques have been studied to obtain adaptive thresholding that copes with changes in illumination conditions. The two-dimensional local memory shown in Fig. 5 provides a method to access multiple pixels simultaneously. In addition, logical filters can be combined with this local memory to extract pattern features and parameters in the real-time mode. Some examples of such logical filters are shown in Fig. 6.

These basic principles can be combined for certain applications in industry, as previously shown in Table 1; however, as mentioned above, most of these applications are still restricted to dedicated systems.

Method of providing vision

It seems, at present, that vision methods can be classified into four categories from the viewpoint of actual industrial applications:

Table 1. Object features and examples of usage

Feature category		Main usage	Typical method	Examples
Geometric features	Shape Size	Classification	Parameter extraction	Diode chip, Cucumber, Fish, Tablet, Capsule, etc.
	Position Orientation	Assembly	Pattern matching Windowing Slit-light	Semiconductor, Bolting robot, Pump-hose robot, Welding, Sealing, etc.
Qualitative features	Flaws and cracks (Blur) (Color tone) (Texture)	Inspection	Expansion and contraction Feature matching Size measurement Two-chip comparison	Printed board, IC, LSI, Photomask, Fruits, Solder joint, Black matrix, etc.
Supplemental features	Figures Symbols Marks	Sorting	Feature extraction Pattern matching	Character reader, Mark reader.

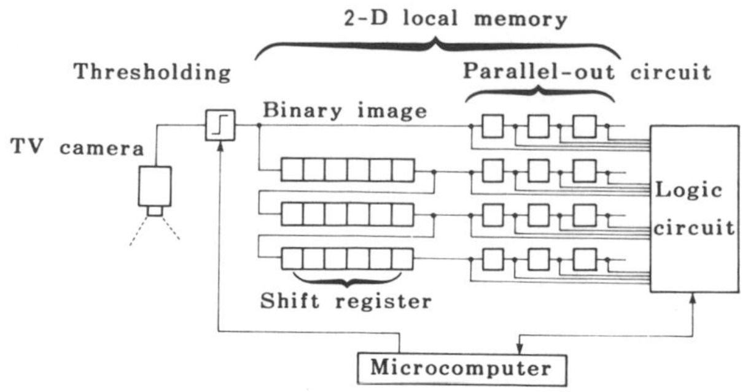

Fig. 5 A simple image processor utilizing 2-D local memory.

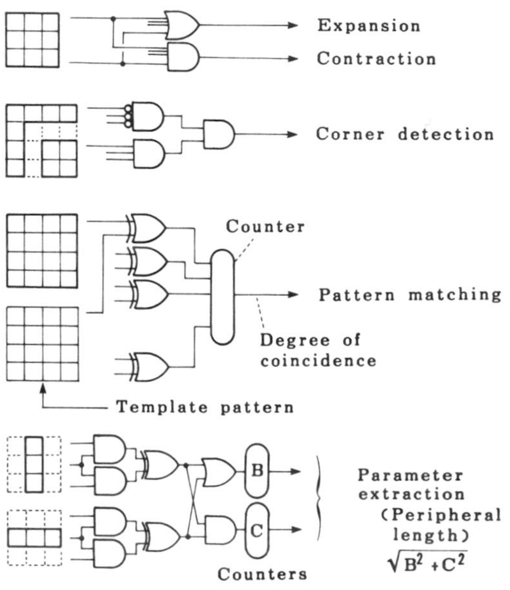

Fig. 6 Examples of logical filtering circuits.

(1) Pattern matching method

A method called rotational pattern matching [Yoda et al., 1973] was the first attempt to recognize 3-D objects flowing on a conveyor from their top views. This method utilized a binary image to find the center of gravity of the object in the image, and then converted the object image into polar coordinates. Thus, one-dimensional matching in the angular direction was executed to find the object type, its position and orientation. A recognition time of less than one second per object was achieved for 32 types of objects. This, however, has not been widely used, although the basic concept of one-directional viewing and teaching by showing has been inherited by most vision modules now available.

To avoid the matching of total view of an object, and to obtain finer positional accuracy, a multiple local pattern matching method has been developed [Kashioka et al., 1976]. This method is now widely used not only for the assembly of transistors but also for assembly of ICs, LSIs and VLSIs. This method utilizes characteristic portions of the object image as templates to be matched. Using these templates, only two template pattern positions must normally be detected to specify the object position. Therefore, the reliability of recognition can be very high both theoretically and in practice.

(2) Windowing method

Geometric information about an object can be found by setting windows in the field of view, and counting the number of pixels of the object in those windows. The balance of the number of pixels in the windows set at the edges of the object image can also give precise position and orientation information [Mese et al., 1977]. For moving objects, the degrees of shape matching and positional timing can also be detected using this windowing technique [Uno et al., 1976]. As this method is based on pixel counting, which is integration-type processing, it gives an algorithm that is strong against image noise.

(3) Slit-light method

Three-dimensional information can be directly obtained by observing a slit-light image projected on an object. This method can be regarded as an active method in the sense that the media for carrying of distance information are actively added on the object surface. Basic research on this method originated 15 years ago at the Electro-technical laboratory in Japan, and wide applications are now being developed. These include welding robots, a sealing robot [Sawano et al., 1983] (Fig. 7), and a system to inspect soldering state for flat-pack devices in high-density circuit boards [Nakagawa, 1982] (Fig. 8).

(4) Parameter extraction method

This method can be used for the recognition of object shapes, and is considered to be effective in classification. In this method, the center of gravity is first calculated from a binary object image, then such parameters as area,

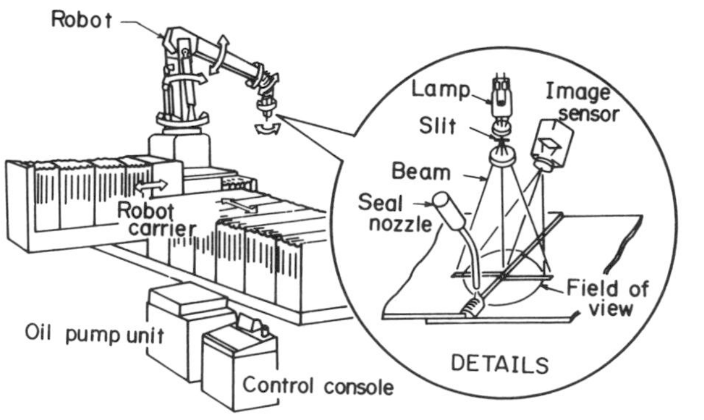

Fig. 7 A sealing robot.

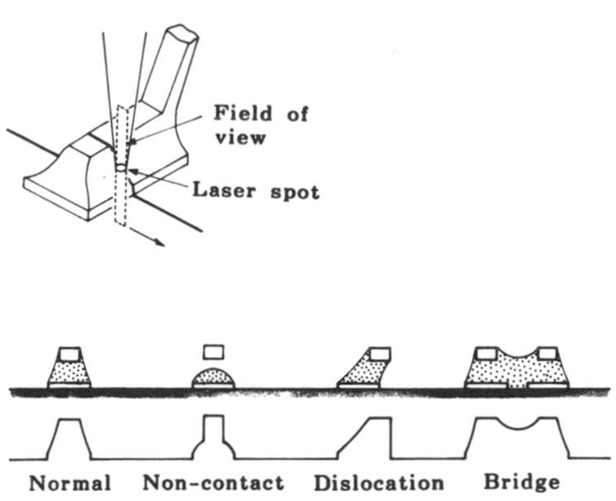

Fig. 8 Solder joint inspection for flat-package devices.

peripheral length, moment of inertia on the principal axes, number of holes, etc., are detected. Averages and variations in these parameters are calculated and memorized during the teaching process, where sample objects are shown to the vision system several times by changing their positions and orientations.

When an object is observed by the vision system, its parameters are extracted and compared in a parameter space with those of pre-memorized objects to find the best-matching object with minimum distance. This parameter extraction method can provide a general-purpose vision system. However, a general-purpose system is usually slower than a special-purpose system developed as a dedicated system. Therefore, problem-oriented extraction of more effective and specific parameters has usually been attempted to obtain faster recognition performance. Machines to classify diode chips, fish, agricultural products, and medicine tablets are examples of this approach.

What is needed in the future?

In every vision application, processing speed and cost/performance ratio have been the center of consideration. One-directional viewing and image thresholding are two traditional keys to increase speed. However, recent semiconductor technology is now forming an environment where even a gray-scale image can be processed at fairly high speed. One main stream in recent years is the development of LSIs for image processing. This also affects the vision system by decreasing the cost/performance ratio.

An example of such an LSI is shown in Fig. 9. This LSI is especially suited for pipelined pattern matching. Here, the spatial filtering of an 8-bit gray image is executed in the real-time mode by synchronizing standard TV scanning. To achieve more effective vision modules, a family of LSIs for image processing and feature extraction will be required.

Another primary effort in future vision technology should be focused on inspection problems for industrial automation. There are a tremendous number of inspection problems to be solved in the future. Present vision technology does not have the potential to solve these problems. One reason for this is that image sensors available now do not have a sensitivity range as good as that of the human eye, which can recognize subtle disorder or degradation. A rough comparison of this range is shown in Table 2 together with other simple parameters. It may be concluded from this table that we have only achieved one trillionth the ability of the human eye to date.

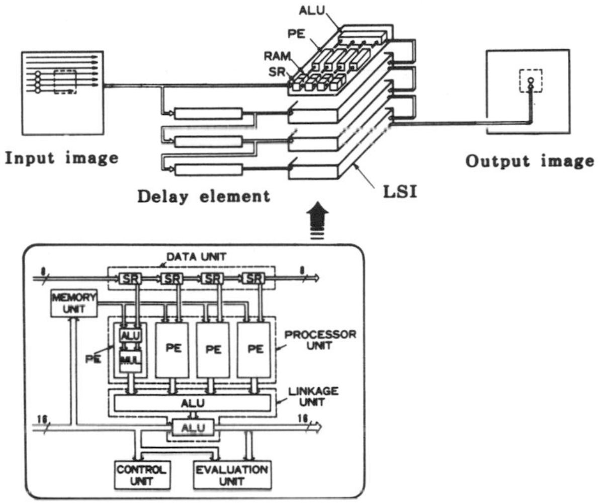

Fig. 9 An example of LSIs for image processing.

Table 2. Comparison of vision

	Robot vision	Human eye
Number of pixels	$10^5 \sim 10^6$	$\sim 10^8$
Processor scale (gates)	$10^4 \sim 10^6$	$\sim 10^{10}$
Sensitivity range	$\sim 10^2$	$> 10^6$
Weight (grams)	$10^2 \sim 10^3$	~ 10
Total ratio	$10^{-11} \sim 10^{-15}$	1

The speed of processing also becomes rather critical in inspection processes. In the case of the inspection of 4 inch IC wafers, for example, image sampling at 6 MHz with a resolution of 1 micron gives at least 10 Gigabytes of data and reqires 30 minutes for only one scan. Therefore, memorizing an image for subsequent analysis does not make sense if we are to meet the production requirement of high speed processing. Pipelined, on-site processing may therefore be the only solution. The inspection machine shown in Fig. 10 has been developed along these lines [Yoda et al.

1984]. In this machine, a multiple number of standard images corresponding to each layer of the IC are generated from its design data in the real-time mode, and the sensed image and the generated standard images are registered and compared to find defective portions. The fatal degree of these portions is also checked here. The total processing speed of this machine is more than 10 GOPS (Giga-operations per second), which exceeds the fastest existing super-computer by 20 fold.

In the case of an LSI or VLSI wafer, the scale of image processing and the speed required will be beyond usable limits. No suitable method exists at present, and if no revolution occurs in inspection methods, higher-resolution products may not be realized, not because of any limitation in lithography, but because of limitation in industrial inspection.

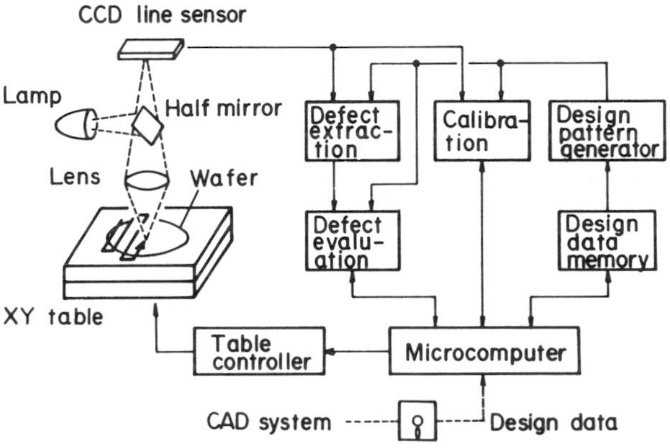

Fig.10 An inspection machine for IC wafer.

The larger the image matrix is, the higher the reliability usually attained in the inspection process. This also reduces image processing speed. In IC wafer inspection, the number of pixels in the image matrix already exceeds the total population of the world, and for an LSI wafer, it will exceed the number of synapses in the brain.

Another aspect of required speed is shown in Fig. 11. This is based on the present view, and as technology improves, demand will become even greater. Therefore, the number of required operations in the ordinate will become higher. Thus, the speed requirement will not be fulfilled for possibly another 20 years. We may need a revolution in architecture before image processing can overcome the speed problems.

DECISION MAKING

Decision-making can be regarded as part of the problem-solving technique. It is regarded as a process that finds the route from the starting state to the goal. The goal is usually designated in the task-understanding process, and the starting state is usually determined by the vision recognition process. If frequent situation changes in the outside world are expected during robot operation, the vision process is operated continuously to determine the most recent state and substitute it for the starting state. This technique is called visual feedback.

To make an effective decision, it is essential to find out how to efficiently search for possible solutions utilizing knowledge about the world. Geometric modelling is one form of knowledge describing the world. Declarative description is another possible form of knowledge representation. In this case, logical inference is one of the key technologies now being extensively investigated in the AI field.

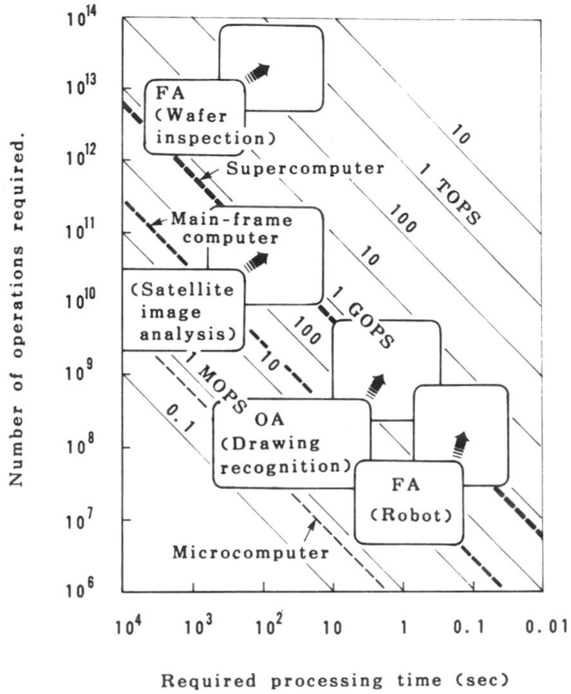

Fig.11 Requirements for image processing.

Future problems concerning the decision-making capability of robots will include how the knowledge can be aquired and implemented, how it can be improved through experience, and how it can be organized to make its later use effective and speedy. Today's inference scheme usually searches the knowledge-base on a one-by-one basis. Therefore, the time required for searching tends to become enormous as the quantity of knowledge increases. Highly-parallel inference machines based on ULSI technology may be one solution to this problem.

The robot acts upon the outside world according to the result of the decision-making process. To do so, manipulation and locomotion are essential. Today's robots seem to be built only to spend their power moving their arms. Low cost, new, ceramic materials and fiber-reinforced plastics should be extensively utilized in future robots. Direct-drive arms simply will not solve the problems.

LSI technology may also invoke a revolution for controlling robots. For example, a single-chip LSI for matrix calculation will help transform coordinate data in the near future, thus shortening the time required for coordinate calculation, and resulting in higher control quality with finer motion resolution.

Robots conceived for use in hazardous environments will be a target for development in the next 10 years. Here, success depends on whether an efficient locomotion scheme is realized. Quick communication between human and robots for cooperative decision-making may be a central part of the technologies. Manipulators in these robots should probably have more degrees of freedom of motion; thus, control of arms with redundant axes will be extensively studied.

Additional views on robotics for future industry use are summarized in Table 3, although there are few obvious reasons and evidence seen of them yet.

CONCLUSIONS

Problems with robotics for future industry use have been discussed in this article. Recent activities in robotics research seem to be facing not only technical difficulty but also difficulty arising from the lack of a firm philosophy in pursuing such research. Possible targets for new frontiers in robotics in industry may be to try to:

(1) connect CAD data as an input to the robot system (in relation to the task understanding function),
(2) develop new sensors and new processor architectures for image processing through the use of VLSI and ULSI technology (in relation to the visual recognition function), and
(3) investigate the horizon of rule-based control of robots for complicated tasks (in relation to the decision-making function).

There are, of course many, other important areas that should be addressed in the future. These include investigation of new materials, new actuators, new control schemes, new components, and new algorithms.

REFERENCES

[1] Ejiri, M. et al. 1972. A prototype intelligent robot that assembles objects from plan drawings, IEEE Trans. Comput., C-21, pp. 161-170.
[2] Ejiri, M. et al. 1984. Automatic recognition of design drawings and maps, Proc. of 7th International Conference on Pattern Recognition, Montreal.
[3] Kakumoto, S. et al. 1983. Development of auto-digitizer using multi-color drawings recognition method, Proc. CVPR'83, IEEE Comp. Society.
[4] Kashioka, S., Ejiri, M. and Sakamoto, Y. 1976. A transistor wire-bonding system utilizing multiple local pattern matching techniques, IEEE Trans. Syst., Man and Cybern., SMC-6, pp. 562-570.
[5] Mese, M. et al. 1977. An automatic position recognition technique for LSI assembly, Proc. 5th International Joint Conf. on Artificial Intelligence, Cambridge, pp. 685-693.
[6] Nakagawa, Y. 1982. Automatic visual inspection of solder joints on printed circuit boards, Proc. of SPIE, 336, robot vision, pp. 121-127.
[7] Sawano, S. et al. 1983. A sealing robot system with visual seam tracking, Proc. International Conf. on Advanced Robotics, Tokyo.
[8] Uno, T., Ejiri, M. and Tokunaga, T. 1976. A method of real-time recognition of movin objects and its application, Pattern Recognition, 8, pp. 201-208.
[9] Yoda, H., Ikeda, S. and Ejiri, M. 1973. A new attempt of selecting objects using a hand-eye system, Hitachi Review, 22, 9, pp. 362-365.
[10] Yoda, H. et al. 1984. An automatic IC wafer pattern inspection system, Proc. National Conf. of Inst. Electr. and Comm. Engrs. of Japan, (in Japanese)

Table 3. Industrial robots in future

		1984	1989	1994	1999
Manipulation	·Main materials	Aluminum alloy	+FRP	+Ceramics	+Compound
	·Load/weight	0.05	0.1	0.2	0.25
	·Arm speed (max.)	1.5 m/s	3 m/s	5 m/s	8 M/S
Locomotion	·Type	Wheels	Wheels	Wheels	Wheels
	·Speed	<0.5 m/s	0.8 m/s	1.5 m/s	3.0 m/s
System control	·Type of control	Unit	Group	CAD connection	Total FMS
	·CPU utilized	16-bit	32-bit	+Dedicated	New architecture
	·Main memory	100 KB	1 MB	5 MB	10 MB
Image processor	·Image type	Binary	+Gray	+Color	Color
	·General purpose	10 MOPS	100 MOPS	500 MOPS	1 GOPS
	·Special purpose	1-10 GOPS	10-100 GOPS	100-500 GOPS	>500 GOPS

ROBOTIZATION IN SHIPBUILDING INDUSTRY
(Present Situation and Projected Schemes)

Ryoichiro Sasano

Mitsubishi Heavy Industries, Ltd.
Kobe Shipyard & Engine Works
1-1, 1-chome, Wadasaki-cho, Hyogo-ku Kobe 652 Japan

In recent years, the trend of automation and labor-saving activity has been remarkable in mass production industries, such as automobile industry, who actively introduced various industrial robots for practical use.

Meanwhile, the shipbuilding industry was far behind the mass production industries owing to such inherent characteristics of shipbuilding work as;

(1) Very large and heavy parts and components
(2) Many work items but a small number per each item
(3) Intricate structure with limited workable range
(4) Rough accuracy in production

Presently, however, the situation is changing, now positively introducing robots from the market to each workshop since the techniques of robots show rapid progress resulting in ready adaptation to the industry and because that the shipbuilding industry confronts serious difficulties in the recession, thus being strongly requested to enhance the cost competitiveness, requiring robotization in the area of production for man-saving by automation.

The shipbuilding industry is, therefore, concentrating potentials altogether for development of robots readily fittable for various work in the industry. This paper summarizes the required functions, the present situation of development of the robots and the projected schemes for the future, such as hull assembling robots, welding robots, painting robots, etc. that are expected to be developed gradually but steadily.

1. Introduction

Japanese shipbuilding industry confronts various difficulties, such as, the gradual change of industrial structure, the abrupt rise of Korea and the other third nations, the trend of advancing of the workers' average age and the hard recruiting of young workers, etc. that threaten the industry to lose the position of the main ship supplier of the world and to become an inferior industry even domestically if the industry is left without any measure to overcome these difficulties.

Under the above circumstances, it is imperative for the shipbuilding industry to enhance the cost competitiveness aiming at survival and future prosperity of the industry by positively driving mechanization in the area of production for improvement of productivity and for labor saving factories.

Meanwhile, the shipbuilding industry was hitherto far behind mass-production industries in robotization owing to such peculiar and inherent characteristics of shipbuilding work as;

(1) Very large and heavy parts and components
(2) Many work items but a small number per each item
(3) Intricate structure with limited workable range
(4) Rough accuracy in production

Recently, however, micro-computers, sensors and the utility techniques of them showed remarkable progress enabling adaptation of robots hopefully in the area of ship construction. And, the shipbuilding industry necessitated man-saving and unattended factory as described above for realizing of drastic productivity improvement. All these have accelerated the development of robotization in the shipbuilding industry. With the above in the background, several shipyards already started the introduction of welding robots from the market to their workshops.

In parallel with the above movement, the shipbuilding industry has been earnestly wrestling with the development of most fittable robots for the workshops, i.e. 7 Major shipbuilders altogether contemplated the research and development of 12 items for super-modernization of production engineering, and entrusted the R & D with "The Shipbuilding Research Association of Japan" (SR co-development) with 5-year - plan since April, 1982, where the development of the shipbuilding robots, e.g. welding robots, undergo presently.

This paper reports the required function and the present situation of the development and utilization of the shipbuilding robots and projected schemes for the future.

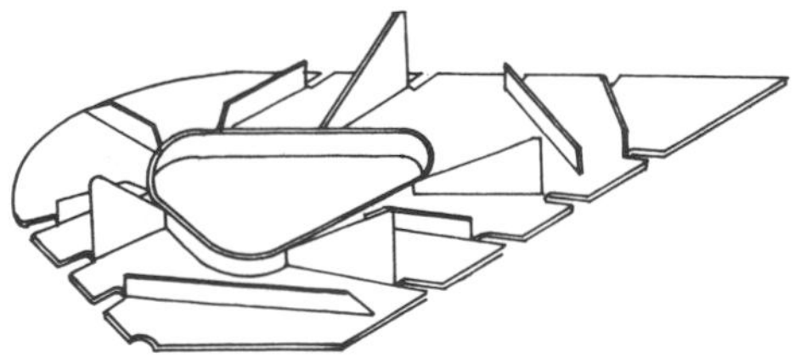

Fig. 1 Sub-assembly block

2. Direction of Robotization

Shipbuilding robots developed and utilized hitherto are yet seldom for the reasons of technical difficulty and low return of the investment due to the peculiarity of the shipbuilding work.

Objectives of robotization, therefore, should be considered taking account of such peculiarity, for example, for the work that can create higher productivity by utilizing robots, for the work that is used to be executed in poor environment and for the work that introduction and utilization can anyhow be expected even if such peculiarity of the shipbuilding work is taken into consideration.

At present, the following 3 items may presumably be the right direction of robotization in the context:

1. Welding robots
2. Hull assembling robots
3. Painting and blasting robots

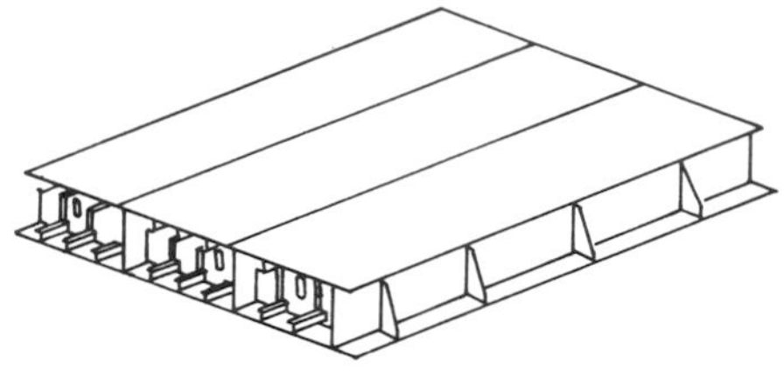

(Double Bottom Block)

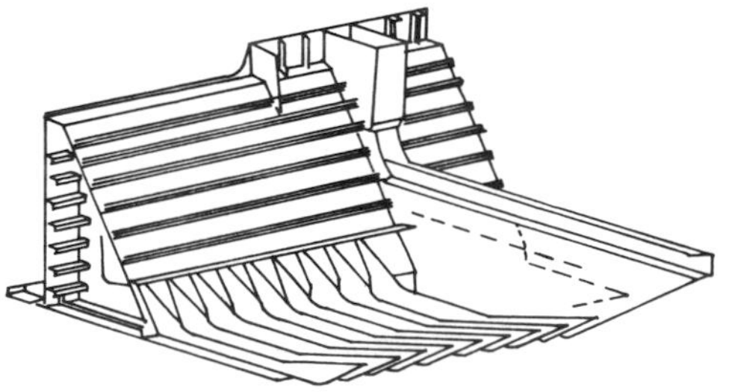

(Side Shell Block)

Fig. 2 Assembly block

3. Welding Robots

3.1 Characteristics of work of welding robots

Hull structures that the welding work is performed have the following characteristics;

1) Very large and heavy parts and components

Sizes vary according to the work stages. Each block is sized about 10M x 4 ∿ 5M at the sub-assembly stage and about 20M x 15M at the assembly stage.
Accordingly, it is extremely difficult to easily move and position the blocks in such a manner as flow-line manufacturing system.
At the sub-assembly stage, sometimes the tact production system may partially be applicable, but usually the work progresses while the objects are fixed in the position. Also, the welding joints almost equally scatter over the surface of these large objects, and most of the joints can be welded by one-path fillet welding resulting in comparatively small work density per unit area.
Fig. 1 and Fig. 2 show sub-assembly block and assembly block.

2) Many work items but a small number per each item

There is not a single case that thousands of thousands of same products are manufactured in sequence as in mass-production industry.
Ten to twenty ships are the maximum.
And, for ships, there is little possibility of repetitive work on account of the type and the arrangement of ships, and of many parts and components of same shape in one ship.
At the best, a hundred of similar type or alike can be seen at the sub-assembly stage.
As an example of number of similar shape, Table 1 denotes the number of Double Bottom Floors of a 34,000 DWT Bulk carrier, a 1,900 TEU Container ship and a 4,900 unit Car carrier.
From this point of view, the shipbuilding industry cannot take such production style that the tremendous numbers of the same parts are welded simultaneously by robots.

Table 1 Number of D.B. floors

Kind of ship	Number of D.B. floors
Bulk carrier (34,000DWT)	120
Container ship (1,900TEU)	110
Car carrier (4,900Unit)	60

However, since the object is large enough, there may be the case that nearly a hundred of joints of similar shape or alike are processed in one unit work and the repetitive work may become an object of robotics. Fig. 3 and Table 2 show the shape of collar plate of section penetrating part of a tank part of a 60,000 DWT oil tanker and its number per ship.

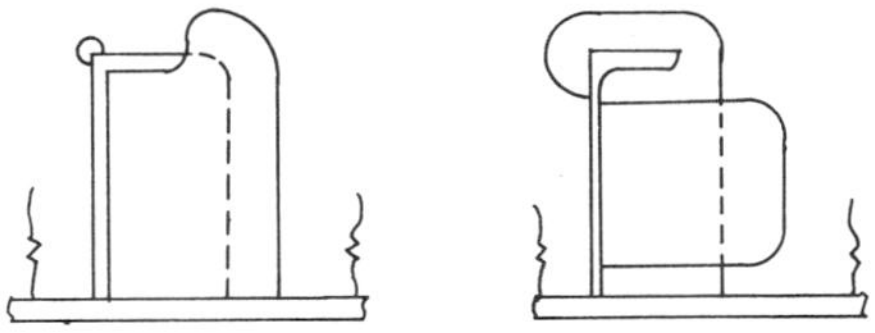

Fig. 3 Shape of callar plate

Table 2 Number of collar plates

Type / Size of Section / Structure	Collar and filler plates					
	250	300	350	400	450	500
Upper Deck		410	110			
Side Shell		360	130	210	320	320
Longl Bulkhead	50	80	290	220	420	400
Bottom Shell		20				

3) Intricate structure with limited workable range

The hull is, in principle, a panel structure comprising plates and frames and these connecting parts are welding joints. In case of sub-assembly blocks, parts are few and welding is feasible in an open condition, while, in case of assembly blocks, many parts are involved and working space is narrow and confined, difficult for welding work.
Also, in case of sub-assembly blocks, welding work is conducted in down-hand position, but in case of assembly blocks, mostly vertical or overhead position.

4) Rough accuracy in production

Ships are large enough, similar to other large structures, and consequently the work accuracy is in the order of millimeters in view of shape, dimensions and production procedure.

Accuracy of cutting, gas cutting or plasma cutting, is much rough than that of machining.
Positioning of parts and components in assembling work is done by sighting of a human, thus, accuracy of assembling becomes also in the order of millimeters.

Table 3 shows an example of a tolerance of dimensions used in the shipbuilding industry.
Besides a problem of accuracy in cutting and assembling, there is a problem of distortion by heat.
It may not be worthwhile, however, to improve the accuracy level than the present level as it necessitates a considerable amount of investment and labor work.
Presently, it may be a wise way to accept the present accuracy and to develop robots to cover this accuracy.

Table 3 Example of tolerance (from J.S.Q.S. 1982 Edition)

Division		Gas Cutting UNIT: mm		
Section	Sub-section	Item	Standard range	Tolerance limits
Dimension	Depth of groove		±1.5	±2.0
	Size of member	General members compared with correct sizes	±3.5	±5.0
		Especially for the depth of floor and girder of double bottom compared with correct sizes	±2.5	±4.0
		Breadth of face bar, compared with correct sizes	±2.0	-3.0∿+4.0

3.2 Equipment type robots and portable robots

There are two types of welding robots for shipbuilding according to the relative positions of the object works.
One is an Equipment type robot that is a large scale one working upon the welding joints of the object structure from outside of the structure, applicable to the objects of open workable range. Straight objects are sub-assembly blocks and assembly blocks.
The other is a Portable robot, that can readily enter the object structure, and that a single worker can operate multiple units simultaneously, applicable to the objects of specific work of comparatively large volume. This portable robot is presumed to be widely applicable for assembly stage and erection stage. More utility can be expected if this portable robot is properly combined with material handling equipment.

Optimum type robot that can enter the object structure is envisaged as to perform completely unmanned operation, contoured in such a way that it moves inside the object structure by numerical information and sensing function, that it checks the welding line and welds in sequence under an appropriate welding conditions.
However, as this involves so much of R & D

factors, necessitating a long period for development until it offers practical use. So, for the time being, the above portable robot is considered more practical.

3.3 Functions required for welding robots

The shipbuilding robots should possess the functions inherent to shipbuilding work considering the peculiarity of the object work.
Necessary functions of both equipment type and portable welding robots are stated below.

3.3.1 Applicable for large structures

A. Common

1) It must be feasible that the robot should move and approach the object work by himself.

B. Equipment type robots

1) In case that sub-assembly blocks are objects, it should be large and self-running type enabling to cover the work of about 10m long and about 4 ∿ 5m wide.

C. Portable robots

1) It must be light-weighted (less than about 20kg), easily portable by a man.

2) Software and environing equipment must be possessed so that one worker may operate multiple units.

3.3.2 Applicable for many work items but a small number per each item

B. Equipment type robots

1) Programming, on-line or off-line, in robotic language must be available.

2) Robots can be operated by the above program.

3) Software can be possessed to utilize the data of similar form such as XY shift, mirror image shift, etc.

4) CAD data can be taken into it.

C. Portable robots

1) Setting at the workshop must be easy, and repetitive work, i.e. correction of positions after setting, etc. must be easy.

2) Repetitive work must be available by only one teaching.

3.3.3 Applicable for intricate structure with limited workable area

A. Common

1) Flexibility of wrist action must be sufficient.

2) Structure and shape of the wrist must be simple.

3) Interferance with the work must be avoided.

4) Welding in all postures must be feasible.

5) Automatic setting of welding conditions and torch action must be available.

C. Portable robots

1) It must be small and transportable to confined compartments.

2) It must be easily set in confined compartments.

3) It must possess cable handling mechanism.

3.3.4 Applicable for rough accuracy in production

A. Common

1) It can cover work accuracy and setting accuracy of the robot and its work.

2) It can be properly controlled by sensors.

3) It can identify the work position in short time.

4) Start-point sensing and close-end sensing are possible. Also, close end sensing can be done at real time.

5) Regardless of any welding posture, it can weld directly sensing weld joints. (It must have an automatic weld line sensing device.)

Of the required functions as above described, Items 3.3.2B1) & 2) and 3.3.3A1), 2) & 4) have already been developed, while, the rest still remains undeveloped or some partially developed.

3.4 Application of welding robots and present situation of development

3.4.1 Equipment type welding robots

Trial of the cross axis type medium size robots introduced from the market has been conducted by several shipyard for application to sub-assembly blocks. Refer to Fig. 4.

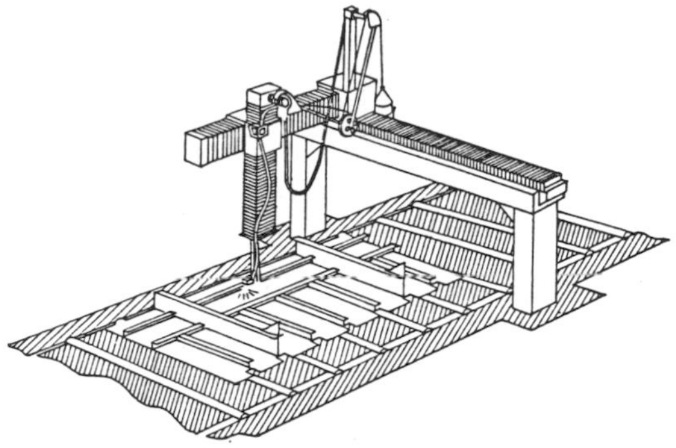

Fig. 4 Cross axis type medium size robot

With the clue of this cross axis type medium size robots, there started a movement of developing and adding the required functions to the robots.
However, it has not reached the stage of practical application.
Large robots of this kind that apply to assembly blocks yet remain undeveloped for the reason of cost-effectiveness.

3.4.2 Portable welding robots

(1) For assembly stage

Portable welding robots for assembly stage are treated as one of major themes of SR co-development developed by combinations of shipyards and robot makers.
At the beginning, development of these robots commenced for application to the section penetrating parts and the collar plates, but, later, necessary function for practical use in shipbuilding workshops have in turn added to the robots for wider application.
It might be called like common type robots.
As to the above robots, trial manufacture was already completed and at the stage of field testing. But, these trial products are somehow heavy not to reach the level of one man handling, needing more improvement for incorporating other necessary functions.

Leading particulars and functions of one of these robots are specified below;

°Leading particulars

Weight	30 kg
Size	500 x 350mm manhole passable
Movable axis	Simultaneous control of 5 axis plus wrist assisting axis
Setting posture	All postures
Weldable range	Range encompassed by: Height 0 ∿ abt.700mm Side abt.450mm Forward 0 ∿ abt.500mm

°Functions

- All posture welding is possible.
- Cubic shift is possible for distance correction of setting position. (Up to ±100mm distance)
- It possesses a start point sensing function, but a close-end sensing function is under development.
- As to weld line sensing device, down hand and vertical have already been developed, and overhead is under development.
- Filing of welding conditions is possible.
- If teaching is done and filed per unit work, welding work of combined unit works can be performed without any more teaching.

Fig. 5 shows the outline of the portable welding robot.

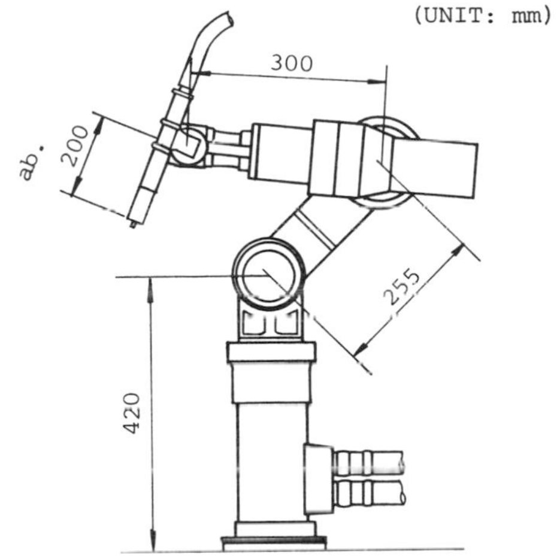

Fig. 5 Portable welding robot

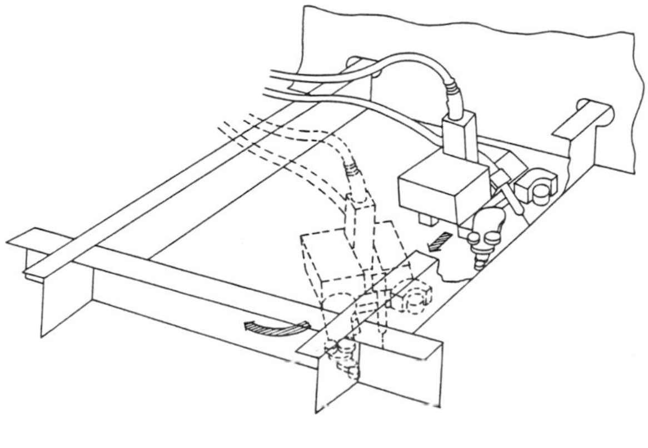

Fig. 6 Horizontal fillet welding machine

Some shipyards have been developing the robots that can perform horizontal fillet welding of so called "lattice structure" surrounded by frames and frames (generally transverse and longitudinals) which is found anywhere as repetitive work at the assembly stage. This is that welding work is performed by sensors incorporated into the robot and by micro-computer control.
This may better be called automatic welding machine because its object is only horizontal fillet welding.

Fig. 6 shows a horizontal fillet welding machine for "lattice structure".

(2) For erection stage

Welding joints at the erection stage scatter widely and solidly. So, there are stronger needs for easily portable robots than at the assembly stage. Erection stage robots tend toward specialized robots of lighter weight by defining their object work.
As the portable robots for the erection stage, at present, development of section butt welding robots has been in progress as one of the major themes of SR co-development by shipyards and robot makers. Characteristics of the robots are as follows:

- Butt joint welding (one side) of sections up to 500mm deep is possible.
- It weighs 19kg and 500 x 350mm, manhole passable.
- All posture welding is possible.
- It is provided with contact sensors to sense the welding line itself and start point and close-end prior to welding work.
- It is also provided with contact sensors to sense a gap of edge preparation prior to welding work.
- It possesses a simple numerically inputting functions.

3.5 Future schemes of welding robots

Development and utilization of welding robots for shipbuilding work are far behind the other manufacturing industries.
In order to maintain the prominent position of Japanese shipbuilding industry in the world, it is indispensable to improve work efficiency and to save work hands of the welding work that occupies about 1/4 of the total man-hours.

And, among others, robotization is one of the major technical themes that should be realized earliest possible.
For immediate approach to practical use of welding robots having various difficult problems for development, development and improvement of the followings are prerequisite.

(1) Prompt development of the required functions

The above described required functions are developed by degrees supported by the progress of the relative technology, but there still are unsettled items that are needed to be developed promptly.

(2) Development of proper controlling system of welding conditions

The robots that are now being developed or intended to be developed are mostly for fillet joints. In case that the object of development is butt welding joints it is necessary to adjust welding conditions while welding as shapes and sizes of edge vary.
It is, therefore, necessary to develop the sensors to sense shapes of edge and to develop the system and argolism that control the welding conditions according to the changes feed back from the sensors.

(3) Development of shape-identifying sensors

Welding line sensors, start-point and close-end sensors etc. have already been developed or are being developed, but identification of shape of joints of many kinds are yet done by human judgement.
Accordingly, it is necessary to develop the system of automatic identification of joint shape and of implementation of welding.
For this purpose, it is necessary to develop shape identifying sensors making possible such a system that various shapes of joints will be patternized in advance, actual shapes of joints are automatically identified per pattern by shape-idenfying sensors, that teaching data which is preset to meet each pattern previously made and filed are retrieved based on pattern identification, and that welding work is performed accordingly.
So, it is necessary to develop sensor technology so that it can continuously and automatically identify the contact points and contact lines of the parts.

(4) Improvement of structural design

When welding was introduced and applied to shipbuilding work, structural design was developed to meet the welding. However, it is necessitated, henceforth, that designers should think of how robots should be best utilized at the time of designing, and that structure and arrangement should be modularized to best fit robotization.
In short, it will be the best way "to design best fittable for robots and best utilizing of robots".
It is no exaggeration to say that this will decide the fate of robotization.

(5) Speed-up of welding

Robots can perform intricate actions speedily and accurately that cannot be attained by manual work.
Therefore, it is one of the most important schemes to pursue the extremity of welding speed so that the features of the robots can be developed to the maximum.

(6) Development of environing equipments

Though the robots are of high specification and high performance, ability of the robots cannot be displayed alone.
This can be attained by combining with the environing equipments, e.g. device for transportation of the works in and out, work positioners realizing optimum workability, robot handling equipment, setting jigs, all of above are properly arranged and organically combined to show the real performance of the robots.
Accordingly, best efforts should be made to develop and devise these environing equipment in parallel with development of the robots.
Above is applicable also to hull assembling robots and painting robots.

4. Hull Assembling Robots

4.1 Image of hull assembling robots

Present image of hull assembling robots is as follows:
The robots are applied to sub-assembly blocks and assembly blocks.
Main plates are fixed on the assembly platen at the predetermined positions, and the robots transfer, position and tentative fit frames to the plates giving pressure-constraint by numerical control and sensor control.

4.2 Specific features of work of hull assembling robots

Specific features are almost similar to those of the welding robots. So, the detailed descriptions are dispensed with. Here shows only the features peculiar to the objects of the assembling robots.

(1) Very large and very heavy

The frames that the robots actually handle are smaller than main plates, but still the objects are very large and heavy in the size of about 800 ∿ 4,000mm long and about 100 ∿ 1,000mm wide for sub-assembly blocks and about 15,000mm long and about 4,000mm wide for assembly blocks.

(2) Many items but small in number

Sizes and shapes of frames are diverse and there is little similarity of shapes.

(3) Intricate structure

(4) Rough accuracy in production

4.3 Required functions for hull assembly robots

Similar to the welding robots, the hull assembling robots are needed to have functions inherent to shipbuilding work for such peculiarity.

4.3.1 Applicable for large structures

In case that the objects are sub-assembly blocks.

(1) The robots must be large and self-running type that can cover the objects of about 10m long (about 20m) and about 4 ∿ 5m wide. (about 15m)

(2) Transferable weight must be about 500kg (several tons)

(3) They must have plural hands and can deal with long size parts of up to about 4m long (about 15m)

Note: Figures in ( ) show the case of objects of assembly blocks.

4.3.2 Applicable for many items but small in number

(1) Programming, on-line or off-line, in robotic language is possible.

(2) CAD data can be taken into them.

(3) Handling of frames of various particular shapes can be possible.

4.3.3 Applicable for rough accuracy in production

(1) Fitted positions of frames can be fine adjusted by sensors.

(2) It possesses the function of pressure-constraining of frames.

(3) It possesses the function of correcting distortion of frames and tentative fitting at the right positions.

(4) It identifies the fitting positions of main plates in short time.

4.4 Present situation of development of hull assembling robots

Needs for hull assembling robots are strong from the viewpoint of man power saving for this kind of work or of relieving workers from heavy labor, but the robotizing involves the nature of development that is technically difficult, causing, at present, no practical use yet.
At present, as one of the themes of SR co-development, the development is yet at the conception stage of drafting and checking real specification of the assembling robots

to satisfy the above described required functions with the objects of assembly work, i.e. transferring and fitting, for flat plate sub-assembly blocks that have the most simple structures.
It is expected that the plan will soon be realized.

Fig. 7 shows the concept plan of a flat plate sub-assembling robot.

The assembling robots of this kind but with the object of large blocks is at the stage that even a concept is not made yet as it involves big barriers technically and economically because of too large objects.

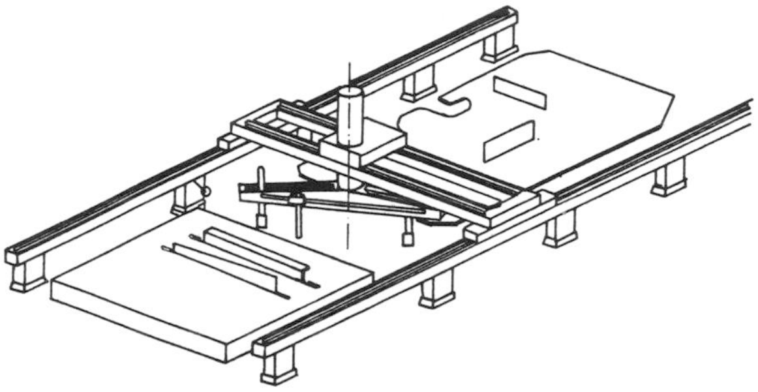

Fig. 7 Concept plan of a flat plate sub-assembling robot

4.5 Future scheme of hull assembling robots

Similar to the welding robots, the hull assembling robots should be developed for practical use for man-saving and for productivity improvement in shipbuilding workshops. But, different from the welding robots, burdensome function of directly handling large objects is meant very difficult technically.
Accordingly, the development should, as the prerequisite, start with the robots for the most simple flat plate sub-assembly blocks with developing of the required functions in parallel.
It is presumed very reasonable procedure that, after the said simple robots are developed, studies and conceptions are consolidated to those robots for the objects of larger and structually intricate hull blocks, such as large assembly blocks, curved blocks, etc. based on the accumulated techniques and valuable experiences with the said simple robots.
Meanwhile, improvement of structural design is also an important scheme for the assembling robots, as stated in the case of the welding robots.
There is a limit of robotization viewing of structures and arrangements of things of today, and consequently it is necessary to materialize modularization of structures and arrangements to suit robotization for perfection of the assembling robots and to realize standardization of the parts.
From this point of view, development of super large robots is not mature yet at present.

5. Painting and Blasting Robots

5.1 Characteristics of painting work and image of painting and blasting robots

Painting work in shipbuilding industry is performed in very inferior environment with dusts and dirts, and is a simple work that can not expect development of faculty of workers.
In this sense, this is one of the most difficult work item to recruit young workers.
Accordingly, the painting work whick is different from welding work or hull assembling work should be replaced from men by machines or robots.

The objects of painting work cover widely, such as hull structures, outfits, pipes, etc., but, here takes up painting work for hull structures as it is the mojor work.
Above described hull assembly work is to form blocks by combining many parts of the hull, while the welding work is to work upon some parts (weld joints) of already shaped objects. Thus both types of work are quite different fundamentally.
Painting work is close to welding in type of work as it works upon the already shaped object though some difference is found as welding works upon a part of the structure, while painting works upon the whole surface of the structure.
Accordingly, the painting and blasting robots are, similar to the welding robots, classified to two types considering relative positions.
One is for the object of blocks, so called single hull, that workable range is open. This is the robot that works upon the surface of the object structure from outside.
The other is for the object of solid blocks so called double hull that workable range is closed, and, for the object of on-board that workable range is also closed.
Naturally, development starts with the robots for the single hull blocks involving little problem technically.
As described in the welding robots, those robots that work inside assembly blocks involve much of elements of development needing long time for development, and these painting and blasting robots are also in a similar situation.

Image of the painting and blasting robots for single hull blocks is such that is described below.
They are large and self-running robots that perform each of painting and blasting work to the object structures set at each predetermined positions with a painting hand and a blasting hand installed at the end of the arms and operated by numerical control and sensor control.

5.2 Specific features of work of painting and blasting robots

Detailed descriptions are omitted because that the form of the painting and blasting robots is close to that of the welding robots and that the features of the robots are similar to those of the welding robots.

5.3 Required functions of painting and blasting robots

Major functions required for the robots for single hull block when robotizing painting and blasting in shipbuilding work are as follows.

(1) They must be large and self-running type to cover the objects of about 20m long and about 15m wide.

(2) Programming, on-line or off-line, in robotic language is possible and they can be operated by this program.

(3) CAD data can be utilized.

(4) Flexibility of wrist action must be sufficient, that is the painting hand and the blasting hand must sufficiently possess head-shaking and direction changing functions necessary for each work.

(5) Both painting hand and blasting hand must be simple enough in construction and shape, and can easily enter narrow and confined space.

(6) Interference with the object work must be avoided. They must have abnormality sensing sensors for continuous operation.

5.4 Present situation of development of painting and blasting robots

As explained above, needs for painting and blasting robots are very strong as a measure to eliminating dirty work, but they are not materialized yet because there involves much of technically difficult development work.

At present, this has been selected as one of the themes of SR co-development that is now in progress by shipyards and robot makers for the painting and blasting robots (impeller type) of NC controlled, hanging and self running type with the objects of single hull blocks.

5.5 Future schemes of painting and blasting robots

(1) It is imperative to develope and utilize those robots equipped with basically required functions described in 5.3 earliest possible.

(2) It is burdensome to make inputs if the system of controlling all movements only by numerical information is to be adapted. It is necessary to develop sensors to identify shapes of hull structures enabling automatic identification of shapes of parts and shapes of surface of the structures by non-contact type sensors, and also enabling implementation of fine movements based on the above.

(3) As in the case of the welding robots and the hull assembling robots, it is necessary to thoroughly improve the structural design aiming at modularization of structures and arrangements to fit robotizing so that painting and blasting work can be easily performed by robots.

(4) It is one of the future schemes that small and highly efficient shot bursting equipments are to be developed and improved in order to more effectuate robotizing of blasting work.

6. Demand for Development of Robotization

(1) Industrial robots have hitherto been mass production type, and it is eagerly hoped that, from now on, various robots fittable for the industries of large scale products of many kinds but small quantity such as shipbuilding industry will be developed speedily.

(2) Common type robots in the market are useful in a sense for study of robots or familiarity to robots, but since their function are limited, it may not be satisfactory in function for enhancement of productivity in shipbuilding industry.
Thus, the development of the special purpose robots for shipbuilding industry is earnestly awaited.

(3) It is the prerequisite that, whatever type or specification may be, the robots should anyhow be lighter in weight for improvement of ability of robots.
For this reason, it is a way to adopt new material, such as carbon-fibre, for the robots.

(4) As the objects are large steel structures, major actions are done by numerical information, but minute actions or fine adjustments should be done by judgement of the robots themselves. For this purpose, it is important to develop shape-identifying sensors for visibility by the robots.

(5) The robots under development for the use in shipbuilding industry at present are either fixed type, or only those move on fixed tracks, similar to common industrial robots.
In the future, it might be possible that, besides the welding robots, there may appear such robots that enter inside the object structure and proceed with work, judging the track by themselves according

to numerical information and sensing function, and walking along the track by themselves even striding over any obstacle if low in height.
However, it should be prudently considered if such robots could be applicable to shipbuilding industry from the viewpoint of cost-performance and if they match the environing conditions, even if technically it might be feasible.

7. Conclusion

This paper has described the direction of robotization in shipbuilding industry, the required functions, the present situation of development and utilization and the future schemes, each for welding robots, hull assembling robots and painting and blasting robots that should presumably be developed for practical use, and the demand for development of robots.
Robotization in shipbuilding industry is far behind the other industries.
Development just began but energetically by concentrating all potentials of the industry for early realization.
From now on, robotization should be accelerated, overcoming various technical difficulties and fully taking into account of the cost-effectiveness and man-machine collaboration and reconciliation.
Anyhow, shipbuilding industries should be prosperous ever in the future by attaining the goal of robotization.

Valuation of the practical use of SCARA type robots on assembly lines and the future robotized assembly systems

Akitaka Kato

Pioneer Electronic Corporation
Production Engineering Division
4-1, Meguro 1-chome, Meguro-ku, Tokyo 153, Japan

The following operations have been done by SCARA type robots on assembly lines: Screw fastening, Insertion of variously shaped electric parts, Assembly of mechanical parts, and Automatic tuning and testing of electric circuit.
The results allow the following comclusion to be drawn.
1) Picking and placing operations for mechanical parts from various taped or palletized sources are possible. The operation effect is equal to 0.8 man power. 2) Hooking operations for coil springs can be made with some modifications to the fingers. 3) Automatic tuning operations by rotating screws on electronic parts are very effective. The operation effect is equal to 1.5 man power. 4) One work station consisting of one robot and the additional equipment costs approximately 7,000,000 Yens. To return the investment in two years by one shift operation, we have to reduce the cost to 5,000,000 Yens. 5) Cost reduction by the standardization of additional equipment is very important. 6) The future robotized assembly system will be as follows:
Simple jobs such as picking and placing and adjustment will be performed by SCARA type robots. Meanwhile, the jobs requiring the ability of image sensing such as wiring and handling freely positioned parts will be done by Puma type robots.
Consequently, the robotization ratio on assembly lines will be increased to 80%, and multi-shift operation involving few workers will be realized. The current manned assembly methods will be changed in processing industries.

1. Introduction

The manufacturers of consumer electronic appliances have recently entered into severe price competition. To cope with regular model changes and to meet the changing needs of consumers, they have been forced to employ a production system of "multi-kind products in small lot sizes". It has also become increasingly difficult to employ workers in monotonous jobs.
Production Engineering Departments of the manufacturers have to put out timely high quality and low-priced products required by consumers.
The whole production system has been reviewed, and robots have been introduced to realize a flexible manufacturing system(FMS). Here we will discuss the application of the SCARA type robot to assembly lines, its evaluation and its future.

2. The adaptability of the SCARA to assembly lines

The SCARA has various features which make it particularly suitable for assemby work.

1) By designing robot-oriented products and assembly lines, 70% of assembling jobs can be reduced to Pick and Place(P&P) operations.

2) High precision assembly with high productivity is possible because the arm moves quickly and precisely.

3) Composing a system is easy because the area of arm movement is larger than that of its base.

4) Being simple, its reliability and cost performance are high, and its maintenance is easy. Fig. 1 shows the side view of a SCARA.

With the above features, the SCARA has been widely adapted for P&P operations. The assembly system shown here has a line of work stations. Each station consists of three blocks: a SCARA, feeders and a conveyer. Most of these have standardized component blocks. Various jobs can be performed by modifying some tools and chucks.

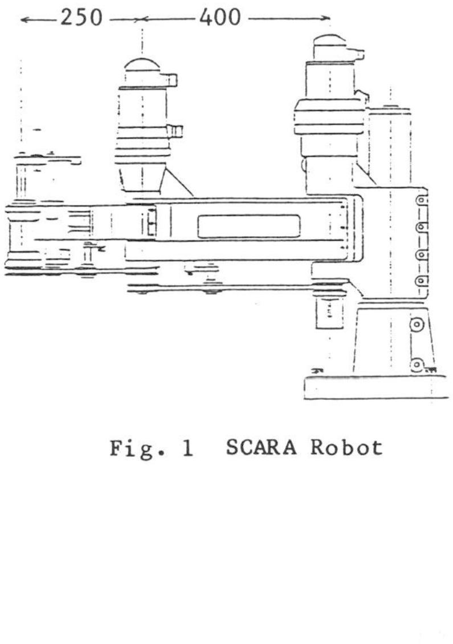

Fig. 1 SCARA Robot

3. Application examples

3-1 An example of a screwing system

This system mounts speaker components in an enclosure placed on a conveyor. It can handle ten kinds of speaker systems and eight kinds of screws. One line has three work stations, and each station consists of a conveyer, a robot and a screwing unit. Fig. 2 shows the standard screwing system. The screws are separated by a hopper shown in Fig. 3, are conveyed by an air hose and sequentially secure the speaker in its enclosure using a single-axis screw driver as the preliminary programmed.

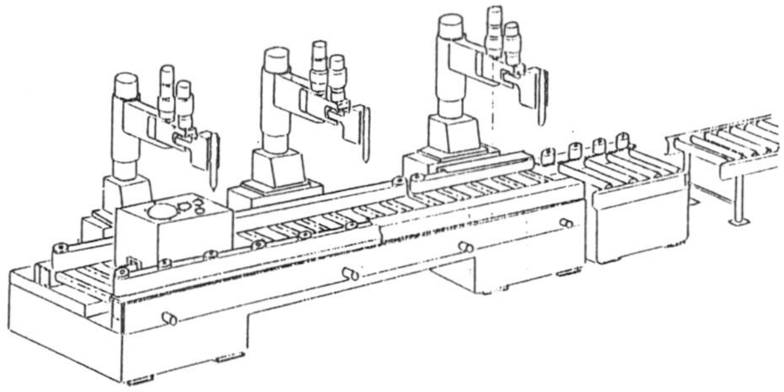

Fig. 2 Screwing System

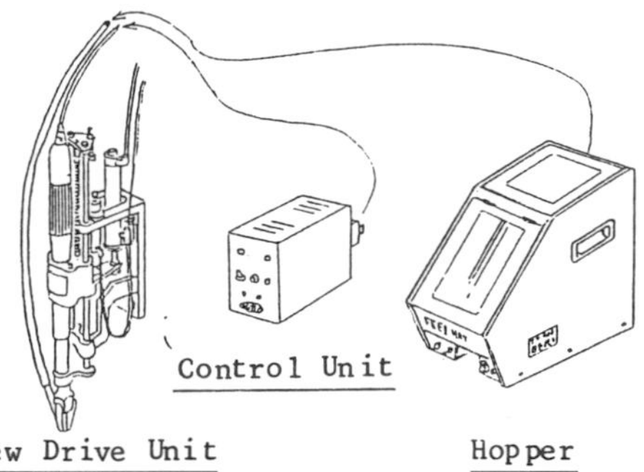

Fig. 3 Standard Unit for Screwing

1) Features

a) Adaptation to various models

Shape and dimensions of speaker and enclosure

Screwing position can be changed by changing the computer program.
The height can be adjusted by varying the height of the robot.
The width can be readjusted by varying the width of the conveyer.

Shape and dimensions of screws

M4 and M5 screws are used, with a head with a hexagonal socket or cross groove head and a length between 16mm and 38mm. Handling these different screws is possible only by replacing the screwdriver-bit and nails.

b) Signal for completion of screwing

The enclosure is made of particle boards. The boards are made by compressing small particles of wood mixed with some adhesive resin. The necessary screwing torque varies by more than twice the minimum value depending on the hardness of the board, the quantity of the adhesive resin, etc. The signal for completion is obtainable by sensing the rapid change of torque. Fig. 4 shows how rapidly the torque varies when tightness is reached. When tightening the screw, the torque varies gradually. It is easy to obtain the completion signal because the presetting allowance is high.

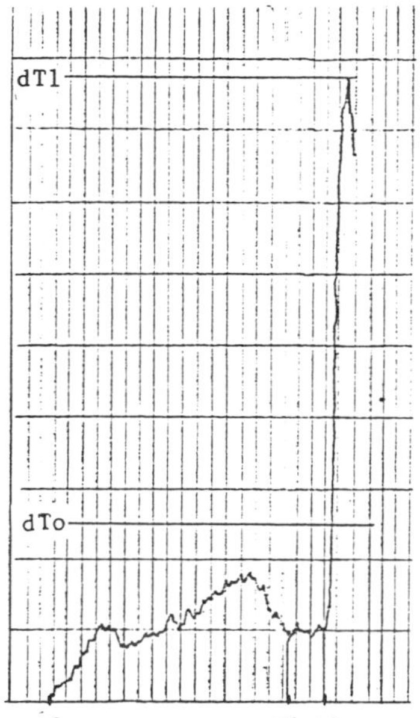

dTo: Variation rate of preset torque for sensing completion signal
dT1: Torque variation rate at the breakdown point of the board
to: Starting point of screwing
t1: The moment the screw goes through the board
t2: The moment when the screw-head touches the board

Fig. 4 Characteristic of increasing torque

3-2 An example of inserters for electronic parts of various shapes

1) SCARA on assembly lines

Fig. 6 shows the process in which SCARA was employed. The SCARA was used in the process between ARI / ACI and the automatic solderer for inserting parts of different shapes into the printed circuit board shown in Fig. 5. It was also used after a special automatic parts inserter to increase the automation ratio.

ARI: automatic resistor inserter or axial-lead parts inserter

ACI: automatic capacitor inserter or radial-lead parts inserter

This system is required to handle various kinds of parts. Even when inserting only a single part of one type, it must be able to work efficiently to reduce the manual jobs shown in Fig. 6. By decreasing the number of assembly workers to 2 or 3 persons, multi-shift operation became possible.

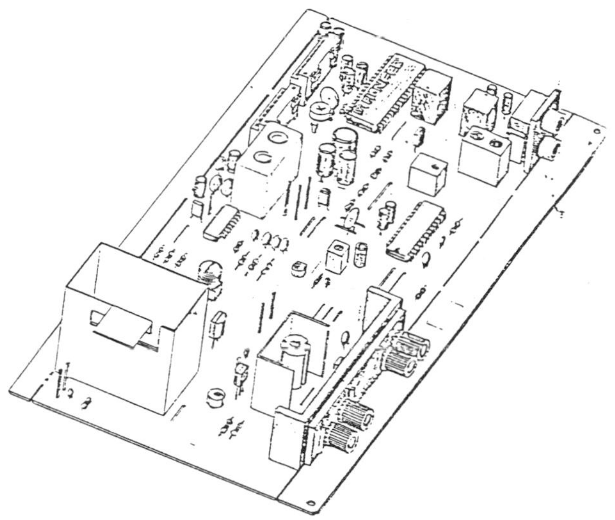

Fig. 5 Printed Circuit Board

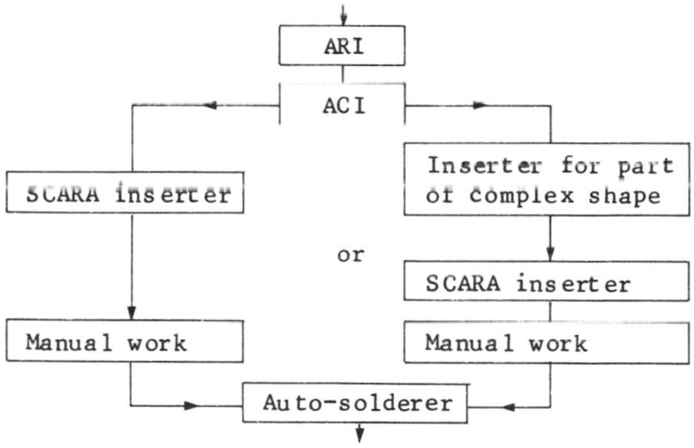

Fig. 6 Processes employing the SCARA inserter

2) SCARA system

This system is composed of a circuit board conveyer which holds the boards in precisely the correct position, a SCARA which moves from the point where it receives parts to the point of insertion, an automatic tool changer(ATC) which changes the chuck and part feeders which determine the feeding point of parts, and a controller. Fig. 7 shows a system comprising three work stations. Table 1 shows its specifications.

The system allows SCARA a large space by installing it above the conveyer. The layout provides a large area alongside the conveyer for parts feeders and machine minders who will attend in cases of trouble. By employing the ATC and compact parts feeders, inserting up to 9 different shapes of parts was possible and efficient assembly lines could be realized.

Changing the type of parts must be done often when the production system of multi-kind products of small lot sizes is pursued. To meet these requirements and to save resetting time, several feeders must be installed. The model on the line can be quickly reset with the help of the peripheral equipment because the motion program of the SCARA can be instantly changed.

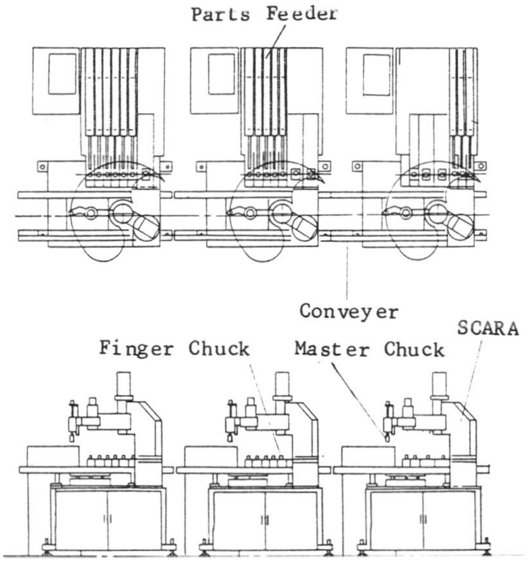

Fig. 7 Various Parts inserting SCARA system

Specification of each work station

Arm-length of the SCARA type robt(mm)robot(mm)	250 x 165
Chuck type	ATC(automatic tool changer)
Conveyer domentions(mm)	Length: 1,200 Width: adjustable automatically
Dimensions of board(mm)	Max. 330x250, Min. 150x80
Max. number of parts feedable	9 kinds in shape
Inserting direction	0 - 360 , 0.225 /step
Inserting time/piece (sec)	3-4.5 depending on inseting conditions
Loading condition of parts	Stick, taped, bulk, hoop
Program input system overall dimensions(mm)	MDI, teaching 1,200(w) x 1,550(d) x 1,500(h)

Table 1 Specifications of the assembly line for installing various shapes of parts

3) ATC(automatic tool changer)

As shown in Fig. 8, a master chuck is installed on the robot and a finger chuck on the feeder. By employing the ATC, the system has become particulaly versatile. Its features are:

a) It handles many kinds of parts.

b) It has parts feeders equipped with chucks.

c) Replacing chuck is unnecessary.

d) Development of new chucks can be expected. The chuck itself has been standardized. Only the nails are not compatible and must be replaced for particular parts. So the picking method, inserting force, etc. can be preset at their optimum. If the feeder has been adjusted when being manufactured so that the relationship between the finger chuck and parts becomes the optimum, teaching the robot the relationship between the master chuck and finger chuck is sufficient for operating the system.

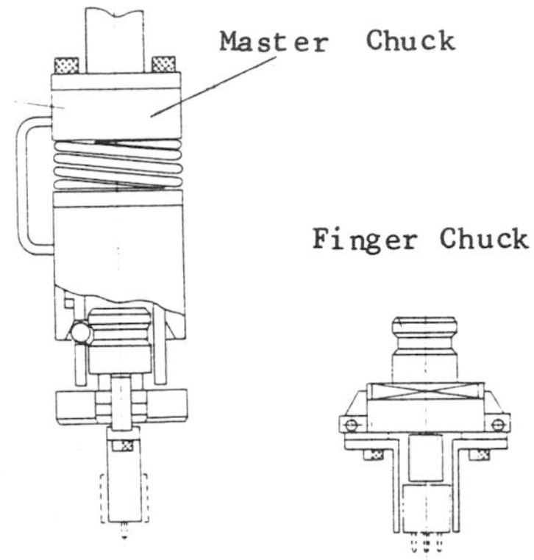

Fig. 8 ATC Units

4) Rotary multi-chuck

Among the chucks which are capable of handling many parts, there is a rotary chuck that can be used instead of ATC. Fig. 9 shows a 4-segment type of rotary chuck. The number of segments and chucks can be increased. The correct chuck and exact position can be found quickly with the help of a pulse motor and locating pin. The control signal from the robot calls out the chuck. Although heavy, this chuck makes the system work quicker than the ATC when the number of kinds of parts of different shapes is small.

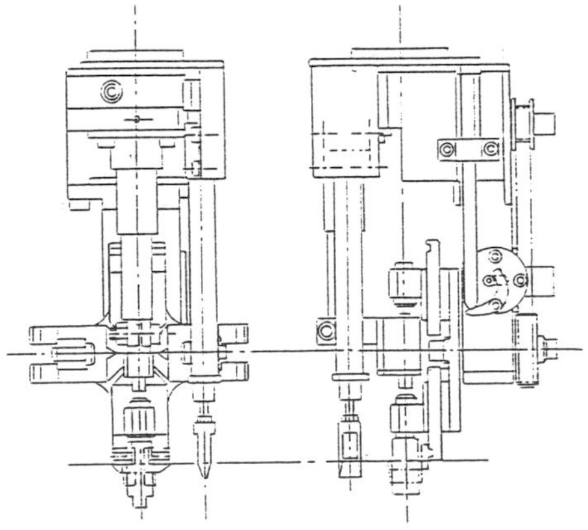

Fig. 9 Rotary multi-chuck

3-3 <u>An example of assembling a mechanical block</u>

Fig. 10 shows a mechanical block assembling system. This is a square loop type assembler for five different types of mechanical blocks of turntables. This system has 16 stations and is capable of assembling 31 parts in all. The system is composed of 7 SCARA robots, a special greaser, a screwing robot and several feeders, and is attended by a worker. The feeders installed on both sides of the SCARA carry parts to a predetermined position. The SCARA picks up and assemble them on a pallet placed at a predetermined position on the conveyer. The motion is mostly P&P and partially horizontal sliding after placing.

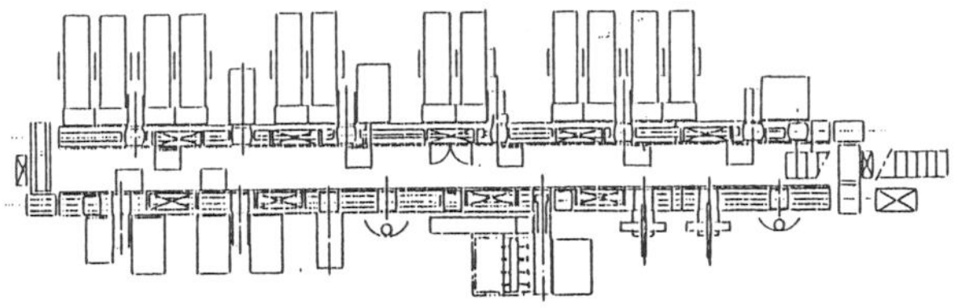

Fig. 10 Mechanical block assembling system

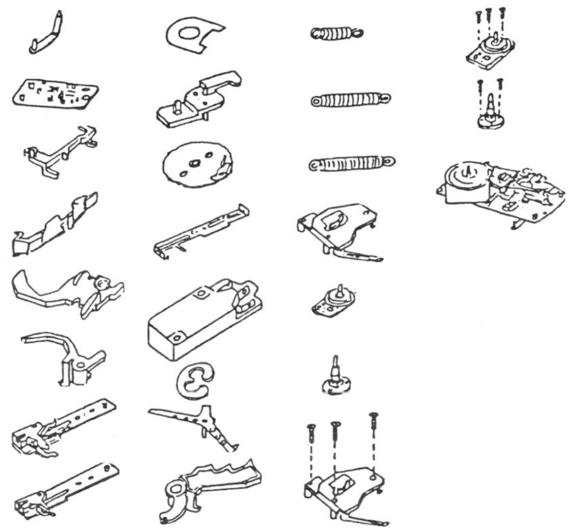

Fig. 11 These parts can be assembled by the above system

Type	Parts	Packing condition of components
Vibrating feeder	Small plastic items	Loose
Drum "	Spring	"
Stick "	Switch	Aligned in sticks
Bucket "	Semi-assembled or medium-sized items	" " buckets
Hopper	Screw	Loose

Table 2 Selected types of feeders

1) Features

a) Flexible manufacturing

In accordance with the schedule programmed in a computer, information is memorized for pallet switching at the information input station. At each assembly station, the system reads out the informaton and changes the robot's programs automatically to proceed with flexible production.

b) Centralized watch/control system

In accordance with the production plan, the control system makes a schedule efficiently and gives model numbers to the information input device. The system always watches to check that there are sufficient parts at each station, measures the quantity produced and displays it on a screen.

c) More than 80% versatility

Including the robot, most of the blocks of this system are standardized. Even if total change is required, more than 80% of the system can be used again costwise.

d) Uni-directional assembly

The system has been designed to assemble parts from the top.

2) Specifications

This mechanism assembler handles various kinds of parts in shape such as semi-assembled blocks, plastic plates, pressed metal pieces, springs, washers, stoppers and screws. Fig. 11 shows the parts it handles. It assembles five models with these parts. The cycle time is from 8.6sec. to 11.6sec.

3) Parts feeder

The type and compatibility of the feeder depend on the manufacturing process, the shape and packed conditon of parts, etc. Further standardization on this point is required. Among various kinds of feeders, those shown in Table 2 have been selected taking the cost, versatility, space and efficiency into consideration.

a) Bucket feeder

Every 10 or 20 parts must first be aligned in each bucket. The buckets are arranged in 3 lines and 15 stacks in the feeder as shown in Fig. 12. The parts in the buckets are picked up in the order which has been programmed.

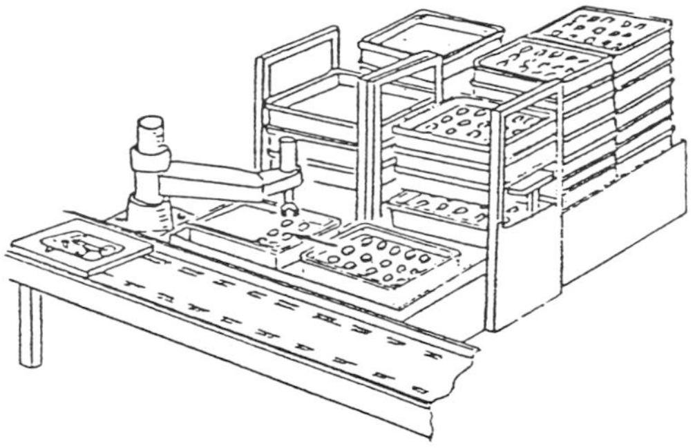

Fig. 12 Bucket feeder

b) Drum feeder

Fig. 13 shows a drum feeder. As the drum turns, a blade slowly stirs the springs loaded in the drum and drops them on a linear chute one by one. Each spring is placed in the optimum position so that it becomes straight with the hook at each end in the same plane.

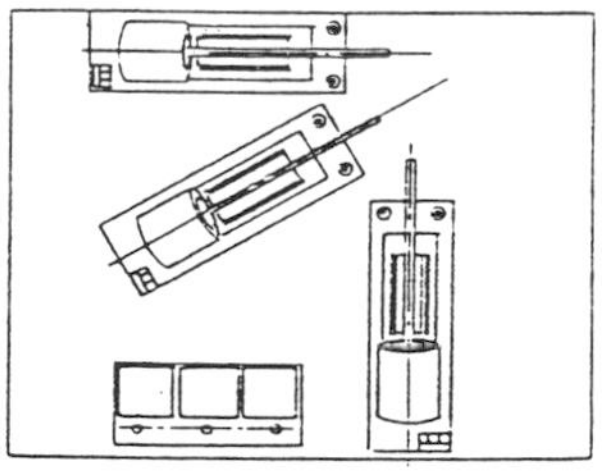

Fig. 13 Drum feeder

c) Stick feeder

Fig. 14 shows a stick feeder in which parts are aligned in a stick. The feeder determines the position of the stick and removes the stick leaving the parts in an arranged position. The robot assembles the parts in the manner programmed and demands another stick after inserting all the parts.

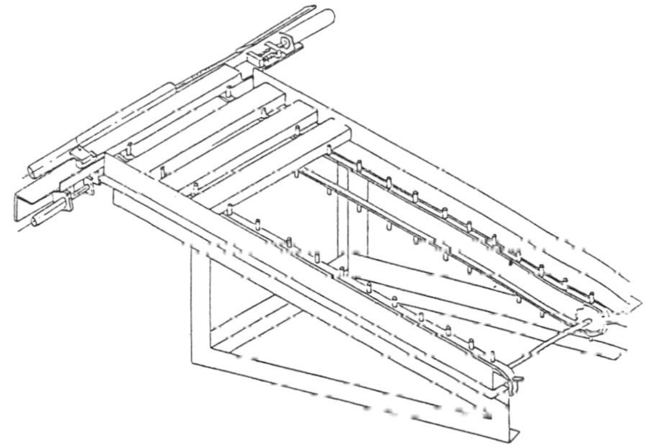

Fig. 14 Stick feeder

4) Chuck

a) Standard chuck

Fig. 15 shows a standard chuck for plastic pieces and pressed metal plates. This chuck can

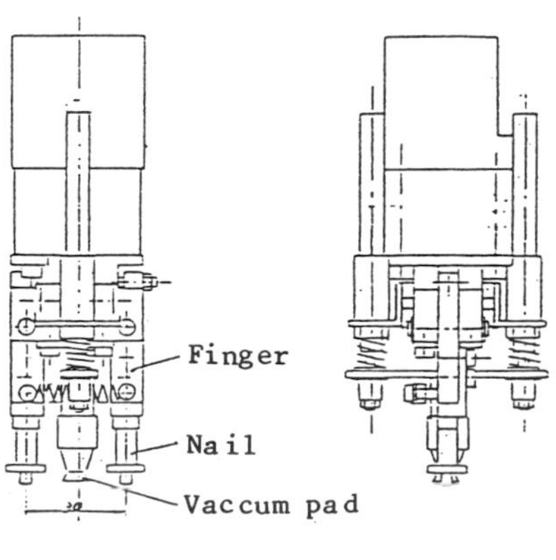

Fig. 15 Standard Chuck

hold a part without applying a force to the device in horizontal direction even when the part is out of position by ±1mm horizontally. The chuck picks up a part by suction, its nails hold the part by the holes in the part after the arm has been raised, and then it places the part in the correct position. A vacuum senser checks if the chucking has been perfectly done or not. The shape and pitch of the holes in the parts have been standardized so that the chuck can find the correct position of the parts when chucking and placing them with the help of its nails. The chuck can hold various kinds of parts.

b) Spring chuck

Figs. 16 and 17 show spring chucks and their motion. These have been designed to chuck and position a part easily. By adding hooks to the plate which receives springs, the springs can be prevented from coming off when raising the chuck pin. Thus the motion of the chuck can be simplified to an up and down movement only.

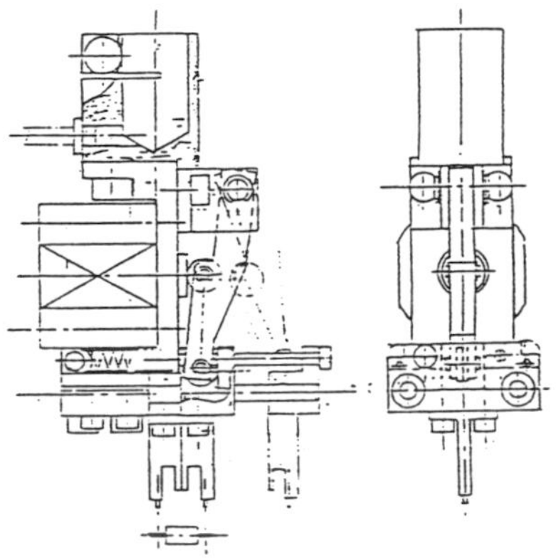

Fig. 16 Spring Chuck

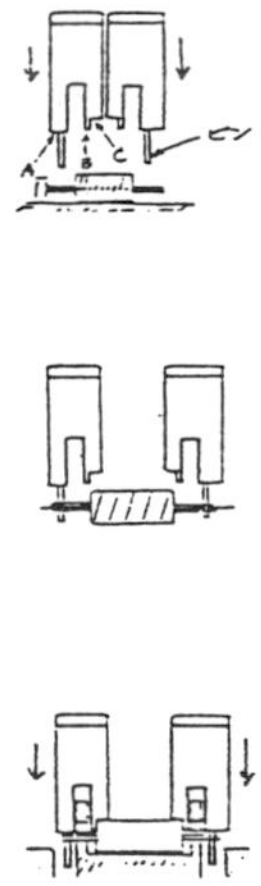

Fig. 17 Motion of Spring Chuck

3-4 An example of automatic adjustment/inspection

This system inspects the functions of each part mounted on the printed circuit board of an AM/FM tuner and automatically adjusts semi-fixed resistors to their optimum values. Four stations have been arranged on a line. One station consists of a conveyer, a robot, an adaptor, measuring equipment and a computer. The robot inspects and adjust the unit in programmed order with the help of the adaptor. The computer controls the system and processes the data. Changing the model can be done by changing the software and replacing the adaptor.

1) Features

a) Easier model changing

Changing the model is easy because the robot is flexible, and processing the parameters and operating the system can be done with the appropriate software. Keeping a preset spare adaptor helps to operate the system more effectively.

b) Quality improvement

Mistakes in adjustment and inspection have been greatly decreased because perfect adjustment can be made by an algorithm that can avoid deviation and misoperation.

c) Saving time

The time to process parameters, etc. can be greatly saved by employing a computer, and thus labour cost can be saved.

2) Specifications

a) Measurement and adjustment

Table 3 shows the items for adjustment and inspection

Adjustment	Inspection
Tracking	DC voltage
FM sensitivity	Switch operation
FM IF	Frequency
MPX	Control functions
	LED operation
	7-segment operation

Table 3 Adjustment and inspection

Figs. 18 and 19 show the side view of the whole adjustment/inspection system and its adaptor block.

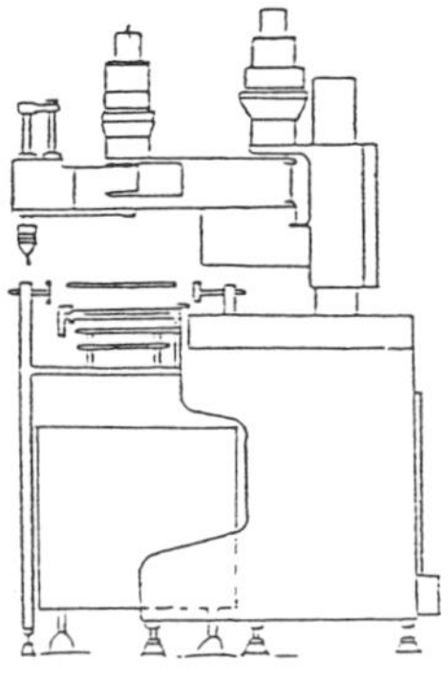

Fig. 18

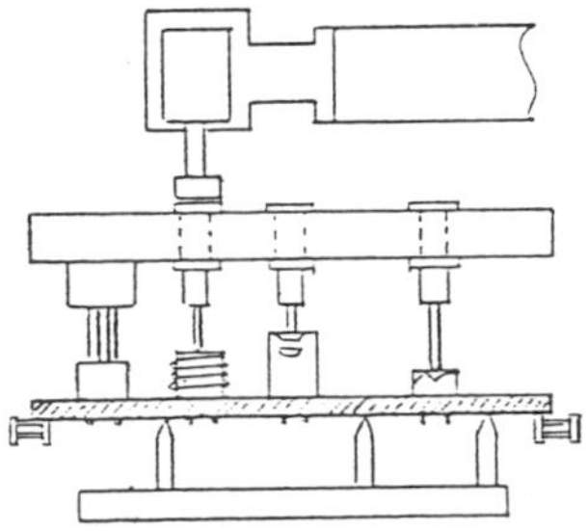

Fig. 19

4. Evaluation

4-1 Application to P&P operation

1) Applicable field

The SCARA has been successfully applied to assembly lines because it is suitable for P&P operation. Its application will be further expanded by designing SCARA-oriented products and peripheral equipment. The ability to assmble products will be improved, and the peripheral equipement will be able to handle variations of the shape and packing condition of parts. There are four main ways of packing parts; loose in a bag or box, palletizing, loading in sticks, and taping or hooping. If the arrangement of parts can be further improved, the application will be extended.

2) Saving labour cost

Fig. 20 shows the number of workers which would have been needed without the robot. For the P&P jobs, one robot is equivalent to 0.8 workers.

4-2 Application to automatic adjustment/inspection

Robots, computers and peripheral equipment have superseded adjusters and inspectors. Changing models on an assembly line has become easy simply by changing the software. This has made it possible to do multi-kind production and to improve the product quality and productivity. This device is equivalent to 1.5 workers.

4-3 Capital cost

The average cost of each station for P&P work including the above cases is 7 million yen as shown in Fig. 21. One station is equivalent one person. However, the productivity must be further improved because a 2-year pay-back period is only possible with a 5 million yen capital cost.

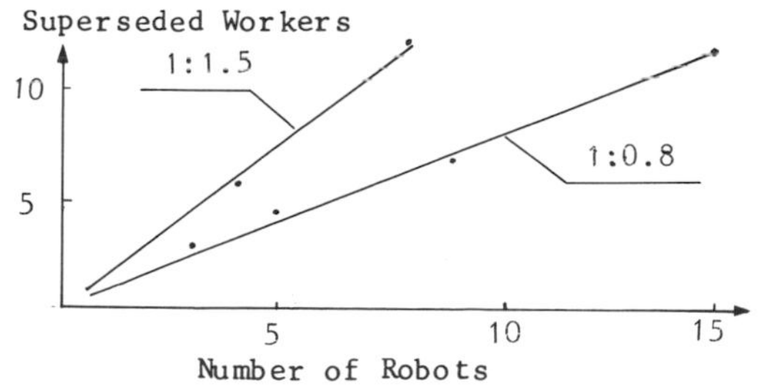

Fig. 20

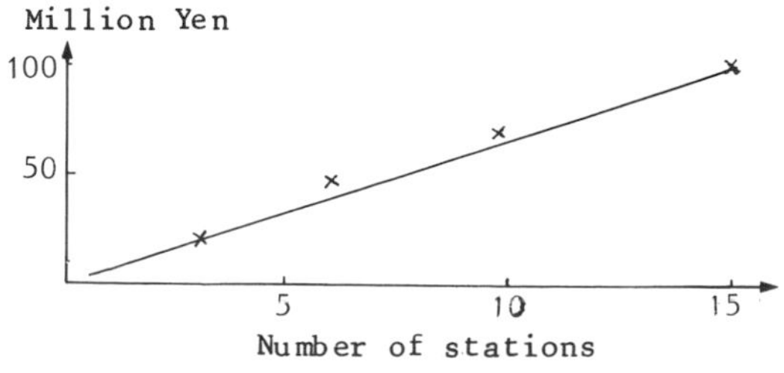

Fig. 21

4-4 Standardization of peripheral equipment

Such peripheral equipment as parts feeders and chucks, in addition to the SCARA, are required for assembling mechanical and electronic parts of different shapes. As shown in Fig. 22, the peripheral equipment carries much weight in the total cost of one station. The cost of feeders and chucks will increase when the number of models and kinds of parts is increased, so that low-priced feeders and chucks must be developed. This will be possible by standardising small blocks in the system as much as possible. For example:

1) Integrating and standardising the functions

Decreasing the number of actuators.

2) Minimizing the component blocks in the system

Classifying the loading method of parts and standardizing feeders

3) Special/versatile equipment

Parts modification can be handled by changing a small block in the system. Clear classification of special blocks and universal blocks will improve matters.

4) Minimizing equipment and making easy presetting.

When changing the model, exchanging the program and replacing some blocks in the system should be made easily with few motions. The new blocks must be easily mounted at the exact position with the help of locating pins, etc. thorough standardization like this, higher versatility and cost reduction can be achieved.

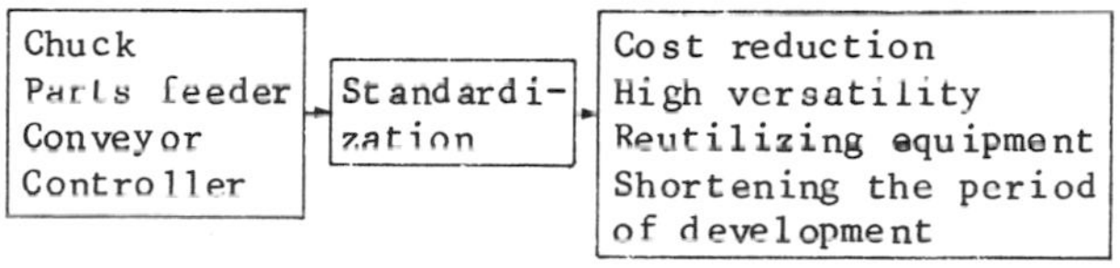

5) Example: Assembling coil springs

As discussed, special jobs can be easily done by modifying a small block of standardized equipment in the system. This can be achieved by analyzing the functions of small portions in the system and not by trying to improve the complete system.

6) Versatility of the system

The versatility of robots can be achieved by standardizing the peripheral equipment.

7) Product design suitable for automation

To reduce the cost of peripheral equipment, it is necessary to design products which fit automation methods, and to standardize and simplify the assembly lines. Fig. 22 shows the expected cost reduction for peripheral equipment.

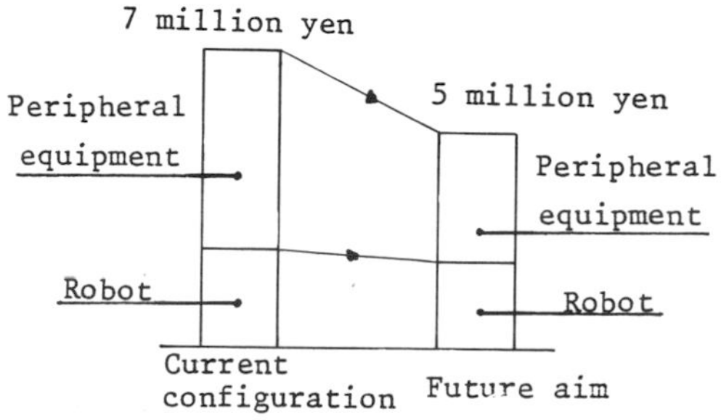

Fig. 22 Capital cost reduction

4-5 Future

The experience of employing the SCARA, operation examples and its evaluation have been discussed. It is clear that SCARA will be more widely employed on assembly lines because of its high adaptability. But it is necessary to save more labour cost by multi-shift operation in manufacturing the multi-kind products of small lot sizes. PUMA type robots and sensors will do any jobs difficult for SCARA such as assembling parts that are difficult to feed or work which requires more flexible motion. By introducing these systems, about 80% of the flexible assembly jobs can be automated, and the assembly lines can be operated by a multi-shift system, using only a few workers for watching the whole line.

Panel Discussion: Robotics for Future Industry

Chairman: Yoji Umetani, Tokyo Institute of Technology

Panelists: Minoru Morita, Matsushita Electric Industrial Co., Ltd.
Masakazu Ejiri, Hitachi Ltd.
Ryoichiro Sasano, Mitsubishi Heavy Industry, Ltd.
Akitaka Kato, Pioneer Electric Corp.

Brief Summary of Panelists' Presentation

1. M. Morita, "Design Concept of Factory Automation System"

Innovating approach to the factory automation to meet the requirement of the time to come should be considered. The requirement should be;

(1) integrated production know-how,
(2) flexibility of automated systems, and
(3) harmonization of the system with human capability of works.

The designing concept of futural automated production will be summarized as following;

(1) to apply the most advanced technology to the system
(2) to be compatible for any component machines to the automated system, and
(3) to design the system with a basic concept of flexibility.

2. M. Ejiri, "Views on Robotics for Future Industry"

An overview on futural directions for R & D of robots are discussed from the three essential robot capabilities; task-understanding, vision, and dicision-making.

(1) To integrate CAD-processed data directly with robot system will be fruitful in the task-understanding.
(2) To increase the speed of image processing for visual recognition, a revolution in the architecture of VLSI visual processor will be essential,
(3) In relation to the decision-making or problem-solving, investigation of rule-based control of robots will be effective even for complicated tasks.

3. R. Sasano, "Robotization in Ship-building Industry (Present Situation and Projected Schemes)"

The shipbuilding industry in Japan is now confronting serious difficulties in the recession, thus it is strongly requested to enhance the cost competitiveness and consequently the robotization of shipbuilding works is required under the specific and inherent characteristics of the work.

Kinds of robots having been developed collaborately at shipbuilders are two types of welding robots for hull structure, the equipment type and the portable type,

°hull assembling robots,
°painting and blasting robots.

4. A. Kato, "Valuation on the Practical Use of SCARA Type Robots on Assembly Lines and the Future Robotized Assembly Systems"

Operating stations in the assembly line automatized by introducing SCARA robots are stated, and the effect of cost reduction is also considered.

Automated stations are

°screwing of speaker components,
°inserting of electronic parts onto the printed circuit board,
°assembling of mechanical blocks for turn-table sub-assembly,
°automatic operation of the adjustment and the inspection for the circuit board.

With respect to the economic and cost evaluation of the whole assembly line robotized with the ratio of 80%, it is recommended to reduce the capital cost of a robotized unit station including peripheral equipments from 7 millions yen to 5 millions yen.

Discussion and Comment

Q: J.P. Trevelyan
All the speakers have dealt with robotics at big companies, but I suspect there are many small and medium-sized enterprises. How do you think about the specific requirement in introducing robots to those small companies?

A: M. Morita
I think there is no difference in the requirement between big and small companies, and I believe it will be enough to apply the robot to the FAS so long as we can provide an effective stand-alone work-cell with a robot from the technical aspect.

Q: D.E. Whitney
I have a question to Mr. Kato at Fig.22 of your paper. You have shown us the cost of each work-station. Does it include the cost of salary of engineers or not?

A: A. Kato
The cost includes those of conveyers, parts feeders, chucking devices, and sequence controllers, as well as its R & D engineering cost. I should stress that, in designing, assembling and making up the total system, each parts or unit devices for work-stations are to be provided in standardized version, or else the R & D cost will be increased due to costing a lot of money for developing such system as being assembled with un-standardized parts or unit devices.

Q: D.E. Whitney
Mr. Kato, on your Fig. 11, we see different types of feeder and finger. Will they handle all the necessary parts?

A: A. Kato
We provide several standardized types of chucks. which can handle not only parts with the same shape but also those with another shape.

Q: P. Davey
When I visited your factory, I remember you want to have a half of your researchers thinking about robots and another half about feeders. Do you still think so?

A: A. Kato
Yes, I do. In addition to this, I am confident that the standardization of peripheral devices around robots is as important as that of robot itself in order to reduce the design cost of the work cell of the automated manufacturing system.

Q: ?
Dr. Ejiri, you have demonstrated a sophisticated design of LSI chips for image processing, and I agree with your way. It is available at the market?

A: M. Ejiri
Unfortunately no, at this moment. But I suppose we will perhaps cooperate with another company in developing such LSI chips.

Q: Y. Shirai
I think there are few chips applicable to gray scale image processing, and I hope you perhaps expect to make such chips in practical use. Well, what is the typical application expected by the chips you mentioned?

A: M. Ejiri
The most interesting application is to the inspection work rather than assembly work, because in the inspection work the traditional binary image processing is becoming less useful and the gray scale processing is still more so.

Q: Y. Shirai
What kind of inspection?

A: M. Ejiri
For example, we are looking at the inspection of electronics parts, such as IC and LSI, where we have to find failure, fault, or damage before shipping.

Q: Y. Shirai
I think the vision system will be essential in robotizing the shipbuilding factory. What kind of visual sensor or system will be demanded or desired there, Mr. Sasano?

A: R. Sasano
As I've mentioned, they usually deal a big scale of work with rough accuracy in dimension, say a few milimeters. However, we require such intelligent processing that the shape and the dimension of work are observed by a visual system and they are automatically compared with their design data on a digital computer to generate command work signals (information file) for the robot.

Q: Y. Umetani
Mr. Sasano, you have little stressed about the utilization of moving robots. I suppose they will be necessary in the shipbuilding industry, particularly your portable robots should be carried on the moving legged robot. How do you think about it?

A: R. Sasano

There are many varieties in our portable robots, and among them such a simple one as the human worker can carry with him. But we are considering to design the most advanced one which moves by itself to the working point with the moving mechanism, and as time goes on, we probably should use a legged robot.

Q: ?

I have two questions directed to Dr. Ejiri, about the automatic digitizer system. The first is how much interactions are there, that you mean in the establishment of the CAD data-base, and the second is that are you capable of 2D or 3D modelling?

A: M. Ejiri

At present, we are dealing with 2D, as 3D picture can be reduced in 2D one by projecting. We are now developing two types of digitizers; one is for LSI drawing composed of at least 18 layers, and the second is for the game watch.

Q: J. Jarvis

Why do you need to digitizer?

A: M. Ejiri

There are many arguments about that. There are two ways. The one is to reduce the designing time, maybe in the United States the same situation, but Bell Telephone Laboratory may be the only one exception.

Q: R. Taylor

When you design an automated manufacturing system, what is the law of design systems?

A: M. Morita

As to the designing of products, the products are now diversifying the variety, so that it seems to me to make designing fitting to any automated system.

10 Key Issues of Robotics Research

Key Issues in Robot Vision

Thomas O. Binford

Artificial Intelligence Laboratory
Stanford University
Stanford, CA 94305, USA

I will discuss key issues in vision motivated by our research. One area of research is inference rules for interpretation of surfaces; a second area is autonomous mobile robots; a third is identification of industrial parts. These problems might be called: 1) a search for meaning; 2) determining unique consistent descriptions; 3) missing information; 4) needle in a haystack; 5) similarity vs identity; 6) computation; 7) building large systems.

Inference Rules for Surface Interpretation

Projection from three dimensions to two dimensions raises the problem of missing information. Image elements are areas, curves, and points (junctions). In space there are volumes, surfaces, curves, and points. Interpretation assigns correspondence between image elements and space elements, e.g. image curves and space curves. These correspondences are nonunique locally, they are disambiguated by global consistency. For images with moderate complexity, combinatorics lead to high complexity.

New geometric constraints implemented as inference rules provide local interpretations with little ambiguity. Global consistency is quasi-local, i.e. consistency is usually resolved over short chains of connected elements.

A worldwide concern is high speed symbolic computation for AI and high level vision. In interpretation with these inference rules, these graph structures have local connectivity to few elements. Information flow is over small neighborhoods. The analysis seems to transform interpretation to a structure favorable for parallel implementation, and to reduce the complexity of interpretation so that simple scenes have low complexity. The important issue is understanding the geometric structure of vision algorithms and their realization in machines.

Another issue is representation of these geometric elements, not only surfaces, curves, and junctions, but geometric operations and constraints on them.

Mobile Robots

One current scenario for much of mobile robot research is an autonomous vehicle outdoors on roads and cross country. When we got a new mobile robot, we had thought also of parts loading and unloading in an FMS. We have had a visit from a large company involved in autonomous vehicles for warehousing who want the next generation to be more flexible than the current generation which follow a wire or a line painted on the floor. Here the issue is real-time computation with vast amounts of data. Moravec's robot in 1980 moved 15 minutes per meter. A current target is 10 km per hour, or 3 m per second. That is about a factor of 2700 too slow. But we want to improve performance considerably to implement improved reliability, accomodate variability, and provide accuracy in identification. We are far from our goals of reliability. For a 20 km traverse with pictures every 3 m, there are 7000 pictures. How many sophisticated research systems have interpreted 20 pictures?

Outdoors scenes have predominatly textured regions. Edge segmentation has had limited success with uniform regions, and little with textured regions. This domain is far from the research problems with man-made or geometric objects with uniform surfaces. One issue is fast, dense range maps with resolution of several cm over a range of 20 m. For outdoors scenes, it is an aid, not a solution. For industrial parts, ranging with resolution of 0.05 mm over a range of 1 to 2 meters would be valuable. Rumors of suitable ranging devices are frequent, but they seem to be still several years away.

A central issue is high speed computation, of the order of 50 to 100 mega OPS (MOPS). Some current processors are able to do convolutions, to transform an image into another image. We need processors not only for these low level operations but programmable processors which can extract connected boundaries and segmented, symbolic descriptions. In figure 1 we compare computation power of some systems. The VAX has about 0.5 MFLOPS; the 68000 has about 0.16 MOPS (16 bit fixed point multiply). The Mercury array processor is planned for about 12 MFLOPS.

Frame buffers have ALUs which do an 8 bit multiply/add per 100 nsec, 20 MOPS. To make the comparison a little more even, we made a second scale, byte OPS (BOPS). Crudely, a 32 bit operation is four times the computation of a 16 bit operation. Some of the high points of the figure are the Star ST-100 array processor, and the WARP processor of CMU which Kung and Kanade are involved with. These are both capable of 32 bit floating point at 100 MFLOPS.

Identification of Industrial Parts

The scenario here is identification of industrial parts presented in trays; they can overlap and may be tilted, but they are usually in stable states or neary so. In the photographs we see some complexities. Because these parts have shiny surfaces and because of extended light sources, large specular reflections are prominent for cylinders. Edges of cylinders are difficult to determine because the brightness on the shadowed edge slopes steeply into the shadow; on the other edge, there is substantial reflection from the tray, so this edge fades out also. For the spring, the tops of the coils have specular reflection and are not visible to the edge operator used. We instead see the bottom coils of the spring. This example suggests requirements for complex segmentation. Prediction of intensity, specularity, range, and geometric relations are important for model-based vision.

In ACRONYM, matching took from one second to minutes for uncluttered scenes. Key issues for matching are: a) the search for meaning: aggregation of image features into canonical structures which are candidate objects, the figure/ground problem; aggregation decreases combinatorial explosion of matching all tuples of features; b) formalization and analysis of matching algorithms: the most usual formalism now is subgraph isomorphism. It is not adequate because it does not deal with partial matches caused by missing, or spurious data, e.g. a match with one leg missing may be acceptable because of obscuration or unacceptable. It appears that matching reqires substantial interpretation and context to measure quality of match and that simple counting of matching and missing features is inadequate. c) indexing: the need in a haystack: Model-based systems typically consider only a few objects in any one context. General systems have very large numbers of objects in visual memory; it is useful to index into the visual memory to select subsets of similar objects for detailed matching.

The quality of segmentation at discontinuities in intensity, range, or on curves still limits the performance of vision systems. The scale problem is one aspect of the problem of determining unique descriptions from multiple appearances in scale, orientations, etc.

For our work toward general vision systems, the definition of object classes is a major problem which involves quantifying similarity among objects which are not identical. We seldom encounter the same object twice. We meet a friend after twenty years; he has changed greatly yet we recognize him. Current systems with few exceptions match individuals, i.e. they may test that a scene contains a 747 or a L-1011, but they don't have much ability to say that it looks like an aircraft, even if it is none that I know. They may not have a good way to represent generic aircraft and to say that it looks more like an aircraft than a car.

The best of current systems have of order 50,000 lines of code. Future systems may be 100 times larger. The familiar problems of building large systems are intensified here because of the complexity of the AI tasks, because of our limited knowledge of the solution, and because of the strong interconnection among vision modules.

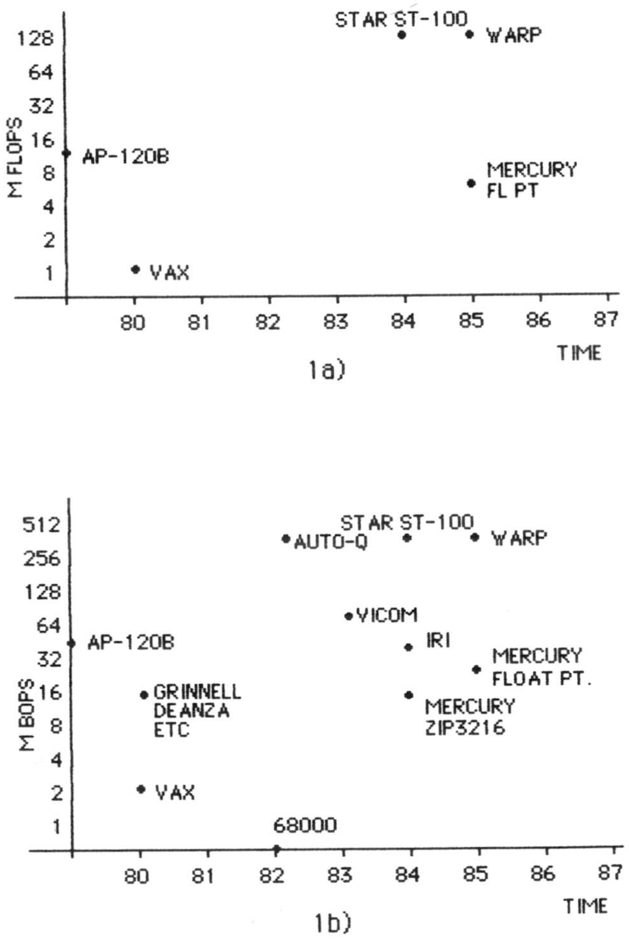

FIGURE 1: PERFORMANCE VS TIME

1a. MEGA FLOPS; 1b. MEGA BYTE OPS

TWO KEY PROBLEMS IN ROBOTICS RESEARCH

R. W. Daniel
Oxford University Engineering Laboratory
Parks Road, Oxford OX1 3RH, England

P. G. Davey
Meta Machines Ltd
9 Blacklands Way, Abingdon Industrial Park
Abingdon, Oxford OX14 1DY, England

This paper attempts to summarise user requirement in two areas:

* Off-line and on-line programming for robot sensors.
* Measurement and control of flexible arms.

It reviews relevant improvements in specifications of commercially available equipment and software, and early research contributions. Some key topics for future research are identified.

INTRODUCTION

It may seem capricious that we have chosen two apparently disparate topics, namely the programming of robot sensors and the measurement and control of flexible robot arms as the subject for this paper.
For several reasons, we regard both topics as particularly important in their own right. The use of imaging sensors is becoming commercially important in a few selected applications, and off-line programming of sensors is coming to be seen as an increasingly essential part of off-line programming for robot systems generally. This latter is gradually becoming more favoured by industrial users. Robot arms are being driven with progressively higher acceleration in the search for shorter cycle times, and it will soon no longer be possible to ignore compliance, either in the links or in the joints, resulting in unwanted degrees of freedom and resonance modes. Strong economic pressures forcing the price of robot arms downwards, while still demanding high accuracy, may well have a similar effect.

On top of all this, however, we see the two topics as linked. This is because in order to provide the exteroceptive data required for better control of flexible arms, sensors must be used increasingly to ensure accurate relative measurements between the end effector and the objects among which it is moving.

It seems to us therefore that programming of robot sensors will become increasingly important not only in its own right but also as an essential adjunct to accurate control of cheaper lightweight structures.

1. Off-line programming of sensors

The use of sensors, especially imaging sensors of various kinds, together with autonomous computer decision-making and a programmable manipulator, has always been implicit in academic robotics research. Most academic researchers would not accept that a machine without (exteroceptive) sensors was robot at all - unlike the production engineers who for 15 years have accepted "industrial robots" with no sensors at all expect primitive interlocks.

An early goal of robotics research was off-line programming at least of an arm and gripper, for complete tasks, eg, [Lieberman 1976] on the grounds that is was expensive, as well as sometimes dangerous for the operator, always to use the robot arm as its own multi degree of freedom digitiser. The emergence of robot arms, like Cincinnati T3 with TCP and Unimation PUMA with VAL, having coordinate transformations an integral part of the controller has made it perfectly feasible to program mechanical movement of the end effector entirely off-line for at least 8 years. However, customer acceptance of this procedure has been small, most preferring interactive use of the real arm and workpieces even when using textual programming methods. Major reasons for this must be the gross inadequacy of the best graphics displays for visualising complex 3D detail, relatively slow progress in adapting existing CAD systems to support robot programming efficiently, and reluctance of industrial robot manufactures to provide parameters and performance sufficient to ensure absolute accuracy of end-effectors position in the workspace. During the last 5 years it has been increasingly realised by researchers that

substantial progress from manipulator level, through object level, toward objective level languages for off-line programming of arms probably cannot be made without fully incorporating off-line programming of sensor systems also. This belief appeared to be an important underlying motive for early work at Stanford on ACRONYM eg, [Binford 1979] and has been stressed in recent work by the Edinburgh group also [Yin 1983].
The main reasons for it are:

(a) It is realised that the very best kinematic program prepared off-line can only serve as a first approximation. It provides definition of the major task structure, normal exception conditions, and trajectories accurate perhaps to 0.5 mm in space, but reqluires much "fine tuning" on-line. This must still be done by the commissioning engineer at present. In future, sensing systems giving relative position, forces and torgues could not only provide an automatic solution to fine tuning, but also accommodate variations in the workplace, fixtures and parts as time goes on.

(b) Accommodating conditionality based on variable information derived from sensors instead of a fixed, even if complicated, sequence of instructions, requires major changes in implementing off-line trajectory programming which ceases even in principle to be a straightforward compilation.

(c) The more progress is made toward automatic planning of tasks like assembly, and especially tasks involving flexible workpieces [Inoue 1983], the more dependent the system becomes on sensor-based checks to ensure that each step has been properly completed.

It is for the above reasons that we have chosen to highlight the need for more work on off-line programming of sensors as one of the two topics of this paper.
Most effort has gone so far into work on visual (camera) images but all that we describe can equlally well be applied to other sensors-eg, ultrasound or eddy current.

1.1 Methods used so far.

As has been mentioned, off-line trajectory programming has not become exactly widespread in industry even since availability of VAL as a commercial product.
Still less has the use of imaging sensors - probably because too many "vision boxes" have been conceived without being sufficiently well adapted to the target industrial process. Nevertheless the training method used in the SRI (later MIC) box, ie, the learning of statistical parameters for each connected "blob" such as area, MI, principal axes, etc, from "teach-by-showing" [Gleason 1979] has become the classic at least for 2-D object recognition and location. For 3D objects it becomes cumbersome when the user must present a large number of diffrent objects in different poses, and is a strictly on-line method requiring all the physical parts to be handled at training time. The next route is to use a high-level image system applications language such as GE's VPL or Automatix'RAIL. This still requires rather intensive labour to define each object by the operator producing the programme and hardly seems a step nearer J C Latombe's vision "Towards the non-programming of robots"! The favoured method for the future must be to base off-line sensor programming upon 3-D representations of objects already held in CAD files, as exemplified by [Gruver 1984]. In this work, by Calma and GE, CAD wireframe models of objects to be grasped can be "exposed" in simulation to the vision system using functions providing correct camera perspective, sensor-to-world spatial calibration, etc. The usual statistical parameters (for each connected blob designated by the operator) are then calculated by the off-line system and passed down for use by the vision system when recognising real objects presented during the on-line process later.

1.2 Future Trends

In attempting to identify some of the key questions for future research work in offline programming of sensors, we take two particular industrial applications as paradigms - these are first, parts handling, that is identification and grasping of assorted parts [cf Gleason, Gruver] and second, welding and seam sealing processes which have received a little less attention in the context of offline programming but where this is becoming increasingly important [Clocksin 1982, Kremers 1983]. It is in fact a commonly held misconception amongst robotic researchers that the only application fit for offline programming, is mechanical assembly; so far from that being the case, there is pressure from users to use offline programming both for the process and for sensors feeding back information about it, even in apparently "simple" applications such as paint spraying.
A first key research issue will continue to be deriving the maximum possible amount of geometric information from the CAD database, not just for deriving statistical blob parameters as mentioned above in binary images, but for 3D model-driven object recognition and position measurement in grey levels. Work in this direction has been a central part of the ACRONYM project at Stanford and also that of Shirai at ETL [Oshima 1981] -- mainly with an eye on the parts handling paradigm.
Interesting though, it has also become crucial in recent developments by Meta Machines in Oxford, to obtain more secure guidance information in our structured light technique used in the arc welding environment.
Especially in the seam following paradigm, users require the ability to specify special features

on the CAD representation of the parts being joined which will define start points, finish points and intermediate discontinuities as for example when arc welding or sealing is required to be continuous around a sharp corner.

Second, not just parts, but also full details of the illumination being used, should be included as a 3D geometrical model drawn from the CAD database. In the normal case of diffused lighting a combination of knowledge about the light source geometry and illumination properties with colour and reflectivity information the typical parts being handled would allow considerably enhanced prediction of interaction between lighting objects, and hence of actual shading different areas of a grey level camera picture. Point-source and strctured lighting should simply be taken as a special case of this, with the result that structured light seam following sensors could dispense with the preliminary "vision teach" phase.

Third, offline programming systems for sensors will have to include facilities for specifying tolerances on the parts being handled. These are particularly important on dimensions but also on other physical properties such as the illumination and surface reflectivities. The operator will normally wish to specify alternative tactics when tolerances are found to be outside certain bounds. In the parts handling paradigm, for instance, the operator will wish to ensure that assemblies for which the mating force is outside a certain tolerance band are not continued but the parts are instead passed for rectification. In he seam following paradigm, when a gap to be welded exceeds, say, twice the thickness of the base metal "weaving" should be initiated to ensure that sufficient filler metal is introduced to make a sound joint across the gap. Should the gap grow greater still, it would be better not to weld at all but to flag that part for rectification instead.

Fourth, radical and extensive research is required to produce appropriate technologies for vastly improved high-resolution 3D visual, force and tactile "displays", virtually giving the operator tele-existence during the off-line programming task.

To summarise, future research in offline sensor programming will increasingly be concerned with deriving the maximum possible amount of information about workpieces, tools and fixtlures from the CAD database and then using that information in support of model-driven object recognition and location and in various strategies for exception-handling and "graceful degradation". Not only 3D dimensions in physical space but also many other physical attributes of both parts and illumination systems will be required ranging from colour and reflectivity through to resistive and magnetic properties. This information will be required not only for vision sensing but for other imaging sensors; for example both resistive and magnetic properties will be of the greatest importance to an imaging eddy current sensor.

2. Control of Flexible Arms

Much research effort has been expended over the past decade on the analysis and control of idealised rigid robot arms. Robot links have been viewed as perfect rigid bodies, subject to torques and forces from actuators or the external world. There is a growing awareness that real robots do not in general fit this form of description unless their links are made to be massive and the robot to move slowly. Some researchers are now modelling the flexlure that occurs in real mechanical components when subject to loads(static or dynamic); we will now consider some of the various approaches that have been used and try to outline possible future avenues of research.

The reason for studying the behaviour of flexible robot arms is the need for fast, cheap robots to satisfy future demands on performance. As has been observed in [Book 1983] the cross sectional areas of robot links necessary to support the dynamic stresses within a robot can be considerably less than those required for it to behave as a "stiff" structure.
Reducing the cross sections of a robot's links results in lower masses and inertias for the robot arm and a commensurate increase in its efficiency as a load carrying device.

Early interest in the control of flexible mechanical systems came from the area of space structure control. Such systems used in space do not in general have to support their own weights, the only significant loads arising from inertial effects. The premium that is placed on payload, together with the lack of gravitational constraint in situ, has led to a number of investigations into the control of extremely flexible structures. Typically, such structures have very little damping and can have significant natural reasonances at a number of frequencies. One major constraint on the control of flexible space systems is the possible excitation of unmodelled modes leading to its eventual destruction (referred to as control or observer "spillover"). All this is in contrast with practical robot arms which must:

(a) be sufficiently strong to support their own weight;

(b) have significant amounts of damping within the physical structure so that vibration is kept to a minimum.

2.1 Methods used so far.

The majority of authors have used one or two

popular methods for deriving the eqluations of motion of a flexible arm. One approach is to try and approximate a continuously deformable structure as a discrete set of lumped spring-mass-damper systems, as for example in the finite element technique used in [Usoro 1984]. The second approach is to use a Modal analysis technique, such as that of Rayleigh-Ritz, to obtain approximate solutions to the partial differential equations describing the distributed system, this method being favoured by Truckenbrodt [Truckenbrodt 1979]. The models obtained by the two approaches are then inserted into a Lagrangian for the whole robot to obtain the equations of motion. Both approaches require judgement on when it is valid to apply the results obtained to the full distributed system.

The main problem with controlling flexible systems using the two approaches outlined above appears to be the high order of the models obtained, eg, for each link, Truckenbrodt requires 12 variables (states) to describe the robot's behaviour with any accuracy [Truckenbrodt 1981]. Another is that only small deviations about a fixed trajectory may be considered and no justificaition in terms of control theory is given for the applicability of results to an arm executing trajectories anywhere within its entire working volume. Apart from the notable exception of Truckenbrodt, the effects of model order reduction have not been considered.
Truckenbrodt uses singular perturbation analysis to obtain error bounds for the truncation problem inherent in using a finite model expansion. There are other methods available in the literature of control engineering for the analysis of effects due to errors between the model used and the actual system; no authors used these methods for flexible arm control.

2.2. Future Trends

There have been recent advances in multivariable control theory in the area of "uncertain" systems - that is, systems where the model used is incomplete or inaccurate because a low order model has been used to approximate a higher order one, or because of uncertainty in measuring the system's parameters. Most of the impetus has been in the frequency domain, and methods are becoming available to analyse certain classes of uncertain non-linear systems. The advantage of frequency domain design techniques is that the method is amenable to the design of low order controllers for potentially high order systems; it also provides predictions of the efficiency of control action. There also exist results on the control of certain classes of uncertain distributed systems [Postlethwaite 1984]. This work needs to be extended from continuous time to sampled data systems, as any realistic controller for a robot would be computer based. Algorithms have to be developed for flexible systems which are recursive, eg, [Featherstone 1983] rather than generating a complete Lagrangian in terms of rigid body inertias and shape functions. The full non-linear nature of the problem needs to be considered and whether approaches outlined by the authors above are really applicable over a robot's entire work volume.

The aim of a robot control system is to generate signals so that there exists a predetermined combination of position and force at the end effector; results are needed on the closed loop control of these parameters using absolute position and force measurement.
Robots form a new class of system to be controlled, they are time varying, non-linear, parameter dependent, and distributed. They are semi-rigid, with tight constrains on the behaviour of the end effector. Future research in robot control will try to address these intractable problems

References

Binford T. O, Brooks R. A.
"Geometric Reasoning in ACRONYM"
Proc. ARPA Image Understanding Workshop, Menlo Park, April 1979

Book W. J, Majett M,
"Controller Design for Flexible Distributed Parameter Mechanical Arms via Combined State Space and Frequency Domain Techniques". ASME Journal Dynamic Systems, Measurement and Control, Vol 105, No 4, December 1983.

Book J. W., Maizza-Meto O., Whitney D. E.,
"Feedback Control of Two Beam Two Joint Systems with Distributed Flexibility" Journal of Dynamic Systems Measurement and Control, Transactions of the ASME Vol 97, pp 424-431, December 1975.

Clocksin W. F., Davey P. G.,
Morgan C. G., Vidler A. R., "Progress in Visual Feedback for Robot Arc Welding of Thin Sheet Steel", Robot Vision, A Pugh (ed) IFS Pubs 1982.

Featherston R, "The Calculation of Robot Dynamics using Articulated Body Inertias", IJRR 2, No 1, Spring 1983.

Gleason G. J., Agin G., "Modular Vision System for Sensor Controlled Manipulation and Inspection". Proc 9 ISIR March 1979.

Gruver W. A. et al "off-line Robot Vision Sytem programming by CAD" Proc Robots 8 Conference, Detroit June 1984.

Inoue H., Inaba M., "Hand Eye Coordination in Rope Handling" Proc ISRR Bretton Woods August 1983.

Lieberman L. I., Wesley M. A.
"AUTOPASS, An Automatic Programming System for Computer Controlled Mechanical Assembly". IBM Yorktown Heights Internal Report, 1976.

Oshima M., Shirai Y.
"Object Recognition using 3D Information". Proc IJCAI Vancouver, August 1981.

Postlethwaite I., Foo Y. K.
"A Robustness Test for Distributed Feedback Systems", Oxford University Engineering Laboratory Report No. 1522/84, April 1984.

Truckenbrodt A.
"Dynamics and Control Methods for Moving Flexible Structures and Their Application to Industrial Robots", Proceedings of the 5th World Congress on Theory of Machines and Mechanisms, 1979.

Truckenbrodt A.
"Truncation Problems in the Dynamics and Control of Flexible Mechanical Systems", 1981 IFAC, p 1909-14, Vol 4, Kyoto 1981.

Usoro P. B., Nadira R., Mahil S. S.
"Control of Lightweight Flexible Manipulators: A Feasibility Study", Transactions of the 1984 American Control Conference, San Diego California, June 6-8 1984.

Yin Baolin
"A Framework for Handling Vision Data in an Object Level Robot Language RAPT" Proc. IJCAI, Karlsruhe 1983.

Key Issues of Robotics Research

Brian Carlisle

Adept Technology, Inc.
Mountain View, CA 94043, USA

I am talking about complexity of programming robots. In 1978, we delivered the first PUMA robot to General Motors. At that time, the programming language which was called VAL was consisted of very simple instructions. Typical PUMA programs are something like this: MOVE A; MOVE B; MOVE C;,,. In 1979, we had extended the control of VAL language, so that the program looks something like this and pretty straighforward but not easiest thing for operator to understand at that time.

In 1982, we created VAL-II which looked much more like Pascal and which began to interact with the environment. It involves some communication routines, some network routines and a great number of control features. Here is an example of the program. It has 50 instructions, and only 8 of those do robot motion.

Today, in 1984, we have just created a program for Robot-8 demonstration which I would like to show to you. I have a video tape. The point is: this program utilizes not only sensors but also multiple robots. There are parallel asynchronous tasks going on. Robot is working on moving coordinate system and we have asynchronous communication for simultaneous operations.

I will talk a little bit of demonstration. There was a vision system to upstream. The vision system recognize the casting. It also recognizes the cassette of PC board. It sends the vison data and location of the cassette over a serial link to the downstream. So, the downstream robots get the vision information asynchronously over communication link. This is a very complicated program. This program consists of about 100 pages of VAL-II codes and adds some 62 routines. The resulting program looks like this. There were 62 routines. Sixteen routines of which are involved in communication. Some 12 routines involve to initialize various constants which will be executed in system start up. Some 10 routines involve with the control, orchestration of events, and sequencing. Actual motion task had 9 routines. The sensor related routines were 4. Actually, vision routine is 4 routines, there was digital sensing routines and so forth. At the points here is the task of programming a robot in real world. System can become extensively complex, far beyond the capacity of operators. We need to figure out something about that.

I think that there is a good deal of task about automatic programming and that it is a very long way off. So, we need near term goals to reduce the complexity of programming a robot. I would suggest a few of areas of focus. The first of those is task oriented language development. Tasks would be high level task that would perform functions or operations. The first job should be to define what the task should be and then we need to develop the task themselves both in sensing areas and control areas. The sequence of tasks might be something like locate, approach, grasp, insert, and so on. The second thing we need to do is to work on aids for event orchestration and system design. As the robot system become more complex, asynchronous timing and unexpected events will tend to dominate the control problems. Finally, we need to have some way to simulate the response of operations of these complex systems. We should be able to simulate the response to sensors, errors, and real world tolerances. We should be able to simulate time varing external input and asynchronous communication.

To talk a little bit more about my concept of task oriented language development, the first thing we would do is to define several types of physical tasks, which the robot is interacting with the environments to sensors, to motions, and to control tasks, which we are trying to sequence physical task and communication tasks. I think, in near term, industries will use ad hoc procedures to some of the tasks. But I think there is a good opprotunity for study in University to develop generalized strategies of the tasks. I would like to encourage some of the work of Mason, Lozano Perez who look at the matter. People of the Draper Lab. who are looking at some of these sort of problems. I think, once we have developped strategies for these tasks, we have to define the position

---

This paper is transcribed and edited from the recorded tape of Carlisle's presentation at the panel.

input and the output of what sort of errors we might expect. To talk about representation of errors, we must consider the monitoring and verification strategies. Moreover, we need some concept about what data the CAD system should supply to our task strategies. We also need to consider logical and geometric reasoning abilities, and we must have some concept how do we initialize these systems. When we have all the above, we can start the work on planning systems.

An example task might be the insertion of a generalized cylinder. Generalized cylinder is defined by cross section and some kind of sweeping function. Tasks might have preconditions associated with it such that the robot holding the cylinder, and aligning the hole within some tolerance. There is certain number of degree of freedom in position. Certain physical data might be supplied to this strategy of the task including the cross section of links and sweeping functions, coefficient of friction, tolerances, and matching the materials. It would have some termination conditions, reaching a position threshold, force threshold, certain degree of freedom that is defined in the position or force, and certain initialization conditions. The important things of those is strategy for the task.

The summary of insertion task procedure is: approaching to the top surface of the hole, stopping on force, doing force based search for hole, using a strategy perhaps RCC strategy to actually perform insertion, verifying the success of insertion, finding the degrees of freedom, and finally releasing the grip. However we have discovered the very little understanding of this sort of physical processes involved in performing of sensor based operation.

Talk about second subject. I would like to discuss event orchestration and system design. Some of the problems concern how should we generate control program for parallel asynchronous tasks. In general, if you have robot working in certain time window, you can imagine the task of picking part off the conveyer. It is important to interrupt the task without some kind of disaster happening. You should like to be able to predict or prevent resource when more than one robot is demanding information for vision system to develop control interlocks.

Secondly, from this system design standpoint, we need to be able to answer such questions how many robots do you need to achieve the certain system: throughput, the system performance, what sort of interactions in space and in time with the robots. How do we optimize between parallel and serial tasks. Serial tasks are so easy to control. Parallel tasks are more effiicient. How do we design buffers based upon the probability of success in a given task. And finally, designing safety interlocks is needed too.

My final comment will relate to system simulation. I think we need modelling capability to debug robot program in off-line. We need to be able to model multiple robots, and fixtures associated with them on a moving coordinate system. We need to be able to model the response to the control input to system in hierarchical level. We need to be able to simulate sensors. The errors associated with the sensors would be nice to be able to simulate the error propagation to the system. What happens in a downstream is asynchronous communication.

Most importantly, a random control of time variations, and sequence the external inputs and we would like to be able to perturb the system to a random way or controlled way to debug the software. This modelling system should monitor the kinematics and dynamics of the robot, and to look for limits of joint excursion. It should dètect collisions. It should detect delays caused by timing problem. It should detect resource complex. And finally, it should work with error propagation.

NEED: Reduce the Complexity of Programming Robots.

NearTerm Goal: Continuing improvements in interactive off-line programming.

Suggested Areas of Focus:

1. Task-oriented language development.
2. Event orchestration & system design
3. Simulation of system response to:
   - sensors
   - errors, tolerances
   - time varying external inputs
   - asynchronous communication

Physical Tasks

Interact with world: Action achieved through strategy and feedback.

Utilize:
- Sensors
- Physical Data
- PhysicalReasoning
- Geometric Data
- Geometric Reasoning
- Position & Force Constraints
- Motion Control
- Error Descriptors

Inputs:
- Preconditions
- Initialization Conditions, Commands
- Physical & Geometric Data
- Termination Conditions

Outputs:
- Post Conditions
- Error Representations

System Simulation

Model: Multiple Robots, Fixtures
Moving Coordinate Systems

Response to:
System Control Inputs
System Control Program
Simulated Sensors
Error Propagation
Asynchronous Communication
Random or Controlled Time Variation
& Sequence of External Inputs

Monitor: Robot Kinematics, Dynamics
Collisions
Delays
Resource Conflicts
Error Propagation

Exampla Task: Generalized Cylinder Insertion

Preconditions: Holding peg, peg aligned with hole within tolerance
6 DOF in position...

Physical Data: Cross section, spine, sweeping function
Coefficient of friction
Tolerances
Material

Termination Condition:
Position threshold
Force threshold
DOF in position
DOF in force

Initialization: Tool length
Error branch address

Strategy: Approach surface
Stop on force
Search for hole
Use RCC strategy to insert
Verify success
Release grip

Event Orchestration & System Design

Problems:

1.Generating Control Programsfor Asynchronous, Parallel Tasks
a) Time windows for action.
b) May not be able to interrupt task without disaster.
c) Predict/prevent resource conflicts.
d) Design interlock.

2. System Design
a) How many robots to perform tasks.
b) Interactions in spsce, time.
c) Optimize between parallel & serial tasks.
d) Buffer design and throughput estimates based on probability of success.
e) Interlock design.

Evolution of Task-oriented Language

1. Definition of Tasks:
Physical, Control, Communication
2. Research
3. Ad Hoc Strategy (Industry:procedures)
4. General Strategies (University)
Study processes
5. Define: Input, output
Errors...representation, recovery
Monitoring, verification
Physical data
Reasoning ability....logical & geometric
Initial conditions

When we have 1--5 we can start work on planning systems.

KEY ISSUES OF ROBOTICS RESEARCH

Yoshiaki Shirai

Electrotechnical Laboratory
1-1-4 Umezono, Sakuramura, Niiharigun
Ibaraki, Japan

In the course of describing the Japanese big project "Advanced Robot Technology, some of the key issues of robotics is discussed. The goal of the project is to develop fundamental technologies and applied systems. This paper focuses on the fundamental technology and raise important problems in the following elements: locomotion, manipulation, sensing, autonomous control, tele-operator, tele-existence, and support technology.

1. Introduction

Recently many industrial robots are used in various fields and strenuous efforts are devoted to research and development of practical robots in many countries. The spread of practical robots does not solely depend on the progress of robotics research. Rather, it mainly depends on the reduction of the hardware cost or the labor system of factories.

On the other hand, there are many area where conventional industrial robots can not be applied because of technical limitations: size, weight, speed, accuracy, sensing ability, flexibility, intelligence, etc. In this panel, we are going to discuss technological and scientific problems for the development of advanced robots in the future (several years ahead).

Since robotics is an integrated research field, we can pick up many important issues. It may be worthwhile to introduce, at first, the Japanese big project "Advanced Robot Technology: JUPITER", which is conducted by Agency of Industrial Science and Technology of MITI with the participation of private companies and two national laboratories, the Mechanical Engineering Laboratory (MEL) and the Electrotechnical Laboratory (ETL). In the course of describing important technologies to be developed in the project, some of the key issues will be discussed.

2. Advanced Robot Technology: JUPITER

It is said that the application of robots is most advanced in Japan. In industry, the working condition is well prepared for robots with less flexibility. Such robots can not be used for works in hazardous conditions such as works in nuclear plants, undersea operations and rescue operation in disaster area because the working condition can not be prepared beforehand by humans.

The project of the MITI called JUPITER (Juvenescent Pioneering Technology for Robots) aims at the R&D of advanced robot technology for works in critical environment. The direct translation of the project is "Robots for Critical Work". Such robots may work fully automatically or guided by human operators depending on the situation. Although the direct aim of the project is not to develop technology for industrial robots, the outcome is expected to be applied to flexible industrial robots, too.

Works in critical condition have the following characteristics:

1. The working area is wide.
2. The working environment is complex.
3. Recognition of the environment and decision making based on the recognition result are required.
4. Adaptation to hazardous conditions such as radioactivity, water pressure, or high temperature is required.

The outline of the R&D for the project is shown in Figure 1. Most of the fundamental technologies are to be developed mainly by the two national laboratories. Note that the actuator system and adaptation technology are not included in the figure, for they are not proper to robotics. The development of the applied systems is to be undertaken by private companies. Various mechanisms and integrated robots will be made for works in particular environments.

3. Technologies Developed in the Project

This chapter focuses on fundamental technologies to be developed in the project and points out important problems of robotics. Since the R&D of application systems is mainly composed by fundamental technologies, it will be described in the corresponding parts.

3.1 Locomotion

The main goal is to develop robots that can move in various environments efficiently. One promising approach is multi-legged locomotion. Although there have been some research works on multi-legged locomotion with two, four, or six

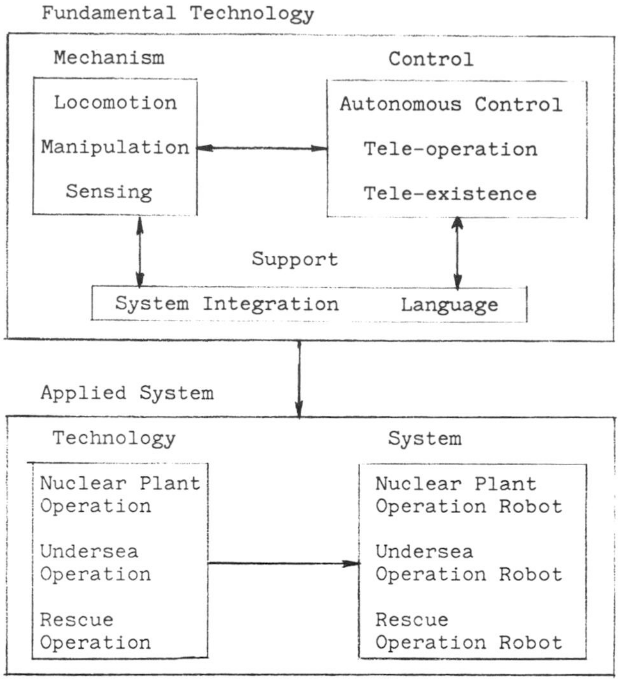

Figure 1. Concept of R & D of JUPITER project.

legged mechanisms, no practical systems have been developed except special purpose robots such as the one for underwater construction (Ishino et al., 1983). The main difficulty with multi-legged is a low energy efficiency and a low speed.

Hybrid robots with both wheels and legs were also proposed so that an efficient locomotion may be attained on a flat floor [Ozaki et al., 1983]. An important difficulty is a slow speed for ascending stairs (typically 1 minute/step).

In the project, a multi-legged walking machine is going to be developed which may be able to move on stairs and on rough terrains at a reasonable speed (more than 4km/hour) with a load comparable to the locomotion mechanism. In order to attain a high energy efficiency, the mass center of the machine must move smoothly independent of the movement of legs. The MEL has already built a six-legged machine that moves on a flat floor without a vertical movement of the mass center [Kimura, 1983]. Further development is required for adaptation to stairs and rough terrains.

Locomotion on rough terrains involves a problem of path finding and that of obstacle avoidance. This problem is very important for nuclear plant operation because there are many pipes and attachments. The solution to the problem needs the development of the following three techniques: (1) a mechanical mechanism for flexible movement, (2) control of the mechanism, and (3) planning according to the information provided by the sensing system. The last problem will be dealt with by sensing and autonomous control.

A wall climbing robot is also going to be developed. A typical one with sucking disks can climb a smooth flat wall. However, no robots have been made that can move across a discontinuous border of planes of different levels. In the project, the goal is to develop a mechanism that can move a wall with difference in level at a speed of about 0.5m/sec. The problem also includes the development of the three techniques described above.

3.2 Manipulation

Research of manipulation is aiming at the realization of multi-joint manipulators whose position and force can be controllable, and the development of the control method for skillful manipulation.

The force (torque) control is indispensable for performing skillful manipulation in various working conditions. Since most of industrial robots are position-controlled, they can not easily adapt to the change of working conditions. There have been some approach to force-related tasks by using adaptive tools which are designed for specific tasks. In order to make a flexible manipulator, however, force must be reliably controlled by software [Takase, 1979].

At the ETL, torque controlled manipulators have been studied [Takase et al., 1974]. It has turned out that a precise torque control can be attained with direct drive method. An experimental manipulator ETA-2 has proved the versatility of this approach [Takase, 1983]. The next version has been designed (see Table 1) and will be completed in 1985.

Table 1. Comparison of ETA−II and ETA−III

	ETA−II	ETA−III
Resolution of encorder	16384/rev	65536/rev
servo stiffness	4.8kg/cm	48kg/cm
maximum acceleration	3.48rad/sec	7.98rad/sec

The manipulator is going to be controlled by software so that it may perform skillful tasks such as decomposing machines, repairing mechanical devices, or assembling mechanical products. There have been many attempts at realization of skillful tasks by force control: turning a handle, inserting a rod in a hole, or coordination of two manipulators. Most of them adopted simple control methods; for example, just to keep the force along a certain direction constant. In order to replace human experts by robots, we must know how position and force are controlled in performing complicated tasks.

A general approach to this problem is to analyze various tasks to decompose them into basic operations and accumulate control patterns of these operations to be used by computer. Some of basic operations for assembly and decomposition are illustrated in Figure 2, where the constraint (the degree of freedom in translation, that in rotation) is given for each operation. For example, the constraint for inserting a rod into a hole consists of two

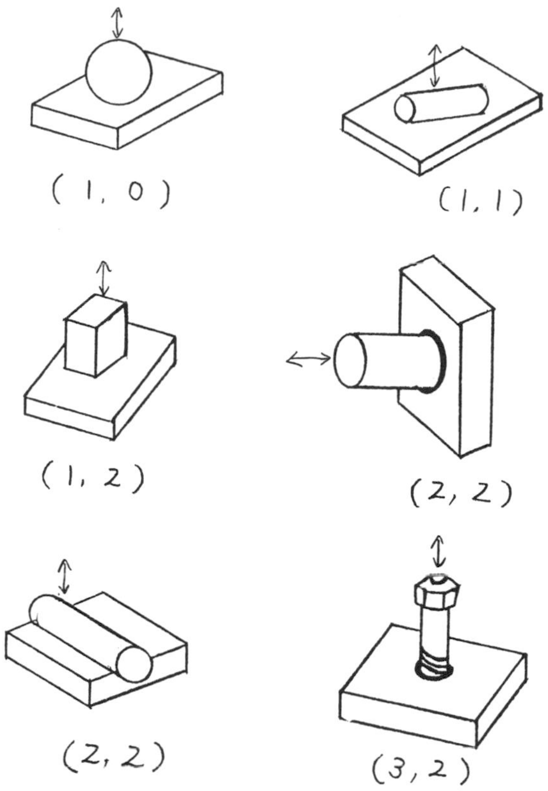

Figure 2. Some basic operations for assembly and decomposition.

degrees of translation and two degrees of rotation. The control of position and force for a assembly or disassembly task depends greatly on the constraint imposed by the spatial relation of the associated bodies. Once a kind of database for these skills of basic operations, many assembly and disassembly tasks will be programmed easily by a higher level language.

Another aspect of manipulation research is a remote control using master and slave manipulators. The MEL is working on master and slave manipulators of different configurations (see Figure 3) with the force sense as well as the position sense. The configuration of the master is designed for the ease of human operation, while that of the slave is for the efficiency of object handling. This method will facilitate the flexibility in the selection of various types of remote manipulation.

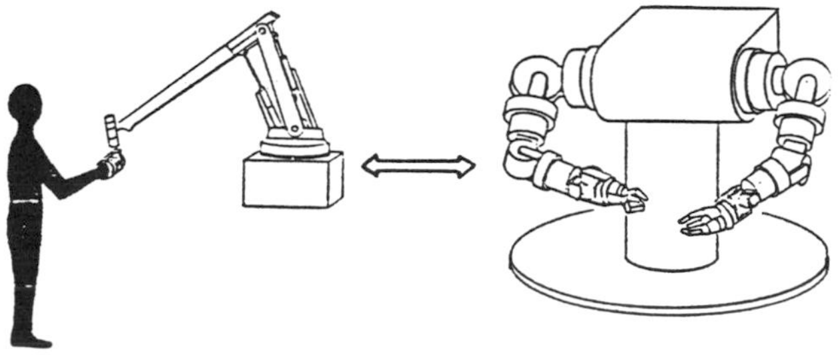

Figure 3. Master and slave manipulators of different configurations.

3.3. Sensing

Robots may have to sense two kinds of state: the internal state of robots and the external state of the environment. An important information of the internal state is the orientation of robots. In the project, the orientation sensor is to be developed which can detect the orientation change ranging from 0.01 to 600 deg/sec.

Among external state sensors, visual sensors and tactile sensors are most important. Conventional imaging devices will not be dealt with in the project, for they may be developed for other uses. The target of tactile sensing in the project is a two-dimensional integrated pressure sensor with density of approximately 100 point/cm . Processing of tactile information will be studied in the application field (manipulation and locomotion).

Visual sensing is the main theme of the sensing technology. Although vision alone can be used for supervision and inspection, it is often used for path finding, obstacle avoidance, or object recognition in locomotion and manipulation. Robot vision research is divided into four subthemes:

1. Sensors.
2. Feature extraction.
3. Scene description building.
4. Model representation and matching.

In the first subtheme, a ranging system will be the main target, for there is no practical one for robots. One promising approach is an active triangulation: projecting light beams and observing the image by a imaging device. The problem with this method is that ranging takes long time and that a strong light beam is necessary for ranging distant objects.

Another approach is a stereo vision method. Although the stereo vision has been studied for a long time, only few systems are practically used. The difficulty is that the mechanism of matching left and right images is not completely known and that the computation time is expected to be enormous. Now we hope that the latter problem will be overcome by the development of the VLSI technology. The key problem of matching is how to determine the correspondence of local images based on the similarlities between candidate pairs.

The second subtheme focuses on feature extraction for recognition of three-dimensional scenes. Recently, many image processors have been developed for local feature extraction. The extension along this line is the development of high speed processors for more global feature extraction such as detection of lines or vanishing points. Another important direction is the development of three-dimensional data processors for extraction of geometrical edges or surfaces from range data or surface normals.

In those two subthemes, the hardware development takes an important role, for many algorithms for those low-level processings have already been proposed. On the other hand, more research is required for the latter two subthemes. The problem with the third subtheme (scene description building) is how to represent complex scenes such as the one that includes multiple objects with curved surfaces occluding one another.

We may need a hierarchical representation; for example, a scene consists of objects, an object consists of surfaces, and a surface is approximated by a quadratic surface. Is it possible to make this hierarchy by a bottom up process? Often objects can not be segmented without the knowledge of the objects. Then, we can not expect that objects are segmented in the scene description before we try to match to the object models.

Another problem is that the scene description may be built differently for the same object if the viewer's direction or an occlusion condition is different. This may happen very easily for curved objects. In order to avoid the influence of those conditions, we need a good way for segmenting a complex surface (body) into simpler primitive surfaces (bodies).

The last subtheme (model representation and matching) is most closely related to the application. For example, the main function of robot vision for locomotion in a known building is to verify expected objects or features such as edges of corridors, doors, or stairs. Then simple wire frame models can be matched to edges in the scen description. Even, detection of vanishing points is useful for determining the position of the robot since most of edges are vertical or parallel horizontal,

In the project, we are taking a more general approach; a basic model of an object is a three-dimensional geometric model which can reconstruct the shape of the object completely, and it may be modified for efficient matching. The geometric model is suitable for representing manufactured objects. It is often provided by CAD/CAM systems. Once a three-dimensional shape is represented in computer, many useful properties for recognizing it can easily be derived from the representation. These properties may be calculated beforehand or when necessary. Figure 4 shows an example of the data structure of GEOMAP [Kimura and Hosaka, 1978]. It is shown that arbitrary information can be attached to the body, faces, or vertices through user pointers. Examples of the use of the geometric model is described in [Shirai et al., 1983].

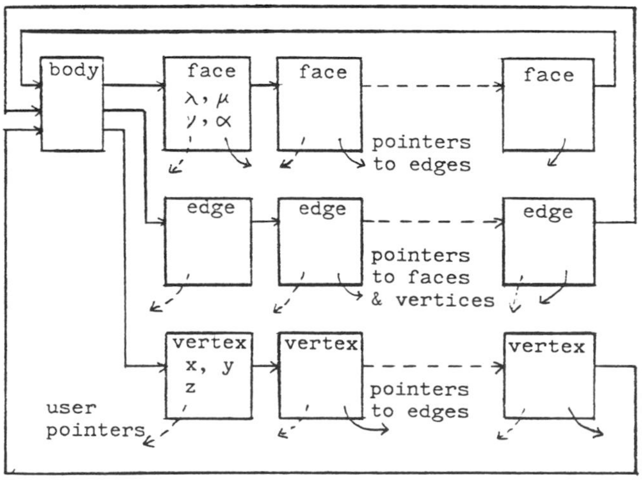

Figure 4. Data structure of GEOMAP.

The next problem is the matching of the scene description to object models. We should consider the case where the scene includes many objects occluding one another and the number of object models is large. Then a method of selecting candidate models or the candidate orientations must be developed. It may depend on what kind of constraints are imposed on the scene and what kind of input information is available.

3.4. Autonomous Control

The name "autonomous control" is used in contrast to man-machine interaction. In this theme, the control of an autonomous robot with locomotion and sensing ability, and that of with manipulation and sensing ability will be studied. The necessary function for the former robot is to plan the path based on a stored map, and to proceed to the destination, verifying the path, detecting obstacles, and avoiding them. The latter robot requires hand-eye coordination and plan generation ability. The temporary goal is automatic assembly and disassembly of machines or equipments for plants such as pumps or valves. The necessary function is similar to that of the former robot except the plan of assembly or disassemly sequences.

The realization of those functions involves the manipulation of the geometry. The optimal solution to such problems may be influenced by the detail of the geometry of the environment or objects. Finding the optimal solution is often NP complete. We may need a heuristic procedure to get an appropriate solution. This problem has an interesting aspect to robotics in that a robot can sense the environment in the middle of locomotion or manipulation.

Again modelling of environment becomes a key issue. Now, we should consider three kinds of models of the environment or objects: the one that is stored beforehand, the one that is built by sensing, and the one that is used for locomotion or manipulation. A unified representation of model or smooth interaction between different kind of models is desired.

3.5 Tele-operation

Robots for hazardous conditions must sometimes work in an unknown environment. The example includes the work for accidents or for fixing troubles. It is not effective to prepare software for all kinds of possibility. Instead, man-machine systems are more effective. However, operation of a conventional tele-operation system is very tiring. Usually human operators can continue complicated work only a few hours.

In the project, a more advanced tele-operation system will be developed, where although the entire course of tasks is conducted by the command or the operation of human operators, each sub-task will be conducted autonomously by robots. In order to realize a smooth man-machine interaction, the system must be based on the model of objects for executing sub-tasks and for the interaction. The manipulator control may be performed by using the software of skills described in manipulation.

One important problem is how to teach the environment to robots. A system has been developed for the interactive modelling of a real world [Hasegawa, 1982]. The main purpose is to build geometric models by commands of human operators and by input information obtained by a ranging system. Photograph 1 shows the image of the objects superimposed by the models of the main parts created by the interaction process.

Photograph 1. Real image superimposed by model image.

3.6. Tele-existence

Tele-existence technology is a kind of tele-operator technology, but it focuses on man-machine interaction that enables a human operator to perform remote manipulation tasks with the feeling that the operator exists in the slave anthropomorphic robot in the remote environment. One of the most important problems is to present a human operator with realistic sensory information of the slave robot's environment.

The MEL is working on the remote-presence of visual information [Tachi et al., 1984]. Figure 5 shows a concept of a display system being developed. Robot sensors are constructed anthropomorphically in function and geometrical relation. Movements of a operator's head and eyeballs are measured in real time, and the robot sensors are controlled to follow the operator's movement. The pictures taken by the robot sensors are displayed directly to human eyes through head-mounted CRT displays. Thus the operator can get the realistic view of the environment and slave manipulators.

The final version will include a sensory augumentation system, which allows an operator to use ultrasonic, infrared, and other invisible sensory information with computer-generated sensation presence.

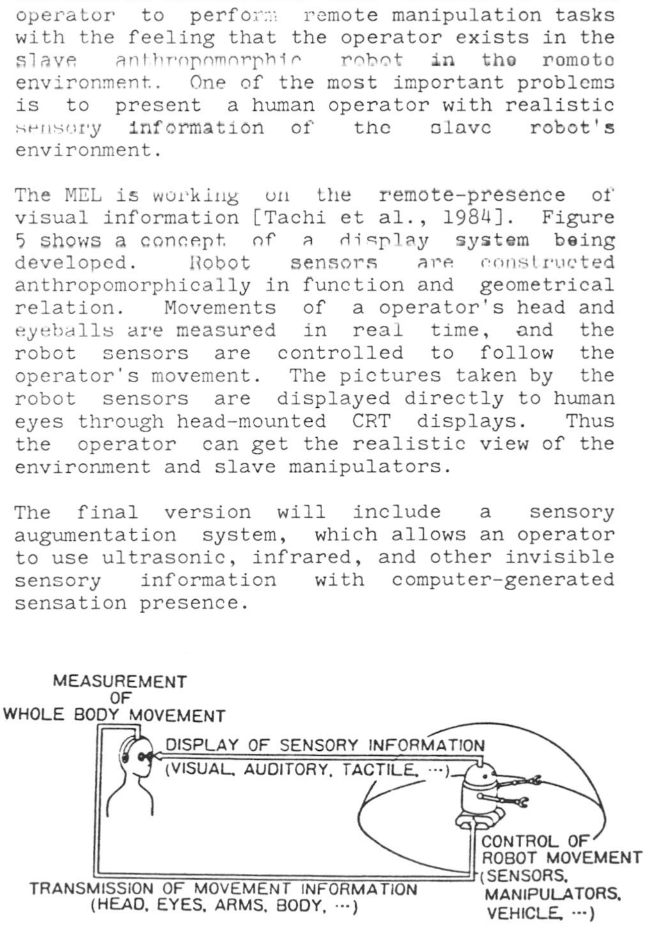

Figure 5. Concept of tele-existence display.

3.7 Support

The main themes of the support technology are system integration techniques and robot languages. The research at the ETL will focus on an operating system for integration of robot subsystems (manipulators, eyes, etc.) and that of multiple robots. The robots developed in the project will be interconnected by a network for communication and sharing common hardware and software resources. Each robot consists of many subsystems such as the one for locomotion, manipulation, sensing, and tele-operation. Each subsystem may have its own processors, communicating one another and sharing a common database. A robot operating system is expected to support the development of each subsystem and an efficient operation of the total system.

The robot operating system consists of the following four functional layers [Tsukamoto et al., 1983].

1. Distributed kernel for integrating physically separated nodes into a logical unit and providing sufficient computation power for real-time robot control.
2. Distributed system description language with a high level description capability (such as LISP).
3. Robot kernel for the cooperation of robot subsystems (that includes database and model manager).
4. Programming environment for the development of a robot system, and operation environment.

The main goal of the development of a robot language in the project may be to recommend a standard robot language. Since the robot language must reflect the state of the robot technology, it should not be fixed in the early stage. First, many languages will be developed in each subfield independently, and then the standardization will be considered. Compared with manipulator languages, there are few vision or locomotion languages.

An attempt has been made to make a robot vision language for a hand-eye system [Matushita et al., 1983]. The language called RVL (Robot Vision Language) supports range data processing for verification vision and model building by showing. It should be extended so that it may be able to deal with a variety of input data for verifying and recognizing objects.

It is difficult to determine whether we should make efforts to develop a unified language or try to realize higher functions in our respective fields. In an appropriate period, the scope of the robot language may be fixed and a standard language will be developed.

Acknowledgements: The author would like to thank Drs. S. Tachi and K. Tani at the MEL, and K. Takase and T. Hasegawa at the ETL for providing him materials for the paper.

Reference

Ishino, Y. et al. 1983. Walking Robot for Underwater Construction. Proceedings of International Conference on Advanced Robotics, Tokyo, pp. 107-114.

Hasegawa, T. 1982. An Interactive system for modeling and monitoring a manipulation environment. IEEE Trans. SMC, SMC-12, 3, pp. 250-258.

Kimura, F. and Hosaka, M. 1978. Program package GEOMAP. Proceedings of Geometric Model Project Meeting, Saint-Louis: CAM-I, Inc.

Kimura, M. 1983. R&D Programs for Advanced Robot Technology. Proceedings of International Conference on Advanced Robotics, Tokyo, pp. 41-46.

Matsushita, T. et al. 1983. An attempt to describe visual functions of the hand-eye system with an robot vision language: RBA/A. Proceedings of International Conference on Advanced Robotics, Tokyo, pp. 327-334.

Ozaki, N. et al. 1983. Tele-Operated Mobile Robot for Remote Maintenance in Nuclear Facilities. Proceedings of International Conference on Advanced Robotics, Tokyo, pp. 67-74.

Shirai, Y. et al. 1983. An approach to object recognition using 3-d solid model. Proceedings of ISRR.

Takase, K. et al. 1974. The Design of an Articulated Manipulator with Torque Control Ability. Proceedings of 4th International Symposium of Industrial Robots, Tokyo.

Takase, K. et al. 1979. Skill of Intelligent Robot. Proceedings of 6th International Conference on Artificial Intelligence, Tokyo, pp. 1095-1100.

Takase, K. et al. 1983. Design of torque cntrolled manipulators composed of direct and low reduction-ration drive joints. Proceedings of ISRR.

Tsukamoto, M. et al. 1983. Conceptual design of a distributed operating system for intelligent robots. Proceedings of International Conference on Advanced Robotics, Tokyo,pp. 399-406.

RESEARCH TRENDS IN DECISIONAL AND MULTISENSORY ASPECTS OF THIRD GENERATION ROBOTS

Georges Giralt

L.A.A.S - C.N.R.S.
7, Avenue du Colonel Roche
31400 Toulouse, FRANCE

In this presentation we discuss the issues and trends of robotics research during the late 1980's and early 1990's in view of current needs to develop robots able to operate in a flexible manner and/or in an unstructurated environment. We therefore deal with third generation robots also referred to as intelligent robots. Two broad application areas are chosen as a framework for the analysis: multi-robot flexible manufacturing cells ; autonomous mobile robots for general purpose tasks. Among the open problems we consider important are those comprising the domains of decision and perception :
- multisensory perception systems. Here is involved environment and task modelling, signal and information processing, feature localisation, pattern and shape recognition, control, monitoring,...
- planning and decision making. Here is involved knowledge representation, plan generation, geometric and space reasoning, off-line programming, error recovery, on-line decision processes, learning,...

I - INTRODUCTION

It is matter-of-fact to say that research in the field of Robotics undergoes in the early 80's an explosive growth. This is clearly the case when numbers are considered : new research groups from university to industry joining the race, new journals, many more workshops, conferences and meetings of all kinds every year. We believe that another and more important aspect is a dramatic qualitative change. What is at stake is indeed the dawning of the third generation robots, also referred to as intelligent robots, which will exhibit "intelligent connection of perception to action" /Brady, 1984/. Three main causes appear to be the driving forces of this process :

1) There are very strong social and economical demands, not without contradictory aspects, for advanced automation in a fast expanding domain of applications ranging from the well-established car-making industry to unmanned underwater workstations. To be open to robotics, most of the new areas require high operating flexibility, efficiency and reliability as well as improved ergonomics for man-machine interfaces.

2) Micro-electronics technology which offers enormously increased possibilities in signal and information processing from general purpose microprocessors to specialized VLSI units.

3) A built-on research power created by previous work results in Manipulator Modelling, System Theory, Control, Decision Making, Computer Programming, Algorithmics, Artificial Intelligence,. ... and their merging to constitute a prime set of concepts, methods and tools of Robotics as a new field.

In this paper we discuss some of the issues and trends of robotics research during the late 1980's and early 1990's in view of current needs to develop robots able to operate in a flexible manner and/or in an unstructurated environment. At the core of this process, two factors will play a very central role. First, System and Processing Complexity : a distributed processing structure will support multisensory perception, distributed decision-making and control. Second, knowledge based, multi-sensor dependent task-planning and task-execution. Bearing this in mind, we will not attempt by any means to give a comprehensive survey of the state-of-the-art of the entire subject nor to cover the complete leading edge of the field but rather outline what we believe to be the main stream of a process rapidly heading towards a major breakthrough. As a framework for the analysis, the following two applications are considered : a multi-robot flexible assembly cell and an autonomous mobile robot for general purpose tasks. Throughout the paper they will be used as generic cases of 3rd generation complex robot systems. The assembly cell should possess flexibility in a fairly structured environment while we would like to have the autonomous mobile robot to move around and fulfill given orders in an almost entirely unstructured environment. In section II we briefly describe two laboratory implemented systems of this kind. On this basis we develop in section III the analysis and the discussion of Planning, Decision-Making, Multi-sensory Perception and Execution Control both in well engineered and in unstructured environments.

Finally, we sumarize the salient points of the thesis we defend here in section IV.

II - GENERIC CASES DESCRIPTION

II-1 Complex multi-robot assembly cell

Let us introduce as an illustrating example the Flexible Assembly Cell (FAC) of the French research program, Advanced Robotics and Automation (A.R.A.) /Giralt, 1983/ which is intended to serve as a realistic experimental main frame for testing, validating and developing hardware and software contributions to advanced robotics. Thus a salient feature of this system is that it is diversified and in constant evolution (fig.1). In this regard, a LISP-based interactive programming environment, NNS, has been developed to establish a framework for integrating various sub systems into a programmable system, and experimentally demonstrating the execution of assembly tasks /Alami, 1984/. This proves to be a very efficient characteristic. A similar system is COSMOS /Inoue, 1983/.
In its present status the cell's basic equipement is composed of a 32-bit Gould-SEL mini-computer system, several microprocessors (INTEL 8086, LSI 11/23), two six-degrees-of-freedom electrical manipulators (RENAULT ACMA-TH8, SCEMI), an image processing system (GRINNEL) and several peripheral effectors and devices (conveyor belt, vise, "left hand"* fixtures,...). The cell structure parameters can easily be modified so to create configurations in which the two robot manipulators have or have not a common work space. The cell's sensory system consists of vision (two grey scale cameras), proximity ultrasonic and magnetic sensors, force and contact measure devices, infrared presence detectors (fig.2),... Color vision /Bajon 1983/ and a "3D-Camera" /Monge, 1983/ are being installed and should be in operation before the end of September 1984. The system's programming and decisional environment is composed of several modules :3D graphics and CAD system, EUCLID and CATIA (remote access mode) ; robot programming language (LM) /Latombe and Mazer, 81/, obstacle avoidance ; part location and identification ; part-mating planning;.. We will consider as a generic case study the assembly of some complex industrial objects : the electrical circuit breaker in fig.3. Some relevant features which concern our analysis are :

a) the parts have a wide range of sizes, forms and rigidity characteristics (part 4 is plastic, parts 5 and 6 are metallic).

b) there is not a set of almost identical objects with only tolerance differences but rather a family of objects with specified part or subpart functional modifications including parameters other than geometrical (spring rigidity,...).

c) several different end-effectors are needed (e.g. for parts 1 and 2 concerning size and part 3 for functional requirements).

d) regardless of accuracy aspects, contact and force control are necessary to perform several sub-assemblies such as parts-group ((4), (5), (6)).

Furthemore, we shall assume that we possess basic knowledge in a formalized way about the object family: 3D geometrical models, assembly conditions, functional and quality requirements.

II-2 General-purpose autonomous mobile robot

Again, we will use an illustrating example, the HILARE project, as a basis for analysis and discussion. The project's purpose is to perform general research in robotics and robot perception and planning /Giralt, Chalila, and Vaisset, 1983/. The present physical structure of HILARE is shown in fig.4. The environment domain considered is a world of flat or near flat smooth floor with walls which include rooms, hallways, corridors, various portable objects and mobile or fixed obstacles. The computer system supporting the various robot functions has a distributed multilevel architecture : several (currently six) robot-borne microprocessors are radio-linked to a ground 32-bit computer accessing one or more other larger or similar processors. To date, the perception system is composed of :

a) fourteen ultrasonic emitter-receivers distributed around the vehicle which provide the range data up to two meters.

b) a camera and a laser range-finder which are mounted on a pan and tilt platform. The laser can be used in scanning mode, or it can measure ranges within the camera's field using a retractable mirror.

c) two optical shaft encoders for odometry path-control

d) an infrared triangulation location system which operates in areas where fixed beacons are installed.

The robot planning and decision-making system is composed of a small number of specialized decision modules (SDM), /Chatila, 82/. The SDM that will compose the decision-making system of HILARE include : general planner (GPL), navigation and motion control system (NMCS), object modelling and scene comprehension, natural language communication, manipulator control. NMCS deals with all that concerns the robot's mobility and for this will use basic procedures such as Routing, Navigation, local obstacle avoidance,... Let us now set up a "world" for a generic study with this kind of mobile robot. The environment general layout is given in fig.5. It is composed of four rooms, R_i , a corridor, C_1 and seven doors, D_i . Within some of the rooms exist specific purpose oriented sites (POS) : 3 work-stations, WS_i ; two storages, S_i , and one refueling-station, RS_1 . Non transportable objects of various kinds, such as boxes, tables,

*"left hand" : mechanism of 2 to 6 degrees of freedom for controlled fine motions with limited range, aimed to operate jointly with a standard manipulator as a part-mating system.

machine-tools may lay on the floor of every room. Some will be only occasionally present, some others will have a more permanent location, but still changing from time to time. They will be considered as obstacles to be avoided in an experiment. Finally, there are transportable objects, O_i ,that can be moved by the robot, often from or to some WS_i or S_i . Here too, we shall assume that the robot, when operating in a normal mode, will have access to some basic knowledge -possibly obtained through previous experiments- about the environ ment structures, e.g. a connectivity graph, fig.6, the specific sites POS and about objects O .

III - CASE STUDIES ANALYSIS

III-1 Task definition

We have defined two different generic tasks to be carried out, the first one in the very well structured environment of a flexible assembly cell and the second one in the fuzzy structure of an ever changing indoors world for an autonomous mobile robot. Let us consider the following robot goals :

1) G1 : Assemble repeatedly over time the elementary circuit-breaker parts progressively supplied to the FAC in a number of partially assembled objects, e.g. sub-assembly ((4), (5), (6)),...

2) G2 : Pick-up object O_K and carry it to WS_i .

III-1-1 Robot goal G1.

When facing the problem of making the ARA FAC (AFAC) execute the tasks necessary to fulfill G1, explicit information about parts, part mating conditions, prototype, assembly sequences should be available and also the set of parameters defining the various similar objects belonging to the same class. This, of course, was obtained at the product design phase, possibly using some CAD system. At this stage we need also to know that G1 can be indeed executed by AFAC. We believe that in the near future, CAD systems must be extended to possess explicit expertise on robots, peripheral devices and flexible assembly cells technology /Paul,83/. Let us call this kind of system an Assembly Expert System, AES. Now, a specific version of the kind of AES (GP-AES) completed with a 3D and functional model of AFAC is required to plan the actual set of operations $\mathcal{P}(P_i)$ to perform G1. However fascinating the prospect to automatically produce the executable program may seem, we already view as an exciting objective enough, meeting efficiency constraints, to have this sort of system included in an interactive decisional structure (IDS) used as a Robot assembly task-oriented programming environment /Lozano-Pérez, 82/, /Latombe, 84/. Production Rule systems appear to be a very promising solution for this part of the decision structure used in an off-line programming mode. At this level, we should have obtained a set of partially ordered sequences of primitive actions or operators, P_i, including parameter values to be acquired by sensing and perception. The primitive actions are : part routing through AFAC, part identification and location, grasping, robot's end-effectors and auxiliary devices status (e.g. gripper changes,...), part-mating, inspection,... Task plan generation also involves the detection of potential concurrent execution ; independent sequences of primitive actions should be considered, taking into account AFAC configuration, execution time estimation, availability of effecors and sensors. To complete task-planning, lower level plans for several of the primitive actions P_i have to be generated. Among these, important planning problems arise in free motion, grasping and part-mating which all imply 3D-models, geometric reasoning and dealing explicitly with inaccuracies and occasional errors. For free motion actions, we need to obtain good collision free trajectories /Lozano-Péres, 83/, /Brooks,83/, /Brooks and Lozano-Pérez, 83//Gouzenes, 84/, which will have to be guided or at least monitored by sensors (e.g. in the case of 2 robots with a common work-space). Whether or not the part-feeding system in actual use requires the gross location of the object to be processed and its explicit identification, in robot working environments like AFAC, we shall precisely estimate the object pose and achieve grasping within tolerances previously defined at the higher task-planning level. Hence the problem is, with or without changing the initial object pose, to plan a sequence of guarded motions guided by proximity and touch sensors until this grasping position is obtained. /Salisbury, 83/, /Latombe, 83/, /Grimson and Lozano-Pérez, 84/. Part-mating will require in several cases a complex sequence of compliant motions, i.e. fine motions, that will necessarily rely on sensor control most often using large bandwith closed-loop control (e.g. force feedbadk in real world applications) /Giraud 83/, /Lozano-Pérez, Mason, and Taylor,83/, /Mason,84/. The SDM corresponding to every primitive action, including the above three software modules should be integrated in a distributed interactive decisional structure, thus completing with GP-AES the high level programming ressources. Another very important issue here concerns the nature of the plan obtained. This plan has to be executed repeatedly in a physical world. There are many branches in $\mathcal{P}$ as well as within the scope of some P_i whose activation is controlled by conditions to be matched to data derivated from the perceived state of the system /Nitzan, Barrouil, Cheesman, and Smith, 83/. The sensing processes and the effectors operating modes implied in $\mathcal{P}(P_i)$ are defined during the planning phase. They constitute the set of specialized processing modules (SPM) which will actually perform the planned task /Chatila, 82 /. SPM's characteristics, the set of the branching conditions, the sensor signals and patterns constitute the Task-Execution Model. Let us stress the fact that this model should be inferred directly from the models of parts, objects and systems (AFAC). At the operating level on-line parameter identification and learning processes can possibly be devised to improve efficiency /Dufay and Latombe 83/. A Flow Chart for AFAC's off-line task-planning structure is given in figure 7.

III-1-2 Robot goal G2.

The robot must carry out the task G2 only once in the best way it can, given the current status of its environment, partly discovered while it proceeds. A first decision-level must lead HILARE to understand the order given and to produce an execution plan. Let us consider that the syntax and the semantics of G2 are consistent with HILARE's world model. The General Planner, GPL, starts the goal oriented search and finds out from the current state of the world data-base, that there is an object of the class O_k in storage S_1. Several consequent sub-goals are produced :

G_1^2 : "Move Robot Room R_1 (RS_1) to Room R_2(S_1)"

G_2^2 : "Load Object O_k from Storage S_1 "

G_3^2 : "Move Robot Room R_2 (S_1) to Room R_4(WS_1)

Further search will attempt to find feasible routes to solve G_1^2 and G_3^2. GPL will use a ROUTING expert module based on the topological model of fig.7. Nodes and arcs in this connectivity graph may be labelled with information, e.g. the "door D is closed", "Room R is void of obstacles",...

G_1^2 and G_3^2 are finally transformed in a sequence of elementary point-to-point moves.

G_1^2 : "Move to door D_2 "

"Move along D_2 D_3 "

"Move to S_1 "

G_3^2 : "Move to door D_3 "

"Move to door D_4 "

"Move to WS_1 "

They will be passed on to the decision module which deals with matters of robot mobility, NMCS. Every move becomes a goal and further planning is made by NMCS to generate a path between the initial location of the robot L_0 to the final one, L_F, going through D_2 D_3 S_i D_3 and D_4. Depending on data some of the moves will be executed within places (i.e. rooms, corridors) whose internal obstacles layout is unknown. Let's say this is the case for rooms R_1 and R_2. All actual moves will be of course environment-dependent and sensory-guided. The following aspects appear to be important :

i) for efficiency reasons, the high level decision making structure, i.e. the planning system, must be organized in a modular distributed structure. Heterarchical organization is here an open and possibly most rewarding issue to investigate.

ii) we believe that an interesting approach for the General Planner consists in an efficient automatic inference system based on Production Rules formalism.

iii) during the next five to ten years, mobile robots will often operate in a man-supervised mode, in application domains such as those involving extreme conditions environments (See projects JUPITER in Japan and RAM in France). This leads to an approach for planning similar to the one advocated in section II-1-1, with conditional steps resolved during actual operations. Notwithstanding this, we believe that the autonomous mode presented in this section stands both as the most important research trend for mobile robots and the crucial issue in robot planning.

iv) all plans here are conditional. Uncertainties and state-of-the-world changes are the rule. They lay everywhere along the robot's errands. This clearly shows the utmost importance of the Execution Model and the Execution-Control system. Likewise in the previous case study, the Execution Model is here one of the outputs of the task-planning structure. It has to be entirely created in an autonomous mode.

III-2 Task sensor-based execution control

III-2-1 Robot goal G 1.

We now consider the normal operating mode of the robot flexible manufacturing cell, AFAC, when a flow of parts and objects is to be dealt with throughout the system according to task planning. Sensors are needed for instantiating and branching program primitives, servoing signals, as well as overall system monitoring.

To possess the sort of flexibility implied by G 1, the AFAC perception system must provide information about :

i) shape and position of parts
ii) Local environment sensing for part-gripper and part-workpiece relationships
iii) joint and end-effector forces
iv) actuator state variables
v) plant supervision

The variety and the multiplicity of sensors lead to a very important characteristic : information redundancy. This can be used in several modes : cooperative, monitoring and cross-checking.

According to their function, sensors can be included in the execution control structure at three levels : procedure parameter feeding, feedback control loops, and fault and emergency interruptions.

Some sensors happen to play a quite versatile role in AFAC ; it seems appropriate to design and implement them as autonomous sub-systems. We can then view each of them as a member of the broader class of specialized processing modules (SPM), which are the means used by the system to physically interact with the environment and perform the planned task. During an actual task, the current status and role of a perception SPM is under the control of the Task-Execution system.

We view these aspects of sensor redundancy, modularity and task dependent integration, to be outstanding research problems for sensor-based robots in manufacturing.

This does not preclude, of course, the interest to develop and improve modular sensors. General 3D vision stands out as a central problem in robotics and a very important research issue for all the interacting questions established between signal processing, knowledge representation, learning, and inference mechanisms, more than for practical usefulness in manufacturing /Binford, 81/, /Faugeras and al., 83/, /Shirai, 83/, /Brady, 84/, /Horaud and Bolles, 84/.

With the late purpose in mind, we consider as very interesting the following developments :

i) lighter, less expensive solid-state cameras combined with specialized VLSI processors will allow for a much broader use of grey and color vision : robot carried cameras for proximity detection and local inspection, cameras or 3D work-space supervision, end-effector positioning and motion control...

ii) reliable tactile sensors (i.e. distributed contact forces measurements) for grippers, "dexterous hands", work-plans and fixtures.

Throughout the task execution, the execution control system has to take into account in addition to environment features plus uncertainties predicted by the execution model, the various inaccuracies induced by sensors /Brooks ,82/.

The interaction of the system's various modules must be organized and coordinated. We want this to be a dynamic process. A convenient model for this is to use predicates and decision rules thus imbedding the task-execution control system in a Rule-Based Pattern-Directed Inference System. An advantage to this approach consists in its extreme flexibility. On the other hand, excessive processing time represents its most serious drawback, since we are concerned by an on-line decision process. This could be an overriding difficulty.

Fortunately, it appears feasible to cope with this problem using a compiled Production Rule System. Moreover, the modulor distributed nature of the planning system leads directly through the Task-Plan and the Execution Model structures to a modulor task-execution control system. This provides the possibility to reduce the control of sub-second process steps to a search in a simple decision tree /Ghallab, 84/.

We must emphasize the fact that in normal operating mode, all the events are expected and model led. Furthermore, occasional out of range sensor readings implie either a defective part or some functional error. Hence they have to be dealt as such and their processing included in an automatic error-recovery mode at task-execution control level.

Recurrent errors due to some system component defect should whenever possible be handled via system reconfiguration and re-planning (graceful degradation). To which extent the latter can be achieved in the near future in an automatic way using the on-line version of the planning structure is a truly open question (fig.9).

When interactive re-planning and/or system repairing will be necessary, the Decisional and Execution control structure must be designed with the capacity to furnish failure diagnoses and systems aids for operational recovery.

All the planning and processing modules SDM and SPM, must inter-communicate efficiently. An on-line processing oriented local network communication structure appears as an appropriate ressource for real world application as well as an interesting research area in connection with distributed decisional topics.

III-2-2 Robot goal G .

In contrast with AFAC's task execution discussed in the previous section, HILARE's actual errands will have to be carried out in a context of unknown facts and unexpected events. At the execution level, plans are produced whose main reason is to acquire lacking information. For HILARE striving to accomplish G this is for instance the case when executing the first step

$$G_1^2 : \text{"Move to door } D_2 \text{ "}$$

The SDM Navigation and Motion Control System (NMCS), does not possess any information about a possible obstacle layout within R_1. It will assume there are obstacles and start a conditional sequence of "Look arounds" and moves that will eventually take it to D if there exists a feasible path between the starting point 1 and this door. Meanwhile, it will have created and memorized a topological and a geometrical model for the "explored" partial obstacle layout /Giralt, Chatila, and Vaisset, 83/.

In order to model its environemnt layout, mobile robots perception systems must have the capacity to perform 3D scene analysis. For this, the system can afford to spend an order of magnitude more time than it was the case for AFAC. Hence, stereovision has here a good application field /Moravec, 81/ most likely to be used in combination with other range sensors, e.g. laser and ultrasonic range-finders.

Two important facts should be noticed :

i) Environment maps are created from a sequence of partial robot centered views, which brings in the problem of how to combine in an efficient way these partial maps taking into account sensor errors /Chatila and Laumond, 84/.

ii) At every information gathering step, the Execution model is up-dated so that expected values for several other sensors, e.g. local environment perception, can be inferred and execution control conditions instantiated.

In HILARE's world, this can be illustrated with the examples of controlling position and motion in the most efficient way in critical space configurations such as going through door D and following the right wall when moving along corridor C

So far, unexpected situations, contradictory at some level to planning and/or the execution model have not arisen yet. Let's first consider the sub-goal

"Move to WS_1 "

HILARE's starting situation is door D and the information that Room R is empty has been transmitted by the General Planner to NMCS. Hence NMCS will devise a direct trajectory leading HILARE to WS and attempt to carry it out. Proximity sensors will alert HILARE that something is in the way.

Given context, this unexpected event will be analyzed as most likely to be an occasional and isolated obstacle. Plan repair will be performed locally at the execution control level. In this case, HILARE will move around the obstacle using ultrasonic feedback control and resume progression towards the goal according to odometry.

What if Door D had been found closed ? In this case, local plan repair cannot cope with the situation and the problem must be passed on from Execution Control System to NMCS and GPL. Replanning will be automatically performed considering the pending part of the initial plan and the up-dated state-of-the-world (fig.10).

Although several other capacities that allow a number of tasks to be accomplished are likely to be included in a mobile robot, the mobility capacity stands out as a very specific and important characteristic which brings to attention a score of research issues linked to navigation-planning and execution-control.

i) Multisensory perception has to operate in an unstructured and not <u>a priori</u> defined environment. Sensor integration and sensing consistency have to be obtained under these conditions.

ii) Navigation planning belongs to the class of conditional planning. Furthermore, when the robot environment is completely unknown, the goal-oriented search can be modelled as a dynamic decision-making, information-gathering, process controlled by a set of decision rules.

iii) The Execution control system must allow for unexpected and yet very normal events. His role must be extended to include decision-making capacities for local plan-mending and to contribute to data-base up-dating (environment models, objects and environment items statuses,...). We believe this is a clear case for a Rule-Based PDIS including efficient compiling /Dufresne,84/, /Sobek, 84/.

iv) Most of the information concerning the robot environment has to be acquired during a sequence of experiments and/or normal operations : efficient algorithms for parameter identification (geometrical model) and structure characterization (topological model) are consequently needed.

If merely in view of this, "learning" must be considered as a basic function for "intelligent" mobile robots. Beyond this, they furnish a very convenient setting for further research in higher levels of learning such as those connected with decision rules for problem-solving and the function or the semantics of some environment items. See for instance /Laumond, 84/ on anthropomorphic environment structure semantics acquisition : rooms, doors, corridors.

We believe that results in those directions will represent a breakthrough for third generation robots.

IV - <u>CONCLUSION</u>

All along this presentation we have endeavoured to express our personal views on near-future perspectives for third generation robots. To conclude, we will attempt to summarize what we believe to be relevant and most interesting aspects, guide-lines for third generation robots and the corresponding trends and research issues for the forthcoming years.

Third generation robots are going to be highly complex signal and processing systems with much better ergonomics for man-machine interaction (Programming, supervision,...).

This complexity is not a "researcher's dream" but the price to be paid to meet the needs for a wide range of real-world applications from flexible work-stations in production lines to intervention robots operating in hostile environments.

Two important aspects appear to be the key to meet the challenge of efficiency and ergonomics versus complexity :

i) distributed processing hardware including dedicated VLSI supporting distributed decision structures and multisensory perception,

ii) knowledge based, sensor guided task-planning and execution-control.

Third generation robots must exhibit an "intelligent connection between perception and action" to cope with ever-increasing levels of flexibility in work environments.

Two robot-systems appear to be highly interesting both as front-line real-world applications and generic research cases :

i) Flexible Assembly Cells which are good test-beds for new robotics concepts in well engineered operating conditionss.

ii) Autonomous mobile robots which constitute a paradigm for decisional and perception research for robot operation in unstructured environments and the key to novel application fields looking ahead, beyond today's gadget phase, to domestic service robots in a not-too-far future.

In production line operating conditions robots must repeatedly perform sequences of actions which are similar or partly similar. The key factors are speed and product quality. In order to combine those imperative factors and flexibility off-line programming and multisensory task execution control appear to be the most convenient approach. Planning and Decision-Making modules have to be integrated in the robot programming environment. Specific on-line versions must be associated to the task-execution control system for error-recovery and fault-tolerant operation.

Autonomous mobile robots have to be able to perform unique tasks in largely unknown work conditions. Robot planning particularly for problems linked to mobility and navigation must be faced here as an autonomous dynamic process including information acquisition, automatic environment mapping, and higher levels of learning as a very central aspect.

For both mobile robots and flexible assembly cells multisensory perception offers the only reasonable way towards efficiency. How to integrate different sensor modules and use redundancy, when to operate them, what sort of functions they can fulfill one with respect to others, are all key research issues at the core of the Execution Control System organization.

Production-Rule based Pattern Directed Inference Systems with structures and algorithms adapted to robot operation could provide a succesful framework for efficient sensor-driven Execution control systems.

BIBLIOGRAPHY

Alami R., "NNS : a lisp-based environment for the integration and operating of complex robotics systems", IEEE Int. Conf. on Robotics, Atlanta (USA), 13-15 March 84.

Bajon J., and al, "Structure et performances du module de vision de GTTSI", 2èmes Journées ARA, Besançon, France, 16-17 Nov. 83.

Binford, T.O., "Inferring Surfaces from Images", Art. Int., Vol. 17, Numb. 1-3, Aug. 81.

Brady M., "Representing Shape", Pro. IEEE Conf. on Robotics, Atlanta, (USA), 13-15 March 84.

Brady M., "Artificial Intellignece and Robotics", 4ème Congrès Reconnaissance des Formes et Intelligence Artificielle, Paris, 23-27 Jan. 84.

Brooks R.A., "Symbolic Error Analysis and Robot Planning", The Int. Journal of Robotics Research, Vol. 1, N° 4, Winter 82.

Brooks R.A., Lozano-Pérez T., "A sub-division algorithm in configuration space for findpath with rotation". Proc. of the 8th IJCAI Karlsruhe, W. Germany, 83.

Brooks R.A., "Planning Collision Free Motions for Pick and Place Operations", 1st Int. Symp. on Robotics Research, Bretton Woods (USA), Aug 28-Sept 2, 83.

Chatila R., "Path Planning and Environment learning in a mobile Robot System", Pro. ECAI 82, Orsay, France, July 1982.

Chatila R., Laumond JP., "Controle et mise à jour de la position et du modèle de l'espace d'un robot mobile", Note Tech., LAAS, Aug. 84.

Dufay B., Latombe JC., "An Approach to Automatic Robot Programming Based on Inductive Learning", 1st Int. Symp. on Robotics Research, Bretton Woods (USA), Aug 28-Sep 2, 1983.

Erman L.D. and al., "The Hearsay-II speech understanding system : integrating knowledge to resolve uncertainty", ACM Computing Surveys, Vol. 12, N°2, June 80.

Dufresne P., "Contribution algorithmique à l'inférence par Règles de Production", These Doc.Ing, Toulouse, France, Juin 84.

Faugeras O.D., Hebert M., Pauchon E., and al., "Object Representation, Identification and Positioning from Range DATA", 1st Int. Symp. on Robotics Research, Bretton Woods (USA), Aug 28-Sep 2, 83.

Ghallab M., "Task Execution Monitoring by Compiled Production Rules in an Advanced Multi-Sensor Robot", 2nd Int. Symp of Robotics Research, Kyoto, Japan, 20-23 Aug, 84.

Giralt G., Chatila R., Vaisset M., "An Integrated Navigation and Motion Control System for autonomous Multisensory Mobile Robots", 1st Int. Symp. on Robotics Research, Bretton Woods (USA), Aug 28-Sep 2, 83.

Giralt G., "ARA : A French National Program for Advanced Robotics and Automation", '83 Int. Conf. on Advanced Robotics, Tokyo, (JAPAN), 12-13 Sep 83.

Giraud A., "Generalized Active Compliance for Part Mating with Assembly Robots", 1st. Int. Sym. on Robotics Research, Bretton Woods (USA), Aug 28-Sep 2, 83.

Gouzenes L., "Collision Avoidance for Robots in an Experimental Flexible Assembly Cell", IEEE Int. Conf. on Robotics, Atlanta (USA), 13-15 March 84.

Grimson W.E.L., Lozano-Pérez T., "Model-Based Recognition and Localization from Tactile DATA", IEEE Int. Conf. on Robotics, Atlanta (USA), 13-15 March 84.

Horaud P., Bolles R.C., "3DPO's strategy for Matching Three Dimensional Objects in Range DATA", IEEE Int. Conf. on Robotics, Atlanta (USA), 13-15 March 84.

Inoue H., Inaba M., "Hand Eye Coordination in Rope Handling", 1st. Int. Sym. on Robotics Research, Bretton Woods (USA), Aug 28-Sep 2,83.

Latombe JC., Mazer E., "LM 1981 : a high-level programming language for controlling assembly robots", 11th Int. Sym. on Ind. Robots, Tokyo, (JAPAN), Oct 81.

Latombe JC., "Toward Automatic Robot Programming" '83 Int. Conf. on Advanced Robotics, Tokyo (JAPAN) 12-13 Sept. 83.

Latombe JC, "Information Processing for Robots", Int. Sym, on Design and Synthesis, Tokyo, 11-13 July, 84.

Lozano-Pérez T., "Robot Programming", A.I. Memo n° 698, MIT, Dec. 82.

Lozano-Pérez T., "Spatial Planning : a Configuration Space Approach", IEEE Trans. Comp. C-32, 2 (February 83).

Lozano-Pérez T., Mason M.T., Taylor R.H., "Automatic Synthesis of Fine-Motion Strategies for Robots", 1st. Int. Sym. on Robotics Research, Bretton Woods (USA), Aug 28-Sep 2, 83.

Mason M.T., "Automatic Planning of Fine Motions : Correctness and Completeness", IEEE Int. Conf. on Robotics, Atlanta (USA), 13-15 March 84.

Monge J. and al., "Capteur de Vision 3D pour la Robotique", 2èmes Journées ARA, Besançon, France, 16-17 Nov. 83.

Moravec H., "Rover Visual Obstacle Avoidance", IJCAI 81, Vancouver, Canada, 24-28 Aug.81.

Nitzan D., Barrouil C., Cheeseman P., and al., "Use of Sensors in Robot Systems", '83 Int. Conf. on Advanced Robotics, Tokyo (JAPAN), 12-13 Sep.83.

Paul R.P., "Sensors and the Off-Line Programming of Robots", '83 Int. Conf. on Advanced Robotics, Tokyo (JAPAN), 12-13 Sept. 83.

Salisbury J.K.Jr., "Interpretation of Contact Geometries from Force Measurements", 1st. Int. Sym. on Robotics Research, Bretton Woods (USA), Aug 28-Sep 2,83.

Shirai Y.,Koshikawa K.,Oshima M.and Ikeuchi K., "An approach to object recognition using 3D Solid Model", 1st Int. Sym. on Robotics Research, Bretton Woods, (USA), Aug 28-Sep 2,83.

Sobek R.P., "Compiling patterns for a production system : implementation considerations", Tech-Note, LAAS, Toulouse, (forthcoming).

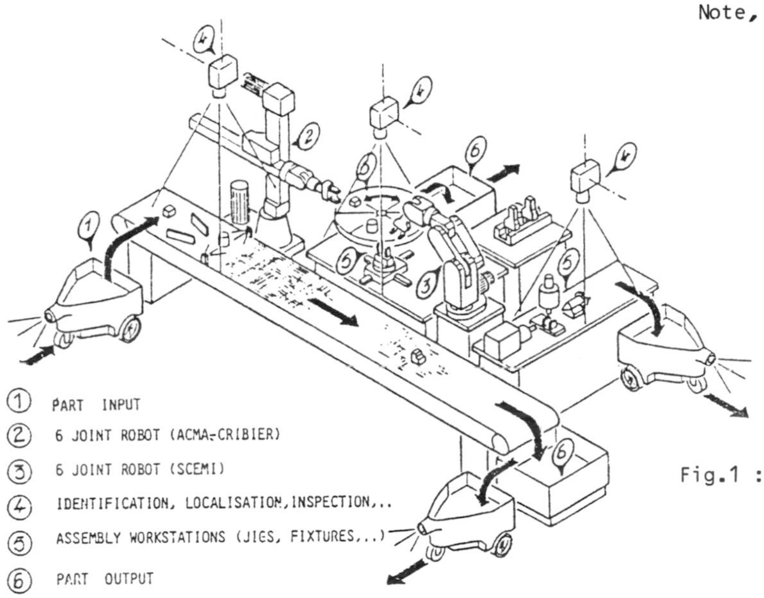

Fig.1 : ARA Flexible Experimental Assembly Cell

■ Presence detectors : switches, LED,...

[F] Force sensors

[P] Proximity sensors

[V] Vision : . grey and color
. 3D (structural light)

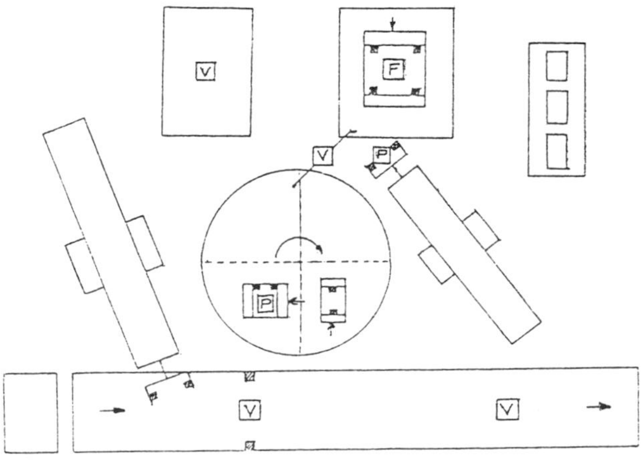

Fig.2 : Current Layout and Sensor Configuration

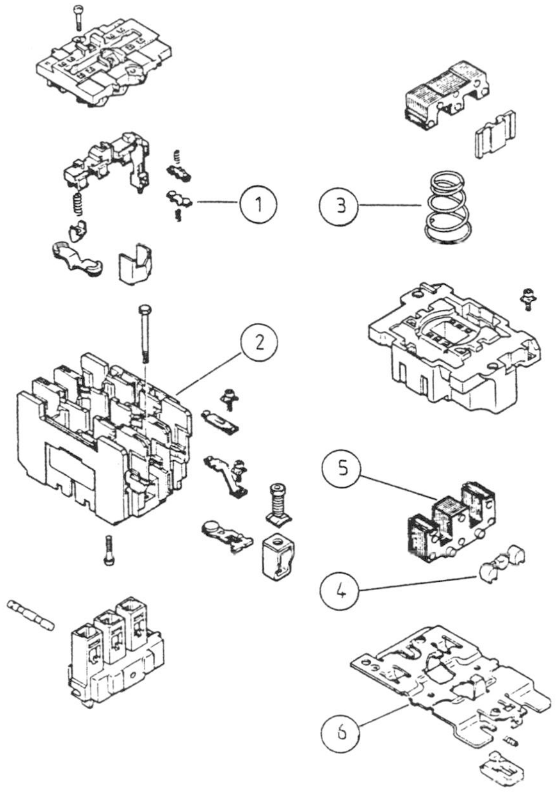

Fig.3 : Electrical Circuit Breaker

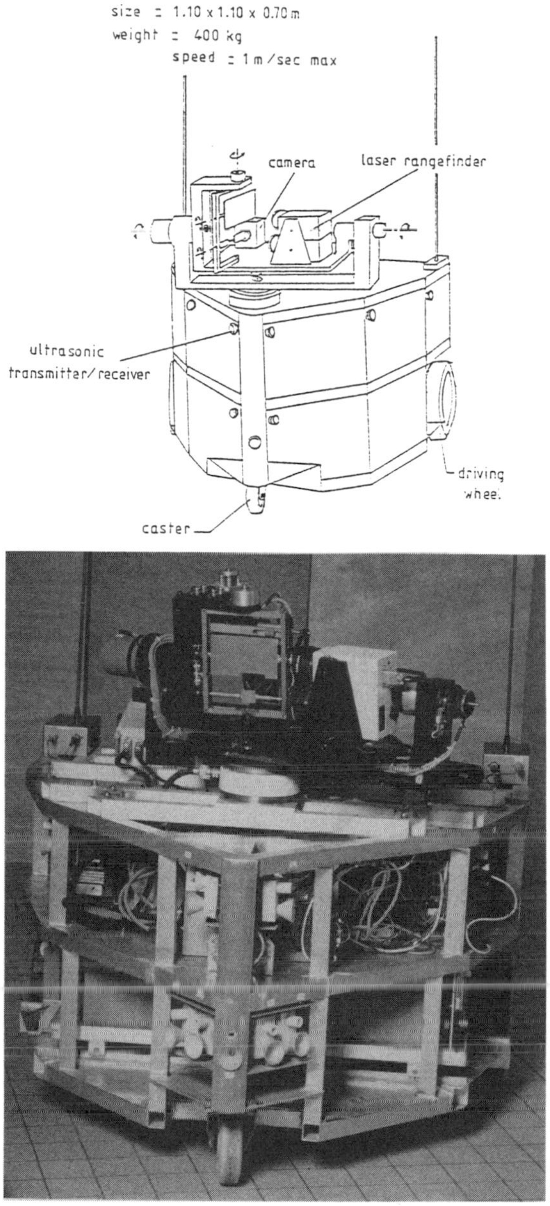

Fig.4 : Mobile Robot HILARE

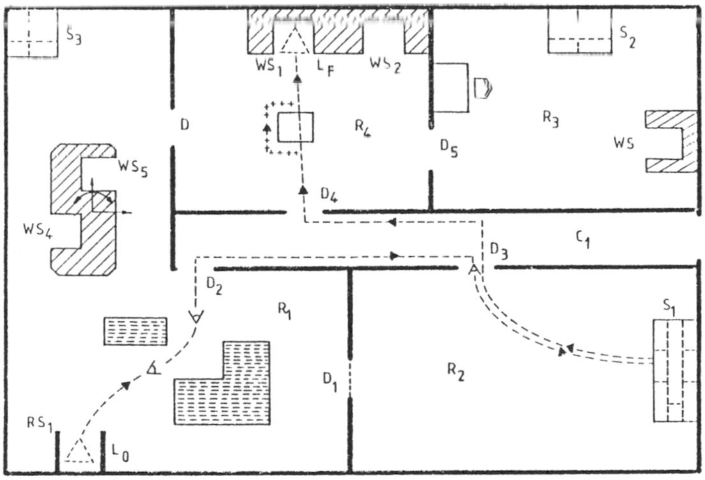

Fig.5 : HILARE'S World Layout

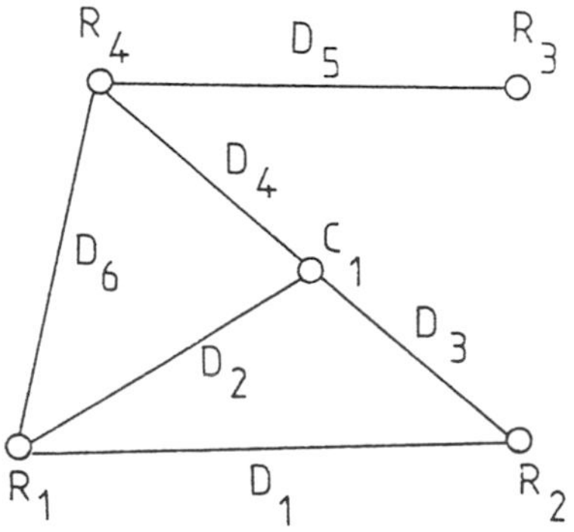

Fig.6 : Topological Representation of Space for the environment layout of fig.5 : a connectivity graph whose nodes are places (rooms, corridors,...) and arcs are transversible boundaries between places (Doors,...)

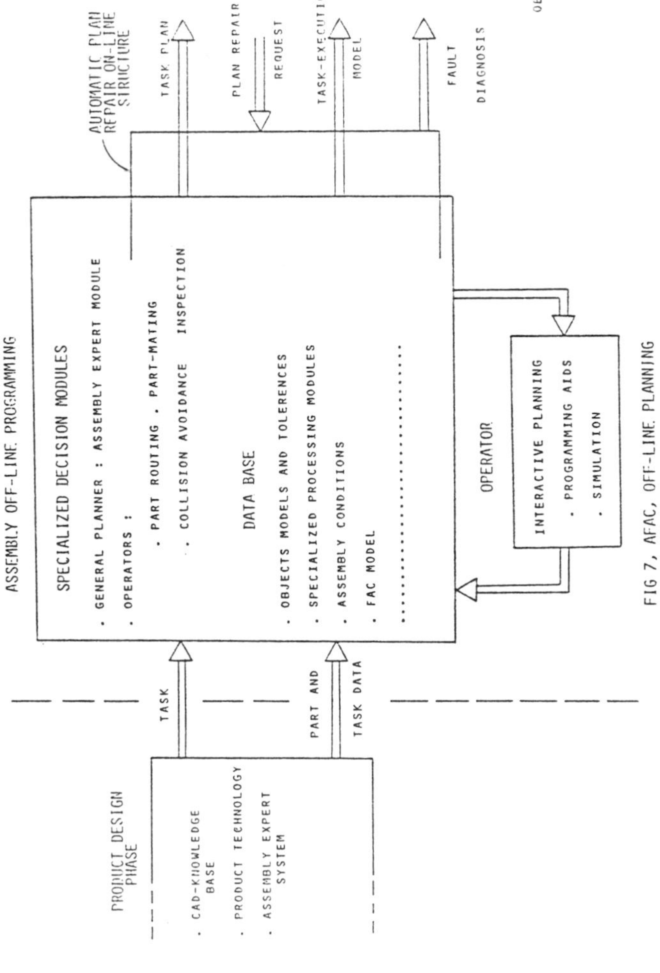

FIG 7, AFAC, OFF-LINE PLANNING

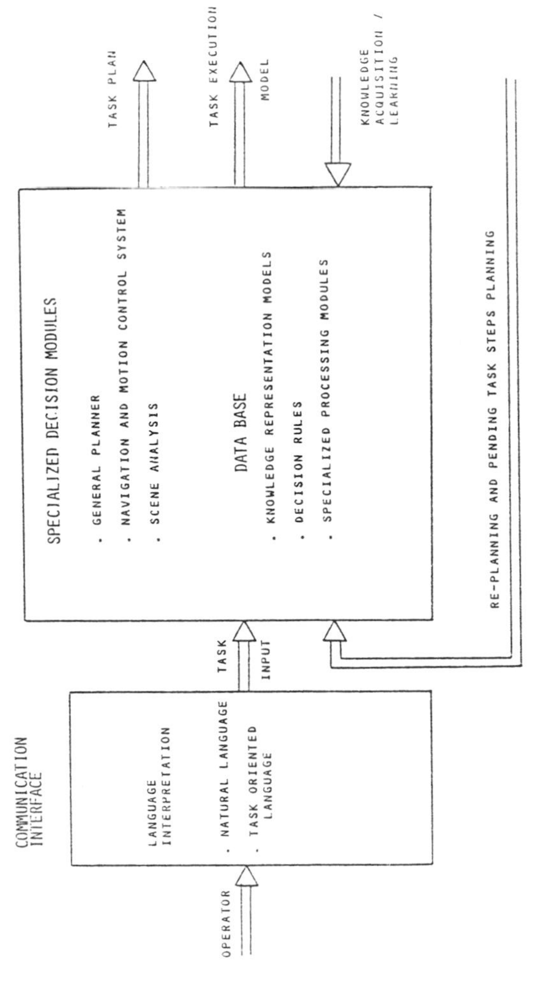

FIG 8, HILARE, AUTOMATIC PLANNING

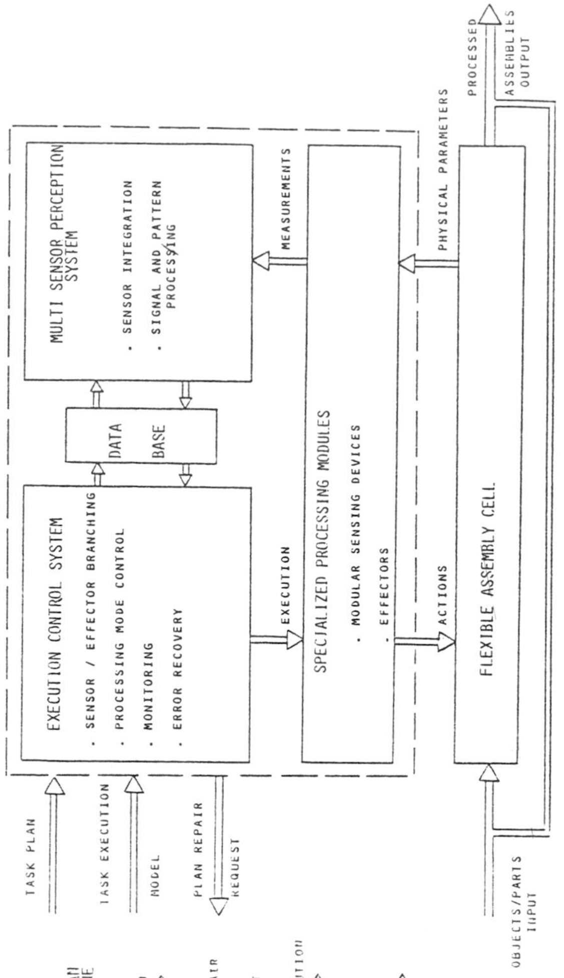

FIG 9, AFAC, TASK-EXECUTION CONTROL SYSTEM

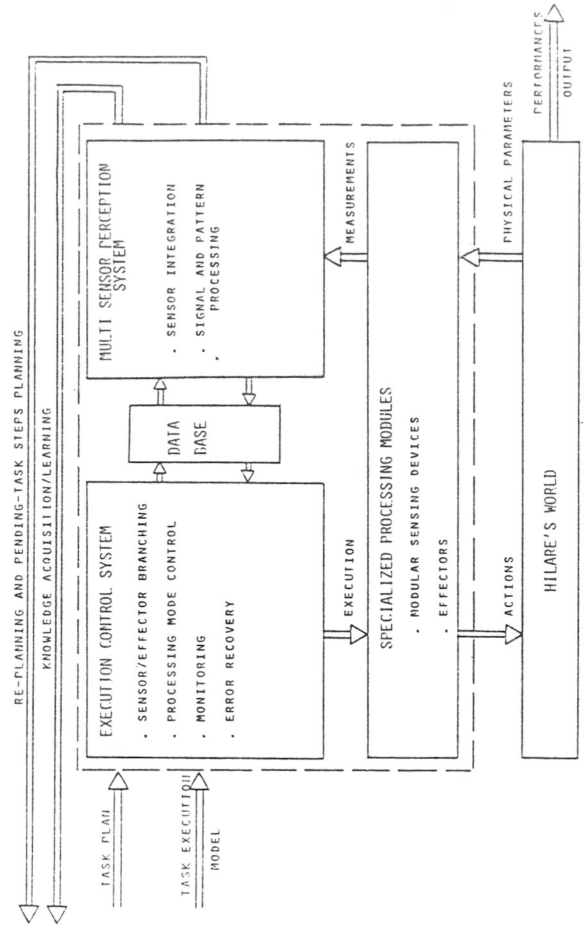

FIG 10, HILARE, TASK EXECUTION CONTROL SYSTEM

Panel Discussion:
Key Issues of Robotics Research

Chairman: B. Roth (Stanford University, U.S.A.)
Panelists: T. Binford (Stanford University, U.S.A.)
P. Davey (Meta Machines, U.K.)
B. Carlisle (Adept Technology, U.S.A.)
G. Giralt (LAAS, CNRS, France)
Y. Shirai (Electrotechnical Lab., Japan)

Roth..... First, I will try to sum up the panelists' talks. Binford emphasized vision, inference systems, mobile robots, recognition and all sorts of vision based processes. Davey spoke about the need to handle sensor data, he was specifically interested in off-line handling. Although the issue of sensor data was common to all the panelists, he was the only one to mention flexible arms relating with sensors. Carlisle, referring to specific types of applications, spoke about the need for simplified programming, also the need for handling of objects that arms interact with. Shirai spoke from the prospective of a specific project which hopes to move into new areas, and said that we need better recognition and sensing. And then, Giralt spoke about the flexible assembly cell, which he felt, would be useful in industrial applications and also emphasized the importance of the autonomous mobile system. There has been much consensus, the panelists have had a lot in common. As I told you, there is a belief that the Buddha is in everyone; certainly, all the people here are as qualified as our panelists to tell us what the key issues are and what the future might be. And I think it might be useful. We don't have to reach a consensus or anything like that. You don't have to agree with everything or anything. Now, I would really welcome comments from the floor.

J.Jarvis..... Many things are mentioned about the state of sensors, tactile sensors, range sensors. Range sensor have been mentioned as adequate, at least the array type, and vision sensors adequate. Nothing has been said about tactile sensors. However, I am commenting that I think we are still lacking good sensors and I am wondering if other people feel the same way.

Carlisle..... I will agree in at least one area. I think that is dense range sensors. And to the extent that people are trying to do three dimensional vision. There seems to be a general lack of dense range sensors. I would say that with respect to tactile sensors, I think, that work is useful, but I don't think it is a major impediment to the near term progress in robotics. I think the key thing that we are trying to do in robotics in the next three to five years are to pick up parts, somehow put them together, and to control that process in a very general way. And so, I think that vision and force sensing are crucial issues, I think in vision the interpretation of the visual data is a crucial issue. I think in force sensing it is not the sensor per se, but the control algorithms which is the crucial issue. I think, in general, system control is a major problem.

Giralt..... Considering vision I do agree in the very high importance of having better sensors for ranging and tactile measurements in flexible manufacturing cells for instance. I would like to say vision will play other roles than the ones it is now playing. I would like to say vision using very light cameras are coming up to do proximity sensing for grasping. We do have good work now in proximity sensors, but still we need to know more about proximity, about relations between end effectors and workparts, and between parts. I also believe a lot in having ways of really detecting end effectors and some other points on the robot arms, detecting them for a general scene analysis with cameras which will also use structured light. I would like to have some kind of safety system that will prevent collision or will allow for redundancy.

Binford..... I agree certainly about the dense range and about touch. I think that is very interesting from a research point of view, and I agree with Brian about the applications of touch. I think we will find that once the sensors are available we'll just begin to find

---

This summary is transcribed and edited from the recorded tape by editors. Editors wish to thank Prof. Roth, the chairman of the panel, for his kind proofreading.

out how inadequate our perception based on these sensors will be. I think also that force will be important and that control is a major issue. Finally, I think a major issue will be actuators, because they are just too weak, and once we have force sensing and control methods we'll be very frustrated by the arms we are trying to control.

Raibert..... I was surprised that so little was said about mechanical design and mechanisms. I remember when I first started in robotics, I thought that the whole problem was getting a computer program that did the right thing. And, I guess my view couldn't be further from that now. And like the works of Asada's direct drive and Jacobson's dexterous hand, we remember something about trying to come up with mechanisms with intrinsic properties that do what you want them to do rather than relying on control sytems or a computer to do what you want to do. I think those are superb general ideas. Davey mentioned flexible arms and Tom just talked about actuators. I think that's a very important piece in the future, a goldmine really.

Whitney..... I would say that there is a paradox of there being an inverse relationship between flexibility and efficiency. You can be efficient, but when you are efficient, you are rigid. Or, you can be flexible, and when you are flexible, you are not efficient. Your cycle times are long. And the result is that you have a very great difficulty deciding which you want. Do you want the efficiency or do you want the flexibility? And no one has yet resolved that problem, and there is always the assumption that in robotics flexibility is the goal. And you pay and pay and pay to get flexibility and no one will buy your robot. And so it becomes a very important problem to distinguish whether we are dealing with Brian Carlisle's environment or Shirai's environment. But if there is an engineered environment, then suddenly, all the assumptions change, all the research priorities change. And then you face this very very serious paradox of flexibility vs efficiency which up to now has been evaluated on rather nebulous economic grounds. So, I would suggest that a lot more attention be paid to what is on the other side of the wall.

Lozano-Perez..... I want to diverge from the tradition and say that what I think really important is something that we are not doing at all. When I did my bachelor's thesis on vision, everybody was using intensity data. But, in the last few years, when you look around at what people talk about at conference regarding vision, almost overnight it seems to have changed, almost everybody talks about 3D data. But, within the context of recognition of parts a wonderful ideal recognition is limited to a well defined problem. We are going back to looking at really more general vision. It seems that we are still far off from really understanding images and we are as far off as we were ten years ago. I don't know what the answer is but I think it's a key issue.

Book..... I have a question for the speakers or perhaps the chairman. What is the definition of a Key Issue? Is it something that defines what I'm doing now or is it something that is good science or does it mean commercial applicability?

Roth..... Well, I think the answers depend of course on what universe you live in, and that's what comes out here. It's a key issue for whom and for what and where? I think there are as many key issues as there are people here. You could not arrive at something you'd call a key issue unless we all have the same goal.

Taylor..... If we take as an issue something where you have to make a choice, there are two sides to an issue. I would like to raise the other side of the issue to Dan Whitney. He was saying we are inventing solutions for which nobody is asking. The other side is that you have to look for opportunities if the technology creates a particular technology for automation with economic justification. If you change the technical assumptions, the design changes and you create new opportunities for products. I think one area where robotics is searching for extensive versatility is to create opportunities for makers of products to exploit the versatility of the manufacturing technology to make products cheaper or functionally better.

Trevelyan..... I think the key issue of robotics research today is a lack of good ideas. When you look around the room, you see the people who were doing robotics research ten or fifteen years ago, they were already playing around with very much the same ideas being classed as new at this conference. And I think that illustrates that there is a basic shortage of good ideas and that the mechanisms which are being followed in robotics research at the moment are not producing good ideas quickly enough. Now, within my own research group we recognize this as being a problem. It is very difficult to find new ways of getting ideas. There are plenty of ways for this but I think we should think about how we can get more cross fertilization between research groups, beyond the context of a conference like this, to get these new ideas in, to get people working on them.

Raibert..... Many people seem to come pretty close to equating automation and industrial concerns with robotics. However, I think robotics has so much more to offer than that, the intellectual problem of intelligent action, intelligent sensor perception and action, whatever you want to call it , is a much broader and exciting thing. And if this conference can't embrace that, then I find that a little bit of a disappointment. I see people nodding, so that everone, apparently, doesn't equate it.

Lacombe..... I have come on things in the same way as my colleage. First, we didn't distinguish clealy the design and the utilization of robotics during this symposium. There is no paper concerning economy and economic prospects. Of couse, robotics is also a matter of economy and there is no micromodel of economics, or a micromodel of insertion of a robot in flexible manufacturing cells and other places, and this lack of information is probably significant due to the limited point of view with respect to the consequence of the problem of robotics.

R.A. Jarvis..... I just wanted to say that I agree with James to some extent about the lack of new ideas but I would also say that there is some degree of general apology. I think that this is a symptom of human nature that we have unrealistic expectations when a field is new and that we tend to look forward, to begin extrapolating all our dreams into actualities. As we get closer, we see that the problems are more difficult than we first thought. This is true of pattern recognition, this is true of many fields in science. I'm not disagreeing but I think we should moderate our views about the effectiveness of our discussions by realising that to discover the problems in more detail as we get along is just part of what we have to tolerate.

Roth..... Thank you. Well, let me turn now to the panelists and give them a chance. I'll give you each two minutes to say anything you'd like to say.

Davey..... I want to pick up on this issue of versatility versus efficiency. Now I think this issue affects robots, it affects sensors, and it also affects conferences. So, let's look at it like this. Robots are already substantially differentiated among themselves. In fact, if you are talking about industrial robots, you do not use the same robot to spray paint, or to do arc welding or to carry out assembly. You use three substantially differentiated machines. Sensors also, if you talk about industrial robotics, the actual sensor itself has got to be highly differentiated. However, the good news is the software. Such things as the software for image understanding, software for reasoning about 3D bodies, software for control in general, these things are what robotics as such is all about. Now, I believe therefore that if we say the best, if we are talking about robotics research, then surely the best research is where the most generality is and there are many beautiful areas within robotics where the generality is almost complete. Now, finally, about versatility vs efficiency. I believe it is rather efficient sometimes to have a conference that is to some extent differentiated. As somebody already pointed out this is not a conference of flexible manufacturing systems, it is not even the conference on industrial robots. This conference, I believe, is and should be about the unifying general principles behind the marvelous discipline of robotics. And I am rather happy that a number of papers that we have heard have stressed those general aspects.

Shirai..... I'll propose only one subject, that is the unified three dimensional model. We have been working on the recognition of objects using a three dimensional CAD models and recently we realized that model can be used for modelling the scene. We can extract the features and try to model the actual scenes and if we can represent it in a similar manner, then manipultion of the three dimensional data becomes very easy. In our laboratory, not only the vision group, but also the manipulation group are going to use that model. So, I propose to you the unified model, if possible, all over the world. If you have some plan to use such a modeller, we are very happy to share the same model.

Giralt..... I will concentrate on the point that we are really lacking good ideas, or are we going too slow in our way. I would say I don't think so. For the last five years I have looked around not only in France but in other countries, and my understanding of the situation is that we are making progress. Of course this progress takes much much more time that anyone of us believed when we started. When I started doing something about automatic plan mapping for mobile robots I thought that was going to be over in two years, and still I have many many doubts about actually at what time it will be finished. So, that's clear, we are slow by ourselves and by the difficulty of the task, but we are making progress. And I have a transparency I am now going to show you, saying that we are facing very exciting problems. And we are going to make it!

Carlisle..... I thought I'd respond to two comments. The first was Marc Raibert's comment about the lack of discussion about mechanisms. I think that's certainly true. We aren't visualizing robots as mechanisms and it has been perhaps only in the last ten years or so that we have begun to visualize them as control system and sensors and distributed systems, much more than mechanisms. There has not been a great deal of development in robot mechanisms, perhaps the only significant recent work has been some of the development of the direct drive robots. I think there is a substantial lack of good actuators for robots, as we try to make robot faster, eventually we will need better actuators. And I think that, if we try to have effective mobile robots or walking robots, they will never be able to carry their power plants today. So I certainly think there is a great deal to be done in that area and I would encourage work in research in mechanisms and I think, very specifically in actuators. My second comment relates to economics. I think that economics in a conference such as this tends not to be so much an issue, we are not all here because of economic reasons, but certainly in the industrial robot world it's a very important issue. One of the things that we used to do at our company was plot the cost of human labor vs the equipment cost of robot labor. Over the last twenty years the cost of labor in the automotive industry has risen from $4 an hour to some 24 or 25 dollars an hour. An equivalent cost of labor for a robot has been roughly five or six dollars an hour, and it is flat essentially over the last twenty years in real dollars. What's happening is that the performance of the robot for a unit cost has been improving. The speed of the robots are improving. We have now one second cycle times which are achievable with robots. The generality of the robots is improving through the use of sensors, so that there is less demand for system engineering; vision systems are an example. The versatility of the robot for flexible automation systems allows us to reduce the capital cost associated with building large automated systems. So, I think the economics are improving, they have improved over the last twenty years and the economic drivers are continuing to improve.

Binford..... I want to respond to the comment about "Well, it was all done in 1970." Also the comment about robotics as a general study of intelligent capabilities. I think from that prospective, when we look at the nature of the problems that we are trying to solve in two years or four years, we are in reality very impatient. These are our internal schedules for solving problems; if you go by the leisurely schedule of psychology or mathematics, we can look forward to decades of research and gradual development. So, I think we are dealing with very hard and very fundamental problems, including ones that are deep mathematical problems, and that we can expect that there will be little steps along the way, and that it will take us considerable time.

Roth..... Well, I want to thank you all for coming here, I certainly want to thank the panelists. I'd just say in closing, one thing that impressed me is in a sense the sameness of it all. I don't mean it in a negative way, but, anywhere you go in the world, it is impossible to distinguish where you are in terms of the work being done in robotics. Years ago I used to be able to close my eyes at a conference and then open them, and I'd see a slide and say that's a Japanese person talking, I'd see a slide and say it's an American, or Frenchman, or Russian. At this meeting I really got the feeling that at our work converging. It has lost a national identity. It is a really interesting thing that the way we all do science has gotten down to be about the same. And the community of problems seem to be about the same all over the world; it is a sign of a maturing field. That is maybe the good news, but this gets back to what Jim is saying. We all have defined terms and we have defined areas and have headings for our conference sections. There is manipulation, vision and all of that. And in one sense, that may lead to progress, in the other sense it is making it all academic and helps people in forgetting what the problems are really all about. I think it's important to be aware of these affects and to be a little bit self conscious about it and to step out of it in some way and look at what we are doing. Anyway, I do thank you all for coming and I thank you for sitting through this, and I thank my panelists for being punctual and for doing much better than could have reasonably been expected. Thank you.

List of Contributors

Tadashi Akita
Fujitsu Laboratories Ltd.
Kawasaki, Japan

Peter Allen
Department of Computer and Information Science
University of Pennsylvania
Philadelphia, Pennsylvania

A. P. Ambler
Department of Artificial Intelligence
University of Edinburgh
Edinburgh, Scotland

Makoto Araki
Fujitsu Laboratories Ltd.
Kawasaki, Japan

Suguru Arimoto
Department of Mechanical Engineering
Faculty of Engineering Science
Osaka, Japan

Haruhiko Asada
Department of Mechanical Engineering and
Laboratory for Manufacturing and Productivity
Massachusetts Institute of Technology
Cambridge, Massachusetts

Haruo Asada
Toshiba Research and Development Center
Kawasaki, Japan

Ruzena Bajcsy
Department of Computer and Information Science
University of Pennsylvania
Philadelphia, Pennsylvania

P. Bidaud
Laboratoire de Mécanique et Robotique
Université de Pierre et Marie Curie
Paris, France

K. B. Biggers
Center for Biomedical Design
Department of Mechanical and Industrial
Engineering and Department of Bioengineering
Salt Lake City, Utah

Thomas O. Binford
Artificial Intelligence Laboratory
Computer Science Department
Stanford University
Stanford, California

Robert C. Bolles
SRI International
Menlo Park, California

Wayne J. Book
School of Mechanical Engineering
Georgia Institute of Technology
Atlanta, Georgia

P. Borrel
Laboratoire d'Automatique et de
Microélectronique de Montpellier
Montpellier, France

Michael Brady
Artificial Intelligence Laboratory
Massachusetts Institute of Technology
Cambridge, Massachusetts

Rodney A. Brooks
Computer Science Department
Stanford University
Stanford, California

Andre B. By
Department of Mechanical Engineering and
Laboratory for Manufacturing and Productivity
Massachusetts Institute of Technology
Cambridge, Massachusetts

Brian Carlisle
Adept Technology, Inc.
Mountain View, California

R. W. Daniel
Engineering Laboratory
Oxford University
Oxford, England

P. G. Davey
Meta Machines Ltd.
Oxford, England

E. Dombre
Laboratoire d'Automatique et de
Microeléctronique de Montpellier
Montpellier, France

Steven Dubowsky
Department of Mechanical Engineering
Massachusetts Institute of Technology
Cambridge, Massachusetts

Alexander C. Edsall
The Charles Stark Draper Laboratory, Inc.
Cambridge, Massachusetts

Masakazu Ejiri
Central Research Laboratory
Hitachi Ltd.
Tokyo, Japan

Bernard Espiau
IRISA
Campus de Beaulieu
Rennes, France

O. D. Faugeras
INRIA
Domaine de Voluceau
Le Chesnay, France

E. Freund
Chair of Automation and Information Processing
Fern Universität
Hagen, West Germany

Yasushi Fukuda
Tokyo Institute of Technology
Tokyo, Japan

Malik Ghallab
Laboratoire d'Automatique et d'Analyse des
Systèmes du CNRS
Toulouse, France

Georges Giralt
Laboratoire d'Automatique et d'Analyse des
Systèmes du CNRS
Toulouse, France

W. Eric L. Grimson
Artificial Intelligence Laboratory
Massachusetts Institute of Technology
Cambridge, Massachusetts

J. C. Guinot
Laboratoire de Mécanique et Robotique
Université de Pierre et Marie Curie
Paris, France

Kyojiro Hakomori
Department of Precision Engineering
Tohoku University
Sendai, Japan

Hideo Hanafusa
Automation Research Laboratory
Kyoto University
Kyoto, Japan

Kensuke Hasegawa
Department of Control Engineering
Tokyo Institute of Technology
Tokyo, Japan

Toshiro Higuchi
Institute of Industrial Science
University of Tokyo
Tokyo, Japan

Shigeo Hirose
Tokyo Institute of Technology
Tokyo, Japan

John M. Hollerbach
Artificial Intelligence Laboratory
Massachusetts Institute of Technology
Cambridge, Massachusetts

Ralph L. Hollis
Manufacturing Research Center
IBM T. J. Watson Research Center
Yorktown Heights, New York

John Hopcroft
Department of Computer Science
Cornell University
Ithaca, New York

Patrice Horaud
Laboratoire d'Automatique de Grenoble
Saint-Martin d'Hères, France

Hiroshi Hoshino
Information Systems Laboratory
Toshiba Research and Development Center
Kawasaki, Japan

H. Hoyer
Chair of Automation and Information Processing
Fern Universität
Hagen, West Germany

Hirochika Inoue
Department of Mechanical Engineering
University of Tokyo
Tokyo, Japan

E. K. Iversen
Center for Biomedical Design
Department of Mechanical and Industrial Engineering and Department of Bioengineering
University of Utah
Salt Lake City, Utah

S. C. Jacobsen
Center for Biomedical Design
Department of Mechanical and Industrial Engineering and Department of Bioengineering
University of Utah
Salt Lake City, Utah

John F. Jarvis
Bell Laboratories
Holmdel, New Jersey

R. A. Jarvis
Department of Computer Science
Australian National University
Canberra, Australia

Feng Kaihua
Faculty of Physics
Nanjing University
Nanjing, People's Republic of China

Takeo Kanade
Department of Computer Science
Carnegie-Mellon University
Pittsburgh, Pennsylvania

Akitaka Kato
Production Engineering Division
Pioneer Electronic Corporation
Tokyo, Japan

Sadao Kawamura
Department of Mechanical Engineering
Faculty of Engineering Science
Osaka University
Osaka, Japan

Y. Kida
Sumitomo Electric Industries Ltd.
Osaka, Japan

Masatsugu Kidode
Information Systems Laboratory
Toshiba Research and Development Center
Kawasaki, Japan

Hidekazu Kikuchi
Tokyo Institute of Technology
Tokyo, Japan

Hiroshi Kimura
Department of Mechanical Engineering
Faculty of Engineering
University of Tokyo
Tokyo, Japan

Charles A. Klein
Department of Electrical Engineering
Ohio State University
Columbus, Ohio

D. F. Knutti
Center for Biomedical Design
Department of Mechanical and Industrial Engineering and Department of Bioengineering
University of Utah
Salt Lake City, Utah

Hiroaki Kobayashi
Department of Precision Engineering
Meiji University
Kawasaki, Japan

Kiyoshi Komoriya
Mechanical Engineering Laboratory
MITI
Ibaraki, Japan

Roy Kornbluh
Department of Mechanical Engineering
Massachusetts Institute of Technology
Cambridge, Massachusetts

Jean-Louis Lacombe
SA MATRA—SPACE BRANCH—EPT/DT/068
Velizy, France

J. P. Lallemand
Laboratoire de Mécanique et Robotique
Université de Pierre et Marie Curie
Paris, France

J. C. Latombe
Laboratoire LIFIA
Saint-Martin d'Hères, France

C. Laugier
Laboratoire LIFIA
Saint-Martin d'Hères, France

Mark A. Lavin
Manufacturing Research Center
IBM T. J. Watson Research Center
Yorktown Heights, New York

J. M. Lefebvre
Laboratoire LIFIA
Saint-Martin d'Hères, France

A. Liegeois
Laboratoire d'Automatique et de Microeléctronique de Montpellier
Montpellier, France

Tomás Lozano-Pérez
Artificial Intelligence Laboratory
Massachusetts Institute of Technology
Cambridge, Massachusetts

Matthew T. Mason
Computer Science Department and Robotics Institute
Carnegie-Mellon University
Pittsburgh, Pennsylvania

Tomoyuki Masui
Production Engineering Research Laboratory
Hitachi Ltd.
Yokohama, Japan

E. Mazer
Laboratoire LIFIA
Saint-Martin d'Hères, France

J. F. Miribel
ITMI
Meylan, France

Mamoru Mitsuishi
Department of Mechanical Engineering
Faculty of Engineering
University of Tokyo
Tokyo, Japan

Hirofumi Miura
Department of Mechanical Engineering
Faculty of Engineering
University of Tokyo
Tokyo, Japan

Fumio Miyazaki
Department of Mechanical Engineering
Faculty of Engineering Science
Osaka University
Osaka, Japan

Hiroshi Mizoguchi
Department of Mechanical Engineering
University of Tokyo
Tokyo, Japan

Takashi Mizutani
Department of Control Engineering
Tokyo Institute of Technology
Tokyo, Japan

Minoru Morita
Corporate Production Engineering Division
Matsushita Electric Industrial Company Ltd.
Osaka, Japan

Makoto Nagao
Department of Electrical Engineering
Kyoto University
Kyoto, Japan

Yoshihiko Nakamura
Automation Research Laboratory
Kyoto University
Kyoto, Japan

K. Ogi
Sumitomo Electric Industries Ltd.
Osaka, Japan

Takushi Okada
Production Engineering Research Laboratory
Hitachi Ltd.
Yokohama, Japan

Tokuji Okada
Electrotechnical Laboratory
Ibaraki, Japan

K. Okamoto
Sumitomo Electric Industries Ltd.
Osaka, Japan

Kiyoshi Okazaki
Toshiba Ltd.
Kawasaki, Japan

A. Ooka
Sumitomo Electric Industries Ltd.
Osaka, Japan

Richard P. Paul
School of Electrical Engineering
Purdue University
West Lafayette, Indiana

Jean Ponce
Artificial Intelligence Laboratory
Massachusetts Institute of Technology
Cambridge, Massachusetts

Marc H. Raibert
Computer Science Department and Robotics Institute
Carnegie-Mellon University
Pittsburgh, Pennsylvania

Bernard Roth
Department of Mechanical Engineering
Stanford University
Stanford, California

Ryoichiro Sasano
Kobe Shipyard & Engine Works
Mitsubishi Heavy Industries Ltd.
Kobe, Japan

Kunitoshi Shimizu
Sony Corporation
Atsugi, Japan

Isao Shimoyama
Department of Mechanical Engineering
Faculty of Engineering
University of Tokyo
Tokyo, Japan

Yoshiaki Shirai
Electrotechnical Laboratory
Ibaraki, Japan

Youkio Shiraogawa
Information Systems Laboratory
Toshiba Research and Development Center
Kawasaki, Japan

Takashi Suehiro
Automatic Control Division
Electrotechnical Laboratory
Ibaraki, Japan

Noboru Sugie
Department of Information Science
Faculty of Engineering
Nagoya University
Nagoya, Japan

Kōkichi Sugihara
Department of Information Science
Faculty of Engineering
Nagoya University
Nagoya, Japan

Koichi Sugimoto
Production Engineering Research Laboratory
Hitachi Ltd.
Yokohama, Japan

Hajime Sugiuchi
Department of Mechanical Engineering
University of Tokyo
Tokyo, Japan

Susumu Tachi
Mechanical Engineering Laboratory
MITI
Ibaraki, Japan

Masaharu Takano
Faculty of Engineering
University of Tokyo
Tokyo, Japan

Kunikatsu Takase
Automatic Control Division
Electrotechnical Laboratory
Ibaraki, Japan

A. Takemoto
Sumitomo Electric Industries Ltd.
Osaka, Japan

Russell H. Taylor
Manufacturing Research Center
IBM T. J. Watson Research Center
Yorktown Heights, New York

Fumiaki Tomita
Department of Computer Science
Carnegie-Mellon University
Pittsburgh, Pennsylvania

James P. Trevelyan
Department of Mechanical Engineering
University of Western Australia
Nedlands, Western Australia

Saburo Tsuji
Department of Control Engineering
Osaka University
Osaka, Japan

Masaru Uchiyama
Department of Precision Engineering
Tohoku University
Sendai, Japan

Takashi Uchiyama
Fujitsu Laboratories Ltd.
Kawasaki, Japan

Yoji Umetani
Tokyo Institute of Technology
Tokyo, Japan

Y. Wada
Sumitomo Electric Industries Ltd.
Osaka, Japan

Daniel E. Whitney
The Charles Stark Draper Laboratory, Inc.
Cambridge, Massachusetts

Gordon Wilfong
Department of Computer Science
Cornell University
Ithaca, New York

J. E. Wood
Center for Biomedical Design
Department of Mechanical and Industrial Engineering and Department of Bioengineering
University of Utah
Salt Lake City, Utah

K. Yoshida
Sumitomo Electric Industries Ltd.
Osaka, Japan

Tsuneo Yoshikawa
Automation Research Laboratory
Kyoto University
Kyoto, Japan

Kenichi Yoshimoto
Department of Mechanical Engineering
University of Tokyo
Tokyo, Japan

Alan Yuille
Artificial Intelligence Laboratory
Massachusetts Institute of Technology
Cambridge, Massachusetts

Hong Zhang
School of Electrical Engineering
Purdue University
West Lafayette, Indiana